MODERN EQUI

AUSTRALIA
LBC Information Services
Sydney

CANADA and USA
Carswell
Toronto

NEW ZEALAND
Brooker's
Auckland

SINGAPORE and MALAYSIA
Thomson Information (S.E.Asia)
Singapore

HANBURY & MARTIN

MODERN EQUITY

FIFTEENTH EDITION

BY

JILL E. MARTIN, LL.D. (Lond.)

Professor of Law, Kings College, London

Barrister, Lincoln's Inn

London
Sweet & Maxwell Ltd
1997

First Edition	1935	Third Impression	1973
Second Edition	1937	Fourth Impression	1974
Third Edition	1943	Fifth Impression	1975
Fourth Edition	1946	Tenth Edition	1976
Fifth Edition	1949	Second Impression	1979
Sixth Edition	1952	Eleventh Edition	1981
Seventh Edition	1957	Twelfth Edition	1985
Eighth Edition	1962	Thirteenth Edition	1989
Ninth Edition	1969	Second Impression	1990
Second Impression	1971	Fourteenth Edition	1993
		Fifteenth Edition	1997

Published by
Sweet & Maxwell Limited of
100 Avenue Road, London NW3 3PF
Computerset by Interactive Sciences Ltd, Gloucester
Printed in England by
Clays Ltd, St. Ives plc.

*A CIP catalogue record
for this book is available
from the British Library*

ISBN 0 421 57860 2

*No natural forests were destroyed
to make this product, only farmed timber
was used and re-planted.*

©
Sweet & Maxwell Ltd
1997

PREFACE

The four years since the publication of the fourteenth edition in 1993 have seen many important developments, both in caselaw and legislation, in the field of equity and trusts. After a period of stagnation on the law reform front, many significant proposals have recently been implemented or are likely to be during the lifetime of this edition.

The basic structure of the book remains similar to previous editions save that there is a new chapter (Chapter 16) on trusts of pension funds to reflect the Pensions Act 1995, the general caselaw and the interest generated by the Maxwell pensions scandal. Space has been found by general pruning, and in particular by a substantial reduction in Chapter 27 (the equitable doctrines of conversion, election, satisfaction and performance).

In the early chapters on the general law of trusts important decisions include *Hunter v. Moss* on certainty of subject-matter and the rulings of the House of Lords in *Tinsley v. Milligan* and the Court of Appeal in *Tribe v. Tribe* on transfers for unlawful purposes. In Chapter 11 (the family home) attention has centred on what might be called the post-*Rosset* decisions, in particular those of the Court of Appeal in *Midland Bank plc v. Cooke* and *Drake v. Whipp*. The section on co-ownership and the trust for sale has been rewritten in the light of the Trusts of Land and Appointment of Trustees Act 1996. Chapter 12 (constructive trusts) needs a thorough overhaul in every edition. Of major interest on this occasion has been the decision of the Privy Council in *Royal Brunei Airlines v. Tan* concerning liability for assisting in a breach of trust. In Chapter 15 (charities) the consolidating Charities Act 1993, which was just too late for the last edition, is included.

Chapters 17 to 20 on the powers and duties of trustees have been the areas most affected by reforms and reform proposals. In the former category are those introduced by the Trusts of Land and Appointment of Trustees Act 1996. An overhaul of the Trustee Investment Act 1961 is under way. Many other proposals aimed at updating the law on trustees to meet modern conditions, such as the power to delegate investment discretions, have emanated from the Law Commission and the Trust Law Committee.

In Chapter 21 (fiduciaries) the focus of attention has been the decision of the Privy Council in *Att.-Gen. for Hong Kong v. Reid* (bribe held on constructive trust), while in Chapter 22 (variation) it has been the decision of the House of Lords in *Brooks v. Brooks*. Chapter 23 (breach) has required substantial rewriting to accommodate the decision of the House of Lords on liability for loss and the assessment of compensation in *Target Holdings Ltd v. Redferns* and the important developments in tracing, many of which have resulted from the Maxwell pensions litigation and the ultra vires "interest-rate swap" transactions entered into by local authorities. New sections have been written on subrogation, "backwards tracing" and the evolving change of position defence. Noteworthy cases in this area include *Re Goldcorp Exchange Ltd*, *Boscawen v. Bajwa*, *Bishopsgate Investment Management Ltd v. Homan*, *Jones (F.C.) & Sons (Trustee) v. Jones* and the long-awaited decision of the House of Lords in *Westdeutsche Landesbank Girozentrale v. Islington London Borough Council* from which (as in *Tinsley v. Milligan*) two of their Lordships dissented.

Of most interest in Chapters 24 and 25 (specific performance and injunctions) have been the continuing debate on the measure of damages under Lord Cairns' Act, highlighted by the decisions of the Court of Appeal in *Jaggard v. Sawyer* and *Surrey County Council v. Bredero Homes Ltd*, and the majority decision of the Court of Appeal in *Co-operative Insurance Society Ltd v. Argyll Stores (Holdings) Ltd*, upholding the enforcement by specific performance of a "keep open" covenant in a lease of retail premises. In Chapter 26 the focus has been on the rulings of the House of Lords in *Barclays Bank plc v. O'Brien* and *CIBC Mortgages plc v. Pitt* (undue influence) and their application in numerous subsequent decisions. Finally, there has been some restructuring of the estoppel section of Chapter 28 to deal with the many recent cases. Throughout the book mention has been made of relevant Commonwealth decisions, periodical literature and Law Commission reports.

I am grateful to all those at King's College and elsewhere who have made helpful suggestions or brought material to my attention, and to the editorial staff of Sweet & Maxwell for their efficiency.

My intention has been to state the law as at January 1, 1997, incorporating such later developments as could be accommodated during the processing of proofs.

Jill Martin
King's College London
March 1st 1997

CONTENTS

	PAGE
Preface	v
Table of Abbreviations	ix
Table of Cases	xii
Table of Statutes	lxxv

PART I

INTRODUCTION

CHAP.	PAGE
1. History and Principles	3
2. Nature and Classification of Trusts	45

PART II

TRUSTS AND POWERS

	PAGE
3. Requirements of a Trust	73
4. Constitution of Trusts. Equity will not Assist a Volunteer	111
5. Testamentary Gifts not Complying with the Wills Act 1837. Secret Trusts	143
6. Powers	165
7. Protective Trusts	185
8. Discretionary Trusts	195
9 Taxation and Trusts	211
10. Resulting Trusts	229
11. Trusts of the Family Home	259
12. Constructive Trusts	285

13. Trusts which Contravene the Law   325
14. Non-Charitable Purpose Trusts   347
15. Charitable Trusts   375
16. Trusts of Pension Funds   455

PART III

TRUSTEES

17. General Principles: Capacity: Appointment: Removal:
    Retirement: Control   479
18. Duties of Trustees in Relation to the Trust Property   511
19. Duties of Trustees in Relation to the Beneficiaries   537
20. Powers of Trustees   553
21. The Fiduciary Nature of Trusteeship   585
22. Variation of Trusts   611
23. Breach of Trust   631

PART IV

EQUITABLE REMEDIES

24. Specific Performance   693
25. Injunctions   733
26. Rescission and Rectification   817

PART V

MISCELLANEOUS EQUITABLE DOCTRINES AND EQUITIES

27. Equitable Doctrines of Conversion, Election, Satisfaction and
    Performance   849
28. Licences and Estoppel   867

Index   897

TABLE OF ABBREVIATIONS

Books

Annual Report	*Annual Report of the Charity Commissioners.*
A.S.C.L.	*Annual Survey of Commonwealth Law.*
Cheshire	Cheshire and Burn, *The Modern Law of Real Property* (15th ed., 1994).
Farrand	Farrand, *Contract and Conveyance* (4th ed., 1983).
Farwell	*Farwell on Powers* (3rd ed., 1916).
Goff and Jones	Goff and Jones, *The Law of Restitution* (4th ed., 1993).
Harris	Harris, *Variation of Trusts.*
Hayton and Marshall	Hayton and Marshall, Commentary and Cases on the Law of Trusts and Equitable Remedies (10th ed., 1996).
Heydon, Gummow & Austin	Heydon, Gummow & Austin, *Cases and Materials on Equity & Trusts* (4th ed., 1993).
Holdsworth *H.E.L.*	Holdsworth, *History of English Law.*
Lewin	*Lewin on Trusts* (16th ed., 1964).
Maitland	*Maitland's Equity* (2nd ed., 1936).
M. & W.	Megarry and Wade, *The Law of Real Property* (5th ed., 1984).
Meagher, Gummow & Lehane	Meagher, Gummow & Lehane, *Equity: Doctrines & Remedies* (3rd ed., 1992).
Morris and Leach	Morris and Leach, *The Rule Against Perpetuities* (2nd ed., 1962).
Oakley	Oakley, *Constructive Trusts* (3rd ed., 1997).
Parker and Mellows	Parker and Mellows, *The Modern Law of Trusts* (6th ed., 1994).

Pettit   Pettit, *Equity and the Law of Trusts* (7th
                          ed., 1993).
Preston and Newsom   Preston and Newsom, *Limitation of Actions*
                          (3rd ed., 1953).
Scott   Scott, *Trusts* (4th ed., 1988).
Snell   Snell, *Principles of Equity* (29th ed.,
                          1990).
Spry   Spry, *Equitable Remedies* (4th ed., 1990).
Tudor   *Tudor on Charities* (8th ed., 1995).
Underhill and Hayton   Underhill and Hayton, *Law Relating to
                          Trusts and Trustees* (15th ed., 1995).

Journals

All E.R. Rev.   All England Law Reports Annual Review.
B.T.R.   British Tax Review.
C.F.L.Q.   Child and Family Law Quarterly.
C.L.J.   Cambridge Law Journal.
C.B.R.   Canadian Bar Review.
Col. L.R.   Columbia Law Review.
Conv.   Conveyancer and Property Lawyer.
Conv. (N.S.)   Conveyancer and Property Lawyer (New
                          Series).
Crim. L.R.   Criminal Law Review.
C.L.P.   Current Legal Problems.
E.G.   Estates Gazette.
Fam. Law.   Family Law.
H.L.R.   Harvard Law Review.
I.C.L.Q.   International and Comparative Law Quar-
                          terly.
J.B.L.   Journal of Business Law.
J.L.H.   Journal of Legal History.
K.C.L.J.   King's College Law Journal.
L.Q.R.   Law Quarterly Review.
L.S.   Legal Studies.
L.S.Gaz.   Law Society's Gazette.
M.L.R.   Modern Law Review.
N.L.J.   New Law Journal.
R.L.R.   Restitution Law Review.
S.J.   Solicitors' Journal.
U.W.A.L.R.   University of Western Australia Law
                          Review.

Acts of Parliament

A.E.A	Administration of Estates Act.
F.A.	Finance Act.
I.C.T.A.	Income and Corporation Taxes Act.
I.H.T.A.	Inheritance Tax Act.
L.C.A.	Land Charges Act.
L.P.A.	Law of Property Act.
L.P.(A).A.	Law of Property (Amendment) Act.
S.L.A.	Settled Land Act.
T.A.	Trustee Act.
T.C.G.A.	Taxation of Chargeable Gains Act.
T.I.A.	Trustee Investments Act.
V.T.A.	Variation of Trusts Act.

General

B.S.	Building Society.
Comm.	Commissioners.
I.R.C.	Inland Revenue Commissioners.
R.S.C.	Rules of the Supreme Court.
S.	Section.
S.E.	Settled Estates.
S.T.	Settlement Trusts.
W.T.	Will Trusts.

TABLE OF CASES

A. v. B. Bank (Governor and Company of the Bank of England intervening) [1993] Q.B. 311; [1992] 3 W.L.R. 705 .... 739, 797
—— v. C. [1981] Q.B. 956 .... 791, 815
—— (No. 2) [1981] Q.B. 961 815
Aas v. Benham [1891] 2 Ch. 244 .... 603, 606
Abbey Malvern Wells Ltd v. Minister of Local Government and Housing [1951] Ch. 728; [1951] 1 T.L.R. 1050 394
Abbey National v. Moss (1993) 26 H.L.R. 249; [1994] 1 F.L.R. 307 281
Abbey National Building Society v. Cann [1991] 1 A.C. 56; [1990] 2 W.L.R. 833 .... 37, 278, 279
Abbott (A Bankrupt), Re, ex p. The Trustee of the Property of the Bankrupt v. Abbott (PM) [1983] Ch. 45, D.C.; [1982] 3 W.L.R. 86 342
Abdallah v. Rickards (1888) 4 T.L.R. 622 558
Aberconway's Settlement Trusts, Re, McLaren v. Aberconway [1953] Ch. 647; [1953] 3 W.L.R. 183 371
Aberdeen Railway Co. v. Blaikie Bros. (1854) 1 Macq. 461 .... 595, 596
Abrahams, Re [1911] 1 Ch. 108 575
Abrahams' Will Trusts, Re, Caplan v. Abrahams [1969] 1 Ch. 463; [1967] 3 W.L.R. 1198 .... 168, 169, 175, 200, 331, 353, 581, 582
Abram (dec'd), Re [1996] 2 F.L.R. 379 188
Ackerley, Re [1913] 1 Ch. 510 .... 171, 172
Acrow (Automation) Ltd v. Rex Chainbelt Inc. [1971] 1 W.L.R. 1676; 115 S.J. 642 .... 739, 748, 753
Adams, Re [1893] 1 Ch. 329 574
Adams and the Kensington Vestry, Re (1884) 27 Ch.D. 394 91
Adderly v. Dixon (1824) 1 Sim. & St. 607 .... 703, 730
Adhous, Re [1955] 1 W.L.R. 459 535
Adlard, Re, Taylor v. Adlard [1954] Ch. 29; [1953] 3 W.L.R. 914 .... 116, 134, 160
Agip (Africa) v. Jackson [1991] Ch. 547; [1991] 3 W.L.R. 116 .... 296, 300, 302, 305, 657, 659, 660, 661, 663, 664
Agip S.p.A. v. Navigazione Alta Italia S.p.A. [1984] 1 Lloyd's Rep. 353, C.A. 842
Agnew v. Belfast Banking Co. [1896] 2 I.R. 204 138
Agricultural Mortgage Corporation plc v. Woodward (1995) 70 P. & C.R. 53 339
Ailion v. Spiekermann [1976] Ch. 158; [1976] 2 W.L.R. 556 717
Ainsbury v. Millington [1987] 1 W.L.R. 379; (1987) 131 S.J. 361 735
Air Canada and M. & L. Travel Ltd, Re (1994) 108 D.L.R. (4th) 592 596
Aitken v. Aitken, 1927 S.C. 374 369
Ajayi v. R. T. Briscoe (Nigeria) Ltd [1964] 1 W.L.R. 1326; 108 S.J. 857 .... 884, 885
Al Nahkel for Contracting and Trading Ltd v. Lowe [1986] Q.B. 235; [1986] 2 W.L.R. 317 .... 30, 745, 810
Alan (W.J.) & Co. Ltd v. El Nasr Export and Import Co. [1972] 2 Q.B. 189; [1972] 2 W.L.R. 800 .... 884, 885
Albany Home Loans Ltd v. Massey, The Times, February 14, 1997 835

Alcock v. Sloper (1833) 2 My. & K. 699 .... 542, 543
Aldous v. Southwark Corporation [1968] 1 W.L.R. 1671; 112 S.J. 687 382
Alec Lobb (Garages) Ltd v. Total Oil G.B. Ltd. *See* Lobb (Alec) Garages v. Total Oil
    Great Britain.
Ali v. London Borough of Southwark [1988] I.R.L.R. 100; [1988] I.C.R. 567 790
Ali (Mohram) v. Tower Hamlets London Borough Council [1993] Q.B. 407; [1992] 3
    W.L.R. 208 800
Allcard v. Skinner (1887) 36 Ch.D. 145 .... 646, 829
Allen, *Re*, Faith v. Allen [1953] Ch. 810; [1953] 3 W.L.R. 637 .... 90, 109, 328, 331
—— v. Distillers Co. (Biochemicals) Ltd, *The Times*, July 3, 1973 .... 615, 619, 624, 628
—— v. Greenhi Builders Ltd [1979] 1 W.L.R. 156; (1978) 123 S.J. 112 769
—— v. Jackson (1875) 1 Ch.D. 399 329
—— v. Jambo Holdings Ltd [1980] 1 W.L.R. 1252; (1979) 124 S.J. 742 .... 809, 814
—— v. Snyder [1977] 2 N.S.W.L.R. 685 .... 42, 324
Allen-Meyrick's Will Trusts, *Re*, Mangnall v. Allen-Meyrick [1966] 1 W.L.R. 499; 109
    S.J. 957 .... 181, 191, 208, 534
Allhusen v. Whittell (1867) L.R. 4 Eq. 295 546
Allied Arab Bank Ltd v. Hajjar [1988] Q.B. 787; [1988] 2 W.L.R. 942 .... 21, 30, 745,
                                                                                  810, 811
Allied Dunbar Assurance plc v. Fowle [1994] 1 E.G.L.R. 122; [1994] 2 B.C.L.C.
    197 89
Allied Irish Bank plc v. Byrne [1995] 2 F.L.R. 325; [1995] 1 F.C.R. 430 .... 833, 834
Allsop, *Re* [1914] 1 Ch. 1 650
Alsop Wilkinson v. Neary [1996] 1 W.L.R. 1220 .... 513, 586
Altertext Inc. v. Advanced Data Communications Ltd [1985] 1 W.L.R. 457; (1985)
    F.S.R. 21 806
Aluminium Industrie Vaassen B.V. v. Romalpa Aluminium Ltd [1976] 1 W.L.R. 676;
    120 S.J. 95 .... 46, 596, 663, 664, 681, 682, 684
Amalgamated Investment and Property Co (in Liquidation) v. Texas Commerce Inter-
    national Bank Ltd [1982] Q.B. 84; [1981] 3 W.L.R. 565 .... 882, 883, 884, 892
Amec Properties Ltd v. Planning Research & Systems plc [1992] 1 E.G.L.R. 70 699
American Cyanamid Co. v. Ethicon Ltd [1975] A.C. 396; [1975] 2 W.L.R. 316 746,
                752, 753, 754, 755, 757, 758, 759, 760, 761, 762, 763, 764, 765,
                                                              766, 767, 794, 809
Ames' Settlement, *Re* [1946] Ch. 217 232
Anchor Brewhouse Developments Ltd v. Berkley House (Docklands Developments)
    Ltd [1987] 2 E.G.L.R. 173; (1988) 138 N.L.J. 23 .... 747, 763, 781, 792
Andrabell Ltd, *Re* [1984] 3 All E.R. 407 .... 596, 664, 682, 685
Andrew's Trust, *Re* [1905] 2 Ch. 48 .... 234, 348
Anker-Petersen v. Anker-Petersen (1991) 88/16 L.S. Gaz. 32 .... 526, 530, 567, 616, 620
Ankerson v. Connelly [1907] 1 Ch. 678 792
Ansah v. Ansah [1977] Fam. 138; [1977] 2 W.L.R. 760 .... 739, 752, 801
Anson v. Anson [1953] 1 Q.B. 636; [1953] 1 W.L.R. 573 247
Aquaculture Corporation v. New Zealand Green Mussel Co. Ltd [1990] 3 N.Z.L.R.
    299 24
Anton Piller KG v. Manufacturing Processes [1976] Ch. 55; [1976] 2 W.L.R. 162 32,
                42, 735, 752, 760, 765, 767, 794, 802, 804, 805, 806, 807, 808,
                                                                           809
Appleby v. Cowley, *The Times*, April 14, 1982 .... 292, 596, 882
Arab Monetary Fund v. Hashim [1989] 1 W.L.R. 565 745
—— v. —— (No. 2) [1990] 1 All E.R. 673 .... 809, 815
Arbuthnot Leasing International Ltd v. Havalet Leasing (No. 2) [1990] B.C.C. 636 ... 340
Archbold v. Scully (1861) 9 H.L.C. 360 772
Archer v. Brown [1985] Q.B. 401; [1984] 3 W.L.R. 350 825
Arden, *Re* [1935] Ch. 326 66
Argyll (Duchess) v. Argyll (Duke) [1967] Ch. 302; [1965] 2 W.L.R. 790 .... 26, 735,
                                                                                  744, 775, 795

Armitage, *Re*; Ellam v. Norwich Corporation [1972] Ch. 438; [1972] 2 W.L.R.
    503 .... 451, 445
Armour v. Thyssen Edelstahl-Werke A.G. [1991] 2 A.C. 339; (1991) 141 N.L.J.
    537 681
ARMS (Multiple Sclerosis Research Ltd), *Re*, *The Times*, November 29, 1996 434
Armstrong v. Reeves (1890) 25 L.R.Ir. 325 406
Armstrong v. Sheppard and Short [1959] 2 Q.B. 384; [1959] 3 W.L.R. 84 .... 746, 888
Arning v. James [1936] Ch. 158 587
Arnold's Trusts, *Re*, Wainwright v. Howlett [1947] Ch. 131; [1947] L.J.R. 227 63
Ashburn Anstalt v. Arnold [1989] Ch. 1, C.A. 41, 42, 77, 321, 323, 877, 878, 880, 894
Ashby, *Re* [1892] 1 Q.B. 872 .... 188, 194, 196
Ashby v. Ebdon [1985] Ch. 394; [1985] 2 W.L.R. 279 .... 742, 797
Ashtiani v. Kashi [1987] Q.B. 888 813
Associated Artists Ltd v. I.R.C. [1956] 1 W.L.R. 752; 100 S.J. 450 391
Associated Japanese Bank International Ltd v. Credit du Nord SA [1989] 1 W.L.R. 255;
    [1988] 3 All E.R. 902 .... 819, 823, 824, 825
Astor's Settlement Trusts, *Re*, Astor v. Schofield [1952] Ch. 534; [1952] 1 T.L.R.
    1003 .... 90, 351, 354, 355, 357, 358, 367, 368, 373
Astro Exito Navegacion S.A. v. Southland Enterprise Co. Ltd (No. 2) [1983] 2 A.C.
    787; [1983] 3 W.L.R. 130 .... 696, 712, 766
Atkinson, *Re* [1904] 2 Ch. 160 .... 530, 547
Atkinson's Will Trusts, *Re*; Atkinson v. Hall [1978] 1 W.L.R. 586; (1977) 122 S.J.
    148 .... 351, 428
Atlas Maritime Co. S.A. v. Avalon Maritime Ltd [1991] 4 All E.R. 769; 1 Lloyd's Rep.
    563 815
Attenborough v. Solomon [1913] A.C. 76 .... 54, 55
Att.-Gen. v. Alford (1855) 4 De G.M. & G. 843 .... 637, 639
——— v. Barker [1990] 3 All E.R. 257; *The Independent*, August 24, 1990 .... 755, 763, 784
——— v. Bastow [1957] 1 Q.B. 514; [1957] 2 W.L.R. 340 .... 741, 798
——— v. Blake [1996] 3 W.L.R. 741; (1996) 146 N.L.J. 727 .... 596, 608
——— v. British Broadcasting Corp. [1981] A.C. 303; [1980] 3 W.L.R. 109 .... 760, 793
——— v. Chaudry [1971] 1 W.L.R. 1623; [1971] 1 W.L.R. 1614; 115 S.J. 792 ...... 741, 798
——— v. City of London (1790) 3 Bro. C.C. 121 430
——— v. Cocke [1988] Ch. 414; [1988] 2 W.L.R. 542 .... 379, 651, 655
——— v. Colchester Corporation [1955] 2 Q.B. 207 .... 736, 774
——— v. Colney Hatch Lunatic Asylum (1868) L.R. 4 Ch.App. 146 774
——— v. Dean and Chapter of Ripon Cathedral [1945] Ch. 239 744
——— v. Goddard (1929) 45 T.L.R. 609 597
——— v. Guardian Newspapers [1987] 1 W.L.R. 1248; (1987) 131 S.J. 1122 . 756, 795, 796
——— v. ——— (No. 2) [1990] 1 A.C. 109 .... 24, 596, 753, 756, 770, 795, 796
——— v. Harris [1961] 1 Q.B. 74; [1960] 3 W.L.R. 532 .... 741, 798
——— v. Heywood (1887) 19 Q.B.D. 326 221
——— v. Ironmongers Co. (1834) 2 My. & K. 526 387
——— v. Jacobs-Smith [1895] 2 Q.B. 341 122
——— v. Jonathan Cape [1975] 756, 796
——— v. London and Home Counties Joint Electricity Authority [1929] 1 Ch. 513 804
——— v. London Weekend Television Ltd [1973] 1 W.L.R. 202; (1972) 116 S.J.
    902 804
——— v. Manchester Corporation [1893] 2 Ch. 87 769
——— v. Margaret and Regius Professors in Cambridge (1682) 1 Vern. 55 389
——— v. National Provincial and Union Bank Ltd [1924] A.C. 262 175, 380, 399, 422, 426
——— v. News Group Newspapers [1987] Q.B. 1; [1986] 3 W.L.R. 365 793
——— v. Nottingham Corporation [1904] 1 Ch. 673 .... 737, 770
——— v. P.Y.A. Quarries [1957] 2 Q.B. 169; [1957] 2 W.L.R. 770 797
——— v. Plowden [1931] W.N. 89 406
——— v. Ross [1986] 1 W.L.R. 252; (1985) 130 S.J. 184 394
——— v. Schonfeld [1980] 1 W.L.R. 1182; [1980] 3 All E.R. 1 449
——— v. Sharp [1931] 1 Ch. 121 .... 741, 798

—— v. Smith [1958] 2 Q.B. 173; [1958] 3 W.L.R. 81 798
—— v. The Cordwainers Co. (1833) 3 Myl. & K. 534 53
—— v. Times Newspapers Ltd. [1974] A.C. 273; [1973] 3 W.L.R. 298 804
—— v. ——, *The Times*, June 27, 1975 .... 747, 756
—— v. —— [1992] 1 A.C. 191; [1991] 2 W.L.R. 994 .... 740, 762, 814
—— v. Wilson (1840) Cr. & Ph. 1 642
—— v. Wright [1988] 1 W.L.R. 164; [1987] 3 All E.R. 579 .... 379, 768
Att.-Gen. for the Dominion of Canada v. Ritchie Contracting and Supply Co. Ltd [1919]
    A.C. 999 769
—— for New South Wales v. Sawtell [1978] 2 N.S.W.L.R. 200 406
—— v. Trethowan [1932] A.C. 526 804
—— for Ontario v. Stavro (1994) 119 D.L.R. (4th) 750 550
—— for Tovalu v. Philatelic Distribution Corporation Ltd [1990] 1 W.L.R. 926 739
—— of Hong Kong v. Humphreys Estate (Queen's Gardens) Ltd [1987] A.C. 114;
    [1987] 2 W.L.R. 343 .... 891, 892
—— v. Reid [1994] 1 A.C. 324; [1993] 3 W.L.R. 1143 .... 28, 48, 289, 597, 603, 608,
                                                                                    609, 633, 666, 667, 812
—— of the Bahamas v. Royal Trust Co. [1986] 1 W.L.R. 1001; (1986) 130 S.J.
    526 .... 384, 426
Att.-Gen's Reference (No. 1 of 1985), *Re* [1986] Q.B. 491 .... 607, 608, 609, 643, 667
Austin v. Keele (1987) 61 A.L.J.R. 605 .... 262, 263, 268, 271
Australian Blue Metal Co. v. Hughes [1963] A.C. 74; [1962] 3 W.L.R. 802 869
Australian Hardwoods Pty. Ltd v. Railways Commissioner [1961] 1 W.L.R. 425; 105
    S.J. 176 717
Australian Postal Corporation v. Lutak (1991) 21 N.S.W.L.R. 584 667
Avon Finance v. Bridger [1985] 2 All E.R. 281, C.A. 833
Avondale Printers & Stationers Ltd v. Haggie [1979] 2 N.Z.L.R. 124 324
Ayerst v. Jenkins (1873) L.R. 16 Eq. 275 .... 251, 330, 333
Ayliffe v. Murray (1740) 2 Atk. 58 589

B. v. B. (1976) 65 D.L.R. (3d) 460 248
BICC v. Burndy Corp [1985] Ch. 232; [1985] 2 W.L.R. 132 .... 22, 715
Babanaft International Co. S.A. v. Bassatne [1990] Ch. 13; [1989] 2 W.L.R. 232 809,
                                                                                                                    813
Bacharach's Will Trusts, *Re*, Minden v. Bacharach [1959] Ch. 245; [1959] 2 W.L.R.
    1 .... 840, 845
Backhouse v. Backhouse [1978] 1 W.L.R. 243; [1978] 1 All E.R. 1158 830
Bacon, *Re* [1907] 1 Ch. 475 166
Baden's Deed Trusts, *Re* (No. 2) [1973] Ch. 9; [1972] 3 W.L.R. 250 .... 64, 101, 102,
                                                                                                                    107, 110
Baden, Delvaux and Lecuit v. Société Générale pour Favoriser le Développement du
    Commerce et de l'Industrie en France SA [1983] B.C.L.C. 325 296
Bahin v. Hughes (1886) 31 Ch.D. 390 .... 485, 632, 641, 642
Bailey (A Bankrupt) (No. 25 of 1975), *Re*; Bailey v. Trustee of the Property of the
    Bankrupt [1977] 1 W.L.R. 278; [1977] 2 All E.R. 26, D.C. 282
Baillie, *Re* (1886) 2 T.L.R. 660 .... 159, 162
Baird v. Baird [1990] 2 A.C. 548; [1990] 2 W.L.R. 1412 .... 48, 88
Baird v. Wells (1890) 44 Ch.D. 661 803
Baker, *Re* [1924] 2 Ch. 271 540
Baker v. Archer-Shee [1927] A.C. 844 19
Baker v. Baker [1993] 2 F.L.R. 247; (1994) 144 N.L.J. 264 .... 889, 890
Baker v. Medway Building and Supplies Ltd [1958] 1 W.L.R. 1216 .... 654, 688
Baker v. Monk (1864) 4 De G.J. & S. 388 830
Baker v. Read (1854) 18 Beav. 398 654
Baker's W.T. *Re* (1948) 64 T.L.R. 273 398
Baldry v. Feintuck [1972] 1 W.L.R. 552; (1971) 115 S.J. 965 .... 394, 452
Balfe v. Halfpenny [1904] 1 Ir.R. 486 155
Balfour's Settlement Trust, *Re*, [1938] Ch. 928 190

Ball's Settlement Trusts, *Re* Ball v. Ball [1968] 1 W.L.R. 899; 112 S.J. 445 .... 183, 199, 624
Banco Exterior Internacional v. Mann [1995] 1 All E.R. 936; (1995) 27 H.L.R. 329 .... 835, 836
Banco Exterior Internacional SA v. Thomas [1997] 1 W.L.R. 221 [1997] 1 F.L.R. 156; [1997] 1 All E.R. 46 .... 830, 834
Banfield, *Re*, Lloyd's Bank v. Smith [1968] 1 W.L.R. 846; (1967) 112 S.J. 396; [1968] 2 All E.R. 276 402
Bank Mellat v. Kazmi [1989] Q.B. 541; [1989] 2 W.L.R. 613 .... 740, 814, 815
Bank Mellat v. Nikpour (Mohammad Ebrahim) [1982] Com.L.R. 158; [1985] F.S.R. 87 808
Bank Melli Iran v. Samadi-Rad [1995] 2 F.L.R. 367; [1995] 3 F.C.R. 735 835
Bank of Baroda v. Rayarel [1995] 2 F.L.R. 376; [1995] 27 H.L.R. 387 .... 835, 836
Bank of Credit and Commerce International S.A., *Re* [1994] 1 W.L.R. 708 813
Bank of Montreal v. Stuart [1911] A.C. 120 830
Bank of Nova Scotia v. Hellenic Mutual War Risks Association (Bermuda) Ltd [1992] 1 A.C. 233; [1991] 2 W.L.R. 1279; [1990] 1 Q.B. 818 826
Bank Tejarat v. Hong Kong and Shanghai Banking Corporation (CI) Ltd [1995] 1 Lloyd's Rep. 239, Q.B.D. 661
Bankers Trust Co. v. Shapira [1980] 1 W.L.R. 1274; (1980) 124 S.J. 480 ..... 662, 666, 810
Bankes v. Salisbury Diocesan Council of Education [1960] Ch. 631; [1960] 2 W.L.R. 916 490
Banks v. Ripley [1940] Ch. 719 844
Bannister v. Bannister [1948] 2 All E.R. 133; [1948] W.N. 261 .... 77, 87, 231, 315, 323, 879
Banque Belge pour L'Etranger v. Hambrouck [1921] 1 K.B. 321 .... 659, 660, 664
Banque Keyser Ullman S.A. v. Skandia (U.K.) Insurance Co. Ltd [1990] 1 Q.B. 665; [1989] 3 W.L.R. 25 826
Barber, *Re* (1886) 34 Ch.D. 77 585
Barber v. Guardian Royal Exchange Assurance Group [1991] 1 Q.B. 344; [1991] 2 W.L.R. 72 475
Barbour's Settlement Trusts, *Re*; National Westminster Bank v. Barbour [1974] 1 W.L.R. 1198; (1973) 118 S.J. 681 .... 558, 587, 615
Barclay v. Barclay [1970] 2 Q.B. 677; [1970] 3 W.L.R. 82 274
Barclay-Johnson v. Yuill [1980] 1 W.L.R. 1259 .... 810, 812
Barclays Bank v. Sumner [1996] E.G.C.S. 65 835
—— v. Eustice [1995] 4 All E.R. 511; [1995] 1 W.L.R. 1238 .... 339, 340
—— v. Hendricks [1996] 1 F.L.R. 258 282
—— v. O'Brien [1994] 1 A.C. 180 .... 37, 38, 832, 833, 834, 835, 836
—— v. Quistclose Investments Ltd [1970] A.C. 567; [1968] 3 W.L.R. 1097 ..... 42, 50, 51, 52, 230
—— v. Quincecare Ltd [1992] 4 All E.R. 363 300
—— v. Schwartz, *The Times*, August 2, 1995, C.A. 837
—— v. Simms (W.J.) Son and Cooke (Southern) Ltd [1980] Q.B. 677; [1980] 2 W.L.R. 218 823
—— v. Thomson [1997] 1 F.L.R. 156 836
—— v. Willowbrook International Ltd [1987] 1 F.T.L.R. 386; [1987] BCLC 717, C.A. 49, 53, 124
Baring's Settlement Trust, *Re* [1940] Ch. 737 190
Barlow v. Grant (1684) 1 Vern. 255 .... 234, 583
Barlow's Will Trusts, *Re*; Royal Exchange Assurance v. National Council of Social Service [1979] 1 W.L.R. 278; (1978) 122 S.J. 646 .... 90, 102, 104, 109, 328
Barlow Clowes International Ltd v. Vaughan [1992] 4 All E.R. 22; [1992] BCLC 910, C.A. 673
Barnado's (Dr) Homes v. Income Tax Special Commissioners [1920] 1 K.B. 468 57
Barnes v. Addy (1874) L.R. 9 Ch.App. 244 .... 293, 294, 295, 604
Barney, *Re* [1892] 2 Ch. 265 288
Barnhart v. Greenshields (1853) 9 Moo. P.C. 18 34
Barret v. Beckford (1750) 1 Ves. Sen. 519 860
Barrowcliff, *Re* [1927] S.A.S.R. 147 316

Barrs v. Bethell [1982] Ch. 294; (1982) 80 L.G.R. 269 .... 741, 797
Bartlett v. Barclays Bank Trust Co. Ltd (No. 1) [1980] Ch. 515; [1980] 2 W.L.R.
 430 .... 482, 521, 527, 540, 633, 639, 640, 649, 650, 654
Barton v. Armstrong [1976] A.C. 104 828
Basham, *Re* [1986] 1 W.L.R. 1498 .... 320, 881, 886, 892, 894, 895
Bateman's Will Trusts, *Re*, Brierley v. Perry [1970] 1 W.L.R. 1463; 114 S.J. 707 155
Bates, *Re* [1928] Ch. 682 547
Bates v. Lord Hailsham of St. Marylebone [1972] 1 W.L.R. 1373; 116 S.J. 584 751,
 771, 804
Bates (Thomas) & Son Ltd v. Wyndham's (Lingerie) Ltd [1981] 1 W.L.R. 505; (1980)
 125 S.J. 32 .... 843, 844
Bath and Montague's Case (1693) 3 Ch. Cas. 84 173
Baumgartner v. Baumgartner (1988) 62 A.L.J. 29 .... 268, 324
Baxter v. Connolly (1820) 1 J. & W. 576 730
Baxter v. Four Oaks Properties Ltd [1965] Ch. 816; [1965] 2 W.L.R. 1115 .... 776, 783
Bayer A.G. v. Winter [1986] 1 W.L.R. 497; (1985) 130 S.J. 246 745
—— v. —— (No. 2) [1986] 1 W.L.R. 540; (1985) 130 S.J. 373 745
Beale v. Kyte [1907] 1 Ch. 564 845
Beale's Settlement Trust, *Re* [1932] 2 Ch. 15 616
Beaman v. A.R.T.S. [1949] 1 K.B. 550; 65 T.L.R. 389 654
Beaney, decd., *Re*; Beaney v. Beaney [1978] 1 W.L.R. 770; (1977) 121 S.J. 832 74
Beard, *Re* [1908] 1 Ch. 383 .... 333, 334
Beatty v. Guggenheim Exploration Co. 225 N.Y. 380 .... 286, 318
Beatty's Will Trusts, *Re* [1990] 1 W.L.R. 1503; [1991] Conv. 138 .... 105, 168, 175,
 353, 586
Beaumont, *Re* [1902] 1 Ch. 886 140
Beaverbrook Newspapers Ltd v. Keys [1978] I.R.L.R. 34; [1978] I.C.R. 582 761
Beckett's Settlement, *Re* [1940] Ch. 279 .... 583, 611
Beddoe, *Re*; Downes v. Cottam [1893] 1 Ch. 547 513
Beddow v. Beddow (1878) 9 Ch.D. 89 .... 734, 744
Beesly's Will Trust, *Re*, [1966] Ch. 223 166
Begg-McBrearty (Inspector of Taxes) v. Stilwell [1996] 1 W.L.R. 951 571
Behbehani v. Salem [1989] 1 W.L.R. 723; [1989] 2 All E.R. 143, C.A. 807, 810
Behnke v. Bede Shipping Co. [1927] 1 K.B. 649 702
Behrens v. Richards [1905] 2 Ch. 614 .... 747, 792
Bekhor (A.J.) & Co. Ltd v. Bilton [1981] Q.B. 923 .... 810, 812
Belchier, *ex p.* (1754) Amb. 218 560
Bell v. Lever Bros. [1932] A.C. 161 .... 819, 821, 823, 825
Bell Concord Educational Trust Ltd v. Customs and Excise Commissioners [1989]
 S.T.C. 264; [1989] 1 C.M.L.R. 845 382
Bell's Indenture, *Re*; Bell v. Hickley [1980] 1 W.L.R. 1217; (1979) 123 S.J. 322; [1980]
 3 All E.R. 425 .... 297, 304, 305, 634, 637
Belmont Finance Corporation v. Williams Furniture Ltd (No. 1) [1979] Ch. 250 299
—— v. —— (No. 2) [1980] 1 All E.R. 393 .... 299, 638, 639, 651
Beloved Wilkes' Charity (1851) 3 Mac. & G. 440 .... 197, 505
Bendall v. McWhirter [1952] 2 Q.B. 466; [1952] 1 T.L.R. 1332 877
Benjamin, *Re* [1902] 1 Ch. 723 .... 534, 687
Bennett, *Re*, Sucker v. Att.-Gen. [1960] Ch. 18; [1959] 3 W.L.R. 427 .... 379, 425
Bennett v. Bennett (1879) 10 Ch.D. 474 249
Bentley v. Bishop of Ely (1729) 1 Barn. 192 446
Bentley-Stevens v. Jones [1974] 1 W.L.R. 638; 118 S.J. 345 753
Beresford v. Royal Insurance Co. [1938] A.C. 586 .... 315, 316
Berger (dec'd), *Re*; *sub nom.* Englander v. Berger [1990] Ch. 118; [1989] 2 W.L.R.
 147 145
Berkeley Applegate (Investment Consultants) Ltd, *Re* [1989] Ch. 32; [1989] BCLC
 28 588
Berkeley Leisure Group Ltd v. Williamson [1996] E.G.C.S. 15 845
Berkley v. Poulett (1976) 120 S.J. 836 .... 700, 728
—— v. —— (1977) 242 E.G. 39 .... 313, 314

Bernard v. Josephs [1982] Ch. 391; [1982] 2 W.L.R. 1052 .... 247, 262, 269, 270, 271
Berry, *Re*, Lloyds Bank v. Berry [1962] Ch. 97; [1961] 2 W.L.R. 329 .... 540, 541, 543
Berry v. Berry [1929] 2 K.B. 316 15
—— v. Green [1938] A.C. 575 611
—— v. St Marylebone B.C. [1958] Ch. 406; [1957] 3 W.L.R. 1029 395
Bersel Manufacturing Co. Ltd v. Berry [1968] 2 All E.R. 552; H.L. 166, 494
Besant v. Wood (1879) 12 Ch.D. 605 775
Best *Re* [1904] 2 Ch. 354 426
Bestobell Paints Ltd v. Bigg (1975) 119 S.J. 678; [1975] F.S.R. 421 .... 760, 794
Beswick v. Beswick [1968] A.C. 58; [1967] 3 W.L.R. 932 .... 123, 125, 128, 130, 131,
                          132, 307, 694, 703, 704, 709, 712, 729, 730, 731, 732, 874
Bethell v. Abraham (1873) L.R. 17 Eq. 24 517
Bevan v. Webb [1905] 1 Ch. 620 593
Beyfus v. Lawley [1903] A.C. 411 711
Bhimji v. Chatwani [1991] 1 W.L.R. 989; [1991] 1 All E.R. 705 .... 806, 807
Biggin v. Minton [1977] 1 W.L.R. 701; (1976) 121 S.J. 254 698
Bignold's Settlement Trust, *Re* (1872) L.R. 7 Ch.App. 223 497
Bilston Corporation v. Wolverhampton Corporation [1942] Ch. 391 804
Binions v. Evans [1972] Ch. 359; [1972] 2 W.L.R. 729 .... 69, 77, 78, 231, 315,
                                                      320, 321, 323, 879, 881
Birch v. Treasury Solicitor [1951] Ch. 298; [1951] 1 T.L.R. 225 138
Bird v. Luckie (1850) 8 Hare 301 106
Birmingham v. Renfrew (1937) 57 C.L.R. 666 .... 161, 310
Biscoe v. Jackson (1887) 35 Ch.D. 460 .... 387, 422, 435
Bishop, *Re*, National Provincial Bank v. Bishop [1965] Ch. 450; [1965] 2 W.L.R.
  188 248
Bishopsgate Investment Management v. Homan [1995] 1 W.L.R. 31 (Pet. dis.), H.L.
  [1995] Ch. 211 .... 669, 672
—— v. Maxwell (No. 2) [1994] 1 All E.R. 261; [1993] BCLC 1282 .... 641, 664
Biss, *Re* [1903] 2 Ch. 40 .... 292, 592
Black v. Homersham (1878) 4 Ex.D. 24 117
—— v. S. Freedman & Co. (1910) 12 C.L.R. 105 664
Blackett v. Bates (1865) L.R. 1 Ch.App. 117 704
Blacklocks v. J. B. Developments (Godalming) Ltd [1982] Ch. 183; [1981] 3 W.L.R.
  554 845
Blackwell v. Blackwell [1929] A.C. 318 .... 148, 153, 154, 158, 159
Blair v. Duncan [1902] A.C. 37 .... 351, 425
Blandy v. Widmore (1716) 1 P. Wms. 323 864
Blathwayt v. Lord Cawley [1976] A.C. 397; [1975] 3 W.L.R. 684 .... 90, 328, 330,
                                                                331, 332
Blausten v. I.R.C. [1972] Ch. 256; [1972] 2 W.L.R. 376 .... 105, 180, 181, 182, 199
Bloxham v. Metropolitan Ry. (1868) L.R. 3 Ch.App. 337 756
Blue Town Investments Ltd v. Higgs & Hill plc [1990] 1 W.L.R. 696 .... 768, 774
Blundell, *Re* [1906] 2 Ch. 222 862
Blyth v. Fladgate [1891] 1 Ch. 337 304
Boardman v. Phipps [1967] 2 A.C. 46; [1966] 3 W.L.R. 1009 .... 68, 289, 292, 293, 480,
                          587, 588, 589, 593, 596, 599, 601, 603, 604, 605, 606, 607, 608,
                                                                609, 676
Boe v. Alexander (1988) 41 D.L.R. (4th) 520 509
Boles and British Land Co.'s Contract, *Re* [1902] 1 Ch. 244 590
Bolivinter Oil S.A. v. Chase Manhattan Bank [1984] 1 W.L.R. 392; (1984) 128 S.J.
  153 752
Bolton v. Curre [1895] 1 Ch. 544 .... 647, 648
Bonar Law Memorial Trust v. I.R.C. (1933) 49 T.L.R. 220 .... 393, 407
Bond Worth Ltd, *Re* [1980] Ch. 228; [1979] 3 W.L.R. 629 .... 682, 683
Bonhote v. Henderson [1895] 1 Ch. 742; [1895] 2 Ch. 202 845
Bonnard v. Perryman [1891] 2 Ch. 269 .... 760, 793, 794
Bonsor v. Musician's Union [1956] A.C. 104; [1955] 3 W.L.R. 788 802
Booker v. Palmer [1942] 2 All E.R. 674 .... 701, 874

Booth, *Re* [1906] 2 Ch. 321 858
Booth v. Booth (1838) 1 Beav. 125 647
Boots The Chemist Ltd v. Street (1983) 268 E.G. 817 .... 840, 845
Borden U.K. v. Scottish Timber Products Ltd [1981] Ch. 25; [1979] 3 W.L.R. 672 ... 684
Borrowman v. Rossell (1864) 16 C.B. (N.S.) 58 846
Borwick, *Re* [1933] Ch. 657 330
Boscawen v. Bajwa [1996] 1 W.L.R. 328 .... 663, 675, 677, 680
Bosomworth v. Faber (1995) 69 P. & C.R. 288 781
Bostock's Settlement, *Re* [1921] 2 Ch. 469 66
Bouch v. Sproule (1887) 12 App.Cas. 385 547
Boulter, *Re* [1922] 1 Ch. 75 330
Boulton's Settlement Trusts, *Re* [1928] Ch. 703 .... 176, 581
Bourne v. Keane [1919] A.C. 815 .... 356, 419
Boustany v. Piggott (1995) 69 P. & C.R. 298 836
Bowden, *Re* (1890) 45 Ch.D. 444 652
——, *Re* [1936] Ch. 71 .... 116, 134
Bowen, *Re* [1893] 2 Ch. 491 380
Bower v. Bantam Investments Ltd [1972] 1 W.L.R. 1120; 116 S.J. 633 .... 748, 785, 786
Bowes, *Re* [1896] 1 Ch. 507 356
Bowman v. Secular Society [1917] A.C. 406 .... 326, 337, 393, 395
Boyce v. Boyce (1849) 16 Sim. 476 93
Boyer v. Warbey [1953] 1 Q.B. 234; [1952] 2 T.L.R. 882 22
Boyes, *Re* (1884) 26 Ch.D. 531 .... 147, 149, 150, 241
Boyes v. Cook (1880) 14 Ch.D. 53 172
Brace, *Re*, Gurton v. Clements [1954] 1 W.L.R. 955; 98 S.J. 456 52
Bracewell v. Appleby [1975] Ch. 408; [1975] 2 W.L.R. 282 .... 772, 781
Bradshaw, *Re* [1902] 1 Ch. 436 174
Bradshaw v. Huish (1889) 43 Ch.D. 260 860
Bradstock Trustee Services Ltd v. Nabarro Nathanson (a firm) [1995] 1 W.L.R. 1405;
    [1995] 4 All E.R. 888, Ch.D. 19, 513, 586
Braithwaite, *Re* (1882) 21 Ch. D. 121 517
Bramblevale Ltd, *Re* [1970] Ch. 128; [1969] 3 W.L.R. 739
Brandon v. Robinson (1811) 18 Ves. Jr. 429 186
Bray v. Ford [1896] A.C. 44 596
Breadalbane v. Chandos (1837) 2 My. & Cr. 711 841
Breed's Will, *Re* (1875) 1 Ch. D. 226 577
Breen v. A.E.U. [1971] 2 Q.B. 175; [1971] 2 W.L.R. 742 802
Bremer Vulkan Schiffbau und Maschinenfabrik v. South India Shipping Corp. [1981]
    A.C. 909; [1981] 2 W.L.R. 141 .... 734, 744
Brennan v. Morphett (1908) 6 C.L.R. 22 135
Brenner v. Rose [1973] 1 W.L.R. 443; (1972) 117 S.J. 245 592
Brewer v. Brewer [1989] 2 F.L.R. 251; [1989] Fam. Law 352 739
Brewer's Settlement, *Re* [1896] 2 Ch. 503 .... 187, 190
Brice v. Stokes (1805) 11 Ves. Jr. 319 565
Bridge v. Campbell Discount Co. Ltd [1962] A.C. 600; [1962] 2 W.L.R. 439 4
Bridges v. Mees [1957] Ch. 475; [1957] 3 W.L.R. 215 313
Brier, *Re* (1884) 26 Ch.D. 238 .... 560, 564
Brierly, *Re* (1894) 43 W.R. 36 63
Brimican Investments Ltd v. Blue Circle Heating Ltd [1995] E.G.C.S. 18; [1995] N.P.C.
    18, Ch. D. 844
Brine and Davies' Contract, *Re* [1935] Ch. 388 722
Brinks Ltd v. Abu-Saleh [1995] 1 W.L.R. 1478; [1995] 4 All E.R. 65 667
—— v. —— (No. 3), *The Times*, October 23, 1995, Ch.D 295
Brink's MAT Ltd v. Elcombe [1988] 1 W.L.R. 1350; (1988) 132 S.J. 1555 810
Brinnand v. Ewens (1987) 19 H.L.R. 415; (1987) 284 E.G. 1052, C.A. 891
Brisbane City Council v. Att.-Gen. for Queensland [1979] A.C. 411; [1978] 3 W.L.R.
    299 .... 399, 410
Bristol and West Building Society v. Henning [1985] 1 W.L.R. 778; (1985) 129 S.J.
    363 .... 34, 37, 266, 279
—— v. May May & Merrimans [1996] 2 All E.R. 801 .... 635, 636
—— v. Mothew [1996] 4 All E.R. 698 .... 636, 663

Bristol's Settled Estates, *Re*, Bristol v. Jermyn [1965] 1 W.L.R. 469; 109 S.J. 236;
[1964] 3 All E.R. 939 617
Bristow v. Warde (1794) 2 Ves. Jr. 336 857
Britannia Building Society v. Pugh [1996] E.G.C.S. 128 834
British Airways Board v. Laker Airways Ltd [1985] A.C. 58; [1984] 3 W.L.R.
413 744
British Broadcasting Corporation v. Hearn [1977] 1 W.L.R. 1004; (1977) 121 S.J.
374 .... 747, 755, 756, 761
British Coal Corp. v. British Coal Staff Superannuation Scheme Trustees Ltd [1995] 1
All E.R. 912; [1994] I.C.R. 537 .... 182, 459, 463, 595
British Data Management plc v. Boxer Commercial Removal plc [1996] 3 All E.R.
707 770
British Museum Trustees v. White (1826) 2 Sm. & St. 594 388
British Red Cross Balkan Fund, *Re* [1914] 2 Ch. 419 .... 236, 437, 673
British School of Egyptian Archaeology, *Re* [1954] 1 W.L.R. 546; 98 S.J. 216 .... 388, 390
Brockbank, *Re* [1948] Ch. 206; [1948] L.J.R. 952 .... 166, 494, 496, 509
Brocklehurst, *Re* [1978] Ch. 14 .... 829, 830, 831
Brogden, *Re* (1888) 38 Ch. D. 546 .... 512, 513
——, *Re* [1948] Ch. 206 559
Bromage v. Genning (1617) 1 Rolle 368 12
Brooke Bond and Co. Ltd's Trust Deed, *Re* [1963] Ch. 357; [1963] 2 W.L.R. 320 489
Brooker, *Re* [1926] W.N. 93 543
Brooks v. Brooks [1996] 1 A.C. 375 .... 457, 459, 474, 476, 618
—— v. Muckleston [1909] 2 Ch. 519 772
Brooks Settlement Trusts, *Re* [1939] Ch. 993 .... 134, 167, 176, 177, 206, 625
Brotherton v. I.R.C. [1978] 1 W.L.R. 610; (1977) 122 S.J. 164 .... 572, 573, 579
Brown, *Re*, District Bank v. Brown [1954] Ch. 39; [1953] 3 W.L.R. 877 .... 186, 332
—— v. Burdert (1882) 21 Ch.D. 667 .... 326, 369
—— v. Gellatly (1867) L.R. 2 Ch.App. 751 .... 541, 543
—— v. Higgs (1803) 8 Ves. 561 59
—— v. I.R.C. [1965] A.C. 244; [1964] 3 W.L.R. 511 .... 594, 596, 597
—— v. Pourau [1995] 1 N.Z.L.R. 352 .... 149, 159, 162
—— v. Smith (1878) 10 Ch.D. 377 632
Brown's Settlement, *Re* [1939] Ch. 944 183
Brown & Root Technology Ltd v. Sun Alliance and London Assurance Co. Ltd [1996]
Ch. 51 119
Browne, *Re* [1944] Ir.R. 90 155
Browne v. Browne [1989] 1 F.L.R. 291; [1989] Fam. Law 147, C.A. 204
Broxtowe Borough Council v. Birch [1983] 1 W.L.R. 314; [1983] 1 All E.R. 641 382,
396
Bryanston Finance Ltd v. de Vries (No. 2) [1976] Ch. 63; [1976] 2 W.L.R. 41 759,
763, 793, 803
Buchanan-Wollaston's Conveyance, *Re* [1939] Ch. 738 281
Buck, *Re* [1896] 2 Ch. 727 413
Buckinghamshire Constabulary Widows' and Orphans' Fund Friendly Society (No. 2),
Re, [1979] 1 W.L.R. 936; (1978) 122 S.J. 557 .... 235, 236, 237, 238, 240,
360, 364, 645, 648
Budge, *Re* [1942] N.Z.L.R. 356 366
Bulkeley v. Stephens [1896] 2 Ch. 241 547
Bulkley v. Wilford (1834) 2 Cl. & F. 102 147
Bull v. Bull [1955] 1 Q.B. 234; [1955] 2 W.L.R. 78 .... 264, 274
—— v. Mannin (1829) 3 Bli. (N.S.) 1 74
Bullivant (Roger) Ltd v. Ellis [1987] 1 C.R. 464; [1987] I.R.L.R. 491 795
Bullock, *Re* (1891) 64 L.T. 736 .... 194, 196
Bullock v. Lloyd's Bank [1955] Ch. 317; [1955] 2 W.L.R. 1 .... 829, 831
Bulmer H.P. Ltd & Showerings Ltd v. Bollinger J., S.A. [1977] 2 C.M.L.R. 625; [1978]
F.S.R. 79, C.A. 29, 772, 773, 774
Bunn v. Markham (1816) 7 Taunt. 224 140
Burdick v. Garrick (1870) 5 Ch.App. 233 .... 638, 651
Burgess v. Burgess [1996] 2 F.L.R. 34 805
—— v. Rawnsley [1975] Ch. 429; [1975] 3 W.L.R. 99 .... 28, 232

—— v. Wheate (1757–59) 1 Eden 177 486

Burney v. MacDonald (1845) 15 Sim. 6 152

Burney's Settlement Trusts, *Re* [1961] 1 W.L.R. 545; 105 S.J. 207; [1961] 1 All E.R.
  856 .... 619, 625

Burns v. Burns [1984] Ch. 317; [1984] 2 W.L.R. 582 ...... 68, 261, 262, 266, 270, 271, 319

Burrell v. Burrell's Trustees 1915 S.C. 33 590

Burris v. Azadani [1995] 1 W.L.R. 1372; [1995] 4 All E.R. 802 .... 745, 791, 801

Burrough v. Philcox (1840) 5 Myl. & Cr. 72 .... 62, 63, 93, 109, 205

Burroughes v. Abbott [1922] 1 Ch. 86 842

Burroughs-Fowler, *Re* [1916] 2 Ch. 251 187

Burrows v. Sharp (1991) 23 H.L.R. 82 890

Burton v. Winters [1993] 1 W.L.R. 1077; [1993] 3 All E.R. 847, C.A. 792

Burton's Settlements, *Re*, Scott v. National Provincial Bank [1955] Ch. 82; [1954] 3
  W.L.R. 581 .... 134, 179

Bushnell (dec'd), *Re*; Lloyds Bank v. Murray [1975] 1 W.L.R. 1596; (1974) 119 S.J.
  189 .... 393, 407

Butler v. Broadhead [1975] Ch. 97; [1974] 3 W.L.R. 27 688

—— v. Sheffield and Manchester Rly. Co. (1888) 21 Q.B.D. 207 871

Butlin's Settlement Trusts, *Re*; Butlin v. Butlin [1976] 251; [1976] 2 W.L.R. 547 486,
  841, 845, 846

Butlin-Sanders v. Butlin (1985) 15 Fam. Law 126 837

Butt v. Kelsen [1952] Ch. 197; *sub nom.*, *Re*, Butt, Butt v. Kelson [1962] W.N. 34;
  [1952] 1 T.L.R. 214 .... 118, 506

Butterworth, *Re*, *ex p.* Russell (1882) 19 Ch.D. 588 .... 338, 340

Buttle v. Saunders [1950] 2 All E.R. 193 .... 513, 557, 791

Button v. Button [1968] 1 W.L.R. 457; 112 S.J. 112; [1968] 1 All E.R. 1064 264

Buxton v. Buxton (1835) 1 My. & Cr. 80 512

Byrchall v. Bradford (1822) 6 Madd. 235 637

Byron's Settlement, *Re* [1891] 3 Ch. 474 .... 102, 109, 168, 172

C., *Re* [1960] 1 W.L.R. 92; 104 S.J. 129 75

C. (A Minor) (Wardship: Jurisdiction), *Re* [1991] 2 F.L.R. 168; [1991] Fam. Law
  525 .... 747, 801

C. (a patient) *Re* [1991] 3 All E.R. 866; [1992] 1 F.L.R. 51 75

C. (Adult: Refusal of Treatment) *Re* [1994] 1 W.L.R. 290; [1994] 1 All E.R. 819 740,
  745

C.E.F.D., *Re* [1963] 1 W.L.R. 329; 107 S.J. 217 75

C.L., *Re* [1969] 1 Ch. 587; [1968] 2 W.L.R. 1275 628

C.W.M., 1941, No. 2396, *Re* [1951] 2 K.B. 714; [1951] 2 All E.R. 707 75

C. v. S. [1988] Q.B. 135; [1987] 2 W.L.R. 1108 744

CBS Songs Ltd v. Amstrad Consumer Electronics plc [1988] A.C. 1013; [1988] 2
  W.L.R. 1191 .... 741, 797

CBS United Kingdom Ltd v. Lambert [1983] Ch. 37; [1982] 3 W.L.R. 746 .... 806, 810

CIBC Mortgages plc v. Pitt [1994] 1 A.C. 200; [1993] 3 W.L.R. 802 .... 832, 834, 836

C.N. Marine Inc. v. Stena Line A/B, *The Times*, June 12, 1982 702

Caborne, *Re* [1943] Ch. 224 330

Cadman v. Bell [1988] E.G.C.S. 139 270

Cadogan v. Cadogan [1977] 1 W.L.R. 1041; [1977] 3 All E.R. 831 .... 341, 346

Caffoor v. Income Tax Commissioner, Colombo [1961] A.C. 584; [1961] 2 W.L.R.
  794 417

Cain v. Moon [1896] 2 Q.B. 283 137

Caird v. Moss (1886) 33 Ch.D. 22 846

Caldy Manor Estate Ltd v. Farrell [1974] 1 W.L.R. 1303; 118 S.J. 681 332

Callaghan v. Callaghan (1841) 8 Cl. & F. 374 720

Calow, *Re* [1928] Ch. 710 851

Campbell Discount Co. Ltd v. Bridge [1961] 1 Q.B. 445; [1961] 2 W.L.R. 596 4

Cambridge Nutrition Ltd v. British Broadcasting Corporation [1990] 3 All E.R. 523,
  C.A. 754, 755, 758, 762

Camilla M. (The) [1979] 1 Lloyd's Rep. 26; (1979) 42 M.L.R. 458 761

Camille and Henry Dreyfus Foundation Inc. v. I.R.C. *See* Dreyfus (Camille and Henry) Foundation Inc. v. IRC.
Campbell v. Walker (1800) 5 Ves. Jr. 678 589
Canada Trust Company v. Ontario Human Rights Commission (1990) 69 D.L.R. (4th) 321 .... 327, 331, 430
Canadian Aero Service Ltd v. O'Malley (1973) 40 D.L.R. (3d) 371 (S.C.C.) 599
Canadian Pacific Ry. Co. v. R. [1931] A.C. 414 869
Canning v. Temby (1905) 3 C.L.R. 419 718
Cannon v. Hartley [1949] Ch. 213; [1949] L.J.R. 370 .... 29, 123, 126, 131, 133, 704
Canson Enterprises Ltd v. Boughton (1991) 85 D.L.R. (4th) 129 .... 21, 24, 634
Carew's Trusts, *Re* (1910) 103 L.T. 658 193
Carl Zeiss Stiftung v. Smith (Herbert) & Co. (No. 2) [1969] 2 Ch. 276; [1969] 2 W.L.R. 427 .... 285, 290, 294
Carly v. Farrelly [1975] 1 N.Z.L.R. 356 324
Carne v. Long (1860) 2 De G.F. & J. 75 .... 360, 362
Carpenters Estates v. Davies [1940] Ch. 160 707
Carr-Saunders v. Dick McNeill Associates Ltd [1986] 1 W.L.R. 922 781
Carreras Rothmans Ltd v. Freeman Mathews Treasure Ltd [1985] Ch. 207; [1984] 3 W.L.R. 1016 .... 48, 50, 230
Carrington, *Re* [1932] 1 Ch. 1 851
Carruthers v. Carruthers [1896] A.C. 659 565
Carter v. Carter (1857) 3 K. & J. 617 34
Carver v. Bowles (1831) 2 R. & M. 301 855
Carver v. Duncan (Inspector of Taxes) [1985] A.C. 1082; [1985] 2 W.L.R. 1010 214
Cash, *Re* (1911) 30 N.Z.L.R. 571 315
Cassel v. Inglis [1916] 2 Ch. 211 803
Casson v. University of Aston in Birmingham [1983] 1 All E.R. 88 446
Castle v. Wilkinson (1870) L.R. 5 Ch. 534 722
Castle Phillips Finance v. Piddington (1995) 70 P. & C.R. 592; [1995] 1 F.L.R. 783 .... 675, 835
Catt v. Marac Australia Ltd (1986) 9 N.S.W.L.R. 639 24
Catt v. Tourle (1869) 785
Caunce v. Caunce [1969] 1 W.L.R. 286; (1968) 113 S.J. 204 277
Cavalier v. Cavalier (1971) 19 F.L.R. 199 (S.C.N.S.W.) 246
Cavendish-Browne's Settlement Trusts [1916] W.N. 341; (1916) 61 S.J. 27 .... 125, 126, 127
Caws, *Re* [1934] Ch. 162 356
Cayne v. Global Natural Resources plc [1984] 1 All E.R. 225, C.A. 755, 761, 762
Cedar Holdings Ltd v. Green [1981] Ch. 129 at p. 147 .... 720, 721
Celsteel Ltd v. Alton House Holdings Ltd [1986] 1 W.L.R. 512 769
Central & Metropolitan Estates Ltd v. Compusave (1983) 266 E.G. 900 .... 840, 843
Central London Property Trust Ltd v. High Trees House Ltd [1947] K.B. 130; [1956] 1 All E.R. 256 .... 884, 885
Chadwick's Trusts, *Re* [1939] 1 All E.R. 850 178
Chaine-Nickson v. Bank of Ireland [1976] I.R. 393 548
Chalinder & Herington, *Re* [1907] 1 Ch. 58 586
Chalmers v. Pardoe [1963] 1 W.L.R. 677; 107 S.J. 435 889
Chamberlain, *Re* (unreported) 623
Chamberlaine v. Chamberlaine (1678) Free. Ch. 34 147
Chan v. Zacharia (1984) 154 C.L.R. 178, High Ct. of Australia 591, 604
Chance's Will Trusts, *Re*, Westminster Bank v. Chance [1962] Ch. 593; [1962] 1 W.L.R. 409 541
Chancellor, Masters and Scholars of the University of Oxford v. Permagon Press (1977) 121 S.J. 758; *The Times*, October 19, 1977, C.A. 756, 757
Chandler v. Kerley [1978] 1 W.L.R. 693 875
Channel Tunnel Group Ltd v. Balfour Beatty Construction Ltd [1993] A.C. 334; [1993] 1 Lloyd's Rep. 291 .... 734, 739, 766, 811
Chaplin, *Re* [1933] Ch. 115 402

Chapman, *Re* [1896] 2 Ch. 763 (1895) 72 L.T. 66 .... 481, 513, 526, 530, 560, 637
Chapman v. Brown (1801) 6 Ves. 404 .... 333, 522, 528
—— v. Chapman [1954] A.C. 429; [1954] 2 W.L.R. 723 .... 613, 614
—— v. Gibson (1791) 3 Bro. C.C. 229 173
—— v. Michaelson [1909] 1 Ch. 238 31
Chapman's Settlement Trusts, *Re. See* Chapman v. Chapman 614
Chappell v. Times Newspapers Ltd [1975] 1 W.L.R. 482; [1975] I.C.R. 145 26,
    709, 775, 790
Chardon, *Re* [1928] Ch. 464 .... 371, 611
Charrington v. Simons & Co. Ltd [1971] 1 W.L.R. 598; 115 S.J. 265 .... 747, 748, 750,
    774, 784
Chartered Bank v. Daklouche [1980] 1 W.L.R. 107 .... 752, 812
Chartered Insurance Institute v. London Corporation [1957] 1 W.L.R. 867; 121 J.P.
    482 393
Charteris, *Re* (1917) 2 Ch. 379 56
Chase Manhattan Bank NA v. Israel-British Bank (London) Ltd [1981] Ch. 105; [1980]
    2 W.L.R. 202 665
Chattey v. Farndale Holdings Inc. [1997] 06 E.G. 152 881
Chaytor, *Re* [1905] 1 Ch. 233 543
Cheadle, *Re* [1900] 2 Ch. 620 95
Cheese v. Thomas [1994] 1 W.L.R. 129; [1994] 1 All E.R. 35 .... 26, 829, 832, 839
Chelsea Cloisters, *Re* (1981) 41 P. & C.R. 98, C.A. 51, 120
Chelsea (Viscount) v. Muscatt [1990] 2 E.G.L.R. 48 784
Cheltenham and Gloucester Building Society v. Ricketts [1993] 1 W.L.R. 1545; [1993]
    4 All E.R. 276 768
Chettiar v. Chettiar [1962] A.C. 294 251
Chetwynd's Settlement, *Re* [1902] 1 Ch. 692 503
Chichester v. Coventry (1867) L.R. 2 H.L. 71 859
Chichester Diocesan Fund and Board of Finance v. Simpson [1944] A.C. 341 .... 232, 351,
    425, 428, 662
Chick v. Commissioner of Stamp Duties of New South Wales [1958] A.C. 435; [1958]
    3 W.L.R. 93 221
Chief Constable of Hampshire v. A. Ltd [1985] Q.B. 132; [1984] 2 W.L.R. 954 743
Chief Constable of Kent v. V. [1983] Q.B. 34; [1982] 3 W.L.R. 462 .... 20, 664,
    735, 741, 743
Chief Constable of Leicestershire v. M. [1989] 1 W.L.R. 20 743
Chillingworth v. Chambers [1896] 1 Ch. 685 .... 633, 643, 647
China and South Sea Bank Ltd v. Tan Soon Gin [1990] 1 A.C. 536; [1990] 2 W.L.R.
    56 21
Chinn v. Collins [1981] A.C. 533; [1981] 2 W.L.R. 14 86
Chitty's Will Trusts, *Re*, Ransferd v. Lloyd's Bank [1970] Ch. 254; [1969] 3 W.L.R.
    643 428
Chohan v. Saggar [1992] B.C.C. 306; [1991] N.P.C. 111 340
Cholmondeley v. I.R.C. [1986] S.T.C. 384; (1986) 83 L.S.Gaz. 2243 228
Chrimes, *Re* [1917] 1 Ch. 30 114
Christ's College, Cambridge, case of (1757) 1 Wm. Bl. 90 389
Christ's Hospital (Governors) v. Grainger (1849) 1 Mac & G. 460 .... 370, 380, 381
Christchurch Inclosure Act, *Re* (1888) 38 Ch.D. 520 422
Christie-Miller's Marriage Settlement, *Re*; Westminster Bank v. Christie-Miller [1961]
    1 W.L.R. 462; 105 S.J. 256 .... 181, 183, 622, 624
Christophers v. White (1847) 10 Beav. 523 589
Churchill, *Re* [1909] 2 Ch. 431 575
Churchill v. Churchill (1867) L.R. 5 Eq. 44 .... 176, 855
Cigna Life Insurance NZ v. Westpac Securities Ltd [1996] 1 N.Z.L.R. 80 302
Citro, Domenico (A Bankrupt), *Re*; Citro, Carmine (A Bankrupt), *Re* [1991] Ch. 142;
    [1990] 3 W.L.R. 880 .... 282, 283
City Equitable Fire Insurance Co., *Re* [1925] 1 Ch. 407 564
City of London Building Society v. Flegg [1988] A.C. 54; [1987] 2 W.L.R. 1266 36,
    261, 274, 276
City of London Corporation v. Bovis Construction Ltd [1992] 3 All E.R. 697; 49 BLR
    1 799

Cityland and Property (Holdings) Ltd v. Dabrah [1968] Ch. 166; [1967] 3 W.L.R.
605 837
Civilian War Claimants Association Ltd v. R. [1932] A.C. 14 .... 70, 486, 487
Clack v. Carlon (1861) 30 L.J. Ch. 639 589
Claremont, *Re* [1923] 2 K.B. 718 59
Clarke, *Re* [1923] 2 Ch. 407 371
Clarke v. Chadburn [1985] 1 W.L.R. 78; (1984) 128 S.J. 767 .... 739, 740
—— v. Turner (1694) Free Ch. 198 100
Clarke's Will Trusts, *Re* [1961] 1 W.L.R. 1471; 105 S.J. 1085 .... 530, 619
Clavering v. Ellison (1859) 7 H.L.Cas. 707 186
Clayton v. Ramsden [1943] A.C. 320 .... 90, 327, 331
Clayton's Case (1817) 1 Mer. 572 .... 670, 671, 673
Cleaver, (dec'd), *Re*; Cleaver v. Insley [1981] 1 W.L.R. 939; (1980) 125 S.J. 445 97,
161, 162, 305, 306, 309, 310, 311, 320, 893
Cleaver v. Mutual Reserve Fund Life Association Ltd [1892] 1 Q.B. 147 316
Clegg v. Fishwick (1849) 1 Mac. & G. 294 .... 292, 596
—— v. Hands (1890) 44 Ch.D. 503 785
Clifford, *Re* [1912] 1 Ch. 29 95
Clifford Davis Management Ltd v. W.E.A. Records Ltd [1975] 1 W.L.R. 61 788
Clipper Maritime Co. Ltd of Monrovia v. Mineralimportexport [1981] 1 W.L.R. 1262;
[1981] 3 All E.R. 664 815
Clitheroe's Settlement Trusts, *Re* [1959] 1 W.L.R. 1159; 103 S.J. 961 .... 621, 622, 627
Clore v. Theatrical Properties Ltd [1936] 3 All E.R. 483 .... 877, 878
Clore's Settlement Trusts, *Re*, Sainer v. Clore [1966] 1 W.L.R. 955; 110 S.J. 252 580,
581
Clough v. Bond (1838) 3 My. & Cr. 490 .... 560, 635
—— v. London and North Western Rail Co. (1871) L.R. 7 Ex. Ch. 26 838
Clough Mill Ltd v. Martin [1985] 1 W.L.R. 111; (1984) 128 S.J. 850 .... 683, 684
Clout and Frewer's Contract [1924] 2 Ch. 230 491
Cloutte v. Storey [1911] 1 Ch. 18 .... 176, 180
Cluett Peabody & Co. Inc. v. McIntyne Hogg Marsh and Co. Ltd [1958] R.P.C.
335 773
Coates, *Re*, Ramsden v. Coates [1955] Ch. 495; [1954] 3 W.L.R. 959 103
Coates to Parsons, *Re* (1886) 34 Ch.D. 370 494
Coates' Trusts, *Re* [1959] 1 W.L.R. 375; 103 S.J. 273 619
Coatsworth v. Johnson (1886) 54 L.T. 520 (1886) 55 L.J.Q.B. 220 .... 26, 717
Coca-Cola Co. v. Gilbey [1995] 4 All E.R. 711; (1995) 145 N.L.J. Rep. 1688 806
Cochrane v. Cochrane [1922] 2 Ch. 230 177
—— v. Moore (1890) 25 Q.B.D. 57 115
Cochrane, *Re*, Shaw v. Cochrane [1955] Ch. 309; [1955] 2 W.L.R. 267 232
Cockburn's Will Trusts, *Re*, Cockburn v. Lewis [1957] Ch. 438; [1957] 3 W.L.R.
212 .... 55, 498
Cocks v. Manners (1871) L.R. 12 Eq. 574 361
—— v. Thanet District Council [1983] 2 A.C. 286; [1982] 3 W.L.R. 1121 .... 764, 800
Codd's Will Trusts, *Re*; National Westminster Bank v. Codd [1975] 1 W.L.R. 1139; 119
S.J. 530 587
Cogent v. Gibson (1864) 33 Beav. 557 700
Cohen, *Re* [1911] 1 Ch. 37 179
——, *Re*, Cowan v. Cohen [1973] 1 W.L.R. 415; (1972) 117 S.J. 222 .... 61, 90, 379,
386, 387, 388, 412
Cohen v. Roche [1927] 1 K.B. 169 .... 701, 702
Cohen's Settlement Trusts, *Re*, Eliot-Cohen v. Cohen [1965] 1 W.L.R. 1229; 109 S.J.
680 .... 622, 629
Cole, *Re*, Westminster Bank v. Moore [1958] Ch. 877; [1958] 3 W.L.R. 447 .... 384, 410
Cole, *Re* (A Bankrupt), *ex p.* The Trustees of the Property of the Bankrupt [1964] Ch.
175; [1963] 3 W.L.R. 621 .... 115, 138
Colebrook's Conveyance, *Re* [1972] 1 W.L.R. 1397; 116 S.J. 784 840
Coleman, *Re* (1888) 39 Ch. 443 .... 194, 196, 198
Coleman v. Harvey [1989] 1 N.Z.L.R. 723 667
Coles v. Trecothick (1804) 9 Ves. Jr. 234 .... 591, 720

Collard's Will Trusts, *Re*, Lloyds Bank v. Rees [1961] Ch. 293; [1961] 2 W.L.R.
　415 576
Collett v. Morrison (1851) 9 Hare 162 844
Collier v. Hollinshead (1984) 272 E.G. 941 54
Collins v. Elstone [1893] P. 1 845
Colls v. Home and Colonial Stores Ltd [1904] A.C. 179 .... 748, 778
Coloroll Pension Trustees Ltd v. Russell [1995] I.C.R. 179; [1995] All E.R. (EC)
　23 475
Columbia Picture Industries Inc. v. Robinson [1987] Ch. 38; [1986] 3 W.L.R. 542 807,
　　　　　　　　　　　　　　　　　　　　　　　　　　　　　　　　　　　　　　810
Combe, *Re* [1925] 1 Ch. 210 63
Combe v. Combe [1951] 2 K.B. 215; [1951] 1 T.L.R. 811 .... 23, 141, 884, 885
Comiskey v. Bowring-Hanbury [1905] A.C. 84 91
Commission for the New Towns v. Cooper (Great Britain) Ltd [1995] Ch. 259 843
Commissioners for Special Purposes of Income Tax v. Pemsel [1891] A.C. 531 376,
　　　　　　　　　　　　　　　　　　　　　　　　　　　　　　　　　　　　380, 383
Commissioner of Stamp Duties of New South Wales v. Perpetual Trustee Co. Ltd
　[1943] A.C. 425 221
Commissioner of Stamp Duties (Queensland) v. Livingston [1965] A.C. 694; [1964] 3
　W.L.R. 963 .... 57, 58, 59, 663
Commonwealth of Australia v. Verwayen (1990) 65 A.L.J.R. 540 .... 883, 886
Company's Application, *Re* [1989] Ch. 477; [1989] 3 W.L.R. 265 796
Compaq Computer Ltd v. Abercorn Group Ltd [1991] B.C.C. 484 .... 682, 685
Competitive Insurance Co. Ltd v. Davies Investments Ltd [1975] 1 W.L.R. 1240; 119
　S.J. 559 .... 294, 304
Compton, *Re* [1945] Ch. 123 .... 412, 414
Connolly Bros Ltd, *Re* [1911] 1 Ch. 731 803
Conservative and Unionist Central Office v. Burrell [1982] 1 W.L.R. 522; [1982] 2 All
　E.R. 1 .... 235, 359, 364, 370
Construction Industry Training Board v. Att.-Gen. [1973] Ch. 173; [1972] 3 W.L.R.
　187 .... 393, 447
Conway v. Fenton (1888) 40 Ch.D. 512 614
Coode, *Re* (1913) 108 L.T. 94 .... 500, 501
Cook v. Cook [1962] P. 235; [1962] 3 W.L.R. 441 256
—— v. Fountain (1676) 3 Swan. 585 .... 13, 90
Cook Industries Inc. v. Galliher [1979] Ch. 439; [1978] 3 W.L.R. 637 .... 738, 806
Cook's Settlement Trusts, *Re*, Royal Exchange Assurance v. Cook [1965] Ch. 902;
　[1965] 2 W.L.R. 179 .... 122, 123, 124, 127, 128, 130, 131, 729
Cooke, *Re* [1922] 1 Ch. 292 174
Cooke v. Head [1972] 1 W.L.R. 518; 116 S.J. 298 .... 68, 231, 262, 266, 318
Cookes' Contract, *Re* (1877) 4 Ch.D. 454 182
Coomber, *Re* [1911] 1 Ch. 723 831
Coombes v. Smith [1986] 1 W.L.R. 808; (1986) 130 S.J. 482 .... 263, 319, 330,
　　　　　　　　　　　　　　　　　　　　　　　　　　　　　　　　　　　875, 887, 891
Cooper (Colin), *Re* [1939] Ch. 811 150
Cooper v. Cooper (1874) L.R. 7 H.L. 53 .... 57, 853, 858
—— v. Phibbs (1867) L.R. 2 H.L. 149; (reversing (1865) 17 Ir. Ch. Rep. 73) 819
Cooper's Settlement, *Re*; Cooper v. Cooper [1962] Ch. 826; [1961] 3 W.L.R.
　1029 .... 530, 619
Co-operative Bank plc v. Tipper [1996] 4 All E.R. 366 839
Co-operative Insurance Society Ltd v. Argyll Stores (Holdings) Ltd [1996] Ch.
　286 .... 694, 705, 736, 748, 774
Corbett *v.* Commissioners of Inland Revenue [1938] 1 K.B. 567 .... 57, 546
Corbyn, *Re* [1941] Ch. 400 410
Coregrange Ltd, *Re* [1984] B.C.L.C. 453 313
Corelli, *Re* [1943] Ch. 332 410
Corin v Patton (1990) A.L.J.R. 256; 169 C.L.R. 540 .... 84, 118
Cork v. McVicar, *The Times*, October 31, 1984 796
Cornish, *Re* [1896] 1 Q.B. 99 652
Cornish v. Brook Green Laundry Ltd [1959] 1 Q.B. 394; [1959] 2 W.L.R. 215 ... 717, 732

Corporation Nacional del Cobre de Chile v. Sogemin Metal Ltd, *The Times*, December 24, 1996 24
Corsellis, *Re* (1887) 34 Ch.D. 675 589
Costello v. Costello (1995) 70 P. & C.R. 297; (1995) 27 H.L.R. 12 .... 879, 896
Cottam, *Re*, Midland Bank Executor and Trustee Co. v. Huddersfield Corporation [1955] 1 W.L.R. 1299; 99 S.J. 889 .... 387, 401, 422
Cotter, *Re* [1915] 1 Ch. 307 500
Coulls v. Bagot's Trustee (1967) 40 A.L.J.R. 471 .... 126, 131, 132, 730, 731
Coulthurst, *Re* [1951] Ch. 661; 95 S.J. 188 .... 386, 387, 422
Countess Fitzwilliam v. I.R.C. [1993] 1 W.L.R. 1189; [1993] 3 All E.R. 184 212
Courage Group's Pension Schemes, *Re* [1987] 1 W.L.R. 495; (1987) 131 S.J. 507 .... 182, 459, 469
Courtauld's Settlement, *Re*, Courtauld v. Farrer [1965] 1 W.L.R. 1385; 109 S.J. 739; [1965] 2 All E.R. 544 .... 181, 183, 624
Courtenay v. Courtenay (1846) 3 Jo. & La. T. 519 503
Cousins v. Dzosens (1984) 81 L.S. Gaz. 2855 271
Cowan v. Scargill; Mineworkers' Pension Scheme Trusts, *Re* [1985] Ch. 270; [1984] 3 W.L.R. 501 .... 465, 504, 522, 523
Cowan de Groot v. Eagle Trust [1992] 4 All E.R. 700 301
Cowcher v. Cowcher [1972] 1 W.L.R. 425; (1971) 116 S.J. 142 42
Cowell v. Rosehill Racecourse Co. (1937) 56 C.L.R. 605 .... 870, 871
Cowley, *Re* (1885) 53 L.T. 494 53
Cowley (Earl) v. I.R.C. [1899] A.C. 198 .... 203, 217
Coxen, *Re* [1948] Ch. 747; [1948] L.J.R. 1590 .... 103, 424, 427
Crabb v. Arun District Council [1976] Ch. 179; [1975] 3 W.L.R. 847 .... 883, 886, 888
Craddock Bros. v. Hunt [1923] 2 Ch. 136 .... 717, 840, 844
Cradock v. Piper (1850) 1 Mac. & G. 664 588
Craig, *Re*, Meneces v. Middleton [1971] Ch. 95; [1970] 2 W.L.R. 829, 831
Cranmer's Case (1702) 2 Salk. 508 860
Crane v. Hegeman-Harris Co. Inc. [1939] 4 All E.R. 68, C.A. 149, 841, 844
Craven's Estate, *Re* [1937] Ch. 423 .... 137, 138
Craven (Inspector of Taxes) v. White [1989] A.C. 398 212
Crawshay, *Re* [1948] Ch. 123; [1948] L.J.R. 586 .... 177, 178, 179
Credit Lyonnais Bank Nederland NV v. Burch [1997] 1 All E.R. 144 ... 830, 833, 836, 837
Cresswell v. Potter [1978] 1 W.L.R. 255 .... 830, 836
Crest Homes Ltd v. Ascolt, *The Times*, February 4, 1975 793
—— v. Marks [1987] A.C. 829; [1987] 3 W.L.R. 293 808
Cretanor Maritime Co. Ltd v. Irish Marine Management Ltd [1978] 1 W.L.R. 966; (1978) 122 S.J. 298 .... 739, 752, 814
Crichton v. Crichton [1895] 2 Ch. 853 860
Crippen, *In the Estate of* [1911] P. 108 315
Cross v. Cross (1982) 12 Fam. Law 182; [1983] F.L.R. 235 .... 717, 720
Crowden v. Aldridge [1993] 1 W.L.R. 433 .... 58, 79
Croydon London Borough Council v. Gladden (1994) 68 P. & C.R. 300; (1994) 1 P.L.R. 30 765
Cuckmere Brick Co. Ltd v. Mutual Finance Ltd [1971] Ch. 949; [1971] 2 W.L.R. 1207 21
Cud (or Cuddee) v. Rutter (1720) 1 P.Wms. 570 701
Cuddon v. Tite (1858) 1 Giff 395 313
Cull's Trusts, *Re* (1875) L.R. 20 Eq. 561 534
Cullen v. Att.-Gen. for Northern Ireland (1866) L.R. 1 H.L. 190 159
Cumberland Consolidated Holdings Ltd v. Ireland [1946] K.B. 264 312
Cummins v. Perkins [1899] 1 Ch. 16 734
Cundy v. Lindsay (1878) 3 App. Cas. 459 818
Cunnack v. Edwards [1896] 2 Ch. 679 237
Cunningham and Fray, *Re* [1891] Ch. 567 69
Cunningham v. Brown, 265 U.S. 1. 44 Sup. Ct. 424; 68 L. Ed. 873 (1923) 670
Customs and Excise Commissioners v. Automobile Association [1974] 1 W.L.R. 1447; 118 S.J. 221 382
—— v. Richmond Theatre Management Ltd [1995] S.T.C. 257; [1995] B.T.R. 332 ... 51, 90

Cutsforth v. Mansfield Inns Ltd [1986] 1 W.L.R. 558; (1986) 130 S.J. 314 .... 745, 756

D. (J.), *Re* [1982] Ch. 237; [1982] 2 W.L.R. 373 75
D. (A Minor) (Adoption Order: Validity), *Re* [1991] Fam. 137; [1991] 2 W.L.R.
    1215 802
—— v. D. (County Court Jurisdiction: Injunctions), *Re* [1993] 2 F.L.R. 802; [1994]
    Fam. Law 8; *The Times*, July 29, 1993 735
D.H.N. Food Distributors Ltd v. Tower Hamlets L.B.C. [1976] 1 W.L.R. 852 84,
                                                                                86, 321, 879
D.P.R. Futures Ltd, *Re* [1989] 1 W.L.R. 778; (1989) 133 S.J. 977 .... 662, 769
Dacre, *Re* [1915] 2 Ch. 480; affirmed [1916] 1 Ch. 344 633
Dale (dec'd), *Re* [1994] Ch. 31 .... 158, 305,
                                                                     307, 308, 309, 310, 311, 711
Dale v. I.R.C. [1954] A.C. 11; [1953] 3 W.L.R. 448 585
Daly v. Sydney Stock Exchange (1986) 160 C.L.R. 371 666
Dalziel, *Re* [1943] Ch. 277 371
Dance v. Goldingham (1873) L.R. 8 Ch.App. 902 .... 557, 791
D'Angibau, *Re* (1880) 15 Ch.D. 228 .... 123, 124, 134
Danish Bacon Co. Staff Pension Fund Trusts, *Re* [1971] 1 W.L.R. 248; [1971] 1 All
    E.R. 486 .... 79, 88
Daniel v. Ferguson [1891] 2 Ch. 27 765
Darbey v. Whitaker (1857) 4 Drew. 134 .... 712, 730
Darby, *Re* [1939] Ch. 905 546
Darling, *Re* [1896] 1 Ch. 56 .... 386, 398
Darlington Borough Council v. Wiltshier Northern Ltd [1995] 1 W.L.R. 68; [1995] 3
    All E.R. 895 125
Darlow v. Sparks [1938] 2 All E.R. 235 138
Davenport v. Bishopp (1843) 2 Y & C.C.C. 451 123
Davey, (dec'd), *Re* [1981] 1 W.L.R. 164; (1980) 124 S.J. 810 75
David (Lawrence) Ltd v. Ashton [1991] 1 All E.R. 385 762
Davies v. Otty (No. 2) (1865) 35 Beav. 208 .... 8, 77
Davies (Paul A.) (Australia) Pty. Ltd v. Davies [1983] 1 N.S.W.L.R. 440 667
Davis, *Re* [1902] 2 Ch. 314 638
—— v. Foreman [1894] 3 Ch. 654 785
—— v. Hutchings [1907] 1 Ch. 356 650
—— v. Lisle [1936] 2 K.B. 434 867
—— v. Richards & Wallington Industries Ltd [1990] 1 W.L.R. 1511; [1991] 2 All E.R.
    563 .... 27, 66, 230, 237, 238, 239, 240, 243, 459, 471, 474
—— v. Vale [1971] 1 W.L.R. 1022; 115 S.J. 347 270
Davitt v. Titcomb [1990] Ch. 110 316
Dawkins v. Antrobus (1881) 17 Ch.D. 615 803
—— v. Crown Supplier's (PSA) Ltd, *The Times*, February 4, 1993; [1993] I.C.R.
    517 327
Dawson, *Re* [1966] 2 N.S.W.L.R. 211 635
Day v. Brownrigg (1878) 10 Ch.D. 294 .... 734, 744
—— v. Mead [1987] 2 N.Z.L.R. 443 24
—— v. Wells (1861) 30 Beav. 220 716
De Bussche v. Alt (1878) 8 Ch.D. 286 .... 175, 292, 596
De Carteret, *Re* [1933] Ch. 103 387
De Falco v. Crawley Borough Council [1980] Q.B. 460; [1980] 2 W.L.R. 664 756,
                                                                                      764, 765
De Francesco v. Barnum (1890) 45 Ch.D. 430 708
De Mattos v. Gibson (1859) 4 De. G. & J. 276 785
De Mestre v. West [1891] A.C. 264 122
De Sommery, *Re* [1912] 2 Ch. 622 .... 166, 492
Dean, *Re* (1889) 41 Ch.D. 552 .... 46, 337, 348, 355, 356, 366, 367, 402
Delamere's Settlement Trusts, *Re* [1984] 1 W.L.R. 813; (1984) 128 S.J. 318 573
Delgoffe v. Fader [1939] Ch. 922 .... 137, 138
Delius, *Re*, Emanuel v. Rosen [1957] Ch. 299; [1957] 2 W.L.R. 548 ..... 380, 388, 390, 391
Denby (William) & Sons Sick and Benevolent Fund, *Re*, Rowling v. Wilks [1971] 1
    W.L.R. 973 .... 236, 239

Denley's Trust Deed, *Re*, Holman v. Martyn (H.H) & Co. [1969] 1 Ch. 373; [1968] 3
    W.L.R. 457 .... 101, 349, 350, 352, 361, 362, 365, 368, 370
Denne v. Light (1857) 8 De G.M. & G. 774 720
Dennis v. McDonald [1982] Fam. 63; [1982] 2 W.L.R. 275 275
Dennis's Settlements Trusts, *Re* [1942] Ch. 283 .... 190, 191
Denny v. Hancock (1870) L.R. 6 Ch.App. 1 716
Densham (A Bankrupt), *Re*; *ex p*. Trustee of the Property of the Bankrupt v. Bankrupt,
    The [1975] 1 W.L.R. 1519; [1975] 3 All E.R. 726 .... 69, 77, 78,
                                                     231, 262, 282, 319, 342
Dent v. Dent [1996] 1 W.L.R. 683 817
Department of Social Security v. Butler [1995] 1 W.L.R. 1528; [1995] 4 All E.R.
    193 811
Derby & Co. Ltd v. Weldon [1990] Ch. 48; [1989] 2 W.L.R. 276 .... 754, 755, 809,
                                                      810, 813
—— v. —— (Nos. 3 and 4) [1990] Ch. 65; [1989] 2 W.L.R. 412 .... 740, 813, 814
—— v. —— (No. 6) [1990] 1 W.L.R. 1139; [1990] 3 All E.R. 263 814
—— v. —— (No. 7) [1990] 1 W.L.R. 1156; [1990] 3 All E.R. 161 765
Derry v. Peek (1889) 14 App. Cas. 337 825
Deschamps v. Miller [1908] 1 Ch. 856 .... 695, 738
Des Salles d'Epinoix v. Des Salles d'Epinoix [1967] 1 W.L.R. 553; 111 S.J. 94 801
Detmold, *Re* (1889) 40 Ch.D. 585 .... 185, 187
Dewar v. Dewar [1975] 1 W.L.R. 1532; 119 S.J. 681 89
Dibbs v. Goren (1849) 11 Beav. 483 533
Dicey, *Re*, Julian v. Dicey [1957] 145; [1956] 3 W.L.R. 981 854
Dick, *Re*, Knight v. Dick [1953] Ch. 343; [1953] 2 W.L.R. 477 .... 178, 179, 538
Diggles, *Re* (1888) 39 Ch.D. 253 91
Digital Equipment Corporation v. Darkcrest Ltd [1984] Ch. 512; [1984] 3 W.L.R.
    617 .... 767, 806
Dillwyn v. Llewelyn (1862) 4 De G.F. & J. 517 .... 889, 894
Dimbleby & Sons Ltd v. National Union of Journalists [1984] 1 W.L.R. 427 .... 761, 763
Dimes v. Scott (1828) 4 Russ. 195 .... 541, 640
Dingle v. Turner [1972] A.C. 601; [1972] 2 W.L.R. 523 .... 377, 378, 387,
                            411, 412, 413, 415, 416, 421
Diplock. *See* Ministry of Health v. Simpson.
Director General of Fair Trading v. Buckland [1990] 1 W.L.R. 920; [1990] 1 All E.R.
    545 739
—— v. Pioneer Concrete (U.K.); *sub nom*. Supply of Ready Mixed Concrete (No. 2),
    Re [1995] 1 A.C. 456; [1994] 3 W.L.R. 1249 739
—— v. Tobyward Ltd [1989] 1 W.L.R. 517; (1989) 133 S.J. 184 769
Distillers Co. (Biochemicals) v. Times Newspapers; Same v. Phillips [1975] Q.B. 613;
    [1974] 3 W.L.R. 728 797
Distributori Automatici India SpA v. Holford General Trading Co. Ltd [1985] 1 W.L.R.
    1066; (1985) 129 S.J. 685 804
Dive, *Re* [1909] 1 Ch. 328 .... 529, 650
Diwell v. Farnes [1959] 1 W.L.R. 624; 103 S.J. 431 .... 247, 256
Dixon, *Re* [1900] 2 Ch. 561 654
Dixon v. Olmius (1787) 1 Cox. Eq. 414 147
Dodsworth v. Dodsworth (1973) 228 E.G. 1115, C.A. 889, 896
Dodwell & Co. Ltd's Trust Deed, *Re* [1979] Ch. 301 199
Doherty v. Allman (1878) 3 App. Cas. 709 .... 763, 783, 784
Doland's Will Trusts, *Re*, Westminster Bank v. Phillips [1970] Ch. 267; [1969] 3
    W.L.R. 614; *sub nom*. Doland's Will Trusts, *Re*, 113 S.J. 798; *sub nom*. Doland,
    Re, Westminster Bank v. Phillips [1969] 3 All E.R. 713 .... 840, 845
Doleman & Sons v. Ossett Corporation [1912] 3 K.B. 257 712
Domb v. Isoz [1980] Ch. 548; [1980] 2 W.L.R. 565 728
Dominion Coal Co. Ltd v. Dominion Iron & Steel [1909] A.C. 293 701
Dominion Students' Hall Trust, *Re* [1947] Ch. 183; [1947] L.J.R. 371 .... 327, 332, 430
Donnell v. Bennett (1883) 22 Ch.D. 835 783
Doughty, *Re*, Burridge v. Doughty [1947] Ch. 263; 176 L.T. 173 547

Douglas, *Re* (1887) 35 Ch.D. 472 .... 371, 406
Dover Coalfield Extension Ltd, *Re* [1908] 1 Ch. 65 594
Downshire Settled Estates, *Re*, Marquess of Downshire v. Royal Bank of Scotland
  [1953] Ch. 218; [1953] 2 W.L.R. 94 .... 558, 614, 616, 617
Downsview Nominee Ltd v. First City Corporation Ltd [1993] A.C. 295; [1993] 2
  W.L.R. 86 21
Dowson & Mason Ltd v. Potter [1986] 1 W.L.R. 1419; (1986) 130 S.J. 841 24
Dowty Boulton Paul Ltd v. Wolverhampton Corporation [1971] 1 W.L.R. 204; (1970)
  115 S.J. 76 748
Doyle v. Northumbria Probation Committee [1991] 1 W.L.R. 1340; [1992] I.C.R.
  121 800
Drake v. Whipp [1996] 1 F.L.R. 826 .... 256, 263, 265, 270, 271, 287, 319
Drakeford v. Wilks (1747) 3 Atk. 539 147
Drane v. Evangelou [1978] 1 W.L.R. 455; 121 S.J. 793 739
Draper's Conveyance, *Re* [1969] 1 Ch. 486; [1968] 2 W.L.R. 166 274
Drexel Burnham Lambert UK Pension Plan, *Re* [1995] 1 W.L.R. 32, Ch.D. 463, 595
Dreyfus (Camille and Henry) Foundation Inc. v. I.R.C. [1956] A.C. 39; [1955] 3 W.L.R.
  451 384
Driffill, (dec'd), *Re*, Harvey v. Chamberlain [1950] Ch. 92; 66 T.L.R. (Pt 1) 80; [1949]
  2 All E.R. 933 .... 401, 410
Drimmie v. Davies [1899] 1 Ir. R. 176 730
Druce's Settlement Trusts, *Re*, Pothecary v. Druce [1962] 1 W.L.R. 363; 106 S.J.
  112 .... 622, 627
Druiff v. Lord Parker (1868) L.R. 5 Eq. 131 844
Drummond, *Re* [1914] 2 Ch. 90 .... 360, 387
——, *Re*; Foster v. Foster [1988] 1 W.L.R. 234; [1988] 1 All E.R. 449 334
Du Boulay v. Raggett (1989) 58 P. & C.R. 12; [1989] 1 EGLR 229 77
Du Sautoy v. Symes [1967] Ch. 1146; [1967] 2 W.L.R. 342 719
Dudman, *Re* [1925] 1 Ch. 553 138
Duffield v. Elwes (1827) 1 Bli (N.S.) 497 .... 137, 139
Dufour v. Pereira (1769) Dick 419 .... 305, 306, 308, 309
Dugdale, *Re* (1883) 38 Ch.D. 176 .... 186, 332
Duke of Beaufort v. Neeld (1845) 12 Cl. & F. 248 716
—— v. Patrick (1853) 17 Beav. 60 .... 878, 889, 894
Duke of Norfolk's Case (1683) 2 Swan. 454 13
Duke of Norfolk's Settlement Trusts, *Re* [1982] Ch. 61 .... 587, 589
Duke of Somerset v. Cookson (1735) 3 P. Nms. 390 701
Dunbar Bank plc v. Nadeem [1997] 2 All E.R. 253 .... 834, 835
Duncuft v. Albrecht (1841) 12 Sim. 189 701
Dundee General Hospitals v. Walker [1952] 1 All E.R. 896; [1952] W.N. 180 ..... 507, 508
Dunford & Elliott Ltd v. Johnson & Firth Brown Ltd [1977] 1 Lloyd's Rep. 505; (1976)
  121 S.J. 53 .... 755, 764
Dunlop (dec'd), *Re* (1984) 19 *Northern Ireland Judgments Bulletin* 401, 420, 421
Dunne v. Byrne [1912] A.C. 407 .... 396, 417, 424
Duport Steels Ltd v. Sirs [1980] 1 W.L.R. 142; (1980) 124 S.J. 133 762
Dupree's Deed Trusts, *Re* [1945] Ch. 16 .... 392, 403
Durant v. Heritage [1994] E.G.C.S. 134; [1994] NPC 117 .... 886, 892
Duxbury's Settlement Trusts, *Re* [1995] 1 W.L.R. 425; [1995] 3 All E.R. 145 490
Dyer v. Dyer (1788) 2 Cox 92 .... 254, 272
Dyster v. Randall [1926] Ch. 932 717

E. v. E. (Financial Provision) [1990] 2 F.L.R. 233; [1989] F.C.R. 591 .... 503, 504, 618
EMI v. Pandit [1975] 1 W.L.R. 302; (1974) 119 S.J. 136 805
—— v. Sharwar and Haider [1977] F.S.R. 146, C.A. 805
EMI Records v. Kudhail [1983] Com. L.R. 280; [1985] F.S.R. 36 738
EVTR Ltd, *Re* [1987] B.C.L.C. 647 .... 50, 230
Eades, *Re* [1920] 2 Ch. 353 426
Eads *v.* Williams (1854) 4 De. G.M. & G. 674 718
Eagle Trust plc v. SBC Securities [1993] 1 W.L.R. 484; [1991] BCLL 438 .... 300, 301
Earl Beauchamp v. Winn (1873) L.R. 6 H.L. 223 819
Earl of Chesterfield's Trust, *Re* (1883) 24 Ch.D. 643 .... 539, 541, 543, 545, 546

Earl of Sefton v. Tophams Ltd [1966] Ch. 1140 720
Earl of Stamford, *Re* [1896] 1 Ch. 288 500
Earl of Stafford, (dec'd), *Re*, Royal Bank of Scotland v. Byng [1980] Ch. 28; [1979] 2
    W.L.R. 459 559
East v. Maurer [1991] 1 W.L.R. 461; [1991] 2 All E.R. 733, C.A. 827
East India Co. v. Vincent (1740) 2 Atk. 83 887
Eastbourne Mutual Building Society v. Hastings Corporation [1965] 1 W.L.R. 861; 129
    J.P. 300 58
Eastern Capital Futures (In Liquidation), *Re* [1989] BCLC 371 674
Eastgate, *Re* [1905] 1 K.B. 465 839
Easton v. Brown [1981] 3 All E.R. 278 719
Eaton v. Buchanan [1911] A.C. 253 558
Eaves v. Hickson (1861) Beav. 136 .... 295, 533, 649
Eddis v. Chichester Constable [1969] 2 Ch. 345; [1969] 3 W.L.R. 48 .... 654, 688
Edmonds v. Edmonds [1965] 1 W.L.R. 58; 108 S.J. 1047 .... 192, 852
Edwards, *Re*, Macadam v. Wright [1958] Ch. 168; [1957] 3 W.L.R. 131 .... 852, 854
Edwards' Will Trusts, *Re* [1948] Ch. 440 146
Edwards' Will Trusts, *Re*, Edwards v. Edwards [1982] Ch. 30; [1981] 3 W.L.R. 15 .. 55,
                                                                                                            57, 504, 591
Edwards v. Carter [1893] A.C. 360 73
—— v. Jones (1836) 1 My. & Cr. 226 140
—— v. SOGAT [1971] Ch. 354; [1970] 3 W.L.R. 713 802
Egan v. Egan [1975] Ch. 218; [1975] 2 W.L.R. 503 801
Egerton v. Brownlow (1853) 4 H.L. 1 333
—— v. Egerton [1949] 2 All E.R. 238; C.A. 330
Egg v. Devey (1847) 10 Beav. 444 646
Eighmie, *Re* [1935] Ch. 524 397
El Ajou v. Dollar Land Holdings plc [1994] 2 All E.R. 685; [1994] BCC 143 295,
                                                                                                            300, 661, 666, 672
—— (No. 2) [1995] 2 All E.R. 213: *The Times*, January 3, 1995, Ch.D. 298,
                                                                                                            301, 639, 670
Ellenborough, *Re* [1903] 1 Ch. 697 .... 116, 134, 135, 160
Eller v. Grovecrest Investments Ltd [1995] Q.B. 272; [1995] 2 W.L.R. 278 22
Ellerman Lines v. Read [1928] 2 K.B. 144 803
Ellerman's Settlement Trusts, *Re*, Hitch v. Ruegg (1984) 81 L.S.Gaz. 430 547
Elliott, *Re*, Lloyds Bank v. Burton-on-Trent Hospital Management Commitee [1952]
    Ch. 217; [1952] 1 T.L.R. 298 334
—— v. Islington London Borough Council [1991] 1 E.G.L.R. 167 .... 738, 777, 779
Elliott and Elliott H. (Builders) v. Pierson [1948] Ch. 452; [1948] L.J.R. 1452 695
Ellis v. I.R.C. [1949] T.R. 273; 42 R. & I.T. 372; 31 T.C. 178 .... 384, 424
Elwes v. Payne (1879) 12 Ch.D. 468 767
Emanuel v. Emanuel [1982] 1 W.L.R. 669; [1982] 2 All E.R. 342 .... 805, 808
Emery's Investment Trusts, *Re*, Emery v. Emery [1959] Ch. 410; [1959] 2 W.L.R.
    461 251
Emmet's Estate, *Re* (1881) 17 Ch.D. 142 639
Endacott, *Re*, Corpe v. Endacott [1960] Ch. 232; [1959] 3 W.L.R. 799 .... 46, 348,
                                                                                                            355, 357, 358
Engels, *Re* [1943] 1 All E.R. 506 380
England's Settlement Trusts, *Re* [1918] 1 Ch. 24 513
Englebach's Estate, *Re*, Tibbetts v. Englebach [1924] 2 Ch. 348 128
English v. Dedham Vale Properties Ltd [1978] 1 W.L.R. 93; (1977) 121 S.J. 320 292,
                                                                                                            596
Ensign Tankers (Leasing) v. Stokes (Inspector of Taxes) [1992] 1 A.C. 655; [1992] 2
    All E.R. 275 212
Equiticorp Industries Group Ltd v. Hawkins [1991] 3 N.Z.L.R. 700 .... 291, 300
—— (In Statutory Management) v. The Crown (Judgment No. 47; Summary) [1996] 3
    N.Z.L.R. 586 300
Equity & Law Home Loans Ltd v. Prestidge [1992] 1 W.L.R. 137; [1992] 1 All E.R.
    909 .... 37, 279
Erinford Properties Ltd v. Cheshire County Council [1974] Ch. 261: [1974] 2 W.L.R.
    749 752

Erlanger v. New Sombrero Phosphate Co. (1873) 3 App. Cas. 1218 .... 772, 818, 838
Errington v. Errington and Woods [1952] 1 K.B. 290; [1952] 1 T.L.R. 231 .... 877, 878
Erskine's Settlement Trusts, *Re*, Hollis v. Pigott [1971] 1 W.L.R. 162; (1970) 115 S.J.
    113 572
Essery v. Cowlard (1884) 26 Ch.D. 191 232
Esso Petroleum v. Kingswood Motors [1974] Q.B. 142; [1973] 3 W.L.R. 780 767
——— v. Mardon [1976] Q.B. 801; [1976] 2 W.L.R. 583 827
Etablissement Esefka International Anstalt v. Central Bank of Nigeria [1979] 1 Lloyd's
    Rep. 445, C.A. 810
Euro Hotel (Belgravia) Ltd, *Re* [1975] 3 All E.R. 1075; (1975) 51 T.C. 293 763
Evans, *Re* [1940] Ch. 629 331
——— v. Benyon (1888) 37 Ch.D. 329 648
——— v. B.B.C. and I.B.A., *The Times*, February 26, 1974 .... 748, 753, 767
——— v. Hayward [1995] 2 F.L.R. 511; [1995] 2 F.C.R. 313 270
Evans Marshall & Co. Ltd v. Bertola S.A. [1973] 1 W.L.R. 349; (1972) 117 S.J.
    225 756
Evans Settlement, *Re* [1967] 1 W.L.R. 1294 579
Evans Will Trusts, *Re* [1921] 2 Ch. 309 .... 539, 543
Evening Standard Co. Ltd v. Henderson [1987] I.R.L.R. 64; (1989) 139 N.L.J.
    1716 789
Evers' Trust, *Re*, Papps v. Evers [1980] 1 W.L.R. 1327; (1980) 124 S.J. 562 281
Evered, *Re* [1910] 2 Ch. 147 .... 172, 174, 183
Eves v. Eves [1975] 1 W.L.R. 1338; 119 S.J. 394 .... 42, 68, 69, 231,
                                                                          262, 263, 267, 270, 286, 318
Ewing v. Orr-Ewing (No. 1) (1883) 9 App. Cas. 34 18
Express Newspapers Ltd v. Keys [1980] I.R.L.R. 247 .... 746, 756, 757, 766
——— v. Liverpool Daily Post and Echo [1986] E.C.C. 204; [1985] 1 W.L.R. 1089 771
——— v. Macshane [1980] A.C. 672; [1980] I.C.R. 42 762
Eykyn's Trusts, *Re* (1877) 6 Ch.D. 115 247
Eyre, *Re* (1883) 49 L.T. 259 182
Ezekiel's Settlements, *Re* [1942] Ch. 230 .... 513, 559

Falcke v. Gray (1859) 4 Dr. 651 701
Falconer v. Falconer [1970] 1 W.L.R. 1333; 114 S.J. 720 266
Faraker, *Re* [1912] 2 Ch. 488 .... 433, 434, 435
Farley v. Westminster Bank [1939] A.C. 430 423
Farmer v. Dean (1863) 32 Beav. 327 591
Farrar v. Farrar's Ltd (1889) 40 Ch.D. 395 590
Faruqui v. English Real Estates [1979] 1 W.L.R. 963; (1978) 123 S.J. 321 723
Fawcett, *Re* [1940] Ch. 402, 407 540
Fawcett and Holmes' Contract, *Re* (1889) 42 Ch.D. 150 722
Featherstonhaugh v. Fenwick (1810) 17 Ves. Jr. 298 .... 292, 596
Fellowes & Son v. Fisher [1976] Q.B. 122; [1975] 3 W.L.R. 184 .... 754, 755,
                                                                              756, 757, 758, 762
Fells v. Reed (1796) 3 Ves. Jr. 70 701
Felton v. Callis [1969] 1 Q.B. 200; [1968] 3 W.L.R. 951 .... 21, 26, 30
Femis-Bank (Anguilla) v. Lazar; Singh (Dinesh Kumar) v. Lazar [1991] Ch. 391;
    [1991] W.L.R. 80 794
Fenwick v. East London Railway (1875) L.R. 20 Eq. 544 737
Ferris v. Weaven [1952] W.N. 318; [1952] 2 All E.R. 233 877
Fielden v. Cox (1906) 22 T.L.R. 411 792
Figg v. Clark (Inspector of Taxes), *The Times*, March 11, 1996 .... 204, 612, 629
Figgis, *Re*, Roberts v. MacLaren [1969] 1 Ch. 123; [1968] 2 W.L.R. 1173 ... 247, 248, 255
Films Rover International v. Cannon Film Sales; *Financial Times*, June 10, 1988; C.A.
    reversing [1987] 1 W.L.R. 670 766
Finers (a firm) v. Miro [1991] 1 W.L.R. 35; [1991] 1 All E.R. 182 .... 294, 297, 533, 796
Finger's Will Trusts, *Re*, Turner v. Ministry of Health [1972] 1 Ch. 286; [1971] 3
    W.L.R. 775 .... 433, 434
First National Bank plc v. Thompson [1996] Ch. 231 .... 23, 883
Fishenden v. Higgs and Hill (1935) 153 L.T. 128 778
Fisk v. Att.-Gen (1867) L.R. 4 Eq. 521 333

Fizgerald v. National Bank [1929] 1 K.B. 394 860
Flavel's Will Trusts, *Re* [1966] 1 W.L.R. 445 .... 66, 97
Fleetwood, *Re* (1880) 15 Ch.D. 594 .... 154, 159
Fletcher, *Re* (1888) 38 Ch.D. 373 860
—— v. Ashburner (1779) 1 Bro. C.C. 497 849
—— v. Bealey (1885) 28 Ch.D. 688 737
—— v. Collis [1905] 2 Ch. 24 646
—— v. Fletcher (1844) 4 Hare 67 .... 93, 125, 127, 128, 129, 130, 132, 133
—— v. Green (1864) 33 Beav. 426 .... 639, 640, 641
Flight v. Bolland (1828) 4 Russ. 298 713
—— v. Booth (1834) 1 Bing. N.C. 370 722
Flinn, *Re*, Public Trustee v. Griffin [1948] Ch. 241; [1948] L.J.R. 923 .... 417, 423
Flint (a bankrupt), *Re* [1993] Ch. 319; [1993] 2 W.L.R. 537 342
Flynn, *Re* [1948] Ch. 24 396
Foord, *Re* [1922] 2 Ch. 519 .... 53, 241, 348
Foot Clinics (1943) v. Cooper's Gowns [1947] K.B. 506; [1947] L.J.R. 938 884
Foran v. Wight (1989) 168 C.L.R. 385 .... 883, 885
Forder, *Re* [1927] 2 Ch. 291 188
Forest of Dean Coal Mining Co., *Re* (1878) 10 Ch.D. 450 .... 598, 632
Forster, *Re* [1939] Ch. 22 397
—— v. Silvermere Golf and Equestrian Centre Ltd (1981) 125 S.J. 397 125
—— v. Williams Deacon's Bank Ltd [1935] Ch. 359 .... 489, 587
Forster's Settlement, *Re* [1942] Ch. 199 583
——, *Re* [1954] 1 W.L.R. 1450; 98 S.J. 852 616
Foster v. Spencer [1996] 2 All E.R. 672 .... 586, 587, 588
Forthergill v. Rowland (1873) L.R. 17 Eq. 132 786
Fountaine, *Re* [1909] 2 Ch. 382 653
Four Point Garage v. Carter [1985] 3 All E.R. 12 682
Foveaux, *Re* [1895] 2 Ch. 501 441
Fowkes v. Pascoe (1875) L.R. 10 Ch. App. 343 .... 245, 249, 254
Fowler v. Fowler (1859) 4 De G. & J. 250 .... 149, 841
—— v. Wyatt (1857) 24 Beav. 232 536
Fox, *Re* [1904] 1 Ch. 480 583
—— v. Fox (1870) L.R. 11 Eq. 142 791
Frame, *Re* [1939] Ch. 700 52
Francis, *Re* (1905) 92 L.T. 77 594
—— v. Cowcliff Ltd (1976) 33 P. & C.R. 368; 239 E.G. 977 D.C. 707, 720
Francome v. Mirror Group Newspapers [1984] 1 W.L.R. 892; (1984) 128 S.J.
    484 .... 741, 796
Fraser v. Evans [1969] 1 Q.B. 349; [1968] 3 W.L.R. 1172 .... 744, 793, 794, 795
—— v. Thames Television Ltd [1984] Q.B. 44; [1983] 2 W.L.R. 917 .... 24, 786, 795
Freeland, *Re*, Jackson v. Rogers [1952] Ch. 110; 95 S.J. 802 136
Freeman's Settlement Trusts, *Re* (1887) 37 Ch.D. 148 500
Freer v. Unwins Ltd [1976] Ch. 288; [1976] 2 W.L.R. 609 840
Freevale Ltd v. Metrostore (Holdings) Ltd [1984] 1 All E.R. 495; (1984) 47 P. & C.R.
    481 .... 313, 699
Friends' Provident Life Office v. Hillier Parker May & Rowden (a firm) [1996] 2
    W.L.R. 123 642
Fry, *Re* [1946] Ch. 312 [92 S.J. 332] 117, 118
—— v. Fry (1859) 27 Beav. 144 636
—— v. Lane (1888) 40 Ch.D 312 .... 720, 836
—— v. Tapson (1884) 28 Ch.D. 268 .... 530, 560
Fuller v. Knight (1843) 6 Beav. 205 647
Fullwood v. Fullwood (1878) 9 Ch.D. 176 .... 29, 772
Fung Kai Sun v. Chan Fui Hing [1951] A.C. 489; [1951] 2 T.L.R. 47 883
Funnell v. Stewart [1996] 1 W.L.R. 288 .... 390, 396, 402, 424
Furniss v. Dawson [1984] A.C. 474; [1984] 2 W.L.R. 226 212

G v. G (Ouster: Ex parte Application) [1990] 1 FLR 395; [1990] Fam. Law 254 752
G. K. N. Bolts and Nuts Ltd (Automotive Division) Birmingham Works, Sports and
    Social Club, *Re* [1982] 1 W.L.R. 774 .... 236, 241

G.K.N. (Cwmbran) Ltd v. Lloyd [1972] 1 C.R. 214; 13 K.I.R. 224 790
GKN Distributors Ltd v. Tyne Tees Fabrication Ltd [1985] 2 E.G.L.R. 181; (1985) 50
    P. & C.R. 403 699
Gaiman v. National Association for Mental Health [1971] Ch. 317; [1970] 3 W.L.R.
    42 802
Galaxia Maritime S.A. v. Mineralimportexport [1982] 1 W.L.R. 539; (1982) 126 S.J.
    115 815
Garden Cottage Foods Ltd v. Milk Marketing Board [1984] A.C. 130; [1983] 3 W.L.R.
    143 757
Gardner, *Re* [1920] 2 Ch. 523 .... 147, 150, 151, 154, 161
——, *Re* (No. 2) [1923] 2 Ch. 230 .... 161, 308
Gardner v. Coutts & Co. [1968] 1 W.L.R. 173; [1967] 3 All E.R. 1064 786
—— v. Rowe (1828) 5 Russ. 258 76
Gardom, *Re* [1914] 1 Ch. 662 .... 152, 153, 387
Garth v. Townsend (1869) L.R. 7 Eq. 220 173
Garthshore v. Chalie (1804) 10 Ves. Jr. 1 864
Gartside v. I.R.C. [1968] A.C. 553; [1968] 2 W.L.R. 277 .... 204, 217, 581
Gascoigne v. Gascoigne [1918] 1 K.B. 223 251
Gates, *Re* [1933] Ch. 913 589
Gee, *Re* [1948] Ch. 284; [1948] L.J.R. 1400 .... 586, 594
Gee v. Pritchard (1818) 2 Swan. 402 14
Geering, *Re* [1964] Ch. 136; [1962] 3 W.L.R. 1541 574
General Accident Fire and Life Assurance Corporation Ltd v. I.R.C. [1963] 1 W.L.R.
    1207, 107 S.J. 870 .... 192, 193
General Nursing Council for England and Wales v. St. Marylebone Borough Council
    [1959] A.C. 540; [1959] 2 W.L.R. 308 .... 393, 424
George Whichelow Ltd, *Re* [1954] 1 W.L.R. 5; 98 S.J. 12 .... 118, 509
George, *Re* (1877) 5 Ch.D. 837 575
George v. Havard (1819) 7 Price 646 245
Gess, *Re* [1942] Ch. 37 534
Gestetner Settlement, *Re* [1953] Ch. 672; [1953] 2 W.L.R. 1033 .... 98, 108, 167,
                                   169, 198, 208, 504
Ghana Commerical Bank v. C, *The Times*, March 3, 1997 .... 294, 300, 664
Ghani v. Jones [1970] 1 Q.B. 693; [1969] 3 W.L.R. 1158 765
Ghoth v. Ghoth [1992] 2 All E.R. 920; [1992] 2 FLR 300 .... 805, 811
Gibbard's Will Trusts, *Re*, Public Trustee v. Davis [1967] 1 W.L.R. 42; *sub nom.*
    Gibbard, *Re*, Public Trustee v. Davis, 110 S.J. 871 .... 102, 104
Gibbon v. Mitchell [1990] 1 W.L.R. 1304; [1990] 3 All E.R. 338 .... 190, 612, 620,
                                    627, 817, 845
Gibbon's Trusts, *Re* (1882) 30 W.R. 287 498
Gibson v. Bott (1802) 7 Ves. Jr. 89 .... 539, 542
—— v. South American Stores (Gath & Chaves) Ltd [1950] Ch. 177; 66 T.L.R. (Pt. 1)
    83 .... 387, 388, 413
Gilbert v. Overton (1864) 22 H. & M. 110 117
Gilbey v. Cossey [1911–13] All E.R. 644 710
Giles, *Re* [1972] Ch. 544; [1971] 3 W.L.R. 640 316
Giles (C.H.) & Co. Ltd v. Morris [1972] 1 W.L.R. 307; (1971) 116 S.J. 176 ...... 705, 709,
                                    712, 785
—— v. Perkins (1807) 9 East. 12 659
Gillett's Will Trusts, *Re*, Barclays Bank v. Gillet [1950] Ch. 102; 65 T.L.R. 727 574
Gillies v. Keogh [1989] 2 N.Z.L.R. 327 .... 268, 883
Gillingham Bus Disaster Fund, *Re* [1959] Ch. 62 .... 233, 238, 348,
                             365, 428, 429, 534
Gillott's Settlements, *Re* [1934] Ch. 97 133
Gilmour v. Coats [1949] A.C. 426; [1949] L.J.R. 1034 .... 361, 396, 411, 417, 418, 419
Girls' Public Day School Trust, *Re* [1951] Ch. 400; 95 S.J. 76 394
Gisborne v. Gisborne (1877) 2 App. Cas. 300 507
Gissing v. Gissing [1971] A.C. 886, [1970] 3 W.L.R. 255 .... 42, 97, 260,
                      261, 265, 266, 271, 318, 878
Glynn v. Keele University [1971] 1 W.L.R. 487; [1971] 2 All E.R. 89 .... 747, 775, 803

Goddard v. Nationwide Building Society [1987] Q.B. 670; [1986] 3 W.L.R. 734 .... 795, 797
Godden v. Crowhurst (1842) 10 Sim. 642 196
Golay's Will Trusts, *Re* [1965] 1 W.L.R. 969; 109 S.J. 517 .... 93, 97
Goldcorp Exchange (In Receivership), *Re* [1995] 1 A.C. 74; (1994) 53 C.L.J. 443 .... 46, 94, 96, 290, 596, 666, 668, 669, 672
Goldschmidt, *Re* [1957] 1 W.L.R. 524; 101 S.J. 285 435
Goldsworthy v. Brickell [1987] Ch. 378; [1987] 2 W.L.R. 133 .... 829, 830, 831, 838
Gonin (dec'd), *Re*, Gonin v. Garmeson [1979] Ch. 16; [1977] 3 W.L.R. 379 .... 135, 136
Gooch, *Re* (1890) 62 L.T. 384 248
Good, *Re* [1905] 2 Ch. 60 410
Goodchild (dec'd) *Re* [1996] 1 W.L.R. 694 .... 305, 306, 307, 310
Goode Durrant Administration v. Biddulph (1994) 26 H.L.R. 625 [1994] 2 F.L.R. 551 835
Gooden v. Ketley (1997) 73 P. & C.R. 305 .... 772, 779
Goodman v. Gallant [1986] Fam. 106 .... 261, 271
—— v. Mayor of Saltash (1882) 7 App. Cas. 633 .... 380, 422
Goodson v. Richardson (1874) L.R. 9 Ch. App. 221 746
Gordon, *Re* [1978] Ch. 145 190
Gordon v. Douce [1983] 1 W.L.R. 563; (1983) 127 S.J. 324 .... 269, 270, 271
—— v. Gonda [1955] 1 W.L.R. 885; 99 S.J. 525 639
—— v. Gordon (1816) 3 Swan 400 .... 818, 820, 826
—— v. Selico Ltd [1986] 1 E.G.L.R. 71 707
Gordon's Will Trusts, *Re* [1978] Ch. 145 .... 852, 857, 858
Gorman (A Bankrupt), *ex p.* Trustee of The Bankrupt v. The Bankrupt [1990] 1 W.L.R. 616; [1990] 1 All E.R. 717 .... 272, 282
Gosling, *Re* (1900) 48 W.R. 300 .... 401, 413
Goss v. Chilcott [1996] A.C. 788; [1997] 2 All E.R. 110 680
Gough, *Re* [1957] Ch. 323; [1957] 2 W.L.R. 961 543
Goulding v. James [1997] 2 All E.R. 239 626
Gouriet v. Union of Post Office Workers [1978] A.C. 435; [1977] 3 W.L.R. 300 .... 734, 741, 742, 743, 797, 798
Gourju's Will Trusts, *Re* [1943] Ch. 24 .... 191, 194, 199, 207
Gower's Settlement, *Re* [1934] Ch. 365 617
Grainge v. Wilberforce (1889) 5 T.L.R. 436 .... 84, 114
Granstown, *Re* [1932] 1 Ch. 537 410
Grant v. Dawkins [1973] 1 W.L.R. 1406; 117 S.J. 665 726
—— v. Edwards [1986] Ch. 638; [1986] 3 W.L.R. 114 .... 261, 262, 263, 267, 268, 270, 271, 887
Grant's Will Trusts, *Re* [1980] 1 W.L.R. 360; (1979) 124 S.J. 84 .... 337, 350, 362
Gravesham Borough Council v. British Railways Board [1978] Ch. 379; [1978] 3 W.L.R. 494 .... 706, 736, 748, 774, 797
Gray, *Re* [1925] Ch. 362 .... 403, 410
Gray v. Barr, Prudential Assurance Co. (Third Party) [1971] 2 Q.B. 554; [1971] 2 W.L.R. 1334 .... 316, 317
—— v. Perpetual Trustee Co. [1928] A.C. 391 306
—— v. Richards Butler (a Firm), *The Times*, July 23, 1996 680
—— v. Siggers (1880) 15 Ch.D. 74 543
Greasley v. Cooke [1980] 1 W.L.R. 1306; (1980) 124 S.J. 629 .... 262, 882, 886
Great Britain Steamboat Co., *Re* (1884) 26 Ch.Div. 616 .... 253, 326
Greaves, *Re* [1954] Ch. 434; [1954] 2 W.L.R. 557 .... 176, 179
Green, (dec'd), *Re*, Linder v. Green [1951] Ch. 148; 66 T.L.R. (Pt. 2) 819 ... 305, 306, 309
Green v. Russell [1959] 2 Q.B. 226; [1959] 3 W.L.R. 17 .... 45, 128
—— v. Spicer (1830) 1 Russ. & M. 395 .... 196, 204
—— v. Whitehead [1930] 1 Ch. 38 562
Green's Will Trust, *Re* [1985] 3 All E.R. 455; (1984) 81 L.S.Gaz. 3590 .... 380, 406, 534
Greenwood, *Re* [1901] 1 Ch. 887 191
——, *Re* [1903] 1 Ch. 749 186

——, *Re* (1911) 105 L.T. 509 .... 513, 559
Grey v. I.R.C. [1960] A.C. 1 .... 69, 79, 80, 84, 112, 114, 624
Griffith v. Owen [1907] 1 Ch. 195 593
Griffiths v. Griffiths [1974] 1 W.L.R. 1350; [1973] 1 W.L.R. 1454 270
—— v. Williams (1977) 248 E.G. 947, C.A. 889, 896
Grimston v. Cuningham [1894] 1 Q.B. 125 783
Grimthorpe, *Re* [1958] Ch. 615; [1958] 1 W.L.R. 381 586
Grindey, *Re* [1898] 2 Ch. 593 649
Grist v. Bailey [1967] Ch. 532; [1966] 3 W.L.R. 618 .... 26, 716, 819, 820,
                                                                                                    821, 822, 824, 840
Group Josi, Re v. Walbrook Insurance Co. Ltd [1996] 1 W.L.R. 1152 760
Grove-Grady, *Re* [1929] 1 Ch. 557 406
Guardian Ocean Cargoes; Transorient Ship Cargoes, Middle East Agents S.A.L. and
       Med. Lines S.A. v. Banco do Brasil S.A. (No. 3) [1992] 2 Lloyd's Rep. 193; *The*
       Times, March 19, 1992 .... 638, 639
Guild v. I.R.C. [1992] 2 A.C. 310; [1992] 2 W.L.R. 397 .... 378, 404, 405, 425
Guinness v. Saunders [1990] 2 A.C. 663; [1990] 2 W.L.R. 324 .... 588, 599, 607, 818, 826
Gulbenkian's Settlements, *Re*, Hacobian v. Maun [1968] Ch. 126; [1967] 3 W.L.R.
       1112 108
Gulbenkian's Settlement Trusts (No. 2), *Re*, Stephens v. Maun [1970] Ch. 408; [1969]
       3 W.L.R. 450 203
Gulf Oil (Great Britain) Ltd v. Page [1987] Ch. 327; [1987] 3 W.L.R. 166 .... 760, 794
Gunning v. Buckfast Abbey Trustees Registered, *The Times*, June 9, 1994 448
Gurlitz, 105 Misc. 30. 172 N.Y. Supp. 523 (1918) 135
Gurtner v. Circuit [1968] 2 Q.B. 587; [1968] 2 W.L.R. 668 .... 703, 704, 731
Gwyon, *Re* [1930] 1 Ch. 255 .... 327, 332, 384, 387, 422

H (dec'd), *Re* [1990] 1 F.L.R. 441 .... 316, 317
Habib Bank Ltd v. Habib Bank A.G. Zurich [1981] 1 W.L.R. 1265; (1980) 125 S.J.
       512 773
Hadden, *Re* [1932] Ch. 133 403
Hadmor Productions Ltd v. Hamilton [1983] 1 A.C. 191; [1982] I.C.R. 114 761,
                                                                                                                762, 763
Hagger, *Re* [1930] 2 Ch. 190 .... 306, 308, 309, 310
Haigh v. Kaye (1872) 7 Ch. App. 469 250
Haines, *Re*, *The Times*, November 7, 1952 366
Haiti (Republic of) v. Duvalier [1990] 1 Q.B. 202; [1989] 2 W.L.R. 261 .... 811, 813
Halford v. Brookes [1992] P.I.Q.R. P175; *The Times*, October 3, 1991 317
Halifax Building Society v. Brown [1996] 1 F.L.R. 103 265
—— v. Thomas [1996] Ch. 217 .... 291, 292, 314, 666
Halifax Mortgage Services Ltd v. Stepsky [1996] Ch. 207 834
Hall, *In the estate of*, Hall v. Knight & Baxter [1914] P. 1 316
Hall, *Re* [1944] Ch. 46 .... 190, 191
Hall v. Derby Sanitary Authority (1885) 16 Q.B.D. 163 414
—— v. Hall [1971] 1 W.L.R. 404; [1971] 1 All E.R. 762 801
—— v. May (1857) 3 K. & J. 585 182
Hallet's Estate, *Re* (1880) 13 Ch.D. 696 .... 13, 289, 662, 664, 667, 670, 673, 676, 682
Hallows v. Lloyd (1888) 39 Ch.D. 686 512
Halsall v. Brizell [1957] Ch. 169; [1957] 2 W.L.R. 123 852
Halsey v. Esso Petroleum Co. Ltd. [1961] 1 W.L.R. 683; [1961] 2 All E.R. 145 747,
                                                                                                                750, 792
Halsted's Will Trusts, *Re* [1937] 2 All E.R. 570 .... 578, 580, 581
Halton Borough Council v. Cawley; Middleton v. Mardon; North v. Sandell Perkins
       [1985] 1 W.L.R. 15 791
Hambleden's Will Trusts, *Re* [1960] 1 W.L.R. 82; 104 S.J. 127 .... 623, 624
Hambro v. Duke of Marlborough [1994] Ch. 158; [1994] 3 W.L.R. 341 .... 188, 617
Hamilton, *Re* [1895] 2 Ch. 370 91
Hamilton-Snowball's Conveyance, *Re* [1959] Ch. 308; [1958] 2 W.L.R. 951 312
Hamlin v. Hamlin [1986] Fam. 11; [1985] 3 W.L.R. 629 .... 29, 738

Hammersmith and Fulham London Borough Council v. Monk; Barnet London Borough
    Council v. Smith [1992] 1 A.C. 478; [1990] 3 W.L.R. 1144 486
Hammersmith London Borough Council v. Magnum Automated Forecourts [1978] 1
    W.L.R. 50; [1977] 1 All E.R. 401 798
Hammond v. Allen [1994] 1 All E.R. 307; (1992) 65 P. & C.R. 18 707
—— v. Mitchell [1991] 1 W.L.R. 1127; [1992] 2 All E.R. 109 .... 263, 267, 271
Hampstead & Surburban Properties Ltd v. Diomedous [1969] 1 Ch. 248; [1968] 3
    W.L.R. 990 .... 763, 784
Hampton Fuel Allotment Charity, *Re* [1989] Ch. 484, C.A. 448
Hancock, *Re* [1905] 1 Ch. 16 858
Hancock v. Watson [1902] A.C. 14 92
Hanley v. Pearson (1870) 13 Ch.D. 545 844
Hanson v. Lorenz [1987] 1 F.T.L.R. 23; (1986) 136 New L.J. 1088, C.A. 596
Harakas v. Baltic Mercantile & Shipping Exchange Ltd [1982] 1 W.L.R. 958; (1982)
    126 S.J. 414 793
Harari's Settlement Trusts, *Re*, Wordsworth v. Fanshawe [1949] W.N. 79; [1949] 1 All
    E.R. 430 517
Harben v. Harben [1957] 1 W.L.R. 261; 101 S.J. 150 802
Harbottle R.D. (Mercantile) Ltd v. National Westminster Bank Ltd [1978] Q.B. 146;
    [1977] 3 W.L.R. 752 752
Harding, *Re* [1923] 1 Ch. 182 .... 166, 492, 494
Harding v. Glyn (1739) 1 Alk. 469 63
Hardoon v. Belilios [1901] A.C. 119 69
Hardwick v. Johnson [1978] 1 W.L.R. 683; (1977) 122 S.J. 162 875
Hardy v. Shaw [1976] Ch. 82; [1975] 2 W.L.R. 1002 577
Hargrave v. Newton [1971] 1 W.L.R. 1611; [1971] 3 All E.R. 866 266
Harington v. Sendall [1903] 1 Ch. 921 803
Harold Stephen and Co. Ltd v. Post Office [1977] 1 W.L.R. 1172; (1977) 121 S.J.
    707 .... 749, 766, 771
Harper v. Secretary of State for the Home Department [1955] Ch. 238; [1955] 2 W.L.R.
    316 804
Harpur's Will Trusts, *Re*, Haller v. Att.-Gen. [1962] Ch. 78; [1961] 3 W.L.R. 924 428
Harries v. Church Commissioners for England [1992] 1 W.L.R. 1241; [1993] 2 All E.R.
    300 .... 450, 524, 525
Harris, *Re* [1945] Ch. 316 191
Harris v. Black (1983) 46 P. & C.R. 366, C.A. 512, 591
—— v. Goddard [1983] 1 W.L.R. 203; (1983) 127 S.J. 617 274
—— v. Harris (1996) 72 P. & C.R. 408 281
Harrison's Settlement Trusts, *Re* [1965] 1 W.L.R. 1492; 109 S.J. 997 504
Harrow London Borough Council v. Donohue [1995] 1 E.G.L.R. 257 ... 737, 747, 777, 792
—— v. Johnstone [1997] 1 All E.R. 929 740
Hart v. Emelkirk Ltd [1983] 1 W.L.R. 1289; (1983) 127 S.J. 156 765
—— v. Hart (1881) 18 Ch.D. 670 716
—— v. Herwig (1873) L.R. 8 Ch. App. 680 702
—— v. O'Connor [1985] A.C. 1000 836
Hartigan Nominees Pty Ltd v. Rydge (1992) 29 N.S.W.L.R. 405 .... 506, 507,
    548, 550, 551
Hartog v. Colin and Shields [1939] 3 All E.R. 566 .... 716, 818
Harvell v. Foster [1954] 2 Q.B. 367; [1954] 3 W.L.R. 351 56
Harvey v. Harvey [1982] Fam. 83; [1982] 2 W.L.R. 283 275
—— v. Oliver (1887) 57 L.T. 239 512
Harwood, *Re* [1936] Ch. 285 435
Harwood v. Harwood [1991] 2 F.L.R. 274; [1991] Fam. Law 418 .... 246, 272
Hasham v. Zenab [1960] A.C. 316 696
Haslemere Estate Ltd v. Baker [1982] 1 W.L.R. 1109; (1982) 126 S.J. 463 .... 448, 895
Hastings-Bass (dec'd), *Re*; Hastings v. I.R.C. [1975] Ch. 25; [1974] 2 W.L.R. 904 170,
    507, 581, 582
Hauxwell v. Barton-on-Humber U.D.C. [1974] Ch. 432; [1973] 3 W.L.R. 41 379
Haves, (dec'd), *Re*, Haves v. Haves [1951] W.N. 550; [1951] 2 All E.R. 928 860
Hawkesley v. May [1956] 1 Q.B. 304; [1955] 3 W.L.R. 569 .... 505, 551

Hawkesley's Settlement, *Re* [1934] Ch. 384 .... 147, 150
Hawkins v. Blewitt (1798) 2 Esp. 663 138
—— v. Kemp (1803) 3 East 410 172
Hawthorne, *Re* (1883) 23 Ch.D. 743 .... 695, 738
Hayes' Will Trusts, *Re*, Pattinson v. Hayes [1971] 1 W.L.R. 758; 115 S.J. 310 .... 56, 58
Hay's Settlement Trusts, *Re*, Grieg v. McGregor [1982] 1 W.L.R. 202 .... 61, 102, 105,
           106, 107, 109, 168, 169, 172, 175, 176, 180, 200, 208, 209, 353
Hayman v. Governors of Rugby School (1874) L.R. 18 Eq. 28 803
Haynes' Will Trusts, *Re*, Pitt v. Haynes [1949] Ch. 5; [1948] L.J.R. 1745 133
Hayward, *Re*, Kerrod v. Hayward [1957] Ch. 528; [1957] 3 W.L.R. 50 861
Haywood v. Brunswick Building Society (1881) 8 Q.B.D. 403 706
—— v. Cope (1858) 25 Beav. 140 .... 694, 699
Head v. Gould [1898] 2 Ch. 250 .... 485, 633, 643, 502
Healey v. Healey [1915] 1 K.B. 938 19
Heard v. Pilley (1869) L.R. 4 Ch. App. 548 256
Heath v. Rydley (1614) Cro. Jac. 335 12
Heathcote v. Hulme (1819) 1 Jac. & W. 122 638
Heather, *Re* [1906] 2 Ch. 230 862
Heilbut Symons & Co. v. Buckleton [1913] A.C. 30 826
Hellewell v. Chief Constable of Derbyshire [1995] 1 W.L.R. 804; [1995] 4 All E.R.
     473 797
Hembury v. Peachey (1996) 72 P. & C.R. 271
Hemingway Securities Ltd v. Dunraven Ltd [1995] 1 E.G.L.R. 61, Ch.D. 765, 767
Hemmens v. Wilson Browne [1995] Ch. 223; [1993] 4 All E.R. 826 96
Henderson, *Re* [1940] Ch. 764 .... 453, 497
Hendy Lennox (Industrial Engines) Ltd v. Grahame Puttick Ltd [1984] 1 W.L.R. 485
     (1984) 128 S.J. 220 .... 682, 683, 685
Henley v. Wardell, *The Times*, January 29, 1988 583
Henning v. Church of Jesus Christ of Latter-Day Saints [1964] A.C. 420 [1962] 1
     W.L.R. 1091 382
Henry Wood Memorial Trust, *Re* [1966] 1 W.L.D. 1601; 110 S.J. 871 442
Henty v. Wrey (1882) 21 Ch.D. 332 177
Henty and Constable (Brewers) Ltd v. I.R.C. [1961] 1 W.L.R. 1504 86
Hepplewhite Will Trusts, *Re*, *The Times*, January 21, 1977 .... 328, 330, 333, 334
Herbage v. Pressdram Ltd (1984) 1 W.L.R. 1160; (1984) 128 W.J. 615 .... 760, 794
Hercy v. Birch (1804) 9 Ves. 357 710
Hermann Loog v. Bean (1884) 26 Ch.D. 306 793
Heron Garage Properties Ltd v. Moss [1974] 1 W.L.R. 148; (1973) 117 S.J. 697 713
Herring v. Templeman [1973] 3 All E.R. 569; (1973) 117 S.J. 793 .... 446, 803
Heseltine v. Heseltine [1971] 1 W.L.R. 342; (1970) 114 S.J. 972 .... 231, 247, 248,
                                          253, 264, 319
Hetherington (dec'd), *Re* [1990] Ch. 1 .... 356, 378, 379, 419
Hetley, *Re* [1902] 2 Ch. 866 155
Hetling and Merton's Contract, *Re* [1893] 3 Ch. 269 175
Heys, Goods of, [1914] P. 192 .... 305, 308
Heyworth's Contingent Reversionary Interest [1956] Ch. 364; [1956] 2 W.L.R.
     1044 .... 571, 618
Hichinbroke (Lord) v. Seymour (1789) 1 Bro. C.C. 395 177
Higginbottom, *Re* [1892] 3 Ch. 132 .... 498, 501
Highway Foods International Ltd, *Re* [1995] 1 B.C.L.C. 209 682
Hill, *Re* [1934] Ch. 623 589
Hill v. Langley, *The Times*, January 28, 1988 591
—— v. C.A. Parsons & Co. Ltd [1972] Ch. 305; [1971] 3 W.L.R. 995 .... 709, 785, 790
—— v. Permanent Trustee Co. of N.S.W. [1930] A.C. 720 548
Hillel v. Christoforides (1992) 63 P. & C.R. 301 698
Hilliard v. Fulford (1876) 4 Ch.D. 389 533
Hillier's Trusts, *Re*, Hillier v. Att.-Gen. [1954] 1 W.L.R. 700; [1954] 1 W.L.R. 9 238,
                                                                  442
Hinves v. Hinves (1884) 3 Hare 609 542
Hivac v. Park Royal Scientific Instruments [1946] Ch. 169 785

Hoare v. Hoare (1983) 13 Fam. Law 142, C.A. 254, 417, 419
—— v. Osborne (1866) L.R. 1 Eq. 585 .... 397, 422, 427
Hobourn Aero-Components Air Raid Distress Fund's Trusts, *Re* [1946] Ch. 194 387,
    236, 240
Hobson, *Re* (1855) 55 L.J.Ch. 422 541
Hochster v. De la Tour (1853) 2 E. & B. 678 696
Hodges, *Re* (1878) 7 Ch.D. 754 .... 507, 508
Hodgson, *Re* [1913] 1 Ch. 34 193
Hodgson v. Duce (1856) 28 L.T. (O.S.) 155 745
—— v. Marks [1971] Ch. 892; [1971] 2 W.L.R. 1263 .... 69, 77, 87, 231, 241, 244, 315
Hoffman-La Roche (F.) & Co. v. Secretary of State for Trade and Industry [1975] A.C.
    295; [1974] 3 W.L.R. 104 .... 751, 754, 768, 769
Hoggart v. Scott (1830) 1 Russ. & M. 293 714
Hohler v. Aston [1920] 2 Ch. 420 730
Holder v. Holder [1968] Ch. 353; [1968] 2 W.L.R. 237 .... 491, 590, 591, 645, 647
Holding & Management Ltd v. Property Holding & Investment Trust plc [1989] 1
    W.L.R. 1313; [1990] 1 All E.R. 938 .... 485, 513, 586
Holland, *Re* [1914] 2 Ch. 595 .... 173, 177, 179
Holland v. German Property Administrator [1937] 2 All E.R. 807 651
Holliday (A Bankrupt), *Re*, *ex p.* Trustee of the Bankrupt v. Bankrupt, The [1981] Ch.
    405; [1981] 2 W.L.R. 996 282
Hollington Brothers v. Rhodes [1951] 2 All E.R. 578n.; [1951] W.N. 437 35
Holmes v. Att.-Gen., *The Times* February 12, 1981 .... 396, 417
—— v. Coghill (1806) 12 Ves. Jr. 206 173
Holmes v. Penney (1856) 3 K. & J. 90 196
Holt's Settlement, *Re*, Wilson v. Holt [1969] 1 Ch. 100; [1968] 2 W.L.R. 653 .... 86, 88,
    619, 623, 624, 628, 629
Homs v. Murphy (1997) 73 P. & C.R. 26 698
Honeywell Information Systems Ltd v. Anglian Water Authority, *The Times*, June 29,
    1976 755
Hood, *Re* [1931] 1 Ch. 240 394
Hooper, *Re* [1932] 1 Ch. 38 .... 354, 355, 366
Hooper v. Rogers [1975] Ch. 43; [1974] 3 W.L.R. 329 .... 769, 771, 776, 778, 780
Hopgood v. Brown [1955] 1 W.L.R. 213; 99 S.J. 168 .... 867, 888, 894
Hopkins v. Hopkins (1739) 1 Atk. 581 11
Hopkins' Will Trusts, *Re*, Naish v. Francis Bacon Society Incorporated [1965] Ch. 669;
    [1964] 3 W.L.R. 840 .... 388, 389
Hopkinson, *Re*, Lloyds Bank v. Baker [1949] W.N. 29; 1 All E.R. 346 .... 393, 407
Horcal Ltd v. Gatland, *The Times*, April 16, 1984 .... 596, 821
Horlock, *Re* [1895] 1 Ch. 516 860
Horne, *Re* [1905] 1 Ch. 76 533
Horrocks v. Forray [1976] 1 W.L.R. 230 875
Horsler v. Zorro [1975] Ch. 302; [1975] 2 W.L.R. 183 .... 725, 727
Hounslow London Borough Council v. Twickenham Garden Developments [1971] Ch.
    233; [1970] 3 W.L.R. 538 .... 706, 871
Houston v. Burns [1918] A.C. 337 .... 175, 351, 422, 425
Howard, *Re*, *The Times*, October 30, 1908 367
Howard v. Harris (1681) 1 Vern. 33 13
Howard E. Perry & Co. Ltd v. British Railways Board [1980] 1 W.L.R. 1375 702
Howe v. Earl of Dartmouth (1802) 7 Ves. 137 .... 28, 527, 538, 539,
    540, 543, 544, 546, 556, 640
Howlett, *Re* [1906] 1 Ch. 793 653
Hubbard v. Pitt [1976] Q.B. 142; [1975] I.C.R. 308 .... 755, 756, 759, 793
—— v. Vosper [1972] 2 Q.B. 84; [1972] 2 W.L.R. 389 .... 26, 755, 760, 775, 795
Hughes v. London Borough of Southwark [1988] I.R.L.R. 55; (1988) 85/5 L.S.Gaz.
    28 .... 709, 791
—— v. Metroplitan Railway Co. (1877) 2 App. Cas. 439 884
Huguenin v. Baseley (1807) 14 Ves. 273 .... 152, 646, 829
Hummeltenberg, *Re* [1923] 1 Ch. 237 390
Huning v. Ferrers (1711) Gilb. Eq. 85 887

Hunt v. Carew (1649) Nels. 46 883
—— v. Luck [1902] 1 Ch. 428; [1901] 1 Ch. 45 34
Hunter v. Moss [1994] 1 W.L.R. 452 .... 95, 96, 97
Hunter's Will Trusts, *Re*, Gilks v. Harris [1963] Ch. 372; [1962] 3 W.L.R. 1442 .... 175, 176, 581
Huntingdon Copper Co. v. Henderson (1872) 4 R. (Court of Session) 294 594
Huntingford v. Hobbs [1993] 1 F.L.R. 736; (1992) 24 H.L.R. 652 .... 254, 264, 270, 272
Hurst v. Picture Theatres Ltd [1915] 1 K.B. 1 .... 871, 872, 873, 874
Hussain v. Hussain [1986] Fam. 134; [1986] 2 W.L.R. 801 .... 739, 768
Hussey v. Palmer [1972] 1 W.L.R. 1286; 116 S.J. 567 .... 52, 68, 69, 231, 256, 270, 286, 318, 879
Hutton v. Watling [1948] Ch. 398; 64 T.L.R. 326; 92 S.J. 297; [1948] 1 All E.R. 803; C.A.; affirming [1948] Ch. 26 .... 699, 874
Huxham v. Llewellyn (1873) 21 W.R. 570 718
Huxtable, *Re* [1902] 2 Ch. 793 .... 154, 155
Hyde, *Re* [1932] 1 Ch. 95 326
Hyde v. Pearce [1982] 1 W.L.R. 560; (1982) 125 S.J. 119; [1982] 1 All E.R. 1029, C.A. 313
Hytrac Conveyors Ltd v. Conveyors International Ltd [1983] 1 W.L.R. 44; (1982) 126 S.J. 728 806

I (a minor), *Re*, *The Times*, May 22, 1987 .... 745, 802
IBM United Kingdom v. Prima Data International [1994] 1 W.L.R. 719; [1994] 4 All E.R. 748 808
IDC Group v. Clark (1992) 65 P. & C.R. 179; [1992] 1 E.G.L.R. 187 .... 321, 880, 881
ITC Film Distributors v. Video Exchange [1982] Ch. 431 806
Imperial Group Pension Trust v. Imperial Tobacco [1991] 1 W.L.R. 589; [1991] 2 All E.R. 597 .... 48, 460
Incorporated Council of Law Reporting for England and Wales v. Att.-Gen. [1972] Ch. 73; [1971] 3 W.L.R. 853 .... 376, 378, 384, 389, 399, 410, 424, 447
Indian Oil Corp. v. Greenstone Shipping Co. S.A. (Panama); Ypatianna, The [1988] Q.B. 345 [1987] 2 Lloyd's Rep. 286 667
Industrial Development Consultants Ltd v. Cooley [1972] 1 W.L.R. 443; [1972] 2 All E.R. 162 .... 599, 607
Industrial Properties (Barton Hill) v. Associated Electrical Industries [1977] Q.B. 580; (1977) 2 W.L.R. 726 .... 17, 710
Ingram (Executors of the Estate of Lady Ingram) v. Inland Revenue Commissioners [1995] S.T.C. 564 221
—— v. Little [1961] 1 Q.B. 31; [1960] 3 W.L.R. 504 818
I.R.C. v. Angus (1889) 23 Q.B.D. 579 79
—— v. Baddeley [1955] A.C. 572 [1955] 2 W.L.R. 552 .... 403, 404, 405, 411, 417, 420, 422, 424
—— v. Bernstein [1961] Ch. 399; [1961] 2 W.L.R. 143 .... 572, 579
—— v. Broadway Cottages Trust, Same v. Sunnylands Trust [1955] Ch. 20; [1954] 3 W.L.R. 438 .... 64, 98, 99, 358, 372
—— v. Burmah Oil Co. (1983) 54 T.C. 200; [1982] S.T.C. 30 212
—— v. Educational Grants Association Ltd [1967] Ch. 993; [1967] 3 W.L.R. 41 ...... 381, 415, 416, 424
—— v. Fitzwilliam. *See* Countess Fitzwilliam v. I.R.C. 212
—— v. Glasgow (City) Police Athletic Association [1953] A.C. 380; [1953] 2 W.L.R. 625 .... 403, 405, 410, 424
—— v. McMullen [1981] A.C. 1; [1980] 2 W.L.R. 416 .... 378, 391, 402, 405, 447
—— v. Macpherson [1989] A.C. 159 H.L 225
—— v. Oldham Training and Enterprise Council [1996] S.T.C. 1218 .... 378, 393
—— v. Slater (Helen) Charitable Trust [1982] Ch. 49; [1981] 3 W.L.R. 377 381
—— v. Stype Investments (Jersey) [1982] Ch. 456 504
—— v. Westminster (Duke) [1936] A.C. 1 212
—— v. Yorkshire Agricultural Society [1928] 1 K.B. 611 410

Innes, *Re* [1910] Ch. 188 136
Institute of Civil Engineers v. I.R.C. [1932] 1 K.B. 149 393
Instone v. Schroeder Music Publishing Co. *See* Schroeder Music Publishing v.
   Macaulay 788
International General Electric Co. Ltd v. Commissioner of Customs and Excise [1962]
   Ch. 784; [1962] 3 W.L.R. 20 740
International Sales and Agencies Ltd v. Marcus [1982] 3 All E.R. 551; [1982] 2
   C.M.L.R. 46 299
Inverugie Investments Ltd v. Hackett [1995] 1 W.L.R. 713; [1995] 3 All E.R. 841 781
Inwards v. Baker [1965] 2 Q.B. 29; [1965] 2 W.L.R. 212 .... 882, 888, 894
Iraqi Ministry of Defence v. Arcepey Shipping Co. S.A. and Gillespie Bros. & Co.
   [1981] Q.B. 65; [1979] 2 Lloyd's Rep. 491 .... 752, 815
Ironmongers' Co. v. Att.-Gen. (1844) 10 Cl. & F. 908 430
Irvine v. Sullivan (1869) L.R. 8 Eq. 673 156
Isaac v. Defriez (1754) 2 Amb. 595 412
Isaacs, *Re* [1894] 3 Ch. 506 851
Islamic Republic of Iran Shipping Lines v. Denby [1987] 1 Lloyd's Rep. 367 (1986)
   136 New L.J. 1162 596
Island Export Finance Ltd v. Umunna [1986] B.C.L.C. 460 600
Istel (A.T. & T.) Ltd v. Tully [1993] A.C. 45 808
Ives (E.R.) Investments Ltd v. High [1967] 2 Q.B. 379: [1967] 2 W.L.R. 789 852,
                                                                               870, 888, 891, 894
Ivin v. Blake (1994) 67 P. & C.R. 263 267
Ivory v. Palmer [1975] I.C.R. 340; 119 S.J. 405, C.A. 873

J (a minor) (medical treatment), *Re* [1993] Fam. 15; [1992] 3 W.L.R. 507 760
—— v. J. (C. intervening). *See* Jones v. Jones & Croall 204
J. T. Developments Ltd v. Quinn (1990) 62 P. & C.R. 33; [1991] 2 E.G.L.R. 257,
   C.A. 883, 894
Jackson, *Re* (1882) 21 Ch.D. 786 614
—— v. Cator (1800) 5 Ves. 688 887
—— v. Dickinson [1903] 1 Ch. 947 641
—— v. Horizon Holidays [1975] 1 W.L.R. 1468; 119 S.J. 759 .... 125, 703, 729
—— v. Normanby Brick Co. [1899] 1 Ch. 438 736
Jacobs, *Re*, Westminster Bank v. Chinn (1970) 114 S.J. 515 385
Jacomb v. Harwood (1751) 2 Ves. Sen. 265 54
Jaffa v. Taylor Gallery; Jaffa v. Harris, *The Times*, March 21, 1990 115
Jaffray v. Marshall [1993] 1 W.L.R. 1285; [1994] 1 All E.R. 143 .... 547, 635
Jaggard v. Sawyer [1995] 1 W.L.R. 269; [1995] 2 All E.R. 189 .... 725, 728, 750,
                                                                               777, 779, 781, 782
Jagger v. Jagger [1926] P. 93 812
Jakeman v. South West Thames Regional Health Authority and London Ambulance
   Service [1990] I.R.L.R. 62 757
James, *Re* [1935] Ch. 449 .... 135, 136
—— v. Dean (1808) 15 Ves. Jr. 236 292
James Jones & Son Ltd v. Tankerville [1909] 2 Ch. 440 869
James's Will Trusts, *Re*, Peard v. James [1962] Ch. 226; [1960] 3 W.L.R. 1031 106
Jane Tyrell's Case (1557) 11
Jankowski v. Petek Estate (1995) 131 D.L.R. 153
Jansen v. Jansen [1965] P. 478; [1965] 3 W.L.R. 875 270
Jarvis, *Re*, Edge v. Jarvis [1958] 1 W.L.R. 815; 102 S.J. 546 .... 587, 638, 655
Jeffrey S. Levitt, *Re* [1992] Ch. 457; [1992] 2 W.L.R. 975 30
Jefferys v. Jefferys (1841) Cr. & Ph. 138 116
Jenkins (Inspector of Taxes) v. Brown; *sub nom.*, Warrington (H.M. Inspector of Taxes)
   v. Brown, 62 TC 230; [1989] 1 W.L.R. 1163 216
Jenkins v. Livesey (formerly Jenkins) [1985] A.C. 424; [1985] 2 W.L.R. 47 826
Jenkin's Will Trusts, *Re*, Public Trustee v. British Union for the Abolition of Vivisec-
   tion [1966] Ch. 249; [1966] 2 W.L.R. 615 436
Jenkin's and Randell's Contract, *Re* [1903] 2 Ch. 362 .... 636, 639
Jenner v. Turner (1880) 16 Ch.D. 188 329
Jervis v. Howle & Talke Colliery Co. [1937] Ch. 67 842

Jeune v. Queens Cross Properties [1974] Ch. 97; [1973] 3 W.L.R. 378 707
Job v. Job (1877) 6 Ch.D. 562 15
Joblin v. Watkins and Roseveare (Motors) 64 T.L.R. 464 [1949] 1 All E.R. 47 35
Jobson v. Palmer [1893] 1 Ch. 71 .... 482, 514
Joel's Will Trusts, *Re*, Rogerson v. Brudenell-Bruce [1967] Ch. 14; [1966] 3 W.L.R.
    209 .... 545, 573, 576
John v. George [1995] 1 E.G.L.R. 9 .... 232, 892
Johnson, *Re* (1880) 15 Ch.D 548 485
——, *Re* [1904] 1 K.B. 134 187
——, *Re* [1939] 2 All E.R. 458 91
—— v. Agnew [1980] A.C. 367; [1979] 2 W.L.R. 487 .... 31, 697, 698, 724, 725,
    726, 727, 776, 782, 780, 781, 817
—— v. Ball (1851) 5 De G. & Sm. 85 155
—— v. Bragge [1901] 1 Ch. 28 840
—— v. Wyatt (1863) 2 De G.J. & S 18 771
Johnson & Co. (Barbados) Ltd v. N.S.R. Ltd [1996] 3 W.L.R. 583 728
Johnson's Will Trusts, *Re*, National Provincial Bank v. Jeffery [1967] Ch. 387; [1967]
    2 W.L.R. 152 .... 328, 330
Johnstone v. Hall (1856) 2 K. & J. 414 783
Joliffe v. Baker (1883) 11 Q.B.D. 255 722
Jones, *Re* [1898] 1 Ch 438 93
——, *Re* [1942] Ch. 328 .... 145, 146
——, *Re* [1945] Ch. 105 168
——, *Re*, Midland Bank Executor and Trustee Co. v. Jones [1953] Ch. 125; [1953] 2
    W.L.R. 283 .... 103, 330
—— v. AMP Perpetual Trustee Company N.Z. Ltd [1994] 1 N.Z.L.R. 690 .... 522, 525,
    526, 594, 600
—— v. Att.-Gen. [1974] Ch. 148; [1973] 3 W.L.R. 608 .... 451, 504
—— v. Badley (1868) L.R. 3 Ch. App. 362 .... 149, 152
—— v. Foxall (1852) 15 Beav. 388 639
—— v. Gwent County Council [1992] I.R.L.R. 521 790
—— v. Jones (1876) 1 Q.B.D. 279 329
—— v. Lipman [1962] 1 W.L.R. 832; 106 S.J. 531 695
—— v. Lock (1865) L.R. 1 Ch. App. 25 .... 76, 118, 119, 132
—— v. Roberts [1995] 2 F.L.R. 422; [1995] Fam. Law 673, Ch.D. 316
—— v. Selby (1710) Prec. Ch. 300 140
—— v. Shipping Federation of British Colombia (1963) 37 D.L.R. (2d) 273 .... 484, 509
—— v. Jones & Croall [1989] Fam. 350; [1989] 2 W.L.R. 852 204
—— v. Lee and Guilding [1980] I.C.R. 310; [1980] I.R.L.R. 67 790
—— v. Pacaya Rubber and Produce Co. [1911] 1 K.B. 455 736
Jones (A.E.) v. Jones (F.W.) [1977] 1 W.L.R. 438; (1976) 33 P. & C.R. 147 .... 275, 888
Jones (F.C.) & Sons (Trustee) v. Jones [1996] 3 W.L.R. 703 .... 659, 660,
    661, 663, 664, 666
Jones & Sons Ltd v. Tankerville [1909] 2 Ch. 440 .... 785, 787
Jones' WIll Trusts, *Re*, Soames v. Att.-Gen. [1947] Ch. 48; 115 L.J.Ch. 307 572
Jordan v. Norfolk County Council [1994] 1 W.L.R. 1353; [1994] 4 All E.R. 218 748
Jorden v. Money (1845) 5 H.L.C. 185 .... 883, 885
Joscelyne v. Nissen [1970] 2 Q.B. 86; [1970] 2 W.L.R. 509 .... 149, 841, 844
Joseph v. National Magazine Co. [1959] Ch. 14; [1958] 3 W.L.R. 366 .... 704, 714
Joseph's W.T., *Re* [1959] 1 W.L.R. 1019; 103 S.J. 833 623
Joyce v. Joyce [1978] 1 W.L.R. 1170; (1978) 122 S.J. 745 719
—— v. Liverpool City Council [1996] Q.B. 252 .... 732, 735

K. (dec'd), *Re* [1986] Fam. 180; [1985] 3 W.L.R. 234 .... 58, 316, 317
K. v. P. [1993] Ch. 140; [1992] 3 W.L.R. 1015 642
Karak Rubber Co. Ltd v. Burden (No. 2) [1971] 299
Kaunas v. Smyth (1977) 75 D.L.R. 368 727
Kay, *Re* [1897] 2 Ch. 518 649
Kay's Settlement Trusts, *Re* [1939] Ch. 329 .... 124, 126, 130, 133
Kaye v. Robertson [1991] 18 F.S.R. 62 794

Kayford (In Liquidation) *Re* [1975] 1 W.L.R. 279; (1974) 118 S.J. 752 .... 42, 51, 76, 92, 120, 342, 668

Keech v. Sandford (1726) Sel. Cas. Ch. 61 .... 68, 591, 593

Keeler's Settlement Trusts, *Re*, Keeler v. Gladhill [1981] Ch. 156; [1981] 2 W.L.R. 499 594

Keen, *Re* [1937] Ch. 236 .... 150, 155, 157, 160

Keenan v. Handley (1864) 2 De. G.J. & A. 283 10 L.T. 800 730

Kekewich v. Manning (1851) 1 De G.M. & G. 176 117

Kelly, *Re* [1932] I.R. 255 367

—— v. Cooper [1993] A.C. 205; [1992] 3 W.L.R. 936 484

—— v. Solari (1841) 9 M. & W. 54 822

Kelsen v. Imperial Tobacco Co. [1957] 2 Q.B. 334; [1957] 2 W.L.R. 1007 .... 748, 772, 776, 779, 793

Kemp v. Burn (1863) 4 Giff. 348 548

—— v. Kemp (1801) 5 Ves. Jr. 849 100

—— v. Neptune Concrete [1988] 48 E.G. 71; (1989) 57 P. & C.R. 369, C.A. 843

—— v. The Public Curator of Queensland [1969] Qd.R. 145 316

Kemp's S.E., *Re*. (1883) 24 Ch. D. 485 500

Kennard v. Kennard (1872) L.R. 8 Ch. App. 227 173

Kennaway v. Thompson [1981] Q.B. 88; [1980] 3 W.L.R. 361 .... 738, 776, 779, 792

Kent County Council v. Batchelor (1977) 33 P. & C.R. 185; (1976) 75 L.G.R. 151 ... 739

—— (No. 2) [1979] 1 W.L.R. 213 .... 742, 798

Keren Kayemeth Le Jisroel Ltd v. I.R.C. [1931] 2 K.B. 465; [1932] A.C. 650 .... 385, 395, 399, 420

Kerr's W.T., *Re* (1878) 4 Ch.D. 600 179

Kershaw v. Whelan (No. 2), *The Times*, February 10, 1997 655

Kershaw's Trusts, *Re* (1868) L.R. 6 Eq. 322 580

Ketchum International plc v. Group Public Relations Holdings Ltd [1997] 1 W.L.R. 4 752

Ketley v. Gooden (1997) 73 P. & C.R. 305 .... 772, 779

Kewal Investments Ltd v. Arthur Maiden [1990] 1 E.G.L.R. 193 321

Khashoggi v. I.P.C. Magazines [1986] 1 W.L.R. 1412; (1986) 130 S.J. 862 793

Khoo Cheng Teow, *Re* [1932] Straits Settlements L.R. 226 .... 357, 367

Khoo Tek Keong v. Ching Joo Tuan Neuh [1934] A.C. 529 514

Kidney v. Coussmaker (1806) 12 Ves. 136 858

Kilpin v. Raltey [1892] 1 Q.B. 582 115

King, *Re* [1923] 1 Ch. 243 .... 397, 422, 437

——, *Re* [1928] Ch. 330 .... 573, 576

—— v. David Allen & Sons, Billposting Ltd [1916] 2 A.C. 54 .... 877, 878, 880

—— v. Denison (1813) I.V. & B. 260 .... 53, 241

—— v. Mullins (1852) 1 Drew 536

King-Ansell v. Police [1979] 2 N.Z.L.R. 531 327

King's Trusts, *Re* (1892) 29 L.R. Ir. 401 186

King's Will Trusts, *Re*, Assheton v. Boyne [1964] Ch. 542; [1964] 2 W.L.R. 913 ...... 57, 493, 498

Kingdom of Spain v. Christie Manson & Woods Ltd [1986] 1 W.L.R. 1120; (1986) 130 S.J. 484 745

Kingsnorth Finance Co. v. Tizard [1986] 1 W.L.R. 783; (1985) 130 S.J. 244 .... 33, 34, 37, 277, 279

Kingsnorth Trust Ltd v. Bell [1986] 1 W.L.R. 119 830

Kingswood Estate Co. Ltd v. Anderson [1963] 2 Q.B. 169; [1962] 3 W.L.R. 1102 ...: 732

Kinlock v. Secretary of State for India (1882) 7 App. Cas 619 70

Kirklees Metropolitan Borough Council v. Wickes Building Supplies; Mendip District Council v. B. & Q. [1993] A.C. 227; [1992] 3 W.L.R. 170 .... 742, 755, 769, 799

Kirwan, *Re* (1884) 25 Ch.D. 373 178

Kitchen v. Royal Air Force Association [1958] 1 W.L.R. 563; 102 S.J. 363 654

Kleinwort Benson v. Birmingham City Council [1996] 3 W.L.R. 1139 679

Klug v. Klug [1918] 2 Ch. 67 .... 171, 506, 508

Knapp, *Re* [1929] 1 Ch. 341 380

Knight, *Re*, Wynn, *Re*, Midland Bank Executor and Trustee Co. v. Parker [1957] Ch. 441; [1957] 2 W.L.R. 987 172
Knight v. Bowyer (1858) 2 De G. & J. 421 773
—— v. Knight (1840) 3 Beav. 148 89
Knight's Trust, *Re* (1859) 27 Beav. 45 534
Knocker v. Youle [1986] 1 W.L.R. 934 621
Knott v. Coltee (1852) 16 Beav. 77 .... 633, 636
Knox v. Mackinnon (1888) 13 App. Cas. 753 483
Koeppler Will Trusts, *Re*, Barclays Bank Trust Co. v. Slack [1986] Ch. 423; [1985] W.L.R. 765 .... 378, 379, 394, 399, 408, 409, 434, 436
Koettgen's Will Trust, *Re*, Westminster Bank v. Family Welfare Association Trustees [1954] Ch. 252; [1954] 2 W.L.R. 166 .... 388, 416, 417
Kolb's Will Trusts, *Re*, Lloyds Bank v. Ullman [1962] Ch. 531; [1961] 3 W.L.R. 1034 .... 530, 531, 619, 620
Kumar (A Bankrupt), *Re*, *ex p.* Lewis v. Kumar [1993] 1 W.L.R. 224; [1993] 2 All E.R. 700 .... 339, 342

Labouchere v. Earl of Wharncliffe (1879) 13 Ch.D. 346 803
Lac Minerals Ltd v. International Corona Resources Ltd (1989) 61 D.L.R. 14 24, 290, 291
Lackersteen v. Lackersteen (1864) 30 L.J.Ch. 5 845
Laidlaw Foundation, *Re* (1985) 48 O.R. (2d) 549 403
Laing (J.W.) Trust, *Re* [1984] Ch. 143 .... 431, 437, 441
Lake, *Re* [1903] 1 K.B. 439 636
Lake v. Bayliss [1974] 1 W.L.R. 1073; 118 S.J. 532 312
—— v. Lake [1989] S.T.C. 865 .... 840, 842
Lall v. Lall [1963] 1 W.L.R. 1249 58
Lamare v. Dixon (1873) L.R. 6 H.L. 414 .... 694, 699, 717
Lambe v. Eames (1871) L.R. 6 Ch. 597 91
Lamshed v. Lamshed (1963) 109 C.L.R. 440 719
Lane, *Re* [1908] 2 Ch. 581 172
Lane v. Newdigate (1804) 10 Ves. Jr. 192 788
Lang v. Lang (1837) 8 Sim. 451 865
Langton v. Langton [1995] 2 F.L.R. 890; [1995] 3 F.C.R. 521 .... 829, 836, 837
Lankow v. Rose [1995] 1 N.Z.L.R. 277 268
Lansdowne's Will Trusts, *Re*, Lansdowne (Marquis) v. Shelburne (Earl) [1967] Ch. 603; [1967] 2 W.L.R. 992 .... 617, 619, 624
Lansing Linde Ltd v. Kerr [1991] 1 W.L.R. 251; [1991] 1 All E.R. 418 762
Lanyon, *Re* [1927] 2 Ch. 264 329
Lashmar, *Re* [1891] 1 Ch. 258 84
Lassence v. Tierney (1849) 1 Mac. & G. 551 92
Laurence v. Lexourt Holdings [1978] 1 W.L.R. 1128 .... 716, 822, 824, 827
Lavery v. Pursell (1888) 39 Ch.D. 508 .... 710, 725, 777
Law Society v. Shanks (1987) 131 S.J. 1626; (1988) 18 Fam. Law 206; [1988] 1 F.L.R. 504 .... 805, 815
Lawes v. Bennett (1785) 1 Cox 167 851
Lawlor v. Union of Post Office Workers [1965] Ch. 712; [1965] 2 W.L.R. 579 802
Lawrence's Will Trusts, *Re*, Public Trustee v. Lawrence [1972] Ch. 418; [1971] 3 W.L.R. 188 .... 168, 171, 172
Laws v. Florinpace Ltd [1981] 1 All E.R. 659 .... 756, 792
Lawson v. Hartley-Brown (1996) 71 P. & C.R. 243 782
Layton v. Martin [1986] 2 F.L.R. 277; (1986) 16 Fam. Law 212 .... 266, 319, 320, 893
Lazard Bros. & Co. Ltd v. Fairfield Property Co. (Mayfair) Ltd (1977) 121 S.J. 793 . 718
Leach, *Re* [1912] 2 Ch. 422 332
Lead Workmens Fund Society, *Re* [1904] 2 Ch. 196 241
Leaf v. International Galleries [1950] 2 K.B. 86; 66 T.L.R. (Pt. 1) 1031 838
League Against Cruel Sports Ltd v. Scott [1986] Q.B. 240; [1985] 3 W.L.R. 400 792
Leahy v. Att.-Gen. for New South Wales [1959] A.C. 457; [1959] 2 W.L.R. 722 ...... 352, 361, 428, 429

Leakey v. National Trust for Places of Historic Interest and National Beauty [1980]
    Q.B. 485; [1980] 2 W.L.R. 65 .... 747, 792
Leaper, *Re* [1916] 1 Ch. 579 140
Learoyd v. Whiteley (1887) 12 App. Cas. 727 .... 481, 521, 522, 529, 560
Le Cras v. Perpetual Trustee Co. Ltd [1969] 1 A.C. 514 387
Lee v. Brown (1798) 4 Ves. 362 632
—— v. Cox and d'Aranda (1747) 3 Atk. 419 865
—— v. Lee [1952] 2 Q.B. 489; [1952] 1 T.L.R. 968 .... 280, 877
—— v. Sankey (1873) L.R. 15 Eq. 204 564
—— v. Showmen's Guild [1952] 2 Q.B. 329; [1952] 1 T.L.R. 1115 802
Leeds Industrial Co-operative Society Ltd v. Slack [1924] A.C. 851 ..... 725, 776, 777, 780
Leek, *Re*, Darwen (Baron) v. Leek [1969] 1 Ch. 563; [1968] 2 W.L.R. 1385 .... 61, 63,
                                                                                103, 108
Legh v. Lillie (1860) 6 H. & N. 165 694
Legione v. Hateley (1983) 57 A.L.J.R. 292 .... 720, 883
Leigh v. Burnett (1885) 29 Ch.D. 231 292
Leigh's Will Trusts, *Re*, Handyside v. Durbridge [1970] Ch. 277 58
Lemann's Trust, *Re* (1883) 22 Ch.D. 633 497
Lemos v. Coutts & Co. [1992–93] Cayman I.L.R. 400 548
Lennox Industries (Canada) Ltd v. The Queen (1987) 34 D.L.R. 297 664
Leong v. Lim Beng Chye [1955] A.C. 648; [1955] 3 W.L.R. 303 329
Le Page v. Gardom (1915) 84 L.J.Ch. 749 153
Lepton's Charity, *Re*, Ambler v. Thomas [1972] Ch. 276; [1971] 2 W.L.R. 659 440
Les Affréteurs Réunis Société Anonyme v. Leopold Walford (London) Ltd [1919] A.C.
    801 .... 19, 124, 132
Leslie (J.) Engineers Co. Ltd, *Re* [1976] 1 W.L.R. 292; (1975) 120 S.J. 146 .... 658, 688
Letterstedt v. Broers (1884) 9 App. Cas. 371 504
Levy, *Re*, Barclays Bank v. Board of Guardians and Trustees for the Relief of the Jewish
    Poor [1960] Ch. 346; [1960] 2 W.L.R. 278 380
Lewin v. Guest (1826) 1 Russ. 325 713
Lewis, *Re* [1904] 2 Ch. 656 551
——, *Re* (1910) 103 L.T. 495 594
——, *Re*, Public Trustee v. Allen [1955] Ch. 104; [1954] 3 W.L.R. 610 401
—— v. Averay [1972] 1 Q.B. 198 818
—— v. Heffer [1978] 1 W.L.R. 1061; (1978) 122 S.J. 112 .... 757, 759
—— v. Nobbs (1878) 8 Ch.D. 591 564
Lewis's of Leicester Ltd, *Re* [1995] 1 B.C.L.C. 428; [1995] B.C.C. 514, Ch.D 51,
                                                                                  92, 344
Liddell's Settlement Trust, *Re* [1936] Ch. 365 .... 738, 802
Liddiard, *Re* (1880) 14 Ch.D. 310 500
Life Association of Scotland v. Siddal (1861) 3 De G.F. & J. 58 .... 645, 646, 838
Lillingston, *Re*, Pembery v. Pembery [1952] W.N. 338; [1952] 1 T.L.R. 1622; 96 S.J.
    462; [1952] 2 All E.R. 184 .... 137, 138, 140
Lim Teng Huan v. Ang Swee Chuan [1992] 1 W.L.R. 113 .... 888, 889, 892
Lind, *Re* [1915] 2 Ch. 345 133
Lindsay and Forder's Contract, *Re* (1895) 72 L.T. 832 721
Lindsay Petroleum Co. v. Hurd (1874) L.R. 5 P.C. 221 655
Lindsay's Executor v. Forsyth, 1940 S.C. 568 369
Lion Laboratories Ltd v. Evans [1985] Q.B. 526; [1984] 3 W.L.R. 539 .... 756, 796
Lipinski's Will Trusts, *Re* [1976] Ch. 235 .... 349, 350, 356, 360,
                                                          361, 362, 364, 370, 406, 420
Lipkin Gorman v. Cass, *The Times*, May 29, 1985 30
—— v. Karpnale [1991] A.C. 548; [1991] 3 W.L.R. 10 .... 297, 300, 303, 657, 659, 660,
                                                            664, 679, 681, 689
Lister v. Hodgson (1867) L.R. 4 Eq. 30 845
Lister & Co. v. Stubbs (1890) 45 Ch.D. 1 .... 608, 812
Lister's Will Trusts, *Re* [1962] 1 W.L.R. 1441; 106 S.J. 1011 .... 619, 621

Livesey v. Livesey (1827) 3 Russ. 287 687
Liverpool and District Hospital for Diseases of the Heart v. Att.-Gen. [1981] Ch. 193;
    [1981] 2 W.L.R. 379 .... 430, 433
Liverpool City Council v. Att.-Gen., *The Times*, May 1, 1992 403
Llandudno Urban District Council v. Woods [1899] 2 Ch. 705 792
Llewellin's Will Trusts, *Re*, Griffiths v. Wilcox [1949] Ch. 225; [1949] L.J.R. 724 594
Llewellyn's Settlement, *Re* [1921] 2 Ch. 281 63
Lloyd v. Lloyd (1852) 2 Sim. (N.S.) 255 .... 329, 397
Lloyd's v. Harper (1880) 16 Ch.D. 290 .... 124, 127, 128
Lloyd's Settlement, *Re*, Lloyds v. Leeper [1967] 2 W.L.R. 1078; 111 S.J. 258 624
Lloyd's Bank v. Bundy [1975] Q.B. 326; [1974] 3 W.L.R. 501 .... 829, 830, 837
—— v. Carrick [1996] 4 All E.R. 630 .... 35, 268, 313, 888, 892, 894
—— v. Duker [1987] 1 W.L.R. 1324; (1987) 131 S.J. 1358 537
—— v. Marcan [1973] 1 W.L.R. 1387; 117 S.J. 761 340
—— v. Rosset [1991] 1 A.C. 107; [1990] 2 W.L.R. 867 ...... 256, 261, 262, 263, 264, 267,
    268, 291, 319
Lloyd's Bowmaker Ltd v. Britannia Arrow Holdings plc [1988] 1 W.L.R. 1337; (1988)
    132 S.J. 1527 810
Lobb (Alec) Garages Ltd v. Total Oil Great Britain [1985] 1 W.L.R. 173; (1985) 129
    S.J. 83 .... 654, 831, 836, 838
Locabail International Finance Ltd v. Agoexport [1986] 1 W.L.R. 657 .... 703, 753,
    765, 766
Lock International plc v. Beswick [1989] 1 W.L.R. 1268; [1989] 3 All E.R. 373 794,
    807
Lockhart v. Reilly (1856) 25 L.J.Ch. 697 643
Locker's Settlement, *Re*; Meachem v. Sachs [1977] 1 W.L.R. 1323; (1977) 121 S.J. 796;
    [1978] 1 All E.R. 216 .... 60, 101, 199, 207
Loffus v. Maw (1862) 3 Giff 592 884
Logicrose Ltd v. Southend United Football Club Ltd [1988] 1 W.L.R. 1256 597,
    817, 838
London Assurance Co. v. Mansel (1879) 11 Ch.D. 363 826
London Borough of Hounslow v. Hare (1992) 24 H.L.R. 9 449
London Hospital Medical College v. I.R.C. [1976] 1 W.L.R. 613; 120 S.J. 250 394,
    402, 424
London & Manchester Assurance Co. Ltd v. O. & H. Construction Ltd [1989] 2
    E.G.L.R. 185 .... 763, 765, 793
London Regional Transport v. Wimpey Group Services Ltd (1987) 53 P. & C.R. 356;
    [1986] 2 E.G.L.R. 41 841
London University v. Yarrow (1857) 1 De G. & J. 72 406
London University's Charitable Trusts, *Re* [1964] Ch. 282; [1963] 3 W.L.R. 1081 450
London Wine Co., *Re* (1986) PCC 121 .... 94, 95
Londonderry's Settlement, *Re*, Peat v. Walsh [1965] Ch. 918; [1965] 2 W.L.R.
    229 .... 460, 506, 507, 533, 550
Long's Settlement, *Re* (1868) 38 L.J.Ch. 125 577
Longman, *Re*, Westminster Bank v. Hatton [1955] 1 W.L.R. 197; 99 S.J. 169 191
Lonrho v. Fayed [1992] 1 A.C. 448; [1991] 3 W.L.R. 188 290
—— v. —— (No. 2) [1992] 1 W.L.R. 1; [1991] 4 All E.R. 961 .... 287, 290, 314, 666
—— v. Shell Petroleum Co. (No. 2) [1982] A.C. 173; [1980] 1 W.L.R. 627 .... 741, 797
Lonrho Exports Ltd v. Export Credits Guarantee Department [1996] 4 All E.R.
    673 .... 70, 674
Lopes, *Re* [1931] 2 Ch. 130 .... 388, 407
Lord v. Bunn (1843) 2 Y. & C. Ch. 98 194
Lord Advocate v. The Scotsman Publications Ltd [1990] 1 A.C. 812; [1989] 3 W.L.R.
    358 795
Lord Cable, *Re* [1977] 1 W.L.R. 7 755
Lord Chesham, *Re* (1886) 31 Ch.D. 466 854
Lord Chichester v. Coventry (1867) L.R. 2 H.L. 71 862
Lord Darlington v. Pulteney (1797) 3 Ves. Jr. 384 172
Lord de Clifford's Estate, *Re* [1900] 2 Ch. 707 .... 649, 651
Lord Inglewood v. I.R.C. [1983] 1 W.L.R. 366 .... 225, 226, 227

Lord Lechmere v. Lady Lechmere (1733) 3 P. Wms. 211; (1735) Cas. T. Talb. 80 863
Lord Provost etc. of Edinburgh v. Lord Advocate (1879) 4 App. Cas. 823 .... 638, 676
Lord Strathcona S.S. Co. v. Dominion Coal Co. [1926] A.C. 108 876
Loscombe v. Wintringham (1850) 13 Beav. 87 387
Lough v. Ward [1945] 2 All E.R. 338 801
Love v. Herrity (1991) 23 H.L.R. 217 .... 753, 763
Lovell, *Re* [1920] 1 Ch. 122 .... 329, 330
Lovesy v. Smith (1880) 15 Ch.D. 655 842
Low v. Bouverie [1891] 3 Ch. 82 883
Lowe v. Dixon (1885) 16 Q.B.D. 455 15
Lowe's Will Trusts, *Re*; More v. Att.-Gen. [1973] 1 W.L.R. 882; [1973] 2 All E.R.
    1136 534
Lowrie, *Re, ex p.* The Trustee of the Bankrupt v. The Bankrupt [1981] 3 All E.R. 353,
    D.C. 282
Lowther v. Bentinck (1874) LR 19 Eq. 166 .... 577, 578
Lucas, *Re*, [1922] 2 Ch. 52 386
——, *Re*, Sheard v. Mellor [1948] Ch. 424; [1948] L.J.R. 1914 433
Lucking's Will Trusts, Renwick v. Lucking [1968] 1 W.L.R. 866; (1967) 112 S.J.
    444 .... 512, 527, 563
Luganda v. Service Hotels [1969] 2 Ch. 209; [1969] 2 W.L.R. 1056 .... 765, 873, 874
Luke v. South Kensington Hotel Ltd (1879) 11 Ch.D. 121 486
Lumley v. Ravenscroft [1895] 1 Q.B. 683 713
Lumley v. Wagner (1852) 1 De. G.M. & G. 604 .... 708, 709, 787, 788, 790, 803
Lupton v. White (1808) 15 Ves. Jr. 432 667
Lyme Valley Squash Club Ltd v. Newcastle under Lyme Borough Council [1985] 2 All
    E.R. 405 .... 778, 845
Lyon v. Baker (1852) 5 De. G. & Sm. 622 588
—— v. Fishmongers Co. (1876) 1 App. Cas. 662 797
—— v. Home (1868) L.R. 6 Eq. 655 828
Lysaght, *Re*, Hill v. Royal College of Surgeons: [1966] 1 Ch. 191; [1965] 3 W.L.R.
    391 .... 166, 331, 432, 492
Lysaght v. Edwards (1876) 2 Ch.D. 499 312
Lyus v. Prowsa Developments [1982] 1 W.L.R. 1044; (1982) 126 S.J. 102 .... 42, 77, 78,
                                                                                                    315, 321, 322, 881

M. v. Home Office; *sub nom.* M., *Re* [1994] 1 A.C. 377; [1993] 3 W.L.R. 433 740
M. v. M. (Custody) [1983] 13 Fam. Law 112, C.A. 801
M. C. Bacon, *Re* [1991] Ch. 127; [1990] B.C.L.C. 324 .... 340, 342, 343, 344
M.E.P.C. Ltd v. Christian-Edwards [1981] A.C. 205 [1979] 3 W.L.R. 713 .... 718, 723
Macadam, *Re* [1946] Ch. 73; [1945] 2 All E.R. 664 594
Macartney, *Re* [1918] 1 Ch. 300 856
Macaulay v. O'Donnell [1943] Ch. 435 360
Macaulay's Estate, *Re* [1943] Ch. 435 395
McBride, *Re* (1980) 107 D.L.R. (3d) 233 330
McCaig v. University of Glasgow, 1907 S.C. 231 369
McCaig's Trustees v. Kirk-Session of United Free Church of Lismore, 1915 S.C.
    426 369
McCarthy, A Bankrupt, *Re. Ex p.* Trustee of the Property of the Bankrupt v. McCarthy,
    A Bankrupt [1975] 1 W.L.R. 807; (1975) 2 All E.R. 857 282
McCarthy and Stone v. Hodge & Co [1971] 1 W.L.R. 1547; 115 S.J. 607 33
McCormick v. Grogan (1868) L.R. 4 H.L. 82 .... 77, 147, 148, 149, 162
McDonald v. Horn [1995] 1 All E.R. 961; [1995] I.C.R. 685 .... 460, 586, 632
—— v. Irvine (1878) 8 Ch.D. 101 542
—— v. Scott [1893] A.C. 642 122
McDougall, *Re* [1957] 1 W.L.R. 81 .... 388, 393
Macduff, *Re* [1896] 2 Ch. 451 .... 390, 399, 401, 425
McEacharn, *Re* (1911) 103 L.T. 900 557
McEven, *Re* [1913] 2 Ch. 704 546
McEvoy v. Belfast Banking Co. [1935] A.C. 24 248
M'Fadden v. Jenkyns (1842) 1 Ph. 153 76
McGeorge, *Re*, Ratcliffe v. McGeorge [1963] Ch. 544; [1963] 2 W.L.R. 767 .... 572, 574

McGovern v. Att.-Gen. [1982] Ch. 321; [1982] 2 W.L.R. 222 ...... 384, 385, 389, 393, 399, 408, 409, 421, 447
McGrath v. Wallis [1995] 2 F.L.R. 114 .... 248, 251, 255, 256
McHardy and Sons (a firm) v. Warren [1994] 2 F.L.R. 338; [1994] 2 F.C.R. 1247 ..... 248, 265
McHenry v. Lewis (1882) 22 Ch.D. 407 803
McIntosh v. Dalwood (No. 4) (1930) 30 S.R. (N.S.W.) 415 703
MacJordan Construction v. Brookmount Erostin [1992] B.C.L.C. 350, *The Times*, October 29, 1991, C.A. 95, 96, 97
Mackay, *Re* [1906] 1 Ch. 25 551
——, *Re* [1911] 1 Ch. 300 651
—— v. Douglas (1872) L.R. 14 Eq. 106 340
Mackintosh v. Pogose [1895] 1 Ch. 505 187
Mackintosh's Judicial Factor v. Lord Advocate, 1935 S.C. 406 369
Mackneth v. Symmons (1808) 15 Ves. Jr. 329 313
Maclaine Watson & Co. Ltd. v. International Tin Council (No. 2) [1989] Ch. 286 ..... 734, 745
MacLaren's Settlement, *Re*, Royal Exchange Assurance v. Maclaren [1951] W.N. 394; [1951] 2 All E.R. 414 547
Macleay, *Re* (1875) 20 Eq. 186 332
McMahon v. McMahon [1996] 3 N.Z.L.R. 334 268
Macmillan Inc. v. Bishopsgate Investment Trust plc (No. 3) [1995] 1 W.L.R. 978 ..... 35, 229, 287, 293, 301
McPhail v. Doulton [1971] A.C. 424; [1970] 2 W.L.R. 1110 .... 60, 61, 62, 63, 64, 94, 97, 98, 99, 100, 104, 105, 107, 108, 109, 166, 169, 171, 198, 205, 206, 207, 208, 209, 358, 504
McRae v. Commonwealth Disposals Commission (1951) 84 C.L.R. 377 .... 819, 821
Maddock, *Re* [1902] 2 Ch. 230 .... 158, 159, 160
Madeley v. Booth (1845) 2 De G. & Sm. 718 722
Magee v. Pennine Insurance Co. [1969] 2 Q.B. 507; [1969] 2 W.L.R. 1278 .... 819, 820, 821, 822, 824
Mahoney v. Purnell [1996] 3 All E.R. 61 .... 634, 829, 832, 839
Mair, *Re* [1935] Ch. 562 .... 192, 616, 624
Maharaj (Sheila) v. Chand (Jai) [1986] A.C. 898; [1986] 3 W.L.R. 440 262
Mahesan v. Malaysia Government Officers Co-operative Housing Society [1979] A.C. 374; [1978] 2 W.L.R. 444 597
Makin (William) & Sons Ltd, *Re* [1993] B.C.C. 453 .... 459, 463
Malcolm v. Chancellor, Masters and Scholars of the University of Oxford (t/a Oxford University Press); *The Times*, December 19, 1990, C.A.; reversing, *The Times*, March 23, 1990 704
Malhotra v. Choudhury [1980] Ch. 52; [1978] 3 W.L.R. 825 .... 719, 724, 725, 728
Malins v. Freeman (1837) 2 Keen 25 .... 716, 717
Mallott v. Wilson [1903] 2 Ch. 494 114
Malmesbury v. Malmesbury (1862) 31 Beav. 407 840
Malone v. Metropolitan Police Commissioner [1980] Q.B. 49; [1978] 3 W.L.R. 936 .... 743, 765, 775, 812
Manches v. Trimborn (1946) 115 L.J.K.B. 305 74
Manchester Brewery Co. Ltd v. Coombs [1901] 2 Ch. 608 710
Manchester Corporation v. Connolly [1970] 1 Ch. 420; [1970] 2 W.L.R. 746 753
Manchester Ship Canal v. Manchester Racecourse Co. [1901] 2 Ch. 37 786
Mander v. Falcke [1891] 3 Ch. 488 32
Mandla v. Lee [1983] 2 A.C. 548; [1983] 2 W.L.R. 620 327
Manisty's Settlement, *Re*, Manisty v. Manisty [1974] Ch. 17; [1973] 3 W.L.R. 341 .... 105, 106, 107, 108, 168, 169, 171, 175, 199, 200, 209, 353, 507
Manners, *Re* [1949] Ch. 613; [1949] L.J.R. 1574 860
Manser, *Re* [1905] 1 Ch. 68 .... 396, 397
Mara v. Browne [1896] 1 Ch. 199 .... 304, 305, 648, 652
Marco Productions Ltd v. Pagola [1945] 1 K.B. 111 .... 730, 746, 783
Mareva Compania Naviera S.A. of Panama v. International Bulk Carriers S.A. (1975) 119 S.J. 660; [1975] 2 Lloyd's Rep. 509, C.A. 32, 42, 697, 735, 738, 739, 752, 760, 767, 802, 808, 809, 810, 811, 812, 813, 814, 815

Mariette, *Re* [1915] 2 Ch. 284 .... 391, 402
Marks v. Lilley [1959] 1 W.L.R. 749; 103 S.J. 658 696
Marlay, *Re* [1915] 2 Ch. 264 851
Marlees v. Franklin (1818) 1 Swans. 13 255
Marley v. Mutual Security Merhcant Bank and Trust Co. Ltd [1991] 3 All E.R. 198,
    P.C. 534
Marquess of Abergavenny's Estate Act Trusts, *Re*, Marquess of Abergavenny v. Ram
    [1981] 1 W.L.R. 843; (1980) 125 S.J. 291 582
Marsden v. Regan [1954] 1 W.L.R. 423; 98 S.J. 144 .... 649, 650, 651
Marsden's Trusts, *Re* (1859) 4 Drew. 594 178
Marshal v. Crutwell (1875) L.R. 20 Eq. 328 247
Marshall, *Re* [1920] 1 Ch. 284 191
Marshall (Inspector of Taxes) v. Kerr [1995] 1 A.C. 148; [1994] 3 W.L.R. 299 58
Marshall (Thomas) (Exports) v. Guinle [1979] Ch. 227; [1978] 3 W.L.R. 116 ..... 708, 756,
    785, 787, 795
Marshall's Will Trusts, *Re* [1945] Ch. 217 45
Martin, *Re*, *The Times*, November 19, 1980 417
—— v. City of Edinburgh District Council [1988] S.L.T. 329 .... 524, 525
—— v. Martin (1987) 54 P. & C.R. 238 271
—— v. Nutkin (1724) 2 P. Wms. 266 783
Mary Clark Home Trustees v. Anderson [1904] 2 K.B. 745 387
Maryon-Wilson's Estate, *Re* [1912] 1 Ch. 55 517
Mascall v. Mascall (1984) 49 P. & C.R. 119; (1984) L.S.Gaz. 2218, C.A. 115, 118
Masich v. Masich (1977) 121 S.J. 645; (1977) 7 Fam. Law 245, C.A. 752
Mason, *Re* [1929] 1 Ch. 1 487
—— v. Armitage (1806) 13 Ves. Jr. 25 701
—— v. Farbrother [1983] 2 All E.R. 1078 .... 465, 530, 531, 532, 615, 616, 619, 620
Massey v. Crown Life Insurance Co. [1978] 1 W.L.R. 676; [1978] I.C.R. 590 708
—— v. Midland Bank plc [1995] 1 All E.R. 929; (1995) 27 H.L.R. 227 ...... 833, 835, 836
Massingberd's Settlement, *Re* (1890) 63 L.T. 296 .... 529, 637, 645
Matharu v. Matharu [1994] 2 F.L.R. 597; (1994) 68 P. & C.R. 93 .... 887, 888, 891
Mathew v. Bobbins (1980) 124 S.J. 479; (1980) 41 P. & C.R. 1 829
—— v. T. M. Sutton [1994] 1 W.L.R. 1455; [1994] 4 All E.R. 793 .... 21, 596, 638
Matthews, *Re* (1859) 26 Beav. 463 497
May's Settlement, *Re* [1926] Ch. 136 .... 176, 581
May's Will Trusts, *Re* [1941] Ch. 109 498
Mayo, *Re* [1943] Ch. 302 .... 279, 486
Maythorn v. Palmer (1864) 11 L.T. 261 .... 775, 787
Mead, *Re* (1880) 15 Ch.D. 651 138
Mead's Trust Deed, *Re*, Briginshaw v. National Society of Operative Printers and
    Assistants [1961] 1 W.L.R. 1244; 105 S.J. 569 .... 387, 415, 428
Meade v. London Borough of Haringey [1979] 1 W.L.R. 637 .... 741, 750, 757,
    764, 766, 797
Measures v. Measures [1910] 2 Ch. 248 775
Medlock, *Re* (1886) 54 L.T. 828 575
Medway v. Doublelock [1978] 1 W.L.R. 710; (1977) 122 S.J. 248 797
Meek v. Kettlewell (1842) Hare 464 134
Meinertzhagen v. Davis (1844) 1 Coll. 353 501
—— v. Walters (1872) L.R. 7 Ch. App. 670 862
Mellody, *Re* [1918] 1 Ch. 228 392
Meng Leong Development Pte. v. Jip Hong Trading Co. Pte. [1985] A.C. 511 [1984]
    3 W.L.R. 1263 697
Mengel's Will Trusts, *Re*, Westminster Bank v. Mengel [1962] Ch. 791; [1962] 3
    W.L.R. 311 .... 852, 853
Mercantile Group (Europe) A.G. v. Aiyela [1994] Q.B. 366; [1993] 3 W.L.R.
    1116 .... 809, 811, 815
Mercedes-Benz A.G. v. Leiduck [1996] 1 A.C. 284 .... 809, 812
Mercier v. Mercier [1903] 2 Ch. 98 247
Merton, *Re*, Public Trustee v. Wilson [1953] 1 W.L.R. 1096; 97 S.J. 572 177
Metall und Rohstoff A.G. v. Donaldson Lufkin & Jenrette Inc. [1990] 1 Q.B. 391;
    [1989] 3 W.L.R. 563 .... 23, 290

Metcalfe v. Metcalfe [1891] 3 Ch. 1 188
Metropolitan Electric Supply Co. v. Ginder [1901] 2 Ch. 799 786
Mettoy Pension Trustees v. Evans [1990] 1 W.L.R. 1587; [1991] 2 All E.R. 513 .... 61, 62,
        101, 106, 168, 169, 170, 171, 173, 180, 182, 209, 459, 469, 503,
        507, 508
Meux, *Re*, Gilmour v. Gilmour [1958] Ch. 154; [1957] 3 W.L.R. 377 .... 617, 618
Mewburn's Settlement, *Re* [1934] Ch. 112 .... 176, 581
Meyers, *Re*, London Life Association v. St. George's Hospital [1951] Ch. 534; [1951]
    1 T.L.R. 435 410
Michaels (Furriers) (M.) v. Askew (1983) 127 S.J. 597, C.A. 738
Michelham's Will Trusts, *Re*, [1964] Ch. 550; [1963] 2 W.L.R. 1238 625
Middleton v. Clitheroe (1798) 3 Ves. 734 397
—— v. Pollock (1876) 2 Ch.D. 104 .... 121, 338
Midland Bank plc v. Cooke [1995] 4 All E.R. 562; (1995) 27 H.L.R. 733 .... 256, 262,
        265, 267, 269, 270, 272
—— v. Dobson and Dobson [1986] 1 F.L.R. 171; (1985) F.L.R. 314 .... 78, 87, 261,
        262, 319
—— v. Farmpride Hatcheries (1980) 260 E.G. 493; C.A. 880
—— plc v. Serter (1996) 71 P. & C.R. 264 835
—— plc v. Shephard [1988] 3 All E.R. 17; C.A. 830
—— plc v. Wyatt [1995] 1 F.L.R. 697; [1995] 3 F.C.R. 11 .... 92, 338, 339, 340
Midland Bank Trust Co. v. Green [1981] A.C. 513 .... 33, 35, 322, 704
Midland Marts Ltd v. Hobday [1989] 1 W.L.R. 1143; 133 S.J. 1109 768
Millennium Productions v. Winter Garden Theatre (London). *See* Winter Garden
    Theatre (London) v. Millennium Productions.
Miller v. I.R.C. [1987] S.T.C. 108. Ct. of Session 222
—— v. Jackson [1977] Q.B. 966; [1977] 3 W.L.R. 20 .... 738, 739, 779, 792
—— v. Lakefield Estates (1989) 57 P. & C.R. 104; 19 E.G. 67, C.A. 279
Miller's Trust Deed, *Re* (1978) 75 L.G.Gaz. 454 .... 511, 528, 634
Mills, *Re* [1930] 1 Ch. 654 180
—— v. Haywood (1877) 6 Ch.D. 196 .... 718, 719
—— v. Winchester Diocesan Board of Finance [1989] Ch. 428; [1989] 2 W.L.R.
    976 448
Milroy v. Lord (1862) 4 De G.F. & J. 264 .... 83, 114, 115, 117, 118, 132
Ministry of Health v. Simpson [1951] A.C. 251; 66 T.L.R. (Pt. 2) 1015; [1950] 2 All
    E.R. 1137; *sub nom. Re*, Diplock, Minister of Health v. Simpson, 94 S.J. 777,
    H.L.; affirming *sub nom. Re*, Diplock, Diplock v. Wintle [1948] Ch. 465; [1948]
    L.J.R. 1670; 92 S.J. 484; *sub nom. Re*, Diplock's Estate; Diplock v. Wintle
    [1948] 2 All E.R. 318; C.A.; reversing [1947] Ch. 716; [1947] L.J.R. 1158; 177
    L.T. 40; 91 S.J. 248; [1947] 1 All E.R. 522 .... 3, 32, 232, 289, 298,
        299, 300, 425, 533, 534, 653, 654, 656, 662, 663, 664, 669, 673,
        674, 675, 677, 678, 679, 686, 687, 688, 689
Milford v. Reynolds (1842) 1 Ph. 185 .... 333, 355
Moate v. Moate [1948] 2 All E.R. 486 .... 247, 256
Moggridge v. Thackwell (1792) 1 Ves. Jr. 464; (1802) 7 Ves. Jr. 36 379
Mohram Ali v. Tower Hamlets London Borough Council. *See* Ali (Mohram) v. Tower
    Hamlets L.B.C.
Molyneux v. Fletcher [1898] 1 Q.B. 648 577
Moncrieff's Settlement Trusts, *Re* [1962] 1 W.L.R. 1344; 106 S.J. 878 .... 621, 622
Monro's Settlement Trust, *Re* [1963] 1 W.L.R. 145 622
Monson v. Tussaud's [1894] 1 Q.B. 671 794
Montagu, *Re* [1897] 2 Ch. 8 614
Montague's Settlements, *Re*, Duke of Manchester v. National Westminster Bank [1987]
    Ch. 264; [1987] 2 W.L.R. 1192 .... 299, 300
Montecchi v. Shimco (U.K.): Navone v. Same [1979] 1 W.L.R. 1180; (1978) 123 S.J.
    551 810

Montgomery v. Montgomery [1965] P. 46; [1964] 2 W.L.R. 1036 744
Moodie v. I.R.C.; Sotnick v. I.R.C. [1993] 1 W.L.R. 266; [1993] 2 All E.R. 49 212
Moody, *Re* [1985] 1 Ch. 101 575
Moon v. Franklin, *The Independent*, June 22, 1990 .... 339, 340, 341
Moon's Will Trusts, *Re*, Foale v. Gillians [1948] W.N. 55; [1948] L.J.R. 778 397,
398, 437
Moor, *Re* (1888) 39 Ch.D. 116 .... 186, 328, 334
Moore v. I.R.C. [1985] Ch. 32; [1984] 3 W.L.R. 341 .... 196, 204, 222
—— v. M'Glynn [1894] 1 Ir.R. 74 .... 504, 595
—— v. Moore (1874) L.R. 18 Eq. 474 140
Moorgate Merchantile Co. v. Twitchings [1977] A.C. 890 H.L. 883, 886
Morgan, *Re* (1881) 18 Ch.D. 93 .... 33, 34
——, *Re* [1955] 1 W.L.R. 738 403
Morice v. Durham (Bishop) (1805) 10 Ves. 522 .... 231, 348, 351, 352, 376, 398, 424
Morley v. Loughnan [1893] 1 Ch. 736 828
—— v. Morley (1678) 2 Ch. Cas. 2 .... 49, 481
Morning Star Co-operative Society v. Express Newspapers, *The Times*, October 18,
1978 .... 755, 756
Morris v. Murjani [1996] 1 W.L.R. 848 745
Morris' Settlement, *Re* [1951] 2 All E.R. 528 .... 175, 176, 581
Morse v. Royal (1806) 12 Ves. Jr. 355 .... 591, 654
Mortimer v. Beckett [1920] 1 Ch. 571 786
Mortlock v. Buller (1804) 10 Ves. Jr. 292 .... 716, 722
Mosely v. Mosely (1673) Fin. 53 100
Moss, *Re* [1949] 1 All E.R. 495 406
—— v. Cooper (1861) 1 J. & H. 352 .... 147, 152, 153, 155
Mossop v. Mossop [1989] Fam. 77, C.A. 247, 260, 264, 269
Mouat v. Clark Boyce [1992] 2 N.Z.L.R. 559 24
Mountford v. Scott [1975] Ch. 258 .... 26, 704, 716, 717, 720, 836
Movitex v. Bulfield [1988] B.C.L.C. 104 .... 589, 590, 606
Moxon's Will Trusts, *Re*, Downey v. Moxon [1958] 1 W.L.R. 165; 102 S.J. 124 578,
581
Muckleston v. Brown (1801) 6 Ves. 52 .... 250, 251
Muetzel v. Muetzel [1970] 1 W.L.R. 188; (1969) 114 S.J. 32 264
Muir v. I.R.C. [1966] 1 W.L.R. 1269 .... 181, 182
Mulholland's Will Trusts, *Re*, Bryan v. Westminster Bank [1949] W.N. 103; [1949] 1
All E.R. 460 590
Multi Guarantee Co. *Re* [1987] B.C.L.C. 257 .... 51, 230
Multiservice Bookbinding v. Marden [1979] Ch. 84; [1978] 2 W.L.R. 535 837
Mumford v. Bank of Scotland (1996) S.L.T. 392 833
Munro v. Commissioner of Stamp Duties of New South Wales [1934] A.C. 61 221
—— v. Meyer [1930] 2 K.B. 312 821
Munro's Settlement Trusts, *Re* [1963] 1 W.L.R. 145; [1963] 1 All E.R. 209 188
Murawski's Will Trusts, *Re*, Lloyd's Bank v. Royal Society for the Prevention of
Cruelty to Animals [1971] 1 W.L.R. 707, 115 S.J. 189 447
Murcutt v. Murcutt [1952] P. 266; [1952] 2 T.L.R. 274 803
Murray v. Parker (1854) 19 Beav. 305 841
Muschinski v. Dodds (1985) 160 C.L.R. 583 .... 291, 292, 323, 324
Musgrave, *Re* [1916] 2 Ch. 417 533
Mussett v. Bingle [1876] W.N. 170 .... 46, 348, 354, 355, 366
Mussourie Bank v. Raynor (1882) 7 App. Cas. 321 .... 90, 91
Mutton v. Peat [1899] 2 Ch. 556 673
Mutual v. Welton (John) & Sons [1937] 2 Q.B. 389 828
Myhill, *Re* [1928] Ch. 100 491
Mylne, *Re* [1941] Ch. 204 397

N. (No. 2), *Re* [1967] Ch. 512; [1967] 2 W.L.R. 751
N.W.L. Ltd v. Woods [1979] 1 W.L.R. 1294; [1979] I.C.R. 867 .... 761, 762
Nant-y-glo and Blaina Ironworks Co. v. Grave (1879) 12 Ch.D. 738 633
Nash, *Re* [1910] 1 Ch. 1 855

National Anti-Vivisection Society v. Inland Revenue Commissioners [1948] A.C.
31 .... 400, 407, 412, 422, 441
National Funds Assurance Co., *Re* (1878) 10 Ch.D. 118 3
National Provincial Bank Ltd v. Ainsworth [1965] A.C. 1175 [1965] 3 W.L.R. 1 33,
878, 895
National & Provincial Building Society v. British Waterways Board [1992] E.G.C.S.
149, C.A. 712, 717
National Trustee Co. of Australasia Ltd v. General Finance Co. of Australasia [1905]
A.C. 373 .... 483, 533, 650, 651
National Westminster Bank plc v. Morgan [1985] A.C. 686; [1985] 2 W.L.R. 588 829,
831, 832, 837
Neale v. Willis (1968) 19 P. & C.R. 839 .... 77, 78
Neave, *Re* [1938] Ch. 793 855
Neeld, *Re*, Carpenter v. Inigo-Jones [1962] Ch. 643: [1962] 2 W.L.R. 1097 .... 59, 333
Nelson, *Re* [1928] Ch. 920n. 60, 166, 206, 611
Nelson v. Hannam and Smith [1943] Ch. 59 292
Nelson v. Larholt [1948] 1 K.B. 339; [1948] L.J.R. 340 .... 35, 688
Nelson v. Nelson (1995) 132 A.L.R. 133 .... 249, 251
Nelson v. Rye [1996] 1 W.L.R. 1378 655
Neptune (Vehicle Washing Equipment) Ltd v. Fitzgerald [1996] Ch. 274 .... 598, 607
Nestlé v. National Westminster Bank plc [1993] 1 W.L.R. 1260 [1994] 1 All E.R. 118 ....
481, 521, 522, 537, 538, 634, 638
Neville v. Wilson [1996] 3 W.L.R. 460 .... 87, 312
Neville Estates v. Madden [1962] Ch. 832; [1961] 3 W.L.R. 999 .... 361, 362, 396,
397, 417, 418
New, *Re* [1901] 2 Ch. 534 614
New Brunswick and Canada Railway and Land Company (The) v. Muggeridge (1860)
1 Dr. & Sm. 363 826
New, Prance and Garrard's Trustee v. Hunting [1897] 2 Q.B. 19 120
New Zealand Land Development Co. Ltd v. Porter [1992] 2 N.Z.L.R. 462 24
New Zealand Netherlands Society "Oranje" Incorporated v. Kuys (Laurentius Cornelis)
[1973] 1 W.L.R. 1126; [1973] 2 All E.R. 1222 .... 596, 602
Newbigging v. Adam (1886) 34 Ch.D. 582 838
Newey, *Re* [1994] 2 N.Z.L.R. 590 305
Newport Association Football Club Ltd v. Football Association of Wales Ltd [1995] 2
All E.R. 87; (1994) 144 N.L.J. Rep. 1351 .... 745, 771
Newport Borough Council v. Khan [1990] 1 W.L.R. 1185; [1991] 1 E.G.L.R. 287 799
News Group Newspapers Ltd v. SOGAT 82 [1986] I.C.R. 716; (1986) 130 S.J.
407 362
Nichols and Von Joel's Contract, *Re* [1910] 1 Ch. 43 723
Nicholson, (dec'd), *Re* Nicholson v. Perks [1974] 1 W.L.R. 476; (1973) 118 S.J.
133 270
Nicholson's Settlement, *Re* [1939] Ch. 11 178
Nicrotherm Electrical Co. Ltd v. Percy [1956] R.P.C. 272 24
Nimmo v. Westpac Banking Corporation [1993] 3 N.Z.L.R. 218 .... 302, 661
Nippon Yusen Kaisha v. Karageorgis [1975]1 W.L.R. 1093; [1975] 3 All E.R. 282 ... 809
Nisbet and Pott's Contract, *Re* [1906] 1 Ch. 386 .... 32, 34, 723
Nixon v. Nixon [1969] 1 W.L.R. 1676; 113 S.J. 565 266
Niyazi's Will Trusts, *Re* [1978] 1 W.L.R. 910; (1978) 122 S.J. 129 .... 384, 387
Norris, *Re* (1884) 27 Ch.D. 333 .... 500, 501
—— v. Le Neve (1743) 3 Atk. 26 593
North and South Trust Co. v. Berkeley; Berkeley v. North and South Trust Co. [1971]
1 W.L.R. 471; [1971] 1 All E.R. 980 606
North American Land Co. v. Watkins [1904] 1 Ch. 242; [1904] 2 Ch. 233 652
North Devon and West Somerset Relief Fund Trusts, *Re*. Hylton v. Wright [1953] 1
W.L.R. 1260; 97 S.J. 728 .... 387, 429, 437
North London Railway v. Great Northern Railway (1883) 11 Q.B.D. 30 734
Northcliffe, *Re* [1925] Ch. 651 135
Northcote's Will Trusts, *Re*, Northcote v. Northcote [1949] W.N. 69; [1949] 1 All E.R.
442 585
Nottage, *Re* [1895] 2 Ch. 657 .... 348, 392, 402

O. (Infants), *Re* [1962] 1 W.L.R. 724; 106 S.J. 429 802
Oakacre Ltd v. Claire Cleaners (Holdings) [1982] Ch. 197; [1981] 3 W.L.R. 761 696,
    718, 724, 725, 726
Oakes v. Commissioner of Stamp Duties of New South Wales [1954] A.C. 57; [1953]
    3 W.L.R. 1127 .... 202, 221
—— v. Sidney Sussex College, Cambridge [1988] 1 W.L.R. 431 446
—— v. Turquand (1867) L.R. 2 H.L 325 .... 826, 839
Oatway, *Re*, Hertslet v. Oatway [1903] 2 Ch. 356 .... 671, 673
O'Brien v. Condon [1905] Ir.R. 51 159
Oceanica Castelana Armadora S.A. of Panama v. Mineralimportexport [1983] 1 W.L.R.
    1294 .... 811, 815
Occeleston v. Fullalove (1874) L.R. 9 Ch. App. 147 326
Oddy, *Re* [1911] 1 Ch. 532 549
Official Assignee v. NZI Life Superannuation Nominees Ltd [1995] 1 N.Z.L.R.
    684 187
Official Custodian for Charities v. Mackay [1985] Ch. 151; [1984] 3 W.L.R. 915 763
Official Receiver in Bankruptcy v. Schulz (1990) 179 C.L.R. 306 (High Court of
    Australia) 59
Ogden, *Re* [1933] Ch. 678 .... 98, 393, 407
—— v. Fossick (1862) 4 De G. F. & J. 426 .... 712, 713
Ogilvie, *Re* [1918] 1 Ch. 492 855
O'Hanlon v. Logue [1906] 1 I.R. 247 .... 418, 419
Oldham, *Re* [1925] Ch. 75 .... 306, 309, 310
Oldham Borough Council v. Att.-Gen. [1993] Ch. 210; [1993] 2 W.L.R. 224 ...... 403, 440,
    441, 449
Oliphant, *Re* (1917) 86 L.J.Ch. 452 176
Oliver, *Re* (1890) 62 L.T. 533 53
——, *Re* [1927] 2 Ch. 323 653
——, *Re* [1947] 2 All E.R. 161 574
—— v. Brickland (1732) cited 3 Atk. 420 865
Oliver's Settlement, *Re* [1905] 1 Ch. 191 855
Ontario Securities Commission, *Re* (1986) D.L.R. (4th) 1 673
Oppenheim v. Tobacco Securities Trust Co. [1951] A.C. 297; [1951] 1 T.L.R. 118 414,
    417, 421
Oppenheim's Will Trusts, *Re*, Westminster Bank v. Oppenheim [1950] Ch. 633; 66
    T.L.R. (Pt. 1) 1040 191
Orde, *Re* (1883) 24 Ch.D. 271 500
O'Reilly v. Mackman; Millbanks v. Secretary of State for the Home Department [1983]
    2 A.C. 237; [1982] 3 W.L.R. 1096 799
Oriental Credit Ltd, *Re* [1988] Ch. 204; [1988] 2 W.L.R. 172 745
O'Rourke v. Darbishire [1920] A.C. 581 549
Orr v. Ford (1988–89) 167 C.L.R. 316 655
Orr-Lewis v. Orr-Lewis [1949] P. 347; [1949] L.J.R. 682 803
Orwell Steel (Erection and Fabrication) v. Asphalt and Tarmac (U.K.) [1984] 1 W.L.R.
    1097; [1984] 128 S.J. 597 809
Orwell's Will Trusts, *Re* [1982] 1 W.L.R. 1337; (1982) 126 S.J. 593 594
Osborne v. Amalgamated Society of Railway Servants [1911] 1 Ch. 540 802
Oscar Chess v. Williams [1957] 1 W.L.R. 370; 101 S.J. 186 821
Osoba (dec'd), *Re*, Osoba v. Osoba [1979] 1 W.L.R. 247; (1978) 123 S.J. 35 .... 53, 234,
    241, 348
O'Sullivan v. Management Agency and Music [1985] Q.B. 428; [1984] 3 W.L.R.
    448 .... 587, 588, 606, 638, 639, 828, 829, 838
Ottaway v. Norman [1972] Ch. 698; [1972] 2 W.L.R. 50 .... 97, 147, 149, 151, 154,
    157, 159, 160, 162, 311
Ottley v. Gilbey (1845) 8 Beav. 602 548
Oughtred v. I.R.C. [1960] A.C. 206; [1959] 3 W.L.R. 898 .... 79, 84, 86, 87, 312, 314, 624
Overton v. Bannister (1884) 3 Hare 503 645
Owen, *Re* [1912] 1 Ch. 519 541
Oxford Group v. I.R.C. [1949] W.N. 343; [1949] 2 All E.R. 537 424
Oxley, *Re* [1914] 1 Ch. 604 485

Oxy Electric v. Zainuddin [1991] 1 W.L.R. 115; [1990] 2 All E.R. 902 .... 768, 773, 777

P. v. Liverpool Daily Post & Echo Newspapers. *See* Pickering v. Liverpool Daily Post
    and Echo Newspapers.
PCW (Underwriting Agencies) v. Dixon (P.S.) [1983] 2 All E.R. 697; [1983] 2 All E.R.
    158 815
PSM International and McKechnie v. Whitehouse and Willenhall Automation [1992]
    IRLR 279; [1992] F.S.R. 489 .... 775, 787
Packe, *Re* [1918] 1 Ch. 437 435
Pacol v. Trade Lines (1982) 126 S.J. 312; [1982] 1 Lloyd's Rep. 456 ... 882, 883, 884, 892
Paddington Building Society v. Mendelsohn (1985) 50 P. & C.R. 244; (1987) 17 Fam.
    Law 121, C.A. 279
Page, *Re* [1893] 1 Ch. 304 653
—— v. Way (1840) 3 Beav. 20 196
Page One Records v. Britton [1968] 1 W.L.R. 157; 111 S.J. 944 .... 789, 790
Paget v. Marshall (1882) 28 Ch.D. 255 843
Paice v. Archbishop of Canterbury (1807) 14 Ves. 364 379
Paine v. Meller (1801) 6 Ves. Jr. 349 312
Palmer v. Bank of N.S.W. (1975) 7 A.L.R. 671 310
—— v. Emerson [1911] 1 Ch. 758 .... 529, 650
—— v. Simmonds (1854) 2 Drew. 221 93
Paradise Motor Co., *Re* [1968] 1 W.L.R. 1125; 112 S.J. 271 .... 88, 89, 117, 248
Paramount Airways, *Re* [1993] Ch. 223 344
Pardoe, *Re* [1906] 2 Ch. 184 397
Park, *Re* [1932] 1 Ch. 580 .... 168, 175, 353
Parker v. Camden London Borough Council; Newman v. Camden London Borough
    Council [1986] Ch. 162; [1985] 3 W.L.R. 47 .... 696, 707, 739, 750, 766
—— v. Judkin [1931] 1 Ch. 475 53
—— v. Sowerby (1854) 4 De G.M. & G. 321 853
Parker-Tweedale v. Dunbar Bank plc. [1991] Ch. 12 .... 19, 21, 124, 513
Parkin, *Re* [1892] 3 Ch. 510 .... 126, 174, 711
Parry, *Re*, Brown v. Parry [1947] Ch. 23; [1947] L.J.R. 81 541
Parsons, *Re* [1940] Ch. 764 .... 493, 497, 500, 501
—— v. Nasar [1990] 2 F.L.R. 103; (1990) 23 H.L.R. 1 .... 765, 771
Partington, *Re* (1887) 57 L.T. 654 643
Pascoe v. Turner [1979] 1 W.L.R. 431; (1978) 123 S.J. 164 .... 886, 890, 894
Pass v. Dundas (1880) 43 L.T. 665 483
Passant v. Jackson (Inspector of Taxes) (1987) 59 T.C. 230; [1986] S.T.C. 164 57
Passee v. Passee [1988] 1 F.L.R. 263; (1988) 18 Fam. Law 132, C.A. 68, 231, 270, 271
Patel v. Ali [1984] Ch. 283; [1984] 2 W.L.R. 960 .... 718, 720
—— v. Patel [1981] 1 W.L.R. 1342; (1981) 125 S.J. 693 594
—— v. Smith (W.H.) (Eziot) [1987] 1 W.L.R. 853; (1987) 131 S.J. 888 .... 746, 747,
    763, 772, 792
—— v. University of Bradford Senate [1979] 1 W.L.R. 1066; (1979) 123 S.J. 436 ... 446
Paton v. British Pregnancy Advisory Service Trustees [1979] Q.B. 276; [1978] 3
    W.L.R. 687 .... 734, 744, 802
Patten, *Re* [1929] 2 Ch. 276 402
Paul, *Re* [1921] 2 Ch. 1 582
—— v. Constance [1977] 1 W.L.R. 527; [1977] 1 All E.R. 195 . 65, 76, 92, 120, 129, 132
—— v. Paul (1882) 20 Ch.D. 742 .... 116, 310
Pauling's Settlement Trusts, *Re*, Younghusband v. Coutts & Co. [1964] Ch. 303; [1963]
    3 W.L.R. 742 .... 483, 571, 579, 583, 644, 645, 646, 651, 652, 654, 831
—— (No. 2) [1963] Ch. 576; [1963] 2 W.L.R. 838 .... 504, 648
Pavlou (a Bankrupt), *Re* [1993] 1 W.L.R. 1046; [1993] 3 All E.R. 955 .... 271, 275
Pawson's Settlement, *Re* [1917] 1 Ch. 541 650
Peachdart Ltd, *Re* [1984] Ch. 131; [1983] 3 W.L.R. 878 .... 683, 684, 685
Peacock, *Re*, Midland Bank Executor and Trustee Co. v. Peacock [1957] Ch. 310;
    [1957] 2 W.L.R. 793 317
Peake v. Highfield (1826) 1 Russ. 559 839
Pearce (C.H.) & Sons Ltd v. Stonechester, *The Times*, November 17, 1983 841
Pearse v. Green (1819) 1 Jac. & W. 135 548

Pearson v. I.R.C. [1981] A.C. 753 .... 217, 222
Pechar, *Re*, [1969] N.Z.L.R. 574 316
Peco Arts Inc. v. Hazlitt Gallery [1983] 1 W.L.R. 1315; (1983) 127 S.J. 806 838
Peczenik's Settlement Trusts, *Re*, Cole v. Ingram [1964] 1 W.L.R. 720; 108 S.J.
  462 517
Peel's Release, *Re* [1921] 2 Ch. 218 .... 380, 438
Peffer v. Rigg [1977] 1 W.L.R. 285; [1978] 3 All E.R. 745 .... 42, 315, 322
Peggs v. Lamb [1994] Ch. 172; [1994] 2 W.L.R. 1 .... 422, 441
Pells v. Brown (1620) Cro. Jac. 590 335
Peninsular Maritime v. Padseal (1981) 259 E.G. 860, C.A. 696, 748, 765
Penn v. Lord Baltimore (1750) 1 Ves. Sen. 444 .... 18, 29, 486, 694, 738
Pennant's Will Trusts, *Re*, Pennant v. Rylands [1970] Ch. 75; [1969] 3 W.L.R. 63 591
Pennine Raceway v. Kirklees Metropolitan Council [1983] Q.B. 382; [1982] 3 W.L.R.
  987 .... 41, 879
Penrose, *Re* [1933] Ch. 793 .... 167, 176
Percival v. Wright [1902] 2 Ch. 421 598
Permanent Trustee Co. v. Scales (1930) 30 S.R. (N.S.W.) 391 135
Perowne, *Re*, Perowne v. Moss [1951] Ch. 785; [1951] 1 T.L.R. 1135 63
Perpetual Executors and Trustees Association of Australia v. Wright (1917) 23 C.L.R.
  185 252
Perrin v. Lyon (1807) 9 East. 170 329
Perrins v. Bellamy [1898] 2 Ch. 521 650
Peso Silver Mines v. Cropper (1966) 58 D.L.R. (2d.) 1 601
Peter v. Beblow (1993) 101 D.L.R. (4th) 621 .... 266, 268, 291
Peter Pan Manufacturing Corporation v. Corsets Silhouette [1964] 1 W.L.R. 96; 108
  S.J. 97 795
Peters v. Chief Adjudication Officer (1989) 19 Fam. Law 318 578
Peterson v. Peterson (1866) L.R. 3 Eq. 111 689
Pettifor's Will Trusts, *Re*, Roberts v. Roberts [1966] Ch. 257; [1966] 2 W.L.R.
  778 629
Pettingall v. Pettingall (1842) 11 L.J.Ch. 176 .... 46, 355
Pettitt v. Pettitt [1970] A.C. 777; [1969] 2 W.L.R. 966 .... 246, 247, 248, 251, 254, 255,
                                                    257, 260, 261, 264, 271, 272, 318
Pettkus v. Becker (1980) 117 D.L.R. 257 .... 291, 324
Peyman v. Lanjani [1985] Ch. 457; [1985] 2 W.L.R. 154 838
Pfeiffer (E.) Weinkellerei-Weineinkauf GmbH & Co. v. Arbuthnot Factors [1988] 1
  W.L.R. 150; (1988) 132 S.J. 89 682
Pfrimmer Estate, *Re* (1936) 2 D.L.R. 460 92
Philips v. Lamdin [1949] 2 K.B. 33 701
Phillipo v. Munnings (1837) 2 Myl. & Cr. 309 59
Phillips, *Re* (1884) 41 Ch.D. 417 172
—— v. Bury (1694) Skinn. 447 445
—— v. Phillips (1861) 4 De. G. F. & J. 208 33
—— v. —— (1885) 29 Ch.D. 673 593
—— v. —— [1973] 1 W.L.R. 615; 117 S.J. 323 801
—— v. —— [1993] 3 N.Z.L.R. 159 268
Phillipson v. Galty (1848) 7 Hare 516 637
Phipps v. Ackers (1842) 9 Cl. & Fin. 583 573
—— v. Boardman. *See* Boardman v. Phipps.
Pickering v. Ely (Bishops) (1843) 2 Y. & C. Ch. 249 713
—— v. Liverpool Daily Post and Echo Newspapers [1991] 2 A.C. 370; [1991] 2 W.L.R.
  513 .... 741, 743, 797
Pickersgill v. Rodger (1876) 5 Ch.D. 163 858
Pilcher v. Rawlins (1872) L.R. 7 Ch.App. 250 .... 32, 34, 311
Pilkington v. I.R.C. [1964] A.C. 612; [1962] 3 W.L.R. 1051 .... 176, 201, 570, 571, 577,
                                                    578, 579, 580, 581, 582, 613, 624
Pilkington's Will Trusts, *Re* [1961] Ch. 486 580
Pinckney v. Pinckney [1966] 1 All E.R. 121n; [1965] C.L.Y. 1327 801
Pinion, *Re*, Westminster Bank v. Pinion [1965] Ch. 85; [1964] 2 W.L.R. 919 ...... 326, 388,
                                                                          390, 391
Piper, *Re* [1946] 2 All E.R. 503 .... 330, 334

Pips (Leisure Productions) v. Walton (1981) 260 E.G. 601 723
Pirbright v. Salwey [1896] W.N. 86 .... 354, 366
Pitcairn, *Re* [1896] 2 Ch. 199 .... 539, 542, 543
Pitt-Rivers, *Re* [1902] 1 Ch. 403 148
Pittortou (A Bankrupt), *Re*, *ex p.* Trustee of the Property of the Bankrupt [1985] 1
    W.L.R. 58; (1985) 129 S.J. 42 282
Playfair, *Re*, Palmer v. Playfair [1951] Ch. 4; 66 T.L.R. (Pt. 1) 1203 147
Plimmer v. Wellington Corporation (1884) 9 App. Cas. 699 .... 882, 889
Plumptre's Marriage Settlement, *Re* [1910] 1 Ch. 609 .... 123, 124, 134
Pollock, *Re* [1941] Ch. 219 316
Polly Peck International plc v. Nadir (No. 2) [1992] 4 All E.R. 769; [1993] BCLC
    187 .... 300, 301, 302, 791, 809, 811, 814
—— (No. 3) *sub nom.* Secretary of State for Trade and Industry v. Ellis [1994] 1
    B.C.L.C. 661; *The Times*, March 22, 1993 301
Ponder, *Re* [1921] 2 Ch. 59 55
Pooley, *Re* (1888) 40 Ch.D. 1 586
Popat v. Shonchhatra [1995] 1 W.L.R. 908; [1995] 4 All E.R. 646 593
Port Line v. Ben Line Steamers [1958] 2 Q.B. 146; [1958] 2 W.L.R. 551 876
Portland v. Topham (1864) 11 H.L.Cas. 32 176
Posner v. Scott-Lewis [1987] Ch. 25; [1986] 3 W.L.R. 531 .... 705, 709
Poster v. Slough Estates Ltd [1968] 1 W.L.R. 1518 37
Postlethwaite, *Re* (1888) 60 L.T. 514 590
Potters v. Loppert [1973] Ch. 399; [1973] 2 W.L.R. 469 .... 49, 51
Poulton's Will Trusts, *Re* [1987] 1 W.L.R. 795; (1987) 131 S.J. 412 104
Powell v. London Borough of Brent [1987] I.R.L.R. 466, C.A. 709, 756, 791
—— v. Smith (1872) L.R. 14 Eq. 85 716
—— v. Thompson [1991] 1 N.Z.L.R. 579 .... 291, 295, 300
Powell-Cotton's Resettlement, *Re*, Henniker-Major v. Powell-Cotton [1956] 1 W.L.R.
    23; 100 S.J. 13 .... 615, 616
Power's Will Trusts, *Re*, Public Trustee v. Hastings [1947] Ch. 572; 177 L.T. 245 514,
                                                                                                        517, 616
Pozot's Settlement Trusts, *Re*, Westminster Bank v. Guerbois [1952] Ch. 427; [1952] 1
    T.L.R. 1042 191
Practice Direction [1960] 1 W.L.R. 17 622
—— [1970] 1 W.L.R. 259 75
—— [1974] 1 W.L.R. 576 768
—— [1976] 1 W.L.R. 884 622
—— [1980] 1 W.L.R. 741 751
—— [1980] 1 W.L.R. 751 736
—— [1983] 1 W.L.R. 433 .... 736, 751
—— [1983] 1 W.L.R. 558 802
—— [1987] 1 W.L.R. 63 488
—— [1996] 1 W.L.R. 1552 .... 807, 810
Practice Note [1978] 1 W.L.R. 925 .... 752, 801
—— [1983] 1 W.L.R. 1077 75
Price, *Re* [1943] Ch. 422 360
Price v. Hartwell [1996] E.G.C.S. 98 .... 886, 892
—— v. Strange [1978] Ch. 337; [1977] 3 W.L.R. 943 ... 701, 706, 709, 713, 714, 724, 725
Pride v. Fooks (1840) 2 Beav. 430 637
Pride of Derby and Derbyshire Angling Association v. British Celanese [1953] Ch. 149;
    [1953] 2 W.L.R. 58 .... 736, 750
Priestley's Will Trusts, *Re*, Hambros Bank Executors and Trustees Co. v. Rabagliali
    [1971] Ch. 858; [1971] 2 W.L.R. 1119; S.J. 350; [1971] 2 All E.R. 817,
    C.A. 172
Prince Albert v. Strange (1849) 1 H. & T. 1 744
Printers and Finishers Ltd v. Holloway [1965] 1 W.L.R. 1 795
Printers and Transferrers Amalgamated Trades Protection Society, *Re* [1899] 2 Ch.
    184 .... 236, 237, 241
Pritchard v. Briggs [1980] Ch. 338; [1979] 3 W.L.R. 868 .... 700, 786
Protheroe v. Protheroe [1968] 1 W.L.R. 519 593

Provident Financial Group and Whitegates Estate Agency v. Hayward [1989] I.C.R.
160; [1989] 3 All E.R. 298 .... 708, 783, 785, 789
Prudential Assurance Co. Ltd v. Newman Industries Ltd (No. 2) [1981] Ch. 257 598
Pryce, *Re* [1917] 1 Ch. 234 .... 124, 126
Public Trustee v. Ferguson [1947] N.Z.L.R. 746 194
—— v. I.R.C. [1960] A.C. 398; [1960] 2 W.L.R. 203 586
Puckett and Smith's Contract, *Re* [1902] 2 Ch. 258 .... 721, 722
Pugh, *Re* [1887] W.N. 143 527
—— v. Heath (1882) 7 App. Cas. 235 15
—— v. Howells (1984) 48 P. & C.R. 298 .... 747, 778, 792
Pugh's Will Trusts, *Re*, Marten v. Pugh [1967] 1 W.L.R. 1262; [1967] 3 All E.R.
337 .... 92, 149, 157, 241
Pullan v. Koe [1913] 1 Ch. 9 .... 113, 122, 123, 128, 133
Pusey v. Pusey (1684) 1 Vern. 273 701
Pyke, *Re* [1895] 1 Ch. 724 851
Pym v. Lockyer (1841) 5 Myl. & Cr. 29 861

Quadrant Visual Communications v. Hutchison Telephone (U.K.) [1993] BCLC 442;
The Times, December 4, 1991, C.A. 717
Quartz Hill Consolidated Gold Mining Co. v. Beall (1882) 20 Ch.D. 501 793
Queensland Mines Ltd v. Hudson (1978) 18 A.L.R. 1 600
Quennell v. Maltby [1979] 1 W.L.R. 318; (1978) 122 S.J. 812 43

R. v. Barrick (1985) 149 J.P. 705; (1985) 129 S.J. 416; (1985) 81 Cr.App.R. 78 643
—— v. British Broadcasting Corporation, ex p. Lavelle [1983] 1 W.L.R. 23; [1983]
I.C.R. 99 790
—— v. Chief National Insurance Commissioner, *ex p.* Connor [1981] 1 Q.B. 758 315,
316
—— v. Clowes (No. 2) [1994] 2 All E.R. 316 .... 51, 92, 643, 671
—— v. Commissioner of Police of the Metropolis, *ex p.* Blackburn [1968] 2 Q.B. 118;
[1968] 2 W.L.R. 893 743
—— v. Deputy Governor of Parkhurst Prison, *ex p.* Hague; Weldon v. Home Office
[1992] 1 A.C. 58; [1991] 3 W.L.R. 340 .... 741, 797
—— v. District Auditor, *ex p.* West Yorkshire Metropolitan County Council [1986] 26
R.V.R. 24, D.C. 101, 105, 106, 350
—— v. Doncaster Metropolitan Borough Council, *ex p.* Braim (1989) 57 P. & C.R.
1 403
—— v. Dunsheath, *ex p.* Meredith [1951] 1 K.B. 127; 66 T.L.R. (Pt. 2) 584 446
—— v. Her Majesty the Queen in Council, *ex p.* Vijaytunga [1990] 2 Q.B. 444; [1989]
3 W.L.R. 13 446
—— v. Her Majesty's Treasury, *ex p.* Smedley [1985] Q.B. 657; [1985] 2 W.L.R.
576 .... 743, 799
—— v. Hull University Visitor, *ex p.* Page [1993] A.C. 682 446
—— v. I.R.C., *ex p.* National Federation of Self-Employed and Small Businesses Ltd
[1982] A.C. 617; [1981] 2 W.L.R. 722 .... 743, 799
—— v. I.R.C., *ex p.* Rossminster Ltd [1980] A.C. 952; [1980] 2 W.L.R. 1 740
—— v. Kensington and Chelsea Royal London Borough Council, *ex p.* Hammell
[1989] Q.B. 518 764
—— v. London Borough of Harrow; *ex p.* Coker, *The Times*, March 14, 1989 254
—— v. Preddy [1996] A.C. 815 661
—— v. Radio Authority, ex. p. Bull, *The Times*, January 21, 1997 409
—— v. Registrar General, *ex p.* Segerdal [1970] 2 Q.B. 697; [1970] 3 W.L.R. 479 ... 397
—— v. Secretary of State for Health, *ex p.* Generics (U.K.) Ltd, *The Times*, February
25, 1997 760
—— v. Secretary of State for the Home Department, *ex p.* Dew [1987] 1 W.L.R. 881;
(1987) 131 S.J. 658 800
—— v. Secretary of State for Transport, *ex p.* Factortame Ltd [1990] 2 A.C. 85; [1989]
2 W.L.R. 997 740

—— v. —— (No. 2) [1991] 1 A.C. 603; [1990] 3 W.L.R. 818 .... 740, 760
—— v. Senate of the University of Aston, *ex p.* Roffey [1969] 2 Q.B. 538; [1969] 2
    W.L.R. 1418 803
—— v. Visitors to the Inns of Court, *ex p.* Calder [1993] Q.B. 1; [1993] 3 W.L.R.
    287 445
—— v. Westminster City Council, *ex p.* Augustin [1993] 1 W.L.R. 730; (1993) 25
    H.L.R. 281 764
R.C.A. Corp. v. Pollard [1983] Ch. 135; [1982] 3 W.L.R. 1007 .... 42, 741
R.H.M. Foods Ltd v. Bovril Ltd [1982] 1 W.L.R. 661; [1982] 1 All E.R. 673; [1983]
    R.P.C. 275 810
Rabin v. Gerson Berger Association Ltd [1986] 1 W.L.R. 526; (1986) 130 S.J. 15 89
Raby v. Ridehalgh (1855) 7 De G. M. & G. 104 .... 538, 647, 648
Racal Group Services Ltd v. Ashmore [1995] S.T.C. 1151, C.A. 842, 844
Radford v. De Froberville [1977] 1 W.L.R. 1262 .... 727, 728
Raffaele v. Raffaele [1962] W.A.R. 29 889
Rahman v. Chase Bank (C.I.) Trust Co. Ltd [1991] J.L.R. 103 (Jersey) 92
Rahman (Prince Abdul) Bin Turki Al Sudairy v. Abu-Taha [1980] 1 W.L.R. 1268;
    [1980] 3 All E.R. 409 .... 812, 815
Raikes v. Lygon [1988] 1 W.L.R. 281; (1988) 132 S.J. 126 617
Raine, *Re* [1929] 1 Ch. 716 575
——, *Re*, Walton v. Att.-Gen. [1956] Ch. 417; [1956] 2 W.L.R. 449 397
Raineri v. Miles [1981] A.C. 1050; [1980] 2 W.L.R. 847 .... 696, 718
Ralli's Will Trusts, *Re*, Ralli's Marriage Settlement, *Re*, Calvocoressi v. Radocanachi
    [1964] Ch. 288; [1964] 2 W.L.R. 144 .... 111, 116, 133, 134, 135, 136, 160, 310
Rama v. Millar [1996] 1 N.Z.L.R. 257 639
Ramsay (W.T.) v. I.R.C. [1982] A.C. 300; [1981] 2 W.L.R. 449 212
Ramsden v. Dyson (1866) L.R. 1 H.L. 129 .... 141, 883, 890
Ramskill v. Edwards (1885) 31 Ch.D. 100 641
Randell, *Re* (1888) 39 Ch.D. 213 438
Randall v. Russell (1817) 3 Mer. 190 593
Rank Film Distirbutors Ltd v. Video Information Centre [1982] A.C. 380; [1981] 2
    W.L.R. 668 .... 805, 806, 807
Rank's Settlement Trusts, *Re*, Newton v. Rollo [1979] 1 W.L.R. 1242; (1979) 123 S.J.
    720 619
Ransome, *Re*, Moberly v. Ransome [1957] Ch. 348; [1957] 2 W.L.R. 556 .... 572, 579
Rasmanis v. Jurewitsch (1970) 70 S.R. (N.S.W.) 407 316
Rasu Maritima S.A. v. Perusahaan Pertambangan Minyak Dan Gas Bumi Negara
    (Pertamina) [1978] Q.B. 644; [1977] 3 W.L.R. 518 .... 735, 809, 810
Rattenberry, *Re* [1906] 1 Ch. 667 860
Raven, *Re*, [1915] 1 Ch. 673 .... 103, 508
Raw v. Meek (1889) 14 App. Cas. 558 483
Rawlins v. Powel (1718) 1 P. Wms. 297 860
Rawluk v. Rawluk (1990) 65 D.L.R. 161 .... 291, 292
Rawsthorne v. Rowley [1909] 1 Ch. 409 .... 526, 637
Rayner v. Preston (1881) Ch.D. 1 312
Reading v. Att.-Gen. [1951] A.C. 507; [1951] 1 T.L.R. 480 .... 289, 597
Recher's Will Trusts, *Re*, National Westminster Bank v. National Anti-Vivisection
    Society [1972] Ch. 526 .... 361, 363, 365, 370
Record v. Bell [1991] 1 W.L.R. 853; [1991] 4 All E.R. 471 701
Redgrave v. Hurd (1881) 20 Ch.D. 1 .... 818, 827
Redland Bricks Ltd v. Morris [1970] A.C. 652; [1969] 2 W.L.R. 1437 .... 706, 736, 737,
    739, 747, 769, 770, 775, 778
Rees' Will Trusts, *Re*, Williams v. Hopkins [1950] Ch. 204; 66 T.L.R. (Pt. 1) 23 53,
    155, 157, 188, 193, 241
Refson (P.S.) & Co. Ltd v. Saggers [1984] 1 W.L.R. 1025; (1984) 128 S.J. 152 767
Regal (Hastings) Ltd v. Gulliver [1942] 1 All E.R. 378; [1967] 2 A.C. 134n 596, 598,
    601
Registered Securities, *Re* [1991] 1 N.Z.L.R. 545 673
Rehden v. Wesley (1861) 29 Beav. 213 483

Reid v. Shergold (1805) 10 Ves. Jr. 370 172
Rely-a-Bell Burglar and Fire Alarm Co. v. Eisler [1926] Ch. 609 788
Remnant's Settlement Trusts, *Re*, Hooper v. Wenhaston [1970] 1 Ch. 560; [1970] 2
    W.L.R. 1103 .... 331, 626, 628
Rena K (The) [1979] Q.B. 377; [1978] 3 W.L.R. 431 814
Rennell v. I.R.C. [1962] Ch. 329; [1961] 3 W.L.R. 1322 122
Resch's Will Trusts, *Re*, Le Cras (Vera Caroline) v. Perpetual Trustee Co., Far West
    Children's Health Scheme v. Perpetual Trustee Co. [1969] 1 A.C. 514; [1968]
    3 W.L.R. 1153; *sub nom.* Le Cras. Perpetual Trustee Co., Far West Children's
    Health Scheme v. Perpetual Trustee Co. [1967] 1 All E.R. 915 .... 384, 402
Rhoden v. Joseph [1990] E.G.C.S. 115 .... 267, 272
Rhodesia Goldfields Ltd, *Re* [1910] 1 Ch. 239 643
Rhone v. Stephens [1994] 2 A.C. 310; [1994] 2 W.L.R. 429 .... 21, 26
Richard v. The Hon. A. B. Mackay (1987, unreported) 623, 501
Richard West and Partners (Inverness) Ltd v. Dick [1969] Ch. 424; [1969] 2 W.L.R.
    1190 .... 18, 694
Richards v. Delbridge (1874) L.R. 18 Eq. 11 .... 119, 120
—— v. Dove [1974] 1 All E.R. 888 266
—— v. Revitt (1877) 7 Ch.D. 224 773
—— v. Richards [1984] A.C. 174; [1983] 3 W.L.R. 173 735
Richardson, *Re* [1920] 1 Ch. 423 653
Richardson v. Chapman (1760) 7 Bro. P.C. 318 100
Richardson's Will Trusts, *Re*, Public Trustee v. Llewellyn Evans' Trustee [1958] Ch.
    504; [1958] 2 W.L.R. 414 .... 192, 193
Richmond upon Thames London Borough Council v. Rogers [1988] 3 W.L.R. 513;
    [1988] 2 All E.R. 761 448
Rickless v. United Artists Corp. [1988] Q.B. 40; [1987] 2 W.L.R. 945 .... 741, 797
Ridgeway Motors (Isleworth) Ltd v. Charles [1996] E.G.C.S. 105 719
Ridsdel, *Re*, Ridsdel v. Rawlinson [1947] Ch. 597; [1947] L.J.R. 1486 487
Rignall Developments Ltd v. Halil [1988] Ch. 190; [1987] 3 W.L.R. 394 723
Riordan v. Banon (1876) 10 Ir.R.Eq. 469 155
Risch v. McFee (1990) 61 P. & C.R. 42; [1991] 1 FLR 105 .... 52, 263, 271
Rissik, *Re* [1936] Ch. 68 348
Riverlate Propeties Ltd v. Paul [1975] Ch. 133; [1974] 3 W.L.R. 564 ... 716, 819, 842, 843
Roadley, *Re*, [1930] 1 Ch. 524 402
Robb, *Re*, Marshall v. Marshall [1953] Ch. 459; [1953] 2 W.L.R. 819 611
Robb v. London Borough of Hammersmith and Fulham [1991] I.R.L.R. 72; [1991]
    I.C.R. 514 790
Roberts, *Re*, [1946] Ch. 1 248
——, *Re*, [1963] 1 W.L.R. 406 .... 433, 434
—— v. Roberts [1990] 2 F.L.R. 111; [1991] Fam. Law 65 739
Roberts (A) and Co. Ltd v. Leicestershire County Council [1961] Ch. 555; [1961] 2
    W.L.R. 1000 .... 842, 843
Robertson v. Minister of Pensions [1949] 1 K.B. 227; [1949] L.J.R. 323 884
Robertson's Will Trusts, *Re* [1960] 1 W.L.R. 1050; 104 S.J. 726 .... 177, 625
Robinson, *Re* [1911] 1 Ch. 502 688
——, *Re* [1921] 2 Ch. 332 430
——, *Re* [1931] 2 Ch. 122 384
——, *Re*, Davis v. Robinson [1951] Ch. 198; [1951] 1 T.L.R. 132 401
—— v. Harkin [1896] 2 Ch. 415 641
—— v. Ommanney (1883) 23 Ch.D. 285 .... 307, 711
—— v. Pett (1734) 3 P. Wms. 249 585
Robinson & Co. Ltd v. Heuer [1898] 2 Ch. 451 789
Robinson's Settlement Trusts, *Re*, [1976] 1 W.L.R. 806; 120 S.J. 525 629
Rochdale Canal Co. v. King (1851) 2 Sim. (N.S.) 78 .... 730, 746, 888
Roche, *Re* (1842) 2 Dr. & War 287 .... 493, 494
Roche v. Sherrington [1982] 1 W.L.R. 599; (1982) 126 S.J. 212 829
Rochefoucauld v. Boustead [1897] 1 Ch. 196 .... 77, 78, 162, 315
Rochford v. Hackman (1852) 9 Hare 475 .... 187, 188
Roffey v. Shallcross (1819) 4 Madd. 227 713
Rogers v. Ingham (1876) 3 Ch.D. 451 820

Rogers v. Jones (1876) 3 Ch.D. 688 858
Roger's Question, *Re* [1948] 1 All E.R. 328, C.A. 264
Rootkin v. Kent County Council [1981] 1 W.L.R. 1186; (1980) 125 S.J. 496 .... 884, 888
Roper-Curzon v. Roper-Curzon (1871) L.R. 11 Eq. 452 577
Roper's Trust, *Re* (1879) 11 Ch.D. 272 .... 507, 508
Ropner's Settlement Trusts, *Re*, *Re* Ropner's Will Trusts, Ropner v. Ropner [1956] 1
    W.L.R. 902; 100 S.J. 530 581
Roscoe v. Winder [1915] 1 Ch. 62 .... 668, 671, 672
Rose, *Re*, Midland Bank Executor and Trustee Co. v. Rose [1949] Ch. 78; [1949] L.J.R.
    208 117
——, *Re*, Rose v. I.R.C. [1952] Ch. 499; [1952] 1 T.L.R. 1577 .... 117, 118
Rose (Frederick E.) (London) v. Pim (William H.) Junior & Co. [1953] 2 Q.B. 450;
    [1953] 3 W.L.R. 497 841
Rosemary Simmons Memorial Housing Association Ltd v. United Dominions Trust Ltd
    [1986] 1 W.L.R. 1440; (1986) 130 S.J. 923 394
Rosenthal, *Re*, Schwarz v. Bernstein [1972] 1 W.L.R. 1273; 116 S.J. 666 .... 482, 649
Rosher, *Re* [1884] 25 Ch. 801 332
Rosling v. Pinnegar (1987) 54 P. & C.R. 124, C.A. 792
Ross v. Lord Advocate [1986] 1 W.L.R. 1077; (1986) 130 S.J. 612 667
Rosseel N.V. v. Oriental Commercial Shipping (U.K.) Ltd [1990] 1 W.L.R. 1387;
    [1990] 3 All E.R. 545, C.A. 813
Rowbotham v. Dunnett (1878) 8 Ch.D. 430 152
Rowland v. Witherden (1851) 3 Mac. & G. 568 560
Rowlandson v. National Westminster Bank Ltd [1978] 1 W.L.R. 798; (1977) 122 S.J.
    347 118
Rowlls v. Bebb [1900] 2 Ch. 107 543
Rowntree (Joseph) Memorial Trust Housing Association v. Att.-Gen. [1983] Ch. 159;
    [1983] 2 W.L.R. 284 .... 387, 401, 447
Roy v. Kensington and Chelsea and Westminster Family Practitioner Committee [1992]
    1 A.C. 624; [1992] 2 W.L.R. 239 800
—— v. Roy [1996] 1 F.L.R. 541 .... 76, 271
Royal Bristol Permanent Building Society v. Bomash (1887) 35 Ch.D. 390 312
Royal Brunei Airlines Sdn. Bhd. v. Tan [1995] 2 A.C. 378 294,
                                                                                                                295, 301
Royal Choral Society v. I.R.C. [1943] 2 All E.R. 101 .... 388, 390, 391
Royal College of Nursing v. St. Marylebone Borough Council [1959] 1 W.L.R. 1077;
    124 J.P. 49 393
Royal College of Surgeons v. National Provincial Bank Ltd [1952] A.C. 631; [1952] 1
    T.L.R. 978 .... 380, 381, 388, 389, 392, 424
Royce, *Re* [1940] Ch. 514 397
Royscott Spa Leasing Ltd v. Lovett [1994] N.P.C. 146; [1995] B.C.C. 502 340
Royscot Trust Ltd v. Rogerson [1991] 2 Q.B. 297 827
Rumball (dec'd), *Re*, Sherlock v. Allan [1956] Ch. 105; [1955] 1 W.L.R. 1037 423
Runnymede Borough Council v. Ball [1986] 1 W.L.R. 353; (1986) 130 S.J. 111 798,
                                                                                                                        799
—— v. Harwood (1994) 68 P. & C.R. 300; [1994] 1 P.L.R. 22 .... 760, 798
Russell v. Jackson (1852) 10 Hare 204 152
Rushton v. Smith [1976] Q.B. 480; [1975] 3 W.L.R. 70 732
Ryall v. Rolls (1750) 1 Ves. Sen. 348 115
Ryan, *Re* [1911] W.N. 56 75
—— v. Mutual Tontine Westminster Chambers Association [1893] 1 Ch. 116 704,
                                                                                                                705, 707
Rymer, *Re* [1895] 1 Ch. 19 .... 432, 434, 435

S. (dec'd), *Re* [1996] 1 W.L.R. 235 .... 316, 317
——, *Re*, S (Gifts by Mental Patient) [1997] 1 F.L.R. 96 75
S. (Hospital Patient; Court's Jurisdiction), *Re* [1996] Fam. 1 745
S.C.F. Finance Co. Ltd v. Masri [1985] 1 W.L.R. 876; (1985) 129 S.J. 450 811
SEDAC Investments Ltd v. Tanner [1982] 1 W.L.R. 1342; (1982) 126 S.J. 609 ... 707, 748
Sahal's Will Trusts, Alliance Assurance Co. v. Att.-Gen. [1958] 1 W.L.R. 1243; 123 J.P.
    73 410

Sainsbury v. I.R.C. [1970] Ch. 712; [1969] 3 W.L.R. 760 204
Sainsbury J. plc v. O' Connor (Inspector of Taxes) [1991] S.T.C. 318; [1991] 1 W.L.R.
    963 .... 57, 313
Sainsbury Settlement, *Re*, Sainsbury v. First C.B. Trustee (Practice Note) [1967] 1
    W.L.R. 476; 111 S.J. 177 627
St. Andrew's Allotment Association, *Re* [1969] 1 W.L.R. 229; (1968) 112 S.J. 927 .. 241
St. Aubyn v. Att.-Gen. [1952] A.C. 15; [1951] 2 All E.R. 473 221
Salisbury v. Salisbury (1848) 6 Hare 526 865
Salt v. Cooper (1880) 16 Ch.D. 544 20
Salting, *Re* [1932] 2 Ch. 57 .... 192, 616
Saltman Engineering Co. Ltd v. Campbell Engineering Co. Ltd [1963] 3 Al E.R. 413;
    65 R.P.C. 203 795
Salusbury v. Denton (1857) 3 K. & J. 529 426
Sampson v. Hodson-Pressinger [1981] 3 All E.R. 710; (1981) 125 S.J. 623 777
Sandbrook, *Re* [1972] 2 Ch. 471 330
Sanders v. Ernest A. Neale Ltd [1974] 1 C.R. 565; [1974] 3 All E.R. 327 790
Sanders Lead Co. Inc. v. Entores Metal Brokers Ltd [1984] 1 W.L.R. 452; (1983) 127
    S.J. 840 814
Sanders' Will Trusts, *Re*, Public Trustee v. McLaren [1954] Ch. 265; [1954] 2 W.L.R.
    487 387
Sanderson's Trust, *Re* (1857) 3 K. & J. 497 .... 186, 234, 622
Sang Lee Invesment Co. Ltd v. Wing Kwai Investment Co. Ltd, *The Times*, April 14,
    1983 .... 27, 718
Sargeant v. National Westminster Bank plc (1991) 61 P. & C.R. 518; *The Times*, May
    10, 1990 .... 589, 591
Satterthwaite's Will Trust, *Re* [1966] 1 W.L.R. 277; 110 S.J. 92 436
Saul v. Pattinson, (1886) 55 L.J.Ch. 831 182
Saunders v. Edwards [1987] 1 W.L.R. 1116; (1987) 131 S.J. 1039 825
—— v. Vautier (1841) 4 Beav. 115, affirmed Cr. & Ph. 240 .... 69, 166, 205,
                                                                              551, 555, 611, 612, 615
Savage v. Dunningham [1974] Ch. 181 .... 256, 592
Savill v. Goodall [1993] 1 F.L.R. 755; (1993) 23 Fam. Law 290 .... 270, 272
Saxone Shoe Co. Ltd's Trust Deed, *Re* [1962] 1 W.L.R. 943 428
Sayer, *Re*, [1957] Ch. 423 167
Sayers v. Collyer (1885) 28 Ch.D. 103 .... 773, 774
Sayre v. Hughes (1868) L.R. 5 Eq. 376 249
Scandinavian Trading Tanker Co. A/B v. Flota Petrolera Ecuatoriana [1983] 2 A.C.
    694 .... 709, 725
Scarisbrick, *Re*, Cockshott v. Public Trustee [1951] Ch. 622; *sub nom. Re*, Scarisbrick's
    Will Trusts, Cockshott v. Public Trustee, 95 S.J. 299 .... 61, 386,
                                                                                   387, 388, 412
Scarisbrick's Re-Settlement Est., *Re* [1944] Ch. 229 617
Schaefer v. Schuhmann [1972] A.C. 572; [1972] 2 W.L.R. 481 .... 346, 711
Schalit v. Nadler Ltd [1933] 2 K.B. 79 19
Schär, (dec'd), *Re*, Midland Bank Executor and Trustee Co. v. Damer [1951] Ch. 280;
    94 S.J. 804 491
Schebsman, *Re* [1944] Ch. 83 128
Schering Chemicals Ltd v. Falkman Ltd [1982] Q.B. 1; [1981] 2 W.L.R. 848 756,
                                                                                       795, 796
Schintz's Will Trusts, *Re*, Lloyd's Bank v. Moreton [1951] Ch. 870; 95 S.J. 369 146
Schmidt v. Air Products of Canada Ltd (1994) 115 D.L.R. 631 240
Schnieder v. Mills [1993] 3 All E.R. 377; [1993] STC 430 840
Schobelt v. Barber (1966) 59 D.L.R. (2d) 519, Ontario High Ct. 316
Schroeder (A.) Music Publishing Co. v. Macaulay (formerly Instone) [1974] 1 W.L.R.
    1308; 118 S.J. 734 788
Scotlife Home Loans (No. 2) Ltd v. Hepworth (1996) 28 H.L.R. 771 834
Scott v. Bradley [1971] Ch. 850 713
—— v. Brownrigg (1881) 9 L.R.Ir. 246 398
—— v. Coulson [1903] 2 Ch. 249 819
—— v. Frank F. Scott (London) Ltd [1940] Ch. 794 844

—— v. Scott (1963) 37 A.L.J.R. 345 676
—— v. Sorman (1742) Willes 400 .... 658, 659
Scottish Burial Reform and Cremation Society v. Glasgow Corporation [1968] A.C.
    138; [1967] 3 W.L.R. 1132 .... 378, 383, 399
Scottish Petroleum Co., *Re* (1883) 23 Ch.D. 434 838
Scowcroft, *Re* [1898] 2 Ch. 638 .... 394, 407
Scruttons Ltd v. Midland Silicones Ltd [1962] A.C. 446; [1962] 2 W.L.R. 186 .... 128, 729
Seager v. Copydex Ltd [1967] 1 W.L.R. 923; 111 S.J. 335 .... 23, 24, 795
—— v. —— (No. 2) [1969] 1 W.L.R. 809; 113 S.J. 281 23
Seale's Marriage Settlement, *Re* [1961] Ch. 574; [1961] 3 W.L.R. 262 .... 500, 501, 623
Searle, *Re* [1900] 2 Ch. 829 538
Searose Ltd v. Seatrain (U.K.) Ltd [1981] 1 W.L.R. 894; (1980) 125 S.J. 287 815
Sechiari, *Re*, Argenti v. Sechiari [1950] W.N. 133; 66 T.L.R. (Pt. 1) 531; 94 S.J. 194;
    [1950] 1 All E.R. 417 547
Second East Dulwich Building Society, *Re* (1899) 79 L.T. 726 649
Secretary of State for Education and Science v. Tameside Metropolitan Borough
    Council (1977) A.C. 1014 743
Securities and Investments Board v. Lloyd-Wright [1993] 4 All E.R. 210 769
—— v. Pantell S.A. [1990] Ch. 426; [1989] 3 W.L.R. 698 743
Sedac Investments Ltd v. Tanner [1982] 1 W.L.R. 1342 .... 707, 748
Sefton v. Tophams (No. 2) [1967] A.C. 50; [1966] 2 W.L.R. 814 783
Segelman, *Re* [1996] Ch. 171 .... 412, 844, 845
Seifert v. Pensions Ombudsman [1997] 1 All E.R. 214 483
Sekhon v. Alissa [1989] 2 F.L.R. 94; [1989] Fam. Law 355 .... 249, 252
Selangor United Rubber Estates v. Cradock (No. 3) [1968] 1 W.L.R. 1555; 112 S.J.
    744 298
—— v. (No. 4) [1969] 3 All E.R. 965; [1969] 1 W.L.R. 1773 643
Selby's Will Trusts, *Re*, Donn v. Selby [1966] 1 W.L.R. 43; 110 S.J. 74 331
Selkirk v. Romar Investments Ltd [1963] 1 W.L.R. 1415; 107 S.J. 907 723
Sen v. Headley [1991] Ch. 425 .... 139, 285, 889, 893, 894
Sergeant v. National Westminster Bank (1991) 61 P. & C.R. 518 .... 513, 557
Series 5 Software Ltd v. Clarke [1996] 1 All E.R. 853 .... 754, 758
Settlement Corporation v. Hochschild [1966] Ch. 10 803
Seven Seas Properties Ltd v. Al-Essa [1988] 1 W.L.R. 1272; (1988) 132 S.J. 1269 ... 697,
    721, 809
Sevenoaks District Council v. Paltullo & Vinson Ltd [1984] Ch. 211; [1984] 2 W.L.R.
    479 .... 738, 777, 779, 791, 792
Seymour v. Seymour, *The Times*, February 16, 1989 .... 840, 842
Shakespeare Memorial Trust, *Re* [1923] 2 Ch. 398 .... 388, 389
Sharman's Will Trusts, *Re*, Public Trustee v. Sharman [1942] Ch. 311 491
Sharp, *Re* [1906] 1 Ch. 793 653
—— v. Harrison [1922] 1 Ch. 502 784
Sharp's Settlement Trusts, *Re*, Ibbotson v. Bliss [1973] Ch. 331; [1972] 3 W.L.R.
    765 573
Sharpe, *Re* [1892] 1 Ch. 154 654
——, *Re*, *ex p.*, Trustee of the Bankrupt's Property v. Bankrupt, The [1980] 1 W.L.R.
    219; (1979) 124 S.J. 147 .... 52, 290, 321, 880, 881
Shaw, *Re*, Public Trustee v. Day [1958] 1 All E.R. 245n., C.A. 358, 371, 372, 390
—— v. Applegate [1977] 1 W.L.R. 970; (1977) 121 S.J. 424 .... 749, 751, 773,
    774, 777, 783, 891
—— v. Cates [1909] 1 Ch. 389 .... 481, 525, 529, 530, 650
—— v. Fitzgerald [1992] 1 F.L.R. 357; [1992] F.C.R. 162 264
—— v. Foster (1872) 5 H.L. 321 .... 312, 313
Shaw's Settlement, *Re*, Shaw v. Shaw, Wisely's Settlement, *Re*, Wisely v. Public
    Trustee [1951] Ch. 833; [1951] 1 T.L.R. 470 .... 188, 193
Shaw's Will Trusts, *Re*, National Provincial Bank v. National City Bank [1952] Ch.
    163; [1951] 2 T.L.R. 1249 389
Shelfer v. City of London Electric Lighting Co. [1985] 1 Ch. 287 .... 739, 772, 774,
    775, 776, 777, 778, 779, 792
Shell U.K. Ltd v. Lostock Garage Ltd [1976] 1 W.L.R. 1187; 120 S.J. 523 .. 720, 774, 775

Shelley v. Shelley (1868) L.R. 6 Eq. 540 92
Shenton, *Re* [1935] Ch. 651 559
Shephard v. Cartwright [1955] A.C. 431; [1954] 3 W.L.R. 967 .... 248, 249
Shephard Homes Ltd v. Sandham [1971] Ch. 340; [1970] 3 W.L.R. 348 ...... 749, 753, 757,
765, 766, 771, 774, 784
Shepherd v. Moulis (1845) 4 Hare 500 638
Sheppard, *Re* [1911] 1 Ch. 50 563
Sherman, *Re*, Walters, *Re*, Trevenen v. Pearce [1954] Ch. 653; [1954] 2 W.L.R.
903 590
Shield's Will Trusts, *Re*, [1974] 2 W.L.R. 885 104
Shiloh Spinners Ltd v. Harding [1973] A.C. 691; [1973] 2 W.L.R. 28 .... 26, 33,
37, 705, 895
Shipley U.D.C. v. Bradford Corpn. [1936] Ch. 375 841
Shipman v. Shipman [1991] 1 F.L.R. 250; [1991] Fam. Law 145 805
Shipwrecked Fishermen and Mariners' Royal Benevolent Society, *Re* [1959] Ch. 220;
[1958] 3 W.L.R. 701 616
Shotton v. Hammond (1976) 120 S.J. 780 .... 764, 765, 772, 802
Sichel's Settlements, *Re* [1916] 1 Ch. 358 .... 492, 494
Sick and Funeral Society of St. John's Sunday School, Golcar, *Re* [1973] Ch. 51; [1972]
2 W.L.R. 962 240
Sifton v. Sifton [1938] A.C. 656 186
Sigsworth, *Re*, [1935] Ch. 89 316
Silkstone & Haigh Moor Coal Co. v. Edey [1900] 1 Ch. 167 590
Simpson, *Re*, [1897] 1 Ch. 256 500
——, *Re* [1952] Ch. 412; 96 S.J. 262 179
Simpson v. Simpson [1992] 1 F.L.R. 601; [1989] Fam. Law 20 .... 74, 133, 136,
231, 246, 247, 264, 829, 830
Simson, *Re*, Fowler v. Tinley [1946] Ch. 299; [1947] L.J.R. 183 .... 398, 423
Sinclair v. Brougham [1914] A.C. 398 .... 18, 665
—— v. Lee [1993] Ch. 497; [1993] 3 W.L.R. 498 548
Singh v. Beggs (1996) 71 P. & C.R. 120 700
—— v. Nazeer [1979] Ch. 474; [1978] 3 W.L.R. 785 698
Siskina (The) [1979] A.C. 210; [1977] 3 W.L.R. 818 .... 734, 808, 811, 812
Skinner v. Att.-Gen. [1940] A.C. 350 57
Sky Petroleum v. V.I.P. Petroleum [1974] 1 W.L.R. 576 (1973) 118 S.J. 311 .... 696, 702,
706, 736, 767, 786
Slatter's Will Trusts, *Re*, Turner v. Turner [1964] Ch. 512; [1964] 3 W.L.R. 18 433
Sledmore v. Dalby (1996) 72 P. & C.R. 196 .... 882, 886, 889
Slevin, *Re* [1891] 2 Ch. 236 437
Slocock's Will Trusts, *Re* [1979] 1 All E.R. 358 840
Smethurst v. Hastings (1885) 30 Ch.D. 490 529
Smirthwaite's Trust, *Re* (1871) L.R. 11 Eq. 251 .... 492, 497
Smith, *Re* [1896] 1 Ch. 71 .... 517, 594, 642
——, *Re* [1904] 1 Ch. 139 .... 166, 492
——, *Re* [1914] 1 Ch. 937 361
——, *Re* [1928] Ch. 915 .... 60, 64, 166, 194, 204, 205, 206, 611
——, *Re* [1932] 1 Ch. 153 .... 379, 411, 423
——, *Re* (1971) 18 D.L.R. (3d) 405 .... 538, 539
—— v. Cooke [1891] A.C. 297 241
—— v. Hughes (1871) L.R. 6 Q.B. 597 818
—— v. Inner London Education Authority [1978] 1 All E.R. 411, C.A. 754,
755, 757, 759
Smith v. Jones [1954] 1 W.L.R. 1089; 98 S.J. 540 .... 33, 35, 845
—— v. Kay (1875) 7 H.L.Cas. 750 828
Smith New Court Securities v. Scrimgeour Vickers (Asset Management) [1996] 3
W.L.R. 1051 827
Smith's Trusts, *Re* (1872) 26 L.T. 820 501
Smith's Will Trust, *Re* [1962] 2 All E.R. 563 402
—— (1981) 131 N.L.J. 292 189
Snell & Prideaux Ltd v. Dutton Mirrors Ltd [1995] 1 E.G.L.R. 259 768
Snelling v. Snelling (John G.) [1973] Q.B. 87; [1972] 2 W.L.R. 588 130

Snowden, *Re*, Shackleton v. Eddy; Henderson, *Re*, Henderson v. Att.-Gen. [1970] Ch.
   700; [1969] 3 W.L.R. 273 453
Snowden. (dec'd), *Re* [1979] Ch. 528; [1979] 2 W.L.R. 654 .... 144, 149, 156
Soar v. Ashwell [1893] 2 Q.B. 390 .... 286, 287
Société Des Industries Metallurgiques S.A. v. Bronx Engineering Co. [1975] 1 Lloyd's
   Rep. 465, C.A. 701, 702
Société Nationale Industrielle Aérospatiale v. Lee Kui Jak [1987] A.C. 871; [1987] 3
   W.L.R. 59 804
Solicitor, *Re*, A (1951 M. No. 234) [1952] Ch. 328; 96 S.J. 59 39
Solicitor to the Treasury v. Lewis [1900] 2 Ch. 812 140
Solihull Metropolitan Borough Council v. Maxfern [1977] 1 W.L.R. 127; (1976) 120
   S.J. 802, 803 798
Solle v. Butcher [1950] 1 K.B. 671; 66 T.L.R. (Pt. 1) 448 .... 26, 43,
                     716, 818, 819, 820, 822, 824, 825, 840, 843
Solomon, *Re.*, A Bankrupt, *ex p.* The Trustee of the Bankrupt v. Solomon [1967] Ch.
   573; [1967] 2 W.L.R. 172 .... 282, 530
Soltau v. de Held (1851) 2 Sim. (N.S.) 133 791
Somerset, *Re* [1894] 1 Ch. 231 .... 530, 647, 648
Somes, *Re* [1896] 1 Ch. 250 179
Sorochan v. Sorochan (1986) 29 D.L.R. 1 291
South African Territories Ltd v. Wallington [1898] A.C. 309 701
South Carolina Insurance Co. v. Assurantie Maatshappij "De Zeven Provincien" N.V.
   Same v. Al Ahlia Insurance Co. [1987] A.C. 24; [1986] 3 W.L.R. 398 744
South Place Ethical Society, *Re*, Barralet v. Att.-Gen. [1980] 1 W.L.R. 1565; (1980) 124
   S.J. 774 .... 389, 395, 397, 399, 411, 420, 424, 428
South Tyneside Metropolitan Borough Council v. Svenska International plc [1995] 1
   All E.R. 545, Q.B.D. 680
Southcomb v. Exeter (Bishop) (1847) 6 H. 213 718
Space Investments Ltd v. Canadian Imperial Bank of Commerce Trust Co. (Bahamas)
   [1986] 1 W.L.R. 1072; [1986] 3 All E.R. 75 .... 96, 586, 667, 668, 669, 679
Specialist Plant Services v. Braithwaite [1987] B.C.L.C. 1, C.A. 684
Speight v. Gaunt (1883) 9 App.Cas 1 .... 481, 482, 521, 527, 560, 565
Spence, *Re*, Quick v. Ackner [1949] W.N. 237 152
Spence, (dec'd), *Re*, Ogden v. Shackleton [1979] Ch. 483; [1978] 3 W.L.R. 483 . 432, 435
Spence v. Brown (1988) 18 Fam. Law. 291, C.A. 52, 270
Spence v. Crawford [1939] 3 All E.R. 271 .... 31, 838
Spencer's S.E., *Re* [1903] 1 Ch. 75 500
Spens v. I.R.C.; Holdsworth Hunt v. I.R.C. [1970] 1 W.L.R. 1173; 114 S.J. 668 624
Spiller v. Maude (1881) 32 Ch.D. 158 413
Spiro v. Lintern [1973] 1 W.L.R. 1002 .... 695, 700
Sport International Bussum B.V. v. Inter-Footwear [1984] 1 W.L.R. 776; (1984) 128
   S.J. 383 717
Sprague, *Re* (1880) 43 L.T. 236 63
Sprange v. Barnard (1789) 2 Bro.C.C. 585 93
Springette v. Defoe (1992) 24 H.L.R. 552; (1992) 65 P. & C.R. 1   254, 262, 265, 270, 272
Spurling's Will Trusts, *Re* [1966] 1 W.L.R. 920 586
Stackhouse v. Barnston (1805) 10 Ves. Jr. 453 .... 646, 647
Stafford Borough Council v. Elkenford [1977] 1 W.L.R. 324; (1976) 75 L.G.R. 337 .   799
Standard Chartered Bank v. Walker; TSB Bank v. Same [1992] 1 W.L.R. 561; [1992]
   BCLC 603 811
Standing v. Bowring (1885) 35 Ch.D. 282 .... 121, 245
Stanford, *Re* [1924] 1 Ch. 73 .... 388, 437
—— v. Hurlstone (1873) L.R. 9 Ch.App. 116 792
Staniland v. Willott (1852) 3 Mac. & G. 664 140
Stanley v. I.R.C. [1944] K.B. 255 573
Stannard v. Fisons Pensions Trust [1991] I.R.L.R. 27; *The Times*, November 19, 1991,
   C.A. 507
Stapylton Fletcher Ltd (In Administrative Receivership), *Re*, Ellis Son & Vidler Ltd (In
   Administrative Receivership) *Re* [1994] 1 W.L.R. 1181; [1995] 1 All E.R.
   192 94

State Bank of India v. Sood [1997] 1 All E.R. 169 36
Stead, *Re* [1990] 1 Ch. 237 152
Steed's Will Trusts, *Re*, Sandford v. Stevenson [1960] Ch. 407; [1960] 2 W.L.R.
    474 .... 619, 625, 626, 628
Steedman v. Drinkle [1916] 1 A.C. 275 720
Steel v. Wellcome Custodian Trustees [1988] 1 W.L.R. 167; (1987) 131 S.J.
    1589 .... 450, 483, 531, 561, 620
Steele's Will Trusts; National Provincial Bank v. Steele [1948] Ch. 603; [1948] L.J.R.
    1888 92
Stemson's Will Trusts, *Re*, Carpenter v. Treasury Solicitor [1970] Ch. 16; [1969] 3
    W.L.R. 21 433
Stenning, *Re* [1895] 2 Ch. 433 673
Stephens v. Avery [1988] Ch. 449; [1988] 2 W.L.R. 1280 .... 24, 797
Stevens v. Chown [1901] 1 Ch. 894 741
Stevens & Cutting v. Anderson [1990] 1 E.G.L.R. 95 .... 838, 887
Stevenson (Inspector of Taxes) v. Wishart [1987] 1 W.L.R. 1204; (1987) 131 S.J.
    744 .... 215, 225
Stewart, *Re* [1908] 2 Ch. 251 .... 135, 136
Stiles v. Cowper (1748) 3 Atk. 692 .... 883, 887
Stimpson's Will Trusts, *Re* [1931] 2 Ch. 77 193
Stoke-on-Trent City Council v. B. & Q. (Retail); Wolverhampton Borough Council v.
    B. & Q.; Barking & Dagenham London Borough Council v. Home Charm Retail
    [1984] A.C. 754; [1984] 2 W.L.R. 929 .... 742, 798, 799
—— v. W. & J. Wass [1988] 1 W.L.R. 1406; (1988) 132 S.J. 1458 .... 779, 781
Stokes v. Anderson [1991] 1 F.L.R. 391; [1991] Fam. Law 310 ...... 97, 262, 263, 268, 271
Stone v. Hoskins [1905] P. 194 .... 306, 308, 309
—— v. Stone (1869) 5 Ch. App. 74 123
Stonegate Securities Ltd v. Gregory [1980] Ch. 576; [1980] 3 W.L.R. 168 764
Stoneham Settlement Trusts, *Re*, Popkiss v. Stoneham [1953] Ch. 59; [1952] 2 T.L.R.
    614 .... 493, 504
Stott v. Milne (1884) 25 Ch.D. 710 586
—— v. Ratcliffe (1982) 79 L.S.Gaz. 634 279
Strahan, *Re* (1856) 8 De. G.M. & G. 291 .... 512, 632
Strakosch, *Re*, Temperley v. Att.-Gen. [1949] Ch. 529; [1949] L.J.R. 1477 .... 399, 422
Stratford (J.T.) & Son v. Lindley [1965] A.C. 307; [1964] 3 W.L.R. 541 753
Stratton's Disclaimer, *Re*, Stratton v. I.R.C. [1958] Ch. 42; [1957] 3 W.L.R. 199 89
Street v. Mountford [1985] A.C. 809; [1985] 2 W.L.R. 877 868
Strickland v. Aldridge (1804) 9 Ves. Jr. 516 .... 147, 162
Strickland's Will Trusts, *Re* [1936] 3 All E.R. 1027 396
Strong v. Bird (1874) L.R. 18 Eq. 315 .... 135, 136
Stroud Architectural Services v. John Laing Construction [1994] B.C.C. 18; [1994] 2
    B.C.L.C. 276 684
Stuart, *Re* [1987] 2 Ch. 583 .... 530, 649, 650
Sudbrook Trading Estate v. Eggleton [1983] 1 A.C. 444; [1982] 3 W.L.R. 315 .... 700, 712
Sudeley (Lord) v. Att.-Gen. [1897] A.C. 11 57
Suenson-Taylor's Settlement Trusts, *Re*, Moores v. Moores [1974] 1 W.L.R. 1280; 118
    S.J. 757 556
Suffert's Settlement, *Re* [1961] Ch. 1; [1960] 3 W.L.R. 796 .... 621, 622
Sugden v. Crossland (1856) 3 Sm. & G. 192 594
Suleman v. Shahsavari [1988] 1 W.L.R. 1181; (1988) 132 S.J. 1243 .... 727, 728
Sullivan, *Re* [1930] 1 Ch. 84 539
—— v. Henderson [1973] 1 W.L.R. 333; (1972) 116 S.J. 969 720
Supply of Ready Mixed Concrete (No. 2). *See* Director General of Fair Trading v.
    Pioneer Concrete
Surrey County Council and Mole District Council v. Bredero Homes [1993] 1 W.L.R.
    1361; [1993] 3 All E.R. 705 .... 724, 725, 728, 776, 781
Suttill v. Graham [1977] 1 W.L.R. 819; (1977) 121 S.J. 408 260
Sutton, *Re* (1885) 28 Ch.D. 464 426
—— v. Sutton [1984] Ch. 184; [1984] 2 W.L.R. 146 714
Sutton Housing Trust v. Lawrence (1988) 55 P. & C.R. 320; (1987) 19 H.L.R. 520,
    C.A. 783

Swain v. The Law Society [1983] 1 A.C. 598; [1982] 3 W.L.R. 261 .... 92, 128,
                                                         129, 132, 292, 597
Swales v. I.R.C. [1984] 3 All E.R. 58; [1984] S.T.C. 413 222
Sweeting (dec'd), *Re* [1988] 1 All E.R. 1016 851
Swires (Inspector of Taxes) v. Renton [1991] S.T.C. 490; *The Times*, July 18, 1991 .. 216
Swiss Bank Corporation v. Lloyds Bank [1982] A.C. 584; [1981] 2 W.L.R. 893 .... 50, 704
Sybron Corp. v. Rochem [1984] Ch. 112 821
Synge v. Synge [1894] 1 Q.B. 466 .... 126, 711

T's Settlement Trusts, *Re* [1964] Ch. 158; [1963] 3 W.L.R. 987 .... 624, 628
T.B., *Re* [1967] Ch. 247; [1967] 2 W.L.R. 15 75
TDK Tape Distributors (U.K.) v. Videochoice Ltd [1986] 1 W.L.R. 141; (1985) 129 S.J.
    574 .... 811, 815
TSB Bank plc v. Camfield [1995] 1 W.L.R. 430; [1995] 1 All E.R. 951 .... 818, 835
T.S.B. Private Bank International S.A. v. Chabra [1992] 1 W.L.R. 231; [1992] 2 All
    E.R. 245, P.C. 811
Tacon, *Re*, Public Trustee v. Tacon [1958] Ch. 447; [1958] 2 W.L.R. 66 .... 435, 437
Tadcliffe, *Re* [1892] 1 Ch. 227 183
Taddy & Co. v. Sterious [1904] 1 Ch. 354 876
Taittinger v. Allbev [1994] 4 All E.R. 75 745
Tamplin v. James (1880) 15 Ch.D. 215 716
Tancred's Settlement, *Re* [1903] 1 Ch. 715 191
Tang Man Sit (Personal Representatives) v. Capacious Investments [1996] 1 A.C.
    514 .... 609, 633
Tanner v. Tanner [1975] 1 W.L.R. 1346; 119 S.J. 391 .... 330, 701, 872, 873, 874, 875
Target Holdings v. Redferns [1996] 1 A.C. 421; [1995] 3 W.L.R. 352 .... 21, 69, 547,
                                                      560, 633, 634, 635
Tate v. Hilbert (1793) 2 Ves. 111 140
—— v. Williamson (1866) 2 Ch. App. 55 828
Tate Access Floors Inc. v. Boswell [1991] Ch. 512; [1991] 2 W.L.R. 304 .... 807, 808
Tatham v. Drummond (1864) 4 De. G.J. & Sm. 484 406
Tatung (U.K.) v. Galex Telesure [1989] 5 B.C.C. 325 683
Taylor, *Re* [1969] 2 Ch. 245 534
—— v. Johnson [1982–1983] 151 C.L.R. 422 842
—— v. Meads (1865) 4 De G.J. & S. 597 174
—— v. National Union of Mineworkers (Derbyshire Area) [1985] I.R.L.R. 99; *The
    Times*, December 29, 1984 763
—— v. Newham London Borough Council [1993] 1 W.L.R. 444; [1993] 2 All E.R.
    649 737
—— v. Plumer (1815) 3 M. & S. 562 .... 658, 660
—— v. Salmon (1838) 4 Myl. & Cr. 134 78
—— v. Taylor (1875) L.R. 20 Eq. 155 577
Taylor Fashions v. Liverpool Victoria Friendly Society; Old & Campbell v. Same
    [1981] Q.B. 133; [1981] 2 W.L.R. 576 .... 141, 891
Tee v. Ferri (1856) 2 K. & J. 357 152
Tempest, *Re* (1866) L.R. 1 Ch. App. 485 500
—— v. Lord Camoys (1882) 21 Ch.D. 571 .... 486, 505
Tepper's Will Trusts, *Re*, Kramer v. Ruda [1987] Ch. 358; [1987] 2 W.L.R. 729 97,
                                                        103, 109, 328, 331
Tetley v. Chitty [1986] 1 All E.R. 663; (1985) 135 New L.J. 1009 792
Texaco v. Mulberry Filling Station [1972] 1 W.L.R. 814; (1971) 116 S.J. 119 ..... 771, 784
Thames Guaranty v. Campbell [1985] Q.B. 210; [1984] 3 W.L.R. 109 .... 712, 720
Thames Launches v. Trinity House Corporation (Deptford Strond) [1961] Ch. 197;
    [1961] 2 W.L.R. 16 803
Thanet District Council v. Ninedrive (1977) 121 S.J. 706; [1978] 1 All E.R.
    703 .... 757, 798
Tharp v. Tharp [1916] 1 Ch. 142; [1916] 2 Ch. 205 147
Thavorn v. Bank of Credit & Commerce International SA [1985] 1 Lloyd's Rep.
    259 245
The Port Caledonia and The Anna [1903] P. 184 837
Themehelp Ltd. v. West [1996] Q.B. 84 811

Third Chandris Shipping Corp. v. Unimarine S.A.; Aggelikai Ptera Compania Maritima
    S.A. v. Same; Western Sealanes Corp. v. Same; Genie The; Pythia The; Angelic
    Wings The [1979] Q.B. 645; [1979] 3 W.L.R. 122 .... 809, 810
Thomas, *Re* [1930] 1 Ch. 194 616
—— v. Fuller-Brown [1988] 1 F.L.R. 237; (1988) 18 Fam. Law 53, C.A. 270
—— v. National Union of Mineworkers (South Wales Area) [1986] Ch. 20; [1985] 2
    W.L.R. 1081 762
—— v. Sorrell (1673) Vaugh. 330 867
—— v. Times Book Co. Ltd [1966] 1 W.L.R. 911; 110 S.J. 252 115
—— v. University of Bradford [1987] A.C. 795; [1987] 2 W.L.R. 677 .... 445, 446
Thomas Marshall (Exports) Ltd v. Guinle. *See* Marshall (Thomas) (Exports) v.
    Guinle
Thompson, *Re* [1930] 1 Ch. 203 595
——, *Re* [1934] Ch. 342 .... 348, 357
—— v. Finch (1856) 25 L.J. Ch. 681 642
—— v. Mechan [1958] O.R. 357 138
—— v. Park [1944] 1 K.B. 408 .... 870, 871, 873
—— v. Thompson (1844) 1 Coll. 381 387
—— v. Whitmore (1860) 1 J. & H. 268 845
Thompson's Settlment, *Re* [1986] Ch. 99 590,
    591, 592
Thomson's Trustee in Bankruptcy v. Heaton [1974] 1 W.L.R. 605; 118 S.J. 295 593
Thomson v. Clydesdale Bank [1893] A.C. 282 679
—— v. Eastwood (1877) 2 App. Cas. 215 591
Thorley, *Re* [1891] 1 Ch. 613 586
Thorndike v. Hunt (1859) 3 De G. & J. 563 .... 33, 679
Thorne v. British Broadcasting Corporation [1967] 1 W.L.R. 1104; 111 S.J. 478 741
—— v. Heard [1895] A.C. 495 .... 651, 653
Thornton v. Howe (1862) 31 Beav. 14 .... 326, 396
—— v. Stokill (1855) 1 Jur. (N.S.) 751 636
Thorpe v. Fasey [1949] Ch. 649; [1949] L.J.R. 1613 838
Thrells Ltd v. Lomas [1993] 1 W.L.R. 456; [1993] 2 All E.R. 546 .... 171, 181, 459, 469
Throckmorton v. Finch (1598) Third Institute 124 12
Thrupp v. Collett (1858) 26 Beav. 125 .... 326, 333
Thynn v. Thynn (1684) 1 Vern. 296 148
Thynne v. Glengall (1848) 2 H.L.C. 131 859
Tiger v. Barclays Bank [1952] W.N. 38; [1951] 2 K.B. 556 512
Tilley's Will Trusts, *Re*, Burgain v. Croad [1967] Ch. 1179; [1967] 2 W.L.R.
    1533 .... 289, 638, 656, 667, 671, 673, 676
Timmis, *Re* [1902] 1 Ch. 176 653
Timpson's Executors v. Yerbury [1936] 1 K.B. 645 113
Tinker v. Tinker [1970] P. 136; [1970] 2 W.L.R. 331 .... 247, 253
Tinker's Settlement, *Re* [1960] 1 W.L.R. 1011; 104 S.J. 805 .... 619, 628
Tinsley v. Milligan [1994] 1 A.C. 340; [1993] 3 W.L.R. 126 .... 18, 22, 26,
    250, 251, 252, 253
Tito v. Waddell (No. 2) Tito v. Att.-Gen. [1977] Ch. 106; [1977] 2 W.L.R. 496 ...... 31, 70,
    90, 487, 549, 590, 591, 632, 651, 655, 694, 705, 706, 728, 852
Tollemache, *Re* [1903] 1 Ch. 457 .... 614, 649
Tollet v. Tollet (1728) 2 P. Wms. 489 173
Tool Metal Manufacturing Co. v. Tungsten Electric Co. [1955] 1 W.L.R. 761; 99 S.J.
    470 885
Topfell Ltd v. Galley Properties [1979] 1 W.L.R. 446; (1978) 123 S.J. 81 .... 721, 723
Tottenham Hotspur Football and Athletic Co. v. Princegrove Publishers [1974] 1
    W.L.R. 113; (1973) 118 S.J. 35 .... 15, 710
Tout & Finch, *Re*, [1954] 1 W.L.R. 178; 98 S.J. 62 84
Towli v. Fourth River Property Co.; Michaelides v. Cormican Properties, *The Times*,
    November 24, 1976 719
Town Investments v. Department of Environment [1978] A.C. 359; [1977] 2 W.L.R.
    450 70
Townley v. Bedwell (1808) 14 Ves. Jr. 591 851
—— v. Sherborne (1634) J. Bridg. 35 .... 565, 632

Trafford's Settlement, *Re. See* Moore v. I.R.C.
Transatlantic Life Assurance Co. Ltd [1980] 1 W.L.R. 79; (1979) 123 S.J. 859 118
Tree, *Re* [1945] Ch. 325 414
Trenberth (John) v. National Westminster Bank (1979) 123 S.J. 388; (1979) 39 P. &
    C.R. 104 .... 746, 750, 766, 770, 793
Trevor (J.) & Sons v. Solomon (P.R.) (1978) 248 E.G. 779, C.A. 760, 794
Tribe v. Tribe [1996] Ch. 107 .... 251, 252
Trident General Insurance Co. v. McNiece Bros. Pty (1988) 165 C.L.R. 107 125, 132, 729
Triffitt's Settlement, *Re*, Hall v. Hyde [1958] Ch. 852; [1958] 2 W.L.R. 927 175
Trimmer v. Danby (1856) 25 L.J. Ch. 424 .... 354, 355
Triplex Safety Glass Co. v. Scorah [1938] Ch. 211; [1937] 4 All E.R. 693 596
Trollope, *Re* [1927] 1 Ch. 596 544
Troop v. Gibson [1986] 1 E.G.L.R. 1, C.A. 882, 883
Trustees of the British Museum v. Att.-Gen. [1984] 1 W.L.R. 418 .... 450, 522,
                                     531, 532, 620
Trusts of the Abbott Fund, *Re* [1900] 2 Ch. 326 .... 233, 234, 348
Tse Kwong Lam v. Wong Chit Sen [1983] 1 W.L.R. 1394; (1983) 127 S.J. 632 590
Tucker v. Burrow (1865) 2 H. & M. 515 248
Tuck's Settlement Trusts; Public Trustee v. Tuck, *Re* [1978] Ch. 49; [1978] 2 W.L.R.
    411 .... 101, 103, 109, 186, 328, 329, 331, 508
Tufnell, *Re* (1902) 18 T.L.R. 705 653
—— v. Constable (1838) 7 Ad. & E. 798 490
Tufton v. Sperni [1952] W.N. 549; [1952] 2 T.L.R. 516 .... 829, 830
Tulk v. Moxhay (1848) 18 L.J. Ch. 88 .... 29, 785, 786, 876
Turkington, *Re* [1937] 4 All E.R. 501 349
Turner, *Re* [1897] 1 Ch. 536 .... 485, 643, 649, 650
——, *Re* [1974] 1 W.L.R. 1556 282
—— v. Clowes (1869) 20 L.T. 214 710
—— v. Corney (1841) 5 Beav. 515 560
—— v. Turner [1984] Ch. 100; [1983] 3 W.L.R. 896 .... 61, 170, 180,
                                  197, 202, 209, 480, 507
Turner's Will Trusts, *Re* [1937] Ch. 15 .... 562, 572
Tussaud's Estate, *Re* (1878) 9 Ch.D. 363 862
Turton v. Turton [1988] Ch. 542; [1987] 3 W.L.R. 622 271
Tweddle v. Atkinson (1861) 1 B. & S. 393 132
Tyborn Productions v. Conan Doyle [1991] Ch. 75; [1990] 3 W.L.R. 167 738
Tyler, *Re*, Graves v. King [1967] 1 W.L.R. 1269; 111 S.J. 794 .... 80, 112, 157,
                               241, 370, 380, 381

Ulrich v. Ulrich and Felton [1968] 1 W.L.R. 180; 111 S.J. 889 247
Ulverston and District New Hospital Building Trust, *Re*, Birkett v. Barrow and Furness
    Hospital Management Committee [1956] Ch. 622; [1956] 3 W.L.R. 559 ... 238, 438
Ungurian v. Lesnoff [1990] Ch. 206; [1989] 3 W.L.R. 840 .... 263, 896
Union Eagle Ltd v. Golden Achievements Ltd [1997] 2 W.L.R. 341; [1997] 2 All E.R.
    215 720
United Bank of Kuwait plc v. Sahib [1996] 3 W.L.R. 372 86
United Grand Lodge of Ancient Free and Accepted Masons of England and Wales v.
    Holborn B.C. [1957] 1 W.L.R. 1080; 121 J.P. 595 395
United Kingdow Nirex v. Barton; Central Electricity Generating Board v. Crampton,
    The Times, October 14, 1986 738
United Scientific Holdings v. Burnley Borough Council; Cheapside Land Development
    Co. v. Messels Service Co. [1978] A.C. 904; [1977] 2 W.L.R. 806 .... 20, 718
Unity Joint Stock Mutual Banking Association v. King (1858) 25 Beav. 72 889
Universal City Studios Inc. v. Hubbard [1984] Ch. 225; affirming [1983] Ch. 241 808
—— v. Mukhtar & Sons Ltd [1976] 1 W.L.R. 568 805
Universal Thermosensors v. Hibben [1992] 1 W.L.R. 840; [1992] 3 All E.R. 257 807

VDU Installations v. Integrated Computer Systems & Cybernetics, *The Times*, August
    13, 1988 807
Vadasz v. Pioneer Concrete (S.A.) Pty Ltd (1995) 184 C.L.R. 102 .... 818, 835
Vallance, *Re* (1884) 26 Ch.D. 353 330

Van den Bergh's Will Trusts, *Re*, Van den Bergh v. Simpson [1948] W.N. 177; [1948]
 1 All E.R. 935 860
Van Gestel v. Cann, *The Times*, August 7, 1987, C.A. 717, 821, 826
Van Gruisen's Will Trusts, *Re*, Bagger v. Dean [1964] 1 W.L.R. 449; 108 S.J. 237 ... 626
Van Praagh v. Everidge [1902] 2 Ch. 266 716
Van Straubenzee, *Re* [1902] 2 Ch. 779 .... 527, 539
Vandepitte v. Preferred Accident Insurance Corp. of New York [1933] A.C. 70 ... 128, 129
Vandervell v. I.R.C. [1967] 2 A.C. 291; [1967] 2 W.L.R. 87 .... 67, 69, 78,
 80, 82, 83, 84, 114, 117, 241, 242, 243
Vandervell's Trusts, *Re* White v. Vandervell Trustees and I.R.C. [1971] A.C. 912;
 [1970] 3 W.L.R. 452 .... 82, 242
—— (No. 2); White v. Vandervell Trustees [1974] Ch. 269; [1974] 3 W.L.R. 256 67,
 82, 84, 92, 97, 121, 230, 243
Vane v. Fletcher (1717) 1 P. Wms. 352 173
Vardon's Trusts, *Re* (1885) 31 Ch.D. 273 .... 123, 857
Vatcher v. Paull [1915] A.C. 372 .... 176, 177
Vaughan, *Re* (1866) 33 Ch.D. 187 427
Vaux, *Re* [1939] Ch. 465 (C.A.) 862
Veracruz Transportation v. V.C. Shipping Co. Inc. and Den Norske Bank A/S; Veracruz
 The [1992] 1 Lloyd's Rep. 353; *The Times*, November 14, 1991 811
Verge v. Somerville [1924] A.C. 496 .... 384, 413
Vernon's Will Trusts, *Re* [1972] Ch. 300; [1971] 3 W.L.R. 786n. 433
Verrall, *Re* [1916] 1 Ch. 100 410
—— v. Great Yarmouth Borough Council [1981] Q.B. 202; [1980] 3 W.L.R. 258 701,
 710, 724, 787, 870, 874
Vestey v. I.R.C.; Lord Vestey v. I.R.C.; Baddeley v. I.R.C.; Payne v. I.R.C. [1980] A.C.
 1148; [1979] 3 W.L.R. 915 .... 60, 61, 171
Vestey's Settlement, *Re*, Lloyds Bank v. O'Meara [1951] Ch. 209; [1950] 2 All E.R.
 891 .... 507, 571
Vickery, *Re* [1931] 1 Ch. 572 .... 483, 561, 562, 564, 567
Vine Products v. Mackenzie & Co. [1966] F.S.R. 426; [1967] R.P.C. 193 772
Vinogradoff, *Re* [1936] W.N. 68 .... 230, 245, 246, 248, 486
Viscount Hambleden's Will Trusts. *See* Hambleden's Will Trusts
Von Joel v. Hornsey [1895] 2 Ch. 774 765
Voyce v. Voyce (1991) 62 P. & C.R. 290, C.A. 890, 894
Vynior's Case (1609) 8 Co. Rep. 81 307

W (a Minor) *Re* [1981] 3 All E.R. 401; (1981) 11 Fam. Law, C.A. 802
W. v. Egdell [1990] Ch. 395; [1990] 2 W.L.R. 471 797
Wachtel v. Wachtel [1973] Fam. 72; [1973] 2 W.L.R. 366 .... 260, 264, 266
Wakeham v. Mackenzie [1968] 1 W.L.R. 1175; (1968) 112 S.J. 504 .... 711, 714
—— v. Wood (1981) 125 S.J. 608; (1982) 43 P. & C.R. 40 .... 749, 777
Waldron v. Sloper (1852) 1 Drew. 193 883
Wale, *Re*, Wale v. Harris [1956] 1 W.L.R. 1346; 100 S.J. 800 136
Walia v. Naughton (Michael) [1985] 1 W.L.R. 1115; (1985) 129 S.J. 701 569
Walker, *Re* (1890) 62 L.T. 449 .... 529, 530
——, *Re* [1901] 1 Ch 259 493
——, *Re* [1939] Ch. 974 188
—— v. Boyle; Boyle v. Walker [1982] 1 W.L.R. 495; (1981) 125 S.J. 724 .... 723, 828
—— v. Hall (1984) 14 Fam. Law. 21 271
—— v. Symonds (1818) 3 Swan 1 647
Wall, *Re* (1889) 52 Ch.D. 570 .... 387, 401
Wallace, *Re* [1920] Ch. 274 329
Wallace's Settlements, *Re*; Fane v. Wallace; Chance v. Wallace; Wallace v. Beaumont
 [1968] 1 W.L.R. 711; (1968) 112 S.J. 381 .... 177, 625
Waller v. Waller [1967] 1 W.L.R. 451; 111 S.J. 94 .... 280, 791
Wallersteiner v. Moir; (No. 2) Moir v. Wallersteiner (No. 2) [1975] Q.B. 373; [1975] 2
 W.L.R. 389 .... 540, 638, 639
Wallgrave v. Tebbs (1855) 2 K. & J. 313 147
Walpole v. Lord Orford (1797) 3 Ves. Jr. 402 305
Walsh v. Lonsdale (1882) 21 Ch.D. 9 .... 15, 20, 27, 710, 717

Waltons Stores (Interstate) v. Maher (1988) 62 A.L.J.R. 110 .... 883, 885, 886
Warburton v. Warburton (1702) 4 Bro. P.C. 1 100
Ward v. Audland (1847) 16 M. & W. 863 126
—— v. Kirkland [1967] Ch. 194; [1966] 1 W.L.R. 601 867
—— v. Turner (1752) 2 Ves. Sen. 431 .... 138, 140
—— v. Ward (1843) 2 H.L.C. 777 512
Wareham, *Re* [1912] 2 Ch. 312 542
Warman International Ltd v. Dwyer (1995) 69 A.L.J.R. 362 .... 587, 595, 605
Warmington v. Miller [1973] Q.B. 877; [1973] 2 W.L.R. 654 .... 15, 720
Warner Bros. Pictures Inc. v. Nelson [1937] 1 K.B. 209 .... 788, 789, 790
Warren v. Gurney [1944] 2 All E.R. 472 255
—— v. Mendy [1989] 1 W.L.R. 853; [1989] 3 All E.R. 103 790
—— v. Warren (1783) 1 Bro. C.C. 305 861
Wasserberg, *Re* [1915] 1 Ch. 195 138
Waterman's Will Trusts, *Re*, Lloyd's Bank v. Sutton [1952] W.N. 538; [1952] 2 All E.R.
    1054 .... 482, 595, 639, 651
Watkin v. Watson-Smith, *The Times*, July 3, 1986 .... 716, 836
Watson, *Re*, (dec'd); Hobbs v. Smith [1973] 1 W.L.R. 1472; 117 S.J. 792 .... 396, 417, 419
—— v. Burton [1957] 1 W.L.R. 19; 101 S.J. 45 .... 721, 722
—— v. Holland [1985] 1 All E.R. 290; [1984] S.T.C. 372 .... 92, 200, 214
Watts v. Spence [1976] Ch. 165; [1975] 2 W.L.R. 1039 720
Waverley Borough Council v. Hilden [1988] 1 W.L.R. 246; (1988) 132 S.J. 192 742,
                                                                                750, 799
Wayling v. Jones [1995] 2 F.L.R. 1029; (1995) 69 P. & C.R. 170 .... 886, 887, 889, 892
Webb v. Ledsam (1855) 1 K. & J. 385 528
—— v. O'Doherty (1991) 3 Admin. L.R. 731; *The Times*, February 11, 1991 394
—— v. Paternoster (1619) Palm 71 869
—— v. Webb [1994] Q.B. 696; [1994] 3 W.L.R. 801 .... 18, 29
Webber, *Re*, Barclays Bank v. Webber [1954] 1 W.L.R. 1500; 96 S.J. 871 392
Webster v. Cecil (1861) 30 Beav. 62 .... 31, 716
—— v. Lord Advocate (1984) S.L.T. 13 .... 779, 792
Webster v. Newham London Borough Council, *The Times*, November 22, 1980 701
Wedgewood, *Re* [1915] 1 Ch. 113 .... 406, 418
Weeds v. Blaney (1977) 247 E.G. 211; (1977) 121 S.J. 794 840
Weekes' Settlement, *Re* [1897] 1 Ch. 289 .... 62, 63
Weinberger v. Inglis [1919] A.C. 606 803
Weir v. Crum-Brown [1908] A.C. 162 .... 378, 386
Weir Hospital, *Re* [1910] 2 Ch. 124 430
Weir's Settlement Trusts, *Re*, MacPherson and Weir (Viscount) v. I.R.C. [1971] Ch.
    145; [1969] 3 W.L.R. 860; *sub nom.* Weir's Settlement, *Re*, McPherson v. I.R.C.
    [1970] 1 All E.R. 297; *sub nom.* Weir (Lord)'s Settlement, *Re*, T.R. 369,
    C.A. 204
Welby v. Rockcliffe (1830) 1 Russ. & M. 571 49
Weld v. Petre [1929] 1 Ch. 33 .... 654, 655
Weldtech Equipment Ltd, *Re* [1991] B.C.C. 16 685
Wellesley v. Wellesley (1828) 2 Bli. (N.S.) 124 583
Wellesley (Lady) v. Earl Mornington (1855) 2 K. & J. 143 177
Welsh Hospital (Netley) Fund, *Re* [1921] 1 Ch. 655 .... 238, 437
Wenlock (Baroness) v. River Dee Company (1887) 19 Q.B.D. 155 674
West, *Re* [1900] 1 Ch. 84 .... 53, 241
West Mercia Constabulary v. Wagener [1982] 1 W.L.R. 127 743
West Sussex Constabulary's Widows, Children and Benevolent (1930) Fund Trust, *Re*
    [1971] Ch. 1; [1970] 2 W.L.R. 848 .... 233, 237, 429
Westby's Settlement, *Re* [1950] Ch. 296 191
Westdeutsche Landesbank Girozentrale v. Islington London Borough Council [1996]
    A.C. 669; [1996] 2 All E.R. 961 .... 21, 30, 68, 230, 232, 243, 246, 287, 288,
                                        291, 294, 300, 639, 663, 664, 665, 666, 688
Western Fish Products v. Penwith District Council (1978) 122 S.J. 471; [1981] 2 All
    E.R. 204 .... 884, 886, 888

Westminster Bank Limited's Declaration of Trust, *Re* [1963] 1 W.L.R. 820; [1963] 2
  All E.R. 400n 629
Weston, *Re* [1902] 1 Ch. 680 .... 138, 140
Weston's Settlements, *Re*, Weston v. Weston [1969] 1 Ch. 234; [1968] 3 W.L.R. 786;
  sub nom. Weston's Settlements, *Re* (1968) 112 S.J. 641; [1968] 3 All E.R.
  338 .... 330, 500, 501, 612, 622, 627
Wharton v. Masterman [1895] A.C. 186 380
Wheatly v. Westminster Brymbo Coal Co. (1869) L.R. 9 Eq. 538 706
Wheeler and De Rochow, *Re* [1896] 1 Ch. 315 .... 492, 494
Wheelwright v. Walker (1883) 23 Ch.D. 752 .... 500, 557
Whigham's Settlement Trusts, *Re*; Whigham v. Johnston [1971] 1 W.L.R. 831n; [1971]
  2 All E.R. 568n. 622
Whishaw v. Stephens [1970] A.C. 508; [1968] 3 W.L.R. 1127; 112 S.J. 882; *sub nom.*
  Gulbenkian's Settlement Trusts, *Re*, Whishaw v. Stephens [1968] 3 All E.R.
  785, H.L. 61, 64, 97, 99, 101, 102, 104, 108, 169, 208, 353
Whistler v. Webster (1794) 2 Ves. Jr. 367 857
White, *Re* [1898] 2 Ch. 217 586
—— v. Bijou Mansions [1937] Ch. 610; [1938] Ch. 531 34
—— v. Kuzych [1951] A.C. 585; [1951] 2 T.L.R. 277 802
—— v. White (1872) L.R. 15 Eq. 247 840
—— v. Wilson (1852) 1 Drew. 298 175
White-Popham's Settled Estates, *Re* [1936] Ch. 727 617
White's Will Trusts, *Re*, Tindall v. United Sheffield Hospitals (Board of Governors)
  [1951] 1 All E.R. 528 .... 402, 435
Whitecomb v. Jacob (1710) Salk. 160 658
Whitehead's Will Trusts, *Re*, Burke v. Burke [1971] 1 W.L.R. 833; 115 S.J. 389 500,
  501, 623, 633
Whiteley, *Re* (1886) Ch.D. 347 522
——, *Re* [1910] 1 Ch. 600 .... 451, 486
Whiteside v. Whiteside [1950] Ch. 65; 66 T.L.R. (Pt. 1) 126 842
Whiting's Settlement, *Re* [1905] 1 Ch. 96 329
Whittall, *Re*; Whittall v. Faulkner [1973] 1 W.L.R. 1027; 117 S.J. 567 622
Whitwood Chemical Co. Ltd v. Hardman [1891] 2 Ch. 416 .... 785, 786, 788
Wicks v. Firth [1983] A.C. 214; [1983] 2 W.L.R. 34 349
Wightwick's Will Trusts, *Re*, Official Trustees of Charitable Funds v. Fielding-Ould
  [1950] Ch. 260; 66 T.L.R. (Pt. 1) 592 .... 380, 650
Wild v. Pensions Ombudsman [1996] P.L.R. 275 .... 462, 507
Wilde v. Wilde [1988] 2 F.L.R. 83; (1988) 18 Fam. Law. 202 735
Wilkes v. Allington [1931] 2 Ch. 104 .... 137, 138
—— v. Spooner [1911] 2 K.B. 473 32
Wilkins v. Hogg (1861) 31 L.J. Ch. 41 483
Wilkinson v. Clements (1872) L.R. 8 Ch. App. 96 .... 712, 714
William Sindall plc v. Cambridgeshire County Council [1994] 1 W.L.R. 1016 727,
  824, 825, 827
William Denby & Sons Ltd Sick and Benevolent Fund. *See* Denby (William) & Sons
  Sick and Benevolent Fund, *Re*.
William Makin & Sons Ltd, *Re* [1993] B.C.C. 453; [1993] O.P.L.R. 171 171
Williams, *Re* [1897] 2 Ch. 12 91
——, *Re* [1915] 1 Ch. 450 858
——, *Re* [1927] 2 Ch. 283 397
—— v. Barton [1927] 2 Ch. 9 594
—— v. C.I.R. [1965] N.Z.L.R. 395 .... 127, 133, 134, 135
—— v. Greatrex [1957] 1 W.L.R. 31; 101 S.J. 49 719
—— v. Kershaw (1835) 5 Cl. & F. 111n. 426
—— v. Scott [1900] A.C. 499 591
—— v. Staite [1979] Ch. 291 873
—— v. Tedcastle [1994] 1 N.Z.L.R. 85 287
—— Williams (1881) 17 Ch.D. 437 .... 294, 304
Williams (J.W.) v. Williams (M.A.) [1976] Ch. 278; [1976] 3 W.L.R. 494 .... 260, 281

Williams-Ashman v. Price and Williams [1942] Ch. 219 304
Williams & Glyn's Bank Ltd v. Boland [1981] A.C. 487; [1980] 3 W.L.R. 138 274,
                                                              277, 278, 279, 322, 720
Williams' Trustees v. I.R.C. [1947] A.C. 447; [1948] L.J.R. 644 .... 399, 403,
                                                              405, 420, 422, 428
Williams' Will Trusts, *Re*, Chartered Bank of India, Australia and China v. Williams
     [1953] Ch. 138; [1953] 2 W.L.R. 418 577
Williamson v. Codrington (1750) 1 Ves. Sen. 511 .... 125, 127
Willis (J.) & Son v. Willis [1986] 1 E.G.L.R. 62, C.A. 873
Willmott v. Barber (1880) 15 Ch.D. 96 .... 141, 890
Wills, *Re* [1915] 1 Ch. 769 546
Wills' Trust Deeds, *Re*, Wills v. Godfrey [1964] Ch. 219; [1963] 2 W.L.R. 1318 167,
                                                              180, 181, 182, 183
Wills' Will Trusts, *Re*, Wills v. Wills [1959] Ch. 1; [1958] 3 W.L.R. 101 ..... 176, 580, 581
Wilson, *Re* [1913] 1 Ch. 314 435
Wilson v. Law Debenture Trust Corp. plc [1995] 2 All E.R. 337 .... 460, 469, 506
—— v. Paniani [1996] N.Z.L.R. 378 .... 137, 138
—— v. Thomas [1958] 1 W.L.R. 422; 102 S.J. 270 723
—— v. Turner (1883) 22 Ch.D. 521 571
—— v. Wilson (1848) 1 H.L.C. 538 330
Wilton Group plc v. Abrams, *The Times*, February 23, 1990 718
Wimbush, *Re* [1940] Ch. 92 117
Windeatt's Will Trusts, *Re*, Webster v. Webster [1969] 1 W.L.R. 692; 113 S.J. 450 ... 500,
                                                                           501, 623
Windeler v. Whitehall [1990] 2 F.L.R. 505; (1990) 154 J.P.N. 29 266
Windle (A Bankrupt), *Re*, *ex p.* Trustee of the Property of the Bankrupt v. Bankrupt
     [1975] 1 W.L.R. 1628; [1975] 3 All E.R. 987 342
Windsor Steam Coal Co. Ltd, *Re* [1929] 1 Ch. 151 .... 483, 651, 652
Winkworth v. Edward Baron Development Co. Ltd [1986] 1 W.L.R. 1512; [1987] 1 All
     E.R. 114 .... 264, 319
Winter Garden Theatre (London) Ltd v. Millenium Productions Ltd [1948] A.C. 173;
     [1947] L.J.R. 1422 .... 701, 710, 867, 869, 870, 872, 873, 874
Winterstoke's Wills Trust, *Re* [1938] Ch. 158 547
Wiseman v. Simpson [1988] 1 W.L.R. 35; (1987) 131 S.J. 1423 801
Wishart v. National Association of Citizens Advice Bureaux Ltd [1990] 1 C.R. 794;
     [1990] I.R.L.R. 393, C.A. 709, 790
Wittke, *Re* [1944] Ch. 166 .... 189, 191
Wokingham Fire Brigade Trust, *Re*, Martin v. Hawkins [1951] Ch. 373; [1951] 1 T.L.R.
     446 .... 410, 438
Wollaston v. King (1869) L.R. 8 Eq. 165 855
Wolverhampton & Walsall Ry. Co. v. London and North Western Ry. (1873) L.R. 16 Eq.
     433 785
Wolverhampton Corporation v. Emmons [1901] 1 K.B. 515 .... 706, 707
Wombwell, *Re* (1921) 125 L.T. 437 187
Wood, *Re*, Barton v. Chilcott [1949] Ch. 498; [1949] L.J.R. 1509 .... 97, 352
—— v. Griffith (1818) 1 Swans 43 712
—— v. Leadbitter (1845) 13 M. & W. 838 .... 870, 871, 872
—— v. Marley (1839) 11 A. & E. 34 869
—— v. Scarth (1855) 2 K. & J. 33 (in equity); (1858) 1 F. & F. 293 .... 31, 716, 818
—— v. Sutcliffe (1851) 2 Sim. (N.S.) 163 746
Woodar Investments Developments Ltd v. Wimpey Construction (U.K.) Ltd [1980] 1
     W.L.R. 277; (1980) 124 S.J. 184 .... 125, 703, 729
Woodard v. Woodard [1995] 3 All E.R. 980 138
Woodford v. Smith [1970] 1 W.L.R. 806; 114 S.J. 245 .... 753, 803
Woodford Estates v. Pollack (1978) 93 D.L.R. (3d) 350, Ont. H.C.J. 727
Woodhams, (dec'd), *Re*; Lloyd's Bank v. London College of Music [1981] 1 W.L.R.
     493; (1980) 125 S.J. 275 .... 432, 492
Woodhouse, *Re* [1941] Ch. 336 541
Woodhouse A.C. Israel Cocoa Ltd v. Nigerian Produce Marketing Co. Ltd [1972] A.C.
     741; [1972] 2 W.L.R. 1090 885
Woodin, *Re* [1895] 2 Ch. 349 575

Woodstead Finance Ltd v. Petrov, *The Times*, January 23, 1986 837
Woodward v. Hutchins [1977] 1 W.L.R. 760; (1977) 121 S.J. 409 .... 793, 797
Wookey v. Wookey; S (A Minor), *Re* [1991] Fam. 121; [1991] 3 W.L.R. 135 ...... 739, 801
Woollerton and Wilson Ltd v. Richard Costain Ltd [1970] 1 W.L.R. 411; 114 S.J.
    170 .... 746, 750, 776, 779
Woolridge v. Woolridge (1859) Johns. 63 855
Woolwich Equitable Building Society v. I.R.C. [1993] A.C. 70; [1992] 3 W.L.R.
    366 .... 657, 686
Worboys v. Carter [1987] 1 E.G.L.R. 1; (1987) 283 E.G. 307 695
Wordingham v. Royal Exchange Trust Co. Ltd [1992] Ch. 412; [1992] 2 W.L.R.
    496 845
Worthing Rugby Football Club Trustees v. I.R.C. [1987] 1 W.L.R. 1057; (1987) 131 S.J.
    976 359
Worthington, *Re*, Leighton v. MacLeod [1954] 1 W.L.R. 526; 98 S.J. 196 587
Wragg, *Re* [1919] 2 Ch. 58 514
——, *Re*, Hollingsworth v. Wragg [1959] 1 W.L.R. 922; 103 S.J. 716 611
Wray v. Steele (1814) 2 V. & B. 388 256
Wright, *Re*, Blizzard v. Lockhart [1954] Ch. 347; [1954] 2 W.L.R. 972 437
—— v. Ginn [1994] O.P.L.R. 83 526
—— v. Goff (1856) 22 Beav. 207 845
—— v. Morgan [1926] A.C. 788 .... 590, 636, 639
—— v. Wilkin (1862) 2 B. & S. 232 49
Wright's Wills Trust, *Re* (1981) 78 L.S.Gaz. 841 103
Wrightson, *Re* [1908] 1 Ch. 789 .... 504, 505
Wroth v. Tyler [1974] Ch. 30; [1973] 2 W.L.R. 405 .... 280, 718, 724, 725, 726, 727, 780
Wrotham Park Estate v. Parkside Homes Ltd [1974] 1 W.L.R. 798; (1973) 118 S.J.
    420 .... 730, 731, 747, 749, 751, 776, 780, 781, 782, 783, 784
Wu Koon Tai v. Wu Yau Loi [1996] 3 W.L.R. 778 59
Wykes, *Re*, Riddington v. Spencer [1961] Ch. 229; [1961] 2 W.L.R. 115 428
Wynn, (dec'd), *Re*, Public Trustee v. Newborough [1952] Ch. 271; [1952] 1 T.L.R.
    278 .... 103, 508
—— v. Skegness Urban District Council [1967] 1 W.L.R. 52; 130 J.P. 404 405
Wynne v. Tempest (1897) 13 T.L.R. 360 485

X. (A Minor), *Re* [1984] 1 W.L.R. 1422; [1985] 1 All E.R. 53 740
X. (Minors) v. Bedfordshire County Council; M. (A Minor) v. Newham London
    Borough Council; E. (A Minor) v. Dorset County Council; Christmas v. Hamp-
    shire County Council; Keating v. Bromley County Council [1995] 2 A.C. 633;
    [1995] 3 W.L.R 152 800
X. v. Y. [1988] 2 All E.R. 648 .... 795, 797
—— v. Morgan Grampian (Publishers) Ltd [1991] 1 A.C. 1; [1990] 2 W.L.R. 1000 . 796

Yeap Cheah Neo v. Ong Chen Neo (1875) L.R. 6 P.C. 381 .... 397, 419
Youde v. Cloud (1874) L.R. 18 Eq. 634 512
Young, *Re*, Young v. Young (No. 2) [1951] Ch. 344; [1951] 1 T.L.R. 262 .... 147, 151,
                                                                                                    152, 159, 387
Young v. Sealey [1949] Ch. 278; [1949] L.J.R. 529 255
Younghusband v. Gisborne (1846) 15 L.J. Ch. 355 186
Yousif v. Salama [1980] 1 W.L.R. 1540; (1980) 124 S.J. 480 .... 765, 805, 806

Z. (A Minor) (Identification: Restrictions on Publication), *Re* [1997] Fam. 1 .... 740, 802
Z. v. A.-Z. and AA-LL [1982] Q.B. 558; [1982] 2 W.L.R. 288 .... 808, 809,
                                                                                                810, 811, 814, 815
Zucker v. Tyndall Holdings plc [1992] 1 W.L.R. 1127; [1993] 1 All E.R. 124 ..... 743, 811
Zamet v. Hyman [1961] 1 W.L.R. 1442; 105 S.J. 911 830
Zandfarid v. Bank of Credit and Commerce International S.A. (in liquidation) [1996] 1
    W.L.R. 1420 835

TABLE OF STATUTES

1535   Statute of Uses (27 Hen. 8,
      c. 10) 10

1601   Charitable Uses Act (43 Eliz. 1,
      c. 4) 376, 409

1660   Tenures Abolition Act (12 Car.
      2, c. 24) .... .11

1677   Statute of Frauds (29 Car. 2,
      c. 3)—
      s. 7 76
      s. 9 78

1688   Bill of Rights (1 Will. & Mar.
      Sess. 2, c. 2)—
      s. 1 804
      Art. 9 804

1701   Act of Settlement (12 & 13
      Will. 3, c. 2) 331

1829   Friendly Societies Act (10 Geo.
      4, c. 56) 237

1837   Wills Act (7 Will. 4 & 1 Vict.
      c. 26) 78, 139,
             143, 144, 148, 153, 154,
             158, 159, 163, 174, 254
      s. 9 .... 76, 89, 143, 155
      s. 10 174
      s. 15 159
      s. 27 .... 168, 172
      s. 33 161

1854   Common Law Procedure Act
      (17 & 18 Vict. c. 125) 14, 734
      s. 78 657

1855   Places of Worship Registration
      Act (18 & 19 Vict. c. 81)   397

1858   Chancery Amendment Act (21
      & 22 Vict. c. 27) 14, 23,
             24, 696, 697, 698, 714,
             725, 726, 728, 731, 738,
             745, 748, 750, 773, 774,
             776, 777, 778, 779, 780,
             781, 782, 783, 792
      s. 2 .... 724, 727

1861   Larceny Act (24 & 25 Vict.
      c. 96) 643

1869   Debtors Act (32 & 33 Vict.
      c. 62) 25
      s. 4 644

1870   Apportionment Act (33 & 34
      Vict. c. 96) 545
      s. 2 545

1873   Supreme Court of Judicature
      Act (36 & 37 Vict. c.
      66) 3, 4, 5, 14, 15,
             16, 20, 21, 23, 696, 725,
             734, 776, 870
      s. 16 776
      s. 24 15
      s. 25 15
         (1) 15
         (6) 15
         (8) 734

1874   Real Property Limitation Act
      (37 & 38 Vict. c. 57) 77

1875   Supreme Court of Judicature
      Act (38 & 39 Vict. c.
      77) 5, 14, 15, 16,
             21, 734, 870

1882   Bills of Exchange Act (45 & 46
      Vict. c. 61)—
      s. 31 115
      Married Women's Property Act
      (45 & 46 Vict. c. 75)—
      s. 17 280

1889   Factors Act (52 & 53 Vict.
      c. 45)—
      s. 1(4) 35
      s. 2 19
      s. 8 19
      s. 9 19

1890   Partnership Act (53 & 54 Vict.
      c. 39)—
      s. 30 595

1893   Sale of Goods Act (56 & 57
      Vict. c. 71) 702

1894   Finance Act (57 & 58 Vict.
      c. 30)—
      ss. 1–2 .... 217, 203

1896 Judicial Trustees Act (59 & 60
         Vict. c. 35) 487
      s. 1 587
         (1)–(6) 487
         (7) 488
      s. 4(1) 487
      s. 5 487
1906 Public Trustee Act (6 Edw. 7, c.
         55) 488, 489
      s. 1 488
      s. 2(1)(*d*) 487
         (2)–(3) 488
         (4)–(5) 489
      s. 3 488
      s. 4 .... 488, 587
         (2)–(3) 489
         (2)(*g*) 490
         (3) 489, 490, 549
      s. 5(1) 488
      s. 7 488
      s. 8(1) 488
         (1A) 488, 587
      s. 9 .... 480, 488, 587
      s. 13 549
1914 Bankruptcy Act (4 & 5 Geo. 5,
         c. 59)—
      s. 42 342
1916 Larceny Act (6 & 7 Geo. 5,
         c. 50) 643
1925 Settled Land Act (15 & 16 Geo.
         5, c. 18) 36, 40, 272,
               273, 491, 557, 579, 896
      s. 38(1) 555
      s. 64 619
         (1) 616
         (2) 617
      s. 73 .... 518, 543
         (1)(xi) 540
      s. 94(1) 556
      Trustee Act (15 & 16 Geo. 5, c.
         19 .... 201, 490, 495,
               499, 554, 560, 568
      s. 4 .... 526, 538, 637
      s. 8(1)(*a*)–(*c*) 529
      s. 9 .... 530, 638
      s. 11(1) 637
      s. 12 556
      s. 13(1)–(2) 557
      s. 14 .... 55, 490, 556, 557, 564
         (2)–(3) 557
         (2) 491
      s. 15 .... 513, 558
      s. 16(1) 556
      s. 18 .... 167, 492
         (1) 166, 494
         (2) 492
      s. 19 .... 557, 558
         (2) 558
      s. 20 558
         (4)–(5) 558

1925 Trustee Act—*cont.*
      s. 21 514
      s. 22 559
         (4) 549
      s. 23 481
         (1)–(2) 566
         (1) 560, 561,
               562, 563, 564, 567
         (2)–(3) 565
         (3) 562, 564
      s. 25 .... 493, 526,
            565, 566, 567, 467, 568,
               569, 570
         (2)–(3) 570
         (5) 467, 566
      s. 26 535
      s. 27 .... 535, 687
         (2)(*a*) 535
      s. 30 .... 481, 483, 632
         (1) 560, 561,
               562, 563, 564, 567
         (2) 586
      ss. 31–32 570
      s. 31 .... 199, 227, 572, 574
         (1) **571**
         (ii) 227
         (2) 571, **572**
         (*a*)(i) 574
         (ii) 576
         (3) 571, 575
      s. 32 .... 193, 576,
               578, 579, 580, 581
         (2) 579
      s. 33 ...... 185, 188, 190, 191, 332
         (1) 189
         (2) 189
      s. 34 .... 451, 491
         (3)(*a*) 491
      s. 36 .... 56, 498, 500, 502, 504
         (1)–(2) **493**
         (1) 496, 502
         (3) 493
         (6) 491, 495
         (*a*)–(*b*) 496
         (7) 498
         (8) 493, 494
         (9) 493
      s. 37(1)(*c*) 495, 502
      s. 38 494
      s. 39 .... 56, 490, 502
         (1) 502
      s. 40 .... 56, 57, 493, 499
         (1) 498, 499
         (2) 503
         (4) 498
      s. 41 ...... 498, 499, 503, 504, 627
         (1) 497
         (4) 497
      s. 42 587
      s. 43 498

1925 Trustee Act—*cont.*

ss. 44–56 499
s. 44(vi) 700
s. 50 700
s. 53 .... 583, 617
s. 57 .... 192, 530, 531,
 615, 617, 619, 620, 624
 (1) 616, 617
ss. 61–62 644
s. 61 ...... 482, 483, 535, 567, 648
s. 62 .... 647, 648
 (1) 647
s. 63 .... 181, 534
 (3) 486
s. 64 617
s. 68(17) 54, 648, 651
 (18) 490
s. 69 .... 54, 201
 (2) 492, 554, 572, 573
Law of Property Act (15 & 16
 Geo. 5, c. 20) 272
s. 1(1) 36
 (6) 74, 141, 486, 493
s. 2 .... 268, 276, 556, 895
 (1) 36
 (2) 490
s. 20 .... 486, 493
s. 22(2) 493, 569
s. 26 280
s. 27(2) 55, 490, 491, 556
s. 28(1) 518, 543
 (2) 543
s. 29 566
s. 30 .... 280, 281
s. 34 273
s. 36 273
 (2) 274
s. 40 699
s. 41 .... 15, 718
s. 44(3) 34
s. 47 312
s. 52(1) 115
s. 53 .... 67, 80, 86, 87,
 88, 114, 286, 314
 (1) 245
  (*b*) 76, 78, 79, 143,
  159, 171, 245, 261, 262,
  319
  (*c*) 78, 79, 80,
  83, 84, 87, 88, 117, 244,
  362, 623, 624
  (2) 65, 76, 84,
  85, 87, 139, 160, 230,
  262, 314, 319, 624
s. 60(1) 66
 (3) 244, 245, 251
s. 63 845
s. 99 339
s. 105 292
s. 136 15
s. 155 181

1925 Law of Property Act—*cont.*

s. 157 180
s. 159 .... 172, 174
s. 160 181
s. 172 338
s. 174(1) 837
s. 175 574
s. 198(1) 35
s. 199 34
 (1)(i) 35
s. 205 33
 (1)(ii) 89
 (1)(x) 79
 (1)(xxviii) 490
Land Registration Act (15 & 16
 Geo. 5, c. 21) 35, 115,
 276, 322, 528, 840
s. 19 119
s. 29 322
s. 34(4) 322
s. 47 499
s. 49 728
s. 59(6) 322
s. 70(1) 32, 278
 (g) 245, 278, 280,
 728, 845, 880, 895
s. 74 322
s. 123 32
Land Charges Act (15 & 16
 Geo. 5, c. 22) 33, 34, 35
Administration of Estates Act
 (15 & 16 Geo. 5, c. 23)—
s. 1–3 492
s. 2(2) 55
s. 9 489
s. 33 .... 54, 538, 555, 556
s. 34(1) 15
s. 35 851
s. 36(4) 55
s. 43(2) 700
s. 44 540
s. 46 54
s. 49 54
s. 55(1)(xxvi) 490
Supreme Court of Judicature
 (Consolidation) Act (15 &
 16 Geo. 5, c. 49) 734, 870
ss. 36–44 15
s. 45 734
1926 Law of Property (Amendment)
 Act (16 & 17 Geo. 5,
 c.11) 491
s. 3 490
s. 164 199
1935 Law Reform (Married Women
 and Tortfeasors) Act (25 &
 26 Geo. 5, c. 30) 186
1939 Limitation Act (2 & 3 Geo. 6, c.
 21) 655

1943 Settled Land and Trustee Acts (Court's General Powers) Act (6 & 7 Geo. 6, c. 25) 617

1947 Crown Proceedings Act (10 & 11 Geo. 6, c. 44)—
s. 21 740
(1)(a) 696
Companies Act (11 & 12 Geo. 6, c. 38) 688
s. 95(1) 684

1949 Married Women (Restraint upon Anticipation) Act (12, 13 & 14 Geo. 6, c. 78) 186
Intestates' Estates Act (15 & 16 Geo. 6 & 1 Eliz. 2, c. 64) 54
s. 415(2) 242

1954 Charitable Trusts (Validation) Act (2 & 3 Eliz. 2, c. 58) 403, 427, 428

1957 Public Trustee (Fees) Act (5 & 6 Eliz. 2, c. 12) . 480, 488, 587
Cheques Act (5 & 6 Eliz. 2, c. 36)—
s. 1–2 115

1958 Recreational Charities Act (6 & 7 Eliz. 2, c. 17) 392, 402
s. 1(1)–(3) 404
(2)(b)(i) 405
(3) 405
s. 2 405
Variation of Trusts Act (6 & 7 Eliz. 2, c. 53) 86, 88, 521, 530, 558, 612, 613, 615, 616, 617, 619, 620, 629
s. 1 .... 183, 620, 625, 626
(1) 619, 623
(b) 621
Finance Act (6 & 7 Eliz. 2, c. 56) 200
s. 22 180

1960 Charities Act (8 & 9 Eliz. 2, c. 58) 399, 430, 431, 439, 440, 441, 444, 453
s. 4 377
s. 14 442
s. 29 449
s. 38 377
(4) 402

1961 Suicide Act (9 & 10 Eliz. 2, c. 60) 138
Trustee Investments Act (9 & 10 Eliz. 2, c. 62) 450, 466, 481, 515, 517, 519, 528, 531, 532, 539, 556, 615, 619

1961 Trustee Investments Act —*cont.*
s. 1(3) 519, 525
s. 2 519
(1) 519
(3) 520
(b) 520
(4) 521
s. 3(1) 521, 525
s. 6(1) 466, 522
(b) 524
(2) 525, 637
(3) 526
(5) 525
(6) 525
s. 15 530
Sched 1 526
Pts II–III 526
Part II 528
para 13 528
Pt. IV 520
para. 2 520
para 2A 520
para. 3 520
Sched 2 521
para 2 521

1963 Stock Transfer Act (c. 18)—
s. 1 .... 115, 117
Wills Act (c. 44) 174
s. 2 174

1964 Married Women's Property Act (c. 19) 247
Perpetuities and Accumulations Act (c. 55) 334, 336, 362, 368, 371, 381, 473
s. 1 .... 198, 335, 368
s. 3 .... 336, 368, 582
(1) 438
s. 4(4) 362
s. 7 .... 167, 168
s. 12 438
s. 13 199
s. 15(4) 368
(5) 624

1965 Administration of Justice Act (c. 2)—
s. 2 .... 488, 587
Finance Act (c. 25) 215

1967 Misrepresentation Act (c. 7) 23, 826
s. 1 838
s. 2(1)–(2) 827
(2) 838
General Rate Act (c. 9)—
s. 40 406
Matrimonial Homes Act (c. 75) 724, 726, 878

1968 Finance Act (c. 44)—
s. 35 217
Theft Act (c. 60) 643, 661
s. 2(1)(c) 644

1968 Theft Act—*cont.*
    s. 4(2)(*a*) 644
    s. 5(2) 643, 644
    s. 31 809
        (1) 644
    Civil Evidence Act (c. 64) 157
    Race Relations Act (c. 71) 327
1969 Administration of Justice Act
    (c. 3) 75
    Finance Act (c. 32) 217
    ss. 36–37 217
    s. 37(3)(*b*) 217
    Family Law Reform Act (c.
    46) 571
    15 326
        (7) 326
    s. 17 533
    Law of Property Act (c. 59)—
    s. 23 34
1970 Parish Councils and Burial Authorities (Miscellaneous Provisions) Act (c. 29)—
    s. 1 355
    Administration of Justice Act
    (c. 31) 39
    s. 1 15
    Law Reform (Miscellaneous Provisions) Act (c. 33)—
    s. 2 257
        (1) 247, 260, 269
    Matrimonial Proceedings and Property Act (c. 45)—
    s. 37 .... 269, 270
1971 Powers of Attorney Act (c. 27)—
    s. 9 565
    Finance Act (c. 68) 216
    Industrial Relations Act (c. 72) 709, 790
    Town and Country Planning Act (c. 78)—
    s. 164 879
1972 Land Charges Act (c. 61) 33, 35, 36, 528
    s. 2 895
        (4) 35, 728
        (7) 37
    s. 4 35
    Local Government Act (c. 70)—
    s. 222 .... 743, 798, 799
1973 Matrimonial Causes Act (c. 18) 192, 260, 269
    ss. 23–25 618
    s. 24 618
        (1) 192
        (*c*)–(*d*) 618
        (*c*) 476
    s. 25 .... 204, 826
        (1) 826

1973 Matrimonial Causes Act —*cont.*
    s. 25B–D 476
    s. 31(2)(*e*) 618
    s. 33 .... 192, 193
        (1) 193
        (ii) 193
    s. 37 .... 345, 801
        (2)(*a*) 345
        (4)–(6) 345
    s. 39 342
    s. 57 193
1974 Consumer Credit Act (c. 39) ... 837
    Sched. 4 19
    para. 22 .... 19, 47
    Friendly Societies Act (c. 46)—
    s. 49(1) 238
    s. 54(1) 360
    Solicitors Act (c. 47)—
    s. 37 598
1975 Finance Act (c. 7) 195, 216, 224
    Sched. 5 209
    para. 15 209
    Inheritance (Provision for Family and Dependants) Act (c. 63) 345, 893
    s. 2 346
    ss. 10–13 346
    s. 10(2) 346
    s. 25(1) 167
    Sex Discrimination Act (c. 65) 327, 392
    s. 43 .... 327, 392
    Local Land Charges Act (c. 76) 35
1976 Race Relations Act (c. 74) 326, 331, 332
    s. 34 .... 327, 430
        (1)–(3) 327
1977 Torts (Interference with Goods) Act (c. 32)—
    ss. 2–3 657
    Finance Act (c. 36)—
    s. 57 382
    Unfair Contract Terms Act (c. 50) 723, 837
    s. 2(3) 484
    s. 3 828
    s. 11(1) 828
1978 Civil Liability (Contribution) Act (c. 47) 641
    s. 2(1)–(2) 642
    s. 6(1) 642
    s. 7(3) 642
1979 Estate Agents Act (c. 38)—
    s. 13 49
    Finance (No. 2) Act (c. 47)—
    s. 5 213
    s. 23(1)(*b*) 209

1979 Sale of Goods Act (c. 54) 94
 s. 19 681
 s. 21 .... 19, 47
 ss. 24–25 682
 s. 24 .... 19, 47
 s. 52 702
1980 Limitation Act (c. 58) 29, 654
 s. 21 .... 29, 655
  (1)–(2) 54
  (1) 653, 655
   (a)–(b) 652
   (b) 655
  (2) 652
  (3) 54, 651, 653, 655
 s. 22 .... 54, 653, 687
 s. 23 655
 s. 28 654
 s. 32 654
  (1)(c) 838
 s. 36 771
  (1)–(2) 718
  (1) 29, 654
  (2) 655, 773
 s. 38(1) 651
1981 Contempt of Court Act (c.
 49) 739
 Supreme Court Act (c. 54) 734
 s. 31 .... 799, 800
  (2)–(3) 799
  (6) 773
 s. 33(1) 806
 s. 37 809
  (1) 734, 735, 810, 813
  (3) 811, 812, 813
 s. 39 700
 s. 49 15
  (11) 15
 s. 50 .... 727, 776
 s. 61 38
  (6) 39
 s. 65 39
 s. 72 .... 808, 809
  (3)–(5) 808
 s. 128 490
 Sched. 1 .... 15, 38
 para. 3 39
1982 Civil Jurisdiction and Judgments Act (c. 27) 814
 s. 25 811
 s. 30 738
 s. 49 804
 Forfeiture Act (c. 34) 317
 s. 1(2) 317
 s. 2(1)–(4) 317
  (7) 58
 ss. 3–5 317
 Finance Act (c. 39) 195, 224
 s. 129 .... 378, 382
 Employment Act (c. 46) 761

1982 Administration of Justice Act
 (c. 53)—
 s. 17 89
 s. 20 .... 845, 859
  (2)–(3) 845
 s. 57 549
  (1)–(2) 487
1983 Matrimonial Homes Act (c.
 19) 35,
      276, 277, 280
 Mental Health Act (c. 20) .. 74, 497
 s. 95 75
 s. 96(1)(d) 75, 619
  (e) 75
  (3) 619
 s. 97 75
 s. 106(6) 191
 s. 148 493
 Sched. 4 493
 Part VII 488, 489
1984 County Courts Act (c. 28)—
 s. 23 732
 s. 38 .... 732, 735
 Matrimonial and Family Pro-
 ceedings Act (c. 42)—
 s. 24 801
 Finance Act (c. 43)—
 s. 17(2) 213
 Sched. 7 213
 Inheritance Tax Act (c. 51) 216
 s. 1–4 218
 s. 2 219
  (3) 218
 s. 3A 219, 227
 s. 4 223
 s. 5(2) 167
 s. 6 218
 s. 7 .... 117, 219, 612
  (4) 219
 ss. 10–11 224
 s. 11 219
 s. 17 .... 89, 613
 s. 18 218
 s. 19 219
 s. 23 382
 ss. 25–26 382
 s. 29(5) 378
 ss. 38–39 220
 s. 43(2) 222
 ss. 48–49 222
 s. 48(3) 623
 s. 49(2) 223
 s. 50(1)–(2) 223
  (5) 223
 ss. 51–52 223
 s. 52(1)–(3) 223
 s. 53(2) 224
 s. 54(1)–(2) 224
 s. 55 224
 s. 57 224
 s. 58 224

1984 Inheritance Tax Act—*cont.*
s. 58(1)(*a*) 228, 382
(*b*) 227
(*c*)–(*e*) 228
s. 64 225
s. 65(1)(*a*)–(*b*) 225
(*a*) 227
(4)–(8) 225
s. 66 225
s. 68 226
(6) 226
s. 69 226
s. 70 .... 227, 228
s. 71 226
(2) 227
(3)(*a*) 227
(4) 227
s. 76 381
ss. 86–89 228
s. 86 474
s. 88 193
s. 90 223
s. 91 57
s. 141 224
s. 151 228
s. 201 223
(1)(*d*) 623
s. 267 501
Sched. 4 228
Part III 218, 222, 613
1985 Companies Act (c. 6)—
s. 2 516
s. 56(1) 745
ss. 182–183 .... 115, 117
s. 183(3) 55
s. 192 484
s. 195 703
s. 360 .... 40, 565
ss. 395–404 684
s. 557 688
s. 558 433
Part VII 449
Charities Act (c. 20) 443, 454
Enduring Powers of Attorney
Act (c. 29) 566, 568
s. 2(8) 568, 569
s. 3(3) 568, 569
Finance Act (c. 54)—
s. 82 79
Administration of Justice Act
(c. 61) 488
s. 48 533
s. 50 .... 56, 487, 493, 502
(4) 488
Landlord and Tenant Act
(c. 70)—
s. 17 .... 707, 713
1986 Finance Act (c. 41) 217, 218,
219, 220, 222
s. 101 .... 196, 218, 219
s. 102 .... 202, 220

1986 Finance Act—*cont.*
s. 102(3)–(5) 221
s. 104 221
Sched. 19 219
Sched. 20 202
Insolvency Act (c. 45) 282, 283,
338, 342
s. 8 685
ss. 10–11 685
s. 15 685
(5) 686
s. 43 685
s. 91(3) 473
s. 95 473
ss. 238–239 344
s. 240(3) 344
s. 241 345
s. 251 685
s. 283 656
s. 284 342
s. 323 50
s. 333 745
s. 335A 282
ss. 336–337 283
s. 338 270
s. 339 342
s. 340 342
ss. 341–342 343
A–C 342, 473
ss. 423–425 341
s. 423 .... 338, 342
(1) 339
(2) 341
s. 425 343
(2) 341
s. 435 343
Sched. 14 342
Part 1 341
Part II 341
Part VIII 341
Public Trustee and Administra-
tion of Funds Act (c.
57) 488
s. 1 488
s. 3(5) 489
(6) 488
Financial Services Act (c. 60) . 467,
520, 526, 532, 567
s. 3 .... 514, 525, 567
s. 84 484
s. 191(2) 467
Sched. 1
para. 22 .... 514, 567
1987 Recognition of Trusts Act
(c. 14) 43
Sched. 1
Art. 6–8 .... 43, 504, 623
Article 11 43
Banking Act (c. 22) 461, 797

1987 Landlord and Tenant Act
         (c. 31)—
       s. 42 51
       Family Law Reform Act (c.
         42) 122, 248, 861
       s. 1 .... 189, 326
       s. 19 326
            (7) 326
       s. 20 533
       Sched. 2
       para. 2 189
       Finance (No. 2) Act (c. 51)—
       s. 96 .... 196, 219,
                            222, 223, 577, 612
       Sched. 7 .... 219, 222
1988 Income and Corporation Taxes
         Act (c. 1)—
       s. 1(2) 213
       ss. 15–20 213
       s. 19(1) 474
       s. 22 200
       s. 86 378
       s. 189 474
       s. 202 381
       ss. 209–211 547
       s. 234 547
       s. 254 547
       s. 257 214
       s. 339 .... 378, 381, 383
       s. 427 383
       ss. 505–506 383
       s. 505 381
            (1) 381, 416
       s. 506(1) 381
       s. 577 378
       s. 590(2)–(3) 473
       s. 592(2) 474
            (4) 474
            (7)–(8) 474
       ss. 601–603 475
       s. 640A 475
       s. 660 378
            (3) 381
       ss. 663–664 576
       ss. 663–665 227
       s. 663 214
       ss. 671–675 180
       s. 671 378
       s. 673 168
       s. 674 180
            A 200
       s. 683 .... 168, 383
       ss. 684–685 .... 81, 83
       s. 685 242
       s. 686 .... 198, 214, 575
            (6) 54
       s. 687 214
            (1) 215
       s. 835 213
       Sched. 22 475

1988 Income and Corporation Taxes
         Act—*cont.*
       Sched. 29
       para. 26 474
       Scheds. A–F 213
       Scheds. B–C 213
       Part XV 214
       Criminal Justice Act (c. 33)—
       Part VI 291
       Finance Act (c. 39) ... 195, 210, 215
       s. 24(1) 213
            (3) 198, 214
       s. 136 226
       Education Reform Act
         (c. 40)—
       s. 202 446
       s. 206 446
       Local Government Finance Act
         (c. 41)—
       s. 43(5)–(6) 382
       s. 47 .... 382, 406
       s. 64(10) 382
       Sched. 5
       para. 11 .... 382, 397
       Copyright Designs and Patents
         Act (c. 48)—
       s. 90(3) 115
1989 Finance Act (c. 26)—
       s. 109 200
       s. 124 215
       Law of Property (Miscellane-
         ous Provisions) Act
         (c. 34) 27
       s. 1(3) 570
       s. 2 .... 85, 86, 261, 699, 700, 711
            (5) 262
       Companies Act (c. 40) 684
1990 Town and Country Planning
         Act (c. 8)—
       s. 187B 743, 760, 798
       Social Security Act (c. 27) 462
       Finance Act (c. 29)—
       ss. 25–26 381
       s. 82 576
       Courts and Legal Services Act
         (c. 41)—
       s. 3 735
1992 Taxation of Chargeable Gains
         Act (c. 12) 215
       s. 3 215
       s. 4 215
       ss. 22–24 215
       s. 35 215
            (3) 215
       s. 62 215
            (6) 613
       s. 64(2) 215
       s. 70 216
       s. 71 216
       s. 72 216
       s. 77 216

1992 Taxation of Chargeable Gains
Act—*cont.*
s. 87 216
s. 115 .... 215, 515
s. 222 215
ss. 256–257 382
s. 262 215
Sched. 1 215
Local Government Finance Act
(c. 14)—
Sched. 10
para. 3 397
Finance Act (c. 20)—
s. 9(2) 213
Cheques Act (c. 32)—
s. 1 120
Friendly Society Act (c. 40) ....
238, 360
Charities Act (c. 41) 444
s. 15 442
s. 29 445
Finance (No. 2) Act (c. 48)—
s. 26 381
Trade Union and Labour Rela-
tions (Consolidation) Act
(c. 52)—
s. 10 359
ss. 20–23 763
s. 176 802
s. 219 761
s. 221(1) 760
(2) 751, 760, 761, 762
s. 236 .... 708, 787
s. 295(1) 708
1993 Charities Act (c. 10) 402, 431,
439, 444, 449, 454
s. 1 .... 379, 444
(3) 444
(5) 444
s. 2 445
s. 3 .... 377, 446
(7) 447
s. 4(1)–(3) 447
s. 8 .... 449, 451
s. 10 449
s. 13 .... 440, 441
(1)–(2) 439
(1) 441
(a) 441
(d) 441
(e)(i) 440
(ii) 441
(iii) 441
(5) 448
s. 14 .... 233, 438, 442
(2) 442
(5) 442
s. 16 379
(1)–(2) 448
(6) 448
s. 18 .... 449, 451, 504

1993 Charities Act—*cont.*
s. 18(4) 452
ss. 21–23 445
s. 24 450
s. 25 450
s. 26 449
s. 27 453
s. 29 .... 421, 448
ss. 32–33 379
s. 33 448
s. 36 449
(2)–(3) 449
(5)–(7) 449
(9) 449
s. 37(4) 449
s. 38 449
ss. 41–49 449
ss. 42–44 .... 449, 549
s. 45 450
s. 46 449
ss. 47–49 450
s. 64 433
ss. 72–73 451
ss. 74–75 443
ss. 76–78 453
s. 85 445
s. 87 .... 447, 450
s. 96 379
Sched. 1
para. 1(1)–(3) 444
Sched. 2 446
Finance Act (c. 34)—
s. 67 381
Criminal Justice Act (c. 36)—
ss. 52–53 598
Pension   Schemes   Act
(c. 48)—
s. 112 468
ss. 146–151 462
s. 163 473
1994 Insolvency (No. 2) Act (c. 12)   343
s. 1 345
Value   Added   Tax   Act
(c. 23)—
Sched. 8–9 382
Law of Property (Miscellane-
ous   Provisions)   Act
(c. 36)—
s. 14 .... 489, 492
s. 16 55
Deregulation and Contracting
Out Act (c. 40)—
s. 1 532
1995 Pensions Act (c. 26) 456, 458,
461, 463, 469, 470, 471,
506, 507, 618
s. 1 461
ss. 3–6 462
s. 3 .... 461, 464, 466, 468, 469
s. 10 ...... 462, 465, 466, 468, 469
s. 11 .... 462, 470

1995 Pensions Act—*cont.*
ss. 13–15 462
ss. 16–18 463
s. 19(5) 463
ss. 22–25 464
s. 23(3) 464
s. 25(2) 170, 183, 471
(6) 464
ss. 27–28 465
s. 29 464
(3)–(4) 464
s. 30(3) 464
(5) 464
(7) 464
s. 31 462
s. 32 464
(2)(b) 465
s. 33 .... 467, 484
s. 34 .... 526, 567
(1) 465
(2) 467
(4)–(6) 467
(5)(a)–(b) 467
(6) 484
s. 35 466
s. 36(2)–(6) 466
s. 37 475
(2) 469
(4)–(5) 470
s. 39 .... 463, 595
s. 40 468
s. 41 .... 465, 471, 549
ss. 47–48 465
s. 49 461
(8) 461
s. 51 469
ss. 56–59 468
s. 60 469
s. 62 475
s. 65 475
ss. 67–69 461
ss. 73–75 470
ss. 76–77 471
s. 78 471
(4) 472
ss. 80–84 472
s. 81(3)(d) 472
(5) 472
s. 83(1) 472
ss. 91–92 472
s. 95 342
s. 117 461
s. 157 462
s. 166 476
Sched. 1 461
Sched. 2 471
Sale of Goods (Amendment)
Act (c. 28) 94, 96, 668
Landlord and Tenant (Covenants) Act (c. 30)—
s. 28(1) 728

1995 Landlord and Tenant (Covenants) Act—*cont.*
Sched. 1 535
Law Reform (Succession) Act
(c. 41)—
s. 1(2) 861
Charities (Amendment) Act
(c. 48)—
s. 96(6) 450
1996 Finance Act (c. 8)—
s. 72 213
s. 73 213
s. 109 381
s. 183 219
Employment Rights Act
(c. 18)—
ss. 114–115 708
s. 117 790
Arbitration Act (c. 23)—
s. 9 712
Family Law Act (c. 27) 35, 41,
260, 276, 277, 280, 476,
618, 724, 726, 739, 801,
878
s. 33 .... 283, 801
ss. 35–36 801
s. 40(1)(b) 276
s. 42 801
s. 45 801
s. 47 801
Trusts of Land and Appoint-
ment of Trustees Act (c.
47) 273, 279, 555,
617, 881, 896
s. 1 554
(1)–(2) 36
(2) 555
s. 2(5) 36, 449
ss. 3–4 273
s. 3 274
(1) 850
s. 4 .... 539, 556
s. 6 .... 280, 449, 554
(1)–(2) 555
(1) 554, 558
(2) 281, 611
(3)–(4) 514
(3) 517, 544
(4)–(6) 518
(5)–(8) 554
(5) 280
(8) 518
ss. 7–8 555
s. 8 518
(3) 449
s. 9 .... 565, 566
(2)–(9) 566
(6) 568
s. 11 .... 280, 505
(1) 554
ss. 12–13 .... 274, 281

1996 Trusts of Land and Appointment of Trustees Act
—*cont.*
ss. 12–14 275
s. 12(2) 274
s. 13(1) 275
(3)–(7) 275
s. 14 .... 280, 282
(1)–(3) 281
s. 15 281
(1)–(3) 281
(2) 275
s. 16(1)–(3) 554
(1) 280, 555
(4)–(5) 555
s. 17 517
s. 18 554
ss. 19–20 .... 497, 498
ss. 19–22 501
s. 19 .... 496, 503, 509
(3)–(4) 503

1996 Trusts of Land and Appointment of Trustees Act
—*cont.*
s. 20 .... 493, 496
s. 21(1)–(2) 496
(3) 498
(5)–(6) 496, 503
Sched. 1
para. 1 .... 74, 141
Sched. 2 .... 274, 538, 556
Sched. 3 .... 556, 557
para. 3(8) 579
(13) 502
para. 4 558
Part 1 36
Theft (Amendment) Act
(c. 62) 661
1997 Land Registration Act 32
Civil Procedure Act—
s. 7 807
(7) 808

PART I

INTRODUCTION

Chapter 1

HISTORY AND PRINCIPLES

1. General 3
2. Historical Outline 5
   A. The Medieval Chancellor 5
   B. Petitions to the Chancellor 5
   C. The Chancellor's Discretion 6
   D. Attendance of the Defendant 7
   E. Enforcement 7
   F. The Use 8
   G. The Advantages of the Use 9
   H. The Statute of Uses 1535 10
   I. A Use upon a Use. The Trust 10
   J. The Struggle over Injunctions 11
   K. The Transformation of Equity into the Modern System 12
   L. The Nineteenth Century and the Judicature Acts 1873 and 1875 14
3. The Nature of Equitable Rights 17
4. The Relationship between Law and Equity; Fusion 20
5. The Maxims of Equity 25
6. Equitable Remedies 30
7. The Bona Fide Purchaser of the Legal Estate for Value without Notice 32
   A. Purchaser for Value 33
   B. Legal Estate 33
   C. Notice 33
      i. Meaning of Notice...................... 33
      ii. Duty to Make Inquiries 34
        (a) Land 34
        (b) Personalty 35
      iii. Registration 35
   D. Overreaching 36
   E. Other Applications of the Doctrine of Notice.. 37
8. The Subject-Matter of Equity................. 38
9. The Trust in Modern Law 39
10. The Creativity of Equity......................... 41
11. The Recognition of Trusts Act 1987 43

1. GENERAL

EQUITY is a word with many meanings. In a wide sense, it means that which is fair and just, moral and ethical; but its legal meaning is much narrower. Equity is the branch of the law which, before the Judicature Act of 1873 came into force, was applied and administered by the Court of Chancery.[1] It is not synonymous with justice in a broad sense. A plaintiff asserting some equitable right or remedy must show that his claim has "an ancestry founded in history and in the practice and precedents of the court administering equity jurisdiction. It is not sufficient that because we may think that the 'justice' of the present case requires it, we should invent such a jurisdiction for the first time."[2]

---

[1] This is "but a poor thing to call a definition"; Maitland, p. 1.

[2] *Re Diplock* [1948] Ch. 465 at pp. 481, 482. See also Jessel M.R. in *Re National Funds Assurance Co.* (1878) 10 Ch.D. 118 at p. 128: "This court is not, as I have often said, a Court of Conscience, but a Court of Law."

Developed systems of law have often been assisted by the introduction of a discretionary power to do justice in particular cases where the strict rules of law cause hardship.[3] Rules formulated to deal with particular situations may subsequently work unfairly as society develops. Equity is the body of rules which evolved to mitigate the severity of the rules of the common law. Its origin was the exercise by the Chancellor of the residual discretionary power of the King to do justice among his subjects in circumstances in which, for one reason or another, justice could not be obtained in a common law court.

Principles of justice and conscience are the basis of equity jurisdiction, but it must not be thought that the contrast between law and equity is one between a system of strict rules and one of broad discretion. Equity has no monopoly of the pursuit of justice. As Harman L.J. has said, equitable principles are "rather too often bandied about in common law courts as though the Chancellor still had only the length of his own foot to measure when coming to a conclusion. Since the time of Lord Eldon, the system of equity for good or evil has been a very precise one, and equitable jurisdiction is exercised only on well-known principles."[4] In similar vein Lord Radcliffe, speaking of common lawyers, said that equity lawyers were "both surprised and discomfited by the plenitude of jurisdiction and the imprecision of rules that are attributed to 'equity' by their more enthusiastic colleagues."[5] Just as the common law has escaped from its early formalism, so over the years equity has established strict rules for the application of its principles. Indeed, at one stage the rules became so fixed that a *"rigor aequitatis"*[6] developed; equity itself displayed the very defect which it was designed to remedy. We will see that today some aspects of equity are strict and technical, while others leave considerable discretion to the court.

The field of equity is delineated by a series of historical events, and not by a pre-conceived theory; an outline of these events will be given in the next section. We will then see that, until the Judicature Act 1873, the Court of Chancery had almost exclusive equity jurisdiction[7]; rules of equity were not enforced in the common law courts. If a defendant to a common law action had an equitable defence to it, he had to go to Chancery to obtain an injunction to stay the proceedings in the common law court and then start a new action

---

[3] The Praetor performed such a function in Roman Law: Buckland and McNair, *Roman Law and Common Law* (2nd ed.), pp. 1–6.

[4] *Campbell Discount Co. Ltd v. Bridge* [1961] 1 Q.B. 445 at p. 459.

[5] *Bridge v. Campbell Discount Co. Ltd* [1962] A.C. 600 at p. 626.

[6] Allen's *Law in the Making* (7th ed.), p. 417.

[7] For the equity jurisdiction of the Court of Exchequer, see Radcliffe and Cross, *English Legal System* (6th ed.), p. 171. The Common Law Procedure Act 1854 had given common law courts a limited power to issue injunctions.

in Chancery to establish his equitable rights. This complicated system led to a number of difficulties, as we shall see. The Judicature Acts of 1873 and 1875 created the Supreme Court of Judicature, all of whose branches exercise common law and equity jurisdiction. The division between law and equity is less marked, therefore, than it was prior to those Acts, but it is still necessary for various reasons to know whether a rule has its origins in law or in equity.[8]

2. HISTORICAL OUTLINE

The long history of the Court of Chancery is a fascinating story, the details of which must be sought elsewhere[9]; it is not possible here to do more than mention, in broad outline, those aspects which are essential to the understanding of modern equity.

A. The Medieval Chancellor

In the medieval period the Chancellor was the most important person in the country next to the King himself: Maitland described him as "the king's prime minister,"[10] "the king's secretary of state for all departments."[11] One very important function of the Chancery was to issue the royal writs which began an action at law.[12] By varying existing writs or inventing new ones, the Chancellor could have some influence on the development of the law; a limited influence, however, for the decision to issue a writ did not create a new form of action. The litigant could not proceed without it; but the common law court could still decide that the writ disclosed no claim recognised by the law.

B. Petitions to the Chancellor[13]

An injured plaintiff could only sue at common law if his complaint came within the scope of an existing writ. In the thirteenth century the available writs covered very narrow ground. Even if the

---

[8] *Post*, pp. 17 *et seq.*
[9] Maitland Lectures I–IV; Holdsworth; *H.E.L.* i, Chap. 5; iv, pp. 407–480; v, pp. 215–338; vi, pp. 518–551, 640–671; ix, pp. 335–408; xii, pp. 178–330; xiii, pp. 574–668; xvi, pp. 5–135; Plucknett, *Concise History of the Common Law* (5th ed.), Part V; Milsom, *Historical Foundations of the Common Law* (2nd ed.), Chaps. 4, 9; Jones, *The Elizabethan Court of Chancery*; (1965) 81 L.Q.R. 562; (1966) 82 L.Q.R. 215 (J. Barton); Keeton and Sheridan's *Equity* (3rd ed.), Chap. 2.
[10] Maitland, p. 3.
[11] Maitland, p. 2.
[12] See Maitland, *Forms of Action at Common Law.*
[13] Holdsworth, *H.E.L.* i, pp. 402 *et seq.*; Milsom, at pp. 82 *et seq.*

claim came within the scope of an existing writ, it may have been that for some reason, such as the power and influence of the defendant, the plaintiff could not get justice before a common law court. The King in his Council still retained wide discretionary power to do justice among his subjects, and the plaintiff could petition to the King and Council praying for a remedy.

Petitions were addressed to the Chancellor in situations in which a petitioner complained that his case was beyond the ordinary mechanism, and he sought another way. Milsom points out that, in its origins, this would not be regarded as an application of a separate and superior body of rules to those applied by the common law courts. "Not only was there no equity as a nascent body of rules different from those of the common law. There was no common law, no body of substantive rules from which equity could be different."[14] If the mechanism appeared to work unfairly, as where juries were misled, corrupted or intimidated, the petitioner would seek another way. The Chancery "was the head office of the organisation, and it was here that application was made when the ordinary mechanisms appeared to be incapable of working. The approach to the chancellor has no more mysterious origin than that."[15]

Later the petition was used to obtain relief in cases where the common law was inflexible and incapable of providing a remedy. The common law developed into a comprehensive system, but an injured plaintiff could only sue at common law if his complaint came within the scope of an existing writ. By the sixteenth century local jurisdictions, where many matters not covered by common law writs had been dealt with, played a much smaller part. The common law was taking on the aspect of a substantive as well as a comprehensive system, and the application to Chancery was ceasing to look like a request for the same justice, withheld below by some mechanical fault. There seemed to be two parallel systems, and the relationship between them had to be explained in theory and worked out in practice.

C. The Chancellor's Discretion

Maitland points out that in the thirteenth and fourteenth centuries the Chancellor probably did not regard himself as administering a new body of law.[16] He was trying to give relief in hard cases, and the medieval Chancellor was peculiarly well fitted for this work. He was usually an ecclesiastic, generally a bishop, and learned in the civil

---

[14] Milsom, at p. 84.
[15] *Ibid.*
[16] Maitland, p. 5.

and canon law.[17] The Chancellor would give or withhold relief, not according to any precedent, but according to the effect produced upon his own individual sense of right and wrong by the merits of the particular case before him. No wonder that Seldon could say that "Equity is a roguish thing. For law we have a measure . . . equity is according to the conscience of him that is Chancellor, and as that is longer or narrower, so is equity. 'Tis all one as if they should make the standard for the measure a Chancellor's foot."[18]

D. Attendance of the Defendant

In exercising this jurisdiction, the Chancellor was faced with the problem of ensuring the attendance of the defendant without the issue of a royal writ. "The Chancellor, having considered the petition or bill as it is called, orders the (defendant) to come before him and answer the complaint. The writ whereby he does this is called a *subpoena*—because it orders the man to appear upon pain of forfeiting a sum of money—*e.g. subpoena centum librarum*."[19] The examination was made under oath; it did not need to be restricted to specific questions raised in the complaint; and issues of fact as well as issues of law were decided by the Chancellor.

E. Enforcement

A further question was that of enforcement. If the petition was successful, the Chancellor's conclusion would usually be different from that which the common law court would have reached; otherwise the matter would have been litigated at common law. If the Chancellor found that Blackacre was owned by A, but that, in conscience, it should be beneficially owned by B, he could order A to convey the land to B, or to hold the legal estate for the exclusive benefit of B. The Chancellor did not and could not in these circumstances hold that B was the owner. A's right at law was undoubted, and the Chancellor could not change the law. What the Chancellor did was to issue an order to A either to convey the land to B, or to refrain from action interfering with B's right. The Chancellor's jurisdiction was against the person; *in personam*,[20] and directed to the conscience of the individual in question. The Chancellor had the power to back up his orders with the threat of imprisonment for those in contempt. Although there was, theoretically, no interference

---

[17] There were some lay Chancellors at this period; see Trevelyan, *England in the Age of Wycliffe* (1899).
[18] *Table Talk of John Selden* (ed. Pollock, 1927), p. 43; quoted Holdsworth, *H.E.L.* i, pp. 467–468.
[19] Maitland, p. 5.
[20] *Post*, p. 17.

with common law property rights, there was in substance an interference with common law jurisdiction. This was the subject of
dispute later on.[21]

F. The Use[22]

"If we were asked what is the greatest and most distinctive
achievement performed by Englishmen in the field of jurisprudence
I cannot think that we should have any better answer to give than
this, namely the development from century to century of the trust
idea."[23] Such was the view of Maitland. A more recent statement is
that "Trust law is the finest legal concept we have given to a
civilised world."[24] Let us now examine the origins of that concept.

In medieval times, the Chancellor's jurisdiction was vague and
undefined; as wide as the subject-matter of the petitions which
invoked it. The basis of intervention was that it was necessary on
grounds of conscience. His authority was unquestioned in cases of
fraud and breach of confidence. As stated above, the most significant and far-reaching sphere of his jurisdiction was the enforcement of the use of land.

If land was given to A on A's undertaking to hold the land to the
use and benefit of B, it was unconscionable for A to keep it for his
own benefit. B however had no legal claim or title to the land. The
conveyance to A gave him whatever legal estate was conveyed, and,
at common law, A could exercise all the rights which that estate
gave him.

Land might be given to A to the use of B for various reasons. If
B were going on a crusade, then there had to be someone to perform
and receive the feudal services. If B were a community of Franciscan friars which, because of the rule of poverty, was incapable of
holding property, it was necessary for someone to hold the land for
its benefit.[25] Perhaps, however, B was trying to escape from his
creditors; or feared that a conviction for felony would result in the
loss of his lands.[26] For various reasons it may have been advisable
or necessary to put the legal title to B's land in A. If B conveyed to
A subject to an undertaking to hold to the use of B, B would have
no protection at common law beyond that given in the fourteenth
century to covenants under seal; and if a third party conveyed the

[21] *Post*, p. 11.
[22] Holdsworth, *H.E.L.* iv, pp. 407–480; Ames, *Lectures on Legal History*, pp. 233–247;
　　 Plucknett, *Concise History of the Common Law*, p. 575; Milsom, Chap. 9; (1965) 81 L.Q.R.
　　 562; (1966) 82 L.Q.R. 215 (J. Barton).
[23] *Selected Essays*, p. 129.
[24] (1995) 9 *Trust Law International* 33 (J. Quarrell).
[25] Maitland, p. 25; Holdsworth, *H.E.L.* iv, p. 415; Milsom, pp. 203 *et seq.*
[26] *Davies v. Otty (No. 2)* (1865) 35 Beav. 208.

land to A to hold to the use of B, no relationship recognised by the common law existed between A and B.

The Chancellor interfered to compel A to hold the land for the exclusive use and benefit of B. The Chancellor could not say that B was the owner; A was. But all the beneficial interest in the land could be given to B by compelling A to keep the legal title only, and to give all the benefit of the land to B. This is what happened when the use was enforced. And, although the jurisdiction against A was a jurisdiction *in personam*, the Chancellor would enforce B's rights, not only against A, but against other persons who took the land from A.[27] It was not long before it was said that A was the owner at law, B the owner in equity. In the terminology of the time, A was the feoffee to uses, B the *cestui que use*. The use was the forerunner, as we will see, of the trust.

Gradually the Chancellors established the circumstances in which uses would be enforced. They had to decide also what equitable estates they would recognise; for example, if land were conveyed to A to the use of B for life and then to the use of C, should this be enforced? Broadly, the answer was that, in accordance with the maxim that equity follows the law, the estates and interests which could be created in equity corresponded with those which existed at law.

G. The Advantages of the Use

The employment of the use made it possible to avoid some of the feudal incidents. Under feudal law, the lord was entitled to a payment when an heir succeeded to feudal land, and to other valuable rights arising when the land was held by a minor heir, and the right of escheat where there was no heir.[28] These burdens could be avoided if the land was vested in a number of feoffees to uses. They were unlikely to die together or without heirs. Those who died could be replaced, and the feoffees would never be minors. Thus, the use, to feudal land owners, had something of the appeal of tax planning techniques at the present day. It was possible also, in spite of the rule that freehold land could not be devised, to create effective dispositions of equitable interests on death by vesting the land in feoffees and declaring the uses on which the land was to be held after the settlor's death. Further, uses made possible the creation of new types of interests in land which were not possible at common law.[29] For a time also, until prevented by statute, land held to uses could be

---

[27] Except a bona fide purchaser of a legal estate for value without notice, *post*, p. 32; Maitland, pp. 113–115.

[28] Cheshire and Burn, pp. 12 *et seq.*

[29] *e.g.* springing and shifting interests; M. & W., pp. 1169, 1179; Cheshire and Burn, p. 69.

enjoyed by religious houses in defiance of the Statutes of Mort-
main,[30] or be placed beyond the reach of creditors.

H. The Statute of Uses 1535

Henry VIII found that his purse was being emptied by the avoidance of feudal incidents which the system of uses made possible. To
small tenants who had no tenants of their own, the system of uses
was entirely beneficial. To large landowners, it was beneficial in so
far as they were tenants, and harmful in so far as they were lords. To
the King, it was entirely harmful, because he was lord of all and
tenant of none. The first part of Henry VIII's reign had been
expensive, and he was determined to restore the revenues of the
Crown by attacking uses. The Statute of Uses of 1535 was intended
to reduce greatly the scope of the use. After a grandiloquent preamble it provided, according to Maitland's summary of the first
clause[31]: "where any person or persons shall be seised of any lands
or other hereditaments to the use, confidence, or trust of any other
person or persons, in every such case such person and persons that
shall have any such use, confidence or trust in fee simple, fee tail,
for term of life or for years or otherwise shall stand and be seised
deemed and adjudged in lawful seisin estate and possession of and
in the same lands and hereditaments in such like estates as they had
or shall have in the use." In other words, the feoffees to uses were
to disappear. The *cestui que use* was to have the legal estate.

The Statute did not however suppress all uses.[32] It only applied
where the feoffee was *seised* to the use of another. If the feoffee held
only a lease, he would not be seised, and the Statute would not
apply. Again it did not apply to situations where the feoffees had
active duties to perform. The feoffees were then necessary participants, and the Chancellor held that a duty to sell the land, or to
collect the rents and profits of the land and pay them to X, was a
sufficiently active duty to exclude the Statute.[33]

I. A Use upon a Use. The Trust

It was possible, after the Statute, to create equitable interests in
land by imposing a use upon a leasehold, or by requiring the legal
owners of freehold land to collect the rents and profits and to pay
them over to the beneficiaries. Such uses were not executed; nor

---

[30] Which forbade the conveyance of land to religious houses without permission of the
Crown. Milsom, p. 204.
[31] Maitland, p. 35.
[32] Holdsworth, *H.E.L.* iv, pp. 467–473.
[33] Maitland, pp. 38–41; M & W., p. 1167.

were they invalid.[34] Passive uses of freehold land were, however, executed by the Statute, so that the beneficiary held the legal estate. What would happen if a second use were imposed? If land were limited to A to the use of B to the use of C, is it possible to argue that the first use will be executed, and that B will hold the legal estate to the use of C? Such a solution was reached by about 1700[35]; the second use is called a trust. A shorter form, which became settled practice, was to omit A, and to make the disposition "unto and to the use of B in trust for C."

The story of this development is confused and uncertain.[36] Most accounts start with the proposition that through the sixteenth century, the second use was repugnant to the first, and void.[37] When the turning-point came is unsettled, but it is clear that after the Restoration in 1660, a number of factors combined to facilitate the recognition of passive trusts of freeholds. The abolition of military tenures[38] and the consequent freedom to devise all freehold land,[39] the reduction in the value of money which followed the development of the New World, and the changes in the constitutional and financial structure of the country in the seventeenth century, all helped to make the collection of feudal dues a minor factor in the royal revenues. The Civil War determined once and for all that the Government was to be financed by Parliamentary vote. There was now no reason of policy why passive trusts of freeholds should not be enforced as were active trusts and trusts of leaseholds. The enforcement of the second use as a trust was so similar to that of the enforcement of the use against a feoffee to uses centuries before that Lord Hardwicke was able to say, in 1738, in a remark of greater dramatic power than legal or mathematical accuracy: " . . . by this means a statute made upon great consideration, introduced in a solemn and pompous manner, by this strict construction, has had no other effect than to add at most, three words to a conveyance."[40]

J. The Struggle over Injunctions

The story of the use and of the trust has taken us away from the chronological sequence. For it was at the close of the sixteenth century that the quarrel over the power of the Chancery to issue

---

[34] Simpson, *Introduction to the History of Land Law* (2nd ed.), p. 195.

[35] Simpson, *loc. cit.*, p. 203.

[36] Milsom, p. 208 suggests that the origin is in a situation in which a settlor wishes to settle upon himself with remainders over; (1977) 93 L.Q.R. 33 (J. Baker).

[37] Maitland, p. 42; Ames, *Lectures on Legal History*, pp. 243–247; Holdsworth, *H.E.L.* iv, pp. 471–473; *Jane Tyrell's Case* (1557) Dyer 155a.

[38] Tenures Abolition Act 1660.

[39] Previously only two-thirds of land held by knight service could be devised.

[40] *Hopkins v. Hopkins* (1739) 1 Atk. 581 at p. 591; see Holdsworth, *H.E.L.* iv, pp. 449 *et seq.*

injunctions came to a head. The use of the injunction had the effect
of rendering the common law inoperative. That the clash did not
come earlier was due partly to the statesmanlike qualities of men
like More; and no doubt also to the reluctance to challenge the
powers of royal officers in Tudor times. Chief Justice Coke was not
willing to see the common law treated in this way, and in a number
of cases decided that imprisonment for disobedience to injunctions
issued by Chancery was unlawful.[41] In one case it was said that "if
any court of equity doth inter-meddle with any matters properly
triable at the common law, or which concern freehold, they are to be
prohibited."[42] Lord Chancellor Ellesmere, equally determined,
claimed that he was in no sense interfering with the common law; he
was merely acting *in personam*, directing the individual that, on
equitable grounds, he must not proceed to sue at law or enforce a
judgment already obtained at law.

James I stepped in and referred the matter to Bacon, then
Attorney-General, and others learned in the law. Acting on their
recommendations, and no doubt in accordance with his own political views and interests, he decided in favour of the Chancery.[43] The
victory did not remain long unchallenged. The success of the Parliament and of the common lawyers in the political struggles of the
seventeenth century provided further impetus for the attack on the
Chancery. As late as 1690, following the Revolution, a Bill was
introduced in the House of Commons to restrain the interference by
Chancery in any suit for which the proper remedy was at common
law.[44] The Bill was not passed, and from that time the Chancellor's
jurisdiction was not seriously challenged. Thereafter, law and equity
worked together, as parts of a consistent whole; and this enabled
Maitland to say that Equity had come, not to destroy the law, but to
fulfil it.[45]

K. The Transformation of Equity into the Modern System[46]

From the beginning of the Chancellorship of Lord Nottingham in
1673 and to the end of that of Lord Eldon in 1827, equity was
transformed from a jurisdiction based upon the personal interference
of the Chancellor into a system of established rules and principles.
We have seen that the early Chancellors were ecclesiastics. Lawyers
and others were sometimes appointed during the Tudor and Stuart

---

[41] *Heath v. Rydley* (1614) Cro.Jac. 335; *Bromage v. Genning* (1617) 1 Rolle 368; *Throckmorton v. Finch* (1598) Third Institute 124 at p. 25.
[42] *i.e.* liable to be subject to the writ of Prohibition; *Heath v. Rydley* (1614) Cro.Jac. 335.
[43] *Reports of Cases in Chancery*, App. 1, p. 49; 21 E.R. 588.
[44] Holdsworth, *H.E.L.* i, pp. 463–465.
[45] *Equity*, p. 19.
[46] Pollock, *Essays in Legal History*, p. 286.

periods. The retirement of Lord Shaftesbury[47] in 1672 was the last occasion on which a non-lawyer held the Great Seal. This factor influenced the development of the system into one based on rules and precedents rather than on individual conscience. The first reported Chancery cases are dated 1557[48] and these cases are treated as authorities and followed.[49]

Lord Nottingham did much to weld together and consolidate the whole system. To him we owe the doctrine that there can be no "clog on the equity of redemption,"[50] a classification of trusts,[51] and the modern rule against perpetuities.[52] Throughout the eighteenth century, equity, in a period of legislative stagnation, became the great force that moulded the progress of the law right up to the beginning of the nineteenth century. In this period the modern law of trusts developed and was shaped to meet entirely new conditions of social life; equity took in hand the administration of the estates of deceased persons, on which depended the doctrines of election,[53] satisfaction,[54] ademption,[55] marshalling of assets,[56] and perform-ance,[57] and in many cases it is possible to point to the Chancellor who first applied them.[58] In this period there were many great Chancellors, culminating in Lord Eldon (1801–06, 1807–27), one of the greatest equity lawyers. His decisions were thorough, painstak-ing, learned and clear. As Holdsworth said: "He had a thorough grasp of existing rules and principles; but he looked as anxiously into all the facts and circumstances of each case . . . as if there were no such rules and as if, therefore, he was under the necessity of determining each case as one of first impression."[59] The judgments were masterly. But it is hardly surprising that the business of the court was scandalously in arrears. The pattern and principles of equity were now established. "Nothing would inflict on me greater pain in quitting this place," he said, "than the recollection that I had

---

[47] A member of the Cabal of Charles II; he had been educated as a lawyer, but never practised; Holdsworth, *H.E.L.* i, p. 411; vi, pp. 525–526.

[48] "Choyce Cases in Chancery"; Holdsworth, *H.E.L.* v. pp. 274–278; Jones, *The Elizabethan Court of Chancery*, p. 3.

[49] In the preface to Nelson's reports, at pp. 2–3, the author said that "Equity became artificial Reason, and hath ever since such a mixture of law in it, that it woud be much easier now for a Lawyer to preach, than for a Prelate to be a Judge of that Court"; Holdsworth, *H.E.L.* vi, p. 669.

[50] *Howard v. Harris* (1681) 1 Vern. 33.

[51] *Cook v. Fountain* (1676) 3 Swan. 585.

[52] *Duke of Norfolk's Case* (1683) 2 Swan. 454.

[53] *Post*, Chap. 27.

[54] *Ibid.*

[55] *Ibid.*

[56] Snell, p. 336.

[57] *Post*, Chap. 27.

[58] *Re Hallet's Estate* (1880) 13 Ch.D. 696 at p. 710.

[59] Holdsworth, *H.E.L.* i, p. 468.

done anything to justify the reproach that the equity of this court varies like the Chancellor's foot."[60]

L. The Nineteenth Century and the Judicature Acts 1873 and 1875

The nineteenth century was a period of great development of the equitable jurisdiction, based upon the principles established by the end of Lord Eldon's tenure. The enormous industrial, international and imperial expansion of Britain in this period necessitated developments in equity to deal with a host of new problems. The accumulation of business fortunes required rules for the administration of companies and partnerships; and the change in emphasis from landed wealth to stocks and shares necessitated the development of new concepts of property settlements.

Clearly the old organisation of the Chancery Court, overloaded in Lord Eldon's time, could not hope to deal with the mass of business. "Remember this," said Maitland to his students at the turn of the twentieth century, "that until 1813 there were only two judges in the Court of Chancery. There was the Lord Chancellor, and there was the Master of the Rolls, and it was but by degrees that the latter had become an independent judge; for a long time he appears merely as the Chancellor's assistant. In 1813 a Vice-Chancellor was appointed. In 1841 two more Vice-Chancellors. In 1851 two Lords Justices of Appeal in Chancery. When the Court was abolished in 1875, it had seven judges. Cases in the first instance were taken before the Master of the Rolls, or one of the three Vice-Chancellors, and there was an Appeal Court constituted by the Chancellor and the two Lords Justices; but the Chancellor could sit as a judge of first instance if he pleased and sometimes did so."[61] At least however, the judges could deal with their work without the fear of opposition from the common law. The two courts had now become, "not rivals but partners in the work of administering justice."[62] The time had come for the fusion of these jurisdictions into a single Supreme Court.

Some limited steps were taken towards this fusion in the middle of the nineteenth century. The Common Law Procedure Act 1854 gave to the common law courts a certain power to give equitable remedies, and the Chancery Amendment Act 1858, commonly known as Lord Cairns' Act, gave to the Court of Chancery power to award damages in addition to, or in substitution for, an injunction or

---

[60] Holdsworth, *H.E.L.* i, pp. 468–469; *Gee v. Pritchard* (1818) 2 Swan. 402 at p. 414.

[61] Maitland, p. 14. There are now 17 judges, headed by the Vice-Chancellor, allocated to the Chancery Division.

[62] Holdsworth, *H.E.L.* v. p. 668.

a decree of specific performance.[63] The major change however came with the Judicature Acts 1873 and 1875. These Acts abolished the old separate Courts of Queen's Bench, Exchequer, Common Pleas, Chancery, Probate, the Divorce Court, and the Court of Admiralty; it created the Supreme Court of Judicature with a High Court divided into Divisions known as the Queen's Bench Division, Chancery Division, and the Probate, Divorce and Admiralty Division. The latter was re-named the Family Division in 1970.[64] Its Admiralty jurisdiction was assigned to the Queen's Bench Division, and Probate business, other than non-contentious and common form probate business, to the Chancery Division. Each Division exercises both legal and equitable jurisdiction.[65] Thus any issue can be adjudicated in any Division; and any point of law or equity can be raised and determined in any Division; but, for the sake of administrative convenience, cases are allocated to the Divisions according to their general subject-matter.[66] Thus the court "is now not a Court of Law or a Court of Equity, it is a Court of complete jurisdiction."[67]

It was foreseen that a court which applied the rules both of common law and of equity would face a conflict where the common law rules would produce one result, and equity another. Section 25 of the Supreme Court of Judicature Act 1873 therefore provided for the solution of many problems in which those rules would conflict.[68] Subsection 11 contained a general residual clause:

"Generally, in all matters not hereinbefore particularly mentioned in which there is any conflict or variance between the rules of equity and the rules of common law with reference to the same matter, the rules of equity shall prevail."

The effect of the Judicature Act is best shown by the leading case of *Walsh v. Lonsdale*.[69]

The landlord (defendant) agreed in writing to grant to the tenant (plaintiff) a lease of a mill for seven years. The agreement

---

[63] *Post*, pp. 724, 776.

[64] Administration of Justice Act 1970, s.1.

[65] Judicature Act 1873, s.24; Judicature Act 1925, ss.36–44; Supreme Court Act 1981, s.49.

[66] See Supreme Court Act 1981, Sched. 1, *post*, p. 38.

[67] *Pugh v. Heath* (1882) 7 App.Cas. 235 at p. 237 (*per* Lord Cairns). Thus the three-fold division of the content of equity into the exclusive, concurrent and auxiliary jurisdictions lost importance after the Judicature Acts; Snell, pp. 13–14.

[68] Now Supreme Court Act 1981, s.49. Examples are found in s.25(1) of the Act of 1873, dealing with the order of priority of payment of debts of a person dying insolvent; and the refusal of common law but not of equity to recognise the assignment of debts and choses in action (s.25(6)). These matters are now dealt with by A.E.A. 1925, s.34(1) and L.P.A. 1925, s.136 respectively. See *Job v. Job* (1877) 6 Ch.D. 562; *Lowe v. Dixon* (1885) 16 Q.B.D. 455; *Berry v. Berry* [1929] 2 K.B. 316. See also L.P.A. 1925, s.41.

[69] (1882) 21 Ch.D. 9; *Warmington v. Miller* [1973] Q.B. 877; *Tottenham Hotspur Football and Athletic Co. Ltd v. Princegrove Publishers Ltd* [1974] 1 W.L.R. 113; (1974) 90 L.Q.R. 149 (M. Albery); (1987) 7 O.J.LS. 60 (S. Gardner).

provided that the rent was payable in advance if demanded. No grant by deed of the lease—as required for a lease exceeding three years *at law*—was ever made.

The tenant entered and paid rent quarterly, not in advance. He became in arrears and the landlord demanded a year's rent in advance. It was not paid, and the landlord distrained. The tenant brought this action for illegal distress.[70]

The action failed. The distress would have been illegal at law, because no seven-year lease had been granted, and the yearly legal tenancy which arose because of the entering into possession and payment of rent did not include the provision for payment of rent in advance.[71] In equity, however, the agreement for the lease was as good as a lease. The tenant was liable to pay a year's rent in advance and the distress was lawful.

It will be seen that the effect of the Act is procedural only.[72] The rights of the parties, whether dependent on the rules of law or of equity, were under the Act determined at a single trial. But the same result would ultimately have been reached if the case had arisen before 1875; the procedure only would have differed. The claim, being one for damages for illegal distress, would have been brought at common law. To the tenant's argument that he held only on a lease from year to year, of which the covenant to pay rent a year in advance was not a term, the landlord would have had no reply in a court of law. The claim to specific performance of the agreement to take a lease was one that could only have been made in equity. The landlord would have had to obtain an injunction to stop the tenant's action at law, and then to obtain specific performance of the agreement; and then to have returned to the common law court with the lease duly created by deed in conformity with the decree of Chancery. The landlord would then have had a good defence in the common law court. The effect of the Judicature Acts was to enable the court to treat as done that which ought to be done, and to allow the landlord to use his equitable defence (based on his right to specific performance) to the common law claim. The principle that equity treats as done that which ought to be done was not new. The significance of the case is the recognition of that principle in a case involving a legal claim. The principle is not limited to agreements for leases, but is applicable to all cases where there is a specifically enforceable contract by a legal owner to convey or create a legal

---

[70] A landlord may distrain (*i.e.* issue a distress) upon a tenant who is in arrear, and in doing so may take and sell sufficient goods of the tenant (with exceptions) as are necessary to pay the arrears; M. & W., p. 709.

[71] A yearly tenancy which arises in these circumstances includes only such terms of any agreement as are consistent with a yearly tenancy. An agreement to pay a year's rent in advance is not consistent with a yearly tenancy; M. & W., p. 641.

[72] See (1966) 4 Alberta L.R. 134 (J. Coté).

estate, such as a contract to sell, to grant a lease or a mortgage. The principle has been applied "once removed"; as where A agreed to sell Blackacre to B who had agreed to grant a lease to C. C was treated as the lessee in equity of the land.[73] C would not become a lessee at law until the legal lease had been properly granted.

Whether developments in the century following the Judicature Acts have had the effect of fusing not only the jurisdictions but law and equity themselves is a disputed question which can best be considered after looking into the nature of equitable rights.

3. THE NATURE OF EQUITABLE RIGHTS

There has for many years been a learned and unsettled controversy on the question of the nature of equitable rights; and particularly of the nature of the interest of a beneficiary under a trust. In its simplest form, one view emphasises the fact that a beneficiary's remedy, historically and practically, is in the form of an action against the trustee; a right *in personam*. On the other hand, equitable interests under trusts are equitable proprietary interests, corresponding to legal estates, and the beneficiary can properly be regarded as the owner of the beneficial interest; and ownership is a right *in rem*. The controversy attracted many great scholars; with Langdell, Ames, Maitland and Holland on one side, and Austin, Salmond, Pomeroy and Scott on the other.[74]

Much of this controversy centred upon whether the beneficiary's right was a right *in personam* or a right *in rem*. This was because Austin, following the classifications of Roman law, laid down that rights must be of one type or the other. But, for the discussion to become meaningful, it is necessary to know what these terms mean. They mean different things in different contexts. It seems that the proper meaning of a right *in rem* in the present context is "a right enforceable against the world with respect to a particular thing."[75] It is assumed throughout that a legal owner does have rights *in rem*. Rights, that is, against all the world with respect to property. How, then, does a beneficiary under a trust measure up to this test?

The basis of equitable jurisdiction, historically and presently, is that, in accordance with the maxim, equity acts *in personam*, equitable rights grew up where the Chancellor was willing to intervene. The use has its origin in the insistence of the Chancellor that the feoffees to uses should administer the property for the

---

[73] *Industrial Properties (Barton Hill) Ltd v. Associated Electrical Industries Ltd* [1977] Q.B. 580; (1977) 40 M.L.R. 718 (P. Jackson).

[74] (1967) 45 C.B.R. at p. 221 (D. Waters); (1917) 17 Col.L.R. 269 (A. Scott); (1917) 17 Col.L.R. 467 (H. Stone); (1962) 40 C.B.R. at p. 270 (E. Mockler).

[75] (1962) 40 C.B.R. at p. 279.

benefit of the *cestui que use*. Similarly with the trust. "Equity did not say that the *cestui que trust* was the owner of the land, it said that the trustee was the owner of the land, but added that he was bound to hold the land for the benefit of the *cestui que trust*."[76] This raised the question of the effect of the sale of the land by the trustee. The answer was that the beneficiary's interest was effective against everyone except a bona fide purchaser for valuable consideration without notice, actual or constructive, of the equitable interest.

Indeed equity could not have done differently. Its remedies of specific performance and injunction were decrees *in personam*. They ordered the defendant to do something or to refrain from doing something; and behind them was the threat that a recalcitrant defendant would be put in prison for contempt.

There is no space here to run through every aspect of equity jurisdiction to establish the point that equity acts *in personam*. One practical application of this proposition is the fact that a court of equity will exercise jurisdiction to decree specific performance of a contract for the sale of land abroad,[77] or to administer assets abroad if the executors are in England.[78] Where a father bought a flat in France in his son's name and sought a declaration that the son was a trustee and an order to vest the property in the father, his action was classified as *in personam* for the purposes of the 1968 Brussels Convention, so that the son's claim that only the French courts had jurisdiction failed.[79]

But this does not prevent us from treating a beneficiary under a trust as having equitable ownership. A beneficiary's interest behind a trust has long been treated as having the basic characteristics of a proprietary interest in that it can be bought, sold, mortgaged, and devised or bequeathed. Even though, historically, the protection of the beneficiary was based on the Chancellor's willingness to proceed *in personam* against the trustee, that protection has ended up by creating rights in the nature of ownership.[80] To argue that a beneficiary's rights are proprietary is not to say that legal rights are the same as equitable, or that equitable ownership is the same as legal. Rather, it is to accept the basic peculiarity of ownership under the English law of trusts. The trustee is the owner at law; and the beneficiary is the owner in equity.

---

[76] Maitland, p. 17.

[77] *Penn v. Lord Baltimore* (1750) 1 Ves.Sen. 444; *Richard West and Partners (Inverness) Ltd v. Dick* [1969] Ch. 424; *post* p. 694.

[78] *Ewing v. Orr-Ewing (No. 1)* (1883) 9 App.Cas. 34.

[79] *Webb v. Webb* [1994] Q.B. 696; (1994) 110 L.Q.R. 526 (A. Briggs); (1994) 53 C.L.J. 462 (P. Rogerson); (1994) 8 *Trust Law International* 99 (P. Birks); All E.R. Rev. 1994 p. 81 (J. Collier); [1996] Conv. 125 (C. MacMillan).

[80] *Sinclair v. Brougham* [1914] A.C. 398 at p. 444; (1954) 70 L.Q.R. 326 at p. 331 (Lord Evershed M.R.); *Tinsley v. Milligan* [1994] 1 A.C. 340 at p. 371.

In relation to some claims affecting the trust property, the trustee is able to sue and not the beneficiary. Thus, the trustee sues for rent,[81] or for possession; and, with personalty, the trustee, not the beneficiary, sues for conversion of the trust property.[82] The beneficiary's right is to compel the trustee to take action; though he may, in some cases, take action himself on behalf of the trust, joining the trustee as defendant.[83] This right may sometimes be inadequate; as where the trustee has sold the property to a bona fide purchaser of the legal estate for value without notice, who will defeat the equitable ownership of the beneficiary.[84] Does this require us to say that his rights are personal against the trustee, and are not properly regarded as proprietary? This was the deciding test for the supporters of the theory that equitable rights must be regarded as being *in personam*. But it shows the inadequacy of the test which is being applied as a means of distinguishing equitable ownership from legal ownership; which is accepted as being a right *in rem*. For legal rights of ownership are not good against all the world. There are many ways in which the legal owner of a chattel or chose in action may be involuntarily deprived of legal ownership.[85] The situation of the bona fide purchaser is not determinative of the question whether the beneficiary's interest is proprietary; or whether his rights are *in rem* or *in personam*. It demonstrates simply that legal and equitable ownership may have different effects.

From a practical point of view, it can be said that where the problem involves the working of the trust machinery, so that the beneficiary asserts his rights by an action against the trustees to enforce their duties, the old theory that equity acts *in personam* is wholly acceptable.[86] But, in other cases, usually tax cases,[87] the theoretical view is overtaken by a pragmatic approach; and the result determined by the language of the statute and a number of policy questions relating to the purposes of the particular statute. This is an area where Austin's theoretical analysis is the least helpful. Perhaps the better view is that the beneficiary's interest is *sui generis*.[88]

---

[81] *Schalit v. Nadler Ltd* [1933] 2 K.B. 79.

[82] The beneficiary can sue if he has a right to immediate possession; *Healey v. Healey* [1915] 1 K.B. 938.

[83] See *Les Affréteurs Réunis Société Anonyme v. Leopold Walford (London) Ltd* [1919] A.C. 801; *Parker-Tweedale v. Dunbar Bank plc.* [1991] Ch. 12; *Bradstock Trustee Services Ltd v. Nabarro Nathanson (a firm)* [1995] 1 W.L.R. 1405.

[84] The beneficiary will have a personal right against the trustee for compensation and may be able to trace the proceeds; *post*, Chap. 23.

[85] Sale of Goods Act 1979, ss. 21, 24; Factors Act 1889, ss.2, 8, 9; Consumer Credit Act 1974, Sched. 4, para. 22.

[86] (1967) 45 C.B.R. at p. 280 (D. Waters).

[87] See *Baker v. Archer-Shee* [1927] A.C. 844.

[88] Pettit, p. 76.

4. THE RELATIONSHIP BETWEEN LAW AND EQUITY: FUSION

The Judicature Act clearly "fused" the administration of law and equity by the creation of the High Court of Judicature exercising both law and equity and gave supremacy to equity in cases of conflict. A disputed question is whether that Act, or the subsequent development of law and equity, should be regarded as having effected the fusion of law and equity themselves.

The orthodox view is that only the jurisdictions have been fused. The changes made by the Judicature Act gave rise to no new cause of action, remedy, or defence, which was not available before. In a famous "fluvial" metaphor, Ashburner said "the two streams of jurisdiction, though they run in the same channel; run side by side, and do not mingle their waters."[89] Thus, legal rights remain legal rights, and equitable rights remain equitable rights, though administered in the same court. Other bills which were introduced prior to the Judicature Act would indeed have fused law and equity; but they failed, and the Judicature Act was a more cautious measure.[90]

There are, however, statements by great judges to the effect that law and equity are fused. Sir George Jessel said, as early as 1881; "there are not two estates as there were formerly, one estate in common law by reason of the payment of rent from year to year, and an estate in equity under the agreement. There is only one court, and equity rules prevail in it."[91] More recently, Lord Diplock[92] discussed Ashburner's metaphor, and declared:

> "By 1977, this metaphor has in my view become most mischievous and deceptive. The innate conservatism of English lawyers may have made them slow to recognise that by the Supreme Court of Judicature Act 1873, the two systems of substantive and adjectival law formerly administered by courts of law and Courts of Chancery (as well as those administered by Courts of Admiralty, Probate and Matrimonial Causes), were fused."

Others, less extreme, have expressed views to the effect that we ought to be addressing our minds to the *combined effect* of the systems of law and equity, and that to keep the systems always

---

[89] *Principles of Equity* (2nd ed.), p. 18. See also (1954) 70 L.Q.R. 326 (Lord Evershed M.R.); (1961) 24 M.L.R. 116 (V. Delaney); (1977) 6 A.A.L.R. 119 (T. Watkin).

[90] (1977) 93 L.Q.R. 529 at p. 530 (P. Baker); (1870) 14 S.J. 548.

[91] *Walsh v. Lonsdale* (1882) 21 Ch.D. 14. He had previously expressed the orthodox view of the effect of the Act, in *Salt v. Cooper* (1880) 16 Ch.D. 544 at p. 549.

[92] *United Scientific Holdings Ltd v. Burnley Borough Council* [1978] A.C. 904 at p. 925. All the members of the House indicated their general acceptance of the principle of fusion. Lord Diplock is described as "the most forceful exponent of the fusion fallacy," in Heydon, Gummow and Austin, *Cases and Materials on Equity and Trusts* (4th ed.), p. 27. See also *Chief Constable of Kent v. V.* [1983] Q.B. 34 at p. 41.

distinct is pedantic, and an impediment to the natural development of the law.[93]

It is important, in this discussion, to be clear as to what is meant by the claim that law and equity are fused. If it means that there is now no distinction or difference between legal rights and remedies and equitable rights and remedies, it cannot be supported.[94] It is still clear that legal ownership is different from equitable ownership; all the provisions of the legislation of 1925, dealing with unregistered land, are based on that assumption.[95] Again, the law of trusts assumes a distinction between legal and equitable rights. The equitable nature of the duties of a mortgagee has recently been emphasised.[96] Further, as discussed below,[97] it is still basically true to say that an equitable claim will provide only an equitable remedy. An equitable claim is required for the newly revived writ *ne exeat regno*.[98] The common law and equitable rules for tracing property are different, as explained in Chapter 23; likewise the rules concerning payment of interest,[99] and the transmission of the burden of a restrictive covenant.[1] Although common law damages and compensation in equity share the requirement of causation, they differ on remoteness and foreseeability.[2] The illustrations could be multiplied.

Nor is it true, at the other extreme, to say that rights exercisable in the High Court today are the same as those existing in 1875; nor that the application of equitable doctrines in the court has not had the effect of refining and developing the common law rules.[3] Both legal and equitable rules have developed since 1873; and the development of legal rules has sometimes been influenced by established equitable doctrine, with the effect that a situation which would at

---

[93] See (1948) J.S.P.T.L. 180 (Lord Evershed); (1952) C.L.P. 1 (Lord Denning); *The Court of Appeal in England*, p. 13 (Lord Evershed); (1961) 24 M.L.R. 116 (V. Delaney); Lord Denning, *Landmarks in the Law*, p. 86 ("the fusion is complete").

[94] (1977) 93 L.Q.R. 529 at p. 532 (P. Baker).

[95] The distinction between legal and equitable ownership is of little significance in registered land. But that is due to the classification of interests for the purposes of the system, and is unconnected with any question of fusion.

[96] *China and South Sea Bank Ltd v. Tan Soon Gin* [1990] 1 A.C. 536; *Parker-Tweedale v. Dunbar Bank plc* [1991] Ch. 12, criticising *Cuckmere Brick Co. Ltd v. Mutual Finance Ltd* [1971] Ch. 949 (common law damages and duty of care in tort imported); *Downsview Nominees Ltd v. First City Corporation Ltd* [1993] A.C. 295.

[97] *Post*, p. 23.

[98] See *Felton v. Callis* [1969] 1 Q.B. 200; *Allied Arab Bank Ltd v. Hajjar* [1988] Q.B. 787.

[99] *Mathew v. T.M. Sutton Ltd* [1994] 1 W.L.R. 1455; *Westdeutsche Landesbank Girozentrale v. Islington London Borough Council* [1996] A.C. 669.

[1] See *Rhone v. Stephens* [1994] 2 A.C. 310, especially at p. 321.

[2] *Target Holdings Ltd v. Redferns (a firm)* [1996] 1 A.C. 421 at p. 438, *post*, p. 634, approving the views of McLachlin J. in *Canson Enterprises Ltd v. Boughton* (1991) 85 D.L.R. (4th) 129.

[3] (1977) 93 L.Q.R. 536 (P. Baker); (1994) 110 L.Q.R. 238 (Sir Anthony Mason); [1994] Conv. 13 (J. Martin); (1995) 9 *Trust Law International* 35 at p. 37 (Sir Peter Millett).

one time have been treated differently at law and in equity is now treated in the same manner. If that is what is meant by fusion, there is evidence of it, as shown below. It is a healthy and welcome development; and there are other situations which might be candidates for future inclusion.

In *Boyer v. Warbey*,[4] the question arose whether covenants in a lease bound assignees, not only where the lease was by deed, but also where the lease was a valid written lease (not exceeding three years). The Court of Appeal held that, whatever the position before 1875, this was not an area where distinctions based on formalities were now acceptable, and that the covenant should bind. It was further suggested that the same result would follow if there was merely a contract for a lease which was enforceable in equity. Whether it was law or equity that regarded the lease as effective, the rule as to the running of covenants should be the same. In a limited sense this is "fusion" in that the reasons why a particular lease is effective are ignored in favour of a uniform consequential rule.

In *Tinsley v. Milligan*[5] the question was whether an equitable interest could be asserted in spite of an element of illegality in its acquisition. Lord Browne-Wilkinson explained that legal and equitable interests had different incidents for historical reasons, but that "fusion" resulted in the adoption of a single rule as to the circumstances in which the court would enforce interests acquired under an illegal transaction. Thus the rule is the same whether the claim is to a legal or equitable title, and can be fully stated without reference to its origins. In *Napier and Ettrick (Lord) v. Hunter*[6] the nature of an insurer's subrogation right was in issue. Lord Goff examined the origins of subrogation at law and in equity and concluded that "No doubt our task nowadays is to see the two strands of authority, at law and in equity, moulded into a coherent whole."[7] Similarly, it has been held that set-off, whether legal or equitable, can be raised as a defence whether the relief sought by the plaintiff is legal or equitable.[8]

Much of the modern development of the law of estoppel, especially promissory estoppel and proprietary estoppel, has been achieved without enquiring whether the doctrines are doctrines of equity, or of law or of both. The doctrine of promissory estoppel works negatively; to give protection to the party who relied on the

---

[4] [1953] 1 Q.B. 234, especially at pp. 245–247, *per* Denning and Romer L.JJ. See also *Australian Blue Metal Ltd v. Hughes* [1963] A.C. 74 at pp. 101–102.

[5] [1994] 1 A.C. 340 at pp. 371, 375, 376.

[6] [1993] A.C. 713.

[7] *Ibid.* at p. 743.

[8] *B.I.C.C. plc v. Burndy Corp.* [1985] Ch. 232; (1985) 101 L.Q.R. 145; *Eller v. Grovecrest Investments Ltd* [1995] Q.B. 272.

promise, but not to give a new cause of action.[9] But proprietary estoppel operates positively[10] and is capable of creating new rights. Such rights are recognised in equity only, and, in unregistered land, cannot bind a bona fide purchaser of a legal estate for value without notice. Proprietary estoppel must be regarded as a development in equity. Other estoppels can be regarded as being based on common law or equity.[11]

One indication of fusion is a situation where the legal remedy of damages may be given for breach of an equitable right. The converse, an equitable remedy for breach of a legal right, such as an injunction to restrain a tort, or specific performance of a contract, is explicable as the exercise of equity's concurrent jurisdiction and is not an example of fusion. Prior to the Judicature Act, Lord Cairns' Act authorised, in certain circumstances, courts of common law to grant specific performance or an injunction instead of damages, and courts of equity to award damages. As will be seen, this Act, although overtaken by the Judicature Act, still has scope for operation.[12]

Generally, however, the breach of an equitable right will provide an equitable remedy only. Thus, a breach of a restrictive covenant by a non-contracting party is remedied by an injunction, not damages; innocent misrepresentation, apart from the Misrepresentation Act 1967, by rescission and not damages; and breach of trust[13] or other fiduciary duty by various equitable remedies. The stages has not yet been reached at which it is immaterial whether a breach is of a legal or equitable duty. This situation was approached in *Seager v. Copydex Ltd*,[14] where the defendants had used a technical idea communicated to them in confidence by the plaintiff in marketing a carpet grip. Equity's remedies in such cases are an injunction and an account of profits. But the circumstances of this case suggested that the most just solution was an assessment of damages. Can an action for common law damages lie, however, for a breach of confidence, which is protected only in equity? The Court of Appeal held that the appropriate remedy must be granted; fictions of implied contracts or

---

[9] *Combe v. Combe* [1951] 2 K.B. 215, *post*, p. 884.

[10] *Post*, p. 885.

[11] These distinctions are no longer drawn in Australia; *post*, p. 882. See, however, *First National Bank plc v. Thompson* [1996] Ch. 231, emphasising the common law origin of certain types of estoppel.

[12] *Post*, p. 724.

[13] See *Metall und Rohstoff A.G. v. Donaldson Lufkin & Jenrette Inc.* [1990] 1 Q.B. 391 at p. 473 (common law damages not available).

[14] [1967] 1 W.L.R. 923, and (*No. 2*) [1969] 1 W.L.R. 809. Heydon, Gummow and Austin, *Cases and Materials on Equity and Trusts* (4th ed.), pp. 13 *et seq.*, treat this case as an example of "fusion fallacies," *i.e* cases where the results are explicable by the application of neither law nor equity, and could only result from a legislative change in substantive principles which is not found in the Judicature Act.

notional injunctions were not now necessary[15]; damages were thus ordered to be assessed.

Lord Goff has recently said that damages are available for breach of confidence, despite the equitable nature of the wrong, "through a beneficent interpretation of the Chancery Amendment Act 1858 (Lord Cairns' Act)".[16] Commonwealth courts have gone further, regarding it as now settled that damages may be awarded for breach of confidence[17] or other fiduciary duty[18]: "equity and common law are now mingled or merged . . . a full range of remedies should be available as appropriate, no matter whether they originated in common law, equity or statute".[19] But the compensation in such cases has been classified not as common law damages, but as "equitable compensation".[20] On the New Zealand approach, exemplary damages[21] or damages for mental distress[22] could be awarded for breach of equitable duties, and equitable compensation reduced for contributory negligence.[23] Whether this is acceptable depends on whether the policy of the common law on which such concepts are based is the same policy as that on which equitable compensation is founded. This, it is submitted, is not necessarily so.[24] We should heed the warning of Stevenson J.: "I greatly fear that talk of fusing law and equity only results in confusing and confounding the law."[25]

---

[15] *i.e.* to enable damages to be granted in lieu under Lord Cairns' Act, *post*, p. 724. See *Seager v. Copydex Ltd, supra*, at pp. 931–932. *cf. Nicrotherm Electrical Co. Ltd v. Percy* [1956] R.P.C. 272. See also *Fraser v. Thames Television Ltd* [1984] Q.B. 44, where damages were awarded for breach of confidence without any argument on this point; *Stephens v. Avery* [1988] Ch. 449; *Dowson & Mason Ltd v. Potter* [1986] 1 W.L.R. 1419. In employment cases, of course, use of confidential information may be a breach of contract sounding in damages.

[16] *Att.-Gen. v. Guardian Newspapers Ltd (No. 2)* [1990] 1 A.C. 109 at p. 286. See (1994) 14 L.S. 313 (D. Capper).

[17] *Catt v. Marac Australia Ltd* (1986) 9 N.S.W.L.R. 639; *Lac Minerals Ltd v. International Corona Resources Ltd* (1989) 61 D.L.R. (4th) 14; (1990) 106 L.Q.R. 207 (G. Hammond).

[18] *Day v. Mead* [1987] 2 N.Z.L.R. 443; (1989) 105 L.Q.R. 32 (M. McGregor Vennell); *New Zealand Land Development Co. Ltd v. Porter* [1992] 2 N.Z.L.R. 462.

[19] *Aquaculture Corporation v. New Zealand Green Mussel Co. Ltd* [1990] 3 N.Z.L.R. 299 at p. 301; (1991) 107 L.Q.R. 209 (J. Beatson).

[20] *Day v. Mead, supra.*

[21] Differing views were expressed in the *Aquaculture* case, *supra*. See (1995) 69 A.L.J. 773 (P. McDermott).

[22] Accepted by Cooke P. in *Mouat v. Clark Boyce* [1992] 2 N.Z.L.R. 559 (not discussed on appeal at [1994] 1 A.C. 428).

[23] Also accepted by Cooke P. in *Mouat, supra*, and in (1995) 9 *Trust Law International* 35 at p. 38 (Sir Peter Millett). Differing views were expressed in *Canson Enterprises Ltd v. Boughton* (1991) 85 D.L.R. (4th) 129. English Courts have rejected the defence in cases of deceit and dishonest assistance in a breach of trust, unless the plaintiff is "the author of his own misfortune"; *Corporacion Nacional del Cobre de Chile v. Sogemin Metals Ltd, The Times*, December 24, 1996.

[24] [1994] Conv. 13 at pp. 21–22 (J. Martin); *cf.* Cooke P. in *Mouat v. Clark Boyce, supra*, at p. 569. Differing views were expressed in *Canson Enterprises Ltd v. Boughton, supra.*

[25] *Canson Enterprises Ltd v. Boughton, supra*, at p. 165.

Sufficient examples have been given to show that law and equity are not fused. What can be said is that a century of fused jurisdiction has seen the two systems working more closely together; each changing and developing and improving from contact with the other; and each willing to accept new ideas and developments, regardless of their origin. They are coming closer together. But they are not yet fused.

5. THE MAXIMS OF EQUITY

The maxims of equity embody the general principles which evolved in the Court of Chancery. They are not rules which must be rigorously applied in every case, but are more in the nature of general guidelines illustrating the way in which equitable jurisdiction is exercised. A few examples of their operation must suffice,[26] but they should be borne in mind when considering the various rules and doctrines of equity.

i. Equity will not suffer a wrong to be without a remedy. The principle behind this maxim is that equity will intervene to protect a right which, perhaps because of some technical defect, is not enforceable at law. It is not sufficient that the defendant may be guilty of some moral wrong: the plaintiff's right must be suitable for enforcement by the court. The classic example is the enforcement of trusts. The beneficiary had no remedy at common law if the trustee claimed the property for himself, as the trustee was the legal owner, but he could enforce his rights in equity. The maxim is also reflected in the area of equitable remedies, which may be granted where the defendant's wrong is one not recognised by the common law. In the field of injunctions, for example, the plaintiff may obtain a *quia timet* injunction to restrain a threatened wrong although he has no cause of action at law until the wrong is committed.[27]

ii. Equity follows the law. Clearly equity may not depart from statute law, nor does it refuse to follow common-law rules save in exceptional circumstances.[28] Thus equitable interests in land correspond with the legal estates and interests.[29] Similarly, the writ *ne exeat regno*, applicable to equitable debts, will not be granted unless the conditions of the Debtors Act 1869, allowing arrest in the case

---

[26] For a more detailed survey, see Snell, Chap. 3.
[27] *Post*, p. 769.
[28] For the conflicts between the rules of law and equity, see *ante*, p. 15.
[29] Equity, however, recognised certain future interests which were not recognised at law. See Megarry and Wade, *The Law of Real Property* (5th ed.), p. 1179.

of a legal debt, are satisfied.[30] Nor will equity depart from the
common law rule that a third party cannot be made to perform a
contract.[31]

iii. He who seeks equity must do equity. A plaintiff who seeks
equitable relief must be prepared to act fairly towards the defendant.
The operation of this principle can be seen where equity, in allowing
rescission of a contract for mistake, puts the plaintiff on terms which
appear to the court to be just and equitable.[32] A plaintiff seeking an
injunction will not succeed if he is unable or unwilling to carry out
his own future obligations.[33] This maxim is also the foundation of
the doctrine of election.[34]

iv. He who comes to equity must come with clean hands.[35] This
principle is closely related to the last one, save that the latter looks
to the plaintiff's future conduct, while the "clean hands" principle
looks to his previous conduct. Thus equity will not grant relief
against forfeiture for breach of covenant where the breach in question was flagrant.[36] Examples abound in the field of equitable
remedies: a tenant cannot get specific performance of a contract for
a lease if he is already in breach of his obligations[37]; nor could a
purchaser if he had taken advantage of the illiteracy of the vendor
who was not separately advised[38]; so also in the case of injunctions,[39] but equitable relief will only be debarred on this ground if
the plaintiff's blameworthy conduct has some connection with the
relief sought. The court is not concerned with the plaintiff's general
conduct. Thus in *Argyll (Duchess) v. Argyll (Duke)*,[40] the fact that
the wife's adultery had led to the divorce proceedings was no
ground for refusing her an injunction to restrain her husband from
publishing confidential material. Nor will unclean hands debar a
claim which does not involve reliance on one's own misconduct.[41]
If both parties have "unclean hands," the court should consider only

---

[30] *Felton v. Callis* [1969] 1 Q.B. 200.
[31] *Rhone v. Stephens* [1994] 2 A.C. 310 (positive covenant relating to land).
[32] See the terms imposed in *Solle v. Butcher* [1950] 1 K.B. 671 and *Grist v. Bailey* [1967] Ch.
532, *post*, p. 820. See also *Cheese v. Thomas* [1994] 1 W.L.R. 129 (undue influence).
[33] See *Chappell v. Times Newspapers Ltd* [1975] 1 W.L.R. 482, where employees failed to get
an injunction to restrain their dismissal where they refused to undertake not to become
involved in strikes.
[34] *Post*, Chap. 27.
[35] [1990] Conv. 416 (P. Pettit).
[36] See *Shiloh Spinners Ltd v. Harding* [1973] A.C. 691.
[37] *Coatsworth v. Johnson* (1886) 54 L.T. 520.
[38] *Mountford v. Scott* [1975] Ch. 258.
[39] See *Hubbard v. Vosper* [1972] 2 Q.B. 84.
[40] [1967] Ch. 302.
[41] *Tinsley v. Milligan* [1994] 1 A.C. 340; *post*, p. 250.

those of the applicant, and need not balance the misconduct of one against that of the other.[42]

v. Where the equities are equal the law prevails.

vi. Where the equities are equal the first in time prevails.

These two related maxims, dealing with the priorities of competing interests, may be dealt with together. They provide the foundation for the doctrine of notice.[43] Thus a prior equitable interest in land can only be defeated by a bona fide purchaser of a legal estate without notice. If the purchaser is bona fide and without notice, then the equities are equal and his legal estate prevails. If he took with notice the position is otherwise, as the equities are not equal. If he does not acquire a legal estate then the first in time, *i.e.* the prior equitable interest, prevails, as equitable interests rank in order of creation. The two maxims have lost some of their importance since the introduction in 1925 of the system of registration of certain interests in land.[44]

vii. Equity imputes an intention to fulfil an obligation.

Where a person is obliged to do some act, and does some other act which could be regarded as a performance of it, then it will be so regarded in equity. This is the basis of the doctrines of performance and satisfaction.[45] For example, if a debtor leaves a legacy to his creditor (of an amount at least as great as the debt), this is presumed to be a repayment of the debt so that, unless the presumption is rebutted, the creditor cannot take the legacy and sue to recover the debt.

viii. Equity regards as done that which ought to be done.

Where there is a specifically enforceable obligation equity regards the parties as already in the position which they would be in after performance of the obligation. Therefore in equity a specifically enforceable contract for a lease creates an equitable lease. This is the doctrine of *Walsh v. Lonsdale*.[46] Similarly, a specifically enforceable contract for the sale of land transfers the equitable interest to the purchaser, the vendor holding the legal title on constructive trust until completion.[47] The maxim is also the basis of the doctrine of

---

[42] *Sang Lee Investment Co. Ltd v. Wing Kwai Investment Co. Ltd, The Times*, April 14, 1983.

[43] *Post*, p. 32.

[44] *Post*, p. 35.

[45] *Post*, Chap. 27.

[46] (1882) 21 Ch.D. 9, *ante* p. 15. A contract relating to land must be in writing; Law of Property (Miscellaneous Provisions) Act 1989.

[47] *Post*, p. 000. See also *Davis v. Richards & Wallington Industries Ltd* [1990] 1 W.L.R. 1511 (obligation to execute pension trust deed).

conversion,[48] and the rule in *Howe v. Dartmouth*,[49] concerning the duty to sell unauthorised investments. The maxim has recently been invoked by the Privy Council and House of Lords. In *Att.-Gen. for Hong Kong v. Reid*[50] the issue was whether a fiduciary who took a bribe became constructive trustee of it or was merely personally accountable. Because he was under a duty to hand over the bribe to his principal, it was held that the property belonged to the principal in equity. The difficulty in this is that an obligation to pay money is not normally specifically enforceable.[51] Similarly, in *Napier and Ettrick (Lord) v. Hunter*[52] it was considered that the duty of an insured person to hand over any damages from the wrongdoer to the insurer was specifically enforceable, so that the insurer had immediate proprietary rights in the form of a lien over the money.

ix. Equity is equality. Where two or more persons are entitled to an interest in the same property, then the principle of equity is equal division, if there is no good reason for any other basis for division. Equity, therefore, dislikes the joint tenancy where, by the doctrine of survivorship, the last survivor takes all. This may be contrasted with the tenancy in common, where the interest of each party devolves upon his personal representative on his death. In the absence of an express declaration to the effect that the equitable interest is held jointly, equity presumes a tenancy in common in certain cases where at law the parties are joint tenants: for example, where the purchase money has been provided in unequal shares, equity presumes a tenancy in common in shares proportionate to the contributions. Even where the equitable interest is held jointly, equity leans in favour of severance, meaning that equity is ready to regard an act or dealing as an act of severance, whereby the equitable interest is converted to a tenancy in common, thus excluding the possibility of survivorship.[53]

x. Equity looks to the intent rather than the form. This principle does not mean that formalities may be ignored in equity, but rather that equity looks at the substance rather than the form. Thus equity will regard a transaction as a mortgage even though it is not so described, if in substance it appears that the property was transferred by way of security. Similarly a trust may be created although

---

[48] *Post*, Chap. 27.
[49] (1802) 7 Ves. 137, *post*, Chap. 19.
[50] [1994] 1 A.C. 324 (P.C.); *post*, p. 608.
[51] [1994] 2 R.L.R. 57 (D. Crilley); (1994) 53 C.L.J. 31 (A. Oakley); (1994) 110 L.Q.R. 178 (P. Watts); All E.R.Rev. 1994 pp. 252 (P. Clarke) and 365 (W. Swadling); (1995) 54 C.L.J. 60 (S. Gardner); (1995) 58 M.L.R. 87 (T. Allen).
[52] [1993] A.C. 713.
[53] See *Burgess v. Rawnsley* [1975] Ch. 429.

the word "trust" has not been used.[54] A covenant will be regarded as a restrictive covenant if negative in substance even if it is worded in a positive form.[55] Although a party to a covenant can enforce the contract at law even though no consideration has been given, equity regards such a party as a volunteer and will not decree specific performance in his favour.[56]

xi. Delay defeats equities. Equity aids the vigilant and not the indolent. This is the foundation of the doctrine of laches, whereby a party who has delayed cannot obtain equitable relief. This doctrine is superseded where the Limitation Act 1980 deals with the matter.[57] For example, actions against trustees for breach of trust must, by section 21, be brought within six years, and delay short of this will not bar relief. Where, however, the plaintiff has a legal right, for example, upon a contract, delay may prevent the grant of an equitable remedy such as specific performance even though the legal right is not statute-barred.[58] Interlocutory injunctions must always be sought promptly, but it seems that delay may not prevent the grant of a final injunction where the cause of action is not statute-barred.[59]

The doctrine of laches continues to apply to those equitable claims which are outside the Limitation Act 1980, for example a claim to set aside a purchase of trust property by a trustee.[60] Similarly, claims to rescission and rectification may be barred by delay.[61]

xii. Equity acts *in personam*. Equity has jurisdiction over the defendant personally. The personal nature of the jurisdiction is illustrated by the fact that failure to comply with an order, such as specific performance or an injunction, is a contempt of court punishable by imprisonment. Provided that the defendant is within the jurisdiction (or can be served outside it), it is no objection that the property which is the subject-matter of the dispute is outside it. Thus in the leading case of *Penn v. Lord Baltimore*,[62] specific performance was ordered of an agreement relating to land boundaries in Pennsylvania and Maryland, the defendant being in this country.

---

[54] *Post*, p. 90.
[55] *Tulk v. Moxhay* (1848) 18 L.J.Ch. 83 (covenant "to keep uncovered by buildings" held negative).
[56] *Cannon v. Hartley* [1949] Ch. 213.
[57] Either expressly or by analogy; *post*, p. 654.
[58] *Post*, p. 718. See Limitation Act 1980, s.36(1).
[59] *Fullwood v. Fullwood* (1878) 9 Ch.D. 176; *H. P. Bulmer Ltd & Showerings Ltd v. J. Bollinger S.A.* [1977] 2 C.M.L.R. 625, *post*, p. 771.
[60] *Post*, p. 654.
[61] *Post*, pp. 838, 845.
[62] (1750) 1 Ves.Sen. 444, *post* p. 000; *Hamlin v. Hamlin* [1986] Fam. 11; *Webb v. Webb* [1994] Q.B. 696; *ante*, p. 18. See also Civil Jurisdiction and Judgments Act 1982, s.30(1).

6. EQUITABLE REMEDIES

At common law, the normal form of relief is an award of damages, to which a plaintiff who has proved his case is entitled as of right. One of the greatest contributions of equity has been to supplement the limited range of legal remedies by introducing wide range of equitable remedies,[63] which can be awarded both to enforce rights which are exclusively equitable and those which are legal. Their common features are that they are discretionary, their availability depends upon the inadequacy of common law remedies (which, in the case of exclusively equitable rights, will not be available at all) and they are governed by the doctrine that equity acts *in personam*.

The most significant of these remedies are specific performance, whereby the court orders a party to a contract to perform his contractual obligations, and an injunction, whereby the court orders a person to do, or, more commonly, to refrain from doing, some particular act. These, plus the remedies of rescission and rectification of contracts, will be examined in Part IV. Other equitable remedies include delivery up and cancellation of documents,[64] account[65] and receivers.[66] Mention might also be made of certain procedural remedies, equitable in origin, which have now been incorporated into the general rules of litigation. Examples include discovery of documents[67] and suits for the perpetuation of testimony.[68] Equity's jurisdiction to award compound interest is not, however, regarded as an equitable remedy in the sense of being exercisable in aid of common law remedies.[69]

The ancient prerogative writ *ne exeat regno*,[70] later adapted by equity, has recently enjoyed something of a revival. The writ prevents the defendant from leaving the jurisdiction, its purpose being to coerce him to give security for an equitable debt, on pain of arrest. The stringent conditions for its grant were laid down in *Felton v. Callis*,[71] but recent cases have tended to relax them,[72] perhaps

---

[63] See generally Meagher, Gummow and Lehane, *Equity—Doctrines and Remedies*; Heydon, Gummow and Austin, *Cases and Materials on Equity and Trusts*; Spry, *Equitable Remedies*, Chap. 1.

[64] Snell, pp. 24 *et seq.*

[65] Snell, pp. 637 *et seq.*

[66] Snell, pp. 689 *et seq.*

[67] R.S.C. Ord. 24; Snell, p. 582.

[68] R.S.C. Ord. 39, r. 15; Snell, p. 582; Pettit, p. 76.

[69] *Westdeutsche Landesbank Girozentrale v. Islington London Borough Council* [1996] A.C. 669 (Lords Goff and Woolf dissenting).

[70] For its history, see *Allied Arab Bank Ltd v. Hajjar* [1988] Q.B. 787.

[71] [1969] 1 Q.B. 200; Snell, p. 583.

[72] *Lipkin Gorman v. Cass, The Times*, May 29, 1985; *Al Nahkel for Contracting and Trading Ltd v. Lowe* [1986] Q.B. 235; *cf. Allied Arab Bank Ltd v. Hajjar, supra.* See also *Thaha v. Thaha* (1987) 17 Fam.Law 234; *Re Jeffrey S. Levitt Ltd* [1992] Ch. 457.

unjustifiably.[73] The conditions may also be sidestepped by the grant of an interlocutory injunction against leaving the jurisdiction.[74]

The remedy of the declaration had some connection with equity in origin,[75] but the jurisdiction to grant it is now governed wholly by statute.[76] Finally, although not remedies in the traditional sense, the constructive trust and the doctrine of tracing are sometimes so described. These will be examined elsewhere.[77]

The differing character of equitable remedies must be appreciated. First, it is obvious that factors such as fraud, misrepresentation and mistake are relevant to the exercise of a discretionary jurisdiction to issue injunctions and decrees of specific performance. Here, the question is ordinarily one of the manner in which an already existing legal or equitable right is enforced.[78] The right itself is not affected. Thus if equity refuses to decree specific performance of a contract due to a defendant's mistake, the plaintiff's right to sue for damages still subsists[79]: it is merely that a supplementary method of enforcement is denied to a plaintiff. But secondly, other equitable remedies are larger in their effect; if equity rescinds a deed or a contract, a right to sue on that contract or deed ceases to be available at law. Equity will exercise this jurisdiction on grounds on which law takes no similar action, for instance, in cases of constructive fraud or wholly innocent misrepresentations, so that the equitable remedy affects the substance of a plaintiff's rights, and not merely the manner of their enforcement. This is also true when the equitable remedy of rectification is called into operation, a remedy by which a term of a document is varied so as to make it accord with the parties' real intentions. Thirdly, it should be noted that an equitable remedy may fulfil a task intermediate between the situations so far considered, the task of enabling a plaintiff to take full advantage of a right at common law. A plaintiff may, for instance, have a right at common law to rescind a contract for fraud, but may be at common law unable to exercise that right[80] because a precise *restitutio in integrum* is not possible. Equity has a wider discretion to rescind in such a case by devising a fair, if not a precise, return of the parties to something approaching their original positions.[81]

---

[73] See (1986) 45 C.L.J. 189 (C. Harpum); (1987) 103 L.Q.R. 246 (L. Anderson); (1988) 47 C.L.J. 364 (N. Andrews); (1990) 20 U.W.A.L.R. 143 at 160 (J. Martin).

[74] *Post*, p. 745.

[75] See de Smith, *Judicial Review of Administrative Action*, (4th ed.), pp. 517–518.

[76] *Tito v. Waddell (No. 2)* [1977] Ch. 106 at p. 259 (Megarry V.-C.). See also *Chapman v. Michaelson* [1909] 1 Ch. 238; Snell, pp. 583–584.

[77] *Post*, pp. 289, 656.

[78] *Post*, pp. 716, 771.

[79] *Wood v. Scarth* (1855) 2 K. & J. 33 (in equity); (1858) 1 F. & F. 293 (at law); *Webster v. Cecil* (1861) 30 Beav. 62; *Johnson v. Agnew* [1980] A.C. 367, *post*, p. 697.

[80] And would be confined to an action for damages.

[81] *Spence v. Crawford* [1939] 3 All E.R. 271; a decision showing that equity may be more willing to do so in cases of actual fraud than in others.

As we shall see, it is in the field of remedies that equity displays perhaps the greatest inventiveness and capacity for development, providing relief in new situations as they arise.[82]

7. THE BONA FIDE PURCHASER OF THE LEGAL ESTATE FOR VALUE WITHOUT NOTICE

As we have seen, the use was enforceable against the feoffee to uses because the feoffee's conscience was bound by the undertaking which he had given to hold the property to the use and benefit of the *cestui que use*. Similarly with a trustee and beneficiary. So long as the same person remained trustee, this theory works quite simply. But if the legal estate passes from him to another person, how is the conscience of the transferee affected? The question is then one of determining, as a matter of policy, whether this new holder of the legal estates is to be bound by the trust.[83] Any way in which the equitable ownership of a beneficiary is destroyed is of course a serious weakening of the position of the beneficiary; and equity strives always to protect him.[84]

Thus, a trust is binding on a person to whom the trustee gave the property[85]; or a mere occupier[86] or adverse possessor,[87] and also on a purchaser who bought it if he knew or could by reasonable inquiries have found out about the existence of the trust.[88] In short, the trust is binding on everyone coming to the land except the bona fide purchaser of a legal estate for value without notice actual, constructive or imputed.[89]

The doctrine applies to land and personalty. As far as land is concerned, its importance has diminished now that the system of registration of title applies throughout England and Wales. Under this system the doctrine of notice has no application.[90] But much unregistered land remains, because there is no duty to register the title until a conveyance after the area has become one of compulsory registration of title.[91] Even with unregistered land, the doctrine of notice was largely replaced, as will be seen, by the Land Charges

---

[82] See particularly the *Anton Piller* and *Mareva* injunctions, *post*, pp. 804, 808.

[83] Maitland, pp. 111 *et seq.*

[84] *Ibid.* at p. 220.

[85] *Re Diplock* [1948] Ch. 465, at pp. 544–545.

[86] *Mander v. Falcke* [1891] 2 Ch. 554.

[87] *Re Nisbet and Pott's Contract* [1906] 1 Ch. 386; affirming [1905] 1 Ch. 391.

[88] *Pilcher v. Rawlins* (1872) L.R. 7 Ch.App. 250.

[89] Such a purchaser can pass his good title to a purchaser with notice under the rule in *Wilkes v. Spooner* [1911] 2 K.B. 473.

[90] Minor interests protected on the register and overriding interests (L.R.A. 1925, s.70(1)) are binding on a purchaser of registered land, regardless of notice, and whether legal or equitable.

[91] L.R.A. 1925, s.123. The occasions for registration have been increased; Land Registration Act 1997 (mortgages, gifts and assents on death included).

Act 1925 (now the Act of 1972). In the account which follows, it should thus be borne in mind that in the case of registered land, the traditional doctrine applies only to transactions occurring before the title was registered, although some aspects of the doctrine have wider application.[92]

A. Purchaser for Value

The purchaser must have given consideration in money, or money's worth,[93] or the consideration of marriage.[94] Otherwise he is a donee, and bound by the trust regardless of notice. A purchaser includes a mortgagee[95] or lessee.

B. Legal Estate

This doctrine is based on the maxim that when the equities are equal the law prevails. In the case of a purchase of a legal estate for value without notice, the equities are equal between the purchaser and the beneficiaries; the purchaser's legal estate is allowed to prevail.

The position is different where the purchaser is a purchaser of an *equitable* interest only. The competition then is between two equitable interests; and the rule here is that the first in time prevails.[96] By way of exception, a purchaser of an equitable interest can defeat prior "mere equities", such as rights to rectification or to set aside a conveyance.[97] It seems that a bona fide purchaser of an equitable interest in the land for value without notice will take free of mere equities,[98] and, *a fortiori*, a purchaser of a legal estate.[99]

C. Notice

i. Meaning of Notice. Apart from legislation[1] a purchaser is taken to have notice of an equitable interest unless he can show that "he took all reasonable care and made inquiries, and that, having taken that care and made inquiry, he received no notice of the trust

---

[92] *Post*, p. 37.

[93] *Thorndike v. Hunt* (1859) 3 De G. & J. 563; *Midland Bank Trust Co. Ltd v. Green* [1981] A.C. 513.

[94] *i.e.* a future marriage. An ante-nuptial settlement is deemed to be made for value in respect of the spouses and the issue of the marriage, *post*, p. 122.

[95] *Kingsnorth Finance Co. v. Tizard* [1986] 1 W.L.R. 783; see L.P.A. 1925, s.205(xxi).

[96] *Phillips v. Phillips* (1862) 4 De G. F. & J. 208 at p. 218; *Re Morgan* (1881) 18 Ch.D. 93; *McCarthy and Stone Ltd v. Hodge & Co.* [1971] 1 W.L.R. 1547.

[97] *Shiloh Spinners Ltd v. Harding* [1973] A.C. at p. 721.

[98] *National Provincial Bank Ltd v. Ainsworth* [1965] A.C. 1175 at p. 1238; *Phillips v. Phillips, supra.*

[99] *Smith v. Jones* [1954] 1 W.L.R. 1089.

[1] Especiallly L.C.A. 1972, *post*, p. 35.

which affected the property."[2] He must show that he had no notice actual, constructive or imputed.

Actual notice is the simple case where the purchaser subjectively knew of the equitable interest. Constructive notice exists where knowledge of the equitable interest would have come to him if he had made all such inquiries as a prudent purchaser would have made. Imputed notice covers actual or constructive notice to his agent who was acting as such in the transaction in question.[3]

ii. Duty to Make Inquiries. The inquiries which should be made will depend on the type of property in question. A purchaser, however, should always inspect the premises, and has notice of the interest of a person in occupation of the property.[4]

(a) *Land.* With the unregistered title system, a vendor satisfied a purchaser of his ownership of the land by producing title deeds which traced the history of the ownership of the land. The title had to start with a good root of title[5] at least 15 years old.[6] A prudent purchaser would examine that document and every one subsequent to it; he would normally be held to have constructive notice of every equitable interest which appeared on the title,[7] but not of those disclosed by earlier deeds with which he was not concerned. If he agreed to accept a title which began later than the statutory period of 15 years, he did so at his own risk, and would be bound by equitable interests disclosed by documents which were within the statutory period but prior to the agreed date.[8] There was an exception where there were in fact deeds which disclosed an equitable interest, but the vendor was able to produce an apparently perfect title after suppressing some of them.[9]

A person intending to enter into a lease is not entitled to examine the title of the lessor (the freeholder),[10] and does not have constructive notice of equitable interests which he would have discovered if he had examined it.[11] The lessee is however bound by land charges which are registered under the Land Charges Act.[12]

---

[2] *Per* Fry J. in *Re Morgan* (1881) 18 Ch.D. 93 at p. 102.

[3] L.P.A. 1925, s.199.

[4] *Barnhart v. Greenshields* (1853) 9 Moo.P.C. 18; *Hunt v. Luck* [1902] 1 Ch. 428; *Kingsnorth Finance Co. Ltd v. Tizard* [1986] 1 W.L.R. 783; cf. *Bristol and West Building Society v. Henning* [1985] 1 W.L.R. 778.

[5] *i.e.* "a document which describes the land sufficiently to identify it, which shows a disposition of the whole legal and equitable interest contracted to be sold, and which contains nothing to throw any doubt on the title"; M. & W., p. 608.

[6] L.P.A. 1969, s.23.

[7] *Carter v. Carter* (1857) 3 K. & J. 617.

[8] *Re Nisbet and Pott's Contract* [1906] 1 Ch. 386; affirming [1905] 1 Ch. 391.

[9] *Pilcher v. Rawlins* (1872) L.R. 7 Ch.App. 259.

[10] L.P.A. 1925, s.44(3).

[11] *Ibid.*

[12] *White v. Bijou Mansions* [1937] Ch. 610 at p. 619.

(b) *Personalty.* The doctrine of notice in the strict conveyancing sense does not apply to personalty, because there is no duty on the purchaser to examine the seller's title; and usually there are no documents of title.[13] A purchaser of shares is not required to inquire about beneficial ownership, nor may notice of any trust affecting the shares be entered on the company's register of shareholders. However, where some equitable interest or charge is disclosed to a purchaser of personalty or presents itself to his notice, he will be bound by it if it is not satisfied out of the purchase money.[14] The doctrine of constructive notice applies even to commercial dealings with personalty, where the facts known to the purchaser make it imperative to seek an explanation, without which it is obvious that the transaction is probably improper.[15]

iii. Registration. The Land Charges Act 1925 introduced a system of registration of various interests in unregistered land.[16] Local land charges are dealt with in the Local Land Charges Act 1975. Most of the registrable interests are equitable, but a legal mortgage where the mortgagee does not take possession of the title deeds is included,[17] and one is a statutory creation.[18] Registration is deemed to be actual notice to all persons so long as the registration remains in force[19] whereas failure to register makes the charge void against a purchaser.[20]

It will be seen that this enactment has vitally affected the old doctrine of notice. A purchaser is deemed to have notice of a charge if it is registered. If the charge is not registered, it has been held that he takes free even if he actually knows about it,[21] or if the interest in question is that of a person who is in actual occupation of the land,[22] and the House of Lords has held that the court cannot enquire into the good faith of the purchaser, nor into the adequacy of the consideration paid by him.[23]

---

[13] See Factors Act 1889, s.1(4). The registration book of a car is not a document of title: *Joblin v. Watkins and Roseveare (Motors) Ltd* [1949] 1 All E.R. 47.

[14] *Nelson v. Larholt* [1948] 1 K.B. 339.

[15] *Macmillan Inc. v. Bishopsgate Investment Trust plc (No. 3)* [1995] 1 W.L.R. 978 at p. 1014 (shares); affirmed [1996] 1 W.L.R. 387.

[16] L.C.A. 1972 does not apply to registered land; but all the interests contained in it can be protected by notice or caution under L.R.A. 1925.

[17] L.C.A. 1972, s.2(4) Class C(i).

[18] Class F. See Family Law Act 1996, re-enacting Matrimonial Homes Act 1983.

[19] L.P.A. 1925, s.198(1).

[20] L.C.A. 1972, s.4; L.P.A. 1925, s.199(1)(i).

[21] *Hollington Brothers v. Rhodes* [1951] 2 All E.R. 578n.

[22] *Smith v. Jones* [1954] 1 W.L.R. 1089; *Lloyd's Bank plc v. Carrick* [1996] 4 All E.R. 630.

[23] *Midland Bank Trust Co. Ltd v. Green* [1981] A.C. 513; (1981) 97 L.Q.R. 518 (B. Green); (1981) 40 C.L.J. 213 (C. Harpum); [1981] Conv. 361 (H. Johnson); (son, holding unregistered option to purchase valuable land granted by father, not protected when father sold to mother for £500).

D. Overreaching

More important for our present purposes than the Land Charges Act 1972 are the equitable interests enjoyed by beneficial owners under trusts of land. Under the Law of Property Act 1925, s.1(1), the only legal estates which can exist in land after 1925 are the fee simple absolute in possession and the term of years absolute. Thus, in every case in which the beneficial ownership of land is split into successive interests (other than leases), the interests are equitable.

The 1925 legislation provided that all successive beneficial interests in land must be held either behind a trust for sale or under a strict settlement under the Settled Land Act 1925. Under Part I of the Trusts of Land and Appointment of Trustees Act 1996, this dual system is replaced by the single system of the "trust of land". Although existing strict settlements are unaffected,[24] no new ones may be created. The 1996 Act applies to other trusts of land, whenever created. The "trust of land" now embraces situations (primarily co-ownership and intestacy) where statutory trusts for sale were imposed before the 1996 Act, expressly created trusts for sale, and bare trusts of land (where the land is held for an adult beneficiary absolutely entitled).[25] The legal estate is vested in trustees, who have a power of sale. When the land is sold by the trustees (or by the tenant for life of an existing strict settlement, in whom the legal estate is vested), the purchaser takes free from the beneficial interests, which are transferred to the proceeds of sale.[26] Thus the beneficiaries have interests in the proceeds which are equivalent to those which they had in the land. This is so whether the title is registered or unregistered.

This process of transfer of beneficial interests from the land to the purchase money is called "overreaching." Provided that any capital money which is payable is paid to at least two trustees, the purchaser takes free of the beneficial interests even if he knew of them. There is no room for the application of the doctrine that occupation by the beneficiaries gives constructive notice to the purchaser.[27] Nor, in unregistered land, is there any machinery for the registration of such interests.

Where, however, the purchase money is paid to a sole trustee (for example, a husband who is sole legal owner of a house in which his wife has a share in equity), the doctrine of overreaching cannot apply. In such a case the doctrine of notice remains applicable in

---

[24] Save that no land held on charitable trusts may be settled land; s.2(5).
[25] s.1(1), (2).
[26] L.P.A. 1925, s.2(1), as amended by the 1996 Act.
[27] *City of London Building Society v. Flegg* [1988] A.C. 54; *cf.* Law Com. No. 188 (1989). Overreaching can occur even if no capital money is payable at the time of the conveyance; *State Bank of India v. Sood* [1997] 1 All E.R. 169. (Mortgage to secure past and future debts).

unregistered land, so that occupation by the wife is likely to give constructive notice to a purchaser or mortgagee.[28] In the case of an acquisition mortgage, however, where the legal owner could not have bought the property without the mortgage loan, it has been held that a person claiming an equitable interest has no rights against the mortgagee but only against the legal owner, even if in occupation.[29]

The doctrine in its conveyancing sense therefore applies only in the cases of equitable interests in unregistered land which are neither registrable nor overreachable, such as a restrictive covenant entered into before 1926 and a few other examples.[30] The cases seem "to show that there may well be rights, of an equitable character outside the provisions as to registration and which are incapable of being overreached."[31]

It is important to appreciate, however, that the doctrine of notice still operates in the context of beneficial interests under a trust of unregistered land where the doctrine of overreaching cannot apply because there is only one trustee.[32] Although such interests cannot be registered, a wife's statutory right to occupy the matrimonial home is registrable.[33] This, however, has no effect on the enforceability of any equitable interest she may have.

E. Other Applications of the Doctrine of Notice

We have seen that the traditional doctrine is now restricted in its application. The doctrine in its wider form, however, remains significant. As discussed above, it can apply even to commercial dealings with personalty.[34] The defence of purchaser without notice operates in the context of personal claims arising from the receipt of trust property transferred in breach of trust and of proprietary tracing claims, as will be explained in Chapters 12 and 23 respectively.

The House of Lords applied the doctrine in its wider sense in *Barclays Bank plc v. O'Brien*,[35] where the question was whether a wife could set aside a mortgage or guarantee entered into with the

---

[28] *Kingsnorth Finance Co. Ltd v. Tizard* [1986] 1 W.L.R. 783; *cf. Bristol and West Building Society v. Henning* [1985] 1 W.L.R. 778; *Abbey National Building Society v. Cann* [1991] 1 A.C. 56; *Equity & Law Home Loans Ltd v. Prestidge* [1992] 1 W.L.R. 137. (Equitable owner who acquiesced in or impliedly authorised mortgage by legal owner deemed to intend to cede priority to mortgagee).

[29] *Abbey National Building Society v. Cann, supra.*

[30] *Poster v. Slough Estates Ltd* [1968] 1 W.L.R. 1518 (right to enter to remove fixtures); *Shiloh Spinners Ltd v. Harding* [1973] A.C. 691 (equitable right of entry).

[31] *Per* Lord Wilberforce in *Shiloh Spinners v. Harding* [1973] A.C. 691 at p. 721.

[32] *Ante*, p. 36.

[33] Land Charges Act 1972, s.2(7) (Class F).

[34] *Ante*, p. 35.

[35] [1994] 1 A.C. 180; *post*, p. 832.

bank as a result of her husband's misrepresentation or undue influence. This was not the traditional doctrine because there was only
one transaction. The issue was not whether the bank could take free
of a prior interest but whether enforcement of the transaction by the
bank would be taking advantage of the husband's equitable fraud.[36]
The solution lay in the doctrine of constructive notice, whether the
land had a registered or unregistered title. This was "not the same
'doctrine of notice' so beloved of property lawyers and now largely
replaced by registration of title."[37] Thus the doctrine has a role to
play beyond the confines of unregistered land. Indeed, it "lies at the
heart of equity."[38]

8. The Subject-Matter of Equity

In this Introduction, it has only been possible to mention certain
heads of equitable jurisdiction as they became relevant, and it may
be helpful to the understanding of equity to list the subjects which
should properly be included within it. No list can be exhaustive.
Certain matters however are assigned to the Chancery Division by
the Supreme Court Act 1981.[39] They are:

> The sale, exchange or partition of land, or the raising of
> charges on land;
>
> The redemption or foreclosure of mortgages[40];
>
> The execution of trusts;
>
> The administration of the estates of deceased persons;
>
> Bankruptcy;
>
> The dissolution of partnerships or the taking of partnership
> or other accounts;
>
> The rectification, setting aside or cancellation of deeds or
> other instruments in writing;
>
> Probate business, other than non-contentious or common
> form business;

---

[36] (1995) 15 L.S. 35 (G. Battersby).
[37] [1994] Conv. 421 at p. 423 (M. Dixon and C. Harpum). See also All E.R. Rev. 1993 p. 367
(W. Swadling); [1994] Conv. 140 (M. Thompson); (1994) 144 N.L.J. 765 (P. O'Hagan);
[1995] Conv. 250 (P. Sparkes); (1995) 54 C.L.J. 280 (A. Lawson) and 536 (J. Mee); [1996]
Conv. 34 (J. Howell).
[38] *Barclays Bank plc v. O'Brien, supra,* at p. 195 (Lord Browne-Wilkinson).
[39] s.61 and Sched. 1. For the transfer of business to the Mayor's and City of London County
Court, see *Practice Direction (Chancery: Transfer of Business)* [1988] 1 W.L.R. 741.
[40] See also R.S.C. Ord. 88, r. 2.

Patents, trade marks, registered designs or copyright;

The appointment of a guardian of a minor's estate[41];

All causes and matters involving the exercise of the High Court's jurisdiction under the enactments relating to companies.

All divisions of the High Court, however, exercise co-ordinate jurisdiction. Where a matter arises which has not been assigned to one division, it should go to whichever division is the more appropriate and convenient; in many cases the plaintiff's counsel will be able to choose. If the action is brought in the wrong division, it may be retained or transferred at the discretion of the judge.[42]

9. THE TRUST IN MODERN LAW[43]

Trusts are primarily about money and the preservation of wealth. The idea of the trust developed as a means for providing for the family. Although the trust still plays a significant role in establishing ownership of property on family breakdown,[44] it "can no longer be doubted that equity has moved out of the family home and the settled estate and into the market-place".[45] A major area of activity is in the holding of the property of charities and other non-profit making bodies. A modern and significant role has emerged for the trust in the constitution of pension funds,[46] although such trusts differ from traditional trusts in so far as there is a contractual relationship of employment and the beneficiaries have given consideration.[47] Unit trusts and investment trusts[48] are designed to spread investment risks. Thus the trust continues to be a form of property-holding of ever-increasing importance because of its adaptability and convenience in effecting complicated forms of settlement. Indeed, "as the principles of equity permeate the complications of modern life, the nature and variety of trusts ever grow."[49]

---

[41] This work was transferred from the Chancery Division to the Family Division by the Adminsitration of Justice Act 1970. Now see Supreme Court Act 1981, Sched. 1, para. 3.

[42] Supreme Court Act 1981, ss.61(6), 65.

[43] See Moffat. *Trust Law Text and Materials* (2nd ed.); p. 21; (1990) 106 L.Q.R. 87 (D. Hayton); (1994) 110 L.Q.R. 238 (Sir Anthony Mason); (1996) 10 *Trust Law International* 38 (W. Goodhart).

[44] *Post*, Chap. 11.

[45] (1995) 9 *Trust Law International* 35 at p. 36 (Sir Peter Millett).

[46] *Post*. Chap. 16.

[47] *Post*, p. 459.

[48] *Post*, p. 516.

[49] *Re a Solicitor* [1952] Ch. 328 at p. 332 (*per* Roxburgh J.).

If a settlor wishes to give property to his wife for life and after her death to various other members of the family, it would be possible to arrange a system of law by which it could be done without using a trust. Indeed, the early common law did so, in an elementary form. Roman law did so[50]; as do those countries which have followed modernised systems of Roman law.[51]

In England, full use has been made of the convenience of the system whereby the legal estate is in the trustees and the equitable or beneficial ownership is kept separate. We have seen that this is insisted upon for the creation of successive or concurrent interests in land under the 1925 legislation.[52] The legal title can be kept clear of beneficial interests; the land can be sold free of them to a purchaser, who can overreach them. Thus a most elaborate system of beneficial interests can be created without complicating the title to the land.

The same advantages exist with personalty. Most modern settlements deal wholly or partly with personalty in the form of investments. No system of legal future interests in personalty ever developed; for settlements of personalty did not arise until the system of trusts was well advanced. In this sphere also, it is most convenient to separate legal and equitable ownership; by doing so, the trustees can buy and sell shares without the purchaser being concerned with the beneficial interests.[53] The beneficial interests attach to whatever is held by the trustees for the time being.

Those are the simple cases. Settlors may wish to create other forms of settlement.[54] With a gift for charitable purposes, for example, there is no beneficial owner; such a gift is effected by a special form of trust.[55] A settlor may wish to protect a beneficiary from his own extravagance by making it impossible for creditors to proceed against his limited interest; this is done by protective trust.[56] The settlor may wish to allow his trustees to determine from time to time how the capital and income shall be distributed among the beneficiaries; this is done by a discretionary trust.[57] He may wish to provide for someone, such as his lover, by will without identifying her in that document; this is done by a secret trust.[58] Each sort of

---

[50] Buckland and McNair: *Roman Law and Common Law* (2nd ed.), pp. 173 *et seq.*

[51] See (1980) *Journal of Legal History*, p. 6 (B. Beinart); (1974) 48 Tulane L.Rev. 917 (J. Merryman).

[52] *Ante*, p. 36. Similarly a trust is necessary where there is incapacity to hold a legal estate in land, as in the case of a minor.

[53] No notice of any trust can be entered on the register of shareholders (Companies Act 1985, s.360).

[54] It should not be forgotten that the trust may also be created unintentionally. See Resulting and Constructive Trusts, *post*, Chaps. 10, 12.

[55] *Post*, Chap. 15. Also a gift for a non-human object, such as the maintenance of an animal or a tombstone; *post*, pp. 354 *et seq.*

[56] *Post*, Chap. 7.

[57] *Post*, Chap. 8.

[58] *Post*, Chap. 5.

trust will be considered in its proper place. It will in each case be seen that the desired result could have been effected without the existence of a trust; but that the trust is a very satisfactory and convenient way of effecting it; and that this has become the only way in which it can now be effected in English law. In some cases, however, the trust has not afforded a solution, for example, in the case of gifts for abstract non-charitable purposes.[59] Theoretical difficulties have also been encountered with the property of unincorporated associations.[60] Finally, it should never be forgotten that there is one factor which dominates all others in the context of the creation of trusts in modern law: taxation. Although the law of equity and trusts can be understood without it, it will be appreciated that the popular forms of trust in recent years have been those which reduce to a minimum the liability to tax. The Chancery lawyer's job is to be able to advise on these matters and to create the most appropriate trusts to meet the wishes of the settlor.

10. THE CREATIVITY OF EQUITY

One question which has arisen is whether the category of equitable interests is closed, or whether new ones might be created.[61] One clear example is the restrictive covenant, which, since Lord Eldon's day, has evolved from a contractual right to an equitable interest enforceable against the covenantor's successors in title. Another possibility is the contractual licence, although the matter awaits clarification in the House of Lords.[62] One view is that the modern machinery for law reform should be relied upon in preference to judicial creativity.[63]

Bagnall J., in a case concerning matrimonial property, warned against unwarranted extensions of equitable jurisdiction in the following words:

"In any individual case the application of these propositions may produce a result which appears unfair. So be it; in my view that is not an injustice. I am convinced that in determining rights, particularly property rights, the only justice that can be obtained by mortals, who are fallible and are not omniscient, is justice

---

[59] *Post*, Chap. 14.

[60] *Post*, p. 359.

[61] Eveleigh L.J. in *Pennine Raceway Ltd v. Kirklees Metropolitan Council* [1983] Q.B. 382 at p. 392, said, "There has ben a considerable development in the law in relation to equitable interests and I do not think that it is right to regard the category as closed." But at p. 397, Stephenson L.J. preferred to express no view.

[62] *Post*, p. 876. See *Ashburn Anstalt v. Arnold* [1989] Ch. 1.

[63] As in the case of the matrimonial homes legislation (now Family Law Act 1996), replacing Lord Denning's "deserted wife's equity."

according to law; the justice which flows from the application of
sure and settled principles to proved or admitted facts. So in the
field of equity, the length of the Chancellor's foot has been
measured or is capable of measurement. This does not mean that
equity is past childbearing; simply that its progeny must be
legitimate—by precedent out of principle. It is well that this
should be so; otherwise no lawyer could safely advise on his
client's title and every quarrel would lead to a law suit."[64]

Throughout this book it will be seen that the principles of equity
have constantly developed and found new fields of application.[65]
The reader, when examining these developments, might consider
whether the words of Bagnall J. have been heeded. A few examples
must suffice here.

Many new developments have been seen in the field of injunctions, notably the evolution of the so-called *Anton Piller* and *Mareva*
injunctions, designed respectively to prevent removal or destruction
of evidence and to prevent the assets of the defendant from being
dissipated.[66] Equity's excursions into the criminal law, however,
have been restricted.[67]

The constructive trust has also proved to be a fertile field, assisting in the enforcement of contractual licences against third parties[68];
and allowing unprotected minor interests to be enforced against
purchasers of registered land.[69] Constructive and resulting trusts
have operated to give security to unsecured creditors[70]; and to
determine the ownership of matrimonial and "quasi-matrimonial"
property.[71] Here we have seen the "new model constructive trust,"
a term first used by Lord Denning M.R. in the case concerning the
claim of a cohabitant to a share in the home, where he said, "Equity
is not past the age of childbearing. One of her latest progeny is a
constructive trust of a new model. Lord Diplock brought it into the
world[72] and we have nourished it".[73]

---

[64] *Cowcher v. Cowcher* [1972] 1 W.L.R. 425 at p. 430.
[65] In some fields, however, the role of equity has declined. The entitlement to the funds on
dissolution of an unincorporated association, for example, is today treated as more a matter
of contract than of trusts. See *post*, p. 235.
[66] *Post*, pp. 804–815.
[67] *R.C.A. Corp. v. Pollard* [1983] Ch. 135; *post*, p. 741.
[68] *Ashburn Anstalt v. Arnold, supra; post*, p. 879.
[69] *Peffer v. Rigg* [1977] 1 W.L.R. 285; *Lyus v. Prowsa Ltd* [1982] 1 W.L.R. 1044, *post*, p.
322.
[70] *Barclays Bank Ltd v. Quistclose Investments Ltd* [1970] A.C. 567, *post*, p. 50. See also *Re
Kayford* [1975] 1 W.L.R. 279.
[71] *Post*, Chap. 11.
[72] In *Gissing v. Gissing* [1971] A.C. 886.
[73] *Eves v. Eves* [1975] 1 W.L.R. 1338 at p. 1341; *cf. Allen v. Snyder* [1977] 2 N.S.W.L.R. 685
at p. 701: "the legitimacy of the new model is at least suspect; at best it is a mutant from
which further breeding should be discouraged." It seems that the "new model" is in
decline; *post*, p. 317.

Other areas where equity's creativity has shown itself in modern times include proprietary estoppel,[74] the rescission of contracts on the ground of mistake,[75] and the restriction of the rights of a mortgagee.[76] This brief survey indicates the dynamism of equity. The developments discussed above, and others, will be examined in the relevant parts of the book.

11. THE RECOGNITION OF TRUSTS ACT 1987[77]

The trust is an English concept which has spread to common law, but not civil law, jurisdictions.[78] The 1984 Hague Convention on the Law applicable to Trusts and their Recognition establishes common principles between states on the law governing trusts and provides guidelines for their recognition. The United Kingdom, by means of the Recognition of Trusts Act 1987, has ratified the Convention.

The ratification does not have the effect of changing the substantive law of trusts of the United Kingdom, nor of importing trusts into civil law jurisdictions. The Convention seeks to establish uniform conflict of laws principles and to assist civil law states to deal with trust issues arising within their jurisdiction. Recognition implies, for example, that the trustee may sue and be sued in his capacity as trustee, and that the trust property is a separate fund and is not part of the trustee's estate.[79] A trust is to be governed by the law chosen by the settlor, expressly or by implication. In the absence of any such choice, the trust is to be governed by the law with which it is most closely connected.[80] The applicable law governs the validity and construction of the trust, and its effects and administration.[81]

---

[74] *Post*, p. 885.

[75] *Solle v. Butcher* [1950] 1 K.B. 671; *post*, p. 820.

[76] *Quennell v. Maltby* [1979] 1 W.L.R. 318 (right to possession must be exercised bona fide and to protect security).

[77] (1987) 36 I.C.L.Q. 260 (D. Hayton); Underhill, Chap. 23.

[78] A Bill drafted by the French Ministry of Justice sought to introduce "La Fiducie", a device similar to the trust, into French law, but it was not enacted. See [1992] Conv. 407 (H. Dyson).

[79] Article 11, as set out in the Schedule to the 1987 Act.

[80] Articles 6 and 7.

[81] Article 8.

CHAPTER 2

NATURE AND CLASSIFICATION OF TRUSTS

1. Distinctions 45
   A. Bailment 46
   B. Agency 47
   C. Contract 48
      i. Settlements and Covenants to
         Settle 48
      ii. Third Party Rights Under a
         Contract 48
      iii. Unincorporated Associations 48
      iv. Contractual Licences 49
   D. Debt 49
   E. Conditions and Charges 52
   F. Interest under a Will or Intestacy 53
      i. Whether a Personal Representa-
         tive is a Trustee 54
         (a) Different Periods of Limita-
            tion Apply 54
         (b) Power of Disposition of
            Personalty 54
         (c) Tenure of Office 55
         (d) Duty to Estate: Duty to
            Beneficiaries 56

      (e) Vesting of a Legal Estate 56
      ii. The Nature of the Interest of a
         Legatee or Devisee 57
   G. Powers 59
      i. Trusts Imperative; Powers Dis-
         cretionary 59
      ii. Terminology 62
      iii. Significance of the Distinction ... 62
         (a) Whether the Class takes if the
            Discretion is not Exercised .. 62
         (b) The Test of Certainty 63
         (c) Terminating the Trust 64
2. Classification of Trusts 64
   A. Express Trusts 65
      i. Executed and Executory 65
      ii. Completely and Incompletely
         Constituted Trusts 66
   B. Resulting Trusts 67
   C. Constructive Trusts 68
   D. Bare Trusts 69
   E. Trusts in the Higher Sense and Trusts
      in the Lower Sense 70

1. DISTINCTIONS

MANY attempts have been made to define a trust, but none of them has been wholly successful.[1] It is more useful to describe than to define a trust, and then to distinguish it from related but distinguishable concepts.

A trust is a relationship recognised by equity which arises where property is vested in (a person or) persons called the trustees, which those trustees are obliged to hold for the benefit of other persons called *cestuis que trust*[2] or beneficiaries. The interests of the beneficiaries will usually be laid down in the instrument creating the trust, but may be implied or imposed by law.[3] The beneficiary's

---

[1] Co.Litt. 272b; Underhill (15th ed.), p. 3; used in *Re Marshall's W.T.* [1945] Ch. 217 at p. 219 and in *Green v. Russell* [1959] 2 Q.B. 226 at p. 241; Snell, p. 89; *Halsbury's Laws of England* (4th ed.), Vol. 48, p. 272; (1955) 71 L.Q.R. 39 (A. Scott).

[2] This is the correct plural; (1910) 26 L.Q.R. 196 (C. Sweet).

[3] *Post*, pp. 67, 68.

interest is proprietary[4] in the sense that it can be sold, given away or disposed of by will; but it will cease to exist if the legal estate in the property comes into the hands of a bona fide purchaser for value without notice of the beneficial interest.[5] The subject-matter of the trust must be some form of property. Commonly, it is legal owner-ship of land or of invested funds; but it may be of any sort of property—land, money, chattels, equitable interests,[6] choses in action,[7] etc. There may also be trusts for charitable purposes; such trusts are enforced at the suit of the Attorney-General.[8] There is much doubt and uncertainty as to the status and validity of trusts for non-charitable purposes—as a trust for the building of a monument[9] or for the maintenance of the testator's horses, dogs, and cats.[10]

A trust must be distinguished from certain other legal phenomena which resemble the trust, but which must be kept separate from it. The point of such distinguishing is threefold: first, to compare the different legal consequences of a trust and the related concept; secondly, to identify the circumstances in which the one concept must exist to the exclusion of the other; and thirdly, to identify the circumstances in which a trust may co-exist with the related con-cept, as may be the case, for example, with certain contracts and debts.

A. Bailment

Bailment is a relationship recognised by the common law, and arises where a chattel owned by A is, with A's permission, in the possession of B.[11] The rights of the parties may or may not be governed by a contract. A is entitled to a certain standard of care by B in his stewardship of A's chattel. But this is very different from a trust. For there is no transfer of ownership from A to B; B's duties are dependent on the rules of common law and not upon equity; and these duties are entirely different from, and minimal in character as compared with, those which would exist if B held the property as trustee for A. The bailor, A, could lose his legal ownership only

---

[4] *Ante*, p. 17. Discretionary trusts and trusts for persons for particular purposes need separate consideration: *post*, Chaps. 8 and 14.

[5] *Ante*, p. 32.

[6] For example, where a beneficiary under a settlement makes a settlement of his beneficial interest.

[7] For example, a trust of the benefit of a covenant, or of a debt, or of a bank balance.

[8] See *post*, Chap. 15.

[9] *Mussett v. Bingle* [1876] W.N. 170; *Re Endacott* [1960] Ch. 232; *post*, p. 354.

[10] *Pettingall v. Pettingall* (1842) 11 L.J.Ch. 176; *Re Dean* (1889) 41 Ch.D. 552; *post*, p. 355.

[11] Bridge, *Personal Property Law*, pp. 23–30; *Aluminium Industrie Vaassen B.V. v. Romalpa Aluminium Ltd* [1976] 1 W.L.R. 676, *post*, p. xxx; *Re Goldcorp Exchange Ltd* [1995] 1 A.C. 74 at p. 97.

through one of the ways in which legal owners may be deprived.[12] But if the property was held by B on trust for A, A's equitable title could be defeated by the transfer of the legal title in the property to a bona fide purchaser for value without notice of the trust.[13]

B. Agency

The relationship of principal and agent, which is normally contractual, is governed by rules of common law and equity, while the relationship of trustee and beneficiary, which is rarely contractual, is exclusively equitable. The function of an agent is to represent the principal in dealings with third parties, while a trustee does not bring the beneficiaries into any relationship with third parties. There are, however, many similarities.[14] The relationship of trustee and beneficiary is fiduciary; that of principal and agent is normally fiduciary, but not inevitably so.[15] Both trustees and agents must act personally and not delegate their duties[16]; neither may make unauthorised profits from their office.[17]

A significant distinction arises from the fact that the relationship of principal and agent is primarily debtor/creditor, while a trust is proprietary: the trust property vests in the trustee and the beneficiaries are the equitable owners. The crucial point here is that a proprietary right (so long as the property or its proceeds can be identified) is not affected by the defendant's insolvency, whereas a personal claim will abate with the claims of other creditors if the defendant cannot pay in full.

An agent does not necessarily hold any property for the principal. Even if he does, he may merely have possession rather than title. The principal will have proprietary rights against the agent only if the agent has acquired title to property for the benefit of the principal. "That proposition is clear enough in the abstract, but it is often extremely difficult to gauge, especially where the subject matter is money ... (i) whether the agent has acquired title or mere possession, and (ii) if he has acquired title, whether there is an intention to create a trust or to allow the agent to take an absolute title subject to a merely personal monetary obligation."[18]

The above discussion relates to assets lawfully received by the agent on behalf of the principal. Where property is received in

---

[12] *e.g.* through estoppel, or the operation of the Factors Act 1899, ss.2, 8, 9; Sale of Goods Act 1979, ss.21, 24, or the Consumer Credit Act 1974, Sched. 4, para. 22.

[13] *Ante*, pp. 32 *et seq.*

[14] See Fridman's *Law of Agency* (6th ed.), pp. 20–21.

[15] *Post*, p. 596.

[16] *Post*, p. 559.

[17] *Post*, Chap. 21.

[18] Heydon, Gummow and Austin, *Cases and Materials on Equity and Trusts* (4th ed.), p. 467.

breach of fiduciary duty, as in the case of a bribe, it is now settled that the agent holds the property on trust for the principal.[19] The consequence is that the principal's remedy does not depend on the agent's solvency, and the principal will be entitled to any increase in value of the property.

C. Contract

Trust and contract are quite different concepts. A contract is a common law personal obligation resulting from agreement between the parties. A trust is an equitable proprietary relation which can arise independently of agreement. However, there are various situations in which the distinction may be difficult to draw, or where the facts may give rise to both[20]; contracts and trusts are not mutually exclusive.[21]

i. Settlements and Covenants to Settle. Property which is vested in the trustees of a settlement is held upon the trusts of the settlement, and the beneficiaries are the owners in equity of their interests under the settlement. But if the property has not yet been conveyed to the trustees, and is merely subject to a covenant to settle, then the beneficiaries will only be able to enforce the covenant if they have given consideration or are parties to the deed. Equity will not assist a volunteer.[22]

ii. Third Party Rights under a Contract. There has been much discussion of the question whether the inability of a third party to sue upon a contract can be overcome by finding that one of the parties to the contract contracted as trustee for him. This is not really a question of distinguishing a trust from a contract. The question is whether there is a trust of the benefit of the contract. The answer to that question depends on whether there is an intention to create a trust of the benefit of the contract; this question is discussed elsewhere.[23]

iii. Unincorporated Associations. An unincorporated association is not a legal entity. Where there is a gift to an unincorporated

---

[19] *Att.-Gen. for Hong Kong v. Reid* [1994] 1 A.C. 324; *post*, p. 608.

[20] As, for example, in the case of a constructive trust arising out of a specifically enforceable contract for sale, *post*, p. 312; or possibly in the case of a contractual licence, discussed below. Consideration does not negative a trust; *Carreras Rothmans Ltd v. Freeman Mathews Treasure Ltd* [1985] Ch. 207.

[21] *Baird v. Baird* [1990] 2 A.C. 548 at p. 560; *Imperial Group Pension Trust Ltd v. Imperial Tobacco Ltd* [1991] 1 W.L.R. 589 at p. 597. These employee pension fund cases are an important illustration of the co-existence of contractual and trust relationships.

[22] *Post*, Chap. 4.

[23] *Post*, p. 127.

association, there is often doubt whether the property is held on trust for the members of the association, or for the purposes of the association, or subject to the members' contractual rights.[24] On the dissolution of such an association the ownership of its funds has sometimes been determined by applying trust principles, but today the matter is more commonly treated as one of contract.[25]

iv. Contractual Licences. A contractual licence, normally involving the occupation of land, is created by agreement of the parties, applying the normal principles of the law of contract. There is authority,[26] however, especially in the context of enforceability against third parties, that a contractual licence may give rise to a constructive trust, thus giving the licensee an equitable interest in the land in addition to his contractual rights. The development of this theory is discussed elsewhere.[27]

D. Debt

A debt may or may not be contractual. Whether the obligation is contractual or not, the duty of the debtor is to pay money to the creditor; that of a trustee is to hold the trust property on trust for the beneficiary. The debtor's obligation is personal. The trust is proprietary. We have seen that the distinction becomes crucial on insolvency. Further, a trustee must invest the trust funds, and the beneficiaries are entitled to the income. With a debtor, or a stakeholder, this is a matter of agreement, express or implied.[28]

On the other hand, it may be to a person's own advantage to be a trustee rather than a person subject to a personal obligation. If money is borrowed and then stolen from the borrower, it must still be repaid; but a trustee may not be liable for a loss which is not due to his own lack of care.[29]

A debt may, of course, be the subject-matter of a trust,[30] but the question here considered is whether the making of a loan can create a trust in favour of the lender, either initially or at some later stage. Sometimes a form of words is construed as creating both forms of obligation.[31] There is no reason why, in certain circumstances, a

---

[24] *Post*, p. 359.
[25] *Post*, p. 235.
[26] See *Ashburn Anstalt v. Arnold* [1989] Ch. 1.
[27] *Post*, p. 879.
[28] *Potters v. Loppert* [1973] Ch. 399 (estate agent held entitled to retain interest earned by deposit held as stakeholder). See now Estate Agents Act 1979, s.13.
[29] *Morley v. Morley* (1678) 2 Ch.Cas. 2.
[30] For an unusual example, see *Barclays Bank plc v. Willowbrook International Ltd* [1987] 1 F.T.L.R. 386, C.A., holding that where A charges to B a debt owed to A by C, any money paid by C to A is held by A on constructive trust for B.
[31] *Welby v. Rockcliffe* (1830) 1 Russ. & M. 571; *Wright v. Wilkin* (1862) 2 B. & S. 232 at p. 260.

debt and a trust cannot co-exist; a loan to be held by the borrower on trust is repayable in debt if the purpose for which the money was lent is carried out, and may be held in trust for the lender if performance is impossible. In *Barclays Bank Ltd v. Quistclose Investments Ltd*[32]:

> Rolls Razor Ltd, very much indebted to Barclays Bank, was in need of £209,719 to pay dividends which had been declared on its shares. This sum was borrowed from Quistclose under an arrangement whereby the loan was to be used only for that purpose. The money was paid into a separate account at Barclays bank, the Bank having notice of the nature of the arrangement.
>
> Before the dividend was paid, Rolls Razor went into liquidation. The question was whether the money in the account was owned beneficially by Rolls Razor in which case Barclays Bank claimed to set it off against the overdraft,[33] or whether Rolls Razor had received the money as trustee and still held it on trust for Quistclose.
>
> The House of Lords unanimously decided that the money had been received upon trust to apply it for the payment of dividends; that purpose having failed, the money was held on trust for Quistclose. The fact that the transaction was a loan, recoverable by an action at law, did not exclude the implication of a trust. The legal and equitable rights and remedies could co-exist. The Bank, having notice of the trust, could not retain the money against Quistclose.

The principle is that "equity fastens on the conscience of the person who receives from another property transferred for a specific purpose only and not therefore for the recipient's own purposes, so that such person will not be permitted to treat the property as his own or to use it for other than the stated purpose."[34] The principle applies also where only part of the money lent is used for the specific purpose: the part not so applied is held on trust for the lender.[35]

---

[32] [1970] A.C. 567; (1980) 43 M.L.R. 489 (W. Goodhart and G. Jones). For other circumstances where an unsecured creditor can acquire a proprietary interest, see *Swiss Bank Corporation v. Lloyds Bank Ltd* [1982] A.C. 584.

[33] See Insolvency Act 1986, s.323.

[34] *Carreras Rothmans Ltd v. Freeman Mathews Treasure Ltd* [1985] Ch. 207 at p. 222. See generally (1985) 101 L.Q.R. 269 (P. Millett). It seems that the parties must have had a common intention to create the primary trust; see (1991) 107 L.Q.R. 608 (C. Rickett).

[35] *Re EVTR Ltd* [1987] B.C.L.C. 647 (loan for buying equipment, part of which was never delivered and money refunded to debtor by vendor).

The court in *Re Kayford Ltd (In Liquidation)*[36] went one step further, holding that circumstances apparently giving rise to a debt in fact created a trust which did not co-exist with the debt but excluded it. In that case, customers of a mail-order company paid in advance when ordering goods. The company, being in financial difficulties, decided to protect its customers in the event of its insolvency by opening a separate bank account, called "Customers' Trust Deposit Account," into which the purchase money was paid. In liquidation proceedings it was held that the money was held on trust for the customers and did not form part of the assets of the company. The customer could create a trust by using appropriate words or, as here, the company could do it by taking suitable steps on or before receiving the money, thus transforming the obligations from debt to trust. The customers never became creditors, so no question of a fraudulent preference[37] of creditors could arise.[38]

Re Kayford Ltd was not referred to in *Customs and Excise Commissioners v. Richmond Theatre Management Ltd,*[39] where a different, and somewhat surprising, result was reached in the context not of insolvency but of liability to value added tax. The theatre sold tickets in advance on terms which expressly imposed a trust on the money for the purchasers until the performance took place. Dyson J. held that no trust was created because the terms also provided that the theatre was "not accountable for interest or otherwise in respect of the use of the ticket money after its receipt." It was considered that the effect of this clause was that the purchasers accepted the risk of insolvency and that it would be inequitable to put them in a better position than unsecured creditors in that event. There was no reference to *R. v. Clowes (No. 2)*[40] where, in the context of theft, the Court of Appeal said that the requirement to keep money separately normally indicates a trust, and the absence of such a requirement normally negatives it *if there were no other indicators of a trust*; the

---

[36] [1975] 1 W.L.R. 279; distinguished in *Re Multi Guarantee Co. Ltd* [1987] B.C.L.C. 257, where a separate account was designated but no trust of the money was established because the company contemplated having further resort to the money. The decision is criticised at (1988) 85 L.S.Gaz. No. 36, p. 14 (I. Hardcastle).

[37] The preference rules are now found in Insolvency Act 1986, s.239.

[38] *Cf.* (1980) 43 M.L.R. 489 at pp. 494 *et seq.* (W. Goodhart and G. Jones). The point that the customers never became creditors seems unconvincing. For this to be so, the trust must already have existed when the company received the money. In *Re Chelsea Cloisters* (1981) 41 P. & C.R. 98, tenants' deposits against damage were paid into a separate bank account, any balance to be credited to them at the end of the lease. The Court of Appeal held that a trust had been created, but doubted (on the authority of *Potters v. Loppert* [1973] Ch. 399, *supra*, n. 28), whether it had arisen at the outset. (See now Landlord and Tenant Act 1987, s.42). See also Heydon, Gummow and Austin, *Cases and Materials on Equity and Trusts* (4th ed.), p. 475, suggesting that *Re Kayford Ltd* and the *Quistclose* case "provide startling opportunities for well-advised lenders to obtain protection against the prospect of the borrower's insolvency."

[39] [1995] S.T.C. 257; criticised [1995] B.T.R. 332 (P. Matthews).

[40] [1994] 2 All E.R. 316. See also *Re Lewis's of Leicester Ltd* [1995] 1 B.C.L.C. 428.

fact that the transaction contemplates the mingling of money is not necessarily fatal to a trust. There the terms of an investment brochure were held to establish that investors' money was received on trust for them, to the exclusion of a debtor/creditor relationship.

In the context of informal family transactions, it may be difficult to determine whether a payment was intended to create a debt or not. Thus in *Hussey v. Palmer*,[41] where the plaintiff paid £607 for an extension to her son-in-law's house, Cairns L.J. held that it was a loan, Lord Denning M.R. held that it was not, and Phillimore L.J. thought that it "might be" a loan. The decision of the majority was that the payment gave rise to a resulting (or constructive) trust on the basis that it would be inequitable for the son-in-law to deny that she had an interest in the house.[42] If the payment was neither a gift nor a loan, this conclusion is not surprising, but Phillimore L.J. held that a resulting trust could arise even if it was a loan.[43] There is much force in the dissenting judgment of Cairns L.J., holding that a resulting trust of money paid by way of a loan could not arise. The question arose again in *Re Sharpe*,[44] where an aunt lent money to her nephew towards the purchase of a house on the understanding that she could live with him for the rest of her life. On the nephew's bankruptcy, the aunt claimed an interest in the house. Although her claim succeeded on other grounds,[45] the argument that the loan gave rise to a resulting trust was rejected, *Hussey v. Palmer* being distinguished as a case on "very special" facts.

E. Conditions and Charges

It is sometimes difficult to determine whether a gift of property is subject to a trust or whether it is conditional upon, or charged with, the duty of making certain payments. Thus a bequest to X "but he is to pay £50 to Y" could give rise to several possible constructions, each of them having different consequences.[46]

The bequest could be construed as a gift to X upon trust to pay Y £50.[47] In that situation, Y would immediately become entitled in equity to the £50, provided that the property bequeathed was of sufficient value; a trustee is not required to produce money of his

---

[41] [1972] 1 W.L.R. 1286.

[42] See *post*, p. 231.

[43] This would not be within the principle of *Barclays Bank Ltd v. Quistclose Investments Ltd*, *supra*, as the money *was* applied to the purpose for which it was paid. The trust was apparently of a proportionate share of the house.

[44] [1980] 1 W.L.R. 219. See also *Spence v. Brown* (1988) 18 Fam.Law. 291; *Risch v. McFee* (1991) 61 P. & C.R. 42.

[45] *Post*, p. 880.

[46] (1952) 11 C.L.J. 240 (T. Thomas).

[47] *Re Frame* [1939] Ch. 700 (devise to housekeeper "on condition that she adopt my daughter Alma and also gives to my daughters Jessie and May the sum of £5 each, and a like sum to my son Alexander."); *cf. Re Brace* [1954] 1 W.L.R. 955.

own to make up deficiencies in the trust property.[48] If there is a surplus, a trustee is not, on principle, entitled to obtain any benefit from the trust and the surplus will usually be held upon a resulting trust.[49] But a possible construction is that, even if there was a trust of the £50, X was intended to take the surplus beneficially, the trust being applicable only to the £50.[50]

The bequest might also be construed as a gift to X conditional upon his performing the obligation. In that situation, Y obtains no interest in the £50; X has the choice of keeping the property and paying £50 or of declining both.[51] It could also be construed so as to impose a charge on the property. Here again, X will only be obliged to make the payment if he receives the property. His obligation will be limited to the value of the property,[52] and he will be entitled to retain any surplus.[53] Y will have an equitable right by virtue of the charge,[54] but this right is a different one from that of a beneficiary under a trust.[55]

The House of Lords has held that equity will protect the right of an insurer to be subrogated to the insured person's rights against the wrongdoer by imposing an equitable lien or charge, although not a trust, in favour of the insurer on the damages payable by the wrongdoer.[56] The imposition of a trust would be onerous, commercially undesirable and unnecessary to the protection of the insurer.

F. Interest under a Will or Intestacy

The relationship between a personal representative and a legatee or devisee bears many similarities to that of trustee and beneficiary. The origins of the relationship, however, are quite distinct, the former originating in the Ecclesiastical Court and the latter in Chancery and their basic function is different. The trustee's duty is to manage the trust so long as it continues. The personal representative's duty is to liquidate the estate and distribute the assets; either

---

[48] *Re Cowley* (1885) 53 L.T. 494.

[49] *King v. Denison* (1813) 1 V. & B. 260 at p. 272; *Re West* [1900] 1 Ch. 84; *Re Rees' W.T.* [1950] Ch. 204; *post*, p. 156.

[50] *Re Foord* [1922] 2 Ch. 519 ("To my sister, Margaret Juliet, absolutely on trust to pay my wife per annum" £300); distinguished in *Re Osoba* [1979] 1 W.L.R. 247.

[51] *Att.-Gen. v. The Cordwainers Co.* (1833) 3 Myl. & K. 534.

[52] *Re Cowley* (1885) 53 L.T. 494.

[53] *Re Oliver* (1890) 62 L.T. 533.

[54] *Parker v. Judkin* [1931] 1 Ch. 475.

[55] See, however, *Barclays Bank plc v. Willowbrook International Ltd* [1987] 1 F.T.L.R. 386, C.A., holding that where a debt due to a company was charged by the company to the bank, the company held the money paid to it by the debtor on constructive trust for the bank.

[56] *Napier and Ettrick (Lord) v. Hunter* [1993] A.C. 713.

to individual beneficiaries, or, if a trust is established by the will, to the trustees. Commonly, the executors and the trustees are the same persons, and, as we shall see,[57] in the case of personalty the transfer to themselves is notional; in the case of land an assent is required. Although the two relationships often coalesce or overlap, there are important distinctions between them.

i. Whether a Personal Representative is a Trustee. The definition of trustee in the Trustee Act 1925 includes a personal representative[58] where the context so admits; and the Act, except where otherwise expressly provided, applies to executorships and administratorships.[59] A personal representative is sometimes treated in Administration of Estates Act 1925 as a trustee.[60] A personal representative is under fiduciary duties which are very similar to those of a trustee. There are, however, a number of ways in which a personal representative has been held not to be a trustee:

(a) *Different Periods of Limitation Apply.* Generally, an action for the recovery of trust property or for a breach of trust must be brought against a trustee within six years.[61] An action against a personal representative in respect of a claim to personal estate must be brought within 12 years, and an action for the recovery of arrears of interest on legacies within six years.[62]

(b) *Power of Disposition of Personalty.* The power of personal representatives to dispose of pure personalty is *several*; that of trustees is *joint*.[63] This means that one of several executors can pass title to a chattel; but in a sale by trustees, all must combine. It thus becomes important to ascertain when a personal representative becomes a trustee. Where, of course, a will appoints certain persons as executors and other persons as trustees, the executors, on the completion of the administration, must assent to the vesting of the property subject to the trust in the trustees. In the case of personalty the assent may be oral, or even implied,[64] in the case of a legal estate

---

[57] *Post*, p. 55.
[58] s.68(17); A.E.A. 1925, s.33; *contra*, I.C.T.A. 1988, s.686(6).
[59] s.69.
[60] A.E.A. 1925, ss.33, 46, 49; Intestates' Estates Act 1952.
[61] Limitation Act 1980, s.21(3); for exceptions, see s.21(1) and (2).
[62] Limitation Act 1980, s.22.
[63] *Jacomb v. Harwood* (1751) 2 Ves.Sen. 265; *Attenborough v. Solomon* [1913] A.C. 76; *Collier v. Hollinshead* (1984) 272 E.G. 941. The Law Reform Committee on Powers and Duties of Trustees (23rd Report, Cmnd. 8733 (1982)) recommended that the power should be joint in the case of personal representatives also.
[64] *Attenborough v. Solomon* [1913] A.C. 76. See [1990] Conv. 257 (C. Stebbings).

in land however an assent must be in writing, and it becomes an essential document of title in the case of unregistered land.[65]

When however, the executors are appointed trustees also, or where no provision is made for the appointment of trustees in a will which provides for property to be held in trust after the completion of administration, the question arises of the way in which, and of the time at which, the executors become trustees. The principle is that the transition from executors to trustees occurs automatically after completion of the administration, but as far as powers of disposition of property are concerned, there must also have been a sufficient assent by the executors in their own favour as trustees.

In *Attenborough v. Solomon*,[66] the House of Lords held that a pledge of silver plate by one of two executors, which was made 13 years after the completion of the administration of the estate, passed no title to the pledgee. The executors had long since become trustees; an assent in their own favour could be inferred from their conduct; and trustees must act jointly.

A similar view was taken in the cases allowing a personal representative to act as a trustee in the exercise of the statutory power of appointing new trustees.[67]

There is no distinction with regard to the power of disposition of land, the power being joint in both cases.[68] Formerly one of two or more personal representatives could enter into a contract to sell land, but this is no longer possible.[69] Where there is only a single personal representative, he may give a receipt for capital money arising on the sale,[70] while at least two trustees or a trust corporation are required in the case of a conveyance by a tenant for life or trustees of land.[71] It is necessary for all personal representatives who are registered shareholders of a company to execute any transfer of the shares.[72]

(c) *Tenure of Office*. Formerly a personal representative held his office for life (unless the grant was for a limited period) and could

---

[65] "An assent to the vesting of a legal estate shall be in writing, signed by the personal representative, and shall name the person in whose favour it is given and shall operate to vest in that person the legal estate to which it relates; and an assent not in writing or not in favour of a named person shall not be effectual to pass a legal estate." A.E.A. 1925, s.36(4). This does not apply to the vesting of an equitable interest in land; *Re Edwards's W.T.* [1982] Ch. 30.

[66] [1913] A.C. 76.

[67] *Re Ponder* [1921] 2 Ch. 59; *Re Cockburn* [1957] Ch. 438. See also [1984] Conv. 423 (C. Stebbings).

[68] A.E.A. 1925, s.2(2).

[69] Law of Property (Miscellaneous Provisions) Act 1994, s.16.

[70] L.P.A. 1925, s.27(2).

[71] T.A. 1925, s.14; *post*, p. 557.

[72] Companies Act 1985, s.183(3). For electronic transfer, see *post*, p. 115.

not retire. Now, however, the court may discharge an executor or administrator and appoint a substitute.[73] A trustee, on the other hand, may retire without a court order.[74] Subject to the above, a personal representative's duties terminate with the completion of the administration of the estate, but his liabilities are limited only by effluxion of time. Thus solicitors who were sureties of an administrator and who handed over the residue of the estate to the administrator (who then absconded) were held liable on their bond.[75]

(d) *Duty to Estate: Duty to Beneficiaries.* Executors and trustees are both subject to fiduciary duties. A trustee's duty is to the beneficiaries, and he must "hold the balance evenly between the beneficiaries to whom the property belongs."[76] With an unadministered estate, no legatee, devisee or next of kin, has, as will be seen[77] beneficial ownership of the assets. The executor's duty is to the estate as a whole.[78] In *Re Hayes' Will Trusts*,[79] a testator appointed four persons, including his son, executors and trustees of his will, and gave power to "my trustees . . . to sell . . . to any person . . . including my son despite his being a trustee and in his case at the value placed upon the same for purposes of estate duty." In agreeing the estate duty valuation of the farm, it was held that the executors were not obliged to consider the implications of the fact that a low valuation benefited the son, a high one benefited the other beneficiaries. They negotiated in the usual way with the District Valuer and agreed as low a valuation for tax purposes as they could obtain. This was the usual correct procedure, and they were right to sell to the son at that price.

(e) *Vesting of a Legal Estate.* A further question arises, however, with a legal estate in land. Where trustees under an existing trust make an appointment of a new trustee under a statutory power given to them by Trustee Act 1925, s.36,[80] the legal estate in the trust property vests in the new trustee under section 40.[81] Although personal representatives cannot appoint successors to their offices, they may, after they have become trustees following the completion of the administration of the estate,[82] appoint additional or successor

---

[73] Administration of Justice Act 1985, s.50.
[74] T.A. 1925, ss.36, 39; *post,* p. 502.
[75] *Harvell v. Foster* [1954] 2 Q.B. 367.
[76] *Re Hayes' W.T.* [1971] 1 W.L.R. 758 at p. 764.
[77] *Post,* p. 57.
[78] *Re Charteris* [1917] 2 Ch. 379, where a postponement of sale of some assets acted to the disadvantage of the life tenant, although it was in the interest of the estate.
[79] [1971] 1 W.L.R. 758; (1971) 36 Conv.(N.S.) 136 (J. Mummery).
[80] *Post,* p. 493.
[81] Registration is necessary in the case of registered land.
[82] *Supra,* n. 67. See also Parry and Clark, *The Law of Succession* (10th ed.), pp. 489–493.

trustees. But in *Re King's Will Trusts*,[83] Pennycuick J. held that Trustee Act 1925, s.40 did not apply to an appointment of a new trustee by the surviving executor and trustee of a will, who had not previously assented in writing to the vesting of the legal estate in himself in his capacity as trustee. We have seen that an assent in writing is necessary for the vesting of a legal estate in land, and that it constitutes an essential document of title.[84] The executor could have assented to the vesting of the legal estate in himself and the new trustee after the appointment; or he could have assented, before the appointment, to the vesting in himself as trustee; in which case s.40 would have applied.

This decision has been criticised,[85] and it may have upset a number of titles which have relied on the practice established by earlier cases, but it is consistent with the principle of the 1925 legislation that every dealing with a legal estate in land should be supported by a document of title. An assent to the vesting of an equitable interest in land need not, however, be in writing, and may be inferred from conduct.[86]

ii. The Nature of the Interest of a Legatee or Devisee. A legatee or devisee does not, on the testator's death, become equitable owner of any part of the estate. The executor takes full title to the testator's property, not merely a bare legal estate.[87] He is, by virtue of his office, subjected to various fiduciary duties, which can be enforced against him by persons interested; and these duties are inconsistent with his holding the property on trust for the legatee or devisee.[88] The equitable ownership is "in suspense."[89]

The fiduciary duties of the personal representatives are "to preserve the assets, to deal properly with them, and to apply them in a due course of administration for the benefit of those interested

---

[83] [1964] Ch. 542; Mellows, *The Law of Succession* (5th ed.), pp. 326–327.

[84] *Ante*, p. 55.

[85] (1964) 28 Conv.(N.S.) 298 (J. Garner); (1964) 80 L.Q.R. 328 (R. Walker); (1976) 29 C.L.P. 60 (E. Ryder). But see Law Com. No. 184 (1989), para. 1.6., suggesting that *Re King's Will Trusts* is now accepted in practice and causes no problems.

[86] *Re Edwards's W.T.* [1982] Ch. 30. But see [1982] Conv. 4 (P. Smith) for the view that only an executor, and not an administrator, can make such an implied assent.

[87] *Commissioner of Stamp Duties (Queensland) v. Livingston* [1965] A.C. 694 at pp. 707, 708, 712. But, for the purposes of inheritance tax, a person who would become entitled to a residuary estate (or part thereof) on the completion of the administration is treated as having become entitled at the death of the deceased. Inheritance Tax Act 1984, s.91.

[88] *Sudeley (Lord) v. Att.-Gen.* [1897] A.C. 11; *Barnado's (Dr.) Homes v. Income Tax Special Commissioners* [1920] 1 K.B. 468 at p. 479; [1921] 2 A.C. 1; *Corbett v. Commissioners of Inland Revenue* [1938] 1 K.B. 567 at pp. 575–577; *Passant v. Jackson (Inspector of Taxes)* [1986] S.T.C. 164; see also *Cooper v. Cooper* (1874) L.R. 7 H.L. 53; *Skinner v. Att.-Gen.* [1940] A.C. 350. For a full discussion of Commonwealth cases, see (1967) 45 C.B.R. 219 (D. Waters).

[89] *J. Sainsbury plc v. O'Connor (Inspector of Taxes)* [1991] S.T.C. 318 at p. 326.

according to that course, creditors, the death duty authorities, legatees of various sorts, and the residuary beneficiaries. They might just
as well have been termed 'duties in respect of the assets' as trusts.
What equity did *not* do was to recognise or create for residuary
legatees a beneficial interest in the assets in the executor's hand
during the course of administration."[90] It may be, as with an insolvent estate, that nothing is left which can be applied for the beneficiaries. Even if the estate is solvent, the devisee or legatee is not
the owner in equity of any asset in the estate. He has a chose in
action, a right to compel the administration of the estate. In *Commissioner of Stamp Duties (Queensland) v. Livingston*,[91] the question
was whether succession duty was payable under a Queensland
statute which applied to property situated in Queensland. A widow
died domiciled in New South Wales, and was residuary legatee
under her husband's will. The estate, which was not administered at
the date of the widow's death, contained land in Queensland. The
Privy Council held that succession duty was not payable on that
property. The widow was not the owner of it. She was the owner of
a chose in action, and that was situated in New South Wales, the
state of her domicile. In *Eastbourne Mutual Building Society v.
Hastings Corporation*,[92] a husband occupied a house on his wife's
intestacy. He was unable to claim compensation for the value of the
house on compulsory purchase, because the estate was not administered, and he had no interest in the house. Similarly, in *Lall v.
Lall*,[93] a widow wished to defend an action for possession of the
matrimonial home, which had been owned by her deceased husband.
No grant of administration of his estate had yet been made, and so
she had no *locus standi* to defend the action. In *Re K. (deceased)*[94]
residuary beneficiaries under an unadministered estate had not
acquired an "interest in property" within section 2(7) of the Forfeiture Act 1982 so as to preclude the court from giving relief under
the Act from the forfeiture rule in favour of an applicant who had
killed the testator. On the other hand, in *Re Leigh's Will Trust*,[95] a
bequest by a widow of "all the shares which I hold and any other
interest or assets which I may have" in a particular company was
held to be wide enough to include a claim to her husband's unadministered estate which contained such shares; and her claim passed
under her will. Similarly, where a person entitled under an unadministered estate is bankrupt, the chose in action and its fruits are

---

[90] *Per* Lord Radcliffe [1965] A.C. 694 at p. 707; *Re Hayes' Will Trusts* [1971] 1 W.L.R.
758.
[91] [1965] A.C. 694. See also *Crowden v. Aldridge* [1993] 1 W.L.R. 433; [1994] Conv. 446
(J. Ross Martyn); *Marshall (Inspector of Taxes) v. Kerr* [1995] 1 A.C. 148.
[92] [1965] 1 W.L.R. 861.
[93] [1965] 1 W.L.R. 1249; (1965) 23 C.L.J. 144 (S. Bailey).
[94] [1986] Ch. 180; *post*, p. 317.
[95] [1970] Ch. 277; (1970) 86 L.Q.R. 20 (P.V.B.).

property of the bankrupt capable of passing to his trustee in bankruptcy.[96]

While it is settled that a residuary legatee or devisee or an intestate successor has no equitable interest in any particular assets of an unadministered estate, the position of a specific legatee or devisee is less clear. While there is some authority that such a legatee or devisee does have an equitable interest in the property in question as from the testator's death,[97] some statements in the *Livingston* case cast doubt on this.[98] The view of the Law Commission is that a specific legatee or devisee has no equitable interest during the period of administration.[99] After all, the assets in question may need to be used for the discharge of debts even if the estate is solvent.

A devisee or legatee may be said to become the equitable owner of specific property once property has been allocated by the executor for the purpose.[1] In the case of a residuary gift or a claim on intestacy, the allocation cannot occur until the residuary accounts are prepared.[2] That is the time at which the executors are turning into trustees. The interest of the person entitled then becomes that of a beneficiary under a trust.

G. Powers[3]

i. Trusts Imperative; Powers Discretionary. The distinction between trusts and powers is fundamental. Trusts are imperative; powers are discretionary. Trustees must perform the duties connected with their trusts. A donee of a power may exercise it, or not, at his choice. If the donee of a power created by will predeceases the testator then the power lapses, but it is otherwise in the case of a trust, which does not fail for lack of a trustee.[4]

---

[96] *Official Receiver in Bankruptcy v. Schultz* (1990) 170 C.L.R. 306 (High Court of Australia); [1992] Conv. 92 (J. Maxton).

[97] See *Re Neeld* [1962] Ch. 643 at p. 688.

[98] [1965] A.C. 694 at pp. 707, 708. See also *Official Receiver in Bankruptcy v. Schultz, supra,* at p. 312.

[99] Law Com. No. 188 (1989), para. 2.16; *cf.* Snell, p. 342. Pending administration a specific devisee may make a valid contract to sell the land, which becomes specifically enforceable when his interest becomes proprietary; *Wu Koon Tai v. Wu Yau Loi* [1996] 3 W.L.R. 778.

[1] *Phillipo v. Munnings* (1837) 2 Myl. & Cr. 309.

[2] *Re Claremont* [1923] 2 K.B. 718.

[3] *Farwell on Powers* (3rd ed.); Halsbury's *Laws of England* (4th ed.), Vol. 36, p. 529; (1957) 35 C.B.R. 1060 (O. Marshall); (1953) 69 L.Q.R. 334 (D. Gordon); (1949) 13 Conv.(N.S.) 20 (J. Fleming); (1954) 18 Conv.(N.S.) 565 (F. Crane); (1971) C.L.J. 68 (J. Hopkins); (1971) 87 L.Q.R. 31 (J. Harris). For views on the changing nature of trusts and powers, see [1970] A.S.C.L. 187 (J. Davies); (1974) 37 M.L.R. 643 (Y. Grbich). *Post,* Chap. 6.

[4] *Brown v. Higgs* (1803) 8 Ves. 561.

Trustees are under a duty to hold the trust property for the beneficiaries in accordance with the terms of the trust. The beneficiaries under a trust are the owners in equity of the trust property. Objects of a power own nothing, unless and until the donee of the power makes an appointment in their favour.[5] They merely have a hope that the power will be exercised in their favour. Until the power is exercised, equitable ownership in such a case is in those who will take in default of an appointment, their interest being subject to defeasance on its exercise. Thus, if a testator by his will leaves property to his widow for life and after her death to his children in equal shares, the widow and the children obtain vested interests in the property. Compare this with a gift to the widow for life and after her death as she shall appoint among the children, and, in default of appointment, to charity. Then the children obtain nothing unless and until an appointment is made in their favour.

Whether a trust or a power has been created is dependent upon the construction of the language of the instrument. A properly drafted instrument will leave no room for doubt.

The distinction is however complicated by the fact that a trust may give to the trustees considerable discretion. A trustee may be given a discretion to select beneficiaries from a specified class, or to determine the proportions in which specified beneficiaries are to take. This is the basis of a discretionary trust. Under such a trust no member of a class of the discretionary beneficiaries has an interest in a specific part of the trust property until the discretion of the trustees has been exercised in his favour. The beneficiaries as a whole, however, are the owners of the trust property. If all are adult and under no disability, they may combine together to terminate the trust and demand a distribution of the property.[6] The trustees throughout are under an obligation to perform the trust; that is to say, in the context of a discretionary trust, to exercise their discretion; and so to make a selection after proper consideration. "If the trustees fail to exercise their discretion, the court can compel them to exercise the trust."[7] Thus a beneficiary under a discretionary trust cannot demand payment. He has, however, the right to demand that the trustees exercise their discretion in accordance with the trust. What happens if the trustees refuse to do so is one of the matters discussed in *McPhail v. Doulton*.[8] The court could replace obstructive trustees with willing ones; and, if no suitable trustees would act, the court ultimately would need to make a selection. The point is

---

[5] *Vestey v. I.R.C.* [1980] A.C. 1148.
[6] *Re Smith* [1928] Ch. 915; *Re Nelson* (1918) Ch. 926; *Vestey v. I.R.C. (Nos. 1 and 2)* [1980] A.C. 1148.
[7] *Per* Lord Guest in *McPhail v. Doulton* [1971] A.C. 424 at p. 444; *Re Locker's S.T.* [1977] 1 W.L.R. 1323.
[8] [1971] A.C. 424; *post*, p. 99.

that a discretionary trust puts the trustees under an obligation. Their duty is to make a selection. This is very different from a mere power to appoint; for in that case there is no duty to make a selection. It has been held, however, that the court has similar powers of intervention in the case of a fiduciary power where there is nobody to exercise it.[9]

Although the donee of a mere power of appointment is not obliged to exercise it, he does have certain duties. Thus he must consider periodically whether to exercise it, consider the range of objects, and the appropriateness of individual appointments. If he does decide to exercise the power, he must do so in a responsible manner according to its purpose and, of course, refrain from making any appointment which is not within the terms of the power.[10] This is the case where the power is given to a trustee as such; the duties described above are necessary to the performance of his fiduciary role. Where, however, the donee of the power is not a fiduciary, he is not subjected to these fiduciary duties, although he must, of course, keep within the terms of the power.

But it is difficult in borderline cases to draw a dividing line between discretionary trusts and powers,[11] and between fiduciary and personal powers. The decision turns on the proper construction of the language of the instrument.[12]

The matter is made more difficult by reason of the fact that a discretionary trust may be "exhaustive" or "non-exhaustive." An exhaustive discretionary trust is one where the trustees' duty to exercise their discretion can only be satisfied by making a distribution. A non-exhaustive discretionary trust, on the other hand, is one where the settlor has given the trustees power to decide not to distribute all of the income, for example, by giving them power to accumulate it for a certain period.[13] It must be admitted that the identification of the precise duty in the case of a non-exhaustive discretionary trust is a difficult task. The distinction from a power of appointment is a fine one, and the matter will be further discussed in Chapter 8. For present purposes the position may be summarised as follows: whereas the donee of a fiduciary power of appointment

---

[9] *Mettoy Pension Trustees Ltd v. Evans* [1990] 1 W.L.R. 1587; *post*, p. 170.

[10] *Re Hay's S.T.* [1982] 1 W.L.R. 202; [1982] Conv. 432 (A. Grubb); *Turner v. Turner* [1984] Ch. 100.

[11] *Re Leek* [1969] 1 Ch. 563; *Re Gulbenkian's Settlements* [1970] A.C. 508 at p. 525, *per* Lord Upjohn. *McPhail v. Doulton, supra*, at p. 448; *Vestey v. I.R.C., supra*. See also, in the context of charity, *Re Cohen* [1973] 1 W.L.R. 415.

[12] *Re Scarisbrick's W.T.* [1951] Ch. 622 at p. 635, *per* Lord Evershed M.R.; *Mettoy Pension Trustees Ltd v. Evans* [1990] 1 W.L.R. 1507.

[13] This led some commentators to take the view that there is no longer any analytical distinction between trusts and powers. See [1970] A.S.C.L. 187 (J. Davies); (1974) 37 M.L.R. 643 (Y. Grbich); (1976) 54 C.B.R. 229 (M. Cullity).

need only consider exercising the power, the trustee of a discretionary trust must actually exercise it, although in the case of a non-exhaustive discretionary trust this duty may be satisfied by deciding to accumulate rather than to distribute.

ii. Terminology. Nor is the matter helped by the terminology. Discretionary trusts have been referred to as a "power in the nature of a trust", or "a power coupled with a duty", or even as a "trust power". Terminology of this type adds to confusion. The situation is that if the limitation, on its proper construction, is held to impose a duty, then the limitation creates a trust—though one in which the trustees have a power of selection.

iii. Significance of the Distinction. The question may be material in a number of circumstances.

(a) *Whether the Class Takes if the Discretion is not Exercised.* If there is a gift in favour of such members of a class as X shall select, and X fails to make a selection, will the gift take effect in favour of the class, or will it fail? If the power is construed as a mere power, the non-exercise of the power will cause it to fail,[14] and the property will then pass on default of appointment, or go on resulting trust for the grantor. But if the gift is construed as a gift to the class subject to X's power of selection, the trust in favour of the class will take effect.

In *Burrough v. Philcox*[15] a testator provided that the survivor of his children should have power, by will, "to dispose of all my real and personal estates amongst my nephews and nieces, or their children, either all to one of them or to as many of them as my surviving child shall think proper." No appointments were made and the members of the class were held to take equally as a trust had been created. On the other hand in *Re Weekes' Settlement*,[16] a testatrix gave her husband a life interest and a power "to dispose of all such property by will amongst our children." He died intestate. There was held to be no trust, and so the children took nothing. In neither case was there a gift over in default.

The question is whether, on the proper construction of the limitation, it is possible to show an intention to benefit the objects in the

---

[14] Subject to *Mettoy Pension Trustees Ltd v. Evans* [1990] 1 W.L.R. 1587; *post*, p. 170.
[15] (1840) 5 Myl. & Cr. 72. Such a trust, it is submitted, should be regarded as a fixed trust subject to defeasance by exercise of the power of selection, and thus unaffected by *McPhail v. Doulton*, *infra*. See *post*, p. 109.
[16] [1897] 1 Ch. 289.

event of no appointment being made.[17] It has been said that the courts are more inclined to such a construction when the objects are small in number, such as children under a marriage settlement.[18] But in *McPhail v. Doulton*[19] a deed was held to create a trust which provided that the trustees "shall apply the net income in making at their absolute discretion" grants to employees, past and present, and their dependants. The principle to be applied was laid down by Lord Cottenham in *Burrough v. Philcox*.[20] "When there appears a general intention in favour of a class, and a particular intention in favour of individuals of a class to be selected by another person, and the particular intention fails, from that selection not being made, the Court will carry into effect the general intention in favour of the class." The presence of a gift over in default of appointment destroys any such implication; the gift over shows that the settlor is providing for a situation where the donee does not appoint to the class; and this is inconsistent with a trust in favour of the class.[21] But there is no hard and fast rule that a trust is intended if there is no gift over.[22]

Where the court finds that there is a trust, the question arises of the share which each of the beneficiaries will take. In the nineteenth century cases, where the question usually arose in the context of division among a family group, the rule of equal division was applied, on the principle that equality was equity.[23] Such a solution would be particularly inappropriate in the context of modern trusts in favour of employees of companies and their dependants. In *McPhail v. Doulton*,[24] the House of Lords, as we have seen, was more courageous, and accepted the obligation, where necessary, of itself making a decision on division.

(b) *The Test of Certainty.* With both trusts and powers, it is necessary for the beneficiaries, or the objects, to be defined with sufficient certainty to enable the trustees or the donees to exercise their functions, and for the court to supervise them. Before the

---

[17] *Harding v. Glyn* (1739) 1 Atk. 469; *Re Llewellyn's Settlement* [1921] 2 Ch. 281; *Re Arnold* [1947] Ch. 131.

[18] *Re Perowne* [1951] Ch. 785 at p. 790.

[19] [1971] A.C. 424.

[20] (1840) 5 Myl. & Cr. 72 at p. 92.

[21] This is so even if the gift is void; *Re Sprague* (1880) 43 L.T. 236. But it would not be so because of a residuary gift, or a gift over in default of there being any objects of the power; *Re Brierly* (1894) 43 W.R. 36; *Re Leek* [1969] 1 Ch. 563.

[22] *Re Weekes* [1879] 1 Ch. 289; *Re Combe* [1925] Ch. 210; *Re Perowne* [1951] Ch. 785; *McPhail v. Doulton* [1971] A.C. 424.

[23] This will still be the result if such was the settlor's intention; *post*, p. 109.

[24] [1971] A.C. 424. Equal division would not be possible in any event if the total membership of the class was not known. As will be seen, the certainty test propounded in *McPhail v. Doulton* does not require all the objects to be ascertained.

decision of the House of Lords in *McPhail v. Doulton*,[25] it was necessary to draw a distinction between the requirement of certainty in the case of trusts (fixed and discretionary) and that required for mere powers. *McPhail v. Doulton*, however, decided that the test was the same for discretionary trusts and mere powers. The test came from *Re Gulbenkian's Settlements*,[26] a case on a power, and is whether "it can be said with certainty that any given individual is or is not a member of the class."[27] This test will be discussed in detail in Chapter 3. But it may be said here that the assimilation of the test of certainty for discretionary trusts and mere powers has greatly reduced the practical significance of the distinction between them. Prior to *McPhail v. Doulton*,[28] most of the litigation on the distinction between discretionary trusts and mere powers concerned the question whether a limitation had to comply only with the above test; or whether it was void for failure to comply with a stricter test which had earlier been applicable to all trusts.[29] That test was whether the description of the beneficiaries enabled the trustee to draw up a full list of the beneficiaries. That test still remains applicable to "fixed" as opposed to discretionary trusts; that is to say trusts which give a specific share to each beneficiary. Unless the court could make a complete list of all the beneficiaries, it would be impossible to make a division, or to supervise the trustees if they failed to distribute.

(c) *Terminating the Trust.* Where all the beneficiaries of a discretionary trust are adult and under no disability they may determine the trust and require the trust property to be shared out.[30] On the other hand, objects of a power can never claim any proprietary interest in the property until the power has been exercised in their favour.

2. CLASSIFICATION OF TRUSTS

Trusts have been variously classified and subdivided. The categories are not exclusive; some trusts could appear in more than one category. The basic division is between private trusts, and public or charitable trusts. Charitable trusts, which are dealt with in Chapter 15, are trusts for certain purposes which are so beneficial to the

---

[25] *Supra.*
[26] [1970] A.C. 508.
[27] *Per* Lord Wilberforce in *McPhail v. Doulton, ante,* at p. 456; *Re Baden's Deed Trusts (No. 2)* [1973] Ch. 9, *post,* p. 99.
[28] [1971] A.C. 424.
[29] *I.R.C. v. Broadway Cottages Trust Ltd* [1955] Ch. 20.
[30] *Re Smith* [1928] 1 Ch. 915.

community that the Attorney-General undertakes responsibility for their enforcement. They are accorded special privileges in terms of non-liability to tax, and in terms of perpetual duration. Private trusts, on the other hand, are trusts for persons, the beneficiaries; and the beneficiaries can enforce the trust. It may also be noted here that there are a few anomalous cases in which trusts for non-charitable purposes, usually for the building of monuments or the upkeep of particular animals, have been upheld. Such trusts are usually called non-charitable purpose trusts, or trusts of imperfect obligation. The latter name indicates one of their main anomalies; who will enforce such a trust? These trusts are dealt with in Chapter 14.

Private trusts are divided into express, constructive and resulting trusts; and express trusts may be divided into executed and executory, and into completely constituted and incompletely constituted trusts. Sometimes implied trusts are included as a further category of private trusts.[31] This classification serves little purpose, and the examples commonly given might preferably be regarded as express, resulting or constructive trusts, as the case may be. Trusts have often been established although express words to that effect have not been used,[32] yet such trusts are "express" because the settlors intended to create them. Trusts based on the presumed intention of the settlor as, for example, in the case of a voluntary conveyance, are sometimes described as implied trusts, but will here be treated as resulting trusts. Mutual wills are also sometimes described as implied trusts,[33] but will here be treated as constructive trusts. The term may be used as meaning any private trust which is not express, but the matter is purely one of terminology.

A. Express Trusts

An express trust is one intentionally declared by the creator of the trust, who is known a the settlor, or, if the trust is created by will, the testator. A trust is created by a manifestation of an intention to create a trust; though certain formalities, as will be seen, are required in the case of lifetime trusts of land and of all testamentary trusts.

Two subdivisions of express trusts should be mentioned.

(i) Executed and Executory. An executed trust is one in which the testator or settlor has marked out in appropriate technical expressions what interests are to be taken by all the beneficiaries. On the other hand, in an executory trust, the execution of some further instrument is required, in order to define the beneficial interests with

---

[31] Such a classification at times appears in statutes, for example, L.P.A. 1925 s.53(2).

[32] See *Paul v. Constance* [1977] 1 W.L.R. 527, and the cases discussed under the heading "Certainty of Intention," *post*, p. 90.

[33] Snell, p. 191.

precision. The property is immediately subject to a valid trust, but it remains executory until the further instrument is duly executed.

The practical significance of the distinction is that while the language of executed trusts is governed by strict rules of construction, executory trusts are construed more liberally. Where, in the case of an executed trust, the settlor has made use of technical expressions, as to the interpretation of which the law has laid down rules, equity will follow the law and give effect to such interpretation.[34] In the case of an executory trust, however, equity will attach less importance to the use or omission of technical words, but will seek to discover the settlor's true intention, and order the preparation of a final deed which gives effect to such intention. It is necessary, however, for the court to be able to ascertain, from the language of the instrument, the trusts which are intended to be imposed on the property.[35]

Executory trusts appeared most commonly in marriage articles, which often provided that certain property belonging to one of the parties should be settled upon them and their issue, and in wills. They are rarely met at the present day; due no doubt to the fact that many modern trusts have tax-saving implications, and it is necessary, for such purposes, to be precise and specific in drafting the trust.

A pension fund trust provides a more modern example. In *Davis v. Richards & Wallington Industries Ltd*[36] the question arose as to entitlement to surplus funds. A pension scheme had been established by an interim trust deed, which provided for the execution of a definitive trust deed. This deed was later executed, and contained rules as to the entitlement to any surplus, but there was doubt as to its validity. In fact the definitive deed was upheld, but if it had not been, the court would have held the interim deed to be a valid executory trust. This could have been executed by a court order bringing into effect rules corresponding to those in the definitive deed, thereby resolving the issue as to the surplus.

(ii) Completely and Incompletely Constituted Trusts.

There cannot be a trust unless the trust is completely constituted. This heading is therefore irrational; it is dealing, not with two different types of trust, but with a rule for distinguishing what is a trust from something that is void. Nevertheless, it is convenient to make the point here, and to deal in more detail with the matter below.[37]

---

[34] *Re Bostock's Settlement* [1921] 2 Ch. 469; see also L.P.A. 1925, s.60(1); *cf. Re Arden* [1935] Ch. 326.

[35] *Re Flavel's Will Trusts* [1966] 1 W.L.R. 445 at p. 447 ("for formation of a superannuation and bonus fund for the employees").

[36] [1990] 1 W.L.R. 1511.

[37] *Post*, Chap. 4.

A trust is only valid if the title to the property is in the trustee and if the trusts have been validly declared. A declaration that A holds on trust for B is ineffective if the property is not vested in A. The trust becomes constituted and valid when the property is vested in A. The form of transfer to A depends on the nature of the property —land, chattel, money, shares in a company, copyrights, patents, debts or other choses in action—and the appropriate method must of course be used.[38] In the case of a trust of land there must also be written evidence of the declaration of trust.[39] The settlor may of course declare himself trustee, and there is then an automatic constitution, because title was in the settlor throughout. Testamentary trusts are always completely constituted; for the executors, if not the trustees themselves, are under a duty to transfer the trust property to the nominated trustees.

Although no trust is created unless the trust is completely constituted, there are situations where intended beneficiaries under an incompletely constituted trust may compel the transfer of the property to the trustees. In general, they can do so if they have given consideration, but not if they are volunteers, for there is yet no trust and "equity will not assist a volunteer."[40]

B. Resulting Trusts[41]

A resulting trust exists where property has been conveyed to another, but the beneficial interest returns, or "results" to the transferor. This may happen in various situations; the simplest one is where the property is conveyed to trustees upon certain trusts which fail or which do not exhaust the whole beneficial interest. The part undisposed of results to the settlor. For example, if there is a gift on trust for A for life and then on trust for X if X attains the age of 21, but X dies under 21 in A's lifetime, the property will result on A's death to the settlor.

Such a resulting trust has been described as "automatic,"[42] meaning that it arises by operation of law, without depending on the intention of the settlor. Indeed it may be what he most wished to avoid, because, for example, it imposes a tax liability upon him.[43] Resulting trusts of this kind are akin to constructive trusts in so far as they appear to arise independently of intention. Indeed, some

---

[38] *Post*, pp. 114 *et seq.*
[39] L.P.A. 1925, s.53; *post*, p. 76.
[40] *Post*, Chap. 4.
[41] *Post*, Chap. 10.
[42] *Per* Megarry J. in *Re Vandervell's Trust (No. 2)* [1974] Ch. 269 at p. 291.
[43] *Vandervell v. I.R.C.* [1967] 2 A.C. 291.

cases treat the two kinds of trust as almost synonymous.[44] The better view, however, is that the so-called "automatic" resulting trust gives effect to the settlor's presumed intention, as is shown by the fact that the beneficial interest goes to the Crown as *bona vacantia* if the settlor has expressly or impliedly abandoned it.[45]

Another category, clearly based on the presumed intention of the settlor, is the "presumed" resulting trust in favour of the transferor where property is conveyed to a volunteer. The presumption is rebuttable by evidence of an intention to make a gift or, where the volunteer is the transferor's wife or child, by the presumption of advancement.[46]

C. Constructive Trusts[47]

While express trusts arise from the act of the parties, constructive trusts arise by operation of law. Equity says that in certain circumstances the legal owner of property must hold it on trust for others. The absence of the need for formalities in such circumstances is obvious. There is, however, much dispute and uncertainty as to the occasions on which constructive trusts arise, and also as to their nature.

The term has indeed been used in different senses. It can cover the duty of a trustee who has obtained benefits by fraud; the obligation of a transferee from an express trustee, unless he proves he was a bona fide purchaser for value without notice, to hold the transferred property on the trusts previously applicable; the obligation of a trustee who has made a profit, however innocently, through his office, to hold such profit for the benefit of his beneficiaries[48]; the position of a stranger to the trust who has dishonestly assisted in a breach of trust[49]; the relationship of vendor and purchaser between the contract and the execution of the conveyance[50]; and other relationships, such as licensees, and claimants to a matrimonial home, where the introduction of a constructive trust was considered to be

---

[44] *Per* Lord Denning M.R. in *Hussey v. Palmer* [1972] 1 W.L.R. 1286 at p. 1289; *Cooke v. Head* [1972] 1 W.L.R. 518; *Eves v. Eves* [1975] 1 W.L.R. 1338; *Burns v. Burns* [1984] Ch. 317; *Passee v. Passee* [1988] 1 F.L.R. 263 at p. 269. A claim based on a constructive trust can give a greater share than one based on a resulting trust in the context of the family home; *post*, p. 270.

[45] *Westdeutsche Landesbank Girozentrale v. Islington London Borough Council* [1996] A.C. 669 at p. 708.

[46] *Post*, p. 246.

[47] *Post*, Chap. 12. Waters, *The Constructive Trust*; Oakley, *Constructive Trusts* (3rd ed.).

[48] *Keech v. Sandford* (1726) Sel.Cas.t. King 61; *Boardman v. Phipps* [1967] 2 A.C. 46.

[49] *Post*, p. 294.

[50] *Post*, p. 312.

necessary to enable the court to reach a just solution.[51] A controversial question is whether the "remedial" constructive trust, favoured in some commonwealth jurisdictions, is available to prevent unjust enrichment whenever the personal remedy is inadequate.

Lord Denning M.R. pioneered a constructive trust "of a new model,"[52] to be imposed "whenever justice and good conscience required it ... " as an equitable remedy "by which the court can enable an aggrieved party to obtain restitution."[53] The implications of these developments will be discussed in Chapter 12.

D. Bare Trusts

A distinction is sometimes made between bare or simple trusts, on the one hand, and "special" trusts on the other. There is said to be a bare trust when the trustee holds trust property in trust for an adult beneficiary absolutely. In such a situation the beneficiary may call for a conveyance of the legal estate at any time, and the trustee must comply.[54] In the meantime the trustee has no duties to perform and must deal with the trust property in accordance with the instructions of the beneficiary.[55]

It is said that all other trusts are "special" trusts. The description however, is not generally used except as a mode of contrast with a bare or simple trust.

A bare trust may arise at the outset, as where an absolute owner puts shares into the name of trustees[56] or some other third party[57] to hold for himself. This may arise in a commercial context, as where a solicitor holds money for a client.[58] A trust which was not originally a bare trust may become one when an adult beneficiary becomes absolutely entitled, as on the death of A in a trust for A for life, remainder to B. A bare trust need not be express, but can take the form of a resulting or constructive trust, as where the settlor fails to declare the beneficial interests[59] or did not intend any beneficial interest to pass to the fraudulent transferee.[60]

A bare trustee into whose name an absolute owner transfers property is sometimes called a nominee. This must be distinguished

---

[51] *Binions v. Evans* [1972] Ch. 359 (licensee); *Eves v. Eves* [1975] 1 W.L.R. 1338 (cohabitant); *Re Densham* [1975] 1 W.L.R. 1519 (wife). See *post*, p. 317.
[52] *Eves v. Eves* [1975] 1 W.L.R. 1338.
[53] *Hussey v. Palmer* [1972] 1 W.L.R. 1286 at p. 1289.
[54] As, indeed, could a multiplicity of beneficiaries, all adult and under no disability; *Saunders v. Vautier* (1841) 4 Beav. 115; *post*, p. 612.
[55] *Re Cunningham and Fray* [1891] 2 Ch. 567; Pettit, p. 65; (1992) 1 J.I.P. 3 (D. Hayton).
[56] *Grey v. I.R.C.* [1960] A.C. 1.
[57] *Hardoon v. Belilios* [1901] A.C. 119.
[58] *Target Holdings Ltd v. Redferns (a firm)* [1996] 1 A.C. 421; *post*, p. 634.
[59] *Vandervell v. I.R.C.* [1967] 2 A.C. 291.
[60] *Hodgson v. Marks* [1971] Ch. 892.

from the situation where the trustees vest securities in a nominee in order to facilitate share dealings. Such a person is in effect an agent of the trustees.[61]

E. Trusts in the Higher Sense and Trusts in the Lower Sense

The word "trust" is used in various contexts which have no relationship to the legal meaning of the term.[62] The Crown may entrust ministers or officials with property, perhaps providing that they shall hold it "in trust" for the benefit of some person or body of persons. While such a situation is capable of creating a trust in the legal or "lower" sense, " 'trust" is not a term of art in public law and when used in relation to matters which lie within the field of public law, the words 'in trust' may do no more than indicate the existence of a duty owned to the Crown by the officer of state as servant of the Crown, to deal with the property for the benefit of the subject for whom it is expressed to be held in trust, such duty being enforced administratively or by disciplinary sanctions and not otherwise; *Kinlock v. Secretary of State for India*.[63]"[64] Similarly, where it is alleged that the Crown is trustee for members of the public. In *Tito v. Waddell*[65] phosphate had been mined on Ocean Island by a British company until 1920, when the mining rights were acquired by the governments of the United Kingdom, Australia and New Zealand. The Ocean Islanders claimed, *inter alia*, that the Crown stood in a fiduciary position to them and was liable for various breaches of trust. The claim failed. Although the relevant documents and Mining Ordinances used the word "trust", their wording was, as a matter of construction, consonant with the creation of a governmental obligation, for the breach of which the court was powerless to give relief. This governmental obligation, or "trust in the higher sense", was not a true trust in the conventional sense. It created no fiduciary obligation, and was not justiciable in the courts.

---

[61] *Post*, p. 568 (delegation of powers). See also custodian trustees; *post*, p. 489.
[62] See [1996] Conv. 186 (R. Bartlett), discussing National Health Service Trusts.
[63] (1882) 7 App.Cas. 619.
[64] *Per* Lord Diplock in *Town Investments Ltd v. Department of the Environment* [1978] A.C. 359 at p. 382. But the Crown can be a trustee in the "lower sense"; *Civilian War Claimants Association Ltd. v. R.* [1932] A.C. 14; *Lonhro Exports Ltd v. Export Credits Guarantee Department* [1996] 4 All E.R. 673.
[65] (*No. 2*) [1977] Ch. 106.

PART II

TRUSTS AND POWERS

CHAPTER 3

REQUIREMENTS OF A TRUST

1. Capacity to Create a Trust 73
   A. Minors 73
   B. Mentally Incapacitated Persons 74
2. Formalities 75
   A. *Inter Vivos* 75
      i. Creation 75
      ii. The Instrument of Fraud
          Principle 76
      iii. Disposition 78
          (a) Assignment of Equitable
              Interest 79
          (b) Direction to Trustees to Hold
              on Trust for Another 79
          (c) Conveyance of Legal Estate
              by Trustee 80
          (d) Declaration of Trust with Con-
              sent of Beneficial Owner 82
          (e) Declaration by Equitable
              Owner of Himself as Trustee .. 84
          (f) Specifically Enforceable Oral
              Contracts for Sale 84
          (g) Variation of Trusts Act
              1958 88
          (h) Right of Nomination under
              Staff Pension Fund 88
          (i) Disclaimer 88
   B. By Will 89

3. Certainty 89
   A. Certainty of Intention 90
   B. Certainty of Subject-Matter 93
   C. Certainty of Objects; The Bene-
      ficiaries 97
      i. Fixed Trusts 98
      ii. Discretionary Trusts 99
      iii. Conceptual Uncertainty and
           Evidential Difficulties 101
      iv. Problems with the Test 102
          (a) What is Conceptually
              Certain? 102
          (b) Proof of Inclusion and
              Exclusion; Proving Neg-
              atives 103
          (c) Width of the Class; Admin-
              istrative Unworkability 104
          (d) Capriciousness 106
          (e) Duty to Survey the Field 107
          (f) Many Certain Categories; One
              Uncertain 108
      v. Effect of Certainty Test on Rights
         of Objects 108
      vi. Trust Powers in the Old Sense;
          Trusts with a Power of Selection 109
      vii. Gifts Subject to a Condition
           Precedent 109

1. CAPACITY TO CREATE A TRUST

CAPACITY to create a trust is, generally speaking, co-extensive with the ability to hold and dispose of a legal or equitable interest in property, but there are two special situations to consider.

A. Minors

A settlement made by a minor is voidable; he may repudiate it during minority, or within a reasonable time of attaining his majority,[1] which is the age of 18.

[1] *Edwards v. Carter* [1893] A.C. 360.

A minor may not hold a legal estate in land.[2] If a minor becomes entitled to a freehold or leasehold, the land is held in trust for the minor.[3]

B. Mentally Incapacitated Persons

Mental incapacity may affect the ability of a person to make a will, or a gift or to create a trust. In the case of a lifetime gift, it seems that the test varies according to the size of the gift and its relationship to the sum of the assets owned by the donor. In *Re Beaney*[4] a mother who was suffering from senile dementia made a gift of her house, the only substantial asset of her estate, to one daughter, Valerie, who had stayed at home to look after her mother for many years; but this had the effect of virtually disinheriting the other two (married) children. The position was summarised as follows[5]:

"The degree or extent of understanding required in respect of any instrument is relative to the particular transaction which it is to effect. In the case of a will the degree required is always high. In the case of a contract, a deed made for consideration or a gift *inter vivos*, whether by deed or otherwise, the degree required varies with the circumstances of the transaction. Thus, at one extreme, if the subject-matter and value of a gift are trivial in relation to the donor's other assets a low degree of understanding will suffice. But, at the other, if its effect is to dispose of the donor's only assets of value and thus for practical purposes to pre-empt the devolution of his estate under his will or on his intestacy, then the degree of understanding required is as high as that required for a will, and the donor must understand the claims of all potential donees and the extent of the property to be disposed of."

It was held that Mrs Beaney's gift to Valerie was void, because she was not capable of understanding the conflicting claims of her other children. These problems can be avoided if steps are taken to place the affairs of the donor under the control of the Court of Protection.

Under the Mental Health Act 1983 the Court of Protection has wide powers of dealing with the property and affairs of a person

---

[2] L.P.A. 1925, s.1(6).

[3] Trusts of Land and Appointment of Trustees Act 1996, Sched. 1, para. 1.

[4] [1978] 1 W.L.R. 770; [1978] Conv. 387 (F. Crane). See also *Simpson v. Simpson* [1992] 1 F.L.R. 601 (life-time gift which upset the balance of the will held void for want of mental capacity. Transferee of bank deposits held them on resulting trust).

[5] At p. 774. See *Ball v. Mannin* (1829) 3 Bli.(N.S.) 1; *Manches v. Trimborn* (1946) 115 L.J.K.B. 305.

whom the judge is satisfied is incapable, by reason of mental disorder, of managing and administering his property and affairs.[6]

The guiding principle for the court is the consideration of what the patient would be likely to do if he were not subject to the disability. Thus, in *Re T.B.*,[7] the court approved the creation of a revocable trust in favour of the patient's illegitimate child; the property would otherwise have passed on intestacy to remoter relatives. If the matter had arisen after 1969, the court could have authorised the making of a will for the patient. Since that date,[8] the court has had power to make a will for an adult mental patient, if the judge has reason to believe that the patient lacks testamentary capacity. The judge must make such a will as the actual, and not a hypothetical patient, acting reasonably, would have been likely to make if restored to full mental capacity, memory and foresight, taking into account the beliefs, affections and antipathies he had (provided they were not "beyond reason") before losing testamentary capacity.[9] If the patient has never had capacity, the court will assume that he would have been a normal, decent person who would have acted in accordance with contemporary standards of morality.[10]

Applications to the court for the approval of schemes affecting the patient's property have commonly been brought in circumstances in which it was desirable in the interests of the family to reduce the tax liability of a rich patient. The applicant must show that the scheme is for the benefit of the patient.[11] It is sufficient that it is the sort of settlement which the patient would be likely to make in favour of other members of the family if he had been subject to no mental abnormality.[12]

2. FORMALITIES[13]

A. Inter Vivos

i. Creation. The basic rule is that a settlor may create a trust by manifesting an intention to create it. No formalities are required for

---

[6] M.H.A. 1983, s.95. A settlement may be ordered under s.96(1)(*d*).

[7] [1967] Ch. 247. See also *Re S (Gifts by Mental Patient)* [1997] 1 F.L.R. 96.

[8] A.J.A. 1969, adding the provisions now found in M.H.A. 1983, ss.96(1)(*e*) and 97; (1970) 34 Conv.(N.S.) 150 (D. Hart and M. Reed); *Practice Direction* [1970] 1 W.L.R. 259; *Practice Note* [1983] 1 W.L.R. 1077. See *Re Davey* [1981] 1 W.L.R. 164.

[9] *Re D. (J.)* [1982] Ch. 237.

[10] *Re C (a patient)* [1991] 3 All E.R. 866.

[11] See *Re Ryan* [1911] W.N. 56.

[12] See *Re C.W.M.* [1951] 2 K.B. 714; *Re C.* [1960] 1 W.L.R. 92; *Re C.E.F.D.* [1963] 1 W.L.R. 329. For the variation of existing trusts, see Chap. 22.

[13] A Law Commission review is proposed; Law Com. No. 239, para. 5.20.

the creation of an *inter vivos* trust of personalty.[14] Evidence in writing is required for the creation of a trust of land, and all testamentary trusts must be in writing, signed by the testator and attested by two witnesses as required by the Wills Act 1837, s.9.[15]

It is necessary, however, to observe literally every word of the basic rule. The intention must be to *create a trust*; a general intention to benefit someone will not suffice.[16] The words or acts of the settlor must be sufficient to establish an intention that either another person (or persons), or the settlor himself, shall be trustee of property for the beneficiary. In practice *inter vivos* trusts are created in writing and usually by deed. Such trusts usually have as one of their objects the saving of tax, and this can only be achieved where there is clear documentary proof of the date and terms of the trust.

With regard to trusts of land, the Law of Property Act 1925, s.53(1)(*b*), provides:

> "A declaration of trust respecting any land or any interest therein must be manifested and proved by some writing signed by some person who is able to declare such trust or by his will."[17]

The writing is required as evidence of intention; the declaration need not itself be in writing. Failure to comply with the requirements of s.53(1)(*b*) renders the trust unenforceable, and not void.[18] The signature will normally be that of the settlor, although there is authority that the transferee of the land may sign.[19]

These requirements apply to express trusts only, and not to resulting, implied or constructive trusts,[20] although, as will be seen from the case-law discussed below, dispositions of interests arising under such trusts are subject to the formality requirements.

ii. The Instrument of Fraud Principle. The question which next arises concerns the effect, if any, of an oral declaration of a trust of land. What should be done if a transferee procures a conveyance of land to him on the strength of a oral agreement to hold on trust for the transferor or a third party, and then seeks to shelter behind the statute?

---

[14] *M'Fadden v. Jenkyns* (1842) 1 Ph. 153; *Paul v. Constance* [1977] 1 W.L.R. 521; *Re Kayford* [1975] 1 W.L.R. 279.

[15] *Post*, p. 89.

[16] *Jones v. Lock* (1865) L.R. 1 Ch.App. 25; *post*, p. 119; *Paul v. Constance* [1977] 1 W.L.R. 521.

[17] Replacing Statute of Frauds 1677, s.7.

[18] *Gardner v. Rowe* (1828) 5 Russ. 258.

[19] *Ibid.*

[20] L.P.A. 1925, s.53(2). Nor do they apply to trusts arising from co-ownership; *Roy v. Roy* [1996] 1 F.L.R. 541.

Equity, where possible, will not permit a statute to be a cloak for fraud. The question is whether equity can, by acting *in personam* against the fraudulent party, prevent the fraud without disregarding the statute.

In *Rochefoucauld v. Boustead*,[21] the plaintiff was the mortgagor of the Delmar Estates in Ceylon. They were sold by the mortgagee to the defendant, who had orally agreed to hold the estates on trust for the plaintiff subject to the repayment to the defendant of the purchase price, and expenses. The defendant sold the land at a profit, but did not account to the plaintiff. The defendant became bankrupt.

The plaintiff obtained an order for an account. The Court of Appeal refused to allow the Statute of Frauds to prevent the proof of fraud; and " . . . it is a fraud on the part of a person to whom land is conveyed as a trustee, and who knows it was so conveyed, to deny the trust and claim the land himself. Consequently, notwithstanding the statute, it is competent for a person claiming land conveyed to another to prove by parol evidence that it was so conveyed upon trust for the claimant, and that the grantee, knowing the facts, is denying the trust and relying upon the form of conveyance and the statute, in order to keep the land himself."[22]

The principle of this decision is that in the case of fraud oral evidence is admissible to establish the trust in spite of the statute. On this basis trust is express,[23] although modern cases have tended to treat trusts established in this way as constructive.[24]

Where the conveyance is by A to B on an oral trust for A, the effect of this doctrine is clearly that B holds on trust for A. The more difficult case is where the conveyance is by A to B on an oral trust for C. Should the beneficial interest be enjoyed by C, or held on resulting trust for A? The latter is all that is necessary to prevent B's unjust enrichment; to give the benefit to C looks like a disregard of the statute. It is a question of balancing the policy of the formality requirement against the injustice which may be caused by relying on the formality rule. If the trust is properly to be classified as express,

---

[21] [1897] 1 Ch. 196. See also *Davies v. Otty (No. 2)* (1865) 35 Beav. 208; *McCormick v. Grogan* (1869) L.R. 4 H.L. 82; *Bannister v. Bannister* [1948] 2 All E.R. 133; *Hodgson v. Marks* [1971] Ch. 892; *Binions v. Evans* [1972] Ch. 359; *Lyus v. Prowsa Ltd* [1982] 1 W.L.R. 1044; *Du Boulay v. Raggett* (1989) 58 P. & C.R. 12.

[22] *Per* Lindley L.J. at p. 206.

[23] So held in *Rochefoucauld v. Boustead, supra,* but specifically in the context of the Limitation Act 1874.

[24] *Bannister v. Bannister, supra; Binions v. Evans, supra; Re Densham* [1975] 1 W.L.R. 1519; *Neale v. Willis* (1968) 19 P. & C.R. 839; *Ashburn Anstalt v. Arnold* [1989] Ch. 1. See further Elias, *Explaining Constructive Trusts,* pp. 106–113.

it is easier to say that C should benefit, especially as the effect of section 53(1)(*b*) is that the trust is not void but merely unenforceable. There are authorities tending to support C's claim,[25] and some commentators favour this view.[26] More compelling is the view that B should hold on trust for A.[27] To go further leaves section 53(1)(*b*) applying only where A orally declares himself trustee. The fraud doctrine cannot be invoked here, and it has been held that the beneficiary cannot assert a constructive trust and thereby avoid section 53(1)(*b*) unless he has acted to his detriment in reliance on the declaration.[28]

A similar question arises where a prospective legatee or devisee agrees with the testator to hold the property on trust for C. Here the doctrine of secret trusts allows C to benefit in spite of the requirements of the Wills Act 1837. Here the resulting trust solution is less appropriate because it is too late for the testator to make other provision for C. This is discussed in Chapter 5.

iii. Disposition.[29] A disposition of an equitable interest is required to be in writing; otherwise, the disposition is void. Section 53(1)(*c*) provides.[30]

> "A disposition of an equitable interest or trust subsisting at the time of the disposition must be in writing signed by the person disposing of the same, or by his agent thereunto lawfully authorised in writing or by will."

"The subsection . . . " said Lord Wilberforce,[31] "is certainly not easy to apply to the various transactions in equitable interests which now occur." Such transactions include attempts to avoid stamp duty on share transfers, and the practice of putting shareholdings in nominees. Modern litigation has established some fine, and not always logical, distinctions.

---

[25] *Taylor v. Salmon* (1838) 4 Myl. & Cr. 134; *Binions v. Evans, supra; Neale v. Willis, supra; Lyus v. Prowsa Ltd, supra. Rochefoucauld v. Boustead* itself should not be regarded as such a case because effectively A arranged with B that B would buy from the mortgagee and hold on trust for A.

[26] (1915) 28 H.L.R. 237 at p. 366 (G. Costigan); (1984) 43 C.L.J. 306 and [1988] Conv. 267 (T. Youdan). See also Elias, *Explaining Constructive Trusts*, pp. 103 *et seq.* (supporting C's claim in the context of a wider view that formality rules should be abolished).

[27] [1987] Conv. 246 (J. Feltham). But as the oral declaration is not void, B may convey to C unless A has revoked his authority to do so.

[28] *Midland Bank Ltd v. Dobson* [1986] 1 F.L.R. 171; *cf. Re Densham* [1975] 1 W.L.R. 1519.

[29] (1966) 24 C.L.J. 19 (G. Jones); (1967) 31 Conv.(N.S.) 175 (S. Spencer); [1975] Ottawa L.R. 483 and [1979] Conv. 17 (G. Battersby); (1978) 94 L.Q.R.. 170 (D. Sugarman and F. Webb).

[30] Re-enacting Statute of Frauds 1677, s.9, with some alterations, the most significant one being that s.9 applied to "all grants and assignments of any trust or confidence" while s.53(1)(*c*) applies to a "disposition of an equitable interest."

[31] In *Vandervell v. I.R.C.* [1967] 2 A.C. 291 at p. 329.

Of course, it might be said that the equitable interest is disposed of whenever an absolute owner declares himself trustee of the property. Such a view would, however, make section 53(1)(*b*) meaningless. The word "subsisting" in section 53(1)(*c*) indicates that the subsection only applies where the equitable interest has already been separated from the legal estate.

(a) *Assignment of Equitable Interest.* The simple case is where a beneficiary under a trust assigns his interest to another. This is a disposition of an equitable interest, and is void unless in writing. This is so, whether the beneficial interest is a limited interest, such as a life interest, or an absolute interest which is held on a bare trust by a nominee. The subsection applies to equitable interests in both land and personalty.[32] The disposition must actually be in writing, and not merely evidenced in writing,[33] but a number of connected documents can provide the necessary writing.[34]

(b) *Direction to Trustees to Hold on Trust for Another.* Where a beneficiary directs the trustee to hold his interest upon other trusts, there is a disposition of the beneficiary's interest. This is the basis of *Grey v. I.R.C.*,[35] which was concerned with an attempt by the settlor to save stamp duty on shares being put into the settlement. At that time *ad valorem* stamp duty (*i.e.* varying with the value of the interest transferred) was payable on deeds of gift, although this is no longer the position.[36] Where stamp duty is payable, it is payable upon instruments whereby property is transferred, and not upon transactions.[37]

In *Grey v. I.R.C.*,[38] the settlor made six settlements of nominal sums in favour of his grandchildren. Later, he transferred shares of substantial value to the trustees, as his nominees, on trust for himself. That transfer attracted only nominal stamp duty. Then he orally instructed the trustees to hold that property upon the trusts of the six settlements. Finally, the trustees executed documents confirming that they held the shares upon the trusts of the settlements. The settlor, though not expressed to be a party, executed the documents.

It was accepted that the trusts were validly declared. The question was whether they were declared by the settlor's oral

---

[32] See (1984) 47 M.L.R. 385 at 388 (B. Green), discussing L.P.A. 1925, s.205(1)(x).
[33] *cf.* L.P.A. 1925, s.53(1)(*b*). See further n. 39, *infra*.
[34] *Re Danish Bacon Co. Staff Pension Fund Trusts* [1971] 1 W.L.R. 248 at p. 255.
[35] [1960] A.C. 1; (1960) C.L.J. 31 (J. Thornley); [1979] Conv. 17 (G. Battersby); (1984) 47 M.L.R. 385 (B. Green). See also *Crowden v. Aldridge* [1993] 1 W.L.R. 433.
[36] F.A. 1985, s.82.
[37] *I.R.C. v. Angus* (1889) 23 Q.B.D. 579; *Oughtred v. I.R.C.* [1960] A.C. 206 at p. 227.
[38] See note 35, *supra*.

declaration, in which case the subsequent documents were truly confirmatory, and passed no beneficial interest; or whether, as the Revenue argued, the documents effected a disposition of an existing equitable interest within section 53(1)(c), in which case they were subject to *ad valorem* duty.[39]

In argument, Pennycuick Q.C. posed the question thus[40]: "If X holds property in trust for A as absolute owner and A then directs X to hold the property on the settlement trusts for the benefit of B, C, and D, and X accepts the trust, is that direction a 'disposition' of a subsisting equitable interest within the meaning of section 53?" The House of Lords answered affirmatively. While the trustees held the shares as nominees for the settlor, the settlor owned the entire beneficial interest. When the trustees held them upon the trusts of the settlements, the beneficial interest passed from the settlor to the beneficiaries under the settlements. That, according to the natural meaning of the word, was a disposition. *Ad valorem* stamp duty was payable on the documents.

It seems that the settlor's objectives would have been achieved if he had orally declared himself trustee of the shares for the beneficiaries while still the legal owner; following the declaration with a confirmatory document; and retiring, when he wished, in favour of other trustees.

It appears that section 53(1)(c) is satisfied if the equitable owner writes to the trustee in terms which refer to prior oral instructions to hold on new trusts, even though the writing does not include the particulars of the new trusts.[41]

(c) *Conveyance of Legal Estate by Trustee.* The subsection does not apply where the trustee or nominee conveys the legal estate to a third party with the consent or at the direction of a beneficiary absolutely entitled. In that situation, "prima facie a transfer of the legal estate carries with it the absolute beneficial interest in the property transferred."[42]

In *Vandervell v. I.R.C.*,[43] Vandervell wished to give sufficient money to the Royal College of Surgeons to found a Chair of Pharmacology. He decided to do so by arranging for the transfer to the College of shares in Vandervell Products Ltd., subject to an

---

[39] It was conceded that the documents should be regarded as dispositive in the event of the oral directions being held ineffective. See (1984) 47 M.L.R. 385 at 391 (B. Green).

[40] [1960] A.C. 1 at p. 4.

[41] *Re Tyler* [1967] 1 W.L.R. 1269. *Grey v. I.R.C.*, *supra*, was cited in argument but not referred to in the judgment.

[42] *Per* Diplock L.J. [1966] Ch. 261 at p. 287.

[43] [1967] 2 A.C. 291; (1966) 24 C.L.J. 19 (G. Jones); (1967) 31 Conv.(N.S.) 175 (S. Spencer); (1967) 30 M.L.R. 461 (N. Strauss); (1975) 38 M.L.R. 557 (J. Harris).

option exercisable by Vandervell Trustees Ltd., a company which acted as trustee for various Vandervell family trusts, to repurchase the shares for £5,000. The shares were held by the National Provincial Bank Ltd as nominee for Vandervell.

The Bank transferred the shares to the College subject to the option. Dividends amounting to £250,000 were declared on the shares and paid to the College, and the income in the hands of the College, being a charity, was not subject to income tax. But the Revenue claimed surtax from Vandervell on the ground that he had not completely divested himself of the beneficial interest in the property.[44] The Revenue succeeded on the ground that there had been no declaration of the trusts on which the option was held by Vandervell Trustees Ltd, and accordingly they held it on a resulting trust for Vandervell. This aspect of the case is considered in Chapter 10 below.

A second argument of the Revenue was that, since the Bank had held the shares on trust for Vandervell, the transfer by the Bank to the College transferred only the bare legal estate; and the equitable interest could not leave Vandervell except by a disposition in writing signed by him. If A holds property on trust for B, and A transfers the legal title to X, a volunteer, the ordinary rule would suggest that X took subject to B's beneficial interest; that the beneficial interest, in short, did not pass on the transfer of the legal title by A. Certainly this would be the case if the transfer was in breach of trust, or was only the appointment of a new trustee. On the other hand, there could be no argument in favour of the application of the section in the case of a transfer by an absolute owner, at law and in equity[45]; and the House of Lords held that the section was similarly not applicable in the case of a transfer by a trustee on the directions of a beneficial owner of the whole interest. Lord Upjohn explained the object of the section as being to prevent hidden oral transactions relating to equitable interests. "But when the beneficial owner owns the whole beneficial estate and is in a position to give directions to his bare trustee with regard to the legal as well as the equitable estate there can be no possible ground for invoking the section where the beneficial owner wants to deal with the legal estate as well as the equitable estate."[46]

Presumably, however, the subsection would apply if the beneficial owner were to direct that the legal title should be transferred to X, who should hold on trust for Y. In such a case the equitable

---

[44] The current legislation is I.C.T.A. 1988, ss.684, 685.

[45] Such a transfer would include the equitable interest unless there is evidence that such was not intended, or where the presumption of resulting trust applies; *post*, p. 244.

[46] [1967] 2 A.C. 291 at p. 311.

interest, although passing at the same time as the legal title, would remain separated from it.[47]

(d) *Declaration of Trust with Consent of Beneficial Owner.* That decision did not exhaust the subtleties of the section in its application to Mr Vandervell's affairs. Faced with the surtax claim in 1961 in respect of the dividends paid to the Royal College of Surgeons, he instructed Vandervell Trustees Ltd to exercise the option. They did so, in the same year, using £5,000 from the Vandervell children's settlement for the purpose, manifesting an intention with Vandervell's consent that the shares which they thereby acquired should be held on the trusts of the children's settlement, and so informing the Revenue. In 1965, Vandervell executed a deed formally assigning to Vandervell Trustees Ltd any right or interest he might still have in the option or the shares.

The Revenue assessed Vandervell to surtax in respect of the years 1961–65. Up to 1961, there was a resulting trust in his favour of the option. He had not, until 1965, they argued, disposed of that beneficial interest in writing, and therefore he must still have it; though now in the shares into which the option had been converted.

The executors of Vandervell's estate stepped in before the Revenue's claim was litigated, and claimed from Vandervell Trustees Ltd the dividends paid during 1961–65.[48] They applied to join the Revenue as second defendants, but Vandervell Trustees Ltd successfully objected.[49] The executors' claim to the dividends succeeded before Megarry J. on the ground that the resulting trust which applied to the option applied also to the shares, and there had been no valid declaration of trust in favour of the children's settlement. This was reversed by the Court of Appeal, holding that the trustee company held the dividends on the trusts of the children's settlement. Four reasons were given[50]: first, that the trustees used funds of the children's settlement to exercise the option; secondly, that the trustees and Vandervell showed an intention that the shares should be held on the trusts of that settlement; thirdly, that there had been a perfect gift of the dividends to the children's settlement; and fourthly, that the resulting trust attached to the option and not to the shares, and the trust of the option came to an end with the exercise

---

[47] But compare the position in *Re Vandervell's Trusts (No. 2)*, *infra*, where the subsection did not apply to a transaction whereby the legal title passed to the trustees and the equitable interest to the children's settlement, having previously been united in the Royal College of Surgeons. On the latter point it is distinguishable from the example in the text, and is in fact the converse of *Vandervell v. I.R.C.*

[48] *Re Vandervell's Trust (No. 2)* [1974] Ch. 269; (1975) 38 M.L.R. 557 (J. Harris).

[49] *Vandervell Trustees Ltd v. White* [1971] A.C. 912.

[50] Lord Denning also considered that Vandervell, having arranged for the exercise of the option and the payment of dividends to the children's settlement, was estopped from claiming any interest; [1974] Ch. 269 at p. 321.

of the option. Neither the extinction of the trust of the option nor the creation of the new trust of the shares, nor the two, viewed as a whole, amounted to a disposition by Vandervell of an interest within section 53(1)(c).

The subsection did not apply where a trustee, with the consent of the beneficiary, declared new trusts of what could be regarded as new property.

The decision of the Court of Appeal leaves many problems in its wake. Essential to the decision was the finding of a valid declaration of trust in favour of the children's settlement, but the three things relied on as constituting the declaration are unconvincing.[51] Surely an element of intention is necessary in the declaration of a trust, yet none of the parties had such an intention, but merely acted on the assumption that the children's settlement was entitled. It is difficult to accept the proposition that the use of the money from the settlement resulted in the acquisition of the beneficial ownership of the shares. Is not the owner of an option entitled to the fruits of it? The fact that it was exercised with X's money gives rights to X, but not equitable ownership.[52] Equally doubtful is the point that there was a "perfect gift" of the dividends to the children's settlement. A valid gift requires a donative intention and capacity to give. Here the dividends were paid to the children's settlement not with a donative intention but on the assumption that the children were already entitled to them.[53]

Other criticisms can be directed at the proposition that Vandervell had no interest in the shares but only in the option, so that when the option terminated (upon its exercise) there was no question of any interest in the shares passing from him to the children's settlement. Underlying the entire decision is the supposition that, if the children's claim failed, there would be a resulting trust of the shares to Vandervell. How could this be if he had no interest in them? Indeed, the House of Lords, in *Vandervell v. I.R.C.*,[54] had held that he had. He was liable to surtax on the dividends because his beneficial ownership of the option meant that he retained some interest in the *shares*.[55] Certainly this was not the entire beneficial interest, but it cannot be said that he had no interest in the shares.

Even assuming a valid declaration of trust for the children, it would have to occur no later than the exercise of the option in order to avoid a resulting trust to Vandervell, whereby any subsequent

---

[51] *Post*, p. 121.
[52] *Ibid.*
[53] See, however *Milroy v. Lord* (1862) 4 De G.F. & J. 264 at 277 (dividends irrecoverable although gift of shares invalid).
[54] [1967] 2 A.C. 291.
[55] See I.C.T.A. 1988, ss.684, 685.

declaration would be a disposition of his interest.[56] Yet two of
the three acts relied on as constituting the declaration occurred after
the exercise of the option. Finally, how did the equitable interest in
the shares pass from the college to the children's settlement without
satisfying the subsection?[57] As the college was at that time also the
legal owner, presumably section 53(1)(c) did not apply.[58]

(e) *Declaration by Equitable Owner of Himself as Trustee.* A
further aspect of the matter which has not yet been worked out is the
situation in which the beneficiary declares himself trustee of his
equitable interest for another. On the one hand, it can be argued that
this is, on its face, a declaration of trust, and not a disposition. It is
a sub-trust, the subject-matter not being identical to that of the
original trust.[59] On the other hand, it was said in *Grainge v. Wilberforce*[60] that "where A was trustee for B, who was trustee for C, A
holds in trust for C, and must convey as C directed." Thus, B
"disappears from the picture,"[61] and C becomes the beneficiary.
This looks like a disposition. It may be otherwise where B retains
active duties, as where he declares a trust of his interest for such of
a class as he shall select.[62]

(f) *Specifically Enforceable Oral Contracts for Sale. Oughtred v.
I.R.C.*,[63] like *Grey*, concerned an attempt to avoid stamp duty on a
share transfer.

Mrs Oughtred was the owner of 72,700 shares in a company
and was also tenant for life under a settlement which contained
100,000 preferences shares and 100,000 ordinary shares. Her son,
Peter, was entitled in remainder. In order to reduce the estate duty

---

[56] As in *Grey v. I.R.C.* [1960] A.C. 1, *supra.*
[57] See (1975) 38 M.L.R. 557 (J. Harris).
[58] On the basis that there was no "subsisting" separate equitable interest. Compare the
reasoning of *Vandervell v. I.R.C.*, *supra.* It might also be argued that the exercise of the
option gave rise to a contract, which gave rise to a constructive trust, as in the *Oughtred*
argument. Thus the equitable interest passed from the college, by virtue of s.53(2), without
the need for a written disposition. But this would not solve the problem of where it went
to. Presumably it would go to the beneficial owner of the option unless he had disposed of
his interest elsewhere, which was the very issue.
[59] Compare the reasoning of *Re Vandervell's Trusts (No. 2)*, *supra.*
[60] (1889) 5 T.L.R. 436 at p. 437; *post*, p. 114; see also *Re Tout & Finch* [1954] 1 W.L.R. 178;
D.H.N. Food Distributors Ltd v. Tower Hamlets L.B.C. [1976] 1 W.L.R. 852; (1977) 93
L.Q.R. 171 (D. Sugarman and F. Webb); *Corin v. Patton* (1990) A.L.J.R. 256 at p. 272.
[61] *Per* Upjohn J. in *Grey v. I.R.C.* [1958] Ch. 375 at p. 382.
[62] *Re Lashmar* [1891] 1 Ch. 258 at p. 268; see (1958) 74 L.Q.R. 180 (P.V.B.); (1984) 37
M.L.R. 385 at p. 396 (B. Green), suggesting that all sub-trusts are within the subsection.
[63] [1960] A.C. 206.

which would be payable on Mrs Oughtred's death, an oral agreement was made in 1956 under which Peter would surrender his remainder interest in the settled shares in consideration for the transfer to him of his mother's 72,700 shares.

A deed was executed by Mrs Oughtred and Peter which recited that the settled shares were then held in trust for Mrs Oughtred absolutely. The trustees then transferred the shares to Mrs Oughtred; and she transferred the 72,700 shares to Peter. The question was whether *ad valorem* stamp duty was payable on the transfers. The document selected for the purpose of the claim was the transfer of the shares from the trustees to Mrs Oughtred.

The question depended on whether or not Mrs Oughtred was owner in equity of the shares before the legal transfer. Provided a contract is specifically enforceable, a constructive trust is said to arise as soon as the contract is entered into, whereby the equitable interest passes to the purchaser by virtue of his right to specific performance.[64] Contracts for the sale of land are normally specifically enforceable, provided they are in writing, as required by section 2 of the Law of Property (Miscellaneous Provisions) Act 1989. Contracts for the sale of personalty are specifically enforceable only if the remedy of damages would be inadequate. Thus contracts to sell shares in a public company are not normally specifically enforceable, but the position is otherwise in the case of shares in a private company, which are not available for purchase on the market. Mrs Oughtred was accordingly able to claim that the equitable interest had passed to her by virtue of her right to specific performance of the contract; or, putting the same point another way, that Peter, after the agreement, held his interest as constructive trustee for her (constructive trusts being exempted from the writing requirement by section 53(2)). The later document would then be only a transfer of the bare legal estate.

The House of Lords, however, by three to two, held to the contrary. For the majority, Lord Jenkins, with whose speech Lord Keith expressed entire agreement, accepted that Mrs Oughtred's interest, after the agreement, was similar to that of a purchaser of land between contract and conveyance. The purchaser's interest "is no doubt a proprietary interest of a sort, which arises, so to speak, in anticipation of the execution of the transfer for which the purchaser is entitled to call. But its existence has never (so far as I know) been held to prevent a subsequent transfer, in performance of the contract, of the property contracted to be sold from constituting for stamp duty purposes a transfer on sale of the property in

---

[64] *Post*, p. 312.

question."[65] So here, the transfer of the legal estate was an instrument attracting duty.

Lord Radcliffe, dissenting, took the view that Mrs Oughtred became equitable owner of the reversionary interest in the settled shares by virtue of the specifically enforceable agreement to exchange. She became the absolute owner in equity. "There was . . . no equity to the shares that could be asserted against her, and it was open to her, if she so wished, to let the matter rest without calling for a written assignment, from her son. . . . It follows that, in my view, this transfer cannot be treated as a conveyance of the son's equitable reversion at all."[66] This argument is compelling, and it points out a number of questions relating to the nature of the interest which Mrs Oughtred held before the legal transfer from the trustees; the majority speeches leave these questions unanswered. It has always been held that stamp duty is payable on a conveyance of land, even though the beneficial interest in the property passed on the signing of the contract; similarly with a purchase of shares. This factor may have influenced the court's approach to the application of section 53. *Oughtred* may thus be viewed as a policy decision.

Later decisions in varying contexts have tended to support the view that an equitable interest can pass under a contract without formality, although the point is rarely fully argued. In *Re Holt's Settlement*,[67] concerning the Variation of Trusts Act 1958, Megarry J., relying on the minority judgments in *Oughtred*, accepted the proposition that where there is a specifically enforceable agreement, the beneficial interest passes to the purchaser under a constructive trust without writing. Similarly in *D.H.N. Food Distributors Ltd v. Tower Hamlets London Borough Council*,[68] concerning compulsory purchase, the Court of Appeal assumed that an equitable interest in land could pass without writing where the transaction was contractual.[69] In *Chinn v. Collins*,[70] concerning a capital gains tax avoidance scheme, Lord Wilberforce said that

> "The legal title to the shares was at all times vested in a nominee . . . and dealings related to the equitable interest in these required no formality. As soon as there was an agreement for their sale accompanied or followed by payment of the price, the equitable title passed at once to the purchaser . . . and all that was

---

[65] [1960] A.C. 206, at p. 240. See also *Henty and Constable (Brewers) Ltd v. I.R.C.* [1961] 1 W.L.R. 1504, at p. 1510.

[66] [1960] A.C. 206 at p. 228.

[67] [1969] 1 Ch. 100, at p. 116.

[68] [1976] 1 W.L.R. 852, at pp. 865, 867.

[69] This argument is no longer tenable in the case of land because the contract must be in writing; Law of Property (Miscellaneous Provisions) Act 1989, s.2. See *United Bank of Kuwait plc v. Sahib* [1996] 3 W.L.R. 372.

[70] [1981] A.C. 533, at p. 548.

needed to perfect his title was notice to the trustees or the nominee . . . "

The shares were in a public company, but Lord Wilberforce did not appear to consider a specifically enforceable contract to be essential to this proposition which, it should be noted, led to the establishment of capital gains tax liability. Neither *Oughtred* nor even section 53 itself was cited. Tax liability was not involved in *Neville v. Wilson*,[71] where nominees held shares in U Ltd on trust for J Ltd, a family company. The shareholders of J Ltd agreed informally to liquidate the company and to divide its equitable interest in the U Ltd shares amongst themselves in proportion to their existing shareholdings. The question was whether section 53(1)(c) invalidated this agreement (in which case the equitable interest would have passed to the Crown when J Ltd was struck off the register). The Court of Appeal held that each shareholder's agreement gave rise to an implied or constructive trust so that section 53(2)[72] applied. Thus the agreement was effective to vest the equitable interest in the shareholders without writing. The analysis of Lord Radcliffe in his dissent in *Oughtred v. I.R.C.*[73] that a specifically enforceable agreement to assign passed the equitable interest to the assignee was correct. It was noted that Lords Jenkins and Keith had left the point open and that Lord Denning (with whom Lord Cohen appeared to agree) had rejected the application of section 53(2) without giving reasons.

It is probable that section 53(2) was intended to embrace the kind of constructive trust which is imposed to prevent fraud,[74] and did not envisage the anomalous constructive trust arising on a specifically enforceable contract for sale. The latter is in any event only a qualified trust (under which the vendor retains valuable rights until the conveyance).[75] In favour of the *Oughtred* decision it might also be said that in the case of a contract there is a transfer of the equitable interest from the vendor to the purchaser, whereas in the case of resulting trusts and constructive trusts imposed to prevent fraud, contemplated by section 53(2), there is no *passing* of the equitable interest, which remains throughout in the true beneficial owner. It seems that the acceptance of the argument that a contract

---

[71] [1996] 3 W.L.R. 460; (1996) 55 C.L.J. 436 (R. Nolan); [1996] Conv. 368 (M. Thompson). *Cf. United Bank of Kuwait plc v. Sahib* [1995] 2 W.L.R. 94, where Chadwick J. held that a contract to assign an equitable interest by way of mortgage required writing to satisfy s.53(1)(c) and doubted whether s.53(2) could apply. The point was not argued on appeal at [1996] 3 W.L.R. 372.

[72] "This section does not effect the creation or operation of resulting, implied or constructive trusts."

[73] [1960] A.C.206.

[74] As in *Bannister v. Bannister* [1948] 2 All E.R. 133; *Hodgson v. Marks* [1971] Ch. 892. See also *Midland Bank Ltd v. Dobson* [1986] 1 F.L.R. 171, *post*, p. 262.

[75] *Post*, p. 312.

can shift the equitable interest without formality under the constructive trust principle depends very much on the context, and that
it is more likely to be accepted in the tax context where this would
result in liability.

(g) *Variation of Trusts Act 1958.* We shall see in Chapter 22 that
the Variation of Trusts Act 1958 gave power to the court to approve,
on behalf of categories of persons unable to make the decision for
themselves, variations of the existing beneficial interests under
trusts where it is for the benefit of the beneficiaries to do so. Many
variations had been approved by the courts when suddenly, in *Re
Holt's Settlement*,[76] Megarry J. asked whether it was not necessary
for the disposition of each existing beneficial interest to be in
writing under section 53. Megarry J. was able to satisfy himself that
writing was not necessary, and the threat of invalidity to most of the
variations previously approved was removed. The details of the
matter are best postponed until the Act is explained.[77]

(h) *Right of Nomination under Staff Pension Fund.* The rules of
the pension fund of the *Danish Bacon Co. Ltd* provided that employees could nominate a person to receive moneys due in the case of
death in service. Such a nomination could be regarded as a disposition, *inter vivos*, of an equitable interest under the pension fund
trust; or as a testamentary disposition in that it took effect only in the
event of the employee's death. In *Re Danish Bacon Co. Staff
Pension Fund Trusts*,[78] Megarry J. held that it was not a testamentary disposition. He very much doubted "whether the nomination
falls within section 53(1)(c)"[79]; but held that, even if it did, the
necessary writing was supplied by two connecting documents.

(i) *Disclaimer.* In *Re Paradise Motor Co. Ltd*,[80] a stepfather made
a gift of shares to his stepson. The transfer, though technically
defective, was sufficient to make the stepson equitable owner of the
shares. The stepson knew nothing of the transfer. When he became
aware of the circumstances, he stated in unmistakable language that
he wished to make no claim to the shares. But when the company
was in liquidation, he changed his mind and claimed his share of the
proceeds. On the question whether there could be a disclaimer of an
equitable interest without compliance with section 53, it was held

---

[76] [1969] 1 Ch. 590.
[77] *Post*, p. 619.
[78] [1971] 1 W.L.R. 248. Followed by the Privy Council in *Baird v. Baird* [1990] 2 A.C. 548
    (application of Wills Act depends on each scheme); [1990] Conv. 458 (G. Kodilinye).
[79] *Ibid.* at p. 256.
[80] [1968] 1 W.L.R. 1125.

that "a disclaimer operates by way of avoidance and not by way of disposition."[81] The disclaimer was effective and the claim failed.

However, the position seems otherwise as far as tax matters are concerned,[82] where it has been found necessary to make express provision that a disclaimer shall not be treated as a disposition for inheritance tax purposes.[83]

B. By Will

Additional formalities are required for the creation of a testamentary trust. Wills Act 1837, s.9, as amended by Administration of Justice Act 1982, s.17, provides:

"No will shall be valid unless:

(a) it is in writing, and signed by the testator, or by some other person in his presence and by his direction; and
(b) it appears that the testator intended by his signature to give effect to the will; and
(c) the signature is made or acknowledged by the testator in the presence of two or more witnesses present at the same time; and
(d) each witness either—

    (i) attests and signs the will; or
    (ii) acknowledges his signature,

        in the presence of the testator (but not necessarily in the presence of any other witness),

but no form of attestation shall be necessary."

No attempt will be made here to deal with the details of this enactment. The question of the validity of trusts taking effect on a testator's death which fail to comply with these provisions—the so-called "secret trusts"—will be discussed in Chapter 5.

3. CERTAINTY

A private express trust cannot be created unless the three certainties[84] are present; certainty of intention; certainty of subject matter;

---

[81] *Re Paradise Motor Co. Ltd, supra*, at p. 1143; *Dewar v. Dewar* [1975] 1 W.L.R. 1532; *Allied Dunbar Assurance plc v. Fowle* [1994] 1 E.G.L.R. 122. But see L.P.A. 1925, s.205(1)(ii). A surrender appears to be a disposition, but *cf.* [1960] B.T.R. 20 (J. Monroe).

[82] *Re Stratton's Disclaimer* [1958] Ch. 42 (estate duty).

[83] Inheritance Tax Act 1984, s.17.

[84] See Lord Langdale in *Knight v. Knight* (1840) 3 Beav. 148 at p. 173. Extrinsic evidence is not generally admissible to aid the construction of a trust deed; *Rabin v. Gerson Berger Association Ltd* [1986] 1 W.L.R. 526.

and certainty of beneficiaries. Each of these heads will be considered below. Different considerations apply to each; yet they are
inter-related. "Uncertainty in the subject of the gift has a reflex
action upon the previous words, and shows doubt upon the intention
of the testator, and seems to show that he could not possibly have
intended his words of confidence, hope, or whatever they may
be—his appeal to the conscience of the first taker—to be imperative
words."[85]

Similar, but distinct, questions about certainty may arise in relation to a conditional gift; whether a condition precedent to taking,[86]
or a condition of defeasance.[87] Further, the requirement of certainty
of beneficiaries operates differently with discretionary as opposed to
fixed trusts, and with trusts for purposes as opposed to trusts for
people. A trust for a non-charitable purpose is normally invalid; but
where such a trust has been upheld, the court has insisted that the
purpose be described with sufficient certainty.[88] With charitable
trusts, there is no need to specify in any way which charity is to be
benefited; but the language of the gift must clearly establish that the
gift is applicable for charitable purposes only.[89]

A. Certainty of Intention

We have already seen that a trustee is under an obligation, but that
the obligation may be inferred from the nature of the gift, considered
as a whole.[90] Technical words are not required. The question is
whether, on the proper construction of the words used, the settlor or
testator has shown an intention to create a trust. A trust may be
created without using the word "trust," and, conversely, the use of
the word "trust" does not conclusively indicate the existence of a
trust.[91] A "precatory" expression of hope or desire, or suggestion or
request, is not sufficient. The words in each case must be examined
to see whether the intention was to impose a trust upon the
donee.

The Court of Chancery at one time leaned in favour of construing
expressions of desire as intended to create a binding trust.[92] This
was because an executor who had administered an estate was entitled to keep for himself any surplus which was undisposed of by the

---

[85] *Mussourie Bank v. Raynor* (1882) 7 App.Cas. 321 at p. 331.
[86] *Re Allen* [1953] Ch. 810; *Re Barlow's W.T.* [1979] 1 W.L.R. 278.
[87] *Clayton v. Ramsden* [1943] A.C. 320; *Blathwayt v. Lord Cawley* [1976] A.C. 397.
[88] *Re Astor's S.T.* [1952] Ch. 534; *post*, p. 357.
[89] *Post*, p. 379.
[90] *Ante*, p. 59. In the context of charity, see *Re Cohen* [1973] 1 W.L.R. 415.
[91] *Tito v. Waddell (No. 2)* [1977] Ch. 106, *ante*, p. 70; *Customs and Excise Commissioners v. Richmond Theatre Management Ltd* [1995] S.T.C. 257, *ante*, p. 51.
[92] See, however, *Cook v. Fountain* (1676) 3 Swan. 585.

will, and the court was ready to find that he took as trustee in order to prevent this. This approach then spread beyond executors. In 1830, however, the Executors Act provided that undisposed-of residue should be held on trust for the next-of-kin; and from about the middle of the nineteenth century, a stricter construction was placed upon these "precatory words". Where, however, an express trust is construed from precatory words, it is, of course, just as much a trust as any other.[93]

The older cases are therefore unhelpful as guides to construction. *Lambe v. Eames*[94] is usually regarded as the case which marks the "turning of the tide". There the testator gave his estate to his widow "to be at her disposal in any way she may think best, for the benefit of herself and her family." By her will she gave part of the estate outside the family; it was held that she had been absolutely entitled to the property and that the gift was valid. Similarly in *Re Adams and the Kensington Vestry*,[95] where a testator gave his estate "unto and to the absolute use of my dear wife, Harriet . . . in full confidence that she will do what is right as to the disposal thereof between my children, either in her lifetime or by will after her decease." The Court of Appeal held that she took absolutely.

But a trust will be found from precatory words if on a proper construction of the language such was the intention of the testator. In *Comiskey v. Bowring-Hanbury*,[96] a testator gave to his wife "the whole of my real and personal estate . . . in full confidence that . . . at her death she will devise it to such one or more of my nieces as she may think fit and in default of any disposition by her thereof by her will . . . I hereby direct that all my estate and property acquired by her under this my will shall at her death be equally divided among the surviving said nieces." A majority of the House of Lords held that the testator intended to make a gift to his wife, with a gift over of the whole property at her death to such of her nieces as should survive her, shared according to the wife's will, and otherwise equally.

Where a form of words has once been held to create a trust, the testator's intention may be held to be such as to reach the same result, at any rate where the words have been used as a precedent,

---

[93] In *Re Williams* [1897] 2 Ch. 12 at p. 27 Rigby L.J. protested against the use of the term "precatory trust," calling it a "misleading nickname."

[94] (1871) L.R. 6 Ch. 597. See also *Re Hamilton* [1895] 2 Ch. 370 at p. 374.

[95] (1884) 27 Ch.D. 394; *Mussourie Bank v. Raynor* (1882) 7 App.Cas. 321 ("feeling confident that she will act justly to our children in distributing the same"); *Re Diggles* (1888) 39 Ch.D. 253 ("it is my desire that she allows . . . an annuity of £25); *Re Johnson* [1939] 2 All E.R. 458 ("I request that my mother will on her death leave the property or what remains of it . . . to my four sisters").

[96] [1905] A.C. 84.

even though the words used, when subjected to the stricter modern construction, might be expected to produce a different result.[97]

Where the words used are held not to create a trust, the donee of the property take beneficially.[98] This must be distinguished from the situation where there is certainty of intention to create a trust, but uncertainty as to the objects or the shares they are to take. In such cases, as we shall see, there is a resulting trust.

The question of certainty of intention may also arise where there is no document to construe. The question then is whether the acts or words of the parties indicate an intention to create a trust; as where a man tells his cohabitant that she can share his bank account[99]; or where a mail order company puts money sent by customers into a separate bank account.[1] This aspect of the problem will be discussed in Chapter 4, where the requirements of the declaration of trust are examined.[2]

Finally, the intention to create a trust must be genuine, and not a sham, as where the "settlor" did not intend the trust to be acted upon, but entered into it for some ulterior motive, such as deceiving creditors or the Inland Revenue. In *Midland Bank plc v. Wyatt*[3] a declaration of trust was executed by a husband and wife in 1987 (when the husband was contemplating a new business) whereby the family home, their only real asset, was apparently settled on the wife and daughters. The document was kept in a safe and the couple continued to act as absolute owners of the property, in particular by mortgaging it. The husband's business failed and the bank obtained a charging order against the house. The husband then revealed the trust document. This was held to be a sham. The inference was that the husband had "kept it up his sleeve for a rainy day" in order to defeat future creditors and had not otherwise intended it to have any effect. This principle does not require a finding of fraud, and can apply if the transaction is the result of merely mistaken advice.

---

[97] *Re Steele's W.T.* [1948] Ch. 603; following *Shelley v. Shelley* (1868) L.R. 6 Eq. 540; (1968) 32 Conv.(N.S.) 361 (P. Langan).

[98] *Lassence v. Tierney* (1849) 1 Mac. & Cr. 551; *Hancock v. Watson* [1902] A.C. 14; *Watson v. Holland* [1985] 1 All E.R. 290; *cf. Re Pugh's W.T.* [1967] 1 W.L.R. 1261.

[99] *Paul v. Constance* [1977] 1 W.L.R. 527. See also *Re Vandervell's Trusts (No. 2)* [1974] Ch. 269; *Swain v. The Law Society* [1983] 1 A.C. 598.

[1] *Re Kayford Ltd (in Liquidation)* [1975] 1 W.L.R. 279, *ante*, p. 51. See also *R. v. Clowes (No. 2)* [1994] 2 All E.R. 316 (terms of investment brochures indicated a trust); *Re Lewis's of Leicester Ltd* [1995] 1 B.C.L.C. 428 (company created trust by paying takings of concessionnaires into separate account, although its commission had not been deducted from the payments, thus the company was also a beneficiary).

[2] *Post*, p. 120.

[3] [1995] 1 F.L.R. 696; *post*, p. 340; (1994) 8 *Trust Law International* 68 (J. Mowbray). See also *Re Pfrimmer Estate* (1936) 2 D.L.R. 460; *Rahman v. Chase Bank (C.I.) Trust Co. Ltd* [1991] J.L.R. 103 (Jersey).

B. Certainty of Subject-Matter

The subject-matter may be an interest in land; it may be chattels or money; it may be a chose in action, such as a covenant[4] or a debt. Whatever form it takes, it must be specified with reasonable certainty. Testamentary gifts have failed where they concerned "the bulk of my estate,"[5] or "such parts of my estate as she shall not have sold,"[6] or "anything that is left,[7] or "the remaining part of what is left"[8] or "all my other houses"[9] *i.e.* those remaining after a choice had been made by another beneficiary who died before choosing. These cases should be contrasted with one where the subject-matter of the gift is to be determined in the discretion of a trustee. In *Re Golay's Will Trusts*,[10] a gift directing the executors to allow a beneficiary to "enjoy one of my flats during her lifetime and to receive a reasonable income from my other properties" was upheld. The executors could select the flat. The words "reasonable income" were not intended to allow the trustees to make a subjective decision: but they provided a sufficient objective determinant to enable the court, if necessary, to quantify the amount. The problem, however, is that no objective determination of words such as "reasonable" can be made unless the context is known. In *Re Golay's Will Trusts*[11] it was assumed that the criterion was the beneficiary's previous standard of living. The word "reasonable" in isolation has little meaning. If a testator were to give "a reasonable legacy" to X, then no doubt the gift would fail, unless it was clear that the amount was to be fixed by the executors.

Where the subject-matter of the trust is uncertain, then no trust is created. There is nothing to form the subject-matter of a resulting trust. If the purported trust has been attached to an absolute gift, then the absolute gift takes effect. It may be, however, that the property itself is certain, but the beneficial shares are not. Unless the trustees have a discretion to determine the amounts, then the trust will fail, and the property will be held on a resulting trust for the settlor. This was the case in *Boyce v. Boyce*,[12] where the determination was to be made by a beneficiary who died before choosing. Sometimes the problem will be solved by the principle that equity is equality,[13] or

---

[4] *Fletcher v. Fletcher* (1844) 4 Hare 67; *post*, p. 128.
[5] *Palmer v. Simmonds* (1854) 2 Drew. 221.
[6] *Re Jones* [1898] 1 Ch. 438.
[7] *In the Estate of Last* [1958] P. 137.
[8] *Sprange v. Barnard* (1789) 2 Bro.C.C. 585.
[9] *Boyce v. Boyce* (1849) 16 Sim. 476.
[10] [1965] 1 W.L.R. 969.
[11] *Supra.*
[12] (1849) 6 Sim. 476.
[13] *Burrough v. Philcox* (1840) 5 Myl. & Cr. 72; (1967) 31 Conv.(N.S.) 117 (A. Hawkins).

by the court determining what is the proper division according to the circumstances.[14]

Certainty of subject matter has been in issue recently not only in relation to express trusts but also in the commercial context of the sale of goods. Where purchasers have paid for goods but have not taken delivery prior to the seller's insolvency, they may seek to gain priority over general creditors by claiming a trust of the goods in their favour. Where the goods have not been segregated but form part of a bulk, these claims failed (prior to a legislative reform mentioned below) on the ground that there cannot be a trust of unidentified chattels. Thus in *Re London Wine Co.*[15] the buyers of wine stored in a warehouse and not segregated from the general stock of similar wine could not establish a trust. It was otherwise where the wine had been segregated for a group of customers (even though not appropriated to each individual customer), as in *Re Stapylton Fletcher Ltd*,[16] although the judge warned that the court "must be very cautious in devising equitable interests and remedies which erode the statutory scheme for distribution on insolvency. It cannot do it because of some perceived injustice arising as a consequence only of the insolvency."[17] In that case the legal title had passed to the customers and there was no need to consider the trust argument.

The leading authority is *Re Goldcorp Exchange Ltd*,[18] where purchasers of bullion, who had paid but had not taken delivery, asserted proprietary rights on the insolvency of the company. Save for a group of customers whose bullion had been segregated, these claims were rejected by the Privy Council. Legal title had not passed, nor was there any trust, as there was no identifiable property to which any trust could attach. Thus the customers were unsecured creditors.

Although no doubt some chattels can be regarded as identical to other chattels of the same description, the rationale of the rule that there cannot be a trust of chattels which have not been segregated from a mass of similar chattels is that they are not necessarily identical.[19] Even bottles of wine of the same label may not be identical; some may be "corked" and undrinkable. Now, however, the Sale of Goods (Amendment) Act 1995[20] provides that purchasers who have paid for unascertained goods forming part of an

---

[14] *McPhail v. Doulton* [1971] A.C. 424 (selection of beneficiaries); *post*, p. 101.
[15] (1986) Palmer's Company Cases 121.
[16] [1994] 1 W.L.R. 1181 (tenancy in common); considered "eminently sensible and fair" in (1995) 48 C.L.P. 117 at p. 131 (A. Clarke).
[17] *Ibid.* at p. 1203 (Paul Baker Q.C.).
[18] [1995] 1 A.C. 74; (1994) 53 C.L.J. 443 (L. Sealy); *post*, p. 668.
[19] *cf.* All E.R. Rev. 1994 p. 250 (P. Clarke), doubting the distinction in an age of mass-produced goods.
[20] Amending the Sale of Goods Act 1979.

identified bulk (where the goods are interchangeable) acquire property rights as tenants in common of the bulk, subject to any contrary agreement. Thus they will prevail over general creditors in an insolvency. This provision will not, of course, apply to the creation of express trusts of chattels.

The chattels rule does not apply to money, shares and other choses in action because, in the nature of things, there is no difference between one pound and another pound, or one share and another share of the same class in the same company. Difficult problems do, however, arise.

In *Hunter v. Moss*[21] the settlor owned 950 shares in M Co., which had an issued share capital of 1,000. He orally declared a trust of 5 per cent of the share capital, *i.e.* 50 shares. The Court of Appeal upheld the trust. Provided the shares were of the same class and in the same company, there was no need to segregate 50 shares before declaring the trust. *Re London Wine Co.*[22] was distinguished as involving chattels. Cases upholding bequests[23] of part of a larger shareholding showed that the chattels rule did not apply to choses in action. Thus a declaration of trust of part of a larger shareholding or £50 out of a designated bank account with a larger balance would be valid. In fact the settlor had subsequently sold the shares to B Co. in exchange for shares in B Co. and cash, and the judgment was for 5 per cent of the consideration.

The decision has been criticised, but before considering the criticisms it is necessary to examine a different situation, where a settlor attempts to create a trust of money but (unlike in the bank account example above) does not designate the source of the money. In *MacJordan Construction Ltd v. Brookmount Erostin Ltd*[24] a building contract provided that the employer would retain 3 per cent of the contract price as trustee for the builder (pending confirmation that the work was satisfactory). The retention fund was never set up. On the employer's insolvency the builder claimed entitlement to the retention money in priority to a bank which had a floating charge over all the assets. This claim failed because no identifiable assets had been impressed with a trust for the builder. There was merely a contractual right, which did not "carry with it any equitable interest of a security character in the assets for the time being of the

---

[21] [1994] 1 W.L.R. 452; [1996] Conv. 223 (J. Martin).

[22] *Supra.*

[23] *Re Cheadle* [1900] 2 Ch. 620; *Re Clifford* [1912] 1 Ch. 29. These are considered distinguishable in (1994) 53 C.L.J. 448 (M. Ockelton).

[24] [1992] B.C.L.C. 350.

employer."[25] This is clearly correct, being in effect no different from an attempt by X to declare himself trustee of £100 for Y without identifying the source of the money. Thus in *Hemmens v. Wilson Browne (a firm)*[26] a document purporting to give A the right to call on B for payment of £110,000 at any time did not create a trust (or any other right) because there was no identifiable fund to form its subject matter.

Of course, there is no difficulty in a trust of a co-owned share, but that solution was rejected in *Hunter v. Moss*[27]: the plaintiff did not have a tenancy in common interest in the whole but was equitable owner of 50 shares. Criticisms of *Hunter v. Moss* point to the difficulties which could arise on subsequent dealings with the shareholding or bank account of which an unsegregated part is subject to a trust. Before any such dealings, the beneficiary could call for a transfer of the money or shares. But what would happen if, after declaring a trust of 50 out of 950 shares, the settlor then sold 50 shares and invested the proceeds (disastrously or profitably)? Whose 50 shares were they? There seems no reason why the tracing rules relating to mixed assets should not apply.[28] Those rules normally deal with trust property which has subsequently become mixed with other property, but there seems no reason why they should be so confined. In any event, it could be said that a settlor who declares a trust of part of his shareholding or bank balance becomes under a duty to segregate the trust assets from his own. Tracing will not work, on the other hand, in a case like *MacJordan*[29] because there is no identifiable mixed fund; the employer there had only one bank account in credit at the insolvency but had never assumed an obligation to set up the retention fund out of that account.[30] It may be that the tracing rules will not always work in a case like *Hunter v. Moss*,[31] but inability to trace need not mean that there was no valid trust in the first place.

It has been said that the approval of *MacJordan*[32] by the Privy Council in *Re Goldcorp Exchange Ltd*[33] shows by inference that

[25] *Ibid.* at p. 360.
[26] [1995] Ch. 223 (a professional negligence action).
[27] [1994] 1 W.L.R. 452. Co-ownership is preferred in (1994–95) 5 K.C.L.J. 139 (P. Oliver). It is also the legislative solution for goods; Sale of Goods (Amendment) Act 1995, *supra.*
[28] *Post*, p. 667.
[29] *Supra.*
[30] To claim a charge over the general assets would go beyond even the unorthodox dicta in *Space Investments Ltd v. Canadian Imperial Bank of Commerce Trust Co. (Bahamas)* [1986] 1 W.L.R. 1072; *post*, p. 667.
[31] See criticisms in All E.R. Rev. 1994 p. 250 (P. Clarke).
[32] *Supra.*
[33] [1995] 1 A.C. 74; *supra.*

Hunter v. Moss is incorrect.[34] This would be so only if *Hunter* and *MacJordan* were indistinguishable, but the discussion above sought to establish that *Hunter* may be distinguished on the basis that the larger asset from which the trust was carved was identified. It is submitted that the *Hunter v. Moss* solution is fair, sensible and workable.[35] Unlike the other cases, it did not involve a claim by unsecured creditors to gain priority in insolvency. It is an example of the court's policy of preventing a clearly intended trust from failing for uncertainty.[36]

Before leaving the question of certainty of subject-matter, it might be said that uncertainty as to the precise scope of property subjected to a secret trust,[37] a trust arising under mutual wills,[38] or a constructive trust of a family home,[39] has not proved fatal to its validity. Insistence on strict rules in these contexts could facilitate fraud or unjust enrichment.

C. Certainty of Objects: The Beneficiaries[40]

"It is clear law that a trust (other than a charitable trust) must be for ascertainable beneficiaries."[41] In the case of future interests, the beneficiaries must be ascertainable within the period of perpetuity.[42] The test to be applied to determine certainty of objects depends upon the nature of the trust. With a "fixed" trust, it is, and always has been, that a trust is void unless it is possible to ascertain every beneficiary. With a discretionary trust, the House of Lords decided in *McPhail v. Doulton*[43] that the test was: can it be said with certainty that any individual is or is not a member of the class?[44] That is the same test as was established for certainty of objects of a mere power in *Re Gulbenkian's Settlements*.[45] This assimilation of the tests for powers and discretionary trusts destroys what used to be

---

[34] (1994) 110 L.Q.R. 335 (D. Hayton); (1995) 9 *Trust Law International* 43 at p. 45 (P. Birks).

[35] See (1995) 48 C.L.P. 117 (A. Clarke).

[36] See *Re Golay's W.T.* [1965] 1 W.L.R. 969; *ante*, p. 93; *Re Tepper's W.T.* [1987] Ch. 358; *post*, p. 103.

[37] *Ottaway v. Norman* [1972] Ch. 698, *post*, p. 151.

[38] *Re Cleaver* [1981] 1 W.L.R. 939, *post*, p. 310.

[39] *Gissing v. Gissing* [1971] A.C. 886 at 909; *Stokes v. Anderson* [1991] 1 F.L.R. 391; *post*, p. 271.

[40] (1971) 24 C.L.P. 133 (H. Cohen); (1971) 87 L.Q.R. 31 (J. Harris); (1971) 29 C.L.J. 68 (J. Hopkins); (1973) 5 N.Z.U.L.R. 348; (1974) 37 M.L.R. 643 (Y. Grbich); (1973) 7 V.U.W.L.R. 258 (L. McKay); (1975) 4 Anglo-American L.R. 442 (S. Fradley); (1982) 98 L.Q.R. 551 (C. Emery); Law Com. No. 58 para. 63.

[41] *Per* Lord Denning in *Re Vandervell's Trusts (No. 2)* [1974] Ch. 269 at p. 319; *Re Wood* [1949] Ch. 498.

[42] *Re Flavel's W.T.* [1969] 1 W.L.R. 444 at pp. 446–447.

[43] [1971] A.C. 424.

[44] *Per* Lord Wilberforce [1971] A.C. 424 at pp. 454, 456.

[45] [1970] A.C. 508; *post*, p. 99.

one of the most important reasons for distinguishing between trusts and powers.[46]

i. Fixed Trusts. A fixed trust is one in which the share or interest of the beneficiaries is specified in the instrument. The beneficiary is the owner of the equitable interest allocated to him. This situation is contrasted with a discretionary trust; where the trustees hold the trust property on trust for such member or members of a class of beneficiaries as they shall in their absolute discretion determine. In that situation, no beneficiary owns any part of the trust fund unless and until the trustees have exercised their discretion in his favour.[47]

Commonly, but not necessarily, there is a fixed trust where there are successive interests in favour of individual beneficiaries; such as a trust for A for life and then for B absolutely. Where there is a gift for a class, it is necessary in the case of a fixed trust to lay down what share each beneficiary is to take; a discretionary trust will provide for the trustees to exercise a discretion in the selection of a beneficiary. The requirement of certainty in discretionary trusts is considered in (ii) below. The point here is that if trust property is to be divided among a class of beneficiaries in equal (or in any other fixed) shares, the trust cannot, in the nature of things, be administered unless the number and identify of beneficiaries are known. Some of the language in *McPhail v. Doulton*[48] might suggest the decision applied to all trusts. But it concerned a discretionary trust and the cases which it examines are cases of discretionary trusts.[49] Although the rule of certainty should be the minimum necessary to make the trust workable, a stricter rule is needed for fixed trusts. How could the trustee or the court administer a trust for "my employees, ex-employees and their relatives and dependants in equal shares"?[50]

To summarise the position, what is required of a fixed trust is that the description of beneficiaries should involve neither conceptual nor evidential uncertainty.[51] But the court will strive to uphold the trust and a common-sense approach will be taken. Furthermore, provided the identity of the beneficiaries is known, it is no objection that their whereabouts or continued existence is not discoverable, as their shares can be paid into court.[52] The requirement is that a list

[46] *Re Gestetner Settlement* [1953] Ch. 672.
[47] *Post*, p. 203.
[48] [1971] A.C. 424.
[49] *Re Ogden* [1933] Ch. 678; *I.R.C. v. Broadway Cottages Trust* [1955] Ch. 678.
[50] *McPhail v. Doulton, supra.* See [1984] Conv. 22 (P. Matthews), suggesting that complete ascertainment is not necessary in the case of fixed trusts. This is doubted at [1984] Conv. 304 (J. Martin) and 307 (D. Hayton).
[51] *Post*, p. 101.
[52] (1982) 98 L.Q.R. 551 (C. Emery); *cf.* [1984] Conv. 22 (P. Matthews).

will be able to be drawn, which is on balance of probabilities complete, as to the maximum number of shares, at the time for distribution.

ii. Discretionary Trusts. The rule of certainty should be no stricter than is necessary to permit trustees to perform their duties. We have seen that, where the trust property is to be divided into specific shares, it is necessary for the trustees to know exactly how many beneficiaries there are. Until 1971, the same rule applied to discretionary trusts[53] (sometimes confusingly called "trust powers"[54]). If the trustees should fail or refuse to carry out their duty to select the beneficiaries and distribute, the court must be able to do so; and, it was argued, the court would necessarily distribute equally on the basis that equality is equity and, for that purpose, the beneficiaries must be identifiable.[55] The fallacy of this argument was shown in *McPhail v. Doulton*.[56]

> Bertram Baden executed a deed establishing a fund to provide benefits for the staff of a company and their relatives and dependants.
> Clause 9(*a*) provided as follows: "The trustees shall apply the net income of the fund in making at their absolute discretion grants to or for the benefit of any of the officers and employees or ex-officers or ex-employees of the company or to any relatives or dependants of any such persons in such amounts at such times and on such conditions (if any) as they think fit."
> The trustees were not obliged to exhaust the income of any year. Capital could be realised for the purpose of making grants if the income was insufficient.

The deed created a discretionary trust not a mere power. It was not possible to make a list of all the members of the class of beneficiaries. The House of Lords, however, held that the test for certainty in discretionary trusts was that applied to fiduciary powers in *Re Gulbenkian's Settlements*.[57] "Can it be said with certainty that any given individual is or is not a member of the class?"[58] The case was referred to the Chancery Division to determine whether the test was satisfied. The Court of Appeal held that it was.[59]

---

[53] *I.R.C. v. Broadway Cottages Trust* [1955] Ch. 678.
[54] For a possible distinction between these two terms, see *post*, p. 109.
[55] [1971] A.C. 424 at p. 442, *per* Lord Hodson.
[56] *Supra*, (1970) 34 Conv.(N.S.) 287 (F. Crane). One result of the decision is to confirm that a trust may be valid although it is impossible to state who is entitled to the equitable interest. See [1982] Conv. 118 (A. Everton).
[57] [1970] A.C. 508.
[58] *Per* Lord Wilberforce [1971] A.C. 424 at pp. 454, 456.
[59] [1973] Ch. 9; *post*, p. 101.

In reaching a decision on the question of the test to be applied, it was necessary to deal with two main arguments in favour of the stricter test. First, that a trustee's duty to distribute could only be performed if he was able to consider every possible claimant; and secondly, that the court could only execute the trust, on failure of the trustees to do so, by equal division of the fund. If these arguments could be answered, there was much to be said for assimilating the test with that for powers; for, although the distinction between trust and power is, in some contexts, basic to a lawyer, it is often difficult to ascertain which exists in any particular case. Thus a relaxation of the test was needed to save many trusts from failure.

A trustee's duty to distribute requires a consideration of the claims of possible recipients. "If [a trustee] has to distribute the whole of a fund's income, he must necessarily make a wider and more systematic survey than if his duty is expressed in terms of a power to make grants"[60]; and later, "a wider and more comprehensive range of inquiry is called for in the case of a trust power than in the case of a power."[61] But the difference is only one of degree; there is no need for a trustee of a discretionary trust to "require the preparation of a complete list of names."[62] The difference does not justify a stricter rule for certainty in discretionary trusts.

The main question is whether the court can execute the trust upon the failure of the trustees to do so. This is primarily a theoretical problem. In the reported cases there have been no examples of trustees refusing to execute a discretionary trust; if a trustee did so, he could be removed and replaced. Secondly, "it does not follow that execution is impossible unless there can be equal division."[63] There are a number of cases, prior to 1801,[64] in which the court exercised a discretion in relation to distribution, deciding in accordance with guidance given by the circumstances of the case.[65] In many of these situations equal division would have been inappropriate. As indeed it would be in modern forms of discretionary trusts for the benefit of employees and their dependants. It would have been paradoxical if the trust in *McPhail v. Doulton*[66] had failed because of the court's inability to divide equally; for equal division would have been a nonsensical solution. Thus, the court, if called upon to execute a discretionary trust, will do so in the manner best calculated to give effect to the testator's intentions. "It may do

---

[60] [1971] A.C. 424 at pp. 449, 457; (1971) 87 L.Q.R. 31 at pp. 61–62.
[61] [1973] Ch. 9 at p. 27.
[62] [1971] A.C. 424 at p. 449.
[63] *Ibid.* at p. 451.
[64] *Kemp v. Kemp* (1801) 5 Ves.Jr. 849.
[65] *Mosely v. Mosely* (1673) Fin. 53; *Clarke v. Turner* (1694) Free Ch. 198; *Warburton v. Warburton* (1702) 4 Bro.P.C. 1; *Richardson v. Chapman* (1760) 7 Bro.P.C. 318.
[66] [1971] A.C. 424.

so by appointing new trustees, or by authorising or directing representative persons of the classes of beneficiaries to prepare a scheme
of distribution, or even, should the proper basis for distribution
appear, by itself directing the trustees so to distribute."[67] In cases
where the trustees have failed to exercise their discretion within a
reasonable time, the court may direct them to do so, provided there
is no evidence of bias or obstinacy.[68] There is no need therefore to
require a stricter rule for discretionary trusts than that accepted in
Gulbenkian[69] as applicable to powers.

It is thought that this less stringent test will also apply to purpose
trusts upheld on the principle of *Re Denley's Trust Deed*[70] as being
for the benefit of ascertainable individuals.

iii. Conceptual Uncertainty[71] **and Evidential Difficulties.** In
Re Baden's Deed Trusts (No. 2), Brightman J.,[72] and then the Court
of Appeal,[73] had to apply the test laid down by the House of Lords,
and consider in particular whether the words "dependants" and
"relatives" were too uncertain. In applying the test "it is essential to
bear in mind the difference between conceptual uncertainty and
evidential difficulties."[74] The test is concerned with the former; "the
court is never defeated by evidential uncertainty."[75] The illustration
given of a conceptual question is that of the contrasting cases
"someone under a moral obligation", which is conceptually uncertain and "first cousins", which is conceptually certain.[76] It would be
possible in the latter case, but not in the former, to say with certainty
"that any given individual is or is not a member of the class."[77] It
is no objection that it may be difficult to establish whether or not any
given person satisfies the description, so long as the description is

---

[67] *Ibid.* at p. 457, *per* Lord Wilberforce. See also *Mettoy Pension Trustees Ltd v. Evans* [1990]
1 W.L.R. 1587, holding that the court has similar powers of intervention in the case of
fiduciary powers.

[68] *Re Locker's Settlement* [1977] 1 W.L.R. 1323; (1978) 94 L.Q.R. 177. The distribution must
be in favour of those who were objects at the time the discretion should have been
exercised. It is otherwise in the case of a mere power, where the default gift will operate
if the power is not exercised within the proper time limits.

[69] [1970] A.C. 508.

[70] [1969] 1 Ch. 373, *post*, p. 349. See *R. v. District Auditor, ex p. West Yorkshire Metropolitan
County Council* (1986) 26 R.V.R. 24, holding that "administrative unworkability" (*infra*)
was fatal to a *Re Denley* type of purpose trust.

[71] Sometimes called linguistic or semantic uncertainty.

[72] [1972] Ch. 607.

[73] [1973] Ch. 9; (1973) 36 Conv.(N.S.) 351 (D. Hayton).

[74] *Per* Sachs L.J. [1973] Ch. 9 at p. 19; see also, *per* Lord Wilberforce [1971] A.C. 424 at
p. 457.

[75] *Ibid.* at p. 20; in *Re Tuck's S.T.* [1978] Ch. 49 at p. 59, Lord Denning M.R. in the context
of a condition precedent, confessed that he found "the dichotomy most unfortunate."

[76] *Ibid.*

[77] *Ante*, p. 99.

conceptually clear.[78] In each case the precise words must of course be examined to see whether the test is satisfied. Once the class is determined as being conceptually certain the question of inclusion is an issue of fact. "Relatives" and "dependants" were both sufficiently certain.

Provided the class is certain in the above sense, it does not matter that the whereabouts or continued existence of an object is not known.[79]

iv. Problems with the Test. The test is not without its difficulties, theoretical and practical.

(a) *What is Conceptually Certain?* Different minds may take different views on the question of whether a particular description is conceptually certain or not. Indeed, the illustrations referred to in the previous paragraph, which were selected to make the point, are not wholly persuasive. The problem is that few descriptions of the kind likely to be encountered in trusts and powers are so clear as to admit of no borderline cases. Most fall between those which are indisputably certain, for example "Nobel prize winners", and those which are conceptually unclear, for example "friends." To insist on complete certainty would be to defeat most gifts. Dispositions ought if possible to be upheld and "should not be held void on a peradventure."[80] Words such as "relatives" may cause difficulties[81] but trustees can be expected to act sensibly and not to select a remote kinsman.[82] The best solution, it is submitted, is to regard such words as conceptually certain, leaving it to the claimant to establish his case, as discussed below. Words such as "friends", on the other hand, must fall on the wrong side of the line. Although "old friends" was upheld in *Re Gibbard*,[83] this was the result of applying a test which has not survived later decisions,[84] namely that it was sufficient that there was some person who could be shown to be within the class. Browne-Wilkinson J., in *Re Barlow's Will Trusts*,[85] attempted to clarify who a "friend" was. But that was in the context of a gift subject to a condition precedent, which, as we shall see,[86] is governed by a less strict test.

---

[78] This is discussed further below. Such evidential difficulties would, however, invalidate a fixed trust; *ante*, p. 98.

[79] *Re Gulbenkian's Settlement Trusts* [1970] A.C. 508; (1982) 98 L.Q.R. 551 (C. Emery). This point is more significant in the case of fixed trusts.

[80] *Re Hay's Settlement Trusts* [1982] 1 W.L.R. 202 at p. 212.

[81] *Infra.*

[82] *Re Baden's Deed Trusts (No. 2)* [1973] Ch. 9.

[83] [1967] 1 W.L.R. 42. See also *Re Byron's Settlement* [1891] 3 Ch. 474 (bare power).

[84] See *Gulbenkian's Settlement Trusts (No. 1)* [1970] A.C. 508.

[85] [1979] 1 W.L.R. 278. It was said that a trust or power in favour of "friends" would probably fail. See also *Re Byron's Settlement* [1891] 3 Ch. 474.

[86] *Post*, p. 109.

Conceptual uncertainty may in some cases be cured by a provision that the opinion of a third party (the trustees or another person) is to settle the matter. In *Re Coxen*[87] it was held that the testator could validly make the trustees' opinion the criterion provided he had sufficiently defined the state of affairs on which they were to form their opinion. The question whether the testator's wife had "ceased permanently to reside" at a property passed this test, whereas in *Re Jones*[88] the question whether X should at any time have a "social or other relationship" with Y in the "uncontrolled opinion" of the trustees was insufficiently defined to enable the trustees to come to a proper decision. A gift to persons "having a moral claim" on the donor would be conceptually uncertain, but a gift to "such persons as the company may consider to have a moral claim" on the donor would satisfy the test.[89] Similarly, any uncertainty in the requirement of being of the Jewish faith and married to an "approved wife" could be cured by a provision that disputes were to be decided by a chief rabbi.[90] The settlor or testator cannot, however, purport to oust the jurisdiction of the court by giving the trustees conclusive power to construe the words used.[91] Such a clause will be void as contrary to public policy. Assuming the power to resolve an uncertainty has been validly given to trustees, the court may intervene if it is exercised in bad faith and possibly on other grounds.[92]

(b) *Proof of Inclusion and Exclusion; Proving Negatives.* Read strictly, the test means that it must be possible to show either that any person is within the class or that he is not within it. But, how could you show that a person is, for example, not your relative? Sachs L.J.[93] said that the claimant needs to show that he is within the class; if he cannot do that, he is not within it. His Lordship was here referring to evidential uncertainty. Clearly conceptual uncertainty

---

[87] [1948] Ch. 747 at pp. 761–762 (condition subsequent).

[88] [1953] Ch. 125 (condition subsequent).

[89] *Re Leek* [1969] 1 Ch. 563; *cf. Re Wright's W.T.* (1981) 78 L.S.Gaz. 841 (gift to trustees "for such people and institutions as they think have helped me or my late husband" uncertain. See also *Re Coates* [1955] Ch. 495 (for any friends the testator's wife might feel he had forgotten). In the case of a discretionary trust, difficulties might arise if the court is called upon to execute it.

[90] *Re Tuck's Settlement Trusts* [1978] Ch. 49 (in fact the condition was held certain). For a contrary view, see Underhill and Hayton (15th ed.), p. 71. See also *Re Tepper's Will Trusts* [1987] Ch. 358, holding that the meaning of "Jewish faith" could be elucidated by extrinsic evidence of the faith as practised by the testator; All E.R. Rev. 1987, p. 159 (P. Clarke) and 260 (C. Sherrin). *Cf.* A.J.A. 1982, s.21.

[91] *Re Wynn* [1952] Ch. 271; *Re Raven* [1915] 1 Ch. 673.

[92] *Post*, p. 508.

[93] [1973] Ch. 9; and see (1973) 32 C.L.J. 36 (J. Hopkins).

cannot be cured by casting the onus of proof on to the claimant, because the matter would not be susceptible of proof.[94] Megaw L.J. said that the test was satisfied[95] "if, as regards at least a substantial number of objects, it can be said with certainty that they fall within the trust; even though, as regards a substantial number of other persons . . . the answer would have to be, not 'they are outside the trust,' but 'it is not proven whether they are in or out.'" His Lordship suggested that to require proof that every person was or was not within the class would return to the old rule requiring the making of a list. This seems doubtful. To be in a position to accept or reject the claim of any given person does not require ascertainment of the whole class. The "substantial number" test might be thought to be a return to the *Gibbard*[96] test which was rejected in *Gulbenkian.*[97] This is not so, as the *Gibbard*[98] test allowed a degree of conceptual uncertainty, while the statement of Megaw L.J. quoted above concerns evidential uncertainty. It is submitted that the majority view is to be preferred to the somewhat stricter test laid down by Stamp L.J., which seems to require that the trustees be in a position to say affirmatively whether any given person is within or outside the class. His Lordship considered that the validity or invalidity of a discretionary trust depended on[99] "whether you can say of any individual—and the accent must be on that word 'any' for it is not simply the individual whose claim you are considering who is spoken of—[that he] 'is or is not a member of the class,' for only thus can you make a survey of the range of objects or possible beneficiaries." If Stamp L.J. had not been able to construe "relatives" as meaning "next-of-kin" or "nearest blood relations" he would have held the trust void for uncertainty.[1]

(c) *Width of the Class; Administrative Unworkability.*[2] Lord Wilberforce in *McPhail v. Doulton*[3] indicated that there might be a

---

[94] *Cf. Re Barlow's Will Trusts* [1979] 1 W.L.R. 278, *post*, p. 109.

[95] [1973] Ch. 9 at p. 24.

[96] [1967] 1 W.L.R. 42.

[97] [1970] A.C. 508.

[98] *Supra.*

[99] [1973] Ch. 9 at p. 28.

[1] The view of the majority was that it meant "descendants from a common ancestor." It has long been established that "relatives" should be confined to next of kin only if this is necessary to save the gift, *e.g.* where the "list test" applies. See *Re Shield's W.T.* [1974] 2 W.L.R. 885; *Re Barlow's W.T.* [1979] 1 W.L.R. 278; *Re Poulton's W.T.* [1987] 1 W.L.R. 795.

[2] See (1991) 107 L.Q.R. 214 at 218 (S. Gardner): "it is not easy to see just what difficulty it is aimed at pre-empting."

[3] [1971] A.C. 424; criticised on this point in (1974) 38 Conv.(N.S.) 269 (L. McKay); (1974) 37 M.L.R. 643 (Y. Grbich).

difference in one situation between the test to be applied to discretionary trusts and that for mere powers. A description of beneficiaries which might comply with the certainty test laid down might be "so hopelessly wide as not to form 'anything like a class,' so that the trust is administratively unworkable,"[4] and he hesitatingly gave as an example a class consisting of "all the residents of Greater London." This was said in the context of a discretionary trust. The question has arisen whether this concept applies also to mere powers. Buckley L.J. assumed *obiter* that it did in *Blausten v. I.R.C.*[5] This was doubted in *Re Manisty's Settlement*,[6] where Templeman J. held that a mere power could not be invalid on the ground of width of numbers, preferring the view that its validity should depend on whether or not it was capricious. This point is discussed below. *Manisty* was preferred to *Blausten* by Megarry V.-C. in *Re Hay's Settlement Trusts*.[7] A mere power, whether or not fiduciary, was not invalid on the ground of the size of the class. Mere numbers could not prevent the trustee from considering whether to exercise the power nor from performing his other duties,[8] nor prevent the court from controlling him. But it was suggested that a discretionary trust in favour of the same wide class[9] as the mere power would have been void as administratively unworkable, as the duties of a discretionary trustee were more stringent, and the objects of a discretionary trust had rights of enforcement which objects of a mere power lacked. A similar view was taken in *R. v. District Auditor, ex p. West Yorkshire Metropolitan County Council*,[10] where a local authority, purporting to act under statutory powers, resolved to set up a trust "for the benefit of any or all or some of the inhabitants of the County of West Yorkshire."[11] There were 2,500,000 potential beneficiaries. The court was prepared to assume that "inhabitant" was sufficiently certain, but held the trust void for administrative unworkability as the class was far too large, applying Lord Wilberforce's dictum in *McPhail v. Doulton*.[12] *Re Manisty's Settlement*[13] was distinguished as concerning a power, where the function of the

[4] *Ibid.* at p. 427.
[5] [1972] Ch. 256. The power was upheld because the trustees' power to include any other person as an object was subject to the settlor's consent. The settlor had, therefore, put "metes and bounds" on the otherwise unrestricted class.
[6] [1974] Ch. 17. In *Re Beatty's W.T.* [1990] 1 W.L.R. 1503, [1991] Conv. 138 (J. Martin), a fiduciary power given to trustees in favour of "such person or persons as they think fit" was upheld without mention of the concept of administrative unworkability.
[7] [1982] 1 W.L.R. 202.
[8] *i.e.* to make no unauthorised appointment; to consider the range of objects; to consider the appropriateness of any individual appointment.
[9] Any person except the settlor, settlor's spouse or trustees.
[10] (1986) 26 R.V.R. 24 (Q.B.D.); (1986) 45 C.L.J. 391 (C. Harpum).
[11] The details of the trust, which was not charitable, are given in Chap. 14, *post*, p. 350.
[12] *Supra.*
[13] *Supra.*

court was more restricted. The weight of authority, therefore, supports the view that "administrative unworkability" can invalidate discretionary trusts but not mere powers.[14]

(d) *Capriciousness.* There is no general principle of English law that a capricious disposition is invalid. Wigram V.-C. in *Bird v. Luckie*[15] said, "No man is bound to make a will in such a manner as to deserve approbation from the prudent, the wise, or the good. A testator is permitted to be capricious and improvident, and moreover is at liberty to conceal the circumstances and the motives by which he has been actuated in his dispositions."

But while a capricious legacy may be valid, the position may be otherwise in a discretionary trust or power. Unlike an outright gift, discretionary trusts and powers involve fiduciary obligations, the performance of which may be rendered impossible if their terms are capricious. In upholding a power of great width in *Re Manisty's Settlement*[16] Templeman J. held that the terms of the power need not provide guidance to the trustees; an absolute discretion did not preclude a sensible consideration of whether and how to exercise the power. The example of a class comprising "residents of Greater London" would be capricious and void, not on the basis of numbers, but on the ground that the terms of the power negatived any sensible intention on the settlor's part and any sensible consideration by the trustees. The objects must either be unlimited, in which case the trustees can perform their obligations sensibly, or limited to a "sensible" class. The disposition would be void if membership of the class of objects was accidental and irrelevant to any purpose or to any method of limiting or selecting beneficiaries.[17]

Is "capriciousness" the same notion as "administrative unworkability?"[18] The latter, as we have seen, has been held inapplicable to mere powers, while the former has been held applicable to both mere powers and discretionary trusts.[19] In *R. v. District Auditor, ex p. West Yorkshire Metropolitan County Council*[20] a trust for the

---

[14] *Cf.* [1982] Conv. 432 at p. 434 (A. Grubb), (1982) 98 L.Q.R. 551 (C. Emery) and [1990] Conv. 24 (I. Hardcastle), taking the view that it applies also to powers, and Riddall, *The Law of Trusts* (4th ed.), p. 25, taking the view that it applies also to fixed trusts. It has been suggested that one result of *Mettoy Pension Trustees Ltd v. Evans* [1990] 1 W.L.R. 1587, which adapts discretionary trust remedies to fiduciary powers, may be to make the concept of administrative unworkability appicable to powers; (1991) 107 L.Q.R. 214 (S. Gardner).

[15] (1850) 8 Hare 301. See also *Re James's Will Trusts* [1962] Ch. 226.

[16] [1974] Ch. 17.

[17] *Ibid.* at p. 26. See [1982] Conv. 432 at p. 435 (A. Grubb) explaining that the "appointment criteria", necessary to avoid invalidity on the ground of capriciousness, need not be apparent from the power itself.

[18] See (1982) 98 L.Q.R. 551 (C. Emery) for the view that they are the same.

[19] See *Re Manisty's Settlement, supra*; *Re Hay's Settlement Trusts* [1982] 1 W.L.R. 202.

[20] (1986) 26 R.V.R. 24, (1986) 45 C.L.J. 391 (C. Harpum); *ante*, p. 105.

benefit of 2,500,000 inhabitants of West Yorkshire was held void for administrative unworkability (as being too large a class) even though it was not capricious because the local authority (the settlor) had every reason to wish to benefit the inhabitants in the ways specified. Thus it appears that the two concepts are distinct, although the same example may give rise to invalidity on both grounds. Capriciousness has no necessary connection with width of numbers, which is the characteristic of administrative unworkability.

It might also be mentioned that the capricious exercise of a fiduciary power or trust, as where objects are chosen by height or complexion, will be invalid even though the power or trust is valid.[21]

(e) *Duty to Survey the Field.* Clearly the trustees of a discretionary trust are not obliged to consider every object, as the trust may be valid although the identity of all the objects is not known. But as we have seen, Lord Wilberforce in *McPhail v. Doulton*[22] considered that the trustees ought to make such a survey of the range of objects as would enable them to carry out their fiduciary duty, and that a wider or more comprehensive range of enquiry was called for in the case of discretionary trusts than in the case of powers. In the case of a wide-ranging discretionary trust, where the number of objects may run to hundreds of thousands, the trustees' duty is to assess in a businesslike way "the size of the problem."[23] Megarry V.-C. in *Re Hay's Settlement Trusts,*[24] said:

"The trustee must not simply proceed to exercise the power in favour of such of the objects as happen to be at hand or claim his attention. He must first consider what persons or classes of persons are objects of the power... there is no need to compile a complete list of the objects, or even to make an accurate assessment of the number of them: what is needed is an appreciation of the width of the field, and thus whether a selection is to be made merely from a dozen or, instead, from thousands or millions. ... Only when the trustee has applied his mind to the 'size of the problem' should he then consider in individual cases whether, in relation to other possible claimants, a particular grant is appropriate. In doing this, no doubt he should not prefer the undeserving to the deserving; but he is not required to make an exact calculation whether, as between deserving claimants, A is more deserving than B."

---

[21] *Re Manisty's Settlement, supra; Re Hay's Settlement Trusts, supra.*
[22] [1971] A.C. 424; criticised in (1974) 37 M.L.R. 643 (Y. Grbich).
[23] *Re Baden's Deed Trusts (No. 2)* [1973] Ch. 9 at p. 20 (*per* Sachs L.J.).
[24] [1982] 1 W.L.R. 202 at pp. 209–210.

This was the duty which had emerged from cases concerning discretionary trusts, but "plainly the requirements for a mere power cannot be more stringent than those for a discretionary trust."[25] The duties of a trustee of a discretionary trust are more stringent than those of the donee of a fiduciary power because of the obligation to distribute. The precise scope of the less onerous duty to survey in the case of a power awaits clarification.[26]

(f) *Many Certain Categories; One Uncertain.* Further difficulties could arise with a definition of a class of beneficiaries which contained a long series of categories which complied with the *McPhail v. Doulton* test, but to which there was added one category which did not. What, for example, would the court say to a trust in the same language as that in *McPhail v. Doulton* but to which there was added "any other person to whom I may be under a moral obligation and any of my old friends"? . . . which is, let it be assumed, conceptually uncertain. The same problem could arise in a case of power.

In this situation, the class as the whole does not satisfy the test. It would however be unfortunate to declare the whole trust void because of the final addition. After all, the trust is workable as it is. Such a trust, however, may be held void unless it is possible to excise the offending phrase by severance; a suggestion which is made on more than one occasion,[27] but which cannot yet be relied on.

v. Effect of Certainty Tests on Rights of Objects. When, prior to *McPhail v. Doulton*,[28] complete ascertainment of objects was required in the case of a discretionary trust, it was thought that each object had a right to be considered, and to share in the fund if the trustees failed in their duty to exercise their discretion. Clearly this is no longer accurate, now that the trust may be valid without the necessity of ascertaining the full membership of the class. The question of equal division in default of exercise has already been

---

[25] *Ibid.* This may be contrasted with the view of Harman J. in *Re Gestetner* [1953] Ch. 672 at p. 688: " . . . there is no obligation on the trustees to do more than consider from time to time the merits of such persons of the specified class as are known to them. . . . " See also Templeman J. in *Re Manisty's Settlement* [1974] Ch. 14 at p. 25.

[26] See [1982] Conv. 432 at p. 437 (A. Grubb), suggesting that the duty is merely to consider those who press claims and present themselves for inspection; there is no need to "go forth and search out worthy candidates." Presumably this duty arises only if the donee has decided to exercise the power.

[27] *Per* Sachs L.J. in *Re Leek* [1969] 1 Ch. 563 at p. 586 (assuming, however, that legislation would be required); and in the case of a power, by Winn L.J. in *Re Gulbenkian's Settlements* [1968] Ch. 126 at p. 138 (C.A.). *Cf.* decisions on trusts which are not exclusively charitable; *post*, p. 423.

[28] [1971] A.C. 424.

dealt with.[29] Any right to be considered must be confined to the situation where the claim is brought to the attention of the trustees. The right of the object is simply to require that the trustees perform their obligation to allocate the fund after surveying the range of objects, as described above.[30] If the unknown or unascertainable object is not considered by the trustees, at any rate he is no worse off than he would have been prior to *McPhail v. Doulton*,[31] when the possibility of his existence would have caused the discretionary trust to fail.

vi. Trust-Powers in the Old Sense; Trusts with a Power of Selection. If, as a matter of construction, it can be inferred that the settlor's intention was that the entire class should take if the trustee failed to make a selection, then no doubt equal division is still appropriate, in which case the "complete ascertainment" test must still be satisfied. This is more likely to be the case in a family trust, where the objects are not large in number, as in *Burrough v. Philcox*.[32] It may be that the minority and the majority in *McPhail v. Doulton*[33] were talking at cross-purposes, the former having in mind the more old-fashioned trust-power as described above, while the latter analysed the modern discretionary trust in favour of a large class, where the settlor could not have contemplated equal division.[34]

vii. Gifts Subject to a Condition Precedent. A less strict test applies where there is a gift subject to a condition precedent as opposed to a discretionary trust or power. A degree of conceptual uncertainty does not invalidate such a gift.[35] The test, as laid down in *Re Allen*,[36] is that the gift is valid if it is possible to say that one or more persons qualify, even though there may be difficulty as to others. This test may also apply to personal (non-fiduciary) powers.[37]

This test fell to be considered by Browne-Wilkinson J. in *Re Barlow's Will Trust*,[38] where the testatrix left a valuable collection of

---

[29] *Ante*, p. 100.

[30] See generally *Re Hay's Settlement Trusts*, *supra*; *Turner v. Turner* [1984] Ch. 100.

[31] *Supra*.

[32] (1840) 5 Myl. & Cr. 72; *ante*, p. 62.

[33] *Supra*.

[34] See (1974) 37 M.L.R. 643 (Y. Grbich); (1982) 98 L.Q.R. 551 (C. Emery). For the proper meaning of "trust power", see [1984] Conv. 227 (R. Bartlett and C. Stebbings).

[35] A stricter test applies to a condition subsequent. The distinction, though criticised by Lord Denning M.R. in *Re Tuck's Settlement Trusts* [1978] Ch. 49, was acknowledged by the House of Lords in *Blaithwayt v. Lord Cawley* [1976] A.C. 397 at p. 425; *post*, p. 328. See also *Re Tepper's Will Trusts* [1987] Ch. 358.

[36] [1953] Ch. 810.

[37] (1982) 98 L.Q.R. 551 (C. Emery); *Re Byron's Settlement* [1891] 3 Ch. 474.

[38] [1979] 1 W.L.R. 278; criticised [1980] Conv. 263 (L. McKay). (1982) 98 L.Q.R. 551 (C. Emery). See also Underhill and Hayton (15th ed.), pp. 80–82.

paintings, directing her executor to sell those not specifically bequeathed, subject to a proviso that "any friends of mine who may wish to do so" be allowed to purchase any of them at a price below the market value. This disposition was held sufficiently certain. Total ascertainment of the testatrix's friends was not required. A "friend" was a person who had a relationship of long standing with the testatrix, which was a social as opposed to a business or professional relationship; and who had met her frequently when circumstances permitted.[39] The effect of the gift was to confer on her friends a series of options to purchase. There was no legal necessity to inform them of their rights, although this would be desirable. The claimant must prove "by any reasonable test" that he qualified.[40] In case of doubt, the executors could apply to the court for directions. The justification for this less strict test was that in the case of individual gifts, unlike trusts and powers, uncertainty as to some beneficiaries did not affect the quantum of the gift in respect of those who clearly qualified. To uphold the gift in the case of the latter gave effect, at least in part, to the donor's intention.[41]

Although the "condition precedent" test is now settled, this decision illustrates the difficulties inherent in it. The trustees could be in real difficulty in giving effect to such a disposition. The solution that trustees could apply to court in cases of doubt is unsatisfactory. How can the court be in any better position than the trustees to pronounce on the question whether X is a "friend" of Y?

---

[39] [1979] 1 W.L.R. 278 at p. 282.
[40] *Cf. Re Baden's Deed Trusts (No. 2)* [1973] Ch. 9, where the onus of proof on the claimant concerns evidential, and not conceptual, uncertainty.
[41] This has not been regarded as sufficient to justify a less strict test in the case of trusts and powers.

CHAPTER 4

CONSTITUTION OF TRUSTS
EQUITY WILL NOT ASSIST A VOLUNTEER

1. The General Problem 111
  A. Requirements of Conveyance and
    Declaration 111
  B. Methods of Benefiting an Intended
    Donee 112
    i. Outright Transfer 112
    ii. Transfer to Trustee 112
    iii. Declaration of Self as Trustee 112
  C. Contracts to Convey or to Create a
    Trust 113
  D. Beneficial Owner under a Trust 113
2. Transfer of the Property to Trustees upon
  Trust 114
  A. Legal Interests 114
  B. Equitable Interests 116
  C. Act of Third Party Required to Perfect
    Title 117
3. Declaration of Self as Trustee 119
4. Covenants to Settle 121
5. Action for Damages by the Trustees.
  Trusts of Choses in Action 124
  A. Suit by the Trustees 125
    i. Decision to Enforce 125

    ii. Nominal or Substantial Dam-
      ages 125
  B. Trust of the Benefit of the Covenant . 127
  C. Specific Performance at the Suit of the
    Contracting Party 130
  D. Summary 133
6. Trusts of Future Property 133
7. Exceptions to the Rule that Equity Will
  not Assist a Volunteer 135
  A. The Rule in *Strong v. Bird* 135
  B. *Donatio Mortis Causa* 137
    i. The Principle 137
    ii. Contemplation of Death 137
    iii. Delivery of Subject-Matter 138
      (a) Chattels 138
      (b) Choses in Action 138
      (c) Land 139
    iv. The Intention of the Donor 140
    v. Revocation 140
    vi. Exceptions 140
  C. Statutory Exception; Conveyance to
    Minor 141
  D. Proprietary Estoppel 141

1. THE GENERAL PROBLEM

A. Requirements of Conveyance and Declaration

We have seen that the interest of the beneficiary under a trust is a proprietary interest. The legal title is in the trustee; the equitable and beneficial title is in the beneficiary. The trust may be of any form of property—land, chattels, money, choses in action—and for any interest known to the law, whether legal or equitable, in possession, remainder[1] or reversion. An intention to create a trust is, as we have seen, one of the requirements for the creation of an express trust,[2] but it is not sufficient in itself. To declare that A is to hold Blackacre on trust for B does not create a trust unless Blackacre is

---

[1] *Re Ralli's W.T.* [1964] Ch. 288.
[2] *Ante*, p. 90.

conveyed to A. Similarly, a conveyance to A does not create a trust of Blackacre for B unless the trust is properly declared. In short, it is necessary both to declare the trust *and* to convey the property to the trustee.

Many difficulties have been caused by failure to observe these basic propositions. Even where they are observed, complications can arise, and a number of questions are left open. Is it necessary that the conveyance and the declaration be contemporaneous? If X conveys Blackacre to A to hold upon trust for B, a trust is created in favour of B; also if X conveys to A upon trust and later declares the trusts.[3] If X conveys Blackacre to A, he cannot then tell A to hold on trust for B, because after the conveyance A became the absolute owner. May the declaration precede the conveyance? May X create a trust for B by declaring that A is to hold on trust for B; and later convey Blackacre to A? This question raises a number of difficulties as we will see; they will be discussed in this chapter and also in Chapter 5.

B. Methods of Benefiting an Intended Donee

If X is the owner at law and in equity, he can make B the beneficial owner in any one of three ways:

i. Outright Transfer. He can transfer legal and equitable owner-ship to B. In the case of land, this transaction is called a conveyance. With a chattel, it is called a sale or gift; with a chose in action, it is called an assignment; with shares it is usually called a transfer. Whatever type of transaction, X, by following the correct procedure appropriate to the type of property, can transfer his absolute interest, legal and equitable, to B. Obviously if X does not follow the correct procedure, he will not transfer the legal or beneficial interest to B. This self-evident proposition is stated here because arguments have unsuccessfully been raised that an unsuccessful transfer to B might be construed as a declaration of trust for B. It is not.[4]

ii. Transfer to Trustee. X may transfer the property to A to hold on trust for B. Provided that the legal title is correctly transferred to A, according to the type of property concerned, A will become legal owner; and provided that an intention to create a trust in favour of B is sufficiently manifested, B will become equitable and beneficial owner. A holds on trust for B.

iii. Declaration of Self as Trustee. X may declare that he holds the property on trust for B. In this situation all that is necessary is a

---

[3] *Re Tyler* [1967] 1 W.L.R. 1269; *Grey v. I.R.C.* [1960] A.C. 1; *ante*, p. 79.
[4] *Post*, pp. 119 *et seq.*

declaration of trust in favour of B. There is no problem of the legal estate being vested in the trustee. It was, and remains, in X, who is the trustee, holding on trust for B. These three situations should be borne in mind in the discussion which follows.

C. Contracts to Convey or to Create a Trust

Situations (ii) and (iii) above concern the creation of trusts in the strict sense. B in each case will obtain an equitable proprietary interest. In such a situation, it is immaterial whether B gave consideration or not. A gift confers title just as effectively as a sale.

If, however, the transaction in question had been *in*effective to transfer the legal title from X to B in situation (i), what is B's position? If B gave no consideration there is nothing more that he can do; the gift fails, just as it would fail if a Christmas present were promised and not given. Equity will not assist a volunteer. If B gave consideration, the position is different. B could either sue X for damages for breach of contract, or, in appropriate circumstances, obtain specific performance of the contract.[5] If, in situation (ii), B gave consideration for the promise by X to convey to A on trust for B, or—more realistically, for this question usually arises in connection with marriage settlements—if B is treated as being within the marriage consideration,[6] B can compel A to take proceedings against X, either to obtain the property or damages for breach, and to hold the property or the damages on the trusts declared. Thus, B, not being a volunteer, is entitled to enforce the promise; and, in accordance with the principle that equity considers as done that which ought to be done, may be treated as entitled in equity to the property which was the subject of the promise.[7]

D. Beneficial Owner under a Trust

Reference should also be made here to the way in which an equitable owner (the legal title being in trustees) may create interests in favour of other persons out of his equitable interest.

In *Timpson's Executors v. Yerbury*,[8] Romer L.J. said: "Now the equitable interest in property in the hands of a trustee can be disposed of by the person entitled to it in favour of a third party in any one of four . . . ways. The person entitled to it (1) can assign it to the third party directly; (2) can direct the trustees to hold the property in trust for the third party (see *per* Sargant J. in *Re*

[5] *Post*, Chap. 24.
[6] *Post*, pp. 122 *et seq.*
[7] *See Pullan v. Koe* [1913] 1 Ch. 9; *post*, p. 122.
[8] [1936] 1 K.B. 645 at p. 664.

Chrimes[9]); (3) can contract for valuable consideration to assign the equitable interest to him; or (4) can declare himself to be a trustee for him of such interest." Category (2), as Lord Evershed pointed out in *Grey v. I.R.C.*[10] "appears . . . to have been regarded as distinct from both an assignment, on the one hand, and a declaration of trust of the interest in the beneficial owner's hands, on the other."

We know however that such a direction is a "disposition" within Law of Property Act 1925, s.53, according to the wide construction put upon that word by the House of Lords,[11] and required therefore to be in writing. If the beneficial owner authorises the trustees to transfer the legal estate to donees, then the beneficial interest passes to the donees without express mention.[12]

It should also be noted that category (4) creates what is usually called a sub-trust; a situation in which A holds property on trust for B, and B declares himself to be trustee of his interest for C. Unless B has specific duties to perform, he is a bare trustee and apparently drops out, the original trustee A holding on trust for C.[13]

2. Transfer of the Property to Trustees upon Trust

A. Legal Interests

The classic statement of the law relating to the requirement of a transfer of the property to trustees is that of Turner L.J. in *Milroy v. Lord*[14]:

"I take the law of this Court to be well settled, that, in order to render a voluntary settlement valid and effectual, the settlor must have done everything which, according to the nature of the property comprised in the settlement, was necessary to be done in order to transfer the property and render the settlement binding upon him. He may, of course, do this by actually transferring the property to the persons for whom he intends to provide, and the provision will then be effectual, and it will be equally effectual if he transfers the property to a trustee for the purposes of the settlement, or declares that he himself holds it in trust for those purposes; and if the property be personal, the trust may, as I apprehend, be declared either in writing or by parol; but, in order to render the settlement binding, one or other of these modes must, as I understand the law of this court, be resorted to, for there

[9] [1917] 1 Ch. 30.
[10] [1958] Ch. 690 at p. 709 (C.A.).
[11] *Grey v. I.R.C.* [1960] A.C. 1; *ante*, p. 79.
[12] *Vandervell v. I.R.C.* [1967] 2 A.C. 291; *ante*, p. 80.
[13] *Grainge v. Wilberforce* (1889) 5 T.L.R. 436; *ante*, p. 84.
[14] (1862) 4 De G.F. & J. 264 at pp. 274–275. For the position where the trustee disclaims, see *Mallott v. Wilson* [1903] 2 Ch. 494; [1981] Conv. 141 (P. Matthews).

is no equity in this court to perfect an imperfect gift. The cases, I think, go further to this extent, that if the settlement is intended to be effectuated by one of the modes to which I have referred, the Court will not give effect to it by applying another of those modes. If it is intended to take effect by transfer, the court will not hold the intended transfer to operate as a declaration of trust, for then every imperfect instrument would be made effectual by being converted into a perfect trust."

The transfer to the trustees must accord with the rules applicable to the property concerned. Legal estates in land must be transferred by deed,[15] equitable interests[16] and copyright[17] by writing, chattels by deed of gift[18] or by an intention to give coupled with a delivery of possession,[19] a bill of exchange by endorsement,[20] and shares by the appropriate form of transfer followed by registration.[21] Since July 1996 it has been possible to transfer shares in certain quoted companies electronically, thereby avoiding the need for transfer forms and share certificates, but this does not detract from the principle that legal title passes only on registration.[22]

In *Milroy v. Lord*,[23] a settlor executed a voluntary deed purporting to transfer shares in the Bank of Louisiana to Samuel Lord to be held on trust for the plaintiff. The shares, however, could only be transferred by the appropriate transfer form followed by registration of the name of the transferee in the books of the Bank. Lord held a power of attorney to act on behalf of the settlor, and it would have enabled him to take all necessary further steps to obtain registration. But this was not done. The Court of Appeal in Chancery held that there was no trust, although the intention clearly was to benefit the intended beneficiary.

---

[15] L.P.A. 1925, s.52(1). Registration of freeholds and long leases is necessary under the registered title system; L.R.A. 1925. See *Mascall v. Mascall* (1985) 49 P. & C.R. 119, *post*, p. 118.

[16] L.P.A. 1925, s.53(1).

[17] Copyright Designs and Patents Act 1988, s.90(3).

[18] Thus it has been held that a trust of a painting was validly constituted without physical delivery to the trustees (one of whom was in Ireland) on the ground that the formal declaration of trust transferred the property in the painting to the trustees, each of whom had a copy of the document and agreed to act; *Jaffa v. Taylor Gallery Ltd*, *The Times*, March 21, 1990.

[19] *Ryall v. Rolls* (1750) 1 Ves.Sen. 348; *Cochrane v. Moore* (1890) 25 Q.B.D. 57; *Kilpin v. Raltey* [1892] 1 Q.B. 582; *Re Cole* [1964] Ch. 175; *Thomas v. Times Book Co. Ltd* [1966] 1 W.L.R. 911; (1953) 12 C.L.J. 355 (J. Thornely); (1964) 27 M.L.R. 357 (A. Diamond).

[20] Bills of Exchange Act 1882, s.31; see, however, Cheques Act 1957, ss.1, 2.

[21] See Companies Act 1985, ss.182, 183; Stock Transfer Act 1963, s.1.

[22] This is the CREST system. It is not compulsory for companies or investors to use this system, and in July 1996 it did not extend to gilts or unit trusts. It is designed for speedy and economic transfer, and will eventually achieve immediate ownership on payment. See (1996) 146 N.L.J. 964 (R. Pinner).

[23] (1862) 4 De G.F. & J. 264.

On the other hand, once the property has been vested in the trustees, and the trusts declared, the trust is constituted, and the settlor is unable to reclaim the property, even though the beneficiaries may be volunteers.[24] It has been held that the trust may be constituted where the property is vested in the trustees, even though it reached them in a capacity distinct from their office as trustees of the trust in question.

In *Re Ralli's Will Trusts*,[25] a testator left his residuary estate on trust for his widow for life and then for his two daughters Irene and Helen. Helen's marriage settlement included a covenant to settle existing and after-acquired property in favour of (in the events which happened) volunteers. Helen predeceased her mother and so never transferred her remainder interest pursuant to her covenant. The plaintiff was the trustee both of the testator's will and also of Helen's marriage settlement. Buckley J. had to decide on what trusts the residue was held. He concluded, as one ground for his decision, that the vesting of the property in the plaintiff was sufficient to constitute the trusts of the remainder interest even though the property came to him in his other capacity as trustee of the will. "The circumstances that the plaintiff holds the fund because he was appointed a trustee of the will is irrelevant. He is at law the owner of the fund, and the means by which he became so have no effect upon the quality of his legal ownership."[26]

This may be contrasted with *Re Brooks' Settlement Trusts*,[27] where a settlor made a voluntary settlement under which he purported to assign after-acquired property to the trustee, Lloyds Bank. Subsequently a power of appointment under another settlement of which Lloyds Bank was also trustee was exercised in the settlor's favour. It was held that the settlor was entitled to be paid the appointed sum by the Bank because the assignment of a mere expectancy was ineffective. Thus the beneficiaries had no claim.

B. Equitable Interests
The same general principle applies where the settlor's interest is equitable. A correct transfer of the equitable interest to a trustee upon properly declared trusts is necessary to create a trust of that

---

[24] *Paul v. Paul* (1882) 20 Ch.D. 742; *Jefferys v. Jefferys* (1841) Cr. & Ph. 138; *Re Ellenborough* [1903] 1 Ch. 697 (the assets received under her sister's will); *Re Bowden* [1936] Ch. 71; similarly for voluntary covenants to settle: *Re Adlard* [1954] Ch. 29.
[25] [1964] Ch. 288.
[26] *Ibid.* at p. 301.
[27] [1939] 1 Ch. 993, not cited in *Re Ralli's W.T.*

equitable interest. A disposition of an equitable interest must, as has been seen, be in writing.[28] In *Kekewich v. Manning*,[29] shares were held on trust for A for life and then for B. B assigned his equitable interest in remainder to trustees to hold on certain trusts, and this was held to create a trust of the equitable interest in remainder.

C. Act of Third Party Required to Perfect Title

Difficulties can arise where the act of a third party is necessary to perfect the transfer of legal title. The problem commonly involves shares, the legal title to which is transferable by the execution of the form of transfer required by the company's articles, followed by registration in the share register of the company.[30] If the transaction is for consideration, the purchaser becomes equitable owner of the shares from the date of the execution of the document of transfer, and is entitled to dividends declared after that date.[31] The position is the same where shares are transferred electronically.[32] The purchaser becomes equitable owner on generation of the instruction to the registrar and legal owner on registration.

The transfer of shares in a private company is restricted, and the Articles usually provide that the directors may refuse to register the transfer. A difficult situation arises where a settlor makes a voluntary settlement of such shares, executing a transfer which purports to transfer the shares to trustees to be held on the trusts of the settlement. The expectation is that the registration of the transfer will follow and the trust become constituted. The directors however may refuse to register the transfer. In that case, under the strict rule of *Milroy v. Lord*,[33] the trust will be incompletely constituted and a nullity. The validity of the trust would be dependent upon the uncontrollable discretion of the directors. Even if they do register it, the date on which this happens may be crucial in determining whether the transfer is liable to inheritance tax at the full death rate applicable to gifts made within three years of death or at the lower rates for gifts made three to seven years before death.[34]

In *Re Rose*,[35] a settlor by voluntary deed transferred shares in a private company to trustees to be held on certain trusts. The directors, who had power to refuse to register transfers, registered

---

[28] L.P.A., s.53(1)(c); *ante*, p. 78.

[29] (1851) 1 De G.M. & G. 176; *Gilbert v. Overton* (1864) 22 H. & M. 110.

[30] See Companies Act 1985, ss.182, 183. Stock Transfer Act 1963, s.1.

[31] *Black v. Homersham* (1878) 4 Ex.D. 24; *Re Wimbush* [1940] Ch. 92.

[32] *Ante*, p. 115.

[33] (1862) 4 De. G.F. & J. 264. There, however, the correct transfer form was not used.

[34] I.H.T.A. 1984, s.7; *post*, p. 219.

[35] [1952] Ch. 499; *Re Fry* [1946] Ch. 312; *Re Rose* [1949] Ch. 78; *Re Paradise Motor Co. Ltd* [1968] 1 W.L.R. 1125; *Vandervell v. I.R.C.* [1967] 2 A.C. 291 at p. 330.

this transfer some two months later. The settlor died at a time at which the shares would be treated as part of his estate for tax purposes if the date of the transfer were the date of registration; but would not be so treated if the date was the date of the deed. The Court of Appeal held that the relevant date was that of the deed; for the settlor had at that time done everything possible to divest himself of the property. All that was needed in addition was the formal act of registration by the third party.

Evershed M.R. went so far as to say that after the execution of the transfer, the settlor held the shares as trustee for the beneficiaries.[36] He did not however give any convincing answer to the Crown's argument that, consistently with *Milroy v. Lord*,[37] the transfer was either a valid transfer at law; or a declaration of trust; or it was ineffective. The settlor clearly did not intend to declare himself a trustee,[38] and would have been surprised to have been told that, if the directors had refused to register, he was unable to withdraw from the transfer because he was a trustee; or that he was required to exercise the voting powers conferred by the shares in the interests of the beneficiaries.[39] *Re Rose* thus creates a number of theoretical difficulties.[40] It is submitted, however, that it is an eminently sensible decision in a context in which the liability to tax may be affected by the date on which the transfer is treated as being effective. *Re Rose* can be contrasted with *Re Fry*,[41] where the donor was domiciled abroad, and had not, at the critical time, done everything that was needed of him, as he had not obtained Treasury consent to the transfer.

The *Re Rose* principle was applied to a transfer of registered land in *Mascall v. Mascall*,[42] where a father executed a transfer of a house to his son, a volunteer, and handed over the land certificate. After the transfer had been sent to the Inland Revenue for stamping,

---

[36] "If a man executes a document transferring all his equitable interest, say, in shares, that document, operating, and intended to operate, as a transfer, will give rise to and take effect as a trust; for the assignor will then be a trustee of the legal estate in the shares for the person in whose favour he has made an assignment of his beneficial interest." [1952] Ch. 499 at p. 510. See Oakley, *Constructive Trusts* (3rd ed.), p. 318, suggesting that a constructive trust arises in these circumstances.

[37] (1862) 4 De G.F. & J. 264.

[38] See *Jones v. Lock* (1865) L.R. 1 Ch.App. 25.

[39] *Butt v. Kelsen* [1952] Ch. 197; *cf. Re George Whichelow Ltd* [1954] 1 W.L.R. 5.

[40] (1976) 40 Conv.(N.S.) 139 (L. McKay), criticising the reasoning. *Re Rose* was described in *Rowlandson v. National Westminster Bank Ltd* [1978] 1 W.L.R. 798 at p. 802 as a "gloss" on the principle of perfect gifts.

[41] [1946] Ch. 312 (he had applied for consent, but further information might have been required); *Re Transatlantic Life Assurance Co. Ltd* [1980] 1 W.L.R. 79; Keeton & Sheridan's *Equity* (3rd ed.), p. 246.

[42] (1985) 49 P. & C.R. 119. *cf. Corin v. Patton* (1990) 169 C.L.R. 540 (gift incomplete where transferor had not requested mortgagee to produce land certificate, without which transferee could not be registered).

and returned, the father (having fallen out with the son), sought a declaration that the transfer was ineffective. The son had not yet sent the documents to the Land Registry in order to become registered proprietor and had, therefore, not acquired legal title.[43] It was held that the gift was complete. The father had done all that he could, as the application to the Land Registry could be made by the son, from whom the father had no right to recover the transfer and land certificate. Similarly in the case of an assignment of a lease which had not been completed by registration.[44]

3. DECLARATION OF SELF AS TRUSTEE

There is no difficulty if a settlor wishes to declare himself trustee of some or all of his property. All that is needed is a manifestation of an intention to declare a trust; and, if the property is land, evidence in writing of such intent. The settlor "need not use the words, 'I declare myself a trustee,' but he must do something which is equivalent to it, and use expressions which have that meaning; for, however anxious the Court may be to carry out a man's intention, it is not at liberty to construe words otherwise than according to their proper meaning."[45] It is necessary to show, not only an intention to benefit someone; but an intention to be trustee for that person. "Men often mean to give things to their kinsfolk, they do not often mean to constitute themselves trustees. An imperfect gift is no declaration of trust."[46]

The issues which arise in this section are quite different from those discussed in section 2. There, the question was whether the property was vested in the trustee. Here, there is no such problem; if there is a trust the settlor is trustee. The question here is whether a trust has properly been declared. The problems usually arise in cases where the settlor's intention was to make a gift to a donee but the gift failed, and the question is whether the intent to benefit the donee can be construed as a declaration of trust in his favour.

The rule is that equity will not construe a void gift as a declaration of trust. What is needed is a manifestation of an intention to declare a trust.

In *Jones v. Lock*,[47] a father, being chided for failing to bring a present from Birmingham for his baby son, produced a £900

---

[43] L.R.A. 1925, s.19.
[44] *Brown & Root Technology Ltd v. Sun Alliance and London Assurance Co. Ltd* [1996] Ch. 51 (assignor retained no rights under the lease).
[45] *Richards v. Delbridge* (1874) L.R. 18 Eq. 11 at p. 14, *per* Jessel M.R.
[46] Maitland, p. 72.
[47] (1865) L.R. 1 Ch.App. 25.

cheque payable to himself, saying: "Look you here, I give this to baby; it is for himself." He gave it to the child, who was about to tear it up, and the father took it away and put it in a safe. The father died and the cheque was found among his effects.

The question was whether the child was entitled to the cheque or whether it formed part of the father's estate. It would belong to the father unless he gave it to the child, or declared himself trustee of it. Clearly, he had not given it to the child, because a gift of a non-bearer cheque requires endorsement.[48] Had he declared himself trustee? No. He intended to give it to the child. There was no evidence that he intended to declare himself trustee of it, and to burden himself with a trustee's duties, including that of investing it in trustee securities and being personally liable for failure to do so. There was no such intention here; nor was there an effective gift. The child took nothing.

Similarly, in *Richards v. Delbridge*,[49] a grandfather who was entitled to leasehold premises endorsed on the lease a memorandum as follows: "This deed and all thereto belonging I give to [R who was a minor] from this time forth, with all the stock-in-trade." He delivered the document to R's mother, and then died, making no mention of the property in his will. Jessel M.R. held that no interest passed; not at law, because the endorsement was ineffective to assign a lease; and not in equity, for the words were inappropriate for the declaration of a trust.

These cases may be contrasted with the situation where the legal owner has not attempted to transfer the property to the third party, but has shown that he considers himself to hold the property as trustee for the third party. Whether or not, in any case, the evidence is sufficient will depend on the facts; it has been held that the intent can be implied from conduct where the evidence is clear.[50]

So in *Paul v. Constance*[51] the conduct of the parties was sufficient to establish an intention to declare a trust. Mr Constance was separated from his wife, and lived with the plaintiff. He received, as damages for an injury suffered at work, a cheque for £950 and he and the plaintiff decided to put it into a deposit account at Lloyds Bank. The account was opened in the name of

---

[48] Under the Cheques Act 1992, s.1, cheques are no longer transferable if they are crossed and the words "account payee" appear.

[49] (1874) L.R. 18 Eq. 11.

[50] *New, Prance and Garrard's Trustee v. Hunting* [1897] 2 Q.B. 19. See also *Re Kayford Ltd* [1975] 1 W.L.R. 279; *Re Chelsea Cloisters Ltd* (1981) 41 P. & C.R. 98; *ante*, p. 51.

[51] [1977] 1 W.L.R. 54; convincingly criticised in Heydon, Gummow and Austin, *Cases and Materials on Equity and Trusts* (4th ed.), p. 142: "The law of express trusts normally requires an intention to benefit the *cestui que trust* specifically by way of trust—a mere intention to benefit him in some way is insufficient."

Mr Constance only; because he and the plaintiff felt an embarrassment in opening a joint account in different names. Mr Constance indicated on many occasions that the money was as much the plaintiff's as his. On his death, the widow claimed the money in the account as part of her husband's estate. The question was whether the account was owned beneficially by Mr Constance, or whether, on the particular facts, he had shown an intention to hold the property as trustee for the plaintiff, or as trustee for the two of them in equal shares. The Court of Appeal found that the evidence was sufficient to support an intention in Mr Constance to declare himself a trustee; although it was not easy to pinpoint a specific moment of declaration.[52] The plaintiff was thus able to recover half of the proceeds of the account.

A lenient view of the requirements of a declaration of trust was taken by the Court of Appeal in *Re Vandervell's Trusts (No. 2)*.[53] An option to purchase certain shares was held by trustees on a resulting trust for Vandervell. The trustees exercised the option, using money from Vandervell's children's settlement. It was held that the shares were henceforth held on trust for the children's settlement. There was no declaration of trust by Vandervell, but such a declaration could be inferred from certain acts of the trustees[54]: first, the use of the money from the children's settlement; secondly, the subsequent payment of the dividends to that settlement; and thirdly, the trustees' notification to the Revenue that they now held the shares on trust for that settlement. The inadequacy of these three acts as establishing a declaration of trust lies in the fact that the second and third merely indicate what the trustees thought the position to be, while the first ignores Vandervell's beneficial ownership of the option. This has already been examined.[55]

It will be noted that it is not necessary that the beneficiary should be aware of the declaration of trust.[56] The beneficiary becomes equitable owner just as he would become legal owner if the property had been transferred by conveyance *inter vivos*.

4. Covenants to Settle

If a settlor has neither conveyed the property to trustees nor declared himself a trustee, no trust is created. If he has covenanted by deed

---

[52] This could cause problems. See Heydon, Gummow and Austin, *op. cit.*, at p. 142.
[53] [1974] Ch. 269.
[54] Trustees cannot normally declare a trust, but here it was accepted that the option was held on such trusts as might thereafter be declared by Vandervell or the trustees.
[55] *Ante*, p. 83.
[56] *Middleton v. Pollock* (1876) 2 Ch.D. 104; *Standing v. Bowring* (1885) 31 Ch.D. 282.

to settle the property, the crucial question is whether or not the intended beneficiary can compel him to carry out the covenant and settle it. The general rule is that a third party cannot sue upon a contract.[57] A beneficiary who has given consideration can enforce the covenant by obtaining specific performance; one who has not given consideration cannot do so. Equity will not assist a volunteer.

For this purpose, "consideration" has a wider meaning than at common law. The term includes everything which would be included by the common law[58]; but equity also treats as having given consideration, in the case of a covenant in a marriage settlement, the husband and wife and issue of the marriage.[59] They are said to be "within the marriage consideration."[60] It appears that the "issue" of the marriage refers not only to children but also to more remote issue.[61] It seems, however, that illegitimate children,[62] children by a former marriage, and children to whom one of the parties stands *in loco parentis*, cannot be included unless their interests are so closely intertwined with those of the natural issue of the marriage that the latter may be said to take only on terms which admit the former to a participation with them.[63]

In *Pullan v. Koe*,[64] a marriage settlement of 1859 settled property on the husband and wife and prospective children, and also contained a covenant by the wife to settle on the same trusts any property she later acquired of the value of £100 and upwards. In 1879 the wife received £285, part of which was used for her own purposes and part invested in bearer bonds, which remained at the bank in the husband's name until his death in 1909. The question was whether the trustees could then take steps to obtain the bonds from his executors and hold them on the trusts of the settlement.

---

[57] But see Law Com. No. 242 (1996), proposing that third parties identified in the contract by name, class or description should be able to sue if such a right is given by an express term of the contract or if the contract purports to confer a benefit on the third party unless, in the latter case, the contracting parties did not intend the third party to have enforcement rights.

[58] Cheshire, Fifoot and Furmston, *The Law of Contract* (13th ed.), Chap. 4; Treitel, *The Law of Contract* (9th ed.), Chap. 3.

[59] *De Mestre v. West* [1891] A.C. 264; *Att.-Gen. v. Jacobs-Smith* [1895] 2 Q.B. 341.

[60] This is so whether the settlement is made on the marriage, or made before but in consideration of the marriage, or a post-nuptial settlement in pursuance of an ante-nuptial agreement.

[61] *MacDonald v. Scott* [1893] A.C. 642.

[62] This principle seems unaffected by the Family Law Reform Act 1987, which in general equates the rights of children of married and unmarried parents.

[63] See *Att.-Gen. v. Jacobs-Smith* [1895] 2 Q.B. 341; *Rennell v. I.R.C.* [1962] Ch. 329 at p. 341, affd. [1964] A.C. 173; *Re Cook's S.T.* [1965] Ch. 902 at p. 914.

[64] [1913] 1 Ch. 9. See (1979) 32 C.L.P. 1 at pp. 4–5 (C. Rickett).

Swinfen-Eady J. held that it was the duty of the trustees to enforce the covenant on behalf of those who were within the marriage consideration. Indeed, the beneficiaries could have taken action themselves if the trustees had refused to do so. Here, however, the common law action on the covenant was barred by the lapse of time; but the court held that the £285 was impressed with the trust at the moment the wife received it, and that the trust could be enforced against the bonds.

Such a covenant would not however be enforceable in favour of next-of-kin, for they are volunteers.[65] Thus, if a marriage settlement contained a similar covenant to settle after-acquired property, and there were no children of the marriage, there is no way in which the husband and wife could be prevented from ignoring the covenant and keeping after-acquired property for themselves. The next-of-kin, or other persons who take in default of children, will not be able to enforce the covenant. It was however suggested in one case that the wife could not keep both her interest under the settlement and also the after-acquired property, but should be put to her election.[66] It is doubtful whether the doctrine of election would be applied so generally.

Where the covenant is enforced by persons within the marriage consideration, the court may order the covenantor to settle the property in accordance with the covenant[67]; or, as in *Pullan v. Koe*,[68] declare that the property is subject to the trusts of the settlement. However where one of the intended beneficiaries is a party[69] to the covenant, even though a volunteer, there is no reason why an action on the covenant for damages should not be brought, although the equitable remedy of specific performance would not lie.

In *Cannon v. Hartley*,[70] a settlement upon a separation, to which the spouses and a daughter were parties, provided that the father should pay to the daughter any sum exceeding £1,000 which he might inherit from his parents. Having inherited, he failed to make the payment. The daughter was a volunteer. She

---

[65] *Re D'Angibau* (1880) 15 Ch.D. 228; *Re Plumptre's Marriage Settlement* [1901] 1 Ch. 609; *Re Cook's S.T.* [1965] Ch. 902. Nor will it be enforceable on this principle if, although for consideration, the covenant is not specifically enforceable, as in the case of a covenant to pay money; *Stone v. Stone* (1869) 5 Ch.App. 74.

[66] *Re Vardon's Trusts* (1885) 31 Ch.D. 275; *post*, p. 857.

[67] This may have the effect of benefiting volunteers, as in *Davenport v. Bishopp* (1843) 2 Y. & C.C.C. 451 (life interest to husband, remainder to volunteers).

[68] [1913] 1 Ch. 9, *supra*.

[69] For the meaning of which, see *Beswick v. Beswick* [1968] A.C. 58 at p. 102.

[70] [1949] Ch. 213. See generally (1988) 8 L.S. 172 (M. Macnair), suggesting that there is some historical support for allowing specific performance of covenants in favour of volunteers.

could however sue upon her father's covenant, and recover damages for breach of covenant at common law.

5. ACTION FOR DAMAGES BY THE TRUSTEES. TRUSTS OF CHOSES IN ACTION

There is no difficulty in enforcing a completely constituted trust of a chose in action.[71] Where a contractual right is held by A on trust for B, A may sue and obtain damages or a decree of specific performance on behalf of B[72]; or B may obtain such relief on his own account if A refuses to act, joining A as a co-defendant in the action.[73]

The question is whether this principle can assist a volunteer in the case of a covenant to settle existing or after-acquired property.[74] If a husband or wife covenants with a trustee A to settle after-acquired property in favour of the children of the marriage, and in default in favour of the next-of-kin, we have seen that the next-of-kin, being volunteers, are unable to sue on the covenant.[75] Could not the trustees sue, recover damages, and hold them in trust for the next-of-kin?[76] Or could not the next-of-kin argue that there is already a completely constituted trust of the benefit of the covenant, a trust of a chose in action for which they are the beneficiaries, and thus entitled to enforce?[77]

The courts have given volunteers no comfort in this respect. In *Re Pryce*,[78] Eve J. held that the trustees should not be compelled to pursue whatever remedy they may have at law on the covenant, and in *Re Kay's Settlement*,[79] Simonds J. decided that they should be instructed not to do so. In *Re Cook's Settlement Trusts*,[80] Buckley J.

---

[71] *Post*, p. 127. See *Barclays Bank plc v. Willowbrook International Ltd* [1987] 1 F.T.L.R. 386.

[72] *Lloyd's v. Harper* (1880) 16 Ch.D. 290.

[73] *Les Affréteurs Réunis Société Anonyme v. Leopold Walford Ltd* [1919] A.C. 801; *Parker-Tweedale v. Dunbar Bank plc* [1991] Ch. 12. This exception to the privity rule would not be affected by the Law Commission's proposals, but would be made less important; Law Com. No. 242, para. 12.2.

[74] *i.e.* property which might come subsequently to the settlor. It was common in a marriage settlement for the spouses to covenant to add to the settlement any property which they subsequently might acquire.

[75] *Ante*, p. 123; *Re D'Angibau* (1880) 15 Ch.D. 228; *Re Plumptre's Marriage Settlement* [1910] 1 Ch. 609.

[76] (1960) 76 L.Q.R. 100 (D. Elliott).

[77] (1962) 78 L.Q.R. 228 (J. Hornby); *Perspectives of Law* (ed. R. Pound), p. 239; (1969) 85 L.Q.R. 213 (W. Lee); (1975) 91 L.Q.R. 236 (J. Barton); (1976) 92 L.Q.R. 427 (R. Meagher and J. Lehane); (1979) 32 C.L.P. 1 and (1981) 34 C.L.P. 189 (C. Rickett); Gardner, *An Introduction to the Law of Trusts*, Chap. 4.

[78] [1917] 1 Ch. 234.

[79] [1939] Ch. 329.

[80] [1965] Ch. 902; (1965) 24 C.L.J. 46 (G. Jones); (1966) 29 M.L.R. 397 (D. Matheson); (1966) 8 Malaya L.R. 153 (M. Scott); [1967] A.S.C.L. 387 *et seq.* (J. Davies).

distinguished *Fletcher v. Fletcher*,[81] *Williamson v. Codrington*[82] and *Re Cavendish-Browne's Settlement Trusts*,[83] and refused to allow volunteers to enforce a covenant even though another person had given consideration. These however are all decisions of courts of first instance, and the matter should be analysed more closely.

A. Suit by the Trustees

There are certain difficulties which lie in the way of the proposition that the trustees, as parties to the covenant, can sue to recover damages with a view to holding the money received on trust for the (volunteer) beneficiaries.

i. Decision to Enforce. If the trustees were able to recover damages, but could not be compelled by the beneficiaries to sue, the trustees would be left with the decision whether or not to constitute the trust. It might be argued that to give the trustee, as a party to the covenant, the right to decide whether anything shall be done for the beneficiaries is undesirable, but this overlooks the fact that the covenantee is not yet a trustee.[84]

ii. Nominal or Substantial Damages. The next question is whether the trustee would recover substantial damages in an action at law on the covenant. If he can recover only nominal damages, the action will be of no help to the beneficiary.[85]

The general rule is that the plaintiff may recover in an action for breach of contract damages sufficient to compensate him for his loss. Just as third parties cannot normally sue upon a contract,[86] damages suffered by third parties are not recoverable by the plaintiff: unless, as explained below, the plaintiff contracted as trustee for the third parties. An attempt by the Court of Appeal in *Jackson v. Horizon Holidays Ltd.*[87] to permit the plaintiff to recover damages in respect of the loss suffered by third parties has been firmly disapproved by the House of Lords.[88]

The real question, however, is this: what does the common law regard as the plaintiff's own loss? In the context of a voluntary

[81] (1844) 4 Hare 67.
[82] (1750) 1 Ves.Sen. 511.
[83] [1916] W.N. 341.
[84] Todd, *Textbook on Trusts*, p. 63.
[85] See (1950) 3 C.L.P. 30 at p. 43 (O. Marshall).
[86] *Cf. Trident General Insurance Co. Ltd v. McNiece Bros. Pty. Ltd* (1988) 165 C.L.R. 107 (third party could sue under insurance policy).
[87] [1975] 1 W.L.R. 1468.
[88] *Woodar Investment Developments Ltd v. Wimpey Construction (U.K.) Ltd* [1980] 1 W.L.R. 277. See also (1976) 39 M.L.R. 202 (D. Yates); *Forster v. Silvermere Golf and Equestrian Centre Ltd* (1981) 42 P. & C.R. 255; *Beswick v. Beswick* [1968] A.C. 58; *post*, p. 130; *Darlington Borough Council v. Wiltshier Northern Ltd* [1995] 1 W.L.R. 68.

covenant to settle, it has been said that "for breach of a covenant to pay a certain sum the measure of damages (if that is the appropriate expression) is the certain sum; and for breach of a covenant to transfer property worth a certain sum, it is the value of the property.[89] There is no doubt that this is the usual rule, as shown by the cases where the volunteer beneficiary is a party to the covenant.[90] Applying this rule, substantial damages should be recoverable at law by B where A covenants to pay a certain sum (or to transfer Blackacre) to B to be held on trust for C. It is no answer at common law to say that B suffers no loss by the breach of such a covenant. At law the position is no different from that of a trustee of a completely constituted trust, who may recover substantial damages for the breach of any contract he may make as trustee even though he personally suffers no loss. There is, however, little direct authority in the context of an incompletely constituted trust. Of the cases usually quoted on this question, *Re Cavendish-Browne's Settlement Trusts*[91] is most clearly in point.

The covenantor was absolutely entitled under two wills to a share of real estate in Canada, which he entered into a voluntary covenant to settle. The trustees sued for damages and were awarded a sum equivalent to the value of the property which would have come into their hands if the covenant had been performed, and this money was to be held on the trusts of the settlement.

This, then, supports the view that a covenantee may recover substantial damages at law for breach of a covenant to pay money or to transfer specific property, although he has suffered no loss personally. But even if this be correct, it may not follow that the same view would prevail in the context of cases like *Re Pryce*[92] and *Re Kay's Settlement*.[93] The covenant in those cases was not to pay a sum of

---

[89] (1960) 76 L.Q.R. 100 at p. 112 (D. Elliott); (1975) 91 L.Q.R. 236 at p. 238 (J. Barton); [1988] Conv. 19 at p. 21 (D. Goddard). See also [1982] Conv. 280 at p. 281 (M. Friend), agreeing that substantial damages are available on the basis of debt in the case of a voluntary covenant to pay money, but suggesting that this is less clear in the case of specific property other than money.

[90] *Cannon v. Hartley* [1949] Ch. 213; *Synge v. Synge* [1894] 1 Q.B. 466.

[91] [1916] W.N. 341; (1916) 61 S.J. 27; *Re Parkin* [1892] 3 Ch. 510; *Ward v. Audland* (1847) 16 M. & W. 863. *cf. Perspectives of Law* (ed. R. Pound), p. 243; (1969) 85 L.Q.R. 213 at p. 219. The decision was prior to the cases holding that a trustee cannot sue; *ante*, p. 124. See, however, (1979) 32 C.L.P. 1 (C. Rickett), suggesting that the decision was based on the "trust of the promise" theory (discussed below).

[92] [1917] 1 Ch. 234.

[93] [1939] Ch. 329. In this case and in *Re Pryce, supra*, it was assumed that the trustees, if they sued at law, would recover substantial damages. See also *Coulls v. Bagot's Trustee* (1967) 40 A.L.J.R. 471; *Cannon v. Hartley* [1949] Ch. 213.

money or to transfer specific property, but to transfer after-acquired property to the covenantee.[94]

Even though substantial damages may be available at law in an action by the trustee-covenantee, this would not be the end of the difficulties, for it may be argued that any such damages would be held on a resulting trust for the covenantor (settlor) and not for the volunteer beneficiaries.[95] The argument (as yet untested) is that, in the absence of any completely constituted trust of either the property or the benefit of the covenant (discussed below), the volunteers would have no claim. The trustee-covenantee, it need hardly be added, could not keep the money himself.

B. Trust of the Benefit of the Covenant

If there is a completely constituted trust of the benefit of the covenant, there is no difficulty, as has been seen,[96] in enforcing it, either by the trustees on behalf of the beneficiaries, or by the beneficiaries themselves. It was said, however, in *Re Cook's Settlement Trusts*,[97] that a covenant to settle future property cannot be the subject-matter of a trust, because it does not "create a debt enforceable at law . . . that is to say, a property right."[98] It is submitted that this restriction is not supportable.[99] Of course, future property itself, or unascertained property, or a mere *spes*, cannot be the subject-matter of a trust.[1] But a covenant to pay a sum to be ascertained in the future is just as good a chose in action as a covenant to pay a specified sum, and it creates legal property of value. The trust *res* is the benefit of the covenant, the chose in action; not the property which will be obtained by its performance.[2] There is no difficulty in a trust of a bank account, which is a chose in action, its value varying with the state of the account from day to day; nor in a trust of an insurance policy under which the obligation is to pay an undetermined sum on a future event which may not happen. The

---

[94] See, however, [1988] Conv. 19 at p. 21 (D. Goddard), suggesting that *Re Cavendish-Browne's S.T.* did involve after-acquired property. The testators from whom the property in question derived had died, but their estates were unadministered at the date of the covenant.

[95] See Underhill and Hayton, *Law of Trusts and Trustees* (15th ed.), p. 156. *cf. Re Cavendish-Browne's S.T., supra.*

[96] *Ante,* p. 124; This narrow exception to the privity rule is rarely of assistance today; Law Com. No. 242, paras. 2.8–2.9.

[97] [1965] Ch. 902.

[98] [1965] Ch. 902 at p. 913; (1976) 92 L.Q.R. 427 (R. Meagher and J. Lehane).

[99] (1965) 24 C.L.J. 46 at p. 49 (G. Jones); *cf.* (1969) 85 L.Q.R. 213 at p. 223 (W. Lee). See also (1979) 32 C.L.P. 1 and (1981) 34 C.L.P. 189 (C. Rickett); (1982) 98 L.Q.R. 17 (J. Feltham); [1982] Conv. 280 (M. Friend); [1982] Conv. 352 (S. Smith).

[1] *Post,* p. 133; *Williams v. C.I.R.* [1965] N.Z.L.R. 395.

[2] *Williamson v. Codrington* (1750) 1 Ves.Sen. 511; *Fletcher v. Fletcher* (1844) 4 Hare 67; *Lloyd's v. Harper* (1880) 16 Ch.D. 290; *Re Cavendish-Browne's S.T.* [1916] W.N. 341; (1975) 91 L.Q.R. 236 at p. 238 (J. Barton); (1976) 92 L.Q.R. at p. 428.

decision in *Re Cook's Settlement Trusts*[3] is justifiable, however, on the basis that there was no manifestation of an intention to create a trust of the benefit of the covenant.

On the assumption that there is no difficulty in the concept of a trust of the benefit of a covenant, there is nevertheless considerable difficulty in any particular case in deciding whether or not there was an intention to create one.[4] The critical case is *Fletcher v. Fletcher*,[5] a decision which presents certain difficulties.

> Ellis Fletcher entered into a voluntary covenant with trustees to pay to them £60,000 to be held on trust, in the events which happened, for his illegitimate son Jacob. The trustees did not wish to accept the trust or to receive the money unless they were required to do so. Vice-Chancellor Wigram held that Jacob was able to claim the money, saying that equity would either allow Jacob to use the name of the trustee to sue at law, or to recover in his own name in a court of equity.

Wigram V.-C. was of course fully aware of the rule forbidding aid being given to a volunteer, and this argument was pressed upon him:

> "According to the authorities, I cannot, I admit, do anything to perfect the liability of the author of the trust, if it is not already perfect. This covenant, however, is already perfect. The covenantor is liable at law, and the Court is not called upon to do any act to perfect it. One question made in argument has been whether there can be a trust of a covenant the benefit of which shall belong to a third party; but I cannot think that there is any difficulty in that. ... The proposition, therefore, that in no case can there be a trust of a covenant is too large, and the real question is whether the relation of trustee and *cestui que trust* is established in the present case."[6]

There was, then, a trust of the benefit of the covenant, and the plaintiff, as beneficiary, could enforce it. The trustees were, analytically, in the same position as Lloyd's were in *Lloyd's v. Harper*.[7] It was there decided that Lloyd's had contracted with Harper (who

---

[3] [1965] Ch. 902.

[4] *Re Engelbach's Estate* [1924] 2 Ch. 348; *Vandepitte v. Preferred Accident Insurance Corp. of New York* [1933] A.C. 70; *Re Schebsman* [1944] Ch. 83; *Green v. Russell* [1959] 2 Q.B. 266; *Scruttons Ltd v. Midland Silicones Ltd* [1962] A.C. 446; *Beswick v. Beswick* [1968] A.C. 58; *Swain v. Law Society* [1983] 1 A.C. 598.

[5] (1844) 4 Hare 67.

[6] *Ibid.* at p. 74. The position will be otherwise if the covenant is statute-barred. *cf. Pullan v. Koe* [1913] 1 Ch. 9; *ante*, p. 122, where the beneficiaries' interest, owing to the presence of consideration, was not merely in the covenant but in the property itself.

[7] (1880) 16 Ch.D. 290.

guaranteed the debts of his son as a Lloyd's underwriter) as trustee for the persons insured, and that, therefore, Lloyd's could sue, on behalf of the persons insured, and recover the damages which they, the beneficiaries, had suffered on the son's bankruptcy. The crucial question in these cases is whether or not there has been a manifestation of an intention to declare a trust of a chose in action, and this is a matter in which the courts have not, over the years, maintained a consistent approach. There are some difficulties in holding that there was a trust of the chose in action on the facts of *Fletcher v. Fletcher*.[8] In the first place, positive evidence of intention is lacking. Ellis Fletcher, the covenantor, covenanted that he would pay the £60,000 to trustees "to be held on the following trusts." There is clearly a trust which will affect the money once it is received by the trustee, but no evidence of an intention by either party to create a trust of a chose in action. It cannot be assumed from the fact that the property itself is to be subjected to a trust that an immediate trust of the benefit of the covenant was also intended.[9]

Another question is whether the relevant intention is that of the covenantor (settlor) or the covenantee (trustee). Certainly there was no intention to create a trust of the chose in action on the part of the trustees, if that is the requirement, in *Fletcher v. Fletcher*[10]: they did not know about the arrangement, and wished to decline the trust upon hearing of it. A trust of tangible property is declared by the owner of the property, whether he declares himself trustee or transfers it to another on trust. As a general rule, a trust of a debt is declared by the creditor. Thus in *Paul v. Constance*[11] the question whether a trust of a bank account had been created was determined by examining the intention of the account-holder (creditor), Mr Constance. It is submitted, however, that a distinction must be drawn between covenants supported by valuable consideration and those which are not. Where there is consideration, the relevant intention to create a trust of the chose in action is that of the covenantee.[12] This will usually be proved by showing that the latter covenanted as trustee for the persons nominated by the covenantor. Where, on the other hand, the covenant is voluntary, as in *Fletcher*

---

[8] (1844) 4 Hare 67.

[9] *cf.* (1982) 98 L.Q.R. 17 (J. Feltham), suggesting that such an assumption should be made, in order to avoid the absurdity that voluntary covenants to settle are otherwise unenforceable.

[10] (1844) 4 Hare 67.

[11] [1977] 1 W.L.R. 54; *ante*, p. 120.

[12] See the insurance cases: *Vandepitte v. Preferred Accident Insurance Corp. of New York* [1933] A.C. 70; *Swain v. The Law Society* [1983] 1 A.C. 598. The question in these cases is whether the policy-holder intended to hold the company's obligation on trust. See (1982) 98 L.Q.R. 17 (J. Feltham).

v. Fletcher,[13] the better view is that "the promisor is the creator of
the trust, and if he manifests an intention that the promisee's rights
under the promise shall be held in trust, the promisee immediately
becomes trustee of his rights under the promise".[14]

C. Specific Performance at the Suit of the Contracting Party

Beswick v. Beswick[15] suggests the possibility of another approach
to this problem. If the administratrix of old Mr Beswick could in that
case obtain specific performance against young Mr Beswick and
compel him to perform his promise to make payments to the widow
Beswick (a volunteer), can it not be argued that the trustee-cove-
nantees should be able to obtain specific performance of the promise
to settle after-acquired property in favour of volunteers? At least in
Beswick v. Beswick the House of Lords saw no objection to a
solution which permitted the widow to obtain by this indirect
method what she could not obtain directly,[16] Simonds J. in *Re Kay's
Settlement*[17] had taken the opposite view.

It is submitted however that the principle of *Beswick v. Beswick*[18]
does not apply to the case of voluntary covenants. In that case, old
Mr Beswick gave consideration for the promise of young Mr Beswick and had a right of action for damages against him. When the
loss was shown to be nil, and the damages therefore nominal,
specific performance became available instead. That remedy is
available where the legal remedy of damages is inadequate.[19] Where
valuable consideration has been given, the remedy of nominal damages is inadequate, although there is no loss to the contracting party,
because the result is the unjust enrichment of the defendant. In the
case of a voluntary covenant to pay to trustees the situation (assuming that damages would be nominal[20]) is different. There is no unjust
enrichment of the covenantor; nominal damages are therefore adequate. Specific performance in any event is not available to a
volunteer, and most trustees are volunteers.[21] Furthermore, the

---

[13] *Supra.*
[14] *The Restatement of Trusts* (2nd ed.), para. 26. See also (1979) 32 C.L.P. 1 at p. 13 (C.
Rickett); Heydon, Gummow and Austin, *Cases and Materials on Equity and Trusts* (4th
ed.), p. 606. Difficulties could arise in cases such as *Re Cook's S.T.* [1965] Ch. 902, where
the covenant is made with persons of whom some, but not all, have given consideration.
[15] [1968] A.C. 58; *post*, pp. 729 *et seq.*; [1967] A.S.C.L. 387 *et seq.* (J. Davies); (1988) 8 L.S.
14 (N. Andrews).
[16] *Per* Lord Pearce [1968] A.C. 58 at p. 89.
[17] [1939] Ch. 329 at p. 342.
[18] [1968] A.C. 58. See also *Snelling v. John G. Snelling Ltd* [1973] Q.B. 87.
[19] *Post*, p. 694.
[20] Which may not be correct; *ante*, p. 126.
[21] Nominal consideration is not sufficient in equity. See (1966) 8 Malaya L.R. 153 at p. 158
(M. Scott).

availability of specific performance in *Beswick v. Beswick*[22] was not hampered by the principle that trustees are not allowed to sue,[23] because the plaintiff there was not a trustee.[24]

We have seen that it made no difference in *Re Cook's Settlement Trusts*[25] that one of the parties had given consideration.

> In *Re Cook's Settlement Trusts*, property including a Rembrandt was settled on H for life, remainder to his son, F. Under the terms of a resettlement the property became F's absolutely and he covenanted to pay to the trustees the proceeds of sale of the Rembrandt (and other pictures) if sold in H's lifetime, to be held on trust for F's children (volunteers). F gave the Rembrandt to his wife, who wished to sell it. Buckley J. held that the trustees could not enforce the covenant if the Rembrandt were sold.

The decision preceded *Beswick v. Beswick*,[26] in which it was apparently not cited. A similarity between the two cases appears on close analysis. H entered into a contract for consideration with F, one of the terms of which was that F would confer a benefit on X. If H had sued F, could he succeed, as in *Beswick v. Beswick*, by saying that the damages awardable for the breach were inadequate, and that specific performance of the covenant to pay should be decreed in favour of X? The covenant was not in terms to pay to the volunteers, but to the trustees, who would hold the money in trust for them; but this seems immaterial. It is H who, on this reasoning, could sue (although he would not be obliged to) and not the trustees; but the action should not be dependent upon H's physical survival, for his estate, on the reasoning of *Beswick*, should be able to do so.[27]

It was suggested in *Coulls v. Bagot's Trustee*,[28] where the contract was not in the form of a covenant, that where the promise is made jointly to H (who gave the consideration) *and* to X (who gave none), *both of whom* are parties to the contract or covenant, X can sue by joining H (irrespective of H's wishes) although X personally has

[22] [1968] A.C. 58.
[23] *Ante*, p. 130.
[24] She was a personal representative, but the position was exactly the same as if Mr Beswick senior had been in a position to bring the action himself. There was no trust.
[25] [1965] Ch. 902; *ante*, p. 124.
[26] [1968] A.C. 58.
[27] *cf.* (1979) 32 C.L.P. 1 at p. 14 (C. Rickett).
[28] (1967) 40 A.L.J.R. 471 at p. 477, *per* Barwick C.J.; [1967] A.S.C.L. at p. 395 (J. Davies); (1978) 37 C.L.J. 301 (B. Coote). Compare the facts of *Cannon v. Hartley* [1949] Ch. 213, *ante*, p. 123, where another party to the covenant had given consideration.

provided no consideration. Enforcement would then be on the basis of contract.[29]

It has been said that "The dicta in *Coulls'* case and the decision in *Beswick v. Beswick* may be the most important developments in specific performance this century."[30] But there was no trust involved in either of those cases and hence no need to surmount the obstacle that trustees cannot sue.[31] Both were cases where valuable consideration had been furnished to the promisor. It is doubtful whether they will enable trustees to enforce voluntary covenants to settle. But in the case of a covenant with a third party in a marriage settlement to settle after-acquired property, that person, or his estate after his death, having provided consideration, and being a party to the transaction, may, on the authority of *Beswick v. Beswick*[32] be able to obtain specific performance for the benefit of the volunteers.

That line of reasoning is wholly separate from the question of the enforcement of a covenant in the *Fletcher v. Fletcher* type of situation.[33] There, no consideration was given. The covenant was voluntary. It would be enforceable by, or on behalf of the beneficiaries if, and only if, there was found to be a trust of the chose in action. That brings us back to the most basic question of all in relation to the creation of trusts: whether the settlor has manifested an intention to create a trust.

The question whether such an intention can be found has been the subject of much litigation since the privity rule was established by *Tweddle v. Atkinson*,[34] and it is well known, both that the courts have been inconsistent in their decisions, and that, since *Walford's* case,[35] they have been more reluctant to find such an intention.[36] It was very different in Jacob Fletcher's day which predated *Milroy v. Lord*,[37] *Jones v. Lock*[38] and *Tweddle v. Atkinson*.[39] There is little

---

[29] The promisee is the entity (H+X). This entity has provided consideration, it being irrelevant whether it was actually furnished by H or X. So viewed, this complies with the normal contract rules. Judgment would be for (H+X). See (1989) 48 C.L.J. 243 (P. Kincaid). The problems of joint parties are discussed in Law Com. No. 242, paras. 6.9–6.12.

[30] Heydon, Gummow and Austin, *Cases and Materials on Equity and Trusts* (4th ed.), p. 947.

[31] *Ante*, p. 124.

[32] [1968] A.C. 58.

[33] (1844) 4 Hare 67.

[34] (1861) 3 B. & S. 393.

[35] *Les Affréteurs Réunis Société Anonyme v. Leopold Walford (London) Ltd* [1919] A.C. 801. See *Swain v. The Law Society* [1983] 1 A.C. 598 (the Law Society did not contract as trustee by using words "on behalf of all solicitors" in insurance contract). Outside the contract area, however, an intention to create a trust has been upheld without strong evidence; see *Paul v. Constance* [1977] 1 W.L.R. 54, *ante*, p. 120.

[36] *Cf. Trident General Insurance Co. Ltd v. McNiece Bros. Pty. Ltd* (1988) 165 C.L.R. 107; (1989) 48 C.L.J. 243 (P. Kincaid).

[37] (1862) 4 De G.F. & J. 264.

[38] (1865) L.R. 1 Ch.App. 25.

[39] *Supra.*

doubt that a modern court would fail to find the necessary intention on the facts of *Fletcher v. Fletcher.*

D. Summary

The proper solution depends on the question of policy, whether the covenantor should or should not be made to implement his undertaking on behalf of the volunteers. If it is thought that he should, the means are at hand, whether by finding a trust of the chose in action, or by allowing specific performance of the covenant or, indeed, by abrogating the rule that third parties cannot sue on a contract, as has been proposed.[40] But if it is thought that he should not, cases like *Re Kay's Settlement*[41] must stand; they are at least consistent with the established rules requiring strict construction of expressions of intention to create trusts, and of the older principles relating to the availability of specific performance.

6. TRUSTS OF FUTURE PROPERTY

A contract for consideration to convey future property to trustees upon trust is valid[42] and, in most cases, specifically enforceable.[43] A voluntary covenant to convey future property to trustees is actionable at law by a beneficiary who is a party to the covenant.[44] If the beneficiary is not a party he is unable to sue, being in no better a position than the volunteer in the case of a covenant relating to present property. Indeed, he may be worse off if it is correct to say that the argument that there is a trust of the benefit of the covenant is not available in the case of future property.[45] A purported assignment of an expectancy[46] cannot be a conveyance because there is nothing to convey. Nor can there be a valid declaration of trust of property not yet existing.[47] If consideration is given for a purported

---

[40] See Law Com. No. 242 (1996).
[41] [1939] Ch. 329; (1975) 91 L.Q.R. 236 (J. Barton).
[42] *Re Lind* [1915] 2 Ch. 345; *Re Gillott's Settlements* [1934] Ch. 97; *Re Haynes' W.T.* [1949] Ch. 5.
[43] *Pullan v. Koe* [1913] 1 Ch. 9.
[44] *Cannon v. Hartley* [1949] Ch. 213; *ante*, p. 123.
[45] *Ante*, p. 127.
[46] *Williams v. C.I.R.* [1965] N.Z.L.R. 345; ("the first £500 of the net income which shall accrue to the assignor . . . from the Trust."). An assignment of the assignor's life interest under the trust would, of course, have been valid.
[47] *cf. Re Ralli's W.T.* [1964] Ch. 288 (valid declaration of trust of remainder interest, which is not future property). See also *Simpson v. Simpson* [1992] 1 F.L.R. 601 (share of proceeds of sale of cottage which was not yet sold).

conveyance, it will be construed as a contract to assign and enforceable as such.[48] But if it is made gratuitously it is a nullity.[49]

In *Re Ellenborough*,[50] the sister of Lord Ellenborough purported to convey by voluntary settlement the property which she
would receive under her brother's will. On his death she declined
to transfer the property to the trustees, and Buckley J. held that the
trustees could not compel her to do so.

A further question is whether such a gratuitous covenant, assignment or declaration in respect of future property can subsequently be
treated as an effective declaration of trust if the property does later
vest in the trustee. The situation can arise if the property, on
materialising, is transferred to trustees without a further declaration
of the trusts, or where the property vests in the settlor after he has
declared the trusts on which he is to hold it.

We have seen that a covenant in a marriage settlement to settle
after-acquired property is not enforceable at the suit of the next-
of-kin because they are volunteers[51]; and that a deed purporting to
convey future property upon trust is ineffective.[52] But if, in either of
these cases, the property found its way into the hands of the trustees,
it would presumably be held upon the trusts declared in the relevant
documents.[53] If the settlor, in either case, conveyed the property to
the trustees, that action could be construed as a further declaration
of the trusts; but if the property reached the trustees by another
route, being conveyed perhaps by the executors of the testator from
whom the property came,[54] or coming into the hands of the trustee
in a different capacity,[55] the possibility of finding that there was a
further declaration of trust is less strong. There appear to be three
possible solutions to such a case: that the trustees take beneficially,
that they hold on trust for the settlor, or that they hold on the trusts
declared in the previous document. The first is obviously untenable.
The second involves the proposition that the settlor could claim
back in equity property which he had covenanted or purported to
settle.[56] The third avoids the necessity of making the ultimate

---

[48] *Re Burton's Settlement* [1955] Ch. 82.
[49] *Meek v. Kettlewell* (1842) 1 Hare 464; *Re Brooks' S.T.* [1939] Ch. 993; *Williams v. C.I.R.* [1965] N.Z.L.R. 345.
[50] [1903] 1 Ch. 697; *cf. Re Bowden* [1936] Ch. 71; *Re Adlard* [1954] Ch. 29.
[51] *Re D'Angibau* (1880) 15 Ch.D. 228; *Re Plumptre's Settlement* [1910] 1 Ch. 609.
[52] *Re Ellenborough* [1903] 1 Ch. 697; *Re Brooks' S.T.* [1939] Ch. 993.
[53] *Re Ellenborough, supra.* Miss Emily Towry Law had already handed over to the trustees the property which she received under her sister's will; and no attempt was made to recover it; *Re Adlard* [1954] Ch. 29; *Re Ralli's W.T.* [1964] Ch. 228.
[54] *Re Adlard* [1954] Ch. 29.
[55] *Re Ralli's W.T.* [1964] Ch. 288.
[56] Dicta in *Re Ralli's W.T.* [1964] Ch. 288, indicate that this could be regarded as unconscion-able. *Cf. Re Brooks' S.T.* [1939] Ch. 993.

destination of the property depend upon the route by which it reached the trustees; it is consistent with the expressed intention of the parties and appears to be the most satisfactory solution.[57]

Where the property comes to the settlor himself, it is possible for the court to hold that a previous declaration of trust,[58] followed by the vesting of the property in him, constitutes the trust. It is clear that a previous declaration is not of itself sufficient[59]; subsequent confirmation of a previous declaration is sufficient.[60] In less obvious cases it is no doubt a question of construction to determine whether or not the settlor is to be taken to have made a subsequent declaration or to have affirmed a previous one. If he made the declaration every day, the last declaration being made the moment before he received the property, this would no doubt be sufficient. But in the absence of authority, it is unsafe to predict to what extent an argument on these lines might be acceptable. What is clear in these cases is that the beneficiaries must show that the trust was properly declared and properly constituted. There appears to be nothing intrinsically wrong in holding that the declaration of a trust may precede its constitution, as in the secret trusts cases.[61]

7. Exceptions to the Rule that Equity will not Assist a Volunteer

A. The Rule in Strong v. Bird[62]

Where an incomplete gift is made during the donor's lifetime, and the donor appointed the donee as executor,[63] or, in the case of an intestacy, the donee is appointed administrator,[64] the vesting of the property in the donee in his capacity as executor or administrator may be treated as the completion of the gift, overriding the claims of the beneficiaries under the will or intestacy. Similarly with the release of a debt owed to the donor. At common law the appointment of the debtor as executor released the debt. In equity such a

---

[57] So held in *Re Ralli's W.T., supra*, discussed *ante*, p. 116.

[58] As opposed to a mere covenant to settle or purported assignment; *Re Ellenborough*, *supra*.

[59] *Matter of Gurlitz*, 105 Misc. 30, 172 N.Y. Supp. 523 (1918); *Brennan v. Morphett* (1908) 6 C.L.R. 22; *Permanent Trustee Co. v. Scales* (1930) 30 S.R. (N.S.W.) 391 at p. 393; *Williams v. C.I.R.* [1965] N.Z.L.R. 345.

[60] *Re Northcliffe* [1925] Ch. 651.

[61] Chap. 5.

[62] See [1982] Conv. 14 (G. Kodilinye).

[63] (1874) L.R. 18 Eq. 315. It is sufficient if he is appointed one of the executors; *Re Stewart* [1908] 2 Ch. 251.

[64] *Re James* [1935] Ch. 449; *Re Gonin* [1979] Ch. 16 (where, however, doubts were expressed by Walton J.); (1977) 93 L.Q.R. 485. In *Strong v. Bird* itself, the rule was said only to apply to an executor.

debtor had to account to the estate unless the testator intended in his lifetime to release the debt, such intention continuing until death.

In *Strong v. Bird*,[65] B borrowed £1,100 from A, his stepmother, who lived in his house, paying £212 10s. a quarter for board, and it was agreed that the debt should be paid off by a deduction of £100 from each quarter's payment. Deductions of this amount were made for two quarters; but on the third quarter-day and thereafter, A paid the full amount. Thus on her death, some four years later, £900 remained owing. B was appointed her sole executor, and proved the will. Later A's next-of-kin claimed for the balance of the debt. It was held that the appointment of B as executor released the debt.

It is necessary to show that the donor intended to make an immediate *inter vivos* gift[66] (or to release a debt, as the case may be), and also that he had a continuing intention until the date of his death. Thus, an intention to make a testamentary gift is not sufficient.[67] The intention must relate to a specific item of property. It is not sufficient that there was a vague desire to provide something for the donee. In *Re Gonin*[68] a mother wished to leave her house to her daughter, who had given up a career to look after her parents, but thought for some reason that she could not do so because the daughter was illegitimate. Instead, she wrote a cheque for £33,000 in the daughter's favour, which was found after her death. (The cheque could not be cashed, as the death terminated the bank's mandate to pay it.) The daughter became administratrix, but failed in her claim to the house. There was no evidence of a continuing intention that the daughter should have an immediate gift of the house. The drawing of the cheque, as a substitute, pointed the other way. Nor will the rule apply if the testator, subsequently to the act on which the executor relies as establishing the intention to give a chattel, acted inconsistently with that intention by giving or lending the chattel to someone else,[69] nor if the testator, having once had an intention to give, forgot the gift, and treated the property as his own.[70]

---

[65] (1874) L.R. 18 Eq. 315; *Re James* [1935] Ch. 449 (a gift of realty).
[66] *cf. Re Ralli's W.T.* [1964] Ch. 288, *ante*, p. 116 (covenant to settle in the future). See also *Simpson v. Simpson* [1992] 1 F.L.R. 601 (future gift of proceeds of sale of cottage which was not yet sold).
[67] *Re Stewart* [1908] 2 Ch. 251; *Re Innes* [1910] Ch. 188.
[68] [1979] Ch. 16; (1977) 93 L.Q.R. 488.
[69] *Re Freeland* [1952] Ch. 110.
[70] *Re Wale* [1956] 1 W.L.R. 1346.

B. Donatio Mortis Causa

i. The Principle. A *donatio mortis causa* is a lifetime gift which is conditional upon, and which takes effect upon, death. It must be distinguished on the one hand from a normal lifetime gift, under which title passes immediately to the transferee; and, on the other hand, from a testamentary gift which takes effect under the provisions of a will.[71] It may therefore be regarded as an exception either to the rules governing lifetime gifts, or to the rules governing testamentary gifts. In the present context, we are concerned with the former aspect. But the assistance of equity will not be required by the donee in all cases. Where the subject-matter is a chattel which has been delivered to the donee, the donee's title is complete on the donor's death, no further act being necessary. In the case of a chose in action or land, on the other hand, the donee's title is not complete on the donor's death as the legal title vests in the donor's personal representatives. The donee can seek the assistance of equity to compel the personal representatives to do whatever is necessary to perfect the donee's title.[72] It is in this latter situation that the doctrine of *donatio mortis causa* can be seen as an exception to the rule that equity will not assist a volunteer to perfect an imperfect gift.

The three essentials for a valid *donatio mortis causa* were laid down by Lord Russell C.J. in *Cain v. Moon*.[73]

(a) The gift must have been in contemplation, though not necessarily in the expectation, of death[74];

(b) the subject-matter of the gift must have been delivered to the donee[75];

(c) the gift must have been made under such circumstances as to show that the property is to revert to the donor if he should recover.[76]

ii. Contemplation of Death. The donor must have been contemplating death more particularly than by merely reflecting that we must all die some day. Commonly, *donationes mortis causa* are made in reference to a particular illness, but the principle applies

---

[71] For the distinction between a *donatio mortis causa* and a legacy, see Snell's *Principles of Equity* (29th ed.), p. 385. As to availability to meet deceased donor's debts, see [1978] Conv. 130 (S. Warnock-Smith).

[72] *Duffield v. Elwes* (1827) 1 Bli.(N.S.) 497; *Re Lillingston* [1952] 2 All E.R. 184.

[73] [1896] 2 Q.B. 283; *Re Craven's Estate* [1937] Ch. 423 at p. 426; *Delgoffe v. Fader* [1939] Ch. 922. The requirements should be stringent as claims are often made without independent evidence; *Wilson v. Paniani* [1996] 3 N.Z.L.R. 378.

[74] *Wilkes v. Allington* [1931] 2 Ch. 104.

[75] *Cain v. Moon* [1896] 2 Q.B. 283.

[76] *Re Lillingston* [1952] 2 All E.R. 184.

equally to other causes such as a hazardous journey,[77] or possibly even to the contemplation of active service in war.[78] If death occurs, the *donatio* may still be valid even though it comes from a cause different from that contemplated.

In *Wilkes v. Allington*[79] the donor was suffering from an incurable disease, and made a gift in the knowledge that he had not long to live; as things turned out, he had an even shorter time than he imagined, for he died two months later of pneumonia. It was held that the gift remained valid.

iii. Delivery of Subject-matter. A *donatio mortis causa* will not be valid without a delivery of the property to the donee[80] with the intention of parting with the "dominion" over it. It will not suffice if the property is handed over merely for safe custody.[81]

(a) *Chattels.* The donor must hand over either the chattel itself or the means of getting control over it such as, for example, a key to the box or place where the subject-matter is located.[82] In the case of a car, it is not necessary that the log book be handed over.[83]

(b) *Choses in Action.* The position is more difficult if the title to the chose in action does not pass by mere delivery of any document. The donor must hand over such documents as constitute "the essential indicia or evidence of title, possession or production of which entitles the possessor to the money or property purported to be given.[84] Thus the delivery of a bank deposit pass-book,[85] a Post Office Savings Bank-book,[86] national savings certificates[87] or a cheque or promissory note payable to the donor[88] have been held to create a *donatio mortis causa* of the chose in action represented by

---

[77] *cf. Thompson v. Mechan* [1958] O.R. 357: the ordinary risks of air travel do not suffice.

[78] *Agnew v. Belfast Banking Co.* [1896] 2 I.R. 204 at p. 221.

[79] [1931] 2 Ch. 104. A valid *donatio mortis causa* cannot be made in contemplation of suicide; *Re Dudman* [1925] 1 Ch. 553. This is probably not affected by the Suicide Act 1961, whereby suicide is no longer a crime.

[80] *Ward v. Turner* (1752) 2 Ves.Sen. 431.

[81] *Hawkins v. Blewitt* (1798) 2 Esp. 663.

[82] *Re Wasserberg* [1915] 1 Ch. 195; *Re Lillingston* [1952] 2 All E.R. 184; *Re Cole* [1964] Ch. 175. It may not suffice if the donor retains a duplicate key; *Re Craven's Estate* [1937] Ch. 423, at p. 428. *Cf. Woodard v. Woodard* [1995] 3 All E.R. 980 (possible retention of second set of car keys by donor who was too ill to use them held insignificant).

[83] *Woodard v. Woodard, supra;* [1992] Conv. 53 (J. Martin).

[84] *Birch v. Treasury Solicitor* [1951] Ch. 298 at p. 311. *cf. Re Weston* [1902] 1 Ch. 680; *Delgoffe v. Fader* [1939] Ch. 922.

[85] *Birch v. Treasury Solicitor* [1951] Ch. 298.

[86] *Re Weston* [1902] 1 Ch. 608. It is otherwise if withdrawals may be made without producing the book; *Delgoffe v. Fader* [1939] Ch. 922.

[87] *Darlow v. Sparks* [1938] 2 All E.R. 235.

[88] Even though unendorsed and therefore not transferable by delivery. See *Re Mead* (1880) 15 Ch.D. 651; *Wilson v. Paniani* [1996] 3 N.Z.L.R. 378 (where the claim failed because there was no delivery).

the document in question, so that, on the death of the donor, the donee can compel the personal representatives to perfect his legal title.

(c) *Land*. It had long been considered that land could not be the subject-matter of a *donatio mortis causa*. Although there was no English authority directly in point, Lord Eldon had doubted the possibility.[89] The reason may have been the supposed difficulty of parting with the "dominion" over land. The matter was reviewed by the Court of Appeal in *Sen v. Headley*.[90]

> The plaintiff and the deceased, who was separated from his wife, had lived together for ten years until 1964, after which they remained on close terms. When the deceased was terminally ill in hospital he said to the plaintiff "The house is yours, Margaret. You have the keys. They are in your bag. The deeds are in the steel box." The plaintiff had always had a set of keys to the house. After the deceased died (intestate), she found the box in a cupboard, used the key (which the deceased had slipped into her bag) and took possession of the deeds.

The plaintiff's claim to the house was upheld. The title deeds were essential indicia of title to the house (which had an unregistered title[91]), and had been constructively delivered to her. As in the case of a chose in action, parting with dominion over the essential indicia of title sufficed. The donor's continuing theoretical ability to deal with the property, and his retention of keys to the house to which he knew he would not return, did not amount to a retention of dominion. Every *donatio mortis causa*, whether or not of land, circumvented the Wills Act. The additional statutory formalities for lifetime transfers of land provided no greater obstacle than the Wills Act, as the trust on the donor's death was implied or constructive. The exception to the formality rule now contained in section 53(2) of the Law of Property Act 1925 was not as well developed in Lord Eldon's day as now. The policy of the law that formalities were required for the transfer of land should be upheld, but it should be acknowledged that that policy had been substantially modified by the developments in estoppel and constructive trusts.[92] The doctrine

---

[89] *Duffield v. Elwes* (1827) 1 Bli.(N.S.) 497 (where a *donatio mortis causa* of a mortgage of land was upheld).

[90] [1991] Ch. 425; [1991] Conv. 307 (M. Halliwell); (1991) 50 C.L.J. 404 (J. Thornely); All E.R. Rev. 1991, p. 207 (P. Clarke); (1991) 1 Carib.L.R. 100 (G. Kodilinye); (1993) 109 L.Q.R. 19 (P. Baker); (1994) 144 N.L.J. 48 (M. Pawlowski).

[91] The result would be the same if the land certificate of registered land had been delivered.

[92] See generally (1995) 15 L.S. 356 (M. Howard and J. Hill).

of *donatio mortis causa* was anomalous, but to except land from it would be a further anomaly.

iv. The Intention of the Donor. The donor's intention must be to make a gift which is conditional upon death, and revocable upon recovery by the donor. Thus, there is no *donatio mortis causa* if the intention is to make an immediate unconditional gift, even though the gift may fail,[93] nor where the intention is to make a future gift.[94] The conditional nature of the gift need not be expressed, but may be implied from the circumstances.[95]

v. Revocation. In addition to automatic revocation upon the donor's recovery,[96] the donor may revoke expressly, or by recovering dominion over the subject-matter,[97] but he cannot revoke by will, the reason being that the donee's title is complete before the will takes effect.[98] It might be added that the gift fails if the donee predeceases the donor.[99]

vi. Exceptions. It has been held that a *donatio mortis causa* cannot be made of the donor's own cheque[1] or promissory note.[2] The former is merely a revocable mandate to the bank,[3] while a gift of the latter is merely a gratuitous promise, thus they are not the "property" of the donor at all. It may be otherwise if the cheque is actually paid in the donor's lifetime, or before the bank has been informed of his death, or if it has been negotiated for value.[4]

There is some authority that stocks and shares cannot form the subject-matter of a *donatio mortis causa*. It was held in *Ward v. Turner*[5] that South Sea annuities could not be the subject-matter of such a gift. The decision may have been based on the inadequacy of the transfer on the facts, but it has been applied in cases concerning railway stock[6] and building society shares.[7] On the other hand, it has been held that shares in a public company can be the subject-matter of a *donatio mortis causa*.[8] This exception is, therefore, a doubtful one.

---

[93] *Edwards v. Jones* (1836) 1 My. & Cr. 226.
[94] *Solicitor to the Treasury v. Lewis* [1900] 2 Ch. 812.
[95] *Re Lillingston* [1952] 2 All E.R. 184.
[96] *Staniland v. Willott* (1852) 3 Mac. & G. 664.
[97] *Bunn v. Markham* (1816) 7 Taunt. 224.
[98] *Jones v. Selby* (1710) Prec.Ch. 300 at p. 303.
[99] *Tate v. Hilbert* (1793) 2 Ves. 111 at p. 120.
[1] *Re Beaumont* [1902] 1 Ch. 886.
[2] *Re Leaper* [1916] 1 Ch. 579.
[3] Only a holder for value can sue.
[4] *Tate v. Hilbert* (1793) 2 Ves. 111.
[5] (1752) 2 Ves.Sen. 431.
[6] *Moore v. Moore* (1874) L.R. 18 Eq. 474.
[7] *Re Weston* [1902] 1 Ch. 680.
[8] *Staniland v. Willott* (1852) 3 Mac. & G. 664.

C. Statutory Exception; Conveyance to Minor

For the sake of completeness, the position concerning conveyances to minors is mentioned, although the exception arises from statute and not from the rules of equity.

A conveyance (whether it is for value or not) which purports to convey a legal estate to a minor[9] operates as a declaration that the land is held in trust for the minor.[10]

D. Proprietary Estoppel

It has long been settled that promissory estoppel works as a shield and not as a sword.[11] In other words, where one person has been led to act upon the statement of another, he can prevent that other person from acting inconsistently with his statement.

There is another doctrine of long standing, which received its modern formulation in the dissenting speech of Lord Kingsdown in *Ramsden v. Dyson*,[12] and a more precise formulation by Fry J. in *Willmott v. Barber*,[13] and which can have the effect of creating a proprietary interest in a volunteer although there was no valid gift or trust in his favour. The doctrine is based on acquiescence and has in modern times acquired the name of Proprietary Estoppel.

Most of the modern applications of this doctrine have been in the context of licences to occupy land, and the matter will be fully discussed in Chapter 28. It will there be seen that, in applying the doctrine, the court exercises a wide discretion in reaching a solution which is appropriate to the facts of a particular case. Solutions will be seen to vary from finding, in some cases, that a volunteer has acquired a proprietary interest; in others that a mere licence is appropriate, with many variations in between.

---

[9] Who is incapable of holding a legal estate; L.P.A. 1925, s.1(6).

[10] Trusts of Land and Appointment of Trustees Act 1996, Sched. 1, para. 1 (replacing earlier legislation).

[11] *Combe v. Combe* [1951] 2 K.B. 215; (1952) 15 M.L.R. 1 (Denning L.J.).

[12] (1866) L.R. 1 H.L. 129 at p. 170.

[13] (1880) 15 Ch.D. 96 at p. 105. See now *Taylors Fashions Ltd v. Liverpool Victoria Trustees Co. Ltd* [1982] Q.B. 133, where a broader approach is formulated.

CHAPTER 5

TESTAMENTARY GIFTS NOT COMPLYING
WITH THE WILLS ACT 1837, SECRET TRUSTS

1. General 143
2. Incorporation by Reference 145
3. Fully Secret Trusts 147
   A. Informal Disclosure of the Existence
      and the Terms of the Trust 147
   B. Proof 149
   C. Disclosure to the Legatee of the Ex-
      istence of the Trust but not its Terms   149
   D. Methods of Communication 150

   E. Additions to the Secret Trust 150
   F. Undertaking to Leave by Will 151
   G. Tenants in Common and Joint
      Tenants 151
4. Half-Secret Trusts 153
5. Can the Secret Trustee Take a Benefit? ... 156
6. Theoretical Basis of Secret Trusts 158
   A. *Inter Vivos* Trust Outside the Will 158
   B. Express or Constructive Trust 162
   C. Conclusion 163

1. GENERAL[1]

WE have seen that certain formalities are necessary for the creation of *inter vivos* trusts of land and for testamentary dispositions. A trust of land must be evidenced in writing,[2] and all testamentary dispositions must be in writing and signed by the testator, in the presence of two or more attesting witnesses present at the same time.[3] We now have to consider the effect of intended dispositions which fail to comply with the necessary formalities.

The problem over the enforcement of secret trusts is the fact that the terms of the trusts are not expressed in a form which complies with the Wills Act; though, in cases in which the testator's intention is clear and there is no possibility of doubt or fraud, there is a real compulsion to enforce the secret trust. The question is whether the enforcement of the secret trust infringes the Wills Act; or whether there is recognised doctrine which allows secret trusts to be enforced in spite of the Wills Act. What should be done, for example, where a legatee or devisee persuades the testator to make a will in his favour in reliance on an oral promise to hold on trust for a third

---

[1] (1947) 12 Conv.(N.S.) 28 (J. Fleming); (1951) 67 L.Q.R. 314 (L. Sheridan); (1963) 27
   Conv.(N.S.) 92 (J. Andrews); (1972) 36 Conv.(N.S.) 113 (R. Burgess).
[2] L.P.A. 1925, s.53(1)(*b*); *ante* p. 76.
[3] Wills Act 1837, s.9; *ante*, p. 89.

party? Or an intestate successor similarly persuades the intending
testator not to make a will at all?

We saw in Chapter 3 that there is an established principle that
equity will not allow a statute to be used as an instrument of fraud.
It was there suggested, in the context of formalities for the creation
of an *inter vivos* trust, that the better solution was to require the
trustee to hold on resulting trust for the settlor where land had been
conveyed to the trustee pursuant to an oral declaration of trust for a
third party.[4] In the case of wills, it is more complicated; for the
solution of a resulting trust for the settlor is less satisfactory; in the
inter vivos case a living settlor can think again; with a will he is
dead, and a resulting trust for the residuary estate is often what the
testator most wished to avoid.

There may be many reasons why a testator wishes to be secret
about his testamentary dispositions. In many of the older cases, the
reason was that he wished to make a gift to support an illegitimate
child and its mother. To include the gift in the will would give
unwanted publicity; either among members of the family when its
provisions are disclosed, or to any person who makes official application to examine the will. At the present day, the usual reason is
that the testator cannot make up his mind upon all the details of the
disposition of his estate.[5] By using a secret trust, he is able to escape
from the policy of the Wills Act, and to retain for himself a power
to make future gifts which do not comply with the Act. There seems
to be no good reason why he should be able to do so. It is also
common to make a settlement *inter vivos* and then, by will, to add
further property to the settlement. The details of the disposition do
not in that case appear in the will; but this is not a proper case of a
secret trust, but of incorporating the other document into the will by
reference.

To create a secret trust the testator will usually arrange to leave a
legacy to a trusted friend (often his solicitor) who undertakes to hold
it upon certain trusts; or the will may give it to him "to be held upon
such trusts as I have declared to him." The question in the former
case is whether the friend could keep the legacy for himself; if not,
and clearly in the latter case he cannot, who can claim it: the
intended beneficiaries, or the estate?

Different considerations apply to these two situations, as will be
seen. The former case is known as a fully secret trust; the latter a
half- or semi-secret trust. Before attempting to answer these questions in the context of secret trusts, it is necessary to mention other
ways in which a trust or gift may be created by will although the will

---

[4] *Ante*, p. 77.
[5] This has been described as an abuse of the doctrine, as secrecy is irrelevant; [1981] Conv.
335 (T. Watkin). See *Re Snowden* [1979] Ch. 528.

does not spell out the precise terms. First, the details may be supplied by extrinsic evidence, the admissibility of which is governed by the principles relating to the construction of wills. Thus if the testator creates a trust in favour of "my grandchildren" or "my partners" their identity can be established by extrinsic evidence. The trust is an ordinary testamentary trust, not a secret trust. What the testator cannot do is to make a gift in favour of persons named in an unattested document, unless that document is incorporated into the will. This leads us to the second way of creating a trust, the details of which do not appear in the will itself. This is the doctrine of incorporation by reference, which bears superficial similarity to the doctrine of half secret trusts, but which must be distinguished from it.

2. INCORPORATION BY REFERENCE

" . . . if a testator, in a testamentary paper duly executed, refers to an existing unattested testamentary paper, the instrument so referred to becomes part of his will; in other words it is incorporated into it; but it is clear that, in order that the informal document should be incorporated in the validly executed document, the latter must refer to the former as a written instrument then existing—that is at the time of execution—in such terms that it may be ascertained."[6] It is not sufficient that the document was in existence; it must be *referred to as an existing document.* Where the doctrine of incorporation applies, the incorporated document is admitted to probate, and the advantage of secrecy is lost. We will see that this doctrine appears to be in the minds of some judges when they are dealing with cases of secret trusts, and that the rules applicable to this doctrine have sometimes been applied to secret trust cases.[7]

It is common practice to make a bequest to trustees of an existing settlement to be held by them upon the trusts of that settlement. There is no difficulty in doing so if the existing settlement is incorporated by reference in the will.

However, the requirement that only an existing document may be incorporated causes difficulty where an *inter vivos* settlement is amended after the date of the will. In *Re Jones*,[8] a testamentary gift which attempted to include future alterations of the settlement was held void even though no alterations were made. The testator was there attempting to reserve for himself a power to dispose of his

---

[6] *Per* Gorell-Barnes J. in *In bonis Smart* [1902] P. 238 at p. 240. For an unusual example, see *Re Berger (decd.)* [1990] Ch. 118.

[7] For differing views as to whether this doctrine is the basis of half secret trusts, see [1979] Conv. 360 (P. Matthews); [1980] Conv. 341 (D. Hodge); [1981] Conv. 335 (T. Watkin).

[8] [1942] Ch. 328.

property by future unattested document.[9] Is this so whenever there
is a testamentary addition to a settlement which includes a power of
revocation or amendment? A strict application of the rules of incorporation by reference would suggest that it is; but the courts have
been willing, where possible, to find a construction which will allow
the testamentary gift to be upheld.[10]

In *Re Schintz's Will Trusts*,[11] a settlor made a settlement in
which he expressly reserved a power to amend or to revoke. His
will provided that the residuary estate should be held on the trusts
of the settlement and those which might be created by future
deeds executed under the power of amendment or revocation "or
as near thereto as the situation will admit." No new trusts were
declared. Wynn-Parry J. upheld the gift, finding, as a matter of
construction, that the words referring to the future deeds were
"otiose and . . . really no more than descriptive of the terms of the
settlement."[12] *Re Jones*[13] was distinguished on that ground.

It is not common for a settlor to reserve a power of revocation and
amendment, for tax reasons. But the point is important because it is
common to include in settlements a provision for the trustees to
have power to amend the trusts, or to appoint upon new trusts, or to
terminate the settlement; and it is necessary to know the effect of
these factors upon a testamentary addition to the settlement.

If the settlement has not been changed at the date of the testator's
death, the question is whether the testamentary addition is valid or
not. Where the settlement has been altered, there are three possible
solutions; first, that the testamentary addition is void; secondly, that
it takes effect upon the settlement in its original form; thirdly, that
it takes effect upon the settlement as amended. The testator's intention would in most cases be the third choice. He will know of the
amendment of the trust made before his death, and which may have
been made for tax or for family reasons. But clearly the doctrine of
incorporation by reference is incapable of incorporating an amendment made after the date of the will. We have seen that the courts
can sometimes escape the necessity of holding the gift void. But the
second solution is not satisfactory on any argument.

The third solution could be achieved by legislation, such as the
Uniform Testamentary Additions to Trusts Act 1960 in the United
States, which enables the testamentary gift to be held on the trusts

---

[9] The gift was to the trustees of the settlement "or any substitution therefor or modification
thereof or addition thereto which I may hereafter execute."
[10] *Re Edwards'* W.T. [1948] Ch. 440.
[11] [1951] Ch. 870.
[12] *Ibid.* at p. 877.
[13] [1942] Ch. 328.

of the settlement in accordance with any amendments made to those trusts prior to the testator's death. In England the matter must be resolved by applying the doctrine of incorporation by reference, with all its limitations.[14]

3. FULLY SECRET TRUSTS

A. Informal Disclosure of the Existence and the Terms of the Trust

Where an absolute gift has taken effect in favour of the donee, it is too late to impose a trust. This is so whether the disposition is a lifetime transfer or a gift by will, which takes effect on the testator's death. Thus in *Wallgrave v. Tebbs*[15] no secret trust was established where the testator's instructions were not communicated to the legatees, who took absolutely on the face of the will, but were found among his papers after his death. Where, however, a testator makes a gift by will to a legatee in reliance upon the legatee's express or implied[16] undertaking to hold the property upon certain trusts, or to dispose of it in a certain way by his will,[17] it would not be satisfactory to permit the legatee to take advantage of the requirement of testamentary formality and to keep the property for himself.[18] The doctrine applies also where the deceased failed to revoke an existing gift,[19] or revoked a codicil so as to revive a previous testamentary gift,[20] or where an intestate, in reliance on the undertaking of those entitled on intestacy, failed to make a will,[21] or where a legatee used force[22] or undue influence.[23] "It is altogether immaterial whether the promise is made before or after the execution of the will, that being a revocable instrument."[24]

If the legatee or intestate successor is not allowed to take the property beneficially, the next question is whether the oral trust

---

[14] For other possibilities, see *Re Playfair* [1951] Ch. 4.

[15] (1855) 2 K. & J. 313; *McCormick v. Grogan* (1869) L.R. 4 H.L. 82; *Re Boyes* (1884) 26 Ch.D. 531; *Re Hawkesley's Settlement* [1934] Ch. 384.

[16] "Acquiescence either by words of consent or by silence": *per* Wood V.-C. in *Moss v. Cooper* (1861) 1 J. & H. 352 at p. 366. The communication may be by the testator or by his agent.

[17] *Re Gardner* [1920] 2 Ch. 523; *Re Young* [1951] Ch. 344; *Ottaway v. Norman* [1972] Ch. 698.

[18] *Drakeford v. Wilks* (1747) 3 Atk. 539; *Stickland v. Aldridge* (1804) 9 Ves.Jr. 516; *Wallgrave v. Tebbs* (1855) 2 K. & J. 313 at p. 320. For the position where the trustee revokes his acceptance during the testator's lifetime, see Hayton and Marshall, *Cases and Commentary on the Law of Trusts and Equitable Remedies* (10th ed.), pp. 106–107.

[19] *Chamberlaine v. Chamberlaine* (1678) Free. Ch. 34; *Moss v. Cooper, supra.*

[20] *Tharp v. Tharp* [1916] 1 Ch. 142; [1916] 2 Ch. 205.

[21] *Stickland v. Aldridge, supra*, at p. 519; (1948) 12 Conv.(N.S.) 28 (J. Fleming).

[22] *Dixon v. Olmius* (1787) 1 Cox. Eq. 414.

[23] *Bulkley v. Wilford* (1834) 2 Cl. & F. 102.

[24] *Per* Wood V.-C. in *Moss v. Cooper* (1861) 1 J. & H. 352 at p. 367.

should be enforced, or whether the legatee or intestate successor should hold on resulting trust for the estate. The rule in these cases is that the secret trust is enforced in favour of the beneficiary.[25]

This result is justifiable if it is correct to say, as explained below,[26] that a secret trust is enforced because the testator validly declared an *inter vivos* trust during his lifetime, and the trust became constituted by the vesting of the property on his death in the trustee. That, as will be seen below, is the modern theoretical explanation of the enforcement of secret trusts. That is not, however, the reason which has been relied on historically to enforce fully secret trusts. Without that theory, the courts were in real difficulty in that the Wills Act laid down the requirements for the creation of a testamentary trust, and those requirements were not met. If, therefore, the trusts were enforced, was not the Wills Act being disregarded? Or, as they said, did the courts not "give the go-by" to it?[27] The courts searched for a justification in not observing the terms of the Wills Act, and found it in the doctrine of fraud: it would be fraudulent if the legatee were to take beneficially in the circumstances. The fraud theory was laid down in the clearest terms by Lord Hatherley L.C. and Lord Westbury in *McCormick v. Grogan*,[28] although the House of Lords held in that case that the testator had not intended to impose an obligation on Grogan, the sole executor, and that, therefore, no trust existed on the facts of the case. To base the court's intervention on the ground of fraud could well be a sufficient justification for not applying the Wills Act; but the next step was not so obvious; it would be wrong for the legatee to keep the property, but it was difficult to see how the prevention of fraud would justify the projection forward of the beneficial interest to the beneficiary. As we will see, this matter became all the more clear when the courts were dealing with the question of half-secret trusts, where the testator requires the legatee to take the property as trustee, without saying in the will who the beneficiaries are. In that situation, there was no possibility of the legatee being fraudulent, in the sense of enriching himself, because he was expressed to take as trustee. In *Blackwell v. Blackwell*[29] the leading case on half-secret trusts, the enforcement of the half-secret trust was justified by saying that the intention of the testator was clear, and that it was communicated to and acquiesced in by the legatee. As explained above, the modern view is to justify the enforcement of secret trusts upon the theory that the trust has

---

[25] *Thynn v. Thynn* (1684) 1 Vern. 296.
[26] *Post*, p. 158.
[27] *Re Pitt-Rivers* [1902] 1 Ch. 403 at p. 407; *Blackwell v. Blackwell* [1929] A.C. 318 at p. 337.
[28] (1869) L.R. 4 H.L. 82.
[29] [1929] A.C. 318.

been declared *inter vivos* and that it is constituted by the testamentary gift to the legatee. There are, as will be seen, some theoretical difficulties in this view also.[30]

B. Proof

Related to the question whether the doctrine is based upon fraud is the question of the standard of proof required to establish a secret trust. A high standard of proof is required to prove fraud, and there are dicta in many cases indicating that a secret trust can only be proved where there is "clear evidence,"[31] and suggesting that the standard is the same as that required to support the rectification of a written instrument.[32] In *Re Snowden*,[33] however, Megarry V.-C. disregarded the historical connection of the doctrine of secret trusts and the requirement of fraud; and laid down that the standard required to prove communication and acceptance is the ordinary civil standard of proof required to establish an ordinary trust.[34] The evidence may, of course, establish an intention to create a trust, and its acceptance by the legatee, without establishing who the beneficiaries were. The legatee would then hold on resulting trust.[35] If questions of fraud or other special factors arose, the standard required would rise. The onus is on the person contending that the trust exists.[36]

C. Disclosure to the Legatee of the Existence of the Trust but not its Terms

If the testator discloses to the legatee the fact that he is to hold the legacy on trust, but does not disclose the terms of the trust before his death, the legatee will hold on resulting trust for the estate.[37] The intended trust, not being declared before the death, cannot be enforced. The imposition of the resulting trust will prevent the unjust enrichment of the legatee.

---

[30] *Post*, p. 158.
[31] See *McCormick v. Grogan* (1869) L.R. 4 H.L. 82 at p. 87, *per* Lord Westbury; *Ottaway v. Norman* [1972] Ch. 698 at p. 699.
[32] *Fowler v. Fowler* (1859) 4 De G. & J. 250 at p. 264; *Crane v. Hegeman-Harris Co. Inc.* [1939] 4 All E.R. 68 at p. 71; *Joscelyne v. Nissen* [1970] 2 Q.B. 86 at p. 98; *Ottaway v. Norman*, *supra*.
[33] [1979] Ch. 528; (1979) 38 C.L.J. 260 (C. Rickett); (1991) 107 L.Q.R. 194 (B. Robertson).
[34] *Ibid.* at p. 537.
[35] *Re Boyes* (1884) 26 Ch.D. 531.
[36] *Jones v. Badley* (1868) L.R. 3 Ch.App. 362.
[37] Similarly if the terms, although disclosed, are unlawful or uncertain. See *Re Pugh's W.T.* [1967] 1 W.L.R. 1262; *Brown v. Pourau* [1995] 1 N.Z.L.R. 352.

In *Re Boyes*,[38] a legacy was given to the testator's solicitor, who had undertaken to hold the property according to directions which he would receive by letter. The letter was found only after the death. The solicitor accepted that he held as trustee, and wished to carry out the trust. Kay J. held that there was a resulting trust in favour of the next-of-kin; and explained the rule by saying: "The essence of all these decisions is that the devisee or legatee accepts a particular trust which thereupon becomes binding upon him, and which it would be a fraud in him not to carry into effect.[39]

This situation is similar to that of half-secret trusts in that the legatee takes as a trustee. But there is an important difference. In *Re Boyes*,[40] the gift was absolute on its face; the trust could have been enforced if the terms had been declared before death.[41] Where the existence of a trust is disclosed on the face of the will, the communication, as we shall see, must be prior to or contemporaneous with the execution of the will.[42]

D. Methods of Communication

We have seen that the trust must be communicated before the testator's death. The communication may be made orally or in writing; and it appears that, just as "a ship which sails under sealed orders, is sailing under orders though the exact terms are not ascertained by the captain till later,"[43] a testator may, during his lifetime, give to the legatee a sealed envelope which is not to be opened until the testator's death. This is sufficient provided the legatee knows that it contains details of the trust.

E. Additions to the Secret Trust

A testator must communicate not only the trust and the terms, but also the identity of the property to be held on trust.

In *Re Colin Cooper*,[44] the testator left £5,000 to two persons as trustees, and informally communicated to them the terms of the trust. By a later codicil he purported to increase the sum to be devoted to the secret trust to £10,000, they "knowing my wishes

---

[38] (1884) 26 Ch.D. 531; *Re Hawkesley's Settlement* [1934] Ch. 384.
[39] *Ibid.* at p. 536.
[40] (1884) 26 Ch.D. 531.
[41] *Re Gardner* [1920] 2 Ch. 523.
[42] *Post*, p. 154.
[43] *Per* Lord Wright in *Re Keen* [1937] Ch. 236 at p. 242; *Re Boyes, supra*, at p. 536.
[44] [1939] Ch. 811.

regarding that sum." This addition was not communicated to the trustees. It was held that the first instalment could be devoted to the secret trusts; but the later instalment went on a resulting trust.[45]

F. Undertaking to Leave by Will

A secret trust may impose an obligation not only to hold on trust for a beneficiary on the testator's death; but also an obligation to make provision for an intended beneficiary after the legatee's death.

In *Re Gardner (No. 1)*,[46] a wife left her estate to her husband for life, and there was an agreement that the property should be divided among certain beneficiaries on his death. The husband died intestate, and the Court of Appeal decided that he held the property, after his life interest, on trust for the beneficiaries.

Ottaway v. Norman[47] took the matter a stage further. The testator agreed with his housekeeper that she should have a bungalow after his death, and she agreed to leave it to the testator's son by her will. The testator left the bungalow (plus its contents and some money) to her absolutely. She first made a will in favour of the testator's son; but she then changed that will, and left the bungalow to the defendant. Brightman J. held that the son was entitled to the bungalow and its contents, although not to the money.

The enforcement of a secret trust in this situation creates a number of problems concerning the status of the trust during the housekeeper's lifetime, and the theoretical basis on which secret trusts are enforced. This question is discussed in section 6 below, but some of the questions arising from *Ottaway v. Norman*[48] are more conveniently considered in Chapter 12.

G. Tenants in Common and Joint Tenants

Where a testamentary gift is made to two or more persons as tenants in common, and secret trusts are communicated to some but not all of the tenants in common, those to whom the communication

---

[45] Had it been a fully secret trust, the legatees would have been beneficially entitled to the addition.

[46] [1920] 2 Ch. 523; *Re Young* [1951] Ch. 344; *post*, p. 159.

[47] [1972] Ch. 698; (1972) 36 Conv.(N.S.) 129 (D. Hayton).

[48] *Supra.*

was made are bound, the others taking beneficially.[49] To hold otherwise would enable one beneficiary to deprive the rest of their
benefits by setting up a secret trust."[50]

But where a gift is made to them as joint tenants, a distinction is
made between the case where the trust is communicated before the
making of the will, and where the communication is between the
will and the death. In the former case, all joint tenants are bound.[51]
In the latter, only those who have accepted the trust are bound by
it,[52] "the reason being that the gift is not tainted with any fraud in
procuring the execution of the will."[53]

Farwell J. was dissatisfied with his own explanation. He confessed that he was "unable to see any difference between a gift made
on the faith of an antecedent promise and a gift left unrevoked on the
faith of a subsequent promise."[54] It has been suggested that gifts
upon secret trusts to joint tenants and tenants in common should be
decided on the principle of *Huguenin v. Baseley*,[55] that "no man may
profit by the fraud of another."[56] Thus "if A induces B to make or
leave unrevoked a will leaving property to A and C,"[57] whether as
joint tenants or tenants in common, C will be bound "if the testator
would not have made any gift to C unless A had promised. . . . If the
testator would still have left property to C even if A had not
promised, C is not bound. . . . Whether A and C are joint tenants or
tenants in common, and whether A's promise was before or after the
making of the will are matters of evidence that may help to determine whether or not there was such an inducement, but of themselves both matters are inconclusive."[58] The argument is persuasive;
but the cases say otherwise. The wrong turning was taken in
Rowbotham v. Dunnett.[59]

The principles discussed above have emerged from cases concerning fully secret trusts. Of course, in the case of half-secret trusts
there could be no question of the legatees taking beneficially. The
issue would be whether a valid half-secret trust could be created by
communication to fewer than the whole number of trustees. It seems
that the principles applicable to fully secret trusts would be applied
by analogy, bearing in mind that half-secret trustees will invariably
be joint tenants, and that communication after the will is ineffective

[49] *Tee v. Ferri* (1856) 2 K. & J. 357.
[50] *Re Stead* [1900] 1 Ch. 237 at p. 241.
[51] *Russell v. Jackson* (1852) 10 Hare 204; *Jones v. Badley* (1868) L.R. 3 Ch.App. 362; *Re
     Gardom* [1914] 1 Ch. 662; *Re Spence* [1949] W.N. 237; *Re Young* [1951] Ch. 344.
[52] *Burney v. MacDonald* (1845) 15 Sim. 6; *Moss v. Cooper* (1861) 1 J. & H. 352.
[53] *Per* Farwell J. in *Re Stead* [1900] 1 Ch. 237 at p. 241.
[54] *Ibid.*
[55] (1807) 14 Ves. 273.
[56] (1972) 88 L.Q.R. 225 at p. 226 (B. Perrins).
[57] *Per* Farwell J. in *Re Stead* [1900] 1 Ch. 237 at p. 241.
[58] (1972) 88 L.Q.R. 225 at p. 226 (B. Perrins).
[59] (1878) 8 Ch.D. 430.

in the case of half-secret trusts, as explained below. Hence communication to one of the trustees prior to the making of the will is effective.[60]

4. HALF-SECRET TRUSTS

Where the will gives property to a legatee *upon trust*, without, however, saying what the intended trusts are, the question of the enforcement of a secret trust communicated to the legatee has been treated very differently from the case where the property was given to the legatee *absolutely* in the will. The courts have found it more difficult to enforce a secret trust in the former case—where the legatee takes expressly as trustee—than in the latter case. It is difficult to see any sense, however, in a rule which allows a secret trust to be enforced if the trust is nowhere mentioned in the will; but holds it void if the testamentary gift discloses the fact that the legatee takes as trustee. If it is right that secret trusts are express trusts operating wholly outside the scope of the Wills Act, it is difficult to see why the two situations should not be treated alike.

But there is a historical explanation. We saw that the nineteenth century judges said that secret trusts were enforced to prevent fraud[61]; to prevent the legatee taking for himself what he had promised the testator to hold upon trust. The element of fraud, however, was not present in the case of the gift to a legatee as trustee. As he took in a fiduciary capacity, he could in no circumstances take the property for himself. There was no possibility of fraud, and no justification, so the argument ran, for not applying the Wills Act. And it was at one time held that the mention of the existence of a trust did prevent the operation of the doctrine of secret trusts.[62] The validity of half-secret trusts was not finally established until the House of Lords decision in *Blackwell v. Blackwell*[63] in 1929.

The testator by a codicil gave a legacy of £12,000 to legatees upon trust to apply the income "for the purposes indicated by me

---

[60] See *Re Gardom* [1914] 1 Ch. 662.
[61] *Ante*, p. 148.
[62] *Moss v. Cooper* (1861) 1 J. & H. 352 at p. 367; *Le Page v. Gardom* (1915) 84 L.J.Ch. 749 at p. 752; (1937) 53 L.Q.R. 501 (W. Holdsworth).
[63] [1929] A.C. 318. If the words in the will are insufficient to impose a trust, any secret trust will be fully secret; *Jankowski v. Petek Estate* (1995) 131 D.L.R. (4th) 717 (gift to executor "to deal with as he may in his discretion decide upon").

to them." The trust had been accepted prior to the execution of
the codicil. The House of Lords enforced the trust. They were
assisted by *Re Fleetwood*[64] and *Re Huxtable*[65] where it was held
that the secret trust doctrine applied although the gift was in terms
a gift upon trust, and where therefore there was no question of
fraud in the legatee. Lord Sumner concluded that "it is communication of the purpose to the legatee, coupled with acquiescence
or promise on his part, that removes the matter from the provision
of the Wills Act and brings it within the law of trusts, as applied
in this instance to trustees, who happen also to be legatees."[66] The
effect of the bequest "remains to be decided by the law as laid
down by the Courts before and since the [Wills] Act, and does not
depend on the Act itself."[67] Thus the trust operated outside the
Act and could be enforced without proof of fraud.

In *Blackwell v. Blackwell*[68] the trusts were communicated before
the will and were stated to have been so communicated. Will the
same rule apply where the trusts are or may be declared in the
future? On the one hand, there is logically no difference between
declarations of trusts before and after the will; for the will is
ambulatory and of no effect until the death.[69] The distinction is not
made, as we have seen, with fully secret trusts.[70] If the trust operates
independently of the Wills Act, the date of the will should be
immaterial. On the other hand, it is more difficult to *assume* acquiescence where the communication is after the will; in the absence of
proof of express agreement, the fact of non-revocation may be the
only basis on which to presume acquiescence. More importantly, "a
testator cannot reserve to himself a power of making future unwit-
nessed dispositions by merely naming a trustee and leaving the
purposes of the trust to be supplied afterwards. . . . "[71] To allow that
to be done by half-secret trust would be to give a wider rule for
secret trusts (which might be oral) than that which as we have seen
is applied in the case of incorporation of documents by reference.[72]
It would be surprising if the law of wills permitted this; but, if the
proper explanation of the enforcement of secret trusts is that they
operate outside the will and independently of the Wills Act, then the

---

[64] (1880) 15 Ch.D. 594.
[65] [1902] 2 Ch. 793.
[66] [1929] A.C. 318 at pp. 339–340; *Ottaway v. Norman* [1972] Ch. 698 at p. 711.
[67] *Ibid.* at p. 339.
[68] [1929] A.C. 318.
[69] (1937) 53 L.Q.R. 501 (W. Holdsworth).
[70] *Ante,* p. 147; *Re Gardner* [1920] 2 Ch. 523.
[71] *Per* Lord Sumner in *Blackwell v. Blackwell* [1929] A.C. 318 at p. 339.
[72] *In bonis Smart* [1902] P. 238; [1979] Conv. 360 (P. Matthews).

rules relating to incorporation by reference are, as has been pointed out, quite irrelevant.[73] And what Lord Sumner feared can always be achieved by a fully secret trust.

With half-secret trusts however the distinction appears to be made.

In *Re Keen*[74] the testator gave a sum of money to trustees "to be held upon trust and disposed of by them among such person, persons or charities as may be notified by me to them or either of them during my lifetime. . . . " Previously, one of the trustees had been given a sealed envelope containing the name of the beneficiary of the intended trust. In deciding in favour of the residuary legatees, the Court of Appeal held that the handing over of the sealed envelope was a communication of the trust, but that this, being *prior* to the date of the will,[75] was inconsistent with the terms of the will which provided for "a future definition . . . of the trust subsequent to the date of the will," while "the sealed letter relied on as notifying the trust was communicated . . . before the date of the will."[76]

The trust would, however, have failed independently of the question of inconsistency. The disposition contained a power to declare trusts in the future. This was void, for it "would involve a power to change a testamentary disposition by an unexecuted codicil and would violate section 9 of the Wills Act."[77]

The criticisms of this rule have been discussed. The contrary rule exists in Ireland[78] and in most of the American jurisdictions.[79] The matter is still open to the House of Lords; it may be that the true ratio of *Re Keen*[80] is the narrow point of inconsistency; but it was followed in *Re Bateman's Will Trusts*,[81] where, it seems, the rule was not challenged. The present position is unsatisfactory; there is no sense in a rule which (in the case of communication between the will

---

[73] (1937) 53 L.Q.R. 501 (W. Holdsworth); *Moss v. Cooper* (1861) 1 J. & K. 352 at p. 367.
[74] [1937] Ch. 236; *Johnson v. Ball* (1851) 5 De G. & Sm. 85; (1972) 23 N.I.L.Q. 263 (R. Burgess).
[75] *Re Huxtable* [1902] 2 Ch. 793.
[76] *Re Keen, supra*, at p. 248; *Re Rees' W.T.* [1950] Ch. 204.
[77] *Re Keen, supra*, at p. 247; *Johnson v. Ball* (1851) 5 De G. & Sm. 85; *Re Hetley* [1902] 2 Ch. 866.
[78] *Riordan v. Banon* (1876) 10 Ir.R.Eq. 469; *contra Balfe v. Halfpenny* [1904] 1 Ir.R. 486; *Re Browne* [1944] Ir.R. 90; (1951) 67 L.Q.R. 413 (L. Sheridan); [1992] Conv. 202 (J. Mee); (1991) 5 *Trust Law International* 69 (P. Coughlan).
[79] *Restatement of Trusts*, § 55, comment (*c*), (*h*).
[80] [1937] Ch. 236.
[81] [1970] 1 W.L.R. 1463.

and the death) enforces a trust in a bequest "to X" but disregards the trust in a bequest "to X upon trust."[82]

Other views are that the distinction is justified because wills creating half-secret trusts are invariably drawn up by solicitors, and so stricter rules are appropriate[83]; or that consistency should be achieved by requiring the communication to be before the will even in the case of a fully secret trust. If the trusteeship was accepted after the will, the legatee would hold on trust for the residuary legatee or next-of-kin. This would have the advantage of preventing reliance on the doctrine of secret trusts by testators who are merely indecisive[84] and thus not within the rationale of the doctrine.[85]

5. Can the Secret Trustee Take a Benefit?

The legatee may claim that the testator intended him to take some benefit from the gift, perhaps, for example, a specific sum, or possibly any surplus after performing the trust. Two separate questions arise here; first, was this the testator's intention? Secondly, how far is evidence of such an intention admissible in favour of the trustee?

To consider first the question of intention, it is necessary to construe the language of the will to determine whether the testator's intention was to make the legatee a trustee of the whole of the property given, or to make a beneficial gift to him subject to his performing certain obligations.[86] In the former case, any surplus left after carrying out the trusts is held upon resulting trusts[87]; in the latter, the legatee may keep it.[88] There is thus no difficulty in a case where the will itself makes it clear that the trust does not extend to the whole of the legacy, but the will may be silent on the matter, and the only evidence extrinsic. This leads us to the second question, namely whether the trustee may be permitted to prove his claim to benefit by relying on documentary or even oral evidence.

The difficulty, whether the trust be fully or half-secret, is the danger of fraud by the secret trustee. A further problem in the case

---

[82] But see [1985] Conv. 248 (B. Perrins), supporting the communication rules as being based on the extrinsic evidence rule.

[83] [1995] Conv. 366 (D. Wilde).

[84] As in *Re Snowden* [1979] Ch. 528.

[85] [1981] Conv. 335 (T. Watkin). See also the discussion of how the suggested reform would operate in the case of a person who refrains from making a will in reliance upon the acceptance of a trust by the next-of-kin.

[86] *Ante*, p. 52. This construction is more likely where the legatee is a relative for whom the testator may be supposed to have been intending to provide. See *Irvine v. Sullivan* (1869) L.R. 8 Eq. 673 (fiancée).

[87] *Ante*, p. 53.

[88] *Ante*, p. 53; *Irvine v. Sullivan* (1869) L.R. 8 Eq. 673.

of a half-secret trust is that the evidence would contradict the terms of the will, which impose a trust on the entire legacy.[89]

In *Re Rees' W.T.*[90] the testator by will appointed a friend and his solicitor (thereinafter called his trustees) to be executors and trustees. He left the whole estate "unto my trustees absolutely they well knowing my wishes concerning the same."

The testator had told the trustees that he wished them to make certain payments and to retain any surplus for themselves. A substantial surplus remained. It was held that the trustees were not entitled to the surplus, which passed as on intestacy. The will, on its true construction, imposed a trust on the whole, and evidence was not admissible to show that the trustees were to take a benefit. It was not without significance that the trustee was the testator's solicitor. As Evershed M.R. said, "In the general public interest it seems to me desirable that, if a testator wishes his property to go to his solicitor and the solicitor prepares the will, that intention on the part of the testator should appear plainly in the will and should not be arrived at by the more oblique method of what is sometimes called a secret trust."[91]

In *Re Tyler*,[92] however, there are suggestions that evidence is admissible as to all the terms of a trust, including any in favour of the trustee himself, although such evidence will not lightly be admitted. Pennycuick J. found difficulty in the reasoning of *Re Rees*. But evidence contained in the (now deceased) trustee's own written memorandum did not suffice.[93]

Finally, we have seen that if a secret trust fails for non-compliance with the communication rules, or for uncertainty, the secret trustee holds on trust for the residuary legatee or next-of-kin. He could not claim the legacy for himself if the trust was half-secret, or, although fully secret, if he had accepted trusteeship. A question might arise to whether the secret trustee could take the property if he himself was the residuary legatee or next-of-kin. There is no reason in principle why he should not, as he would be claiming in a

[89] We have seen, in the context of communication, that evidence inconsistent with the will is not admissible; *Re Keen* [1937] Ch. 236, *ante*, p. 155.

[90] [1950] Ch. 204. See also *Re Pugh's W.T.* [1967] 1 W.L.R. 1262, suggesting that it is easier to infer an intention that a sole trustee should take beneficially than that two or more trustees should do so.

[91] [1950] Ch. 204 at p. 211.

[92] [1967] 1 W.L.R. 1269 (concerning an *inter vivos* trust). See also *Ottaway v. Norman* [1972] Ch. 698, *ante*, p. 151, where the secret trustee took a benefit in the form of a life interest. This was clearly the testator's intention and the point was not discussed. In any event, the interest had already been enjoyed.

[93] Although generally such a memorandum is *admissible* under the Civil Evidence Act 1968 to prove the terms of the trust.

different capacity, but the court might intervene if he disclaimed the legacy in order to benefit.[94]

6. THEORETICAL BASIS OF SECRET TRUSTS

A. Inter Vivos Trust Outside the Will

The formal requirements for a will, contained in the Wills Act 1837, are based upon a sound policy. It is important to avoid doubt, fraud and uncertainty in connection with testamentary dispositions; and it is essential to rely upon written formalities as there is no other way of ascertaining the intention of the testator. If secret trusts, which effectively create dispositions of property on death, are to be allowed, it is important to justify the failure to apply the provisions of the Wills Act. In terms of policy, it is easy to favour an exception in cases in which the intention of the testator is clear, and is opposed only by the formalities which were set up in the hope of establishing it. But further justification is needed. The Wills Act is a statute, and not merely an expression of policy. The question is whether some theory can be found to justify the enforcement of secret trusts.

We have seen that the early cases were explained on the ground of fraud[95]; the fear that the legatee would otherwise keep the property for himself. There is substantial authority for a refusal to allow a statute to be used as an instrument of fraud, but the fraud theory appears not to justify the enforcement of half-secret trusts, because the legatee, being named as a trustee, cannot claim. On the other hand, it may be said that a secret trustee who relies on the Wills Act to defeat the testator's expectation commits a fraud against the testator and the secret beneficiary even in the absence of personal benefit, and recent authority on mutual wills has confirmed that fraud can be perpetrated without gain.[96] On this view the fraud theory can explain both kinds of secret trust. What is clear, however, is that it is not sufficient to say as did Lord Sumner in *Blackwell v. Blackwell*[97] that secret trusts are based upon the essential elements of intention, communication and acquiescence, for this assumes a new basis for the enforcement of testamentary dispositions which is wholly inconsistent with the Wills Act, and suggests that a testator

---

[94] See *Blackwell v. Blackwell* [1929] A.C. 318 at p. 341. Disclaimer might in any event not cause a half-secret trust to fail, by reliance on the maxim that a trust does not fail for want of a trustee; but it has been said that a fully secret trust will fail if the trustee disclaims; *Re Maddock* [1902] 2 Ch. 220 at p. 231; *cf. Blackwell v. Blackwell, supra*; Oakley, *Constructive Trusts* (3rd ed.), p. 252.

[95] *Ante*, p. 148; doubted in Oakley, *Constructive Trusts* (3rd ed.), pp. 252–253.

[96] *Re Dale (deceased)* [1994] Ch. 31; (1995) 58 M.L.R. 95 (A. Brierley); *post*, p. 309. See generally [1980] Conv. 341 (D. Hodge), supporting the fraud theory as the basis of half secret trusts.

[97] [1929] A.C. 318 at p. 340.

could "contract out of" the Wills Act, and create testamentary dispositions by a different method. The modern view is that secret trusts can be enforced because they are not trusts created by will; but are trusts arising outside and independently of the will[98]; that they arise by reason of the personal obligation accepted by the legatee.[99]

In *Re Young*,[1] the testator made a bequest to his wife with a direction that on her death she should leave the property for the purposes which he had communicated to her. One of the purposes was that she would leave a legacy of £2,000 to the chauffeur. The chauffeur had witnessed the will. A witness may not normally take a legacy, and the question was whether he had thereby forfeited his interest.[2] Danckwerts J. held that he had not; the trust in his favour was not a trust contained in the will but one created separately and imposed upon the legatee.[3]

It is one thing to say that the trust operates outside the will, but it is another to say just how and when the trust takes effect. If some of the propositions discussed in Chapter 4[4] are sound, the most natural way for this to occur is to treat the communication to the trustee as the declaration of trust, and the vesting of the property in the trustee by the will as the constitution of the trust. If this is so, the declaration is *inter vivos*, and the Wills Act has no effect upon it; the only statutory formalities that are relevant are Law of Property Act 1925, s.53(1)(*b*),[5] which requires that declarations of trusts of land should be evidenced in writing; but this would not affect the rule requiring a fraudulent trustee in a fully secret trust of land to hold on a

---

[98] *Per* Lord Westbury in *Cullen v. Att.-Gen. for Northern Ireland* (1866) L.R. 1 H.L. 190 at p. 198; *per* Lord Sumner in *Blackwell v. Blackwell* [1929] A.C. 318 at p. 340.

[99] "I think the solution is to be found by bearing in mind that what is enforced is not a trust imposed by the will, but one arising from the acceptance by the legatee of a trust communicated to him by the testator, on the faith of which acceptance the will was made or left revoked, as the case might be": *per* Lord Warrington of Clyffe in *Blackwell v. Blackwell* [1929] A.C. 318 at p. 342. For New Zealand views, see *Brown v. Pourau* [1995] 1 N.Z.L.R. 352.

[1] [1951] Ch. 344; *Cullen v. Att.-Gen. for Northern Ireland* (1866) L.R. 1 H.L. 190.

[2] Wills Act 1837, s.15. *cf. Re Fleetwood* (1880) 15 Ch.D. 594; *O'Brien v. Condon* [1905] Ir.R. 51. If it is the secret trustee who attests there should be no difficulty if it is a half-secret trust, as he takes no beneficial interest on the face of the will. If it is fully secret, the position is less clear. For the view that it would fail, see Oakley, *Constructive Trusts* (3rd ed.), p. 250.

[3] To the contrary is *Re Maddock* [1902] 2 Ch. 220, where the property subject to a fully secret trust was treated as being subject to a specific bequest for the purpose of the payment of debts out of the estate. No doubt the legacy would be treated as part of the estate for tax purposes and for the purposes of the Inheritance (Provision for Family and Dependants) Act 1975, rather than as property disposed of prior to the death.

[4] *Ante*, pp. 111 *et seq.*

[5] *Ante*, p. 76. *Re Baillie* (1886) 2 T.L.R. 660 at p. 661; but there was no writing in *Ottaway v. Norman* [1972] Ch. 698; *post*, p. 160.

constructive trust.[6] There would be no awkward distinction between declarations prior to and subsequent to the will in half-secret trusts[7]; the sole question would be whether or not a trust was declared of the property before the death, and whether that trust became properly constituted by the vesting of the property in the trustee.

We have seen that the usual rule in the case of property coming to a person who had previously declared himself trustee of it was that the trust did not become constituted without a further manifestation of intention.[8] It was submitted that where a third person accepted an instruction to hold the property on certain trusts and the settlor subsequently transferred the property to him without further declaration, the trust would be constituted. It should make no difference whether the property passed to the trustee by conveyance *inter vivos* or by a will.[9] It will probably fail however if the trustee predeceases the testator, at any rate in the case of a fully secret trust.[10] Assuming its terms were known, it may be that a half-secret trust could be saved by the maxim "a trust does not fail for want of a trustee."[11]

Ottaway v. Norman[12] raises a further complication. There the secret trust was upheld as to the bungalow (and its contents). Assuming that it is correct to say that the testator made an *inter vivos* declaration that the bungalow was to be held on trust for his son after the housekeeper's death, and that the trust was constituted by the vesting of the property in the housekeeper as trustee, then the trust of the bungalow arose on the testator's death, the housekeeper's interest effectively being a life interest. But the son also claimed entitlement to so much of the money left to the housekeeper as remained at her death. This claim failed. The testator had not intended to impose an obligation on the housekeeper as to *all* her money, nor had he intended to impose an obligation as to the money derived from his will, because this would be unworkable unless this money was to be kept separately, which was not envisaged. But Brightman J. was content to assume, without deciding, that if property was given on the understanding that the primary donee would

---

[6] L.P.A. 1925, s.53(2). As to whether he should hold on trust for the secret beneficiaries, see *post*, p. 162.

[7] *Re Keen* [1937] Ch. 236; *ante*, p. 155.

[8] *Ante*, p. 135.

[9] As with the property received by Miss Towry Law from her sister and conveyed to the trustees: *Re Ellenborough* [1903] 1 Ch. 697; *Re Adlard* [1954] Ch. 29; *Re Ralli's W.T.* [1964] Ch. 288.

[10] *Per* Cozens-Hardy L.J. in *Re Maddock* [1902] 2 Ch. 220 at p. 251; Oakley, *Constructive Trusts* (3rd ed.), p. 250.

[11] Unless the particular trustee is regarded as essential to the trust. For the view that a half secret trust would also fail, see [1995] Conv. 366 at p. 373 (D. Wilde). The question of disclaimer by the secret trustee has already been considered; *ante*, p. 158.

[12] [1972] Ch. 698; (1972) 36 Conv.(N.S.) 129 (D. Hayton); (1972) 36 Conv.(N.S.) at p. 115 (R. Burgess); [1971] A.S.C.L. 375 at p. 384 (J. Hackney).

dispose of such assets, if any, as he may still have at his death in favour of a secondary donee, there would be a valid trust, "in suspense"[13] during the lifetime of the primary donee but attaching to the estate of the primary donee on the latter's death. This would be a "floating trust,"[14] such as was recognised by the High Court of Australia in *Birmingham v. Renfrew*[15] but which can hardly be said to be a recognised legal concept. The situation during the primary donee's lifetime would be similar to that existing during the lifetime of the survivor of makers of mutual wills. But the origin of the trust is of course quite different. In the former case it is based upon the declaration of the trust, followed by communication and acquiescence and the vesting of the property in the trustee; in the case of mutual wills, it is based on the contract between the parties followed by the death of the first testator in reliance upon non-revocation by the survivor. Once the trust has attached, however, the problems are similar, and will be discussed in Chapter 12.

Until the property has so vested, there is no completely constituted trust; the declaration can have no effect, and cannot create property rights. The will can be revoked or altered, or the property may be disposed of during the testator's lifetime. The testator can revoke his instructions to the secret trustee at any time,[16] and if he acts as if he had forgotten the declaration or assumed it to be no longer existent, no doubt it will be treated as having expired. No rational theory, it is suggested, can be found which will justify the remarkable decision in *Re Gardner (No. 2)*.[17] We have seen that a wife left her estate to her husband for life,[18] and that after his death it was to be held on secret trust for five named beneficiaries. One of the beneficiaries pre-deceased the wife. The representatives of the deceased beneficiary successfully claimed the share.

A gift by will normally lapses if the donee predeceases the testator,[19] and the estate of the donee can only claim if the donee acquired some interest in the property before he died. No such interest could exist in this case; and the theory which suggests that a secret trust can be treated as a declaration of trust *inter vivos* does not suggest that any interest is obtained by any beneficiary prior to

---

[13] *Ibid.* at p. 713.

[14] (1972) 36 Conv.(N.S.) at p. 132 (D. Hayton).

[15] (1937) 57 C.L.R. 666. Applied in *Re Cleaver* [1981] 1 W.L.R. 939.

[16] But any substituted instructions given after the will is executed will be invalid in the case of a half secret trust.

[17] [1923] 2 Ch. 230. See Oakley, *Constructive Trusts* (3rd ed.), p. 251, suggesting that there is no clear rule against a non-testamentary trust for a dead person. This is doubtful, as such a beneficiary has no legal personality, unless it is clear that his estate is intended to take.

[18] *Re Gardner (No. 1)* [1920] 2 Ch. 523; *ante*, p. 151.

[19] A special exception is made in the case of children of the testator who predecease him, leaving issue: Wills Act 1837, s.33. Such a gift takes effect in favour of the issue.

the constitution of the trust by vesting of the legal estate in the trustee.

B. Express or Constructive Trust

Closely connected with the theoretical basis of secret trusts is the question whether a secret trust is properly categorised as an express or constructive trust.[20] The question is not merely academic, for, as we have seen,[21] constructive trusts of land are excepted from the requirement of written evidence. Is an oral secret trust of land valid?

An express trust is one declared by the settlor; a constructive trust is one imposed by the law.[22] The analysis of secret trusts as being declarations outside the will categorises them as express trusts, whether they are fully or half secret. In the case of a half secret trust the will itself expressly declares a trust. While this element is absent with a fully secret trust, such a trust may claim to be express on the basis of the testator's express declaration to the secret trustee. There is authority that a half-secret trust of land is not enforceable without written evidence.[23] In *Ottaway v. Norman*,[24] however, a fully secret trust of land was upheld without written evidence, but the point was not discussed.

Fully secret trusts however have, as it were, another string to their bow. They were enforced long before secret trusts were thought of as taking effect outside the will. We have seen that they have been said on high authority to be enforceable on the ground of fraud,[25] and they can claim also to be constructive trusts.[26] It is submitted that fully secret trusts can be enforced under either head.

If it becomes established that even a fully secret trust is express, it does not follow that the secret trustee would take beneficially if the trust fails for lack of compliance with the formality requirements. The result in such a case would be that, having accepted trusteeship, he would hold on trust for the residuary beneficiary or next-of-kin.[27]

---

[20] One view is that the attempt to classify as express or constructive is misguided because the secret trust doctrine is concerned with the procedural question of admitting evidence of a trust and not with the nature of the trust itself; [1985] Conv. 248, at p. 253 (B. Perrins).

[21] *Ante*, p. 76.

[22] *Post*, p. 285.

[23] *Re Baillie* (1886) 2 T.L.R. 660 at p. 661.

[24] [1972] Ch. 698. See also *Strickland v. Aldridge* (1804) 9 Ves.Jr. 516; *Brown v. Pourau* [1995] 1 N.Z.L.R. 352; [1996] Conv. 302 (C. Rickett). Similarly with *inter vivos* transfers; *Rochefoucauld v. Boustead* [1897] 1 Ch. 196.

[25] *McCormick v. Grogan* (1869) L.R. 4 H.L. 82; *ante*, p. 148.

[26] This is assumed *obiter* in *Re Cleaver* [1981] 1 W.L.R. 939 at 947.

[27] [1985] Conv. 248 (B. Perrins); (1986) 36 N.I.L.Q. 358 (M. Thompson). Another view is that both fully and half-secret trusts are constructive, as both are imposed to prevent fraud on the testator, which may occur without any benefit to the secret trustee; [1980] Conv. 341 (D. Hodge). *cf.* (1951) 67 L.Q.R. 413 (L. Sheridan).

C. Conclusion

Ultimately, the enforcement of secret trusts is a matter of policy relating to testamentary dispositions. The rules of the Wills Act 1837 are intended to achieve a reasonable degree of certainty in respect of testamentary dispositions. Secret trusts have, in effect, created a wide gap in the law relating to testamentary formalities. It is possible to take the view that secret trusts should not be enforced beyond preventing the unjust enrichment of the fraudulent legatee; or, on the other hand, to hold that the testator's intention should be upheld in every case. This is really a matter for the legislature, and it is submitted that it would be more satisfactory to review the whole matter and to incorporate into the statutory scheme as much of the secret trust doctrine as it is desired to retain.

CHAPTER 6

POWERS

1. Powers and Trusts 165	(b) Appointment by Will 174
2. Bare Powers and Fiduciary Powers 166	D. Contract to Exercise 174
3. Powers of Appointment 167	5. Delegation of Powers 174
A. General, Special and Intermediate (or	6. Fraud on a Power 176
Hybrid) Powers 167	A. Prior Agreement 177
B. The Requirement of Certainty; Wide	B. Benefit to Appointor 177
Powers; Capricious Powers 168	C. Non-Objects 177
C. Duties of Donee of Power; Rights of	D. Excessive Exercise; Severance 179
Objects 168	E. Releases 179
D. Power to Apply for Purposes 171	F. Position of Third Parties 180
4. Exercise of Powers of Appointment 171	7. Release of Powers 180
A. General Rule 171	A. Why Release? 180
i. *Inter Vivos*..................................... 171	B. How to Effect a Release 181
ii. By Will 172	C. Validity of Release 181
B. Excessive Execution 172	i. Trusts 182
C. Defective Execution 173	ii. Fiduciary Powers 182
i. In Equity 173	iii. Bare Powers 183
ii. By Statute 174	iv. Variation of Trusts Act
(a) Appointment *Inter Vivos* 174	1958 183

1. POWERS[1] AND TRUSTS

A POWER is an authorisation to do certain things which affect property to which the appointor is not solely entitled, and in which he may have no beneficial interest at all. A person may hold a power in a personal or an official capacity, a distinction relevant to the question whether he has fiduciary obligations. The source of the power may be express grant or a statute. Thus trustees have by statute powers of investment, sale, and so on. They may also be given other powers by the terms of the trust instrument, such as a power of appointment which enables those holding the power to effect the disposal of the settlor's property by "appointing" it to other people. It is with "powers" in the latter sense that this chapter is concerned.

---

[1] See Farwell; Halsbury (4th ed.), Vol. 36, p. 529; Keeton & Sheridan's *Equity* (3rd ed.), Chap. 9.

It has been seen that there are important points of distinction between powers and trusts.[2] Essentially a trust is imperative and a power discretionary. The dividing line is not always clear; for many trusts contain discretionary elements; and many powers are given to trustees who are governed by fiduciary duties in the exercise of their powers.

The practical importance of the distinction lies in the extent of the obligations imposed on a trustee as compared with the donee of a power, for example, the question how far he is obliged to consider the claims of possible recipients,[3] also the extent of the rights of objects of a trust as compared with a mere power, including the question of entitlement to the property in default of exercise and the question whether the beneficiaries, all being adult and under no disability, can terminate the trust and either divide the trust property[4] or alienate it.[5]

Whether a particular disposition creates a mere power or a discretionary trust is a question of construction. This has already been discussed.[6]

2. Bare Powers and Fiduciary Powers

A distinction must also be made between a bare power (sometimes called a personal power) and a power to which some fiduciary obligation is attached, such as a power given to trustees of property exercisable in relation to that property. Several manifestations of this distinction will be explained in connection with powers of appointment. Of general application however is the rule that a bare power given to an individual can only be exercised by him,[7] and a "bare power given to two or more by name cannot be executed by the survivor."[8] But a power given to trustees is prima facie given to them *ex officio*, and may be exercised by the survivor,[9] or by their successors in office,[10] and powers given to two or more trustees jointly may be exercised by the survivor or survivors of them, or by

[2] *Ante*, pp. 59 *et seq.*
[3] *McPhail v. Doulton* [1971] A.C. 424; *esp.* at p. 456; *ante*, p. 107.
[4] *Saunders v. Vautier* (1841) 4 Beav. 115; *Re Brockbank* [1948] Ch. 206; *ante*, p. 64, *post*, p. 204.
[5] *Re Smith* [1928] Ch. 915; *Re Nelson* (1918) [1928] Ch. 920 n.
[6] *Ante*, p. 60.
[7] *Re Harding* [1923] 1 Ch. 182; *Re Lysaght* [1966] Ch. 191.
[8] Farwell, p. 514; Halsbury (4th ed.), Vol. 36, § 861; *Re Beesly's W.T.* [1966] Ch. 223 (contrary inention).
[9] *Re Bacon* [1907] 1 Ch. 475; *Bersel Manufacturing Co. Ltd v. Berry* [1968] 2 All E.R. 552; T.A. 1925, s.18(1).
[10] *Re Smith* [1904] 1 Ch. 139; *Re De Sommery* [1912] 2 Ch. 622.

the personal representatives of the last of them, pending the appointment of new trustees.[11]

3. Powers of Appointment

A power of appointment is one given (by the donor of the power) to the donee of the power (the appointor) to appoint property to some person (the appointee). Such powers are useful in that they make it possible for the donee of the power to take into consideration circumstances existing at the date of the appointment which the settlor or testator could not have foreseen. Thus, a husband may give his estate to his widow for her life, and after her death to their children. He may leave his widow to decide upon the shares which each child is to receive by giving to her a power to appoint among the children in such shares as she shall in her absolute discretion select, with a gift in default of appointment to the children in equal shares. Powers feature in trusts of all sorts, and modern trusts commonly give various powers of appointment to the trustees in addition to imposing the obligation to hold the property upon trust. In such situations the property is owned by the beneficiaries who are entitled in default of appointment, subject to defeasance upon the exercise of the power.[12]

A. General, Special and Intermediate (or Hybrid) Powers

A gift to A for life with remainder to whomsoever he shall appoint is a general power; A may appoint to himself and become absolute owner. A general power is in most cases equivalent to ownership.[13] If, however, in the illustration given above, the power were exercisable only by will, it would still be a general power even though A would then be unable to appoint to himself. A special power is one in which the choice of appointees is restricted by the terms of the power: for example a power to appoint in favour of one's own children, or of the employees of a company and their families and dependants.[14] The power is special even though the appointor is himself a member of the restricted group.[15] A power which does not fit neatly into these categories is one where the donee is given power to appoint to anyone except certain people or

---

[11] T.A. 1925, s.18, and see *ibid.* s.36(7); *Re Wills' Trust Deeds* [1964] Ch. 219, *post*, p. 182.

[12] *Re Brooks' S.T.* [1939] Ch. 993 at p. 997; Farwell, p. 310.

[13] See, for example, Inheritance Tax Act 1984, s.5(2); Inheritance (Provision for Family and Dependants) Act 1975, s.25(1).

[14] *Re Gestetner* [1953] Ch. 672; *Re Sayer* [1957] Ch. 423.

[15] *Re Penrose* [1933] Ch. 793. See, however, Perpetuities and Accumulations Act 1964, s.7.

groups of people, for instance himself,[16] or all persons except the settlor and his wife,[17] or to all persons living at the death of the donee[18]; such powers are called intermediate or hybrid powers,[19] and they may be treated as general powers for some purposes, and special for others.[20] Intermediate powers are classified as special powers for the purpose of the Wills Act 1837, s.27,[21] and for the purposes of the rule against perpetuities.[22]

A power may be exercisable *inter vivos*, or by will, or by either method. A power which is exercisable by will only is called a testamentary power; and may be general or special.

B. The Requirement of Certainty; Wide Powers; Capricious Powers

These matters have been dealt with in Chapter 3, where the requirements of trusts and powers are compared.[23]

C. Duties of Donee of Power; Rights of Objects

A donee of a power is not, as such, under any fiduciary duties. In the example given above of the power given to the wife to determine the shares in which the children shall receive the property from their father's estate, the widow is under no obligation to exercise the power or even to consider its exercise, although if she does exercise it, then she owes a duty to the default beneficiaries to keep within the terms of the power.[24] This is a bare, or personal power of appointment. This must be contrasted with a fiduciary power held by a trustee *virtute officii*, which in turn must be distinguished from the obligation of a trustee of a discretionary trust.

A discretionary trust is a trust in which the property is held by the trustees on trust, not for named beneficiaries in fixed proportions,

---

[16] *Re Park* [1932] 1 Ch. 580; *Re Byron's Settlement* [1891] 3 Ch. 475 (except "her husband or any friend or relative of his.") *Re Abraham's W.T.* [1969] 1 Ch. 463 at p. 474; *Re Lawrence's W.T.* [1972] Ch. 418 (except his "wife's relatives").

[17] To avoid aggregation of the income of the trust with that of the settlor; I.C.T.A. 1988, ss.673, 683. Also to avoid "reservation of benefit" under the inheritance tax system.

[18] *Re Jones* [1945] Ch. 105.

[19] *Re Lawrence's W.T.* [1972] Ch. 418; *Re Manisty's Settlement* [1974] Ch. 17; *Re Hay's S.T.* [1982] 1 W.L.R. 202; *Re Beatty's W.T.* [1990] 1 W.L.R. 1503.

[20] "This division (*i.e.* of powers into general and special) is neither precise nor exhaustive, for these are some powers which may be general for some purposes and not for others." (Halsbury (4th ed.), Vol. 36, § 805.)

[21] *Post*, p. 172.

[22] P.A.A. 1964, s.7; *Re Earl of Coventry's Indentures* [1974] Ch. 77. For the significance of the distinction in the contect of perpetuity, see Maudsley, *The Modern Law of Perpetuities*, pp. 60–64, 162–166.

[23] See also Chap. 2, pp. 63 *et seq.*

[24] *Re Hay's S.T.* [1982] 1 W.L.R. 202; *Mettoy Pension Trustees Ltd v. Evans* [1990] 1 W.L.R. 1587.

but on trust for such members of a class of beneficiaries as the trustees shall in their absolute discretion select. That situation has many points of similarity with a power of appointment held by trustees to appoint among a group of objects. The distinction however remains that a trust is obligatory, a power permissive. In many aspects the distinction is theoretical only. We have seen that the test for certainty of objects has been assimilated, but clear distinctions remain in the area of the rights and duties of the parties.

Although a power is discretionary and permissive, a trustee who is the donee of a power must act in accordance with his fiduciary duty. The duties in the case of a fiduciary power arise, as it were, not from the power, but those inherent in the office of trustee. Thus, a trustee may not disregard a power, or forget about it, or release it. His fiduciary duty requires him to give consideration to the exercise of the power, and particularly to any application made to him by an object of the power requesting an exercise in his favour.[25] "Trustees of a power must consider from time to time whether and how to exercise the power."[26] "A settlor or testator who entrusts a power to his trustees must be relying on them in their fiduciary capacity so they cannot simply push aside the power and refuse to consider whether it ought in their judgment to be exercised."[27]

The duties of the donee of a fiduciary power were analysed by Megarry V.-C. in *Re Hay's Settlement Trusts*.[28] He must make no unauthorised appointment; he must consider periodically whether to exercise the power; he must consider the range of objects[29]; and he must consider the appropriateness of individual appointments. These duties, which were not intended to be exhaustive,[30] were further explained as follows: the donee, if he exercises the power, must do so "in a responsible manner according to its purpose. It is not enough for him to refrain from acting capriciously; he must do more. He must 'make such survey of the range of objects or possible beneficiaries' as will enable him to carry out his fiduciary duties."[31] He must not simply exercise the power in favour of those objects who happen to be at hand or to claim his attention. He must first consider who the objects are. He need not compile a list or assess the number: ". . . what is needed is an appreciation of the width of the

---

[25] *Re Gestetner* [1953] Ch. 672 at p. 688, *per* Harman J.; *Re Manisty's Settlement* [1974] Ch. 17 at p. 25.

[26] [1974] Ch. 17 at p. 22, *per* Templeman J.; *Re Gestetner (supra); Re Abraham's W.T.* [1969] 1 Ch. 463 at p. 474; *Re Gulbenkian's Settlements* [1970] A.C. 508 at p. 518; *McPhail v. Doulton* [1972] A.C. 424 at p. 456; *Mettoy Pension Trustees Ltd v. Evans* [1990] 1 W.L.R. 1587.

[27] *Re Gulbenkian's Settlements, supra,* at p. 518.

[28] [1982] 1 W.L.R. 202.

[29] Further discussed in Chap. 3.

[30] For the duty not to delegate, and to appoint in good faith, see *post,* pp. 174, 176.

[31] [1982] 1 W.L.R. 202 at p. 209, quoting from *McPhail v. Doulton* [1971] A.C. 424 at p. 449.

field, and thus whether a selection is to be made merely from a dozen or, instead, from thousands or millions. . . . Only when the trustee has applied his mind to 'the size of the problem' should he then consider in individual cases whether, in relation to other possible claimants, a particular grant is appropriate. In doing this, no doubt he should not prefer the undeserving to the deserving; but he is not required to make an exact calculation whether, as between deserving claimants, A is more deserving than B."[32]

The question arises of what the court will do if the trustees fail in their duty to consider the exercise of the power. "Normally the trustee is not bound to exercise it, and the court will not compel him to do so. That, however, does not mean that he can simply fold his hands and ignore it, for normally he must from time to time consider whether or not to exercise the power, and the court may direct him to do this."[33] A recalcitrant trustee may be removed. Where the power has been exercised, the court "will intervene if the trustees exceed their power, and possibly if they are proved to have exercised it capriciously."[34] The court will also intervene if the trustees have failed in any other respect to discharge the duties described above. Thus, in *Turner v. Turner*,[35] the exercise of a power of appointment was invalid when the trustees, who were not professional trustees, failed to appreciate their powers and duties and left all the decision-making to the settlor (who was not a trustee). They executed documents of appointment at his behest without reading them, and without understanding that they had a discretion. The settlor "held the reins", and the trustees acted as a "rubber-stamp." This was a breach of their duty to consider the exercise of the power and the appropriateness of the appointments made. There was no effective exercise at all, and the appointments accordingly were null and void, save to the extent that one appointment concerned land and was effective to transfer the legal title, which was held on trust by the appointee for the trustees of the settlement.

A further question is whether the court may intervene in a more positive way than merely removing a trustee or setting aside an appointment made in breach of duty. It was held in *Mettoy Pension Trustees Ltd v. Evans*[36] that where the court was called upon to intervene (because of breach of duty or where there was nobody left to exercise a fiduciary power),[37] it could adopt any of the methods

---

[32] *Ibid.* at p. 210.

[33] *Ibid.* at p. 209.

[34] [1971] A.C. 424 at p. 456, *per* Lord Wilberforce.

[35] [1984] Ch. 100. See also *Re Hastings-Bass* [1975] Ch. 25.

[36] [1990] 1 W.L.R. 1587; (1991) 107 L.Q.R. 214 (S. Gardner); [1991] Conv. 364 (J. Martin); K.C.L.J. 2 (1991–92), p. 127 (R. Ellison); (1994) 8 *Trust Law International* 35 at p. 36 (Vinelott J.).

[37] See now Pensions Act 1995, s.25(2) (fiduciary powers exercisable by independent trustee of pension fund on employer's insolvency); *post*, p. 464.

suggested by Lord Wilberforce in *McPhail v. Doulton*[38] in the context of discretionary trusts. Thus it could appoint new trustees, authorise the beneficiaries to prepare a scheme of distribution, or itself order a distribution.[39]

Whatever the form of the court's intervention, it is based upon the breach by the trustee of his fiduciary duty, and not upon any property right or entitlement among the objects of the power to compel a payment to them. The right of an object is not to compel an exercise of the power, in his own favour or at all, but merely to insist that the trustees consider the exercise of the power, to restrain any invalid exercise of the power, and, of course, to retain any property duly appointed to him.[40]

D. Power to Apply for Purposes

There seems to be no reason why a power should not permit the application of money for specific purposes, as opposed to being paid to persons. The purposes must be sufficiently certain to enable a court to determine whether any particular application is within the terms of the power or not. Such a power may be useful as a means of permitting the application of money to non-charitable purposes; a trust for non-charitable purposes lacks a means of enforcement and is void. That is a problem which is not faced by a power. The matter is discussed in Chapter 14.

4. EXERCISE OF POWERS OF APPOINTMENT

A. General Rule

i. Inter Vivos. No technical words are required for the exercise of a power. "All that is requisite is an intention on the part of the donee that the fund shall pass to some one who is an object of the power."[41] If the appointment relates to land, it must comply with Law of Property Act 1925, s.53(1)(b), and be evidenced in writing, signed by the donee of the power; an appointment of personalty may be made orally.[42] The terms of the power may require certain further

---

[38] [1972] A.C. 424, *ante* p. 100.
[39] Reliance was placed on *Klug v. Klug* [1918] 2 Ch. 67, *post*, p. 508, which was not cited in *Re Manisty's Settlement* [1974] Ch. 17, where the appointment of new trustees is said to be the only remedy. The *Mettoy* approach was followed in *Thrells Ltd v. Lomas* [1993] 1 W.L.R. 456 and *In re William Makin & Sons Ltd* [1993] O.P.L.R 171 (pension trust cases).
[40] *Vestey v. I.R.C. (No. 2)* [1979] Ch. 198 (Walton J.). Affirmed [1980] A.C. 1148.
[41] Farwell, p. 218; *Re Ackerley* [1913] 1 Ch. 510; *Re Lawrence's W.T.* [1972] Ch. 418.
[42] Halsbury (4th ed.), Vol. 36, para. 864.

formalities[43] for its exercise, or specific reference to the power or to the property subject thereto,[44] and such requirements must be strictly complied with. Thus, "if a power is to be executed by deed, it cannot be validly exercised by will,"[45] and "a power to be executed by will cannot be validly exercised by any instrument to take effect in the lifetime of the donee of the power."[46]

ii. By Will. Wills Act 1837, section 27, provides, in relation to both realty and personalty, and subject to a contrary intention, that, where a testator shall have a "power to appoint in any manner he may think proper," a general devise[47] or bequest shall operate as an execution of the power. This clearly excludes special powers, and also intermediate or hybrid powers, which in any way restrict the donee's freedom of choice.[48] The section applies even though the will was executed before the power was created.[49]

Any power to which the section does not apply is only exercised by will if "there is an indication of intention to exercise the power," a sufficient indication being "either a reference to the power or a sufficient reference to the property subject to the power."[50] Whether or not this is so in any particular case is often a question of great difficulty.[51]

B. Excessive Execution[52]

The donee has only the power which is given to him by the instrument. Thus he may not exercise it in favour of non-objects; nor in breach of the perpetuity rule; nor impose unauthorised conditions.[53] Any such purported exercise will be void. Difficult questions can arise when an appointment is partly good and partly bad, as where there is an appointment of a sum greater than that authorised; or where some of the appointees are objects and some are not. The rule is that the court will sever the good from the bad where

---

[43] *Hawkins v. Kemp* (1803) 3 East 410; subject to L.P.A. 1925, s.159, *post*, p. 174.

[44] *Re Lane* [1908] 2 Ch. 581; *Re Knight* [1957] Ch. 441; *Re Priestley's W.T.* [1971] Ch. 562, 858; *Re Lawrence's W.T.* [1972] Ch. 418; (1971) 121 N.L.J. 41, 597, 808 (C. Sherrin).

[45] Farwell, p. 197; *Lord Darlington v. Pulteney* (1797) 3 Ves.Jr. 384; *Re Phillips* (1884) 41 Ch.D. 417 at p. 419.

[46] Farwell, p. 198; *Reid v. Shergold* (1805) 10 Ves.Jr. 370; *Re Evered* [1910] 2 Ch. 147 at p. 156.

[47] *e.g.* a devise which refers generally to realty and not specifically to separate pieces; *e.g.* "all my realty."

[48] *Re Ackerley* [1913] 1 Ch. 510; *Re Byron's Settlement* [1893] 3 Ch. 474 (death of excluded persons would make the power general).

[49] *Boyes v. Cook* (1880) 14 Ch.D. 53.

[50] *Re Ackerley, supra*, at p. 513; *Re Priestley's W.T.* [1971] Ch. 858.

[51] *Re Ackerley, supra; Re Priestley's W.T.* [1971] Ch. 562, 858; *Re Lawrence's W.T.* [1972] Ch. 418; (1971) 121 N.L.J. 41, 597, 808 (C. Sherrin).

[52] See Farwell, Chap. 6; Halsbury (4th ed.), Vol. 36, para. 951.

[53] See *Re Hay's S.T.* [1982] 1 W.L.R. 202, *post*, p. 175.

possible: "... if there is a complete execution of the power with the addition of something improper, the execution is good and the excess bad, whereas if there is no complete execution, or if the boundaries between the excess and the execution are not distinguishable, the whole appointment fails. In order to be valid, the appointment must be distinct and absolute."[54] It is believed that this rule will apply where the exercise of a power makes an appointment and contains a release; if the release is invalid, the rest of the appointment may stand.[55]

C. Defective Execution

The donee of a power should exercise it in accordance with the provisions of the instrument creating it. Thus the necessary formalities should be observed, and the required consents obtained. Failure to comply will usually render the exercise void, but there is a jurisdiction in equity and under statute to validate certain cases of defective execution.

i. In Equity. Where the donee, "in discharge of moral or natural obligations, shows an intention to execute [a] power"[56] equity will act upon the conscience of those entitled in default to compel them to make good the defect in the execution. Relief may be obtained in favour of purchasers for value, creditors, charities, and persons to whom the donee is under a natural or moral obligation to provide.[57]

The essential features of the intended execution must be proved; these are "the intention to pass the property ... the persons to be benefited ... the amount of the benefit and ... good consideration."[58] There will not normally be relief against the non-execution of a power,[59] except perhaps in the case of fraud by the person entitled in default.[60]

The jurisdiction applies to the execution of express powers generally, but not to defective execution of statutory powers; for "it is difficult to see how the court can give validity to any such act if done

---

[54] Halsbury, (4th ed.), Vol. 36, para. 951; *Re Holland* [1914] 2 Ch. 595; see also Halsbury, paras. 952–955, for illustrations. The rule applies also where part of the appointment is void under the doctrine of "fraud on a power," *post*, p. 176.

[55] *Post*, p. 181.

[56] Farwell, p. 378; *Chapman v. Gibson* (1791) 3 Bro.C.C. 229 at p. 230.

[57] Halsbury, (4th ed.), Vol. 36, para. 957.

[58] Farwell, p. 379; *Garth v. Townsend* (1869) L.R. 7 Eq. 220; *Kennard v. Kennard* (1872) L.R. 8 Ch.App. 227.

[59] *Tollet v. Tollet* (1728) 2 P.Wms. 489 at p. 490; *Holmes v. Coghill* (1806) 12 Ves.Jr. 206. *Cf. Mettoy Pension Trustees v. Evans* [1990] 1 W.L.R. 1587; *ante*, p. 170.

[60] *Bath and Montague's Case* (1693) 3 Ch.Cas. 84 at pp. 108, 122; *Vane v. Fletcher* (1717) 1 P.Wms. 352 at p. 355; Farwell, pp. 383–385.

otherwise than in accordance with the statutory requirements; to give relief in such a case would be to legislate afresh."[61]

ii. By Statute.

(a) *Appointment Inter Vivos.* Law of Property Act 1925, s.159, provides that the execution of a deed of appointment will be valid if executed in the presence of and attested by two or more witnesses, even though it does not comply with additional formalities stipulated in the instrument. This provision does not however dispense with any necessary consents, nor does it apply to any acts required to be performed which have no relation to the mode of executing and attesting the document. Nor does it require a power to be exercised by deed where another method of exercise complies with the terms of the power.

(b) *Appointment by Will.* Similarly, an appointment by will is valid as regards execution and attestation if the provisions of the Wills Acts relating to the formalities of wills are complied with.[62]

D. Contract to Exercise

A valid contract to exercise a general power, if capable of specific performance, operates as a valid exercise of the power in equity; but there can never be specific performance of a contract to exercise a testamentary power, and the only remedy for breach is an action for damages against the estate.[63] A contract to exercise a special testamentary power is not enforceable[64]; but a release, in appropriate circumstances,[65] can be effective, as can a contract not to exercise the power[66]; the property will then go in default of appointment.

5. Delegation of Powers

In general, a person to whom a discretion has been given, whether personally or by virtue of his being in a fiduciary relationship, may

---

[61] Farwell, p. 394.
[62] Wills Act 1837, s.10; Wills Act 1963, s.2; *Taylor v. Meads* (1865) 4 De G.J. & S. 597 at p. 601.
[63] *Re Parkin* [1892] 3 Ch. 510; *post*, p. 711.
[64] *Re Bradshaw* [1902] 1 Ch. 436; *Re Cooke* [1922] 1 Ch. 292.
[65] *Post*, p. 181.
[66] *Re Evered* [1910] 2 Ch. 147.

not delegate his discretion to others. *Delegatus non potest dele-gare*.[67] A donee may delegate the performance of merely ministerial acts[68]; and the donee of a general power equivalent to absolute ownership may appoint to a class in such proportions as another shall select.[69] But many powers involve a personal discretion and this prevents delegation.[70] There is no objection however to a testator or settlor giving a power of appointment to a trustee.[71] Such a power given by a testator is not to be impugned as a delegation of testamentary disposition. In *Re Beatty's Will Trusts*[72] the testatrix gave her personal estate and £1.5 million to trustees to allocate "to or among such person or persons as they think fit." Hoffmann J. upheld the power, rejecting the supposed "anti-delegation" rule: there was no doubt as to the validity of testamentary powers, whether special, general or intermediate.

In the absence of express provision in the instrument creating a special power, the donee may not appoint on discretionary trust.[73] This question arose in *Re Hay's Settlement Trusts*.[74]

Trustees had a power to appoint to "such persons or purposes" as they should in their discretion select, except the settlor, her husband, or the trustees. Prior to the appointment, the income was to be applied, at the trustees' discretion, for the settlor's nephews and nieces, or for charity. The trustees exercised the power of appointment by appointing the property to themselves on a discretionary trust for similar purposes. Prior to the distribution, the income was to be applied to any person or charity. Megarry V.-C. held that the exercise of the power was void, so that the property vested in the persons entitled in default of appointment (the period during which the power was exercisable having expired). The appointment did not designate the persons appointed, as the settlement required. It merely provided a mechanism whereby the appointees might be ascertained. The power was to appoint persons, and not to nominate persons to make an appointment. Intermediate powers were subject to the rule against unauthorised

---

[67] *Post*, p. 559.

[68] *Re Hetling and Merton's Contract* [1893] 3 Ch. 269; Farwell, pp. 503–504.

[69] Farwell, p. 505; *White v. Wilson* (1852) 1 Drew. 298 at p. 304; *Re Triffitt's Settlement* [1958] Ch. 852 (explained in *Re Hay's S.T.* [1982] 1 W.L.R. 202 as showing that the rule does not apply to bare powers).

[70] *De Bussche v. Alt* (1878) 8 Ch.D. 286; *Re Morris' Settlement* [1951] 2 All E.R. 528; *Re Hunter's W.T.* [1963] Ch. 372; (1954) 23 Conv.(N.S.) 27, 423 (D. Waters).

[71] *Houston v. Burns* [1918] A.C. 337; *Att.-Gen. v. National Provincial Bank* [1924] A.C. 262; *Re Manisty's Settlement* [1974] Ch. 17 at p. 26; *Re Park* [1932] 1 Ch. 580; *Re Abraham's W.T.* [1969] 1 Ch. 463 at p. 475.

[72] [1990] 1 W.L.R. 1503; (1991) 107 L.Q.R. 211 (J. Davies); [1991] Conv. 138 (J. Martin).

[73] *Re Morris' Settlement* [1951] 2 All E.R. 528.

[74] [1982] 1 W.L.R. 202.

delegation, and it was immaterial that the donees of the power were the same persons as the trustees of the discretionary trust.

If the donee appoints on protective trusts,[75] the determinable life interests will be valid, but the discretionary trusts due to take effect on forfeiture of the life interest are void and the trusts in default take effect.[76] There is no objection, however, to the inclusion in an appointment of a power of advancement.[77] Generally, where it is desired that the donee should be able to make an appointment which itself includes a power of appointment or involves any other delegation of discretion, express provision should be made in the instrument creating the power.

6. Fraud on a Power

An appointor, in the typical case of a special power of appointment with a gift over in default, is under no duty to exercise the power; but if he chooses to exercise the power, he must exercise it honestly.[78] Unless he is a fiduciary,[79] he need not weigh the merits of the possible beneficiaries; he may appoint all the available assets to any one beneficiary, who may indeed be himself.[80] But he must exercise it within the limits imposed by the donor or testator who created it.[81] If, of course, he expressly exceeds those limits the exercise of the power will be void unless it can be cut down by severing the invalid excess.[82] But the doctrine of fraudulent exercise of a power goes further than this, for it extends to the intent with which a power is exercised. The theory is that, in the case of a special power, the property is vested in those entitled in default of its exercise subject to its being divested by a proper exercise of the power,[83] and that an exercise of the power for any "sinister object" is not proper, is a fraud on those entitled in default, and void.[84]

---

[75] *Post*, Chap. 7.
[76] *Re Boulton's S.T.* [1928] Ch. 703; *Re Morris' Settlement, supra; Re Hunter* [1963] Ch. 372.
[77] *Re May's Settlement* [1926] Ch. 136; *Re Mewburn's Settlement* [1934] Ch. 112; *Re Morris' Settlement* [1951] 2 All E.R. 528; *Re Wills' W.T.* [1959] Ch. 1; *Pilkington v. I.R.C.* [1964] A.C. 612; *post*, p. 580.
[78] *Cloutte v. Storey* [1911] 1 Ch. 18.
[79] In which case, see *Re Hay's S.T.* [1982] 1 W.L.R. 202, *ante*, p. 169.
[80] *Re Penrose* [1933] Ch. 793.
[81] (1977) 3 Monash L.R. 210 (Y. Grbich), describing the doctrine of fraud on a power as an "*ultra vires* appointments" doctrine.
[82] *Churchill v. Churchill* (1867) L.R. 5 Eq. 44; *Re Oliphant* (1917) 86 L.J.Ch. 452.
[83] *Re Brook's S.T.* [1939] Ch. 993.
[84] *Portland v. Topham* (1864) 11 H.L.Cas. 32 at p. 54; *Vatcher v. Paull* [1915] A.C. 372. *cf. Re Greaves* [1954] Ch. 434 at p. 446.

A. Prior Agreement

The first type of case in which an apparently valid exercise of a power will be void for what in this context is termed fraud[85] is where the appointment is made as the result of a prior agreement with the appointee as to what he will do with the proceeds. Such an exercise of a power will be wholly void save when the appointor is the person entitled in default, or where the person entitled in default is a party to it.[86]

B. Benefit to Appointor

A second type of case is where the power is exercised so as to benefit the appointor. The benefit is usually financial in character, as where an appointment is made to an ailing child by its father, who will benefit on the child's death,[87] but it is not restricted to financial benefit.[88] For the exercise of the power to be void, there must be more than a hope of benefit. Thus an appointment to a healthy child by a father will be valid.[89] For fraud to operate, the appointment must have been made with intent to benefit the appointor. An appointment is sometimes made, however, which in fact benefits the appointor, but which is clearly intended to, and does, benefit the appointees; this is true of many an appointment that forms part of the variation of a trust, for the tax savings achieved will often be a benefit to the appointor. Thus in *Re Merton*,[90] Wynn-Parry J. decided that there was no inflexible rule that forced him to declare such an exercise of a power to be void. The intent that renders an appointment void is a matter "of fact or of inference rather than of law,"[91] and must be ascertained as a single fact after consideration of all the relevant evidence.[92] In the context of variation of trusts however, modern cases have shown a reluctance to apply this benevolent view.[93]

C. Non-objects

An appointment is sometimes drafted so that the intent appears to be to benefit objects of the power, but the real intent is to benefit

---

[85] See the classification in Farwell, p. 460, and also Sheridan, *Fraud in Equity*, pp. 116 *et seq.*

[86] See generally *Vatcher v. Paull* [1915] A.C. 372.

[87] *Lord Hichinbroke v. Seymour* (1789) 1 Bro.C.C. 395; *Lady Wellesley v. Earl Mornington* (1855) 2 K. & J. 143.

[88] *Cochrane v. Cochrane* [1922] 2 Ch. 230.

[89] *Henty v. Wrey* (1882) 21 Ch.D. 332.

[90] [1953] 1 W.L.R. 1096 at p. 1100; *Re Robertson's W.T.* [1960] 1 W.L.R. 1050.

[91] *Re Holland* [1914] 2 Ch. 595 at p. 601, *per* Sargant J.

[92] *Re Crawshay* [1948] Ch. 123.

[93] *Re Wallace's Settlements* [1968] 1 W.L.R. 711; *Re Brook's Settlement* [1968] 1 W.L.R. 1661; *post*, p. 625, [1968] B.T.R. 199 (J.G.M.); (1969) 32 M.L.R. 317 (S. Cretney).

non-objects. It will then be void, even though the appointee was in no sense a party, and might not even have known of the appointment or its intent.[94] Thus, in *Re Dick*:[95]

A widow had a power to appoint amongst her brothers and sisters and their issue, but she wished to provide for a family who were looking after her. She had inadequate free capital to do so. She appointed by will to her favourite sister, but coupling the appointment with a request "without imposing any trust or legal obligation" that the sister should provide an annuity for the family concerned. The Court of Appeal held that the absence of obligation on the appointee was not crucial; but rather that the whole intent in making the appointment was to secure a benefit to non-objects by subjecting the appointee to "strong moral suasion to benefit a non-object, which suasion the [appointee] would in the appointor's opinion, be unable to resist."[96] This intent was enough to constitute the exercise of the power as fraudulent.

Difficulties arise from this rule as to real intent, for it is not easy to distinguish cases such as *Re Dick* from cases where there was a real intent to benefit the appointee but coupled with a hope that the appointee would benefit a non-object, which cases are of course not within the doctrine of fraud on a power. But the intent in many cases is simply dual—genuinely to benefit the appointee but also to subject him to strong moral persuasion as to part of the benefit appointed. It may therefore be relevant in *Re Dick*[97] that a substantial proportion of the sum appointed would have been absorbed by the annuity and that a great deal of planning and discussion had gone into the making of the appointment coupled with the expression of the request in formal memoranda. For the danger inherent in extending the doctrine too far is that, if the appointment is void, the appointee loses all benefit unless the appointor is alive to reappoint,[98] a loss to the appointee which is not justified if intent to

---

[94] *Re Nicholson's Settlement* [1939] Ch. 11. This case decided that the doctrine as to the real intent behind an appointment did not apply to a power exercisable only in favour of one person and so exercised. But see the criticism in Sheridan, *Fraud in Equity*, p. 122 and Keeton & Sheridan's *Equity* (3rd ed.), p. 297.

[95] [1953] Ch. 343; *Re Kirwan* (1884) 25 Ch.D. 373 *cf. Re Marsden's Trusts* (1859) 4 Drew. 594.

[96] The matter was put in this way by Cohen L.J. in *Re Crawshay* [1948] Ch. 123 at p. 135, a case which contained the additional vitiating factor of a covenant by the appointee assigning to non-objects any benefits received by the exercise of the power; (1948) 64 L.Q.R. 221 (H. Hanbury).

[97] *Supra.*

[98] There can be no severance in these cases as there is nothing to sever. But *Re Chadwick's Trusts* [1939] 1 All E.R. 850 shows that a fresh appointment is valid if free from the element that vitiated a prior one.

benefit him was a substantial element in the exercise of the power.

D. Excessive Exercise; Severance

If there is a genuine intent to benefit the appointee, something expressly superadded so as to benefit a non-object can be severed, leaving the appointment valid.[99] But severance will not occur in the absence of such a genuine intent.[1] Again if, in a will by which he exercises a power, a testator makes a gift of *his own* property conditional on the appointee resettling the *appointed* property, this is a valid condition on his own gift and the exercise of the power also is valid, provided there was a genuine intent to benefit the appointee.[2] This would be difficult to reconcile with strict emphasis on the intent with which a power was exercised as being "entire and single."[3]

E. Releases

The doctrine of fraud on a power does not apply to releases, for releases simply benefit those entitled in default. It is irrelevant that the appointor, in releasing his power, is intended to benefit thereby, as he has no duty in respect of the disappointed objects.[4] Nor does the doctrine apply to the revocation of the exercise of a power.[5] An appointment may only be revoked where such right of revocation has been reserved. Where such right exists, it seems that the appointor is under no duty to the appointees. It has even been said that, in revoking, he may stipulate for a benefit, but it would be strange if, by first exercising a power and then revoking it, an appointor could obtain a benefit rightly denied him on an appointment, and it is significant that, in the leading case,[6] the revocation was followed by a release.[7]

---

[99] *Re Kerr's W.T.* (1878) 4 Ch.D. 600; *Re Holland* [1914] 2 Ch. 595; followed in *Re Burton's Settlements* [1955] Ch. 82.

[1] *Re Cohen* [1911] 1 Ch. 37. Severance will not of course occur when there has been a prior agreement with the appointee.

[2] *Re Burton's Settlements* [1955] Ch. 82.

[3] In *Re Simpson* [1952] Ch. 412, Vaisey J. had held that *Re Crawshay* and *Re Dick* impelled him to take this strict view on facts analogous to those in *Re Burton's Settlements* in which case, however, Upjohn J. rightly refused to follow the lead.

[4] *Re Somes* [1896] 1 Ch. 250. Releases may be an important element in the variation of a trust; *Re Ball's Settlement Trusts* [1968] 1 W.L.R. 899, *post*, p. 624.

[5] *Re Greaves* [1954] Ch. 434.

[6] *Ibid.*

[7] *cf.* Evershed M.R. in *Re Greaves, supra*, at p. 448.

F. Position of Third Parties

The position of a bona fide purchaser, for instance a mortgagee, of an interest appointed to his vendor in such a manner as to amount to a fraud on the power is complicated. Those entitled in default of appointment who can challenge the exercise of the power as fraudulent have an interest in the property appointed which in principle prevails over the interest of its bona fide purchasers for value,[8] because no legal title passes under the ordinary power of appointment. The Law of Property Act 1925, s.157, protects such purchasers, but only if the vendor-appointee was at least 25 years of age at the time of sale, and only to the extent to which he was presumptively entitled in default of appointment. Apart from this curious and limited protection, a fraudulent appointment is void even against a bona fide purchaser.

7. RELEASE OF POWERS

A. Why Release?

As a power is discretionary, it may be asked why it becomes advantageous to release it as opposed merely to not exercising it. This may be for various reasons; for example, to create indefeasible interests in those entitled in default,[9] to make a gift charitable by releasing a power to appoint to anyone else,[10] to avoid the "reservation of benefit" rules under the inheritance tax system by excluding the settlor from the class of objects,[11] and especially to avoid the effect of Income and Corporation Taxes Act 1988, ss.671–675. They provide for the income of a settlement to be treated as that of the settlor where, for example, the settlor or his wife may benefit from the exercise of a power of appointment. Until 1958, it had been common to include the wife of the settlor as a member of the discretionary class; and it thus became important to exclude her.[12] This was usually done by exercising the trustees' power to appoint on new trusts which were identical with the old ones except that the wife was omitted. This is in effect a partial release of the earlier

---

[8] *Cloutte v. Storey* [1911] 1 Ch. 18. See also *Turner v. Turner* [1984] Ch. 100, *ante*, p. 170, on the effect of appointments made in breach of the duty to consider; and *Re Hay's S.T.* [1982] 1 W.L.R. 202, *ante*, p. 175, on the effect of an appointment in breach of the duty not to delegate.

[9] *Re Mills* [1930] 1 Ch. 654; *Mettoy Pension Trustees Ltd v. Evans* [1990] 1 W.L.R. 1587 (where default beneficiary insolvent).

[10] *Re Wills* [1964] Ch. 219.

[11] *Post*, p. 221.

[12] F.A. 1958, s.22, now I.C.T.A. 1988, s.674; *Blausten v. I.R.C.* [1972] Ch. 256; (1972) 36 Conv.(N.S.) 127 (D. Hayton).

power, and is treated as such.[13] As we will see, many of the releases which have been made in this way are of doubtful validity.

B. How to Effect a Release

Trustees may in effect surrender their trusts and powers by paying the money into court under the Trustee Act 1925, s.63[14]; or they may apply to the court for an administration order; or they may ask the court for directions as to the way in which they should act on questions arising in the administration of the trust. Usually, however, the court will not give general directions concerning the exercise of discretionary powers in the future.[15]

They may also effect a release of a power, in appropriate circumstances, by executing a deed of release, or by a contract not to exercise the power.[16] A power may also be extinguished by implication by any dealing with the property by the donee which is inconsistent with its further exercise[17]; or by obtaining the approval of the court to an arrangement which is so inconsistent. There is much uncertainty concerning the validity of releases in some circumstances, and it is important that express provision should be made in the instrument creating the power which expressly authorises the donees of the power to release it.[18]

C. Validity of Release

It is not possible to lay down with confidence what are the circumstances in which, in the absence of express provision, a release will be valid. The Law of Property Act 1925, s.155, provides that: "A person to whom any power, whether coupled with an interest or not, is given may by deed release or contract not to exercise, the power."[19]

The question arose whether this provision applied to a situation where the donees of the power were trustees who held the power in a fiduciary capacity. Admittedly they cannot be compelled to exercise it; but can they be allowed to release it? The courts answered

---

[13] *Re Wills, supra; Muir v. I.R.C.* [1966] 1 W.L.R. 251 and 1269; *Blausten v. I.R.C.* (*supra*).

[14] *Post*, p. 534; this is now rare; (1968) 84 L.Q.R. 67 (A. Hawkins). See also *Thrells Ltd v. Lomas* [1993] 1 W.L.R. 456 (exercise of fiduciary power properly surrendered to court to avoid conflict of duties).

[15] *Re Allen-Meyrick's W.T.* [1966] 1 W.L.R. 499; (1967) 31 Conv.(N.S.) 117 (A. Hawkins); *post*, p. 533.

[16] L.P.A. 1925, ss.155, 160.

[17] *Re Christie-Miller's Settlement* [1961] 1 W.L.R. 462; *Re Wills* [1964] Ch. 219; *Muir v. I.R.C.* [1966] 1 W.L.R. 251, 1269; *Re Courtauld's Settlement* [1965] 2 All E.R. 544; *Blausten v. I.R.C.* [1972] Ch. 256; (1968) 84 L.Q.R. 92–93 (A. Hawkins).

[18] *Muir v. I.R.C.* [1966] 1 W.L.R. 1269; *Blausten v. I.R.C.* (*supra*).

[19] Replacing earlier legislation.

this question in the negative[20]; the problem is how to determine which are the cases to which the statute does not apply.

i. Trusts. The first category is that discussed above where the situation is not really a power but a discretionary trust. Here the trustees are under a duty to appoint; if they fail to do so, the court will declare the property to be held on trust for the class of possible appointees.[21] There is no question of release here.

ii. Fiduciary Powers. Where a power is conferred upon a person *virtute officii*, he may not release it. "*In the absence of words in the trust deed authorising [him] so to do.*"[22] Here there may be a gift over in default, either to the class of appointees or to a different class. This is a power proper, and not a trust. But the power is one given to the trustees to be exercised in a fiduciary capacity. They cannot discard it; they are, as has been seen,[23] under a duty to consider from time to time whether and how to exercise the power. This is so whether it is given to them as trustees, or whether it is given to persons by name "if on the true view of the facts, they were selected as donee of the power because they were trustees."[24] Conversely, persons selected as individuals may be described as trustees. In *Re Wills' Trust Deeds*[25] a power of appointment in respect of property which was the subject of a *settlement* was given to the trustees of the settlor's *will*; this was not given *virtute officii*. Modern pension fund cases provide illustrations of the rules as to the release of powers. In *Re Courage Group's Pension Schemes*[26] fiduciary powers were vested in a committee set up to manage a pension scheme. It was held that even if existing members of the committee could release, fetter, or agree not to exercise their powers (which was not decided),[27] they could not deprive their successors of the right to exercise their powers. In *Mettoy Pension Trustees Ltd v. Evans*[28] there was a power in favour of the pension fund beneficiaries, with the employer company taking in default. On the company's insolvency, the liquidator sought to release the power in

---

[20] *Re Eyre* (1883) 49 L.T. 259; *Saul v. Pattinson* (1886) 55 L.J.Ch. 831.

[21] Equal division is not necessary in the case of the modern discretionary trust; *ante*, p. 100.

[22] *Muir v. I.R.C.* [1966] 1 W.L.R. 1269 at p. 1283, *per* Harman L.J.; the italics are original; *Blausten v. I.R.C.* [1972] Ch. 256.

[23] *Ante*, p. 169.

[24] Lewin, p. 387; *Hall v. May* (1857) 3 K. & J. 585; *Re Cookes' Contract* (1877) 4 Ch.D. 454.

[25] [1964] Ch. 219. (The actual decision probably does not survive that of the Court of Appeal in *Muir v. I.R.C.* [1966] 1 W.L.R. 1269).

[26] [1987] 1 W.L.R. 495.

[27] See (1993) 7 *Trust Law International* 69 (H. Arthur).

[28] [1990] 1 W.L.R. 1587. See also *British Coal Corp. v. British Coal Staff Superannuation Scheme Trustees Ltd* [1995] 1 All E.R. 912.

the interests of the creditors. This could not be done because the power was fiduciary. The liquidator could not exercise the power because of a conflict of duties,[29] and so the court could intervene to protect the objects.[30]

iii. Bare Powers. Where the power is given to a person in his private capacity, the donee is prima facie able to release it,[31] even if the release operates in favour of the donee, as where a father releases a power so that the shares of his sons (who are entitled in default) become absolute, and that of a deceased son passes to the donee.[32] A release, or a covenant not to exercise it, (which will be equivalent to a release)[33] may be effective if it refers only to part of the property,[34] or if it relates only to one or more of several objects.[35]

iv. Variation of Trusts Act 1958. Section 1 of the Variation of Trusts Act 1958 makes no express reference to powers. Many powers are vested in trustees, as in the case of discretionary or protective trusts; and a variation of such powers will no doubt be covered by the provisions of the Act. It appears that an arrangement under the Act which recites the release of a power,[36] or one which is inconsistent with the future exercise of the power,[37] will effectively release it.

---

[29] See now Pensions Act 1995, s.25(2).

[30] *Ante*, p. 170.

[31] This is Buckley J.'s fifth category in *Re Wills' Trust Deeds* [1964] Ch. 219.

[32] *Re Radcliffe* [1892] 1 Ch. 227; an appointment in favour of the estate of the deceased son would have been a fraud on the power.

[33] *Per* Buckley L.J. in *Re Evered* [1910] 2 Ch. 147 at p. 161.

[34] *Re Evered, supra.*

[35] *Re Brown's Settlement* [1939] Ch. 944; Farwell, p. 16.

[36] *Re Christie-Miller's S.T.* [1961] 1 W.L.R. 462.

[37] *Re Courtauld's Settlement* [1965] 2 All E.R. 544; *Re Ball's S.T.* [1968] 1 W.L.R. 899.

CHAPTER 7

PROTECTIVE TRUSTS

1. The General Problem	185	A. Determining Events	190
2. Determinable and Conditional Interests	186	B. Order of the Court under Trustee Act	
3. Self-Protection	187	1925, s.57	192
4. Protected Life Interests in Persons Other		C. Order of the Court under Matrimonial	
than the Settlor	188	Causes Acts 1859–1973	192
5. Trustee Act 1925, s.33	188	7. Advancements	193
6. Forfeiture of the Life Tenant's Interest	190	8. Effect of Forfeiture	193

1. THE GENERAL PROBLEM

A DEBTOR'S property is in principle available for the satisfaction of his creditors and, if he becomes bankrupt, it will pass to his trustee in bankruptcy; but it is possible, by making use of a protective trust, to obtain a measure of protection against such an event.

In the development of protective trusts the courts have been torn between two conflicting pressures. On the one hand, nobody should have the power of defeating his creditors by putting his property beyond their grasp; on the other, a settlor should be able to create a trust in any form, so long as it is not unlawful; and there is much to be said for allowing some means of protecting a person's dependants from the ill-effects of his extravagance. The technique of protective trusts involves the giving of a determinable life interest with a gift over upon the happening of certain events. Originally, the gift over was usually in favour of other members of the family[1]; but the modern practice is to provide for a gift over to trustees to hold on discretionary trusts in favour of a class which includes the life tenant and members of his family; and this pattern is provided for by the Trustee Act 1925, s.33.[2] In most American jurisdictions, it is possible to make an equitable life interest inalienable whether voluntarily or involuntarily. This is known as a "spendthrift trust",[3] and

[1] e.g. Re Detmold (1889) 40 Ch.D. 585.
[2] Post, p. 188. See generally Moffat, Trusts Law Text and Materials (2nd ed.), pp. 203 et seq.
[3] Griswold, Spendthrift Trusts.

is justified on the ground that the settlor, in creating the trust, should be allowed to create such equitable interests as he wishes. This has never been allowed in England,[4] but, as will be seen, the technique of the protective trust as at least an equivalent protection. Protective trust clauses are commonly used today in occupational pension schemes, to prevent alienation of pension rights.[5]

2. DETERMINABLE AND CONDITIONAL INTERESTS

A distinction is made in law between an interest subject to a condition subsequent and a determinable interest.[6] The former exists where there is a gift of an absolute interest which is then cut down by the application of a condition; such as a gift to X absolutely, but if he should change his nationality, then over to Y. A determinable interest exists where something less than an absolute interest is given in the first place; as a gift to X until he changes (or so long as he retains) his nationality. The distinction is subtle[7]; it depends entirely upon the language of the gift; but it is a distinction that has importance in several contexts. The relevance in the present context is twofold: first, that a condition against alienation is void[8]; secondly, that a condition subsequent, being one which effects a forfeiture of an existing interest, is strictly construed[9]; if the condition is held void, the interest becomes absolute.[10] The determining event, however, in the case of a determinable interest is less strictly construed; and if it should be held invalid, the whole interest fails.[11]

Thus it is clear that a *condition* so drafted as to terminate an interest upon alienation[12] or bankruptcy[13] is void and the prior

---

[4] But from the early 19th century until 1935 it was possible to create a trust for the separate use of a married woman to impose a restraint upon the anticipation or alienation. See Law Reform (Married Women and Tortfeasors) Act 1935 and Married Women (Restraint upon Anticipation) Act 1949.

[5] *Post,* p. 472.

[6] *Brandon v. Robinson* (1811) 18 Ves.Jr. 429 at p. 433 (Lord Eldon); M. & W., pp. 69 *et seq.*; Cheshire and Burn, pp. 339 *et seq.* The clue to the existence of a determinable limitation is the use of words such as "until," "so long as," "whilst," as distinct from phraseology such as "but if" and "when, if ever."

[7] "Little short of disgraceful to our jurisprudence," *per* Porter M.R. in *Re King's Trusts* (1892) 29 L.R.Ir. 401 at p. 410.

[8] Co.Litt. 223a; *Re Brown* [1954] Ch. 39.

[9] *Clavering v. Ellison* (1859) 7 H.L.Cas. 707; *Sifton v. Sifton* [1938] A.C. 656.

[10] Co.Litt. 206a, b; *Re Greenwood* [1903] 1 Ch. 749.

[11] *Re Moore* (1888) 39 Ch.D. 116. (Gift of a weekly sum to T's sister "whilst . . . living apart from her husband" construed as a gift determinable upon returning to her husband, and held void); *Re Tuck's S.T.* [1978] Ch. 49.

[12] *Brandon v. Robinson* (1811) 18 Ves.Jr. 429; *Re Dugdale* (1888) 38 Ch.D. 176; *Re Brown* [1954] Ch. 39; (1943) 59 L.Q.R. 343 (Glanville Williams).

[13] *Younghusband v. Gisborne* (1846) 15 L.J.Ch. 355; *Re Sanderson's Trust* (1857) 3 K. & J. 497.

interest is absolute. But an interest *determinable* on alienation or bankruptcy is valid.[14] Further, courts place an even more generous construction upon the validity of determining events in the case of life interests.[15] The basis of protective trusts is therefore a determinable life interest.

3. SELF-PROTECTION

A settlor cannot make a settlement which will protect himself against his own bankruptcy.[16]

In *Re Burroughs-Fowler*,[17] the settlor, by ante-nuptial settlement, settled property upon trust to pay the income to himself for life or until one of certain events should occur, including his bankruptcy, after which event the income was to be paid to his wife. The settlor was adjudicated bankrupt during the wife's lifetime. It was held that the life interest vested indefeasibly in his trustee in bankruptcy, who could validly dispose of it.

A settlor may however protect himself against other forms of alienation, voluntary or involuntary. And if the limitation, as is usual, provides for the termination of his interest upon any one of such events *or* upon his bankruptcy, the gift over, as we have seen, is void in the event of bankruptcy, but valid in all other cases.[18] If the gift over has taken effect upon, for example, an attempt to charge the life interest, the subsequent bankruptcy of the settlor has no effect upon it.

In *Re Detmold*,[19] a marriage settlement of the settlor's own property provided for the payment of the income to the settlor for life or "till he shall become bankrupt or shall . . . suffer something whereby the same . . . would . . . by operation of law . . . become . . . payable to some other person . . . " and, after such determination, on trust to pay the income to his wife. In July 1888, an order was made appointing a judgment creditor to be

---

[14] *Post*, p. 188; see also the earlier authorities relied on by Turner V.-C. in *Rochford v. Hackman*, (1852) 9 Hare 475.

[15] Jarman, p. 1486.

[16] *Mackintosh v. Pogose* [1895] 1 Ch. 505; *Re Wombwell* (1921) 125 L.T. 437; this rule is preserved by T.A. 1925, s.33(3). Nor may he settle his property on a third party to prejudice his own creditors; *post*, pp. 337 *et seq.*

[17] [1916] 2 Ch. 251; *Official Assignee v. NZI Life Superannuation Nominees Ltd* [1995] 1 N.Z.L.R. 684.

[18] *Re Detmold* (1889) 40 Ch.D. 585; *Re Brewer's Settlement* [1896] 2 Ch. 503; *Re Johnson* [1904] 1 K.B. 134.

[19] (1889) 40 Ch.D. 585; *Re Brewer's Settlement* [1896] 2 Ch. 503.

receiver of the income; and in September 1888 the settlor was adjudicated bankrupt. It was held that the forfeiture took place upon the involuntary alienation of the income by process of law. The wife then became entitled to the income, and she did not lose the right on the subsequent bankruptcy.

4. Protected Life Interests in Persons Other than the Settlor

Though a person cannot make a settlement of his own property upon himself until bankruptcy, and then over, yet a trust created by A to pay the income to B until B dies or becomes bankrupt alienates or charges his life interest and then over to C is good in the event of the occurrence of any of those events, including B's bankruptcy.[20] The essence of the device of protected life interests[21] is that, on the occurrence of a determining event, such as alienation or bankruptcy, the interest of the life tenant determines, and the trustees then hold the property on discretionary trusts for the benefit of the life tenant and his family.

Some early attempts to reach this result failed, owing to the absence of any clear gift over of the income.[22] Eventually, however, discretionary trusts became accepted,[23] and in recent years quite independently of protective trusts.

The court may exercise its jurisdiction to vary trusts so as to convert a beneficial interest into a protected life interest where it is feared that the beneficiary cannot manage his affairs in a responsible manner.[24]

5. Trustee Act 1925, s.33

Before 1926 it was necessary to set out expressly the terms of the trusts; and a settlor may still do so if he wishes.[25] In relation, however, to trusts coming into operation after 1925, Trustee Act 1925, s.33, "provides a shorthand arrangement whereby a settlor

---

[20] *Re Ashby* [1892] 1 Q.B. 872.

[21] (1957) 21 Conv.(N.S.) 110 (L. Sheridan).

[22] The point is discussed in *Rochford v. Hackman* (1852) 9 Hare 475.

[23] And may take effect where the forfeiture precedes the settlement; as where the bankruptcy began before the testator died: *Metcalfe v. Metcalfe* [1891] 3 Ch. 1. See also *Re Forder* [1927] 2 Ch. 291; *Re Walker* [1939] Ch. 974.

[24] *Hambro v. Duke of Marlborough* [1994] Ch. 158; *post*, p. 617 (unsuitability of Marquess of Blandford to manage Blenheim). See also *Re Abram (deceased)* [1996] 2 F.L.R. 379 (protected life interest ordered under Inheritance (Provision for Family and Dependants) Act 1975, where any capital sum would have gone to applicant's creditors).

[25] *Re Shaw's Settlement* [1951] Ch. 833; *Re Rees (decd.)* [1954] Ch. 202; *Re Munro's S.T.* [1963] 1 W.L.R. 145.

may establish a trust without setting forth in detail all the terms upon which the property is to be held."[26] The section applies although the statutory formula "on protective trusts" may not be used, so long as the intention is clear.[27] The section then applies subject to any modification contained in the instrument creating the trust.[28]

Section 33(1) provides:

"Where any income, including an annuity or other periodical income payment, is directed to be held on protective trusts for the benefit of any person (in this section called 'the principal beneficiary') for the period of his life or for any less period, then, during that period (in this section called the 'trust period') the said income shall, without prejudice to any prior interest, be held on the following trusts, namely:—

(i) Upon trust for the principal beneficiary during the trust period or until he . . . does or attempts to do or suffers any act or thing, or until any event happens, other than an advance under any statutory or express power, whereby, if the said income were payable during the trust period to the principal beneficiary absolutely during that period, he would be deprived of the right to receive the same or any part thereof,[29] in any of which cases . . . this trust of the said income shall fail or determine;

(iii) [and during the remainder of the trust period] . . . upon trust for the application thereof for the maintenance or support, or otherwise for the benefit, of all or any one or more exclusively of the other or others of the following persons[30] (that is to say)—

(a) the principal beneficiary and his or her wife or husband, if any, and his or her children or more remote issue, if any; or

(b) if there is no wife or husband or issue of the principal beneficiary in existence, the principal beneficiary and the persons who would, if he were actually dead, be entitled to the trust property or the income thereof or the annuity fund, if any, or arrears of the annuity, as the case may be;

as the trustees in their absolute discretion, without being liable to account for the exercise of such discretion, think fit."

---

[26] Griswold, *Spendthrift Trusts*, p. 375.

[27] *Re Wittke* [1944] Ch. 166 ("under protective trusts for the benefit of my sister").

[28] T.A. 1925, s.33(2).

[29] See *Re Smith's Will Trusts* (1981) 131 N.L.J. 292.

[30] Relationships are to be construed in accordance with s.1 of the Family Law Reform Act 1987 (*i.e.* without regard to legitimacy); F.L.R.A. 1987, Sched. 2, para. 2.

6. FORFEITURE OF THE LIFE TENANT'S INTEREST

It is necessary in each case to decide whether or not the event which has occurred is sufficient to determine the interest of the life tenant, and thus to bring the discretionary trusts into operation.[31] The question usually arises under trusts governed by the Trustee Act 1925, s.33. Where the question arises in respect of an express protective trust, the question will depend on the construction of the particular trust under consideration.[32] The principles applicable will however be the same.

It will be appreciated that a forfeiture is not in the bankruptcy cases a disaster. The forfeiture deprives the life tenant of his life interest, which would otherwise have become available to his creditors. The effect of the forfeiture is to allow the protective provisions to come into effect, and to keep the principal beneficiary's interest from his trustee in bankruptcy.

A. Determining Events

If the principal beneficiary alienates his interest,[33] or goes bankrupt, a forfeiture obviously occurs. In other circumstances, it is often difficult to draw a clear dividing line between those which will and those which will not effect a forfeiture. The matter is best explained by illustrations. The first three are cases of express protective trusts in which the instrument provided that the life interest should be determinable upon the happening of some event whereby some or all of the income became payable to another person.

In *Re Balfour's Settlement Trusts*,[34] the trustees had, at the life tenant's request, and in breach of trust, advanced parts of the capital to him. They then asserted their right to retain the income of the fund in order to make good the breach. Subsequently, the life tenant became bankrupt. Farwell J. held that the life tenant's interest had determined because the trustees became entitled to the income.[35] The life interest was thus saved from the bankruptcy.

In *Re Baring's Settlement Trusts*,[36] a sequestration order was made against the property of a mother who failed to obey a court order to return her children to the jurisdiction. Morton J. held that

---

[31] *Re Brewer's Settlement* [1896] 2 Ch. 503.

[32] *Ibid.* at p. 507; *Re Dennis' S.T.* [1942] Ch. 283 at p. 286; *Re Hall* [1944] Ch. 46.

[33] *Gibbon v. Mitchell* [1990] 1 W.L.R. 1304, *post*, p. 845 (surrender of protected life interest to remaindermen for tax purposes caused forfeiture, but deed set aside for mistake).

[34] [1938] Ch. 928; *Re Gordon* [1978] Ch. 145; *post*, p. 857.

[35] Distinguishing *Re Brewer's Settlement* [1896] 2 Ch. 503, where bankruptcy took place before the trustees exercised their right.

[36] [1940] Ch. 737.

the order effected a forfeiture, although the mother's loss of income was only temporary.

In *Re Dennis' Settlement Trusts*,[37] the settlor's son was entitled to a protective life interest under a family settlement. A rearrangement took place on his attaining the age of 21, and provided that for the next six years the trustees should pay to him only part of the income and should accumulate the rest for him. The rearrangement caused a forfeiture.

In *Re Gourju's Will Trusts*,[38] the protective trust was one governed by the Trustee Act 1925, s.33. The life tenant ceased to be entitled to receive the income of the trust because she lived in Nice, which became enemy occupied country during the Second World War. This caused a forfeiture. The Custodian of Enemy Property had no claim; nor could the trustees treat the tenant for life is still entitled, and retain income for her until the end of the war. The discretionary trusts came into effect, and the income was payable to one or more members of the class of beneficiaries.

On the other hand, residence in enemy occupied territory did not cause a forfeiture in *Re Hall*,[39] where forfeiture was to take place if the annuitant (*inter alia*) should "do or suffer any act" whereby the annuity should be payable elsewhere. The annuity could no longer be paid to the annuitant; but this was not due to anything that she had done or permitted; the Custodian of Enemy Property was entitled. Nor was there a forfeiture where a life tenant under a protective trust (terminable if the income became "payable to . . . some other person") assigned his interest to the trustees of his marriage settlement (of which he was tenant for life), authorised the trustees to charge their expenses to the fund and appointed them his attorneys to receive the income.[40] Again there was no forfeiture where the life tenant was of unsound mind and a receiver was appointed.[41] Nor does the fact that a receiver's fees become payable out of the estate of such a person effect a forfeiture.[42] An authority to pay to creditors the dividends due from a company for a period of time during which the company declared no dividend did not cause a forfeiture.[43]

---

[37] [1942] Ch. 283.
[38] [1943] Ch. 24; *Re Wittke* [1944] Ch. 166; *Re Allen-Meyrick's Will Trusts* [1966] 1 W.L.R. 499. See also Trading with the Enemy (Custodian) (No. 2) Order, 1945 (S.R. & O. 1945 No. 887) providing that vesting in the Custodian should not take place if it would cause a forfeiture.
[39] [1944] Ch. 46; *Re Harris* [1945] Ch. 316; *Re Pozot's S.T.* [1952] Ch. 427.
[40] *Re Tancred's Settlement* [1903] 1 Ch. 715. Similarly an assignment of income already accrued; *Re Greenwood* [1901] 1 Ch. 887.
[41] *Re Oppenheimer's W.T.* [1950] Ch. 633; *Re Marshall* [1920] 1 Ch. 284.
[42] *Re Westby's Settlement* [1950] Ch. 296; Mental Health Act 1983, s.106(6).
[43] *Re Longman* [1955] 1 W.L.R. 197.

B. Order of the Court under Trustee Act 1925, s.57[44]

The court may make an order under Trustee Act 1925, s.57, which may affect the operation of a trust. If an order is made authorising the trustees to raise money to pay the debts of a life tenant under a protective trust, there is no forfeiture; for the power must be treated as if it had been "inserted in the trust instrument as an over-riding power."[45] If the order provides that the life tenant effects an insurance policy to secure a like amount of money at his death, and that the trustees shall pay the premiums out of the income if the life tenant fails to do so, there is no forfeiture so long as the life tenant makes the payments; but if the life tenant fails to pay and they become payable by the trustees from the income, there would be a forfeiture.[46]

C. Order of the Court under Matrimonial Causes Acts 1859–1973

It is not clear whether a forfeiture is effected when a court order is made which alters a protected life interest under a marriage settlement.[47] In *Re Richardson's Will Trusts*,[48] the court ordered that the principal beneficiary should charge his interest with an annual payment of £50 in favour of his divorced wife. The charge was held to create a forfeiture. On the other hand, in *General Accident Fire and Life Assurance Corporation Ltd v. I.R.C.*[49] an order diverting part of the income from the life tenant in favour of a former wife was held not to effect a forfeiture.

These cases are distinguishable on a narrow ground of construction of section 33.[50] But the broader ground of the decision, that this situation has no relevance to the real purpose of protective trusts, would seem to apply to the charge in *Re Richardson's Will Trusts*[51] as much as to the diversion of part of the income in the *General Accident* case.[52] It is submitted that the principle of the *General Accident* case is sound. As Donovan L.J. said[53]: " . . . the section is

---

[44] *Post*, p. 616.
[45] *Re Mair* [1935] Ch. 562 at p. 565, *per* Farwell J.
[46] *Re Salting* [1932] 2 Ch. 57 at p. 65.
[47] Which the court has power to do under Matrimonial Causes Act 1973, s.24(1).
[48] [1958] Ch. 504; *Edmonds v. Edmonds* [1965] 1 W.L.R. 58. *Re Richardson* illustrates the advantage of establishing a series of protective trusts, "one set until the beneficiary is twenty-five, another from twenty-five to thirty-five, a third from thirty-fie to forty-five, and another for the rest of his life." A forfeiture of, or a charge upon, the principal beneficiary's interest in one of the trusts would not affect his interest in subsequent trusts. He would get a fresh start. (1958) 74 L.Q.R. 182 (R.E.M.).
[49] [1963] 1 W.L.R. 1207.
[50] *Ibid*. See Donovan L.J. at p. 1217 and Russell L.J. at p. 1221; (1963) 27 Conv.(N.S.) 517 (F. Crane).
[51] [1958] Ch. 504.
[52] [1963] 1 W.L.R. 1207.
[53] [1963] 1 W.L.R. 1207, *per* Donovan L.J. at p. 1218.

intended as a protection to spendthrift or improvident or weak life tenants. But it can give . . . no protection against the effect of a court order such as was made here. Furthermore, if such an order involves a forfeiture much injustice could be done." Perhaps the problem can be rationalised with the cases on section 57 by saying with Russell L.J., who made clear, however, that he did not rest his decision on this approach: "the settlement throughout was potentially subject in all its trusts to such an order as was made."[54] *Re Richardson's Will Trusts*[55] was not mentioned; but an earlier case on the Matrimonial Causes Act 1859 in favour of forfeiture, *Re Carew*,[56] was overruled. It is tempting to say that *Re Richardson's Will Trusts* is wrong; but it should be noted that in that case, as in *Re Carew*, the decision in favour of forfeiture forwarded the broad policy of section 33; for the forfeiture in those cases allowed the discretionary trusts to operate when otherwise the trustee in bankruptcy would have claimed the interest.

7. ADVANCEMENTS

Section 33(1) expressly exempts, as a cause of forfeiture, an advancement under any statutory[57] or express power. Thus the fact that the life tenant no longer receives the income of the part of the capital which has been advanced does not effect a forfeiture.[58] It appears that the same rule applies in the case of an express protective trust.[59] *Re Stimpson*[60] is to the contrary, but is regarded as of doubtful authority.

8. EFFECT OF FORFEITURE

When a forfeiture has taken place, the life interest of the principal beneficiary is terminated, and the trusts in section 33(1)(ii), or those expressly contained in the instrument, as the case may be, come into play. The termination is not, however, an occasion of charge to inheritance tax.[61] Under section 33 there are discretionary trusts in

---

[54] *Ibid.* at p. 1222.
[55] [1958] Ch. 504.
[56] (1910) 103 L.T. 658.
[57] T.A. 1925, s.32; *post*, p. 578.
[58] See however *General Accident, etc. v. I.R.C.* [1963] 1 W.L.R. 1207 which suggests that an advancement does not effect a forfeiture and that the proviso to s.33 is *ex abundanti cautela*.
[59] *Re Hodgson* [1913] 1 Ch. 34; *Re Shaw's Settlement* [1951] Ch. 833; *Re Rees (decd.)* [1954] Ch. 202.
[60] [1931] 2 Ch. 77.
[61] Inheritance Tax Act 1984, s.88; *post*, p. 228.

favour of the principal beneficiary and other persons, depending on whether or not a spouse or issue of the principal beneficiary is in existence. The trustees may apply the income for the remainder of the trust period for any member of the discretionary class. The principal beneficiary is not entitled to any income; but the trustees may, if they wish, pay it to him. They must pay the income to one or more of the members.[62] If the trustees decide to pay some income to the principal beneficiary, they face the problem that the money may be claimed by the trustee in bankruptcy as the assignee of his "interest" under the discretionary trust,[63] or perhaps only the surplus above that needed for his "mere support."[64] They may, however, in their absolute discretion, apply the money for his use and benefit.[65] Thus, "if the trustees were to pay an hotel-keeper to give him a dinner he would get nothing but the right to eat a dinner, and that is not property which could pass by assignment or bankruptcy."[66] It is safer to pay the money to third persons in satisfaction of services provided for the bankrupt.

---

[62] *Re Gourju's W.T.* [1943] Ch. 24.

[63] *Re Coleman* (1888) 39 Ch.D. 443; *Lord v. Bunn* (1843) 2 Y. & C.Ch. 98; *Re Bullock* (1891) 64 L.T. 736 at p. 738.

[64] *Re Ashby* [1892] 1 Q.B. 872 at p. 877.

[65] *Re Bullock (supra); Re Coleman (supra); Re Smith* [1928] Ch. 915 at p. 919; *Public Trustees v. Ferguson* [1947] N.Z.L.R. 746.

[66] *Re Coleman, supra,* at p. 451.

CHAPTER 8

DISCRETIONARY TRUSTS

1. General	195	A. Exhaustive and Non-Exhaustive Discretionary Trusts	203
2. Uses of Discretionary Trusts	196		
A. To Protect the Beneficiary Against Creditors	196	B. The Nature of the Interest of the Beneficiaries	203
B. To Continue to Exercise Control Over Young or Improvident Beneficiaries	197	i. Individual Beneficiaries	203
		ii. The Class	204
C. To React to Changes in Circumstances	197	C. Powers and Duties	205
3. Usual Form of Discretionary Trusts	197	i. Fixed Trust	205
A. Trustees' Discretion	197	ii. Trust with a Power of Selection	205
B. The Trust Period	198		
C. Power to Accumulate	198	iii. Discretionary Trusts; Exhaustive and Non-Exhaustive	206
D. Power to Add to, or Exclude from, the Class of Beneficiaries	199	iv. Powers Held as Trustee; Fiduciary Powers	208
E. Power to Appoint Upon New Trusts	200		
F. Miscellaneous Administrative Provisions	201	v. Powers Held in a Non-Fiduciary Capacity	209
4. The Selection of Trustees	201	vi. The Rule of Certainty in Ascertaining Beneficiaries or Objects	209
5. The Nature of the Interest of the Beneficiaries Under a Discretionary Trust	202	vii. Discretionary Trusts Since 1974	209

1. GENERAL

IT has been seen that discretionary trusts were used as a means of dealing with the income of a protective trust after the interest of the principal beneficiary had determined. Conveyancers appreciated the advantages which discretionary trusts could offer, especially in the context of estate duty saving, and they developed into one of the principal tools of estate and tax planners. Estate duty was replaced by capital transfer tax (now inheritance tax) in the Finance Act 1975. An explanation of the current tax position will be delayed until the next chapter, so that the fiscal situation of different types of trusts may be considered together. It will then be seen that discretionary trusts suffered substantially upon the introduction of capital transfer tax, and became at a disadvantage in relation to other trusts.[1] The

---

[1] Although the rules applicable to discretionary trusts were substantially amended and rationalised by the Finance Act 1982. It should be added that the rates of inheritance tax under F.A. 1988 are not high, the maximum being 40 per cent on death and 20 per cent for chargeable lifetime transactions.

disadvantage has been increased now that the discretionary trust is
the only form of trust to be initially chargeable to inheritance tax
upon its creation *inter vivos*. Outright gifts and non-discretionary
trusts are generally potentially exempt (*i.e.* chargeable only if the
transferor dies within seven years).[2] The importance of discretionary
trusts has been reduced, but they need to be examined because they
retain many advantages outside the fiscal field; also because they
raise a number of interesting and important theoretical questions in
the law of trusts.

2. USES OF DISCRETIONARY TRUSTS

There are various reasons why a settlor may prefer to establish
discretionary trusts rather than fixed trusts. As previously indicated,
the most important reason used to be the saving of estate duty, and
this will be referred to in Chapter 9. The emphasis is now on the
other advantages.

A. To Protect the Beneficiary Against Creditors

If one member of a class of beneficiaries under a discretionary
trust goes bankrupt, the trustee in bankruptcy is not entitled to claim
any part of the fund.[3] The trustee in bankruptcy is however entitled
to goods and money paid over by the trustees to the beneficiary in
the exercise of their discretion[4]; or perhaps only to the amount in
excess of that needed for the maintenance of the beneficiary.[5] The
trustee in bankruptcy is however excluded if the trustees make the
maintenance payments to third parties, such as a hotel keeper[6] or
tradesman.[7]

We have already seen that discretionary trusts are employed under
protective trusts as a means whereby a protected life tenant may
continue to receive some benefit from settled funds after his bankruptcy.[8] Indeed, this was their earliest use.

---

[2] See F.A. 1986, s.101, introducing the potentially exempt transfer for lifetime gifts other
than trusts, and Finance (No. 2) Act 1987, s.96, extending this to non-discretionary
trusts.
[3] *Re Ashby* [1892] 1 Q.B. 872 at p. 877; *Re Bullock* (1891) 64 L.T. 736; *Holmes v. Penney*
(1856) 3 K. & J. 90. If the bankrupt is the sole member of the discretionary class, the
interest passes to the trustee in bankruptcy: *Green v. Spicer* (1830) 1 Russ. & M. 395. See
also *Re Trafford's Settlement* [1985] Ch. 32, post. p. 204.
[4] *Re Coleman* (1888) 39 Ch.D. 443.
[5] *Re Ashby, supra,* at p. 877 *per* Vaughan Williams J.; *Page v. Way* (1840) 3 Beav. 20, *per*
Lord Langdale M.R.; *ante*, p. 194.
[6] *Re Coleman, supra,* at p. 451; *ante*, p. 194.
[7] *Godden v. Crowhurst* (1842) 10 Sim. 642 at p. 656.
[8] *Ante*, pp. 185 *et seq.*

B. To Continue to Exercise Control over Young or Improvident Beneficiaries

Many take the view that it is unwise to put large sums of money at the disposal of beneficiaries if they are young or extravagant. This is due not only to the fear of the loss of family capital in case of insolvency; but also because a rich young beneficiary may be encouraged to develop habits of idleness and extravagance, and waste the inheritance; older beneficiaries may already have done so. While the discretionary trust is in operation, each member of the class of beneficiaries is entitled only to the money which the trustees see fit to allocate to him in the exercise of their discretion. The settlor may, whether or not he is a trustee, be able to influence the selection so as to exercise some element of control over the beneficiaries.[9]

C. To React to Changes in Circumstances

The trustees can exercise their discretion in relation to distribution of income and capital according to the circumstances existing at the time. When the trust is set up, there is no way of knowing how the beneficiaries will fare in the future; which of them will be most in need; which will be deserving, which spendthrift, which inebriate; which will marry millionaires, and which missionaries. The trustees can take all these factors into consideration in making their decisions; and will be much influenced by the wishes of the settlor. In making these decisions, they will also take tax factors into consideration; it is more economical to give income to those with smaller incomes; and capital given to rich beneficiaries may bear inheritance tax not only on the distribution but also when disposed of by them. Decisions by trustees which favour one beneficiary over another may of course give rise to criticism and resentment by disappointed beneficiaries.[10] All these factors need to be taken into consideration.

3. USUAL FORM OF DISCRETIONARY TRUSTS

A. Trustees' Discretion

The essential feature of a discretionary trust is that the property is conveyed to trustees to be held by them on trust to apply the income or the capital or both for the benefit of the members of a class of

---

[9] But if he influences the trustees to such an extent that they fail to exercise their discretion independently, the appointment will be void; *Turner v. Turner* [1984] Ch. 100, *post*, p. 209.

[10] The trustees need not disclose the reasons for their decisions; *Re Beloved Wilkes's Charity* (1851) 3 Mac. & G. 440, *post*, p. 505.

beneficiaries in such proportions as the trustees shall, in their absolute discretion, think fit. Most discretionary trusts are concerned
with distribution of income; the distribution of capital is commonly
effected under a power to appoint. It used to be common to include
a wider class of beneficiaries as objects of the power of appointment, and a narrower, more specific class of beneficiaries of the
discretionary trusts.[11] But, since *McPhail v. Doulton*,[12] the test of
certainty of beneficiaries of a discretionary trust has been assimilated, as has been seen,[13] to that of objects of a mere power, and the
wider class can now be employed for both purposes. During the
period of the trust, no individual beneficiary is entitled to any share
of the property, income or capital; he receives what the trustees see
fit to give him and no more.

B. The Trust Period

Provision will be made for the discretionary trust to continue for
the trust period; which can be any desired period which is not in
excess of the perpetuity period. Discretionary trusts provide a special situation for the application of the perpetuity rule. Since no
individual beneficiary has any interest under the trust, property only
vests in a beneficiary upon the exercise of the trustees' discretion in
his favour; and such a vesting is void unless it takes place within the
perpetuity period.[14] A discretionary trust can only exist, therefore,
for the duration of the perpetuity period.

A discretionary trust will therefore be designed to terminate
before the end of the period. This is normally done by postulating
the "trust period" at the conclusion of which the discretionary trust
will terminate, and providing for a gift over on fixed trusts which
will themselves vest within the perpetuity period. Since 1964, a
period of years not exceeding 80 years may be specified.[15]

C. Power to Accumulate

In many cases the income beneficiaries will not need the trust
income each year, and it may be that, because the beneficiaries'
income tax rates are higher than those of the trust, the tax payable
will be higher if the income is paid out than it would be if it were
retained in the trust.[16] The trustees are commonly given a power to
accumulate. Without such a power, they will be obliged to distribute

---

[11] *Re Gestetner* [1953] Ch. 672.
[12] [1971] A.C. 424.
[13] *Ante*, p. 99.
[14] *Re Coleman* [1936] Ch. 521.
[15] P.A.A. 1964, s.1.
[16] Even though the additional rate is payable on the whole of the tust income: I.C.T.A. 1988,
s.686; F.A. 1988, s.24(3).

the income[17]; not to any particular beneficiary, but among the beneficiaries. It was noted above[18] that such a power makes the distinction between exhaustive and non-exhaustive discretionary trusts. The trust is non-exhaustive as to the income if the income is not required to be distributed each year; and non-exhaustive as to the capital if the trustees are not obliged to distribute all the capital during the currency of the trust.

There are, however, statutory restrictions upon powers of accumulation. The permitted periods are (by the Law of Property Act 1925, s.164 as amended by the Perpetuities and Accumulations Act 1964, s.13)[19]:

(*a*) the life of the grantor or settlor; or

(*b*) a term of 21 years from the death of the grantor, settlor or testator; or

(*c*) the duration of the minority or respective minorities of any person or persons living or *en ventre sa mère* at the death of the grantor, settlor or testator; or

(*d*) the duration of the minority or respective minorities only of any person or persons who under the limitations of the instrument directing the accumulations would, for the time being, if of full age be entitled to the income directed to be accumulated; or

(*e*) a term of 21 years from the date of the making of the disposition; or

(*f*) the duration of the minority or respective minorities of any person or persons in being at that date.

The settlor may select whichever period he wishes. If he selects a period which is in excess of those permitted, the accumulation will be invalid only as to the excess. The court will select whichever period is the most appropriate to the settlor's intent.[20] At the conclusion of the period of accumulation, the income must be distributed.

D. Power to Add to, or to Exclude from, the Class of Beneficiaries

The trustees may be given a power to add new members to the class of beneficiaries, or to exclude existing members.[21] The power

[17] *Re Gourju's W.T.* [1943] Ch. 24; *Re Locker's S.T.* [1977] 1 W.L.R. 1323; subject to T.A. 1925, s.31, *post*, p. 571.

[18] *Ante*, p. 61.

[19] The section does not apply to a corporate settlor: *Re Dodwell & Co. Ltd's Trust Deed* [1979] Ch. 301; [1979] Conv. 319 (J.T.F.).

[20] Maudsley, *The Modern Law of Perpetuities*, p. 208; Morris & Leach, p. 272.

[21] *Re Manisty's Settlement* [1974] Ch. 17; *Blausten v. I.R.C.* [1972] 1 Ch. 256.

to exclude members became important when Finance Act 1958[22] provided that a settlor should be liable to income tax upon the income of a settlement if the settlor or the spouse of the settlor might benefit from the income or property of the settlement. Many settlements in existence at that date included the spouse of the settlor as a member of the class of beneficiaries, and the Act provided that the settlor should not be so liable if, *inter alia*, the power to make the payments was not exercisable after April 9, 1959. Similar situations may arise in the future. A difficulty could arise if the trustees decided to exclude a member of the class for no good reason. Arbitrary exclusion will be inconsistent with the trustees' fiduciary duties.[23] It might also be construed as an improper release of a power held in a fiduciary capacity.[24] Yet it is difficult to see how the excluded member could establish that he had suffered loss; because, as a member of a class of beneficiaries under a discretionary trust, he was not entitled to any interest under the trust, and would be deprived of nothing except his hope or expectation of favourable consideration by the trustees.

It may be useful also to give power to the trustees to add new members to the class. Care has to be taken to ensure that the trustees cannot include persons, such as the settlor or his spouse, whose inclusion would have damaging tax consequences.[25] The power to add new members to the class is usually done by defining a class of excepted persons, and giving to the trustees a power to include in the class of beneficiaries any person who was not a member of the excepted class. Such a provision was upheld in *Re Manisty's Settlement*,[26] concerning a power of appointment; the settlor's mother, and any person who should become his widow, were added to the class of beneficiaries. The validity of trusts and powers in favour of very large classes was discussed in Chapter 3.

E. Power to Appoint Upon New Trusts

It is common to give to trustees power to appoint on further trusts, including discretionary and protective trusts, and also in favour of trustees of a foreign settlement[27] and to give them full power of delegation. This makes possible a resettlement on new trusts at the

---

[22] s.22; now I.C.T.A. 1988, s.674; *Watson v. Holland* [1985] 1 All E.R. 290. See also s.674A, added by F.A. 1989, s.109.

[23] *Post*, pp. 206 *et seq.*

[24] *Ante*, p. 182.

[25] Inclusion of the settlor (but probably not the settlor's spouse) would, for example, attract the "reservation of benefit" rules of inheritance tax; *post*, p. 220.

[26] [1974] Ch. 17; the power was described as an "intermediate" power; *ante*, p. 167: *Re Park* [1932] 1 Ch. 580; *Re Abraham's W.T.* [1969] 1 Ch. 463. See also *Re Hay's S.T.* [1982] 1 W.L.R. 202.

[27] *Post*, p. 501.

end of the accumulation period, or at any time at which it becomes advantageous for fiscal or other reasons, to do so. Such an appointment must keep within the perpetuity period as measured from the date of the original settlement,[28] and it may not provide for accumulation for any period beyond that which was available to the original settlor.[29] The periods of perpetuity and of accumulation will only start again if appointments are made to a beneficiary who resettles; but such a course would result in a double transfer of the capital, which may have damaging inheritance tax consequences.

F. Miscellaneous Administrative Provisions

Trustees of every trust need to be given the powers necessary to enable them to perform their duties. Obvious powers which they need are the power to sell, to invest, to apply income for the maintenance of minor beneficiaries, to make advancements, to make payments to, and accept receipts from, guardians of minors, etc. It was at one time necessary to include all such powers in the settlement. But most of the basic necessary powers are given to trustees by the Trustee Act 1925 and amendments thereto, discussed in detail below.[30] The statutory powers can be added to, or restricted, by the terms of the trust instrument[31] This will be necessary in the case of powers not envisaged in 1925, such as the power to delegate investment decisions.[32] It is usual, in the case of a discretionary trust, to give to the trustees the widest and most extensive powers. In terms of bulk, these administrative provisions will form the greater part of the trust instrument.

4. THE SELECTION OF TRUSTEES

The selection of the right trustees is important in the case of any trust; but particularly so in the case of a discretionary trust, where the trustees are given such extensive discretionary powers. The technical aspects of the matter are postponed to Chapter 17; but it may be useful here to anticipate some of that discussion. The settlor, in confiding such broad discretion, will wish to select individuals whose judgment and co-operation he respects. He can select his most trusted friends, but they may have no expertise in investment,

---

[28] *Pilkington v. I.R.C.* [1964] A.C. 612.
[29] Because the appointors cannot be given powers in excess of those available to the settlor.
[30] *Post,* Chap. 20.
[31] T.A. 1925, s.69.
[32] *Post,* p. 567.

accounting or law or taxes.[33] He may thus favour the inclusion of some professionals; who should do the job more efficiently; but they will need to be paid for their work. In a case of executorships or trusts generally, it is common to appoint a corporate trustee, usually the Executor and Trustee Company of a bank, but there may be reluctance to appoint a corporate trustee in a case of a discretionary trust, because it may be felt that the trust officer will not be in as good a position as a personal friend to exercise the broad discretions contained in a discretionary trust. It is common to select a mixture of professionals and non-professionals; and there is no legal reason why a corporation and an individual should not be trustees.

As the disposition of the property is dependent upon the discretion of the trustees, the settlor may wish to be appointed trustee in order to be able to participate in decisions on distribution. Such an appointment has, in the past, been considered unadvisable because it might be possible for him to obtain a benefit under the settlement, and, under the estate duty system, this would have had the effect of treating the trust property as being part of the settlor's estate for estate duty purposes.[34] Under the system of inheritance tax the old estate duty concept of "reservation of benefit" has been reintroduced.[35] In the context of the discretionary trust, this means that the property is treated as remaining part of the settlor's estate if he is within the class of objects.[36] If the settlor is merely a trustee it is unlikely that the "reservation of benefit" rules will apply, but it will be otherwise if he can in fact derive benefit from his trusteeship, for example by way of remuneration. In view of these uncertainties, the appointment of the settlor as trustee is best avoided.

Even if he is not a trustee, it is possible for the settlor to exert some influence upon the trustees in the way in which they exercise their discretion. However, if the settlor effectively dictates the distribution of the property in such a way that the trustees exercise no independent discretion, any appointments so made will be void.[37]

5. THE NATURE OF THE INTEREST OF THE BENEFICIARIES UNDER A DISCRETIONARY TRUST

The nature of the interest of beneficiaries under a discretionary trust raises some important theoretical and practical questions. The discussion will tie in with some of the points made earlier in the

---

[33] For an illustration of the dangers of appointing such persons without the inclusion of professionals, see *Turner v. Turner* [1984] Ch. 100, *post*, p. 209.

[34] *Oakes v. Stamp Duty Commissioner for N.S.W.* [1954] A.C. 51.

[35] F.A. 1986, s.102 and Sched. 20.

[36] See (1986) 83 L.S.Gaz. 3728.

[37] *Turner v. Turner, supra.*

distinction between trusts and powers.[38] In that context, the present discussion will justify the recognition of the basic difference between trusts and powers as being one of obligation or discretion. But it will be clear that the "duty" concept in the case of discretionary trusts is a very different duty from that recognised in the case of fixed trusts.[39]

A. Exhaustive and Non-exhaustive Discretionary Trusts

If the trustees are required to distribute the whole of the income, the discretionary trust is exhaustive. Where, as in the case of most modern discretionary trusts, the trustees may apply the income for some purposes other than distribution among the beneficiaries, as where there is a power to accumulate income not so applied, there is a non-exhaustive discretionary trust. The rights of the beneficiaries are more complex in the case of a non-exhaustive discretionary trust. For the income beneficiaries cannot argue that they are, as a group, *entitled* to the income. The income may be accumulated in whole or in part and added to the capital.

B. The Nature of the Interest of the Beneficiaries

i. Individual Beneficiaries. In the case of a fixed trust, we saw that the beneficiary's interest is regarded as proprietary. He is the owner of an equitable interest under the trust. This is not so in the case of a beneficiary under a discretionary trust. He is dependent upon the exercise by the trustees of their power of selection in his favour.[40] This point was crucial to the success of discretionary trusts in the estate duty days; because estate duty was payable when property "passed" on a death,[41] as on the death of a life tenant.[42] A discretionary beneficiary could not be said to be entitled to any quantifiable share. He therefore owned no part of the property and no property passed on his death. The position is similar under the inheritance tax system. As we will see, the death of a discretionary beneficiary is not an event upon which the trust fund is taxable. Inheritance tax is, however, payable on a payment to a beneficiary and on certain other occasions.[43]

---

[38] *Ante,* p. 59.
[39] (1976) 54 C.B.R. 229 (M. Cullity); [1970] A.S.C.L. 187 (J. Davies); (1974) 37 M.L.R. 643 (Y. Grbich).
[40] He can renounce his position as class member; *Re Gulbenkian's Settlement (No. 2)* [1970] Ch. 408.
[41] F.A. 1894, s.2.
[42] *Earl Cowley v. I.R.C.* [1899] A.C. 198.
[43] *Post,* Chap. 9.

A sole member of a class of discretionary beneficiaries cannot claim entitlement to the income so long as there is a possibility that another member could come into existence.[44] The trust fund may be regarded as financial resources of a sole beneficiary for the purpose of an order for financial provision (in favour of or against the beneficiary) under section 25 of the Matrimonial Causes Act 1973, provided the order would not put improper pressure on the trustees in the exercise of their discretion.[45]

ii. The Class. Whether or not the class of beneficiaries is properly regarded as the owner is a different matter. We have seen that a sole beneficiary of a discretionary trust and the remaindermen expectant upon the determination of the trust on his death, may, if all are adult and under no disability, call for the capital to be paid over to them, or may validly assign to a third party who will become the beneficiary.[46]

Cases on estate duty have indicated that a class of beneficiaries may not hold a proprietary interest which "passes" for estate duty purposes. "Two or more persons," said Lord Reid, "cannot have a single right unless they hold it jointly or in common. But clearly objects of a discretionary trust do not have that: they have individual rights, they are in competition with each other and what the trustees give to one is his alone."[47] This was said in *Gartside v. I.R.C.*[48] which was a case of a non-exhaustive discretionary trust, but in *Re Weir's Settlement*[49] and *Sainsbury v. I.R.C.*[50] the same analysis was applied to exhaustive discretionary trusts. Lord Reid's rejection of the "group or class" interest concept "seems equally applicable, whether the trust is exhaustive or not exhaustive."[51] The question has ceased to be of significance in relation to estate duty, but is relevant to determine where the beneficial interest is in a discretionary trust; and whether the class of beneficiaries, all being adult and under no disability, is able to call for a transfer of the legal title and to terminate the trust. It is submitted that the beneficial ownership should be in all those persons in whose favour the discretion may be exercised, including the beneficiaries of an accumulation provision under a non-exhaustive trust; and that, on the principle of

---

[44] *Re Trafford's Settlement* [1985] Ch. 32. (Capital transfer tax). See also *Figg v. Clark (Inspector of Taxes)*, *The Times*, March 11, 1996.

[45] *Browne v. Browne* [1989] 1 F.L.R. 291 (order against wife who was sole beneficiary); *J. v. J. (C. Intervening) (Minors: Financial Provision)* [1989] Fam. 29 (maintenance of two children, the only beneficiaries, who would become absolutely entitled at majority).

[46] *Green v. Spicer* (1830) 1 Russ. & My. 395; *Re Smith* [1928] Ch. 915.

[47] *Per* Lord Reid [1968] A.C. 553 at pp. 605–606.

[48] [1968] A.C. 553.

[49] [1969] 1 Ch. 657, reversed on a different point [1971] Ch. 145.

[50] [1970] Ch. 712.

[51] [1970] Ch. 712 at p. 724, *per* Ungoed-Thomas J.

Re Smith,[52] they should be able to terminate the trust in appropriate circumstances, if all adult and under no disability.[53]

C. Powers and Duties

It may be useful at this stage to recapitulate some of the points, discussed above,[54] in connection with the nature of rights, duties and discretions in the context of trusts and powers. It will be seen that the basic distinction between trusts and powers continues to be that between obligations and discretions; but it is important to be able to identify what the trustees' duty is in the case of a discretionary trust. There are various contexts in which the question of the distinction between trusts and powers arises.

i. Fixed Trust. At one end of the spectrum is the case of the trustee of a fixed trust. This is clearly an obligation upon the trustee. Having once accepted the trusteeship, he has no choice of whether or not to perform the trust. He is obliged to do so; he can be required by the court to perform, and is personally liable for breach. Some of the trustees' duties will require the exercise of a discretion in their performance. Thus, a trustee is under a duty to invest;[55] but, he will of course exercise a discretion in the selection of investments. The trustees' duty may be seen as a correlative of the beneficiaries' rights. His position is wholly different from that at the other end of the spectrum; that of the donee of a power held in a non-fiduciary capacity. As will be seen, the question whether to exercise such a power is wholly a matter of the donee's discretion.

ii. Trust with a Power of Selection. We have seen that there are cases in which the trustees hold property upon trust for a specified group of persons, subject to a power to select the shares and proportions in which those persons shall take. Thus in *Burrough v. Philcox*[56] the disposition was "among my nephews and nieces, or their children, either all to one or to as many of them as my surviving child shall think proper." We saw that, in the absence of an appointment being made, the nieces and nephews took in equal shares. The nieces and nephews thus held a vested interest under the trust, subject to divestment upon an appointment being made. Their

---

[52] [1928] Ch. 915; *supra*; *Saunders v. Vautier* (1841) 4 Beav. 115, affirmed Cr. & Ph. 240. But see Pettit, p. 70, suggesting that the beneficial interest is in suspense until the discretion is exercised.

[53] This will not be possible unless all members are ascertainable, which may not be the case since *McPhail v. Doulton* [1971] A.C. 424.

[54] *Ante*, p. 59.

[55] *Post*, p. 514.

[56] (1840) 5 My. & Cr. 72.

situation is exactly the same as it would have been if the testamentary provisions had given to a donee a power to appoint, and in default of appointment to my nephews and nieces in equal shares. Those entitled in default are treated as owners in equity subject to divestment on the exercise of the power.[57] The trust in their favour is a fixed trust.[58] The division into equal shares makes it necessary to identify each member, and to know how many there are. This case is the same as that of a fixed trust; but the beneficiaries' interests are subject to defeasance. The trustee's duty to the beneficiaries is clear. It is a question of construction whether the instrument creates such a trust or creates a discretionary trust, discussed below.

iii. Discretionary Trusts: Exhaustive and Non-exhaustive.

A discretionary trust may require the trustees to distribute all the income; or it may give to the trustees a power to accumulate for a period allowed by law. Similarly, it may require the trustees to dispose of the capital during the trust period, or it may provide for a gift over of the assets of the trust at the end of the trust period. Whether the trust is exhaustive or non-exhaustive, an individual beneficiary is not regarded as having any proprietary interest in the trust property.[59] If the trust is exhaustive, there is authority to say the class as a whole, if adult and under no disability, can terminate the trust.[60]

This raises the question: what is the trustee's duty? Clearly, it is different from the case of a fixed trust. Where are the beneficiary's correlative rights? This situation does not fit neatly into the right-duty correlation. The beneficiary has no proprietary rights. Is it correct to describe the situation as a trust; which, by definition, involves a duty? The answer, it is submitted, is: yes; this is a trust, and it involves a duty, although different from that in the case of a fixed trust.

The duty here is to exercise the discretion. In the case of an exhaustive discretionary trust, a selection must be made; whereas if the discretionary trust is non-exhaustive, the discretion may be exercised by deciding to accumulate. As Harris argued[61] persuasively, "the discretionary trust in fact depends on a rule-concept of duty, with no such necessity for correlative rights." Herein is the trustee's duty in a discretionary trust; and here is the point of distinction between a discretionary trust and a mere power. Each member of the class of beneficiaries under a discretionary trust has

---

[57] *Re Brooks' S.T.* [1939] Ch. 993 at p. 997.
[58] And thus not affected by the decision in *McPhail v. Doulton* [1971] A.C. 424, *ante*, p. 98. See (1982) 98 L.Q.R. 551 (C. Emery).
[59] *Ante*, p. 203.
[60] *Re Smith* [1928] Ch. 915; *Re Nelson* [1928] Ch. 920n.; *ante*, p. 205.
[61] (1971) 87 L.Q.R. 231.

standing to sue in order to have the trustees' duty performed. Not that such a beneficiary will necessarily benefit by the performance of the trustees' duty; as it is a duty, not to pay to that beneficiary, but to exercise their discretion as described above.

In *Re Locker's Settlement*,[62] the terms of an exhaustive discretionary trust required the trustees to pay, divide and apply the income for charitable purposes or among the class of beneficiaries as the trustees "shall in their absolute discretion determine." Because of subsequent expressions of wishes by the settlor, the trustees failed to make distributions of income from 1965 to 1968. The question arose in 1975 what should be done with that income, and particularly whether the trustees' discretion had expired.

Goulding J. held that the discretion still continued, and that the trustees should apply their discretion in the distribution of the money among those who were members of the class of beneficiaries in the relevant years. In discussing the question of the trustees' duty and the court's power to enforce the exercise of the discretion, he said,[63] "it is common ground that it was the duty of the trustees to distribute the trust income within a reasonable time. .... A court of equity, where the trustees have failed to discharge their duty of prompt discretionary distribution of income, is concerned to make them, as owners of the trust assets at law, dispose of them in accordance with the requirements of conscience. .... " If the trustees refuse to perform their duty, the court can itself execute the trust—"by appointing new trustees, or by authorising or directing representative persons of the classes of beneficiaries to prepare a scheme for distribution, or even, should the proper basis for distribution appear, by itself directing the trustees so to distribute."[64] The trustees in *Locker*,[65] as is usual in these cases,[66] were ready and willing to perform, and did so.

The point is that the trustees under these circumstances are under a duty to distribute. That is an obligation which is subject to enforcement by the court in one of the ways stated. *Locker*[67] was a case of an exhaustive discretionary trust; though the individuals in the class of beneficiaries were not, as a class, entitled to the whole of the income, because the trustees could make payments to charity. The duty and obligation of the trustees, however, is the same in the

---

[62] [1977] 1 W.L.R. 1323; *Re Gourju's W.T.* [1943] Ch. 241; *McPhail v. Doulton* [1971] A.C. 424.

[63] [1977] 1 W.L.R. 1323 at p. 1325.

[64] *Ibid.* at p. 1325, quoting Lord Wilberforce in *McPhail v. Doulton* [1971] A.C. 424 at p. 457.

[65] *Supra.*

[66] As pointed out by Lord Wilberforce at p. 449.

[67] *Supra.*

case of a non-exhaustive discretionary trust as in *McPhail v. Doulton*[68] itself. The difference is that in a non-exhaustive trust the duty to exercise the discretion can be satisfied by deciding to accumulate.

iv. Powers Held as Trustee. Fiduciary Powers.[69]   The situation is quite different where the trustees, as one of the terms of the trust instrument, are given a power of appointment. Here there is no duty to exercise; and the court will not order the trustee to exercise the discretion. Typical is *Re Allen Meyrick's Trust*[70] where:

> A will gave property to trustees to hold "upon trust that they may apply the income thereof in their absolute discretion for the maintenance of my said husband and subject to the exercise of their discretion on trust for my two godchildren ... in equal shares absolutely." Various difficulties arose. The husband was an undischarged bankrupt. Some of the money was applied in paying the rent and certain debts. The trustees could not agree on the disposal of other income, and attempted to surrender their discretion to the court.

The court refused to accept, and was willing only to hear applications for directions in particular circumstances as they arose. Nor were the trustees ordered to exercise their discretion. The trust here was in favour of the godchildren, subject to the overriding power. If the trustees could not reach unanimity as to the exercise of the power, the godchildren became entitled.

This is not, of course, to say that the trustees in this situation are not subject to duties in relation to the exercise of the power. They hold the power in a fiduciary capacity, and are subject to the highest fiduciary duties in the way in which they make their decision. They must do more than refrain from acting capriciously. Their duty is to consider periodically whether to exercise the power, and to consider the range of objects in such manner as will enable them to carry out their fiduciary duties. If they decide to exercise the power they must, of course, keep within its terms; they must exercise it in a responsible manner according to its purpose and consider the appropriateness of individual appointments.[71] The court will intervene if they exceed their powers or act capriciously.[72] Furthermore, they must

---

[68] *Supra.*
[69] See Chap. 6.
[70] [1966] 1 W.L.R. 499.
[71] *Re Hay's S.T.* [1982] 1 W.L.R. 202; [1982] Conv. 432 (A. Grubb). These duties, which were laid down in *McPhail v. Doulton* [1971] A.C. 424, *Re Gestetner* [1953] Ch. 672, and *Re Gulbenkian's S.T.* [1970] A.C. 508, are not necessarily exhaustive.
[72] *McPhail v. Doulton* [1971] A.C. 424 at 456–457.

not release the power, nor delegate it without authority.[73] They must appreciate that the discretion is theirs and not that of the settlor. If they merely obey the settlor's instructions without any independent consideration, they will be in breach of the duties described above, and any appointment made in such circumstances will be void.[74] These duties stem from the fact that the power is fiduciary; not from any duty to exercise the power. If they decide not to do so, the court will not interfere. It has been held, however, that the court must step in where a fiduciary power is left with no-one to exercise it.[75] In such a case the court can adopt any of the methods indicated by Lord Wilberforce in *McPhail v Doulton*[76] in the context of discretionary trusts, *i.e.* it may appoint new trustees, direct the beneficiaries to prepare a scheme of distribution, or itself direct a distribution.[77]

v. Powers Held in a Non-fiduciary Capacity. As is seen in Chapter 6, no duty is imposed upon a donee who holds a power in a non-fiduciary capacity. If a grandparent leaves property on trust for his grandchildren, and gives his son a power to appoint in favour of charity, the son is under no duty to appoint or even to consider the rival claims of charity or the grandchildren. He is, of course, if he makes an appointment, required to keep within the terms of the power, and to avoid exercising the power for an improper purpose.

vi. The Rule of Certainty in Ascertaining Beneficiaries or Objects. Reference should be made to Chapter 3, where this aspect of discretionary trusts is fully discussed.

vii. Discretionary Trusts Since 1974. Because of the change in tax policy, discretionary trusts of this type became unpopular in tax planning circles. As will be seen, such trusts created after March 1974 suffer higher rates of tax than those existing before the capital transfer tax legislation came into operation.[78] Since the introduction of inheritance tax, we have seen that discretionary trusts have suffered further by reason of their exclusion from the "potentially

---

[73] *Re Hay's S.T., supra.*
[74] *Turner v. Turner* [1984] Ch. 100.
[75] *Mettoy Pension Trustees Ltd v. Evans* [1990] 1 W.L.R. 1587 (fiduciary powers of company directors ceased on appointment of liquidator, but could not be exercised by liquidator or receiver because of conflict of duties); (1991) 107 L.Q.R. 214 (S. Gardner); [1991] Conv. 364 (J. Martin).
[76] *Supra.*
[77] *Mettoy Pension Trustees Ltd v. Evans, supra. Re Manisty's Settlement* [1974] Ch. 17, suggested that the only remedy was the appointment of new trustees, but *Klug v. Klug* [1918] 2 Ch. 67, *post*, p. 508, was not there cited.
[78] Relief was given on distributions before April 1983 from pre-1974 discretionary trusts; F.A. 1975, Sched. 5, para. 15; F.A. (No. 2) 1979, s.23(1)(*b*).

exempt transfer" regime.[79] The lifetime creation of such trusts is, therefore, taxable even if the settlor survives a further seven years. For this reason few discretionary trusts of substantial size (other than "offshore" trusts) are likely to be created under the present tax system,[80] although more modest discretionary trusts falling within the settlor's inheritance tax "nil rate band"[81] may still be attractive.

---

[79] *Ante*, p. 196.

[80] Unless they are within the class of discretionary trusts which are given preferential treatment, *e.g.* accumulation and maintenance trusts, *post*, p. 226.

[81] *Post*, p. 219. The reduction of the maximum lifetime rate to 20 per cent by F.A. 1988 alleviates the position to some extent.

CHAPTER 9

TAXATION AND TRUSTS[1]

1. Estate and Tax Planning	211	
2. The Tax Structure	212	
A. Income Tax	213	
B. Capital Gains Tax	215	
C. Inheritance Tax	216	
i. Estate Duty	217	
ii. Capital Transfer Tax	217	
iii. Inheritance Tax	218	
3. Inheritance Tax and Settlements	222	
A. Settlements in which There is an Interest in Possession	222	
B. Settlements in which There is No Interest in Possession	224	
i. Discretionary Trusts	224	
(a) The "Exit" Charge	225	
(b) The Decennial Charge	225	
(c) Rates of Tax	225	
ii. Accumulation and Maintenance Settlements	226	
C. Protective and Other Trusts	228	

1. ESTATE AND TAX PLANNING

THE most significant factor in the creation of trusts *inter vivos* has been the avoidance of taxation. A wealthy person may benefit the family by making gifts to them, and then leave property to them by will. But tax legislation imposes higher rates on larger accumulations of property, and this wealthy person will seek ways of conferring benefits on the family and at the same time reducing tax liability. The tax payable by 10 people on incomes of £5,000 each is less in total than that payable by one person with an income of £50,000. Similarly, tax on capital is at its highest in large concentrations. More details of the income, and especially of the capital tax system, will be given below. The point here is that a wealthy person can best preserve the family fortune by sharing out, and that this has commonly been done by creating lifetime trusts. This tax planning of an estate is one of the most important and sophisticated functions of trust lawyers.

Until comparatively recently the courts in determining the tax effectiveness of any scheme of tax avoidance applied the principle

---

[1] See Thomas, *Taxation and Trusts*; Shipwright, *Trusts and U.K. Taxation*; Maudsley and Burn, *Trusts and Trustees*; *Cases and Materials* (5th ed.), Part 3; Moffat, *Trusts Law, Text and Materials* (2nd ed.), Chap. 3; *Butterworths U.K. Tax Guide* (14th ed.), Chapter 11 (income tax), Chapter 18 (capital gains tax) and Chapters 41 and 42 (inheritance tax).

laid down by Lord Tomlin in *I.R.C. v. Duke of Westminister*[2]: "every man is entitled if he can to order his affairs so that the tax attaching under the appropriate Acts is less than it otherwise would be."[3] But starting in *W. T. Ramsay v. I.R.C.*,[4] the House of Lords began to elaborate a new and much more restrictive principle to apply in dealing with questions of the effectiveness of complex tax avoidance schemes. Where there occurs a pre-ordained series of transactions designed to reduce tax payable by a particular taxpayer the court is free to disregard any of those transactions if they are inserted for no good commercial purposes other than the reduction of tax. The transactions will be treated as a single composite whole and taxed accordingly. This principle applies to the creation and manipulation of trusts as well as to commercial and corporate dealings.[5]

As the circumstances of each individual differ, so each situation needs individual treatment. The estate- or tax-planner, with the assistance of accountants and other specialists, will present to the client various possible solutions, indicating the tax implications of each. The client must then decide how much to give away immediately and irrevocably, and to whom; and how much to keep; and, in days of inflation, many people will hesitate before making gifts, and thereby running the risk of leaving themselves short of capital in their old age. What is kept will be disposed of by will, and a testamentary trust may be created. Those whose fortunes are insufficient to create tax problems will not be concerned with *inter vivos* tax planning; but may, again, create testamentary trusts on their deaths.

2. The Tax Structure

To explain how best to minimise liability to tax, it is essential to explain the tax system in detail. There is no room to do that here, and only a few highlights can be given. It is in any case dangerous, in a book of this nature, to include too much detail; for each annual Budget may be expected to make some changes in the rates; and, if there is a change of Government, the policy behind the tax system also changes. Tax policy is often dictated more by political philosophy than by the search for a system which is rational and just.

[2] [1936] A.C. 1. The principle is confirmed in H.C.Deb., Vol. 226, col. 765 (1993).
[3] *Ibid.* at p. 19.
[4] [1982] A.C. 300. See also *I.R.C. v. Burmah Oil Co. Ltd* (1981) 54 T.C. 200; *Furness v. Dawson* [1984] A.C. 474; *Craven (Inspector of Taxes) v. White* [1989] A.C. 398 (where the House of Lords refused to extend this principle); *Ensign Tankers (Leasing) Ltd v. Stokes* [1992] 1 A.C. 655; *Moodie v. I.R.C.* [1993] 1 W.L.R. 266.
[5] *I.R.C. v. Fitzwilliam* [1993] 1 W.L.R. 1189 (but *Ramsay* principle did not apply on facts, Lord Templeman dissenting); [1994] Conv. 67 (J. Kirkbride).

The greatest revenue raiser is income tax. The net receipts from capital taxes have been disappointingly small.[6] A Government in need of money has therefore an interest in keeping income tax rates high; though the logic of the matter would seem to be that you should pay lower taxes on the money that you work for, than on inheritances. There was a substantial argument to the effect that income tax rates, reaching up to 83 per cent,[7] resulted in the stifling of initiative and enterprise.[8] The Conservative Government in 1979[9] heeded that argument and reduced the top rate to 60 per cent, and it has since been reduced to 40 per cent.[10] Further changes are likely.[11] The tax system has hitherto been regarded not only as a revenue raiser, but also as a means of promoting the social, economic and political philosophy of the Government.

A. Income Tax

Tax is chargeable upon an individual's taxable income[12] at the rates laid down annually in the Finance Act. At the present time, the first £3,900 of taxable income is subject to the lower rate of 20 per cent. The basic rate of 24 per cent is then payable on taxable income above £3,900 and up to £25,500; thereafter the rate is 40 per cent.[13] The additional rate payable by individuals on investment income has been abolished.[14] There are a number of allowances and reliefs to which individuals are entitled.

We are concerned, however, with the taxation of trusts. Trustees are not individuals for income tax purposes. Trusts as such therefore enjoy no personal allowances. Nor does the lower rate of 20 per cent apply.[15] The income of a trust is chargeable at the basic rate, and the trustees are assessable.[16] In a wider range of circumstances the

---

[6] In 1988/89 income tax raised 43.8 per cent of revenue, capital gains tax 2.4 per cent and inheritance tax 1.1 per cent; Budget speech, *The Times*, March 15, 1989. Income tax raised 25 per cent of revenue in 1995/96; *The Times*, November 29, 1995 (indirect taxation having increased).

[7] On incomes over £21,000 in 1979.

[8] For different views, see Kay and King, *The British Tax System* (5th ed.), Chap. 1.

[9] F.A. 1979 (No. 2), s.5.

[10] F.A. 1988, s.24(1).

[11] A commitment to a basic rate of 20 per cent was expressed in the Budget speech, November 28, 1995.

[12] I.C.T.A. 1988, s.835; and means income calculated in accordance with Scheds. A–F, I.C.T.A. 1988, ss.15–20. Schedules B and C have been abolished.

[13] F.A. 1996, s.72, amending I.C.T.A. 1988, s.1(2): See also F.A. 1996, s.73 (taxation of certain savings at lower rate). The 1996 Budget reduces the basic rate to 23 per cent, extends the 20 per cent band to £4,100 and raises the 40 per cent threshold to £26,100.

[14] F.A. 1984, s.17(2) and Sched. 7. The additional rate payable by trustees is not affected.

[15] F.A. 1992, s.9(2).

[16] There is no specific statutory provision. The higher rates do not apply to trustees because they are not "individuals"; I.C.T.A. 1988, s.1(2). See generally *Butterworth's U.K. Tax Guide* (14th ed.), pp. 590–591; (1991) 5 *Trust Law International*, 143 (M. Jacobs).

income arising under a trust may be treated as the settlor's income.[17]
The trustees need take no action in respect of income from most
stock exchange investments which effectively is paid net of basic
rate tax. The beneficiary who is entitled to the income is responsible
for the payment of any higher rate tax which may be due; and it is
often convenient to arrange for the dividends to be paid direct to
him. The trustees will, however, need to deduct and account for
income tax which is due on any income of the trust which has been
received without deduction of tax at the basic rate, such as income
from land or profits if they carry on a trade, and also for the
additional rate which becomes due in the case of the income of a
trust where there is no person currently entitled to the income.[18]

With such a trust, the income may either be paid out or, if the trust
contains such a power, it may be accumulated. If it is accumulated,
there is no tax liability beyond income tax at the basic rate plus the
additional rate (a total in 1996–97 of 34 per cent). Where the income
is paid to or for the benefit of a beneficiary, the ultimate tax liability
is dependent upon the beneficiary's tax situation.[19] He is treated as
having received the value of the payment grossed up to reflect basic
and additional rate tax.[20] If the beneficiary's taxable income is in
excess of £25,500, he will be liable to make up the difference
between the tax already paid (34 per cent) and the tax due at his
marginal rate (40 per cent). On the other hand, if his other income
does not exhaust his allowances and reliefs and the lower rate of 20
per cent, he may claim a repayment of an appropriate amount on
producing to the Revenue the trustees' certificate of deduction of
tax. It will thus be seen that income tax may be saved if the trustees
have a discretion as to the distribution of income, and use it to make
payments to those on low incomes whose tax rate is lower than the
trust's. Thus, £66 of trust income after tax at 34 per cent,[21] if paid
to a beneficiary whose taxable income, including the payment, is
£30,000, will bear another £6 in tax; but if paid to a child with no
income, the child would get a rebate of £34.[22] There is, of course, no
choice where the beneficiaries are entitled to the income or a
specified share. Moreover none of the above consequences apply if
the sum as received by the beneficiary is capital in his hands, for

---

[17] I.C.T.A. 1988, Part XV. See *Watson v. Holland* [1985] 1 All E.R. 290. These provisions are
intended to prevent and penalise tax avoidance.

[18] I.C.T.A. 1988, s.686; F.A. 1988, s.24(3). This includes income of a disretionary trust or an
accumulation and maintenance trust; *post*, p. 226. The additional rate is 10 per cent. on the
whole income of the trust, after deducting expenses properly chargeable to income under
the general law; *Carver v. Duncan (Inspector of Taxes)* [1985] A.C. 1082.

[19] But where the payment is in favour of the infant and unmarried child of the settlor, the
income is treated as that of the settlor: I.C.T.A. 1988, s.663; *post*, p. 575.

[20] I.C.T.A. 1988, s.687.

[21] Basic income tax at 24 per cent plus additional rate of 10 per cent.

[22] The child is entitled to the personal allowance of £3,765; I.C.T.A. 1988, s.257. The
allowance is raised to £4,045 in the 1996 Budget.

example where it is paid pursuant to a power of appointment restricted to capital or out of accumulated income.[23]

B. Capital Gains Tax

Capital gains tax was introduced by the Finance Act 1965, and originally imposed at a rate of 30 per cent upon the gains accruing upon the disposal of an asset. The Finance Act 1988 wrought significant changes in the tax. The position is now governed by the consolidating Taxation of Chargeable Gains Act 1992. The tax is charged at income tax rates (20, 24 and 40 per cent respectively).[24] In many cases the gain accruing on a disposal of an asset is computed as though the disposer's acquisition cost had been the market value of the asset on March 31, 1982.[25] Thus gains attributable to a period of ownership prior to the 1982 date escape tax.[26] Capital gains tax is payable upon a sale, exchange or gift.[27] The tax is not payable on death, though the deceased's property is deemed to be acquired by his personal representatives on his death at a consideration equal to its then market value.[28] This generally involves a "tax-free uplift" in the notional acquisition cost of the assets in question, since their market value at death is usually greater than the acquisition cost enjoyed by the deceased. When the personal representatives pass the assets to the legatee[29] no disposal is deemed to occur and the legatee acquires the assets with an acquisition cost equal to that of the personal representatives. Finally, capital gains tax is payable where disposals are deemed to occur, as where a capital sum is derived from an asset.[30]

There are many exemptions from liability to capital gains tax, the most important being an annual exemption of gains of £6,500 for individuals and £3,250 for a trust[31] the taxpayer's main or only residence,[32] a chattel worth less than £6,000[33] and dated gilt-edged securities.[34]

---

[23] I.C.T.A. 1988, s.687(1). See also *Stevenson (Inspector of Taxes) v. Wishart* [1987] 1 W.L.R. 1204.

[24] T.C.G.A. 1992, s.4, as amended. The rate for accumulation and discretionary trusts is 34 per cent; s.5.

[25] *Ibid.* s.35. The date is that of the introduction of indexation allowance.

[26] This is not so in all cases; s.35(3).

[27] Relief on gifts was withdrawn (with exceptions) by F.A. 1989, s.124.

[28] T.C.G.A. 1992, s.62.

[29] Defined in s.64(2) to include "any person taking under a testamentary disposition or on an intestacy or partial intestacy, whether he takes beneficially or as trustee ... "

[30] *Ibid.* ss.22–24. See also *Zim Properties v. Proctor* [1985] S.T.C. 90.

[31] *Ibid.* s.3, Sched. 1; Capital Gains Tax (Annual Exempt Amount) Order 1996 (S.I. 1996 No. 2957). The exemptions are index-linked.

[32] *Ibid.* s.222.

[33] *Ibid.* s.262.

[34] *Ibid.* s.115.

The settlor will be liable to capital gains tax on making the settlement since this is a disposal even where the settlor declares himself trustee.[35] Under the settlement, the trustees will be affected in two quite different ways.[36] First, in relation to the disposition of assets of the trust. On a disposal, the trustees are liable to tax on gains, as individuals would be.[37] This situation normally arises where trustees switch investments in the ordinary course of administration of the trust. There is no liability, however, on the trustees of a trust where the majority of the trustees are resident abroad, and the management of the trust is carried on abroad; liability is imposed on resident beneficiaries in relation to their interests under the trust. In certain circumstances gains of a non-resident trust may be attributed to beneficiaries for the purposes of liability.[38]

Secondly, there are certain occasions on which a disposal is deemed to have been made. Disposals are deemed to be made on various occasions, but the only one in this context on which tax is chargeable is that on which a person becomes absolutely entitled against the trustee[39] as, for example, where the beneficiary becomes absolutely entitled upon fulfilling a condition, such as majority, or where an advancement is made to a beneficiary. As originally enacted, tax was chargeable on the death of a life tenant, but that was changed by the Finance Act 1971[40] to bring the settlement provisions in line with the death rule for free estates. The abolition of capital gains tax and inheritance tax is envisaged as soon as resources allow.[41]

C. Inheritance Tax

Inheritance tax is a modified version of its predecessor, capital transfer tax. Estate duty was replaced by capital transfer tax by the Finance Act 1975,[42] with effect from March 26, 1974. This was part of a complete reorganisation of the structure of the taxation of capital, which was extended to lifetime gifts. A wealth tax, in the form of an annual tax on ownership of assets, was planned in 1974, but was never introduced. The application of capital transfer tax to

---

[35] *Ibid.* s.70. See also s.77.

[36] See generally (1991) 88/17 L.S.Gaz. 24 (M. Hutton); (1991) 5 *Trust Law International* 143 (M. Jacobs) and 152 (J. Brown).

[37] Unless the gains are chargeable on the settlor because he has an interest in the settlement; T.C.G.A. 1992, s.77.

[38] T.C.G.A. 1992, s.87.

[39] *Ibid.* s.71. See *Jenkins (Inspector of Taxes) v. Brown* [1989] 1 W.L.R. 1163; *Swires (Inspector of Taxes) v. Renton* [1991] S.T.C. 490. A deemed disposal, whether or not tax is charged, has the effect of establishing the acquisition value in the hands of the recipient.

[40] See now T.C.G.A. 1992, s.72.

[41] Budget speech, 1995 and 1996. A change of government would make this unlikely.

[42] The provisions are now consolidated by the Inheritance Tax Act 1984, hereafter referred to as I.H.T.A. 1984.

lifetime gifts was largely removed by the Finance Act 1986, in which the tax was renamed as inheritance tax.

i. Estate Duty. Before March 26, 1974, estate duty was the only tax on private capital. It was a death tax only, and payable upon property passing on a death.[43] It could therefore be avoided by disposing of property before death; save that transfers made within seven years before death were subject to the tax.[44]

The disposal would often be by the creation of an *inter vivos* trust. The settlor would wish to avoid estate duty, not only on his death, but also upon the deaths of the beneficiaries. It was held that estate duty was payable upon the whole capital of a trust upon the death of a life tenant, or of the holder of some other limited interest.[45] The members of a class of beneficiaries of a discretionary trust owned no interest, however, in the fund[46]; they had no more than a hope that the trustees' discretion would be exercised in their favour. It was possible, therefore, to avoid liability to estate duty, until 1969, on the death of the settlor and of any of the beneficiaries by creating a discretionary trust at least seven years before the death of the settlor.[47] No wonder that the tax was called a "voluntary tax." The Finance Act 1969 imposed a charge upon the death of any beneficiary who had received payments of income in the past seven years.[48] The charge was on a portion of the capital equivalent to the share of the income received by the deceased during the "relevant" period. This system had little time to work, and would not in any case have been very effective because the trustees of a discretionary trust could pay the income to those whom they judged least likely to die in the near future; and so long as the income was thus disposed of, there was no objection to making capital payments to the old and sick beneficiaries.[49]

ii. Capital Transfer Tax. In a White Paper on Capital Transfer Tax[50] and a Green Paper on Wealth Tax,[51] the Labour Government in 1974 announced its intention of imposing both taxes. The policy was to effect a levelling of wealth[52]; estate duty, with all its loopholes, had conspicuously failed to do so. Capital transfer tax was a

---

[43] F.A. 1894, ss.1, 2.

[44] F.A. 1968, s.35.

[45] *Cowley (Earl) v. I.R.C.* [1899] A.C. 198.

[46] Eventually so decided in *Gartside v. I.R.C.* [1968] A.C. 553; *ante*, p. 204.

[47] See *Pearson v. I.R.C.* [1980] Ch. 1, *per* Templeman L.J. at p. 25.

[48] ss.36, 37.

[49] See F.A. 1969, s.37(3)(*b*).

[50] Cmnd. No. 5705 of 1974.

[51] *Ibid.*

[52] "The Government is committed to use the taxation system to promote greater social and economic equality. This requires a redistribution of wealth as well as income." Preface to Green Paper.

tax on capital transfers, whether *inter vivos* or on death, and was planned to tax family capital, whether or not settled, at least once a generation. The Wealth Tax would go further, and impose a tax annually on capital. The imposition of a wealth tax would take some time, and the Government appreciated that it needed to be preceded by capital transfer tax.

Capital transfer tax in its original form was a cumulative tax applying to all transfers of value made by an individual after March 26, 1974 until his final transfer on death. Rates were progressive, and those chargeable on death (or on transfers within three years of death) were double those chargeable on lifetime transfers. The tax was modified by subsequent Conservative Governments, in particular by alleviating the cumulation principle. Instead of cumulating all transfers (made after March 26, 1974), only those made within the previous 10 years had to be cumulated, the figure finally being reduced to seven years.[53] The rates of tax being progressive, these amendments were beneficial to the transferor. Further substantial modifications were made by the Finance Act 1986, which renamed the tax as inheritance tax, to which we now turn.

ii. Inheritance Tax. The most significant changes brought about by the 1986 Act were the introduction of the "potentially exempt transfer" and the reintroduction of the estate duty principle of "reservation of benefit." These are explained in the outline of inheritance tax which follows.

The central concept of inheritance tax is the transfer of value, which may be chargeable, exempt or potentially exempt.[54] There is a transfer of value where a person makes a disposition as a result of which the value of his estate immediately after the disposition is less than it would have been but for the transfer, and the value transferred is the amount by which the estate is the less.[55] On a death, the deceased is treated as making a transfer of value of the whole of his estate immediately before the death.[56] There are special rules relating to settled property,[57] which will be examined below, and a number of exemptions and reliefs. The most important exemptions relate to transfers of any amount between spouses, whether *inter vivos* or on death,[58] certain foreign property,[59] and certain personal

---

[53] F.A. 1986, s.101.
[54] I.H.T.A. 1984, ss.1, 2.
[55] *Ibid.* s.3. It may include an omission to claim an entitlement: s.3(3).
[56] *Ibid.* s.4.
[57] *Ibid.* Pt. III.
[58] *Ibid.* s.18.
[59] *Ibid.* s.6, not strictly an exemption; but effectively so.

exemptions.[60] Other reliefs and exemptions relate to situations which were familiar with estate duty, and include gifts to charities, works of art, agricultural or business property, and woodlands. They cannot be examined here.

The exemptions referred to above may be described as substantive exemptions, to distinguish them from the potentially exempt transfer, introduced by the Finance Act 1986.[61] A lifetime transfer by an individual made on or after March 18, 1986 is potentially exempt. As in the days of estate duty, it becomes chargeable if the transferor does not survive for seven years. If he dies within three years, the rates are those chargeable on a death. If he dies between three and seven years from the transfer, there is a taper relief on a sliding scale.[62] In certain exceptional cases, in particular the creation of a discretionary trust, a lifetime disposition is *immediately* chargeable,[63] although at half the rates applicable on death.[64] If the settlor dies within seven years, the rates are increased as described above.

In the case of a lifetime transfer which is either initially chargeable or which becomes so by reason of death within seven years, and in the case of a transfer on death, the rates of tax are affected by any chargeable transfers within the previous seven years, which must be cumulated.[65] No tax will, however, be payable if the transfer falls within the "nil rate band," which stands at £200,000 at the time of writing.[66] Thereafter the rate is 40 per cent if the transfer was on death or within three years of death, and 20 per cent in the case of an initially chargeable lifetime transfer. As mentioned above, there is a sliding scale applicable to a potentially exempt transfer which becomes chargeable.[67]

In the case of an initially chargeable lifetime transfer, the tax may be paid by the transferor or the transferee. If it is paid by the transferor, the value of the chargeable transfer is the amount by which his estate is reduced, therefore the amount of the transfer for tax purposes must include the tax. It will be necessary to "gross up"

---

[60] *Ibid.* ss.19 *et seq.* These include £3,000 per donor per year; £250 per donee per year; normal expenditure out of income; gifts in consideration of marriage of various permitted amounts up to £5,000; and payments for the maintenance of dependants. (s.11). They give considerable scope for tax saving. It is obviously important for a donor to start his giving early, especially since the introduction of the potentially exempt transfer.

[61] I.H.T.A. 1984, s.3A, introduced by F.A. 1986, s.101 and Sched. 19.

[62] *Ibid.* s.7, as amended.

[63] *Ibid.* s.3A. The lifetime creation of an interest in possession trust was initially chargeable under the 1986 Act, but this rule was abrogated by F.(No. 2)A. 1987, s.96 and Sched. 7.

[64] *Ibid.* s.2.

[65] *Ibid.* s.7.

[66] F.A. 1996, s.183. The nil rate band is increased to £215,000 for transfers on or after April 6, 1997 by the 1996 Budget. 18,000 estates paid the tax in 1995, reducing to 14,000 in 1996/97. The yield for 1997/98 is expected to be £1.55 billion; Budget speech 1996.

[67] I.H.T.A. 1984, s.7(4).

the sum transferred. The amount of tax payable on any sum varies, not only with the size of the sum, but also with the total of prior chargeable transfers within the previous seven years. The calculations in any particular case can be formidable, and will be worked out in each case from grossing up tables. On the other hand, if the transferee pays the tax, the actual amount of the transfer is treated as the gross gift, and added to the transferor's total gifts. The amount of tax payable will be less; but the amount received by the transferee will also be less.

The last transfer which a person makes is that of the estate on death. The rates applicable are those which begin at the total value of any taxable lifetime gifts within the previous seven years, grossed up as necessary. There is no question of grossing up the estate at death. Any tax is deducted prior to distribution. The incidence of tax as between specific and residuary beneficiaries is another problem.[68]

It is thus necessary to keep a "score" of taxable lifetime gifts, pay tax on them as due, and apply the seven-year cumulation rule when calculating the tax liability on subsequent chargeable gifts, and ultimately on death. The tax planner's job is to enable the client to make the best use of available exemptions and reliefs, and of the potentially exempt transfer. The adviser's dilemma is that the calculations have to be made on a number of assumptions about future events and tax liabilities.

Before examining the special rules relating to trusts, mention must be made of the principle of reservation of benefit. Although familiar under the estate duty regime, this concept was not relevant to capital transfer tax. It was reintroduced by the Finance Act 1986 and is a fundamental feature of inheritance tax. The object of this principle is that the donor should not be permitted to take advantage of the potentially exempt transfer rule by making gifts where he effectively retains an interest.

Where an individual makes a gift on or after March 18, 1986 the property is treated as subject to a reservation in two cases. First, where possession and enjoyment of the property is not bona fide assumed by the donee prior to the seven-year period ending with the donor's death (or, if the donor died within seven years of the gift, at the date of the gift). Secondly, where the property is not enjoyed "to the entire exclusion, or virtually to the entire exclusion, of the donor and of any benefit to him by contract or otherwise" at any time during the seven years ending with his death (or, if the donor died within seven years of the gift, at any time after the gift[69]). There are

---

[68] I.H.T.A. 1984, ss.38, 39.
[69] F.A. 1986, s.102.

certain exceptions, for example where the donor occupies the property for full consideration in money or money's worth.[70] Nor does the principle apply where the gift falls within certain of the substantive exemptions, for example the spouse exemption.[71]

The effect of a gift with reservation of benefit is that the property is treated as remaining in the estate of the donor. Hence the making of a gift with reservation normally has no immediate inheritance tax consequence, but the property will be treated as part of the donor's estate on his death (at its value at that time) and taxed accordingly.[72] If during his lifetime there is a change of circumstances so that there is no longer a reservation of benefit, for example where the donor renounces any benefit he has retained, a potentially exempt transfer is treated as made at that time, so that the donor must survive a further seven years if tax is to be avoided.[73] If he dies within seven years, the property is taxed on its value at the date of the release of benefit, not of the prior gift. In the rare case where the lifetime gift is initially chargeable, as in the case of the creation of a discretionary trust, the property subject to a reservation will be treated as part of the settlor's estate on his death and taxed again, but relief is given against this double charge.[74]

There is, as yet, little authority on the interpretation of these provisions, but the cases on estate duty and comparable Commonwealth legislation afford guidance as to what is a reservation of benefit.[75] In the context of trusts, the settlor will be treated as reserving a benefit if he is among the class of objects of a discretionary trust,[76] even though he receives nothing. Similarly if the settlor is a remunerated trustee of the settlement.[77] The settlor does not, however, reserve a benefit by reason of being an unpaid trustee,[78] nor if he has a reversionary or leasehold interest in the settled property, because the subject-matter of the gift does not include the reversion,[79] or the leasehold interest.[80]

---

[70] *Ibid.* Sched. 20, para. 6.

[71] *Ibid.* s.102(5).

[72] *Ibid.* s.102(3).

[73] *Ibid.* s.102(4).

[74] *Ibid.* s.104; Inheritance Tax (Double Charges Relief) Regulations 1987 (S.I. 1987/1130).

[75] See *Chick v. Commissioner of Stamp Duties of New South Wales* [1958] A.C. 435; *Nichols v. I.R.C.* [1975] 1 W.L.R. 534; *Munro v. Commissioner of Stamp Duties of New South Wales* [1934] A.C. 61; *St. Aubyn v. Att.-Gen.* [1952] A.C. 11. See also (1986) 83 L.S.Gaz 3728. These authorities were applied in *Ingram v. I.R.C.* [1995] 4 All E.R. 334.

[76] *Att.-Gen. v. Heywood* (1887) 19 Q.B.D. 326. It does not seem that the inclusion of his spouse would have this effect; (1986) 83 L.S.Gaz. 3728.

[77] *Oakes v. Commissioner of Stamp Duties of New South Wales* [1954] A.C. 57.

[78] *Commissioner of Stamp Duties of New South Wales v. Perpetual Trustee Co. Ltd* [1943] A.C. 425; (1986) 83 L.S.Gaz. 3728.

[79] *Ibid.*

[80] *Ingram v. I.R.C.* [1995] 4 All E.R. 334.

3. Inheritance Tax and Settlements[81]

Family trusts have been used for many years as ways of avoiding tax. Not surprisingly, trusts in general, and discretionary trusts in particular, were treated harshly by the capital transfer and inheritance tax legislation. There are, for inheritance tax purposes, two broad categories of settlements; those in which there is an interest in possession and those in which there is not, these being primarily discretionary trusts. The rules relating to reservation of benefit, discussed above,[82] must be borne in mind in relation to both categories.

When the Finance Act 1986 introduced the potentially exempt transfer, the only type of trust to benefit from it was the accumulation and maintenance trust.[83] The lifetime creation of other settlements was initially chargeable irrespective of seven-year survival. This position was subsequently modified so that the lifetime creation of an interest in possession settlement is now potentially exempt.[84] The lifetime creation of a discretionary trust (other than an accumulation and maintenance trust) remains initially chargeable.

A. Settlements in Which There is an Interest in Possession

This category deals with the standard form situation of a fixed trust for successive beneficiaries, whose interests are specified in the trust instrument; as a trust for Mrs X for her life, and after her death for her children in equal shares. A beneficiary has an interest in possession if he is entitled to the income as it arises. He is so entitled even though the trustees have a power to revoke or to appoint elsewhere, but not if they have a power to accumulate the income, even if unexercised.[85] A person entitled to an interest in possession under such a trust is treated for the purposes of inheritance tax as being beneficially entitled to the property in which his interest subsists.[86] Mrs X would thus be regarded, for purposes of inheritance tax, not merely as the owner of a life interest in the trust property, but as the owner of the property itself. There are special

---

[81] I.H.T.A. 1984, Pt. III. "Settlement" is defined in s.43(2). For foreign elements, see *Butterworths U.K. Tax Guide* (14th ed.), Chapter 49.

[82] *Ante*, p. 220.

[83] *Post*, p. 226.

[84] F.(No. 2)A. 1987, s.96 and Sched. 7.

[85] See *Pearson v. I.R.C.* [1981] A.C. 753; (1980) 43 M.L.R. 712 (W. Murphy); (1980) 39 C.L.J. 246 (J. Tiley); (1981) 97 L.Q.R. 1; *Re Trafford's Settlement* [1985] Ch. 32; *Swales v. I.R.C.* [1984] 3 All E.R. 16; *Miller v. I.R.C.* [1987] S.T.C. 108.

[86] I.H.T.A. 1984, s.49. Accordingly, reversionary interests are "excluded property" (s.48); but there are exceptions (*ibid.*).

provisions to deal with cases where there is a shared entitlement to the income,[87] or where the beneficiary is entitled to a fixed amount,[88] and also for the beneficiary who is entitled to the use and enjoyment of property which does not produce income.[89]

When an interest in possession comes to an end, the person entitled to the interest is treated as having at that time made a transfer of value of his interest. His interest is regarded as coming to an end on his disposing of or surrendering his interest, or on its termination in whole or in part by an appointment being made of the property in which his interest subsisted.[90] Where the interest in possession terminates during the lifetime of the person entitled to it, the transfer is potentially exempt.[91] If the disposal is for a consideration in money or money's worth, the value of the property is treated as reduced by the amount of the consideration,[92] but in determining that amount, the value of a reversionary interest in the property (which the tenant for life may acquire on a partition) must be left out of account.[93] Additionally, depreciatory transactions between the trustees and the persons interested under the settlement (as where the value of the trust property is reduced by granting a long lease of the property at a low rent) are treated as transfers of value.[94] Where a person dies entitled to an interest in possession, he is treated as having made a transfer of value immediately before his death of the property in which the interest subsisted.[95]

As the coming to an end of an interest in possession is treated as a transfer of value by the person beneficially entitled to that interest, the *rate* of any tax chargeable is determined by his personal scorecard.[96] There is, however, no question of grossing up; for the value of the transfer is not the loss to the transferor, but the value of the property in which the interest subsisted.[97]

There are certain reliefs and exemptions.[98] No tax is payable where an interest in possession comes to an end and (subject to

---

[87] *Ibid.* s.50(1).

[88] *Ibid.* s.50(2).

[89] *Ibid.* s.50(5).

[90] *Ibid.* ss.51, 52.

[91] F.(No. 2)A. 1987, s.96.

[92] Which will be less than the value of the property in which the interest subsisted. See I.H.T.A. 1984, s.49(2), dealing with the case where more than the actuarial value is paid.

[93] *Ibid.* s.52(2).

[94] *Ibid.* s.52(3).

[95] *Ibid.*, s.4.

[96] *Ibid.* s.52(1). But the tax is payable out of the settled property, and the trustees are responsible for it, concurrently with the beneficiary; *ibid.* s.201.

[97] *Ibid.* s.52(1).

[98] Terminations under protective trusts are dealt with below. (*post*, p. 228). See also I.H.T.A. 1984, s.90 (trustees' annuities).

certain qualifications) it reverts to the settlor,[99] or to the spouse, widow or widower of the settlor.[1]

There is total or partial relief where the person whose interest comes to an end becomes on the same occasion entitled either to the property or to another interest in possession in the property; there is a potentially exempt transfer only to the extent that the value of the property to which he becomes entitled is less than the value of the property in which his interest subsisted.[2] If, however, the life tenant becomes absolutely entitled by purchasing the reversion, he makes a potentially exempt transfer of the amount of the purchase price.[3] The result of these rules in the case of partition is that there is a potentially exempt transfer of that part of the fund to which the remainderman becomes absolutely entitled.

Some of the general exemptions which apply to transfers of non-settled property apply also to termination of interests in possession, for example, transfers to a spouse or to charity, the annual exemption (£3,000) and marriage consideration[4]; and also transfers for family maintenance.[5] Finally, quick succession relief reduces the rate of tax where tax is payable on the termination of an interest in possession in settled property within five years of a previous chargeable transfer.[6]

B. Settlements in Which There is No Interest in Possession

i. Discretionary Trusts. In the context of inheritance tax, a discretionary trust means a settlement in which there is no interest in possession. Such trusts were hard hit by the original provisions of the 1975 Act, but the position was somewhat rationalised and ameliorated by the modifications of the Finance Act 1982.[7] The present code applies to "relevant property,"[8] meaning settled property in which there is no interest in possession, other than certain types of settlements which are preferentially treated.[9] As explained

---

[99] *Ibid.* s.54(1).
[1] *Ibid.* s.54(2).
[2] *Ibid.* s.53(2).
[3] Otherwise the life tenant could reduce the value of his taxable estate, as his free estate is reduced by the payment, while the value of the trust property in his estate is unaffected. See I.H.T.A. 1984, ss.10, 55.
[4] *Ibid.* s.57. But the small gifts exemption (£250) does not apply. Valuation reliefs on business and agricultural property are also available to settlements.
[5] *Ibid.* s.11.
[6] *Ibid.* s.141.
[7] It has also been mitigated by the reduction in rates; *post*, p. 226.
[8] *Ibid.*, s.58.
[9] *Ibid.* The exceptions include accumulation and maintenance trusts, discussed below, and the special trusts mentioned in section C., *infra*.

above, the lifetime creation of a discretionary trust is initially chargeable, although at half the rate applicable on death.[10]

(a) *The "Exit" Charge.* Tax is chargeable on any part of the funds which ceases to be "relevant property."[11] This covers not only the simple case of a payment of capital to a beneficiary, including the winding-up of the trust, but also the situation where the trustees convert the trust into a settlement with an interest in possession or into an accumulation and maintenance settlement.[12] There are certain exceptions to this rule; for example, no tax is payable in respect of a payment of costs or expenses, nor where the payment is income for income tax purposes in the hands of the recipient.[13] Only a limited number of the general exemptions, such as distributions to charity, are available.[14]

(b) *The Decennial Charge.* The "exit" charge alone is not sufficient, for the capital may not be distributed until the end of the trust period, which, as has been seen, may not occur until just before the end of the perpetuity period.[15] It is provided, therefore, that tax is payable on the whole of the settled funds every 10 years, although only at 30 per cent of the "effective rate," as described below.[16] Thus the capital is fully taxed broadly once a generation, whether the capital is distributed or retained, or the trust is converted into another form.

(c) *Rates of Tax.* Different rules apply to the "exit" charge and the decennial charge, although in both cases the rates applicable to lifetime transfers are used. Only an outline can be given here.

In the case of the decennial charge, tax is charged on the value of the "relevant property" on the day before the 10-year anniversary, at 30 per cent of the "effective rate" which would have been charged on a hypothetical transfer at that time, on the assumption that the hypothetical transferor's cumulative total to be taken into account includes the settlor's chargeable transfers during the seven years preceding the creation of the settlement, plus the amounts, if any, subjected to an "exit charge" in the 10 years before the 10-year anniversary in question.[17]

---

[10] *Ante*, p. 222.

[11] I.H.T.A. 1984, s.65(1)(*a*). Tax is also chargeable where the trustees make a disposition resulting in the reduction in the value of the property; s.65(1)(*b*). See *I.R.C. v. Macpherson* [1989] A.C. 159.

[12] *Post*, p. 226; *Inglewood (Lord) v. I.R.C.* [1983] 1 W.L.R. 366.

[13] I.H.T.A. 1984, s.65(5); *Stevenson (Inspector of Taxes) v. Wishart* [1987] 1 W.L.R. 1204. See also s.65(4), (6)–(8).

[14] The annual exemption (£3,000) is not available, nor does quick succession relief apply. The valuation reliefs, however, available for business and agricultural property, do apply.

[15] *Ante*, p. 198.

[16] I.H.T.A. 1984, ss.64, 66.

[17] *Ibid.* s.66.

In the case of the "exit" charge, the rate depends on whether the charge is payable before or after the first 10-year anniversary. In both cases the amount on which tax is payable is the amount by which the value of the "relevant property" is diminished by the event in question.[18] The rate before the first 10-year anniversary is the "appropriate fraction" of the rate payable on an assumed chargeable transfer made at the time of the "exit" charge, where the amount is the value of the settled property at the date of the settlement, and the hypothetical cumulative total is the settlor's chargeable transfers during the seven years prior to the creation of the settlement. The "appropriate fraction" is $3/10 \times N/40$, where N is the number of completed quarters (*i.e.* three-month periods) between the creation of the settlement and the chargeable event.[19] Different rules apply to settlements made before March 27, 1974.[20]

Where an "exit" charge arises after a 10-year anniversary, tax is charged at the "appropriate fraction" of the rate at which it was charged on the last 10-year anniversary. The "appropriate fraction" is $N/40$, where N is the number of completed quarters between the last 10-year anniversary and the chargeable event.[21] This rule applies also to settlements made before March 27, 1974.

Although discretionary trusts are treated more harshly than other settlements, the rates outlined above are not high. Now that the maximum lifetime rate is 20 per cent,[22] the rate of the decennial charge cannot exceed 6 per cent (being 30 per cent of the rate applicable to an actual transfer, as explained above). Furthermore, a discretionary trust within the nil rate band[23] retains some attraction.

ii. Accumulation and Maintenance Settlements.

An accumulation and maintenance settlement is one in which no interest in possession exists, but one or more beneficiaries will, on attaining a specified age not exceeding 25 years, become entitled to an interest in possession.[24]

It has long been common practice to create accumulation and maintenance settlements in favour of minor relatives, and to give to the trustees power to apply the income at their discretion for the maintenance and education of the minors, and to accumulate any

---

[18] "Grossing-up" occurs, *ibid.* s.65(2).

[19] *Ibid.* s.68.

[20] *Ibid.* s.68(6).

[21] *Ibid.* s.69.

[22] F.A. 1988, s.136.

[23] *Ante*, p. 219. On tax planning for discretionary trusts, see *Butterworths U.K. Tax Guide* (14th ed.), p. 1859.

[24] I.H.T.A. 1984, s.71. There are other conditions. See *Inglewood (Lord) v. I.R.C.* [1983] 1 W.L.R. 366.

income not so applied; and power to advance some or all of the capital for the advancement or benefit of the beneficiaries. The powers are now statutory,[25] subject to the expression of a contrary intention, and are discussed in more detail in Chapter 20.

Such trusts offer some attraction to a settlor who wishes to reduce his tax liability by setting up a trust for members of the family. The income of the trust will be taxed at the basic rate plus the additional rate.[26] Where income is paid to or applied for the maintenance and education of a beneficiary, the income, if the settlement is irrevocable,[27] is taxed according to the tax status of the beneficiary. But there is one important limitation. If the beneficiary is a minor unmarried child *of the settlor*,[28] any income paid to or applied for his maintenance or education is aggregated for tax purposes with the income of the settlor.[29] There is no aggregation, however, if such income is accumulated.

The lifetime creation of an accumulation and maintenance settlement is a potentially exempt transfer.[30] The advantage of such a trust is that it is not taxed under the principles, discussed above, which apply to settlements in which there is no interest in possession.[31] Such trusts are favourably treated because of the difficulties in the way of giving capital or income to a minor absolutely. Hence the decennial charge is not payable; nor is there any charge when a payment of capital is made to a beneficiary, as on an advancement, or when his interest vests; nor on the death of a beneficiary before becoming entitled.[32] Because of these advantages, tax is payable when a discretionary trust is converted into an accumulation and maintenance settlement.[33] In any event, the advantages of such a settlement are not permanently available. The trust will cease to qualify as an accumulation and maintenance settlement after 25 years have elapsed since its commencement, unless all the beneficiaries are grandchildren of a common grandparent.[34] Tax becomes chargeable when the settlement ceases to qualify.[35]

---

[25] T.A. 1925, s.31; *post*, p. 571.

[26] *Ante*, p. 213. The saving is not great when the top rate on unsettled income is only 40 per cent. See (1994) 110 L.Q.R. 84 (R. Kerridge).

[27] I.C.T.A. 1988, ss.663–665.

[28] *cf.* grandchildren of the settlor.

[29] I.C.T.A. 1988, s.663; *ante*, p. 214, n. 19.

[30] I.H.T.A. 1984, s.3A.

[31] *Ibid.* s.58(1)(*b*).

[32] *Ibid.* s.71(4). The beneficiary's interest in the income normally vests at the age of 18; T.A. 1925, s.31(1)(ii).

[33] *Ibid.* s.65(1)(*a*); *Inglewood (Lord) v. I.R.C., supra.*

[34] *Ibid.* s.71(2).

[35] *Ibid.* s.71(3)(*a*). Also where the trustees enter into a "depreciatory transaction." Tax is charged in the same manner as under s.70 (temporary charitable trusts).

C. Protective and Other Trusts

Other forms of trusts which are entitled to special treatment are protective trusts,[36] superannuation schemes,[37] trusts for the benefit of employees[38] and for disabled persons,[39] charitable trusts,[40] newspaper trusts,[41] maintenance funds for historic buildings,[42] and various special compensation funds, such as those maintained by Lloyd's and the Law Society.[43]

A protective trust does not fit neatly into the two categories into which trusts are divided for inheritance tax purposes; for there is an interest in possession during the currency of the interest of the principal beneficiary, but a discretionary trust after the forfeiture. There is a charge to inheritance tax upon the death of the principal beneficiary; but not on the forfeiture of his interest, which, for the purpose of inheritance tax, is deemed to continue during the currency of the discretionary trusts which then arise.[44]

---

[36] I.H.T.A. 1984, s.88; *ante*, Chap. 7.
[37] *Ibid.* ss.58(1)(*d*), 151.
[38] *Ibid.* s.86.
[39] *Ibid.* s.89.
[40] *Ibid.* s.58(1)(*a*). As to temporary charitable trusts, see s.70.
[41] *Ibid.* s.87.
[42] *Ibid.* s.58(1)(*c*) and Sched. 4.
[43] *Ibid.* s.58(1)(*e*).
[44] *Ibid.* s.88. See *Cholmondeley v. I.R.C.* [1986] S.T.C. 384.

CHAPTER 10

RESULTING TRUSTS

1. General 229
   A. Where the Trust is Implied 230
   B. Incompete Disposal 230
   C. Voluntary Conveyance 230
   D. Purchase Money Resulting Trust 231
   E. To Reach the Just Result 231
2. Conveyance to Trustees 231
   A. Where a Trust Fails 231
   B. Incomplete Disposal of Beneficial
      Interest 232
   C. Methods of Disposal of Surplus
      Funds 233
     i. Transfer to Persons for Particular
       Purposes 234
     ii. Surplus Funds on Dissolution of
       Unincorporated Associations 235
       (a) Trust or Contract 235
       (b) Meaning of Dissolution 235
       (c) Resulting Trust for Members . 236
       (d) Contractual Basis 237
        (e) Method of Distribution
         Among the Members 240
     iii. Trust and Charge 241
   D. No Declaration of Trust 241
3. Voluntary Conveyance and the
   Presumptions 244
   A. Presumption of Resulting Trust;
      Conveyance to a Third Party 244
     i. Land 244
     ii. Personalty 245
   B. Presumption of Advancement 246
     i. Husband and Wife 246
      (a) Gift by Husband 246
      (b) Rebuttal 247
     ii. Father and Child 248
     iii. Other Relationships 248
     iv. Admissibility of Donor's
       Statements 249
     v. Transfers for Unlawful
       Purposes 249
4. Purchase Money Resulting Trusts 254
   A. Purchase in the Name of Another 254
     i. Presumption in Favour of the
      Purchaser 254
     ii. Presumption of Advancement 255
   B. Purchase by Several in the Name of
     One 255
5. Reform 257

1. GENERAL

A RESULTING trust is a situation in which a transferee is required by equity to hold property on trust for the transferor; or for the person who provided the purchase money for the transfer. The beneficial interest results, or comes back to the transferor or to the party who makes the payment. In effect the resulting trust is the basis of a claim to recover one's own property.[1] This situation can arise in a wide variety of circumstances, and it has been seen that resulting trusts overlap with other categories.[2]

---

[1] See *MacMillan Inc. v. Bishopsgate Investments Trust plc (No. 3)* [1995] 1 W.L.R. 978 at p. 989.
[2] *Ante*, pp. 65, 67.

Resulting trusts are not subject to all the rules of express trusts. Their creation is not dependent on compliance with formalities[3]; and a minor may be a resulting trustee.[4]

There are five basic types of situation in which resulting trusts arise.

A. Where the Trust is Implied

If A transfers property to B in circumstances in which it is clear from the acts or statements of the parties that A intended that B should hold on trust for him, B will hold on resulting trust. This may be better classified as an express trust. But, like the distinction between express and implied contracts, the precise dividing line between the two is impossible to find. In *Barclays Bank Ltd v. Quistclose Investments Ltd*[5] an intention was found that the Bank should hold the funds on trust for the plaintiffs, who provided them, if they could not be used to pay the Rolls Razor dividend; but there was no formal declaration. This could be regarded as an express or resulting trust.

B. Incomplete Disposal

Where property is conveyed to a person in the capacity of a trustee, there will be a resulting trust for the grantor of any part of the beneficial interest which is not disposed of. This result arises by operation of law. It is sometimes called an automatic[6] resulting trust. Such a resulting trust may be excluded expressly or impliedly.[7] It will be discussed in more detail in section 2.

C. Voluntary Conveyance

A conveyance to a third party will in some circumstances give rise to a resulting trust for the transferor. The trust will be raised by a presumption of a resulting trust. The presumption may of course be rebutted. In the case of a conveyance to the transferor's wife or child or to a person to whom the transferor is *in loco parentis*, the

---

[3] L.P.A. 1925, s.53(2).

[4] *Re Vinogradoff* [1936] W.N. 68.

[5] [1970] A.C. 567; *ante* p. 50. See also *Carreras Rothmans Ltd v. Freeman Mathews Treasure Ltd* [1985] Ch. 207 (contractual arrangement whereby money paid into a special bank account for a specific purpose created a trust); *cf. Re Multi Guarantee Co. Ltd* [1987] B.C.L.C. 257; *Re E.V.T.R. Ltd* [1987] B.C.L.C. 647 (*Quistclose* principle applied to loan for specific purpose which partially failed).

[6] *Re Vandervell's Trusts (No. 2)* [1974] Ch. 269, by Megarry J.

[7] *Davis v. Richards & Wallington Industries Ltd* [1990] 1 W.L.R. 1511, *post*, p. 239. For this reason Lord Browne-Wilkinson has doubted the "automatic" classification; *Westdeutsche Landesbank Girozentrale v. Islington London Borough Council* [1996] A.C. 669 at p. 708. See generally [1996] R.L.R. 3 (P. Birks).

presumption is reversed by the presumption of advancement. These matters are discussed in section 3.

D. Purchase Money Resulting Trust

Closely related to the previous category are conveyances to transferees who provide none or only part of the purchase price. This category includes cases where the conveyance is made to A, but some or all of the purchase price is provided by B, or where the conveyance is to persons jointly, but the purchase price is provided unequally. The complex questions of the division of property ownership between spouses or cohabitants, where the contribution to the family may be in ways other than the payment of money, will be dealt with in outline in Chapter 11.

E. To Reach the Just Result

In some situations, it is necessary in the interests of justice that a transferee should hold property on trust for the transferor; for example if the transfer is obtained by fraud. *Bannister v. Bannister*[8] and *Hodgson v. Marks*[9] may be regarded as coming within this category. There are other situations where, in the absence of fraud, a trust for the transferor is necessary to reach a just result. These situations clearly overlap with constructive trusts. Lord Denning in *Hussey v. Palmer*[10] said "Although the plaintiff alleged that there was a resulting trust, I should have thought that the trust in this case, if there was one, was more in the nature of a constructive trust; but this is more a matter of words than anything else. The two run together." These situations are considered in Chapter 12.

2. Conveyance to Trustees

A. Where a Trust Fails

A resulting trust may arise on the failure, for a variety of reasons, of an express trust. In *Morice v. Bishop of Durham*,[11] the trusts were

---

[8] [1948] 2 All E.R. 133.
[9] [1971] Ch. 892; *post*, p. 244.
[10] [1972] 1 W.L.R. 1286 at p. 1289; *Heseltine v. Heseltine* [1971] 1 W.L.R. 342; *Binions v. Evans* [1972] Ch. 359; *Cooke v. Head* [1972] 1 W.L.R. 518; *Eves v. Eves* [1975] 1 W.L.R. 1338; *Re Densham* [1975] 1 W.L.R. 1519. See also *Passee v. Passee* [1988] 1 F.L.R. 263 at 269, suggesting that a trust arising from a contribution to the acquisition of the home could be called implied, constructive or resulting, the latter being "not inappropriate".
[11] (1804) 8 Ves. 399; (1805) 10 Ves. 522; *post*, p. 351. See also *Simpson v. Simpson* [1992] 1 F.L.R. 601 (transferee of bank deposit held on resulting trust for transferor where the latter lacked mental capacity to make a gift).

void; so also in *Re Diplock*,[12] where a large sum of money was left to be applied for purposes which the executors thought to be charitable, and was distributed among a number of charitable institutions. The trusts were void. The next-of-kin were entitled under a resulting trust; and they were able to recover the bulk of the money from the charities. In *Essery v. Cowlard*,[13] an intending wife executed a pre-nuptial settlement in which she conveyed the trust property to trustees upon trust for herself, the intended husband and the issue of the marriage. The marriage never took place, but the parties cohabited and children were born. Six years later, the plaintiff successfully reclaimed the property. The trusts failed as the "contract to marry had been definitely and absolutely put an end to."

In *Re Ames' Settlement*[14] property had been settled by the husband's father upon the trusts of a marriage settlement, and the marriage took place. Eighteen years later the wife obtained a decree of nullity (which then had the effect of declaring the marriage void *ab initio*).[15] Vaisey J. decided, after the husband's death, that the property was held on a resulting trust for the executors of the settlor.

There is no resulting trust, however, where money is paid under a void transaction, in which case the recipient is subject to personal restitutionary liability.[16]

B. Incomplete Disposal of Beneficial Interest

Unskilful draftsmanship and the failure to foresee and provide for future contingencies may leave the beneficial ownership incomplete.[17] A resulting trust will then arise, although, as will be seen, some sets of circumstances can render this result so inconvenient that other solutions are sought.

The fact that an equitable interest is not fully disposed of may not become apparent until some time has elapsed since the constitution of the trust.

---

[12] [1941] Ch. 253; [1944] A.C. 341; *sub nom. Chichester Diocesan Fund and Board of Finance (Incorporated) v. Simpson*; [1948] Ch. 465; [1951] A.C. 251; *sub. nom. Ministry of Health v. Simpson; post*, p. 662.

[13] (1884) 26 Ch.D. 191; *Burgess v. Rawnsley* [1975] Ch. 429 (if conveyance taken jointly for a purpose which fails, resulting trust to each party of his share. Majority view that must be a common purpose).

[14] [1946] Ch. 217.

[15] A decree of nullity in respect of a voidable marriage now operates to annul the marriage only from the date of the decree absolute; Matrimonial Causes Act 1973, s.16. See also the court's power to make property adjustments under s.24.

[16] *Westdeutsche Landesbank Girozentrale v. Islington London Borough Council* [1996] A.C. 669 (*ultra vires* contract). The judgment in *Re Ames, supra*, was regarded as confused; *ibid.* at p. 715.

[17] See *Re Cochrane* [1955] Ch. 309; *John v. George* [1995] 1 E.G.L.R. 9 (conveyance to trustees on trust for daughter at 18 gave rise to resulting trust until she reached 18).

In *Re Trusts of the Abbott Fund*[18] a sum of money was collected, to be used for the maintenance of two deaf and dumb ladies. It was held by Stirling J. that the ladies had no enforceable interests in the capital sum and that on their death, the sum remaining went on resulting trust to the subscribers.

The consequent problem of distribution on resulting trust among subscribers becomes acute when the number of subscribers is great, and the gifts are mostly anonymous, as in *Re Gillingham Bus Disaster Fund.*[19]

A number of marine cadets were injured or killed when a bus was driven into the rear of a marching column. The mayors of three towns appealed for subscriptions to a fund that would initially care for the disabled and thereafter be available for "worthy causes" in memory of those killed. More money was contributed than could be used for the object (liability at common law for the accident having been accepted) and the second object failed as it had not been confined within the limit of legal charity.[20] Harman J. held that, despite the manifest inconvenience of such a decision, a resulting trust arose. All subscribers, large or small, intended to contribute to a specific purpose; on that purpose being attained or no longer attainable, each donor had an interest by way of resulting trust. There was no evidence on which to arrive at any other conclusion. The suggestion that the money should be treated as *bona vacantia* was regarded by Harman J. as taking the line of least resistance in a manner unauthorised by law. "The resulting trust arises where [the donor's] expectation is for some unforeseen reason cheated of fruition and is an inference of law based on after-knowledge of the event."[21]

C. Methods of Disposal of Surplus Funds

A resulting trust is not, however, the most appropriate solution in many situations; and, although something of a digression, it will be convenient here to examine other solutions. The question arises particularly in two contexts: First, that of gifts to persons for stated

[18] [1900] 2 Ch. 326, *post*, p. 234.
[19] [1958] Ch. 300, *post*, p. 238.
[20] Charities Act 1993, s.14 (*post*, p. 442) provides the most convenient solution to this type of case, but it applies only when the gift is charitable. The fund was finally wound up in 1965, when the remainder of the money was paid into court. It was announced on April 5, 1993, that the money (£7,300) was to be paid out and used for a memorial to the victims. For a different solution, see *Re West Sussex Constabulary's Widows, Children and Benevolent Fund Trust* [1971] Ch. 1, *post*.
[21] [1958] Ch. 300 at p. 310.

purposes, without specifying what is to be done when the purposes are completed; and, secondly, in the context of the dissolution of unincorporated associations.

In determining the correct solution in each of these contexts, two points will be of particular significance. First, did the transferor intend to dispose of his whole interest; or did he intend to transfer for a particular purpose only? Secondly, was the transfer made to a person in a capacity of trustee? If so, a resulting trust may be expected of the surplus.

i. Transfer to Persons for Particular Purposes. If property is given for the care and maintenance of certain persons, what is to happen to the property when the period of maintenance comes to an end? Do the intended beneficiaries (or their estates) keep the property, or does it return on a resulting trust to the donor? The answer will depend on the intention of the donor, which has to be ascertained from all the surrounding circumstances. The construction of the gift in *Re Trusts of the Abbott Fund*[22] may be regarded as unusual. It will be noted that the beneficiaries in that case had died. More commonly, the gift is regarded as absolute. The principle of construction was laid down in *Re Sanderson's Trust*[23] as follows: "If a gross sum be given, or if the whole income of the property be given, and a special purpose be assigned for that gift, the court always regards the gift as absolute, and the purpose merely as the motive of the gift, and therefore holds that the gift takes effect as to the whole sum or the whole income, as the case may be." Thus,

In *Re Andrew's Trust*,[24] a fund was subscribed for the infant children of a deceased clergyman. An accompanying letter showed that the contributions were made "for or towards their education; . . . as being necessary to defray the expenses of all, and that solely in the matter of education." After their formal education was completed, the question arose of the disposal of the surplus. Kekewich J. decided that the children were entitled in equal shares.

In *Re Osoba*[25] there was a gift by will of a residuary estate, consisting, for present purposes, of a freehold house in London, to the testator's widow on trust to be used "for her maintenance and for the training of my daughter up to University grade and for the maintenance of my aged mother . . . " The mother predeceased the testator; the widow died in 1970, and the daughter's education

[22] [1900] 2 Ch. 326.
[23] *Per* Page Wood V.-C. (1857) 3 K. & J. 497 at p. 503; *Barlow v. Grant* (1684) 1 Vern. 255.
[24] [1905] 2 Ch. 48.
[25] [1979] 1 W.L.R. 247.

up to university grade was completed in 1975. The children under an earlier marriage claimed the residue on intestacy.

The Court of Appeal found that the testator's intention was to provide absolute gifts for the beneficiaries, the references to maintenance and to education being expressions of motive. In the absence of words of severance, the beneficiaries took as joint tenants, with the daughter becoming entitled, on her mother's death, to the whole. The result would have been the same if the daughter had not gone to university.

ii. Surplus Funds on Dissolution of Unincorporated Association.[26]

(a) *Trust or Contract.* As will be seen in Chapter 14, funds of such an association will sometimes be held by trustees on an express trust for the members and sometimes by the treasurer or committee on a bare trust; in either case the property rights in the assets of the society are likely to be governed by the rules of the society which operate as a contract between the members. The question whether the property is held upon the terms of any trust created by the donor, or whether it is held by the members absolutely according to their contractual rights is relevant here also. The question commonly arises on a dissolution. It will be seen in the analysis which follows that the distinction between rights governed by a trust and those governed by a contract has not always been kept clear. In the case of a failure of a trust, the most appropriate solution is by way of resulting trust. In a case of dissolution of a society where the rights of the members are governed by a contract (*i.e.* by the rules of the society) the likely solution is in accordance with the terms of the contract; and if the contract is silent; by equal division among the members. The Crown might claim the fund as *bona vacantia*. It may also have to be considered whether any third party contributors may have a claim to participate in the distribution along with the members. Whether the matter is regarded as one of trust or contract affects the question of who is entitled and the calculation of the share. All these solutions will be demonstrated here, although the analysis in the earlier cases was subject to criticism by Walton J. in *Re Bucks Constabulary Fund (No. 2).*[27]

(b) *Meaning of Dissolution.* An association may be wound up in a formal manner, but in the absence of a formal dissolution, the question arises as to the circumstances which will justify a finding

---

[26] See generally Warburton, *Unincorporated Associations: Law & Practice* (2nd ed.); [1992] Conv. 41 (S. Gardner). For the meaning of "unincorporated association" see *Conservative and Unionist Central Office v. Burrell* [1982] 1 W.L.R. 522, *post*, p. 364.
[27] [1979] 1 W.L.R. 936; *post*, p. 238.

that the body has ceased to exist. In *Re G.K.N. Bolts and Nuts Ltd (Automotive Division) Birmingham Works, Sports and Social Club*,[28] the trustees of a social club had purchased a sports ground for £2,200 in 1946. In 1975, membership cards ceased to be issued and the last annual general meeting was held. No further accounts were taken, the stock of drinks was sold and the steward dismissed. A special meeting was convened on December 18, 1975 to deal with an offer to buy the land. Resolutions were passed that the land be sold, but no sale then took place. In 1978, the trustees sold the land for £253,000. One question which arose was the date the club ceased to exist.[29] It was held that mere inactivity did not suffice, unless it was so prolonged or so circumstanced that the only reasonable inference was spontaneous dissolution, in which case the court must select a date. On the facts, it ceased to exist on December 18, 1975, on the basis of inactivity coupled with positive acts to wind it up. This would be so even if the resolution to sell the land was invalid, as by that date the club's activities had ceased and it had become incapable of carrying out its objects.

(c) *Resulting Trust for Members*. In *Re Printers' and Transferrers' Society*,[30] a society was founded to raise funds by weekly contributions to defend and support its members in maintaining reasonable remuneration for their labour, and to provide strike and lock-out benefits for members. The scale of payments varied according to the length of time a claimant had been a member of the society, and different conditions applied to printers and transferrers respectively. No provision was made by the rules for the distribution of the funds of the society on a dissolution. At the time of its dissolution the society consisted of 201 members, and its funds amounted to £1,000. The question arose as to how the sum was to be distributed. The Attorney-General made no claim to the fund as *bona vacantia*. It was held that there was a resulting trust in favour of those who had subscribed to the fund, and that the money was divisible amongst the existing members at the time of the dissolution, in proportion to the amount contributed by each member to the funds of the society irrespective of fines, or payments made to members in accordance with the rules.

In *Re Hobourn Aero Components Air Raid Distress Fund*,[31] a fund was established during the Second World War for employees of

---

[28] [1982] 1 W.L.R. 774; [1983] Conv. 315 (R. Griffith). See also *Re William Denby & Sons Ltd Sick and Benevolent Fund* [1971] 1 W.L.R. 973; *Re Bucks Constabulary Widows' and Orphans' Fund Friendly Society (No. 2)* [1979] 1 W.L.R. 936.

[29] The question of entitlement to the money is dealt with *post*, p. 241.

[30] [1899] 2 Ch. 184.

[31] [1946] Ch. 86 (affirmed *ibid.* at p. 194), see especially pp. 97–98; following *Re British Red Cross Balkan Fund* [1914] 2 Ch. 419, (which is doubted in Tudor, *Charities* (8th ed.), at p. 354, n. 74).

a company who were on war service or who sustained loss in air raids. The fund was financed by voluntary subscriptions among the employees, but it was not charitable. The Crown made no claim to the fund as *bona vacantia*. After the war, the fund was found to have a surplus. It was held that each contributor, past or present, had an interest in the surplus by way of resulting trust in proportion to the amount he had contributed, but subject to adjustment in relation to any benefit he had received from the fund.

This conclusion, although logically consistent with the resulting trust analysis, is less convenient than the decision in *Re Printers' and Transferrers' Society*,[32] in that it concentrates attention on all the contributors to a society, however remote in time past, and not on those who have retained a connection with it. There is much to be said for the simpler solution of the earlier case, which, however, Cohen J. in the present case thought defensible only in cases where the ascertainment of the true entitlements would be too difficult.[33]

(d) *Contractual Basis.* In *Cunnack v. Edwards*,[34] a society governed by the Friendly Societies Act 1829[35] had been established in 1810 to raise a fund, by the subscriptions, fines and forfeitures of its members, to provide annuities for the widows of its deceased members. By 1879 all the members had died. The last widow-annuitant died in 1892, the society then having a surplus of £1,250. A claim to the assets was made by the personal representatives of the last surviving members. It was held that there was no resulting trust in favour of the personal representatives of the members of the society. Each member had paid away his money in return for the protection given to his widow, if he left one. "Except as to this he abandoned and gave up the money for ever."[36] The assets went to the Crown as *bona vacantia*.[37]

In *Re West Sussex Constabulary's Widows, Children and Benevolent (1930) Fund Trust*,[38] a fund had been established to provide benefits to widows and certain dependants of members who died. The income of the fund came from members' subscriptions, the proceeds of entertainments, sweepstakes, raffles and collecting boxes and various donations and legacies. On the amalgamation of

---

[32] [1899] 2 Ch. 184.

[33] *Cf. Davis v. Richards & Wallington Industries Ltd* [1990] 1 W.L.R. 1511, *post*, p. 239, where such difficulties were held to exclude a resulting trust in favour of the *bona vacantia* solution.

[34] [1896] 2 Ch. 679; (1966) 30 Conv.(N.S.) 117 (H. Hickling); (1980) 43 M.L.R. 626 (B. Green). The decision was distinguished in *Re Bucks Constabulary Fund (No. 2)*, *infra*, as turning upon the combined effect of the rules and the 1829 Act.

[35] For the special position of Friendly Societies, see Warburton, *Unincorporated Associations: Law & Practice* (2nd ed.), pp. 5–6.

[36] [1896] 2 Ch. 679 at p. 683.

[37] Ing; *Bona Vacantia.*

[38] [1971] Ch. 1; (1971) 87 L.Q.R. 464 (M. Albery).

the West Sussex Constabulary with other police forces in 1968, the question arose of the distribution of the fund.

Goff J. held that the surviving members had no claim because first, the members had received all that they had contracted for,[39] and secondly, the money was paid on the basis of contract, and not of trust. The funds went as *bona vacantia* to the Crown. The possibility that living members may have a contractual claim on the basis of frustration of the contract or failure of consideration was met by the Crown giving an indemnity to the trustees.

Contributions from outside sources were divided into three categories. The first two, proceeds of entertainments, etc., and collecting boxes, could not be the subject of a resulting trust,[40] they were out-and-out payments.[41] Identifiable donations, however, and legacies were in a different position. The object of the gift had failed, and the property was held on resulting trust. On the latter point, it is difficult to see why third party contributors, even if identifiable, should have any claim in such circumstances. The validity of the initial gift is usually explained on the basis that it is an absolute gift to the members of the association.[42] If that is so, such contributions should be dealt with on the same basis as the rest of the funds. It is submitted that there is no room here for a resulting trust for third parties.

The more acceptable modern solution to the distribution of assets of an unincorporated society is among the members. The matter is regarded as one of contract between the members, express or implied. On this analysis, the resulting trust solution is no longer appropriate. This is so, even though the assets of the society may be vested in trustees; as is indeed required in the case of unincorporated Friendly Societies.[43] The trustees then hold the assets on trust for the members according to the rules of the society. The rules may provide for the distribution upon dissolution. Otherwise, the assets will be divided among the members at the time of the dissolution.

Re Bucks Constabulary Fund (No. 2)[44] was another case of the distribution of a fund established to provide benefits for the widows and orphans of deceased police officers and the provision of payments on the death of a member or during sickness. The

---

[39] *Cf. Davis v. Richards & Wallington Industries Ltd* [1990] 1 W.L.R. 1511, *post.*

[40] Not following *Re Gillingham Bus Disaster Fund* [1958] Ch. 300, *ante*, p. 233.

[41] *Re Welsh Hospital (Netley) Fund* [1921] 1 Ch. 655; *Re Hillier's Trusts* [1954] 1 W.L.R. 9; *Re Ulverston and District New Hospital Building Trust* [1956] Ch. 672.

[42] *Post*, p. 361.

[43] Friendly Societies Act 1974 s.49(1). The Friendly Societies Act 1992 provides for the incorporation of Friendly Societies carrying on mutual insurance business for the members and their families.

[44] [1979] 1 W.L.R. 936; (1980) 39 C.L.J. 88 (C. Rickett); (1980) 43 M.L.R. 626 (B. Green).

Bucks Constabulary amalgamated with other constabularies and in 1968 the fund was wound up.

The question of the proper method of distribution came before Walton J., who held that the assets should be divided equally among members alive at the date of dissolution. If the society was moribund, as where there were no members or only one member left, the property would be ownerless. Only then would the Crown be entitled.[45] Walton J. emphasised the distinction between property held under the terms of the trust, and that governed by contract. In such a case, quoting Brightman J.,[46] "The right of the member of the fund to receive benefits is a contractual right and the member ceases to have any interest in the fund if and when he has received the totality of the benefits to which he was contractually entitled. In other words, there is no possible claim by any member founded on a resulting trust.... If it has been dissolved or terminated, the members entitled to participate would prima facie be those persons who were members at the date of dissolution or termination."[47]

The *West Sussex*[48] decision, although distinguishable on the ground that it did not involve a Friendly Society, was criticised by Walton J. on the basis that the principle of law applicable to the members' club cases should have governed the distribution. It made no difference whether or not the association was for the benefit of the members themselves. They controlled the assets, which were theirs all along. Thus *bona vacantia* was not an appropriate solution in that case.

A different view was taken in *Davis v. Richards & Wallington Industries Ltd*,[49] which concerned entitlement to the surplus funds on termination of a pension scheme. To the extent that any of the surplus derived from employees' contributions, Scott J. considered, obiter,[50] that neither the contractual background nor the fact that the employees had obtained all that they bargained for under the contract, necessarily prevented a resulting trust. Such a trust was, however, excluded by implication, partly because it would be unworkable (because the employees had different rights) and partly because the scheme was based on legislation which placed a maximum on the financial return to which the employees would be

[45] *cf. Davis v. Richards & Wallington Industries Ltd* [1990] 1 W.L.R. 1511, *post.*
[46] *Re William Denby and Sons Ltd Sick and Benevolent Fund* [1971] 1 W.L.R. 973 at p. 978.
[47] [1979] 1 W.L.R. 936 at p. 948.
[48] *Supra.*
[49] *Supra*; [1991] Conv. 366 (J. Martin); [1992] Conv. 41 (S. Gardner); (1992) 6 *Trust Law International* 119 at p. 124 (Lord Browne-Wilkinson); (1994) 8 *Trust Law International* 35 at p. 37 (Vinelott J.). *Re Bucks* was cited but not referred to.
[50] In fact the employers were entitled under the trust deed.

entitled without loss of tax relief: this prevented imputing an intention to them to have any surplus.[51] Thus the *bona vacantia* solution was preferred in relation to the employees, although there was no reason to exclude a resulting trust with respect to the employers' contributions. The decision seems out of line with the modern trend in favour of a contractual *per capita* distribution, but shows that this approach can be sidestepped if it would lead to an inconvenient result.

(e) *Methods of Distribution Among the Members.* If entitlement is on the basis of a resulting trust, the distribution will be made amongst all members, past and present, including personal representatives of deceased members, in shares proportionate to their contributions. Past members will be excluded if the calculation would prove too difficult.[52] We have seen, however, that the resulting trust analysis is not usually favoured today. It is also unlikely, in view of *Re Bucks Constabulary Fund (No. 2)*,[53] that the Crown will establish a claim to the assets as *bona vacantia* in many cases, or, as submitted above,[54] that outside contributors will have any claim. Assuming that the contractual basis is adopted, only those members existing at the date of dissolution will be entitled. Unless the rules provide otherwise, the distribution will be on a *per capita* basis, prima facie in equal shares, and ignoring actual contributions.

In *Re Sick and Funeral Society of St. John's Sunday School, Golcar*,[55] a society was formed in 1866 to provide sickness and death benefits for its members. Those under 13 paid $\frac{1}{2}$d per week, and the others paid 1d. The benefits for those paying the whole subscription were twice those of the smaller subscribers. Upon the winding up of the society, the surplus funds were held distributable among the members as at that date on a *per capita* basis, but as the benefits and burdens differed among the two classes of members, the proper basis for distribution was full shares for full members and half shares for the children. The *per capita* basis did not favour new members at the expense of older ones, as each got what he paid for: the newer members had had the benefits of membership for a short time and the older members for a longer time. The latter could not complain if they did not receive more in the winding up.

In *Re Bucks Constabulary Fund (No. 2)*,[56] Walton J. held that the prima facie rule of equal division applied also to Friendly Society

[51] Criticised as highly artificial in Goff and Jones, p. 567. See also *Schmidt v. Air Products of Canada Ltd* (1994) 115 D.L.R. (4th) 631, where the view of Scott J. was rejected.

[52] *Re Hobourn Aero Components Air Raid Distress Fund* [1946] Ch. 86 at p. 97.

[53] [1979] 1 W.L.R. 936. *Cf. Davis v. Richards & Wallington Industries Ltd, supra.*

[54] *Ante*, p. 238.

[55] [1973] Ch. 51.

[56] *Supra.*

cases, although in the past some of those cases had favoured a distribution in proportion to contributions.[57] this approach was also adopted in *Re G.K.N. Bolts & Nuts Ltd (Automotive Division) Birmingham Works, Sports and Social Club*,[58] where those entitled to share the assets on a *per capita* basis were the full members and the ordinary members. Honorary, temporary and associate members, who neither paid subscriptions nor had voting rights, were excluded.

iii. Trust and Charge. Here also the distinction between a trust and a charge is important.[59] A distinction was drawn by Lord Eldon in *King v. Denison*[60] between devises *charged with payment* of debts, and devises *on trust to pay* debts. In the former case it is assumed that the testator intended a beneficial interest for the devisee, subject to the payment of debts; in the latter case it is assumed that he intended merely to use the devisee as a vehicle for payment of the debts, and not to confer any benefit upon him. In the latter case there will, therefore, be a resulting trust of any surplus for the residuary devisee, or those entitled on intestacy; but there will be no resulting trust in the former case. In construing the language of a gift, it must be remembered that equity will not allow trustees themselves to give evidence that what was intended was a conditional gift.[61]

D. No Declaration of Trust

Where property is conveyed to persons in circumstances in which they are intended to take as trustees, then, if no beneficial interests are declared, they will hold on resulting trust for the grantor; as where a transfer is made to a nominee.[62] We have seen this principle in operation in the case of testamentary gifts to legatees as trustees, without the trusts upon which they are to hold being declared prior to the testator's death.[63]

The *Vandervell* litigation serves as a warning of the crucial importance of attention to detail in tax planning. There were two visits to the House of Lords and three to the Court of Appeal. The

---

[57] *Re Printers' and Transferrers' Society* [1899] 2 Ch. 184; *Re Lead Workmens Fund Society* [1904] 2 Ch. 196.

[58] [1982] 1 W.L.R. 774. The facts have been given, *ante*, p. 236. See also *Re St Andrew's Allotment Association* [1969] 1 W.L.R. 229.

[59] *Ante*, p. 52.

[60] (1813) 1 Ves. & Bea. 260; *Smith v. Cooke* [1891] A.C. 297; *Re West* [1900] 1 Ch. 84; *Re Foord* [1922] 2 Ch. 519, distinguished in *Re Osoba* [1979] 1 W.L.R. 247, *ante*, p. 234.

[61] *Re Rees* [1950] Ch. 204; *Re Pugh* [1967] 1 W.L.R. 1262; *Re Tyler* [1967] 1 W.L.R. 1269; *ante*, p. 157, *cf. Smith v. Cooke (supra)*.

[62] *Hodgson v. Marks* [1971] Ch. 892; *Vandervell v. I.R.C.* [1967] 2 A.C. 291.

[63] *Re Boyes* (1884) 26 Ch.D. 531; *ante*, p. 150; *Re Pugh's W.T.* [1967] 1 W.L.R. 1262.

problem was caused by the fact that Mr. Vandervell's advisers overlooked the possibility of the existence of a resulting trust; when all that Mr. Vandervell was doing was trying to give away a large sum of money to charity.

In 1958 Vandervell decided to found a Chair of Pharmacology at the Royal College of Surgeons with a gift of £250,000. This was to be effected by a scheme under which a block of shares in Vandervell Products Ltd would be transferred to the College, and the necessary dividends subsequently declared on them. Such dividends, in the hands of the College, would be free of liability to income tax and surtax.[64] The shares were to be transferred subject to an option to repurchase for £5,000 in favour of Vandervell Trustees Ltd, a private company whose only function was to act as trustee for various trusts connected with the Vandervell family and business. It was trustee of the Vandervell children's trust.

The transfer of the shares was made in 1958, and between then and 1961 the necessary dividends were paid to the College. The Revenue assessed Vandervell for surtax on the dividends on the ground that he had not entirely disposed of all his interest in the property,[65] because, in the absence of a declaration of trust of the option, it was held on resulting trust for Vandervell. The Revenue succeeded. That was *Vandervell v. I.R.C.*[66] Before discussing the reasoning, it will be best to complete the story.

On receiving the Revenue's claim in 1961, Vandervell ordered Vandervell Trustees Ltd to exercise the option, and they did so, taking £5,000 from the children's settlement to finance it. All the dividends since that date were paid to Vandervell Trustees Ltd, who applied them to the children's settlement. They so informed the Revenue.

The Revenue assessed Vandervell to surtax in respect of the years 1961–65 on the footing that the shares were held on trust for him during that period. In 1965 he at last executed a deed which transferred all or any interest which he may have in the shares in favour of the children's settlement. In 1967 he died.

Before this claim of the Revenue was litigated, Vandervell's estate stepped in and claimed the dividends from Vandervell Trustees Ltd. If the estate succeeded, the Revenue's claim was clearly good; and the Revenue attempted to join the litigation in support. The defendants successfully excluded them.[67] In *Re*

[64] Because the College is a charity.
[65] I.T.A. 1952, s.415(2). Now I.C.T.A. 1988, s.685.
[66] [1967] 2 A.C. 291; (1966) 24 C.L.J. 19 (G. Jones); (1967) 31 Conv.(N.S.) 175 (S. Spencer); (1967) 30 M.L.R. 461 (N. Strauss).
[67] *Re Vandervell's Trusts (No. 1)* [1971] A.C. 912.

Vandervell's Trusts (No. 2) the estate succeeded before Megarry J., but failed before the Court of Appeal.[68]

In the first case, *Vandervell v. I.R.C.*[69] the Revenue succeeded by a majority of three to two. The option was held on trust for Vandervell. He was effectively the grantor of the option, although it was in form granted by the Royal College. It was taken by Vandervell Trustees Ltd upon trust, but no effective trusts of the option were declared, "and so the defendant company held the option on an automatic trust for Mr. Vandervell."[70] In this situation, there was, as Lord Wilberforce said "no need, or room to invoke a presumption. The conclusion, on the facts found, is simply that the option was vested in the trustee company as a trustee on trusts, not defined at the time, possibly to be defined later. But the equitable, or beneficial interest, cannot remain in the air: the consequence in law must be that it remains in the settlor."[71] An indication of the parties' intention, as opposed to what they might be supposed to have desired, would of course have changed the whole situation. But the donor's mere intention not to have the beneficial interest cannot prevail in an automatic resulting trust.[72]

In *Re Vandervell's Trusts (No. 2)*,[73] the Court of Appeal, reversing Megarry J., found that the resulting trust of the option in favour of Vandervell terminated with the exercise of the option; and that a trust of the shares had been declared in favour of the children's settlements. Criticisms of the finding of a declaration of trust have already been made.[74] Another difficulty is that even if the acts of the trustees were sufficient to manifest an intention to create a new trust, how could the option and the shares be separated? Is it right to say: "Before the option was exercised, there was a gap in the beneficial ownership. So there was a resulting trust for Mr. Vandervell. But, as soon as the option was exercised and the shares registered in the trustees' name, there was created a valid trust of the shares in favour of the children's settlement"?[75] Other problems relating to the

---

[68] [1974] Ch. 269.

[69] [1967] 2 A.C. 291.

[70] [1974] Ch. 269 at p. 296, *per* Megarry J.

[71] [1967] 2 A.C. 291 at p. 329. Lord Browne Wilkinson in the *Westdeutsche* case (n. 72, *infra*) considers (at p. 706) that where a transfer by an absolute owner fails to pass full title, the transferor does not "retain" an equitable interest, which arises for the first time when a resulting trust is imposed on the transferee; *post*, p. 246.

[72] [1974] Ch. 269 at p. 298, *per* Megarry J. *Cf. Davis v. Richards & Wallington Industries Ltd* [1990] 1 W.L.R. 1511; *Westdeutsche Landesbank Girozentrale v. Islington London Borough Council* [1996] A.C. 669 at p. 708; *ante*, p. 68.

[73] [1974] Ch. 269; (1974) 38 Conv.(N.S.) 405 (P. Clarke); (1975) 38 M.L.R. (J. Harris); (1975) 7 D.L.R. 483 (G. Battersby).

[74] *Ante*, pp. 83, 121.

[75] *Per* Lord Denning M.R. at p. 320; Lawton L.J. made the same point: "There could not be a resulting trust of a chose in action which was no more": *ibid.* at 325.

formality requirements of Law of Property Act 1925, s.53(1)(*c*) were discussed in Chapter 4.

3. VOLUNTARY CONVEYANCE AND THE PRESUMPTIONS

A. Presumption of Resulting Trust: Conveyance to a Third Party

i. Land. One of the effects of the Statute of Uses was to prevent the operation of resulting uses. Previously, a resulting use arose on a voluntary conveyance which did not declare a use; the beneficial interest reverted to the grantor. After the Statute of Uses, the use was executed, and the grantor retained the legal estate; the conveyance was thus ineffectual. When equitable interests returned under the name of trusts, the beneficial interest might again remain in the grantor in cases both of realty and personalty, where the grantee was not intended to take beneficially. A number of problems remain in the ascertainment of the intention to be ascribed to the grantor.

The Law of Property Act, 1925, s.60(3), helps in solving these problems in relation to land.[76] While before 1926 it was necessary, in a voluntary conveyance, to insert a use in favour of the grantee in order to prevent a resulting trust arising, section 60(3) makes this no longer essential. Section 60(3) however, only prevents the implication of a resulting trust *merely* by reason that the conveyance is not expressed to be for the benefit of the grantee. If it is intended to take effect as a gift, it is still preferable to make this clear in the conveyance, as section 60(3) does not preclude the implication of a resulting trust on general equitable principles.[77] Where the transferor establishes that no gift was intended, section 60(3) does not prevent the finding of a resulting trust.

> In *Hodgson v. Marks*,[78] Mrs. Hodgson was an old lady who was the registered owner of a house. A lodger, Evans, lived there. Mrs. Hodgson developed an affection for Evans, and trusted him to look after all her affairs. Her nephew disapproved of Evans, and tried to persuade Mrs. Hodgson to turn him out. To protect Evans, she transferred the house to him, under an oral agreement that she would continue to be beneficial owner. Evans, as registered owner, sold it to a bona fide purchaser, Marks, and the question was whether Mrs. Hodgson was protected against Marks.

---

[76] "In a voluntary conveyance a resulting trust for the grantor shall not be implied merely by reason that the property is not expressed to be conveyed for the use or benefit of the grantee."

[77] See Parker and Mellows, *The Modern Law of Trusts* (6th ed.), p. 200.

[78] [1971] Ch. 892.

The Court of Appeal held that she remained beneficial owner in equity, and that this was an overriding interest.[79] The express oral agreement in her favour was unenforceable under the Law of Property Act 1925, s.53(1)(*b*). Evidence of her intention was however admissible, and this gave rise to "a resulting trust of the beneficial interest to the plaintiff, which would not, of course, be affected by section 53(1).[80] Section 60(3) was not discussed.

ii. Personalty. In relation to personalty, the initial presumption remains that a voluntary transfer to a third party is accompanied by the inference of a resulting trust.

In *Re Vinogradoff*,[81] the testatrix had transferred a sum of £800 War Loan, then standing in her name, into the joint names of herself and her granddaughter, then four years old. The testatrix continued to receive the dividends until her death.

Farwell J. held that, even though an infant may not be appointed a trustee, the presumption of resulting trust applied, and the granddaughter held that property on resulting trust for the estate of the testatrix.

It is questionable whether such a result coincides with the real intention of the transferor. If, however, as would be one possible construction, her intention was to keep the property as her own during her lifetime and to give it to the granddaughter upon her death, such an attempted disposition would be testamentary, and void for failure to comply with the formal requirements of the Wills Act. A valid gift could be affected if intended to be held by the transferor for her life and after her death for the donee, or if a form of joint tenancy with a right of survivorship was created.[82]

It is even more doubtful whether the presumption accords with the transferor's intention in the case of a transfer to the grantee alone. The majority of such transfers must be intended as gifts. Although it seems correct to say that the presumption of a resulting trust exist in such cases,[83] it gives way to the slightest contrary evidence. The common sense of the transaction frequently prevails, and the rules of evidence do not prevent the sense of the transaction being deduced.

---

[79] Because she was in actual occupation; L.R.A. 1925, s.70(1)(*g*).

[80] *Ibid.* at p. 933.

[81] [1935] W.N. 68; *Standing v. Bowring* (1885) 16 Ch.D. 282 at p. 287; *Fowkes v. Pascoe* (1875) L.R. 10 Ch.App. 343; *Thavorn v. Bank of Credit & Commerce International SA* [1985] 1 Lloyd's Rep. 259 (resulting trust where aunt opened bank account in name of 15 year old nephew).

[82] *Fowkes v. Pascoe* (1875) L.R. 10 Ch.App. 343; *post*, p. 254. See *Thavorn v. Bank of Credit & Commerce International SA*, *supra*, at p. 262.

[83] *George v. Havard* (1819) 7 Price 646 at p. 651, *per* Richards C.B.

Lord Browne-Wilkinson has suggested that the resulting trust in such cases does not arise at the date of the transfer if the transferee was then ignorant of the facts, but arises only when the transferee's conscience becomes affected.[84] It is difficult to see how *Re Vinogradoff* supports this analysis, in view of the infancy of the transferee at all relevant times.

B. Presumption of Advancement

The presumption of advancement is a presumption working in the opposite direction. It arises where certain relationships exist, where the donor or purchaser is under an obligation recognised in equity, to support or provide for the transferee.[85] It arises if the person to whom a voluntary conveyance is made is the wife or child of the donor, or someone to whom he stands *in loco parentis*. It is clear from the cases, however, that adult children are within the presumption. Like the presumption of resulting trust, it is rebuttable by evidence that the donor intended to keep the beneficial interest for himself.

i. Husband and wife.

(a) *Gift by Husband.* The presumption of advancement applies where a husband makes a transfer to his wife. The strength of the presumption is diminished in modern times.[86] "It would in my view," said Lord Diplock in *Pettitt v. Pettitt*, [87] "be an abuse of the legal technique for ascertaining or imputing intention to apply to transactions between the post-war generation of married couples 'presumptions' which are based upon inferences of fact which an earlier generation of judges drew as the most likely intentions of earlier generations of spouses belonging to the propertied classes of a different social era." *Pettitt v. Pettitt* was a case of a claim to a share in the ownership of a matrimonial home, as to which special considerations apply, and will be discussed in Chapter 11.

---

[84] *Westdeutsche Landesbank Girozentrale v. Islington London Borough Council* [1996] A.C. 669 at pp. 705–706. But see [1996] R.L.R. 3 at p. 20 (P. Birks), pointing out the difficulties of this view in tax and other contexts where it is essential to ascertain the date on which property rights arise; (1996) 55 C.L.J. 432 (G. Jones).

[85] See *Cavalier v. Cavalier* (1971) 19 F.L.R. 199 (S.C.N.S.W.) at p. 205, where Carmichael J. considered this statement too narrow; [1974] A.S.C.L. p. 527 (J. Hackney).

[86] *Pettitt v. Pettitt* [1970] A.C. 777; *Gissing v. Gissing* [1971] A.C. 886; *Falconer v. Falconer* [1970] 1 W.L.R. 1333; (1971) N.L.J. 96 at p. 126 (T. Earnshaw).

[87] *Supra*, at p. 824. See also *Simpson v. Simpson* [1992] 1 F.L.R. 601; *Harwood v. Harwood* [1991] 2 F.L.R. 274.

In *Re Eykyn's Trusts*[88] in 1877, Malins V.-C. said: "The law of this court is perfectly settled that where a husband transfers money or other property into the name of his wife only, then the presumption is, that it is intended as a gift or advancement to the wife absolutely at once . . . " Transfers of chattels to a wife are within the presumption; and so is the matrimonial home which is conveyed to the wife although paid for by the husband. In *Tinker v. Tinker*,[89] the presumption was readily applied, in spite of the comments upon the presumption in *Pettitt v. Pettitt*; but there was ample evidence to show that the wife was intended to benefit.

The presumption also applies where the gift is made before marriage, but with a specific marriage (which in fact takes place) in mind.[90] There is no presumption of advancement where a man puts property into the name of his mistress,[91] nor is there such a presumption where a wife puts property into the name of her husband.[92] With a matrimonial home, at least, very little evidence will suffice to establish a sharing of the beneficial interest.[93]

(b) *Rebuttal.* The presumption can be rebutted by evidence which tends to show that no gift was intended. Thus, in *Anson v. Anson*,[94] a husband guaranteed his wife's banking account, and eventually the guarantee was called and he was obliged to pay a sum of money to the bank as a result. Pearson J. held that the husband could recover that sum from the wife, as the transaction was not in the nature of an advancement. There will be no advancement if, for example, a joint account was opened for the purposes of making it easier for the wife to draw money from an account, the husband being ill.[95] A

---

[88] (1877) 6 Ch.D. 115 at p. 118; quoted in *Pettitt v. Pettitt, supra*, at p. 815.

[89] [1970] P. 136.

[90] *Moate v. Moate* [1948] 2 All E.R. 486; *Ulrich v. Ulrich* [1968] 1 W.L.R. 180; (1975) 119 S.J. 108 (E. Ellis). A void marriage is not included. As to engaged couples, see Law Reform (Miscellaneous Provisions) Act 1970, s.2(1). One effect of s.2(1) is that the presumption of advancement applies to resolve disputes between couples whose engagement has ended; *Mossop v. Mossop* [1989] Fam. 77; [1988] Conv. 284 (J.E.M.); *cf. Bernard v. Josephs* [1982] Ch. 391 at 400.

[91] *Diwell v. Farnes* [1959] 1 W.L.R. 624; but the other rules for ascertaining the ownership of the home apply; *post*, p. 269.

[92] *Mercier v. Mercier* [1903] 2 Ch. 98; *Heseltine v. Heseltine* [1971] 1 W.L.R. 342. The Law Commission recommends otherwise; Law Com. No. 175 (1988), *Matrimonial Property*, para. 4.19.

[93] *Per* Lord Upjohn in *Pettitt v. Pettitt* [1970] A.C. 777 at p. 815.

[94] [1953] 1 Q.B. 636. Similarly where the husband lacked mental capacity to make a gift; *Simpson v. Simpson* [1992] 1 F.L.R. 601.

[95] *Marshal v. Crutwell* (1875) L.R. 20 Eq. 328; *Simpson v. Simpson, supra*. Housekeeping money was dealt with by the Married Women's Property Act 1964, under which equality of ownership is presumed in the absence of other evidence; *cf. Re Figgis* [1969] Ch. 123.

joint account, though funded by the husband, will frequently lead to the inference of a joint tenancy in law and equity.[96]

ii. Father and Child. There is a presumption of advancement between a father and his legitimate child. The presumption here is stronger, and "should not . . . give way to slight circumstances."[97]

In *Re Roberts*,[98] a father took out an instance policy on the life of his son and paid the premiums on it. It was contended after the father's death that the amounts paid by way of premium (by the father in his lifetime and by his estate until the son's death) were recoverable by his estate by means of a lien over the policy moneys. Evershed J. held that the presumption of advancement prevailed, and that each premium paid by the father during his lifetime was a separate advancement to the son. The premiums paid after the father's death by his estate were, however, recoverable as the relationship of father and son no longer existed.

iii. Other Relationships. But the moment one passes from this type of case to transfers from a mother to a child (whether or not the father is dead), from a father to an illegitimate child,[99] from grand-parents, aunts and uncles, then the presumptions fade. Whether or not the presumption is technically in favour of a resulting trust, or technically in favour of advancement, the important consideration is whether or not there is evidence that the donor or purchaser regarded himself or herself as being *in loco parentis*, and the donee as being someone for whom an obligation to provide is felt.[1] The issue is treated as one of fact in the modern cases, and it is only in the absence of any evidence that the technical presumptions prevail.[2] Although, therefore, in cases other than that of father and legitimate child, the presumption may technically be in favour of a resulting trust, this is not, for the vast majority of cases, a decisive factor. The point is well brought out by the cases dealing with widowed mothers

[96] *Re Bishop* [1965] Ch. 450; *Re Figgis* [1969] Ch. 123; (1969) 85 L.Q.R. 530 (M. Cullity); *McHardy and Sons (a firm) v. Warren* (1994) 2 F.L.R. 338; *cf. Heseltine v. Heseltine* [1971] 1 W.L.R. 342 (husband had no interest where money provided by wife).

[97] *Per* Viscount Simonds in *Shephard v. Cartwright, infra; cf.* Lord Upjohn in *Pettitt v. Pettitt, supra*, at p. 815; *McGrath v. Wallis* [1995] 2 F.L.R. 114; *post*, p. 256.

[98] [1946] Ch. 1. The policy itself was held on express trust for the son. See also *B. v. B.* (1976) 65 D.L.R. (3d) 460 (purchase of lottery ticket in name of 12-year-old daughter). A case where the presumption was rebutted is *Re Gooch* (1890) 62 L.T. 384 (father purchased shares to qualify son as director, and son handed over dividends to his father). See also *McEvoy v. Belfast Banking Co.* [1935] A.C. 24.

[99] This principle seems unaffected by the Family Law Reform Act 1987, which in general removes the property law disadvantages of children of unmarried parents.

[1] See, *per* Page-Wood V.-C. in *Tucker v. Burrow* (1865) 2 H. & M. 515 at pp. 525–527; *Re Paradise Motor Co. Ltd* [1968] 1 W.L.R. 1125.

[2] *Re Vinogradoff* [1935] W.N. 68.

and their children.[3] In this situation, equity does not recognise in the mother, as it would have done in the father, an obligation to provide, hence there is no presumption of advancement. But the strangeness of this conclusion is wholly mitigated by the ease with which, on very little evidence, the courts will find the intent to advance.[4]

iv. Admissibility of Donor's Statements. In *Shephard v. Cartwright*,[5] C. caused shares in companies he was promoting to be allotted to himself, his wife and his three children in 1929. The companies made considerable profits and in 1934 a public company was formed; the original shareholders received partly new shares and partly cash by way of payment for their old shares. C., in fact, controlled the whole family wealth, and the shares and money were divided between his wife and children for tax reasons. The wife and children at all times acquiesced in C.'s activities, and signed powers or attorney and powers to withdraw money at his wish.

By 1936, the cash had all been withdrawn by C. and spent. Dividends on the shares allotted to the children were, however, treated as the income of the children, not the income of C. To a claim by the children against C.'s estate to recover the cash drawn by him on their bank accounts, it was argued that C.'s conduct showed that he had not intended the beneficial interest to vest in the children, but that they at all times held on resulting trust for C. The House of Lords rejected this contention. The onus of rebutting the presumption of advancement lay on C.'s executors, and there was nothing in C.'s conduct that was truly inconsistent with the presumption. The children had acquiesced in their father's conduct, rather than acted as trustees for him. The House of Lords also applied the rule that evidence of declarations and conduct subsequent to the original transaction is admissible only against the party making them, though those made at the time of the original transaction are admissible for or against him.

v. Transfers for Unlawful Purposes. A further question is whether a transferor who has put property in the name of the transferee to achieve an unlawful purpose may rebut the presumption of advancement by proving his real intention. If the relevant presumption is that of resulting trust, the question is whether he may rely on it in spite of the illegality.

---

[3] *Bennet v. Bennet* (1879) 10 Ch.D. 474, discussing *Sayre v. Hughes* (1868) L.R. 5 Eq. 376 (where there was held to be a presumption). Commonwealth authorities favour extending the presumption of advancement to the mother/child relationship; see Pettit, p. 134; *Nelson v. Nelson* (1995) 132 A.L.R. 133; [1996] Conv. 274 (A. Dowling); *cf. Sekhon v. Alissa* [1989] 2 F.L.R. 94.

[4] See especially Jessel M.R. in *Bennet v. Bennet, supra.*

[5] [1955] A.C. 431. Mellish L.J.'s judgment in *Fowkes v. Pascoe* (1875) L.R. 10 Ch.App. 343, emphasising the sense of the transaction, was expressly approved.

The matter has recently been reviewed by the House of Lords in
Tinsley v. Milligan.[6]

Two women agreed to put a house which they owned jointly
into the name of one of them (the plaintiff) in order to facilitate
fraudulent claims to housing benefit by the other (the defendant).
Both were parties to the fraud, which was perpetrated over several
years, but had now ceased. Eventually the plaintiff sought to evict
the defendant.

The plaintiff's claim was rejected by a bare majority,[7] holding
that the defendant could assert ownership of her equitable interest.
The principle that a litigant cannot rely on his own fraud or illegality
to rebut the presumption of advancement was confirmed.[8] Here,
however, the operative presumption was that of a resulting trust. The
defendant merely had to found her claim on that presumption and
not on any illegality. Nor was she seeking to enforce executory
provisions of an unlawful contract, in which the court would not
assist. This result, according to the majority, promoted harmony
between the approaches of equity and the common law to illegality.
Policy did not require a wider application of the "clean hands"
principle, which would not deter fraudulent conduct. The nineteenth
century authorities supported the plaintiff, but, although the wide
"clean hands" approach favoured by Lord Eldon[9] had never been
overruled, the law on illegality had continued to develop. The reason
why the property had been conveyed to the plaintiff was irrelevant
to the defendant's claim, to which the presumption of resulting trust
was crucial. The illegality only emerged because the plaintiff raised
it; it was not necessary to the defendant's case.[10]

Lords Goff and Keith dissented on the ground that the "clean
hands" principle espoused by Lord Eldon had been consistently
followed. Subject only to the "repentance" exception,[11] once it had
come to the attention of the court that the claimant did not have
clean hands, the court would refuse assistance even though the claim
could be established without relying on the illegality. Both the
majority and the minority agreed, however, that the "public conscience" test adopted by the Court of Appeal[12] (whereby a claim
would succeed in spite of the illegality if the public conscience
would not be offended) was too vague and discretionary, and not

[6] [1994] 1 A.C. 340.
[7] Lords Jauncey, Lowry and Browne-Wilkinson.
[8] Discussed below.
[9] In *Muckleston v. Brown* (1801) 6 Ves. 52.
[10] See also *Haigh v. Kaye* (1872) 7 Ch.App. 469.
[11] Discussed below.
[12] [1992] Ch. 310.

based on authority. Only Parliament could introduce such a reform.[13]

A solution which discourages illegality and also prevents the unjust enrichment of the transferee is not easy to find. It is unfortunate that the majority decision is based on the old presumptions, which are generally regarded as outmoded.[14] The result of *Tinsley v. Milligan* is that if a husband transfers to his wife or a father to his daughter for an unlawful purpose, he will be unable to assert any claim after carrying out the purpose,[15] whereas a wife who transfers to her husband, or a mother to her daughter, or a brother to his sister, will be successful. There seems little merit in this distinction, and in any event even a wife, mother or brother may be unsuccessful in the case of a voluntary conveyance of land, because section 60(3) of the Law of Property Act 1925[16] appears to remove the presumption of a resulting trust, so that the onus of proof of entitlement is on the transferor.

The decision of the House of Lords has been much criticised.[17] Its effect has been said to be that "He who comes to equity should keep unclean hands in his pockets."[18]

It has long been established and, as mentioned above, was confirmed by the House of Lords, that the presumption of advancement cannot be rebutted by evidence of the transferor's illegal purpose. Thus where a husband transferred property to his wife in order to evade tax[19] or to defeat his creditors[20] the property belonged to the wife even if she was a party to the scheme.[21] Similarly where a father transferred property to his son for an unlawful purpose.[22] In these cases it appears that the unlawful purpose had been carried

---

[13] See Illegal Contracts Act 1970 (New Zealand), ss.6, 7, permitting restitution of property at the court's discretion. *Tinsley* has been rejected in Australia in favour of a more flexible public policy approach; *Nelson v. Nelson* (1995) 132 A.L.R. 133. The "public conscience" test is favoured in (1993) 7 *Trust Law International* 114 (M. Lunney). The Law Commission plans to review this area; Law Com. No. 239, para. 2.20.

[14] See *Pettitt v. Pettitt* [1970] A.C. 777; *ante*, p. 246; *McGrath v. Wallis* [1995] 2 F.L.R. 114; *post*, p. 256.

[15] It is otherwise if the purpose has not been carried out; *Tribe v. Tribe* [1996] Ch. 107; *infra*.

[16] *Ante*, p. 244.

[17] (1993) 52 C.L.J. 394 (R. Thornton); [1994] Conv. 62 (M. Halliwell); (1994) 57 M.L.R. 441 (H. Stowe); (1994) 110 L.Q.R. 3 (R. Buckley). For a different analysis, see (1995) 111 L.Q.R. 135 (N. Enonchong).

[18] (1993) 143 N.L.J. 1577 (B. Council).

[19] *Re Emery's Investment Trusts* [1959] Ch. 410.

[20] *Gascoigne v. Gascoigne* [1918] 1 K.B. 223.

[21] *ibid.*

[22] *Chettiar v. Chettiar* [1962] A.C. 294. It was suggested in *Muckleston v. Brown* (1801) 6 Ves. 52 at p. 68 that where the transferor could not recover, an innocent person claiming through him could do so, but this seems contrary to principle: *Ayerst v. Jenkins* (1873) L.R. 16 Eq. 274 at p. 281.

out. The question which arose in *Tribe v. Tribe*[23] was whether the presumption of advancement may be rebutted by evidence of an illegal purpose where that purpose has not been carried out.

A landlord served repair notices on the tenant of two properties. The required works were substantial. If the tenant were to be held responsible, he would need to raise funds by selling his shares in his family company which occupied the premises. He transferred his shares to his son for a stated consideration which was not paid, in order to deceive the landlord as to his assets and thereby safeguard them. In fact the matter of the repairs was resolved without resort to deception, as the landlord agreed to the surrender of one lease and sold the reversion of the other to the tenant. When the son claimed to be entitled to the shares, the Court of Appeal held that the presumption of advancement was rebutted by evidence of the father's intentions, which were not consistent with a gift to the son. Although his purpose was illegal, the illegality had not been carried out.[24]

Tinsley v. Milligan did not decide that there was no exception to the rule that a claim could not be founded on an illegal act. Earlier cases established that the transferor could succeed where he "repented" and withdrew from the illegal transaction, although they were inconsistent as to whether genuine repentance was necessary. In *Sekhon v. Alissa*,[25] for example, a mother who had a house conveyed into her daughter's name was able to rebut the presumption where her alleged purpose of capital gains tax evasion had not been carried out simply because the house had not yet been sold. In *Tribe v. Tribe* there was no "repentance" because the father did not seek to recover the shares until the danger had passed. As the authorities on repentance were conflicting, it was held that a transferor could succeed if he withdrew from the transaction only because it was no longer necessary. The exception (*i.e.* that recovery is permitted where the illegal purpose has not been wholly or partly carried out) mitigates the harshness of the general rule, which could otherwise lead to injustice, and is designed to encourage withdrawal from fraud. The fact that "repentance" is not necessary does not further this policy, but it was felt that a stricter requirement could lead to bizarre results.

---

[23] [1996] Ch. 107; criticised (1996) 26 Fam.Law 30 (S. Cretney); (1996) 55 C.L.J. 23 (G. Virgo); (1996) 112 L.Q.R. 386 (F. Rose); (1996) 10 *Trust Law International* 51 (P. Pettit); [1996] R.L.R. 78 (N. Enonchong).

[24] *Perpetual Executors and Trustees Association of Australia Ltd v. Wright* (1917) 23 C.L.R. 185 was applied.

[25] [1989] 2 F.L.R. 94.

The Court of Appeal noted the arbitrary aspects of the principles laid down in *Tinsley v. Milligan*,[26] where so much depended on the relationship of the parties. As the presumption of advancement has fallen into disfavour, "there seems to be some perversity in its elevation to a decisive status in the context of illegality."[27] Miss Milligan had recovered although she had defrauded. There would be cause for concern if a plaintiff who had not done so could not recover simply because the transferee was his son.

Millett L.J. sought to eliminate these arbitrary aspects by saying that the transferor would not invariably succeed where the presumption of resulting trust applied.[28] The presumption would be rebutted where the transferee led evidence that the transferor's subsequent conduct was inconsistent with any intention to retain a beneficial interest. An example would be where an uncle transferred assets to his nephew to conceal them from creditors and then settled with his creditors on the footing that he did not own the assets. He could not recover as his own conduct would be inconsistent with the retention of any interest. The problem with this is that the example is difficult to distinguish from *Tinsley v. Milligan* itself.

Of course, evidence that property was transferred to protect it from creditors does not alone rebut the presumption of advancement. Rather, it reinforces it, because the only way of protecting the property is for the transferor to divest himself of his interest. *Tinker v. Tinker*,[29] where a husband put a house in his wife's name to protect it from creditors if his new business should fail, was such a case. In fact there were no creditors and the husband in any event was not dishonest as his solicitors had advised the transfer. The evidence strengthened rather than rebutted the presumption of advancement. In order to rebut the presumption, a dishonest transferor must show that he intended to retain an interest and conceal it from his creditors. As Millett L.J. explained, compelling evidence of such an intention would be required. The court would be unlikely to reach such a conclusion where there was no imminent threat from known creditors at the transfer.

The cases discussed above have involved disputes between the transferor and the transferee. The principle that the presumption of advancement cannot be rebutted by evidence of illegality has been

---

[26] [1994] 1 A.C. 340.

[27] [1996] Ch. 107 at p. 118 (Nourse L.J.).

[28] His Lordship considered that *Re Great Berlin Steamboat Co.* (1884) 26 Ch.Div. 616 (no recovery in resulting trust case where illegality carried out) had not been impliedly overruled.

[29] [1970] P. 136; *cf. Heseltine v. Heseltine* [1971] 1 W.L.R. 342 (presumption of resulting trust not rebutted where wife transferred assets to husband to save estate duty and qualify him as a Lloyd's "name", although these purposes would not be achieved unless the husband took beneficially).

held not to apply where the dispute is between the transferee and a third party.[30]

4. PURCHASE MONEY RESULTING TRUSTS

A. Purchase in the Name of Another

i. Presumptions in Favour of the Purchaser. Where a purchaser of realty or personalty takes a conveyance in the name of a third party, but there is nothing to indicate an intention on his part of not having the beneficial interest, then there is a presumption that he intended to obtain the beneficial interest for himself, and a resulting trust will be decreed in his favour. In the words of Eyre C.B.: "The trust of a legal estate . . . results to the man who advances the purchase-money.[31]

The presumption arises when a purchase is made in the joint names of a purchaser and a third party, and where a purchase is made in the name of third party alone; also where property purchased with the contributions of more than one person is conveyed into the name of only one of them, or where unequal contributors become joint legal owners.[32]

The classic case is *Fowkes v. Pascoe*.[33]

Mrs B. purchased stock in the names of herself and the son of her widowed daughter-in-law. The son was outside the relationships where the presumption of advancement would arise, hence he would prima facie be presumed to hold on resulting trust for Mrs B. But the Court of Appeal in Chancery held that the strength of the presumption varied according to the circumstances and that, once there is some evidence to rebut it, the court must look at the facts from a common-sense point of view. In the present case, the only rational inference was that Mrs B. intended the purchase as a gift, so that the presumption of resulting trust was rebutted, though the effect of the gift would not be apparent until Mrs B.'s death, for the court also held that any income declared on the stock during Mrs B.'s lifetime would belong beneficially to her. Such a gift does not infringe the Wills Act 1837, as the legal title passes by the transfer; the legal title carries with it the right

---

[30] *R. v. London Borough of Harrow, ex p. Coker, The Times*, March 14, 1989 (money paid by H into W's bank account to evade exchange control and later paid over by W to H held not to belong to W for purpose of grant assessment by local authority).

[31] *Dyer v. Dyer* (1788) 2 Cox 92 at p. 93.

[32] See *Springette v. Defoe* (1993) 65 P. & C.R. 1; *Huntingford v. Hobbs* [1993] 1 F.L.R. 736.

[33] (1875) L.R. 10 Ch.App. 343; see also *Pettitt v. Pettitt* [1970] A.C. 777; *Hoare v. Hoare* (1983) 13 Fam.Law 142.

of survivorship, and all that happens on the death of Mrs B. is that her equitable right ceases to be outstanding.[34] There is thus no *testamentary* gift provided the transfer *inter vivos* is complete and not revocable.[35]

ii. Presumption of Advancement. As in the case of voluntary conveyances, a purchase in the name of a wife or child or other person to whom the purchaser stands *in loco parentis* raises a contrary presumption, as the purchase is presumed in these cases to be an advancement. As Lord Eldon said in *Marlees v. Franklin*,[36] "The general rule that on a purchase by one man in the name of another, the nominee is trustee for the purchaser is subject to exception where the purchaser is under a species of natural obligation to provide for the nominee." The presumption is weak in the case of husband and wife. It is stronger with a parent and child, at any rate where the house is for the sole occupation of the child,[37] but may be rebutted. In *Warren v. Gurney*[38]

A father bought a house for his daughter, who was shortly to get married, to live in. The conveyance was taken in the name of the daughter, but the father retained the title deeds. On his death 15 years later, the daughter claimed to be the beneficial owner of the house. The Court of Appeal held that there was a presumption of advancement in her favour, but that it had been rebutted by the fact of the retention of the title deeds, accompanied by evidence contemporaneous with the purchase in 1929. Retention of the deeds by itself is probably insufficient evidence, however.

B. Purchase by Several in the Name of One

The general principle is that the legal title is held on trust for the purchasers in the proportions in which they contributed to the

---

[34] *Young v. Sealey* [1949] Ch. 278. The argument is not an easy one, but Romer J. preferred to take this view as no previous English case had taken this point under the Wills Act, and gifts of this sort had not previously been thought to raise difficulties. See (1992) 6 *Trust Law International* 57 (J. Miller).

[35] But in the case of a joint bank account opened by a husband in the name of himself and his wife so that either can draw on it (the account being kept in credit by the husband), there is a gift to the wife of what happens to be in the account at the date of the husband's death. The difficulties of this reasoning are discussed by Megarry J. in *Re Figgis* [1969] Ch. 123, where however *Young v. Sealey, supra*, was followed. (1969) 85 L.Q.R. 530 (M. Cullity).

[36] (1818) 1 Swans. 13 at p. 17.

[37] *cf. McGrath v. Wallis; infra.*

[38] [1944] 2 All E.R. 472; see also *Pettitt v. Pettitt* [1970] A.C. 777.

purchase price,[39] although in some circumstances the court may be able to infer an agreement (giving rise to a constructive trust) to hold in shares which are not proportionate to the contributions.[40] The purchasers thus have a concurrent interest and can claim the due proportion of the proceeds on any eventual sale of the property to include a proportion of any increase in the value of the property.[41] The resulting trust may arise where the land is purchased subject to a mortgage which is paid off by instalments.[42] No resulting trust however arose where one member of a group was tenant of a flat, and all the residents shared the payment of the rent.[43]

Cases of this kind can give rise to serious conveyancing difficulties. The true facts of the purchase may be proved by oral evidence[44] and, not being part of the title, may not be known to a purchaser or mortgagee; who may then find himself dealing with a case of co-ownership without having appreciated this.[45] Many cases under this head are concerned with the question of the ownership of a matrimonial home, and are dealt with in Chapter 11.

Where two people contribute to the purchase of a house for their joint occupation which is conveyed into the name of one, the presumption of advancement, which arises if the legal owner is the wife or child of the other party, is a last resort, and is rebuttable by comparatively slight evidence in both cases.

In *McGrath v. Wallis*[46] a house was acquired for the occupation of a family (parents, son and daughter) but was put in the adult son's name to enable a mortgage loan to be obtained (the father being unemployed). The father contributed £34,500 towards the price of £42,995, the balance being raised by the mortgage. The father's solicitors drew up a declaration of trust whereby the beneficial interest was to be held as to 80 per cent for the father and 20 per cent for the son, but, for reasons which were not established, it was never executed. After the death of the parents, the son claimed absolute entitlement, but the Court of Appeal held that the presumption of advancement was rebutted. The parties' intentions were to hold in shares proportionate to their contributions.

---

[39] *Wray v. Steele* (1814) 2 V. & B. 388. The trust is traditionally regarded as resulting, but Lord Bridge described it as constructive in *Lloyds Bank plc v. Rosset* [1991] 1 A.C. 107 at 133.

[40] *Midland Bank plc v. Cooke* [1995] 4 All E.R. 562; *Drake v. Whipp* [1996] 1 F.L.R. 826; *post*, p. 265.

[41] *Diwell v. Farnes* [1959] 1 W.L.R. 624; *cf. Hussey v. Palmer* [1972] 1 W.L.R. 1286. See further, *post*, p. 271.

[42] *Moate v. Moate* [1948] 2 All E.R. 486.

[43] *Savage v. Dunningham* [1974] Ch. 181; (1973) 37 Conv.(N.S.) 440 (F. Crane).

[44] *Heard v. Pilley* (1869) L.R. 4 Ch.App. 548.

[45] *Cook v. Cook* [1962] P. 235; *post*, p. 276.

[46] [1995] 2 F.L.R. 114; criticised in (1995) 25 Fam.Law 552 (J. Dewar).

The decisive features were that the son alone was acceptable as mortgagor (which alone was probably enough to rebut the presumption); there was no evidence that the father had instructed the solicitors not to proceed with the declaration; and there was no reason why the father, who was only 63 at the time and not ill, should wish to give the house to the son. The observations in *Pettitt v. Pettitt*[47] and elsewhere as to the weakness of the presumption of advancement between husband and wife applied equally to father and child.

5. REFORM

The Law Commission has proposed certain reforms affecting the presumptions and purchase money resulting trusts.[48] These proposals apply to spouses and engaged couples,[49] but not to cohabitants.

The main proposal is that where money is spent to buy property, or property or money is transferred by one spouse to the other, for their joint use or benefit, the property or money should be jointly owned.[50] Where money or property is transferred by one spouse to the other for any other purpose, it should be owned by the transferee. In both cases, this is subject to a contrary intention on the part of the paying or transferring spouse, provided it is known to the other spouse.

The proposal relating to purchases does not apply to land,[51] on the ground that most matrimonial homes are now purchased in joint names and the spouses are likely to have taken legal advice when buying the home. There is no such exclusion regarding the proposal relating to transfers of property from one spouse to the other. Such a transfer which is not for their joint use and benefit will be treated as a gift under the above proposals whether the transferor is the husband or wife. Thus the presumption of advancement will apply equally to both spouses.[52] As the presumption now applies to all kinds of property, any reform must do as well.[53]

---

[47] [1970] A.C. 777.
[48] Law Com. No. 175 (1988), *Family Law; Matrimonial Property*.
[49] By virtue of Law Reform (Miscellaneous Provisions) Act 1970, s.2.
[50] Para. 4.1.
[51] Para. 4.2. Life assurance policies are also excluded.
[52] Para. 4.19.
[53] Para. 4.10.

CHAPTER 11

TRUSTS OF THE FAMILY HOME

1. Introduction 259	iv. Substantial Improvements 269
2. Acquisition of Interests in the Home 259	v. Size of the Share 270
A. Background to the Problem 259	vi. Date for Valuation of the Share ... 271
B. Conveyance to One Party Only 261	C. Legal Estate in Both Parties 271
i. Express Agreement or Declaration 262	3. Consequences of Co-ownership 272
	A. The Trust of Land 272
ii. Presumption of Resulting Trust; Direct Contributions 264	B. Occupation Rights 274
	C. Sale by Sole Trustee 276
iii. Indirect Contributions 266	D. Disputes over Sale 279

1. INTRODUCTION

IN the last chapter we saw the part played by the doctrine of resulting trusts in the acquisition of property interests. Most of the modern cases involve disputes between married or unmarried couples over ownership of the home. In this chapter we will examine the special considerations which apply to the matrimonial or family home. The first part of the chapter will deal with the establishment of a proprietary interest in the home, for example under the doctrines or resulting or constructive trusts. The second part will examine some of the problems of co-ownership of land. To complete the picture, reference should also be made to Chapter 28, where it will be seen that those who cannot establish an interest under a trust of the family home might nevertheless acquire rights as licensees or under the doctrine of estoppel.

2. ACQUISITION OF INTERESTS IN THE HOME

A. Background to the Problem

In the case of a married couple, one problem which arises is that the older rules of property law, which became established at a time when the wife was less likely to be earning her living than is the case today, do not properly recognise her contribution to the relationship.

The modern view is that marriage is a partnership between equals, in which the wife has an economic contribution to make. But she does not always insist on the matrimonial home being conveyed to the spouses jointly; or on a declaration of trust of a share of the house in favour of herself. Nor is justice done to her by the presumption of a resulting trust, based on payment of the purchase money; first, because work in the house is not money-producing, and secondly, because if she has a job, her earnings may be spent on household expenses and not in contributing to the purchase price of the house. "The cock can feather the nest because he does not have to spend most of his time sitting on it."[1]

Another problem stems from the fact that today an increasing proportion of couples cohabit outside marriage. Should their relationship break down, the court has no statutory power to adjust their property interests. Divorcing couples, on the other hand, can invoke the court's discretionary powers to order a distribution of the property of the spouses.[2] This statutory jurisdiction will not be discussed here, but its significance must be emphasised. The following account deals only with the general law, which applies, subject to minor exceptions, equally to married and unmarried couples. A difficulty frequently encountered, as will be seen, is that the parties do not formulate their intention at the time the property is acquired, but consider the matter only when their relationship breaks down.

The question then is how to ensure that the ownership of the home is fairly shared. The possibility of giving the court, in the case of married couples, a wide discretionary power to declare what are the appropriate shares to be held by disputing spouses in any particular case has been rejected[3]; likewise the concept of community of property.[4] A proposal[5] that the matrimonial home should be shared equally was not implemented. The property rights of cohabitants are currently under review.[6] Until the enactment of any reforms, the rights of the parties are determined according to the principles of property law, making whatever use is appropriate of evidence of

---

[1] *Per* Sir Jocelyn Simon, extrajudicially quoted by Lord Hodson in *Pettitt v. Pettitt* [1970] A.C. 777 at p. 811.

[2] Matrimonial Causes Act 1973, as amended by Family Law Act 1996; *Wachtel v. Wachtel* [1973] Fam. 72; (1974) 118 S.J. 431 (S. Cretney). Property disputes between spouses are best settled under this jurisdiction; *Williams v. Williams* [1976] Ch. 278 at p. 286; *Suttill v. Graham* [1977] 1 W.L.R. 819 at p. 824. The statutory jurisdiction does not apply to engaged couples by reason of Law Reform (Miscellaneous Provisions) Act 1970, s.2(1); *Mossop v. Mossop* [1989] Fam. 77; [1988] Conv. 286 (J.E.M.).

[3] *Gissing v. Gissing* [1971] A.C. 886.

[4] Law Com. No. 52, para. 59. See also Law Com. No. 90, para. 5.20.

[5] Third Report on Family Property (Law Com. No. 86). These proposals were flawed by registration requirements.

[6] Law Com. No. 239, para. 6.7.

agreement, declarations of trust (which comply with the necessary formalities applicable to trusts of land) and of inferences and presumptions.

The first question to determine is whether each party owns some share. If so, there is co-ownership, and the house is held upon trust, even though it may be vested only in one.[7] The next question is to determine what is the share of each party.[8] A number of other problems can arise, such as a decision on sale if one party wishes to sell and the other to retain; questions as to the right to possession and the payment of rent; and the protection of an occupying co-owner if the sole legal owner sells to a third party.

B. Conveyance to One Party Only

If the house is conveyed to one party only, to the man, let us assume, for that is the usual case, then he will prima facie be the owner of the whole beneficial interest as well.[9] If the documents of title expressly declare the beneficial interests, that, in the absence of fraud or mistake, is conclusive,[10] although those who were not parties to the deed cannot be prejudiced by such a declaration if they have contributed.[11] Failing that, the woman may claim a share of the beneficial interest in various ways. First, there may be an express contract in writing,[12] or a trust in her favour which is evidenced in writing.[13] Subject to estoppel arguments, an oral contract for the disposition of an interest in land is void. An oral declaration of a trust of land which is not evidenced in writing is unenforceable unless it has been acted upon so as to give rise to a constructive trust.[14] This is discussed below. If there is no express agreement or declaration, direct contributions in money or money's worth have traditionally been regarded as giving rise to a resulting trust, but the House of Lords appears now to regard direct contributions as creating a constructive trust.[15] As we will see, their Lordships considered that no common intention to share (giving rise to a constructive trust) could be inferred from indirect contributions. Finally, a trust

---

[7] *Post*, p. 272.

[8] *Post*, p. 270.

[9] *Gissing v. Gissing* [1971] A.C. 886 at pp. 900, 901, 910; *Burns v. Burns* [1984] Ch. 317.

[10] *Pettitt v. Pettitt* [1970] A.C. 777 at p. 813; *Goodman v. Gallant* [1986] Fam. 106.

[11] See *City of London Building Society v. Flegg* [1988] A.C. 54.

[12] Law of Property (Miscellaneous Provisions) Act 1989, s.2. See (1990) 10 L.S. 325 (L. Bently and P. Coughlan).

[13] L.P.A. 1925, s.53(1)(*b*).

[14] *Midland Bank Ltd v. Dobson* [1986] 1 F.L.R. 171; *Grant v. Edwards* [1986] Ch. 638.

[15] *Lloyds Bank plc v. Rosset* [1991] 1 A.C. 107.

has been imposed in some cases simply in the interests of justice.[16]

i. Express Agreement or Declaration. If the declaration is contained in the documents of title, then it will be conclusive, as stated above. If it is not contained in the documents of title but is nevertheless evidenced in writing, it is enforceable under section 53(1)(*b*) of the Law of Property Act 1925. These formality requirements do not apply to resulting or constructive trusts.[17] Resulting trusts are dealt with below. In the present context, the question arises as to the circumstances necessary for the imposition of a constructive trust where there is an express oral declaration or agreement.

The first point to consider is what constitutes an express oral declaration or agreement. The question is whether prior to the acquisition, or exceptionally at some later date,[18] the parties had an agreement to share, based on evidence of express discussions, however imperfectly remembered and however imprecise the terms.[19] A common intention to renovate a house as a joint venture or to share it as a family home does not amount to a common intention to share the beneficial ownership.[20] An excuse as to why the property is in the man's name will, however, be treated as an express declaration of an intention to share the beneficial ownership.[21] An express common intention means one that is communicated between the parties.[22]

Assuming that an express common intention is established, the claimant must also show that she has acted upon it to her detriment if a constructive trust (or estoppel) is to arise.[23] An oral agreement alone cannot suffice, as this would infringe the formality rules and could prejudice the legal owner's creditors.[24] It is clear that significant contributions in money or money's worth, even though

---

[16] *Cooke v. Head* [1972] 1 W.L.R. 518; (1973) C.L.P. 17 at p. 25 (A. Oakley); *Eves v. Eves* [1975] 1 W.L.R. 1338.

[17] L.P.A. 1925, s. 53(2); Law of Property (Miscellaneous Provisions) Act 1989, s.2(5).

[18] *Bernard v. Josephs* [1982] Ch. 391; *Burns v. Burns* [1984] Ch. 317; *Austin v. Keele* (1987) 61 A.L.J.R. 605; *Lloyds Bank plc v. Rosset* [1991] 1 A.C. 107; *Stokes v. Anderson* [1991] 1 F.L.R. 391.

[19] *Lloyds Bank plc v. Rosset, supra*. But see (1996) 16 L.S. 325 (N. Glover and P. Todd).

[20] *Ibid.*

[21] *Eves v. Eves, supra* (excuse that woman under 21); *Grant v. Edwards* [1986] Ch. 638 (excuse that joint names might prejudice her divorce proceedings); criticised (1987) 50 M.L.R. 94 (B. Sufrin); *cf.* (1993) 3 Carib.L.R. 96 (R. Smith); (1995) 145 N.L.J. 423, 456 (P. Milne).

[22] *Springette v. Defoe* (1993) 65 P. & C.R. 1. See, however, *Midland Bank plc v. Cooke* [1995] 4 All E.R. 562; *post*, p. 265.

[23] The onus is on the legal owner to prove that any detrimental act was not done in reliance upon the common intention; *Greasley v. Cooke* [1980] 1 W.L.R. 1306; *Maharaj v. Chand* [1986] A.C. 898.

[24] *Midland Bank Ltd v. Dobson* [1986] 1 F.L.R. 171; *cf. Re Densham* [1975] 1 W.L.R. 1519.

indirect, will satisfy the requirements of detrimental reliance. Thus in *Grant v. Edwards*[25] a woman was entitled to a half share where, pursuant to an express oral declaration, she had made substantial indirect contributions to the mortgage by applying her earnings to the joint household expenses in addition to keeping house and bringing up the children. The Court of Appeal considered that any detrimental act relating to the joint lives of the parties would have sufficed. Such a view, while requiring clarification, seems to provide an opportunity for a sympathetic treatment of a woman who has made no financial contribution.[26] In similar vein, the Privy Council has said that once a common intention has been established it may not be difficult to find conduct on the part of the woman which is referable to the creation of her beneficial interest.[27]

The House of Lords reviewed these principles in *Lloyds Bank plc v. Rosset*.[28] In that case there was no express common intention. If there had been, the wife's acts of decorating and supervising renovation works would not have constituted detrimental reliance, as they were acts which any wife would do.[29] Acts which have been considered sufficient include refraining from seeking repayment of a loan or interest upon it,[30] and a payment of £12,000 to the man so that he could buy out his estranged wife's share and pay the mortgage on her new house.[31] Where a constructive trust arises from an express common intention coupled with direct and indirect contributions (such as labour and contributions to household expenses) the latter may increase the share beyond that which would otherwise arise under a resulting trust.[32] In *Hammond v. Mitchell*[33] a woman was held entitled to a half share of a bungalow when, pursuant to an oral agreement, she acted as the man's unpaid business assistant and supported him in his business ventures as well as looking after the home and children. The judge also classified her act of agreeing to subordinate her rights to those of a mortgagee as one of detrimental reliance, but this seems inadequate. "Can consent to the possible

---

[25] *Supra.* See also *Eves v. Eves, supra.*
[26] (1987) 50 M.L.R. 94 (B. Sufrin); [1987] Conv. 16 (J. Montgomery); (1996) 16 L.S. 218 (A. Lawson); *cf. Coombes v. Smith* [1986] 1 W.L.R. 808, *post,* p. 875.
[27] *Austin v. Keele* (1987) 61 A.L.J.R. 605 at p. 610.
[28] [1991] 1 A.C. 107; (1990) 106 L.Q.R. 539 (J. Davies); [1990] Conv. 314 (M. Thompson); All E.R.Rev. 1990, p. 138 (S. Cretney); (1991) 50 C.L.J. 38 (M. Dixon); (1991) 54 M.L.R. 126 (S. Gardner).
[29] *cf. Ungurian v. Lesnoff* [1990] Ch. 206; (1990) 49 C.L.J. 25 (M. Oldham) (common intention to create life interest sufficiently acted upon by decorating and refurbishment).
[30] *Risch v. McFee* (1991) 61 P. & C.R. 42.
[31] *Stokes v. Anderson* [1991] 1 F.L.R. 391. The woman had also spent £2,500 on decorating. The parties had drawn up a promissory note, but it was held that the £12,000 was not in fact a loan.
[32] *Drake v. Whipp* [1996] 1 F.L.R. 826; *post,* p. 265.
[33] [1991] 1 W.L.R. 1127; (1992) 22 Fam. Law 523 (L. Clarke and R. Edmunds).

loss of property one does not own make one an owner of that very property?"[34]

ii. Presumption of Resulting Trust; Direct Contributions.
There will be a purchase money resulting trust in favour of a person who has contributed to the purchase price. Beneficial ownership will normally be enjoyed in the proportion in which the purchase money has been provided.[35] If the purchase money is provided equally, the parties are beneficial joint tenants. If the contributions are unequal, they are tenants in common. Payment of, or substantial contributions to the mortgage instalments, will usually suffice[36]; however, such payments do not give rise to a resulting trust unless the payer had assumed liability to make them when the property was purchased (although they may found a constructive trust).[37] For a resulting trust to arise, any payments must be in money or money's worth.[38]

The presumption of advancement may similarly arise in a case where a husband has transferred or arranged for the transfer of the legal estate to his wife; but, as has been seen, statements in *Pettitt v. Pettitt*[39] show that the influence of the presumptions has been much reduced. There is no presumption of advancement where a wife has transferred to her husband[40]; nor in the case of an unmarried couple.[41]

In the case of direct contributions, it does not seem that any actual intention to share must be proved, because the effect of the doctrine of resulting trusts is that such an intention is rebuttably presumed. Unfortunately the House of Lords has made the position uncertain by treating direct contributions as giving rise to a constructive trust.[42]

---

[34] [1992] Conv. 218 at p. 222 (A. Lawson); All E.R.Rev. 1992, p. 210 (P. Clarke); (1993) 56 M.L.R. 224 (P. O'Hagan).
[35] *Re Roger's Question* [1948] 1 All E.R. 328; *Bull v. Bull* [1955] 1 Q.B. 234. A strict view was taken in *Winkworth v. Edward Baron Development Co. Ltd* [1986] 1 W.L.R. 1512, where, however, the protection of creditors was a significant factor. See [1987] Conv. 217 (J. Warburton).
[36] *Springette v. Defoe* (1993) 65 P. & C.R. 1; *Huntingford v. Hobbs* [1993] 1 F.L.R. 736; [1992] Conv. 347 (H. Norman).
[37] *Re Roger's Question* [1948] 1 All E.R. 328; (1994) 8 *Trust Law International* 43 (P. Matthews). See also *Winkworth v. Edward Baron Developments Ltd* [1986] 1 W.L.R. 1512 at p. 1515.
[38] *Button v. Button* [1968] 1 All E.R. 1064; *Muetzel v. Muetzel* [1970] 1 W.L.R. 188; *Wachtel v. Wachtel* [1973] Fam. 72 at p. 92, *per* Lord Denning M.R.
[39] 1970 A.C. 777. See also *Simpson v. Simpson* [1992] 1 F.L.R. 601.
[40] *Heseltine v. Heseltine* [1971] 1 W.L.R. 342 (personalty).
[41] Unless they had agreed to marry; Law Reform (Miscellaneous Provisions) Act 1970, s.2(1); *Mossop v. Mossop* [1989] Fam. 77. As to "agreement to marry," see *Shaw v. Fitzgerald* [1992] 1 F.L.R. 357.
[42] *Lloyds Bank plc v. Rosset* [1991] 1 A.C. 107.

Recent cases display a broad approach to direct contributions. In *McHardy and Sons (a firm) v. Warren*[43] the Court of Appeal held that where a parent pays a deposit on a house as a wedding present, the irresistible conclusion is that all three intended the couple to have equal shares in the house and not shares measured by reference to the percentage which the deposit bore to the price. In *Midland Bank plc v. Cooke*[44] a house was bought in the husband's name with a mortgage loan of £6,450, his savings of £950 and a gift of £1,100 from his parents to the couple. The wife did not pay the mortgage directly but paid other outgoings from her earnings. Both stated that they never discussed their shares. In possession proceedings relating to a later mortgage, the Court of Appeal held that if an equitable interest has been acquired by direct contribution (the money derived from the gift) and there is no express evidence of intention, the court will assess the proportions the parties are assumed to have intended by surveying the course of dealing between them, their sharing of the burdens and benefits of the property, and all conduct throwing light on the question. The court is not bound to find that the shares are proportionate to direct contributions on a strict resulting trust basis and is free to infer an intention to share differently on general equitable principles. On that basis (which seems over generous to the wife) the parties took in equal shares, as they agreed to share everything equally: the profits of the husband's business and the risks of indebtedness if it failed, the upbringing of the children, and the home (which had been put into joint names after the date of the plaintiff's mortgage) which the wife had helped to maintain and improve, coupled with the added commitment of marriage. Similarly in *Drake v. Whipp*,[45] where the woman made a direct contribution of about one fifth to the purchase and conversion of a barn. The parties had a common intention that she should have a beneficial interest, which the Court of Appeal determined as one third, adopting a "broad brush" approach, and taking into account her work on the conversion and contribution to household expenses. The need to distinguish constructive and resulting trust principles was emphasised. Thus the finding of a common intention may enable the court to fix a fair share which differs from the proportionate resulting trust.

[43] [1994] 2 F.L.R. 338, questioned in (1994) 24 Fam. Law 567 (J. Dewar). See also *Halifax Building Society v. Brown* [1996] 1 F.L.R. 103 (loan from mother-in-law for deposit).
[44] [1995] 4 All E.R. 562, applying *Gissing v. Gissing* [1971] A.C. 886. The different approaches of Dillon L.J. in *McHardy, supra*, and in *Springette v. Defoe* (1993) 65 P. & C.R. 1 were "mystifying". See All E.R.Rev. 1995, pp. 286 (S. Cretney) and 312 (P. Clarke); (1996) 112 L.Q.R. 378 (S. Gardner); (1996) 55 C.L.J. 194 (M. Oldham); (1996) 26 Fam. Law 298 (D. Wragg) and 484 (M. Pawlowski); [1996] 8 C.F.L.Q. 261 (G. Battersby); (1996) 16 L.S. 325 at p. 340 (N. Glover and P. Todd); [1997] Conv. 66 (M. Dixon).
[45] [1996] 1 F.L.R. 826.

The next question is whether, in the absence of a direct contributions or express agreement, a common intention to share may be inferred solely from indirect contributions or other conduct.

iii. Indirect Contributions. It is important to appreciate at the outset that, since *Gissing v. Gissing*,[46] the court does not decide how the parties might have ordered their affairs; it only finds how they did. "The court cannot devise agreements which the parties never made. The court cannot ascribe intentions which the parties in fact never had."[47] In that case the House of Lords rejected the claim of a wife who had paid £220 for furnishings and for laying a lawn, plus some household expenses, because she had made no contribution to the purchase price. It was, however, accepted that a wife who contributed indirectly by relieving her husband of household expenses and thereby enabling him to pay the mortgage would be entitled to an interest.[48]

Later decisions in the Court of Appeal, primarily in Lord Denning's time, supported the view that substantial financial contributions, even though indirect, would suffice for the acquisition of a share.[49] Thus interests were acquired by the contribution of physical labour on the property,[50] or by unpaid work in the family business which enabled the husband to put the money saved towards the purchase of property.[51] Domestic duties in the home, on the other hand, have never sufficed. In *Burns v. Burns*[52] the woman's housework, decorating and the purchase of chattels for the home over a period of 17 years gave her no share. If this was unjust, it was suggested that the remedy lay with Parliament. The position is otherwise in Canada, where the view that domestic services do not suffice is now considered untenable. Thus in *Peter v. Beblow*[53] a woman who cared for her own children and those of her partner for some years, did the housework, and contributed to the housekeeping with earnings from a part-time job was held entitled to the house under a constructive trust on the basis that her partner (who was entitled to keep a van and a houseboat acquired during the cohabitation) would otherwise be unjustly enriched by her services, which enhanced his ability to pay off the mortgage and acquire other

---

[46] [1971] A.C. 886.
[47] *Ibid., per* Lord Morris of Borth-y-Gest at pp. 898; *cf. Bristol and West Building Society v. Henning* [1985] 1 W.L.R. 778, *post* p. 279.
[48] [1971] A.C. 886 at pp. 903, 907–908.
[49] *Falconer v. Falconer* [1970] 1 W.L.R. 1333; *Hargrave v. Newton* [1971] 1 W.L.R. 1611; *Wachtel v. Wachtel* [1973] Fam. 72.
[50] *Cooke v. Head* [1972] 1 W.L.R. 518. For improvements, see *post*, p. 269.
[51] *Nixon v. Nixon* [1969] 1 W.L.R. 1676.
[52] [1984] Ch. 317 (unmarried couple). See also *Richards v. Dove* [1974] 1 All E.R. 888; *Layton v. Martin* (1986) 16 Fam. Law 212; *Windeler v. Whitehall* [1990] 2 F.L.R. 505 (housework and business entertaining insufficient).
[53] (1993) 101 D.L.R. (4th) 621; *post*, p. 268.

assets. The free accommodation she had enjoyed was not sufficient compensation.

In English law it appears that, in the absence of an express common intention, indirect contributions will not suffice. In *Lloyds Bank plc v. Rosset*,[54] where the wife had made no substantial contribution, direct or indirect, Lord Bridge took the opportunity to state that direct contributions (whether initially or by payment of the mortgage) were necessary, and that "it is at least extremely doubtful whether anything less will do."[55] The earlier cases of *Eves v. Eves*[56] (extensive decorative work and heavy gardening) and *Grant v. Edwards*[57] (substantial indirect contributions to the mortgage by applying earnings to household expenses, plus running the home) were correctly decided because both involved an express common intention. In the absence of the latter, neither claimant would have succeeded, because the conduct in each case "fell far short" of conduct which would by itself have supported a claim to a share. Applying this principle, it has been held that a woman who acted as the man's unpaid business assistant, supported him in his speculative ventures and looked after the home and children, could not acquire a share in the property in the absence of an express common intention.[58] Likewise where a daughter worked full-time in her mother's public house for pocket money only, assisting her mother to make a profit which facilitated the purchase of a house. The daughter had no interest in the house as there was neither direct contribution nor express agreement.[59] We have seen, however, that where a common intention to share is inferred from a direct contribution, indirect contributions may also be taken into account in assessing the shares the parties are assumed to have intended.[60] This approach reduces the impact of *Lloyds Bank plc v. Rosset*,[61] but the apparent exclusion from any share of a spouse whose only contributions are indirect seems capable of leading to injustice, although mitigated by the ease with which an express common intention may be found to exist.

A preferable solution might be to base such claims on the doctrine of proprietary estoppel, where the act of detrimental reliance need not take the form of financial contributions, and which does not

---

[54] [1991] 1 A.C. 107. These principles were held applicable where the property was in joint names but the beneficial interest was not declared; *Rhoden v. Joseph* [1990] E.G.C.S. 115.

[55] *Ibid.* at p. 133.

[56] [1975] 1 W.L.R. 1338.

[57] [1986] Ch. 638.

[58] *Hammond v. Mitchell* [1991] 1 W.L.R. 1127 (the Spanish house); *ante*, p. 263.

[59] *Ivin v. Blake* (1994) 67 P. & C.R. 263; criticised [1996] Conv. 462 (A. Lawson).

[60] *Midland Bank plc v. Cooke* [1995] 4 All E.R. 562.

[61] *Supra*. See (1995) 25 Fam. Law 633 (P. Wylie).

require a search for an artificial common intention,[62] although estoppel itself has elements of artificiality.[63] Recent cases have tended to assimilate the doctrines of constructive trusts and proprietary estoppel,[64] although the process is not yet complete.[65] It appears that interests under constructive trusts crystallise as soon as a sufficient act of detrimental reliance has occurred, prior to their vindication by the court, so that they can affect third parties.[66] Whether proprietary estoppel interests take effect before the court order is not yet established.[67] If they do, a distinction is that interests under trusts are overreachable, whereas estoppel interests are not.[68]

Other solutions have been found in Commonwealth jurisdictions.[69] In Australia non-financial contributions have been recognised by legislation.[70] The principles of unjust enrichment have been utilised in Australia, New Zealand and Canada,[71] although "unconscionability is not a notion which makes hard cases easier to decide".[72] The majority of the Canadian Supreme Court in *Peter v. Beblow*[73] considered that a constructive trust should be imposed on the basis of unjust enrichment where there was a direct link between substantial indirect contributions and the acquisition or improvement of property; otherwise compensation could be available on a *quantum meruit* basis. The decision also reflects the "reasonable expectation" principle applied in New Zealand in *Lankow v. Rose*,[74] that where a plaintiff has contributed in more than a minor way,

---

[62] *Gillies v. Keogh* [1989] 2 N.Z.L.R. 327 (suggesting also that indirect contributions should suffice for a constructive trust); (1990) 106 L.Q.R. 213 (M. Bryan). See also [1987] Conv. 93 (J. Eekelaar); [1990] Conv. 314 (M. Thompson) and 370 (D. Hayton); *cf.* (1993) 109 L.Q.R. 114 (P. Ferguson); (1993) 109 L.Q.R. 485 (D. Hayton).

[63] *Phillips v. Phillips* [1993] 3 N.Z.L.R. 159, doubting estoppel as the way forward.

[64] *Grant v. Edwards* [1986] Ch. 638; *Austin v. Keele* (1987) 61 A.L.J.R 605; *Lloyds Bank plc v. Rosset, supra* (but see (1991) 54 M.L.R. 126 and (1993) 109 L.Q.R. 263 (S. Gardner)); *Hammond v. Mitchell* [1991] 1 W.L.R. 1127; *Lloyds Bank plc v. Carrick* [1996] 4 All E.R. 630; (1996) 112 L.Q.R. 549 (P. Ferguson).

[65] *Stokes v. Anderson* [1991] 1 F.L.R. 391.

[66] Implicit in *Lloyds Bank plc v. Rosset, supra.* See [1990] Conv. 370 (D. Hayton); (1991) 5 *Trust Law International* 9 (J. Warburton); [1991] Conv. 155 (P. Evans); Presidential Address to the Holdsworth Club, Birmingham University (1991) (Sir Nicolas Browne-Wilkinson), published in (1996) 10 *Trust Law International* 98.

[67] *Post*, p. 894.

[68] L.P.A. 1925, s.2. A further distinction may lie in the onus of proof; (1993) 109 L.Q.R. 114 (P. Ferguson). See also (1993) 3 Carib.L.R. 96 (R. Smith).

[69] See generally Pearce and Stevens, *The Law of Trusts and Equitable Obligations*, pp. 648–653. For the position in Ireland, see [1993] Conv. 359 (J. Mee).

[70] De Facto Relationships Act 1984 (N.S.W.); (1992) 22 Fam. Law 72 at p. 76 (P. Clarke). See also Scottish Law Com. No. 135 (1992), *Report on Family Law*.

[71] *Baumgartner v. Baumgartner* (1988) 62 A.L.J. 29; *Gillies v. Keogh* [1989] 2 N.Z.L.R. 327; *Peter v. Beblow* (1993) 101 D.L.R. (4th) 621.

[72] (1990) 106 L.Q.R. 25 at p. 28 (M. Bryan); (1994) 8 *Trust Law International* 74 (M. Bryan). See also (1993) 109 L.Q.R. 263 (S. Gardner), advocating the "communality" approach based on the relationship itself, with less emphasis on intention or contribution.

[73] *Supra; ante*, p. 266.

[74] [1995] 1 N.Z.L.R. 277; *McMahon v. McMahon* [1996] 3 N.Z.L.R. 334. See also *The Frontiers of Liability*, Vol. 2, p. 204 (J. Eekelaar).

either directly or indirectly, to the acquisition, preservation or enhancement of the defendant's assets, a constructive trust will be imposed on the basis that the parties must reasonably have expected the plaintiff to have an interest. The contribution need not be financial, but must be causally related to the acquisition, preservation or enhancement. This objective test thus replaces the search for an artificial common intention, and gives effect to indirect contributions which, although giving rise to difficulties of proof and quantification, are just as real as direct contributions.[75]

Finally, it seems that the principles applicable to stable relationships between unmarried couples are the same as those applicable between husband and wife,[76] but the nature of the relationship is an important factor when considering what inferences should be drawn from the way the parties have conducted their affairs and in the ascertainment of their common intention.[77] The whole question is of reduced importance in the case of divorcing couples, as mentioned above,[78] because of the wide discretionary powers given to the court to make a distribution of property under the Matrimonial Causes Act 1973.

iv. Substantial Improvements. Some of the problems of indirect contributions arose where one of the parties had made a substantial contribution in time or money to the improvement of the property subsequent to the purchase. The Matrimonial Proceedings and Property Act 1970, s.37, which applies only to married couples,[79] provides that:

"where a husband or wife contributes in money or money's worth to the improvement of real or personal property in which ... either or both of them has or have a beneficial interest, the husband or wife so contributing shall, if the contribution is of a substantial nature and subject to any agreement between them to the contrary express or implied, be treated as having then acquired by virtue of his or her contribution a share or an enlarged share, as the case may be, in that beneficial interest of such an

---

[75] *Ibid.* at p. 295.
[76] There is of course no presumption of advancement; *ante*, p. 246. See generally (1980) 96 L.Q.R. 248 (A. Zuckerman); (1976) 40 Conv. (N.S.) 351 (M. Richards).
[77] *Bernard v. Josephs* [1982] Ch. 391; (1982) 98 L.Q.R. 517 (J. Thomson); [1982] Conv. 444 (J. Warburton); All E.R.Rev. 1982, 150 (R. Deech) and 169 (P. Clarke). (1983) 42 C.L.J. 30 (K. Gray). See also *Gordon v. Douce* [1983] 1 W.L.R. 563; *Midland Bank plc v. Cooke* [1995] 4 All E.R. 562. As to engaged couples, see Law Reform (Miscellaneous Provisions) Act 1970, s.2; *Mossop v. Mossop* [1989] Fam. 77.
[78] *Ante*, p. 260.
[79] And to engaged couples by reason of Law Reform (Miscellaneous Provisions) Act 1970, s.2(1).

extent as may have been then agreed or, in default of such agreement, as may seem in all the circumstances just . . . "[80]

Lord Denning has said that this provision was declaratory of the previous law,[81] indeed the language of the statute is declaratory. As far as unmarried couples are concerned, substantial improvements may give rise to an interest on the basis of common intention or estoppel, even though section 37 does not apply.[82]

v. Size of the Share. The size of the share of each party may be determined on resulting trust principles, or on the basis of the common intention of the parties. The time of acquisition of the property is the starting point for the ascertainment of the shares, but later events, up to and after any separation, can be taken into account.[83] Where entitlement is based on direct contributions (to the purchase price or mortgage repayments[84]), the shares will normally be proportionate to the contributions,[85] although an intention to hold differently may be established expressly[86] or may be inferred from additional indirect contributions and conduct.[87] If it has been agreed that one party will be liable for the mortgage, that party's share will be debited with any outstanding principal.[88] Where entitlement arises from an express common intention coupled with detrimental reliance, the share is not necessarily proportionate to the value of any indirect contributions, and may be greater.[89] Such indirect contributions are in any event difficult to evaluate. If the parties have agreed that the woman is to acquire a specified share if she acts in a particular way, it seems that she will acquire that share by so acting, even though the value of her contribution may be less than

---

[80] *Griffiths v. Griffiths* [1973] 1 W.L.R. 1454; *Re Nicholson (decd.)* [1974] 1 W.L.R. 476.

[81] *Davis v. Vale* [1971] 1 W.L.R. 1021; *Jansen v. Jansen* [1965] P. 478.

[82] *Thomas v. Fuller-Brown* [1988] 1 F.L.R. 237 (where the claim failed because the inference was that the expenditure was in return for rent-free accommodation); *Cadman v. Bell* [1988] E.G.C.S. 139 (licence for life); *Passee v. Passee* [1988] 1 F.L.R. 263; [1988] Conv. 361 (J. Warburton); *Huntingford v. Hobbs* (1992) 24 H.L.R. 652 (joint names); *Drake v. Whipp* [1996] 1 F.L.R. 826. It is otherwise if the money was advanced as a loan; *Spence v. Brown* (1988) 18 Fam. Law 291; *cf. Hussey v. Palmer* [1972] 1 W.L.R. 1286; *ante*, p. 52.

[83] *Bernard v. Josephs* [1982] Ch. 391; *Gordon v. Douce* [1983] 1 W.L.R. 563; *Burns v. Burns* [1984] Ch. 317.

[84] Whether capital or interest; *Passee v. Passee, supra*. See also Insolvency Act 1986, s.338.

[85] See *Springette v. Defoe* (1993) 65 P. & C.R. 1; *Evans v. Hayward* [1995] 2 F.L.R. 511 (discount to council tenant exercising right to buy is a contribution to the price); [1996] 8 C.F.L.Q. 313 (C. Davis and C. Hunter); *Huntingford v. Hobbs* [1993] 1 F.L.R. 736 (cost of building conservatory included); (1993) 23 Fam. Law 176 (P. Wylie). In these cases the property was in joint names.

[86] *Drake v. Whipp, supra*.

[87] *Midland Bank plc v. Cooke* [1995] 4 All E.R. 562; *ante*, p. 265.

[88] *Savill v. Goodall* [1993] 1 F.L.R. 755; (1993) 23 Fam. Law 290 (S. Cretney).

[89] See *Eves v. Eves* [1975] 1 W.L.R. 1338; *Grant v. Edwards* [1986] Ch. 638.

the value of the agreed share.[90] Where there is an express common intention to share but no agreement as to the size of the share, the court will not be defeated by the element of uncertainty. An equal division based on the maxim that "equity is equality" is not the preferred solution.[91] The court will determine what is a "fair share" on a broad approach, taking into account the total contributions.[92] To insist on the level of certainty required by the law of contract could lead to the unjust enrichment of the legal owner. Of course, any express declaration in the title documents as to the size of the shares is conclusive.[93]

vi. Date for Valuation of the Share. If it is established that a person is entitled to a share of the home under a trust (express, constructive or resulting), it follows that he or she is entitled to share proportionately in any increase (or decrease) in its value, although occurring after separation, until such time as the property is sold.[94] This principle has been firmly upheld by the Court of Appeal.[95] Credit will be given by way of "equitable accounting" for expenditure such as mortgage payments and repairs incurred by the occupying spouse after separation.[96]

C. Legal Estate in Both Parties

Where the legal title is in both parties, the beneficial interest will prima facie also be shared.[97] Any express declaration of the beneficial interests in the title documents will be conclusive.[98] A Land Registry transfer form which states that the transferees are entitled

---

[90] This is the "quid pro quo" constructive trust, which distinguishes the situation from proprietary estoppel. See [1990] Conv. 370 (D. Hayton); *cf.* (1993) 109 L.Q.R. 263 at p. 266 (S. Gardner); *Gissing v. Gissing* [1971] A.C. 887 at p. 905; *Grant v. Edwards* [1986] Ch. 638 at p. 652; *Austin v. Keele* (1987) 61 A.L.J.R. 605 at p. 610.

[91] *Gissing v. Gissing, supra,* at pp. 897, 903; *Hammond v. Mitchell* [1991] 1 W.L.R. 1127 (although equal division upheld on facts).

[92] *Gissing v. Gissing, supra,* at p. 909; *Stokes v. Anderson* [1991] 1 F.L.R. 391; *Drake v. Whipp, supra.* See also *Risch v. McFee* (1991) 61 P. & C.R. 42 (loan which claimant had not sought to recover treated as contribution).

[93] *Ante,* p. 261.

[94] Or the co-ownership ends in another way, *e.g.* if one buys the other out.

[95] *Turton v. Turton* [1988] Ch. 542; [1987] Conv. 378 (J. Warburton); (1987) 103 L.Q.R. 500; (1988) 18 Fam. Law 72 (J. Montgomery); (1989) 86/31 L.S.Gaz. 31 (I. Hardcastle); *Gordon v. Douce* [1983] 1 W.L.R. 563; *Walker v. Hall* (1984) 14 Fam. Law 21; *Passee v. Passee* [1988] 1 F.L.R. 263. See also *Cousins v. Dzosens* (1984) 81 L.S.Gaz. 2855; *Bernard v. Josephs* [1982] Ch. 391.

[96] *Re Pavlou (a Bankrupt)* [1993] 1 W.L.R. 1047; [1995] Conv. 391 (E. Cooke).

[97] *Pettitt v. Petitt* [1970] A.C. 777 at pp. 813–814; *Bernard v. Josephs* [1982] Ch. 391; *Burns v. Burns* [1984] Ch. 317.

[98] See *Goodman v. Gallant* [1986] Fam. 106; (1986) 45 C.L.J. 205 (S. Juss); [1986] Conv. 355 (J.E.M.). (Severance of beneficial joint tenancy must result in equal shares even though unequal contributions). See also *Roy v. Roy* [1996] 1 F.L.R. 541; *Hembury v. Peachey* (1996) 72 P. & C.R. Digest 46. For the position where the declaration contains inconsistent provisions, see *Martin v. Martin* (1987) 54 P. & C.R. 238.

for their own benefit and that the survivor can give a valid receipt for capital money will be treated as a declaration of a beneficial joint tenancy.[99] Where, however, the words "for their own benefit" are missing, the statement that the survivor can give a valid receipt is not equivalent to a declaration of a beneficial joint tenancy.[1] The title documents should make the position clear, but if they contain no declaration, shares will be determined by any express common intention of the parties (which has been relied upon).[2] If no express common intention can be established, the parties will normally take shares proportionate to their contributions under resulting trust principles,[3] although an agreement to hold differently may be inferred from indirect contributions or conduct.[4] Where a husband purchases property and has it conveyed into the names of himself and his wife, the presumption of advancement may apply, although of limited strength today.[5] Where a wife is the purchaser, and has the property conveyed into joint names, the presumption of a resulting trust will be easily rebutted. In modern circumstances there would seem to be no explanation other than a wish to hold equally.[6]

3. CONSEQUENCES OF CO-OWNERSHIP

A. The Trust of Land

The two forms of co-ownership existing under the modern law are the joint tenancy and the tenancy in common. Here only a brief outline will be given, as the details may be found in the land law books.[7] Under the Law of Property Act 1925 a trust for sale was imposed on both forms of co-ownership, while successive interests came within the Settled Land Act 1925. This system operated for many years, but was subject to criticism partly because the dual system was perceived as unnecessary and partly because the duty to sell which arose under the trust for sale was not readily understood by co-owners. Furthermore, this duty to sell brought into play the doctrine of conversion,[8] often with inconvenient and artificial results. The effect of this doctrine was that the interests of the

---

[99] *Re Gorman* [1990] 1 W.L.R. 616 (even if the transferees have not signed the form).

[1] *Harwood v. Harwood* [1991] 2 F.L.R. 274; *Huntingford v. Hobbs* [1993] 1 F.L.R. 736.

[2] *Rhoden v. Jospeh* [1990] E.G.C.S. 115; *Hungtingford v. Hobbs, supra*; *Savill v. Goodall* [1993] 1 F.L.R. 755.

[3] *Dyer v. Dyer* (1788) 2 Cox Eq.Cas. 92; *Pettitt v. Pettitt* [1970] A.C. 777 at p. 814; *Springette v. Defoe* (1993) 65 P. & C.R. 1.

[4] *Midland Bank plc v. Cooke* [1995] 4 All E.R. 562; *ante*, p. 265.

[5] *Ante*, p. 246.

[6] *Pettitt v. Pettitt* [1970] A.C. 777 at p. 815. See also *Savill v. Goodall, supra* (unmarried couple).

[7] M. & W., pp. 417 *et seq.*; Cheshire and Burn, pp. 213 *et seq.*

[8] *Post*, Chap. 27.

co-owners were treated as personalty, which gave rise to difficulties, particularly in the interpretation of many legislative provisions.[9]

Following Law Commission proposals,[10] the dual system of the trust for sale and the strict settlement has been replaced by the new "trust of land" under the Trusts of Land and Appointment of Trustees Act 1996, which applies to both concurrent and successive interests. While pre-existing settlements under the Settled Land Act 1925 (other than those relating to charity land) are preserved, no new settlements may be created.[11] The definition of "trust of land"[12] is "any trust of property which consists of or includes land", whether the trust is express, implied, resulting or constructive, including a trust for sale and a bare trust. With the exception of pre-existing strict settlements, the 1996 Act applies to trusts of land created before and after its commencement (January 1, 1997).

Under the trust of land, the trustees have a power of sale, but no duty to sell. (Other powers and duties will be mentioned where relevant in the following sections). The interests of the beneficiaries will be overreached on sale (provided there are at least two trustees), as under the previous legislation.[13] Trusts for sale may still be expressly created, but, as already mentioned, fall within the definition of a "trust of land". All express trusts for sale of land, whenever created, include (despite any provision to the contrary) a power to postpone the sale, and the trustees are not liable in any way for postponing sale for an indefinite period in the exercise of their discretion.[14] Although the duty to sell remains in such a case, the doctrine of conversion is abolished in respect of all trusts for sale of land whenever created, save for those created by the will of a testator dying before the commencement of the 1996 Act.[15] Thus the interests of the beneficiaries are no longer interests in personalty, but are recognised as interests in the land itself.

As already mentioned, the 1925 legislation imposed a trust for sale on co-owned land (and in various other circumstances, such as intestacy). Under the new regime the statutory trust for sale is replaced by the trust of land. While the legal estate, if vested in more than one person, must be held jointly, the beneficial interest may be held either on a joint tenancy or on a tenancy in common. The relevant legislation is Law of Property Act 1925, section 34 (tenancies in common) and section 36 (joint tenancies), as amended by the 1996 Act to reflect the replacement of the trust for sale by the

---

[9] These were discussed at pp. 285–288 of the 14th edition, and will not be repeated here.

[10] No. 181 (1989), *Trusts of Land*. On the 1996 Act see [1996] Conv. 411 (N. Hopkins).

[11] Trusts of Land and Appointment of Trustees Act 1996, s.2. Entailed interests may no longer be created; Sched. 1, para. 5.

[12] *Ibid.*, s.1.

[13] *Ante*, p. 36.

[14] Trusts of Land and Appointment of Trustees Act 1996, s.4.

[15] *Ibid.*, s.3.

trust of land.[16] To facilitate conveyancing, the legal joint tenancy cannot be severed, but severance of any equitable joint tenancy can be effected by any of the means applicable before 1926[17]; and also by notice in writing to the other joint tenants.[18] The purpose of severance is to convert the joint tenancy into a tenancy in common and thereby prevent the application of the doctrine of survivorship (whereby the survivor of joint tenants takes the whole).

B. Occupation rights

Difficulties arose in the past concerning the occupation rights of beneficiaries under a trust for sale, whether imposed expressly or, more commonly, by statute, as in the case of co-ownership. The difficulty stemmed from the old doctrine of conversion, whereby the interests of the beneficiaries were regarded as in the proceeds of sale, not the land. Although the situation was somewhat obscure, modern decisions upheld the occupation rights of the beneficiaries, regarding the doctrine of conversion as artificial.[19] Thus it was held in the leading case of *Bull v. Bull*[20] that a son, who held the legal estate on trust for sale for himself and his mother as equitable tenants in common, was not entitled to evict his mother.

The occupation rights of beneficiaries are now governed by the Trusts of Land and Appointment of Trustees Act 1996, whenever the trust of land arose. The Act abolished the doctrine of conversion.[21] Section 12 provides that a beneficiary beneficially entitled to an interest in possession is entitled to occupy at any time if at that time (a) the purposes of the trust include making the land available for his occupation (or for the occupation of beneficiaries of a class of which he is a member or of beneficiaries in general) or (b) the land is held by the trustees so as to be so available. The section does not confer a right to occupy land if it is either unavailable or unsuitable for occupation by him,[22] and is subject to section 13, discussed below. Thus a beneficiary will normally be entitled to occupy unless, for example, the land has been let, or it is clear that the purpose of the trust is the sale of the property and division of the proceeds among the beneficiaries.[23]

---

[16] *Ibid.*, Sched. 2.
[17] M. & W., pp. 429 *et seq.*; Cheshire and Burn, pp. 217 *et seq.*
[18] L.P.A. 1925, s.36(2); *Re Draper's Conveyance* [1969] 1 Ch. 486; *Harris v. Goddard* [1983] 1 W.L.R. 1203.
[19] *Williams & Glyn's Bank Ltd v. Boland* [1981] A.C. 487; *City of London Building Society v. Flegg* [1988] A.C. 54.
[20] [1955] 1 Q.B. 234; *cf. Barclay v. Barclay* [1970] 2 Q.B. 677 (express testamentary trust for sale).
[21] s.3.
[22] s.12(2).
[23] As in the testamentary trust for sale in *Barclay v. Barclay, supra.*

Section 13(1) of the 1996 Act provides that where two or more beneficiaries are entitled to occupy under section 12, the trustees may, provided they do not act unreasonably, exclude or restrict the entitlement of any one or more (but not all) of them. They may also impose reasonable conditions from time to time on any beneficiary in relation to his occupation.[24] The matters to which the trustees must have regard in exercising these powers include (a) the intention of the person or persons (if any) who created the trust, (b) the purposes for which the land is held, and (c) the circumstances and wishes of each of the beneficiaries who is (or apart from any previous exercise by the trustees of those powers would be) entitled to occupy the land under section 12.[25] The conditions which they may impose include the payment of outgoings or expenses in respect of the land, or the assumption of any other obligation in relation to the land or to any activity which is or is proposed to be conducted there.[26] If the entitlement of any beneficiary has been excluded or restricted under the section, conditions may be imposed on any other beneficiary requiring him to compensate the beneficiary whose rights have been excluded or restricted, or to forgo a benefit under the trust so as to benefit the other beneficiary.[27] The trustees may not exercise their powers so as to prevent any person in occupation (whether or not by reason of any entitlement under section 12) from continuing to occupy, or in a manner likely to have that result, unless he consents or the court gives approval.[28] Disputes concerning the exercise of the trustees' powers under section 13 may be resolved by an application to court under section 14, where the circumstances and wishes of each beneficiary with occupation rights will be considered.[29]

Prior to the 1996 Act occupying co-owners were in certain cases obliged to pay rent to non-occupying co-owners, as where the latter had been "ousted" by the occupier,[30] or where the occupier had presented a divorce petition against the non-occupier,[31] or as a condition of postponing a sale.[32] As a general principle, however, no rent was payable to a beneficiary who chose not to occupy.[33] The position was somewhat uncertain, but the matter now falls within section 13 which, as mentioned above, permits the imposition of

---

[24] s.13(3).

[25] s.13(4).

[26] s.13(5).

[27] s.13(6).

[28] s.13(7). The court will have regard to the matters set out in s.13(4).

[29] See s.15(2); *post*, p. 281.

[30] See *Dennis v. McDonald* [1982] Fam. 63.

[31] *Re Pavlou (a Bankrupt)* [1993] 1 W.L.R. 1047 (discussing also the question of set-off against mortgage interest paid by the occupier).

[32] *Harvey v. Harvey* [1982] Fam. 83.

[33] *Jones (A.E.) v. Jones (F.W.)* [1977] 1 W.L.R. 438.

conditions including the compensation of a non-occupying beneficiary by an occupier.[34]

Finally, a spouse who is not a legal owner may assert occupation
rights under the Family Law Act 1996 (replacing Matrimonial
Homes Act 1983) whether or not he or she has an equitable interest
in the home.[35] This right is registrable, but failure to register will not
affect enforcement against the other spouse, or enforcement of any
rights arising independently by reason of an equitable interest in the
home.

C. Sale by Sole Trustee

Under the trust of land and its predecessor, the trust for sale, at
least two trustees are necessary if the overreaching machinery is to
operate.[36] While there are likely to be at least two trustees in the
case of an expressly created trust of land, the difficulty which arises
in many cases of co-ownership is that the land is vested in one
person only. That person holds on trust for all those who are
beneficially entitled, but the overreaching machinery will not operate. As we saw in the earlier parts of this chapter, the question
whether a person other than the legal owner has acquired an interest
is often difficult, so that the existence of the trust may not be
appreciated, either by the parties or the purchaser (or mortgagee).

Where there are two trustees, the interests of the beneficiaries will
be overreached whether or not they are occupying[37] and whether the
title is registered or unregistered. Where there is a sole trustee, the
principles applicable to registered and unregistered titles must be
considered separately.

If the title is unregistered,[38] the question whether the transferee,
typically a mortgagee, is bound by the equitable interests depends
on whether the mortgagee has notice, actual or constructive, of the
interest of the beneficiary. The equitable co-ownership usually arises
by virtue of one party having contributed to the purchase price, or to
the mortgage payments; and there will be nothing in the documents
of title to indicate this. The question is whether the beneficiary's
occupation gives constructive notice. It was at one time held that a
bank mortgagee dealing with the husband as sole legal owner did

---

[34] See also Family Law Act 1996, s.40(1)(b) (periodical payments while occupation order in
force).

[35] Former spouses, cohabitants and former cohabitants may in certain cases obtain occupation
orders whether or not they have an equitable interest. These are not registrable.

[36] L.P.A. 1925, s.2.

[37] *City of London Building Society v. Flegg* [1988] A.C. 54; *cf.* Law Com. No. 188, *Transfer
of Land; Overreaching; Beneficiaries in Occupation.*

[38] *i.e.* not subject to the provisions of the Land Registration Act 1925 at the time of the
transaction. Many titles remain unregistered even though the registration system applies in
all areas.

not have constructive notice of the wife's equitable interest by contribution, even though the bank knew that the parties lived together in the house.[39] This view is now untenable.[40] So many wives today have a share in the home that a reasonable mortgagee should consider the possibility. If it makes insufficient inquiries, the fact of the wife's (or other beneficiary's) occupation will give constructive notice of her rights. The difficulty which remains is in deciding whether sufficient inquiries have been made. This arose in *Kingsnorth Finance Co. v. Tizard*[41] where a wife had a half share in a house which was vested in her husband alone. When the marriage broke down she slept elsewhere but came to the house every day to look after the children and kept her possessions there. The husband mortgaged the property, falsely stating that he was single. The mortgagee's surveyor inspected the house at a time when the husband had arranged for the wife to be out. He saw evidence of the children's occupation and was told that the wife had left. No further inquiries were made as to her rights. The husband later emigrated, leaving the loan of £66,000 unpaid. It was held that the mortgagee had constructive notice of the wife's interest. In order for physical presence to amount to occupation, it did not need to be exclusive, continuous or uninterrupted, nor was it negatived by regular absences. The wife was accordingly in occupation for the purpose of constructive notice. When the surveyor discovered that the mortgagor was married, he was put on enquiry as to the wife's rights. The mortgagee would not have notice if a reasonable inspection had been made which did not reveal the occupier or evidence of occupation. What amounts to a reasonable inspection depends on the circumstances, but the judge considered that the pre-arranged inspection in the present case did not discharge the obligation. If this is so, there is indeed a heavy onus on the mortgagee.[42]

It should be added that where spouses occupy a matrimonial home, a spouse who has no legal title may protect his or her statutory rights of occupation under the Family Law Act 1996 (replacing Matrimonial Homes Act 1983) by registration, whether or not that spouse has any equitable interest in the home. But there is no possibility of protecting a substantive equitable interest by registration in cases of unregistered title.

In the case of registered land, notice plays no part.[43] Equitable interests are binding on a purchaser only if proper steps have been taken to protect them, as by a notice, restriction or caution; or if the interest is an "overriding interest"; which is binding regardless of

[39] *Caunce v. Caunce* [1969] 1 W.L.R. 286.
[40] *Williams & Glyn's Bank Ltd v. Boland* [1981] A.C. 487.
[41] [1986] 1 W.L.R. 783.
[42] See [1986] Conv. 283 (M. Thompson); (1987) 46 C.L.J. 28 (P. McHugh).
[43] [1981] A.C. 487 at p. 504, *per* Lord Wilberforce.

notice or of any means of discovery. The issue came to a head in
Williams & Glyn's Bank Ltd v. Boland.[44]

Mr and Mrs Boland each contributed towards the purchase of,
and to the mortgage payments due upon, a matrimonial home.
Title was taken in the sole name of Mr Boland, and he was
registered as sole proprietor.

Later, Mr Boland mortgaged the house to the Bank. On default
being made in the mortgage payments, the Bank started proceedings for possession. The wife resisted this claim on the ground
that she was entitled to an equitable interest in the house which
the Bank could not override. She had taken no steps to protect her
interest by restriction or caution.

It was accepted that the wife had, by virtue of her financial
contribution, an equitable interest in the house. The question
whether this interest was valid against the Bank depended on
whether it was an overriding interest under the Land Registration
Act 1925, s.70(1)(g)[45]; it could not be binding as a minor interest,
because the wife had taken no steps to protect it. Nor could it be
overreached by the payment to a sole trustee.

The House of Lords unanimously held that the wife's interest was
an overriding interest. It was a right "subsisting in reference" to
registered land; and, on the plain words of sub-paragraph (g), the
wife was "in actual occupation" at the execution of the mortgage.[46]
Lord Scarman emphasised the importance of construing the legislation in the light of current social policy, and of protecting the
"beneficial interest which English law now recognizes that a married woman has in the matrimonial home."[47] It is thus necessary to
make inquiries of all persons in occupation, whether spouse, cohabitant, or other persons; for their interests are capable of being binding
as overriding interests on the purchaser or mortgagee.

The principles discussed above are subject to an important proviso. An equitable co-owner in occupation can rely neither on
constructive notice (in unregistered land) nor on section 70(1)(g) (in

---

[44] [1981] A.C. 487; [1980] Conv. 361 (J. Martin); (1980) 43 M.L.R. 692 (S. Freeman); (1980)
39 C.L.J. 243 (M. Prichard); (1981) 97 L.Q.R. 12 (R. Smith).
[45] s.70(1) reads: "All registered land shall, unless . . . the contrary is expressed in the register,
be deemed to be subject to such of the following overriding interests as may be for the time
being subsisting in reference thereto . . .
   (g) The rights of every person in actual occupation of the land or in receipt of the rents
and profits thereof, save where enquiry is made of such person and the rights are not
disclosed; . . . "
[46] This is the relevant date for the application of s.70(1)(g), rather than the later date of
registration of the legal charge; *Abbey National B.S. v. Cann* [1991] 1 A.C. 56.
[47] [1981] A.C. 487 at p. 510.

registered land) where he or she was aware of the mortgage transaction and did not bring the equitable interest to the attention of the mortgagee.[48] This seems to be a version of the doctrine of estoppel. The principle is that in such circumstances it is impossible to infer any common intention other than that the equitable owner authorised the legal owner to raise money by mortgage which would have priority to any beneficial interest. Apparently it is not relevant that the mortgagee failed to make the inquiries which might have revealed the interest. As has been said, this seems to be a reversal of the doctrine of notice; the onus has shifted to the occupier to declare his rights to a purchaser (mortgagee) of whom he has notice, or be deemed to concede priority.[49] In the case of an acquisition mortgage, the House of Lords has taken the principle further by holding that a purchaser who depends on a mortgage in order to buy the property acquires on completion only an equity of redemption, (*i.e.* the property already subject to the mortgage). Thus a third party claiming a beneficial interest as against the purchaser can assert no rights against the mortgagee, whether or not the third party was aware of the mortgage.[50] The effect of these principles is to restrict the application of *Williams & Glyn's Bank Ltd v. Boland*[51] and *Kingsnorth Finance Co. v. Tizard*,[52] to subsequent mortgages of which the co-owner was unaware.

D. Disputes over Sale

Disputes commonly arise, primarily on the breakdown of a relationship, as to whether the property should be sold or not. The question may also arise on the death of a co-owner, if his or her share devolves on a third party.[53] Where the legal estate is vested in all the co-owners, they (being trustees) must act unanimously in the exercise of any power.[54] Since the commencement of the Trusts of Land and Appointment of Trustees Act 1996, trustees of land have a power of sale instead of the duty to sell which formerly existed under the statutory trust for sale imposed in cases of co-ownership.

---

[48] *Bristol and West Building Society v. Henning* [1985] 1 W.L.R. 778; *Paddington Building Society v. Mendelsohn* (1985) 50 P. & C.R. 244; criticised [1985] Conv. 361 (P. Todd); [1986] Conv. 57; (1986) 49 M.L.R. 255 and (1986) 6 L.S. 140 (M. Thompson).

[49] (1985) 44 C.L.J. 354 (M. Welstead).

[50] *Abbey National B.S. v. Cann* [1991] 1 A.C. 56; [1991] Conv. 116 (S. Baughen) and 155 (P. Evans). As to remortgages, see *Equity & Law Home Loans Ltd v. Prestidge* [1992] 1 W.L.R. 137; (1992) 108 L.Q.R. 372 (R. Smith); (1993) 56 M.L.R. 87 (M. Lunney); (1993) 23 Fam. Law 231 (J. Dewar).

[51] *Supra.*

[52] [1986] 1 W.L.R. 783, *ante*, p. 277.

[53] See *Stott v. Ratcliffe* (1982) 79 L.S.Gaz. 634.

[54] *Re Mayo* [1943] Ch. 302; *post*, p. 486. The parties may have made express provisions for sale or for one to buy the other out; *Miller v. Lakefield Estates Ltd* (1989) 57 P. & C.R. 104.

Thus the power of sale cannot be exercised unless all agree. In cases of dispute, as explained below, they can apply to court under section 14 of the 1996 Act, replacing section 30 of the Law of Property Act 1925.

It may be that the legal estate is vested in one co-owner only, as where a husband holds the legal estate on trust for himself and his wife as co-owners in equity. In the last section we saw the effect of a sale or mortgage by a sole trustee. Here we will consider the position prior to any such disposition. The question of unanimity does not arise, because there is only one trustee. In the event of a dispute, the wife (or other equitable co-owner) may apply to court under section 14 if she has the opportunity to act in time. In any event, sale will be hampered if she has registered her statutory right of occupation[55] or (in the case of registered land) has protected her equitable interest by the entry of a restriction or caution. Even if she has not done so, her interest is likely to prevail against the purchaser or mortgagee if she is in occupation.[56] She may also seek an injunction to prevent sale without the appointment of a second trustee to safeguard the proceeds of sale, or to restrain the husband from disregarding his statutory duty to consult the beneficiaries.[57] Section 11 of the Trusts of Land and Appointment of Trustees Act 1996 (replacing section 26 of the Law of Property Act 1925) provides that the trustees, in the exercise of any function relating to the land, shall (so far as practicable) consult the beneficiaries of full age and beneficially entitled to an interest in possession, and, so far as consistent with the general interest of the trust, give effect to the wishes of those beneficiaries or of the majority of them, according to the value of their combined interests.[58] Clearly this section is of limited assistance to a beneficiary with a minority interest, and will result in a stalemate if there are two disputing co-owners who are equally entitled. In certain cases, however, it will resolve the situation.

Assuming that the dispute cannot otherwise be resolved, application may be made to court under section 14 of the 1996 Act. The application may be made by a trustee or any person having an

---

[55] Family Law Act 1996, re-enacting Matrimonial Homes Act 1983; *Wroth v. Tyler* [1974] Ch. 30.

[56] Under L.R.A. 1925, s.70(1)(g) (registered land) or under the doctrine of notice (unregistered land); *ante*, p. 276.

[57] *Waller v. Waller* [1967] 1 W.L.R. 451. See also *Lee v. Lee* [1952] 2 Q.B. 489n. (jurisdiction under Married Women's Property Act 1882, s.17).

[58] This duty may be excluded in an express trust. Also, the trustees must have regard to the rights of the beneficiaries when exercising the powers of an absolute owner conferred by s.6 of the 1996 Act; *ibid.*, s.6(5). See also s.16(1) (protection of purchaser of unregistered land). For purchasers of registered land, see [1996] Conv. 411 at pp. 427–428 (N. Hopkins).

interest in the property.[59] Thus the trustee in bankruptcy of a beneficiary (whose position is discussed below) or chargee of a beneficial
interest may apply, as under the previous law. The court may make
such order as it thinks fit (a) relating to the exercise by the trustees
of any of their functions (including an order relieving them of any
obligation to obtain the consent of, or to consult, any person in
connection with the exercise of any of their functions), or (b) declaring the nature or extent of a person's interest in the property; but
may not appoint or remove trustees under this section.[60]

The matters to which the court is to have regard include (a) the
intentions of the person or persons (if any) who created the trust,
(b) the purposes for which the property subject to the trust is held,
(c) the welfare of any minor who occupies or might reasonably be
expected to occupy any land subject to the trust as his home, and
(d) the interests of any secured creditor of any beneficiary.[61] So far
as applications relating to the exercise of the trustees' powers under
section 13 to exclude or restrict occupation rights are concerned,
the court will also consider the circumstances and wishes of each of
the beneficiaries who is (or apart from any previous exercise by the
trustees of those powers would be) entitled to occupy the land under
section 12.[62] In the case of any other application, the court will also
consider the circumstances and wishes of any beneficiaries of full
age and entitled to an interest in possession or (in case of dispute) of
the majority (according to the value of their combined interests).[63]
Different considerations apply to applications by a trustee in bankruptcy, which are discussed below.

Decisions on the predecessor legislation (section 30 of the Law of
Property Act 1925) may afford some guidance, bearing in mind,
however, that those decisions were influenced by the primacy of the
duty to sell which then arose under the statutory trust for sale in
cases of co-ownership. Another distinction is that section 30, unlike
section 15 of the 1996 Act, did not spell out the factors to be taken
into account by the court. As under the previous law, the provision
of a home for the parties' children will continue to be a significant,
although not paramount, consideration in family cases.[64] The width
of section 15, however, makes it unlikely that much resort will need

---

[59] s.14(1).

[60] *Ibid.*, s.14(2), (3).

[61] *Ibid.*, s.15(1). For problems arising in applications by chargees of a beneficiary's interest
under the previous legislation, see *Abbey National plc v. Moss* [1994] 1 F.L.R. 307.

[62] *Ibid.*, s.15(2). For ss.12 and 13, see *ante*, p. 274.

[63] *Ibid.*, s.15(3). This does not apply to applications relating to s.6(2) (power to convey to
adult beneficiaries absolutely entitled without request).

[64] See *Williams v. Williams* [1976] Ch. 278; *Re Evers' Trust* [1980] 1 W.L.R. 1327 (unmarried
couple); *Harris v. Harris* (1996) 72 P. & C.R. 408 (no sale on father's death where deed of
family arrangement had provided for retention as family home for father and son, who still
occupied). For property other than the family home, see *Re Buchanan-Wollaston's Conveyance* [1939] Ch. 738.

to be made to the previous authorities, and they will not be examined here.

Where, however, the sale is requested by the trustee in bankruptcy of one spouse, different considerations arise. "Bankruptcy has, in relation to the matrimonial home, its own claim to protection."[65] The rights of the creditors are in competition with the interests of all the beneficiaries. They do not automatically defeat the interests of the family; but the reported cases indicate that it is only in exceptional circumstances that the trustee in bankruptcy will not succeed,[66] although sale may be deferred for a short time if the spouse has some prospect of buying the bankrupt's share.[67] The fact that the bankrupt's family will be unable to buy a comparable home and that his children's schooling may be disrupted are not exceptional circumstances justifying refusal of an order for sale; they are the "melancholy consequences of debt and improvidence."[68]

The law in this area was amended by the Insolvency Act 1986, following an examination by the Review Committee on Insolvency Law and Practice.[69] The 1986 provisions have in turn been amended by the Trusts of Land and Appointment of Trustees Act 1996. Where an application for sale is made under section 14 of the 1996 Act by the trustee in bankruptcy of a co-owner, the position is governed by section 335A of the Insolvency Act 1986. On such an application the court shall make such order as it thinks just and reasonable, having regard to:

    (a) the interests of the bankrupt's creditors;
    (b) where the application is made in respect of land which includes a dwelling-house which is or has been the home of the bankrupt or the bankrupt's spouse or former spouse,
        (i) the conduct of the spouse or former spouse, so far as contributing to the bankruptcy,
        (ii) the needs and financial resources of the spouse or former spouse, and
        (iii) the needs of any children; and

---

[65] *Re Bailey* [1977] 1 W.L.R. 278 at p. 279 (*per* Megarry V.-C.).

[66] *Re Solomon* [1967] Ch. 573; *Re Turner* [1974] 1 W.L.R. 1556; *Re McCarthy* [1975] 1 W.L.R. 807; *Re Lowrie* [1981] 3 All E.R. 353; *Re Densham* [1975] 1 W.L.R. 1519, *cf. Re Holliday* [1981] Ch. 405 (no order until 1985, where no creditors pressing, more assets than debts, and debtor bankrupt on his own petition); (1981) 97 L.Q.R. 200 (C. Hand); [1982] Conv. 74 (A. Sydenham); [1983] Conv. 219 (C. Hand). For the equity of exoneration, see *Re Pittortou* [1985] 1 W.L.R. 58.

[67] *Re Gorman* [1990] 1 W.L.R. 616.

[68] *Re Citro* [1991] Ch. 142 at p. 157 (bankruptcy prior to Insolvency Act 1986). Sir George Waller dissented. See also *Barclays Bank plc v. Hendricks* [1996] 1 F.L.R. 258.

[69] 1982, Cmnd. 8558. Some jurisdictions offer greater protection by "homestead legislation." See Joint Family Homes Act 1964 (New Zealand); Gray, *Elements of Land Law* (2nd ed.), pp. 605–606.

(c) all the circumstances of the case other than the needs of the bankrupt.

Where, however, the application is made after a year from the vesting in the trustee in bankruptcy, the court must assume that the interests of the creditors outweigh all other considerations save in exceptional circumstances. It has been said that "exceptional circumstances" reflects the same test as has been applied in the case law prior to the 1986 Act.[70] This provision, therefore, gives some protection to the family by delaying the sale, but the trustee will normally succeed after a year. There are similar provisions relating to occupation orders under section 33 of the Family Law Act 1996 in cases of bankruptcy.[71]

---

[70] *Re Citro* [1991] Ch. 142 (in the context of s.336); (1991) 50 C.L.J. 45 (J. Hall); (1991) 107 L.Q.R. 177 (S. Cretney); [1991] Conv. 302 (A. Lawson); (1992) 55 M.L.R. 284 (D. Brown).
[71] Insolvency Act 1986, ss.336, 337, as amended.

Chapter 12

CONSTRUCTIVE TRUSTS

1. General 285	iv. Liability of Partner of Construc-
A. Overlap in Classification 286	tive Trustee 304
B. Establishing the Existence or the	C. Mutual Wills 305
Terms of the Trust 287	i. Agreement Necessary 305
C. The Duties of a Constructive Trustee 287	ii. Remedies on the Contract 307
D. Distinction Between Constructive	iii. Trusts Created by Mutual Wills ... 307
Trusts, Accountability and Proprietary	(a) When does the Trust Arise? .. 308
Remedies 288	(b) To what Property does the
E. The Remedial Constructive Trust 289	Trust Attach? 309
2. When a Constructive Trust Arises 292	(c) The Survivor as Trustee 311
A. Unauthorised Profit by a Trustee or	iv. Conclusion 311
Fiduciary 292	D. The Vendor under a Specifically En-
B. Liability of Third Parties 293	forceable Contract for Sale 312
i. Dishonest Assistance 294	E. Secret Trusts 314
(a) Terminology 294	F. Conveyance by Fraud 314
(b) Nature of Trustee's Breach 294	G. Acquisition of Property by Killing 315
(c) Dishonesty of Third Party 295	i. Type of Killing 315
ii. Liability for Receipt 298	ii. Means of Acquisition 316
(a) Personal and Proprietary	iii. Destination of Property 316
Remedies 298	iv. Statutory Relief 317
(b) Actual or Constructive	H. Constructive Trusts of a New Model:
Knowledge 298	Justice and Good Conscience 317
(c) Ministerial Receipt 302	i. Family Arrangements 318
(d) Common Law Remedy 302	ii. Licences 320
iii. Agent Assuming Trustee's	iii. Registered Land 322
Duties 303	iv. Conclusion 323

1. GENERAL

A CONSTRUCTIVE trust is one which arises by operation of law, and not by reason of the intention of the parties, express or implied. "English law provides no clear and all-embracing definition of a constructive trust. Its boundaries have been left perhaps deliberately vague, so as not to restrict the court by technicalities in deciding what the justice of a particular case may demand."[1] It has been "a ready means of developing our property law in modern times."[2] The principle is that where a person who holds property in circumstances

[1] *Carl Zeiss Stiftung v. Herbert Smith & Co.* [1969] 2 Ch. 276 at p. 300 (*per* Edmund Davies L.J.).
[2] *Sen v. Headley* [1991] Ch. 425 at p. 440 (Nourse L.J.).

in which in equity and good conscience it should be held or enjoyed by another, he will be compelled to hold the property on trust for that other.[3] Such a statement can be criticised as being too general to be helpful. It used to be said that equity had developed pragmatically in this field, relying on the precedents and paying too little attention to the general principle. Subsequently the pendulum swung the other way, and a constructive trust was used as a means of reaching a desired result over a wide variety of cases; constructive trusts of a "new model",[4] "wherever justice and good conscience require it."[5] It now seems, however, that the "new model" has lost momentum.[6] Modern developments have caused Sir Peter Millett to say that "At present the language of constructive trust has become such a fertile source of confusion that it would be better if it were abandoned."[7] The confusion could be avoided if the term were to be confined to "a situation in which it would be unconscionable for one party to deny the other's beneficial proprietary interest in a particular and identified property."[8]

A. Overlap in Classification

We saw, in discussing the classification of trusts,[9] that there is an overlap between resulting and constructive trusts. Normally it makes little practical difference whether a trust is described as constructive or resulting. The formality rules, for example, apply to neither type.[10] But the tendency to merge the two categories makes any definition of a constructive trust even harder to formulate. "It has been suggested that nomenclature in this context is unimportant. There is, however, some risk that confusion of terminology may lead to confusion of thought."[11] Distinctions have been emphasised in the context of the conflict of laws, where it has been said that a resulting trust involves the claim of an equitable owner to assert a continuing proprietary interest in his own property, while a constructive trust may be imposed in appropriate circumstances where a breach of fiduciary obligation has given rise to an equity between

---

[3] See *Beatty v. Guggenheim Exploration Co.*, 225 N.Y. 380 at p. 386 (1919); *Soar v. Ashwell* [1893] 2 Q.B. 390; (1913–14) 27 Harv.L.R. 125 (A. Scott); (1955) 72 L.Q.R. 39 (A. Scott); *Restatement of Restitution*, § 160; Waters, *The Constructive Trust*; Oakley, *Constructive Trusts*; Elias, *Explaining Constructive Trusts*.

[4] *Eves v. Eves* [1975] 1 W.L.R. 1338 at p. 1341.

[5] *Hussey v. Palmer* [1972] 1 W.L.R. 1286 at p. 1290, *per* Lord Denning M.R.

[6] *Post*, p. 318.

[7] (1995) 9 *Trust Law International* 35 at p. 38.

[8] *Ibid.* at p. 39.

[9] *Ante*, p. 67.

[10] L.P.A. 1925, s.53, *ante*, p. 76.

[11] The Child & Co. Oxford Lecture (1984) "The Informal Creation of Interests in Land," at p. 4 (Sir Christopher Slade); *cf.* [1982] Conv. 424 at p. 431 (F. Bates).

the parties.[12] Similarly in the context of family property, where a common intention may found a constructive trust which is quantified differently from the proportionate shares arising under a resulting trust.[13]

The constructive trust is usually regarded as a residual category; one which is called into play where the court desires to impose a trust and no other suitable category is available.

B. Establishing the Existence or the Terms of the Trust

The imposition of a constructive trust is often a determination that previously declared trusts are enforceable against someone other than the original trustee, or extend to additional property.[14] Thus, a wrongful recipient of trust property, not being a bona fide purchaser without notice from a trustee, takes the property subject to the existing trusts. A trustee who makes an improper profit holds the profit on the trusts which had previously been declared of the property out of which the profit was made.[15]

It may be, however, that the constructive trust doctrine will determine the trusts on which a person, admittedly a trustee, will hold the property. Thus, in a case of mutual wills, the executor of the second party to die needs to know whether he holds on the trusts of that party's will, or under the agreement which was the basis of the mutual wills.[16] Thus the constructive trust covers situations in which either the existence of the trusteeship or the terms of the trust or both are determined by operation of law.

C. The Duties of a Constructive Trustee

The duties and liabilities of a constructive trustee are not necessarily the same as those of an express trustee. A decision that X holds as constructive trustee does not necessarily subject him to the usual trustees' duties in respect of investments, etc.[17] If a person purchases property with constructive but not actual notice of a trust, the beneficiaries may enforce the trust against him; but if he is not informed of their claims for some time, it seems that he will not be subjected also to liability for failure to invest in trustee investments

---

[12] *Macmillan Inc. v. Bishopsgate Investment Trust plc (No. 3)* [1995] 1 W.L.R. 978; affirmed on other grounds (to which the distinction was not relevant) at [1996] 1 W.L.R. 387. See also *Williams v. Tedcastle* [1994] 1 N.Z.L.R. 85; *Westdeutsche Landesbank Girozentrale v. Islington London Borough Council* [1996] A.C. 669 at p. 707.

[13] *Drake v. Whipp* [1996] 1 F.L.R. 826; *ante*, p. 265 (lax terminology a "potent source of confusion").

[14] Bowen L.J. in *Soar v. Ashwell* [1893] 2 Q.B. 390 at p. 396.

[15] *Post*, p. 292.

[16] *Post*, p. 305.

[17] See *Lonrho plc v. Fayed (No. 2)* [1992] 1 W.L.R. 1 at p. 12.

and to the usual standard of *exacta diligentia* which is required of express trustees in the performance of their duties. The duties of a constructive trustee have not been made clear; they probably vary with the circumstances and will be greater for a fraudulent trustee than for others.[18]

D. Distinction Between Constructive Trusts, Accountability and Proprietary Remedies

Circumstances giving rise to a constructive trust may give rise to other remedies also. Strictly speaking a person can only be a trustee, express or constructive, if there is vested in him certain property which he holds upon trust.[19] Constructive trusteeship should be distinguished from the equitable proprietary remedy of tracing, and a personal action in equity against a fiduciary for an account. They are considered in more detail below.[20]

Where a trustee (express or constructive) has had trust property vested in him but has wrongfully disposed of it, he will commonly be regarded as retaining his status as trustee.[21] Subject to what is said below concerning tracing, the absence of trust property means that the remedy against him is personal only. Where, however, no trust property has ever been vested in the defendant (as where liability arises from dishonestly assisting the trustees in a breach of trust),[22] he cannot properly be called a trustee, constructive or otherwise. As in the previous example, the remedy against him is personal only. The defendant is *accountable*; he is not a constructive trustee of any property. If he has insufficient assets, the plaintiff will be unable to obtain compensation in full.

There is, however, another possibility. It may be possible to show that the property, wrongly obtained and disposed of, is now represented by money or by some other property in the trustee's or a third party's hands; and, by use of the equitable proprietary remedy, to "follow" the original property into that for which it has been exchanged. This is done by the technique of "tracing".[23]

The advantages of "tracing" the money (or other property) in this way are twofold. First, if the defendant should become insolvent, the

---

[18] *Restatement of Restitution*, §§ 202–204.

[19] *Re Barney* [1892] 2 Ch. 265 at p. 272; *Westdeutsche Landesbank Girozentrale v. Islington London Borough Council* [1996] A.C. 669.

[20] *Post*, Chaps. 21, 23.

[21] See Pettit, p. 60, suggesting that principle is satisified by treating his obligation to restore the trust fund as the trust property.

[22] *Post*, p. 294.

[23] *Post*, p. 656.

plaintiff takes in priority to the general creditors, for the money "traced" is trust money, and is kept out of the defendant's insolvency.[24] Secondly, if the money has been invested successfully by the defendant, the plaintiff is allowed to claim the share of the investments which is proportionate to the share which the trust money contributed to the invested fund.[25] A distinction between constructive trusteeship and liability to the "tracing" process is that the latter may be available against a person who is not liable as constructive trustee. For example, where trust property is transferred to an innocent volunteer, *i.e.* a person who is not a purchaser and who thus takes subject to the trust but who has neither actual nor constructive knowledge of it, the volunteer is apparently not liable as constructive trustee,[26] but the "tracing" remedy lies against him while he still has the property or its identifiable proceeds.[27]

There are thus three separate matters to consider: constructive trusts, proprietary remedies, and personal actions. They are all interrelated, but each is distinct. Many decisions fail to make these distinctions, and fail to make clear whether the issue is one of accountability or one of trust,[28] although the matter has been to some extent clarified by the Privy Council.[29] This chapter will examine constructive trusts properly so called and also certain cases of personal liability which have traditionally (but inappropriately) been treated as constructive trusteeship. Accountability for profits and the question of liability to proprietary remedies are considered later.[30]

E. The Remedial Constructive Trust

We saw that the duties of a constructive trustee differ from those of an ordinary trustee. If the plaintiff merely wishes to have the property returned, the question is whether a constructive trust need be considered as anything beyond a means of demanding the return of the property to which he is entitled in equity. This is the way in which constructive trusts are regarded in most jurisdictions in the United States of America and in the *Restatement*. "Where a person holding title to property is subject to an equitable duty to convey it to another on the ground that he would be unjustly enriched if he

---

[24] *Re Hallett's Estate* (1880) 13 Ch.D. 696.
[25] *Re Tilley's W.T.* [1967] Ch. 1179.
[26] *Post*, p. 300; *Restatement of Restitution*, § 203. The view that the innocent volunteer is personally liable is discussed below, p. 301.
[27] *Re Diplock* [1948] Ch. 465, *post*, p. 662.
[28] *Reading v. Att.-Gen.* [1951] A.C. 507; *Boardman v. Phipps* [1967] 2 A.C. 46.
[29] *Att.-Gen. for Hong Kong v. Reid* [1994] 1 A.C. 324; *post*, p. 608.
[30] *Post*, Chaps. 21, 23.

were permitted to retain it, a constructive trust arises."[31] Thus the duty is to convey to those entitled; not to hold on trust for them.

The constructive trust is regarded as a "remedial rather than substantive" institution.[32] The constructive trust is imposed under this doctrine whenever it is needed to prevent unjust enrichment. Like other equitable remedies, it is available where the legal remedy is inadequate. Thus, in a case of unjust enrichment the plaintiff will sue in quasi-contract; but if the defendant still has the property, and either the plaintiff wants specific recovery, or the defendant is insolvent, or the property has increased in value, the plaintiff will be able to assert a constructive trust.[33]

The English cases have however, traditionally regarded the constructive trust as a substantive institution,[34] vindicating a pre-existing proprietary right.

The Court of Appeal has stated that there is a good arguable case that circumstances may arise in which the court could impose a remedial constructive trust *de novo* as the foundation for the grant of an equitable remedy.[35] The existence of such a doctrine has been left open by the Privy Council.[36] Millett J., however, warned that, while equity must be flexible, "its intervention must be based on principle; there must be some relationship between the relief granted and the circumstances which give rise to it.[37] To which his Lordship has added "there is neither room nor need for the remedial constructive trust. In my view it is a counsel of despair which too readily concedes the impossibility of propounding a general rationale for the availability of proprietary remedies. We need to be more ready to categorise wrongdoers as fiduciaries and to extend the situations in which proprietary remedies are made available, but we can do all this while adhering to established principles."[38] Similarly, "the remedial constructive trust is a judicial discretion to vary property rights and, as such, an object of suspicion."[39] Lord Browne-Wilkinson, on the other hand, has suggested that the introduction of

---

[31] *Restatement of Restitution*, § 160; (1955) 71 L.Q.R. 71 (A. Scott); *Carl Zeiss Stiftung v. Herbert Smith & Co.* [1969] 2 Ch. 276 at p. 300.

[32] (1920) 33 Harv.L.R. 420 (R. Pound). See also (1983) 3 L.S. 283 at p. 292 (R. Goode); [1988] Conv. 259 (D. Hayton); (1991) 107 L.Q.R. 608 (C. Rickett); Elias, *Explaining Constructive Trusts*, pp. 159–163.

[33] See *Lac Minerals Ltd v. International Corona Resources Ltd* (1989) 61 D.L.R. (4th) 14.

[34] See *Re Sharpe* [1980] 1 W.L.R. 219, where the notion of imposing a constructive trust as a remedy was described as a novel concept in English law.

[35] *Metall und Rohstoff A.G. v. Donaldson Lufkin & Jenrette Inc.* [1990] 1 Q.B. 391 at p. 479 (overruled on another point by *Lonrho plc v. Fayed* [1992] 1 A.C. 448).

[36] *Re Goldcorp Exchange Ltd (in receivership)* [1995] 1 A.C. 74.

[37] *Lonrho plc v. Fayed (No. 2)* [1992] 1 W.L.R. 1 at p. 9 (no constructive trust where plaintiff's claim had no proprietary base). See also (1991) 107 L.Q.R. 71 at p. 85 (Sir Peter Millett).

[38] (1995) 9 *Trust Law International* 35 at p. 40.

[39] *The Frontiers of Liability*, Vol. 2, p. 24 (P. Birks); *cf.* at p. 165 (D. Waters) and p. 186 (S. Gardner). See also [1996] R.L.R. 3 (P. Birks).

the remedial constructive trust may provide a satisfactory basis for developing proprietary restitutionary remedies.[40]

The question arose in *Halifax Building Society v. Thomas*,[41] where the defendant obtained a mortgage loan to buy a flat by fraudulent misrepresentation. When he fell into arrears the mortgagee sold the flat. After the repayment of the debt a surplus remained, to which the mortgagee claimed entitlement under a constructive trust in its favour, to prevent the defendant profiting from his fraud. In rejecting this claim the Court of Appeal noted that English law had not followed other jurisdictions where the constructive trust had become a remedy for unjust enrichment. There was no universal principle that there must be restitution of a benefit derived from wrongdoing. The relationship was not fiduciary but was merely one of debtor and secured creditor. The mortgagee had recovered all it was contractually entitled to, and the surplus belonged to the defendant. It was thus available for confiscation under Part VI of the Criminal Justice Act 1988, the enactment of which indicated that the profits of crime did not belong to the victim.

The remedial constructive trust has been widely accepted in Australia,[42] New Zealand[43] and Canada.[44] It has not replaced the traditional institutional constructive trust, but exists alongside it.[45]

One distinction between institutional and remedial constructive trusts may lie in the date from which the plaintiff may assert proprietary rights. This question has significance for third parties acquiring interests in the property before the court makes its order. It seems clear that the traditional institutional constructive trust vindicates a pre-existing proprietary interest which is operative before the date of the court order.[46] The effect of a remedial constructive trust, on the other hand, may be to confer a new proprietary interest on the plaintiff.[47] In such a case it will have prospective

---

[40] *Westdeutsche Landesbank Girozentrale v. Islington London Borough Council* [1996] A.C. 669 at p. 716.

[41] [1996] Ch. 217; (1996) 10 *Trust Law International* 2 (P. Birks); (1996) 112 L.Q.R. 219 (P. Watts); [1996] R.L.R. 92 (P. Jaffey).

[42] *Muschinski v. Dodds* (1985) 160 C.L.R. 583.

[43] *Powell v. Thompson* [1991] 1 N.Z.L.R. 579 at p. 615 ("a broad equitable remedy for reversing that which is inequitable or unconscionable"); *Equiticorp Industries Group Ltd v. Hawkins* [1991] 3 N.Z.L.R. 700.

[44] *Pettkus v. Becker* (1980) 117 D.L.R. (3d) 257; *Sorochan v. Sorochan* (1986) 29 D.L.R. (4th) 1; *Lac Minerals Ltd v. International Corona Resources Ltd* (1989) 61 D.L.R. (4th) 14; (1990) 106 L.Q.R. 207 (G. Hammond); *Rawluk v. Rawluk* (1990) 65 D.L.R. (4th) 161; [1991] Conv. 125 (C. Rickett); (1991) 11 L.S. 304 (G. Fridman); *Peter v. Beblow* (1993) 101 D.L.R. (4th) 621.

[45] *Muschinski v. Dodds, supra*, at pp. 613–615.

[46] This is assumed in the English cases such as *Lloyds Bank plc v. Rosset* [1991] 1 A.C. 107; *ante*, p. 263. See *Westdeutsche Landesbank Girozentrale v. Islington London Borough Council, supra*, at p. 716.

[47] *Lac Minerals Ltd v. International Corona Resources Ltd, supra*, at p. 50.

effect only, operating from the date of the court order which creates it.[48]

We will now examine the circumstances in which a constructive trust has been held to exist.

2. WHEN A CONSTRUCTIVE TRUST ARISES

Constructive trusts can arise over a wide variety of situations. No claim is made that those discussed in this section cover the whole field; they are merely illustrations. It will be seen that some of the selected categories lay down specific rules; others rely on general principles, which have been stated in the widest terms.

A. Unauthorised Profit by a Trustee or Fiduciary

The principle is that a fiduciary may not make use of his position to gain a benefit for himself. Trustees, personal representatives[49] and agents[50] are by their "position debarred from keeping a personal advantage derived directly or indirectly out of his fiduciary or quasi-fiduciary position."[51] With other fiduciaries, such as company directors,[52] partners,[53] mortgagors[54] and mortgagees,[55] the question is one of fact whether the benefit was obtained by reason or independently of, the fiduciary relationship. The category of fiduciaries is not closed.[56]

These matters are dealt with in Chapter 21. We will there see that a trustee must not renew in his own favour any lease held on trust; nor may he purchase the reversion on any such lease; nor may he purchase the trust property. He must not make any incidental profits

---

[48] *Muschinski v. Dodds* (1985) 160 C.L.R. 583 at p. 615; *cf. Rawluk v. Rawluk, supra.* A similar question arises as to the date on which an estoppel interest takes effect, *post*, p. 894.

[49] *James v. Dean* (1808) 15 Ves.Jr. 236.

[50] *De Bussche v. Alt* (1878) 8 Ch.D. 286 at p. 310; *Boardman v. Phipps* [1967] 2 A.C. 67.

[51] *Re Biss* [1903] 2 Ch. 40 at p. 56.

[52] *Post*, pp. 598 *et seq.*

[53] *Featherstonhaugh v. Fenwick* (1810) 17 Ves.Jr. 298; *Clegg v. Fishwick* (1849) 1 Mac. & G. 294.

[54] *Leigh v. Burnett* (1885) 29 Ch.D. 231.

[55] *Nelson v. Hannam and Smith* [1943] Ch. 59. A mortgagee is not a trustee of his power of sale, but is trustee of any surplus proceeds. This trust was originally imposed by equity, but is now statutory; L.P.A. 1925, s.105. Save as to surplus, the relationship is not fiduciary; *Halifax Building Society v. Thomas* [1996] Ch. 217; *ante*, p. 291.

[56] *English v. Dedham Vale Properties Ltd* [1978] 1 W.L.R. 93. See also *Swain v. Law Society* [1983] A.C. 598; *Appleby v. Cowley, The Times*, April 14, 1982.

out of his trusteeship. In the present context, one example must suffice.

In *Boardman v. Phipps*,[57] the trustees held a minority shareholding in a private company which was not being efficiently managed. Boardman had acted as solicitor to the trust, and was therefore a fiduciary. He decided that the beneficiaries would be in a better position if the trustees had control of the company, but no trust money was available to buy the extra shares. Boardman and one of the beneficiaries therefore bought the necessary shares themselves and reorganised the company. All this was done in good faith and with the object of enhancing the trust holding. Both the personal and the trust holdings increased in value. A majority of the House of Lords held that Boardman was constructive trustee of the profit made on his personal shareholding. The opportunity to make the profit arose out of his fiduciary relationship with the trust and certain confidential information had been used in the process. However, compensation was ordered from the trust in recognition of the work and skill involved.

B. Liability of Third Parties

Third parties may incur personal liability (in addition to the trustees' liability) in certain circumstances, in particular where they dishonestly assist the trustee (or other fiduciary) in a breach of duty, or where they receive trust property transferred in breach of trust. Such persons are commonly called constructive trustees,[58] although this is misleading because the liability is personal only. The two categories were until recently known as "knowing assistance" and "knowing receipt".[59] As explained below, the terminology in the first case, and maybe in the second also, is no longer appropriate. The terms "accessory liability" and "recipient liability" may be preferable. Whatever the heading of liability, the existence of the trust must be established. Knowledge of a "doubtful equity" does not suffice; hence a solicitor was not accountable for moneys received in payment of costs and expenses paid by a client for work done in defending an action in which the plaintiff was claiming that

---

[57] [1967] 2 A.C. 67, *post*, p. 601.
[58] Sir Peter Millett considers the "receipt" cases to be examples of resulting trusts; (1995) 9 *Trust Law International* 35 at p. 39; *Macmillan Inc. v. Bishopsgate Investment Trust plc (No. 3)* [1995] 1 W.L.R. 978.
[59] The categories were based on Lord Selborne's speech in *Barnes v. Addy* (1874) L.R. 9 Ch. App. 244 at pp. 251–252.

the client was a trustee of the whole of its assets.[60] It would be otherwise if he knew that the plaintiff's claim was well-founded.

i. Dishonest Assistance

(a) *Terminology.* An agent or other third party may be liable to make good the loss to a trust without the trust property ever vesting in him and without his purporting to act as trustee; as where an agent dishonestly participates with a trustee in a breach of trust. Thus liability does not depend on unjust enrichment.

It is submitted that, as no trust property is vested in him, he should not be called a constructive, or any other kind of trustee.[61] The question at issue is one of personal liability. The matter will nevertheless be dealt with in this Chapter because the constructive trust terminology has been used in much of the caselaw.[62]

(b) *Nature of Trustee's Breach.* In *Barnes v. Addy,*[63] Lord Selborne laid down the test of liability as that of as assisting "with knowledge in a dishonest and fraudulent design on the part of the trustees." This statement was *obiter,* but the principle that the third party could not be liable under this heading unless the breach of trust in which he assisted was dishonest on the part of the trustee became entrenched in the law until the recent clarification by the Privy Council in *Royal Brunei Airlines Sdn. Bhd. v. Tan.*[64]

The plaintiff appointed a company (BLT) to act as its travel agent and to account for the proceeds of ticket sales. It was conceded that BLT committed a breach of trust by using the money in its business. BLT fell into arrears in accounting and the contract was terminated. As BLT was insolvent, the plaintiff sued Tan, the principal shareholder and director. It was conceded that Tan had assisted in the breach with actual knowledge. The Brunei Court of Appeal found for Tan, holding that the breach in which

---

[60] *Carl Zeiss Stiftung v. Herbert Smith & Co. (No. 2)* [1969] 2 Ch. 276; (1969) 85 L.Q.R. 160 (P.V.B.); (1986) 102 L.Q.R. 267 at p. 287 (C. Harpum). See also *Williams v. Williams* (1881) 17 Ch.D. 437; *Competitive Insurance Co. Ltd v. Davies Investments Ltd* [1975] 1 W.L.R. 1240. A solicitor in doubt as to possible liability should apply to court for directions; *Finers v. Miro* [1991] 1 W.L.R. 35.

[61] See McKendrick's *Commercial Aspects of Trusts and Fiduciary Obligations,* Chapter 8 (P. Birks).

[62] See *Westdeutsche Landesbank Girozentrale v. Islington London Borough Council* [1996] A.C. 669 at p. 705; *Ghana Commercial Bank v. C, The Times,* March 3, 1997.

[63] (1874) L.R. 9 Ch.App. 255 at pp. 251, 252.

[64] [1995] 2 A.C. 378; [1995] Conv. 339 (M. Halliwell); (1995) 111 L.Q.R. 545 (C. Harpum); (1995) 54 C.L.J. 505 (R. Nolan); (1995) 3 R.L.R. 105 (J. Stevens); (1996) 112 L.Q.R. 56 (S. Gardner). For criticisms, see (1996) L.M.C.L.Q. 1 (P. Birks); (1996) 59 M.L.R. 443 (A. Berg).

he had assisted had not been shown to be fraudulent on the part of BLT. The appeal to the Privy Council centred upon the question whether accessory liability requires the breach of trust itself to be fraudulent. Tan was held personally liable for dishonestly assisting BLT's breach. There was no further requirement of dishonesty by BLT.[65]

Lord Nicholls of Birkenhead reviewed the authorities prior to *Barnes v. Addy*.[66] Those authorities did not require dishonesty on the part of the trustee whether the third party had procured the breach[67] or merely assisted in it. The law had taken a wrong turning in reliance on Lord Selborne's dictum in *Barnes v. Addy*. The trustee would be liable whether or not the breach was dishonest, but it would make no sense for a dishonest accessory, whose liability is fault-based, to escape simply because the trustee did not also act dishonestly. Although cases where the accessory is dishonest but the trustee is not will be rare, especially where the trustee is a company of which the accessories are directors,[68] this is a welcome clarification of the law.

It might be added that "assistance" requires actual participation. Thus a wife who merely accompanied her husband on holiday trips which also involved money laundering did not assist his breach.[69]

(c) *Dishonesty of Third Party.* The next question is whether the accessory must be shown to have acted dishonestly, or whether constructive knowledge of the breach (*i.e.* negligence) suffices. This is a matter of great importance, because frauds and other breaches of duty in the commercial context are complex, and can involve participants who are unaware of the wrongdoing.

Opinions have differed as to whether dishonesty is required on the part of the accessory or whether it suffices that he ought to have known of the breach. The weight of modern authority supports the view that dishonesty is required, and the matter has now been put beyond doubt by the Privy Council in *Royal Brunei Airlines Sdn.*

---

[65] In fact BLT's breach was dishonest because Tan's state of mind could be imputed to it. See *El Ajou v. Dollar Land Holdings plc* [1994] 2 All E.R. 685 ("directing mind and will").

[66] *Supra.*

[67] See *Eaves v. Hickson* (1861) Beav. 136 (trustees innocently deceived by forgery made wrongful distrubution which the party responsible for the deceit was liable to restore). A modern authority not requiring dishonesty by the trustees is *Powell v. Thompson* [1991] 1 N.Z.L.R. 597.

[68] See n. 65, *supra.*

[69] *Brinks Ltd v. Abu-Saleh (No. 3), The Times*, October 23, 1995; criticised (1996) 59 M.L.R. 443 at pp. 447–448 (A. Berg); (1996) 10 *Trust Law International* 53 (A. Oakley); [1996] Conv. 447 (J. Stevens).

Bhd. v. Tan.[70] Although the main issue, as we have seen, was whether the breach must be dishonest on the part of the trustee, their Lordships considered also the question whether the accessory must have acted dishonestly. In confirming that requirement, Lord Nicholls rejected the label "knowing assistance" because "knowledge" has too many shades of meaning. The five categories of knowledge elaborated by Peter Gibson J. in the *Baden* case[71] were "best forgotten". The word "dishonesty" was also to be preferred to "unconscionable conduct", a term little used save by equity lawyers. Lord Nicholls summarily rejected the view that an accessory could never be directly liable to the beneficiaries, because they are entitled to expect that others will refrain from intentionally intruding in the trustee-beneficiary relationship. Similarly rejected was the view that even an innocent third party could be liable, as that would make commerce impossible. In rejecting the view that negligence was a sufficient basis for liability, Lord Nicholls observed that in the commercial context persons such as bankers, advisers and many other agents would be liable to the trustees if they acted negligently. There was no reason why they should also be liable to the beneficiaries.[72] Thus the conclusion was that dishonesty is the basis of accessory liability.

It remains to consider what is meant by dishonesty. Lord Nicholls explained that it combines the objective standard of not acting as an honest person would in the circumstances with a strong subjective element: the court will assess the conduct in the light of what the defendant actually knew, not what a reasonable person would have known, and will have regard to the defendant's experience, intelligence and reasons for acting as he did. The broad meaning is conscious impropriety. It includes deliberately closing one's eyes or deliberately not asking questions, of which an example is *Agip (Africa) Ltd v. Jackson*:

> Payment orders from Agip to third parties were fraudulently altered by Agip's accountant, Z, who changed the name of the payees to that of B Co. and other companies. B Co. (and the other companies) had been formed by the defendants, who were two accountants in partnership (Jackson & Co.) and their employee. Two of the defendants were the sole directors and shareholders of

---

[70] [1995] 2 A.C. 378; *supra*.

[71] *Baden, Delvaux and Lecuit v. Société Générale pour Favoriser le Développement du Commerce et de l'Industrie en France SA* [1983] B.C.L.C. 325.

[72] This would sidestep the tort principle that there is no liability for negligently causing economic loss. *Cf.* (1995) 9 *Trust Law International* 102 (G. McCormack), suggesting that an accessory to fraud should be liable if negligent.

B Co. The money was transferred to the account of B Co. and thence to Jackson's client account in the Isle of Man. It was then paid to various recipients abroad who had no connection with Agip. B Co. was then put into liquidation. Agip sought to recover from the defendants, who had throughout followed the instructions of their client, a French lawyer acting for unidentified principals.

The claim based on assistance in the breach was successful before Millett J.[73] Z had committed a fraudulent breach of his duty to Agip, which the defendants must have realised was going on. They obviously knew they were "laundering" money, and were consciously helping Z to conceal the fraud. At best, they had been indifferent to it, which amounted to dishonesty. One partner and the employee were liable for assisting the breach, and the other partner was vicariously liable for their acts.[74] The judgment of Millett J. was upheld on appeal[75]: the defendants were liable because they did not act honestly.

The issue arose again in *Lipkin Gorman v. Karpnale Ltd.*

A solicitor, C, wrongly withdrew £200,000 from his firm's client account at the bank and spent it on gambling at the Playboy Club. C's firm sued the bank and the Club. In the present context, we are concerned only with the action against the bank. The bank manager had known that C was a gambler, but made no enquiries about the withdrawals.[76]

The Court of Appeal[77] held that the bank was not liable. It was conceded that the bank could not be liable as accessory if it was not in breach of its contract with the plaintiff firm. There was no breach of contract because the bank had no reason to believe that there was a serious possibility that C was drawing money for his own purposes.

In the absence of a dishonest accessory, the remedy is against the trustees and against those who have received the property, whose position will now be examined.

---

[73] [1990] Ch. 265; (1991) 107 L.Q.R. 71 (Sir Peter Millett). See also *Finers v. Miro* [1991] 1 W.L.R. 35.

[74] *cf. Re Bell's Indenture* [1980] 1 W.L.R. 1217; *post*, p. 304.

[75] [1991] Ch. 547; [1992] Conv. 367 (S. Goulding); (1992) 12 L.S. 332 (H. Norman); (1993–94) 4 K.C.L.J. 82 (P. Oliver).

[76] Any allegation of dishonesty was insufficiently pleaded.

[77] [1989] 1 W.L.R. 1340. The House of Lords dealt only with the Club's position; [1992] A.C. 548; *post*, p. 303.

ii. Liability for Receipt[78]

(a) *Personal and Proprietary Remedies.* A basic principle of property law is that any person who receives trust property, not being a purchaser for value without notice, takes subject to the trust. This is so whether he took with actual or constructive notice. So long as he retains the property he is bound to return it, and the tracing process[79] is available to identify the property or its proceeds. However, this is different from the question whether the recipient should be under a *personal* liability to account. The distinction is important if he no longer has the property. If he is liable to account, his liability remains. If he is not so accountable, his liability is confined to the return of the property or its proceeds while still in his possession. It may be that not every transferee who fails to prove that he was a bona fide purchaser of the legal estate without notice is subjected to the additional personal liability. An "innocent volunteer,"[80] for example, who took without notice that the property was trust property transferred in breach of trust cannot take free of the trust, but may not incur personal liability.[81] Whether the defendant has received the trust property will depend on the application of the tracing rules discussed in Chapter 23.[82]

(b *Actual or Constructive Knowledge.* While constructive knowledge clearly suffices where the question is whether the recipient took the property subject to the trust, the position is less clear where the question is whether he has incurred the personal liability to account. Opinions differ as to whether liability is based on actual knowledge, or constructive knowledge, or whether it is strict, so that even an innocent volunteer is liable. The weight of authority favours the view that constructive knowledge suffices. It is thus important to distinguish "assistance" and "receipt," as actual knowledge is necessary in the former category. Some cases, however, favour the view that actual knowledge is necessary to found personal liability in the "receipt" category also.

The traditional view is that where a third party "has received trust property with actual or constructive notice that it is trust property transferred in breach of trust, or because (not being a bona fide purchaser for value without notice), he acquires notice subsequent to

---

[78] Persons within this category were described in *Selangor United Rubber Estates v. Cradock (No. 3)* [1968] 1 W.L.R. 1555 as trustees *de son tort,* by analogy with executors *de son tort.* The distinction was once significant in the context of the defence of limitation, but is of no significance today; *ibid.* at p. 1579. As to whether the beneficiary may sue for conversion, see (1996) 55 C.L.J. 36 (A. Tettenborn).

[79] *Post,* Chapter 23.

[80] *Re Diplock* [1948] Ch. 465 at pp. 478–479; *ante,* p. 289, *post,* p. 677.

[81] For the view that liability is strict, see *post,* p. 301.

[82] See *El Ajou v. Dollar Land Holdings plc (No. 2)* [1995] 2 All E.R. 213; *post,* p. 670.

such receipt and then deals with the property in a manner inconsistent with the trust,"[83] he is personally liable. Thus in *Belmont Finance Corporation v. Williams Furniture Ltd (No. 2)*[84] company directors who participated in an unlawful share purchase scheme were liable because they had knowledge of all the facts which established the improper use of the funds, and knew or ought to have known that the money which they received was impressed with a trust. It was immaterial that, as the judge found, the directors did not act fraudulently.

A different view was taken in *Re Montagu's S.T.*[85]

Trustees transferred certain settled chattels to the beneficiary (the tenth Duke) absolutely, in breach of trust. The situation resulted from an "honest muddle" by all concerned. The Duke's solicitor had at an earlier stage been aware of the terms of the settlement. The Duke disposed of a number of the chattels during his lifetime. After his death, the eleventh Duke claimed that his predecessor had become a constructive trustee of them. Megarry V.-C. held that, while the tenth Duke's estate must return any remaining chattels or their traceable proceeds, the Duke was not liable as constructive trustee because he had no actual knowledge that the chattels were trust property transferred in breach of trust. Even if he had once understood the terms of the settlement, there was nothing to suggest that he remembered them so as to be aware at the date of receipt that the chattels were trust property. Nor was there any reason to impute the solicitor's knowledge to the Duke, by analogy with the doctrine of imputed notice.

The Vice-Chancellor emphasised that the relevant question was whether the recipient had *knowledge*, not whether he had *notice* according to the rules established under the doctrine of notice which dealt with the question whether an equitable interest was binding on a transferee. The question in the present context was whether a person was to have imposed on him the burdens of trusteeship. His Lordship held that liability should not be imposed unless the conscience of the recipient was affected; this required "want of probity", which includes actual knowledge, shutting one's eyes to the obvious, or wilfully and recklessly failing to make such enquiries as a reasonable and honest man would make; it does not include

[83] *Per* Brightman J. in *Karak Rubber Co. Ltd v. Burden, supra* at p. 632.
[84] [1980] 1 All E.R. 393; see also *(No. 1)* [1979] Ch. 250; (1979) 42 M.L.R. 707 and (1981) 44 M.L.R. 107 (R. Gregory); (1979) 38 C.L.J. 278 and (1980) 39 C.L.J. 276 (L. Sealy); *International Sales and Agencies Ltd v. Marcus* [1982] 3 All E.R. 551 at p. 558. It is also assumed in *Re Diplock* [1948] Ch. 465 at pp. 477–479 that constructive knowledge would suffice.
[85] [1987] Ch. 264 (decided 1985); (1986) 102 L.Q.R. 267 and (1987) 50 M.L.R. 217 (C. Harpum). (1987) 1 *Trust Law & Practice* 130 (M. Brindle and R. Hooley).

knowledge of circumstances which would indicate the facts to an honest and reasonable man or would put the latter on enquiry.

This view gained some support,[86] but subsequent cases in this country[87] and in New Zealand[88] have generally confirmed the view that constructive knowledge suffices for liability in the "receipt" category. As Thomas J. explained in *Powell v. Thompson*,[89] liability in the "assistance" category is based on unconscionable conduct, whereas in the "receipt" category it is based on unjust enrichment, to which dishonesty is not necessary.

Taking the unjust enrichment approach to its logical conclusion, a volunteer should be liable (subject to the change of position defence) if he has received the property of another without any kind of notice, as restitutionary liability is receipt-based, not fault-based.[90] This approach is likely to gain ground, as it is consistent with the common law action for money had and received, which lies against an innocent volunteer,[91] and with the action in equity against an innocent volunteer who has received property to which he is not entitled in the administration of an estate.[92] Lord Browne-Wilkinson, however, recently stated in *Westdeutsche Landesbank Girozentrale v. Islington London Borough Council*[93] (which involved a common law action) that an innocent volunteer is not personally liable to account as constructive trustee because he lacks the necessary knowledge, referring with apparent approval to *Re Montagu's S.T.*[94] This does not preclude the strict liability argument because, as shown by *Re Diplock*[95] itself, personal liability to

---

[86] *Lipkin Gorman v. Karpnale Ltd* [1987] 1 W.L.R. 987 (but the higher courts decided on other grounds, *infra*); *Barlcays Bank plc v. Quincecare Ltd* [1992] 4 All E.R. 363 (decided 1988); (1991) 5 *Trust Law International* 115 (M. Halliwell).

[87] See *Agip (Africa) Ltd v. Jackson* [1990] Ch. 265 at p. 291 (not dealt with in the Court of Appeal [1991] Ch. 547); *Polly Peck International plc v. Nadir (No. 2)* [1992] 4 All E.R. 769 at pp. 781–782; (1990) 49 C.L.J. 217 (C. Harpum); (1991) 107 L.Q.R. 71 (Sir Peter Millett); (1993) 109 L.Q.R. 368 (M. Bryan); *Eagle Trust plc v. S.B.C. Securities Ltd* [1993] 1 W.L.R. 484; *El Ajou v. Dollar Land Holdings plc* [1993] 3 All E.R. 717 (High Court).

[88] *Powell v. Thompson* [1991] 1 N.Z.L.R. 597; *Equiticorp Industries Group Ltd v. Hawkins* [1991] 3 N.Z.L.R. 700; *cf. Equiticorp Industries Group Ltd (In Statutory Management) v. The Crown (Judgment no. 47: Summary)* [1996] 3 N.Z.L.R. 586.

[89] *Supra*, at p. 607.

[90] (1989) 105 L.Q.R. 528 (P. Birks); (1991) 107 L.Q.R. 71 and (1995) 9 *Trust Law International* 35 at p. 39 (Sir Peter Millett); All E.R.Rev. 1992, pp. 270–272 (W. Swadling); (1994) 57 M.L.R. 38 (S. Fennell); Goff and Jones, p. 673; *cf.* (1996) 112 L.Q.R. 56 at p. 89 (S. Gardner). The possibility of imposing strict liability was left open in *Powell v. Thompson* [1991] 1 N.Z.L.R. 597 at p. 608.

[91] *Lipkin Gorman v. Karpnale Ltd* [1991] 2 A.C. 548; *post*, p. 303.

[92] *Ministry of Health v. Simpson* [1951] A.C. 251 (subject to requirement of suing personal representative first); *post*, p. 687. The volunteers were not, however, liable *as constructive trustees* because they were entitled to assume that the executors were acting properly; [1948] Ch. 465 at pp. 477–479.

[93] [1996] A.C. 669 at p. 707. See also *Ghana Commercial Bank v. C, The Times*, March 3, 1997.

[94] [1987] Ch. 264; *ante*, p. 299.

[95] [1948] Ch. 465. Liability based on constructive trusteeship was rejected at p. 478.

account in equity can arise in the absence of constructive trusteeship. It is right that an innocent volunteer should not be a constructive trustee, with consequent liability to repay with interest,[96]
but it does not follow that there should be no restitutionary liability
in equity in the absence of change of position.[97] Otherwise an
equitable owner is denied a remedy in circumstances where a legal
owner will succeed. That recipient liability is restitution-based has
recently been emphasised by the Privy Council.[98] It may be, however, that legislation will be required to achieve coherence in this
area.[99]

Of course, there is no room for strict liability in the case of a
purchaser, whose liability depends on notice, *i.e.* knowledge.
Assuming, as discussed above, that constructive notice is now
accepted as sufficient, it must be emphasised that where the recipient is a purchaser acting in an arm's length commercial transaction
not involving title to land, there is no duty to investigate.[1] Thus the
doctrine of constructive notice, while not inapplicable, is not applied
in its strict conveyancing sense. It has been held that a purchaser in
such a case is not liable unless he had actual knowledge of the
impropriety or acted with wilful or reckless disregard.[2] He will not
be put on inquiry unless he has been made aware of facts making it
obvious that the transaction may be improper.[3] The question arose in
El Ajou v. Dollar Land Holdings plc,[4] where the plaintiff, the victim
of a fraudulent investment scheme, sued the defendant company on
the basis that it had purchased the plaintiff's property from the
fraudsters with knowledge of the fraud. The action succeeded
because a director of the defendant company, who was its "directing
mind and will", had actual knowledge of the fraud, and his knowledge could be attributed to the company. The judgment of Millett J.[5]
was reversed on this point, but it contains a fuller discussion of the

---

[96] Liability to pay compound interest was the issue in the *Westdeutsche* case.

[97] See Goff and Jones, p. 672.

[98] *Royal Brunei Airlines Sdn. Bhd. v. Tan* [1995] 2 A.C. 378 (a case of dishonest assistance).
The receipt-based restitutionary claim was described by Auld L.J. as an "equitable new-
comer" in *Macmillan Inc. v. Bishopsgate Investment Trust plc (No. 3)* [1996] 1 W.L.R. 387
at p. 407.

[99] See (1995) 11 L.Q.R. 545 (C. Harpum).

[1] Banks and other financial institutions must, however, satisfy the Money Laundering
Regulations (S.I. 1993 No. 1933); *Laundering and Tracing* (ed. Birks, 1995), p. 115
(S. Gleeson).

[2] See *Polly Peck International plc v. Nadir (No. 2), supra; Eagle Trust plc v. S.B.C. Securities
Ltd, supra; Cowan de Groot Properties Ltd v. Eagle Trust plc* [1992] 4 All E.R. 700
(knowledge not to be imputed to purchaser unless guilty of commercially unacceptable
conduct).

[3] (1995) 9 *Trust Law International* 35 at p. 40 (Sir Peter Millett). See also *Polly Peck
International plc v. Nadir (No. 3), The Times,* March 22, 1993.

[4] [1994] 2 All E.R. 685; (1994) 53 C.L.J. 453 (G. Virgo). This case was remitted to the
Chancery Division on the question of quantum; *El Ajou v. Dollar Land Holdings plc (No.
2)* [1995] 2 All E.R. 213.

[5] [1993] 3 All E.R. 717.

principles of recipient liability. His Lordship emphasised that a purchaser was not expected to be unduly suspicious and would not be liable unless an honest and reasonable person would have realised that the property was probably trust property which was being misapplied.

(c) *Ministerial Receipt.* Recipient liability cannot arise where the third party has received the trust property merely in his capacity as agent and has dealt with it according to his principal's instructions. In other words, the "receipt" category is confined to third parties who have received the property for their own benefit.[6] Thus in *Agip (Africa) Ltd v. Jackson*[7] the defendants were not liable on the basis of receipt because they had merely received the money as agents and passed it on to third parties according to their principal's instructions. As we have seen, they were liable for dishonest assistance.

It has been said that banks receive merely as agents and so will not normally be liable for receipt unless they use the money to reduce an overdraft, as this amounts to receipt for their own benefit, although the defence of purchaser without notice will normally be available.[8] This reasoning has been convincingly criticised.[9]

(d) *Common Law Remedy.* A discussion of the equitable principles alone would be misleading, because the circumstances giving rise to a receipt claim may also found the common law personal action for money had and received. It is clear that the common law personal action lies against an innocent volunteer who had no knowledge, actual or constructive, of the fact that the money belonged not to the transferor but to the plaintiff. The plaintiff must, however, show title at common law to the money which, by applying the tracing rules, the defendant can be shown to have received. It is not necessary that the money should remain identifiable in the recipient's hands (in which case a proprietary claim might be considered).[10] A recipient of the money in good faith and for value has a defence.

---

[6] Birks, *Introduction to the Law of Restitution*, p. 445; (1986) 102 L.Q.R. 114 (C. Harpum); (1989) 105 L.Q.R. 528 (P. Birks); (1991) 107 L.Q.R. 71 (Sir Peter Millett).

[7] [1990] Ch. 265, affirmed [1991] Ch. 547. The facts have been given, *ante*, p. 296.

[8] *Agip (Africa) Ltd v. Jackson, supra,* at p. 292; (1991) 107 L.Q.R. 71 at p. 83. See also *Polly Peck International plc. v. Nadir (No. 2)* [1992] 4 All E.R. 769 (bank receiving sterling and exchanging it for foreign currency receives the sterling for its own benefit, but could have defence of purchaser without notice); *cf. Nimmo v. Westpac Banking Corporation* [1993] 3 N.Z.L.R. 218 at p. 225; *Cigna Life Insurance NZ v. Westpac Securities Ltd* [1996] 1 N.Z.L.R. 80 at p. 86.

[9] *Laundering and Tracing* (ed. Birks, 1995), p. 126 (S. Gleeson); [1996] J.B.L. 165 (M. Bryan). Money paid to a bank becomes the property of the bank.

[10] It is not clear how far this action lies against a transferee from the recipient. See *Agip (Africa) Ltd v. Jackson* [1990] Ch. 265 at pp. 287–288; (1990) 106 L.Q.R. 20 (A. Burrows); (1991) 107 L.Q.R. 71 (Sir Peter Millett); Goff and Jones, p. 673.

These issues came before the House of Lords in *Lipkin Gorman v. Karpnale Ltd*,[11] where a firm of solicitors sought to recover money paid to the Playboy Club by a member of the firm, Cass, who had withdrawn if from the firm's client account and spent it on gambling. The Club had no knowledge of the source of the money, but had not given consideration: the gaming contract was not legally enforceable, and so the Club had incurred no obligation to honour the bets. The solicitors were held entitled to recover in the common law action, subject to the defence of change of position.

The decision has been criticised on the ground that the plaintiff firm did not have legal title to the money after it was withdrawn from the bank, because the legal title vested in Cass.[12] Lord Goff avoided this difficulty by holding that the firm had a legal chose in action (the debt owed to them by the bank holding their client account) which they could follow into the money drawn by Cass and thence into the hands of the Club (the Club surprisingly conceded that this legal title was not defeated by reason of any mixing of the money by Cass with his own).

Of great significance was the unqualified acceptance by the House of Lords of the defence of change of position, widely recognised in the common law world, which should be left to develop on a case by case basis.[13] The defence is available to an innocent defendant[14] (but not to a wrongdoer) who has so changed his position that it would be inequitable to require restitution or restitution in full. Of course, it will not be available where the recipient has applied the money to normal expenses which would have been incurred in any event. In the present case the Club could invoke the defence to the extent that it had paid out winnings to Cass. These sums could be set off against the total sums received from him.

iii. Agent Assuming Trustee's Duties.[15]

An agent of the trustees may, as we have seen, incur liability under the above rules if he has been dishonest or has received trust property for his own benefit. There will normally be no such liability where trust property is transferred to an agent in the ordinary process of delegation,[16] as his receipt is ministerial and there is no breach of trust. In such a case he will only be subjected to a trustee's liability if he receives the property into his hands in connection with his assumption of the trustee's office and duties. In *Williams-Ashman v. Price and*

---

[11] [1991] 2 A.C. 548; *ante*, p. 297. The plaintiffs were content to bring a personal action as the defendant was not insolvent.

[12] [1992] Conv. 124 (M. Halliwell); (1992) 55 M.L.R. 377 (E. McKendrick).

[13] *Post*, p. 679. The defence existed in limited form, as discussed by the House of Lords.

[14] See Goff and Jones, p. 673.

[15] See (1986) 102 L.Q.R. 114 at pp. 130 *et seq.* (C. Harpum).

[16] *Post*, p. 559.

Williams,[17] Bennett J. treated *Mara v. Browne*[18] as authority for the proposition that "an agent in possession of money which he knows to be trust money, so long as he acts honestly, is not accountable to the beneficiaries interested in the trust money unless he intermeddles in the trust by doing acts characteristic of a trustee and outside the duties of an agent." Thus, where a solicitor received trust money through his own account, and invested it in unauthorised mortgages on the instructions of the trustees, the solicitor was held to be acting in his capacity as a solicitor, and not liable as a constructive trustee.[19] A stockbroker would not incur such liability for receiving trust money and investing it on the trustee's instructions in an unauthorised investment. The remedy is against the trustees.

If the agent does not know that the property is trust property, he is not liable if he acts honestly and within the scope of his agency, even if the facts were such as to put him on enquiry.[20]

iv. Liability of Partner of Constructive Trustee

In *Re Bell's Indenture*,[21] trustee-beneficiaries dissipated nearly £30,000 of the trust fund with the knowledge and assistance of H, a partner in a firm of solicitors acting for the trustees. The beneficiaries sought to make H's partner, who, it was conceded, had acted honestly and reasonably throughout, liable. H's liability was not disputed. Vinelott J. held that a solicitor has the implied authority of his partners to accept trust monies as agent of the trustees, but has no implied authority to accept office as trustee, nor to constitute himself as constructive trustee, and so make his partners liable for any misapplication of the trust property. The monies, which had passed through the firm's client account, had not been received by the partnership as trustees, thus H's partner was not liable as constructive trustee. Nor was he liable under the provisions of the Partnership Act 1980.[22]

The decision in *Blyth v. Fladgate*,[23] where, in similar circumstances, the solicitor's partners were held jointly liable, was treated

---

[17] [1942] Ch. 219 at p. 228.
[18] [1896] 1 Ch. 199.
[19] *Mara v. Browne* [1896] 1 Ch. 199 (any negligence action would have been statute-barred); *Williams-Ashman v. Price and Williams* [1942] Ch. 219.
[20] *Williams v. Williams* (1881) 17 Ch.D. 437; *Competitive Insurance Co. Ltd v. Davies Investments Ltd* [1975] 1 W.L.R. 1240.
[21] [1980] 1 W.L.R. 1217; [1981] Conv. 310 (P. Luxton).
[22] See s.13, providing that if a partner, being a trustee, improperly employs trust property in the business or on the account of the partnership, no other partner is liable for the trust property to the beneficiaries. It is otherwise if the partner has notice of the breach of trust, and nothing in this section prevents the recovery of trust money from the firm while still in its possession or under its control. Nor was the firm liable under ss.10 or 11 of the Act. On this aspect of the decision, see [1981] Conv. 310 (P. Luxton).
[23] [1891] 1 Ch. 337.

as a case on "very special facts," where the partners became trustees because there were no trustees at the time the money was paid into the firm's account, and, consequently, the partners could not be considered to be merely agents of the trustees. That this was the correct explanation was clear from *Mara v. Browne*,[24] where Lord Herschell said "it is not within the scope of the implied authority of a partner in such a business that he should so act as to make himself a constructive trustee, and thereby subject his partner to the same liability."[25]

This may be contrasted with *Agip (Africa) Ltd v. Jackson*,[26] where only two of the three defendants, an accountant and an employee of his firm, had dishonestly assisted in the breach of trust. The other defendant, the accountant's partner, was held vicariously liable (with little discussion) for the acts of the other two.

C. Mutual Wills[27]

Two persons (often husband and wife)[28] may agree that, on the death of the first to die, all their property shall be enjoyed by the survivor, and after his (her) death by nominated beneficiaries; and may make mutual wills to that effect. The survivor may be given a life interest,[29] an absolute interest[30] or no interest at all.[31] The question is whether, and to what extent, such an agreement controls the devolution of their property.

i. Agreement Necessary. Before any remedy can be obtained, an agreement to make wills and not to revoke them[32] between the parties must be proved. The agreement must indicate that the wills are to be mutually binding, whether or not expressed in the language of revocation.[33] The standard of proof is the ordinary civil standard (*i.e.* on balance of probabilities); the evidence must be "clear and satisfactory" and may be extrinsic, as where the agreement is substantiated by family conversations.[34] The mere fact that the wills

---

[24] [1896] 1 Ch. 199, *ante*, p. 304. But see [1981] Conv. 310 (P. Luxton).

[25] *Ibid.* at p. 208.

[26] [1991] Ch. 547; *ante*, p. 296. *Re Bell's Indenture* was not cited.

[27] (1951) 15 Conv.(N.S.) 28 (G. Graham); (1951) 14 M.L.R. 140 (J. Mitchell); (1970) 34 Conv.(N.S.) 230 (R. Burgess); (1989) 105 L.Q.R. 534 (C. Rickett).

[28] *Walpole v. Lord Orford* (1797) 3 Ves.Jr. 402.

[29] *Dufour v. Pereira* (1769) Dick. 419.

[30] *Re Green* [1951] 148.

[31] *Re Dale (deceased)* [1994] Ch. 31.

[32] *In the Goods of Heys* [1914] P. 192.

[33] *Re Goodchild (deceased)* [1996] 1 W.L.R. 694. (mistaken belief of first testator that wills mutually binding may enable intended beneficiary to claim under the Inheritance (Provision for Family and Dependants) Act 1975 on death of survivor).

[34] *Re Cleaver* [1981] 1 W.L.R. 939; *Re Newey* [1994] 2 N.Z.L.R. 590; [1996] Conv. 136 (C. Rickett).

were made simultaneously and in the same form is not, of itself, proof of an agreement although it is a relevant circumstance to be taken into account.[35] The agreement must amount to a contract, not a mere understanding.[36] But the court may infer an agreement from the conduct of the parties, the circumstances and the terms of the wills.[37] Preferably the agreement, if there was one, should be recited in the will.

In *Re Oldham*,[38] a husband and wife made mutual wills in similar form; each spouse left his (or her) property to the other absolutely with the same provisions in the event of the other predeceasing. There was no evidence of an agreement that they should be irrevocable. After the husband's death, the wife married again, and made a new will which was quite different from the earlier one. The second will was upheld; Astbury J. saying: "The fact that the two wills were made in identical terms does not necessarily connote any agreement beyond that of so making them . . . there is no evidence . . . that there was an agreement that the trust in the mutual will should in all circumstances be irrevocable by the survivor who took the benefit." The parties had left their estates to each other "absolutely." They "may have thought it quite safe to trust the other. . . . But that is a very different thing from saying that they bound themselves by a trust that should be operative in all circumstances and in all cases."[39]

In *Re Cleaver*,[40] on the other hand, the evidence of mutual wills was sufficient. An elderly couple married in 1967. The husband had three children. They made wills in each other's favour absolutely, and in default to the three children. In 1974, each of them reduced the share of one daughter, Martha, to a life interest. After the husband's death the wife made a new will consistent with the earlier one. Thereafter she made a further will enlarging Martha's share from a life interest to an absolute interest; and by her last will she left her residue to Martha and her husband, and nothing to the other two children. It was held that the wife's executors held the estate on the trusts of the 1974 will. Sufficient evidence of an agreement to make mutual wills was shown by the simultaneity and similarity of the original wills; the pattern of successive

---

[35] *Ibid.*

[36] *Re Goodchild (deceased), supra*; (1996) 146 N.L.J. 961; (J. Stevens) [1996] 8 C.F.L.Q. 253 (L. Ross); (1996) 10 *Trust Law International* 88 (N. Richardson).

[37] *Dufour v. Pereira* (1769) Dick. 419; *Stone v. Hoskins* [1905] P. 194; *Re Hagger* [1930] 2 Ch. 190; *Re Green* [1951] Ch. 148.

[38] [1925] Ch. 75.

[39] *Ibid.* at pp. 88–89; *Gray v. Perpetual Trustee Co.* [1928] A.C. 391.

[40] *Supra.*

wills made together; the fact that both parties reduced Martha's interest; the faithful terms of the first will made after the husband's death; and the fact that, in family conversations, the wife had regarded herself as under an obligation to leave her estate to the children.

ii. Remedies on the Contract. The agreement is binding between the parties. If it is broken by the first party to die, his estate will be liable in damages to the survivor.[41] If the breach is by the second party to die, as by revocation or alteration of his will, it has always been assumed that no remedy could be obtained against him or his estate under the contract. The law which has developed on the subject is based upon a trust which arises in appropriate cases in favour of the beneficiaries.

It is arguable that the principle of *Beswick v. Beswick*[42] could apply in this situation. The agreement between the testators is a contract, but the beneficiaries are not parties to the contract, and, while the privity rule remains,[43] cannot sue on it. The estate of the first to die, however, is in a similar position to Mrs Beswick, the administratrix. It seems that an action for specific performance of the contract would lie by the estate against the survivor or his estate; and a decree of specific performance would effect the transfer of the property. An examination of the problems which have arisen in treating the interests of the beneficiaries as trusts, as will be seen, makes a contractual solution attractive.[44] The court in *Re Dale (deceased)*[45] rejected the argument that the second testator could be ordered to make a will in accordance with the contract, or restrained from revoking it. It may remain arguable that specific performance could be obtained to enforce a conveyance of the property.[46]

iii. Trusts Created by Mutual Wills. A will is always revocable; an agreement not to revoke it does not make it irrevocable.[47]

---

[41] *Robinson v. Ommanney* (1883) 23 Ch.D. 285; but not where the revocation of the first will is by the subsequent marriage of the covenantor. See further (1991) 54 M.L.R. 581 (C. Rickett). Revocation of the survivor's will by remarriage does not affect any trust if the wills were mutual; *Re Goodchild (deceased)* [1996] 1 W.L.R. 694.

[42] [1968] A.C. 58.

[43] See Law Com. No. 242 (1996), suggesting enforceability by the third parties in certain cases.

[44] See (1979) 29 U. of Toronto L.J. 390 (T. Youdan). The executor must be willing to sue. See [1982] Conv. 228 (K. Hodkinson), suggesting that the ultimate beneficiary should be the executor; (1989) 105 L.Q.R. 534 (C. Rickett).

[45] [1994] Ch. 31; (1995) 58 M.L.R. 95 (A. Brierley). *Beswick v. Beswick* was not discussed.

[46] *Post*, p. 711.

[47] *Vynior's Case* (1609) 8 Co.Rep. 81b.

Thus, if the survivor of an agreement to make mutual wills destroys his will, he will die intestate: and if he makes a new will, that later one will be admitted to probate. But the disposition of his property on his death will be affected by the agreement. For the principle is established that the agreement between the parties, followed by the death of the first party, relying on the undertaking of the other party to observe the agreement, creates trusts in favour of the intended beneficiaries, which are enforceable against the property of the survivor.[48] Of the leading case of *Dufour v. Pereira*,[49] Clauson J. said.[50] *Dufour v. Pereira* decides that where there is a joint will . . . on the death of the first testator the position as regards that part of the property which belongs to the survivor is that the survivor will be treated . . . as holding the property on trust to apply it so as to carry out the effect of the joint will." A number of difficulties arise concerning the operation of such trusts.[51]

(a) *When Does the Trust Arise?* Mitchell says that there are three possibilities.[52] When the agreement was made; when the first testator dies; when the survivor dies. It is clear that no trust exists from the date of the agreement. For either party can revoke before either dies, on giving notice to the other[53]; and even notice is not necessary in the case of the first to die, for the survivor has notice on the first death and will not be prejudiced.[54] The survivor in such circumstances is unable to establish any trust in his favour against the estate of the first to die.[55] Nor can the death of the survivor be the correct time. For where a beneficiary died between the date of the death of the first to die and the survivor, the estate of that beneficiary was able to claim its share on the ground that the interest was vested and there was no lapse.[56] Of these three possibilities, it seems therefore that the trust arises on the death of the first to die.

Until recently a fourth possibility was arguable: that the trust arises when the survivor receives a benefit under the first will. On this question there were dicta both ways. Most of the dicta favoured the view that the trust is imposed only where the survivor takes a

---

[48] *In the Goods of Heys* [1914] P. 192; *Stone v. Hoskins* [1905] P. 194 (later will of first to die).
[49] (1769) Dick 419; interpreted in *Re Dale (deceased)*, *supra*, as not requiring any benefit to pass to the survivor.
[50] *Re Hagger* [1930] 2 Ch. 190 at p. 195.
[51] These difficulties are discussed in (1979) 29 U. of Toronto L.J. at pp. 411–419 (T. Youdan).
[52] (1951) 14 M.L.R. 137 (J. Mitchell).
[53] *Dufour v. Pereira* (1769) Dick. 419 at p. 420.
[54] *Ibid.*
[55] *Stone v. Hoskins* [1905] P. 194.
[56] *Re Hagger* [1930] 2 Ch. 190; *cf. Re Gardner (No. 2)* [1923] Ch. 230.

benefit.[57] Clauson J., however, in *Re Hagger*[58] said *obiter* that the trust would arise "even though the survivor did not signify his election to give effect to the will by taking benefits under it."

It has now been held by Morritt J. in *Re Dale (deceased)*,[59] after a full review of all the authorities, that the doctrine of mutual wills applies even where the survivor does not benefit from the will of the first testator. A husband and wife agreed that each would leave his or her whole estate to their son and daughter equally. The husband died first, leaving his estate of £18,500 in this way. The wife later made a new will leaving her daughter £300 and the rest of her estate of £19,000 to her son. It was held that the son, as executor, held the estate on trust for himself and the daughter equally. Benefit by the survivor was a sufficient but not a necessary requirement for the operation of the doctrine. The survivor committed a fraud on the first testator who died in reliance upon their bargain even if he or she did not benefit from the will. That this was the true basis of the doctrine appeared from *Dufour v. Pereira*[60] "he, that dies first, does by his death carry the agreement on his part into execution. If the other then refuses, he is guilty of a fraud, can never unbind himself, and becomes a trustee of course. For no man shall deceive another to his prejudice."[61] Morritt J. considered that the imposition of the trust was consistent with all the authorities, supported by some of them and was in furtherance of equity's original jurisdiction to intervene in cases of fraud.

(b) *To what Property Does the Trust Attach?*[62] This may be clear from the express terms of the will.[63] Failing that, and subject always to a contrary intention, there are four possibilities; that the trust attaches to the property, if any, which the survivor receives from the estate of the first to die: or to all the property that the survivor owned at that time: or to all the property which the survivor owned at *his* death: or to all property which the survivor owned at any time since the first death.

Clearly the trust must include any property received from the first to die. If the will gave only a life interest, there is no scope for the

---

[57] *Dufour v. Pereira* (1769) Dick. 419 at p. 421; *Stone v. Hoskins* [1905] P. 194 at p. 197; *Re Oldham* [1925] Ch. 75 at p. 87. See also *Re Cleaver* [1981] 1 W.L.R. 939.

[58] [1930] 2 Ch. 190 at p. 195. See (1970) 34 Conv.(N.S.) 230 (R. Burgess); [1982] Conv. 228 at p. 230 (K. Hodkinson).

[59] [1994] Ch. 31; (1993) 7 *Trust Law International* 18 (D. Brown); All E.R.Rev. 1993, p. 415 (C. Sherrin).

[60] As more fully reported in Hargrave's Juridical Arguments, Vol. 2, p. 304.

[61] *Ibid.* at p. 310 (Lord Camden).

[62] See (1977) 15 Alberta L.Rev. 211 (L. Sheridan).

[63] As in *Re Green* [1951] Ch. 148, where the wills provided that if the other spouse predeceased, the residue was to be divided into halves, one half being considered as the testator's personal property and the other as the benefit received from the other spouse. It was held that the trust attached only to the latter.

trust in respect of that property. If the gift is absolute, the imposition of a trust in favour of ultimate beneficiaries will in effect reduce the survivor's interest to a life interest.

The position is more complex in relation to the property of the survivor. *Re Hagger*,[64] suggests that the trust attaches at least to all the property which the survivor had at the time of the first death. Morritt J. held that the trust embraced the survivor's whole estate at his or her death.[65] This means that a disposition *inter vivos* by the survivor would be a breach of trust; indeed it would make nonsense of the trust if he could so dispose of the property.[66] This raises the question of acquisitions by the survivor by his own efforts after the first death. After all, the property acquired after the date of the wills by the first to die was included in his estate; and the agreement, in the absence of a contrary provision, would apply to all property. The agreement thus acts like a covenant to settle after-acquired property, and the property becomes subject to the trust on its becoming vested in the trustee.[67] If this is correct, the effect of mutual wills is to reduce the survivor to the position of a life tenant in respect of all his property. He may use the income, but the capital is held on trust for the ultimate beneficiaries.

In *Re Cleaver*[68] Nourse J., relying on the Australian decision *Birmingham v. Renfrew*,[69] adopted the view there expressed that the survivor could enjoy the property as an absolute owner in his lifetime "subject to a fiduciary duty which, so to speak, crystallised on his death and disabled him only from voluntary dispositions *inter vivos*."[70] This meant dispositions calculated to defeat the agreement. There was no objection to ordinary gifts of small value. The difficulty however, is that any such duty not to dissipate the assets *inter vivos* will be unenforceable if the beneficiary does not discover his rights until the survivor's death. Although Nourse J. affirmed the requirement of certainty of subject-matter, this is not fully consistent with his formulation of the rights and duties of the parties.[71] If, on the other hand, the survivor's obligation is merely not to dispose of the property *by will* inconsistently with the agreement,[72] then the difficulties are all the greater; for the trust property would be

---

[64] [1930] 2 Ch. 190. (Interest of beneficiary vested before death of survivor).
[65] *Re Dale (deceased)* [1994] Ch. 31.
[66] See however Astbury J. in *Re Oldham* [1925] Ch. 75 at pp. 87, 88; suggesting that the trust attaches only to property held by the survivor at death.
[67] *Paul v. Paul* (1882) 20 Ch.D. 742; *Re Ralli's W.T.* [1964] Ch. 288.
[68] [1981] 1 W.L.R. 939. Similarly in *Goodchild v. Goodchild* [1996] 1 W.L.R. 694.
[69] (1936) 57 C.L.R. 666.
[70] (1936) 57 C.L.R. at p. 690. *cf. Palmer v. Bank of N.S.W.* (1975) 7 A.L.R. 671.
[71] See [1982] Conv. 228 (K. Hodkinson).
[72] See *Palmer v. Bank of N.S.W., supra.*

indefinite until his death. These problems were not examined in *Re Dale (deceased)*.[73]

(c) *The Survivor as Trustee.* If it is correct that the survivor becomes a trustee of all the property he owns or acquires before his death, the consequences of the doctrine could be draconian for the survivor, for example if he acquires new dependants after the death of the first testator, or wins the lottery; similarly if the agreed beneficiary acquires a fortune elsewhere or is guilty of misconduct.[74] As far as the beneficiaries are concerned, there is very little opportunity to ensure that proper control over the survivor is maintained. Purchasers have no notice of the trusts, and the trust property may be lost on alienation to them.[75] Also, the survivor may have no idea that he is a trustee. If land is included in the trusts the lack of knowledge of all parties concerned may result in disputes and uncertainties as to title if it is alienated without observing the proper procedures. And, as noted above, further problems arise if the trust is treated as attaching only on the death of the survivor; and as "floating"[76] or as being "in suspense"[77] in the meantime. This is the problem, it should be noted, created in the field of secret trusts by *dicta* in *Ottaway v. Norman*.[78] The possibilities of trouble are unlimited; they have not yet been finally worked out.[79]

iv. Conclusion. It is clear that the imposition by law of a trust in cases of mutual wills is a clumsy and inadequate way of dealing with a complicated problem. A contractual solution under the *Beswick* principle would be much more satisfactory; but this has not been accepted.[80] A solution based on the idea of a floating charge has also been suggested.[81] For the present, persons who wish to leave property by way of mutual wills should be advised to consider most carefully the trusts on which they wish the property to be held; what property is to be included; the position during the survivor's lifetime; who they wish to be trustees; what administrative powers the trustees should have; and how best the scheme desired can be carried out from an inheritance tax point of view. Merely to draft mutual wills and then leave the law to sort out such a host of

---

[73] [1994] Ch. 31; *supra.*
[74] See (1994) 144 N.L.J. 1272 (P. O'Hagan).
[75] *Pilcher v. Rawlins* (1872) L.R. 7 Ch.App. 259.
[76] *Ante,* p. 310; (1972) 36 Conv.(N.S.) 129 at p. 132 (D. Hayton).
[77] *Per* Brightman J. [1972] Ch. 698 at p. 713; *Re Cleaver, supra.*
[78] [1972] Ch. 698 at p. 713 ("suspended trust" where donee obliged to bequeath to X whatever remains at the donee's death), *ante,* p. 160.
[79] (1951) 14 M.L.R. 140–142 (J. Mitchell).
[80] *Re Dale (deceased)* [1994] Ch. 31.
[81] [1982] Conv. 228, at p. 231 (K. Hodkinson). This does not solve the problem that the "beneficiaries" are often unaware of the situation.

problems is no service to the testator. The law in this context, as in most other areas of constructive trusts, imposes a trust in an attempt to prevent one party from committing a fraud on the other. It is a kind of salvage operation; a salvage of a wreck which competent legal advice would have avoided in the first place.[82]

D. The Vendor under a Specifically Enforceable Contract for Sale

A contract for sale is specifically enforceable where the remedy of damages would be inadequate.[83] Contracts relating to personalty are rarely specifically enforceable, as the property may be purchased elsewhere. If this is not so, as in the case of shares in a private company, then the contract will be specifically enforceable.[84] In the present context, however, we are mainly concerned with contracts relating to land. The availability of specific performance means that, in equity, the purchaser is regarded as already the owner. Thus it has many times been said by high authority that a vendor of land, on the conclusion of the contract of sale, becomes a trustee of the land for the purchaser.[85] Opinions have differed as to the time at which the trusteeship arises.[86] Any changes in the nature of the property after that time, for example by fire or flooding, if they occur without the fault of the vendor, are at the purchaser's risk.[87] If the vendor sells to another, he holds the purchase money on trust for the purchaser.[88] Beyond that, however, there is little agreement.[89] It is clear at least that this is not an ordinary trusteeship. Cotton L.J. said that the vendor was trustee only in a qualified sense[90]; Lord Greene M.R. called him a quasi-trustee,[91] and Stamp L.J. a "constructive trustee

---

[82] For a different view, see (1988) 138 N.L.J. 351 (F. Sunnucks).

[83] *Post*, Chap. 24.

[84] See *Oughtred v. I.R.C.* [1960] A.C. 206; *Neville v. Wilson* [1996] 3 W.L.R. 460.

[85] *Lysaght v. Edwards* (1876) 2 Ch.D. 499 at p. 507; (1959) 23 Conv.(N.S.) 173 (V. Wellings); Waters, *The Constructive Trust*, Chap. 2; Oakley, *Constructive Trusts*, Ch. 6.

[86] It may be the date of the contract; or the date the vendor makes title. If the latter, the trust relates back to the contract date. See *Lysaght v. Edwards* (1876) 2 Ch.D. 499; *Rayner v. Preston* (1881) 18 Ch.D. 1; *Oughtred v. I.R.C.* [1960] A.C. 206.

[87] *Paine v. Meller* (1801) 6 Ves.Jr. 349. As to insurance, see L.P.A. 1925, s.47. For the view that the risk does not pass to the purchaser see [1984] Conv. 43 (M. Thompson). See further Law Com. No. 191 (1990), *Transfer of Land; Risk of Damage after Contract for Sale*, para. 2.25, suggesting that the risk should pass only on completion.

[88] *Lake v. Bayliss* [1974] 1 W.L.R. 1073; *Shaw v. Foster* (1872) 5 H.L. 321 at p. 327; (1974) 38 Conv.(N.S.) 357 (F. Crane).

[89] Cotton, Brett and James L.JJ. in *Rayner v. Preston* (1881) Ch.D. 1 expressed different views on the situation.

[90] *Rayner v. Preston, supra*, at p. 6; *Lysaght v. Edwards* (1876) 2 Ch.D. 499 at p. 506; *Royal Bristol Permanent Building Society v. Bomash* (1887) 35 Ch.D. 390 at p. 397 ("a modified sense"); *Re Hamilton-Snowball's Conveyance* [1959] Ch. 308.

[91] *Cumberland Consolidated Holdings Ltd v. Ireland* [1946] K.B. 264 at p. 269.

or a trustee *sub modo*"[92]; and Lord Cairns[93] explained that the trustee was entitled to protect his own interest in the property. Similarly, the vendor is entitled to keep for himself the rents and profits of the land (or dividends in the case of shares[94]) until the date of the completion of the sale,[95] and to retain possession against the purchaser until the purchase price has been paid; and he retains a lien on the land for the price if the land is conveyed before the price is paid,[96] and time runs under the Limitation Act 1980 against the vendor in respect of possession of the land.[97] The relationship between the parties contains a number of aspects in which they are hostile and the vendor self-interested.

Once the date for completion has arrived and the price is paid in full, the vendor must immediately convey. This is an example of a trusteeship arising because the bare legal estate is in one person, and the entire beneficial ownership in another.[98] Until that situation has arisen, it does not seem that any useful purpose is served by stating that the relationship between the parties is one of trustee and beneficiary. The position at law is that they are parties to a contract and no more. In equity additional rights arise by reason of the fact that specific performance is available as a remedy in favour of an innocent party. Equity then treats as done that which ought to be done, and considers the purchaser as being the owner in equity. Hence, where a receiver was appointed upon the vendor company's insolvency before completion, the contract remained specifically enforceable against the receiver as opposed to merely sounding in damages.[99] This is not attributable to any trust, but to the characteristics of a specifically enforceable contract for sale, whereby the equitable interest passes to the purchaser and is not destroyed by the subsequent insolvency of the vendor. The trust cannot be enforced against a purchaser if the contract, being unregistered, does not bind him.[1] In many other respects the contractual nature of the relationship is apparent; each party is continuing to guard his own interests against the other in a way which is quite inconsistent with the existence of the relationship of trustee and beneficiary.

A further question is whether the vendor becomes trustee for a sub-purchaser, if the purchaser has entered into a contract to sell to

---

[92] *Berkley v. Poulett* (1977) 242 E.G. 39 at p. 43.
[93] *Shaw v. Foster* (1872) L.R. 5 H.L. 321 at p. 338.
[94] *J. Sainsbury plc v. O'Connor (Inspector of Taxes)* [1991] S.T.C. 318.
[95] *Cuddon v. Tite* (1858) 1 Giff 395.
[96] *Mackreth v. Symmons* (1808) 15 Ves.Jr. 329. See further (1994) 53 C.L.J. 263 (S. Worthington).
[97] *Bridges v. Mees* [1957] Ch. 475; *cf. Hyde v. Pearce* [1982] 1 All E.R. 1029.
[98] *Lloyds Bank plc v. Carrick* [1996] 4 All E.R. 630; [1996] Conv. 295 (M. Thompson).
[99] *Freevale Ltd v. Metrostore (Holdings) Ltd* [1984] 1 All E.R. 495 (a receiver, unlike a liquidator, has no statutory right to disclaim contracts); [1984] Conv. 446 (D. Milman and S. Coneys); *Re Coregrange Ltd* [1984] B.C.L.C. 453.
[1] *Lloyds Bank plc v. Carrick, supra.*

the sub-purchaser. In such a case, the sub-purchaser, by virtue of his contract with the purchaser, is entitled to specific performance and is treated as the owner in equity. In *Berkley v. Earl Poulett*[2] the vendor, with the concurrence of the purchaser, had allegedly allowed certain fixtures to be taken away. The sub-purchaser claimed that the vendor was in breach of the trustee's duty to take proper care of the property. A majority of the Court of Appeal considered that no fiduciary duty was owed to the sub-purchaser. It was not that the vendor was a trustee and therefore had fiduciary duties; rather that the vendor owed duties to the purchaser and was labelled a trustee. A sub-purchaser's right is to have the purchaser enforce the contract against the vendor.

No doubt it is too late now to say that the relationship between vendor and purchaser is not that of trustee and beneficiary. The terminology must, however, be received with reserve. Unlike other cases of constructive trusts, the element of improper conduct is absent and the situation must, at best, be treated as anomalous.[3]

E. Secret Trusts

It is unsettled whether secret trusts, and more particularly half-secret trusts, are to be regarded as express or constructive. The practical significance of the distinction is that, in the case of land, section 53 of the Law of Property Act 1925 requires written evidence in the case of express trusts, but not in the case of constructive trusts. The matter is examined in detail in Chapter 5.

F. Conveyance by Fraud

Where property has been obtained by the fraud of the defendant, he may be compelled to hold it as a constructive trustee. The trust is not imposed in every case.[4] While it is difficult to define the circumstances in which the trust will be imposed, some broad principles are in practice clear. In the case of a conveyance of land *inter vivos*, the transferee may be prevented, by the imposition of a constructive trust, from setting up the apparently absolute nature of the conveyance in order to defeat a beneficial interest which, by oral

---

[2] (1977) 242 E.G. 39.

[3] (1959) 23 Conv.(N.S.) 1734 (V. Wellings). We have seen that it is not treated as a constructive trust for the purpose of L.P.A. 1925, s.53(2); *Oughtred v. I.R.C.* [1960] A.C. 206, *ante*, p. 84.

[4] For example, if the plaintiff had acquiesced in the fraud; *Lonrho plc v. Fayed (No. 2)* [1992] 1 W.L.R. 1. See *Halifax Building Society v. Thomas* [1996] Ch. 217; *ante*, p. 291.

agreement, was intended to remain in the transferor,[5] or in some third party.[6]

Similarly, situations in which a will is fraudulently revoked, or where the testator is fraudulently prevented from making a will, or fraudulently induced to leave property to a legatee or devisee, are all appropriate for the imposition of a constructive trust. These situations are discussed under the heading of secret trusts.[7]

G. Acquisition of Property by Killing[8]

Where a beneficiary kills the testator, or next of kin kills an intestate, there is good reason to prevent him from benefiting from his crime.[9] The English courts have established a rule to this effect, but they "have worked out no rational theory for their actions in depriving killers[10] . . . there has been little discussion of the theoretical basis for a deprivation . . . and generally they have considered that the killer does not gain legal title."[11] Such a result is contrary to the enactments relating to succession, testate or intestate, but clearly a rule of public policy can override statutory provisions.[12] If the killer does not acquire any title to the property in question, as in the pension and insurance cases, then there is no need for the imposition of a constructive trust. If, on the other hand, the killer acquires legal title, as is arguably the position in some of the succession cases, then he will be subjected to a constructive trust which is imposed to prevent unjust enrichment. A bona fide purchaser from the wrongdoer would then be protected.[13]

Whichever solution is reached, a number of problems remain, on which there is little authority.

i. Type of Killing. Killing may be effected by any means from murder to accident. The deprivation principle only applies to criminal killing. There is much to be said for the view that "the killer should only be deprived when he does or causes to be done a

---

[5] *Rochefoucauld v. Boustead* [1897] 1 Ch. 196; *Bannister v. Bannister* [1948] 2 All E.R. 133; *Hodgson v. Marks* [1972] Ch. 892; *ante*, p. 77.

[6] *Binions v. Evans* [1972] Ch. 359; *Peffer v. Rigg* [1977] 1 W.L.R. 285; *Lyus v. Prowsa Developments Ltd* [1982] 1 W.L.R. 1044; *post*, p. 322. See also [1987] Conv. 246 (J. Feltham).

[7] *Supra.* For a fuller discussion, see Chap. 5.

[8] Goff and Jones, pp. 703–713; (1973) 89 L.Q.R. 235 (T. Youdan), which has been used as the basis of this account; *Restatement of Restitution*, § 187; (1969) 68 Mich. L.R. 65 (W. McGovern).

[9] *In the Estate of Crippen* [1911] P. 108.

[10] (1973) 89 L.Q.R. 235.

[11] *Ibid.* at p. 251.

[12] See, for example, *R. v. Chief National Insurance Commissioner, ex p. Connor, infra.*

[13] *Re Cash* (1911) 30 N.Z.L.R. 571; *Beresford v. Royal Insurance Ltd* [1938] A.C. 586 at p. 600.

dangerous act intending[14] harm to the person whose death occasions his acquisition; and that person dies as a result of that act."[15] Thus the rule does not apply to all cases of manslaughter.[16]

ii. Means of Acquisition. The principle applies when the killer benefits by testamentary gift,[17] or under his intestacy,[18] and also under a life insurance policy on the victim's life[19]; and, in the days when suicide was a crime, the estate of a suicide was held to be unable to claim the benefits of an insurance policy.[20] Similarly, a woman who kills her husband cannot claim a widow's pension.[21] More complicated questions arise where one joint tenant kills another, or a remainderman kills the life tenant. Following Commonwealth decisions[22] it has been held that the joint tenant cannot profit from his wrong. He becomes entitled under the common law rule of survivorship to the whole legal estate, but he holds it as to one half on trust for the victim's estate.[23] In the case of the remainderman killing the life tenant, the best course would be to postpone the killer's enjoyment until the time at which the victim's life expectation would terminate.[24]

iii. Destination of Property. To deprive the wrongdoer does not solve all the problems. Persons claiming through the wrongdoer should not benefit from the crime, but the position is different with the wrongdoer's next of kin if they are also next of kin of the victim. They should not be deprived of an independent right of succession. It is suggested that they should be allowed to take "provided that they would have been as next of kin of the murdered person if the

---

[14] Including recklessness.

[15] (1973) 89 L.Q.R. 235 at p. 240, where the matter is examined in detail; Goff and Jones (4th ed.), p. 704.

[16] *Gray v. Barr* [1971] 2 Q.B. 544; *Re K (deceased)* [1986] Ch. 180; *Re H (deceased)* [1990] 1 F.L.R. 441; [1991] Conv. 48 (J. Martin); *cf. Re Hall* [1914] P. 1; *Re Giles* [1972] Ch. 544; *Jones v. Roberts* [1995] 2 F.L.R. 422; (1995) 111 L.Q.R. 196 (R. Buckley); *Re S. (deceased)* [1996] 1 W.L.R. 235.

[17] *Re Pollock* [1941] Ch. 219.

[18] *Re Sigsworth* [1935] Ch. 89.

[19] *Cleaver v. Mutual Reserve Fund Life Association Ltd* [1892] 1 Q.B. 147; *Davitt v. Titcumb* [1990] Ch. 110; [1991] Conv. 50 (J. Martin) (mortgage protection policy).

[20] *Beresford v. Royal Insurance Ltd* [1938] A.C. 586.

[21] *R. v. Chief National Commissioner, ex p. Connor* [1981] 1 Q.B. 758 (manslaughter); (1981) 44 M.L.R. 718 (St J. Robilliard). See also (1972) 31 C.L.J. 144 (J. Shand). As submitted above, this is not a case of constructive trust, as the claimant acquires no title to any property.

[22] *Schobelt v. Barber* (1967) 59 D.L.R. (2d) 519 (Ont.); *Re Barrowcliff* [1927] S.A.S.R. 147; *Rasmanis v. Jurewitsch* (1970) 70 S.R.(N.S.W.) 407; *Re Pechar* [1969] N.Z.L.R. 574.

[23] *Re K. (deceased), supra,* in the High Court. The Court of Appeal affirmed the decision without discussing this point. See also [1987] Conv. 33 (M. Thompson). For variants, see *Re Barrowcliff, supra; Kemp v. The Public Curator of Queensland* [1969] Qd.R. 145; *Restatement of Restitution,* § 188.

[24] (1973) 89 L.Q.R. 235 at p. 250.

murderer had predeceased his victim."[25] In other cases, the proper solution will be for the property to go to the victim's residuary legatee, or as on his intestacy, or to the other members of a class of which the wrongdoer was one[26]; or, where there are special circumstances to show what the victim's intention was, as where it was shown that the killing took place in order to prevent the victim from changing his will in favour of another, then the flexibility introduced by the concept of the constructive trust should allow the property to be claimed by "the person who, in the eyes of equity, has the best right to it."[27]

iv. Statutory Relief. It is provided by the Forfeiture Act 1982[28] that the court may grant relief from the forfeiture of inheritance and other rights to persons guilty of unlawful killing[29] other than murder,[30] where the court is satisfied that the justice of the case so requires.[31] A convicted person must bring proceedings for this purpose within three months of any conviction.[32] The Act applies to benefits under a will or upon intestacy; nominations; a *donatio mortis causa*; and property held on trust before the death which would devolve on the offender as a result of the death.[33] The Court may grant relief as to all or part of the property.[34] In the case of social security benefits, such as a widow's pension, the Act confers the discretion not on the court but on the Social Security Commissioner.[35] Finally, it is provided that the forfeiture principle does not preclude an application under the Family Provision legislation.[36]

H. Constructive Trusts of a New Model: Justice and Good Conscience

Some cases indicated a wide extension of the operation of constructive trusts by the introduction of what Lord Denning M.R.

---

[25] Goff and Jones (4th ed.), p. 707; *Scott on Trusts*, § 187; *Restatement of Restitution*, § 187.

[26] *Re Peacock* [1957] Ch. 310.

[27] (1973) 89 L.Q.R. 235 at p. 257.

[28] (1983) 46 M.L.R. 66 (P. Kenny); (1983) 80 L.S.Gaz. 910 (A. Mithani and A. Wilton).

[29] Including aiding, abetting, counselling or procuring the death; s.1(2). The Act does not apply to suicide, nor to attempts to kill.

[30] s.5.

[31] s.2(2). Degree of moral blame is significant; *Re K (deceased)* [1986] Ch. 180; *Re H. (deceased)* [1990] 1 F.L.R. 441.

[32] s.2(3). But the Act and the doctrine may apply even in the case of acquittal, because the civil standard of proof is lower; *Gray v. Barr* [1971] 2 Q.B. 544. See, however, *Halford v. Brookes, The Times*, October 3, 1991 (finding of murder in civil action must satisfy criminal standard of proof).

[33] s.2(4). See *Re S. (deceased)* [1996] 1 W.L.R. 235 (joint life insurance).

[34] s.2(1) and (5); *Re K. (deceased), supra.*

[35] s.4, as amended by Social Security Act 1986. See (1984) 81 L.S.Gaz. 288; (1988) 85 L.S.Gaz. 37 (sequel to *Re K. (deceased), supra*).

[36] s.3.

called "a constructive trust of a new model."[37] The broad principle
was that a constructive trust may be imposed, regardless of established legal rules, in order to reach the result required by equity,
justice and good conscience. The principle was thus articulated in
Hussey v. Palmer[38]: "It is a trust imposed by law wherever justice
and good conscience require it. It is a liberal process, founded on
large principles of equity. . . . It is an equitable remedy by which the
court can enable an aggrieved party to obtain restitution." Such a
principle, if it survives, would effect a complete swing on the
pendulum so far as the principles of English law concerning constructive trusts are concerned. The law in this field was once criticised as being too restricted[39]; in that the older cases would find a
constructive trust only where the facts brought the case within one
of the limited and established categories of constructive trust, usually requiring a fiduciary relationship. The new model opened up the
possibility of finding a constructive trust in any situation in which
the established rules lead to a result which would appear to be
inconsistent with equity, justice and good conscience.[40]

Not surprisingly, this doctrine has been applied in cases where
satisfactory solutions under established doctrines have proved particularly difficult to find. Illustrations come from the plight of the
deserted wife or cohabitant; the problem of the licensee of land
whose expectations have been disappointed; and the position of a
bona fide purchaser of registered land. The "new model," however,
has declined since the retirement of Lord Denning M.R.

i. Family Arrangements. In Chapter 11 we saw that, in the
context of claims to an interest in the family home, some decisions
are difficult to reconcile with the principles of *Pettitt v. Pettitt*[41] and
Gissing v. Gissing,[42] to the effect that the interests of the parties
must be determined according to the principles of property law. In
Eves v. Eves,[43] involving an unmarried couple, the man bought a
house as a joint home. He had it conveyed into his sole name, giving
as an excuse the fact that the woman was under 21 years old. She did
a great deal of heavy work in the house and garden, beyond ordinary
housework. When they separated, she claimed a share of the house.
"In strict law she has no claim upon him whatever. She is not his
wife. He is not bound to provide a roof over her head. He can turn

---

[37] *Eves v. Eves* [1975] 1 W.L.R. 1338.
[38] [1972] 1 W.L.R. 1286 at p. 1289. See also Cardozo J. in *Beatty v. Guggenheim Exploration
Co.* (1919) 255 N.Y. 360 at p. 385: "A constructive trust is the formula through which the
conscience of equity finds expression." (1973) 26 C.L.P. 17 at p. 35 (A. Oakley).
[39] Waters, *The Constructive Trust.*
[40] (1977) 28 N.I.L.Q. 123 (R. Maudsley).
[41] [1970] A.C. 777.
[42] [1971] A.C. 886.
[43] [1975] 1 W.L.R. 1338 *ante*, p. 262; *Cooke v. Head* [1972] 1 W.L.R. 518.

her into the street. ... And a few years ago even equity would not have helped her. But things are altered now. ... " It would be "most inequitable for him to deny her any share in the house. The law will impute or impose a constructive trust by which he was to hold it in trust for both of them."[44] Her share was one quarter. A similar principle was applied in *Heseltine v. Heseltine*[45] where a wife gave her husband £40,000 for the purpose of saving estate duty if she predeceased him; and £20,000 for the purpose of enabling him to become a member of Lloyd's. The Court of Appeal decided that the husband held the sums on constructive trust for his wife. The conclusion seems at variance with the principles of resulting trusts.[46] The presumption of a resulting trust should have been rebutted because the stated purposes could only be achieved if the husband became beneficial owner. A constructive trust appears to have been imposed in order to reach what the court regarded as a just solution.

More recent decisions, however, seem to have turned away from this use of the constructive trust. As we have seen, the House of Lords in *Lloyds Bank plc v. Rosset*[47] has restated the principles governing the acquisition of an interest in the home. Insofar as the "common intention" is, in these cases, a somewhat artificial concept, the court retains a measure of discretion. Although a "broad brush" approach has been adopted,[48] the court does not have any discretion to impose a constructive trust simply to achieve a "fair" result. So in *Burns v. Burns*[49] a woman who looked after the home for many years but who made little financial contribution failed in her claim to a share. Where the woman has made no contribution but the parties assert a common intention to share, it was held in *Midland Bank Ltd v. Dobson*[50] that an undocumented common intention cannot give rise to a constructive trust unless the woman has acted to her detriment in reliance upon it. Without such an act, section 53(1)(*b*) of the Law of Property Act 1925 is not displaced by section 53(2).[51] In *Layton v. Martin*[52] a man invited his mistress to live with him, promising to provide for her by will. When he did not,

---

[44] *Ibid.* at p. 1341.
[45] [1971] 1 W.L.R. 342; *Re Densham* [1975] 1 W.L.R. 1519 (constructive trust imposed to meet the parties' undocumented intention to hold jointly). See also (1973) 26 C.L.P. at p. 27. (A. Oakley).
[46] *Ante* p. 253.
[47] [1991] 1 A.C. 107; *ante*, p. 263.
[48] *Drake v. Whipp* [1996] 1 F.L.R. 826; *ante*, p. 265.
[49] [1984] Ch. 317; *ante*, p. 266. A strict view was also taken by the House of Lords in *Winkworth v. Edward Baron Development Co. Ltd* [1986] 1 W.L.R. 1512.
[50] [1986] 1 F.L.R. 171. The wife was attempting to defeat the husband's creditors. *cf. Re Densham, supra.*
[51] *Ante*, p. 76.
[52] [1986] 2 F.L.R. 277. Alternative claims based on contract and proprietary estoppel also failed. See further *Coombes v. Smith* [1986] 1 W.L.R. 808; *post*, p. 875.

she claimed a constructive trust to give effect to his intention. Her
claim failed because she had not contributed to the acquisition or
preservation of any of his assets. In *Re Basham*,[53] on the other hand,
the constructive trust was utilised as a means of filling what were
perceived to be gaps in the proprietary estoppel doctrine. The
plaintiff had acted to her detriment in reliance on her stepfather's
assurances that she would inherit from him. There was little authority on the application of that doctrine where the belief related to a
future right and to non-specific assets.[54] These problems were overcome by holding that if the belief related to a future right, a species
of constructive trust arose. Hence reliance could be placed on other
branches of constructive trusts such as mutual wills, where the
doctrine was not confined to present rights in specific assets.[55]

ii. Licences. The new model constructive trust was once most
active in the context of licences. The matter will be treated in more
detail in Chapter 28. Here let it merely be said that a licensee is a
person who is physically present on land whether in occupation or
not, but without any proprietary interest in the land. In the simplest
case, such as that of a guest invited to dinner, the licensor may
revoke the licence and require the guest to leave, allowing him a
reasonable time to collect his belongings. But more complex cases
arise: as where the licensee has given consideration for the licence;
or where the licensee has been encouraged to act to his detriment in
reliance on promises by the licensor, in such a way as to raise an
estoppel against the licensor. Under the doctrine of proprietary
estoppel,[56] the licensee can obtain a proprietary interest in the land.
In the absence of such proprietary interest, a number of problems
arise concerning the protection of the licensee. He is protected
against the licensor; but how is he protected against third parties?
The constructive trust has been called in aid as a means of enforcing
a contractual licence against a third party, thus circumventing the
rule that contractual rights are not binding on third parties even if
they had notice. Lord Denning M.R. pioneered this use of the
constructive trust in *Binions v. Evans*,[57] where an employer agreed
to allow an employee's widow to reside in a cottage rent free for
life. The cottage was sold at a reduced price, expressly subject to her
interest. Lord Denning M.R. regarded her interest as a licence,
binding on the purchaser under a constructive trust. This principle

---

[53] [1986] 1 W.L.R. 1498; [1987] Conv. 211 (J. Martin); (1987) 46 C.L.J. 215 (D. Hayton); All
E.R.Rev. 1987, p. 156 (P. Clarke) and p. 263 (C. Sherrin); (1988) 8 L.S. 92 at pp. 101 *et
seq.* (M. Davey); *post*, p. 892.

[54] *cf. Layton v. Martin, supra.*

[55] See *Re Cleaver* [1981] 1 W.L.R. 939; *ante*, p. 310.

[56] *Post*, p. 885.

[57] [1972] Ch. 359; (1972) 88 L.Q.R. 326 (P.V.B.); (1972) 37 Conv.(N.S.) 266 (J. Martin);
(1977) 36 C.L.J. 123 (R. Smith). The majority view was that she had a life interest.

was next applied in *D.H.N. Foods Ltd v. Tower Hamlets London Borough Council*,[58] where the constructive trust theory enabled a contractual licensee to be treated as having a sufficient interest to qualify for compensation on compulsory purchase of the land. In *Re Sharpe (a Bankrupt)*[59] the aunt of the bankrupt had lent substantial sums of money to the bankrupt to purchase a shop and maisonette. She had been told that she could remain on the premises as long as she wished. She was held to have an interest by way of constructive trust against the trustee in bankruptcy. The trustee had contracted to sell the premises to a bona fide purchaser. The purchaser was not a party to the proceedings, and no decision was made on the question of her right, if any, against him.

Thus a principle was evolving that a constructive trust could be imposed on a purchaser with notice of a contractual licence, in order to achieve what was perceived as the just result. The Court of Appeal has since clarified and restricted the use of the constructive trust in this context, while leaving it with some scope for operation. In *Ashburn Anstalt v. Arnold*[60] the question arose whether an occupier's rights were binding on a purchaser. In fact the occupier was held to have a tenancy, but the Court of Appeal nevertheless considered *obiter* what the position would have been in the case of a licence. The basic principle that a contractual licence is only a personal right was confirmed, but the constructive trust solution was justified if the facts were appropriate to support it. A purchaser of the land would not automatically be bound by a constructive trust. The test was whether he had so conducted himself that it would be inequitable to allow him to deny the licensee's rights. The mere fact that the purchaser had notice or that property was conveyed "subject to" the licence was not enough.[61] Such a term may be included merely to protect the vendor against claims by the purchaser should it turn out that he is bound by third party rights. The constructive trust solution was appropriate in *Binions v. Evans*[62] because the purchaser paid a low price and was intended to give effect to the widow's rights. In *Re Sharpe (a Bankrupt)*,[63] on the other hand, the constructive trust was not appropriate, because the aunt did not reply to the trustee's enquiries as to her interest. In the instant case the imposition of a constructive trust would not have been justified.

[58] [1976] 1 W.L.R. 852; (1977) 36 C.L.J. 12 (D. Hayton).

[59] [1980] 1 W.L.R. 219; [1980] Conv. 207 (J. Martin).

[60] [1989] Ch. 1; (1988) 104 L.Q.R. 175 (P. Sparkes); (1988) 47 C.L.J. 353 (A. Oakley); (1988) 51 M.L.R. 226 (J. Hill); All E.R.Rev. 1988, p. 177 (P. Clarke); [1988] Conv. 201 (M. Thompson); *post*, p. 880.

[61] *Kewal Investments Ltd v. Arthur Maiden Ltd* [1990] 1 E.G.L.R. 193; *IDC Group Ltd v. Clark* [1992] 1 E.G.L.R. 187 at p. 190 (the point did not arise on appeal at (1993) 65 P. & C.R. 179).

[62] *Supra*. Also in *Lyus v. Prowsa Developments Ltd* [1982] 1 W.L.R. 1044; *post*, p. 322.

[63] *Supra*.

Although the vendor had disclosed the occupier's rights, this was done to protect the vendor, rather than with the intention that the purchaser should give effect to them, and the price was not reduced. The Court of Appeal emphasised that in matters relating to title to land, certainty was of prime importance, and that constructive trusts should not be imposed in reliance on slender materials. Thus the constructive trust survives as a means of achieving justice in appropriate cases, but the wide principle that a contractual licence automatically give rise to a constructive trust binding on a purchaser with notice has gone.[64]

iii. Registered Land. A constructive trust was also found in *Peffer v. Rigg*,[65] where a purchaser with notice of an interest under a trust for sale was held to take subject to it, applying general equitable principles, notwithstanding that the title to the property was registered and the interest was not protected on the register, as required by the Land Registration Act 1925. It has since been affirmed by the House of Lords in *Williams & Glyn's Bank Ltd v. Boland*[66] that the concept of notice has no relevance to dealings with registered land: "The only kind of notice recognised is by entry on the register."[67] The land registration system has provided a code in which, it is submitted, the constructive trust doctrine has no part to play.[68]

Fraudulent or sham transactions would raise different considerations. There is a well known principle that a statute must not be used as an instrument of fraud. This principle was invoked in *Lyus v. Prowsa Developments Ltd*,[69] where land was brought expressly subject to the plaintiff's contractual rights, but the defendants sought to defeat them by relying on the Land Registration Act 1925.[70] A constructive trust was imposed on the defendants on the ground that the statute was not to be used as an instrument of fraud. It has been said, on the highest authority, that it is not fraud to rely on legal rights conferred by an Act of Parliament.[71] Here, however, the defendants had gone further, by reneging on a positive stipulation in favour of the plaintiffs. Where the agreement expressly creates a right which a third party is to have against the purchaser, a constructive trust arises if the purchaser seeks to defeat that right. The

---

[64] See further Gardner, *An Introduction to the Law of Trusts*, pp. 242–246.
[65] [1977] 1 W.L.R. 285; (1977) 93 L.Q.R. 341 (R. Smith); [1978] Conv. 52 (J. Martin); (1977) 36 C.L.J. 227 (D. Hayton); (1977) 40 M.L.R. 602 (S. Anderson).
[66] [1981] A.C. 487. *Peffer v. Rigg* was not cited on this point.
[67] *Ibid.* at p. 504 (*per* Lord Wilberforce).
[68] See especially s.59(6) and s.74 of Land Registration Act 1925.
[69] [1982] 1 W.L.R. 1044.
[70] ss.29, 34(4).
[71] *Midland Bank Trust Co. Ltd v. Green* [1981] A.C. 513 at p. 531.

result would have been the same in unregistered land.[72] The application to these facts of the maxim that a statute cannot be used as an
instrument of fraud has been much criticised.[73] The Court of
Appeal, however, has approved the decision, emphasising that the
parties intended the purchaser to give effect to the contract and that
an assurance to that effect had been given.[74]

iv. Conclusion. The courts, in some of these cases, were "invoking the constructive trust as an equitable remedy to do justice inter
partes."[75] While a liberalisation of the application of equitable
remedies is generally to be welcomed, it is important to appreciate
that the "new model" constructive trust left a number of problems
in its wake. The concept of justice alone is too vague to be used as
the basis for determining property rights, and, inevitably, the imposition of the constructive trust on this basis is impossible to forecast.
Further, a trust creates equitable proprietary rights, and these can
operate more widely than the dispute between the parties. The
question of the rights of third parties arises: whether, in particular, a
bona fide purchaser or mortgagee is bound by a licensee's right of
occupation, or by a woman's claim to share in the home. It may be
possible to find a just solution between the parties on the basis of a
personal decree not affecting the interests or rights of third parties.[76]

It is important also to appreciate that the "new model" constructive trust went far beyond the principle of the remedial constructive trust to prevent unjust enrichment,[77] although some
examples of the remedial constructive trust differ little from Lord
Denning's formulation.[78] The provision of a remedy for unjust
enrichment does not require an unlimited free-wheeling discretion
as to the imposition of a constructive trust. There must at least be
general guide-lines for the exercise of the discretion. The law of
unjust enrichment lays down with reasonable clarity when an action
will lie. Some of the English cases seemed to treat a constructive
trust as a magic formula to reach a just result between the parties,
regardless of existing proprietary rights in them, or of the interests

---

[72] Applying *Bannister v. Bannister* [1948] 2 All E.R. 133, and the judgment of Lord Denning
M.R. in *Binions v. Evans* [1972] Ch. 359.
[73] All E.R.Rev. 1982, p. 165 (P. Clarke); (1983) 46 M.L.R. 96 (P. Kenny); [1983] Conv. 64
(P. Jackson); (1983) 42 C.L.J. 54 (C. Harpum); (1985) 44 C.L.J. 280 (M. Thompson); *cf.*
(1984) 47 M.L.R. 476 (P. Bennett).
[74] *Ashburn Anstalt v. Arnold* [1989] Ch. 1, *ante*, p. 321.
[75] (1973) 26 C.L.P. 17 at p. 35 (A. Oakley). The trend is examined in Oakley, *Constructive
Trusts* (3rd ed.), pp. 59–60.
[76] See *Muschinski v. Dodds* (1985) C.L.R. 583 (constructive trust took effect only from date
of court order); *ante*, p. 291.
[77] *Ante*, p. 289.
[78] See (1994) 8 *Trust Law International* 74 at p. 79 (M. Bryan), discussing Australian
decisions.

of persons who were not parties to the dispute. Present indications, however, are that the "new model" constructive trust will not develop further. The most recent decisions, as we have seen, favour a return to more orthodox principles of property law. Similarly in the Commonwealth, where, although the remedial constructive trust is accepted, it has been said that "the legitimacy of the new model is at least suspect; at best it is a mutant from which further breeding should be discouraged."[79]

---

[79] *Allen v. Snyder* [1977] 2 N.S.W.L.R. 685 at p. 701. The "new model" was also rejected in *Carly v. Farrelly* [1975] 1 N.Z.L.R. 356; (1978) 94 L.Q.R. 347 (G. Samuels); *Avondale Printers & Stationers Ltd v. Haggie* [1979] 2 N.Z.L.R. 124; *Muschinski v. Dodds* (1985) 160 C.L.R. 583. The "new model" was accepted in a modified form in *Pettkus v. Becker* (1980) 17 D.L.R. (3d) 257; (1982) 12 Fam. Law 21 (M. Bryan). See further (1978) 94 L.Q.R. 351 (W. Gummow); (1975) 53 C.B.R. 366 (D. Waters); [1982] Conv. 424 (F. Bates); [1983] Conv. 420 (K. Hodkinson) (reviewing the position also in N. Ireland). The unjust enrichment approach was favoured in *Baumgartner v. Baumgartner* (1988) 62 A.L.J. 29; [1988] Conv. 259 (D. Hayton).

CHAPTER 13

TRUSTS WHICH CONTRAVENE THE LAW

1. Trusts Contrary to the General Policy of
   the Law 325
   A. Purposes Contrary to Law, Public Poli-
      cy or Morality 325
   B. Statutory Provisions Against
      Discrimination 326
      i. Race Relations Act 1976 326
      ii. Sex Discrimination Act 1975 327
   C. Conditions Precedent and Subsequent;
      Determinable Interests 328
      i. Marriage, Separation and
         Divorce 329
      ii. Parental Duties 330
      iii. Religion 331
      iv. Race 332
      v. Alienation 332
      vi. Other Cases 332
   D. The Consequence of Illegality 333
      i. Fraudulent Settlements 333
      ii. Conditional and Determinable
         Interests 333
2. Perpetuity, Duration and Inalienability 334
   A. General 334
   B. Tying up Land 334
   C. Remote Vesting. Life in Being Plus 21
      years 335
   D. Wait and See 335
   E. Duration and Inalienability 337
3. Attempts to Keep Property from
   Creditors 337
   A. General 337
   B. Insolvency Act 1986 338
      i. Transactions Defrauding
         Creditors 338
         (a) Transactions at an under
            value 339
         (b) Intention 340
         (c) Persons who may apply to
            court 341
         (d) Orders to be made 341
         (e) Third parties 341
      ii. Bankruptcy Provisions 342
         (a) Transaction at an under
            value 342
         (b) Preference of creditors 342
         (c) Time limits 343
         (d) Orders to be made 343
         (e) Third parties 343
         (f) Corporate Insolvency 344
   C. Protection of the Spouse and Family . 345
      i. Matrimonial Causes Act 1973,
         s.37 345
      ii. Inheritance (Provision for Family
         and Dependants) Act 1975 345

A TRUST, though otherwise valid, may fail because it contains an element of unlawfulness or immorality, or is contrary to public policy. It is impossible to categorise all the possible grounds of unlawfulness, and only some of the more important ones can be mentioned here.

1. TRUSTS CONTRARY TO THE GENERAL POLICY OF THE LAW

A. Purposes Contrary to Law, Public Policy or Morality

It will be appreciated that such trusts are likely to fail in any event, apart from any question of unlawfulness, on the ground that they are non-charitable purpose trusts.[1] There are, perhaps for this reason, few examples of cases decided on the basis of illegality, but one such is *Thrupp v. Collett*,[2] where a testator attempted to provide for paying the fines of convicted poachers. Sir John Romilly M.R. held the trust void on the ground that it was against public policy. It was held in *Bowman v. Secular Society*[3] that the denial of Christianity was not *per se* an illegal purpose, but it was suggested in *Thornton v. Howe*[4] that a trust whose purpose was adverse to all religion or subversive of morality would be void. It need hardly be added that trusts for the furtherance of illegal or immoral activities, such as, for example, terrorism or prostitution,[5] would fail. Likewise a trust for a fraudulent purpose, such as placing money with a company in order to give it the false appearance of a credit balance.[6]

It was at one time established that gifts by deed or will for future illegitimate children were void as being *contra bonos mores*, on the ground that they would tend to encourage immorality.[7] For dispositions made on or after January 1, 1970,[8] the position was changed by section 15(7) of the Family Law Reform Act 1969 (now replaced by the Family Law Reform Act 1987, section 19).[9]

B. Statutory Provisions Against Discrimination

i. Race Relations Act 1976. Discrimination, as defined by the 1976 Act, on the ground of colour, race, nationality, or ethnic or national origins is unlawful.[10] The 1976 Act applies to certain specified situations, including employment, the provision of goods and services, and the disposal of property. In these situations a person discriminates against another, for the purposes of the Act, if

---

[1] *Post*, Chap. 14. See, for example, *Brown v. Burdett* (1882) 21 Ch.D. 667, where a "useless" trust to seal up a house for 20 years failed.

[2] (1858) 26 Beav. 125.

[3] [1917] A.C. 406 (Lord Finlay L.C. dissenting).

[4] (1862) 31 Beav. 14.

[5] See Harman L.J.'s example of a "school for prostitutes or pickpockets" in *Re Pinion* [1965] Ch. 85.

[6] *Re Great Berlin Steamboat Co.* (1884) 26 Ch.D. 616.

[7] *Occleston v. Fullalove* (1874) L.R. 9 Ch.App. 147; *cf. Re Hyde* [1932] 1 Ch. 95. The claim of an illegitimate beneficiary might have failed in any event on the ground that gifts were generally construed as confined to legitimate relatives. This is no longer the position: Family Law Reform Act 1987, s.19 (replacing F.L.R.A. 1969, s.15).

[8] A disposition made by will is made on the date of the execution of the will; F.L.R.A. 1987, s.19(7).

[9] This Act replaces the concept of the illegitimate child with that of the unmarried parent.

[10] s.1.

on any of the above-mentioned grounds he treats that other less favourably than he treats or would treat other persons. It will be noted that religion as such is not covered by the Act.[11]

Subject to what is said below about charitable trusts, the Act does not extend to discrimination in the making of a gift or trust.[12] But trustees, just as any other individuals, are bound by the provisions relating to employment, disposal of property and so on. This is especially significant in the administration of charitable trusts.

Special provisions relating to charitable trusts are contained in section 34 of the 1976 Act. The general position is that the Act does not affect a provision in a charitable instrument which provides for conferring *benefits* on persons of a class defined by reference to race, nationality, or ethnic or national origins.[13] In other words, it is lawful to discriminate in favour of such groups, but not against them.[14] But it is not permissible to discriminate even in favour of a class defined by reference to colour.[15] Any such provision is to take effect as if it provided for conferring the benefits in question on persons of the class which results if the colour qualification is disregarded.

Finally, it should be noted that even where discrimination in a charitable trust is not made unlawful by the Act, the removal of discriminatory provisions is possible under the *cy-près* doctrine.[16]

ii. Sex Discrimination Act 1975. Sex discrimination is not a ground for invalidating any provision in a private trust. As far as charitable trusts are concerned, section 43 provides that the Act does not apply to any provision in a charitable instrument for conferring benefits on persons of one sex only. Thus there is nothing unlawful in single sex charities, such as the YMCA. Of course, the trustees are bound by the Act in matters such as the employment of staff.

---

[11] The position of the Jewish religion is unclear. See the Race Relations Board First Annual Report. A condition requiring Jewish parentage was considered racial in *Clayton v. Ramsden* [1943] A.C. 320. Jews were held to be an ethnic group in *King-Ansell v. Police* [1979] 2 N.Z.L.R. 531, approved by the House of Lords in *Mandla v. Dowell Lee* [1983] 2 A.C. 548, where Sikhs were held to be a racial group. For the position of Rastafarians, see *Dawkins v. Crown Suppliers (PSA) Ltd, The Times*, February 4, 1993.

[12] For the American position on racially discriminatory trusts, see (1972) A.A.L.R. 101 (L. Sheridan).

[13] s.34(2) and (3).

[14] Thus the provisions contained in *Re Dominion Students' Hall Trust* [1947] Ch. 183 would now be unlawful. (This was also the case under the Race Relations Act 1968). See also *Re Gwyon* [1930] 1 Ch. 255.

[15] s.34(1).

[16] *Post*, p. 430. See *Re Lysaght* [1966] Ch. 191; *Re Dominion Students' Hall Trust, supra; Canada Trust Company v. Ontario Human Rights Commission* (1990) 69 D.L.R. (4th) 321. The promotion of racial harmony is now considered a charitable purpose; Annual Report of the Charity Commissioners for 1983, para. 19.

Special provisions relating to educational charities enable restrictions based on sex to be removed or modified on application to the Secretary of State.[17]

C. Conditions Precedent and Subsequent; Determinable Interests

Questions involving illegality often arise in connection with the validity of conditions imposed upon otherwise valid gifts.[18] A condition precedent is one which must be satisfied before the gift can vest, whereas a condition subsequent operates to defeat an already vested gift by forfeiture. A determinable interest, on the other hand, is one which will automatically determine on the occurrence of the determining event, no question of forfeiture being involved.[19] It is not always easy, as a matter of construction, to decide whether a condition is intended to operate as a condition precedent or subsequent, or to distinguish conditional and determinable interests.[20] It seems that the latter are less susceptible to, although not immune from, attack on the ground of public policy.[21]

Apart from any question of illegality, conditions have frequently failed on the ground of uncertainty. A distinction has been drawn between conditions precedent and subsequent. A stricter test of certainty applies to a condition subsequent, which must be so framed that at the outset the beneficiary knows the exact event which will divest his interest.[22] Lord Denning M.R., has described this distinction as a "deplorable dichotomy," serving only to defeat the settlor's intention.[23] Even in the case of a condition subsequent, however, the court is reluctant to pronounce the condition void for uncertainty. So in *Re Tepper's Will Trusts*,[24] where a condition subsequent required the beneficiaries to remain within the Jewish faith and not to marry outside it, the court regarded as admissible

---

[17] s.78.

[18] Where several conditions are attached to one gift, the valid conditions may be severed from any which are invalid: *Re Hepplewhite Will Trusts, The Times*, January 21, 1977.

[19] *Ante*, p. 186. For a detailed account of the distinctions and their significance, see Cheshire and Burn's *Modern Law of Real Property* (15th ed.), pp. 339 *et seq.*

[20] See, for example, *Re Tuck's Settlement Trusts* [1978] Ch. 49; *Re Johnson's Will Trusts* [1967] Ch. 387; *Re Tepper's Will Trusts* [1987] Ch. 358.

[21] See *Re Johnson's Will Trusts, supra*, at p. 396; *Re Moore* (1888) 39 Ch.D. 116; Megarry and Wade, *The Law of Real Property* (5th ed.), pp. 71–72.

[22] *Re Tepper's Will Trusts, supra*. The test applying to conditions precedent is that laid down in *Re Allen* [1953] Ch. 810: conceptual uncertainty may not defeat such conditions. A modern example is *Re Barlow's Will Trusts* [1979] 1 W.L.R. 278, *ante*, p. 109. See generally Underhill (15th ed.), pp. 80–82; [1980] Conv. 263 (L. McKay).

[23] *Re Tuck's Settlement Trusts* [1978] Ch. 49 at p. 60. But the distinction was acknowledged by the House of Lords in *Blathwayt v. Lord Cawley* [1976] A.C. 397 at p. 425.

[24] *Supra.*

extrinsic evidence of the Jewish faith as practised by the testator, to elucidate the meaning of his words.[25]

Assuming that the condition does not fail for uncertainty, the next question is whether it will be void as being illegal or otherwise contrary to public policy. The categories discussed below involve the types of condition which have been most frequently encountered.

i. Marriage, Separation and Divorce. Where property is given by way of a determinable gift until marriage, and then to other beneficiaries, the limitation is unobjectionable.[26] Conditions, on the other hand, will be void if they are designed to prevent marriage or to encourage divorce or separation.

As far as conditions restraining marriage are concerned, a distinction is drawn between total and partial restraints. A condition subsequent, operating to divest the property on marriage, is void if its object is to restrain marriage altogether.[27] But conditions operating only in the event of a second or subsequent marriage, or merely requiring consent to marriage,[28] are not void.[29] Nor is there any objection to a condition in restraint of marriage with certain persons, or a certain class.[30] The rules relating to partial restraints on marriage differ according to whether the gift is of realty or personalty, the reason being that the personalty rules evolved in the ecclesiastical courts, whereas the realty rules were developed by the common law. The result of this historical distinction is as follows: in the case of personalty a condition imposing a partial restraint on marriage is invalid as being merely "*in terrorem*" if there is no express gift over on the occurrence of the marriage[31] whereas in the case of realty, a partial restraint is never invalid, whether or not there is a gift over.[32]

---

[25] Relying on *Re Tuck's Settlement Trusts, supra,* where, however, the will expressly provided that the Chief Rabbi could determine the meaning of "Jewish faith" and "approved wife." *cf.* A.J.A. 1982, s.21. See All E.R. Rev. 1987, p. 159 (P. Clarke) and p. 260 (C. Sherrin).

[26] *Re Lovell* [1920] 1 Ch. 122.

[27] *Lloyd v. Lloyd* (1852) 2 Sim.(N.S.) 255. This includes a condition which in practice amounts to a general restraint: *Re Lanyon* [1927] 2 Ch. 264. (Condition against marriage with any blood relation). It seems that similar rules would apply to a condition precedent. See *Re Wallace* [1920] Ch. 274.

[28] *Re Whiting's Settlement* [1905] 1 Ch. 96.

[29] *Allen v. Jackson* (1875) 1 Ch.D. 399.

[30] *Jenner v. Turner* (1880) 16 Ch.D. 188; *Perrin v. Lyon* (1807) 9 East. 170; condition against marrying a person born in Scotland or of Scottish parents upheld. See also the cases on religion, discussed below.

[31] *Leong v. Lim Beng Chye* [1955] A.C. 648 (A residuary gift is not a gift over).

[32] Another possible distinction is that in the case of realty, but not personalty, even a general restraint is valid if intended merely to provide for the beneficiary while unmarried, rather than to promote celibacy: *Jones v. Jones* (1876) 1 Q.B.D. 279.

Conditions designed to induce the separation or divorce of a husband and wife are void as being contrary to public policy.[33] But if the parties have already decided upon a separation, the trusts in any deed of separation are not invalid.[34] Nor is there any objection where the true object of a disposition is merely to make provision for a party during the separation.[35]

It will be seen that most of these cases were decided at a time when the sanctity of marriage was perhaps regarded more highly than it is today. A stricter view was taken of relationships outside marriage than is now the case. Thus in the past trusts or covenants to create trusts have been held void if created in consideration of a future immoral association.[36] The modern tendency might be to discover some other form of consideration from the beneficiary.[37]

A question which might arise is the effect of a condition designed to restrain the modern practice of "living in sin."[38] Such a condition might fail for uncertainty,[39] but, in any event, it might be said that while such a practice is not unlawful, "it is not yet a virtue."[40]

ii. Parental Duties. A condition calculated to bring about the separation of parent and child is void as being contrary to public policy,[41] even where the parents are divorced.[42] Similarly, a condition designed to interfere with the exercise of parental duties.[43] In *Blathwayt v. Lord Cawley*[44] a settlement provided for the forfeiture of the interest of any child who became a Roman Catholic. It was argued that the condition was void on the ground that it would hamper parental duties in religious instruction. The House of Lords rejected this argument: "To say that any condition which in any way

---

[33] *Re Johnson's Will Trusts* [1967] Ch. 387; *Re Caborne* [1943] Ch. 224. See also *Re McBride* (1980) 107 D.L.R. (3d) 233; *Re Hepplewhite Will Trusts, The Times,* January 21, 1977.

[34] *Wilson v. Wilson* (1848) 1 H.L.C. 538. It is otherwise if the provision is designed to discourage reconciliation. See also *Egerton v. Egerton* [1949] 2 All E.R. 238 at p. 242: "a settlement which contains provisions as to what should happen in the case of divorce is not contrary to public policy" (*per* Denning L.J.).

[35] *Re Lovell* [1920] 1 Ch. 122. As to the admissibility of any evidence of the settlor's motive, see *Re Johnson's Will Trusts* [1967] Ch. 387.

[36] See *Re Vallance* (1884) 26 Ch.D. 353; *Ayerst v. Jenkins* (1873) L.R. 16 Eq. 275.

[37] See, for example, *Tanner v. Tanner* [1975] 1 W.L.R. 1346 where a contract was inferred between a man and his mistress in consideration of her looking after the house and family; *cf. Coombes v. Smith* [1986] 1 W.L.R. 808.

[38] Another example might be a condition restraining a homosexual relationship.

[39] See *Re Jones* [1953] Ch. 125, where a condition prohibiting a "social or other relationship" with X failed for uncertainty.

[40] Borrowing Lord Denning's description, in a different context (tax avoidance), in *Re Weston's Settlements* [1969] 1 Ch. 223.

[41] *Re Boulter* [1922] 1 Ch. 75.

[42] *Re Piper* [1946] 2 All E.R. 503.

[43] *Re Borwick* [1933] Ch. 657; *Re Sandbrook* [1912] 2 Ch. 471. These two decisions must now be read in the light of the comments made in *Blathwayt v. Lord Cawley* [1976] A.C. 397, discussed below.

[44] [1976] A.C. 397.

might affect or influence the way in which a child is brought up, or in which parental duties are exercised, seems to me to state far too wide a rule."[45]

iii. Religion. It has already been noted that discrimination on religious grounds falls outside the Race Relations Act 1976. Conditions restricting freedom of religion have long been popular with settlors and testators. While such conditions have sometimes failed for uncertainty, especially in the case of conditions subsequent,[46] it has never been held that such provisions are contrary to public policy, even in the case of charitable trusts.[47] In *Blathwayt v. Lord Cawley*,[48] of which the facts have already been given, Lord Cross said that while it may be wrong for the government to discriminate on religion, it does not follow that it is against public policy for an adherent of one religion to distinguish in disposing of his property; any other view amounts to saying that "it is disreputable for him to be convinced of the importance of holding true religious beliefs and of the fact that his religious beliefs are the true ones."[49] It had been argued that the Race Relations Acts and the European Convention of Human Rights showed that the law was now against discrimination. Lord Wilberforce said "I do not doubt that conceptions of public policy should move with the times and that widely accepted treaties and statutes may point the direction in which such conceptions, as applied by the courts, ought to move. It may well be that conditions such as this are, or at least are becoming, inconsistent with standards now widely accepted."[50] But this did not justify the introduction of a new rule, for to do so would reduce another freedom, that of testamentary disposition. "Discrimination is not the same thing as choice: it operates over a larger and less personal area, and neither by express provision nor by implication has private selection yet become a matter of public policy."[51]

---

[45] *Ibid.* at p. 426 (*per* Lord Wilberforce).

[46] *Clayton v. Ramsden* [1943] A.C. 320 (forfeiture on marriage to person not of Jewish parentage and faith); *Re Abraham's Will Trusts* [1969] 1 Ch. 463; *Re Tepper's Will Trusts* [1987] Ch. 358. A condition precedent is less likely to fail on this ground: see *Re Allen* [1953] Ch. 810; *Re Selby's Will Trusts* [1966] 1 W.L.R. 43; *Re Tuck's Settlement Trusts* [1978] Ch. 49 (marriage to "approved wife" of Jewish blood and faith not uncertain). See also *Re Evans* [1940] Ch. 629.

[47] See *Re Lysaght* [1966] Ch. 191. (Discrimination against Jews and Roman Catholics was merely "undesirable"); *cf. Canada Trust Company v. Ontario Human Rights Commission* (1990) 69 D.L.R. (4th) 321.

[48] [1976] A.C. 397. See also *Re Remnant's Settlement Trusts* [1970] 1 Ch. 560; *Clayton v. Ramsden, supra*. For a discussion of racial and religious discrimination in restrictive covenants, see [1978] Conv. 24 (J. Brooke-Taylor). The heir to the throne may not be, or marry, a Roman Catholic: Act of Settlement 1701.

[49] [1976] A.C. 397 at p. 429.

[50] *Ibid.* at p. 426.

[51] *Ibid.*

iv. Race. We have already seen that discrimination on the grounds of race or colour is made unlawful by the Race Relations Act 1976, and that, apart from special provisions relating to charities, the Act has no application to private trusts. It seems that it is not contrary to public policy for a settlor to discriminate on these grounds, although the point is not unarguable.[52] There is little authority on the point, which has arisen mainly in connection with charitable trusts.[53] Many of the comments made by the House of Lords in *Blathwayt v. Lord Cawley*[54] in the context of religion would apply equally to racial discrimination, save that the dictum of Lord Cross[55] loses all conviction if race is substituted for religious beliefs.

v. Alienation. Conditions operating as a complete restraint on the alienation of property are void as being contrary to public policy.

In *Re Brown*,[56] a testator devised realty among his four sons subject to a condition which would have produced forfeiture of his interest by any son who mortgaged or sold his interest other than among his brothers. The condition was held to be equivalent to a general restraint on alienation, and therefore void, since the class of permitted alienees was small and bound to get smaller.

A partial restraint on alienation is valid.[57] Restrictions upon alienation to groups identified by religion may be unobjectionable, but the Race Relations Act 1976 forbids racial discrimination in the disposal of property.[58]

Restraints even of a general nature may be valid if they take the form of a determinable interest.[59] Section 33 of the Trustee Act 1925 itself provides such an example.[60]

vi. Other Cases. Much difficulty has been encountered in the past with "name and arms" clauses, whereby settlors seek to ensure that the beneficiary adopts a specified name and coat of arms,

---

[52] See Underhill, *loc. cit.* at p. 196.

[53] See *Re Gwyon* [1930] 1 Ch. 255; *Re Dominion Students' Hall Trust* [1947] Ch. 183. In neither case was public policy discussed.

[54] [1976] A.C. 397.

[55] *Ibid.* at p. 429; *supra.*

[56] [1954] Ch. 39; *cf. Caldy Manor Estate Ltd v. Farrell* [1974] 1 W.L.R. 1303 (covenant against alienation not unlawful).

[57] See *Re MacLeay* (1875) L.R. 20 Eq. 186. (Doubted in *Re Rosher* [1884] 25 Ch. 801). It is suggested in Cheshire and Burn's *Modern Law of Real Property* (15th ed.), at p. 344, that even partial restraints should be invalid as repugnant to ownership.

[58] s.21.

[59] *Re Dugdale* (1883) 38 Ch.D. 176 at pp. 178–181, *per* Kay J.; *Re Leach* [1912] 2 Ch. 422.

[60] *Ante*, p. 188 (the protective trust).

usually those of the settlor. Such clauses were at one time held to be contrary to public policy, on the ground that, if the beneficiary was a married woman, the taking of another name might lead to dissension between husband and wife. It is now settled that such clauses are neither uncertain nor contrary to public policy.[61]

It was held in *Egerton v. Brownlow*[62] that a condition requiring the beneficiary to obtain a dukedom was contrary to public policy as tending to encourage corruption, but a similar provision involving a baronetcy was upheld in *Re Wallace*,[63] the distinction being that, unlike a dukedom, no legislative powers and duties would be involved, consequently the public interest could not be affected. Conditions forbidding entry into the naval or military services have also been held void.[64] The validity of conditions relating to bankruptcy has already been discussed.[65]

Finally, a condition whereby a beneficiary was to become entitled to property on becoming destitute has been held void as contrary to public policy in that it could encourage irresponsibility with money.[66]

D. The Consequence of Illegality

The general position is that if an express trust fails on the ground of unlawfulness, a resulting trust to the settlor or his estate ensues.[67] This is so even if the trust was designed to encourage an offence prohibited by statute.[68] Where the trust is only partly unlawful, the whole fails if the proportion to be devoted to the unlawful purpose is unascertainable,[69] whereas if that proportion is ascertainable, only that part fails.[70]

i. Fraudulent Settlements. Where the purpose of the trust is not merely unlawful, but also fraudulent, the question arises whether the court will assist the settlor to recover the property. This was discussed in Chapter 10.[71]

ii. Conditional and Determinable Interests. Where a condition subsequent is unlawful, the gift takes effect as an absolute interest:

---

[61] *Re Neeld* [1962] Ch. 643.
[62] (1853) 4 H.L. 1.
[63] [1920] 2 Ch. 274.
[64] See *Re Beard* [1908] 1 Ch. 383.
[65] *Ante,* p. 186.
[66] *Re Hepplewhite Will Trusts, The Times,* January 21, 1977.
[67] *Ante,* p. 231. *cf. Ayerst v. Jenkins* (1873) L.R. 16 Eq. 275.
[68] *Thrupp v. Collett* (1858) 26 Beav. 125.
[69] *Chapman v. Brown* (1801) 6 Ves. 404.
[70] *Mitford v. Reynolds* (1842) 1 Ph. 185. There is some authority that in such a case the whole can go to the lawful part: *Fisk v. Att.-Gen.* (1867) L.R. 4 Eq. 521.
[71] *Ante,* p. 249.

the condition alone is void.[72] In the case of a condition precedent, a distinction is drawn between realty and personality. As far as realty is concerned, the gift itself fails if the condition is bad.[73] Where the gift is of personalty, however, it takes effect free of the condition where the illegality is only a *malum prohibitum*.[74] But where the illegality is a *malum in se*, the gift fails. In the case of a determinable interest, the gift fails if the determining event is unlawful.[75]

2. PERPETUITY, DURATION AND INALIENABILITY

A. General

One of the most common causes over the years of invalidity of interests under a trust has been the failure to comply with the Rule Against Perpetuities. The hazard has been much reduced, and the law simplified by the Perpetuities and Accumulations Act 1964, which applies to dispositions coming into effect after July 15, 1964. Questions may still arise in respect of earlier instruments, as a decision on a will, for example, may be delayed until the death of a life tenant.[76] But the Act has been in operation for over 30 years, and each year which passes will reduce the likelihood of a question arising which is not governed by the Act. There is not space to deal with the subject in detail here. It is covered by books on real property,[77] a practice which can have a historical justification only; the rule grew up in connection with settlements of land, but now applies mainly to trusts of personalty. The subject is one which has caused much confusion, not least in connection with the Act; and a few general comments may be helpful.

B. Tying Up Land

The perpetuity rule is based on a policy against the tying up of lands for an undue length of time. The struggle began in the earliest years of common law. Conditions against alienation were held void. Entails were by statute inalienable, but by 1472 it was recognised

---

[72] *Re Beard* [1908] 1 Ch. 383. This is so whether the gift is realty or personalty.

[73] *Re Elliott* [1952] Ch. 217.

[74] *i.e.* something made unlawful only by statute. See *Re Piper* [1946] 2 All E.R. 503. The distinction was apparently not discussed in *Re Hepplewhite Will Trusts, The Times*, January 21, 1977.

[75] *Re Moore* (1888) 39 Ch.D. 116. For the application of the perpetuity rule to conditional and determinable interests, see Perpetuities and Accumulations Act 1964, s.12: the interest becomes absolute if the determining event or breach of condition does not occur within the perpetuity period.

[76] See *Re Drummond* [1988] 1 W.L.R. 234, concerning a 1924 settlement.

[77] Cheshire and Burn, pp. 275 *et seq.*, M. & W., pp. 231 *et seq.*; Morris and Leach, *The Rule against Perpetuities*; Maudsley, *The Modern Law of Perpetuities*.

that an entail could be barred, turned into a fee simple and alienated.[78] The Old Rule Against Perpetuities prevented a series of
contingent life estates. Alienability was successfully being maintained. But once it was decided that executory interests were valid
and indestructible,[79] it was possible to create interests limited to vest
at an indefinite time in the future. The Rule Against Perpetuities was
designed to restrict the extent to which future vesting could be
postponed.

C. Remote Vesting. Life in Being Plus 21 Years

The permitted period was a life in being plus 21 years; permitting
in effect, a grant to the first son of A to attain the age of 21 years.
For A's son must attain the age of 21 years, if he ever does, within
21 years of A's death.[80] A period of gestation was also allowed in
the case of posthumous children.

One could not wait and see whether the gift vested in time or not.
The common law rule was that the interest was void if it *might* vest
outside the period; even if in fact it vested the next day. The Rule
is:

> "No interest is good unless it must vest, if at all, not later than
> twenty-one years after some life in being at the creation of the
> interest."[81]

Thus, a gift to the first son of A to attain the age of 22 years was
void at common law if A was still alive; even if A had a son of $21\frac{1}{2}$
at the time. For that son might die, another son be born, and A die;
and A's first son to attain the age of 22 might do so more than 21
years after the death of any persons alive at the date of the gift. A
long series of bizarre situations showing the ruthless operation of the
rule has often been catalogued, and need not be repeated. The one
simple example makes the point.

D. Wait and See

The Act deals with this situation in three ways; first, by permitting
a settlor to specify as the perpetuity period for the purpose of the
disposition a period of years not exceeding 80[82]; secondly, by a
number of specific reforms on individual points which had caused

---

[78] *Taltarum's Case* Y.B. 12 Edw. 4, 19.
[79] *Pells v. Brown* (1620) Cro. Jac. 590.
[80] Scientific advances in reproduction have made this statement untrue, but will not be
considered here.
[81] Gray, *The Rule Against Perpetuities* (4th ed.), § 201.
[82] s.1.

difficulty, and thirdly, by introducing a system of wait and see.[83] If the law was unrealistic because it made void an interest which vested in fact within the period merely because it might have vested outside it, an obvious solution would be to make its validity depend on whether or not it does in fact vest within it. That is the theory of wait and see.

There is much disagreement as to the identity of the lives in being at common law.[84] The 1964 Act, however, lays down, in section 3, its own list of statutory lives in being, which must be used where the wait and see rule is invoked. Although certain common law lives in being, such as "royal lives," are not included, the statutory class is generally wider than the class of common law lives in being.

One would have thought it obvious that, on enacting wait and see, the common law rule should be abolished. It no longer has any part to play. If a disposition must vest, if at all, within the period, then it will vest, if at all, within the period. Thus, the common law test is contained within the wait and see test. There is no advantage in knowing that an interest complies with the common law test. The interest remains contingent, and its value is dependent, not on compliance with the common law rule, but upon its likelihood of vesting. Assume that A has a son X aged 21. A gift to A's first son to attain the age of 22 is void under the common law rule, but likely to vest within the period; and would be of greater value than a gift to the first son of A to go to the moon in A's lifetime, which would be valid at common law. Compliance with the common law rule is irrelevant in a system of wait and see.[85]

Nevertheless, the Act retained the common law rule. Wait and see only applies to "void" limitations.[86] So it is necessary to apply the common law rule to test validity, and to apply wait and see, if it fails to comply with the common law rule. It is tempting to ignore the common law rule. Every limitation which was valid at common law would also be valid under wait and see: unless, however, there could be some situation in which a gift was validated by a common law life who is not in the statutory list, and the interest does not in fact vest within 21 years of the death of the survivor of the statutory lives. Because the class of statutory lives does not coincide exactly with the common law lives, that is theoretically possible.[87] But it is

---

[83] s.3.

[84] (1964) 80 L.Q.R. 486 at pp. 495–508 (J. Morris and H. Wade); (1965) 81 L.Q.R. 106 at p. 108 (D. Allan); (1970) 86 L.Q.R. 357 (R. Maudsley), (1975) 60 Cornell L.R. 355 (R. Maudsley); Maudsley, *The Modern Law of Perpetuities*; (1981) 97 L.Q.R. 593 (R. Deech); (1986) 102 L.Q.R. 251 (J. Dukeminier).

[85] (1970) 86 L.Q.R. 357 at p. 372 (R. Maudsley); (1975) 60 Cornell L.R. 355 (R. Maudsley); Maudsley, *The Modern Law of Perpetuities*.

[86] s.3.

[87] As in the case of dispositions governed by a royal lives clause.

absurd to retain all the common law learning in order to save such a rare gift. The common law rule should have been abolished.[88]

If it had been, the application of the wait and see rule would have been simple. In the case of any gift, all that would be necessary would be the writing down of the measuring lives, the recording of their deaths, and the addition of 21 years.[89] The interests which had then vested would be valid; those which had not vested would be void. The Law Commission is considering reform of the rule against remote vesting.[90]

E. Duration and Inalienability

Separate from the perpetuity rule governing remoteness of vesting, but a further manifestation of the same policy, is the rule which declares void trusts which might continue for too long a period; longer, that is, than the perpetuity period.

The matter will be discussed in connection with non-charitable purpose trusts.[91] In so far as they are permitted, they must be limited to the perpetuity period. The restriction upon duration does not apply to charitable trusts, nor to most pension trusts.[92]

It should be added that this rule is not in any way inconsistent with the ownership of property in fee simple by a person or a corporation. Those owners may alienate at any time. They may of course keep the property for ever; but the property is not tied up in any way. Thus in *Bowman v. Secular Society*,[93] a gift to the "Secular Society" a society devoted to furthering anti-Christian beliefs, having survived an attack on the grounds of public policy, had nothing to fear on the score of perpetuity, as the Society was a limited company, and able to deal freely with its property.

3. ATTEMPTS TO KEEP PROPERTY FROM CREDITORS

A. General

A creditor can demand payment from his debtor out of the debtor's property. If the debtor's property is insufficient to pay his debts, he is insolvent, and it will not be possible to pay all the

---

[88] (1975) 60 Cornell L.R. 355 at p. 370 (R. Maudsley).

[89] Even simpler is the approach of the American Uniform Statutory Rule Against Perpetuities, discussed in (1987) 46 C.L.J. 234 (L. Waggoner), whereby the wait and see period is 90 years, without any lives in being. The rule has been abolished in some jurisdictions.

[90] Law Com. C.P. No. 133 (1993); *The Rules against Perpetuities and Excessive Accumulations.* Excessive duration is not dealt with.

[91] *Post*, p. 365; *cf. Re Dean* (1889) 41 Ch.D. 552. For difficulties arising with unincorporated associations, see *Re Grant's Will Trusts* [1980] 1 W.L.R. 360, *post*, p. 362.

[92] *Post*, pp. 380, 473.

[93] [1917] A.C. 406.

creditors in full. Generally speaking, before bankruptcy the debtor may choose which creditors he pays first[94]; but after bankruptcy the bankruptcy law provides for a fair sharing out of his property.

When a person foresees the danger of his own[95] future insolvency—as where he is entering upon a business venture—there is the temptation to put property out of the reach of creditors, by, for example, creating a settlement in favour of the family, in this or other jurisdictions.[96] If the business venture succeeds the profits will flow in; if it fails, the creditors will be unpaid; but the family will be cared for.[97] It may also be that a settlement is made for other reasons, such as the reduction of tax liability,[98] but insolvency subsequently occurs. The question for consideration here is the extent to which a creditor can upset dispositions made by debtors of property which would otherwise be available for the creditors, whether or not there is a bankruptcy.

B. Insolvency Act 1986

i. Transactions Defrauding Creditors. Section 423 of the Insolvency Act 1986, replacing section 172 of the Law of Property Act 1925, provides that a transaction at an undervalue may be set aside if the court is satisfied that the person entering into the transaction (the debtor) did so for the purpose

(a) of putting assets beyond the reach of a person who is making, or may at some time make, a claim against him, or
(b) of otherwise prejudicing the interests of such a person in relation to the claim which he is making or may make.

The court may make such order as it thinks fit for

(a) restoring the position to what it would have been if the transaction had not been entered into, and
(b) protecting the interests of persons who are victims of the transaction (defined as a person who is, or is capable of being, prejudiced by the transaction).

---

[94] *Middleton v. Pollock* (1876) 2 Ch.D. 104.
[95] Where he foresees his beneficiary's insolvency, the protective trust may be employed; *ante*, Chap. 7.
[96] For offshore asset protection trusts, see (1993) 143 N.L.J. 721 (B. Marrache and G. Davis); (1995–96) 6 K.C.L.J. 62 (P. Matthews).
[97] "If I succeed in business, I make a fortune for myself. If I fail, I leave my creditors unpaid. They will pay the loss." *per* Jessel M.R. in *Re Butterworth, ex p. Russell* (1882) 19 Ch.D. 588 at p. 598. See also *Midland Bank plc v. Wyatt* [1995] 1 F.L.R. 696.
[98] *Ante*, p. 211.

The section applies equally to transactions entered into by individuals and by corporate bodies.[99]

(a) *Transaction at an undervalue.* By section 423(1), a person enters into a transaction with another person at an undervalue if

(a) he makes a gift to the other person or he otherwise enters into a transaction with the other on terms that provide for him to receive no consideration; or
(b) he enters into a transaction with the other in consideration of marriage; or
(c) he enters into a transaction with the other for a consideration the value of which, in money or money's worth, is significantly less than the value, in money or money's worth, of the consideration provided by himself.

Thus the section applies where a husband makes a gift of money to his wife, transfers his interest in the matrimonial home to her,[1] or purchases property in the joint names of himself and his wife without any contribution from her.[2] Similarly where a married couple declare a trust of the family home for the wife and children,[3] or where a father grants a tenancy to his sons on favourable terms.[4]

When assessing "undervalue" the court will view the transaction as a whole. In *Agricultural Mortgage Corporation plc v. Woodward*[5] an insolvent farmer, whose land was mortgaged for £700,000, granted a tenancy at the full market rent of £37,250 to his wife, to ensure that the mortgagee could not get vacant possession.[6] It was argued that the full rent prevented the application of section 423. The Court of Appeal set aside the tenancy on the ground that the wife received benefits beyond those granted by the tenancy agreement, namely the safeguarding of her home, the ability to carry on the family business freed from the claims of creditors, and the surrender value of the tenancy, which gave her a "ransom" position against the mortgagee. She had paid nothing for these extra benefits, which were significantly more valuable than the rent. It was argued that such benefits could not be valued in money or money's worth

---

[99] See also I.A. 1986, s.207.
[1] *In re Kumar (a Bankrupt)* [1993] 1 W.L.R. 224 (assumption of sole liability for the mortgage by the wife was worth significantly less than value of share transferred).
[2] *Moon v. Franklin, The Independent,* June 22, 1990.
[3] *Midland Bank plc v. Wyatt* [1995] 1 F.L.R. 696 (the trust was in any event a sham; *ante,* p. 92).
[4] *Barclays Bank plc v. Eustice* [1995] 4 All E.R. 511 (unusual term for payment of annual rent in arrears).
[5] (1995) 70 P. & C.R. 53; applied in *Barclays Bank plc v. Eustice, supra.*
[6] A mortgagor's leasing power under L.P.A. 1925, s.99, cannot be excluded in the case of agricultural land.

and so should be left out of account. However, the surrender value alone was significantly greater than the rent. It was unnecessary to decide whether a detriment to the husband which gave no corresponding benefit to the wife (*i.e.* the diminution by at least 50 per cent of the £1 million freehold value caused by the letting) could be treated as consideration provided by the husband.

The creation of a security in relation to an existing debt does not diminish the debtor's assets and is thus not a transaction at an undervalue.[7]

(b) *Intention.* As stated above, the court must be satisfied that the person entering into the transaction did so for the purpose of putting assets beyond the reach of, or of otherwise prejudicing, an existing or potential claimant.[8] The court was so satisfied where a husband who was threatened with legal actions and who knew there was doubt as to his insurance cover made substantial gifts to his wife upon receiving a large sum from the sale of his practice.[9] Indeed, where a debtor transfers assets to his family at an undervalue when an action by creditors is expected, the retained assets being insufficient, there is a strong prima facie case of intention to prejudice the creditor.[10] It is not necessary, however, to establish dishonesty. Thus the section may apply where the transfer was considered proper by legal advisers.[11] Putting the assets beyond the reach of creditors must be a substantial purpose of the transaction but need not be the sole motive.[12]

As under the previous law, it is not necessary that there should be existing creditors at the time of the transaction. The section preserves the effect of *Re Butterworth, ex p. Russell*,[13] where the court set aside a settlement made by a prosperous baker immediately before purchasing a grocer's business, a trade in which he had no experience. It makes no difference whether the anticipated creditors are those of the settlor himself or of a company he plans to set up.[14]

---

[7] *Re M.C. Bacon Ltd* [1990] B.C.L.C. 324 (examining also the meaning of "money or money's worth").

[8] See, on the previous law, *Lloyds Bank Ltd v. Marcan* [1973] 1 W.L.R. 1387 (sufficient to show intent to deprive creditors of timely recourse to property otherwise applicable for their benefit).

[9] *Moon v. Franklin, The Independent*, June 22, 1990.

[10] *Barclays Bank plc v. Eustice* [1995] 1 W.L.R. 1238.

[11] *Arbuthnot Leasing International Ltd v. Havalet Leasing (No. 2)* [1990] B.C.C. 636. It should be added that legal professional privilege will be overridden on the ground of "iniquity" if a client seeks legal advice as to how to structure a transaction to defeat creditors; *Barclays Bank plc v. Eustice, supra.*

[12] *Chohan v. Saggar* [1992] B.C.C. 306 (varied on another point at [1993] E.G.C.S. 194); *Moon v. Franklin, The Independent*, June 22, 1990; *Midland Bank plc v. Wyatt* [1995] 1 F.L.R. 696; *Royscott Spa Leasing Ltd v. Lovett* [1994] N.P.C. 146.

[13] (1882) 19 Ch.D. 588; *Mackay v. Douglas* (1872) L.R. 14 Eq. 106.

[14] *Midland Bank plc v. Wyatt* [1995] 1 F.L.R. 696.

Nor is it necessary that the person seeking to set aside the transaction should be technically a "creditor."[15]

(c) *Persons who may apply to court.* Where the debtor, being an individual, is now bankrupt, or, being a body corporate, is being wound up or is the subject of an administration order under Part II of the 1986 Act, the application may only be made by the official receiver, the trustee of the bankrupt's estate or the liquidator or administrator of the body corporate. The victim of the transaction, as defined above,[16] may apply with the leave of the court. Where a voluntary arrangement has been approved under Part I (corporate bodies) or Part VIII (individuals) of the 1986 Act, the application may be made by the supervisor of the voluntary arrangement or the victim of the transaction. In any other case, for example where there is no insolvency, the application may be made by the victim of the transaction. These provisions are found in section 424 of the 1986 Act, which further provides that any application made under the section is treated as made on behalf of every victim of the transaction.

(d) *Orders to be made.* Sections 423(2) and 425 of the 1986 Act set out the orders which may be made by the court.[17] These include orders

    (a) requiring any property transferred by the impugned transaction to be vested in any person, either absolutely or for the benefit of all the persons on whose behalf the application is treated as made, or

    (b) requiring any property representing the application of the proceeds of sale of property transferred by the impugned transaction or of money transferred by it to be so vested, or

    (c) requiring any person to pay to any other person in respect of benefits received from the debtor such sums as the court may direct.

(e) *Third parties.* Section 425(2) provides that any order made may affect the property of, or impose an obligation on, any person whether or not he was a party to the transaction, but the order shall not prejudice any interest in property acquired from a person other than the debtor which was acquired in good faith, for value and without notice of the circumstances making section 423 applicable,

---

[15] See *Cadogan v. Cadogan* [1977] 1 W.L.R. 1041.

[16] *Ante*, p. 338.

[17] See *Moon v. Franklin, The Independent*, June 22, 1990 (order compelling return of unspent portion of gift and restraining dealing with land).

or prejudice any interest deriving from such an interest. Nor shall the order require a person who received a benefit from the transaction in good faith, for value and without notice of the circumstances to pay any sum unless he was a party to the transaction. "Value" here bears its ordinary meaning.

ii. Bankruptcy provisions. The Insolvency Act 1986 replaced section 42 of the Bankruptcy Act 1914 with provisions dealing with transactions at an undervalue and preferences by individuals or corporate bodies within a certain time limit prior to insolvency.

(a) *Transaction at an undervalue.* In the case of the insolvency of an individual, section 339 permits the trustee of the bankrupt's estate to apply to court for an order where the individual entered into a transaction at an undervalue within certain time limits discussed below. The court may make such order as it thinks fit for restoring the position to what it would have been but for the transaction. "Undervalue" here bears the same meaning as under section 423.[18] Thus, as under the previous law, the trustee may obtain the wife's share in the matrimonial home to the extent that she has not contributed to its acquisition.[19] A property adjustment order on divorce may be set aside under these provisions.[20] Where the wife has compromised her claim, with the result that the order is made by consent, the compromise is capable of being consideration, but it may be difficult to assess it in money or money's worth. If so, the section is applicable.[21]

(b) *Preference of creditors.* Where an individual is adjudged bankrupt and has given a preference to any person within time limits discussed below, the trustee of the bankrupt's estate may apply to court for an order under section 340. The court may make such order as it thinks fit for restoring the position to what it would have been if that individual had not given that preference. An individual gives a preference to a person if that person is a creditor,[22] surety or guarantor, and the effect is to put that person into a better position than he would otherwise have been in in the event of the individual's

---

[18] *Ante*, p. 339. See *Re M.C. Bacon Ltd* [1990] B.C.L.C. 324. Excessive pension contributions are recoverable under ss.342A, B, C, introduced by Pensions Act 1995, s.95; *post*, p. 473.

[19] *Re Densham* [1975] 1 W.L.R. 1519; Moffat, *Trusts Law, Text and Materials* (2nd ed.), pp. 223–224. See also *Re Windle* [1975] 1 W.L.R. 1628.

[20] I.A. 1986, Sched. 14, amending M.C.A. 1973, s.39. Similarly under s.284; *In re Flint (a bankrupt)* [1993] Ch. 319; (1993) 23 Fam. Law 211 (S. Cretney).

[21] *Re Kumar (a bankrupt)* [1993] 1 W.L.R. 224; [1993] Conv. 310 (G. Ferris); *cf. Re Abbott (a bankrupt)* [1983] Ch. 45.

[22] This result could be avoided if the apparent "creditor" was in reality a beneficiary under a trust who never became a creditor. See *Re Kayford* [1975] 1 W.L.R. 279, *ante*, p. 51.

bankruptcy. An order may only be made if the individual was influenced by a desire to produce the effect mentioned above, but this is presumed where the other person was an associate.[23] A person is not "influenced by a desire" to produce such an effect where he had no choice but to do the act in question if he wanted to continue trading.[24]

(c) *Time limits.* Section 341 provides a five year time limit, ending with the day of the presentation of the bankruptcy petition, in the case of a transaction at an undervalue. In the case of a preference which is not an undervalue, the period is six months save in the case of an associate, where the period is two years.

Except in the case of a transaction at an undervalue made within two years before the bankruptcy, no order may be made with respect to a transaction entered into within the above time limits unless the individual was insolvent at the time or became insolvent in consequence of the transaction or preference.[25] In the case of a transaction at an undervalue entered into with an associate, there is a rebuttable presumption that the individual was or became insolvent at the time of the transaction. A person is insolvent for this purpose if he cannot pay his debts as they fall due, or if the value of his assets is less than his liabilities.

(d) *Orders to be made.* Section 342 sets out the orders which the court may make for the benefit of the bankrupt's estate. These are similar to the orders which may be made under section 425.[26]

(e) *Third parties.* As in the case of section 425,[27] no order may prejudice any interest in property acquired from a person other than the bankrupt and acquired in good faith and for value. Section 342 as originally drafted put a purchaser of land at risk where a gift or transaction at an undervalue appeared on the title and the time limits for setting aside had not expired. This was remedied by the Insolvency (No. 2) Act 1994,[28] amending section 342 so that a purchaser is at risk in only two situations, where he is rebuttably presumed not to be in good faith. The first situation is where he had notice at the time he acquired his interest of the fact that the earlier transaction was at an undervalue (or was a preference) and of the fact that the earlier transferor had been adjudged bankrupt or that the petition on

---

[23] As defined by section 435. The definition includes relatives of the individual or of his spouse, partners, employers, employees and related companies.
[24] *Re M.C. Bacon Ltd* [1990] B.C.L.C. 324; *post*, p. 344.
[25] See further s.341(4) and (5), dealing with criminal bankruptcy orders.
[26] *Ante*, p. 341.
[27] *Ante*, p. 341.
[28] See (1995) 92 L.S.Gaz. No. 2, p. 18 (I. Storey); (1995) 92 L.S.Gaz. No. 35, p. 31.

which he was later adjudged bankrupt had been presented. The second situation is where the purchaser was an associate of, or was connected with, the bankrupt or the person with whom the bankrupt entered into the transaction at an undervalue (or to whom preference was given). Thus mere notice of the fact that the previous transaction was at an undervalue does not suffice. Similar rules apply to a person who has received a benefit from the transaction or preference in good faith and for value. Such a person shall not be required to pay any sum to the trustee unless he was a party to the transaction or was given a preference at a time when he was a creditor of the bankrupt.

(f) *Corporate insolvency.* The 1986 Act lays down similar provisions in the case of transactions at an undervalue and preferences prior to liquidation or the making of an administration order. Section 238 defines "undervalue" as in the case of an individual,[29] but, of course, without any reference to marriage consideration. However, no order will be made concerning a transaction at an undervalue if the court is satisfied that the company entered into it in good faith and for the purpose of carrying on its business, and at that time there were reasonable grounds for believing that the transaction would benefit the company.

Section 239 (preferences) was held inapplicable in *Re M.C. Bacon Ltd*,[30] where the company had been required by its bank to give security for its overdraft shortly before becoming insolvent. The company had no choice but to grant the security if it wanted to continue trading, as the bank's support was necessary to prevent liquidation. No preference had been given, as the company did not "desire" to put the bank in a better position on insolvency, as required by section 239.

The time limits are shorter than in the case of an individual. In the case of a transaction at an undervalue or a preference given to a person connected[31] with the company, the period is two years ending with the onset of insolvency, as defined by section 240(3). In the case of a preference which is neither a transaction at an undervalue nor given to a connected person, the period is six months.[32] But no transaction within these time limits may be set aside unless the company was unable to pay its debts at the time, or became unable to do so in consequence of the transaction.[33]

[29] See *Re M.C. Bacon Ltd* [1990] B.C.L.C. 324, *ante*, p. 343. The section has extra-territorial effect; In *re Paramount Airways Ltd* [1993] Ch. 223.

[30] *Supra.* See also *Re Lewis's of Leicester Ltd* [1995] 1 B.C.L.C. 428.

[31] Defined by s.249.

[32] A transaction at an undervalue or a preference may also be set aside if made between the presentation of a petition for an administration order and the making of the order.

[33] Such inability is presumed in the case of a transaction at an undervalue with a connected person unless the contrary is shown.

Section 241,[34] dealing with the orders which may be made and the protection of third parties, contains provisions similar to those already discussed in relation to individual insolvency.

C. Protection of the Spouse and Family

The previous sections dealt with attempts by a debtor to deprive his creditors of satisfaction by transferring property by way of voluntary settlement to other persons, usually members of his family, whom the debtor wishes to protect. We now deal with what is in effect the converse of that problem; cases where the defendant is trying to deprive his spouse or family of assets which should properly be available to them. This occurs in matrimonial proceedings, and also in relation to the rights of dependants upon a death.

i. Matrimonial Causes Act 1973, s.37.

Section 37 protects a spouse from activities of the other spouse which may diminish the assets available for the purposes of financial relief under the Act. If the court is satisfied that one spouse is about to make a disposition[35] or transfer with the intention of depriving the applicant of financial relief, it may make such order as it thinks fit for the purpose of protecting the applicant's claim.[36] Where the defendant spouse has made a disposition of property, other than one made for valuable consideration to a bona fide purchaser without notice of any intention to defeat the applicant's claim,[37] the disposition may be set aside.

The intention to defeat the applicant's claim must be affirmatively proved, except in cases where the disposition was made within three years before the date of the application, in which case there is a statutory presumption[38] that the intention is to defeat the applicant's claim for financial relief.

ii. Inheritance (Provision for Family and Dependants) Act 1975.

A similar problem arises in connection with statutory schemes which restrict the decedent's powers of free disposal of his property by will, in order to provide for the surviving spouse and children and other dependants. This is an old problem; originally answered by the surviving spouse's right to dower or curtesy, and now governed by a wide variety of provisions (such as "forced heirship") in various parts of the world. A common solution is to

---

[34] As amended by Insolvency (No. 2) Act 1994, s.1 (protection of purchasers in good faith).

[35] The wide definition in s.37(6) includes a trust, but not any provision made in a will.

[36] s.37(2)(a).

[37] Called a "reviewable disposition" and defined in s.37(4).

[38] s.37(5); rebuttable, of course.

give to the surviving spouse, and sometimes to children, a fractional share of the estate. The system in England and Wales is to give to the court a discretionary power to make an award to a surviving spouse and other dependants on the ground that the disposition of the deceased's estate (whether by will or intestacy) is not such as to make reasonable financial provision for the applicant.[39] But these schemes could be thwarted if the decedent who wished to deprive a widow and dependants could give away all his property before death.[40]

Provisions to deal with this problem are contained in sections 10–13 of the Act. In short, the court is given power to require a donee from the decedent to provide sums of money,[41] up to, but not in excess of, the value of the gift,[42] if the gift was made within six years before the death of the decedent, and was made "with the intention of defeating an application for financial provision under this Act."[43] Protection is given to persons who gave full valuable consideration for a transfer. The intention is to be determined on a balance of probabilities,[44] and need not be the sole intention of the decedent in making the gift. Similar provisions in section 11 deal with contracts to leave property by will; and transfers to trustees in section 13.

---

[39] s.2.

[40] See *Schaefer v. Schuhmann* [1972] A.C. 572. It is possible that such transfers could be set aside independently of any statutory provisions in a case of fraud. See *Cadogan v. Cadogan* [1977] 1 W.L.R. 1041.

[41] s.10(2); see also s.10(6), giving the factors which the court shall take into consideration.

[42] Valued, in the case of gifts other than cash, at the date of death of the decedent, or, if the property was disposed of by the donee, the value at the date of disposal.

[43] s.10(2).

[44] s.12.

CHAPTER 14

NON-CHARITABLE PURPOSE TRUSTS

1. The General Problem 347
   A. Private Trusts, Purpose Trusts, Chari-
     table Trusts 347
   B. Trusts for Persons and Purposes 348
2. Objections to Purpose Trusts 351
   A. The Beneficiary Principle,
     Enforceability.................................... 351
   B. Uncertainty 351
   C. Excessive Delegation of Testamentary
     Power 352
   D. Perpetuity 353
3. Exceptional Cases Upholding Purpose
   Trusts 354
   A. Tombs and Monuments 354
   B. Animals 355
   C. Other Purposes 356
4. The Failure of the Astor Trust 357
5. Unincorporated Associations 359
   A. Charitable Purposes 359
   B. Non-Charitable Purposes 359

   C. Property Held on Trust for the
     Members 360
   D. Ownership by Members on Contrac-
     tual Basis 363
6. Mandate or Agency 364
7. Perpetuity 365
   A. Excessive Duration 365
   B. Human Lives Only 366
   C. A Fixed Number of Years 367
8. Useless or Capricious Purposes 368
9. Alternative Solutions 369
   A. By the Draftsman 370
     i. Incorporation 370
     ii. Mandate or Agency 370
     iii. Gift to Members of an Association
       and not for Purposes Only 370
     iv. Conveyancing Devices 370
     v. Draft as a Power; not as a
       Trust 371
   B. By the Legislature 372

1. THE GENERAL PROBLEM

A. Private Trusts, Purpose Trusts, Charitable Trusts

A private trust is essentially a trust in favour of ascertainable individuals. A charitable trust is a trust for purposes which are treated in law as charitable. The question for consideration in this chapter is whether or not it is possible to establish a trust for non-charitable purposes.

We have considered in earlier chapters questions relating to the setting up of trusts for individuals. Charitable trusts are dealt with in Chapter 15. For the present purpose, it will be sufficient to state that charitable purposes are grouped into four categories: trusts for the relief of poverty, trusts for the advancement of religion, trusts for the advancement of education, and trusts for other purposes beneficial to the community. The purpose trusts at present under consideration are those which do not come within these categories. A trust, for example, to provide a cup for a yacht race,[1] to feed the testator's horses and hounds,[2] to set up a monument,[3] or to be applied for useful or benevolent purposes.[4] There is no question of any such trusts having any privilege in relation to taxation or to perpetuity, such as is allowed in the case of charitable trusts. The question is whether they are valid or void.[5]

B. Trusts for Persons and Purposes

With any particular trust, there may be a question of construction to determine whether the trust is for persons or for purposes. Most purposes affect persons, and there is no reason why a trust should not be treated as a trust for persons where the beneficiaries are to be benefited in some way other than by payment of money. Thus, a trust for the education of the children of X can be construed as a trust of which the children of X are the beneficiaries.[6] A trust for the promotion of fox-hunting would be treated as a trust for a purpose, although it might be said that the individual sportsman might benefit from it.[7]

There are various examples of trusts in which the beneficiaries enjoy only a limited proprietary interest. Where, for example, a debtor assigns an asset to trustees for the payment of his debts, his creditors do not, unless there has been an absolute assignment, take any surplus.[8] In *Re the Trusts of Abbott Fund*[9] it was accepted that a trust for the maintenance of two old ladies was valid although it seems that they did not become owners of any proprietary interest; and in *Re Gillingham Bus Disaster Fund*,[10] a fund collected for the benefit of injured cadets and other "worthy purposes" was not invalid although there was no suggestion that the cadets could ever have claimed the assets of the fund. It may be possible to support these latter decisions as examples of discretionary trusts for the benefit of individuals; but they were not so drafted, and it may be preferable to regard them as examples of trusts for persons to be

---

[1] *Re Nottage* [1895] 2 Ch. 649.
[2] *Re Dean* (1889) 41 Ch.D. 554.
[3] *Mussett v. Bingle* [1876] W.N. 170; *Re Endacott* [1960] Ch. 232.
[4] *Morice v. Bishop of Durham* (1804) 9 Ves.Jr. 399.
[5] See generally (1953) 17 Conv.(N.S.) 46 (L. Sheridan); (1953) 6 C.L.P. 151 (O. Marshall); Morris and Leach, Chap. 12; Maudsley, *The Modern Law of Perpetuities*, pp. 166–178 (1970) 34 Conv.(N.S.) 77 (P. Lovell); (1973) 37 Conv.(N.S.) 420 (L. McKay); (1971) 87 L.Q.R. 31 (J. Harris); (1977) 40 M.L.R. 397 (N. Gravells); (1977) 41 Conv.(N.S.) 179 (K. Widdows); *Trends in Contemporary Trust Law* (ed. A. Oakley), Chap. 1 (P. Matthews).
[6] See [1968] A.S.C.L. at p. 439 (J. Davies). See also *Re Osoba* [1979] 1 W.L.R. 247, *ante* p. 234.
[7] *Re Thompson* [1934] Ch. 342, *post*, p. 357.
[8] *Re Rissik* [1936] Ch. 68.
[9] [1900] 2 Ch. 326, *ante*, p. 233; contrast *Re Andrew's Trust* [1905] 2 Ch. 48; *Re Foord* [1922] 2 Ch. 599; *ante*, pp. 53, 234.
[10] [1959] Ch. 62, *ante*, p. 233.

benefited in a particular way. The proper analysis of trusts of this kind was little discussed until the decision of Goff J. in *Re Denley's Trust Deed* in 1969.[11]

> A plot of land was conveyed to trustees to hold, for a period determined by lives, "for the purpose of a recreation or sports ground primarily for the benefit of the employees of the company and secondarily for the benefit of such other person or persons (if any) as the trustees may allow."

Goff J. upheld the trust as one for the benefit of the employees. They were ascertainable, and the trust was one which the court could control. If it had been construed as a trust for non-charitable purposes, it would have been void. "The objection [to non-charitable purpose trusts] is not that the trust is for a purpose or an object per se, but that there is no beneficiary or cestui que trust."[12] Here, however, "the trust deed expressly states that . . . the employees of the company shall be entitled to the use and enjoyment of the land."[13] He contrasted this situation with a "purpose . . . trust, the carrying out of which would benefit an individual or individuals, where that benefit is so indirect or intangible or which is otherwise so framed as not to give those persons any *locus standi* to apply to the court to enforce the trust"[14]; in which case the trust would have been a non-charitable purpose trust, and void.

The same line of reasoning was applied in *Re Lipinski's Will Trusts*,[15] a case of a gift to an unincorporated association.

> The testator bequeathed his residuary estate to trustees in trust as to one-half for the Hull Judeans (Maccabi) Association "in memory of my late wife to be used solely in the work of constructing the new buildings for the association and/or improvements to the said buildings."

At first sight, this would appear to be a gift to an unincorporated association to be applied for its (non-charitable) purposes.[16] We will

---

[11] [1969] 1 Ch. 373. See also *Wicks v. Firth* [1983] A.C. 214 (non-charitable trust to award scholarships assumed valid).

[12] [1969] 1 Ch. 373 at p. 383.

[13] *Ibid.* at p. 383.

[14] *Ibid.* at p. 382. For discussion of *locus standi* to enforce the *Re Denley* type of trust, see [1982] Conv. 118, at p. 124 (A. Everton).

[15] [1976] Ch. 235; (1977) 93 L.Q.R. 167; (1977) 41 Conv.(N.S.) 179 (K. Widdows); (1977) 40 M.L.R. 231 (N. Gravells); *Re Turkington* [1937] 4 All E.R. 501.

[16] In favour of this construction, counsel relied on the reference to the testator's late wife's memory as indicating an intention to create an endowment; and on a requirement that the money was to be used "solely" for the stated purposes.

see,[17] however, that gifts to unincorporated associations are normally upheld as gifts to the members rather than invalidated as purpose trusts. To the extent that the testator's superadded purpose hindered this construction, *Re Denley's Trust Deed*[18] came to the rescue.

The beneficiaries, the members of the association, were ascertainable; there was no problem of perpetuity,[19] because they could, according to the rules of the association, terminate the trust for their own benefit.[20] The implication of these factors will be discussed later in the chapter.

These cases show a more liberal judicial tendency in connection with the construction of gifts of this type.[21] *Re Denley*, however, could not save the trust in *R. v. District Auditor, ex p. West Yorkshire Metropolitan County Council*,[22] where a local authority, purporting to act under statutory powers, resolved to create a trust "for the benefit of any or all or some of the inhabitants of the County of West Yorkshire" in any of four ways: (i) to assist economic development in the county in order to relieve unemployment and poverty; (ii) to assist bodies concerned with youth and community problems in West Yorkshire; (iii) to assist and encourage ethnic and minority groups in West Yorkshire; (iv) to inform all interested and influential persons of the consequences of the abolition (proposed by the Government) of the Council and other metropolitan county councils and of other proposals affecting local government in the county. The capital and income were to be applied within a short period, obviating any perpetuity problems, but the trust was void as a non-charitable purpose trust. It was not within the purpose trust exceptions illustrated by *Re Denley* and *Re Lipinski* because there were no "ascertained or ascertainable beneficiaries." Even if "inhabitant" was sufficiently certain, the class of 2,500,000 potential beneficiaries was so large that the trust was unworkable. It has never been established what certainty test applies to a *Re Denley* trust,[23] but this decision suggests that the class of beneficiaries, even if conceptually certain and not capricious, must not be too wide. A private trust which fails for "administrative unworkability"[24] cannot be rescued by the *Re Denley* principle.

---

[17] *Post*, p. 361.

[18] [1969] 1 Ch. 373.

[19] *Post*, p. 353. *cf. Re Grant's W.T.* [1980] 1 W.L.R. 360, *post*, p. 362.

[20] By altering the constitution of the association. The beneficiaries in *Re Denley*, on the other hand, would seem to have no right to divide up the assets under the *Saunders v. Vautier* principle (*post*, p. 612), but no perpetuity problem arose because the trust was expressly confined to the perpetuity period.

[21] (1970) 34 Conv.(N.S.) 77 (P. Lovell); (1972) 87 L.Q.R. 31 (J. Harris).

[22] [1986] R.V.R. 24; (1986) 45 C.L.J. 391 (C. Harpum). The certainty aspects are discussed in Chap. 3, *ante*, p. 101.

[23] *Ante*, p. 101.

[24] *Ante*, p. 105.

It is necessary now to consider the objections to non-charitable purpose trusts.

2. OBJECTIONS TO PURPOSE TRUSTS

If a disposition is construed as a trust for non-charitable purposes, there are various objections which may be made to it. The first of these objections denies the possibility of existence of non-charitable purpose trusts. It has not however been consistently applied; and purpose trusts for the building of graves and monuments and the care of specific animals, which succeeded in the nineteenth century[25] are now regarded as anomalous exceptions to the rule.[26] The other objections accept the possibility of the existence of non-charitable purpose trusts, but impose restrictions upon them.

A. The Beneficiary Principle; Enforceability

The first objection may be seen in a celebrated dictum of Sir William Grant M.R. in *Morice v. Bishop of Durham*.[27] "Every other [*i.e.* non-charitable] trust must have a definite object. There must be somebody in whose favour the court can decree performance.[28] A trust, as we have seen, is an obligation. The objection is that there cannot be an obligation upon the trustees unless there is a correlative right in someone else to enforce it. With charitable trusts, the Attorney-General is charged with the duty of enforcement. With private trusts, no public official is involved. The trust is void unless there are human beneficiaries capable of enforcing the trust. In effect the objection is that there is no beneficial owner of the property. Acceptance of this principle renders non-charitable purpose trusts void *in limine*.

B. Uncertainty

If non-charitable purpose trusts are recognised at all by the law, they are only valid if the purposes are expressed with sufficient certainty to enable the court to control the performance of the trust. The point commonly arises in the cases where incompetent draftsmanship has failed to create a charitable trust; where, for example, the property is to be applied for charitable or benevolent purposes,[29]

---

[25] *Post*, p. 354.

[26] *Per* Roxburgh J. in *Re Astor's S.T.* [1952] Ch. 534 at p. 547.

[27] (1804) 9 Ves.Jr. 399.

[28] At p. 404.

[29] *Blair v. Duncan* [1902] A.C. 37; *Houston v. Burns* [1918] A.C. 337; *Chichester Diocesan Fund and Board of Finance v. Simpson* [1944] A.C. 341; *Re Atkinson's Will Trusts* [1978] 1 W.L.R. 586.

or, as in *Morice v. Bishop of Durham*[30] for "such objects of benevolence and liberality as the Bishop of Durham in his own discretion
shall most approve of." "Benevolence" and "liberality" are wider
concepts than "charity," and the trust was not therefore applicable
for charitable purposes only. The purposes were uncertain and the
trust void. Indeed, this reason was more clearly emphasised by Sir
William Grant M.R. than was the earlier objection. Having established that the trust was not for charitable purposes, and that the
Bishop did not claim any personal benefit for himself, he said[31]:

> "That it is a trust, unless it be of a charitable nature, too indefinite
> to be executed by this Court, has not been, and cannot be denied.
> There can be no trust, over the exercise of which this Court will
> not assume a control; for an uncontrollable power of disposition
> would be ownership and not trust. If there be a clear trust, but for
> uncertain objects, the property, that is the subject of the trust, is
> indisposed of; and the benefit of such trust must result to those, to
> whom the law gives the ownership in default of disposition by the
> former owner. But this doctrine does not hold good with regard to
> trusts for charity. Every other trust must have a definite object.
> There must be somebody, in whose favour the Court can decree
> performance."

This objection can be met by specifying in sufficient detail the
purposes to which the property is to be applied. Trusts for specific
purposes like feeding the testator's animals, or maintaining a tomb
or monument, usually pass this test. But general projects, even
carefully drafted, are likely to be held void. The point only becomes
significant, of course, if the problem of the beneficiary principle has
been surmounted.

C. Excessive Delegation of Testamentary Power

There have been judicial statements to the effect that purpose
trusts created by will are void because, in the absence of anyone to
enforce the trust, the trustees are left to determine the application of
the property; thus "the testator has imperfectly exercised his testamentary power; he has delegated it, for the disposal of his property
lies with them, not with him."[32] The objection is not relevant to
trusts created *inter vivos*. Of the trust in *Re Denley's Trust Deed*,
Goff J. said[33]: "If this were a will, a question might arise whether

---

[30] (1804) 9 Ves.Jr. 399.
[31] (1804) 9 Ves.Jr. 399 at pp. 404–405.
[32] *Leahy v. Att.-Gen. for New South Wales* [1959] A.C. 457 at p. 484; *Re Wood* [1949] Ch. 498
at p. 501.
[33] [1969] 1 Ch. 373 at p. 387.

this provision might be open to attack as a delegation of the testamentary power. I do not say that would be so, but in any case it cannot be said of a settlement inter vivos." The status of the objection was, however, not established, even with wills. Special, general and intermediate powers are permitted in wills[34]; and "an anti-delegation rule is really an anti-power rule."[35]

In *Re Beatty's Will Trusts*[36] Hoffmann J., upholding a testamentary disposition to trustees to allocate "to or among such person or persons as they think fit", rejected the supposed "anti-delegation" rule. Thus there is no objection on this basis to the validity of purpose trusts. Moreover, the acceptance of the validity of testamentary powers is significant. For one way, as will be seen,[37] of effecting a non-charitable purpose where there are willing trustees, may be to give them *power* to perform, and not attempt to require them to do so.

D. Perpetuity

A charitable trust may last for ever; a non-charitable trust is void if it is to continue beyond the perpetuity period.[38] The reason is that perpetual non-charitable purpose trusts would conflict with the *policy* of the perpetuity rule, which is the prevention of the tying up of property for too long a period.

In its more usual context the rule against perpetuities deals with the limit of time to which the vesting of future interests may be postponed. An outline of this has already been given.[39] In the present context, however, we are not concerned with future vesting. We are concerned with a situation in which the property is vested in the trustees to be applied by them for certain non-charitable purposes for a period which may exceed that of perpetuity. This situation will arise if either the capital or the income of the fund is to be so applied. If the trust relates to income, then the capital must be maintained in order to produce the income. It is no answer to say that, since the trustees may sell the present investments and purchase others, the capital is not inalienable. The objection relates, not only to alienability, but to duration. Whatever happens to individual investments, an obligation to retain the capital as a fund for an excessive period violates the rule. Accordingly, a non-charitable

---

[34] *Re Park* [1932] 1 Ch. 580; *Re Abraham's W.T.* [1969] 1 Ch. 463; *Re Gulbenkian's Settlements* [1970] A.C. 508; *Re Manisty's Settlement* [1974] Ch. 17; *Re Hay's Settlement Trusts* [1982] 1 W.L.R. 202.
[35] (1953) 69 L.Q.R. 334 at p. 342 (D. Gordon).
[36] [1990] 1 W.L.R. 503; [1991] Conv. 138 (J. Martin).
[37] *Post,* p. 371.
[38] Most pension trusts are exempted; *post,* p. 473.
[39] *Ante,* Chap. 13.

purpose trust is valid, if at all, only if it is confined to the perpetuity period. The matter is examined below.[40]

3. EXCEPTIONAL CASES UPHOLDING PURPOSE TRUSTS[41]

Until *Re Astor's Settlement Trusts*[42] in 1952, it was arguable that it was possible to establish a trust for a non-charitable purpose for the period of perpetuity. The authorities cover a narrow field, being nearly all concerned with trusts for building or maintaining monuments or tombs, or for caring for the testator's animals. But the language of the judgments is general, and there are occasional cases outside those fields. As will be seen, *Re Astor's Settlement Trusts*[43] underlined the beneficiary principle; and it is clear now that trusts for non-charitable purposes will fail unless they are kept strictly within the narrow confines of these exceptional cases.

A. Tombs and Monuments

Reasonable provision for the building of a tomb or a gravestone for a testator may be regarded as a funeral expense, and valid independently of any doctrine relating to purpose trusts.[44] But bequests for family burial enclosures have been upheld as purpose trusts[45]; as have bequests for monuments to other people, such as the testator's wife's first husband.[46] Such a gift may be for the building of the monument which, it seems, may be assumed to be done within the period of perpetuity[47]; or for the care or the maintenance of the graves for a period limited to the period of perpetuity. An example is *Re Hooper*,[48] where

> A testator gave a sum of money to trustees for the care and upkeep of certain family graves and monuments, and a tablet in a window in a church so far as the trustees could legally do so. Maugham J. upheld the gift for a period of 21 years.[49]

---

[40] *Post*, p. 365.
[41] Morris and Leach (*op. cit.*), pp. 310–319; Maudsley, *The Modern Law of Perpetuities*, pp. 168–176.
[42] [1952] Ch. 534; *post*, p. 357.
[43] *Supra*.
[44] *Trimmer v. Danby* (1856) 25 L.J.Ch. 424. Gray thought that it was the only justification for upholding such trusts: *The Rule Against Perpetuities*, pp. 310–311.
[45] *Pirbright v. Salwey* [1896] W.N. 86; *Re Hooper* [1932] 1 Ch. 38.
[46] *Mussett v. Bingle* [1876] W.N. 170.
[47] *Post*, p. 366.
[48] [1932] 1 Ch. 38.
[49] Relying on *Pirbright v. Salwey* [1896] W.N. 86.

Similarly, in *Mussett v. Bingle*,[50] Hall V.-C. held that since the executors were ready to carry out a bequest of £300 to erect a monument to the testator's wife's first husband, "it must be performed accordingly." But he held void for perpetuity a further gift for its upkeep.

Such trusts must of course comply with the requirement of certainty. In *Re Endacott*,[51] the Court of Appeal held void a residuary gift amounting to some £20,000 "to the North Tawton Devon Parish Council for the purpose of providing some useful memorial to myself." Such a trust, though specific in the sense that it indicated a purpose capable of expression, was "of far too wide and uncertain a nature to qualify within the class of cases cited."[52] No doubt was cast upon *Re Hooper*[53] and the early cases. Yet *Re Endacott*[54] may illustrate the stricter modern approach to purpose trusts; or perhaps it indicates the willingness of the court to allow reasonable sums to be spent upon these purposes, and a reluctance to uphold such grandiose schemes. This policy, as will be seen, is articulated in *Re Astor*.[55] The Parish Councils and Burial Authorities (Miscellaneous Provisions) Act 1970, s.1, now provides that a burial authority or a local authority may agree by contract to maintain a grave, or memorial or monument for a period not exceeding 99 years.

B. Animals

Gifts for the care of specific animals, though not charitable, have also been upheld. There was no argument on the point in *Pettingall v. Pettingall*[56] where an annuity of £50 to be applied in maintaining the testator's favourite black mare was held valid. In *Re Dean*,[57] the leading case, North J., relying on *Mitford v. Reynolds*[58] and the monument cases, upheld a gift of £750 per annum for the period of 50 years for the maintenance of the testator's horses and hounds if they should so long live. He met head-on the argument that the court will not recognise a trust unless it is capable of being enforced by someone, by pronouncing: "I do not assent to that view."[59] There was no objection to such a provision "provided, of course, that it is

[50] [1876] W.N. 170. See also *Trimmer v. Danby* (1856) 25 L.J.Ch. 424.
[51] [1960] Ch. 232.
[52] At p. 247.
[53] [1932] 1 Ch. 38.
[54] [1960] Ch. 232.
[55] [1952] Ch. 534.
[56] (1842) 11 L.J.Ch. 176.
[57] (1889) 41 Ch.D. 552.
[58] (1848) 16 Sim. 105.
[59] (1889) 41 Ch.D. 552 at p. 556.

not to last for too long a period."[60] It is difficult to see how the gift could be upheld for a 50-year period; for the horses and hounds could not be the measuring lives for the period of perpetuity. This aspect of the matter is discussed below.[61] The case has been accepted as authority for the proposition that trusts for the upkeep of specific animals are valid for the perpetuity period; and it is believed that this exception to the general rule has been relied on in countless cases since *Re Dean*.[62]

A possible difficulty, it has been suggested,[63] is that the fund might be claimed by the person who now owns the animal (*e.g.* as specific or residuary legatee). A fund to maintain another's property can be claimed by that other without applying it to the purpose.[64] Another solution might be to give the fund to the person acquiring the animal on the testator's death, determinable on the death of the animal or on the trustee's decision that it is improperly maintained.[65]

C. Other Purposes

Trusts for other purposes have on occasion been upheld; and others which have failed have been refused on the ground of perpetuity, without any indication that they would not have been valid if confined to the permitted period.

Trusts for the saying of masses for the benefit of private individuals have been considered to come into this category. Until the House of Lords decision in *Bourne v. Keane*, in 1919,[66] such trusts were regarded as being trusts for superstitious uses and void. *Bourne v. Keane* held them valid. Such trusts have now been upheld as charitable in *Re Hetherington*[67] where the masses are said in public. Even where the masses are said in private, the trust is arguably charitable on the basis that public benefit can be found in the endowment of the priesthood. The acceptance of such trusts as charitable makes it unnecessary to consider them in the category of private purpose trusts.

One possible member of this category of miscellaneous purpose trusts is a trust for non-Christian private ceremonies. In *Re Khoo*

---

[60] At p. 557.
[61] *Post*, p. 366.
[62] (1889) 41 Ch.D. 552.
[63] (1983) 80 L.S.Gaz. 2451 (P. Matthews).
[64] *Re Bowes* [1896] 1 Ch. 507 (money directed to be laid out in planting trees on an estate belonged to the owners of the estate absolutely.) See also *Re Lipinski's Will Trusts* [1976] Ch. 235.
[65] See Matthews, *op. cit.*, discussing other possibilities.
[66] [1919] A.C. 815.
[67] [1990] Ch. 1; [1989] Conv. 453 (N. Parry); *post*, p. 419. See also *Re Caus* [1934] Ch. 162.

Cheng Teow,[68] the Supreme Court of the Straits Settlements held valid a gift to be applied for the period of perpetuity in the performance of ceremonies called Sin Chew to perpetuate the testator's memory. The gift was not charitable; but the Court held that it was valid for a period measured by royal lives plus 21 years.

A decision which has perhaps been elevated to a position of importance which it does not merit is *Re Thompson*[69]:

> An alumnus of Trinity Hall, Cambridge, bequeathed a legacy to one Lloyd, an old friend, to be applied in such manner as he should think fit towards the promotion and furtherance of fox-hunting, and gave the residuary estate to Trinity Hall. Lloyd made no claim to any beneficial interest, but desired to carry out the testator's wishes if he should be permitted to do so. Trinity Hall also was anxious that the trust should be performed; but felt it its duty, as a charity, to submit that the trust was void for lack of a beneficiary. There was no problem of perpetuity, and Clauson J. held that the purpose was sufficiently certain. He upheld the gift by ordering the money to be paid to Lloyd upon his giving an undertaking to apply it for these stated objects, and gave to Trinity Hall liberty to apply if the money should be used for other purposes.

The case is one of very limited significance. It does not, as some have claimed,[70] provide a solution to the beneficiary problem, by holding that the party entitled in default can enforce a purpose trust. Enforcement is contrary to the interest of the party entitled in default; he is interested to restrain misapplication, which is a very different matter. In *Re Thompson*,[71] there was no contest, as all parties desired enforcement. The case was only litigated because Trinity Hall, as a charity, could not, without the court's approval, forgo its strict legal claim to the property.

4. THE FAILURE OF THE ASTOR TRUST[72]

Modern decisions have made clear that this line of cases will not be extended.[73] They are regarded as "concessions to human weakness

---

[68] [1932] Straits Settlements L.R. 226.
[69] [1934] Ch. 342.
[70] See Roxburgh J. in *Re Astor's S.T.* [1952] Ch. 534 at p. 543.
[71] *Supra.*
[72] (1953) 6 C.L.P. 151 (O. Marshall); (1953) 17 Conv.(N.S.) 46 (L. Sheridan); (1955) 18 M.L.R. 120 (L. Leigh).
[73] *Re Endacott* [1960] 2 Ch. 232 at p. 246.

or sentiment,"[74] troublesome, anomalous and aberrant,"[75] and as "occasions when Homer has nodded."[76] Purpose trusts generally have failed under the beneficiary principle, and on the ground of uncertainty. In these circumstances, compliance with the perpetuity rule is no escape.

In *Re Astor's Settlement Trusts*,[77] an *inter vivos* settlement was made in 1945, expressly limited to a period of lives in being plus 21 years, under which the trustees were to hold a fund upon various trusts for non-charitable purposes, including "the maintenance of good relations between nations . . . the preservation of the independence of the newspapers," and other similar purposes in favour of independent newspapers. Roxburgh J. held the trust void; both because there was no one who could enforce the trust, and also on the ground of uncertainty.

Re Shaw[78] concerned the will of George Bernard Shaw, which provided that the residue of the estate should be applied to research the utility of the development of a 40-letter British alphabet in the place of the present one, and for the translation of his play "Androcles and the Lion" into the new alphabet. Harman J. held that the trust was not charitable, and that it failed on the beneficiary principle. The trustees were willing to carry out the testator's wishes if they were permitted to do so. But "I am not at liberty to validate this trust by treating it as a power. A valid power is not to be spelled out of an invalid trust."[79]

These cases show the current trend in situations where the gift is construed as a gift for purposes. The insistence upon an ascertained beneficiary reflects the analysis of the law of trusts before the days when discretionary trusts became common. We have seen that a beneficiary under a discretionary trust is not entitled to specific property; only to a limited right to be considered. It has been argued that *McPhail v. Doulton*[80] manifests a basic change in the conceptual development of the law of trusts. "It has broken the stranglehold imposed on the development of trusts . . . by a rigid conception of a framework of fixed equitable interests and correlatively narrow obligations . . . it does not take much crystal-ball gazing to see the

---

[74] *Re Astor's S.T.* [1952] Ch. 534 at p. 547.
[75] *Re Endacott, supra,* at p. 251.
[76] *Ibid.* at p. 250.
[77] [1952] Ch. 534.
[78] [1957] 1 W.L.R. 729. The litigation started when the success of "My Fair Lady" "brought the interpretation of the will into the realm of practical politics"; p. 731.
[79] *Ibid.* at p. 731, relying on *I.R.C. v. Broadway Cottages Trust* [1955] Ch. 20 at p. 36.
[80] [1971] A.C. 424; *ante,* p. 99.

impact this extension will have on all the old sterile purpose trust and unincorporated association debates."[81]

5. UNINCORPORATED ASSOCIATIONS

An unincorporated association exists where two or more persons are bound together for one or more common purposes by mutual undertakings, each having mutual duties and obligations, in an organisation which has rules identifying in whom control of the organisation and its funds is vested, and which can be joined or left at will.[82]

Special problems arise in connection with the holding of property by unincorporated associations.[83] An unincorporated association is not a legal person, and, with the exception of trade unions,[84] cannot be the owner of property or the subject of legal rights and duties.[85] The question we will consider here is the effect of gifts to such associations, and the various ways in which their property is held. The latter is determined by the terms of the gift or by the constitution or rules of the association. The question of entitlement to the funds on the dissolution of the association is dealt with elsewhere.[86]

A. Charitable Purposes

The assets of an unincorporated association may be held upon charitable trusts. For example, a society for the relief of the poor. A charitable trust is valid even though it is a purpose trust; the usual rules of certainty of objects do not apply; it may continue for ever; and it enjoys a number of tax privileges.

B. Non-Charitable Purposes

We have seen that, generally speaking, trusts for the promotion of non-charitable purposes are void. Hence gifts to non-charitable unincorporated associations will fail if construed as purpose trusts. But such a result may be avoided if it is possible to regard the gift

---

[81] (1974) 37 M.L.R. 643 at pp. 655–656 (Y. Grbich); (1972) 89 L.Q.R. 31 (J. Harris); [1970] A.S.C.L. 189 (J. Davies).

[82] *Conservative and Unionist Central Office v. Burrell (Inspector of Taxes)* [1982] 1 W.L.R. 522. (The definition was for tax purposes, but seems to be of general application). See [1983] Conv. 150 (P. Creighton), doubting the last requirement.

[83] See Warburton, *Unincorporated Associations: Law and Practice* (2nd ed.), Chap. 5.

[84] Trade Union and Labour Relations (Consolidation) Act 1992, s.10.

[85] Halsbury (4th ed.), Vol. 7, p. 11. It is otherwise in the context of tax; *Worthing Rugby Football Club Trustees v. I.R.C.* [1987] 1 W.L.R. 1057.

[86] *Ante,* pp. 235 *et seq.*

as in favour of the members, as described below. Such a construction may be adopted even where the donor has expressly stated that
his gift is for particular non-charitable purposes.[87]

C. Property Held on Trust for the Members

The property of an unincorporated association may be held on
trust for the members of the association, and not for its purposes.
Such a trust must comply with the usual rules for the creation of a
trust. There must be an intention to create a trust, and there must be
ascertainable beneficiaries. This will often be made clear by the
terms of the constitution of the society; or, in the case of societies
governed by statute, such as friendly societies, by the terms of the
statute governing them. The Friendly Societies Act 1974, s.54(1)
provides that the property of an unincorporated friendly society shall
vest in the trustees for the time being of the society, for the use and
benefit of the society and the members thereof.[88] It was at one time
thought that there was no need to identify the beneficiaries of
property held by unincorporated associations; and that a gift to
persons holding the property as trustees was good so long as the
trustees had power to spend the capital. A society could then dispose
of any of its assets at any time; there would be no more tendency to
inalienability than in the case of an individual holding property, and,
it was argued, no reason for invalidating it. Thus, in *Re Drummond*,[89] a gift was made to the Old Bradfordians Club, London, to
be utilised as the committee should think best in the interests of the
club or school. Eve J. upheld the gift. It was not, he said, a gift to
the members, but the committee was free to spend the money as it
thought fit on the specified objects. It did not tend to a perpetuity,
and was valid.

If the trustees could spend only the income however—if, in other
words, the capital was tied up as an endowment—the trusts on
which the assets were held would be perpetual and void. This view,
which appeared to have been approved by the House of Lords,[90]
dealt, however, only with the perpetuity aspect of the problem. It
ignored the necessity to analyse the property interests which were
created.

---

[87] *Re Lipinski's Will Trusts* [1976] Ch. 235, *ante*, p. 349.
[88] See *Re Bucks Constabulary Fund (No. 2)* [1979] 1 W.L.R. 937. The Friendly Societies Act
1992 provides for the incorporation of such societies carrying on mutual insurance business.
[89] [1914] 2 Ch. 90; *Re Price* [1943] Ch. 422 ("To the Anthroposophical Society of Great
Britain to be used at the discretion of the Chairman and Executive Council of the Society
for carrying out the teaching of the founder Dr. Rudolf Steiner."); (1937) 53 L.Q.R. 24 at
p. 46 (W. Hart).
[90] *Macaulay v. O'Donnell*, July 10, 1933; reported at [1943] Ch. 435n.; *Carne v. Long* (1860)
2 De G.F. & J. 75.

In *Leahy v. Att.-Gen. for New South Wales*,[91] a testator provided that Elmslea, a sheep station of some 730 acres, should be held upon trust for "such order of nuns of the Catholic Church or the Christian Brothers as my executors and trustees shall select." The gift was not valid as a charitable trust because some of the orders were purely contemplative orders which are not charitable in law.[92]

Nor was it valid as a private trust. In view of the nature of the property and the fact that the members of the selected orders might be very numerous and spread across the world, there was no intention to create a trust in favour of the individual members of selected orders.[93] The testator's intention clearly was to establish an endowment. The gift would have failed if it had not been rescued by a statute of New South Wales which permitted partly charitable trusts to be applied wholly in favour of those parts which were charitable. The trustees' power of selection did not therefore extend to contemplative orders.

Other modern cases, however, have shown a "retreat from *Leahy*"[94] and have found a different construction, enabling the gift to be held valid as being a trust for the members of the association.[95] This has even proved possible, applying the principle of *Re Denley's Trust Deed*,[96] where the donor has stated that his gift is to be applied for specific non-charitable purposes.[97] The position was analysed in *Neville Estates v. Madden*,[98] where Cross J. held that the property interests of the members of an association would fall into one of three categories. There might be a gift to the members at the relevant date as joint tenants, giving each a right of severance of his part; or a gift subject to the contractual rights and liabilities of the members towards each other, which prevent severance and cause a member's interest, on his death or resignation, to accrue to the remaining members; or a gift to present and future members, in which case the gift, unless confined to the perpetuity period, would be void. A fourth possibility is that this situation creates a specialised form of

---

[91] [1959] A.C. 457.
[92] *Gilmour v. Coats* [1949] A.C. 426; *post*, p. 417.
[93] [1959] A.C. 457 at p. 486; *cf. Re Smith* [1914] 1 Ch. 937, where a bequest to the Society of Franciscan Friars of Clevedon County, Somerset was construed as a gift to the members of the community at the date of the testator's death; *Cocks v. Manners* (1871) L.R. 12 Eq. 574 (a share of residue to the "Dominican Convent of Carisbrooke payable to the Superior for the time being").
[94] (1977) 41 Conv.(N.S.) 139 (F. Crane).
[95] (1977) 41 Conv.(N.S.) 179 (K. Widdows); (1980) 39 C.L.J. 88 (C. Rickett); [1985] Conv. 318 (J. Warburton).
[96] [1969] 1 Ch. 373, *ante*, p. 349. This did not involve an unincorporated association, but the reasoning is applicable to gifts to such associations.
[97] *Re Lipinski's Will Trusts* [1976] Ch. 235, *ante*, p. 349.
[98] [1962] Ch. 832 at p. 849; *Re Recher's W.T.* [1972] Ch. 526 at p. 538, *post*, p. 363.

co-ownership, whose rules should be worked out separately, and independently of the law of trusts.[99] All these possible solutions fail to explain how the equitable interest of a member passes on his resignation without compliance with Law of Property Act 1925, s.53(1)(c).[1]

Gifts to unincorporated associations can involve perpetuity problems of two distinct kinds, relating to remoteness of vesting and perpetual duration. To avoid both problems, the trust must be for the benefit of members who are both ascertainable during the perpetuity period and also able to claim a division of the funds before that period expires. If the members are not so ascertainable, the trust will fail, subject to what is said below, for remoteness of vesting. If the capital is to be retained as an endowment, the trust will be void as a perpetual trust.[2]

Cross J. in *Neville Estates v. Madden*[3] referred to the problem of remoteness of vesting in his third category (gift to present and future members). This problem has been resolved by the Perpetuities and Accumulations Act 1964, which excludes from the gift any members not ascertainable within the perpetuity period.[4] The 1964 Act does not remove the problem of perpetual duration (inalienability). The gift will fail if "there is something in its terms or circumstances or in the rules of the association which precludes the members at any time from dividing the subject of the gift between them on the footing that they are solely entitled in equity".[5] This aspect of the perpetuity rule caused the gift to fail in *Re Grant's Will Trusts*.[6] The trust was for the purposes of the Chertsey Labour Party Headquarters, which were not charitable. The members of this local association did not control the property, nor could they change the rules of the association and thereby gain control, because the rules were subject to the approval of, and capable of alteration by, an outside body (the National Executive Committee). Although it seems that a way around this problem could have been found,[7] the

---

[99] Ford, *Unincorporated Non-Profit Associations*, Part 1, especially at pp. 5–8, 21–23.

[1] Morris and Leach, pp. 313–318; [1971] A.S.C.L. p. 379 (J. Hackney). The *Re Denley* approach (*ante*, p. 349), whereby the beneficiary has no proprietary interest, does not encounter these difficulties.

[2] *Carne v. Long* (1860) 2 De G.F. & J. 75.

[3] *Supra.*

[4] s.4(4). The Act applies to dispositions made after July 15, 1964.

[5] *Re Lipinski's Will Trusts*, *supra*, at p. 244, quoting the summary of Cross J.'s categories in *Tudor on Charities* (6th ed., 1967), p. 150.

[6] [1980] 1 W.L.R. 360; (1980) 43 M.L.R. 459 (B. Green); [1980] Conv. 80 (G. Shindler).

[7] See Heydon, Gummow and Austin, *Cases and Materials on Equity and Trusts* (4th ed.), p. 595, suggesting that control by the outside body was not as significant as the case suggests. The beneficiaries could be treated as including the members of that body also. Another possibility is that the members could disaffiliate from the national body. See also *News Group Newspapers Ltd v. SOGAT 82* [1986] I.C.R. 716, where *Re Grant* was distinguished because the members of a local branch of a trade union had control over the branch assets and could in theory secede from the union and divide the assets.

trust was held void for perpetuity, even though the restriction on disposing of the capital was not one imposed by the testator.

D. Ownership by Members on Contractual Basis

The contractual analysis provides a method by which unincorporated associations can validly hold property without the necessity of discovering an intention to create a trust, and by which gifts to the association, in order to escape invalidity as purpose trusts, need not be regarded as taking effect as immediate distributive shares in favour of the members, which is unlikely to have been the donor's intention. Members of an association can "band themselves together as an association or society, pay subscriptions and validly devote their funds in pursuit of some lawful non-charitable purpose. An obvious example is a members' social club"[8]—where it would in most cases be difficult to find an intention to create a trust. Their assets, whether donations or members' subscriptions, are held by the trustees or by the committee or officers of the club on the terms of the constitution or rules of the club, which are themselves a contract among the members *inter se*. A trust is interposed simply because it is normally inconvenient (and impossible in the case of land) for the assets to be vested in all the members. This is a bare trust and does not detract from the contractual analysis.

This solution avoids some of the difficulties which arise from an analysis which regards the members as beneficiaries under a private trust. The members' rights are contractual, and of course they depend upon the rules of the association. A member will not usually be able to claim his share at any time; but the members as a whole control the committee's activities in accordance with the rules, and can usually take the decision to wind up the association and share out the proceeds. A member's rights terminate on death or resignation, and a new member obtains rights in relation to the assets during his period of membership. Questions concerning the contractual rights of members usually arise on the termination of an association, as we have seen.[9]

The fact that the assets are held by the members on a contractual basis of course does not prejudge the construction of a gift by a third party to the association. But the court will lean in favour of validity, and is likely to regard such a gift as an accretion to the funds of the association. In *Re Recher's Will Trust*[10] there was a gift in trust for "The London and Provincial Anti-Vivisection Society." Brightman

---

[8] *Re Recher's W.T.* [1972] Ch. 526 at p. 538, *per* Brightman J.

[9] *Ante*, p. 235.

[10] [1972] Ch. 526; (1972) 35 Conv.(N.S.) 381; (1971) 8 M.U.L.R. 1 (P. Hogg); (1973) 47 A.L.J. 305. The "accretion to funds" solution is adopted by the Queensland Succession Act 1981, s.63.

J. held that the assets of the society were owned by the members in accordance with the rules. "There is no private trust or trust for charitable purposes or other trust to hinder the process."[11] If it was correct that a gift to such an association must be construed as a (void) purpose trust or as distributive shares in favour of the members, then it would be difficult to make a donation in favour of the body, which would contrary to common sense. The solution was that the gift could be construed as a beneficial gift in favour of the members, not so as to entitle them to an immediate distributive share, but as an accretion to the funds of the society subject to the contract of the members as set out in the rules. Such a construction was equally available whether the society existed to promote the interest of its members ("inward-looking") or, as in the present case, to promote some outside purpose ("outward-looking"). If the society had remained in existence, the gift would have been good. In fact, however, it had been dissolved before the date of the gift.

As has been pointed out,[12] the question whether a gift to an association is subject to any restriction on its use depends on the intention of the members as expressed in their contract with each other. Thus whether the gift is one to the members in severable shares or subject to the purposes of the association normally depends not on the donor's intention but on the rules of the association. To be valid, any restrictions imposed by the donor must infringe neither the beneficiary principle nor the perpetuity rule.[13]

6. MANDATE OR AGENCY

The principles described above apply to unincorporated associations, which have already been defined.[14] It may be that an organisation (which is not incorporated) fails to satisfy the requirements of an unincorporated association. This was the case in *Conservative and Unionist Central Office v. Burrell (Inspector of Taxes)*,[15] where the Crown claimed that the Conservative Party was an unincorporated association. If this were so, Central Office would be assessable to corporation tax, as opposed to income tax, on certain income. The Court of Appeal rejected the Crown's claim. The Party was an amorphous combination of various elements, but not an unincorporated association, because the members had no mutual rights and obligations, there were no rules governing control (which lay in the

---

[11] *Ibid.* at p. 539; *Re Bucks Constabulary Fund (No. 2)* [1979] 1 W.L.R. 937.
[12] [1995] Conv. 302 (P. Matthews).
[13] See *Re Lipinski's Will Trusts* [1976] Ch. 235.
[14] *Ante*, p. 359.
[15] [1982] 1 W.L.R. 522. See generally [1987] Conv. 415 (P. Smart).

party leader), and no event in history could be identified as marking the creation of the party as an association.[16]

Of interest in the present context was the analysis of the legal effect of a contribution to such a body. Where the body was not an unincorporated association, the *Re Recher*[17] analysis could not apply. The legal basis was mandate or agency. The contributor gives the recipient (*e.g.* the treasurer) a mandate to use the gift in a particular way. He can demand its return unless the mandate becomes irrevocable, as when the gift is added to a mixed fund with the authority of the contributor. There is no trust, only the fiduciary element inherent in the relationship of principal and agent. Once the mandate has become irrevocable, the contributor's rights are to an account of expenditure, and to restrain a misapplication. Difficulties might arise where there was a change of the office-holder to whom the mandate was given. More seriously, the mandate theory could not explain the validity of bequests to such organisations, as agency cannot be set up at death. No solution to this problem was offered, the Court of Appeal being content to suggest that the answer was "not difficult to find."[18]

It remains to be seen whether the mandate theory will be applied in other situations.[19] In view of its limitations, especially with regard to testamentary gifts, this is perhaps doubtful.

7. PERPETUITY

A. Excessive Duration[20]

It has been said that a non-charitable purpose trust, even though otherwise valid, is void if it may last beyond the period of perpetuity; this being a rule designed to produce an effect analogous to the rule controlling remoteness of vesting, and applying the same general policy. If, therefore, a purpose trust survives an attack under the beneficiary principle, it must be restricted to the period of perpetuity.

---

[16] Convincingly criticised in [1983] Conv. 150 (P. Creighton); "It may be as misleading to deny the organisation its status as an unincorporated association because its origins are obscure as it would be to deny the existence of a living human being on the ground that his birth certificate could not be found."

[17] *Ante*, p. 363.

[18] Perhaps referring to the principle of *Re Denley's Deed Trust* [1969] 1 Ch. 373, *ante*, p. 349, or to the fact that the testator may authorise his executors to give a mandate. See also [1983] Conv. 150 (P. Creighton); [1987] Conv. 415 (P. Smart).

[19] It was referred to in connection with members' subscriptions in *Re Recher's Will Trusts* [1972] Ch. 526 at p. 539. The reasoning might apply to cases such as *Re Gillingham Bus Disaster Fund* [1959] Ch. 62, *ante*, p. 233, involving public donations to non-charitable purposes.

[20] Morris and Leach, pp. 321–327; Maudsley, *The Modern Law of Perpetuities*, pp. 166–178.

In applying the rule against excessive duration, the courts have been more generous than in other aspects of perpetuity law. First, they have assumed that a monument will be erected within the period.

In *Mussett v. Bingle*,[21] a testator gave £300 to be applied in the erection of a monument to his wife's first husband, and £200 the interest on which was to be applied in maintaining it. The latter gift was perpetual and void. The former was upheld. In the absence of any objection on the ground of perpetuity, the court must have assumed that the monument would be erected within the period.

Secondly a trust will be upheld if the instrument provides that it is to continue "so long as the law allows" or some similar period. The gift is good for 21 years.[22] If no such saving phrase is included, the trust is wholly void.[23] The court will not supply the necessary words to meet the testator's obvious intention. The wait and see principle does not apply to purpose trusts.[24] If it did, it would at least have solved this problem.

Thirdly, the courts have on various occasions taken judicial notice of the fact that an animal's life span is limited to 21 years. If the animal could not live that long, the trust could not endure beyond the period. Danckwerts J. in *Re Haines*[25] took judicial notice of the fact that a cat could not live for more than 21 years. Biologists have corrected him, showing that a cat may live for 25 years.[26] It seems that, if the courts are willing to take judicial notice of longevity, it should be permissible to take evidence of the age of the cats in question; for if the youngest cat is over four, the particular trust would not last for more than 21 years.

B. Human Lives Only

Perhaps North J. in *Re Dean*[27] should be taken to have applied some such doctrine. He upheld a gift of an annual sum for the period of 50 years if any of the testator's horses and hounds should so long live. The perpetuity point was not dealt with, and it seems almost as

---

[21] [1876] W.N. 170.

[22] *Pirbright v. Salwey* [1896] W.N. 86; *Re Hooper* [1932] 1 Ch. 38.

[23] *Contra, Re Budge* [1942] N.Z.L.R. 356, where a trust to apply the income in keeping a grave neat and tidy was held valid for 21 years. Morris and Leach, p. 322.

[24] s.15(4); *post*, p. 368; *cf.* New Zealand Perpetuities Act 1964; Maudsley, *The Modern Law of Perpetuities*, App. D.

[25] *The Times*, November 7, 1952.

[26] See Comfort: *The Biology of Senescence*; Morris and Leach, p. 323; Maudsley, *op. cit.* p. 170.

[27] (1889) 41 Ch.D. 552.

if the learned judge assumed that the life of an animal could be used as a measuring life for the purposes of the rule. The better doctrine however was provided by Meredith J. in *Re Kelly*[28]:

"If the lives of dogs or other animals could be taken into account in reckoning the maximum period of 'lives in being and twenty-one years afterwards' any contingent or executory interest might be properly limited, so as only to vest within the lives of specified carp, or tortoises, or other animals that might live for over a hundred years, and for twenty-one years afterwards, which, of course, is absurd. 'Lives' means human lives. It was suggested that the last of the dogs could in fact not outlive the testator by more than twenty-one years. I know nothing of that. The court does not enter into the question of a dog's expectation of life. In point of fact neighbours' dogs and cats are unpleasantly long-lived; but I have no knowledge of their precise expectation of life. Anyway the maximum period is exceeded by the lives of specified butterflies and twenty-one years afterwards. And even, according to my decision—and, I confess, it displays this weakness on being pressed to a logical conclusion—the expiration of the life of a single butterfly, even without the twenty-one years, would be too remote, despite all the world of poetry that may be thereby destroyed . . . there can be no doubt that 'lives' means lives of human beings, not of animals or trees in California."

Re Dean[29] is unsupportable on this point. All other purpose trusts which may last beyond the period of perpetuity have been held void.

C. A Fixed Number of Years

As we are dealing here with a question of duration and not one of remoteness of vesting of beneficial interests, it would be much more convenient to have a perpetuity period which was gauged by a number of years, rather than one measured by lives. It is possible to argue that a court should hold that purpose trusts can last for 21 years only; for no purpose trust, with the exception of *Re Howard*,[30] when a parrot was to be fed during the lives of the survivor of two servants, has been upheld for any other or longer period. Yet a royal lives clause was not challenged in *Re Astor's Trusts*.[31] In *Re Moore*,[32] the objection was to the excessive number of lives chosen and not to the fact that lives were chosen, and in *Re Khoo Cheng*

---

[28] [1932] I.R. 255 at pp. 260–261.
[29] (1889) 41 Ch.D. 552.
[30] *The Times*, October 30, 1908.
[31] [1952] Ch. 534.
[32] [1901] 1 Ch. 936.

Teow,[33] the Supreme Court of the Straits Settlements has upheld a non-charitable purpose trust for the period of royal lives plus 21 years.

It was reasonable therefore to hope that the Perpetuities and Accumulations Act 1964 would provide for a fixed period of years. A restriction to a period of 21 years would have been welcome. The 80-year period would have been an improvement.[34] In fact the Act has left the period at lives plus 21 years.

Section 15(4) provides:

> "Nothing in this Act shall affect the operation of the rule of law rendering void for remoteness certain dispositions under which property is limited to be applied for purposes other than the benefit of any person or class of persons in cases where the property may be so applied after the end of the perpetuity period."

Although the contrary is not unarguable,[35] it appears that the effect of this provision is that neither the 80-year period permitted by section 1 of the Act nor the "wait and see" rule of section 3 applies to purposes trusts.

8. USELESS OR CAPRICIOUS PURPOSES

One question which has to be faced when considering whether, as a matter of policy, purpose trusts should be enforced is that of excluding trusts which are useless, wasteful, capricious, or even harmful or illegal. This aspect of the matter was in the mind of Roxburgh J. in *Re Astor's Trusts* when he said[36]: " . . . it is not possible to contemplate with equanimity the creation of large funds directed to non-charitable purposes which no court and no department of state can control, or in the case of maladministration reform." The question ultimately is that of the extent to which one person, usually deceased, should be allowed to deprive the community or individuals within it, of the beneficial use of capital.[37] The larger the amount, and the longer the period of application, the greater the problem. No attempt has been made to draw a precise line between those which are acceptable and those which are not. We will see that the greatest difficulty has been experienced in trying to draw a line

---

[33] [1932] Straits Settlements Report 226.

[34] See Trusts (Guernsey) Law 1989 (100 years); Belize Trusts Act 1992 (120 years).

[35] See Maudsley, *The Modern Law of Perpetuities*, p. 177; (1965) 29 Conv.(N.S.) 165 (J. Andrews). For the view that s.15(4) does not apply to purpose trusts within the principle of *Re Denley's Trust Deed* [1969] 1 Ch. 373, see Underhill (15th ed.), p. 94; *Trends in Contemporary Trust Law* (ed. A. Oakley), pp. 12, 18 (P. Matthews).

[36] [1952] Ch. at p. 542.

[37] See Gardner, *An Introduction to the Law of Trusts*, pp. 210–211.

between charitable and other trusts.[38] This does not augur well for the creation of a recognisable line between acceptable and non-acceptable non-charitable purpose trusts; but it is no reason for insisting on holding all non-charitable purpose trusts void. "The answer, of course, is that the courts will have to strike down the silly purposes and uphold the sensible ones."[39]

In *Brown v. Burdett*,[40] the testator devised a freehold house to trustees upon trust to block up almost all the rooms of the house for a period of 20 years, and, subject thereto, to a devisee. Bacon V.-C. decided that he must "unseal" this "useless, undisposed of property," and declared that there was an intestacy as to the period of 20 years.

Scottish judges have been forthright in their disapproval of the waste of money on useless projects. "I consider that, if it is not unlawful, it ought to be unlawful, to dedicate by testamentary disposition, for all time, or for a length of time, the whole income of a large estate . . . to objects of no utility, private or public, objects which benefit nobody, and which have no other purpose or use than that of perpetuating at great cost, and in an absurd manner, the idiosyncrasies of an eccentric testator."[41] "The prospect of Scotland being dotted with monuments to obscure persons cumbered with trusts for the purpose of maintaining these monuments in all time coming, appears to me to be little less than appalling. . . . "[42]

9. ALTERNATIVE SOLUTIONS

It seems therefore that non-charitable purpose trusts are void under the beneficiary principle; that there are recognised exceptions in trusts for animals and monuments, which, to be valid, must be certain, not useless or capricious, and confined to the period of perpetuity; and that a trust may be upheld if, although expressed as a purpose trust, it is directly for the benefit of ascertainable individuals. Some take the view that this is too restricted a position. We

---

[38] *Post*, Chap. 15.
[39] (1959) 4 U. of W.A.L.R. at p. 239 (L. Sheridan).
[40] (1882) 21 Ch.D. 667; see also *McCaig v. University of Glasgow*, 1907 S.C. 231; *McCaig's Trustees v. Kirk-Session of United Free Church of Lismore*, 1915 S.C. 426 (bronze statues at £1,000 each); *Aitken v. Aitken*, 1927 S.C. 374 (massive bronze equestrian statue); *Mackintosh's Judicial Factor v. Lord Advocate*, 1935 S.C. 406 (erection of vault); *Lindsay's Executor v. Forsyth*, 1940 S.C. 568 (£1,000 on trust to provide a weekly supply of fresh flowers on the graves of my mother and my own).
[41] *McCaig v. University of Glasgow, supra*, at p. 242.
[42] *McCaig's Trustees v. Kirk-Session of United Free Church of Lismore, supra*, at p. 434.

now consider in what ways the effecting of a non-charitable purpose can be achieved.

A. By the Draftsman

i. Incorporation. A society may be incorporated to advance such purposes. The matter then leaves the law of trusts, and the problem here discussed disappears. This is the simplest practical solution.[43]

ii. Mandate or Agency. Consideration should also be given to the possibility of utilising the mandate or agency theory expounded in *Conservative and Unionist Central Office v. Burrell (Inspector of Taxes)*,[44] discussed in section 6, above. The principle could also be invoked in the case of gifts to unincorporated associations, although it is doubtful whether it has much to offer here, not least because it cannot be the basis of a testamentary gift.[45] Where this principle can be utilised, the matter then leaves the law of trusts, as in the case of incorporation. The problem of purpose trusts disappears, but other problems, as we have seen, take its place.

iii. Gift to Members of an Association and Not for Purposes Only. In *Re Lipinski's Will Trusts*,[46] Oliver J. emphasised the distinction between "the case where a purpose is prescribed which is clearly intended for the benefit of ascertained or ascertainable beneficiaries . . . and the case where no beneficiary at all is intended . . . or where the beneficiaries are unascertainable." This distinction is crucial. A gift to provide recreational facilities may be a gift for beneficiaries if those persons are intended to be benefited[47]; and similarly a gift to an association where it is construed as a gift for the members as an accretion to their funds.[48] The problem of construction was substantial in the cases discussed; but there is no need for any difficulty to arise if the draftsman is aware of the possibilities and the difficulties and drafts the gift accordingly.

iv. Conveyancing Devices. A gift over from one charity to another may validly take place at any time in the future; the rule against perpetuities does not apply.[49] Advantage was taken of this rule in *Re Tyler*,[50] to achieve a non-charitable purpose.

---

[43] Report of the Goodman Committee on Charity Law and Voluntary Organisations, p. 24.
[44] [1982] 1 W.L.R. 522.
[45] *Ante*, p. 365.
[46] [1976] Ch. 235, at p. 246.
[47] *Re Denley's Trust Deed* [1969] 1 Ch. 373.
[48] *Re Recher's W.T.* [1972] Ch. 526; *Re Lipinski's W.T.* [1976] Ch. 235.
[49] *Christ's Hospital (Governors) v. Grainger* (1849) 1 Mac & G. 460.
[50] [1891] 3 Ch. 252.

A gift was made to the London Missionary Society, committing to their care the family vault, and if they failed to comply with the request the money was to go to the Bluecoat School. The gift was upheld. It could last perpetually if the value of the gift was sufficient to encourage the London Missionary Society to perform the task. If the task became unprofitable, as no doubt it would do by the progress of inflation, the gift over would take effect. The Bluecoat School would be under no obligation to perform the task. Indeed, if an attempt was made to impose an obligation on either donee by requiring any part of the income to be applied for the non-charitable purpose, the gift would have been void as not exclusively charitable.[51]

A similar result could have been produced before 1964, even without making the gift in favour of charity. In *Re Chardon*,[52] a gift of income was made to a cemetery company so long as it maintained a grave. This was held valid because the perpetuity rule did not apply to the termination of such interests. Under the Perpetuities and Accumulations Act 1964, the interest would become absolute unless terminated within the perpetuity period.[53] It is still possible however to frame a limitation on these lines which will secure the maintenance of a grave for the perpetuity period.

v. Draft as a Power; not as a Trust. The beneficiary principle applies to trusts. There must be someone who can enforce the trust. With a power, there is no question of enforcement; although questions of certainty and perpetuity arise. Assuming however that these are overcome, could not the purpose be achieved by giving the property, not to a trustee upon trust, but to the ultimate beneficiary subject to a power in a third party to apply the property for the stated purpose for the perpetuity period?

There is little authority on the validity of such a power. Clearly, a power can be something other than a general or special power to appoint to persons.[54] It may be, then, that a power to apply the income for the improvement of land,[55] or for research into the advantages of the 40-letter alphabet,[56] could, if limited to the period of perpetuity, be valid. It seems that the same rule should apply to repairing monuments, feeding animals, or providing a cup for a

---

[51] *Re Dalziel* [1943] Ch. 277. See further [1987] Conv. 415 (P. Smart).
[52] [1928] Ch. 464.
[53] s.12.
[54] See *Re Douglas* (1887) 35 Ch.D. 472; (1902) 15 H.L.R. 67 (J. Gray); (1959) 4 U. of W.A.L.R. at p. 260 (L. Sheridan). See also *Re Clarke* [1923] 2 Ch. 407, where a power to appoint to *uncertain* non-charitable objects failed.
[55] *Re Aberconway's S.T.* [1953] Ch. 647.
[56] *Re Shaw* [1957] 1 W.L.R. 729.

yacht race. The person entitled in default could restrain misapplication.

There seems to be nothing contrary to policy in allowing the purpose to be effected in this way. Policy questions will arise, of course, where an eccentric testator provides for large sums to be applied for useless, capricious or harmful purposes for a substantial period.[57] The problem here is the same as that discussed in section 8 above.

Arguments have been put forward to the effect that an instrument which purports to create a purpose trust should be construed as a power so as to allow the purpose to be carried out.[58] Supporters of this view argued that this is a way of achieving the testator's or settlor's intention without conflicting with any rules of policy. In *Re Shaw*,[59] Harman J. appeared to find some attraction in the argument; but he rejected it, following what Jenkins L.J. had said in *Commissioners of Inland Revenue v. Broadway Cottages Trust*[60]; "We do not think that a valid power is to be spelt out of an invalid trust."

B. By the Legislature

If reform is to come, it will come best from the Legislature. The basic question is whether gifts for non-charitable purposes should be upheld. If so, it is necessary to find a means of overcoming the beneficiary principle, and this would most conveniently be done by enacting that trusts for non-charitable purposes should be construed as powers.[61] The purpose could then be carried out by the trustees if they elected to do so. If they did not, the purpose would fail and the property would go to those entitled in default. The power would be valid only if it was sufficiently certain. It may be thought best to limit such trusts to a period of 21 years,[62] or require them to be restricted to the common law perpetuity rule, or a longer specified period such as 80 years.[63] The danger of maladministration would be no greater than that already encountered in the case of the permitted purpose trusts discussed in section 3 above. Purpose trusts are now permitted by statute in many jurisdictions to facilitate estate planning and asset protection schemes, by exploiting the point that

---

[57] See Morris and Leach (2nd ed.), p. 320.
[58] (1949) 13 Conv.(N.S.) 418 at p. 424 (D. Potter); (1950) 14 Conv.(N.S.) 374 (A. Kiralfy); (1959) 4 U. of W.A.L.R. at pp. 240–244 (L. Sheridan); (1953) 17 Conv.(N.S.) 46 at p. 59.
[59] [1957] 1 W.L.R. 729 at p. 746.
[60] [1955] Ch. 20 at p. 36.
[61] See Ontario Perpetuities Act 1966.
[62] New Zealand Perpetuities Act 1964, s.20.
[63] Maudsley, *The Modern Law of Perpetuities*, App. D.

neither the settlor nor any other person is the beneficial owner of the property.[64]

To the statutory solution, it may be objected that it does not answer the anxiety expressed by Roxburgh J. in *Re Astor's Settlement Trusts*[65] that it was not in the general interest that large sums of money should be applied for non-charitable purposes for long periods of time. The period of perpetuity can be about 100 years, and non-charitable purposes include all those which at one end are nearly charitable and those which are so useless as to be capricious. In validating gifts for purposes, it is important to ensure that funds are made available for purposes which are useful to the public rather than for the satisfaction of the private interests of a settlor or testator. Resources are scarce, and need to be put to good use. The problem is one which exists also in the case of gifts which are drafted in the form of powers. No doubt, the amount of money involved, and the duration of the trust will be factors which will be relevant to a decision. The line is difficult to draw. But capricious trusts are the rare ones. The fact that they exist is no reason for failing to establish a rational method of validating the useful ones.

---

[64] See *Trends in Contemporary Trust Law* (ed. A. Oakley), Chap. 1 (P. Matthews). The Belize Trusts Act 1992 permits purpose trusts, which are enforceable by the "protector" of the settlement (s.15) and can last for up to 120 years (s.6). See also (1997) 1 Jersey Law Review 6 (P. Matthews), examining the Trusts (Amendment No. 3) (Jersey) Law 1996 (purpose trust with an "enforcer" permitted for 100 years).

[65] [1952] Ch. 534.

CHARITABLE TRUSTS

1. Introduction	376	
2. Advantages Enjoyed by Charitable Trusts	378	
A. Purpose Trusts	378	
B. Objects Need not be Certain	379	
C. May be Perpetual	380	
D. Fiscal Advantages	381	
3. The Definition of Charity	383	
A. The Four Categories	383	
i. Lord Macnaghten's Classification	383	
ii. Public Benefit	384	
iii. Exclusively Charitable	384	
iv. Charitable Purpose Overseas	384	
B. The Relief of Poverty	386	
i. Meaning of Poverty	386	
ii. Illustrations	386	
C. The Advancement of Education	388	
i. Meaning of Education	388	
ii. Research	389	
iii. Artistic and Aesthetic Education	390	
iv. Subjective Evaluation	391	
v. Youth. Sports at School and University	391	
vi. Professional Bodies	392	
vii. Political Propaganda Masquerading as Education	393	
viii. Private and Independent Schools	394	
D. The Advancement of Religion	395	
i. What is Religion?	395	
ii. Religious Toleration Within Christianity	395	
iii. Non-Christian Religions	396	
iv. Related Purposes	397	
E. Other Purposes Beneficial to the Community	398	
i. The Spirit and Intendment of the Preamble	398	
ii. The Test is What the Law Treats as Charitable	400	
iii. Examples of Trusts under the Fourth Head	401	
(a) Specific Mention in the Preamble. Age and Sickness	401	
(b) Social, Recreational and Sporting Trusts	402	
(c) Animals	406	

(d) Political Trusts	407	
(e) Miscellaneous	410	
4. Public Benefit	411	
A. Preliminary Points	411	
B. Trusts for the Relief of Poverty	412	
i. A Class of Poor as Opposed to Selected Individuals. Poor Relations	412	
ii. Poor Employees	412	
C. Trusts for the Advancement of Education	413	
i. Benefits to the Public or a Section thereof	413	
ii. Personal Nexus	414	
iii. Benefiting Private Individuals	416	
D. Trusts for the Advancement of Religion	417	
E. The Fourth Head	419	
5. The Interpretation of Charitable Gifts and Purposes	421	
A. The Motive of the Donor	422	
B. The Locality Cases	422	
C. The Charitable Status of the Trustee	423	
D. The Objects Must be Exclusively Charitable	423	
i. Main and Subsidiary Objects	423	
ii. And/Or Cases	425	
(a) Cases of "or"	425	
(b) Cases of "and"	425	
iii. Severance	426	
iv. Charitable Trusts (Validation) Act 1954	427	
E. Disaster Appeals	429	
6. Cy-Près	430	
A. The Cy-Près Doctrine Prior to 1960	430	
B. Initial Failure, Paramount Charitable Intent	431	
i. Width of Charitable Intent	431	
ii. Has the Gift Failed? Continuation in Another Form	432	
(a) Gift in Augmentation of Funds of Defunct Charity	433	
(b) Gift for Purposes. Unincorporated Associations and Charitable Corporations	433	
iii. Projects	435	
iv. Non-Existent Charity	435	

v. A Group of Donees; Mostly
     Charitable 436
C. Subsequent Failure 436
D. Termination in Favour of Non-
     Charity 438
E. The Widening of Cy-Près Jurisdiction,
     Charities Act 1993, s.13 439
     i. General 439
     ii. Section 13 439
     iii. Section 14. Charity Collections .. 442
F. Small Charities 443
7. The Administration of Charities 444
A. Reform 444
B. The Authorities 444
     i. The Charity Commissioners 444
     ii. The Official Custodian for
          Charities 445
     iii. The Visitor 445
C. The Register 446
D. Decisions on Registration 447
E. Advice 447

F. Powers of the Charity Commissioners 448
     i. Schemes 448
     ii. Consent to Proceedings 448
     iii. Dealings with Charity Property .. 448
     iv. Accounts; Inquiries 449
G. Investment 450
     i. Investment Powers 450
     ii. Pooling, C.O.I.F. Common De-
          posit Scheme 450
H. Trustees 451
     i. Capacity 451
     ii. Number, Majority Vote 451
     iii. Retirement 451
     iv. Removal and Suspension 451
     v. Supply of Goods and Services by
          Trustees 452
     vi. Misapplication 452
I. *Ex Gratia* Payments 452
J. Co-operation Between Charities and
     Statutory Services 453

I. INTRODUCTION[1]

CHARITABLE purposes are those which are considered to be of such value and importance to the community that they receive especially favourable treatment. These purposes are the relief of poverty, the advancement of education and religion, and other purposes beneficial to the community. Such a list is vague and old-fashioned. That is because the scope of charity originates in the Preamble to the Charitable Uses Act of 1601, an Act which was passed for the purpose of remedying abuses which had grown up in the administration of charitable trusts. The Preamble contained a general catalogue of the purposes then regarded as charitable. Since that time, purposes which are regarded as being within the "spirit and intendment"[2] or "within the equity"[3] of the statute have been accepted as being charitable. In 1891, Lord Macnaghten summarised these purposes into four categories given above.[4] In 1952, the Nathan Committee[5] recommended that a new statutory definition of charity

---

[1] See generally *Tudor on Charities* (8th ed., 1995); Sheridan and Keeton, *The Modern Law of Charities* (4th ed., 1992); Picarda, *The Law and Practice Relating to Charities* (2nd ed., 1995); Chesterman, *Charities, Trusts and Social Welfare* (1979). See also the Annual Reports and Decisions of the Charity Commissioners. For important reviews of the law and practice, see the Goodman Committee Report on Charity Law and Voluntary Organisations (1976); The Wolfenden Committee Report on the Future of Voluntary Organisations; The Woodfield Report, Efficiency Scrutiny of the Supervision of Charities (1987).

[2] *Morice v. Bishop of Durham* (1805) 9 Ves. 399 at p. 405.

[3] See *Incorporated Council of Law Reporting v. Att.-Gen.* [1972] Ch. 73 at pp. 87–88.

[4] *Commissioners for Special Purposes of Income Tax v. Pemsel* [1891] A.C. 531.

[5] The Committee on the Law and Practice relating to Charitable Trusts (1952) Cmd. 8710, para. 140.

should be enacted, based on that classification. This recommendation was not implemented.[6] In spite of further recommendations from the Expenditure Committee of the House of Commons, the Government decided not to promote a legislative definition of charity.[7] A more recent report advocating the abolition of the concept of charity and concomitant tax relief and its replacement by a state-funded voluntary sector, was rejected by the Government.[8]

The Preamble was, however, repealed by the Charities Act 1960.[9] No definition replaced it. The matter is now governed by the case law, and current developments by the decisions of the Charity Commissioners on the question of the registration of Charities under the Charities Act 1993, s.3.[10]

We will see that charitable trusts are accorded a number of concessions over other trusts in terms of enforcement, perpetuity, certainty and taxation.[11] To earn these concessions, especially in relation to the growing significance of relief from taxation, a trust must be of a public nature; of benefit to the public, and not merely to private individuals. This is obvious in the fourth category. It exists also in connection with trusts for the advancement of religion and education, but only minimally in trusts for the relief of poverty. The policy in question behind most litigation concerning charitable trusts is an examination of whether the purposes are so useful to the public as to earn the concessions. This has to be carried out against a background of cases decided in earlier times when the condition of society was very different. In the days when the State made little or no provision for the poor and uneducated or for other general welfare purposes, and at a time when religious observance was unchallenged, trusts for these four categories were clearly for the public benefit. At the present time, however, many of the welfare and educational needs of society are provided from public sources.[12]

---

[6] The Report of the Commission on the Future of the Voluntary Sector (1996) recommends a statutory definition, but there is much to be said for retaining the flexibility which the present situation provides.

[7] House of Commons Report, Vol. I, paras. 24–34; Goodman Committee, para. 32, App. 1.

[8] *Voluntary Action*, published in 1993 by the Home Office on behalf of the CENTRIS research project.

[9] s.38.

[10] Replacing Charities Act 1960, s.4. The more significant decisions are discussed in the Annual Reports of the Charity Commissioners (referred to hereafter as *Annual Reports*) and, since 1993, in the Decisions of the Charity Commissioners.

[11] *Per* Lord Cross in *Dingle v. Turner* [1972] A.C. 601 at p. 624.

[12] The main categories of recent charitable trusts are for: (i) social welfare, *e.g.* for drug addicts, the consequences of the break-up of family life, counselling for young homosexuals, victim support schemes, care of AIDS sufferers, and the relief of youth unemployment; (ii) cultural purposes; (iii) conservation of the environment; (iv) religious cultural teachings of immigrant communities and the promotion of racial harmony. Annual Report 1978, para. 60; 1980, paras. 74–77; 1981, paras. 65–67; 1982, paras. 28–30; 1983, paras. 12–20; 1986, para. 35; 1987, para. 14; 1989, para. 29; 1991, paras. 73, 78.

Are these purposes so vital to present-day society that trusts for them should receive special encouragement by being permitted to exist as purpose trusts, for ever, supported by the court's *cy-près* power,[13] and tax free?[14] Judicial attitudes to gifts for charitable purposes have varied. In 1908, Lord Loreburn said "now there is no better rule than that a benignant construction will be placed upon charitable bequests."[15] But since the 1940s when taxation became higher the courts have been astute to restrict the scope of charity especially by emphasising the requirement of public benefit.[16] More recently, however, Lord Hailsham of St. Marylebone referred to Lord Loreburn's dictum and said: "In construing trust deeds the intention of which is to set up a charitable trust, and in others too, where it can be claimed that there is an ambiguity, a benignant construction should be given if possible."[17] In similar vein, the Government's intention is to encourage the liberality of the donor, and, within the present financial restraints, the development of the voluntary sector as a whole.[18] The policy changes which have been effected by changing social and economic conditions should be borne in mind when considering the cases relating to the definition of charity.

Harmonisation of non-profit making bodies in the European Union by the introduction of the "European Association", a new legal structure, has been proposed.[19] However, English charity law and the civil law of voluntary organisations are so different that little progress has been made.

2. ADVANTAGES ENJOYED BY CHARITABLE TRUSTS

A. Purpose Trusts

Charitable trusts are purpose trusts. But there is no need for human beneficiaries to enforce them, as there is in the case of non-

---

[13] *Post*, p. 430.

[14] (1956) 72 L.Q.R. 187 at p. 204 (G. Cross); (1977) 40 M.L.R. 397 (N. Gravells); *Scottish Burial Reform and Cremation Society v. Glasgow Corporation* [1968] A.C. 138 at p. 153; *Dingle v. Turner* [1972] A.C. 601 at p. 624.

[15] *Weir v. Crum-Brown* [1908] A.C. 162 at p. 167.

[16] The Royal Commission on the Taxation of Profits and Income (1955) Cmd. 9474, recommended (paras. 168–175) that some charitable trusts should be subject to tax liability. See also [1989] Conv. 28 (S. Bright).

[17] *I.R.C. v. McMullen* [1981] A.C. 1 at p. 14; *Re Koeppler's W.T.* [1986] Ch. 423; *Re Hetherington (deceased)* [1990] Ch. 1; *Guild v. I.R.C.* [1992] 2 A.C. 310. The "benignant" approach applies only where a disposition would otherwise be void; *I.R.C. v. Oldham Training and Enterprise Council* [1996] S.T.C. 1218.

[18] House of Commons, January 24, 1980. The Goodman Committee recommended increasing the fiscal privileges of charities; Chap. 5. Some of these recommendations have been implemented; F.A. 1982, s.129; I.H.T.A. 1984, s.29(5); I.C.T.A. 1988, ss.86, 339, 577, 660, 671. See too *Incorporated Council of Law Reporting v. Att.-Gen.* [1972] Ch. 73 at p. 88, *per* Russell L.J., p. 399, *post*.

[19] See Annual Report 1991, paras. 17–22; 1992, paras. 105–112; 1995, para. 108.

charitable purpose trusts.[20] Individuals who may benefit from a charitable trust have no *locus standi* to enforce them.[21] Charitable trusts are public trusts, and are enforced by the Attorney-General in the name of the Crown,[22] although the general administration of charitable trusts is overseen by the Charity Commissioners.[23] There must of course be an obligation upon the trustees; a mere power to apply to charitable purposes cannot be a trust.[24] It should be emphasised that this Chapter deals with charitable *trusts*. The legal position differs in many ways where the charity is incorporated.[25]

B. Objects Need Not be Certain

There is no requirement, as with other trusts, that the objects of the trust must be certain. Thus, a trust for "charitable purposes" will be valid. The court and the Charity Commissioners[26] have jurisdiction to establish a scheme for the application of the funds for specific charitable purposes. There must, of course, be no doubt that the objects of the trust are exclusively charitable, and the purpose expressed must not be so vague and uncertain that the court could not control the application of the assets.[27] The relaxation of the certainty rule is only in respect of the particular form of charitable purpose intended.[28]

Where no trust has been created, but only a general intention expressed that the property should go to charity, the court has no jurisdiction. In such a case the Crown disposes of the gifts by sign manual.[29] But the Crown acts on principles very similar to those by which the court is governed.

---

[20] *Ante*, Chap. 14.
[21] *Hauxwell v. Barton-on-Humber U.D.C.* [1974] Ch. 432; Charities Act 1993, s.33.
[22] See *Att.-Gen. v. Wright* [1988] 1 W.L.R. 164; *Att.-Gen. v. Cocke* [1988] Ch. 414. The Commissioners may exercise these powers with the consent of the Attorney-General; Charities Act 1993, s.32.
[23] Charities Act 1993, s.1.
[24] *Re Cohen* [1973] 1 W.L.R. 415, where a gift to trustees to apply "the whole or any part" of the fund "in such manner and at such time or times as my trustees shall in their absolute and uncontrolled discretion think fit," was held to create a trust.
[25] For the distinctions, see (1993–94) 2 *Charity Law and Practice Review* 133 (J. Hill). See also Charities Act 1993, s.96. 13,000 registered charities are companies; *The Times*, March 6, 1997.
[26] Charities Act 1993, s.16; *post*, p. 448.
[27] *Re Koeppler's Will Trusts* [1986] Ch. 423, where the formation of an informed international public opinion and the promotion of greater co-operation in Europe and the West were held too vague and uncertain to be charitable in themselves, but these aims did not destroy the charitable nature of the gift, which was to further the work of an educational project.
[28] See *Moggridge v. Thackwell* (1792) 1 Ves.Jr. 464; (1803) 7 Ves.Jr. 36; (1807) 13 Ves.Jr. 416.
[29] *Moggridge v. Thackwell, supra; Paice v. Archbishop of Canterbury* (1807) 14 Ves. 364 at p. 371; *Re Smith* [1932] 1 Ch. 53; *Re Bennett* [1960] Ch. 18; *Re Hetherington* [1990] Ch. 1.

C. May be Perpetual

Statements have often been made by judges to the effect that the Rule against Perpetuities does not apply to charities.[30] That is not so. With the exception of the rule in *Christ's Hospital v. Grainger*,[31] explained below, the rule governs the remoteness of vesting in the case of gifts to charities in the same way that it governs remoteness in the case of other gifts.[32]

Charitable trusts, however, may be perpetual. Indeed, the purpose of many charitable trusts could be said never to be capable of final achievement.[33] Many charitable trusts have existed for centuries. If a perpetual gift of income only is made to a charity, the charity cannot claim the capital, as an individual could do in such circumstances.[34] But where property is given absolutely to a charity with a direction to accumulate the income for a period of time, a charity may terminate the accumulation, and claim the principal forthwith.[35]

The exception to the rule regulating remoteness of vesting is that a gift over from one charity to *another charity* is not subject to the rule.[36] The gift over to the second charity is valid even if it takes effect outside the perpetuity period.[37]

The reason for the exception is that "there is no more perpetuity created by giving to two charities rather than by giving to one."[38] "If the reason for upholding a gift to a charity for an indefinite period is that a charity in its nature is not obnoxious to the rule against perpetuities, I fail to see why the same reason should not apply to a gift over from any one charity to any other charity."[39] The explanation looks to the vesting for charitable purposes, rather than vesting in one specific charity. Once vested in charity, then, subject to express provision to the contrary, a trust will continue, even if the purposes become impossible of fulfilment; the property will be applied *cy-près*.[40] All that is done by the provision for vesting in

---

[30] *Goodman v. Mayor of Saltash* (1882) 7 App.Cas. 633 at p. 642; *Commissioners for Special Purposes of Income Tax v. Pemsel* [1891] A.C. 531 at pp. 580–581; *Att.-Gen. v National Provincial and Union Bank Ltd* [1924] A.C. 262 at p. 266.

[31] (1849) 1 Mac. & G. 460; *Re Tyler* [1891] 3 Ch. 252; *Royal College of Surgeons v. National Provincial Bank Ltd* [1952] A.C. 631.

[32] *Re Wightwick's W.T.* [1950] Ch. 547; *Re Green's W.T.* [1985] 3 All E.R. 455.

[33] *Re Delius* [1957] Ch. 299.

[34] *Re Levy* [1960] Ch. 346.

[35] *Wharton v. Masterman* [1895] A.C. 186; *Re Knapp* [1929] 1 Ch. 341.

[36] A gift from non-charity to a charity is caught: *Re Bowen* [1893] 2 Ch. 291. So also a gift from a charity to a non-charity; *Re Bowen (supra); Re Peel's Release* [1921] 2 Ch. 218; *Re Engels* [1943] 1 All E.R. 506.

[37] *Christ's Hospital v. Grainger* (1849) 1 Mac. & G. 460.

[38] *Per* Shadwell V.-C. in the court below (1848) 16 Sim. 83 at p. 100.

[39] *Per* Lord Morton of Henryton in *Royal College of Surgeons v. National Provincial Bank Ltd* [1952] A.C. 631 at p. 650.

[40] *Post*, p. 430.

another charity is to make expressly the selection of the charity to be benefited when the first gift terminates.

This rule therefore seems logical; and also reasonable when the gift over is to take effect upon the happening of some event related to the carrying out of the purposes of the charity, as was the case in *Christ's Hospital v. Grainger*,[41] and *Royal College of Surgeons v. National Provincial Bank*.[42] In the hands of conveyancers, however as has been seen,[43] it can be used to produce, in effect, a perpetual non-charitable trust by making a gift to one charity conditional upon carrying out a non-charitable purpose, and terminable in favour of another charity upon its failure to do so. This is not a satisfactory use of charity privilege: but this conveyancer's technique was not questioned in the *Royal College of Surgeons* case, and remains possible after the Perpetuities and Accumulations Act 1964.

D. Fiscal Advantages

Charities are exempt from income tax, provided that the income is applied for charitable purposes only.[44] They may recover from the Revenue income tax paid or credited prior to the payment of interest or dividends, and also in respect of income received by charities under "four-year" covenants.[45] Relief is also available with respect to uncovenanted donations.[46] Alternatively, donors who are employees may utilise the payroll deduction scheme.[47] Further, no income tax is chargeable in respect of profits of any trade carried on by the charity, if the profits are applied solely to the purposes of the charity and either the trade is exercised in the course of the actual carrying out of a primary purpose of the charity, or the work in connection with the trade is mainly carried out by beneficiaries of the charity.[48] Again the profits must be applied solely to the purposes of the charity. Similarly, charitable corporations are exempt from paying corporation tax.[49]

Gifts of any amount in favour of charity are exempt from inheritance tax if made by way of payment from a discretionary trust,[50]

---

[41] *Supra.*

[42] [1952] A.C. 631.

[43] *Ante*, p. 370, *Re Tyler* [1891] 3 Ch. 252.

[44] I.C.T.A. 1988, s.505. See *I.R.C. v. Educational Grants Association Ltd* [1967] Ch. 993; *I.R.C. v. Helen Slater Charitable Trust Ltd* [1982] Ch. 49.

[45] I.C.T.A. 1988, s.660(3); [1989] Conv. 321 (D. Morris).

[46] F.A. 1990, ss.25, 26; F.A. 1993, s.67. For company donations, see I.C.T.A. 1988, s.339, as amended by F.(No. 2)A. 1992, s.26.

[47] I.C.T.A. 1988, s. 202; F.A. 1996, s.109. [1989] Conv. 175 (D. Morris).

[48] *Ibid.* s.505(1); (1989) 3 *Trust Law & Practice* 98 (J. Hill and J. de Souza).

[49] *Ibid.* ss.505(1), 506(1).

[50] Inheritance Tax Act 1984, s.76.

or by way of gift by an individual during his lifetime or on death.[51] Similarly, transfers from a charitable trust are exempt from inheritance tax.[52]

No capital gains tax arises where a gain accrues to a charity and the gain is applicable and is applied for charitable purposes.[53] Nor will a donor be under any such liability in respect of a disposal to charity.[54] Charities are also exempt from stamp duty on conveyances,[55] and from National Insurance Surcharge.[56]

Charities, however, do have to bear Value Added Tax on goods and services which they purchase.[57] This liability will be particularly burdensome for many charities in respect of the maintenance and repair of buildings. Also, VAT may be chargeable in respect of goods and services provided, on payment, by some charities.[58]

All charities are entitled to exemption in respect of 80 per cent of the non-domestic rates of the properties which they occupy,[59] wholly or mainly used for charitable purposes. This includes administrative premises,[60] and premises used wholly or mainly for the sale of goods donated to a charity and applied for the purposes of a charity.[61] Relief can also be granted at the discretion of the rating authority up to the whole amount of the rates.[62] Churches, church halls and similar premises used for religious purposes are entitled to relief in respect of the whole of the rates,[63] as are those providing facilities for the disabled.[64]

In view of the extent of income and other assets thus exempted, this is a formidable list of fiscal advantages. In 1989 it was estimated that the value of tax exemptions and other support from public funds

---

[51] *Ibid.* s.23. See also ss.25, 26.

[52] *Ibid.* s.58(1)(*a*).

[53] Taxation of Chargeable Gains Act 1992, s.256.

[54] *Ibid.* s.257.

[55] F.A. 1982, s.129.

[56] F.A. 1977, s.57.

[57] For specific exemptions, see the consolidating Value Added Tax Act 1994, Sched. 9; *Bell Concord Educational Trust Ltd v. Customs and Excise Commissioners* [1989] S.T.C. 264.

[58] See [1972] B.T.R. 346 at p. 356 (G. Glover); *Customs and Excise Commissioners v. Automobile Association* [1974] 1 W.L.R. 1447; Annual Report 1974, paras. 17–21; (1995/96) 3 *Charity Law and Practice Review* 37 (J. Warburton). However, some goods supplied to or by charities are zero-rated under Sched. 8 (Group 15) of the 1994 Act.

[59] Local Government Finance Act 1988, s.43(5), (6).

[60] *Aldous v. Southwark Corporation* [1968] 1 W.L.R. 1671 (the management of Dulwich College Estates).

[61] L.G.F.A. 1988, s.64(10); Hansard, H.L., Vol. 499, col. 874, July 13, 1988.

[62] *Ibid.* s.47.

[63] L.G.F.A. 1988, Sched. 5, para. 11. In *Henning v. Church of Jesus Christ of Latter-Day Saints* [1962] 1 W.L.R. 1091, the Mormon Church failed to obtain exemption in respect of premises to which only selected members of the faith were admitted. Similarly, the Exclusive Brethren in *Broxtowe Borough Council v. Birch* [1983] 1 W.L.R. 314.

[64] *Ibid.* para. 16.

exceeded £2.5 billion.[65] This explains the prominence of Revenue cases in charity litigation.

Measures have been taken to prevent abuse of these tax advantages, for example by requiring charities to take reasonable steps to ensure that payments made to overseas bodies will be applied to genuine charitable purposes and requiring them to justify certain loans or investments as being for the benefit of charity and not for tax avoidance.[66] These provisions restrict tax relief where funds are applied for non-charitable purposes and prevent manipulation of charity tax advantages by individuals. So far they are working well.[67]

3. THE DEFINITION OF CHARITY

A. The Four Categories

i. Lord Macnaghten's Classification. A claim to charitable status is determined by considering whether the purpose in question comes within Lord Macnaghten's classification as exemplified by the cases decided in accordance with it. Lord Macnaghten said; "Charity in its legal sense comprises four principal divisions: trusts for the relief of poverty; trusts for the advancement of education; trusts for the advancement of religion; and trusts for other purposes beneficial to the community."[68] It is obvious that the heads provide no precise definition. Lord Wilberforce had this comment to make[69]: "first, that, since it is a classification of convenience, there may well be purposes which do not fit neatly into one or other of the headings." He might also have added that there are many purposes which overlap.[70] "Secondly that the words used must not be given the force of a statute to be construed; and thirdly, that the law of charity is a moving subject which may well have evolved even since 1891." Indeed, it is continually changing, and as has been explained, the impact of heavy taxation and the resulting significance of tax exemption, and also the development of State agencies to provide education, relief from poverty, and other purposes needed by society

---

[65] *Charities: A Framework for the Future*, para. 1.5. The gross income of registered charities was over £12 billion in 1994; Annual Report 1994, para. 24. The figure for all charities is thought to be £17 billion; Annual Report 1993, para. 29.

[66] I.C.T.A. 1988, ss.339, 427, 505, 506, 683.

[67] Annual Report 1987, para. 28.

[68] *Commissioners for Special Purposes of Income Tax v. Pemsel* [1891] A.C. 531 at p. 583.

[69] *Scottish Burial Reform and Cremation Society Ltd v. Glasgow Corporation* [1968] A.C. 138 at p. 154.

[70] Thus, a gift for the preparation of "poor students for the Ministry" might come under all four heads.

have transformed the concept of charity.[71] It should be appreciated that the Charity Commissioners have a major role in the development of this concept.[72]

ii. Public Benefit. It should also be noted at this stage that each head involves two elements; an element of benefit, such as the advancement of education, and also an element of *public* benefit, that is to say, education being advanced in a way that will benefit the whole community, or a sufficiently substantial part of it. The requirement of public benefit varies from head to head, and will be discussed in detail.[73]

iii. Exclusively Charitable. A trust will not fail to be charitable because it may in its operation incidentally benefit the rich, or other non-objects of charity.[74] But if a non-charitable purpose is an object, the trust cannot be charitable, for then it ceases to be wholly and exclusively "for charitable purposes."[75] A statement of objects which includes non-charitable purposes is not saved by adding "in so far as they are of a charitable nature."[76]

iv. Charitable Purposes Overseas. Special problems arise where the benefits arising from charitable trusts are to be enjoyed abroad. For at least 200 years there has been no rule requiring the benefits to be retained in this country.[77] But, how can the court or the (English) trustees control the application of the funds? What relationship is there between the Preamble of 1601 and the problem of a developing country suffering from drought, floods or earthquake? Should tax privileges be given by the British Revenue for the benefit of communities abroad?[78]

The Charity Commissioners have stated[79] that the relief of poverty[80] and the advancement of education and religion are presumed

---

[71] See *Incorporated Council of Law Reporting v. Att.-Gen.* [1972] Ch. 73 at pp. 88–89.

[72] *Post*, p. 447. The Commissioners take a generous view as to what is charitable, to reflect changes in society; Annual Report 1985, para. 5.

[73] *Post*, p. 411.

[74] *Verge v. Somerville* [1924] A.C. 496; *Re Resch's W.T.* [1969] 1 A.C. 514; *sub nom. Le Cras v. Perpetual Trustee Co.* [1967] 1 All E.R. 915. But a trust for the relief of poverty will fail if it may benefit persons who are not poor; *Re Gwyon* [1903] 1 Ch. 255.

[75] *Post*, p. 423, *Ellis v. I.R.C.* (1949) 31 T.C. 178; *Re Cole* [1958] Ch. 877; *Att.-Gen. of the Bahamas v. Royal Trust Co.* [1986] 1 W.L.R. 1001.

[76] *McGovern v. Att.-Gen.* [1982] Ch. 321.

[77] *Re Robinson* [1931] 2 Ch. 122 at p. 126 (gift to German Government for the benefit of its soldiers disabled in the late war held charitable).

[78] Annual Report 1963, paras. 69–76. See (1965) 29 Conv.(N.S.) 123 (D. Emrys Evans).

[79] Annual Report 1992, paras. 74, 75; Decisions, Vol. 1 (1993), p. 16. See *Camille and Henry Dreyfus Foundation Inc. v. I.R.C.* [1954] Ch. 672 at p. 684.

[80] See *Re Niyazi's Will Trusts* [1978] 1 W.L.R. 910 (trust for construction of working men's hostel in Cyprus charitable). The work overseas of organisations like Oxfam is well known.

beneficial wherever they occur, but this may be challenged by applying criteria adopted by the English courts, for example it would not be charitable to support a religion overseas if it would be considered contrary to public policy to carry it on at home. The fourth head is more difficult. The test of public benefit is the same whether the activity is at home or abroad (as is also the case with the other heads), as our courts cannot judge what is for the benefit of the public in a foreign country. This does not mean that there must be a benefit to the public in this country. The courts should first consider if the activity would be charitable if it operated at home. If so, it is charitable even though operated abroad unless it would be contrary to public policy to recognise it. For example, our courts would not consider an institution operating abroad whose object was contrary to the law of the state in question to be charitable. These views are consistent with Commonwealth authorities, which have held that fourth category purposes may be charitable even though solely of benefit to a foreign community.[81]

It has been said that the court would be bound to take account of the probable results of the execution of the trust on the inhabitants of the country concerned, which would doubtless have a history and social structure quite different from that of the United Kingdom. So in *McGovern v. Att.-Gen.*,[82] a trust to procure the abolition of torture or inhuman or degrading treatment or punishment[83] in all parts of the world was not charitable, one reason being that the court would have no satisfactory means of judging the probable effects of, say, legislation to abolish the death penalty on the local community. If the purpose of a trust was to secure abolition of the death penalty for adultery in Islamic countries, the court would not be competent to deal with it because it would either have to apply English standards as to public benefit, which might not be appropriate in the local conditions, or attempt to apply local standards of which it knew little or nothing.

In *Keren Kayemeth Le Jisroel Ltd v. I.R.C.*,[84] a trust for the purchase of land in Israel and for the settlement there of Jewish people was held not charitable, but the decision turned on the character of the purposes, and not on the fact that the benefit would be enjoyed abroad. In *Re Jacobs* in 1970[85] a trust for the purpose "of

---

[81] *Re Levy Estate* (1989) 58 D.L.R. (4th) 375 (bequest to State of Israel for charitable purposes selected by trustee). For the Australian position, see *Re Stone* (1970) 91 W.N. (N.S.W.) 704 at p. 717.

[82] [1982] Ch. 321, *post*, p. 408.

[83] Including punishment inflicted by process of law.

[84] [1932] A.C. 650.

[85] Annual Report 1970, para. 78.

planting a grove of trees in Israel to perpetuate my name on the eternal soil of the Holy Land" was upheld. Soil conservation is of crucial importance in Israel. It was the benefit to the community abroad which was significant. The Commissioners have recently registered several organisations concerned with the preservation of the environment outside the United Kingdom.[86]

B. The Relief of Poverty

i. Meaning of Poverty. There is no definition of poverty. Its meaning can only be understood by examining the cases on the subject. "It is quite clearly established," said Sir Raymond Evershed M.R., "that poverty does not mean destitution; ... it may not unfairly be paraphrased as meaning persons who have to 'go short' in the ordinary acceptance of that term ..."[87] It is thus a matter of degree. Most of the cases come from a time before welfare payments were available from public funds. Such payments are intended to relieve poverty and hardship, and it could be argued that eligibility for such payments should be the test of poverty. But, if that were so, charity in this area would duplicate the work of a good welfare programme. If relief of poverty is the duty of the State, what scope is there for private charity? This is a problem which is met in many of the areas of charity today, especially in connection with trusts for the relief of poverty and for education and health. Private charity is useful to fill the gaps which the welfare state programme leaves uncovered.[88] But in doing so, it creates some controversies. If a trust's purpose is not appealing enough to justify the expenditure of public money, should it justify the tax exemptions to which charity is entitled?

ii. Illustrations. Gifts for the benefit of the poor are clearly charitable.[89] Also "needy" persons,[90] or "indigent"[91] persons. Often a group of poor is confined to a particular location,[92] or

---

[86] Annual Report 1989, para. 29.

[87] *Re Coulthurst* [1951] Ch. 661 at pp. 665–666.

[88] See Annual Report 1967, paras. 17–21; 1971, paras. 76–79; 1978, paras. 61–63, App. A, suggesting ways in which the income of charities for the relief of poverty may be effectively applied.

[89] *Re Darling* [1896] 1 Ch. 56: "to the poor and the service of God."

[90] *Re Scarisbrick* [1951] Ch. 622; *Re Cohen* [1973] 1 W.L.R. 415.

[91] *Weir v. Crum-Brown* [1908] A.C. 162: "indigent bachelors and widowers who have shown sympathy with science."

[92] *Re Lucas* [1922] 2 Ch. 52 (oldest respectable inhabitants in Gunville).

religion,[93] or to a group which is assumed to be in need of help,[94] or victims of a disaster.[95] Persons of "limited means"[96] are included, and trusts for gentlewomen and distressed gentlefolk.[97] On the other hand, a gift which includes persons who are not in need will be excluded. Thus gifts to employees of a company are not charitable[98] unless the qualification of poverty is clearly imposed.[99] In *Re Sanders' Will Trusts*,[1] a gift for the provision of housing for the working classes was not charitable. In *Re Gwyon*,[2] a fund providing for a gift of clothing to boys in Farnham and district failed on the ground that the conditions for qualification, precise though they were in many ways, failed to exclude affluent children.[3] It is no objection, however, that the scheme operates by way of bargain rather than bounty, *i.e.* that the beneficiaries are required to contribute to the cost of the benefits they receive.[4]

There is no need for the trust to be an endowment. A trust may be charitable although the trustees may distribute the capital. A trust was upheld in *Re Scarisbrick*[5] "for such relations of my . . . son and daughters as in the opinion of the survivor of my . . . son and daughters shall be in needy circumstances . . . as the survivor . . . shall by deed or will appoint." This was a trust for "poor relations," and there is no requirement, in poverty cases, for public benefit.[6] But there can be no charitable trust, even in the poverty category, where

---

[93] *Re Wall* (1889) 52 Ch.D. 570.

[94] *Att.-Gen. v. Ironmongers Co.* (1834) 2 My. & K. 526 (debtors); *Thompson v. Thompson* (1844) 1 Coll. 381 at p. 395 (unsuccessful literary men); *Loscombe v. Wintringham* (1850) 13 Beav. 87 (servants); *Biscoe v. Jackson* (1887) 35 Ch.D. 460 (soup kitchen for the parish of Shoreditch); *Re Coulthurst* [1951] Ch. 661 (widows and orphaned children of employees).

[95] *Re North Devon and West Somerset Relief Fund Trust* [1953] 1 W.L.R. 1260 (flood disaster).

[96] *Re Gardom* [1914] 1 Ch. 664; *Re De Carteret* [1933] Ch. 103.

[97] *Mary Clark Home Trustees v. Anderson* [1904] 2 K.B. 745; *Re Gardom (supra)*; *Re Young* [1951] Ch. 344.

[98] *Re Drummond* [1914] 2 Ch. 90; *Re Hobourn Aero-Components Air Raid Distress Fund* [1946] Ch. 194.

[99] *Gibson v. South American Stores (Gath & Chaves) Ltd* [1950] Ch. 177; *Dingle v. Turner* [1973] A.C. 601.

[1] [1954] Ch. 265. *Re Mead's Trust Deed* [1961] 1 W.L.R. 1244 (membership of a Trade Union). *cf. Re Niyazi's W.T.* [1978] 1 W.L.R. 910 (gift for "the construction of a working men's hostel" in Famagusta, Cyprus held charitable by Megarry V.-C. "although it was desperately near the border-line."). But some homes for working classes have been registered as charities where there were other factors which indicated a requirement of poverty. Annual Report 1965, App. C, para. I. A.9.

[2] [1930] 1 Ch. 255.

[3] They also excluded black boys. This caused no comment at the time; but would no doubt do so today, *ante*, p. 326. See further [1981] Conv. 131 (T. Watkin); Annual Report 1983, para. 19; Annual Report 1987, para. 14.

[4] *Re Cottam's W.T.* [1955] 1 W.L.R. 1299; *Le Cras v. Perpetual Trustee Co. Ltd* [1969] 1 A.C. 514; *Joseph Rowntree Memorial Trust Housing Association Ltd v. Att.-Gen.* [1983] Ch. 159 (dwellings for sale to elderly at 70 per cent cost).

[5] [1951] Ch. 622; *Re Cohen* [1973] 1 W.L.R. 415.

[6] *Dingle v. Turner* [1972] A.C. 601; *post*, p. 413.

the persons to be benefited are specified individuals; and such a construction is more likely where the capital of a trust may be immediately distributed. But it is not decisive.

Nor is it an objection that the persons to be benefited are to be selected at the discretion of the trustees.[7] It is necessary, of course, that there should be a duty and not a mere power to select,[8] and that the discretion is exercisable only in favour of those who are poor. Jenkins L.J. in *Re Scarisbrick* dismissed the words "in the opinion of the survivor" as having no potential bearing on the character of the trust.

C. The Advancement of Education

i. Meaning of Education. The second head has its origin in the phrases in the Preamble which speak of "the maintenance of schools of learning, free schools and scholars in universities" and "the education and preferment of orphans." The endowments, some of course very ancient, of many schools and colleges and universities are based on this provision. Education in school and university is now however accepted as being within the responsibility of the State; and it is not surprising that modern cases have substantially widened the concept of educational charity. It can now cover almost any form of worthwhile instruction or cultural advancement, except for purely professional or career courses.

The following trusts have been held charitable under this head: Education in business management,[9] and in the art of government,[10] the production of a dictionary,[11] the support of London Zoological Society,[12] the establishment and maintenance of museums,[13] the support of learned literary, scientific and cultural societies,[14] a search for the Shakespeare manuscript,[15] choral singing in London,[16] the promotion of the music of Delius,[17] classical drama

---

[7] *Gibson v. South American Stores (Gath & Chaves) Ltd* [1950] Ch. 177; *Re Scarisbrick (supra), Re Cohen (supra).*

[8] *Re Cohen (supra).*

[9] *Re Koettgen's W.T.* [1954] Ch. 252.

[10] *Re McDougall* [1957] 1 W.L.R. 81. But not for the promotion of political causes; *post,* p. 393. The holding of conferences with a "political flavour" but not of a party political nature was upheld in *Re Koeppler's W.T.* [1986] Ch. 423.

[11] *Re Stanford* [1924] 1 Ch. 73.

[12] *Re Lopes* [1931] 2 Ch. 130.

[13] *British Museum Trustees v. White* (1826) 2 Sm. & St. 594; *Re Pinion* [1965] Ch. 85 at p. 105.

[14] *Royal College of Surgeons v. National Provincial Bank Ltd* [1952] A.C. 631; *Re Shakespeare Memorial Trust* [1923] 2 Ch. 398; *Re British School of Egyptian Archaeology* [1954] 1 W.L.R. 546.

[15] *Re Hopkins' W.T.* [1965] Ch. 669.

[16] *Royal Choral Society v. I.R.C.* [1943] 2 All E.R. 101.

[17] *Re Delius* [1957] Ch. 299.

and acting,[18] the publication of the Law Reports,[19] the founding of lectureships and professorships,[20] the study and dissemination of ethical principles and cultivation of a rational religious sentiment[21] and even a "sort of finishing school for the Irish people" where "self-control, oratory, deportment and the art of personal contact" were to be taught.[22] Educational purposes include matters ancillary to the main purposes, such as the payment of teachers and administrative staff.[23]

ii. Research. Education requires something more than the mere accumulation of knowledge. There must be some sharing, or teaching or dissemination, some way of showing that the public will benefit. There is no difficulty in the case of research which is likely to produce material benefit to the community, such as medical or scientific research.[24] Such purposes would in any case come under the fourth head. But, on literary, cultural and scholarly subjects, the matter is less obvious. "I think, therefore," said Wilberforce J. in *Re Hopkins*,[25] "that the word 'education' ... must be used in a wide sense, certainly extending beyond teaching, and that the requirement is that, in order to be charitable, research must either be of educational value to the researcher or must be so directed as to lead to something which will pass into the store of educational material, or so as to improve the sum of communicable knowledge in an area which education may cover—education in this last context extending to the formation of literary taste and appreciation."

In *Re Hopkins*,[26] there was a testamentary gift to the Francis Bacon Society "to be earmarked and applied towards finding the Bacon-Shakespeare manuscripts." A "search, or research, for the original manuscripts of England's greatest dramatist (whoever he was) would be well within the law's conception of charitable purposes. The discovery would be of the highest value to history and to literature."[27] The gift was held to be a valid charitable trust under this head and the fourth head.

---

[18] *Re Shakespeare Memorial Trust (supra).*
[19] *Incorporated Council of Law Reporting for England and Wales v. Att.-Gen.* [1972] Ch. 73.
[20] *Att.-Gen. v. Margaret and Regius Professors in Cambridge* (1682) 1 Vern. 55.
[21] *Re South Place Ethical Society* [1980] 1 W.L.R. 1565.
[22] *Re Shaw's W.T.* [1952] Ch. 163.
[23] *Case of Christ's College, Cambridge* (1757) 1 Wm. Bl. 90.
[24] *Royal College of Surgeons v. National Provincial Bank Ltd (supra).* See also Annual Report 1987, para. 12.
[25] [1965] Ch. 669 at p. 680.
[26] [1965] Ch. 669. See also *McGovern v. Att.-Gen.* [1982] Ch. 321, where research into human rights and dissemination of the results would have been charitable. The trust failed for other reasons. Trusts for research into human rights have been registered; Annual Report 1987, para. 12. Likewise research into terrorism; Annual Report 1988, paras. 27–34.
[27] *Ibid.* at p. 679.

Re Shaw[28] was distinguished.

George Bernard Shaw, by his will, directed that his residuary estate should be devoted to researching the advantages to be gained by a new proposed British alphabet of 40 letters, in which each letter would indicate a single sound; and to translate his play "Androcles and the Lion" into the new alphabet. Harman J. held that the gift was not charitable "if the object be merely the increase of knowledge, that is not in itself a charitable object unless it be combined with teaching or education."[29]

This is thought to be too narrow a view of education. Whether the trust in this case would be held charitable under Wilberforce J.'s test depends on the usefulness of the research, and that is a matter of individual judgment. Not every type of knowledge, whether researched, disseminated or taught is capable of being education. Not schools for prostitutes or pickpockets,[30] nor the training of spiritualistic mediums.[31]

iii. Artistic and Aesthetic Education.

In *Royal Choral Society v. I.R.C.*,[32] the Court of Appeal upheld as charitable a trust to promote the practice and performance of choral works. Lord Greene said of the view that education meant a master teaching a class[33]: "I protest against that narrow conception of education when one is dealing with aesthetic education. In my opinion, a body of persons established for the purpose of raising the artistic state of the country . . . is established for educational purposes."

In *Re British School of Egyptian Archaeology*[34] a trust to excavate and discover Egyptian antiquities, to hold exhibitions and to promote the training and assistance of students in the field of Egyptian history was held educational. In *Re Delius*,[35] there was a gift to increase the general appreciation of the musical work of the composer. Roxburgh J. had no doubt that the trust was for the advancement of education.

But it seems that a trust for "artistic" purposes is not charitable. Upjohn J. dealing with a clause in the Associated Artists Ltd Memorandum which empowered it to present "artistic . . . dramatic

---

[28] [1957] 1 W.L.R. 729.
[29] *Ibid.* at p. 737, referring to Rigby L.J. in *Re Macduff* [1896] 2 Ch. 451.
[30] *Per* Harman J. [1957] 1 W.L.R. 729 at p. 737; and in *Re Pinion* [1965] Ch. 85 at p. 105.
[31] *Re Hummeltenberg* [1923] 1 Ch. 237. *Cf. Funnell v. Stewart* [1996] 1 W.L.R. 288 (faith healing charitable).
[32] [1943] 2 All E.R. 101.
[33] *Ibid.* at p. 104.
[34] [1954] 1 W.L.R. 540.
[35] [1957] Ch. 299.

works' " found it difficult to attach any real charitable concept to an artistic dramatic work; it is too wide and too vague . . ."[36]

iv. Subjective Evaluation. The question whether a purpose is educational or not will depend in many cases upon the evaluation of its quality and usefulness for that purpose. Music, drama, literature, archaeology, museums; these and many more are included. But not bad music, ham acting, pornography, useless digging or collections of rubbish. In *Re Delius*,[37] Roxburgh J. recognised that there would be difficulty if a manifestly inadequate composer had been chosen. A judge may be assisted by expert evidence. But that may not be conclusive, and artistic evaluation changes with the times. It is clear that the court will require to be satisfied of the merit of artistic work.[38] The opinion of the donor that the gift is for the public benefit does not make it so.

In *Re Pinion*,[39] a testator gave his studio, together with its contents, to trustees to enable it to be used as a museum for the display of his collection of furniture and objets d'art, and paintings, some of which were by the testator himself.

Expert opinion was unanimous that the collection had no artistic merit. One expert expressed his surprise that "so voracious a collector should not by hazard have picked up even one meritorious object."[40] The Court of Appeal held the trust void. "I can conceive," said Harman L.J., "of no useful object to be served in foisting upon the public this mass of junk. It has neither public utility nor educational value."[41]

v. Youth. Sports at School and University. Education is specially concerned with the young. In many situations a provision for the young will be held charitable although the same provision for older people would fail.

In *Re Mariette*,[42] there was a gift to provide Eton fives courts and squash rackets courts at Aldenham School. Eve J. upheld this, on the principle that learning to play games at a boarding school was as important as learning from the books.

The sporting facilities need not be limited to a particular school or institution. In *I.R.C. v. McMullen*,[43] a trust to provide facilities for

[36] *Associated Artists Ltd v. I.R.C.* [1956] 1 W.L.R. 752 at p. 758; see also *Royal Choral Society v. I.R.C.* [1943] 2 All E.R. 101 at p. 107.
[37] [1957] Ch. 299.
[38] The same problem arises with many situations under the fourth head.
[39] [1965] Ch. 85.
[40] *Ibid.* at p. 107.
[41] *Ibid.*
[42] [1915] 2 Ch. 284. For sport outside universities and schools, see *post*, p. 402.
[43] [1981] A.C. 1; [1980] Conv. 173, 225 (J. Warburton); (1986) 1 *Trust Law & Practice* 22 (D. Evans).

pupils at schools and universities in any part of the United Kingdom to play association football or other games or sports was held valid by the House of Lords. Lord Hailsham said[44]: "The picture of education when applied to the young . . . is complex and varied . . . It is the picture of a balanced and systematic process of instruction, training and practice containing both spiritual, moral, mental and physical elements . . . I reject any idea which would cramp the education of the young within the school or university campus, limit it to formal instruction, or render it devoid of pleasure in the exercise of skill." But this wide definition of education is not without its limits. Lord Hailsham stated that the mere playing of games or enjoyment or amusement or competition was not *per se* charitable nor necessarily educational; and that a trust for physical education *per se* and not associated with persons of school age or just above was not necessarily a good charitable gift.[45]

Trusts for sport outside educational facilities and the services are not charitable[46] unless they come within the scope of the Recreational Charities Act 1958.[47] But intelligent games like chess are educational for young people; though Vaisey J. in *Re Dupree's Deed Trusts*[48] recognised that here, as with outdoor games, the problem of distinguishing between the influence of one activity and another was very difficult. He foresaw a slippery slope from chess to draughts, to bezique, to bridge and whist, and stamp collecting and acquiring birds' eggs.[49] All that can be said is that purposeful activities for the young receive favourable treatment. The Boy Scout Movement[50] and the National Association of Toy Libraries[51] are charities, and a gift for an annual treat or field day for school children at Turton has been upheld as encouraging a study of natural history.[52]

vi. Professional Bodies. Professional bodies may be charitable if their object is the advancement of education. The object of the Royal College of Surgeons[53] was stated in the royal charter of 1800 to be: "the due promotion and encouragement of the study and practice of the . . . art and science of surgery."

---

[44] *Ibid.* at p. 18.
[45] The Cliff Richard Tennis Development Trust was registered in 1991; Annual Report, para. 74.
[46] *Re Nottage* [1895] 2 Ch. 649 (a prize for a yacht race).
[47] *Post*, p. 404.
[48] [1945] Ch. 16; (a chess contest in Portsmouth for males under 21). This is not contrary to Sex Discrimination Act 1975. Charities are excepted: s.43. Sex Discrimination Act 1975 (Amendment of Section 43) Order 1977 (S.I. 1977 No. 528). A similar trust was established for girls in Portsmouth under 18; see (1977) 41 Conv.(N.S.) 8.
[49] *Ibid.* at p. 20.
[50] *Re Webber* [1954] 1 W.L.R. 1500.
[51] Annual Report 1973, para. 41.
[52] *Re Mellody* [1918] 1 Ch. 228.
[53] *Royal College of Surgeons v. National Provincial Bank Ltd* [1952] A.C. 631.

The fact that the College gives assistance and protection to its members is ancillary only; and the College was held to be a charity. Similarly, the Royal College of Nursing,[54] as the advance of nursing as a profession in all or any of its branches was a charitable purpose. The Construction Industry Training Board was held to be charitable,[55] and subsequently most of the Industrial Training Boards have been registered as charities.[56]

But if the object or one of the objects of the society is to promote the status of the profession or the welfare of its members, it will not be charitable. The General Nursing Council for England and Wales, which is a statutory body, had as its main function the regulation of the nursing profession; and was not therefore charitable.[57]

vii. Political Propaganda Masquerading as Education.[58] Political purposes are not charitable. They may be for the public benefit, but they are partisan. The court cannot determine whether any particular programme is for the public benefit.[59] Nor can such a trust be charitable even where the testator's project has subsequently been endorsed by Parliament.[60] A trust for political purposes will fail. Attempts have been made to foster the doctrines of a political party under the guise of a trust for education by providing for the advancement of adult education on the lines of the principles of that party.[61] In *Re Hopkinson*,[62] Vaisey J. explained the principle as follows: "Political propaganda masquerading ... I do not use the word in any sinister sense ... as education is not education within the statute of Elizabeth ... In other words it is not charitable."[63] But there is no doubt that the prospects of success are greater if purposes

---

[54] *Royal College of Nursing v. St. Marylebone Borough Council* [1959] 1 W.L.R. 1077; *Institute of Civil Engineers v. I.R.C.* [1932] 1 K.B. 149.

[55] *Construction Industry Training Board v. Att.-Gen.* [1973] Ch. 173.

[56] Annual Report 1973, para. 39; *cf. I.R.C. v. Oldham Training and Enterprise Council* [1996] S.T.C. 1218 (not exclusively charitable because promotion of commerce conferred private benefits).

[57] *General Nursing Council for England and Wales v. St. Marylebone Borough Council* [1959] A.C. 540; *Chartered Insurance Institute v. London Corporation* [1957] 1 W.L.R. 867 (promoting the insurance profession).

[58] Annual Report 1966, para. 38 (warning the overworking of the word "education"); 1969, para. 11; 1971, paras. 7–10; 1981, para. 54.

[59] *Bowman v. Secular Society* [1917] A.C. 406 at p. 421.

[60] *Re Bushnell* [1975] 1 W.L.R. 1596 (national health system introduced after testator's death but before the litigation); (1975) 38 M.L.R. 471 (R. Cotterrell).

[61] *Bonar Law Memorial Trust v. I.R.C.* (1933) 49 T.L.R. 220 (Conservative); *Re Hopkinson* [1949] 1 All E.R. 346 (Socialist); *cf. McDougall* [1957] 1 W.L.R. 81. See also *Re Ogden* [1933] Ch. 678, where, however, a trust for Liberal institutions was upheld on other grounds.

[62] [1949] 1 All E.R. 346. See also *McGovern v. Att.-Gen.* [1982] Ch. 321, *post*, p. 408, where an essentially political trust was not saved by educational elements.

[63] *Ibid.* at p. 350.

are presented in the form of education. In *Re Scowcroft*,[64] the gift was of income to be applied "for the furtherance of Conservative principles and religious and mental improvement," and this succeeded. Similarly in *Re Koeppler's Will Trusts*[65] a gift to further the work of an educational project was held charitable even though the testator's express aspirations (the formation of informed international public opinion and the promotion of greater co-operation in Europe and the West) were not regarded as charitable. The project involved conferences with a "political flavour," but did not further the interests of a particular political party, nor seek to change the law or government policies.

While a students' union is a charitable body, as being ancillary to the educational purposes of the college or university,[66] the donation of union funds for political, or indeed for charitable purposes which are not educational, is not permitted. So in *Baldry v. Feintuck*[67] the use of union funds to campaign for the restoration of free school milk was restrained as political, although the fact that a students' union has political clubs is not inconsistent with its charitable status.[68]

viii. Private and Independent Schools. An educational institution cannot be charitable if it is operated for profit.[69] In recent years, the practice has been to operate fee-paying schools as non-profit-making bodies which can then obtain the fiscal benefits available to educational charities.[70]

There has been no challenge in law to the charitable status of public schools. Labour Party policy, however, has been to deprive independent schools of the fiscal benefits of charitable status, on the ground that they exercise a divisive influence on our society, and are

---

[64] [1898] 2 Ch. 638; *cf.* in the field of religion, *Re Hood* [1931] 1 Ch. 240 (spreading Christian principles by extinguishing "the drink traffic").

[65] [1986] Ch. 423; [1985] Conv. 412 (T. Watkin).

[66] *London Hospital Medical College v. I.R.C.* [1976] 1 W.L.R. 613. The National Union of Students is not a charity; see *Att.-Gen. v. Ross, infra.*

[67] [1972] 1 W.L.R. 552. A donation to the charity War on Want was also restrained, as it was not an educational charity. See Annual Report 1983, paras. 95 and 96 and App. A; (1986) 1 *Trust Law & Practice* 47 (J. Warburton). In *Webb v. O'Doherty, The Times,* February 11, 1991, expenditure on a campaign to end the Gulf War was restrained.

[68] *Att.-Gen. v. Ross* [1986] 1 W.L.R. 252; All E.R. Rev. 1985, p. 320 (P. Clarke). (Preliminary issue as to whether Attorney General had *locus standi* to seek injunction to restrain donation of union funds to striking miners and famine aid in Ethiopia). By similar reasoning, a charity cannot guarantee the liabilities of a non-charity; *Rosemary Simmons Memorial Housing Association Ltd v. United Dominions Trust Ltd* [1986] 1 W.L.R. 1440. See further [1988] Conv. 275 (J. Warburton).

[69] *Re Girls' Public Day School Trust* [1951] Ch. 400.

[70] *Abbey, Malvern Wells Ltd v. Minister of Local Government and Housing* [1951] Ch. 728.

hostile to the public, and not beneficial.[71] Such a change could only come by legislation.

D. The Advancement of Religion[72]

i. What is Religion? In *Bowman v. Secular Society*,[73] Lord Parker of Waddington suggested that any form of monotheistic theism will be recognised as a religion, but the restriction to monotheism is probably now outmoded.[74] Religion requires a spiritual belief. It may include, but is greater than, morality, or a recommended way of life. In *Re South Place Ethical Society*,[75] one question was whether the Society's objects, which were the "study and dissemination of ethical principles and the cultivation of a rational religious sentiment," were charitable under this heading. Dillon J. held that they were not. "Religion as I see it, is concerned with man's relations with God, and ethics are concerned with man's relations with man. The two are not the same, and are not made the same by sincere enquiry into the question; what is God?"[76] Similarly, the objects of a body such as the Freemasons, whose rules demand the highest personal, social and domestic standards, do not constitute a religion, even though they insist upon a belief in a divine spirit.[77] Nor did *Keren Kayemeth Le Jisroel*, the organisation whose object was the settlement of Jews in Palestine and neighbouring lands.[78] In any event, to be charitable, a trust must be for the *advancement* of religion; and this means "the promotion of spiritual teaching in a wide sense and the maintenance of the doctrines on which this rests, and the observances that serve to promote and manifest it—not merely a foundation or cause to which it can be related."[79]

ii. Religious Toleration Within Christianity. The advent of religious toleration in the seventeenth century permitted the recognition of Christian sects other than the Established Church, and it

---

[71] Recommended by the Public Schools Commission (1968); see Annual Report 1974, para. 16. See also Chesterman, *Charities, Trusts and Social Welfare*, pp. 336–339.

[72] The only reference to religion in the Preamble is to the repair of churches.

[73] [1917] A.C. 406.

[74] *Tudor on Charities* (8th ed.), pp. 63–64.

[75] [1980] 1 W.L.R. 1565; [1980] Conv. 150 (St. J. Robilliard).

[76] *Ibid.* at p. 1571. The Society was charitable under the second and fourth headings; *ante*, p. 389, *post*, p. 411.

[77] *United Grand Lodge of Ancient Free and Accepted Masons of England and Wales v. Holborn B.C.* [1957] 1 W.L.R. 1080. See also *Re Macaulay's Estate* [1943] Ch. 475n; *Berry v. St. Marylebone B.C.* [1958] Ch. 406. (Theosophy held to be a philosophical or metaphysical conception, rather than the advancement of religion).

[78] *Keren Kayemeth Le Jisroel v. I.R.C.* [1931] 2 K.B. 465; *affd.* [1932] A.C. 650.

[79] *Ibid.*

CHAPTER 15

CHARITABLE TRUSTS

1. Introduction	376
2. Advantages Enjoyed by Charitable Trusts	378
A. Purpose Trusts	378
B. Objects Need not be Certain	379
C. May be Perpetual	380
D. Fiscal Advantages	381
3. The Definition of Charity	383
A. The Four Categories	383
i. Lord Macnaghten's Classification	383
ii. Public Benefit	384
iii. Exclusively Charitable	384
iv. Charitable Purpose Overseas	384
B. The Relief of Poverty	386
i. Meaning of Poverty	386
ii. Illustrations	386
C. The Advancement of Education	388
i. Meaning of Education	388
ii. Research	389
iii. Artistic and Aesthetic Education	390
iv. Subjective Evaluation	391
v. Youth. Sports at School and University	391
vi. Professional Bodies	392
vii. Political Propaganda Masquerading as Education	393
viii. Private and Independent Schools	394
D. The Advancement of Religion	395
i. What is Religion?	395
ii. Religious Toleration Within Christianity	395
iii. Non-Christian Religions	396
iv. Related Purposes	397
E. Other Purposes Beneficial to the Community	398
i. The Spirit and Intendment of the Preamble	398
ii. The Test is What the Law Treats as Charitable	400
iii. Examples of Trusts under the Fourth Head	401
(a) Specific Mention in the Preamble. Age and Sickness	401
(b) Social, Recreational and Sporting Trusts	402
(c) Animals	406

(d) Political Trusts	407
(e) Miscellaneous	410
4. Public Benefit	411
A. Preliminary Points	411
B. Trusts for the Relief of Poverty	412
i. A Class of Poor as Opposed to Selected Individuals. Poor Relations	412
ii. Poor Employees	412
C. Trusts for the Advancement of Education	413
i. Benefits to the Public or a Section thereof	413
ii. Personal Nexus	414
iii. Benefiting Private Individuals	416
D. Trusts for the Advancement of Religion	417
E. The Fourth Head	419
5. The Interpretation of Charitable Gifts and Purposes	421
A. The Motive of the Donor	422
B. The Locality Cases	422
C. The Charitable Status of the Trustee	423
D. The Objects Must be Exclusively Charitable	423
i. Main and Subsidiary Objects	423
ii. And/Or Cases	425
(a) Cases of "or"	425
(b) Cases of "and"	425
iii. Severance	426
iv. Charitable Trusts (Validation) Act 1954	427
E. Disaster Appeals	429
6. Cy-Près	430
A. The Cy-Près Doctrine Prior to 1960	430
B. Initial Failure, Paramount Charitable Intent	431
i. Width of Charitable Intent	431
ii. Has the Gift Failed? Continuation in Another Form	432
(a) Gift in Augmentation of Funds of Defunct Charity	433
(b) Gift for Purposes. Unincorporated Associations and Charitable Corporations	433
iii. Projects	435
iv. Non-Existent Charity	435

pious, religious ceremonies for the gratification of the spirits of the ancestors failed, mainly on the ground that it could be of benefit to the family only and not to the public.[91] That was a decision of the Privy Council on appeal from Penang. The matter is of domestic importance now, because of the increase in the numbers of members of non-Christian religions among the population.

A gift for the promotion of the Jewish religion has been upheld.[92] The reference in Statutory Instruments to "the advancement of religion other than Christianity" clearly implies recognition.[93] It is believed that Sikh temples and other centres of non-Christian worship have been accorded the non-domestic rating privileges applicable to charities,[94] and there seems little doubt that all non-Christian religions will be treated equally. This situation may give rise to a number of difficult questions if charitable status is claimed for some mystical oriental and other cults.[95]

iv. Related Purposes. A large number of purposes have been accepted as charitable, although indirectly connected with the advancement of religion. Again, only a few illustrations can be selected. Many of these relate to the erection of churches or the maintenance of the fabric of religious buildings; which includes a window,[96] a tomb in the church,[97] and bells.[98] A trust for a graveyard, even though restricted to one denomination, is charitable,[99] but not a trust for individual tombs in the churchyard.[1]

Similarly, a trust for the benefit of the clergy,[2] or for the church choir,[3] and also for retired missionaries.[4] It has been held, however, that a gift for missionary work is not charitable on the ground that

---

[91] *Yeap Cheah Neo v. Ong Chen Neo* (1875) L.R. 6 P.C. 381.
[92] *Neville Estates Ltd v. Madden* [1962] Ch. 832. The position of Buddhism was left open in *Re South Place Ethical Society* [1980] 1 W.L.R. 1565.
[93] S.I. 1962 No. 1421; 1963 No. 2074.
[94] Local Government Finance Act 1988, Sched. 5, para. 11, as amended by L.G.F.A. 1992, Sched. 10, para. 3.
[95] On "fringe" religious organisations, see Annual Report 1976, paras. 103–108; and on exorcism, paras. 65–67. The Unification Church (the "Moonies") has also been registered; Annual Report 1982, paras. 36–38, App. C. The Attorney General announced on February 3, 1988, that a High Court action to deprive the "Moonies" of charitable status was being dropped. As to Scientology, see *R. v. Registrar General, ex p. Segerdal* [1970] 2 Q.B. 697 (meeting place not registrable under Places of Worship Registration Act 1855). A decision on registration by the Charity Commissioners is pending; *The Times*, January 10, 1997.
[96] *Re King* [1923] 1 Ch. 243; *Re Raine* [1936] Ch. 417.
[97] *Hoare v. Osborne* (1866) L.R. 1 Eq. 585.
[98] *Re Pardoe* [1906] 2 Ch. 184; an extreme case, as the purpose was to commemorate the restoration of the Monarchy.
[99] *Re Manser* [1905] 1 Ch. 68; *Re Eighmie* [1935] Ch. 524.
[1] *Lloyd v. Lloyd* (1852) 2 Sim.(N.S.) 225.
[2] *Middleton v. Clitheroe* (1798) 3 Ves. 734 (stipends); *Re Williams* [1927] 2 Ch. 283 (education of candidates for Ministry); *Re Forster* [1939] Ch. 22.
[3] *Re Royce* [1940] Ch. 514.
[4] *Re Mylne* [1941] Ch. 204; *Re Moon's W.T.* [1948] 1 All E.R. 300.

the description was too wide.[5] In this situation, however, as with many other phrases like "for God's work,"[6] or "for his work in the parish,"[7] the court will often find circumstances to indicate that the purposes are intended to be limited to charitable religious purposes.[8]

E. Other Purposes Beneficial to the Community[9]

This is the residual head of charity; the most difficult, as Sir Samuel Romilly called it as he presented the formulation.[10] The earlier three heads are in their nature charitable. There is no need in those cases to prove that the relief of poverty or the advancement of education or religion is beneficial. The public element there, as we will see,[11] concerns the extent to which those benefits are made available to the public or a section of the public as opposed to a group of individuals. With the fourth head, however, it must be shown that the selected purposes are beneficial; beneficial, that is, in the way which the law regards as charitable.

i. The Spirit and Intendment of the Preamble. The Preamble has always constituted the general statement of charitable purposes. The purposes were:

" ... the relief of aged, impotent and poor people; the maintenance of sick and maimed soldiers and mariners, schools of learning, free schools, and scholars in universities; the repair of bridges, ports, havens, causeways, churches, sea banks and highways; the education and preferment of orphans; the relief, stock, or maintenance of houses of correction; the marriage of poor maids; the supportation aid and help of young tradesmen, handicraftsmen and persons decayed; the relief or redemption of prisoners or captives; the aid or ease of any poor inhabitants concerning payment of fifteens, setting out of soldiers and other taxes."

Since its repeal, the cases themselves are the source of the principle. A purpose which is expressly included in the Preamble is charitable; and also one covered by case authority. But "not every object of

[5] *Scott v. Brownrigg* (1881) 9 L.R.Ir. 246.
[6] *Re Barker's W.T.* (1948) 64 T.L.R. 273. See also *Re Darling* [1896] 1 Ch. 50.
[7] *Re Simson* [1946] Ch. 299; *post,* p. 423.
[8] *Re Moon's W.T.* [1948] 1 All E.R. 300.
[9] See generally (1983) 36 C.L.P. 241 (H. Cohen). Most new registrations are under this heading; Annual Report 1985, para. 8.
[10] *Morice v. The Bishop of Durham* (1805) 10 Ves. 522 at p. 531.
[11] *Post,* pp. 411 *et seq.*

public general utility must necessarily be a charity."[12] The purpose
need not be *eiusdem generis* with those listed in the Preamble, but
must be charitable in the same sense.[13] When new purposes arise, it
is not sufficient to show that the purpose is beneficial. It must be
shown to be beneficial within the spirit and intendment of the Preamble, or by analogy from the principles established by the cases.[14]
In *Williams' Trustees v. I.R.C.*,[15] a trust for promoting the interests
of the Welsh community in London failed, on the ground that the
objects of the trust, though beneficial to the community, were not
beneficial in the way which the law regards as charitable. Similarly,
trusts for international co-operation have usually failed, either on the
ground that their purposes are not within the spirit and intendment
of the statute,[16] or because they are political.[17] On the other hand, in
*Scottish Burial Reform and Cremation Society v. Glasgow Corpora-
tion*,[18] a non-profit-making cremation society was held charitable by
analogy with cases holding burial grounds to be so, though neither
facility receives specific mention in the Preamble. Over the years, of
course, the law has been developed in a radical manner. There is no
definitional boundary to the fourth class; any purpose can be argued
as coming within it; and Russell L.J. went so far as to say that the
courts are accepting that if a purpose is beneficial to the community,
it is prima facie charitable in law, and that the analogy approach is
too restrictive.[19] The treatment of the problem has been much
improved by the obligation first imposed by the Charities Act 1960
to register charities with the Charity Commissioners.[20] For, as part
of their jurisdiction to register or to refuse registration, the Commissioners have built up a valuable range of precedents by which they
can be guided, and though this has had to be based on the existing
case law, nevertheless the Commissioners feel that they can develop
from it "such a concept of the field of charity as may meet the needs

[12] *Per* Lindley L.J. in *Re Macduff* [1896] 2 Ch. 451 at p. 456; *Att.-Gen. v. National Provincial and Union Bank of England* [1924] A.C. 262 at p. 265.

[13] *Re Strakosch* [1949] Ch. 529.

[14] See *Williams' Trustees v. I.R.C.* [1947] A.C. 447 at p. 455. See also *Brisbane C.C. v. Att.-Gen. for Queensland* [1979] A.C. 411 at p. 422.

[15] [1947] A.C. 447. The trust was later validated under the Charitable Trusts (Validation) Act 1954, p. 427, *post*; Annual Report 1977, paras. 71–80.

[16] *Re Strakosch* [1949] Ch. 529 (the furthering of understanding between the Union of South Africa and the Mother Country); *cf.* Annual Report 1983, para. 18; *Keren Kayemeth Le Jisroel v. I.R.C.* [1932] A.C. 650 (resettlement of Jews). See Picarda, pp. 166–167.

[17] See *McGovern v. Att-Gen.* [1982] Ch. 321, *post*, p. 408; *Re Koeppler's W.T.* [1986] Ch. 423 (formation of an informed international public opinion and promotion of greater co-operation in Europe and the West not regarded as charitable, although gift upheld as being for the furtherance of the work of a charitable educational project).

[18] [1968] A.C. 138.

[19] *Incorporated Council of Law Reporting v. Att.-Gen.* [1972] Ch. 73 at p. 88. *cf. Re South Place Ethical Society* [1980] 1 W.L.R. 1565, where Dillon J. preferred the analogy approach. See Annual Report 1985, paras. 24–27 (analogy required, but strict approach to it undesirable).

[20] *Post*, p. 446.

of the community."[21] There is an appeal from the Commissioners' decision to the court.[22]

ii. The Test is What the Law Treats as Charitable. The question whether a purpose is beneficial to the community is one that the court must decide in the light of all the evidence available. What the donor thought, or what other people think is not the issue. In a sense, the test is objective, yet the judges, as we saw in the case of artistic questions, cannot avoid making a subjective choice.

In *National Anti-Vivisection Society v. Inland Revenue Commissioners*,[23] the question was whether the Society was entitled to relief from income tax on the ground that its object, which was the total suppression of vivisection, was charitable. The protection of animals from cruelty is a charitable purpose.[24] Vivisection, on the other hand, is a necessary part of medical research and, as such, is itself beneficial to the community. The question, as Lord Simonds said "is whether the court, for the purposes of determining whether the object of the society is charitable may disregard the finding of fact that any assumed public benefit in the direction of the advancement of morals and education was far outweighed by the detriment to medical science and research and consequently to the public health which would result if the society succeeded in achieving its object, and that on balance, the object of the society, so far from being for the public benefit, was gravely injurious thereto. The society says that the court must disregard this fact, arguing that evidence of disadvantages or evils which would or might result from the stopping of vivisection is irrelevant and inadmissible."[25]

The court undertook to make the value judgment, "weighing conflicting moral and material utilities." On balance, on the evidence available to it, the suppression of vivisection was not beneficial to the public, and the claim failed.

The American Restatement takes a neutral position.[26] It sees nothing improper in upholding trusts for both armament and disarmament and, by a parity of reasoning, vivisection and anti-

---

[21] Annual Report 1966, paras. 27–41.

[22] *Post*, p. 447.

[23] [1948] A.C. 31. See also Decisions, Vol. 2 (1994) p. 1 (Animal AID, to prevent exploitation of animals by man, not charitable).

[24] *Post*, p. 406.

[25] [1948] A.C. 31 at pp. 60–61.

[26] *Restatement of the Law of Trusts*, § 374, comment 1; "The courts do not take sides or attempt to decide which of two conflicting views of promoting the social interest of the community is the better adapted for the purpose, even though the views are opposed to each other. Thus, a trust to promote peace by disarmament, as well as a trust to promote peace by preparedness for war, is charitable."

vivisection being charitable. This view greatly simplifies the task of the court. The balancing of the merits of two different forms of public benefit is a matter on which opinions may vary, and one on which the court may not be the best judge.

iii. Examples of Trusts under the Fourth Head. The number of cases decided under the fourth head is enormous, and only the main groups can be examined.

(a) *Specific Mention in the Preamble. Age and Sickness.* The Preamble refers to the "relief of aged, impotent and poor people." The phrase is construed disjunctively, and there is no need to show that the purpose of a trust includes all three. Thus, in *Re Robinson*,[27] a gift for old people over 60 years of age was upheld; and also trusts for the provision of housing for the aged.[28] Impotent means physically handicapped; and in *Re Lewis*,[29] a gift of £100 each to 10 blind girls and 10 blind boys in Tottenham was valid, there being no requirement that they should also be poor. "It would be as absurd to require that the aged must be impotent or poor as it would be to require the impotent to be aged or poor, or the poor to be aged or impotent."[30]

But difficulties arise where the rich participate. What would be the effect, it is asked, of a gift for the relief of aged peers or impotent millionaires?[31] The answer is that "The word 'relief' implies that the persons in question have a need attributable to their condition as aged, impotent or poor persons which requires alleviating, and which those persons could not alleviate, or would find difficulty in alleviating, themselves from their own resources. The word 'relief' is not synonymous with 'benefit.' . . . Thus a gift of money to the aged millionaires of Mayfair would not relieve a need of theirs as aged persons."[32]

Some of the other instances given in the preamble occasionally receive mention,[33] but there is reluctance to rely on them if the gift would not otherwise be charitable under Lord Macnaghten's classification. Their effect, now that the preamble is repealed, is obscure,

---

[27] [1951] Ch. 198; *Re Gosling* (1900) 48 W.R. 300 ("old and worn-out clerks" of the bank); *Re Wall* (1889) 42 Ch.D. 510.

[28] *Re Cottam* [1955] 1 W.L.R. 1299; *Joseph Rowntree Memorial Trust Housing Association Ltd v. Att.-Gen.* [1983] Ch. 159, (1983) 46 M.L.R. 782 (R. Nobles), All E.R. Rev. 1983, p. 356 (P. Clarke); *Re Dunlop (deceased)* (1984) 19 *Northern Ireland Judgments Bulletin.* See Annual Report 1967, paras. 22–29 (Homes for old people).

[29] [1955] Ch. 104.

[30] *Joseph Rowntree Memorial Trust Housing Association Ltd v. Att.-Gen.* [1983] Ch. 159 at p. 171.

[31] (1951) 67 L.Q.R. 164; (1955) 71 L.Q.R. 16 (R.E.M.). For the view that the poor cannot be excluded, see *Re Macduff* [1896] 2 Ch. 451.

[32] *Joseph Rowntree Memorial Trust Housing Association Ltd v. Att.-Gen., supra,* at p. 171.

[33] *e.g.* "The setting out of soldiers"; *Re Driffill* [1949] 2 All E.R. 933.

but those that have been acted on by the courts will presumably continue in effect, for the preamble was never a substantive provision and hence its repeal cannot affect the authority of cases based on it.[34]

A trust for the relief of the sick is charitable,[35] and so are trusts for the support of hospitals.[36] Indeed, prior to the introduction of the National Health Service in 1946, such hospitals were probably the greatest beneficiaries of charitable gifts, and the main hospital service of the nation was dependent on charity. It is no objection in this context that the benefits will be received by the rich as well as the poor; nor that the hospital was a private hospital for paying patients.[37] Ancillary purposes consistent with the object of the hospital are included, such as benefits for the sick in hospital[38] or for nurses,[39] which improve the quality of the service, and the provision of accommodation for the relatives of the critically ill,[40] and for rest homes for those suffering from nervous strain.[41] A nursing home privately owned and run for profit is not however a charity.[42]

(b) *Social, Recreational and Sporting Trusts.* Great difficulty has been experienced in establishing a dividing line to determine the validity of trusts for social, recreational or sporting purposes. The uncertainty caused by a series of cases in the 1940s and 1950s created doubts as to the charitable status of a number of institutions which had always been assumed to be charitable, such as the National Playing Fields Association, the Women's Institute and a number of local activities such as village halls. The Recreational Charities Act 1958 rescued them, but made no attempt to deal with the many problems thrown up by these cases. They will provide a useful background to the Act.

A trust to provide sporting facilities was not charitable,[43] unless, as has been seen, the facilities were for pupils of schools or universities, in which case they would be regarded as being for the advancement of education,[44] or within the armed forces, when they

---

[34] See Charities Act 1960, s.38(4), unrepealed by Charities Act 1993.
[35] Including faith healing; *Funnell v. Stewart* [1996] 1 W.L.R. 288.
[36] *Re Smith's W.T.* [1962] 2 All E.R. 563. On charities engaged in fringe medicine, see Annual Report 1975, para. 70.
[37] *Re Resch's W.T.* [1969] 1 A.C. 514; [1978] Conv. 277 (T. Watkin).
[38] *Re Roadley* [1930] 1 Ch. 524.
[39] *Re White's W.T.* [1951] 1 All E.R. 520.
[40] *Re Dean's W.T.* [1950] 1 All E.R. 882.
[41] *Re Chaplin* [1933] Ch. 115; *Re Banfield* [1968] 2 All E.R. 276.
[42] *Re Resch's W.T., supra,* at p. 540.
[43] *Re Nottage* [1895] 2 Ch. 649 (prize for a yacht race); *Re Patten* [1929] 2 Ch. 276 (cricket). See (1956) C.L.P. 39 (O. Marshall); *I.R.C. v. McMullen* [1981] A.C. 1 at p. 15, where the point was expressly left open.
[44] *Re Mariette* [1915] 2 Ch. 284; *ante,* p. 391; *London Hospital Medical College v. I.R.C.* [1976] 1 W.L.R. 613; [1978] Conv. 92 (N. Gravells).

would contribute to the safety and protection of the country,[45] or where the game was itself of an educational nature.[46]

In *I.R.C. v. Glasgow Police Athletic Association*,[47] the Association, whose object was "to encourage and promote all forms of athletic sport and general pastimes" was held not to be charitable. In so far as the objects were concerned with the "encouragement of recruiting, the improvement of the efficiency of the force and the public advantage"[48] they would have been charitable. But the provision of mere recreation was not charitable; nor could it, in the circumstances of the case, be held to be merely incidental to the main purpose. It was therefore fatal to the claim.

Gifts for the establishment of recreation grounds for the public generally or for the inhabitants of a particular area have been held charitable,[49] likewise particular sporting facilities.[50] However, as has been seen, in *Williams' Trustees v. I.R.C.*,[51] a trust for the promotion of Welsh interests in London by various means, most of which were charitable, failed because they involved a "social" and recreational element.[52] Further problems arose in a stamp duty context in *I.R.C. v. Baddeley* in 1955.[53]

Land was conveyed to a Methodist Mission "for the promotion of the religious, social and physical well-being of persons resident in . . . West Ham and Leyton . . . by the provision of facilities for religious services and instruction; and for the social and physical training and recreation of . . . persons who . . . are in the opinion of [local Church] leaders members or likely to become members of the Methodist church . . . and of insufficient means otherwise to enjoy the advantages provided. . . ." By a majority of four to one (Lord Reid dissenting), the House of Lords held that the purposes were not exclusively charitable, because of the inclusion

---

[45] *Re Gray* [1925] Ch. 362.

[46] *Re Dupree's Deed Trusts* [1945] Ch. 16, *ante,* p. 392.

[47] [1953] A.C. 380.

[48] *Per* Lord Normand, *ibid.,* at p. 395.

[49] *Re Hadden* [1932] Ch. 133; *Re Morgan* [1955] 1 W.L.R. 738; *R. v. Doncaster Metropolitan Borough Council, ex p. Braim* (1989) 57 P. & C.R. 1; *Oldham Borough Council v. Att.-Gen.,* [1993] Ch. 210; *cf. Liverpool City Council v. Att.-Gen., The Times,* May 1, 1992 (covenant by council to use donated land as recreation ground did not create charitable trust).

[50] Annual Report 1984, paras. 18–25 (Oxford Ice Skating Association charitable under the 1958 Act and the general law); *Re Laidlaw Foundation* (1985) 48 O.R. (2d) 549 (Athletics). This decision was doubted in Annual Report 1989, para. 53, where Birchfield Harriers Athletics Club was refused registration.

[51] [1947] A.C. 447, *ante,* p. 399.

[52] This element was deleted in 1977, when the Charity Commissioners validated the Trust under Charitable Trusts (Validation) Act 1954, *post,* p. 427; Annual Report 1971, paras. 71–80.

[53] [1955] A.C. 572.

of purely "social" purposes; and three of their Lordships further held that the requirement of public benefit was not satisfied.[54]

The Recreational Charities Act 1958[55] attempted to remove the uncertainty caused by these decisions. The object[56] was to give statutory recognition to a number of trusts which had always been regarded as charitable, "without enlarging the definition of charity or encroaching on existing authorities (including *Baddeley's Case* itself), or making any institution charitable which was not ordinarily regarded as charitable before that decision." It validates prospectively and retrospectively certain cases of the provision of recreational or other leisure-time occupations if the facilities are provided in the interests of social welfare.[57] Section 1 reads:

"—(1) Subject to the provisions of this Act, it shall be and be deemed always to have been charitable to provide, or assist in the provision of, facilities for recreation or other leisure-time occupation, if the facilities are provided in the interests of social welfare:

Provided that nothing in this section shall be taken to derogate from the principle that a trust or institution to be charitable must be for the public benefit.[58]

(2) The requirement of the foregoing subsection that the facilities are provided in the interests of social welfare shall not be treated as satisfied unless—

(a) the facilities are provided with the object of improving the conditions of life for the persons for whom the facilities are primarily intended; and

(b) either—

(i) those persons have need for such facilities as aforesaid by reason of their youth, age, infirmity or disablement, poverty or social and economic circumstances; or

(ii) the facilities are to be available to the members or female members of the public at large.[59]

(3) Subject to the said requirement, subsection (1) of this section applies in particular to the provision of facilities at village halls, community centres and women's institutes, and to the

---

[54] *Post*, p. 420.

[55] (1959) 23 Conv.(N.S.) 15 (S. Maurice); (1958) 21 M.L.R. 534 (L. Price); [1980] Conv. 173 (J. Warburton).

[56] *Halsbury's Statutes*, Vol. 5, p. 806.

[57] Selected as the criterion because the phrase appeared in other similar provisions, and had been judicially interpreted; *Halsbury's Statutes*, Vol. 5, p. 806; House of Commons Official Report, p. 322; February 11, 1958.

[58] *Post*, pp. 411 *et seq.*

[59] It is no objection that the facilities may be reserved for particular groups, thereby excluding the public at certain times; *Guild v. I.R.C.* [1992] 2 A.C. 310.

provision and maintenance of grounds and buildings to be used for purposes of recreation or leisure-time occupation and extends to the provision of facilities for those purposes by the organising of any activity."

It will be seen that the Act has little effect upon the cases previously discussed. The "Welsh people" do not come within section 1(2)(*b*)(i)[60]; nor would the "Methodists or persons likely to become Methodists" in *Baddeley*[61]; nor the Glasgow police, who would presumably not be covered by "social and economic circumstances."[62] The Charity Commissioners have stated that the Act was intended to relieve the "class within a class" problem which arises where a fourth category purpose is available only to a restricted class and consequently may not satisfy the "public benefit" requirement.[63] They take the view that section 1(2)(*b*)(i) may be satisfied by groups having need of the facilities which are further restricted by reference to their race, nationality, ethnic origins or religion. Thus a community centre restricted to such a group could qualify, if the Act is otherwise satisfied.[64]

Village halls, women's institutes and so forth were included in subsection (3) to overcome any argument that their activities were not within the spirit and intendment of the Preamble. Express provision is made also for Miners' Welfare Trusts in section 2.[65]

To meet the "social welfare" qualification, the facilities must be provided with the object of improving the conditions of life for the persons for whom they are primarily intended. In *I.R.C. v. McMullen*[66] (the Football Association Youth Trust case), the majority of the Court of Appeal[67] adopted a restrictive view, considering that the words implied that only "the deprived" can benefit. On the other hand, Bridge L.J. adopted a more liberal approach. Social welfare is not limited to the deprived. "Hyde Park improves the conditions of life for residents in Mayfair as much as for those in Pimlico or the Portobello Road."[68] The approach of Bridge L.J. was adopted by the House of Lords in *Guild v. I.R.C.*,[69] where a gift for the benefit of a public sports centre was held charitable under the Act. Section 1(2) was satisfied where the object of the gift was to

---

[60] *Williams v. I.R.C.* [1947] A.C. 447.
[61] *Supra.*
[62] *I.R.C. v. City of Glasgow Police Athletic Association* [1953] A.C. 380.
[63] *Post*, p. 420.
[64] Decisions, Vol. 4 (1995), p. 17.
[65] *Wynn v. Skegness U.D.C.* [1966] 1 W.L.R. 52.
[66] *Ante*, p. 391.
[67] [1979] 1 W.L.R. 130, especially at p. 138. The point was left open in the House of Lords; [1981] A.C. 1.
[68] At p. 143.
[69] [1992] 2 A.C. 310; [1992] Conv. 361 (H. Norman); (1992) 51 C.L.J. 429 (J. Hopkins). See also Annual Report 1995, para. 95 ("social welfare" has ethical and altruistic elements).

improve the conditions of life of the community generally. The facilities of the centre, which promoted physical well-being, would have this effect.

Further guidance on the construction of social welfare can be obtained from other statutes in which the phrase has been used.[70] There must be something more than a group of individuals combining together, as a club or society, to benefit themselves.[71]

(c) *Animals.* Trusts for the welfare of animals generally are charitable, though gifts for specified animals are not.[72] The charitable status of gifts to animals was originally limited to the welfare of animals which were useful to man,[73] and this rule was justified on the basis of public utility. More recently, the category has widened, although there are no words in the Preamble to support such gifts. The grounds of validity of such gifts have been differently stated in England and in Ireland. In Ireland, it is the simple and obvious good of the welfare of the animals themselves.[74] In England, the cases are justified on the ground that they "tend to promote and encourage kindness towards [animals], and to ameliorate the condition of the brute creation, and thus to stimulate humane and generous sentiments in man towards the lower animals, and by this means to promote feelings of humanity and morality generally, repress brutality, and thus elevate the human race."[75] On this basis, trusts have been upheld for a home for lost dogs,[76] cats and kittens needing care and attention,[77] the Society for the Prevention of Cruelty to Animals,[78] and for hospitals,[79] and humane slaughtering.[80] But there are limits. We have seen that a trust for the abolition of vivisection was not charitable because its purposes would, on balance, cause more harm than good to the public. The borderline in these cases is hard to draw. In *Re Grove-Grady*,[81] the Court of Appeal decided that it had been overstepped, Russell L.J. expressing the view that the

---

[70] General Rate Act 1967, s.40. See now Local Government Finance Act 1988, s.47.
[71] See *Re Lipinski's W.T.* [1976] Ch. 235, *ante*, p. 349; Annual Report 1989, paras. 48–55 (Birchfield Harriers Athletics Club did not satisfy s.1(2)); Decisions, Vol. 1 (1993), p. 4 (rifle club not within s.1(2)); Annual Report 1995, para. 95 (North Tawton Rugby Union Football Club failed public benefit test).
[72] *Ante*, p. 355.
[73] *London University v. Yarrow* (1857) 1 De G. & J. 72.
[74] *Armstrong v. Reeves* (1890) 25 L.R.Ir. 325.
[75] *Re Wedgwood* [1915] 1 Ch. 113, *per* Swinfen-Eady L.J. at p. 122. See also *Re Green's W.T.* [1985] 3 All E.R. 455.
[76] Re *Douglas* (1887) 35 Ch.D. 472.
[77] *Re Moss* [1949] 1 All E.R. 495.
[78] *Tatham v. Drummond* (1864) 4 De G.J. & Sm. 484; *Armstrong v. Reeves* (1890) 25 L.R.Ir. 325. See Annual Report 1979, para. 20.
[79] *London University v. Yarrow* (1857) 1 De G. & J. 72.
[80] *Tatham v. Drummond (supra)*.
[81] [1929] 1 Ch. 557 (compromised on appeal; *Att.-Gen. v. Plowden* [1931] W.N. 89). *Cf. Att.-Gen. (N.S.W.) v. Sawtell* [1978] 2 N.S.W.L.R. 200; Pettit, p. 243.

authorities had reached the furthest admissible point of benevolence in construing as charitable, gifts in favour of animals. There was a trust for the setting up of an animal refuge where the animals, birds and other creatures should be safe from molestation by man. A sanctuary which deprived mankind of all rights of involvement was not for the public benefit, although this view may be outmoded.

The decision does not cast doubt upon the charitable status of animal sanctuaries generally. Many purposes connected with animals could be made charities by being expressed in terms of education[82] or of environmental preservation.[83]

(d) *Political Trusts.* Trusts whose object, direct or indirect, is the support of one political party are clearly not charitable.[84] The borderline between such trusts and trusts where political propaganda was "masquerading as education" has been discussed.[85]

The general principle is that political trusts are not charitable. In *Re Bushnell*,[86] the testator left money for "the advancement and propagation of the teaching of socialised medicine." The trust was neither an educational charity nor charitable under the fourth heading. The testator had died in 1941, and at that time legislation would have been required to achieve the purpose. The desirability of such legislation was a political matter. It made no difference that a national health service had subsequently been introduced, as the relevant time for judging the matter was the testator's death.

A second reason for the failure of the Anti-Vivisection trust[87] was that the objects of the Society required a change in the law. The majority treated this as necessarily being a political purpose. Lord Normand stressed that this should only be so where, as here, the change in the law was a *predominant object*,[88] while Lord Porter, who dissented, would have excluded only trusts which were purely political,[89] that is to say, where the object is to be attained *only* by

---

[82] *Re Lopes* [1931] 2 Ch. 130.

[83] See Annual Report 1973, para. 40.

[84] *Bonar Law Memorial Trust v. I.R.C.* (1933) 49 T.L.R. 220 (Conservative); *Re Ogden* [1933] Ch. 678 (Liberal); *Re Hopkinson* [1949] 1 All E.R. 346 (Socialist: the whole tenor of the gift was to mask political propaganda as education). It is doubtful whether *Re Scowcroft* [1898] 2 Ch. 638 would now be followed; the case itself might have been differently decided had the gift been only for the furtherance of Conservative principles. See also Annual Report 1982, paras. 45–51 (refusal to register Youth Training, whose purpose is to assist the Workers' Revolutionary Party); Annual Report 1991, para. 75 (Margaret Thatcher Foundation was political).

[85] *Ante*, p. 393.

[86] [1975] 1 W.L.R. 1596.

[87] *National Anti-Vivisection Society v. I.R.C.* [1948] A.C. 31; *ante*, p. 400.

[88] *Ibid.* at pp. 77–78.

[89] *Ibid.* at p. 56.

a change in the law. Ultimately "It is a question of degree of a sort well known to the courts."[90]

The treatment as political of any trust requiring a change in the law has been criticised. But whether the proposed change is for the public benefit "is not for the court to judge, and the court has no means of judging."[91] The Legislature decides on changes in the law. The judges' duty is to apply it. The judges should not be put in a position of being asked to hold that a controversial object, often a minority object, is so obviously for the public good that it should be pursued perpetually and tax-free. It is difficult, however, to answer the criticism that organisations campaigning for improvements in the law[92] cannot be registered as charities, while existing charities can and do campaign for and against change.[93]

The matter arose in *McGovern v. Att.-Gen.*,[94] where a non-charitable body, Amnesty International, sought to obtain charitable status for part of its activities by setting up the Amnesty International Trust, to which were transferred those aspects of its work which were thought to be charitable. The objects were: (i) the relief of needy persons who were, or were likely to become, prisoners of conscience, and their relatives; (ii) attempting to secure the release of prisoners of conscience; (iii) the abolition of torture or inhuman or degrading treatment or punishment; (iv) research into human rights and disseminating the results of the research.[95] These objects were to be carried out in all parts of the world. Purposes (i) and (iv), if standing alone, would have been charitable, but the inclusion of the other objects caused the trust to fail on the ground that it was political.[96] A trust could not be charitable if its direct and main object was to secure a change in the law of the United Kingdom or of foreign countries, for example by repealing legislation authoris-ing capital or corporal punishment. The court could not judge whether this would be for the public benefit, locally or internation-ally. Nor could a trust be charitable if a direct and principal purpose was to procure the reversal of government policy or of governmental

---

[90] *Ibid.* at p. 77.
[91] *Per* Lord Simonds [1948] A.C. 31 at p. 62.
[92] National Council for Civil Liberties; Amnesty.
[93] Lord's Day Observance Society; Temperance Societies.
[94] [1982] Ch. 321; [1982] Conv. 387 (T. Watkin); (1982) 45 M.L.R. 704 (R. Nobles); (1983) 46 M.L.R. 385 (F. Weiss); [1984] Conv. 263 (C. Forder). See also *Re Koeppler's W.T.* [1986] Ch. 423; where the formation of an informed international public opinion and the promotion of greater co-operation in Europe and the West were not regarded as charitable, although the gift was upheld as being for the furtherance of the work of a charitable educational project.
[95] See Annual Report 1987, para. 12 (trusts for research into human rights upheld); Annual Report 1988, paras. 27–34 (Institute for the Study of Terrorism registered).
[96] It was not saved by a proviso restricting it to charitable purposes; *post*, p. 421.

decisions at home or abroad.[97] Object (ii) was not simply for the "relief or redemption of prisoners or captives,"[98] but involved putting pressure on foreign governments and authorities. To ascribe charitable status to such a trust could prejudice the relations of this country with the foreign country concerned. This public policy consideration could not be ignored.

A related problem arises where an existing charity is tempted to become involved in pursuing "causes" relating to the work with which it is concerned. It was suggested in *McGovern v. Att.-Gen.*[99] that if the objects had been charitable, it would not have mattered that the trustees had incidental powers to employ political means to further these objects. The Charity Commissioners have offered some revised guidelines to charity trustees, including the following points[1]:

(i) Any political activity must be in furtherance of and ancillary to the charity's stated objects and within its powers. To be ancillary, the activity must serve and be subordinate to the charity's purpose.

(ii) Where these requirements are met, the trustees may enter into a dialogue with the Government on matters relating to their purposes, and may respond to Green and White Papers.

(iii) The trustees may inform and educate the public on issues relevant to the charity and on solutions to its needs. They must not advocate policies nor seek to inform the public on matters having no bearing on their charity, nor indulge in propaganda.

(iv) The trustees may engage in campaigning, by reasoned argument and not on the basis of material which is merely emotive, if the above requirements are satisfied. They may advocate a change in law or policy which they reasonably believe would help to achieve the charity's purpose, or

---

[97] The decision was distinguised in *Re Koeppler's W.T., supra*, where an educational project involving conferences with a "political flavour" was held charitable. The project was not concerned with party politics nor did it seek to change laws or government policies. See also *R. v. Radio Authority, ex p. Bull, The Times*, January 21, 1997.

[98] Preamble to the Charitable Uses Act, 1601.

[99] *Supra.*

[1] *Political Activities and Campaigning by Charities* (1994, 1995). In 1978 the activities of three international relief charities were reviewed (War on Want; Oxfam; and the Christian Aid Division), Annual Report 1978, paras. 21–29; and in 1979 three domestic charities (Abortion, the R.S.P.C.A., and the Howard League for Penal Reform); Annual Report 1979, paras. 18–22; Annual Report 1991, paras. 111–127 (Oxfam; War on Want). Annual Report 1988, paras. 27–34 (strong political views of trustees of the Institute for the Study of Terrorism did not affect charitable status, but warned to maintain objectivity). The RSPCA has been warned not to campaign against animal experiments which benefit mankind; *The Times*, March 28, 1996. See also *The Times*, July 1, 1996 (hunting).

oppose a change which would hinder it. Similarly, they may promote legislation to achieve or further its purpose.

(v) The trustees should not seek to organise public opinion to support or oppose a political party which has a particular policy, nor may a charity participate in party political demonstrations.

(vi) Where the charity operates overseas, it may pursue activities which would be permissible at home even if considered political elsewhere, provided they are not actually illegal in the country where they are undertaken.

(e) *Miscellaneous.* There is no way of explaining the full width of the fourth head. But some miscellaneous examples may be helpful. Gifts for the promotion of the efficiency of the fighting services are charitable. It has been seen that the promotion of sport in the Army is included[2]; so is a gift to the officers' mess,[3] and for the training of officers for the Navy or Merchant Marine,[4] for the protection of the Kingdom against attack by hostile aircraft.[5] On the other hand, a provision for ex-members of the services is not charitable, unless confined to the aged or poor.[6] The efficiency of the police is similarly a charitable purpose,[7] and also a gift to a voluntary fire brigade.[8] The National Trust is charitable,[9] and the Royal National Lifeboat Institution; so also are gifts for the promotion of agriculture,[10] preservation of natural amenities,[11] and for environmental objects.[12] A gift for the founding of a children's home is charitable,[13] but, it seems a gift for the benefit of the children in such a home is too wide, unless expressly confined to the meeting of the children's needs at the home, otherwise it might be applied to the purchase of luxurious amenities.[14] The Incorporated Council of Law Reporting has been held to be charitable under the second and fourth heads[15]; and so has the study and dissemination of ethical principles

---

[2] *Re Gray* [1925] Ch. 362.

[3] *Re Good* [1905] 2 Ch. 60.

[4] *Re Corbyn* [1941] Ch. 400.

[5] *Re Driffill* [1950] Ch. 92.

[6] *Re Meyers* [1951] Ch. 534.

[7] *I.R.C. v. City of Glasgow Police Athletic Association* [1953] A.C. 380. See also Annual Report 1984, para. 17 (Police Memorial Trust to commemorate officers killed on duty).

[8] *Re Wokingham Fire Brigade Trusts* [1951] Ch. 373; Annual Report 1979, paras. 74–81.

[9] *Re Verrall* [1916] 1 Ch. 100.

[10] *I.R.C. v. Yorkshire Agricultural Society* [1928] 1 K.B. 611; *Brisbane C.C. v. Att.-Gen. for Queensland* [1979] A.C. 411.

[11] *Re Granstown* [1932] 1 Ch. 537; *Re Corelli* [1943] Ch. 332.

[12] Annual Report 1973, para. 40; Annual Report 1979, paras. 61–65.

[13] *Re Sahal's W.T.* [1958] 1 W.L.R. 1243.

[14] *Re Cole* [1958] Ch. 877; doubted in *Tudor on Charities* (8th ed.), p. 100.

[15] *Incorporated Council of Law Reporting for England and Wales v. Att.-Gen.* [1972] Ch. 73; (1972) 88 L.Q.R. 171.

and the cultivation of a rational religious sentiment.[16] An appeal for a public memorial may be charitable, as in the case of the statue of Earl Mountbatten of Burma.[17] The Charity Commissioners concluded that "the provision of a statue might be held to have a sufficient element of public benefit where the person being commemorated was nationally, and perhaps internationally, respected and could be said to be a figure of historical importance. In such a case the provision and maintenance of a statue can be held to be charitable as likely to foster patriotism and good citizenship, and to be an incentive to heroic and noble deeds." Finally, a gift "To my country, England,"[18] was upheld, the court taking the view, based on some old "locality" cases that,[19] in the context, the property could be applied only to charitable purposes.

4. PUBLIC BENEFIT[20]

A. Preliminary Points

A gift can only be charitable if it is for the public benefit. A few preliminary points must be made. First, it will be seen that the requirement differs in respect of each category,[21] and that it may differ within the fourth category, dependent upon the purpose concerned. Secondly, we will see that there is disagreement among the Law Lords on the question whether tax exemption is a factor which should be taken into consideration in deciding upon charitable status.[22] Thirdly, it may seem anomalous to speak in terms of a requirement of public benefit in the fourth category, for that category is defined in terms of trusts for the benefit of the community. To establish a trust as charitable within this category, it is necessary that the purposes are beneficial in the way which the law regards as charitable, and also that the benefits are available to a sufficient section of the public. With trusts coming under the first three heads, the matter is rather different. The beneficial aspect of trusts for the

---

[16] *Re South Place Ethical Society* [1980] 1 W.L.R. 1565.

[17] Annual Report 1981, paras. 68–70.

[18] *Re Smith* [1932] 1 Ch. 153.

[19] The restriction of a benefit to a specified locality may enable the judge, by applying a benevolent construction, to find that a trust was charitable; *post*, p. 422.

[20] See generally (1956) 72 L.Q.R. 187 (G. Cross); (1958) 21 M.L.R. 138 (P. Atiyah); (1974) 33 C.L.J. 63 (G. Jones); (1975) 39 Conv.(N.S.) 183 (S. Plowright); (1976) 22 N.I.L.Q. 198 (J. Brady); (1977) 40 M.L.R. 397 (N. Gravells); [1978] Conv. 277 (T. Watkin); Goodman Committee Report Chap. 2 (Benefit to the "Community"); Chap. 3 ("Benefit" to the Community).

[21] *Per* Lord Simonds in *Gilmour v. Coats* [1949] A.C. 426 at p. 429; *per* Lord Somervell in *I.R.C. v. Baddeley* [1955] A.C. 572 at p. 615.

[22] *Dingle v. Turner* [1972] A.C. 601; *post*, p. 413.

relief of poverty, or the advancement of education or religion is assumed.[23] The necessary public element needs to be shown.

B. Trusts for the Relief of Poverty

i. A Class of Poor as Opposed to Selected Individuals. Poor Relations.

The requirement of public benefit has been reduced, in the field of poverty, almost to vanishing point. It is necessary to distinguish between a gift to a class or group of poor persons, and a gift to specified poor individuals. The former will be charitable, even if the group is small, and personally connected with the donor; gifts to poor relations have been upheld since the middle of the eighteenth century.[24] As Jenkins L.J. said: "I think that the true question in each case has really been whether the gift for the relief of poverty amongst a class of persons, or rather, as Sir William Grant, M.R. put it, a particular description of poor, or was merely a gift to individuals, albeit with relief of poverty amongst those individuals as the motive of the gift, or with a selective preference for the poor or poorest amongst those individuals. . . ."[25] Thus, a gift to such of the testator's relatives as shall be poor or "in special need"[26] or "in needy circumstances"[27] is charitable. Similarly a gift to "poor and needy" members of a class of six named relatives of the testator and their issue, there being 26 members at the testator's death and a likelihood of a substantial increase in future.[28] It does not matter that the distribution of capital can be made so as to exhaust the principal.[29]

ii. Poor Employees.

Poor relations trusts are said to constitute an anomalous exception to the requirement of public benefit,[30] and we will see that a personal nexus or relationship between the group of persons to be benefited is fatal to gifts under the other heads.[31] This relaxation in favour of poverty trusts applies also in connection with

---

[23] *Per* Lord Simonds in *National Anti-Vivisection Society v. I.R.C.* [1948] A.C. 31.

[24] *Isaac v. Defriez* (1754) Amb. 595. They are discussed at length in *Re Compton* [1945] Ch. 123, and in *Re Scarisbrick* [1951] Ch. 622. See also *Dingle v. Turner* [1972] A.C. 601; *infra.*

[25] In *Re Scarisbrick* [1951] Ch. 622 at p. 655; see also at pp. 650–651; *Re Cohen* [1973] 1 W.L.R. 415 at p. 426; *Dingle v. Turner* [1972] A.C. 601 at p. 617.

[26] *Re Cohen* [1973] 1 W.L.R. 415.

[27] *Re Scarisbrick* [1951] Ch. 622.

[28] *Re Segelman* [1996] Ch. 171; [1996] Conv. 379 (E. Histed). The inclusion of named persons as objects of charity may be an extension of the rule.

[29] *Re Scarisbrick, supra; Dingle v. Turner, supra.*

[30] *Re Compton* [1945] Ch. 123 at 139, *per* Lord Greene M.R.

[31] *Post*, p. 414.

trusts for the relief of poverty among members of a friendly society,[32] or a professional association,[33] or employees of a company.

In *Dingle v. Turner*,[34] a testator provided a fund upon trust "to apply the income thereof in paying pensions to poor employees of E. Dingle and Co. Ltd who are of the age of 60 years at least or who being of the age of 45 years at least are incapacitated from earning their living by reason of some physical or mental infirmity." At the date of the testator's death, the company employed over 600 persons, and there was a substantial number of ex-employees. The House of Lords upheld the gift as a charitable trust.

The poor relations cases had been recognised for 200 years, and, even if anomalous, should not now be overruled. It would be illogical to draw a distinction between poor relations, and poor employees or poor members. All forms of trusts for the relief of poverty should be treated the same, and there was no need to introduce into the poverty cases the stricter requirements of public benefit applicable to other forms of charitable trusts. Lord Cross suggested that one reason for the different treatment of poverty trusts—a practical justification but not the historical explanation—is that there is for a settlor a "temptation to enlist the assistance of the law of charity in private endeavours"[35] in order to gain the tax benefits, though the danger is not so great in the field of relief of poverty. Three Law Lords[36] doubted whether the fiscal considerations should be given any relevance in deciding whether a gift was charitable. There seems little doubt, however, that they often have done so.[37]

C. Trusts for the Advancement of Education

i. Benefit to the Public or a Section thereof. Much of what is said in this section also applies to the next two following sections. Poverty apart, a trust will only be charitable if it is "for the benefit of the community or an appreciably important class of the community."[38] The principle appears to be that the privileges of charity, and

[32] *Re Buck* [1896] 2 Ch. 727.
[33] *Spiller v. Maude* (1886) 32 Ch.D. 158n. (aged and decayed actors).
[34] [1972] A.C. 601; *Re Gosling* (1900) 48 W.R. 300 (old and worn-out clerks in a banking firm); *Gibson v. South American Stores (Gath & Chaves) Ltd* [1950] Ch. 177 ("necessitous and deserving employees, ex-employes and their dependants").
[35] At p. 625.
[36] Lords Dilhorne, McDermott and Hodson.
[37] *Ante*, p. 378.
[38] *Per* Lord Westbury in *Verge v. Somerville* [1924] A.C. 496 at p. 499.

the loss of public revenue, should only be accorded to trusts which provide a benefit to the public. There is no objection to a parent educating children expensively, nor to isolated religious communities, nor to friendly societies for the benefit of members; but there is no reason why these activities should be supported, indirectly, by the taxpayer. Poor relations trusts, as has been seen, are a long-established anomaly.

ii. Personal Nexus. Not every member of the public can benefit from every charitable trust, and it becomes necessary to determine what is a section of the public for these purposes. Again, this will vary with the different categories. A trust for the advancement of education is charitable if it is for the education of the public or of a section of the public which is not selected on the basis of a personal nexus or connection, either with the donor or between themselves. Thus, a trust for the education of named persons or for descendants of named persons,[39] or the children of employees of a company,[40] or of members of a club is not charitable. But a trust for the education of the residents of a certain borough in 1880 and their descendants is charitable[41]; as are trusts for the education of children of members of a particular profession,[42] and trusts for specified schools and colleges, and even "closed" scholarships from a specified school to a college at Oxford or Cambridge[43]; unless, of course, the number of possible beneficiaries was derisory.

In *Oppenheim v. Tobacco Securities Trust Co.*,[44] income was to be applied in "providing for ... the education of children of employees or former employees of the British-American Tobacco Company Ltd ... or any of its subsidiary or allied companies in such manner ... as the acting trustees shall in their absolute discretion ... think fit" and there was power also to apply capital. The number of employees of the company and the subsidiary and allied companies exceeded 100,000. The House of Lords (Lord McDermott dissenting), following *Re Compton*,[45] held that there was a personal nexus between the members of the class of

---

[39] *Re Compton* [1945] Ch. 123. "A trust established by a father for the education of his sons is not a charity"; *per* Lord Simonds in *Oppenheim v. Tobacco Securities Trust Ltd* [1951] A.C. 297 at p. 306.

[40] *Oppenheim v. Tobacco Securities Trust Ltd* [1951] A.C. 297.

[41] *Re Tree* [1945] Ch. 325.

[42] *Hall v. Derby Sanitary Authority* (1885) 16 Q.B.D. 163, approved in *Oppenheim v. Tobacco Securities Trust Ltd, supra.*

[43] Though it is difficult to see how some of these trusts satisfy the *Oppenheim* rule; see Lord McDermott in *Oppenheim, ante*, at p. 318. See also the anomalous "founder's kin" cases; Picarda, p. 59; Tudor, p. 61.

[44] [1951] A.C. 297.

[45] [1945] Ch. 123.

beneficiaries and they did not constitute a section of the public. The trust failed.

In the leading majority speech, Lord Simonds said that to constitute a section of the community for these purposes the "possible (I emphasize the word 'possible') beneficiaries must be not numerically negligible, and, secondly, that the quality which distinguishes them from members of the community . . . must be a quality which does not depend on their relationship to a particular individual . . . A group of persons may be numerous but, if the nexus between them is their personal relationship to a single propositus or to several propositi, they are neither the community nor a section of the community for charitable purposes."[46]

Lord McDermott, dissenting, pointed out the difficulties which arise in trying to lay down a positive rule in such a situation.[47] "But can any really fundamental distinction, as respects the personal or impersonal nature of the common link, be drawn between those employed, for example, by a particular university and those whom the same university has put in a certain category as the result of individual examination and assessment? Again, if the bond between those employed by a particular railway is purely personal, why should the bond between those who are employed as railwaymen be so essentially different? Is a distinction to be drawn in this respect between those who are employed in a particular industry before it is nationalised and those who are employed therein after that process has been completed and one employer has taken the place of many? Are miners in the service of the National Coal Board now in one category and miners in a particular pit or of a particular district in another? Is the relationship between those in the service of the Crown to be distinguished from that obtaining between those in the service of some other employer? Or, if not, are the children of, say, soldiers or civil servants to be regarded as not constituting a sufficient section of the public to make a trust for their education charitable?[48] The question, he thought, should be one of degree, depending upon the facts of each particular case. All five Law Lords, sitting in *Dingle v. Turner*,[49] supported this view. This does not necessarily mean that *Oppenheim* would be decided differently. Taking all factors into account, these educational trusts for employees are attempts to use charity's fiscal privileges for the benefit of

---

[46] [1951] A.C. 297 at p. 306.
[47] See also Cross J. in *Re Mead's Trust Deed* [1961] 1 W.L.R. 1244 at p. 1249; and Lord Denning M.R. in *I.R.C. v. Educational Grants Association Ltd* [1967] Ch. 993 at p. 1009; "There is no logic in it."
[48] At pp. 317–318.
[49] [1972] A.C. 601; see also Annual Report 1971, para. 21.

the company by providing a tax-free fringe benefit for the employees.[50] Such trusts should fail, not on the ground that the employees, however numerous, can never constitute a class of the public, but because the *purpose* of the trust, being a company purpose, is not charitable.[51] A trust for the advancement of religion among employees might be different[52]; as might an "entirely altruistic educational trust . . . if the size of the company is sufficiently large."[53] It is obvious that it is easier to criticise the "personal nexus" test than it is to improve upon it; and "it may well be that Lord Cross's halfway house creates more problems than it solves."[54]

iii. Benefiting Private Individuals. The question arises as to whether a donor can effectively obtain benefits for a group of private individuals by means of a charitable trust. He cannot do so by setting up a charitable trust in favour of the public and relying on the trustees to make grants in favour of a narrow group.

In *I.R.C. v. Educational Grants Association Ltd*[55] the defendant was an association established for the advancement of education in general terms and was a charitable corporation. It was financially supported by payments under a deed of covenant by the Metal Box Co. Ltd, and by senior executives of the company. The Association claimed the repayment of tax due in respect of payment under the covenant. Between 76 per cent and 85 per cent of the income of the relevant year had been paid towards the education of children of persons connected with the Metal Box Co. Ltd, and the Court of Appeal held that the tax was not recoverable, because the money had not been applied for charitable purposes only.[56]

It is impossible to say what percentage of a trust for charity could properly be spent in favour of a private group. In *Re Koettgen's Will Trusts*,[57] there was a trust for the promotion of commercial education among members of the public unable to acquire it at their own

---

[50] "It is an admirable thing that the children of employees should have a higher education, but I do not see why that should be at the expense of the taxpayer" *per* Harman L.J. in *I.R.C. v. Educational Grants Association Ltd, supra,* at p. 1013; *cf.* Annual Report 1971, para. 21.

[51] *Dingle v. Turner, supra.*

[52] (1974) 33 C.L.J. 63 at p. 66 (G. Jones); *Dingle v. Turner, supra.*

[53] Annual Report 1971, para. 21.

[54] (1974) 33 C.L.J. 63 (G. Jones).

[55] [1967] Ch. 993; Annual Report 1976, paras. 45–49.

[56] See I.C.T.A. 1988, s.505(1), which permits exemption for a charitable body *so far as the income is applied to charitable purposes only.* In the *Educational Grants* case the non-charitable payments were *ultra vires.* If the objects permit such payments, the body is not charitable (subject to *Re Koettgen*) and there will be no tax exemption.

[57] [1954] Ch. 252.

expense; and a direction that preference be given to the families of employees of a named company in respect of a maximum of 75 per cent of the income. This was charitable. Lord Radcliffe in *Caffoor v. Income Tax Commissioner, Colombo*,[58] thought that *Re Koettgen* "edged very near to being inconsistent with" *Oppenheim*.[59] If a preference in favour of a private group is desired, it is essential to make it subsidiary to the trust in favour of the public; and the 75 per cent which succeeded in *Koettgen* should be regarded as the outside maximum.[60] If, however, there is an absolute right in favour of a private group, and not merely a preference, then the trust cannot be charitable. It is a matter of construction into which category the gift falls.[61]

D. Trusts for the Advancement of Religion

The notion of public benefit in religious trusts is very similar to that in education. The advancement of religion among the public or a section of the public is charitable, and there is no room for the argument of the atheists that it is not beneficial. The section of the public may be a sect, whether of the Christian religion, such as the Roman Catholic[62] or the Methodist Church,[63] or of a non-Christian religion, such as the Jewish.[64] And we have seen that the law is especially generous in favour of bona fide religions, even though they have minimal following,[65] similarly a gift to a Church will be charitable even though the congregation is small. A trust is charitable if it makes available a religious activity to the public if they should wish to take advantage of it. It may be that a sufficient benefit to the public is shown by having amongst it persons who have enjoyed the benefit of religious experience. But an enclosed, cloistered, monastic activity is excluded.

In *Gilmour v. Coats*,[66] a gift of £500 was made to a Carmelite Priory "if the purposes of [the Priory] are charitable." The Priory consisted of a community of cloistered nuns, about 20 in number, who devoted their lives to prayer, contemplation and self-sanctification, and engaged in no external work.

---

[58] [1961] A.C. 584.
[59] *Ibid.* at p. 604.
[60] See Annual Report 1978, paras. 86–89, where the Charity Commissioners followed *Re Koettgen* in three cases; 65 per cent and 75 per cent.
[61] *Re Martin, The Times*, November 19, 1980.
[62] *Dunne v. Byrne* [1912] A.C. 407; *Re Flinn* [1948] Ch. 241.
[63] *I.R.C. v. Baddeley* [1955] A.C. 572.
[64] *Neville Estates Ltd v. Madden* [1962] Ch. 832.
[65] *Re Watson* [1973] 1 W.L.R. 1472; (1974) 90 L.Q.R. 4.
[66] [1949] A.C. 426. Likewise services in a private chapel; *Hoare v. Hoare* (1886) 56 L.T. 147. But sufficient public benefit was found in *Holmes v. Att.-Gen., The Times*, February 12, 1981 (Exclusive Brethren). See Annual Report 1982, App. C.

The House of Lords held that the purposes were not charitable because they lacked the necessary public benefit. This could not be found in the benefits conferred upon the public by the prayers and intercessions of the nuns according to the doctrine of the Roman Catholic Church. Such benefit was "manifestly not susceptible of proof"[67] in a court of law, and the doctrinal belief of the Roman Catholic Church would be no substitute[68]; nor in the edification of a section of the public by the example of the spiritual life followed by the nuns, for that was too vague and intangible to constitute a proper test[69]; nor by the availability of the religious life being open to all women of the Roman Catholic faith.

The latter argument provides an interesting comparison with trusts for the advancement of education. Lord Simonds accepted that there was a "speciously logical appearance" in the argument that "just as the endowment of a scholarship open to public competition is a charity, so also is a gift to enable any woman (or, presumably, any man) to enter into a fuller religious life a charity."[70] Yet there is no conflict here. The explanation is that a public benefit is supplied in educational trusts by the presence in society of educated people. A trust for the advancement of religion among the members of Catford Synagogue was held by Cross J. in *Neville Estates Ltd v. Madden*[71] to be charitable because the court was "entitled to assume that some benefit accrues to the public from the attendance at places of worship of persons who live in this world and mix with their fellow-citizens."[72] And "if it can be imagined that it was made a condition of a gift for the advancement of education that its beneficiaries should lead a cloistered life and communicate to no one, and leave no record of the fruits of their study, I do not think that the charitable character of the gift will be sustained."[73]

This suggests that there must be some benefit to the public as a whole, however indirect, rather than the section which decides to participate. This point arises also under the fourth head. It is odd, however, that a gift to enable pious women to spend their life in

---

[67] *Ibid.* at p. 446. But extra-statutory tax concessions have been made; Halsbury (4th ed.), para. 1073.

[68] The Irish courts take a different view and accept the doctrine of the Church: *O'Hanlon v. Logue* [1906] 1 I.R. 247. See generally [1981] J.L.H. 207 (M. Blakeney); [1990] Conv. 35 (C. Rickett).

[69] [1949] A.C. 426 at p. 446. *Cf. Re Wedgwood* [1915] 1 Ch. 113, where the uplifting example of kindness to animals constituted a benefit to the public. The views expressed in *Gilmour v. Coats* seem inconsistent with the acceptance of the advancement of religion as a charitable purpose.

[70] [1949] A.C. 426 at p. 448.

[71] [1962] Ch. 832.

[72] *Ibid.* at p. 853.

[73] *Per* Lord Simonds in *Gilmour v. Coats* [1949] A.C. 426 at p. 450.

religious contemplation is not charitable; while a trust to propagate religious works of no value is.[74] The convent's problem can, however, be overcome by an extension of their activities to include external work.[75]

The decision in *Gilmour v. Coats*[76] cast doubt on the charitable status of gifts for the saying of masses. It had been held in *Bourne v. Keane*[77] that a gift for masses was not illegal as a superstitious use, and in *Re Caus*[78] that it was charitable. This was doubted in *Gilmour v. Coats*,[79] but the charitable nature of such a gift was recently upheld in *Re Hetherington (deceased)*,[80] where the testatrix left £2,000 to the Roman Catholic Bishop of Westminster for "masses for the repose of the souls of my husband and my parents and my sisters and also myself when I die." One reason was that the celebration of a religious rite in public conferred a sufficient public benefit in the edifying effect it had on those attending. Celebration of the rite in private would not suffice because the benefit conferred by prayer was incapable of proof and the edification of the private class attending was not a public benefit.[81] In the present case there was no express term that the masses should be said in public, but in practice they would be and the gift should be so construed. The second reason for upholding the gift was that it provided stipends for the priests saying the masses, and thereby assisted in the endowment of the priesthood. This reason would seem equally applicable to gifts for the saying of masses in private, but assuming such gifts are not charitable it is possible that they are valid as anomalous non-charitable purpose trusts.[82]

E. The Fourth Head

In most of the situations which have been considered under this head, the trust is for the benefit of all the public. This is so with gifts which improve the efficiency of the fighting forces, or the police, or medical research, or public parks and sea walls, or law reporting. It does not matter that it is only a limited number of people who will take advantage of the benefit provided. "A bridge which is available for all the public may undoubtedly be a charity and it is indifferent

---

[74] *Re Watson* [1973] 1 W.L.R. 1472, *ante*, p. 396.
[75] See Annual Report 1989, paras. 56–62; Decisions, Vol. 3 (1995), p. 11 (Society of the Precious Blood).
[76] [1949] A.C. 426.
[77] [1919] A.C. 815.
[78] [1934] Ch. 162; *O'Hanlon v. Logue* [1906] 1 I.R. 247.
[79] *Supra.*
[80] [1990] Ch. 1; [1989] Conv. 453 (N. Parry); (1989) 48 C.L.J. 373 (J. Hopkins); All E.R. Rev. 1989, p. 307 (C. Sherrin).
[81] *Gilmour v. Coats, supra; Hoare v. Hoare* (1886) 56 L.T. 147; *Yeap Cheah Neo v. Ong Chen Neo* (1875) L.R. 6 P.C. 381.
[82] *Ante*, p. 356.

how many people use it. But confine its use to a selected number of persons, however numerous and important: it is then clearly not a charity. It is not of general public utility: for it does not serve the public purpose which its nature qualifies it to serve."[83]

The problem arises where the purposes are restricted to a group of persons. We have seen that trusts for the relief of the aged and the sick are charitable. Not everyone is aged or sick. But if the benefits are generally available, there is some benefit, albeit indirect, to the public generally.[84] Clearly, a trust under the fourth head cannot be charitable if it is confined to persons bound together by a personal nexus.[85] The inhabitants of a geographical area are a section of the public in this context. But there are dicta in *Williams v. I.R.C.*[86] and in *I.R.C. v. Baddeley*[87] which suggest that trusts under the fourth head, even if otherwise charitable, are subject to a stricter rule than trusts under the other three heads in relation to the selection of persons who are to benefit.

In *Williams v. I.R.C.* Lord Simonds suggested that, even if the trust would otherwise have been charitable, the "Welsh people in London," to whom the benefit was confined, would not have constituted a section of the public.[88] He returned to this in *Baddeley*. It is necessary to distinguish between "relief extended to the whole community yet by its very nature advantageous only to the few and a form of relief accorded to a selected few out of a larger number equally willing to take advantage of it."[89] He doubted whether the test could be satisfied "if the beneficiaries are a class of persons not only confined to a particular area but selected from within it by reference to a particular creed."[90] "Who has ever heard of a bridge to be crossed only by impecunious Methodists?"[91] The persons to be benefited must be the whole community, or all the inhabitants of a particular area. Not a "class within a class." Lord Reid disagreed

---

[83] *Per* Lord Simonds in *I.R.C. v. Baddeley* [1955] A.C. 572 at p. 592.

[84] See also *Re Dunlop (deceased)* (1984) 19 *Northern Ireland Judgments Bulletin*; [1987] Conv. 114 (N. Dawson), where a home for "Old Presbyterian Persons" was held charitable. It did not fail on the "bridge for Methodists" principle, as the public generally benefits from having some members housed.

[85] *Ante*, p. 414. This problem is not encountered with learned societies, where the benefit is not confined to the members; *Re South Place Ethical Society* [1980] 1 W.L.R. 1565. *Tudor on Charities* (8th ed.), pp. 34–35, expresses the view that a personal nexus may not defeat trusts for the sick or aged, by analogy with poverty charities.

[86] [1947] A.C. 447.

[87] [1955] A.C. 572.

[88] Similarly with the Jews in *Keren Kayemeth Le Jisroel v. I.R.C.* [1942] A.C. 650. But see Annual Report 1977, para. 79, where the Charity Commissioners, when subsequently registering the *Williams* Trust as a charity under Charitable Trusts (Validation) Act 1954, held that the beneficiary class nevertheless did comprise a sufficient section of the public; *post*, p. 428. See also Decisions, Vol. 4 (1995), p. 8 (preservation of law and order for benefit of Jewish members of community not charitable).

[89] *Ibid.* at p. 592.

[90] *Ibid.* See also *Re Lipinski's Will Trusts* [1976] Ch. 235, *ante*, p. 349.

[91] *Ibid.*

and found no justification in the suggestion that the test for determining what was a section of the community should be different
under the fourth head.[92]

The matter must be considered to be one of uncertainty. The
decision shows the difficulties which arise in this area from an
attempt to lay down positive rules,[93] and Lord Simonds admitted
that it "was often very difficult to draw the line."[94] The only
solution appears to be to accept, in all heads of charity where public
benefit is required, the more general and flexible test proposed by
Lord McDermott,[95] and supported by the House in *Dingle v. Turner*
through Lord Cross.[96] The question whether the beneficiaries constitute a section of the public "is a question of degree and cannot be
by itself decisive of the question whether the trust is a charity. Much
must depend on the purpose of the trust. It may well be that, on the
one hand, a trust to promote some purpose, prima facie charitable,
will constitute a charity even though the class of potential beneficiaries might fairly be called a private class and that, on the other
hand, a trust to promote another purpose, also prima facie charitable,
will not constitute a charity even though the class of potential
beneficiaries might seem to some people fairly describable as a
section of the public."[97]

5. The Interpretation of Charitable Gifts and Purposes

A number of special questions arise in connection with the construction of instruments which are claimed to create charitable trusts. The
problems here discussed provide a further reminder of the importance of proper draftsmanship when setting up a charitable trust. The
Charity Commissioners will help with advice,[98] and they will give
reasons for the refusal to register, and make it possible for the trusts
to be redrafted. The Commissioners warn draftsmen not to draft
object clauses in unnecessarily wide terms, for this may allow non-
charitable purposes to be included.[99] In *McGovern v. Att.-Gen.*,[1] a
trust included political objects, but the deed provided that the
objects were "restricted to those which are charitable according to
the law of the United Kingdom but subject thereto they may be

---

[92] See also *Re Dunlop (deceased), ante*, p. 420, n. 84, which suggests that the test for each
    head is different, and that the test can differ even within the same head.
[93] (1974) 33 C.L.J. 63 (G. Jones).
[94] [1955] A.C. 572 at p. 592.
[95] *Oppenheim v. Tobacco Securities Trust Ltd* [1951] A.C. 197; *ante*, p. 415.
[96] [1972] A.C. 601; *ante*, p. 415.
[97] *Ibid.* at p. 624.
[98] Charities Act 1993, s.29; Annual Report 1966, para. 19.
[99] Annual Report 1971, paras. 70–71; 1966, para. 39.
[1] [1982] Ch. 321, *ante*, p. 408.

carried out in all parts of the world." This proviso did not have the "blue-pencil" effect of cancelling out the non-charitable parts, and hence the trust was not charitable. The restriction was merely intended to make it clear that the trustees, when operating outside the United Kingdom, should be restricted to purposes charitable by United Kingdom law. In so far as the purposes of the trust included political and thus non-charitable objects, the proviso could not save it.

A. The Motive of the Donor

The charitable motive of the donor, even if expressed, is not of major significance. The rule cuts both ways. In *Re King*,[2] a will provided for the erection of a stained-glass window in a church in memory of her parents, her sister and the testatrix herself. This was held to be a valid charitable gift. The fact that the intention was "not to beautify the church or benefit the parishioners, but to perpetuate the memory of the testatrix and her relations"[3] was immaterial. Conversely, a non-charitable gift, such as a gift for the suppression of vivisection, cannot be made charitable by the donor's charitable motive.[4] But a clear charitable intent may help to turn an ambiguity in favour of charity; especially, as has been seen, where it is possible to find an intention to benefit the poor.[5]

B. The Locality Cases

Particular difficulty has been experienced with the "locality cases." The restriction of a benefit to a precise locality seemed at one time to colour the judges' views of the nature of the benefit. By a benevolent construction, the benefits concerned were construed as being charitable. These cases[6] were discussed by Lord Simonds in *Williams' Trustees v. I.R.C.*,[7] by Lord Greene M.R. in *Re Strakosch*,[8] and by the Court of Appeal in *I.R.C. v. Baddeley*.[9] They are to be treated as anomalous and not to be extended.[10] They will, however, be followed in cases directly similar.[11] At the other end of the

---

[2] [1923] 1 Ch. 243, following *Hoare v. Obsorne* (1866) L.R. 1 Eq. 585.

[3] *Ibid.* at p. 245.

[4] *National Anti-Vivisection Society v. I.R.C.* [1948] A.C. 31.

[5] *Biscoe v. Jackson* (1887) 35 Ch.D. 460; *Re Coulthurst's W.T.* [1951] Ch. 193; *Re Cottam* [1955] 1 W.L.R. 1299, *ante*, p. 387.

[6] *e.g. Goodman v. Saltash Corp.* (1882) 7 App. Cas. 633; *Re Christchurch Inclosure Act* (1888) 38 Ch.D. 520.

[7] [1947] A.C. 447 at pp. 459–460.

[8] [1949] Ch. 529 at pp. 539–540.

[9] [1955] A.C. 572.

[10] *Houston v. Burns* [1918] A.C. 337; *Att.-Gen. v. National Provincial and Union Bank of England Ltd* [1924] A.C. 262; *Re Gwyon* [1930] 1 Ch. 255.

[11] A recent example is *Peggs v. Lamb* [1994] Ch. 172.

locality scale, a gift "unto my country England" is a valid charitable gift.[12]

C. The Charitable Status of the Trustee[13]

The charitable nature of a trust is determined by the terms of the trust and not by the status of the trustee. Non-charitable trustees may hold property on charitable trusts, and charity trustees may, subject, in the case of a corporation, to the terms of their incorporation, hold property on non-charitable trusts. But the charitable status of the trustee can in some cases, where the terms of the trust are not spelled out, lead the court to construe the terms of the trust as charitable. A gift to a bishop or vicar, without the purposes being specified, may be charitable. In *Re Flinn*,[14] a gift to "His Eminence the Archbishop of Westminster Cathedral for the time being to be used by him for such purposes as he shall in his absolute discretion think fit" was upheld. So, also, gifts to such officers for their work, for this is treated as being wholly charitable. In *Re Rumball*[15] a gift "to the bishop for the time being of the diocese of the Windward Islands to be used by him as he thinks fit in his diocese" was upheld.

But there is a danger in saying too much; where the terms of the gift specify the purposes and allow any part of the fund to be used for non-charitable purposes, the gift is void. The cases turn on the finest points of construction. "Parish work," for example, includes some extra-charitable activities, and in *Farley v. Westminster Bank*[16] a gift to a vicar "for parish work" was held invalid. But in *Re Simson*,[17] a gift to a vicar "for his work in the parish" was held valid. The former phrase is held to be dispositive, thus enlarging the ambit of the gift and producing the result that a charitable trustee holds on non-charitable trusts, while the latter phrase is held to be merely descriptive of the vicar's responsibilities. The many pages in the reports dealing with these refinements bring no credit to our jurisprudence.

D. The Objects Must be Exclusively Charitable

To be charitable, the funds of a trust must be applicable for charitable purposes only.

i. Main and Subsidiary Objects. A trust may be charitable, however, even if some expenditure is permitted on non-charitable

---

[12] *Re Smith* [1932] 1 Ch. 153.
[13] (1960) 25 Conv. (N.S.) 306 (V. Delaney).
[14] [1948] Ch. 241.
[15] [1956] Ch. 105.
[16] [1939] A.C. 430.
[17] [1946] Ch. 299.

purposes, but only if those non-charitable purposes are entirely subsidiary to the main charitable purposes. The question is whether "The main purpose of the body ... is charitable and the only elements in its constitution and operation which are non-charitable are merely incidental to that purpose."[18]

Failure of a trust for this reason is fairly obvious in cases such as *Morice v. Bishop of Durham*,[19] and *I.R.C. v. Baddeley*[20] where the purposes are patently too widely expressed but it is less obvious in cases where the non-charitable element is latent. In *Ellis v. I.R.C.*,[21] realty was conveyed to trustees for use "generally in such manner for the promotion and aiding of the work of the Roman Catholic Church in the district as the Trustees with the consent of the Bishop may prescribe." The Court of Appeal held that assets could be spent on subsidiary objects which were not necessarily conducive to the main (and undoubtedly charitable) object; such subsidiary objects existed in their own right and prevented the gift from being "for charitable purposes *only.*"

An acute form of this problem occurs where the furtherance of a charitable purpose also benefits particular groups of persons. This may or may not be fatal according to the weight the courts place on it. For instance in *I.R.C. v. City of Glasgow Police Athletic Association*,[22] the House of Lords held that a police athletic association, intended to benefit policemen in Glasgow, was not wholly ancillary to increasing the efficiency of the Glasgow police force and therefore not charitable. Again, while the benefits to the nursing profession as such loomed too large in the constitution of the General Nursing Council in proportion to the advancement of healing,[23] this was not so of surgeons in relation to the advancement of surgery in the constitution of the Royal College of Surgeons.[24] In *Re Coxen*[25] a substantial gift to a charity included provision for an annual dinner for the trustees; and this was held charitable as being ancillary to the better administration of the charity. And in *London Hospital Medical College v. I.R.C.*,[26] a students' union was held to be a charitable

[18] *Per* Lord Cohen in *I.R.C. v. City of Glasgow Police Athletic Association* [1953] A.C. 380 at p. 405. See [1978] Conv. 92 (N. Gravells).

[19] (1804) 9 Ves.Jr. 399; (1805) 10 Ves.Jr. 522 ("objects of benevolence and liberality").

[20] [1955] A.C. 572, *ante*, p. 403.

[21] (1949) 31 T.C. 178, following *Dunne v. Byrne* [1912] A.C. 407. See also *I.R.C. v. Educational Grants Association Ltd* [1967] Ch. 993 at pp. 1010 and 1015; *Oxford Group v. I.R.C.* [1949] 2 All E.R. 537, at pp. 539–540; *Re Cole* [1958] Ch. 877.

[22] [1953] A.C. 380.

[23] *General Nursing Council v. St. Marylebone B.C.* [1959] A.C. 540.

[24] *Royal College of Surgeons v. National Provincial Bank Ltd* [1952] A.C. 631; see also *Incorporated Council of Law Reporting v. Att.-Gen.* [1972] Ch. 73.

[25] [1948] Ch. 747.

[26] [1976] 1 W.L.R. 613. See also *Re South Place Ethical Society* [1980] 1 W.L.R. 1565 (social activities held to be ancillary to the objects of ethical humanist society); *Funnell v. Stewart* [1996] 1 W.L.R. 288.

trust where its predominant object was to further the purposes of the college, even though one of its objects was to confer private and personal benefits on union members.

ii. And/Or Cases. Nowhere is the draftsman's error more obvious than in this group of cases. If a purpose is described as "charitable and benevolent"—philanthropic, useful, or any other such adjective—the purposes are wholly charitable. For the purposes, to qualify, must be, *inter alia*, charitable; and that is enough. But if the draftsman says charitable *or* benevolent, there is prima facie an alternative; and the funds could be applied for purposes which are benevolent, but not charitable. But this is an oversimplification, and the question is one of construction in each case. Is the word conjunctive or disjunctive?

(a) *Cases of "or."* In *Blair v. Duncan*[27] the words were "such charitable or public purposes as my trustee thinks proper"; in *Houston v. Burns*,[28] "public, benevolent, or charitable purposes"; in *Chichester Diocesan Fund and Board of Finance v. Simpson*[29] "charitable or benevolent"; in each of these cases the gift was held not to be charitable, in that the words were wide enough to justify the trustees in disposing of the fund, or an unascertainable part of it, to non-charitable objects.

In *Re Macduff*,[30] a bequest of money "for some one or more purposes, charitable, philanthropic or—" was held to be bad, not by reason of the blank, but because there may be philanthropic purposes that are not charitable.

But in *Re Bennett*[31] the words were "for the benefit of the schools, and charitable institutions, and poor, and other objects of charity, or *any other* public objects," and Eve J. held that the addition of the word "other" entitled him to apply the *ejusdem generis* rule of interpretation and dispensed him from the necessity of reading the word "or" disjunctively; the gift was, therefore, upheld as a charitable gift of the whole.

(b) *Cases of "and."* Lord **Davey** in *Blair v. Duncan*[32] said that if the words had been "charitable *and* public" effect might be given to

---

[27] [1902] A.C. 37.
[28] [1918] A.C. 337.
[29] [1944] A.C. 341; the trustees of the will paid the sums over to various charities, not anticipating the litigation by the next-of-kin which, in the event, occurred and the sequel was *Ministry of Health v. Simpson* [1951] A.C. 251.
[30] [1896] 2 Ch. 451.
[31] [1920] 1 Ch. 305. See also *Guild v. I.R.C.* [1992] 2 A.C. 310 (gift to specified recreational charitable purpose "or some similar purpose in connection with sport" upheld).
[32] [1902] A.C. 37 at p. 4.

them, because they could be construed to mean charitable purposes of a public character. Some cases support this view, the word "and" being regarded as having the power to draw the other word into the orbit of the charitable. This view is borne out by *Re Sutton*[33] and *Re Best*,[34] where gifts to "charitable and deserving objects" and "charitable and benevolent" objects respectively were upheld. In *Att.-Gen. of the Bahamas v. Royal Trust Co.*,[35] on the other hand, a gift for the "education and welfare" of Bahamian children and young people was held void on a disjunctive construction. To construe the words conjunctively would result in a single purpose of educational welfare, but the word "welfare" was regarded as too wide to permit such a construction. The addition of a third word, "without any conjunction, copulative or disjunctive,"[36] was in *Williams v. Kershaw*[37] held fatal to a gift to "benevolent, charitable and religious" purposes, and in *Re Eades*[38] Sargant J. refused to uphold a gift for "such religious, charitable and philanthropic objects" as three named persons should jointly appoint.

In *Att.-Gen. v. National Provincial and Union Bank of England*[39] there was a gift of part of the residuary estate "for such patriotic purposes or objects and such charitable institution or institutions or charitable object or objects in the British Empire" as the trustees should select. The House of Lords interpreted this as a gift for any or all of four categories, two of which might not be charitable, and so held the whole gift void.

So we cannot say more than that prima facie the word "or" causes the words to be read disjunctively; the word "and" causes them to be read conjunctively.

iii. Severance. Where the language permits funds to be applied partly for charitable and partly for non-charitable purposes, the court will, in some cases, apply a doctrine of severance, separating the charitable from the non-charitable, and allow the former to stand although the latter may fail.

In *Salusbury v. Denton*[40] a testator bequeathed a fund to his widow to be applied by her in her will, in part towards the

---

[33] (1885) 28 Ch.D. 464.
[34] [1904] 2 Ch. 354.
[35] [1986] 1 W.L.R. 1001, criticised as too narrow in (1987) 50 N.L.J. *Annual Charities Review* 20 (S. de Cruz).
[36] *Per* Pearson J. in *Re Sutton* (1885) 28 Ch.D. 464 at p. 466.
[37] (1835) 5 Cl. & F. 111n.
[38] [1920] 2 Ch. 353.
[39] [1924] A.C. 262.
[40] (1857) 3 K. & J. 529.

foundation of a charity school, and as to the rest towards the benefit of the testator's relatives. The widow died without making any apportionment, but it was held, relying on the maxim "Equality is Equity," that the court would divide the fund into two halves.

The distinction between this and the "charitable or benevolent" cases is well brought out by Page-Wood V.-C.[41] "It is one thing to direct a trustee to give *a part* of a fund to one set of objects, and the *remainder* to another, and it is a distinct thing to direct him to give 'either' to one set of objects 'or' to another . . . This is a case of the former description. Here the trustee was bound to give a part to each." The crux of the matter is that the whole of a fund cannot be devoted to non-charity; once this is established, the court will endeavour to quantify what proportion of the capital assets is needed to support the non-charitable part,[42] and then hold the remaining part to be validly devoted to charity. In the absence of factors requiring a different division, the court will divide equally.[43] But there may be good reasons for making an unequal division.

In *Re Coxen*,[44] a testator gave the residue of his estate, amounting to more than £200,000 to the Court of Aldermen of the City of London for charitable purposes, providing however that one guinea should be paid to each of the six aldermen chosen to administer the trust on the occasion of his attending any meeting to administer the trust, and that £100 p.a. be used for an annual dinner for the Court of Aldermen when it should meet to discuss the business of the trust. On the assumption that these administrative provisions were not charitable,[45] quantification was desirable, for a division into equal parts would be absurd. Jenkins J. held that the court would find the necessary means to quantify the maximum slice of capital that would be needed to support them.

iv. Charitable Trusts (Validation) Act 1954. If the terms of a trust coming into operation before December 16, 1952,[46] are such that the property could be applied exclusively for charitable purposes, but could also be applied for non-charitable purposes (called in the Act an "imperfect trust provision") then as from July 30,

[41] At p. 539; the italics are the Vice Chancellor's.
[42] In most cases this will produce *pro tanto* voidness.
[43] *Hoare v. Osborne* (1866) L.R. 1 Eq. 585; *Re Vaughan* (1866) 33 Ch.D. 187.
[44] [1948] Ch. 747.
[45] Jenkins J. later decided that they were charitable; *ante*, p. 424.
[46] The date of publication of the Nathan Report; see (1954) 18 Conv.(N.S) 532; (1962) 26 Conv.(N.S.) 200 (S. Maurice).

1954, the terms shall be treated as if they permitted application for charitable purposes only.[47]

The simple case covered by this provision would be a gift, prior to December 16, 1952, for "charitable or benevolent purposes." It would have saved the trusts of the *Diplock* will,[48] and was applied in the case of a trust deed some of whose purposes were charitable and others not.[49] The difficulty arises where there is no express mention of any charitable purposes, but where the purposes are capable of including charitable purposes.[50] It was said in *Re Gillingham Bus Disaster Fund*[51] that a trust for "worthy causes" was covered, and in *Re Wykes' Will Trust*,[52] a trust for welfare purposes was upheld as those purposes are akin to the relief of poverty. On the other hand, a trust for division among institutions and associations, some of which were not charitable, was not validated[53]; nor was a trust providing various benefits for employees because it was essentially a private discretionary trust and contained no indication of an intention to benefit the public.[54] The principle seems to be that where there is a clear flavour of charity present, "a quasi-charitable trust" as Cross J. has put it,[55] the donor of such a gift would not feel that his intentions were being distorted by the whole of his gift being made available to charity. This accords with the view of the Privy Council on a comparable issue of New South Wales legislation.[56] It would thus cover "worthy causes," but not a case involving the mere possibility of charitable benefit.[57]

Commonwealth legislation[58] goes much further, and gives the courts a "blue pencil" power. Where non-charitable purposes are, or are deemed to be, within the ambit of a trust obviously intended to

---

[47] s.1(2); *Re Chitty's W.T.* [1970] Ch. 254. The Act does not apply to assets already distributed; s.2.

[48] *Chichester Diocesan Fund and Board of Finance v. Simpson* [1944] A.C. 341; *ante*, p. 425.

[49] *Re Mead's Trust Deed* [1961] 1 W.L.R. 1244; *Re South Place Ethical Society* [1980] 1 W.L.R. 1565 ("purposes either religious or civil"). The trust in *Williams Trustees v. I.R.C.* [1947] A.C. 447, p. 399, *ante*, was eventually saved by the Act; Annual Report 1977, paras. 71–80.

[50] *Re Gillingham Bus Disaster Fund* [1959] Ch. 62; *Re Wykes* [1961] Ch. 229; *Re Mead's Trust Deed (supra)*.

[51] *Supra*, at p. 80.

[52] *Supra*. Apart from the 1954 Act, such a trust fails: *Re Atkinson's W. T.* [1978] 1 W.L.R. 586.

[53] *Re Harpur's W. T.* [1962] Ch. 78.

[54] *Re Saxone Shoe Co. Ltd's Trust Deed* [1962] 1 W.L.R. 943.

[55] *Ibid.* at pp. 957–958.

[56] *Leahy v. Att.-Gen. for New South Wales* [1959] A.C. 457 at pp. 474–476.

[57] *cf. Re Mead's Trust Deed, supra*, which goes rather far in restricting a trust to "poor" members of a union.

[58] (New South Wales) Conveyancing Act 1919–1969; s. 37D; (New Zealand) Charitable Trusts Act 1957, s.61B; (Victoria) Property Law Act 1958, s.131; (Western Australia) Trustees Act 1962, s.102. See also Charities Act (Northern Ireland) 1964, s.24.

be charitable,[59] the trust is carried out as if the non-charitable elements were not present. The principle of such legislation seems acceptable and it is a pity that the Nathan Committee hesitated to recommend its adoption here.

E. Disaster Appeals

Problems can arise when public appeals for donations are made after some accident or disaster, if insufficient thought has been given to the question whether the fund is to be charitable or not. Such was the case with the loss of Penlee Lifeboat in Cornwall in 1982, when over £2 million was donated by the public to the dependants of the lost crew, numbering eight families. If charitable, the fund would attract tax relief but, contrary to the expectations of some donors, it could not be simply divided amongst the families, as charitable funds, being essentially public in nature, cannot be used to give benefits to individuals exceeding those appropriate to their needs. Any surplus would, under the *cy-près* doctrine, be applied to related charities.[60] If, on the other hand, the fund was not charitable, it would not attract tax relief, but could be distributed entirely among the dependants if, upon construing the terms of the appeal, that was the intention of the donors. If that was not their intention, the surplus would not be applicable *cy-près*, but would result to the subscribers or perhaps devolve upon the Crown as *bona vacantia*.[61] Similar problems can arise if the appeal is on behalf of one specific person, such as a sick child. In the Penlee case[62] it was decided, after negotiations with the Attorney-General and the Charity Commissioners, to forgo tax relief and to treat the fund as private, so that the money could be divided among the families.[63]

The terms of the appeal are all-important in determining the status of the fund, and the consequences flowing from that status. The Attorney-General has issued guidelines for consideration by persons planning to launch a public appeal of this sort.[64] It appears that non-charitable status has most often been chosen.[65]

---

[59] *Leahy v. Att.-Gen. for New South Wales* [1959] A.C. 457.

[60] *Infra.*

[61] *Re Gillingham Bus Disaster Fund* [1959] Ch. 62; *Re West Sussx Constabulary's Widows, Children and Benevolent* (1930) *Fund Trust* [1971] Ch. 1; *ante*, p. 233.

[62] Which was not litigated. See Annual Report 1981, paras. 4–8; (1982) 132 N.L.J. 223 (H. Picarda).

[63] The Charity Commissioners have stated that the fund was not charitable; Annual Report 1981, para. 6. If it had been charitable, as being for the relief of victims of a disaster (*Re North Devon and West Somerset Relief Fund Trusts* [1953] 1 W.L.R. 1260), presumably it would not be possible to forgo that status.

[64] See Annual Report, 1981, App. A. See also Annual Report 1982, paras. 31–35 (South Atlantic Fund); Annual Report 1985, para. 19 (Bradford City Disaster Charitable Trust); Annual Report 1988, para. 25 (Armenian earthquake and Philippines Ferry); Annual Report 1989, paras. 36, 37 (Clapham Junction and Hillsborough).

[65] Annual Report 1988, para. 25; 1989, para. 36.

6. Cy-Près

A. The Cy-Près Doctrine Prior to 1960

Where property is given for charitable purposes and the purposes cannot be carried out in the precise manner intended by the donor, the question is whether the trust should fail, or whether the property should be applied for other charitable purposes. The *cy-près* doctrine, where it applies, enables the court (or the Commissioners) to make a scheme for the application of the property for other charitable purposes as near as possible to those intended by the donor. This is judicial *cy-près*. If a gift is to charity but not upon trust, it is disposed of by the Crown under prerogative *cy-près*.[66] The distinction is not however always observed.

The *cy-près* jurisdiction was very narrow until the reforms of the Charities Act 1960, and was available only where it was "impossible" or "impracticable" to carry out the purposes of the trust.[67] Thus, trusts for the distribution of loaves of bread to the poor or of stockings for poor maidservants continued until modern times. Their performance was cumbersome, uneconomical, inconvenient, but not impossible nor impracticable. But it had at least, by the turn of the nineteenth century, become impracticable to apply money for the advancement and propagation of the Christian religion among the infidels of Virginia,[68] or for "the redemption of British slaves in Turkey or Barbary."[69] *Re Dominion Students' Hall Trust*[70] showed the furthest development of the doctrine by the courts.

> One of the objects of a charity was to promote community of citizenship, culture and tradition among all members of the British Community of Nations; and it maintained a hostel for students in Bloomsbury. But the benefits of the charity were restricted to students of European origin. The *cy-près* power was used to remove the "colour bar." It could not be said that it was "absolutely impracticable" to carry on the charity in its present state; but, by 1947, "to retain the condition, so far from furthering the charity's main object, might defeat it and would be liable to

---

[66] *Ante*, p. 379 (sign manual). But even if there is no trust, the court has jurisdiction if there is an analogous legally binding restriction; *Liverpool and District Hospital for Diseases of the Heart v. Att.-Gen.* [1981] Ch. 193 (charitable corporation); [1984] Conv. 112 (J. Warburton).

[67] See *Re Weir Hospital* [1910] 2 Ch. 124.

[68] *Att.-Gen. v. City of London* (1790) 3 Bro.C.C. 121. Annual Report (1971), paras. 65–69; see also *Re Robinson* [1923] 2 Ch. 332. (The wearing of a black gown by the preacher was impracticable because it was likely to offend the congregation and defeat the main object.).

[69] *Ironmongers' Co. v. Att.-Gen.* (1844) 10 Cl. & F. 908.

[70] [1947] Ch. 183; see Race Relations Act 1976, s.34; *ante*, p. 327; Annual Report 1976, para. 20; Annual Report 1983, para. 19; *Canada Trust Company v. Ontario Human Rights Commission* (1990) 69 D.L.R. (4th) 321.

antagonize those students, both white and coloured, whose support and goodwill it is the purpose of the charity to sustain. The case, therefore, can be said to fall within the broad description of impossibility . . ."[71]

More recently, in *Re J. W. Laing Trust*,[72] concerning a settlement of shares worth £15,000 in 1922, the question was whether the court could delete a term imposed by the settlor that the capital and income should be distributed no later than 10 years after his death. The investment was now worth £24 million. The trust was for Christian evangelical causes, and the individuals and bodies who would be the recipients were unsuited to receive large capital sums. The deletion of this term was approved under the court's inherent jurisdiction, as it had become inexpedient in the very altered circumstances of the charity.

It is convenient also at this stage to note that a distinction is made between the initial failure of a charitable trust, and a failure after the time when the trust has been in operation. Application *cy-près* is much easier in the latter case; for, after application to charity, there is no resulting trust for the donor.[73] If the donor wants the property to pass to a third party, or to return to himself or his estate, he must expressly so provide by a gift over to take effect within the perpetuity period.[74] In the case of initial failure, the gift will lapse unless there is, on the proper construction of the instrument, a paramount intention to benefit charity. These situations will now be examined.

B. Initial Failure. Paramount Charitable Intent

i. Width of Charitable Intent. Where a charitable trust fails as being ineffective at the date of the gift, the gift will either lapse and fall into residue, or the property will be applied *cy-près*. The decision depends on the width of charitable intent manifested by the donor. If the intention was that the property should be applied for a specified purpose, which cannot be carried out, or for one specific charitable institution which no longer exists, the gift will lapse. But if the court finds a wider intent, a paramount or general charitable intention, the property may be applied *cy-près*.

---

[71] [1947] Ch. 183 at p. 186, *per* Evershed J.
[72] [1984] Ch. 143, [1984] Conv. 319 (J. Warburton); [1985] Conv. 313 (P. Luxton). Section 13 of the Charities Act 1960 (now the Act of 1993) did not apply; *post*, p. 439.
[73] *Re Wright* [1954] Ch. 347 at pp. 362–363. But see [1983] Conv. 107 (P. Luxton).
[74] *Post*, p. 438.

In *Re Rymer*,[75] there was a legacy of £5,000 "to the rector for the time being of St. Thomas's Seminary for the education of priests for the diocese of Westminster." At the time of the testator's death, the Seminary had ceased to exist, and the students had been transferred to another Seminary in Birmingham. The Court of Appeal held that the gift failed. It was a gift "to a particular seminary for the purposes thereof." There was no wider intent.

This may be contrasted with *Re Lysaght*,[76] where the testatrix gave funds to the Royal College of Surgeons to found medical studentships. The gift was subject to restrictions, in that the students were to be male, the sons of qualified British-born medical men, themselves British-born, and not of the Jewish or Roman Catholic faith. The Royal College of Surgeons declined to accept the gift on these terms. As it was held that the particular trustee was essential to the gift, the refusal of the College would cause the gift to fail. Buckley J. held that there was a paramount charitable intention. The particularity of the testatrix's directions was not fatal to such a construction, as the directions were not an essential part of her true intention. A scheme was ordered whereby the money was payable to the College on the trusts of the will, but omitting the religious disqualification.

This liberal approach was followed in *Re Woodhams (deceased)*,[77] where the testator left money to two music colleges to found annual scholarships for "the complete musical education of a promising boy who is an absolute orphan and only of British Nationality and Birth from any one of Dr. Barnardo's Homes or the Church of England Children's Society Homes." The two colleges declined the gifts because it would be impractical to restrict the scholarships as required by the testator, but were prepared to accept them if available for boys of British nationality and birth generally. The gift failed for impracticability, but a paramount charitable intention to further musical education was found. The restriction to orphans from the named homes was not essential to the testator's purpose. Thus the gift was applicable *cy-près* under a scheme whereby the restriction was deleted.

ii. Has the Gift Failed? Continuation in Another Form. A gift to a defunct charity may be regarded as not having failed at all, on the basis that it is continuing in another form. It may have been amalgamated with a similar charity by scheme, or have been reconstituted under more effective trusts. In such a case the gift may take

---

[75] [1895] 1 Ch. 19; *Re Spence* [1979] Ch. 483. On the matter generally, see (1969) 32 M.L.R. 283 (J. Hutton).

[76] [1966] Ch. 191. See particularly at pp. 201–202.

[77] [1981] 1 W.L.R. 493.

effect in favour of the body now administering the assets of the old charity. Or the court may construe the gift as being for the purposes of the named charity, so that the nomination of a defunct charity does not cause the gift to fail. Provided the purposes still exist the gift takes effect in favour of a body furthering those purposes. It will be appreciated that the significance of holding that such a gift has not failed is that it is not necessary to find a general charitable intention. A scheme will be ordered to give effect to the gift, but it will not be a *cy-près* scheme.

(a) *Gift in Augmentation of Funds of Defunct Charity*

In *Re Faraker*,[78] there was a gift to "Mrs. Bayley's Charity, Rotherhithe." A charity had been founded by a Mrs. Hannah Bayly in 1756 for the benefit of poor widows in Rotherhithe. This, with a number of other local charities had been consolidated under a scheme by the Charity Commissioners in 1905, and the funds were held in various trusts for the benefit of the poor in Rotherhithe. The Court of Appeal held that the Bayly trusts had not been destroyed by the scheme, and that the consolidated charities were entitled to the legacy. The gift had not failed, because a perpetual charity cannot die.[79]

(b) *Gifts for Purposes. Unincorporated Associations and Charitable Corporations.*

In considering whether a gift is effectively for the purposes of the named institution, a distinction is drawn between gifts to unincorporated societies and to corporations. "Every bequest to an unincorporated charity by name without more must take effect as a gift for a charitable purpose . . . a bequest which is in terms made for a charitable purpose will not fail for lack of a trustee but will be carried into effect either under the Sign Manual or by means of a scheme"[80]; unless the testator's intention was to the contrary. On the other hand, "a bequest to a corporate body . . . takes effect simply as a gift to that body beneficially, unless there are circumstances which show that the recipient is to take the gift as a trustee. There is no need in such a case to infer a trust for any

---

[78] [1912] 2 Ch. 488; *Re Lucas* [1948] Ch. 424; *cf. Re Slatter's W. T.* [1964] Ch. 512; (1964) 28 Conv.(N.S.) 313 (J. Farrand).

[79] Distinguished in *Re Stemson's W.T.* [1970] Ch. 16 (involving a terminable corporate charity), and *Re Roberts* [1963] 1 W.L.R. 406, *infra*.

[80] *Per* Buckley J. in *Re Vernon's W.T.* [1972] Ch. 300n; *Re Finger's W.T.* [1972] Ch. 286; (1972) 36 Conv.(N.S.) 198 (R. Cotterell); (1974) 38 Conv.(N.S.) 187 (J. Martin). See also *Liverpool and District Hospital for Diseases of the Heart v. Att.-Gen.* [1982] Ch. 193 (charitable corporation does not hold as trustee, but court has *cy-près* jurisdiction on winding-up; Companies Act 1985, s.558). See Charities Act 1993, s.64, for the position where a charitable corporation ceases to be charitable or otherwise alters its objects.

particular purpose."[81] Thus a gift to a defunct charitable corporation lapses and fails,[82] and *cy-près* application is possible only if there was a general charitable intention. In *Re Finger's Will Trusts*,[83] there was a gift to the National Radium Commission (unincorporated) and to the National Council for Maternity and Child Welfare (incorporated). Both had ceased to exist by the date of the testatrix's death. The gift to the unincorporated charity was construed as a gift to charitable purposes. As those purposes still existed there was no failure, as a trust does not fail for lack of a trustee. A scheme was ordered to settle the destination of the gift, but this was not a *cy-près* scheme and no general charitable intention was necessary.[84] In the case of the incorporated charity, on the other hand, it was a gift to a legal person which had ceased to exist, and was not a purpose trust. The gift therefore failed, but was saved from lapse by the finding of a general charitable intention, and was accordingly applied *cy-près*.

This is a technical distinction which might not be appreciated by the testator, but it has a certain logic. One difficulty which remains is that the same facts may allow either the *Re Faraker* construction or that adopted in *Re Finger's Will Trusts* in the case of the unincorporated charity, although the results are different. While both constructions avoid the finding of a failure and the need for a general charitable intention, the result of the *Re Faraker* construction is that the gift goes to the body now administering the funds of the defunct charity, even if its purposes are different. In *Re Faraker*[85] itself, the defunct charity was specifically for widows, while the new consolidated charity was for the poor generally, so that it "was not bound to give one penny to a widow,"[86] thus defeating the testator's intention to some extent. The result in *Re Finger's Will Trusts*[87] is that the gift is devoted, by means of a scheme, to the testator's purpose. It may be that the court would decline to apply *Re Faraker* where the purposes of the new body were widely different. Thus in *Re Roberts*,[88] a gift was made to the Sheffield Boys' Working Home,

---

[81] *Ibid.* See [1984] Conv. 112 and [1990] Conv. 95 (J. Warburton). See also *Re ARMS (Multiple Sclerosis Research Ltd)*, *The Times*, November 29, 1996 (no failure where incorporated charity existed at testator's death although insolvent, thus legacy available to its creditors).

[82] Unless the testator has indicated that the corporation was to take as trustee for its purposes.

[83] [1972] Ch. 286; applied by the Court of Apeal in *Re Koeppler's W.T.* [1986] Ch. 423. If the purposes had ceased to exist, the gift to the unincorporated charity would fail, but could be applied *cy-près* if there was a general charitable intention.

[84] It would be otherwise if the donor intended the particular institution and no other, as in *Re Rymer, supra*.

[85] [1912] 2 Ch. 488.

[86] *Ibid.* at p. 496.

[87] [1972] Ch. 286.

[88] [1963] 1 W.L.R. 406. See (1974) 38 Conv.(N.S.) 187 (J. Martin).

which had wound up and transferred most of its assets to the Sheffield Town Trust. The claim of the latter body was rejected as an undesirable extension of the *Re Faraker* principle, as it purposes were different. The money was applied, by means of an ordinary scheme, to the purposes to which the defunct Home had been dedicated.

Both constructions, however, were rejected in *Re Spence*,[89] where money was left to a specified Old Folks Home, "for the benefit of the patients." The home was no longer in use at the testatrix's death. Megarry V.-C. held that the gift failed and could not be applied *cy-près*. It was not a general gift to the old people of the district. following *Re Harwood*,[90] it was said that if a particular institution is correctly identified, then it is that institution and no other which is intended: "It is difficult to envisage a testator as being suffused with a general glow of broad charity when he is labouring, and labouring successfully, to identify some particular specified institution or purpose as the object of his bounty."[91] This, with respect, is a very narrow view of the *cy-près* doctrine. A testator should always be careful to identify his beneficiary correctly. It is difficult to see why this should automatically negative a general charitable intention.

iii. Projects. The cases so far discussed have dealt with gifts to institutions, corporate or unincorporated. The same rules apply in principle also to cases where there is a gift for a purpose or project such as, for example, the payment of a schoolmaster at a school to be built,[92] or a holiday home for clergymen of the Church of England and their wives,[93] or the establishment of a soup kitchen and cottage hospital.[94] In such cases, the question is whether the project is on the balance of probabilities capable or incapable of being implemented. If it is incapable, then, in the absence of wider intent, the gift will fail and will fall into residue. There is no "wait and see" provision.[95]

iv. Non-Existent Charity. In *Re Harwood*,[96] it was said that, where there was a gift for a non-existent charity, it was easier to find a general charitable intent in a case where the institution had never existed than it was in the case where an identifiable institution had ceased to exist.

[89] [1979] Ch. 483.
[90] [1936] Ch. 285, *infra. Re Rymer* [1895] 1 Ch. 19, *ante*, p. 432 was also relied on.
[91] [1979] Ch. 483 at p. 493.
[92] *Re Wilson* [1913] 1 Ch. 314.
[93] *Re Packe* [1918] 1 Ch. 437.
[94] *Biscoe v. Jackson* (1887) 35 Ch.D. 460.
[95] *Re White's W.T.* [1955] Ch. 188; *Re Tacon* [1958] Ch. 447 at pp. 453–455.
[96] [1936] Ch. 285; *cf. Re Goldschmidt* [1957] 1 W.L.R. 524, where a gift to a non-existent charity was not applied *cy-près*, but fell into residue, which was also given to charity.

In that case, a testatrix, who died in 1934, left £200 to the Wisbech Peace Society and £300 to the Peace Society in Belfast. The Wisbech Society had existed prior to 1934, but had ceased by that date to exist. There was no evidence that the Peace Society of Belfast had ever existed. The former failed, but in respect of the latter Farwell J. was able to find an intention to "benefit societies whose object was the promotion of peace,"[97] and the £300 was applied *cy-près*.

Similarly, in *Re Satterthwaite's Will Trusts*,[98] where a testatrix, who hated the whole human race, left her residuary estate to a number of institutions concerned with animal welfare. Most of them were charitable, but a dispute arose over the share left to the London Animal Hospital. There was no charity of that name, but the plaintiff, a veterinary surgeon, carried on a practice under that trade name at a time prior to the date of the will and death. The Court of Appeal considered the gift as being to a non-existent charitable institution, and not to the plaintiff. A sufficiently wide charitable intent was discerned from the nature of the other shares (notwithstanding that one share was to a non-charity), and thus *cy-près* application was ordered.

v. A Group of Donees; Mostly Charitable. It may be that the testator has made a number of gifts, all of which are charitable except one. It can be argued that the intention clearly was to apply all the money for charitable purposes. On the other hand, "if you meet seven men with black hair and one with red hair, you are not entitled to say that here are eight men with black hair."[99] A gift for a non-charitable purpose is not made charitable by being included in a list of other gifts which are charitable. So held Buckley J. in *Re Jenkins' Will Trusts*[1] where a gift for the abolition of vivisection failed and could not be applied *cy-près*. This may be contrasted with *Re Satterthwaite's Will Trusts*,[2] where the gift in question was construed as charitable, and hence the *cy-près* doctrine could apply.

C. Subsequent Failure

Once assets are effectively dedicated to charity, there can be no question of a lapse or a resulting trust save where the gift effectively

---

[97] *Ibid.* at p. 288. But the decision was doubted by the High Court in *Re Koeppler's Will Trusts* [1984] Ch. 243, on the basis that the purpose was political and not charitable. It was not cited in the Court of Appeal [1986] Ch. 423.

[98] [1966] 1 W.L.R. 277.

[99] *Per* Buckley J. in *Re Jenkins' W.T.* [1966] Ch. 249.

[1] *Supra.*

[2] *Supra.*

provides for it. Width of charitable intent is irrelevant. All that is necessary is that the property has been given "out and out" to charity, in the sense that the donor did not envisage its return in any circumstances.

In *Re Wright*,[3] a testatrix who died in 1933 provided for the foundation, on the death of a tenant for life, of a convalescent home for impecunious gentlewomen. The scheme was practicable in 1933, but the balance of probabilities was against it in 1942 when the tenant for life died. The Court of Appeal held that 1933 was the crucial date; at that date the scheme was practicable, dedication to charity occurred, and the possibility of a lapse or resulting trust was excluded. *Cy-près* was available in 1942 irrespective of width of charitable intent.

This rule is now firmly established,[4] but it was not always so, and it is not possible to reconcile some earlier cases on the subject, in particular the "surplus" cases.

In *Re King*,[5] residue worth £1,500 was bequeathed for one stained-glass window in a church. The cost of the window could not exceed £800. Romer J. held that the whole of £1,500 had been dedicated to charity with the necessary consequences that any surplus would be applied *cy-près* (in fact for a second window) irrespective of width of intent.

But in *Re Stanford*,[6] where £5,000 was bequeathed for the purpose of completing and publishing an etymological dictionary and over £1,500 remained unspent when the task was complete, Eve J. held that the surplus fell into residue.

Such a result is only justifiable if the surplus can be regarded as a case of initial impossibility *pro tanto*.[7] Similar confusion can be seen in the cases where the surplus has arisen in the circumstances of a public appeal. In *Re Welsh Hospital (Netley) Fund*[8] and *Re North Devon and West Somerset Relief Fund Trusts*[9] money was collected for purposes which were fulfilled, leaving surplus. The

---

[3] [1954] Ch. 347; *Re Slevin* [1891] 2 Ch. 236, where an orphanage was in existence at the testator's death, but came to an end before the money was paid over. *Cy-près* application was ordered; *Re Moon's W.T.* [1948] 1 All E.R. 300.

[4] *Re Tacon* [1958] Ch. 447, a case of a contingent gift; *cf. Re J. W. Laing Trust* [1984] Ch. 143, [1984] Conv. 319 (J. Warburton).

[5] [1923] 1 Ch. 243.

[6] [1924] 1 Ch. 73.

[7] See Picarda, p. 328; *Tudor on Charities* (8th ed.), pp. 434–436.

[8] [1921] 1 Ch. 655; *cf. Re British Red Cross Balkan Fund* [1914] 2 Ch. 419. The latter case is doubted in *Tudor on Charities* (8th ed.), p. 354, n. 74.

[9] [1953] 1 W.L.R. 1260.

surplus was held applicable *cy-près* on the basis that there was a general charitable intention. If these cases are to be regarded as involving subsequent failure, it is difficult to see why such an intention is necessary. All that is required is an "out and out" gift to charity. Thus in *Re Wokingham Fire Brigade Trusts*[10] a surplus was applicable *cy-près* without the need to discover a general charitable intention. It is submitted that this approach, which was approved *obiter* by the Court of Appeal in *Re Ulverston and District New Hospital Building Trusts*[11] (involving initial failure as insufficient funds were collected) is to be preferred.

D. Termination in Favour of Non-Charity

It was seen that a donor could, if he wished, make express provision for a gift over to a third party or to himself or to his estate upon the failure of a charitable gift within the period of perpetuity.[12] Before the Perpetuities and Accumulations Act 1964, a resulting trust after a determinable interest was immune from the perpetuity rule, although any express gift over was subject to it. Thus a determinable charitable gift could terminate at a remote time and result to the settlor. It could not be applied *cy-près* because, although a subsequent failure, there was no "out and out" gift to charity.[13] However, in the case of a charitable gift subject to a condition subsequent, the gift took effect as absolute if the gift over was void for perpetuity. The *cy-près* doctrine would then apply in the usual way on any subsequent failure, to the exclusion of a resulting trust.[14]

Under section 12 of the 1964 Act, the perpetuity rule became applicable to resulting trusts, but the Act also introduced the "wait and see" rule.[15] Thus in the case of a determinable charitable gift, a gift over or resulting trust will operate to the exclusion of the *cy-près* doctrine if the determining event occurs within the perpetuity period. If it does not, the gift becomes absolute, so that *cy-près* will apply on any subsequent failure. Likewise if the charitable gift is subject to a condition subsequent. On breach of condition within the perpetuity period, the gift over (or resulting trust in default) will take effect. If, however, the condition is not broken within that period, the charitable gift becomes absolute. Thus the *cy-près* doctrine is

---

[10] [1951] Ch. 373.
[11] [1956] Ch. 622. The case illustrates the difficulties now resolved by Charities Act 1993, s.14, *post*, p. 442. s.14 does not apply to the surplus cases unless it becomes established that a general charitable intention is necessary, contrary to the view expressed in the text.
[12] *Ante*, p. 431.
[13] *Re Randell* (1888) 39 Ch.D. 213.
[14] *Re Peel's Release* [1921] 2 Ch. 218.
[15] s.3(1).

available because, whatever the donor's intention, the gift is by statute an "out and out" gift to charity.

E. The Widening of Cy-Près Jurisdiction. Charities Act 1993, s.13

i. General. As part of the policy of modernising charitable trusts, the Charities Act 1960 introduced far-reaching reforms (now found in the consolidating Act of 1993) in the application of the *cy-près* doctrine. Before examining these reforms it must be emphasised that it is the trustees' duty, where some or all of the property may be applied *cy-près*, to take steps to have the property so applied.[16] This situation will arise where there is an existing trust for outdated objects; for purposes which were once useful, but are now unnecessary, or overtaken by statutory services; or where the income of the trust has during the years become inadequate for the purpose, or, perhaps so large that there is a surplus. In short, the policy is to enable the trustees, with the help of the Charity Commissioners, to make the best use, in modern conditions, of funds dedicated to charity.

ii. Section 13. Section 13 provides for application *cy-près* in five situations:

(1) Subject to subsection (2) below, the circumstances in which the original purposes of a charitable gift can be altered to allow the property given or part of it to be applied *cy-près* shall be as follows:
(*a*) where the original purposes, in whole or in part,—
    (i) have been as far as may be fulfilled; or
    (ii) cannot be carried out, or not according to the directions given and to the spirit of the gift; or
(*b*) where the original purposes provide a use for part only of the property available by virtue of the gift; or
(*c*) where the property available by virtue of the gift and other property applicable for similar purposes can be more effectively used in conjunction, and to that end can suitably, regard being had to the spirit of the gift, be made applicable to common purposes; or
(*d*) where the original purposes were laid down by reference to an area which then was but has since ceased to be a unit for some other purpose, or by reference to a class of persons or to an area which has for any reason since ceased to be

[16] s.13(5).

suitable, regard being had to the spirit of the gift, or to be practical in administering the gift; or

(*e*) where the original purposes, in whole or in part, have, since they were laid down,—

    (i) been adequately provided by other means; or

    (ii) ceased, as being useless or harmful to the community or for other reasons, to be in law charitable; or

    (iii) ceased in any other way to provide a suitable and effective method of using the property available by virtue of the gift, regard being had to the spirit of the gift.

(2) Subsection (1) above shall not affect the conditions which must be satisfied in order that property given for charitable purposes may be applied *cy-près*, except in so far as those conditions require a failure of the original purposes.

In the case of subsequent failure, width of charitable intent is of no significance, but the Commissioners endeavour to follow the spirit of the original gift, so far as this is consistent with proper application of the funds. "The paramount principle that the donor's intent must be followed as closely as possibly has been preserved, but his intention is now interpreted in the light of modern conditions and having regard to the spirit of the gift." [17] Nothing in section 13 requires a *cy-près* scheme where such a scheme was not required before the 1960 Act. [18]

Many schemes have been made by the Commissioners under this section and its predecessor. In their Annual Report for 1970, they say that they "have made good use of the powers contained in section 13(1)(*e*)(i) [purpose adequately provided for by other means]. . . . For example, we have made schemes for a number of charities established for the repair of roads and bridges, substituting for those purposes other general purposes for the benefit of local inhabitants which could include, for instance, the promotion of the arts, the provision of seats and shelters, the preservation of old buildings, or the improvement of local amenities." [19]

The first occasion on which the section was litigated was *Re Lepton's Charity*. [20]

A will dating from 1715 instructed trustees to pay £3 per annum to the Minister, and the "overplus of the profits" to the poor. At that time, the income was £5 per annum, and in 1970 the

---

[17] Annual Report 1970, para. 41; see also 1973, para. 11.
[18] *Oldham Borough Council v. Att.-Gen.* [1993] Ch. 210.
[19] Annual Report 1970, para. 43.
[20] [1972] Ch. 276.

income from the proceeds of sale of the land was nearly £800. Pennycuick V.-C. raised the payment to £100 per annum. This was consistent with the spirit of the gift. Subsection (1)(*a*) applied because "the original purposes" covered the purposes as a whole; it was not necessary to consider separately the gift of the annuity and that of the surplus. In any case (1)(*e*)(iii) would have applied.

More recently, in *Re J. W. Laing Trust*,[21] the question which arose was whether section 13 could be utilised in order to dispense with the donor's requirement that the capital and income be distributed no later than 10 years after his death. It was held that the provision could not be deleted under section 13(1), as the "original purposes"[22] which the court could there review meant the objects of the trust, whereas the settlor's direction was merely administrative. The provision was, however, deleted under the court's inherent jurisdiction. In *Peggs v. Lamb*[23] a trust was created in the Middle Ages for the freemen of Huntingdon and their widows. It was charitable on the basis of the anomalous "locality" cases.[24] In the past the freemen were a substantial section of the public and a suitable class of charitable objects. At present there were only fifteen members, and they claimed equal division of the annual income, irrespective of need, which would give them over £30,000 each. A *cy-près* scheme was ordered to enable the money to be distributed amongst the inhabitants of the borough as a whole, in accordance with the spirit of the gift. The case fell within section 13(1)(d), on the basis that the class had ceased to be suitable recipients of charitable funds. It was not necessary to decide whether section 13(1)(*e*)(ii) also applied, on the basis that they were no longer a section of the public.

Subsection (1)(*e*)(ii) may give rise to difficulty at some future time. Clearly, it will apply to the endowments of independent schools if charitable status should be withdrawn.[25] Perhaps also the section would, if then available, have applied to anti-vivisection trusts, for these had been held charitable in *Re Foveaux*,[26] but non-charitable in *National Anti-Vivisection Society v. I.R.C.*[27] in 1948. The same would seem to apply to charities which have been

---

[21] [1984] Ch. 143. The facts were given at p. 431, *ante*.
[22] See further *Oldham Borough Council v. Att.-Gen* [1993] Ch. 210.
[23] [1994] Ch. 172.
[24] *Ante*, p. 422.
[25] See [1996] Conv. 24 (J. Jaconelli).
[26] [1895] 2 Ch. 501.
[27] [1948] A.C. 31. Lord Simonds suggested at pp. 64–65 that application *cy-près* would have been possible before the 1960 Act.

removed from the Register on the ground that they have ceased to be charitable.

iii. Section 14.[28] Charity Collections.

Finally, it is necessary to refer to section 14. This provides that property given for specific charitable purposes which fail shall be applicable *cy-près* as if given for charitable purposes generally, where it belongs—

(*a*) to a donor who after—
    (i) the prescribed[29] advertisements and inquiries have been published and made, and
    (ii) the prescribed period beginning with the publication of those advertisements has expired,[30]
   cannot be identified or cannot be found,[31] or
(*b*) to a donor who has executed a disclaimer in the prescribed form of his right to have the property returned.

In the case of the proceeds of cash collections by means of collecting boxes or other means not adapted for distinguishing one gift from another, or the proceeds of lotteries and similar money-raising activities, the property is conclusively presumed to belong to unidentifiable donors, without any advertisement or inquiry. In other cases the court may direct the property to be treated as belonging to unidentifiable donors, without any advertisement or inquiry, if it appears that it would not be reasonable, having regard to the amounts or the lapse of time since the gifts, to return it.

Section 14 applies only to cases of initial failure, subsection (7) providing that charitable purposes are deemed to fail, for the purposes of the section, where any difficulty in applying the property to those purposes makes it available for return to the donors.[32] In the case of subsequent failure, the property is not so available.

This solution is much more sensible than any attempt to solve the problem by applying the usual *cy-près* doctrine, involving either the

---

[28] Re-enacting s.14 of the 1960 Act, as amended by Charities Act 1992, s.15.

[29] The Charities (Cy-près Advertisements, Inquiries and Disclaimer) Regulations 1993.

[30] The trustees are not liable to any person in respect of the property if no claim is received before expiry of this period; s.14(2).

[31] Such donors may claim from the *cy-près* recipient within six months of the scheme; s.14(5). For an example of the operation of s.14 see *Re Henry Wood Memorial Trust* [1966] 1 W.L.R. 1601 (failure of Mile End Memorial Hall Fund through lack of financial support); Annual Report 1965, paras. 19–21.

[32] See [1983] Conv. 40 (D. Wilson), arguing that this is never the case where the gift is anonymous and indistinguishable, because the property either goes *cy-près* by the imputation of a general charitable intent (see *Re Hillier* [1954] 1 W.L.R. 700) or to the Crown as *bona vacantia*.

imputation of an artificial general charitable intent, or, failing that, a search for the many donors of tiny gifts, with the possibility of a claim by the Crown to the property as *bona vacantia*.

F. Small Charities

The Charities Act 1985 introduced a principle enabling trustees of certain small charities in effect to determine their own *cy-près* application with the concurrence of the Charity Commissioners. The response from trustees was disappointing,[33] and so the Act was repealed and replaced by provisions now found in the 1993 Act which both extend and simplify the principle.

Under section 74 of the 1993 Act, powers are given to trustees of small charities, meaning those having a gross income not exceeding £5,000 in the last financial year and which do not hold land on trusts stipulating that it must be used for the purposes of the charity. If at least two-thirds of the trustees agree, they may resolve to transfer the property to one or more specified charities. They must be satisfied that their charity's resources are no longer being effectively applied and the purposes of the recipient are as similar as is reasonably practicable. Alternatively, they may modify the trusts by replacing all or any of the purposes with other specified charitable purposes which are as similar in character as is practical, if satisfied that the existing purposes have ceased to be conducive to an effective application of their resources.

Section 75 applies to a charity having a permanent endowment which does not include land and a gross income not exceeding £1,000 in the last financial year. If at least two-thirds of the trustees agree, they may resolve to remove the restrictions on spending capital if of the opinion that the property is too small, in relation to the charity's purposes, to achieve a useful purpose by spending income. They must first consider a transfer under section 74.

Under both sections, the trustees must give public notice of their resolution, of which a copy must be sent to the Commissioners. The Commissioners may require further information and must consider any representations from persons interested in the charity. They will then notify the trustees whether or not they concur, and, if they do, the trustees may proceed accordingly. Neither section applies to an exempt or corporate charity. Much use has been made of these provisions.[34]

---

[33] For statistics, see Annual Report 1986, para. 14; 1987, para. 49; 1988, para. 95; 1989, para. 105; 1990, para. 91; 1991, para. 30.
[34] Annual Report 1995, para. 16.

7. THE ADMINISTRATION OF CHARITIES

A. Reform

Reform of the law of charities was long overdue when the Charities Act was passed in 1960. The major problems were: the narrow limits of the *cy-près* doctrine; the gap and the competition which existed between the established charities and the statutory services of the welfare state; the haphazard state of existing charities and the lack of information about them. The Charities Act 1960 contained reforms on these matters.

Reform has recently been directed towards increasing the supervision of charities by the Charity Commissioners in order to minimise abuse and maladministration by charity trustees. To this end the powers of the Commissioners were increased by the Charities Act 1992, following the Woodfield Report.[35] The reforms were mainly directed to increasing the duty of trustees to prepare annual accounts, to disqualifying certain persons from trusteeship, to controlling fundraising and public charitable collections, and to providing effective means of enforcement. The provisions are now found in the consolidating Charities Act 1993.

B. The Authorities

i. The Charity Commissioners. There is a minimum of three Commissioners, and two at least must be solicitors or barristers.[36] They are civil servants appointed by the Secretary of State, Department of National Heritage,[37] but act independently of that Department. They are charged with "the general function of promoting the effective use of charitable resources by encouraging the development of better methods of administration, by giving charity trustees information and advice on any matter affecting the charity and by investigating and checking abuses."[38]

The Commissioners are under a duty to submit an Annual Report to the Secretary of State,[39] and their reports give an excellent picture of the administration of the law of charities, and of the problems of the day. The reports emphasise continually the duty and the desire

---

[35] Efficiency Scrutiny of the Supervision of Charities, 1987; National Audit Office Report, House of Commons Paper 380, 1986–87; Annual Report 1987; (1993) 7 *Trust Law International* 9 (J. Hill).

[36] Charities Act 1993, s.1; First Sched. para. 1(1), (2). There are currently five.

[37] *Ibid.* para. 1(3).

[38] s.1(3). Their two main functions are charity support and charity supervision; Annual Report 1991, para. 6.

[39] s.1(5).

of the Commissioners to be helpful to trustees.[40] Provision is made for the payment of fees to the Commissioners in certain cases.[41]

ii. The Official Custodian for Charities. The Commissioners are required to appoint an Official Custodian for Charities,[42] a corporation sole. The object was that charity trustees could vest trust property in the custodian and thereby avoid "the necessity for periodical transfers of land and securities upon the appointment of new trustees,"[43] and the necessity to reclaim income tax on investments, as dividends are remitted without deduction. One effect of the recent reforms is to reduce the role of the Official Custodian, in order to increase the responsibility of the trustees. The Official Custodian is being divested of property other than land,[44] and may transfer investments to the trustees or persons nominated by them.

iii. The Visitor.[45] Ecclesiastical[46] and eleemosynary[47] corporations are subject to the jurisdiction of the visitor in relation to their internal affairs. Modern decisions illustrate that the visitor has an important role to play in the universities. Ecclesiastical corporations are visitable by the ordinary. In the case of eleemosynary corporations, the founder may appoint a visitor. If none is appointed, the founder (or his heirs) is the visitor by operation of law.[48] A similar principle applies where the Crown is the founder. Where visitatorial powers are exercisable by the Crown, they are in practice exercised by the Lord Chancellor.

The visitor's jurisdiction stems from the power recognised by the common law in the founder of an eleemosynary corporation to provide the law under which it was to be governed and to be sole judge of the interpretation and application of those laws, either

---

[40] Leaflets for the guidance of charity trustees are regularly published by the Commissioners.

[41] s.85.

[42] s.2. See Annual Report 1974, para. 107.

[43] Annual Report 1970, para. 75.

[44] Charities Act 1992, s.29 (unrepealed). For the provisions as to land, see Charities Act 1993, ss.21–23.

[45] See generally (1970) 86 L.Q.R. 531 (J. Bridge); Picarda, Chap. 41; *Tudor on Charities* (8th ed.), pp. 369–388; (1981) 97 L.Q.R. 610 (P. Smith); (1986) 136 N.L.J. 484, 519, 567 and 665 (P. Smith), adopted in *Thomas v. University of Bradford, infra.*

[46] Corporations existing for the furtherance of religion and the perpetuation of the rites of the Church.

[47] The original meaning was corporations whose object was the distribution of free alms, or the relief of individual distress; *Re Armitage's W. T.* [1972] Ch. 438. But for the purpose of visitatorial powers, corporate schools and modern universities are included. Similarly the Inns of Court; see *R. v. Visitors to the Inns of Court, ex p. Calder* [1994] Q.B. 1.

[48] *Phillips v. Bury* (1694) Skinn. 447. If the heirs die out or cannot act, the Crown is the visitor.

himself or via the person appointed as visitor. Thus the visitor has exclusive jurisdiction over matters of internal management, including the admission and removal of students,[49] and the award of prizes and degrees,[50] but not disputes between the foundation and outsiders.[51] The jurisdiction of the visitor in these matters is sole and exclusive.[52] No appeal lies from his decisions unless the statutes of the corporation so provide,[53] but he is subject to the prerogative remedies of prohibition,[54] mandamus[55] and certiorari[56]; although only if he has acted outside his jurisdiction, abused his powers, or acted in breach of the rules of natural justice.[57] The Education Reform Act 1988 abolished the visitor's jurisdiction in relation to appointment, employment and dismissal of university staff.[58]

C. The Register

Section 3 of the 1993 Act requires the Commissioners to maintain a public register on which all charities are to be included except for (*a*) exempt charities,[59] (*b*) any charity excepted by order or regulation,[60] (*c*) any charity having no permanent endowment, nor the use and occupation of land, and whose income does not exceed £1,000 a year, and (*d*) in respect of a registered place of worship. The purpose of the register, now computerised, is to obtain information about charities. Those which are excepted are those which are national institutions (exempt charities), small ones not occupying land, and others such as ecclesiastical charities where provision for obtaining the necessary information already exists.

---

[49] *Patel v. University of Bradford Senate* [1979] 1 W.L.R. 1066; *c.f. Herring v. Templeman* [1973] 3 All E.R. 569.

[50] *R. v. Her Majesty the Queen in Council, ex p. Vijaytunga* [1990] Q.B. 444; *Oakes v. Sidney Sussex College, Cambridge* [1988] 1 W.L.R. 431.

[51] *Casson v. University of Aston in Birmingham* [1983] 1 All E.R. 88 (dispute over contract entered into with student before he was a member). In *Thomas v. University of Bradford* [1987] A.C. 795 this decision was upheld as correct on the facts but criticised as taking too narrow a view of the visitor's jurisdiction.

[52] *Thomas v. University of Bradford, supra.*

[53] *Thorne v. University of London* [1966] 2 Q.B. 237; *Patel v. University of Bradford Senate, supra*; (1974) 37 M.L.R. 324 (D. Christie); (1974) 33 C.L.J. 23 (S. de Smith).

[54] *Bentley v. Bishop of Ely* (1729) 1 Barn. 192.

[55] *R. v. Dunsheath* [1951] 1 K.B. 127 at p. 134.

[56] *Thomas v. University of Bradford, supra.*

[57] *R. v. Hull University Visitor, ex p. Page* [1993] A.C. 682; (1993) 109 L.Q.R. 155 (H. Wade).

[58] s.206. See (1991) 54 M.L.R. 137 (P. Pettit). The Act applies to publicly funded universities and similar institutions; s.202.

[59] Sched. 2.

[60] S.I. 1963 No. 2074; S.I. 1964 No. 1825 (Regligious Charities); S.I. 1961 No. 1044 (Boy Scouts and Girl Guides); S.I 1965 No. 1056 (Armed Forces); S.I. 1966 No. 965 (Non-exempt Universities).

D. Decisions on Registration

It is the duty of trustees of charities to register,[61] enforceable by order of the Commissioners.[62] Registration is much to the advantage of the trustees, for it raises a conclusive presumption of being a charity,[63] and of being entitled therefore to the privileges accorded to charity. Non-entry gives rise to no presumption either way.

The decision to register a claimant is that of the Charity Commissioners, and an account of recent decisions is given in the Annual Reports and Decisions. In this way, the development of charity law is greatly influenced by the Commissioners. Any person who may be affected by registration, such as a residuary legatee in the case of a will charity, may object to registration, or apply for removal.[64] Nearly all these matters are finally disposed of by the Commissioners but there is provision for an appeal to the High Court from any decision of the Commissioners.[65] In making their decision, the Commissioners are aware of the need for flexibility, and for keeping the law of charities in tune with changing circumstances. They have not always been able to satisfy the critics, who assume that charitable purposes should include all useful projects of reform. The Commissioners sometimes have a narrow line to follow between the attacks of the critics and the decisions which bind them.[66] By the end of 1995, over 180,000 charities had been registered, and during that year 6,274 charities were removed from the Register,[67] mainly because they had ceased to operate. On the matter of removal, the Commissioners are not bound by the view of the Attorney-General.[68]

E. Advice

The Commissioners may also give to any charity trustee an opinion or advice on any matter affecting the performance of his duties, and a trustee acting upon it is deemed to have acted in

[61] Charities Act 1993, s.3(7).
[62] *Ibid.*, s. 87.
[63] *Ibid.*, s.4(1); *Re Murawski's W.T.* [1971] 1 W.L.R. 707.
[64] *Ibid.* s.4(2). Annual Report 1978, para. 84.
[65] *Ibid.* s.4(3); *Incorporated Council of Law Reporting for England and Wales v. Att.-Gen.* [1972] Ch. 73; *Re Construction Industry Training Board* [1973] Ch. 173; *I.R.C. v. McMullen* [1981] A.C. 1, where H.L. upheld the decision of the Commissioners to register; *McGovern v. Att.-Gen.* [1982] Ch. 321, where Slade J. upheld the Commissioners' refusal to register; *Joseph Rowntree Memorial Trust Housing Association Ltd v. Att.-Gen.* [1983] Ch. 159, where refusal was reversed.
[66] Annual Report 1966, paras. 27–41.
[67] Annual Report 1995, para. 75. In 1995 8,752 were registered; *ibid.* About 140,000 are small local charities.
[68] See Annual Report 1982, paras. 36–38, App. C, for the Commissioners' refusal to accede to the request of the Attorney-General to remove the Church of Unification (the "Moonies") from the register. (The Attorney-General's action was subsequently dropped).

accordance with the trust.[69] The Commissioners' advice is also available where an application is made to register a new charity. If the application is refused, the reason will be given so that the language may be amended. It is not of course possible to alter the terms of established trusts which fail to be registered.

F. Powers of the Charity Commissioners

i. Schemes. The Charity Commissioners have concurrent jurisdiction with the High Court in establishing schemes for the administration of a charity.[70] This helps the trustees of charities to administer them more efficiently and to make better use of their funds and property. Schemes may cover the appointment of new bodies of trustees, the vesting of property in new trustees, the provision of new *cy-près* objects in place of objects which have become impracticable, the extension of the trustees' investment powers, and the grouping or amalgamation of charities. Schemes are usually made by the Commissioners on the application of a charity, or where the court, on directing a scheme, orders that the Commissioners shall settle the scheme.[71] It is the duty of charity trustees to secure the effective use of charity property.[72] If they unreasonably refuse or neglect to apply for a scheme in circumstances in which they ought, in the interest of the charity, to do so, the Commissioners may proceed as if an application for a scheme had been made in the case of a charity at least 40 years old.[73]

ii. Consent to Proceedings. By section 33 of the Charities Act 1993, no court proceedings relating to the administration of a charity (other than an exempt charity) shall be entertained unless authorised by the Commissioners.[74] This is to prevent the dissipation of charitable funds in legal proceedings over matters which the Commissioners could resolve.

iii. Dealings with Charity Property. Charity trustees are subject to various statutory restrictions on dealings in charity property.

---

[69] Charities Act 1993, s.29. The Commissioners owe no duty of care to potential objects of a charity; *Mills v. Winchester Diocesan Board of Finance* [1989] Ch. 428; (1989) 3 *Trust Law & Practice* 114 (N. Reville).

[70] *Ibid.* s.16(1).

[71] *Ibid.* s.16(2). As to the right of appeal, see *Childs v. Att.-Gen.* [1973] 1 W.L.R. 497.

[72] *Ibid*, s.13(5).

[73] *Ibid.* s.16(6). The restriction to charities 40 years old was introduced in order to protect donors against official intervention to alter the terms of trusts wihtin the donor's lifetime.

[74] See *Haslemere Estates Ltd v. Baker* [1982] 1 W.L.R. 1109; *Re Hampton Fuel Allotment Charity* [1989] Ch. 484; *Richmond upon Thames London Borough Council v. Rogers* [1988] 2 All E.R. 761; *Mills v. Winchester Diocesan Board of Finance* [1989] Ch. 428; *Gunning v. Buckfast Abbey Trustees Registered, The Times*, June 9, 1994.

Of particular importance is section 36 of the Charities Act 1993,[75] restricting the trustees' powers[76] to sell, lease or otherwise dispose of charity land.[77] The trustees require an order of the court or of the Commissioners unless the following conditions are satisfied: (*a*) the trustees have obtained and considered a written report on the proposed disposition from a qualified surveyor; (*b*) they have advertised the proposed disposition as advised by the surveyor; and (*c*) they are satisfied that the terms are the best reasonably obtainable.[78] The requirements are less stringent in the case of a lease not exceeding seven years.[79] Where the trustees hold land on trusts which stipulate that it is to be used for the purposes (or any particular purpose) of the charity, they must also give public notice and invite and consider representations.[80] Such land could be sold in certain circumstances under the previous law.[81]

Under section 26 of the Act of 1993 the Commissioners have a general power to authorise dealings with charity property which the trustees would otherwise have no power to do.

iv. Accounts; Inquiries. The Commissioners oversee the trustees' duty to provide accounts,[82] and, if dissatisfied in any way, may institute inquiries.[83] Ultimately, they may remove trustees from office.[84] The Commissioners may be alerted by the Inland Revenue to the possible misapplication of charity funds.[85]

It is in the area of accounts and audit that much disquiet was felt over the possibility of abuse and maladministration by charity trustees. The Charities Act 1993 imposes more rigorous duties on trustees of unincorporated charities[86] to keep accounting records and to prepare annual accounts, which must be audited.[87] The trustees

---

[75] See also s.38 (mortgages).

[76] Which derive from the Trusts of Land and Appointment of Trustees Act 1996, s.6 (which cannot be excluded by the settlor; s.8(3)), or under the founding instrument or statute.

[77] Such land is no longer settled land but is held on a trust of land; Trusts of Land and Appointment of Trustees Act 1996, s.2(5).

[78] s.36(2), (3). For exceptions, see s.36(9). Neither s.36 nor s.38 (mortgages) applies to exempt charities. A disposition not complying with s.36 is valid in favour of a purchaser in good faith; s.37(4); *cf. London Borough of Hounslow v. Hare* (1992) 24 H.L.R. 9 (on Charities Act 1960, s.29).

[79] s.36(5).

[80] s.36(6). This does not apply if they are acquiring replacement property, or in the case of a lease not exceeding two years; s.36(7).

[81] See *Oldham Borough Council v. Att.-Gen.* [1993] Ch. 210.

[82] Charities Act 1993, ss.41–49; Charities (Accounts and Reports) Regulations (S.I. 1995 No. 2724).

[83] *Ibid.*, s.8. See Annual Report 1979, paras. 24–36. Examples may be found in most of the Annual Reports.

[84] *Ibid.* s.18, *post*, p. 451. See also *Att-Gen. v. Schonfeld* [1980] 1 W.L.R. 1182.

[85] *Ibid.*, s.10.

[86] Companies Act 1985, Part VII, applies to corporate charities. The new rules do not apply to exempt charities, but s.46 of the 1993 Act imposes a duty to keep accounts on them.

[87] ss.42–44.

must send annual reports to the Commissioners of their activities, with a statement of accounts and the auditor's report.[88] The Commissioners may grant a unifying order enabling two or more charities with the same trustees to file consolidated accounts.[89]

G. Investment

i. Investment Powers.[90]

Under the Trustee Investments Act 1961[91] a proportion of the trust fund, recently increased to three quarters,[92] may be invested in equities. Proposed reforms of trustee investment powers (discussed in Chapter 18) will apply to charity trustees, but will not involve major changes in this area because charities are already able to achieve a reasonable spread of investments under the pooling schemes mentioned below.

ii. Pooling. C.O.I.F. Common Deposit Scheme.

Without statutory authority, different bodies of trustees could not pool their funds for investment purposes, for this would involve a delegation of the trustees' investment powers, and was inconsistent with the trustees' duty to act personally. Section 24 of the 1993 Act (re-enacting earlier provisions) gives power to the court or the Commissioners to create common investment schemes under which the investment of property transferred to the fund is invested by trustees appointed to manage the fund, and the participating charities are entitled to shares related to their contributions.[93] Under the predecessor legislation, the Commissioners established the Charities Official Investment Fund, which is open to all charities.

The Charities Act 1993 also authorises the creation of common deposit schemes,[94] whereby money can be deposited at interest.

---

[88] s.45. The reports are subject to public inspection; s.47. The trustees must also send annual returns in prescribed form to the Commissioners; s.48. Persistent default in these duties is an offence; s.49. See also s.87.

[89] s.96(6), inserted by the Charities (Amendment) Act 1995. The order may apply to all or any of the purposes of the 1993 Act.

[90] As to ethical investment by charity trustees, see *Harries v. Church Commissioners for England* [1992] 1 W.L.R. 1241; *post*, p. 524.

[91] *Post*, Chap. 18. Wider powers may be approved by the court; *Trustees of the British Museum v. Att.-Gen* [1984] 1 W.L.R. 418, *post*, p. 530; *Steel v. Wellcome Custodian Trustees Ltd* [1988] 1 W.L.R. 167. Applications to court will rarely be necessary after the reforms of trustee investment powers discussed in Chap. 18 take effect.

[92] Trustee Investments (Division of Trust Fund) Order (S.I. 1996 No. 845).

[93] Annual Report 1970, paras. 68–74; 1971, para. 90; *Re London University's Charitable Trust* [1964] Ch. 284.Alterations to the structure of these funds have been proposed; *The Times*, December 3, 1996.

[94] s.25.

H. Trustees

i. Capacity. One of the means by which the Charities Act 1993 seeks to prevent fraud and maladministration is by the disqualification of certain persons from holding the office of trustee of a charity.[95] Those disqualified include persons convicted of an offence involving dishonesty or deception, undischarged bankrupts and persons previously removed from charity trusteeship on the grounds of misconduct or mismanagement.[96] Also a Local Authority may not be trustee of an eleemosynary charity.[97] We have seen that the appointment of a charity as trustee may colour the construction which a court will place upon the language of the trust, but does not ensure that a trust is charitable.[98]

ii. Number. Majority Vote. There is no limit upon the number of persons who may be trustees of a charity.[99] Too great a number of trustees is an obvious inconvenience. But decisions of trustees of a charity may be taken by majority vote and need not be unanimous.[1]

iii. Retirement. Charity trustees may retire in the same way as trustees of private trusts.[2] In 1982 the Law Reform Committee recommended that the procedure should be facilitated,[3] but this has not been implemented.

iv. Removal and Suspension. The Commissioners may suspend a trustee on being satisfied as a result of inquiries[4] that (*a*) there has been misconduct or mismanagement or (*b*) that it is necessary or desirable for the purpose of protecting the property if the charity,[5] or they may appoint additional trustees or make orders for the protection of the property, such as the appointment of a receiver and manager. Where they are satisfied that both conditions (*a*) and (*b*) are fulfilled, they may order the removal of a trustee or other officer who has been responsible for or privy to the misconduct or mismanagement or has contributed to or facilitated it. They may also (or instead) order a scheme for the administration of the charity. The Commissioners may also, by order made of their own motion,

---

[95] s.72. By s.73, it is an offence to act while disqualified.
[96] The Commissioners are to keep a public register of persons so removed.
[97] *Re Armitage* [1972] Ch. 438.
[98] *Ante*, p. 423.
[99] T.A. 1925, s. 34.
[1] *Re Whiteley* [1910] 1 Ch. 600 at p. 608.
[2] *Post*, p. 502.
[3] 23rd Report, *The Powers and Duties of Trustees* (1982, Cmnd, 8733), para. 6.2.
[4] Under Charities Act 1993, s.8.; *Jones v. Att.-Gen.* [1974] Ch. 148.
[5] s.18.

remove a charity trustee who has been discharged from bankruptcy within the last five years, who is a corporation in liquidation, is mentally incapable, has failed to act, or is abroad or cannot be found.[6] In such cases they may appoint a replacement or additional trustee. These provisions do not apply to exempt charities.

v. Supply of Goods and Services by Trustees. The question arose whether charity trustees should be prohibited from supplying goods or services to a charity. Under the ordinary rule, his fiduciary relationship would not allow him to be in a position where his duty as a trustee might conflict with his interests as an individual.[7] In many cases, however, trustees of a charity may be willing to supply goods and services on terms which are beneficial to the charity. The Commissioners announced in their report for 1971[8] that a trustee should absent himself from any meeting of the trustees at which the provision of goods and services by him was being discussed, and that the other trustees must be satisfied that the transaction is advantageous to the charity.

vi. Misapplication. An application by the trustee for purposes not covered by the terms of the trust is a misapplication of charity funds, which may give rise to personal liability on the trustee, and may be restrained by injunction,[9] or may be the subject of an inquiry by the Charity Commissioners.[10]

I. Ex Gratia Payments

Difficulty and distress has been caused by the fact that a charity was thought to be unable to make *ex gratia* payments for non-charitable purposes, however compelling the moral obligation to do so. Thus, if a testator gave to his family his shares in certain companies, and left his residuary estate to charity, and at the time of the testator's death all the shares had been sold and the proceeds of sale fell into the residuary estate, the charity would be obtaining much more than the testator intended. Cross J. decided that, in appropriate circumstances, the court and the Attorney-General had power to give authority to make *ex gratia* payments from charitable

---

[6] *Ibid.* subs. (4).
[7] *Post*, Chap. 21.
[8] Para. 93. See also, on remuneration, Decisions, Vol. 2 (1994), pp. 14–23.
[9] *Baldry v. Feintuck* [1972] 1 W.L.R. 552. (Resolution to apply Students' Union funds for political purposes). See Annual Report 1983, paras. 95 and 96 and App. A.
[10] *Ante*, p. 449.

funds; but only in case of strong moral obligation.[11] Trustees wishing to make such a payment should apply to the Charity Commissioners, who can authorise such payments under the supervision of the Attorney-General.[12]

J. Co-operation Between Charities and Statutory Services[13]

If the best value is to be obtained from the resources available to charity trustees and local authorities, it is essential that they work in harmony. The social services of the Welfare State have taken over most of the ground of charity work, as it has been understood. This raises the question of the role of charity, which has certainly changed in the last 100 years. If it is argued that all the important needs of the community are now the responsibility of the State, one conclusion is that the State should take over all funds held in charitable trusts. On the other hand, a giant bureaucratic system has its gaps and limitations; and, being users of public money, there is a danger of a lack of enterprise and experiment. Charitable trusts in the context look like a "private enterprise" social system; but it should never be forgotten that charitable trusts are users of public money too; for the fiscal privileges enjoyed by charities mean that the Revenue is losing income which it would otherwise receive. The role of charity is "to seek out the gaps in the statutory services and to pioneer new services."[14] Charities should remain independent, and "co-operation between them and the statutory services should be on the basis of partnership not subordination."[15] These are principles on which sections 76–78 of the 1993 Act, re-enacting provisions of the 1960 Act, are based.

Section 76 authorises a local authority to maintain a public index of local charities. Under section 77, the authority may initiate a review of local charities, and report to the Commissioners and make recommendations. Section 78 permits any local council to make arrangements for the co-ordination of the work of the council and of the charities in the interests of persons who may benefit from the service of either.

---

[11] *Re Snowden* [1970] Ch. 700; *Re Henderson* [1960] Ch. 700; Annual Report 1969, paras. 26–31; Annual Report 1977, paras. 154–156.

[12] Charities Act 1993, s. 27.

[13] See Annual Report 1970, paras. 28–36; 1971, paras. 101 *et seq.*; 1972, para. 49; 1976, paras. 76–84; 1977, paras. 51–56 (Motability: charity in partnership with State); paras. 58–62 (care of disabled); 1978, paras. 61–63, Apps. A and B suggesting ways in which the income of charities for the relief of poverty and sickness may be spent without overlapping the statutory services; 1987, para. 4. See also *Charity and the National Health, The Times,* December 6, 1989.

[14] *Ibid.* para. 28.

[15] *Ibid.* para. 29; 1971, paras. 80, 84.

Although many schemes arising out of local reviews have been made,[16] few local authorities can now afford to initiate a review.[17] The ineffectiveness of many local authority reviews of charities to achieve modernisation and use of resources in co-operation with the welfare services led to the passing of the Charities Act 1985. This Act and the provisions of the Charities Act 1993 which replace it[18] were designed to promote greater accountability to the community by trustees of local charities and to facilitate the modernisation of these and other small charities and the disposal of funds which can no longer be effectively used.

---

[16] H.C. Expenditure Committee Report, Vol. II, pp. 20–21; Goodman Committee Report, paras. 184–185; Annual Report 1979, para. 123.

[17] Annual Report 1980, para. 154.

[18] *Ante*, p. 443.

CHAPTER 16

TRUSTS OF PENSION FUNDS

1. Introduction 455
  A. Types of Pension Scheme 456
  B. Beneficiaries Not Volunteers 459
2. Special Rules Applicable to Pension
  Trusts 461
  A. Pensions Act 1995 461
    i. Regulatory Authority 461
    ii. Trustees 462
      (a) Constitution 463
      (b) Disqualification 464
      (c) Majority Decisions 464
    iii. Professional Advisers 465
    iv. Investment 465
      (a) General Principles 465
      (b) Delegation to Fund
        Manager 466
      (c) Exclusion of Liability 467

      (d) Employer-Related Invest-
        ments 467
     v. Minimum Funding 468
     vi. Surplus 469
     vii. Winding Up 470
     viii. Information to Members 471
     ix. Compensation 471
     x. Alienability; Bankruptcy 472
  B. Other Statutory Provisions 473
    i. Perpetuities 473
    ii. Tax Relief 473
      (a) Tax Relief for Contributions 474
      (b) Tax Relief for the Pension
        Fund 474
      (c) Overfunding 474
3. Equal Treatment 475
4. Pensions on Divorce 476

1. INTRODUCTION

PENSION fund trusts have received much public scrutiny in recent
years, primarily as a result of the misappropriation of about £453
million from the pension funds of the employees of Mirror Group
Newspapers and the Maxwell Communications Corporation by the
late Robert Maxwell.[1] The focus of the ensuing debate was the
question whether pension schemes should continue to be governed
by the law of trusts, and how the scheme members (the beneficiaries) could be better safeguarded against fraud, mismanagement
and insolvency. The matter was referred to the Pension Law Review
Committee, chaired by Professor Roy Goode. The Goode Report[2]
favoured retaining the law of trusts as the most suitable mechanism
for dealing with pension funds, primarily because of the well-
established principles concerning the fiduciary responsibilities of

---

[1] Most of the money has been recovered and all benefits are likely to be paid; *The Times*,
February 20, 1996.

[2] *Pension Law Reform: Pension Law Review Committee Report* (1993), Cmnd. 2342; (1993)
7 *Trust Law International* 91 (D. Chatterton). See also [1993] Conv. 283 (D. Hayton).

trustees and the proprietary rights of beneficiaries, conferring protection from the employer's insolvency. Of course, no legal mechanism can prevent deliberate wrongdoing.

The Committee recommended various ways in which the rights of pension beneficiaries might be enhanced and safeguarded by the enactment of special rules going beyond the protection afforded to beneficiaries of traditional trusts under the general law. In particular, they recommended the introduction of a regulatory body, a compensation scheme to apply in cases of misappropriation, a minimum funding requirement to prevent a shortfall of funds in the case of funded schemes, restrictions on employers' rights to surplus funds, and reforms relating to the appointment, removal and disqualification of trustees. Most of their recommendations, some in modified form, were implemented by the Pensions Act 1995.[3] The special treatment of pension fund beneficiaries reflects the fact that their entitlements arise from their contracts of employment. Unlike traditional beneficiaries, they are not volunteers. In many ways, however, pension trusts are subject to the same principles as any other trusts, and the pension trust caselaw has contributed much to the development of the general law of trusts.[4]

A long-term European goal is cross-border membership of pension schemes through the establishment of European pension funds covering workers in several member states, to reflect the principle of free movement of workers.

The purpose of this chapter is to examine pension funds as an important modern illustration of the law of trusts in operation (about £500 billion is currently invested in pensions[5]), and to consider the ways in which pension fund trusts are treated differently from traditional trusts. Before doing so it is necessary to appreciate the different types of pension schemes available and to understand the terminology.

A. Types of Pension Scheme

Pension provision falls into three broad categories: the state pension, a personal pension (a form of investment made by an individual with an insurance company, to which the employer may contribute) and an occupational pension scheme, which is organised by an employer to provide pensions and other benefits for employees (and usually for their dependants) on leaving employment (by

---

[3] See (1996) 59 M.L.R. 241 (R. Nobles).
[4] See (1993) 56 M.L.R. 471 (G. Moffat), examining whether a separate pensions law is developing, or whether the developments in recent pensions cases are applicable generally. See also (1994) 8 *Trust Law International* 35 (Vinelott J.). For the "property" rights of pension beneficiaries, see (1994) 14 L.S. 345 (R. Nobles).
[5] *Simon's Weekly Tax Intelligence* 1995, p. 7.

retirement or otherwise) or on death.[6] The latter category is the subject of this chapter. Occupational pension schemes themselves take various forms, but in essence trust law will apply where assets are segregated and invested to provide pension benefits. In 1991 10.7 million employees were members of occupational pension schemes.[7] Fewer than 40 per cent of private sector employees were scheme members in contrast with over 70 per cent of public sector employees. Many public sector schemes (such as those for teachers and the civil service) are established by legislation and are unfunded in the sense that there is no trust fund set aside to provide benefits. The employees' security is founded on the statute rather than on the segregation of assets. State pensions are also unfunded, benefits being paid from current contributions. A non-statutory scheme is unfunded where the employer does not set aside and accumulate assets in a separate trust fund in advance of the benefits commencing to be paid. Most private schemes, however, are funded. (There is no obligation on an employer, other than by contract, to provide a funded scheme, or indeed any pension scheme at all). We are concerned with funded schemes, where a fund is held on trust to make provision in advance for future liabilities to members by accumulating assets. The assets are invested and the investments held by the trustees. This may be contrasted with an insured scheme, where the trustees have effected an insurance contract for each member which guarantees benefits corresponding to those promised under the scheme rules. In other words, this is an investment through the medium of an insurance company, the trustees using the contributions to pay the premiums. The insurance is the only significant asset of the scheme. If the sums payable by the insurer are sufficient at all times to cover all benefits, the scheme is said to be fully insured. Most small schemes are run through insurers.

The benefits to which an employee is entitled depend on whether the scheme is earnings-related (a defined *benefit* scheme) or whether it is a "money purchase" scheme (a defined *contribution* scheme). An earnings-related scheme (sometimes called a final salary scheme) is where the benefit is calculated by reference to the member's pensionable earnings for a period of pensionable service ending at or before normal pension date or leaving service. There is normally a restriction on the number of years (*e.g.* 40) which qualify as pensionable service, and not all earnings (*e.g.* a bonus or allowance) are pensionable. The scheme may require contributions from employees (a contributory scheme) or may not (non-contributory). The benefits are usually based on a fraction of the final salary for

---

[6] Another, less common, variant is the "executive pension plan", in which a scheme is established by a private company (the employer) for one employee (the director). Such a scheme was involved in *Brooks v. Brooks* [1996] 1 A.C. 375, *post*, p. 476.

[7] *Pension Law Review Committee Report*, para. 2.2.4.

each year of pensionable service. The cost of providing these defined benefits cannot be accurately predicted, so the employer in a contributory scheme undertakes to pay whatever sum is needed to top up employee contributions. If the fund is in surplus, the employer may be able to take a "contributions holiday", by temporarily suspending its contributions.[8] It follows that the risk of poor investment performance falls on the employer in an earnings-related scheme.

A "money purchase" scheme is where the benefits of an individual member are determined by reference to the contributions paid into the scheme by or on behalf of that member, usually increased by an amount based on the investment return of those contributions. The contributions are fixed (normally a percentage of salary) by the scheme, and the benefits vary according to investment performance. Thus the employee takes the risk of poor investments, but also takes the benefit of a good performance. The fund is either used to purchase an annuity to provide the pension, or a pension may be paid from the fund according to the size of the member's account in the fund. The majority of schemes are earnings-related, but "money purchase" is more popular for new schemes. As explained below, one attraction to employers is that a money purchase scheme is not subject to the minimum funding requirements introduced by the Pensions Act 1995.

When a funded scheme is being set up, the trust deeds are lengthy and take time to prepare. It is, therefore, usual to have an interim trust deed with outline rules, which appoints the first trustees. This enables the scheme to be started without delay, and provisional tax relief to be secured.[9] In due course this is replaced by the final (or definitive) trust deed, and the Inland Revenue normally gives approval (necessary for tax relief) backdated to the execution of the interim deed.

Much of the caselaw deals with entitlement to surplus funds, the contest normally involving beneficiaries, employers, creditors of an insolvent employer, or companies which have taken over the employer company and wish to syphon off the surplus ("takeover raiders" or "predators"). Of course, a surplus cannot arise in the case of a money purchase scheme or an unfunded scheme. In the case of a funded earnings-related scheme, any surplus is notional if the scheme is ongoing. A surplus is said to exist whenever, according to actuarial calculations, the value of the assets exceeds the estimated liabilities. There will be an actual surplus only if the scheme is wound up, leaving an excess after discharge of liabilities.

---

[8] This is one of the permitted methods of reducing an excessive surplus under the pension trust tax regime; *post*, p. 475. A thirty year "holiday" was a breach of trust by the trustees of the British Airways pension fund; (1996) 10 *Trust Law International* 26.

[9] For the fiscal benefits, see *post*, p. 473.

Where a pension scheme is terminated by winding-up, the assets will usually be applied to the purchase of annuities to provide pensions for members, or the assets and liabilities may be transferred to another pension scheme.

B. Beneficiaries Not Volunteers

The fact that pension trust beneficiaries are not volunteers puts them in certain respects in a different position from the beneficiaries of traditional family trusts. The consideration arises from the fact that the pension benefits are a form of deferred remuneration for their services[10] and from their contributions (if any) to the fund. In *Mettoy Pension Trustees Ltd v. Evans*[11] the scheme contained a power of appointment in favour of the members, any surplus not so appointed going to the employer, which was in liquidation. The fact that the members were not volunteers was influential in classifying the power as fiduciary rather than personal. Had it been only personal (*i.e.* a bare power), the unpalatable conclusion would have been that the entire surplus would have gone to the creditors, the power proving to be of illusory benefit to the members. The classification of the power as fiduciary meant that it could not be released[12] (in the interests of the creditors), and, further, that the court could intervene to secure the exercise of the power.[13]

In *Davis v. Richards & Wallington Industries Ltd*[14] there were doubts whether the definitive (final) trust deed had been validly executed. This deed provided that any surplus should belong to the employers after increasing the pension benefits to the statutory maximum. If the deed was invalid the trust would be incompletely constituted. However, as the beneficiaries were not volunteers they could compel the execution of a valid deed and their rights (by applying the maxim that equity regards as done that which ought to be done) were as if such a deed had already been executed. In fact the deed was held valid.

In a pension trust the trustee/beneficiary relationship exists in parallel with the contractual employer/employee relationship and

---

[10] See *Brooks v. Brooks* [1996] 1 A.C. 375. This meant that the husband (the employee) and not the employer was regarded as settlor of the marriage settlement constituted by the pension scheme.

[11] [1990] 1 W.L.R. 1587; *ante*, p. 170. See also *Thrells Ltd v. Lomas* [1993] 1 W.L.R. 456; *In re Makin (William) & Sons Ltd* [1993] B.C.C. 453; *Brtish Coal Corp. v. British Coal Staff Superannuation Scheme Trustees Ltd* [1995] 1 All E.R. 912 at p. 925.

[12] See also *Re Courage Group's Pension Schemes* [1987] 1 W.L.R. 495; *ante*, p. 182.

[13] This controversial aspect of the decision was discussed at p. 170, *ante*. See now Pensions Act 1995, s.25 (fiduciary powers exercisable by independent trusteee on insolvency); *post*, p. 464.

[14] [1990] 1 W.L.R. 1511; *ante*, p. 239.

the pension scheme must be interpreted against this background. In *Imperial Group Pension Trust Ltd v. Imperial Tobacco Ltd*[15] the company had power under the scheme to consent to an increase in benefits. The issue was whether it was under a duty to consider the interests of the members and not just its own interests when granting or withholding consent. It was held that the implied contractual obligation of good faith between employer and employee (meaning that the employer would not act in a manner calculated or likely to destroy or damage the relationship of confidence and trust between employer and employee) applied to the exercise of the employer's rights and powers under the pension scheme just as it applied to its other rights and powers. The power to give or withhold consent was accordingly subject to a restriction that it could not be validly exercised in breach of the obligation of good faith. Thus the pension trust "lies at the interface between trust and employment law."[16]

The fact that pension trust beneficiaries are not volunteers may allow them to be more favourably treated than other beneficiaries in the matter of costs. In *McDonald v. Horn*[17] it was held that, contrary to the usual rule, pension beneficiaries may obtain a "pre-emptive costs order" where there are serious allegations of impropriety and breach of trust against the employers and trustees. Thus the beneficiaries would obtain their costs, and any costs which they might be ordered to pay to the defendants, out of the fund whether or not their action ultimately proved successful. The fact that the beneficiaries had given consideration made the action analogous to an action by a minority shareholder on behalf of a company, where such an order could be made.

As a general proposition, however, the ordinary principles of trust law apply to pension trusts as to other trusts. This was emphasised in *Wilson v. Law Debenture Trust Corp plc*,[18] where it was held that the principle of *Re Londonderry's Settlement*,[19] whereby trustees are not obliged to give reasons for the exercise of their discretions to the beneficiaries, applied equally to pension fund trusts.[20] Although the court must have regard to the fact that the beneficiaries are not volunteers when construing the trust deed, effect must be given to settled principles of trust law in determining the effect of the deed on its true construction.

---

[15] [1991] 1 W.L.R. 589.
[16] (1994) 8 *Trust Law International* 35 (Vinelott J.).
[17] [1995] 1 All E.R. 961.
[18] [1995] 2 All E.R. 337; (1995) 145 N.L.J. 1414 (P. O'Hagan). Member trustees will have access to reasons.
[19] [1965] Ch. 198; *post*, p. 506.
[20] A contrary view is taken in (1992) 6 *Trust Law International* 119 at p. 125 (Lord Browne-Wilkinson) and (1994) 8 *Trust Law International* 27 and 118 (D. Schaffer).

2. SPECIAL RULES APPLICABLE TO PENSION TRUSTS

In view of the special nature of pension fund trusts in terms of the size of the funds, their quasi-public nature, the opportunities for misappropriation by the employer, the non-volunteer status of the beneficiaries, and the public interest in the encouragement of such trusts, there are many statutory provisions which apply special rules to pension trusts. Most of these are contained in the Pensions Act 1995, but others, relating in particular to taxation and the application of the perpetuity rule, are found elsewhere.

A. Pensions Act 1995

As discussed at the beginning of this chapter, the main objective of the Act is to protect the beneficiaries from the effects of maladministration, fraud and insolvency. Illustrations of this objective include the provision that the trustees must keep proper books and records and must keep any money received by them in a separate account at an institution authorised under the Banking Act 1987,[21] and that an employer who fails to pay over any contributions deducted from members within a certain period commits an offence.[22] The 1995 Act seeks also to strike a fair balance between the interests of current employees, pensioners and employers. To the extent that any of the statutory provisions discussed below conflict with the terms of a pension scheme, such terms are overridden by the Act.[23] Provision is also made for modifying pension schemes in order to implement the requirements of the Act.[24]

i. Regulatory Authority. Following the recommendations of the Goode Report, the 1995 Act set up the Occupational Pensions Regulatory Authority[25] (replacing the Occupational Pensions Board) to supervise pension trusts and thereby reduce the likelihood of maladministration and fraud. The Authority may, by an order under section 3 of the Act, prohibit a person from being a trustee of a particular pension trust in various circumstances, as where it is satisfied that the person has been in serious or persistent breach of his duties under the Act while a trustee of the pension trust. Such an order, which is revocable, operates to remove the trustee. Section 4 enables the Authority to make an order suspending a trustee in various circumstances, as where a bankruptcy petition has been

---

[21] Pensions Act 1995, s.49.

[22] s.49(8).

[23] s.117.

[24] ss.68, 69. Schemes often contain express modification powers, the exercise of which is restricted by s.67.

[25] s.1 and Sched. 1.

presented against him or proceedings commenced for an offence involving dishonesty or deception, and such proceedings have not been concluded. While the order is in force, the person is prohibited from exercising any functions as trustee.[26] A person who purports to act as trustee while prohibited or suspended is guilty of an offence, but things done by him while purporting to act are not invalid merely because of the prohibition or suspension.[27] The power of the Authority to disqualify certain persons from acting as trustee of any occupational pension scheme is dealt with below.[28] Section 7 permits the Authority to appoint a new trustee in place of one who has been removed or disqualified, or where the appointment is necessary to secure that the number of trustees is sufficient or that the trustees as a whole have the necessary skills. Such a trustee may be paid fees out of the trust assets.

In addition to the powers discussed above, the Authority has jurisdiction under section 10 to impose financial penalties on trustees and other persons, such as the director of a corporate trustee, in respect of various breaches of their duties under the 1995 Act. It may also seek injunctions to restrain misuse or misappropriation of assets, apply to court for the restitution of assets transferred to the employer or invested in the employer's business in breach of the Act, and give directions to trustees.[29] Trustees must not be indemnified out of the trust assets for any fine imposed for an offence under the Act nor for any civil penalty imposed by the Authority.[30] Nor may the premiums of an insurance policy be paid out of trust assets where the risk is or includes the imposition of such a fine or penalty.

Finally, the Authority may order an occupational pension scheme to be wound up in order to protect the interests of the members or, on the application of the trustees or employer, if the scheme is no longer required or should be replaced by a different scheme.[31]

In addition to the Authority, the Pensions Ombudsman (first created by the Social Security Act 1990) has jurisdiction over occupational and personal pension schemes. He may investigate and determine various complaints and disputes relating primarily to maladministration.[32]

ii. Trustees. The supervisory powers of the regulatory authority over trustees, including the power of removal, suspension and

---

[26] The procedure for making orders under ss.3 and 4 is found in s.5.

[27] s.6.

[28] *Post*, p. 464.

[29] ss.13–15. For information gathering by the Authority, see s.98–102.

[30] s.31.

[31] s.11.

[32] Pension Schemes Act 1993, ss.146–151, as amended by Pensions Act 1995, s.157. See *Wild v. Pensions Ombudsman* [1996] P.L.R. 275.

appointment, were noted above. The 1995 Act contains further important provisions concerning trustees, which are designed primarily to ensure good administration and to dilute the influence of the employer.

(a) *Constitution.* The constitution of the trustee body requires that representatives of the scheme members must be included, and that a trustee who is independent of the employer must be appointed on the employer's insolvency.

The trustees must normally make arrangements for the selection of "member-nominated trustees".[33] There must be at least two (or at least one if the scheme comprises less than 100 members) and they must constitute at least one third of the total number of trustees. A greater number cannot be appointed without the employer's approval. Where the trustee is a company connected with the employer, the requirements is for "member-nominated directors".[34] A person who is not a scheme member cannot be selected as a member-nominated trustee (or director) without the employer's approval, if the employer so requires.[35]

Where a person is both a trustee and a beneficiary, as in the case of member-nominated trustees, difficult problems of conflict of interest and duty might arise. Where, for example, trustees have a discretion to use a surplus to augment the benefits of the members, any balance going to the employer, the question arises whether they can validly exercise their discretion in such a way as to benefit themselves in their capacity as members.[36] This is now resolved by section 39 of the 1995 Act, which provides that "no rule of law that a trustee may not exercise the powers vested in him so as to give rise to a conflict between his personal interest and his duties to the beneficiaries shall apply to a trustee of a trust scheme, who is also a member of the scheme, exercising the powers vested in him in any manner, merely because their exercise in that manner benefits, or may benefit, him as a member of the scheme."

At least one independent trustee must be appointed in circumstances connected with the insolvency of the employer, namely when an insolvency practitioner begins to act in relation to the employer or if the official receiver becomes the liquidator of the

---

[33] Pensions Act 1995, s.16, subject to significant exceptions in s.17. See Occupational Pension Schemes (Member-nominated Trustees and Directors) Regulations (S.I. 1996 No. 1216). The failure to make member trustees mandatory is criticised in (1996) 59 M.L.R. 241 at p.259 (R. Nobles).

[34] s.18.

[35] s.19(5).

[36] See *In re Makin (William) & Sons Ltd* [1993] B.C.C. 453; (1996) 10 *Trust Law International* 15 (M. Milner); *British Coal Corp. v. British Coal Staff Superannuation Scheme Trustees Ltd* [1995] 1 All E.R. 912; *Re Drexel Burnham Lambert UK Pension Plan* [1995] 1 W.L.R. 32.

employer company or the receiver and manager or trustee in bankruptcy of an individual employer.[37] The appointment is the responsibility of the insolvency practitioner or official receiver.[38] Once appointed, and so long as the circumstances requiring the appointment continue, only the independent trustee may exercise any discretionary powers of the trustees under the scheme and any fiduciary powers of the employer.[39]

(b) *Disqualification.* Certain categories of persons are disqualified by section 29 from being trustee of any occupational pension scheme. Broadly, the disqualification applies to a person convicted of any offence involving dishonesty or deception; an undischarged bankrupt; a company of which any director is disqualified under the section; a person who has made a composition with creditors and has not been discharged; and a person disqualified from acting as a company director. There are other circumstances in which the regulatory authority may disqualify a person from acting as trustee of any occupational pension scheme. A person who has been removed by the Authority under section 3 of the Act or by court order on the ground of misconduct or mismanagement may be disqualified if the Authority considers that it is not desirable for him to be a trustee of any occupational pension scheme.[40] The Authority may also disqualify a company which has gone into liquidation or a person it considers incapable of acting as such a trustee by reason of mental disorder.[41]

A trustee who becomes disqualified ceases to be a trustee and commits an offence if he purports to act while disqualified,[42] although things done by him while purporting to act as trustee are not invalid merely because of the disqualification.[43] The Authority must keep a register of persons disqualified by its order.[44]

(c) *Majority Decisions.* Under the general law, trustees (other than charity trustees) must act unanimously, unless the trust instrument provides otherwise.[45] Section 32 of the 1995 Act provides an exception for trustees of an occupational pension scheme, who may,

---

[37] s.22. "Independent" is defined in s.23(3). He may be paid fees from the trust fund; s.25(6). An independent trustee was already required in such circumstances under previous legislation.

[38] s.23. Scheme members may apply to court to enforce this duy under s.24.

[39] s.25. The employer, if previously sole trustee, ceases to be trustee on the appointment of the independent trustee.

[40] s.29(3).

[41] s.29(4). Orders under subsections (3) and (4) are revocable. Any disqualification under the section may be waived by the Authority.

[42] s.30(3).

[43] s.30(5).

[44] s.30(7).

[45] *Post*, p. 485.

unless the trust scheme provides otherwise, make decisions by majority. As a safeguard, the trustees must give notice of occasions at which decisions may be taken to each trustee, so far as reasonably practicable.[46]

iii. Professional Advisers. The trustees or managers of every occupational pension scheme must appoint an individual or a firm as auditor and an individual as actuary.[47] Where the trust assets include investments, an individual or firm must be appointed as fund manager.[48] If the auditor or actuary has reasonable cause to believe that any duty imposed on the trustees or managers, employer or professional adviser relating to the administration of the pension scheme has not been or is not being complied with, he must give a written report to the regulatory authority.[49] If he fails to do so, he may be subjected to a financial penalty under section 10 and may be disqualified by the regulatory authority from being the auditor or actuary of the pension scheme or of any other specified scheme.

The trustees of the pension scheme (and any connected persons and associates) are ineligible to act as auditor or actuary of the scheme.[50]

iv. Investment. Under the general law, pension trusts have been governed by the same investment principles as traditional trusts,[51] although the courts, recognising the need for the trustees of large pension funds to have wide investment powers, have been ready to exercise their jurisdiction to vary trusts by extending these powers.[52] It is now recognised, in the 1995 Act, that the special nature of pension trusts requires special treatment.

(a) *General Principles.* The trustees of an occupational pension scheme have, subject to any restriction in the scheme, the same power to make an investment of any kind as if they were absolutely entitled to the assets.[53] Thus they are no longer subject to the restrictions on the type of investment which may be made by trustees under the general law.[54] They must ensure that a written

---

[46] s.32(2)(b).
[47] s.47. The duty to obtain audited accounts is imposed by regulations, the present source of which is s.41.
[48] *Ibid.* For delegation of investment powers to the fund manager, see below.
[49] s.48 ("blowing the whistle"). Other persons, such as the trustees or professional advisers other than the auditor or actuary, may also report such matters to the regulatory authority.
[50] s.27. Contravention is an offence under s.28.
[51] See *Cowan v. Scargill* [1985] Ch. 270; *post*, p. 523.
[52] See *Mason v. Farbrother* [1983] 2 All E.R. 1078; *post*, pp. 530, 616.
[53] Pensions Act 1995, s.34(1). "Investment" is not defined.
[54] *Post*, p. 518.

statement of the principles governing investment decisions is prepared, maintained and revised from time to time.[55] This statement
must include the trustees' policy for securing compliance with the
minimum funding requirement (discussed below) and on various
other matters such as the kind of investments to be held, the balance
between them, risk, expected return and realisation. They must
obtain and consider the advice of a person they reasonably believe
to be qualified in investment matters and consult the employer
before making or revising this statement, but neither the trust
scheme nor the statement may restrict the investment power by
reference to the employer's consent.

In choosing investments the trustees (or any fund manager to
whom investment powers have been delegated, as discussed below)
must have regard to the need to diversify investments so far as
appropriate to the scheme, and to the suitability to the scheme of
investments of the description of investment proposed and of the
investment proposed as an investment of that description.[56] Before
investing (other than in very safe "narrower range" investments not
requiring advice under the Trustee Investments Act 1961[57]) and at
suitable intervals thereafter, the trustees must obtain and consider
proper advice[58] on the question whether the investment is satisfactory having regard to the factors just mentioned and the principles contained in their policy statement.[59] The trustees or fund
manager must exercise their powers with a view to giving effect to
the principles of their policy statement, so far as reasonably practicable.[60] Failure to comply with these investment duties may result in
removal under section 3 and the imposition of a financial penalty
under section 10.

(b) *Delegation to Fund Manager.* Under the general law a trustee
may not delegate the exercise of his discretions without authority,
and this has led to inconvenient problems over the delegation of
investment decisions to fund managers, which are discussed elsewhere.[61] Pending reform of the general law, the Pensions Act 1995
clarifies the position with regard to occupational pension funds. The
trustees may delegate investment decisions to a fund manager who
is authorised to conduct investment business under the Financial

---

[55] s.35.
[56] s.36(2), modelled on Trustee Investment Act 1961, s.6(1).
[57] A draft Order substantially amending the 1961 Act has been laid before Parliament; *post*,
p. 532. The proposed reforms will not apply to pension trusts.
[58] Defined in s.36(6).
[59] s.36(3), (4).
[60] s.36(5).
[61] *Post*, p. 567.

Services Act 1986.[62] The trustees are not responsible for the act or default of such a fund manager if they have taken all reasonable steps to satisfy themselves that the manager has appropriate knowledge and experience and is carrying out his work competently and in accordance with statutory duties.[63] Alternatively, the trustees may delegate investment decisions by power of attorney under section 25 of the Trustee Act 1925,[64] or to a fund manager not authorised to conduct investment business under the Financial Services Act 1986 (provided that giving effect to the investment decision would not constitute carrying on investment business in the United Kingdom within the meaning of the 1986 Act[65]), or, subject to any restriction in the trust scheme, may authorise two or more of their number to make investment decisions on their behalf.[66] In these three cases, however, the trustees as a whole remain liable for any breaches resulting from any acts or defaults in the exercise of the discretion.[67]

(c) *Exclusion of Liability.* Liability for failure to take care or to exercise skill in the performance of investment functions exercisable by the trustees or the fund manager cannot be excluded or restricted by an instrument or agreement.[68] On the question whether the trustees may be exempted from responsibility for the acts and defaults of fund managers, we have seen that the trustees are not liable for the acts of fund managers who are authorised to conduct investment business under the Financial Services Act 1986, and so the point does not arise in such a case. In the case of delegation to fund managers who are not authorised to conduct investment business, where such delegation is permitted by section 34(5)(b) of the 1995 Act, the trustees are normally liable for the acts and defaults of such a person, as mentioned above. In this case, however, the liability may be validly excluded or restricted provided the trustees have taken all reasonable steps to satisfy themselves that the fund manager has appropriate knowledge and experience and is carrying out his work competently and in accordance with statutory duties.[69]

(d) *Employer-Related Investments.* Investments of pension fund assets in the employer's business, such as the purchase of shares in

---

[62] Pensions Act 1995, s.34(2). The fund manager must fall within s.191(2) of the 1986 Act.
[63] s.34(4).
[64] *Post*, p. 565.
[65] Pensions Act 1995, s.34(5)(b).
[66] s.34(5)(a).
[67] s.34(5); Trustee Act 1925, s.25(5).
[68] s.33. On trustee exemption clauses generally, see p. 483, *post*.
[69] s.34(6).

the employer company or loans to the employer, are subject to restrictions[70] because of the danger they present on the employer's insolvency. If a substantial proportion of the fund could be invested in the employer company, the losses would be great if the employer went into liquidation. Section 40 of the Pensions Act 1995 obliges the trustees or managers of an occupational pension scheme to ensure that current restrictions on employer-related investments are complied with. Failure to do so may result in removal under section 3 and the imposition of a financial penalty under section 10, and a trustee or manager who agrees to invest in contravention of the restrictions commits an offence.

v. Minimum Funding. The minimum funding requirement is designed to ensure that any inadequacies of funding will be revealed by a regular monitoring process and remedied by an increase in contributions or, in the case of serious underfunding, by a payment by the employer. The requirement is that the value of the assets is not less than the amount of the scheme's liabilities.[71] The provisions apply to occupational pension schemes other than money purchase schemes.

The trustees (or managers) must obtain a valuation by the scheme actuary at intervals prescribed by regulations.[72] The actuary must prepare a certificate stating whether or not the contributions are adequate to secure minimum funding. If they are considered inadequate, the trustees must obtain a further valuation within six months unless the assets were certified to be not less than 90 per cent of the liabilities and the contributions have since been increased to eradicate the shortfall.

The trustees must maintain a schedule of contributions showing the rates payable by the employer and members.[73] This must be revised after each actuarial valuation. The rates of contribution must be certified by the scheme actuary as being adequate to secure that the minimum funding requirement will be or will continue to be met.

If the amounts payable under the schedule of contributions are not paid by the due date, the trustees must give notice to the regulatory authority and the scheme members.[74]

If the actuarial valuation shows that the assets are less than 90 per cent of the liabilities, the employer must eliminate the shortfall

---

[70] Currently 5 per cent of the assets by regulations under Pension Schemes Act 1993, s.112. See (1994) 8 *Trust Law International* 56 (I. Greenstreet).

[71] Pensions Act 1995, s.56.

[72] s.57; Occupational Pension Schemes (Minimum Funding Requirement and Actuarial Valuations) Regulations 1996 (S.I. 1996/1536).

[73] s.58.

[74] s.59.

within one year by making a payment to the trustees.[75] If the employer fails to do so, the trustees must inform the regulatory authority and the scheme members. Trustees who fail to take all reasonable steps to secure compliance with the minimum funding requirement may be removed under section 3 or subjected to a financial penalty under section 10.

So far as the valuation of liabilities is concerned, it must be borne in mind that the 1995 Act requires pension rates to be increased annually.[76]

vi. Surplus. Much of the pension trust litigation has involved entitlement to surplus funds. Surpluses arose primarily in the 1980s because of the huge growth in the value of investments at that time. Where the scheme is ongoing, the surplus is notional, and means that the actuarial estimation of the assets at a given time exceeds the actuarial estimation of the liabilities. Such a calculation involves many projections and assumptions. There will be an actual surplus only if the scheme is wound up and all liabilities discharged. Surplus on a winding up is dealt with in the following section. Where the scheme is ongoing, the question is one of rights and duties in the application of the surplus rather than ownership as such.

The application of a surplus (actual or notional) will be crucial where the employer is insolvent,[77] or where the employer company is taken over by a company which proposes to "raid" the surplus,[78] or where, on a partial sale of the employer company, the employees are transferred to the purchaser's pension scheme and dispute the decision of the trustees of the original scheme not to transfer any of the substantial surplus to the purchaser's scheme.[79]

As explained below, the tax regime requires the elimination of excessive surpluses in an ongoing scheme and the taxation of any payments to the employer, to avoid exploitation of pension fund tax reliefs.[80]

The Pensions Act 1995 imposes further restrictions on payments of surplus to the employer from an approved scheme which is ongoing. Where the scheme confers power on any person (including the employer) other than the trustees to make payments to the employer, it can be exercised only by the trustees.[81] The power can be exercised only pursuant to Revenue-approved proposals to

---

[75] s.60; S.I. 1996/1536, *supra.*
[76] s.51.
[77] See *Mettoy Pension Trustees Ltd v. Evans* [1990] 1 W.L.R. 1587; *ante,* p. 459; *Thrells Ltd v. Lomas* [1993] 1 W.L.R. 456.
[78] See *Re Courage Group's Pension Scheme* [1987] 1 W.L.R. 495.
[79] *Wilson v. Law Debenture Trust Corp plc* [1995] 2 All E.R. 337; *ante,* p. 460; *post,* p. 506.
[80] *Post,* p. 474.
[81] s.37(2).

reduce an excessive surplus and is subject to further conditions, such as that the trustees are satisfied that it is in the interest of members to exercise it in the manner proposed, and that the pension rates have been increased annually.[82] In certain circumstances the regulatory authority must confirm that these requirements have been satisfied.[83]

vii. Winding Up. On this event, which may occur on the employer's insolvency and in other circumstances specified in the scheme rules,[84] the members' rights crystallise. Liabilities to them must be discharged and any surplus assets distributed.[85] It has already been noted that a pension scheme may be wound up by the order of the regulatory authority in certain circumstances.[86] The 1995 Act contains other provisions dealing with the discharge of liabilities and distribution of surplus on the winding up of an earnings-related scheme. (The question of insufficient or excess assets will not arise with a money purchase scheme, where the level of benefits is not defined and depends on the performance of the investments). The assets must be applied to discharge liabilities to members in a specified order, for example liability for pension increases ranks last.[87] Liabilities may be discharged in various ways, such as by transferring credits to another scheme, by transfer to certain personal pension schemes, or by the purchase of annuities.[88] If the assets are insufficient to discharge the liabilities, the deficit is treated as a debt from the employer to the trustees, without prejudice to any other right or remedy of the trustees.[89]

Where there are surplus assets, the scheme will normally provide for their allocation, often by requiring payment to the employer after augmenting benefits. In the rare case where the scheme does not deal with surplus, the general law applies. The position is in some ways analogous to the ownership of assets of an unincorporated association, where the modern view favours a contractual solution rather than a resulting trust.[90] Scott J., however, has preferred a resulting trust analysis, leading to *bona vacantia* of any share of the

---

[82] s.37(4).
[83] s.37(5).
[84] For example, a solvent employer may wish to wind up an earnings-related scheme in order to replace it with a money-purchase scheme.
[85] See (1995) 9 *Trust Law International* 127 (P. Docking), considering unknown beneficiaries.
[86] s.11; *ante*, p. 462.
[87] s.73. Any power in the scheme to apply assets to pensions and benefits may be exercised only by the trustees or managers.
[88] s.74.
[89] s.75. Such a debt is not a preferential debt on insolvency.
[90] *Ante*, p. 238.

members where it could be inferred that (primarily for tax reasons) they intended to exclude a resulting trust.[91]

As stated above, on insolvency of the employer any fiduciary powers, including powers relating to the allocation of surplus, are exercisable only by the independent trustee.[92] The 1995 Act makes further provisions for the allocation of surplus assets on the winding up of an approved scheme, of which the rules either permit or prohibit distribution to the employer. If the scheme confers power on the employer or trustees to distribute assets to the employer, the power can only be exercised where all liabilities have been fully discharged and the pension rates increased. In certain circumstances the regulatory authority must confirm that these requirements have been satisfied.[93]

Where a surplus remains after the discharge of all liabilities and the scheme prohibits distribution to the employer, the pension rates must be increased and additional benefits provided, after which the trustees may distribute any surplus to the employer.[94] Sanctions for failure to comply with these provisions include removal of trustees under section 3 and the imposition of a financial penalty under section 10.

viii. Information to Members. As explained in Chapter 19, trustees are under a general law duty to provide information and accounts to the beneficiaries. In addition, section 41 of the 1995 Act provides for regulations requiring the trustees to make copies of various documents available to the members and prospective members and their spouses (and to certain other persons).[95] The documents in question include audited accounts, actuarial valuations of assets and liabilities of the scheme, certificates relating to the minimum funding requirement and reports (required by the Act) concerning any failure to meet that requirement.

ix. Compensation. Although the aim of the 1995 Act is to prevent the misappropriation of pension funds, no statutory mechanism can provide totally effective safeguards. The Act, therefore, provides a compensation scheme to diminish hardships such as those suffered by the victims of Robert Maxwell's fraud. Application may be made to the Pensions Compensation Board[96] in respect

---

[91] *Davis v. Richards & Wallington Industries Ltd* [1990] 1 W.L.R. 1511; *ante*, p. 239. This analysis was doubted by Vinelott J. in (1994) 8 *Trust Law International* 35 at p. 37.

[92] Pensions Act 1995, s.25(2); *ante*, p. 464.

[93] s.76.

[94] s.77.

[95] Occupational Pension Schemes (Disclosure of Information) Regulations 1996 (S.I. 1996/1655); Occupational Pension Schemes (Requirement to Obtain Audited Accounts and a Statement from the Auditor) Regulations 1996 (S.I. 1996/1975).

[96] Set up under s.78 and Sched. 2 of the Pensions Act 1995.

of an occupational pension scheme where the value of the assets has
been reduced (and, in the case of a salary related scheme, is less than
90 per cent of the liabilities) and there are reasonable grounds for
believing that the reduction was attributable to a prescribed offence
(*i.e.* misappropriation). The compensation provisions apply only
where the employer is insolvent.[97] To this extent the scheme is
narrower than that recommended in the Goode Report, and would
not have helped the Maxwell pensioners had the Act been in force
at that time, as the employer companies did not go into liquidation.

The application must be made within the period of twelve months
beginning with the insolvency or, if later, the time when the
scheme's auditor or actuary or the trustees knew or ought to have
known that a reduction of assets had occurred.[98] The compensation
must not exceed 90 per cent of the shortfall and, in the case of a
salary related scheme, must not exceed the amount required to
ensure that the assets are not less than 90 per cent of the scheme's
liabilities.[99] Payments may be made subject to conditions or terms
requiring repayment, for example if the misappropriated money is
recovered.[1] No compensation will be paid, however, until the Board
considers that further recoveries of the lost funds are unlikely.[2] Thus
the trustees must take all reasonable steps to recover the lost assets,
for example by tracing, before compensation will be paid.[3] The
Board may vary or revoke an award if satisfied that there has been
a change of circumstances or that the award was made in ignorance
of a material fact or based on a mistake of fact or law.[4]

x. Alienability; Bankruptcy. Other provisions of the Pensions
Act 1995 deal with the alienability of pension rights and the position
on the bankruptcy of a scheme member. The object of a pension
scheme is not to provide members with a disposable asset but to
ensure an income on retirement. Accrued rights under an occupational pension scheme cannot be assigned, surrendered, charged or
subjected to any right of set-off.[5] This general prohibition, which
reflects the provisions normally found in pension schemes, does not
apply to assignments to or surrenders for the benefit of the member's
widow, widower or dependant, and there are limited exceptions
permitting a charge or set-off by the employer.

---

[97] s.81.
[98] s.82. These dates must have occurred after s.81 came into operation.
[99] s.83. Interim payments may be made under s.84.
[1] s.78(4).
[2] ss.81(3)(d), 83(1).
[3] s.81(5).
[4] s.80.
[5] s.91. Forfeiture, meaning any manner of deprivation or suspension (*e.g.* for misconduct), is
prohibited, subject to certain exceptions, by s.92.

Where a scheme member is made bankrupt, his accrued pension rights are excluded from his estate for the purposes of the Insolvency Act 1986 and are thus unavailable to creditors.[6] The provisions of the 1986 Act relating to the setting aside of certain dispositions made prior to bankruptcy[7] are extended so that contributions to an occupational pension scheme within the period of five years before the bankruptcy may be ordered by the court to be recovered by the trustee in bankruptcy to the extent that the contributions were excessive and unfairly prejudicial to the creditors.[8] The court will consider in particular whether the contributions were made for the purpose of putting assets beyond the reach of creditors.

B. Other Statutory Provisions

i. Rule Against Perpetuities. As explained in Chapter 14, the perpetuity rule prevents the vesting of property at a remote date beyond the perpetuity period (lives in being plus 21 years or a specified period not exceeding 80 years under the Perpetuities and Accumulations Act 1964) and also invalidates non-charitable purpose trusts which are not confined in duration to the perpetuity period. It will be appreciated that the perpetuity rule could prove troublesome if applied to occupational pension schemes. The perpetuity rule is based on public policy, namely that it is undesirable for economic and other reasons to have property tied up for long periods of time save for charitable purposes (to which the rule does not apply). In the case of pension funds there is a countervailing public interest in encouraging the provision of retirement pensions. The Pension Schemes Act 1993[9] provides, therefore, that qualifying occupational pension schemes (primarily those approved by the Inland Revenue for tax relief purposes) are exempted from the perpetuity rule.

ii. Tax Relief. The public interest in the provision of retirement benefits beyond the state pension results in significant tax relief for "exempt approved schemes". To secure this status, pension schemes must satisfy certain conditions,[10] for example the sole purpose of the scheme must be to provide benefits in respect of service as an employee, the normal retirement age must be at least 60, and the

---

[6] s.91(3). See (1996) 10 *Trust Law International* 6 (I. Greenstreet).

[7] *Ante*, p. 342.

[8] s.95, inserting ss.342 A, B and C into the Insolvency Act 1986.

[9] s.163, replacing earlier legislation; Personal and Occupational Pension Schemes (Perpetuities) Regulations 1990 (S.I. 1990/1143), as amended.

[10] I.C.T.A. 1988, s.590(2), (3).

pension must not exceed two thirds of the final salary. A scheme may be approved whether it is earnings-related or money purchase, and whether the investments are held by the trustees or through the medium of an insurer. The benefits are such that an unapproved scheme would not be entertained unless it is inherently impossible for it to satisfy the conditions for exemption. The court will not vary a pension trust in a manner which could put at risk its tax exempt status.[11] The effect of loss of exempt status is so severe that employees have been deemed to intend to exclude a resulting trust of surplus funds in their favour which would put their benefits above the statutory limits for exemption.[12]

(a) *Tax Relief for Contributions.* Provided the scheme is an exempt approved scheme, tax relief is given to both employer and employee contributions. Contributions by the employer are treated as trading expenses and thus deductible from income and corporation tax liability.[13] Contributions by the employee are deductible from taxable income, but must not exceed 15 per cent of annual remuneration.[14] A further benefit is that the employer's contributions are not taxable as remuneration of the employee. Ultimately the pension itself will be subject to income tax whether or not the scheme is approved,[15] although lump sums payable on retirement are tax free.[16]

(b) *Tax Relief for the Pension Fund.* Provided the scheme is an exempt approved scheme, the fund itself attracts significant relief. Neither income tax[17] nor capital gains tax[18] is payable on the investments. Equivalent benefits are available for insured schemes.

(c) *Overfunding.* In view of the above reliefs there might be a temptation to put more money than is required into the pension fund, which could either be used to pay excessive benefits or retrieved by the employer as surplus. The exploitation of tax relief is prevented in various ways. It has already been noted that there is a restriction (15 per cent) on the amount of earnings which an employee may contribute. A minimum of 20 years' service is required to generate the maximum pension of two thirds of final salary. Further, there is

---

[11] *Brooks v. Brooks* [1996] 1 A.C. 375; *post*, p. 476.
[12] *Davis v. Richards & Wallington Industries Ltd* [1990] 1 W.L.R. 1511; *ante*, p. 239.
[13] I.C.T.A. 1988, s.592(4).
[14] *Ibid.*, s.592(7), (8).
[15] *Ibid.*, s.19(1).
[16] *Ibid.*, s.189.
[17] *Ibid.*, s.592(2).
[18] *Ibid.*, Sched. 29, para. 26. For inheritance tax relief, see I.H.T.A. 1984, s.86 (employee trusts).

an inflation-linked earnings cap[19] on the final salary which can be reflected in a pension, to limit the extent to which highly paid employees can secure large pensions and tax free lump sums from a tax exempt scheme. The other way in which pension funds are prevented from being used as tax shelters is by the rule that any surplus funds in an exempt scheme must be reduced so as not to exceed 5 per cent of assets over liabilities.[20] Failure to do so will result in loss of tax exemptions for the investments. The fund must be regularly valued, and any prohibited surplus eliminated in various ways. The first call on the surplus is the increase of benefits, after which contributions may be reduced or suspended. Any payment to the employer (which must be authorised by the scheme or any amendments to it) is taxed at 40 per cent.[21]

3. EQUAL TREATMENT

Article 119 of the Treaty of Rome embodies the principle that men and women should receive equal pay for equal work. Clearly this has no scope for application to traditional trusts conferring benefits by way of bounty, but it does apply to occupational pension schemes because, as we have seen, pension entitlements are a form of deferred remuneration for services. Thus it was held by the European Court of Justice in *Barber v. Guardian Royal Exchange Assurance Group*[22] that pension rights fell within Article 119, with the result that the common practice of conferring pension entitlements on women employees at an earlier age than their male counterparts was no longer permissible. There were doubts as to the precise scope of the *Barber* decision, and so the matter was tested again in the European Court of Justice in *Coloroll Pension Trustees Ltd v. Russell*.[23] It was there held that trustees are bound to do everything within the scope of their powers to ensure compliance with the equal pay principle. Thus the trustees are bound, in the exercise of the powers and the performance of the duties laid down in the trust deed, to observe the principle of equal pay and treatment.

The Pensions Act 1995 now provides that an occupational pension scheme which does not contain an equal treatment rule shall be treated as including one.[24]

---

[19] £82,200 for 1996/97; I.C.T.A. 1988, s.640A (index-linked). This restricts the maximum pension (two thirds of final salary) to £54,800. It is increased to £84,000 in the 1996 Budget.

[20] I.C.T.A. 1988, ss.601–603, Sched. 22.

[21] *Ibid.*, s.601. See also Pensions Act 1995, s.37, *supra* (restrictions on exercise of power to make payments to employer).

[22] [1991] 1 Q.B. 344.

[23] [1995] I.C.R. 179.

[24] s.62. See also s.65 (power to alter schemes to secure conformity).

4. Pensions on Divorce

Another matter of current concern, which will be dealt with only in outline here, is the extent to which the pension entitlement of one spouse (usually the husband) must be shared with the other spouse on divorce. A wife who has brought up a family instead of working may have no pension provision of her own and may be reduced to penury in old age if her former husband's pension (often the most valuable family asset after the matrimonial home) is not available to her. The question whether and how pension benefits should be shared is a matter of government policy. One way it to take the husband's pension into account by giving a greater share of other assets to the wife on divorce. Alternatively, the pension itself may be split or earmarked as a source of payments to the spouse, either on divorce[25] or later, when it comes to be paid. The complexities of pension-splitting cannot be examined here. The House of Lords in *Brooks v. Brooks*[26] held that a pension trust which constituted a marriage settlement within section 24(1)(c) of the Matrimonial Causes Act 1973 could be varied by the court in the wife's favour, but this decision is of limited application because few pension schemes will fall within the 1973 Act.

The matter is dealt with by section 166 of the Pensions Act 1995, which favours the earmarking approach. It inserts sections 25B, C and D into the Matrimonial Causes Act 1973. The broad effect of these provisions is that the court, when making a financial provision order, may require the trustees or managers[27] of a pension scheme to divert all or part of the benefits (including lump sums and periodical payments) to the former spouse. Such an order cannot take effect until the pension benefits have become payable to the scheme member, and the payments to the spouse can come only from the member's entitlements, so that other members are not prejudiced. Where a lump sum is payable on death, the court may require the trustees to pay all or part of it to the former spouse when it becomes due.[28] These provisions apply to occupational and personal pension schemes.

---

[25] Provisions in the Family Law Act 1996 on pension splitting at the time of divorce are unlikely to be implemented until April 2000. A White Paper was published in February 1997.

[26] [1996] 1 A.C. 375; *post*, p. 618. See (1995) 25 Fam. Law 504 (R. Ellison).

[27] Or the insurer in the case of an insured scheme.

[28] Instead of to the person to whom it would otherwise have been paid. The court may require a power of nomination to be exercised in favour of the former spouse.

PART III

TRUSTEES

CHAPTER 17

GENERAL PRINCIPLES: CAPACITY; APPOINTMENT; REMOVAL; RETIREMENT; CONTROL

1. Onerous Nature of Office 479
2. Standards Applicable to Trustees 481
   A. Duties and Discretions 481
   B. Paid and Unpaid Trustees 482
   C. Trustee Exemption Clauses 483
3. Liability to Third Parties 484
4. Unanimity 485
5. Who may be a Trustee 486
   i. Minors 486
   ii. The Crown 486
   iii. Judicial Trustees 487
   iv. The Public Trustee 488
      (a) Functions 488
      (b) Restrictions 489
   v. Custodian Trustees 489
   vi. Trust Corporations 490
6. Disclaimer 491
7. Number of Trustees 491
8. Appointment of Trustees 492
   A. The First Trustees 492
   B. Who May Appoint New Trustees 492
      i. Express Power 492
      ii. The Statutory Power; Trustee Act
          1925, s.36(1) (2) 493
      iii. Exercise of the Statutory Power ... 494
         (a) By Persons Appointed under
             section 36(1)(a) 494
         (b) By the Surviving or Continu-
             ing Trustees under section
             36(1)(b) 494
         (c) Additional Trustees 495
      iv. By Direction of the Beneficiaries . 496

   C. Appointment by the Court 497
      i. Trustee Act, s.41 497
      ii. Circumstances in which the Juris-
          diction will be Exercised 497
9. Vesting of the Trust Property in Trustees 498
   A. Requirement of Vesting 498
   B. Vesting Declaration under section 40 . 498
      i. Subsection (1) 498
      ii. Exceptions under subsection
          (4) 498
   C. Vesting Orders under sections 44 to
      56 499
10. Selection of Trustees 499
    A. On Appointment by the Court under
       section 41 499
    B. On Appointment under Express
       Power or under section 36 500
       i. Choice of Donee of Power 500
       ii. Foreign Trusts 501
       iii. Direction by Beneficiaries 501
    C. On Appointment by the Settlor 502
11. Retirement 502
    A. Under an Express Power in the Trust
       Instrument 502
    B. Under Section 39 502
    C. Under an Order of the Court 503
    D. By Direction of the Beneficiaries 503
12. Removal 503
13. Control of Trustees 505
    A. Giving of Reasons 505
    B. Intervention by the Court 507
    C. Power of Decision 508

1. ONEROUS NATURE OF OFFICE

THE office of trustee is an onerous one. We will discuss in some detail a trustee's duties, powers and liability; there is little to be said as to his rights. In the performance of his office a trustee must act exclusively in the interest of the trust. He stands to gain nothing

479

from his work, unless special provision in the form of a clause authorising remuneration is made.[1] He is required to observe the highest standards of integrity,[2] and a reasonable standard of business efficiency in the management of the affairs of the trust; and he is subjected to onerous personal liability if he fails to reach the standards set. Nor may he compete in business with the trust; or be in a position in which his personal interests conflict with those of the trust. He may thus be forced to forgo opportunities which would be available to him if he were not a trustee.[3]

It may well be asked why people consent to become trustees. To this there are two answers. First, professional trustees undertake the work only where express provision is made in the settlement or will providing for their remuneration. Solicitors, banks (Executor and Trustee Departments) and insurance companies come into this category. The Public Trustee is entitled to charge.[4] Most trusts of any size will have a professional trustee. There may be non-professional trustees also; but in any case the bulk of the work of administration—investment, distribution, accounting, tax payments, etc. —will in fact be done by professionals, either the trustees or others employed by them. Secondly, members of the family of the settlor or testator will often consent to be trustees out of feelings of duty to the settlor or testator. Where there is no professional trustee, the non-professionals will, as will be seen,[5] usually employ professional agents such as a solicitor, investment manager and accountant to perform the technical duties of the trust. It may well be better to have such experts appointed as trustees, with a power to charge, in the first place, so that technical matters will not be overlooked.[6] It is usual and common to appoint a mixture of professional trustees and non-professional. There is much to be said for appointing a corporation such as a bank which has unrivalled facilities, dependability and permanence.

The settlor may also provide for the appointment of a "protector", an independent fiduciary to oversee the exercise of the trustees' powers.[7]

---

[1] *Post*, p. 586. He is entitled to expenses; *post* p. 585.

[2] *Post*, p. 481.

[3] *Phipps v. Boardman* [1967] 2 A.C. 46; *post*, pp. 601 *et seq.*

[4] Public Trustee Act 1906, s.9; as amended by the Public Trustee (Fees) Act 1957.

[5] *Post*, p. 559.

[6] For the dangers inherent in appointing no professional trustees, see *Turner v. Turner* [1984] Ch. 100, *ante*, p. 170. See generally (1988) 2 *Trust Law & Practice* 86 (C. Bell).

[7] See (1993) 90 L.S.Gaz. No. 27, p. 19 (H. Rosen); [1995] 4 J.Int.P. 31 (A. Penney); (1995) 9 *Trust Law International* 108 (P. Matthews); (1996) 2 *Trusts & Trustees* 6 (P. Hobson); Underhill (15th ed.), pp. 23–25.

2. STANDARDS APPLICABLE TO TRUSTEES

A. Duties and Discretions

A distinction must be made between a trustee's duties and his powers or discretions. A duty is an obligation which *must* be carried out. The rules of equity require strict and diligent performance of a trustee's duties. On the other hand, a power is discretionary; it may be exercised, or it may not. This is so whether the power is one given to trustees by statute, or is a power or discretion contained in the instrument creating the trust, or relates to the general management of the affairs of the trust.

Trustees must act honestly; and must take, in managing trust affairs, "all those precautions which an ordinary prudent man of business would take in managing similar affairs of his own."[8] This formula is varied in relation to the trustees' duties concerning investment. A trustee is under a duty to invest; he has a discretion in the selection of investments, but in the exercise of this discretion he is less free than a prudent man would be in investing his own money; for "business men of ordinary prudence may, and frequently do, select investments which are more or less of a speculative character; but it is the duty of a trustee to confine himself to the class of investments which are permitted by the trust [and now by the Trustee Investments Act 1961][9] and likewise to avoid all investments of that class which are attended with hazard."[10] If he properly performs his duties, powers and discretions, he is not liable for loss[11] to or depreciation[12] of the trust property arising from factors beyond his control.

We will see that many of the rules relating to trustees' duties are more strict in their terms than in their practical application. The past 100 years have brought a great alleviation in the lot of the honest trustee. We saw that much of the work of administration of a trust is necessarily done by professionals. This development has led to great relaxation, first by the courts[13] and then by statute,[14] of the requirement that the trustee should act personally. Further, the exemption clauses (discussed below) which were commonly

---

[8] *Per* Lord Blackkburn in *Speight v. Gaunt* (1883) 9 App.Cas. 1 at p. 19; in similar terms, Lord Watson in *Learoyd v. Whiteley* (1887) 12 App.Cas. 727 at p. 733.

[9] *Post*, Chap. 18.

[10] *Per* Lord Watson in *Learoyd v. Whiteley* (1887) 12 App.Cas. 727 at p. 733. The standard was described as "undemanding" in *Nestlé v. National Westminster Bank plc* [1993] 1 W.L.R. 1260.

[11] *Morley v. Morley* (1678) 2 Ch.Cas. 2.

[12] *Re Chapman* [1896] 2 Ch. 763.

[13] *Speight v. Gaunt* (1883) 9 App.Cas. 1: *post*, p. 560; *Learoyd v. Whiteley, supra*; *Shaw v. Cates* [1909] 1 Ch. 389.

[14] T.A. 1925, ss.23, 30; *post*, pp. 560 *et seq.*

inserted into trust instruments excluding the trustees' personal liability in certain circumstances have become statutory[15]; and Trustee
Act 1925, s.61, gives the court a discretion to excuse a trustee who
has acted honestly and reasonably and ought fairly to be
excused.[16]

B. Paid and Unpaid Trustees

As far as the standard of conduct required of trustees is concerned, it appears that a higher standard of care and diligence is
expected of paid professional trustees than is required of unpaid
trustees. The Law Reform Committee[17] described trustees as falling
in practice into three groups:

(i) unprofessional unpaid trustees of the "family friend" type;
(ii) paid, often professionally qualified, trustees such as solicitors
and accountants; and
(iii) professional trustees, such as banks, who advertise themselves as such.

The standard of conduct required of an unpaid trustee is that laid
down in *Speight v. Gaunt*,[18] namely that in the managing of trust
affairs he must take the precautions which an ordinary prudent man
of business would take in managing similar affairs of his own. But
a higher standard is imposed on paid trustees in categories (ii) and
(iii). In *Re Waterman's Will Trusts*[19] Harman J. said "I do not forget
that a paid trustee is expected to exercise a higher standard of
diligence and knowledge than an unpaid trustee and that a bank
which advertises itself largely in the public press as taking charge of
administrations is under a special duty." More recently, in *Bartlett v.
Barclays Bank Trust Co. Ltd (No. 1)*[20] Brightman J. said:

"I am of opinion that a higher duty of care is plainly due from
someone like a trust corporation which carries on a specialised
business of trust management. A trust corporation holds itself out
in its advertising literature as being above ordinary mortals. With
a specialist staff of trained trust officers and managers . . . the

---

[15] *Ibid.*
[16] *Post*, p. 648.
[17] 23rd Report, *The Powers and Duties of Trustees* (Cmnd. 8733 (1982)), paras. 2.12–2.16.
See also (1996) 146 N.L.J. 348 (A. Kenny).
[18] (1883) 9 App.Cas. 1.
[19] [1952] 2 All E.R. 1054 at p. 1055; *cf. Jobson v. Palmer* [1893] 1 Ch. 71; (1969) 33
Conv.(N.S.) 179 (M. Davies); (1973) 37 Conv.(N.S.) 48 (D. Paling).
[20] [1980] Ch. 515 at p. 534. See also *Re Rosenthal* [1972] 1 W.L.R. 1373.

trust corporation holds itself out, and rightly, as capable of providing an expertise which it would be unrealistic to expect and unjust to demand from the ordinary prudent man or woman who accepts, probably unpaid and sometimes reluctantly from a sense of family duty, the burdens of a trusteeship . . . so I think that a professional corporate trustee is liable for breach of trust if loss is caused to the trust fund because it neglects to exercise the special care and skill which it professes to have."

The Law Reform Committee[21] saw no need to incorporate the existing distinction between unpaid and professional trustees into a statutory provision. The distinction is maintained through the application of section 61 of the Trustee Act 1925, under which an unpaid family trustee is more likely to be relieved from liability than a professional trustee.[22] Further, a paid trustee will be expected to do more of the work himself and to delegate less; and a paid trustee will be given less opportunity to rely upon the fact that he acted upon legal advice.[23]

C. Trustee Exemption Clauses[24]

A question on which there appears to be little modern English authority is whether and how far the settlor may effectively exempt a trustee from liability. Before considering express clauses, reference should be made to section 30 of the Trustee Act 1925, which provides that a trustee shall not be answerable for the defaults of co-trustees or other persons with whom trust money or securities are deposited unless the loss results from his own wilful default. The weight of opinion is that "wilful default" in this context includes want of ordinary prudence, although there is authority that it covers only intentional wrongdoing or recklessness.[25]

It appears from pre-1926 English[26] and Scottish[27] authorities that exemption clauses, which are strictly construed against trustees, will not protect them in cases of bad faith, recklessness or deliberate breach of duty. To allow protection in such cases would be contrary

---

[21] *Supra.*
[22] *National Trustee Co. of Australasia Ltd v. General Finance Co. of Australasia* [1905] A.C. 373; *Re Pauling's S.T.* [1964] Ch. 303 at pp. 338, 339.
[23] *Re Windsor Steam Co. (1901) Ltd* [1929] 1 Ch. 151. See also *Steel v. Wellcome Custodian Trustees Ltd* [1988] 1 W.L.R. 167, at p. 174.
[24] [1989] Conv. 42 (P. Matthews). See also Kessler, *Drafting Trusts and Will Trusts*, pp. 35, 36.
[25] *Re Vickery* [1931] 1 Ch. 572; *post*, p. 561. See also *Seifert v. Pensions Ombudsman* [1997] 1 All E.R. 214 at p. 225.
[26] *Wilkins v. Hogg* (1861) 31 L.J. Ch. 41; *Pass v. Dundas* (1880) 43 L.T. 665. See also *Rehden v. Wesley* (1861) 29 Beav. 213.
[27] *Knox v. Mackinnon* (1888) 13 App.Cas. 753; *Raw v. Meek* (1889) 14 App.Cas. 558.

to public policy. It is generally considered possible to confer protection against liability for ordinary negligence,[28] or even gross negligence if the clause is unambiguous.[29] Another view is that exemption clauses should not even be effective in the case of want of ordinary prudence,[30] bearing in mind the possibility of insurance. It has also been held that a provision that only the settlor or employers could sue the trustees of a pension fund was ineffective.[31]

Assuming that an exemption clause may be effective in cases of negligence, a question would then arise as to the application of the Unfair Contract Terms Act 1977 to professional trustees appointed by the settlor. Provided the appointment may be regarded as contractual, the validity of the clause would depend upon its reasonableness, under section 2(3) of the Act.[32]

There is a distinction between clauses which exempt from breach and those which prevent the duty from arising. Such a clause as the latter may be effective where there was no pre-existing fiduciary relationship between the parties, especially in the context of a commercial agreement between parties of equal status.[33]

Finally, special rules apply to pension trusts,[34] unit trusts[35] and debenture trusts.[36]

3. Liability to Third Parties

Persons entering into a contractual relationship with trustees, for example by supplying goods or by lending money, can enforce their rights against the trustees personally, but have no direct right to payment out of the trust assets. But the trustees are entitled to an indemnity out of the trust fund for liabilities properly incurred, to which the third party may be subrogated. The difficulty is that the creditor cannot make any claim against the trust fund which the

---

[28] See Law Com. No. 236 (1995), *Fiduciary Duties and Regulatory Rules*, paras. 2.11, 2.12, 7.3.

[29] See *Trends in Contemporary Trusts Law* (ed. A. Oakley), p. 59 (D. Hayton); (1996) 10 *Trust Law International* 66 (R. Nobles), discussing English and Jersey authorities.

[30] Ontario Law Reform Committee, *Report on the Law of Trusts* (1984), Vol. 1, pp. 40–42; (1995) 9 *Trust Law International* 21 (R. Ham); (1996) 10 *Trust Law International* 38 at p. 43 (W. Goodhart).

[31] *Jones v. Shipping Federation of British Columbia* (1963) 37 D.L.R. (2d) 273.

[32] See [1980] Conv. 333 (W. Goodhart). The Unfair Terms in Consumer Contract Regulations (S.I. 1994 No. 3159) apply only to terms in consumer contracts which have not been individually negotiated.

[33] Law Com. No. 236, *supra*. See also *Kelly v. Cooper* [1993] A.C. 205.

[34] Pensions Act 1995, ss.33, 34(6) (investment functions); *ante*, p. 467.

[35] Financial Services Act 1986, s.84 (exemption for negligence not permitted for manager or trustee).

[36] Companies Act 1985, s.192 (exemption for negligence not permitted for trustee of debenture deed).

trustees could not have made.[37] If the trustees have committed a breach of trust, then of course they are not entitled to an indemnity,[38] and the creditor can be in no better position.

The absence of direct rights against the trust assets may cause difficulties with large commercial trusts, such as pension funds, wishing to borrow money on a large scale. The solution proposed by the Law Reform Committee[39] was that the trust deed should confer on the trustees a power to charge the trust fund in favour of the creditor. The charge would be void if the creditor knew that the trustees were acting in breach of trust.[40]

4. UNANIMITY[41]

Each trustee should be active in the administration of the trust. Equity does not recognise a "sleeping" trustee. A trustee who concurs with his co-trustees has, in so agreeing, as much "acted" as those others, and thus will be equally liable with them to beneficiaries who suffer loss if a breach results.[42] Nor will the concurring trustee necessarily escape liability when his co-trustee was a solicitor, unless he reasonably deferred to what could legitimately be regarded as superior knowledge.[43] But blind trust cannot safely be placed in a co-trustee. For although there is no rule that trustees are vicariously liable for the acts of co-trustees, a non-active trustee may himself be liable for neglecting to take the steps necessary to have prevented the breach.[44]

Trustees (other than trustees of charities and pension trusts[45]) cannot act by a majority, unless expressly authorised in the trust

---

[37] See *Re Johnson* (1880) 15 Ch.D. 548; *Re Oxley* [1914] 1 Ch. 604.

[38] See *Holding & Management Ltd v. Property Holding & Investment Trust plc* [1989] 1 W.L.R. 1313.

[39] 23rd Report, *The Powers and Duties of Trustees* (1982, Cmnd. 8733) paras. 2.17–2.24. See Underhill and Hayton (15th ed.), pp. 802–803.; (1987) 2 *Trust Law & Practice* 51 (D. Goddard); (1992) 6 *Trust Law International* 48 (I. Lambert); (1996) 10 *Trust Law International* 45 (R. Ham). The matter is under review by the Trust Law Committee.

[40] If the creditor was unaware of the breach, the charge would be valid, but the beneficiaries could sue the trustees.

[41] See Law Reform Committee, 23rd Report, *The Powers and Duties of Trustees* (1982, Cmnd. 8733), paras. 3.60–3.65, recommending no change in this rule; *cf.* [1991] Conv. 30 (J. Jaconelli).

[42] *Bahin v. Hughes* (1886) 31 Ch.D. 390; *Re Turner* [1897] 1 Ch. 536; *Wynne v. Tempest* (1897) 13 T.L.R. 360. But the co-trustee who concurs may be able to obtain an indemnity from the active trustee; *post*, p. 641.

[43] See *Head v. Gould* [1898] 2 Ch. 250; *Bahin v. Hughes, supra.*

[44] *Bahin v. Hughes, supra.*

[45] *Ante*, pp. 451, 464.

instrument.[46] A majority binds neither a dissenting minority nor the trust estate.[47] The consequences of this rule need to be appreciated.

In *Re Mayo*,[48] for instance, one trustee of a trust for sale wished to sell, two to postpone. The trustees were by virtue of the trust to sell, under a *duty* to sell, but possessed *power* to postpone. Simonds J. held that their duty to sell prevailed unless they were unanimous in exercising their power to postpone. They were not unanimous on this point; the view of the single trustee who wished to sell prevailed, and the other two were directed to join in the sale.

5. Who may be a Trustee

In principle, any person who is able to hold property may be a trustee. Special rules apply to charity and pension trustees,[49] and other categories need special consideration.

i. Minors. A minor cannot hold a legal estate in land[50]; and Law of Property Act 1925, s.20, provides that the appointment of a minor to be a trustee in relation to any trust shall be void. A child of four years old was, however, held to be able to hold personalty on resulting trust.[51] As will be seen,[52] if a minor is a trustee of personalty, he may be replaced, whether or not he consents.

ii. The Crown. It is usually said that the Crown may be a trustee[53] "if it chooses deliberately to do so,"[54] but attempts to claim funds in the hands of the Crown on the ground that the Crown

---

[46] *Re Butlin's W.T.* [1976] Ch. 251. *Re Whiteley* [1910] 1 Ch. 600 at p. 608. See also T.A. 1925, s.63(3).

[47] *Luke v. South Kensington Hotel Ltd* (1879) 11 Ch.D. 121.

[48] [1943] Ch. 302; *cf. Tempest v. Lord Camoys* (1882) 21 Ch.D. 571; but the unanimity rule did not affect the validity of a notice to quit served by only one of two joint tenants holding on trust for sale, because the characteristic of a periodic tenancy is that all parties must concur in its continuance; *Hammersmith and Fulham L.B.C. v. Monk* [1992] 1 A.C. 478.

[49] *Ante*, pp. 451, 464.

[50] L.P.A. 1925, s.1(6).

[51] *Re Vinogradoff* [1935] W.N. 68; *ante*, p. 245.

[52] *Post*, p. 493.

[53] *Penn v. Lord Baltimore* (1750) 1 Ves.Sen. 444, *per* Lord Hardwicke at p. 453; *Burgess v. Wheate* (1757–59) 1 Eden 177.

[54] *Civilian War Claimants Association Ltd v. R.* [1932] A.C. 14, *per* Lord Atkin at p. 27 (a claim by the Association for payment by the Crown of reparations money received from Germany: "There is nothing so far as I know, to prevent the Crown acting as agent or trustee if it chooses deliberately to do so.")

should be treated as a trustee have not been successful.[55] The circumstances in which the Crown will accept a trusteeship must be rare indeed, and there would be substantial difficulties in enforcing the trust if it did.[56]

iii. Judicial Trustees. The High Court may, on the application of a person creating or intending to create a trust, or by or on behalf of a trustee or beneficiary, appoint a person to be a judicial trustee of that trust.[57] The court may appoint any fit and proper person,[58] and, in the absence of the nomination of such person, may appoint an official of the court.[59] Remuneration may be paid,[60] and the court may direct an inquiry into the administration of the trust by a judicial trustee.[61] The court may give a judicial trustee any general or special directions in regard to the trust or to the administration thereof,[62] not, however, so as to "reduce the administration of an estate by a judicial trustee to very much the same position as where an estate is being administered by the court and every step has to be taken in pursuance of the court's directions. ... The object of the Judicial Trustees Act 1896 ... was to provide a middle course in cases where the administration of the estate by the ordinary trustees had broken down, and it was not desired to put the estate to the expense of a full administration ... a solution was found in the appointment of a judicial trustee, who acts in close concert with the court and under conditions enabling the court to supervise his transactions."[63]

A judicial trustee may also be appointed in respect of the administration of an estate.[64] At the time when there was no machinery whereby a personal representative could retire, this provided a method of replacing one who could no longer act. Now, however, the court may appoint a substitute executor or administrator under section 50 of the Administration of Justice Act 1985. In an application under the 1896 Act for the appointment of a judicial trustee, the

---

[55] *Re Mason* [1929] 1 Ch. 1; *Civilian War Claimants Association Ltd v. R.*, *supra*; *Tito v. Waddell (No. 2)* [1977] Ch. 106; *ante*, p. 70.

[56] Hanbury, *Essays in Equity*, pp. 87–89; Holdsworth H.E.L., Vol. IX, pp. 30–32.

[57] Judicial Trustees Act 1896, s.1(1); Judicial Trustee Rules 1983 (S.I. 1983 No. 370). The procedure has not been much used in practice.

[58] *Ibid.* subs. (3); Public Trustee Act 1906, s.2(i)(*d*).

[59] *Ibid.* subs. (3); usually the Official Solicitor of the court; Judicial Trustees Act 1896, s.5.

[60] Judicial Trustees Act 1896, s.1(5).

[61] *Ibid.* subs. (6), as amended by A.J.A. 1982, s.57(1). On the auditing of accounts, see Judicial Trustees Act 1896, s.4(1), as amended by A.J.A. 1982, s.57(2). See also Judicial Trustee Rules 1983, rr. 2, 13.

[62] *Ibid. subs.* (4); Judicial Trustee Rules 1983, r. 8.

[63] *Re Ridsdel* [1947] Ch. 597 at p. 605.

[64] Judicial Trustees Act 1896, s.1(2).

court may proceed as if it was an application under the 1985 Act, and vice versa.[65]

iv. The Public Trustee

(a) *Functions.* The Public Trustee, established by the Public Trustee Act 1906,[66] may be appointed as trustee alone or jointly with another or others, and may act as a custodian trustee[67] or an ordinary trustee or as a judicial trustee. He may be appointed as sole trustee although there were originally two or more trustees, and although the trust deed stipulates at least two trustees.[68] The Public Trustee is a corporation sole,[69] covered in respect of liability for breach of trust by the State,[70] and entitled to charge fees on a scale fixed by the Lord Chancellor.[71] His special function is the administration of small estates and, although he may decline to accept any trust, he may not do so on the ground "only of the small value of the trust property."[72] He is required to undertake the administration of an estate less than £1,000 on the application of a person entitled to an order for administration by the court.[73] Once appointed, the Public Trustee has the same powers and duties and liabilities, and is entitled to the same rights and immunities as a private trustee.[74] Because the office of Public Trustee was not financially self-supporting, its abolition was recommended in 1972, but the Lord Chancellor announced in 1974 that it had been reprieved.[75] The functions of the Public Trustee have since been extended by the Public Trustee and Administration of Funds Act 1986,[76] which confers on him all the functions conferred on the judge of the Court of Protection by Part VII of the Mental Health Act 1983 with respect to the property and affairs of mental patients. He may act as, or appoint a person to act as a receiver,[77] or carry on, as well as

[65] A.J.A. 1985, s.50(4); Judicial Trustees Act 1896, s.1(7), added by the 1985 Act.

[66] He is appointed by the Lord Chancellor, and may be the same person as the Accountant General of the Supreme Court; Public Trustee Act 1906, s.8(1); Public Trustee and Administration of Funds Act 1986, s.1 and Sched. He is paid such salary or fees as the Lord Chancellor determines; s.8(1A) of the 1906 Act, as amended.

[67] s.4, *post.*

[68] s.5(1); *In re Duxbury's S.T.* [1995] 1 W.L.R. 425; [1996] Conv. 50 (J. Snape).

[69] Public Trustee Act 1906, s.1.

[70] *Ibid.* s.7.

[71] *Ibid.* s.9; Public Trustee (Fees) Act 1957; Administration of Justice Act 1965, s.2; Public Trustee (Fees) (Amendment) Order 1995 (S.I. 1995 No. 1425). See also Public Trustee and Administration of Funds Act 1986, s.3(6).

[72] *Ibid.* s.2(3).

[73] *Ibid.* s.3.

[74] *Ibid.* s.2(2).

[75] *The Times,* August 1, 1974.

[76] s.3. Since the Act the office is called the Public Trust Office. See the report of the National Audit Office, *Looking after the Financial Affairs of People with Mental Incapacity* (1994).

[77] See Practice Direction [1987] 1 W.L.R. 63.

authorise a suitable person to carry on, a patient's profession, trade or business. A new role, taken over from the President of the Family Division, is the holding of the property of a person who has died intestate, pending the appointment of an administrator.[78]

(b) *Restrictions.*[79] There are certain trusts that the Public Trustee may not accept; such as a trust exclusively for religious or charitable purposes,[80] or any trust under a deed of arrangement for the benefit of creditors, or the administration of an estate known by him to be insolvent,[81] and he may only accept a trust involving the management of a business under special restrictions limiting him to a short period of operation and requiring the Treasury's consent.[82]

v. Custodian Trustees.[83] The Public Trustee,[84] the Official Custodian for Charities[85] and a large number of other corporations[86] are authorised by statute to act as custodian trustees, and they may all charge fees not exceeding those chargeable by the Public Trustee.[87] Others may act under the terms of the trust instrument, outside the statutory schemes The custodian trustee holds property and the documents relating thereto while leaving to the managing trustee the day-to-day administration of the trust.[88] The Public Trustee cannot act in both capacities in relation to the same trust.

The advantage of the scheme of custodian trusteeship is that new managing trustees can be appointed without the necessity of undergoing the trouble and expense—which can be considerable in the case of a large trust—of vesting all the trust investments in new trustees whenever there is a death, retirement or new appointment.

---

[78] Law of Property (Miscellaneous Provisions) Act 1994, s.14, amending A.E.A. 1925, s.9.

[79] These are subject to Public Trustee and Administration of Funds Act 1986, s.3(5), whereby functions conferred on the Public Trustee under Part VII of the Mental Health Act 1983 are exercisable notwithstanding any provision of the 1906 Act under which he would be obliged or empowered to decline to accept any trust or other duty.

[80] Public Trustee Act 1906, s.2(5).

[81] *Ibid.* s.2(4).

[82] Public Trustee Rules 1912, r. 7.

[83] (1960) 24 Conv.(N.S.) 196 (S. Maurice).

[84] Public Trustee Act 1906, s.4(3).

[85] *Ante*, p. 445.

[86] Public Trustee Rules 1912, r. 30, as substituted by the Public Trustee (Custodian Trustee) Rules 1975 (S.I. 1975 No. 1189), r. 2. See also Public Trustee (Custodian Trustee) Rules 1976 (S.I. 1976 No. 836), 1981 (S.I. 1981. No. 358) and 1994 (S.I. 1994 No. 2519). Qualifying corporations include those of EU States which comply with the requirements and have a place of business in the U.K. carrying on trust business.

[87] Public Trustee Act 1906, s.4(3).

[88] For the relationship between custodian trustees and managing trustees, see Public Trustee Act 1906, s.4(2); *Forster v. Williams Deacon's Bank Ltd* [1935] Ch. 359; *Re Booke Bond and Co. Ltd's Trust Deed* [1963] Ch. 357.

It should be noted that this advantage cannot be gained by appointing the holder of an office as trustee, as the investments must be transferred to the names of the new holders of the office when a change is made. This can be avoided if the trustee is a corporation sole.[89]

In determining a number of trustees for the purpose of the Trustee Act 1925, the custodian trustee is not included.[90]

vi. Trust Corporations. Trust corporations play a large part in the administration of trusts. Their size, stability, dependability and expertise give them advantages over individual trustees.

They enjoy a special status in that they can often act alone in circumstances in which at least two trustees would otherwise be necessary.[91] A trust corporation can give a valid receipt for capital money arising from the sale of land[92]; and a trust of land has greater overreaching powers if a trust corporation is trustee.[93] Further, trustees may retire and leave a sole trustee only if that trustee is a trust corporation.[94]

In most private trusts, a trust corporation is typically a bank. The legal definition is: "Trust corporation means the Public Trustee or a corporation either appointed by the court in a particular case to be a trustee, or entitled by rules made under subsection (3) of section four of the Public Trustee Act 1906, to act as custodian trustee."[95] The qualifications are contained in the Public Trustee (Custodian Trustee) Rules 1975.[96] The Law of Property (Amendment) Act 1926, s.3 added, *inter alia*, a trustee in bankruptcy, the Treasury Solicitor, and the Official Solicitor. A trust corporation, unless acting as custodian trustee only, has no greater power to charge remuneration than any other trustee has. Fee earning is however their business, and express powers will always be given for a fee to be charged for the service.

---

[89] *Tufnell v. Constable* (1838) 7 Ad. & E. 798; *Bankes v. Salisbury Diocesan Council of Education* [1960] Ch. 631 at pp. 647–649.

[90] Public Trustee Act 1906, s.4(2)(g).

[91] See *In re Duxbury's S.T.* [1995] 1 W.L.R. 425; *ante*, p. 488 (Public Trustee).

[92] T.A. 1925, s.14; L.P.A. 1925, s.27(2).

[93] L.P.A. 1925, s.2(2).

[94] T.A. 1925, s.39; *post*, p. 502.

[95] T.A. 1925, s.68(18); see also L.P.A. 1925, s.205(1)(xxviii); A.E.A. 1925, s.55(1)(xxvi); Supreme Court Act 1981, s.128.

[96] S.I. No. 1189 of 1975. They include any corporation which (i) is constitued under the law of the U.K. or of any other Member State of the E.U.; and (ii) is empowered by its constitution to undertake trust business in England and Wales; (iii) has one or more places of business in the U.K.; and (iv) being a registered company has a capital (in stock or shares) for the time being issued of not less than £250,000 (or its equivalent in the currency of the state where the company is registered), of which not less than £100,000 (or its equivalent) has been paid up in cash. See also the Public Trustee (Custodian Trustee) Rules 1976 (S.I. 1976 No. 836) and 1981 (S.I. 1981 No. 358).

6. DISCLAIMER

Nobody can be compelled to accept the office of trustee against his will.[97] A person appointed as trustee who wishes to disclaim should do so by deed,[98] as this provides clear evidence of the disclaimer. However, a disclaimer may be implied; apathy will be evidence of an intention to disclaim, provided the apathy is consistent.[99] But if the trustee meddles with the estate, his conduct will be construed as an acceptance. Once he has disclaimed, he can no longer accept. Once he has accepted he can no longer disclaim[1] but as we will see, he may retire.[2]

7. NUMBER OF TRUSTEES

There is no restriction upon the number of trustees of personalty. It is inconvenient to have too many; and rare to have more than four, save in the case of charity and pension trustees, who can act by majority.[3] Where additional trustees are appointed under the statutory power, appointments may only be made up to a total of four.[4] A sole trustee is most unsatisfactory because of the opportunities for maladministration and fraud which then arise.

In trusts of land, the Trustee Act 1925, s.34, restricts the number of trustees to four. There are exceptions, the most important of which is that of land vested in trustees for charitable, ecclesiastical or public purposes.[5]

While a sole trustee of land is not forbidden,[6] the Trustee Act 1925, s.14(2), makes it impossible for a sole trustee (not being a trust corporation) to give a valid receipt for the proceeds of sale or other capital money arising under a trust of land, or capital money arising under the Settled Land Act 1925.[7]

The Law Reform Committee[8] recommended that the number of trustees should, unless the settlor provided otherwise, be limited to four, regardless of the nature of the trust property, on the ground that costs, administrative inconvenience and delays are increased if there are more than four.

---

[97] A person can, of course, become a constructive or resulting trustee against his will.

[98] *Re Schär* [1951] Ch. 280; *Holder v. Holder* [1968] Ch. 353 (an executor).

[99] *Re Clout and Frewer's Contract* [1924] 2 Ch. 230.

[1] *Re Sharman's W.T.* [1942] Ch. 311; *Holder v. Holder, supra.*

[2] *Post*, p. 502.

[3] *Ante*, p. 485. The special rules for the constitution of the trustees of pension funds are explained in Chapter 16.

[4] T.A. 1925, s.36(6), *post*, p. 495.

[5] T.A. 1925, s.34(3)(*a*).

[6] *Re Myhill* [1928] Ch. 100.

[7] Also L.P.A. 1925, s.27(2); L.P.(A.)A. 1926, Sched.

[8] 23rd Report, *The Powers and Duties of Trustees* (1982), Cmnd, 8733), para. 2.2.

8. APPOINTMENT OF TRUSTEES

A. The First Trustees

The first trustees will ordinarily be appointed by the settlor or testator in the deed or will creating the trust. In the case of an *inter vivos* trust, the trustees will ordinarily be parties to the deed, and the trust is constituted upon the conveyance of the trust property to them. In a will, the same persons may be appointed executors and trustees. Where they are different persons, the trust is constituted upon the testator's death, for the title of the executors relates back to the death, and they hold on trust pending transfer to the persons appointed trustees in the will.

Trustees hold as joint tenants, and if one of several trustees dies, the survivors are the trustees, and they, and their successors, retain the same powers and duties as the original trustees.[9] On the death of a sole trustee, his personal representatives become trustees.[10] If he dies intestate, the trust estate will vest, pending the grant of administration, in the Public Trustee.[11] A trust does not normally fail for lack of a trustee; hence if the trustees disclaim, the trust still subsists, save in the rare cases where the settlor or testator has himself made the validity of the trust dependent upon the acceptance of office by particular trustees.[12] If all the nominated trustees predecease the testator in the case of a testamentary trust, the personal representatives of the testator will hold until such time as trustees are appointed.[13]

B. Who May Appoint New Trustees

i. Express Power. The trust instrument may include an express power to appoint new trustees, although most settlors now think it sufficient to rely on the statutory power. Where an express power is given, it is often reserved to the settlor. The statutory power will be available in addition, unless a contrary intention appears in the instrument.[14]

---

[9] T.A. 1925, s.18; *contra*, a bare power given to two persons in their individual capacity: *Re Smith* [1904] 1 Ch. 139; *Re de Sommery* [1912] 2 Ch. 622; *Re Harding* [1923] 1 Ch. 182; *ante*, p. 166.

[10] A.E.A. 1925, ss.1–3; T.A. 1925, s.18(2).

[11] Law of Property (Miscellaneous Provisions) Act 1994, s.14. Previously such property vested in the President of the Family Division.

[12] *Re Lysaght* [1966] Ch. 191; *Re Woodhams (deceased)* [1981] 1 W.L.R. 493.

[13] *Re Smirthwaite's Trust* (1871) L.R. 11 Eq. 251.

[14] T.A. 1925, s.69(2). See *Re Wheeler and De Rochow* [1896] 1 Ch. 315; *Re Sichel's Settlements* [1916] 1 Ch. 358.

ii. The Statutory Power: Trustee Act 1925, s.36(1) (2).[15]

"(1) Where a trustee, either original or substituted, and whether appointed by the court or otherwise, is dead,[16] or remains out of the United Kingdom for more than 12 months,[17] or desires to be discharged from all or any of the trusts or powers reposed in or conferred on him,[18] or refuses[19] or is unfit to act therein, or is incapable of acting therein,[20] or is an infant,[21] then, subject to the restrictions imposed by this Act on the number of trustees,—

> (*a*) the person or persons nominated for the purpose of appointing new trustees by the instrument, if any, creating the trust; or
> (*b*) if there is no such person, or no such person able and willing to act, then the surviving or continuing trustees or trustee for the time being, or the personal representatives of the last surviving or continuing trustee;

may, be writing,[22] appoint one or more other persons (whether or not being the persons exercising the power) to be a trustee or trustees in the place of the trustee so deceased remaining out of the United Kingdom, desiring to be discharged, refusing, or being unfit or being incapable, or being an infant, as aforesaid.

(2) Where a trustee has been removed under a power contained in the instrument creating the trust, a new trustee or new trustees may be appointed in the place of the trustee who is removed, as if he were dead, or, in the case of a corporation, as if the corporation desired to be discharged from the trust, and the provisions of this section shall apply accordingly, but subject to the restrictions imposed by this Act on the number of trustees."

---

[15] The statutory power does not apply to personal representatives; *Re King's W.T.* [1964] Ch. 542; *ante*, p. 57. The court, however, may appoint a substitute personal representative under Administration of Justice Act 1985, s.50. Special rules for the appointment of pension trustees are dealt with in Chapter 16.

[16] Which includes the case of a person nominated trustee in a will but dying before the testator: T.A. 1925, s.36(8), and *ante*, p. 492.

[17] The period must be continuous: *Re Walker* [1901] 1 Ch. 259; see also *Re Stoneham S.T.* [1953] Ch. 59. T.A. 1925, s.25, permits a trustee in such a case to delegate his duties by power of attorney for a period not exceeding 12 months; *post*, p. 565.

[18] For retirement of a trustee, see *post*, p. 502.

[19] This includes disclaimer.

[20] "Unfit" has a wider meaning than "incapable." "Incapable" refers to personal incapacity, such as illness or mental disorder; see T.A. 1925, s.36(9). "Unfit" is more general and an absconding bankrupt has been held to be "unfit" but not "incapable": *Re Roche* (1842) 2 Dr. & War. 287. See s.36(3), providing that a corporation is "incapable" from the date of dissolution, and Mental Health Act 1983, s.148 and Sched. 4. L.P.A. s.22(2) requires a mentally incapacitated trustee of land to be discharged before the legal estate is dealt with. See also Trusts of Land and Appointment of Trustees Act 1996, s.20; *post*, p. 496.

[21] L.P.A. 1925, ss.1(6), 20; *Re Parsons* [1940] Ch. 764.

[22] See *post*, p. 498, and T.A. 1925, s.40.

In favour of a purchaser of a legal estate in land, a statement in an instrument appointing a new trustee to the effect that a trustee is unfit, incapable or refuses to act, or has remained out of the United Kingdom for more than 12 months, is conclusive evidence of the matter. Similarly, any appointment of a new trustee depending on that statement, and the consequent vesting of the trust property in the new trustee, is valid in favour of such a purchaser.[23]

iii. Exercise of the Statutory Power. It is usual to appoint someone to exercise the statutory power.

(a) *By Persons Appointed under section* 36(1)(*a*). If two or more persons are given power to exercise it jointly, the power is not, in the absence of a contrary intention, exercisable by the survivor. This is consistent with the usual rule relating to bare powers given to individuals.[24]

Complications can arise if the power is subjected to conditions and limitations.

In *Re Wheeler and De Rochow*,[25] the settlor gave power to donees to appoint a new trustee if one of the existing trustees should be (*inter alia*) "incapable." One of the trustees was bankrupt, and absconded. This made him "unfit" but not "incapable."[26] The question was whether a new trustee should be appointed by the donees under section 36(1)(*a*) or by the continuing trustees under section 36(1)(*b*). It was held that the situation was not within the terms of the power given to the donees and that section 36(1)(*b*) applied.

(b) *By the Surviving or Continuing Trustees under section* 36(1)(*b*). In the case of continuing trustees it is expressly provided by section 36(8) that the provisions of section 36 "relative to a continuing trustee include a refusing or retiring trustee, if willing to act in the execution of the provisions of this section." This provision enables a retiring sole trustee or a retiring group of trustees to appoint their successors. It raises the question, however, whether their participation is essential; whether an appointment in which they did not participate would be void. Such an objection failed in *Re Coates to Parsons*[27]; the retiring trustee is only included if it is

---

[23] T.A. 1925, s.38.

[24] *Re Harding* [1923] 1 Ch. 182; *Bersel Manufacturing Co. Ltd v. Berry* [1968] 2 All E.R. 552; *ante*, p. 166; *contra* where the power is given to persons as trustees: T.A. 1925, s.18(1).

[25] [1896] 1 Ch. 315; followed reluctantly in *Re Sichel's Settlements* [1916] 1 Ch. 358; *cf. Re Brockbank* [1948] Ch. 206.

[26] *Re Roche* (1842) Dr. & War. 287, *ante*, p. 493.

[27] (1886) 34 Ch.D. 370.

shown that he is competent and willing to act. The concurrence of a trustee who is removed on the ground that he remained outside the United Kingdom for more than 12 months[28] is not required.[29] It is advisable, in order to avoid these difficulties, that refusing or retiring trustees should participate in the appointment of new trustees if possible, and this is the usual practice.

Section 37(1)(c) requires the replacement of trustees who are being discharged unless there will be either a trust corporation or at least two persons[30] to act if the vacancy if not filled. The exception is where only one trustee was originally appointed and a sole trustee will be able to give a good receipt for capital money.

The statutory power to appoint a new trustee can be exercised by the executor of a sole trustee appointed by will,[31] but not by the personal representative of the survivor of a body of trustees named in a will, who has died in the testator's lifetime, as the Act does not contemplate the case of all the trustees named in the will predeceasing the testator.[32] Nor can the sole surviving trustee exercise the power by his will, so as thereby to appoint new trustees in succession to himself.[33] The aim of the Act of 1925 is to ensure the making of an appointment in all events. The executors who have proved the will need not have the concurrence of those who have not proved or intend to renounce probate.[34] A sole or last surviving executor who intends to renounce probate can nevertheless fulfil this one function without thereby accepting the office of executor,[35] but the title of an executor to exercise the statutory power can only be proved by a proper grant of administration.[36]

(c) *Additional Trustees.* A broad power is given by section 36(6),[37] restricted only by the limitation to a total number of four trustees, and by the fact that the power is to appoint "another person or other persons" and that consequently (and unlike appointments under subsection (1)) the appointor may not appoint himself.[38] Section 36(6) reads:

[28] *Ante*, p. 493.

[29] *Re Stoneham S.T.* [1953] Ch. 59.

[30] As amended by Trusts of Land and Appointment of Trustees Act 1996, Sched. 3, para. 3(12), substituting "persons" for "individuals". A corporate trustee (whether or not it is a "trust corporation") is a "person" but not an "individual".

[31] *Re Shafto's Trusts* (1885) 29 Ch.D. 247.

[32] *Nicholson v. Field* (1893) 2 Ch. 511.

[33] *Re Parker's Trusts* [1894] 1 Ch. 707.

[34] T.A. 1925, s.36(4).

[35] T.A. 1925, s.36(5).

[36] *Re Crowhurst Park* [1974] 1 W.L.R. 583.

[37] As amended by Trusts of Land and Appointment of Trustees Act 1996, Sched. 3, para. 3(11).

[38] *Re Power's S.T.* [1951] Ch. 1074.

"Where, in the case of any trust, there are not more than three trustees—

    (*a*) the person or persons nominated for the purpose of appointing new trustees by the instrument, if any, creating the trust; or

    (*b*) if there is no such person, or no such person able and willing to act, then the trustee or trustees for the time being;

may, by writing, appoint another person or other persons to be an additional trustee or additional trustees, but it shall not be obligatory to appoint any additional trustee, unless the instrument, if any, creating the trust, or any statutory enactment provides to the contrary, nor shall the number of trustees be increased beyond four by virtue of any such appointment."

iv. By Direction of the Beneficiaries. A new power is given to beneficiaries by section 19[39] of the Trusts of Land and Appointment of Trustees Act 1996, which applies to trusts of land and personalty, whenever created, unless excluded by the settlor.[40] Provided the beneficiaries are of full age and capacity and together absolutely entitled, and there is no person with an express power to appoint, the beneficiaries may direct the trustees in matters of retirement[41] and appointment. They may give directions of either or both of the following kinds:

    (a) a written direction to a trustee or trustees to retire from the trust; and

    (b) a written direction to the trustees or trustee for the time being (or, if there are none, to the personal representative of the last person who was a trustee) to appoint by writing to be a trustee or trustees the person or persons specified in the direction.

The beneficiaries may give joint or separate directions, but they must specify the same person for appointment or retirement.[42] Section 19 has effect subject to the restrictions imposed by the 1925

---

[39] This in effect reverses *Re Brockbank* [1948] Ch. 206. See also s.20 (replacement by direction of beneficiaries where trustee mentally incapacitated and no person entitled, willing and able to act under T.A. 1925, s.36(1)). S. 20 (unlike s.19) contains no provisions on vesting or indemnity. See (1996) 146 N.L.J. 1779 (M. Keppel-Palmer); [1996] Conv. 411 at pp. 428–430 (N. Hopkins).

[40] s.21(5). Living settlors of trusts created before the 1996 Act may exclude the power by deed under s.21(6). The same applies to the power under s.20.

[41] *Post*, p. 503.

[42] s.21(1), (2).

Act on the number of trustees. In the absence of the exercise of the new power by the beneficiaries, the trustees' power of appointment is exercisable in the usual way.

C. Appointment by the Court

i. Trustee Act 1925, s.41.[43] Subsection (1) provides:

"The court[44] may, whenever it is expedient to appoint a new trustee or new trustees, and it is found inexpedient difficult or impracticable so to do without the assistance of the court, make an order appointing a new trustee or new trustees either in substitution for or in addition to any existing trustee or trustees, or although there is no existing trustee.

In particular and without prejudice to the generality of the foregoing provision, the court may make an order appointing a new trustee in substitution for a trustee who is [incapable, by reason of mental disorder within the meaning of the Mental Health Act 1983, of exercising his functions as trustee] or is a bankrupt, or is a corporation which is in liquidation or has been dissolved."

ii. Circumstances in which the Jurisdiction will be Exercised. The section gives the court a discretion. Cases arise in a variety of circumstances, *e.g.* where a sole surviving trustee has died intestate, or where all the trustees of a testamentary trust predeceased the testator,[45] and difficulty is experienced in obtaining administration of his estate,[46] or where the donee is incapable of making an effective appointment because of infancy.[47] The court has power to replace a trustee against his will[48]; and also where the trustees were the life tenant and remainderman and there was friction between them; or where a trustee has, through age or infirmity,[49] become incapable of acting, or who permanently resides abroad.[50] The statutory power of beneficiaries to direct appointments reduces the need to apply to court.[51]

---

[43] The section does not apply to the appointment of personal representatives (s. 41(4)).

[44] *i.e.* the High Court; or where the estate or trust fund does not exceed its financial jurisdiction, the county court.

[45] *Re Sattherthwaite's Trust* (1871) L.R. 11 Eq. 251.

[46] *Re Matthews* (1859) 26 Beav. 463.

[47] *Re Parsons* [1940] Ch. 973; (1941) 57 L.Q.R. 25 (R.E.M.).

[48] *Re Henderson* [1940] Ch. 764.

[49] *Re Lemann's Trust* (1883) 22 Ch.D. 633.

[50] *Re Bignold's S.T.* (1872) L.R. 7 Ch.App. 223.

[51] Trusts of Land and Appointment of Trustees Act 1996, ss.19, 20; *ante*, p. 496.

The court should not be asked to exercise its jurisdiction where a statutory power can be exercised.[52] It has no jurisdiction to appoint a new trustee against the wishes of the persons who have a statutory power to appoint, even in a case where an application has been made to it by a majority of the beneficiaries.[53] Where the beneficiaries are *sui juris*, absolutely entitled and unanimous, they may exercise the statutory power referred to above.

9. Vesting of the Trust Property in Trustees

A. Requirement of Vesting

The trust property must be vested in the trustees to enable them to deal with outside parties. Before and after the vesting, however, a trustee, whether appointed under section 36 or by the court under section 41, or by direction of the beneficiaries under sections 19 or 20 of the Trusts of Land and Appointment of Trustees Act 1996,[54] has "the same powers, authorities, and discretions, and may in all respects act as if he had been originally appointed a trustee by the instrument, if any, creating the trust."[55]

B. Vesting Declaration under Section 40

i. Subsection (1). In order to avoid the necessity of a formal transfer of the trust property from the old trustees to the new, section 40 provides that the vesting may, with important exceptions, be effected automatically if the appointment of the trustees has been made by *deed*.[56] It does not apply, however, where the property is held by personal representatives and not by a trustee.[57]

Subsection (1) of section 40 provides that the deed of appointment shall operate to vest any land, chattel or chose in action subject to the trust in the new trustee, unless the deed expressly provides to the contrary.

ii. Exceptions under subsection (4). These in outline are:

(a) a mortgage of land to secure a loan of trust money;

---

[52] *Re Gibbon's Trusts* (1882) 30 W.R. 287 (where, however, such an appointment was made); *cf. Re May's W.T.* [1941] Ch. 109.

[53] *Re Higginbottom* [1892] 3 Ch. 132.

[54] *Ibid.*, s.21(3).

[55] T.A. 1925, ss.36(7), 43.

[56] *Ante*, p. 493.

[57] *Re Cockburn's W.T.* [1957] Ch. 438; *Re King's W.T.* [1964] Ch. 542; *ante*, p. 57.

   (b) land held under a lease which contains a covenant against
       assignment without consent, and the consent has not been
       obtained prior to the execution of the deed;
   (c) stocks and shares.[58]

These exceptions are necessary. Where trust money is lent on mortgage, no mention is made in the mortgage deed of the existence of the trust, nor upon a transfer of the mortgage, such as would occur on the appointment of a new trustee. If section 40(1) applied, the mortgagor on redeeming would have to investigate the appointments of new trustees to make sure he was paying the right persons. The second exception is included in order to avoid an unintended breach of covenant, such as could occur in the appointment of a new trustee. The most serious exception in practice is the third; for this is the most important and valuable form of property in modern settlements. The provision, however, was necessary, because title to stocks and shares depends on the registration of the owners in the register of shareholders, and it is essential that the current trustees should be registered.[59]

It will be seen that vesting orders relating to registered land are not expressly excepted; however, the legal title cannot pass until registration. By the Land Registration Act 1925, s.47, the registrar is required to give effect on the register to any vesting order or vesting declaration made on the appointment or discharge of a trustee. The provisions of the Trustee Act 1925 relating to the appointment and discharge of trustees and the vesting of trust property apply to registered land subject to proper entry being made on the register.

C. Vesting Orders under Sections 44 to 56

Sections 44 to 56 contain the rules as to vesting orders by the court. These overlap section 40, for vesting orders as to all kinds of property can be made not only where the appointment has been made by the court, but also where it has been made out of court under an express or statutory power. The court is given wide powers to make such orders in a variety of eventualities.

10. SELECTION OF TRUSTEES

A. On Appointment by the Court under Section 41

The factors which a court will take into account when exercising its jurisdiction to appoint a trustee were discussed by Turner L.J. in

---

[58] "Any share, stock, annuity or property which is only transferable in books kept by a company or other body, or in manner directed by or under an Act of Parliament." This includes money in a bank account, for example, but not bearer bonds.

[59] See (1992) 142 N.L.J. 541 (M. Russell). For electronic transfer, see *ante*, p. 115.

Re Tempest.[60] The court should always have regard to three prime requirements: the wishes of the person by whom the trust was created; the interests, which may be conflicting, of *all* the beneficiaries; the efficient administration of the trust. It is important that the trustees act harmoniously together; but Turner L.J. thought it would be going too far to say that the court should refuse to appoint a particular trustee on the ground that the continuing trustee refused to act with him. That would give the continuing trustee a veto; rather, the reasons for the refusal should be examined to see whether the objection is well founded.

The court is reluctant to appoint a person who, though not himself interested, is related to, or connected with, someone who is. Thus a relative of one of the beneficiaries is not a desirable appointment,[61] nor is one nominated by a relative of the testator with whom the testator was on bad terms.[62] Again, the solicitor to the trust,[63] or to one of the beneficiaries[64] or trustees, should not be appointed, as there might be a conflict of duties; unless, of course, no other person can be found to undertake the position. If the solicitor to the trust is a continuing trustee, his partner should not be appointed.[65] Persons out of the jurisdiction will not be appointed[66] except in a case where circumstances require it, or where the beneficiaries are resident outside the jurisdiction also.[67] Even where the trust can be more conveniently administered by trustees resident abroad, the court may exact an undertaking from them that they will consult the court before proceeding to the appointment of new trustees out of the jurisdiction.[68] Trusts administered abroad have enjoyed a number of fiscal advantages, and this has encouraged the movement of many trusts overseas.

B. On Appointment under Express Power or under Section 36

i. Choice by Donee of Power. It is said that the above principles should guide persons exercising their power to appoint under section 36. In practice, however, it is common for beneficiaries and other

[60] (1866) L.R. 1 Ch.App. 485.
[61] *Re Coode* (1913) 108 L.T. 94; *Re Parsons* [1940] Ch. 973 (where an infant purported to appoint his mother).
[62] *Re Tempest* (1866) L.R. 1 Ch. 485.
[63] *Wheelwright v. Walker* (1883) 23 Ch.D. 752; *Re Orde* (1883) 24 Ch.D. 271.
[64] *Re Kemp's S.E.* (1883) 24 Ch.D. 485; *Re Earl of Stamford* [1896] 1 Ch. 288; *Re Spencer's S.E.* [1903] 1 Ch. 75; *Re Cotter* [1915] 1 Ch. 307.
[65] *Re Norris* (1884) 27 Ch.D. 333.
[66] *Re Weston's Settlements* [1969] 1 Ch. 223.
[67] *Re Liddiard* (1880) 14 Ch.D. 310; *Re Simpson* [1897] 1 Ch. 256; *Re Seale's Marriage S.T.* [1961] Ch. 574; *Re Windeatt's W.T.* [1969] 1 W.L.R. 692; *Re Whitehead's W.T.* [1971] 1 W.L.R. 833.
[68] *Re Freeman's S.T.* (1888) 37 Ch.D. 148.

members of the beneficiaries' families, and for solicitors to the beneficiaries, to be appointed. A conflict of interest and duty or of two duties should of course be avoided. However, even if the trustee appointed is one whom the court itself would not have selected, it seems that the court will not rectify it.[69]

ii. Foreign Trusts. Problems have arisen in relation to the appointment of foreign trustees with the intention of enjoying the tax advantages of offshore trusts. The tax advantages are now minimal unless there are beneficiaries who are resident abroad, or the settlor was domiciled[70] abroad at the date of the creation of the settlement. We have seen that the court was unwilling to appoint trustees resident abroad unless the beneficiaries have made their homes in the country in question.[71] It was said in *Re Whitehead's Will Trusts*[72] that trustees or persons with an express power should only appoint foreign resident trustees in similar circumstances (although an appointment inconsistent with this rule would be a valid appointment[73]). More recently, however, Millett J. has held that the *Whitehead* approach is outdated.[74] Where the trustees are exercising their own discretion and are merely seeking the authorisation of the court for their own protection, the test is simply whether the trustees can properly form the view that the proposed transaction is for the benefit of the beneficiaries. Thus Bermudan trustees were sanctioned although the trust had no Bermuda connection. Where it is clear that this test is satisfied, there is no need to apply to court. It is might be added that many settlements now expressly authorise the appointment of non-resident trustees.

iii. Direction by Beneficiaries. We saw that in certain circumstances, beneficiaries may give directions as to the exercise of the statutory power of appointment.[75] It appears that the beneficiaries are under no restrictions in the choice of person they direct to be appointed.

---

[69] In *Re Norris* (1884) 27 Ch.D. 333, the funds were being administered by the court; *Re Higginbottom* [1892] 3 Ch. 132; in *Re Coode* (1913) 108 L.T. 94, an appointment of an infant was held void; *Re Parsons* [1940] Ch. 973; (1941) 57 L.Q.R. 25 (R.E.M.).

[70] Inheritance Tax Act 1984, s.267.

[71] *Re Weston's Settlements* [1969] 1 Ch. 223; *cf. Re Seale's Marriage S.T.* [1961] Ch. 574; *Re Windeatt's W.T.* [1969] 1 W.L.R. 692; *Re Whitehead's W.T.* [1971] 1 W.L.R. 833; (1976) 40 Conv.(N.S.) 295 (T. Watkin). See generally Parker and Mellows, *The Modern Law of Trusts* (6th ed.), Chap. 22.

[72] [1971] 1 W.L.R. 833 at p. 838.

[73] *Meinertzhagen v. Davis* (1844) 1 Coll. 353; *Re Smith's Trusts* (1872) 26 L.T. 820; (1969) 85 L.Q.R. 15 (P.V.B.); *Re Whitehead's W.T., supra,* at p. 837.

[74] *Richard v. The Hon. A.B. Mackay* (1987, unreported), discussed in The Offshore Tax Planning Review (1990/91), Vol. 1, p. 1 (R. Bramwell).

[75] Trusts of Land and Appointment of Trustees Act 1996, ss.19–22; *ante,* p. 496.

C. On Appointment by the Settlor

The settlor is under no restrictions in the selection of the original trustees whether English or foreign. The question is not merely one of selecting efficient, businesslike and fair-minded trustees who will carry out their duties according to law. They are commonly given wide discretions. They therefore should be people who will be relied on to respect the wishes of the settlor on matters on which they are in law virtually uncontrolled; and in circumstances which may have greatly changed since the trust was created.

11. RETIREMENT

A trustee may retire from a subsisting trust in any one of the ways explained below.[76] Retirement means a discharge from further responsibility and liability under the trust. A trustee should not retire when faced with disputes among beneficiaries and leave them to settle their differences among themselves. If he retires in order to facilitate a breach of trust by his successors, he will remain liable.[77]

A. Under an Express Power in the Trust Instrument

This is rare, since (the predecessors of) sections 36 and 39 made express powers unnecessary.

B. Under Section 39

We saw that a trustee desiring to be discharged could be replaced by a newly appointed trustee.[78] He may retire, without being replaced, if he complies with section 39 of the Trustee Act 1925.

"(1) Where a trustee is desirous of being discharged from the trust, and after his discharge there will be either a trust corporation or at least two persons[79] to act as trustees to perform the trust, then, if such trustee as aforesaid by deed declares that he is desirous of being discharged from the trust, and if his co-trustees and such other person, if any, as is empowered to appoint trustees,

---

[76] A personal representative may be discharged by the court; Administration of Justice Act 1985, s.50.

[77] *Head v. Gould* [1898] 2 Ch. 250.

[78] T.A. 1925, s.36(1); *ante*, p. 493. *cf.* (1989) 9 L.S. 323 (Y. Tan), suggesting that s.36 permits retirement without replacement.

[79] A sole trustee other than a trust corporation does not suffice even if he has power to give a valid receipt for capital money, in contrast with the position under T.A. 1925, s.37(1)(c). The word "persons" in s.39(1) was inserted by Trusts of Land and Appointment of Trustees Act 1996, Sched. 3, para. 3(13), in place of "individuals." A corporate trustee (whether or not a "trust corporation") is a "person" but not an "individual."

by deed consent to the discharge of the trustee, and to the vesting in the co-trustees alone of the trust property, the trustee desirous of being discharged shall be deemed to have retired from the trust, and shall, by the deed, be discharged therefrom under this Act, without any new trustee being appointed in his place."

A retirement not complying with the statutory provisions is invalid, hence the trustee remains in office.[80]

C. Under an Order of the Court

The court will only discharge a trustee under its statutory jurisdiction where it replaces him by a new appointment under section 41. It has however an inherent power to discharge him without replacement in the case of an action to administer the trust. While it will not, in the exercise of this jurisdiction, encourage capricious retirement,[81] it will allow a trustee to retire where it is entirely proper for him to do so.[82]

D. By Direction of the Beneficiaries

We saw that section 19 of the Trusts of Land and Appointment of Trustees Act 1996 gives beneficiaries of full age and capacity and together absolutely entitled the power to give directions to the trustees in matters of appointment and retirement.[83] Where a trustee has been given a direction to retire under section 19 and reasonable arrangements have been made for the protection of any rights of his in connection with the trust, he must execute a deed declaring his retirement, provided that after his retirement there will be either a trust corporation or at least two persons to act, and either another person is to be appointed in his place (by direction of the beneficiaries or otherwise) or the continuing trustees by deed consent to his retirement.[84]

12. REMOVAL

We have seen that the court[85] may, on the appointment of a new trustee, remove an existing trustee and that some appointments by a

---

[80] *Mettoy Pension Trustees Ltd v. Evans* [1990] 1 W.L.R. 1587.

[81] *Courtenay v. Courtenay* (1846) 3 Jo. & La.T. 519, 533.

[82] *Re Chetwynd's Settlement* [1902] 1 Ch. 692.

[83] *Ante*, p. 496. The power may be excluded by the settlor under s.21(5), (6).

[84] s.19(3). For vesting and divesting of the trust property, see s.19(4) of the 1996 Act and T.A. 1925, s.40(2), as amended.

[85] Normally the Chancery Division, but the Family Division has such jurisdiction; *E. v. E.* [1990] 2 F.L.R. 233 (post-nuptial settlement).

donee of a power will have this effect.[86] The power of beneficiaries to direct a trustee to retire was discussed above. The court has also an inherent jurisdiction in actions for the administration of trusts to remove a trustee compulsorily; but the principles on which this power is exercised are somewhat vague.[87]

Actual misconduct on the part of a trustee need not be shown, but the court must be satisfied that his continuance in office would be prejudicial to the due performance of the trust, and so to the interests of the beneficiaries.[88] The court has a clear ground for removal in cases where a trustee is ignoring one of his duties. Thus, though it will not necessarily constitute a breach of trust for a trustee of a will carrying on the business of his testator to set up a rival business, yet it will be a ground for his removal,[89] as he has put himself in a position wherein his duty and interest are bound to be in conflict. Similarly if trustees were to persist in an investment policy based on considerations other than the best interests of the beneficiaries.[90] Harman J. has suggested that a member of a discretionary class could procure the removal of a trustee who "deliberately refused to consider any question" relating to the qualification of members to receive payments.[91]

In the case of a foreign settlement, the court has inherent jurisdiction to make *in personam* orders removing and replacing foreign trustees, whether or not the assets are in England, provided that the individual trustee is subject to the jurisdiction of the English courts[92] However, where the applicable law of the trust is not English law, matters such as the appointment, resignation and removal of trustees are governed by the law of the relevant jurisdiction.[93]

In administration actions the powers of the court are very elastic.[94] The court can, at any time during such proceedings, remove the trustees, if it considers such removal necessary for the preservation of the trust estate or the welfare of the beneficiaries, notwithstanding that such removal has not been expressly asked for by the pleadings. But each case must be weighed carefully on its merits;

---

[86] T.A. 1925, ss.36, 41, *ante*, pp. 493, 497; *Re Stoneham S.T.* [1953] Ch. 59; as to removal of a charitable trustee, see Charities Act 1993, s.18; *ante*, p. 451.

[87] *Letterstedt v. Broers* (1884) 9 App.Cas. 371; *Re Wrightson* [1908] 1 Ch. 789; *Re Pauling's S.T. (No. 2)* [1963] Ch. 576; *Jones v. Att.-Gen.* [1974] Ch. 148 (trustee of charitable trust); *Re Edwards' W.T.* [1982] Ch. 30.

[88] See *E. v. E., supra.*

[89] *Moore v. M'Glynn* [1894] 1 Ir.R. 74.

[90] *Cowan v. Scargill* [1985] Ch. 270, *post*, p. 523.

[91] *Re Gestetner Settlement* [1953] Ch. 672 at p. 688; see also *per* Lord Wilberforce in *McPhail v. Doulton* [1971] A.C. 424 at p. 456; *ante*, p. 100.

[92] By reason of service of process in England, or because the trustee has submitted to the jurisdiction, or because the court has assumed jurisdiction under R.S.C. Ord. 11.

[93] Recognition of Trusts Act 1987, Sched., Art. 8. For the applicable law, see Arts. 6, 7; *ante*, p. 43.

[94] *Re Harrison's Settlement Trusts* [1965] 1 W.L.R. 1492. On the removal of an executor, see *I.R.C. v. Stype Investments (Jersey) Ltd* [1982] Ch. 456.

and the court will sometimes find it necessary to place in one scale a minor breach of trust, and in the other the certain expense to the trust estate of a change of trustees.[95]

Special rules relating to the suspension, removal, disqualification and replacement of pension trustees are discussed in Chapter 16.

13. CONTROL OF TRUSTEES

The basic principle governing trustees is that, while duties must be discharged, the exercise of discretions needs only to be considered. The trustee is not obliged to exercise it in any particular manner, or indeed at all. Thus in *Tempest v. Lord Camoys*,[96] one trustee wished to take advantage of a power in a trust instrument to purchase land but his co-trustee would not agree. It could not be shown that he had failed to consider the matter, and the court refused to issue any directive to him.

Nor is there a general principle that trustees should consult beneficiaries, though they should inform them that they have certain rights.[97] Frequently consultation takes place as a matter of practice, but only occasionally does statute[98] impose an obligation on them to do so, and even then their wishes are not mandatory but must be related to the overall welfare of the trust.

But what is the position if trustees exercise a discretion in a manner that appears wholly unreasonable? Is it a satisfactory answer to state simply that the matter has been fully considered? The law on this subject is neither wholly clear not wholly satisfactory.

A. Giving of Reasons

There is a basic rule that trustees cannot be compelled to explain their reasons for exercising or not exercising a discretionary power.

> In *Re Beloved Wilkes' Charity*,[99] trustees were directed to select a boy to be educated for Orders in the Church of England. Their freedom of choice was limited by a preference for certain parishes, if a fit and proper candidate therefrom could be found.
>
> The trustees selected Charles Joyce, a boy who did not come from one of these parishes. It appeared that Charles' brother was a minister who had sought assistance on his behalf from one of

---

[95] *Re Wrightson* [1908] 1 Ch. 789.
[96] (1882) 21 Ch.D. 571.
[97] *Hawkesley v. May* [1956] 1 Q.B. 304; *post,* p. 550.
[98] *e.g.* Trusts of Land and Appointment of Trustees Act 1996, s.11; *ante,* p. 280.
[99] (1851) 3 Mac. & G. 440.

the trustees. The trustees gave no reasons for their choice, but asserted that they had considered the candidates impartially.

Lord Truro refused to set aside the trustees' selection, or to require the trustees to explain how they had arrived at their conclusion.[1]

No distinction exists in this context between oral and documentary evidence, which is a matter of some importance in view of the large amount of trust business which is conducted by correspondence or at meetings with written agenda and minutes. In *Re Londonderry's Settlement*,[2] the court drew a sharp distinction between written material of this nature which related to management of the trust property (which should be disclosed to requesting beneficiaries) and material which related to the exercise of discretions (which need not be disclosed). But if trustees do give reasons, then the courts will look into their adequacy.[3]

The principle that trustees need not give reasons for their decisions is based on the fact that trustees have a confidential role which, it is said, they cannot properly exercise if they are to be subjected to an investigation to see whether they have exercised it in the best possible manner.[4] Documents relating to the trust may contain confidential information, the disclosure of which could cause trouble in the family, out of all proportion to the benefit gained from inspecting them. Thus the principle is designed not to encourage secrecy but to avoid litigation and family disputes.[5]

Whether the principle is appropriate to pension trusts may be doubted,[6] but it was held to apply in *Wilson v. Law Debenture Trust Corporation plc*,[7] even though pension trusts are in many ways treated differently from traditional trusts because the beneficiaries are not volunteers.[8] There the employees failed to obtain disclosure of the trustees' reasons for not transferring a surplus to another scheme to which the employees had been transferred. Any change, it was said, would require legislation.[9] The significance of member

---

[1] For a discussion on policy grounds, see (1965) 28 M.L.R. 220 (A. Samuels); (1965) S.J. 239 (A. Hawkins and F. Taylor).

[2] [1965] 1 Ch. 918; the facts are given *post*, p. 550; *Butt v. Kelson* [1952] Ch. 197.

[3] *Klug v. Klug* [1918] 2 Ch. 67.

[4] *Re Londonderry's Settlement* [1965] Ch. 918 at pp. 935–936.

[5] *Hartigan Nominees Pty Ltd v. Rydge* (1992) 29 N.S.W.L.R. 405, holding that *Londonderry* accorded with principle and common sense; [1994] 3 J.I.P. 60 (J. Lehane).

[6] (1992) 6 *Trust Law International* 119 at p. 125 (Lord Browne-Wilkinson); (1994) 8 *Trust Law International* 27 (D. Schaffer).

[7] [1995] 2 All E.R. 337; criticised (1994) 8 *Trust Law International* 118 (D. Schaffer); All E.R. Rev. 1995, p. 321 (P. Clarke).

[8] *Ante*, p. 459.

[9] The Pensions Act 1995 requires the disclosure of certain documents (*ante*, p. 471), but does not impose any general duty to give reasons.

trustees (required by the Pensions Act 1995) in this context should not, however, be overlooked.[10]

It is otherwise where there is evidence of bad faith or other impropriety. The difficulty is that it may not be possible to establish impropriety without seeing the documents which the trustees are not obliged to disclose. The beneficiaries may obtain discovery of documents to support their case, but may not use that process to ascertain if a case exists.[11] Indeed the order made in the *Londonderry* case was without prejudice to the beneficiary's right to discovery in separate proceedings against the trustees.[12]

B. Intervention by the Court

The cases are not clear, however, on whether the courts will look into the exercise of a discretion that *appears* to be wholly unreasonable. If there is an allegation of fraud or misconduct, the courts must investigate it; but the complainant is in a difficulty in that the evidence which he requires is the personal motivation of the trustees. If fraud is proved, or if the exercise of the discretion is shown to be "capricious,"[13] or if the trustees have blindly followed the settlor's wishes,[14] the court will declare the trustees' decision void. There is some authority that the court will not intervene in the absence of bad faith if the instrument provides that the trustees' discretion is "uncontrollable."[15] It is not clear how far the court has greater powers in the absence of such a statement.[16] Although some nineteenth century decisions[17] asserted a wide jurisdiction, it seems that the court will not intervene simply on the ground that the trustees have exercised their discretion in good faith but unreasonably. The House of Lords in a Scottish appeal[18] indicated that the court could intervene, whether or not the trustees had given their reasons, if it was clear that they had not applied their minds to the right question or had perversely shut their eyes to the facts. This reflects the rule in *Re Hastings-Bass*,[19] applying where trustees exercise a discretion in good faith but their disposition does not have

---

[10] (1995) 145 N.L.J. 1414 (P. O'Hagan).
[11] *Hartigan Nominees Pty Ltd v. Rydge* (1992) 29 N.S.W.L.R. 405.
[12] [1965] Ch. 918 at p. 939.
[13] *Re Manisty's Settlement* [1974] Ch. 17; *ante*, p. 107.
[14] *Turner v. Turner* [1984] Ch. 100.
[15] *Gisborne v. Gisborne* (1877) 2 App.Cas. 300.
[16] See [1989] Conv. 244 (N. Parry).
[17] *Re Hodges* (1878) 7 Ch.D. 754; *Re Roper's Trust* (1879) 11 Ch.D. 272.
[18] *Dundee General Hospitals v. Walker* [1952] 1 All E.R. 896. The trustees accepted that unreasonableness was the test, but this was doubted.
[19] [1975] Ch. 25, *post*, p. 582; *Re Vestey's Settlement* [1951] Ch. 209; *Mettoy Pension Trustees Ltd v. Evans* [1990] 1 W.L.R. 1587; [1991] Conv. 364. (J. Martin); *Stannard v. Fisons Pension Trust Ltd* [1992] I.R.L.R. 27. See also *Wild v. Pensions Ombudsman* [1996] P.L.R. 275 (jurisdiction of ombudsman to deal with maladministration).

the full effect which they intended (due to some rule of law or other cause). The court will set aside the disposition (wholly or partly) if it was outside the terms of the power or if it is clear that the trustees would not have acted as they did had they not taken into account considerations which they should not have taken into account or failed to take into account considerations which they ought to have taken into account. It is not enough to show that the trustees did not fully understand the effect of their act. It must also be clear that, if they had fully understood, they would not have acted as they did.

Where the court does intervene, the result is normally negative: the decision of the trustees may be declared void, or a future course of action restrained. Usually the court makes no positive direction that a discretion must be exercised in a particular way. However, this can be done in an appropriate case, as in *Klug v. Klug*,[20] where a trustee refused to exercise a power of advancement for an extraneous reason (because the beneficiary, her daughter, had married without her consent). The court directed the trustee to agree to the advancement. Alternatively, a trustee may be persuaded by the prospect of removal.

C. Power of Decision

A trust deed may give the trustees or a third party power to decide a particular matter. We saw in Chapter 3 that this may be a means of curing conceptual uncertainty,[21] in which case the question arises whether the court may intervene if the decision appears unreasonable or wrong. Lord Denning in *Re Tuck's Settlement Trusts* would only have accepted the decision of the Chief Rabbi "so long as he does not misconduct himself or come to a decision which is wholly unreasonable."[22]

The trustees cannot be given power to decide legal issues in such manner as to oust the jurisdiction of the court, as this would be contrary to public policy.[23] They may be given power to decide limited issues, such as where the beneficiaries reside, or what is their ancestry or faith. The House of Lords in *Dundee General Hospitals v. Walker*[24] thought it possible, as mentioned above, that the decisions of trustees in such cases could be attacked on the grounds of

---

[20] [1918] 2 Ch. 67. See also *Re Hodges* (1878) 7 Ch.D. 754; *Re Roper's Trust* (1879) 11 Ch.D. 272. The appointment of new trustees is considered preferable to positive intervention (*i.e.* the judicial exercise of fiduciary discretions) in (1990) 107 L.Q.R. 214 at pp. 219–220 (S. Gardner), discussing *Mettoy Pension Trustees Ltd v. Evans, supra.*

[21] *Ante,* p. 103.

[22] [1978] Ch. 49 at p. 62.

[23] *Re Wynn,* [1952] Ch. 271. See also *Re Raven* [1915] 1 Ch. 673 (trustees cannot be given conclusive power to resolve doubts as to identity of beneficiary).

[24] [1952] 1 All E.R. 896 at p. 905. This was a Scottish appeal, but "of the highest persuasive value": *per* Lord Denning M.R. in *Re Tuck's S.T., supra,* at p. 61.

perversity or failure to appreciate the issue, as well as on grounds of bad faith. Where a clause in a trust of a pension fund provided that the determination of matters such as eligibility and the construction of the instrument adopted by the trustees in good faith should be binding on all parties and beneficiaries, the Canadian court held that its jurisdiction was not excluded where the trustees acted in breach of their duty of impartiality, although in good faith.[25]

The general principle that beneficiaries cannot control trustees in the manner in which they exercise their powers applies even though all the beneficiaries are ascertained and *sui juris* and desirous of the power being exercised in a particular way.[26] But in such a case the trust can of course be brought to an end.

---

[25] *Boe v. Alexander* (1988) 41 D.L.R. (4th) 520. See also *Jones v. Shipping Federation of British Columbia* (1963) 37 D.L.R. (2d) 273.

[26] *Re Brockbank* [1948] Ch. 206; *cf. Re George Whichelow Ltd* [1954] 1 W.L.R. 5 at p. 8. See, however, s.19 of the Trusts of Land and Appointment of Trustees Act 1996; *ante*, p. 496.

Chapter 18

DUTIES OF TRUSTEES IN RELATION TO THE TRUST PROPERTY

1. Duty to Collect in the Assets 511
   A. Duty on Accepting Office 511
   B. Extent of Duty 512
   C. Litigation 513
   D. A Continuing Duty 514
2. Duty to Invest 514
   A. Meaning of Investment 514
   B. Types of Investment 515
      i. Loans at a Rate of Interest 515
      ii. Equities 516
         (a) Ordinary Shares 516
         (b) Unit Trusts and Investment
             Trusts 516
   C. Express Powers of Investment 517
   D. The Purchase of Land 517
   E. Authorised Investments 518
      i. Traditional Rule 518
      ii. Trustee Investment Act 1961 519
      iii. The Scheme of the Act 519
      iv. Narrower and Wider Range 519
   F. Alterations to the Fund 520
      i. Accruals 520
      ii. Withdrawals 520
   G. Special Powers and Special Range 521
   H. General Duty in Choosing
      Investments; Ethical Investments 521

I. Advice 525
J. Delegation of Investment
   Powers 525
K. Retention of Investments: Section
   6(3) 526
L. Trustees Holding Controlling Interest
   in a Company 526
M. Mortgages of Land 528
   i. The Security 528
   ii. The Amount 529
N. Extension of Investment Powers by the
   Court 530
O. Reform 532
3. Duty to Distribute. Satisfaction of
   Claims 532
   A. Liability for Wrongful Payments 532
   B. Doubtful Claims 533
      i. Application to Court for
         Directions 533
      ii. Payment into Court 534
      iii. "Benjamin" Order 534
      iv. Distribution after Advertise-
         ment 535
      v. Setting Aside a Fund 535
   C. Relief under Section 61 535
   D. Discharge 535

1. Duty to Collect in the Assets

A. Duty on Accepting Office

Trustees must, on their appointment, make themselves acquainted with the terms of the trust and the state and the details of the trust property, check that the trust fund is invested in accordance with the provisions of the trust deed, and that the securities and any chattels are in proper custody.[1] They should not wait until the trust property is formally vested in them. The discharge of their duties will obviously depend upon circumstances. The trustees of a trust newly

[1] *Re Miller's Deed Trust* (1978) 75 L.S.Gaz. 454.

511

constituted, and with suitable assets, are in an easier situation than personal representatives who find, as part of the estate, assets which are highly speculative or precarious. In the latter case the duty is to consider the best method of protecting the value of the assets, and this may involve delaying a decision to dispose of them. Liability for loss will not be imposed on them if their decision to delay was reasonable, even though subsequent events show it to have been the less wise course.[2]

A replacement trustee must make all reasonable inquiries[3] to satisfy himself that nothing has been done by his predecessor and the continuing trustees which amounts to a breach of trust; and the continuing trustees must provide this information from trust documents.[4] Omission to inquire may render the new trustee liable, but he is not to be fixed with notice of matters that do not appear on any of the trust documents, though the matter may be known to the retiring trustee.[5] On a similar principle, if he is ignorant of the existence of some right forming part of the trust, he is not liable for loss of that right through non-enforcement unless he could have discovered its existence from materials at his disposal.[6]

B. Extent of Duty

The duty to safeguard trust assets is a stringent one; indeed, it has sometimes been almost too strictly applied.

In *Re Brogden*,[7] the trustees of a marriage settlement took what they considered to be all reasonable steps to ensure that a covenant to pay £10,000 to them at the end of a stated period of five years was carried out. They did not sue because the covenantor's estate was the basis of the family partnership, the stability of which might have been imperilled by an action at a time of trade depression. The trustees were held liable. They should have taken

---

[2] *Buxton v. Buxton* (1835) 1 My. & Cr. 80.

[3] *Harvey v. Oliver* (1887) 57 L.T. 239; *Re Lucking's W.T.* [1968] 1 W.L.R. 866. The Law Reform Committee, 23rd Report, *The Powers and Duties of Trustees* (1982, Cmnd. 8733), para. 4.15, takes the view that a new trustee must act as a prudent businessman in ascertaining the details of the trust. If these show nothing unusual, he is not liable for the defaults of his co-trustees. The same standard of care will apply in relation to the acts of his co-trustees during the trustee's office.

[4] *Tiger v. Barclays Bank* [1951] 2 K.B. 556.

[5] *Hallows v. Lloyd* (1888) 39 Ch.D. 686.

[6] *Youde v. Cloud* (1874) L.R. 18 Eq. 634. A similarly reasonable rule governs the inquiries trustees should make in relation to covenants to settle after-acquired property: *Re Strahan* (1856) 8 De. G.M. & G. 291.

[7] (1888) 38 Ch.D. 546. An extreme case, when litigation would have ruined a beneficiary, is *Ward v. Ward* (1843) 2 H.L.C. 777n. See also *Harris v. Black* (1983) 46 P. & C.R. 366 (duty to preserve assets did not require court to compel a trustee-beneficiary to seek the renewal of a business tenancy which he did not want, the partnership with the other trustee-beneficiary having been dissolved).

every possible step to insist on payment, irrespective of the claims of sentiment within a family.

In *Buttle v. Sunders*,[8] trustees had orally agreed to sell a freehold reversion to the leaseholder. Then a beneficiary made a higher offer. The trustees declined to consider it, feeling themselves bound by commercial morality to complete the agreement. Wynn-Parry J. held that, although there may be cases where a trustee should accept a lower offer—as where that offer may be lost if not honoured—and although the honourable course was to stand by the earlier offer, the trustees had an overriding duty to obtain the best price for their beneficiaries.

C. Litigation

In *Re Brogden*,[9] the Court of Appeal laid down that the only excuse for not taking action to enforce payment was a well-founded belief on the part of the trustees that such action would be fruitless; and the burden of proof was on the trustees. Now trustees have extensive powers of compounding liabilities, allowing time for the payment of debts, and compromising doubtful actions, etc., given by the Trustee Act 1925, s.15.[10] Trustees are not liable for loss caused by any acts done by them in good faith in exercise of these powers, provided they have directed their minds to the problem and not just let the matter slide.[11] A trustee will be allowed the costs of litigation from the trust assets if properly incurred,[12] but not where the litigation results from an unreasonable withholding of property from those entitled to it,[13] nor where the litigation is speculative and turns out to be unsuccessful,[14] nor where the trustee has acted in a manner hostile to the beneficiaries.[15] A beneficiary may sue a third party on behalf of the trust where the trustee unreasonably refuses to sue or has disabled himself from doing so.[16] Trustees who discontinue litigation against third parties because the trust fund could be exhausted in indemnifying them for costs do not act unreasonably, and the beneficiaries may not take over the action.[17]

---

[8] [1950] 2 All E.R. 193; (1950) 14 Conv.(N.S.) 228 (E. Bodkin); (1975) 30 Conv.(N.S.) 177 (A. Samuels). See also *Sergeant v. National Westminster Bank* (1991) 61 P. & C.R. 518.
[9] (1888) 38 Ch.D. 546.
[10] *Post,* p. 558.
[11] *Re Greenwood* (1911) 105 L.T. 509. *cf. Re Ezekiel's Settlements* [1942] Ch. 230.
[12] See generally *Alsop Wilkinson v. Neary* [1996] 1 W.L.R. 1220; *post,* p. 586.
[13] *Re Chapman* (1895) 72 L.T. 66.
[14] *Re Beddoe* [1893] 1 Ch. 547; *Re England's S.T.* [1918] 1 Ch. 24.
[15] *Holding and Management Ltd v. Property Holding and Investment Trust plc.* [1989] 1 W.L.R. 1313.
[16] *Parker-Tweedale v. Dunbar Bank plc* [1991] Ch. 12.
[17] *Bradstock Trustee Services Ltd v. Nabarro Nathanson (a firm)* [1995] 1 W.L.R. 1405.

D. A Continuing Duty

Trustees must regard their duty of safeguarding trust assets as a
continuing one. In regard to investment in securities, the point is
dealt with below. In regard to land, there is a duty to consider the
maintenance and general welfare of the property, and in regard to
deeds and chattels, a duty to see that they are kept securely.[18] These
may be deposited with a bank or company whose business includes
the safe custody of documents.[19] There is no duty to insure unless
required by the trust deed, but trustees have a power to insure.[20]

2. DUTY TO INVEST[21]

A. Meaning of Investment

A trustee is under a duty to invest trust money in his hands. To
invest means "to employ money in the purchase of anything from
which interest or profit is expected.[22] From the point of view of an
individual investing his own money, he does not mind whether the
profit comes from income earned by the investment or from capital
appreciation. But trustees often have to consider the interests of a
life tenant, who is entitled to the income, and also of the remaindermen who are interested in the capital.[23] The trustees' duty is to act
fairly between them. The investments should produce income, and
maintain the capital. Thus premium bonds and chattels, such as
antiques or silver, are not investments for this purpose. Similarly a
purchase of a house for occupation by a beneficiary, and which
therefore produces no income, has been held not to be an investment.[24] It is for this reason that power is usually given expressly to
trustees to make such a purchase, and trustees of land have statutory
power to do so.[25] Similarly investments which yield a high rate of
income because the capital is wasting away, as with short leaseholds,[26] or an unsecured loan,[27] should be avoided. The law relating
to authorised trustee investments is an attempt to give the trustees an
area of choice within this principle.

---

[18] *Jobson v. Palmer* [1893] 1 Ch. 71.

[19] T.A. 1925, s.21.

[20] *Post*, p. 557.

[21] Trustees conducting investment business are required by Financial Services Act 1986, s.3,
to be authorised under the Act or exempted. See Sched. 1, para. 22.

[22] *Shorter Oxford English Dictionary; Re Wragg* [1919] 2 Ch. 58 at p. 64, *per* P.O. Lawrence
J. who added: "and which property is purchased in order to be held for the sake of the
income which it will yield."

[23] Compare "percentage trusts," *post*, p. 545.

[24] *Re Power* [1947] Ch. 572.

[25] Trusts of Land and Appointment of Trustees Act 1996, s.6(3), (4); *post*, p. 517.

[26] Trustees of land may now purchase short leaseholds; *post*, p. 518.

[27] *Khoo Tek Keong v. Ch'ng Joo Tuan Neoh* [1934] A.C. 529.

B. Types of Investment

In most general terms, there are basically two types of investment. The first is a loan at a rate of interest. The second is a participation in a profit-making activity; which in the present context means the purchase of ordinary shares in a company ("equities"). The great change made by the Trustee Investments Act 1961 was the inclusion of ordinary shares in the list of permitted investments for trustees. Mention should also be made of "derivatives", such as futures and options. A "future" obliges the holder to buy or sell (shares, currency, commodities etc.) at a set price at a future date. An option gives the holder the right, but not the obligation, to buy or sell at a set price at a set date. Pension fund trustees and others with sufficiently wide powers may make use of derivatives in appropriate circumstances, but they are not presently within the range of authorised trustee investments. Dealing in derivatives can be risky, as illustrated in extreme form by the collapse of Barings Bank in 1995.

i. Loans at a Rate of Interest. In the case of an investment such as a deposit account at a bank or a building society, the capital sum does not alter (save by additions or withdrawals). Interest is earned at a rate which is normally variable.

Most fixed interest securities issued by the Government and local authorities are in the form of stock and pay a fixed rate of interest. The purchaser may sell the stock to other purchasers. The value of the stock is whatever a purchaser will give for it. That depends on many factors; essentially the current rate of interest chargeable on loans. Where interest rates have increased since the stock was issued, the value of the stock declines. A three per cent stock, paying £3 per annum on an investment of £100, needs to pay the current rate of interest in order to be saleable, but the interest is fixed at a lower rate. Assuming a current market rate of return of 10 per cent, a three per cent stock would be worth £30. £3 per annum on an outlay of £30 is a 10 per cent return.

Some stocks however are "dated"; that is, they will be repaid at "par" (100) at a stated date in the future. The nearer the date, the higher the price. Thus in March 1997, Treasury seven and a quarter per cent 1998 was priced at 100. Capital gains on certain government stocks are free of capital gains tax.[28] This and other factors contribute to the price.

A debenture is an acknowledgement of indebtedness by a company, supported in practice by a charge upon the undertaking and assets of a company. This is a floating, as opposed to a fixed, charge. The company is free to deal with any of its specific assets unaffected

---

[28] Taxation of Chargeable Gains Act 1992, s.115; *ante*, p. 215.

by the charge. The charge crystallises when the debenture holders take the necessary steps to enforce their security. The value of a debenture is dependent partly upon the ability of the assets and undertaking of the company to provide sufficient security for the loan, and it is therefore to some extent dependent upon the commercial stability of the company.

Preference shares are shares in a company which have a preference in relation to the payment of a fixed rate of dividend, and may have other preferential rights as well. Being dependent upon the earning by the company of sufficient profits to pay the dividends, they are less secure than government securities (gilts) or debentures, and consequently they normally carry a higher return. That does not mean that the rate of dividend rises. It is the price at which the shares can be purchased on the market which varies. If 5 per cent preference shares, paying £5 per annum on their par value were priced at 50, the dividend of £5 per annum on an outlay of £50 would put the shares on a return of 10 per cent.

ii. Equities.

(a) *Ordinary shares.* The capital of a company is laid down in its Memorandum[29] and its division into classes of shares usually contained in the Articles, and it normally includes ordinary shares. Ownership of an ordinary share entitles the purchaser to vote at the general meeting, to participate in dividends when declared on the ordinary shares, and to participate in a winding up.

The Annual General Meeting will declare the dividend payable for the year, if any. The value of ordinary shares varies with the fortunes of the company. They necessarily contain an element of speculation, and it is for this reason that ordinary shares were not authorised investments for trustees until 1961.

(b) *Unit Trusts and Investment Trusts.*[30] The selection of ordinary shares for investment is a highly specialised matter. Further, it is important that the investment of a trust should be spread over a wide range of companies. But a small trust cannot provide a satisfactory spread. This can be achieved by participating in an investment fund which is managed by investment experts. There are basically two types. First the unit trust, in which the managers receive money from investors, and form a single fund, divided up into units which are owned by the investors. The management is paid expenses and salary. The investors have the advantage of investment expertise, and of the spread of investments. Units in a trust can be bought and

[29] Companies Act 1985, s.2.
[30] See (1995) 92/09 L.S.Gaz. p. 18 (A. Harris).

sold. Secondly, the misleadingly named investment trust. This is a limited company in which shares can be bought and sold like other shares. The company buys shares in other companies, and the investors receive their return in the form of dividends from the investment trust.

C. Express Powers of Investment

A trustee may be given wide power by the trust instrument to select investments; or his selection may be left to investments authorised by the general law. Express clauses at one time were strictly construed, reflecting the court's fear of investment in ordinary shares in the nineteenth century. There was "a good deal of authority . . . to the effect that investment clauses should be strictly construed and should not be construed as authorising investments outside the trustee range unless they clearly and unambiguously indicate any intention to that effect."[31] Thus it seemed to be established that words such as a "power to invest in such securities as they might think fit"[32] gave power merely to select among trustee securities. The modern approach appears from *Re Harari's Settlement Trusts*,[33] where the words "in or upon such investments as to them may seem fit" permitted the trustees to invest in equities.

It remains the usual practice to include a clause giving trustees wide powers of investment in respect of the whole of the fund and thus to exclude the Trustee Investment Act 1961; and the trustees, or other persons, may be given authority to amend the power.[34]

D. The Purchase of Land

As a general rule, trustees may not purchase land unless the trust instrument so permits. Even where the instrument does authorise investment in land, we have seen that the purchase of a house for the occupation of a beneficiary is not an "investment."[35] However, trustees of land have statutory power to purchase a legal estate in any land in England and Wales.[36] The statutory power extends to trustees of a trust of the proceeds of sale of land,[37] so that trustees

---

[31] Jenkins J. in *Re Harari's S.T.* [1949] 1 All E.R. 430 at p. 432; *Re Peczenik's Settlement* [1964] 1 W.L.R. 720.

[32] *Re Braithwaite* (1882) 21 Ch.D. 121; *Bethell v. Abraham* (1873) L.R. 17 Eq. 24; "as (to) the majority shall seem meet": *Re Maryon-Wilson's Estate* [1912] 1 Ch. 55; in *Re Smith* [1896] 1 Ch. 71, Kekewich J. held that such a clause entitled the trustees to invest in debentures of a limited company.

[33] [1949] 1 All E.R. 430.

[34] *Re Harari's S.T., supra*, at p. 434.

[35] *Re Power* [1947] Ch. 572, *ante*, p. 514.

[36] Trusts of Land and Appointment of Trustees Act 1996, s.6(3).

[37] *Ibid.*, s.17.

of land who have sold the land retain the power to purchase land. The power may be exercised to purchase land by way of investment, for occupation of a beneficiary, or for any other reason.[38] As in the case of the statutory powers of trustees of land generally, the power to buy land is subject to the requirements that the trustees must have regard to the rights of the beneficiaries, and must not contravene any enactment or any rule of law or equity.[39] It may be excluded by the settlor in the case of an express trust, or made subject to consent.[40] Where the land is leasehold, the previous restriction to leases with at least 60 years unexpired[41] no longer applies.

E. Authorised Investments

i. Traditional Rule. The rules governing investment by trustees have been governed by the principles, first that trustees must avoid all risk to the capital of the fund, and secondly, that the value of the £ will remain stable. Throughout the nineteenth century, the system worked well enough. At first, trustees were restricted to consols,[42] and were subsequently permitted to choose among a narrow range of fixed interest investments, known as trustee securities. Investment was not yet a technical or specialised matter. The income beneficiaries were assured of an income, and the capital was secure. But progressive inflation changed all that.

Much of the problem of the decline of the value of the currency should be solved by investment in equities. A purchaser of a share in a company owns a share of the operation. If the business prospers, its actual value may increase. Assume, however, that the actual value of the business remains the same; if the value of money is reduced to one-third, the value of the shares will treble, providing "a hedge against inflation".

But in times of recession, the prices of ordinary shares fall even faster than those of gilts. Prices on investment exchanges are established by buyers and sellers, and a number of irrational factors play their part in establishing and undermining confidence. The overall prices of shares are gauged by an index called the *Financial Times Index*.[43] The fluctuations in prices underline the dangers involved in investment in ordinary shares, and emphasise the need for expertise in selecting investments; and the avoidance of speculation.

---

[38] *Ibid.*, s.6(4).
[39] *Ibid.*, s.6(5), (6), (8).
[40] *Ibid.*, s.8.
[41] S.L.A. 1925, s.73; L.P.A. 1925, s.28(1) (now repealed).
[42] Fixed interest Government securities without redemption date.
[43] This is now the FT30-share index. Since 1984 there is also the broader based FT-SE 100 Index.

ii. Trustee Investments Act 1961. Authorised investments are governed by the Trustee Investments Act 1961. The Act applies subject to a contrary intention in an instrument made after the passing of the Act,[44] but regardless of the provisions of such instruments coming into operation previously. The object of the Act was to permit trustees to invest a proportion of trust funds in equities. The original permitted proportion was one-half,[45] but the Treasury has recently increased this to three-quarters, pending a more fundamental reform of trustee investments.[46] Trustees of pension funds are not subject to the restrictions of the 1961 Act.[47]

iii. The Scheme of the Act. Trustees who wish to take advantage of the wider powers of investment given by the Act must divide the fund into two parts, called the narrower-range part (one quarter) and the wider-range part (three quarters).[48] The division sets the two parts of the fund once and for all, and there is no need to ensure that the ratio of three to one is maintained. There is no obligation, however, to invest all or indeed any of the wider-range part in wider-range investments after division. As discussed below, a draft order laid before Parliament at the time of writing removes the need to divide the fund, so that the whole may be invested in equities.[49]

iv. Narrower and Wider Range. The First Schedule, supplemented by numerous statutory instruments, lists the authorised investments. A significant recent amendment facilitates investment in European Union and EFTA states,[50] hereafter referred to as "relevant states". Part I consists of fixed interest investments whose capital value does not fluctuate, and which may be selected without expert advice. Examples are National Savings Certificates and deposits in the National Savings Bank. Part II contains a long list of (mainly) fixed interest investments, most of which may fluctuate in value. Examples are governmental securities in the United Kingdom or relevant states; fixed interest securities issued in the United Kingdom or in a relevant state by nationalised industries, Commonwealth governments or various regional Development Banks; debentures issued by companies incorporated in the United Kingdom or in a relevant state; deposits with a building society or a mutual investment society in a relevant state; gilt-edged unit trusts;

---

[44] *Ibid.* s.1(3).

[45] *Ibid.* s.2.

[46] Trustee Investments (Division of Trust Fund) Order (S.I. 1996 No. 845).

[47] *Ante*, p. 465. As to charity trustees, see p. 450, *ante*.

[48] T.I.A. 1961, s.2(1), as amended.

[49] The draft Deregulation (Trustee Investments) Order 1997. A separate Order will be made to extend the range of trustee investments.

[50] Trustee Investments (Additional Powers) (No. 2) Order 1994 (S.I. 1994/1908).

and mortgages of freeholds or leaseholds with at least 60 years unexpired in the United Kingdom or equivalent securities in relevant states.

Part III contains wider-range investments, and includes ordinary shares in companies incorporated in the United Kingdom or in a relevant state; shares in building societies or mutual investment societies in relevant states; and authorised unit trust schemes within the meaning of the Financial Services Act 1986 and equivalent collective investment schemes in relevant states.

Trustees must take expert advice before investing within Parts II or III. There are further restrictions on ordinary shares within Part III and debentures (and many of the fixed interest securities) within Part II[51]: (i) they must be quoted on a recognised investment exchange within the meaning of the Financial Services Act 1986 or the equivalent in a relevant state; (ii) they must be fully paid up (or required by the terms of the issue to be fully paid up within nine months); (iii) the company must have an issued capital of £1,000,000 or more (or the equivalent in a relevant state); (iv) the company must have paid a dividend in each of the immediately preceding five years on all of its shares ranking for dividend.

F. Alterations to the Fund[52]

i. Accruals. If property accrues to the trustee *as owner of property comprised in either part of the fund*, it shall be treated as belonging to that part.[53] Thus a bonus issue of shares stays in wider-range.

With other accruals, however, the trustee must ensure, by apportionment of the accruing property or by the transfer of property from one part of the fund to another, that three quarters of the value of the accrual goes to the wider-range part.[54] This is also the case with additions to the trust fund. Property which is paid for, such as a "rights issue,"[55] is treated as an investment, not an accrual.[56] Thus it belongs to the part which provided the money.

ii. Withdrawals. Where trustees take property out of the trust fund in the exercise of any power or duty, the property may be taken

---

[51] T.I.A. 1961, Sched. 1, Pt. IV, paras. 2, 2A, 3. The draft order mentioned in n. 49 removes these restrictions.

[52] These rules will not apply if the draft order (above) is implemented.

[53] T.I.A. 1961, s.2(3).

[54] T.I.A. 1961, s.2(3)(b), as amended.

[55] The right, given to shareholders by a company wishing to raise additional capital, to subscribe for newly issued shares, usually at a favourable price.

[56] T.I.A. 1961, s.2(3).

at the trustees' discretion from either part[57]; no compensating transfer is necessary. This permits the balance between the narrower- and wider-range parts to be disturbed; indeed it seems that the narrower-range part might be completely used up.

G. Special Powers and Special Range

The powers of investment conferred by the Act are in addition to express powers of investment. Such powers are referred to in the Act as "special powers."[58]

Property which trustees are authorised to hold apart from the provisions of the Act is called "special range" property, and is held subject to the provisions of the Second Schedule.[59] In effect, special range investments are those authorised under an express power of investment, or under a court order relating to the investment powers of a trust,[60] or under a special statute relating to various corporations and institutions. Common examples of special range investments include shares in private companies and the purchase of land. If the whole property of the trust is governed by any such power, the Act has no relevance. Where, however, the trust contains other property, the Act applies to the remainder.[61] If the trustees then wish to exercise the investment powers under the Act, the trust funds must (pending the reform already mentioned) be divided into three parts; the special range, covering whatever part of the fund is so applicable, and the remainder divided between narrower-range (one quarter) and wider-range (three quarters).

H. General Duty in Choosing Investments; Ethical Investments

Trustees are under a duty not only to ensure that the chosen investments are authorised, but also that they are property selected for the trust in accordance with the standard of a prudent man of business,[62] and "to avoid all investments of that class which are attended with hazard."[63] "The duty of a trustee is not to take such care only as a prudent man would take if he had only himself to

---

[57] T.I.A. 1961, s.2(4).

[58] T.I.A. 1961, s.3(1).

[59] *Ibid.* s.3(3) (to be repealed).

[60] Such as an order made under the Variation of Trusts Act 1958.

[61] *Ibid.* Sched. 2, para. 2 (to be repealed).

[62] *Speight v. Gaunt* (1883) 9 App.Cas. 1; *Learoyd v. Whiteley* (1887) 12 App.Cas. 727; *Bartlett v. Barclays Bank Trust Co.* [1980] Ch. 515; *Nestlé v. National Westminster Bank plc* [1993] 1 W.L.R. 1260 (standard of prudence regarded as "undemanding" and likely to result in complacency and inactivity). See generally [1983] Conv. 127 (P. Pearce and A. Samuels).

[63] *Learoyd v. Whiteley* (1887) 12 App.Cas. 727 at p. 733, *ante*, p. 481.

consider; the duty rather is to take such care as an ordinary prudent
man would take if he were minded to make an investment for the
benefit of other people for whom he felt morally bound to provide."[64] In making an investment for the benefit of persons for
whom he felt morally bound to provide he must show more caution
than a private investor who may well benefit from making wisely
chosen speculations.[65] This is so, however wide a discretion he may
be given by the trust instrument.[66] The Act[67] requires that he shall
have regard "to the need for diversification of investments of the
trust, in so far as is appropriate to the circumstances of the trust" and
"to the suitability to the trust of investments of the description of
investment proposed and of the investment proposed as an investment of that description." He must also consider the competing
interests of the life tenant and the remainderman, investing so as to
provide a reasonable income, and to keep secure the capital.[68] The
modern "portfolio theory"[69] requires the investment decisions of
trustees to be made and evaluated in the context of the portfolio as
a whole rather than in relation to individual assets.

These general investment duties were reviewed in *Nestlé v.
National Westminster Bank plc*,[70] where the remainder beneficiary
complained that the fund of £270,000 would have been worth over
£1m if properly invested. The claim failed because, although the
trustees had failed to appreciate the scope of their investment power
and to conduct regular reviews, the beneficiary had not proved that
these failures had resulted in wrong investment decisions and loss.
Although the investments fell "woefully short" of maintaining the
real value of the fund, failure to maintain the value was not in itself
a breach of trust, as to do so would require extraordinary skill and
luck, and would at times be impossible.[71] Further, the trustees were
entitled and bound to consider tax implications, which justified
investment in government stock rather than equities where the life
tenant was non-resident. In the absence of such special factors,
however, it was accepted that trustees should invest at least half of
the fund in equities.

---

[64] *Re Whiteley* (1886) Ch.D. 347 at p. 355, *per* Lindley M.R.
[65] *Learoyd v. Whiteley* (1887) 12 App.Cas. 727.
[66] *Chapman v. Browne* [1902] 1 Ch. 785.
[67] s.6(1) (not to be repealed). Diversification is especially important with large funds; *Cowan
v. Scargill, infra*; *Nestlé v. National Westminster Bank plc, supra*.
[68] *Post*, Chap. 19. This is unaffected by the investment reforms discussed below.
[69] *Post*, p. 532. This is reflected in Pensions Act 1995, s.35; *ante*, p. 466. See also *Trustees of
the British Museum v. Att.-Gen.* [1984] 1 W.L.R. 418; *Nestlé v. National Westminster Bank
plc*, June 29, 1988 (High Court), reported at 10 *Trust Law International* 112.
[70] [1993] 1 W.L.R. 1260; (1992) 142 N.L.J. 1279 (J. Martin); [1993] Conv. 63 (A. Kenny).
[71] See *Jones v. AMP Perpetual Trustee Company NZ Ltd* [1994] 1 N.Z.L.R. 690 (trustee is
neither insurer nor guarantor of fund).

The question whether trustees may adopt non-financial investment criteria arose in *Cowan v. Scargill*.[72]

A mineworkers' pension fund with large assets and very wide powers of investment was managed by ten trustees, of whom five, including the defendant, were appointed by the National Union of Mineworkers. They were assisted in investment decisions by an advisory panel of experts. An investment plan was submitted, which the union trustees, on the basis of union policy, refused to accept unless it was amended so that there should be no increase in overseas investments; those already made should be withdrawn; and there should be no investment in energies in competition with coal. It was held that the trustees would be in breach of duty if they refused to adopt the investment strategy. They must exercise their powers in the best interests of present and future beneficiaries. If the purpose of the trust was the provision of financial benefit, the best interests of the beneficiaries normally meant their best *financial* interests. This duty to the beneficiaries was paramount. The trustees must exercise their investment powers so as to yield the best return, putting aside personal interests and social and political views. If investments in, for example, armaments, tobacco or South African companies, were beneficial, they must not refrain because of their own views. Honesty and sincerity were not enough to satisfy the "prudent businessman" test, but financial benefit was not *inevitably* paramount. If all the beneficiaries were adults with strict views on, say, tobacco, it might not "benefit" them to make such investments. Here, however, there was no justification for reducing the benefit because the trustees had an investment policy intended to assist the union or the industry. The trustees were pursuing union policy, and the ultimate sanction was removal.[73]

It is difficult to see, however, why the trustees would be failing in their duties if they confined themselves to the investments proposed by the union trustees. In the case of a pension fund, maintenance of the prosperity of the industry must be in the financial interests of the beneficiaries, and to invest in a competing industry may be harmful.[74] Overseas investments may be risky, and there is an ample

---

[72] [1985] Ch. 270; (1984) 81 L.S.Gaz. 2291 (S. Butler); All E.R.Rev. 1984, p. 306 (P. Clarke); Moffat, *Trusts Law, Text and Materials* (2nd ed.), pp. 500–503. See also Uniform Prudent Investor Act 1994, s.5 (U.S.A.), requiring investment solely in the interest of the beneficiaries.

[73] Damages would not be recoverable unless the policy was implemented and caused loss, which is unlikely.

[74] This argument was rejected by Megarry V.-C. on the facts. The miners' pension fund is fully funded and is unusual in that its value far exceeds that of the declining coal industry, and there are many more pensioners than miners.

range of authorised investments at home: "no trust fund is so big as to exhaust the home market."[75] Perhaps the outcome would have been different if the union trustees had not argued their case on ideology rather than law.[76]

Presumably there would be no breach if trustees were to pursue an ethical investment policy only after satisfying themselves that their selected investments were at least as financially sound as those rejected on ethical grounds (a "socially sensitive" policy).[77] The point is that they must not fetter their discretion by adopting a policy which excludes any consideration of the financial merits of a particular class of investments (a "socially dictated" policy). Thus in *Martin v. City of Edinburgh District Council*[78] the Scottish court granted a declaration that a policy to oppose apartheid by disinvesting in companies which had South African interests was a breach of duty, even though no loss was incurred. The trustees (the local authority) had failed to consider whether their policy was in the best financial interests of the beneficiaries. These principles should be adhered to whether the trustees have a negative investment policy (to avoid certain types of investments) or, less commonly, a positive investment policy (to make only certain types of investments). They must remember that their duty is the provision of financial benefits, "not the reform of the world."[79]

In the case of a charity, an additional factor is that the trust is pursuing an aim, so that the question arises whether the trustees can invest in undertakings which are incompatible with their objective. For example, can trustees of a cancer charity invest in the tobacco industry?[80] In *Harries v. Church Commissioners for England*[81] the plaintiff claimed that the Commissioners, whose purpose was to promote the Christian faith through the Church of England, should not invest in a manner incompatible with that purposes even if this involved a risk of significant financial detriment. It was held that they could take non-financial ethical considerations into account only in so far as they could do so without jeopardising the profitabil-

---

[75] [1985] Conv. 52 at p. 53 (P. Pearce and A. Samuels).

[76] (1986) 102 L.Q.R. 32 (J. Farrar and J. Maxton). See also (1980) 79 Mich. L.Rev. 72 (J. Langbein and R. Posner).

[77] See generally (1990) 4 *Trust Law & Practice* 25 (P. Docking and I. Pittaway); (1990) 87/23 L.S.Gaz. 17 (N. Convey); (1991) 5 *Trust Law International* 157 (R. Ellison); (1994) 8 *Trust Law International* 10 (L. Irish and A. Kent); (1995) 9 *Trust Law International* 71 (Lord Nicholls).

[78] [1988] S.L.T. 329.

[79] (1991) 5 *Trust Law International* 157 at pp. 165–166; *Harries v. Church Commissioners for England, infra* (trustees must not make moral statements at the expense of the trust).

[80] See B.M.A. Report on Investment in the U.K. Tobacco Industry; T.I.A. 1961, s.6(1)(b) (suitability to the trust); (1982) 45 M.L.R. 268 (H. Beynon); (1987) 1 *Trust Law & Practice* 162 (J. Thurston); Annual Report of the Charity Commissioners, 1987, paras. 41–45.

[81] [1992] 1 W.L.R. 1241; [1992] Conv. 115 (R. Nobles); (1992) 55 M.L.R. 587 (P. Luxton); (1992) 6 *Trust Law International* 119 at p. 123 (Lord Browne-Wilkinson).

ity of investments. Their charitable purpose would be best served by seeking the maximum financial return. There might be rare cases where certain investments would directly conflict with the objects of the charity (as in the cancer/tobacco example). In these cases the trustees should not make such investments even if this results in financial detriment, but this was unlikely to arise because of the width of other investments. There might also be rare cases where a particular investment might alienate potential donors or recipients. The Commissioners already had a policy which excluded investment in armaments, gambling, tobacco, newspapers and South Africa, considering that there was an adequate width of alternative investments, and the propriety of this was not doubted.[82]

A settlor may secure ethical investments by providing in the instrument that the trustees must or must not make certain kinds of investments.[83] This is unaffected by the reforms discussed below.

I. Advice

Investment by trustees is normally an expert's job. When investing under Part II (narrower-range requiring advice) or Part III (wider-range) of the First Schedule, a trustee must obtain and consider written advice as to its suitability.[84] Such advice must be given by a person who is reasonably believed by the trustee to be qualified to advise.[85] The trustee must, as always, consider the advice, use his own judgment as a prudent man of business, and take his own decision.[86] He must not repose blind faith in his adviser.

These provisions do not apply where the advice is given by one trustee to his co-trustees: nor where the trustees' decisions are taken by an officer competent to advise, as in the case of a trust corporation acting as trustee.[87] As mentioned below, the advice requirements are to be modified by reforms currently before Parliament.

J. Delegation of Investment Powers[88]

We have seen that investment may need expert advice. Trustees may wish to go further and delegate their investment powers to a

---

[82] The Commissioners appeared to have fettered their discretion, but this seems permissible where the excluded investments conflict with the charity's purpose, even if not directly incompatible.

[83] T.I.A. 1961, ss.1(3), 3(1); *Harries v. Church Commissioners for England, supra.*

[84] T.I.A. 1961, s.6(2), (5).

[85] See Financial Services Act 1986, s.3: adviser must be authorised under the Act.

[86] *Shaw v. Cates* [1909] 1 Ch. 389; *Martin v. City of Edinburgh District Council* [1988] S.L.T. 329; *Jones v. AMP Perpetual Trustee Company NZ Ltd* [1994] 1 N.Z.L.R. 690.

[87] T.I.A., 1961, s.6(6).

[88] See Law Reform Committee, 23rd Report, *The Powers and Duties of Trustees* (1982, Cmnd. 8733), paras. 4.16 *et seq.*; (1989) 3 *Trust Law & Practice* 110 (C. Francis); (1990) 106 L.Q.R. 87 (D. Hayton).

professional such as an investment manager authorised under the Financial Services Act 1986. As this involves the delegation of a discretion, it can only be done if permitted by the trust instrument or by power of attorney under section 25 of the Trustee Act 1925,[89] or pursuant to an application to court for an extension of investment powers.[90] This is further discussed in Chapter 20.[91] Legislation should be enacted to enable trustees to take fuller advantage of professional investment skills.[92] This already exists in the case of pension trusts.[93]

K. Retention of Investments: Section 6(3)

A trustee is required, in respect of investments for whose selection advice was required,[94] to determine at what intervals he should take advice on the question of retaining the investment.[95] The extent of this provision is not clear. It suggests that the trustee will be liable if loss occurs by reason of his failure to observe this requirement, or if he makes a determination in an unbusinesslike way.[96] However, Trustee Act 1925, s.4 protects a trustee from liability for breach of trust "by reason only of his continuing to hold an investment which has ceased to be an investment authorised by the trust instrument or by the general law." It is submitted that a trustee who retains an unauthorised investment will be liable if he fails to consider the matter at proper times under advice; the protection of Trustee Act 1925, s.4, only arises where the *only* reason for the breach was the fact that the investment became unauthorised.[97]

L. Trustees Holding Controlling Interest in a Company

Difficult questions arise in relation to the trustees' duties where the trust contains a controlling interest in a company. The first question is whether the shareholding is a proper investment at all. If the company is a private company, as is the usual case in this situation, express authorisation would be needed to purchase such shares. Usually the question is one of retention. A provision

---

[89] *Post*, p. 565.

[90] *Post*, p. 530, *Anker-Petersen v. Anker-Petersen* (1991) 88/16 L.S.Gaz. 32.

[91] *Post*, p. 567.

[92] See Trusts (Guernsey) Law 1989, s.29(2); Uniform Prudent Investor Act 1994, s.9 (U.S.A.).

[93] Pensions Act 1995, s.34; *ante*, p. 466.

[94] *Ante*, p. 525.

[95] T.I.A. 1961, s.6(3); see *Rawsthorne v. Rowley* [1909] 1 Ch. 409n; *Re Chapman* [1896] 2 Ch. 763.

[96] See *Jones v. AMP Perpetual Trustee Company NZ Ltd* [1994] 1 N.Z.L.R. 690 (not liable for mere error of judgment in retaining shares in a falling market).

[97] See *Wright v. Ginn* [1994] O.P.L.R. 83; (1994) 8 *Trust Law International* 56 (I. Greenstreet), considering s.4 in the context of pension trusts.

expressly authorising retention is desirable (whether the holding is a majority or a minority), but the right to retain will be implied where the trust deed or will specifically refers to the property, as in the case of a specific bequest on trust.[98] A right to retain does not impliedly authorise a right to purchase more of the shares.[99]

But that is not the end of the matter. It is not sufficient for the trustees to determine that the investment is suitable, and leave it at that. For the company or its directors may engage in practices which are wholly unsuitable for a trust investment, such as speculative activities. Can the trustees shelter behind the directors, whose acts they are in a position to control?

In *Bartlett v. Barclays Bank Trust Co. Ltd*,[1] the bank was trustee of the Bartlett trust. The sole asset of the trust was a shareholding amounting to virtually all the shares in a family property company, which held some £500,000 worth of rent-producing properties.

Tax would need to be paid on the death of the life tenants, and a suggestion was made that cash would be more easily raised if the company went public; and merchant bankers advised that a public issue would be more successful if the company were not only a manager of existing property, but a developer of new properties also. The bank agreed to a policy of active development, so long as the income available to the income beneficiaries was not prejudiced.

The board then embarked upon speculative developments, one of which was a disaster, because planning permission for the intended office development could not be obtained. This resulted in a large loss to the trust shareholding.

The Bank was held liable. It was not sufficient that they believed the directors to be competent and capable of running a profitable business. Their duty was "to conduct the business of the trust with the same care as an ordinary prudent man of business would extend to his own affairs."[2] To do that it was necessary, especially as the bank was aware that the company was moving into speculative development, to get the fullest information on the conduct of the business; and not merely to be content with the supply of information which they received as shareholders. Cross J. in *Re Lucking's*

---

[98] *Re Pugh* [1887] W.N. 143; *Re Van Straubenzee* [1902] 2 Ch. 779. Where the shares are part of a residuary bequest, sale may be required by the rule in *Howe v. Lord Dartmouth, post*, p. 539.

[99] *Re Pugh, supra.*

[1] [1980] Ch. 515. See (1995) 9 *Trust Law International* 71 at p. 76 (Lord Nicholls).

[2] *Ibid.* at p. 531, quoting *Speight v. Gaunt* (1883) 9 App.Cas. 1.

Will Trusts[3] held that a controlling shareholder should insist on being represented on the board; but Brightman J. treated this as one convenient way of ensuring that all the necessary information was available.[4]

So the controlling shareholder must obtain the necessary information, as a means of "enabling the trustee to safeguard the interests of the beneficiaries."[5] How do the trustees do that? Ultimately, of course, the majority shareholder will get its way; as by adopting "the draconian course of threatening to remove, or actually removing, the board in favour of compliant directors,"[6] which is asking a lot of the trust department of a bank. Brightman J. was able to avoid the practical difficulties of such a course by finding that the members of the board were "reasonable persons, and would (as I find) have followed any reasonable policy desired by the bank had the bank's wishes been indicated to the board."[7]

M. Mortgages of Land[8]

i. The Security. The Act includes in the list of narrower-range investments requiring advice, "mortgages of freehold property in England and Wales or Northern Ireland and of leasehold property in those countries of which the unexpired term at the time of investment is not less than sixty years. . . . "[9] A number of restrictions had previously been established in relation to mortgage investments, and arguably the old rules still stand. They established that trustees should lend money only on a first legal mortgage. Equitable mortgages[10] were unsatisfactory because of the danger of the appearance of a bona fide purchaser for value without notice. This is less likely today, because an equitable mortgage is normally registrable.[11] Second mortgages were not authorised.[12] Nor was a contributory

---

[3] [1968] 1 W.L.R. 866 at p. 874.
[4] [1980] Ch. 515 at p. 533. "Other methods may be equally satisfactory and convenient depending upon the circumstances of the individual case. Alternatives which spring to mind are the receipt of copies of the agenda and minutes of board meetings if regularly held, the receipt of monthly management accounts in the case of a trading concern . . . the possibilities are endless. . . . " See *Re Miller's Trust Deed* (1978) 75 L.S.Gaz. 454, where one of the trustees was a member of a firm of accountants which acted as auditors for the company.
[5] *Ibid.* at p. 534.
[6] *Ibid.* at p. 530.
[7] *Ibid.*
[8] The reforms discussed below do not affect the mortgage rules.
[9] T.I.A. 1961, Sched. I. Part II, para. 13.
[10] *Webb v. Ledsam* (1855) 1 K. & J. 385.
[11] Under L.C.A. 1972, or protected by notice or caution under L.R.A. 1925 in the case of registered land. An equitable mortgage protected by a deposit of title deeds is not registrable.
[12] *Chapman v. Browne* [1902] 1 Ch. 785 at p. 800.

mortgage,[13] for, in spite of their many advantages in widening the spread of risk and choice of security, the trustees, needing to cooperate with strangers, lost effective control. A sub-mortgage, on the other hand, is a perfectly proper form of security.[14]

The Law Reform Committee[15] proposed that second mortgages should be permissible, as their priority can be protected by registration.

ii. The Amount. Guidance to trustees as to the amount of money which should be advanced on mortgage is contained in Trustee Act 1925, s.8.

8.—(1) A trustee lending money on the security of any property on which he can properly lend[16] shall not be chargeable with breach of trust by reason only of the proportion borne by the amount of the loan to the value of the property at the time when the loan was made, if it appears to the court—

(*a*) that in making the loan the trustee was acting upon a report as to the value of the property made by a person whom he reasonably believed to be an able practical surveyor or valuer instructed and employed independently of any owner of the property . . . and

(*b*) that the amount of the loan does not exceed two third parts of the value of the property as stated in the report; and

(*c*) that the loan was made under the advice of the surveyor or valuer expressed in the report.

It is important to take into consideration all relevant factors in determining a valuation for mortgage purposes. The current market value is not a sufficient guide, for example, in a situation in which there may be unusual fluctuations in value, connected perhaps with a business carried on there,[17] but a trustee "is justified in acting on expert advice not only as to the value of the property, but also as to the amount he may properly advance thereon . . . it being, of course, assumed that in giving the advice the expert will consider all the circumstances of the case, including the nature of the property, and will not advise a larger advance than under all the circumstances can be prudently made.[18] It is the trustee's responsibility to select the

---

[13] *i.e.* a mortgage where several mortgagees joined; *Re Massingberd's Settlement* (1890) 63 L.T. 296; *Re Dive* [1909] 1 Ch. 328.

[14] *Smethurst v. Hastings* (1885) 30 Ch.D. 490.

[15] 23rd Report, *The Powers and Duties of Trustees* (1982, Cmnd, 8733), para. 3.13.

[16] See *Re Walker* (1890) 62 L.T. 449; *Shaw v. Cates* [1909] 1 Ch. 389.

[17] *Learoyd v. Whiteley* (1887) 12 App.Cas. 727. The security upon which the trustee may lend is the land and buildings, and not the additional value of a business conducted there. See *Palmer v. Emerson* [1911] 1 Ch. 758.

[18] *Shaw v. Cates, supra*, at p. 398.

valuer,[19] who must be instructed and employed independently of the mortgagor[20]; and his report must be followed. Even then, the mortgage may for other reasons be improper. If wholly unauthorised, and a loss results, the trustee is liable for the whole loss. If the fault is only in respect of the amount of money lent, the mortgage is treated as a proper investment for the smaller sum; and the trustee is only liable to make good the excess.[21]

It is possible that a trustee who fails to comply with the provisions of section 8 will obtain relief under section 61.[22] Section 8 does, however, in the case of investment of trust funds on mortgage, "constitute a standard by which reasonable conduct is to be judged."[23] The trustee will not be liable where the value of the land has decreased through economic circumstances outside the trustee's control, and where the trustee has taken reasonable steps to safeguard the trust property.[24]

N. Extension of Investment Powers by the Court

Trustees may apply to court under section 57 of the Trustee Act 1925[25] or under the Variation of Trusts Act 1958[26] to widen investment powers. An application under section 57 is more convenient provided the beneficial interests are not affected.[27] Although section 15 of the Trustee Investments Act 1961 expressly preserves the power of the court to confer wider powers of investment, applications under the 1958 Act have been rare since the passing of the Act of 1961, the court taking the view (here described as the *Re Kolb* principle[28]), that special circumstances have to be shown to justify an extension beyond the powers conferred by a modern statute. The question arose in *Mason v. Farbrother*,[29] concerning a pension fund which had limited investment powers. By 1982, as a result of inflation, the fund had vastly increased, and the trustees wished to

---

[19] *Fry v. Tapson* (1884) 28 Ch.D. 268.

[20] *Shaw v. Cates, supra; Re Stuart* [1897] 2 Ch. 583; *Re Solomon* [1912] 1 Ch. 261. It is not sufficient that the trustee "reasonably believed" the valuer to be so instructed and employed; see Kekewich J. in *Re Somerset* [1894] 1 Ch. 231 at p. 253.

[21] T.A. 1925, s.9; *Shaw v. Cates* [1909] 1 Ch. 389; *Re Walker* (1890) 62 L.T. 449.

[22] *Post*, p. 648.

[23] *Re Stuart* [1897] 2 Ch. 583 at p. 592; *post*, p. 650.

[24] *Re Chapman* [1896] 2 Ch. 763 (a case of retention while values were falling). Where the security, although proper, diminishes, the loss will be apportioned amongst the beneficiaries under the rule in *Re Atkinson* [1904] 2 Ch. 160, *post*, p. 547.

[25] *Post*, p. 616.

[26] *Post*, p. 619.

[27] *Anker-Petersen v. Anker-Petersen* (1991) 88/16 L.S.Gaz. 32.

[28] *Re Kolb's Will Trusts* [1962] Ch. 531; *Re Cooper's Settlement* [1962] Ch. 826; *Re Clarke's Will Trusts* [1961] 1 W.L.R. 1471.

[29] [1983] 2 All E.R. 1078; [1984] Conv. 373 (H. Norman).

have wider powers. They applied to court under section 57 of the Trustee Act 1925.[30] It was held that there was no absolute rule that the court should not widen investment powers after the 1961 Act. The court approved a wide modern clause, not restricted to investments permitted by the 1961 Act, which was out of date. This could be done if there were special circumstances, which included the effect of inflation and the fact that it was in the nature of a public fund.

A different approach was subsequently taken by Megarry V.-C. in *Trustees of the British Museum v. Att.-Gen.*,[31] where the trustees sought a relaxation of their present scheme, made in 1960, as they needed a wider choice and a power to invest abroad. The trustees were eminent and responsible, and had highly skilled advice. The size of the fund (£5 million–£6 million) made it unlike a private trust and more like a pension fund or large institutional investor. Megarry V.-C. pointed out that there had been significant changes in investment practice in the last twenty years, especially with large funds. Referring to *Mason v. Farbrother*,[32] where, as we have seen, the court treated the *Re Kolb*[33] principle as still binding in the absence of special circumstances, Megarry V.-C. disagreed that inflation could be called a special circumstance, and preferred to say that the *Re Kolb* principle had gone, although if the statutory powers were increased, the principle could apply again. Factors to be considered included the standing of the particular trustees and the width and efficiency of their provisions for advice and control; the size of the fund (wider powers being permissible for larger funds as the spread of investments justifies greater risks); the objects of the fund (here the desirability of increasing the capital value, so that objects for the museum could be acquired despite soaring prices, justified greater risks); and the wider the powers sought, the more important it became that part should be in relatively safe investments.[34] Applying these principles, the trustees' application succeeded. Such applications will be unnecessary when restrictions on trustee investments are relaxed, as discussed below.

---

[30] The application under the 1958 Act did not proceed because of difficulties with the representative parties. The aspect concerning the court's inherent jurisdiction to approve a compromise is dealt with *post*, p. 614.

[31] [1984] 1 W.L.R. 418. See also *Steel v. Wellcome Custodian Trustees Ltd* [1988] 1 W.L.R. 167; [1988] Conv. 380 (B. Dale). (Trustees of large charity with funds of £3,200 million including share capital in W. Ltd which could not be sold sought wider powers of beneficial owner. Variation approved, having regard to size of fund, eminence of trustees and provisions requiring advice).

[32] *Supra*.

[33] [1962] Ch. 531, *supra*.

[34] In *Steel v. Wellcome Custodian Trustees Ltd, supra*, a variation which did not require any narrower-range investments was, however, sanctioned.

O. Reform

Over 35 years have passed since the Trustee Investments Act 1961 and, as we have seen, investment practice has changed and the Act has become out of date.[35] In any event, the Act is usually modified or excluded by the trust instrument. The Law Reform Committee recommended the repeal of the 1961 Act,[36] but this report is itself now outdated in view of changes in investment practice since 1982, especially after the Financial Services Act 1986.[37] A draft Order made under section 3 of the Deregulation and Contracting Out Act 1994 has been laid before Parliament.[38] The proposals do not apply to pension trusts, where reforms have already been enacted.[39] Under the draft Order the 1961 Act is not repealed but the need to divide the fund is removed, enabling free choice of trustee investments (which are to be extended by a separate Order). Restrictions[40] on equities in which trustees may invest are lifted, and trustees need not obtain advice in all cases. Trustees will continue to be under a duty to consider diversification and the suitability to the trust of proposed investments. They will remain subject to the standard of care and general duties imposed by the law of trusts. The new rules will apply to existing trusts, whose trustees will be expected to review and vary investments accordingly, but will not be retrospective in the sense of validating existing breaches. The increased powers will be subject to any restrictions imposed by the settlor, whether the trust was created before or after enactment of the reforms.

The Treasury consultation paper[41] adopted the modern "portfolio theory", whereby trustees' investment decisions must be evaluated not in relation to individual assets in isolation but in the context of the trust portfolio as a whole and as part of an overall investment strategy.[42] This is not referred to in the draft Order, but may now be regarded as part of the general law.

3. Duty to Distribute. Satisfaction of Claims

A. Liability for Wrongful Payments

A trustee is obliged to make payments of income and capital as they become due, and to make them to the persons properly entitled.

---

[35] See *Mason v. Farbrother, supra*; *Trustees of the British Museum v. Att.-Gen., supra*.

[36] 23rd Report, *The Powers and Duties of Trustees* (1982, Cmnd. 8733), para. 3.20.

[37] [1992] Conv. 425 (R. Bartlett).

[38] The draft Deregulation (Trustee Investments) Order 1997.

[39] *Ante*, p. 465.

[40] *Ante*, p. 520.

[41] *Investment Powers of Trustees* (May 1996), paras. 35(ii), 40(iii).

[42] See (1995) 9 *Trust Law International* 71 (Lord Nicholls); (1996) 10 *Trust Law International* 102 (E. Ford).

Failure to do so is a breach of trust, which the trustee must normally make good, such as for example, a payment based on a forged document,[43] or upon an erroneous construction of a document,[44] even if legal advice was taken,[45] or without regard to the entitlement of illegitimate beneficiaries.[46]

Where a trustee makes an overpayment of income or of instalments of capital, the error (whether of fact or law) may be adjusted in later payments.[47] If the payment is to a person who is not entitled, the trustee's right of recovery is a quasi-contractual one, and the money will be recoverable if the mistake is one of fact, but not (so long as this distinction remains significant in the law of restitution) if it is a mistake of law.[48] An unpaid or underpaid beneficiary may, in addition to his right to sue the trustee, proceed against the property in the hands of the wrongly paid recipient not being a bona fide purchaser for value without notice.[49] A trustee-beneficiary who fails to pay himself in full has been held to have no remedy,[50] but this rule is thought to be too extreme.[51]

B. Doubtful Claims

i. Application to Court for Directions.
Where the trustees are in any doubt in relation to the claims of the beneficiaries, they may make an application to the court for directions; and will be protected if they obey the directions of the court.[52] This course can now be taken with a minimum of complication by the procedure of originating summons.[53] In this way problems of construction of the trust instrument and difficulties in administering the trust can be brought before the court, so that the trustees are not forced to take the risk of making decisions upon a false premise.[54] An application to the court can also be helpful in cases where the trustees are in difficulty

---

[43] *Eaves v. Hickson* (1861) 30 Beav. 136.

[44] *Hilliard v. Fulford* (1876) 4 Ch.D. 389.

[45] *National Trustees Company of Australasia Ltd v. General Finance Company of Australasia Ltd* [1905] A.C. 373.

[46] Family Law Reform Act 1987, s.20, reversing the previous position under F.L.R.A. 1969, s.17.

[47] *Dibbs v. Goren* (1849) 11 Beav. 483 (administration by the court); *Re Musgrave* [1916] 2 Ch. 417; [1994] 2 R.L.R. 44 (P. Matthews).

[48] *Re Diplock* [1947] Ch. 716; the rule is different in respect of unpaid or underpaid beneficiaries in the administration of a deceased's estate: *Ministry of Health v. Simpson* [1951] A.C. 251; *post*, p. 686.

[49] *Re Diplock* [1948] Ch. 465.

[50] *Re Horne* [1905] 1 Ch. 76.

[51] *Lewin on Trusts* (16th ed.), p. 262.

[52] *Re Londonderry's Settlement* [1965] Ch. 918; *Finers v. Miro* [1991] 1 W.L.R. 35.

[53] R.S.C., Ord. 85, r. 2, and Ord. 5, r. 4.

[54] See also A.J.A. 1985, s.48, giving the court power to authorise action to be taken in reliance on counsel's opinion respecting the contruction of a will or trust.

in connection with the exercise of a discretion, for instance a discretionary power to make advancements. In such a case the trustees surrender their discretion to the court, and must put all relevant information before it to enable the discretion to be exercised.[55] Trustees cannot, however, surrender the future exercise of discretions to the court.[56] Trustees or beneficiaries may, in suitable cases, apply for the trust to be administered by the court,[57] but an unsuccessful applicant may be liable for costs.

ii. Payment into Court. Where beneficiaries cannot be ascertained, or where for some exceptional reason trustees cannot obtain a good discharge from the trust, there is a residual power in trustees to pay the trust moneys into court.[58] The residue of the fund in *Re Gillingham Bus Disaster Fund*,[59] for instance, was eventually paid into court.

But this will not be tolerated by the court as a means of trustees evading their obligations when difficulties arise.[60] It is a last resort when all other methods of dealing with the problem have proved unsuccessful. Trustees who pay trust funds into court when a different course was preferable, may be liable for costs.[61]

iii. "Benjamin" Order. The court has a power to authorise distribution of the whole of the assets of an estate, although not all the beneficiaries or creditors have made themselves known so as to be able to receive their share. A typical situation is where the whereabouts or continued existence of a certain beneficiary is not known. The procedure is sometimes known as a "Benjamin" order, and its purpose is to protect those distributing the assets,[62] if those entitled who have received nothing under the distribution eventually come forward to establish their claim, they may still be able to proceed, within the period of limitation, against the person wrongly paid,[63] or against the property itself. Such an order will of course only be made after all practicable inquiries have been instituted. A modern example as *Re Green's Will Trusts*,[64] where the testatrix left

---

[55] *Marley v. Mutual Security Merchant Bank and Trust Co. Ltd* [1991] 3 All E.R. 198.
[56] *Re Allen-Meyrick's W.T.* [1966] 1 W.L.R. 499.
[57] R.S.C., Ord. 5, r. 1; (1968) 84 L.Q.R. 68 (A. Hawkins).
[58] Payment into court furnishes an exception to the rule that a majority of trustees cannot defeat a dissentient minority, for T.A. 1925, s. 63, provides that the payment may in certain circumstances be made by a majority of the trustees.
[59] [1959] Ch. 62; *ante*, p. 233.
[60] See *Re Knight's Trust* (1859) 27 Beav. 45.
[61] *Re Cull's Trusts* (1875) L.R. 20 Eq. 561; (1968) 84 L.Q.R. 64 at pp. 65–67 (A. Hawkins).
[62] *Re Benjamin* [1902] 1 Ch. 723; *Re Gess* [1942] Ch. 37; *Re Taylor* [1969] 2 Ch. 245.
[63] *Ministry of Health v. Simpson* [1951] A.C. 251; *Re Lowe's W.T.* [1973] 1 W.L.R. 882 at p. 887.
[64] [1985] 3 All E.R. 455.

her property to her son, providing that it should go to charity if he did not claim it by the year 2020. The son had disappeared on a bombing raid in 1943, and all but his mother were satisfied that he was dead. A "Benjamin" order was made, allowing distribution to the charity, it being no bar to such an order that it was contrary to the intention of the testatrix.[65]

iv. Distribution after Advertisement. Under the Trustee Act 1925, s.27, trustees have themselves the power to advertise for claimants[66] and, after compliance with certain formalities, the power to distribute the whole of their trust assets to claimants who have made themselves known. Those who subsequently demonstrate an entitlement are enabled to proceed against the property distributed, save when it is in the hands of a purchaser.[67]

v. Setting Aside a Fund. The Trustee Act 1925, s.26,[68] provides a procedure whereby trustees can set aside out of trust assets a sum to meet any potential liabilities under a lease or rentcharge, and then to distribute the remainder of the trust assets to those entitled. Again, should the sum set aside prove insufficient, those entitled to the extra sums may still follow the distributed property. In the case of contingent liabilities outside section 26, the trustees can either retain a fund, distribute under a court order, or obtain an indemnity from the beneficiaries and then distribute.[69]

C. Relief under Section 61

A trustee who makes an erroneous distribution may be relieved from liability if he acted honestly and reasonably and ought fairly to be excused.[70]

D. Discharge

On the termination of the trust, the trustees should present their final accounts and obtain a discharge from the beneficiaries. The best protection is provided by a release by deed, for that places on a complaining beneficiary the burden of proving fraud, concealment,

---

[65] Criticised on this point in [1986] Conv. 138 (P. Luxton).
[66] Normally creditors, but also beneficiaries, for example claimants under an intestacy. For the application of s.27 to pension funds, see (1995) 9 *Trust Law International* 127 (P. Docking).
[67] s.27(2)(*a*); and see *Re Aldhous* [1955] 1 W.L.R. 459.
[68] As amended by Landlord and Tenant (Covenants) Act 1995, Sched. 1.
[69] See Mellows, *The Law of Succession* (5th ed.), p. 379.
[70] *Post*, p. 648.

mistake or undue influence.[71] But a trustee is not entitled to a release
by deed.[72] If the beneficiaries are unwilling to give one, the trustees
may apply to the court for the accounts to be taken and
approved.[73]

---

[71] *Fowler v. Wyatt* (1857) 24 Beav. 232.
[72] *King v. Mullins* (1852) 1 Drew. at p. 311, *per* Kindersley V.-C.
[73] Underhill (15th ed.) p. 803.

CHAPTER 19

DUTIES OF TRUSTEES IN RELATION TO THE BENEFICIARIES

1. Duty to Maintain Equality Between the Beneficiaries 537
A. The Rule in *Howe v. Earl of Dartmouth* 538
  i. Life Tenant and Remainderman ... 538
  ii. The Duty to Convert 538
    (a) Express Trust for Sale of Personalty 539
    (b) Rule in *Howe v. Earl of Dartmouth* 539
  iii. Apportionment 540
    (a) Wasting, Hazardous or Un-authorised Investments 540
    (b) Future, Reversionary or other Non-Income Producing Property 541
  iv. Contrary Intention 542
    (a) Express Trust to Convert 542
    (b) No Express Trust to Convert . 543
    (c) Reversionary Interests 543
  v. Leaseholds 543

  vi. *Howe v. Earl of Dartmouth* Today 544
    (a) Exclusion of Duty to Apportion 544
    (b) Effect of Current Investment Situation 544
    (c) Reform 544
B. Other Methods of Apportionment 545
  i. Apportionment Act 1870 545
  ii. The Rule in *Allhusen v. Whittell* .. 546
  iii. The Rule in *Re Atkinson* 547
  iv. Interest on Damages 547
  v. Purchase or Sale of Shares cum Dividend 547
  vi. Company Distributions 547
2. Duty to Provide Accounts and Information 548
A. Accounts 548
  i. Extent of Duty 548
  ii. Audit 549
B. Information. Trust Documents 549

1. DUTY TO MAINTAIN EQUALITY BETWEEN THE BENEFICIARIES

A trustee is under a general duty to maintain equality between the beneficiaries. This duty forms the basis of the specific rules of conversion and apportionment, discussed below, which apply as between life tenant and remainderman. It is not, however, confined to such cases. A modern example of the wider general duty is *Lloyds Bank plc v. Duker*,[1] where a testator's residuary estate included 999 company shares. He left 46/80 to his wife, and the rest to other beneficiaries. In spite of the general rule that a beneficiary is entitled *in specie* to his share of divisible personalty held on trust for sale, it was held that the wife could not claim 574 shares, as such a majority holding would be worth more than 46/80. The only fair solution was

---

[1] [1987] 1 W.L.R. 1324. See also *Nestlé v. National Westminster Bank plc* [1993] 1 W.L.R. 1261.

for the trustees to sell the shares and divide the proceeds in the specified proportions.

A. Rule in Howe v. Earl of Dartmouth[2]

i. Life Tenant and Remainderman. A trustee must act impartially between life tenant and remainderman. This duty applies to the selection of investments[3]; and the rules governing investment by trustees are an attempt to strike a balance between the provision of income for the life tenant and the preservation of the capital for the remainderman.[4] So long as those rules are observed, a trustee is usually under no duty to rearrange the investments so as to balance equally the interests of the life tenant and remainderman.[5] Nor, if there are investments in the fund which have ceased to be authorised, are the trustees under any immediate duty to convert them into authorised investments.[6] However the fund is invested, the normal rule is that the tenant for life takes all the income; the remainderman's interest is in the capital. The capital is not of course available until the life tenant's death; but he may, if he wishes, deal with or dispose of his reversionary interest in the fund.

There are, as we will see, some situations in which there is a duty to convert into authorised investments; and this duty carries with it a duty to apportion the income earned before the conversion is effected.

ii. The Duty to Convert. A duty to convert (i.e. sell) and reinvest in authorised investments may arise by reason of the existence of an express trust to sell or to convert, or, in the case of a bequest of residuary personalty, under the rule in *Howe v. Earl of Dartmouth*.[7]

---

[2] (1943) 7 Conv.(N.S.) 128 and 191 (S. Bailey); (1952) 16 Conv.(N.S.) 347 (L. Sheridan).

[3] *Raby v. Ridehalgh* (1855) 7 De G. M. & G. 104 at p. 109; *Re Dick* [1891] 1 Ch. 423 at p. 431.

[4] *Ante*, p. 514. There is no duty to preserve the real value of the capital; *Nestlé v. National Westminster Bank plc* [1993] 1 W.L.R. 1261 (suggesting also that trustees entitled to incline towards high income investments if rich remainderman and poor life tenant).

[5] "It it perhaps surprising that equity has not cast upon trustees, in every such case, a duty to convert the trust property as soon as practicable into something more likely to produce an equitable result" (1943) 7 Conv.(N.S.) 128 at p. 129 (S. Bailey); *Re Searle* [1900] 2 Ch. 829 at p. 834; *cf. Re Smith* (1971) 18 D.L.R. (3d) 405, (1972) 50 Can.B.R.116 (M. Cullity) (duty to reinvest where authorised shares producing low return because of company policy to pursue capital growth).

[6] T.A. 1925, s.4.

[7] (1802) 7 Ves.Jr. 137. The duty to sell the assets of an intestate has been replaced by a power of sale; A.E.A. 1925, s.33, as amended by Trusts of Land and Appointment of Trustees Act 1996, Sched. 2.

(a) *Express Trust for Sale of Personalty.* The trustees' duties under an express trust, of course, depend on the terms of the trust. It is important to note that an express trust to convert involves, as does a duty to convert under the rule in *Howe v. Earl of Dartmouth*,[8] an apportionment of the income pending conversion.[9] A mere power to sell is not sufficient to create a trust to convert.[10] In the case of an express trust for sale of land, the duty to sell is counterbalanced by a power to postpone sale for an indefinite period, notwithstanding any provision to the contrary in the instrument, and the trustees are not liable in any way for postponing sale in the exercise of their discretion.[11]

(b) *Rule in Howe v. Earl of Dartmouth. Howe v. Earl of Dartmouth* establishes that, subject to a contrary provision in the will, there is a duty to convert where residuary personalty is settled by will in favour of persons in succession. The trustees should convert all such parts of it as are of a wasting[12] or future or reversionary[13] nature or consist of unauthorised securities,[14] into authorised investments.

Thus property such as speculative investments,[15] royalties and copyrights[16] should be converted in the interest of the remainder-man. For these may be of reduced or of no value at the life tenant's death. On the other hand, "future" property such as a remainder or reversionary interest, or other property which at present produces no income, is of no immediate benefit to the tenant for life. In his interest therefore it should be converted into income-bearing proper-ties. And, as we shall see, provision is made for apportionment between the life tenant and remainderman of the value of such property when it falls into possession.[17]

It will be seen that, on its terms, the rule is of limited application. It does not apply to property settled *inter vivos*[18]; nor to specific as opposed to residuary bequests[19] (for the settlor's or testator's inten-tion in such cases is for the specific property settled to be enjoyed

---

[8] *Supra.*
[9] *Gibson v. Bott* (1802) 7 Ves.Jr. 89.
[10] *Re Pitcairn* [1896] 2 Ch. 199.
[11] Trusts of Land and Appointment of Trustees Act 1996, s.4. One effect of this Act is to abolish the statutory trust for sale.
[12] Such as leases, which terminate after a period of time; or mines or ships which will eventually become worthless; or patents or copyrights which expire.
[13] *i.e.* property which will only come into possession after the death of the life tenant.
[14] *i.e.* not authorised by the terms of the will, nor by T.I.A. 1961. *cf. Re Smith* (1971) 18 D.L.R. (3d) 405, *ante*, p. 538 (authorised securities).
[15] *Howe v. Earl of Dartmouth* (1802) 7 Ves.Jr. 137.
[16] *Re Evans' W.T.* [1921] 2 Ch. 309; *Re Sullivan* [1930] 1 Ch. 84.
[17] *Re Earl of Chesterfield's Trust* (1883) 24 Ch.D. 643; *post*, p. 541.
[18] *Re Van Straubenzee* [1901] 2 Ch. 779.
[19] *Ibid.* at p. 782.

successively). Nor does it apply to leaseholds held for a term exceeding 60 years, for these are now authorised investments[20]; the question of its application to shorter leaseholds will be discussed later.[21]

iii. Apportionment. Where there is a duty to convert, whether under an express trust for sale of personalty or under the rule in *Howe v. Earl of Dartmouth*,[22] there is, in the absence of an intention that the life tenant shall enjoy the income until sale, a duty also to apportion fairly between the life tenant and the remainderman the original property pending conversion. The detailed rules appear complicated at first sight; but they are simple if their purpose is understood.

(a) *Wasting, Hazardous or Unauthorised Investments.* It is assumed that wasting, hazardous and unauthorised securities produce income in excess of that which the life tenant should reasonably receive; and do so at the expense of the security of the capital. With such property therefore the object of the apportionment rule is to provide that the life tenant receives an income which represents the current yield on authorised investments,[23] and that the excess is added to capital.[24] If the interest received is less than 4 per cent, the balance should be made up out of subsequent income or from the proceeds of the unauthorised investments when sold.[25]

The question arises of the time at which the capital should be valued for the purpose of calculating the 4 per cent income. A distinction must be made between cases where the trustees are given power to postpone conversion and those where they are not.

First: where there is no power to postpone. In this situation the trustees should convert within the "executor's year"[26] the period during which the administration of the deceased's estate is expected to be completed. If the investments are sold within the year, the net proceeds of sale are taken as their value[27]; if not, these investments

---

[20] S.L.A. 1925, s.73(1)(xi).

[21] *Post*, p. 543.

[22] (1802) 7 Ves.Jr. 137.

[23] The life tenant's income was fixed at 4 per cent in *Re Baker* [1924] 2 Ch. 271, and applied at that figure in *Re Berry* [1962] Ch. 97 at p. 113. However, this became out of line with the return from gilt-edged investments, although interest rates are low at the time of writing. Trustees who have to decide what income to pay may be well advised to take instructions from the court. Interest rates in other contexts have been increased, for example judgment debts; legacies and overdue taxes. See also *Wallersteiner v. Moir (No. 2)* [1975] Q.B. 373; *Bartlett v. Barclays Bank Trust Co. Ltd (No. 2)* [1980] Ch. 515.

[24] The life tenant will of course receive the income from the capital as thus increased.

[25] *Re Fawcett* [1940] Ch. 402.

[26] A.E.A. 1925, s.44.

[27] *Re Fawcett, supra.*

are valued *en bloc* as at the end of one year from the death.[28] In either case the life tenant is entitled, as from the date of the death of the testator, to 4 per cent on that sum.

Secondly: where the trustees postpone sale in the exercise of a power to postpone.[29] The executor's year here has no relevance. There is a duty to convert, but no time within which the conversion should be effected. The date of the valuation is the date of the testator's death.[30]

> In *Brown v. Gellatly*,[31] the estate consisted of (i) some ships (wasting assets) which the testator directed his executors to continue to use until they could be conveniently sold, and (ii) unauthorised securities. Both were retained for more than a year from the death. The question was whether, for the purpose of apportionment, the assets should be valued at the date of death or at a year from the death.
>
> Lord Cairns held that the ships, being subject to a power to postpone sale, should be valued at the death; the unauthorised investments, on the other hand, a year from the death.

(b) *Future, Reversionary or other Non-Income Producing Property.* Where personalty which is subject to a duty to convert includes reversionary property, it is necessary, in the interest of the life tenant, to provide for apportionment[32]; otherwise the life tenant would obtain no benefit from the property until it fell into possession. The reversion should be sold and the proceeds re-invested; until that is done there is no way of producing income for the life tenant. When it has been sold, there is still the problem of determining how much of the proceeds of sale should be apportioned to capital and how much to the life tenant. This is done by[33] ascertaining the sum "which, put out at 4 per cent per annum . . . and accumulating at compound interest at that rate with yearly rests,[34] and deducting income tax at the standard rate, would, with the accumulation of interest, have produced, at the respective dates of receipt, the amounts actually received; and that the aggregate of the sums so ascertained ought to be treated as principal and be applied

---

[28] *Dimes v. Scott* (1828) 4 Russ. 195.

[29] We are here concerned with an administrative power to postpone which is not sufficient to exclude the rule; see *post*, p. 543.

[30] *Brown v. Gellatly* (1867) L.R. 2 Ch. App. 751 (the ships); *Re Owen* [1912] 1 Ch. 519; *Re Parry* [1947] Ch. 23; *Re Berry* [1962] Ch. 97.

[31] (1867) L.R. 2 Ch.App. 751.

[32] The interest may be contingent: *Re Hobson* (1855) 55 L.J.Ch. 422. The rule also applies where the sum in question is itself a mixture of capital and income; *Re Chance's W.T.* [1962] Ch. 593. A reversionary interest in land is not within the rule (*Re Woodhouse* [1941] Ch. 336).

[33] *Re Earl of Chesterfield's Trusts* (1883) 24 Ch.D. 643.

[34] *i.e.* the income is transferred to capital at the end of each year.

accordingly, and the residue should be treated as income." In other words, the proceeds of sale of the reversion, are part principal, part interest. The principal is the sum which, if invested at 4 per cent at the date of the testator's death, would have produced the sum now received. The balance goes to the tenant for life.[35]

iv. Contrary Intention. All the rules above discussed are subject to a contrary intention by the testator.[36] A number of very fine points of construction arise; but the matter can only be discussed in outline here. The onus is on the person alleging that the equitable rules are excluded.[37]

(a) *Express Trust to Convert.* An express trust to convert personalty normally carries with it the duty to apportion the income received pending conversion.[38] There is no question in this situation of a contrary intention with regard to conversion; but there may be a contrary intention with regard to apportionment. This will arise where there is an indication of intention that, although the property should be converted, the life tenant is to enjoy the whole income produced by it pending conversion.

Such an intention is commonly indicated by the inclusion of a provision to the effect that "the income of so much of the residue as for the time being shall remain unsold, shall be applied as if the same were income arising from investments of the proceeds of sale thereof."[39]

It may of course be indicated in other ways. The question depends upon the construction of the particular instrument. A power in the trustees to postpone a sale in their discretion is not a sufficient

---

[35] The calculation can be made by taking the value of the reversion on sale or on falling in (£x), and working backwards year by year until the date of the testator's death. If the standard rate of income tax is 25 per cent, the net income earned at 4 per cent on £100 of capital is £3.00. The sum needed to produce £x after *one* year of investment can be found by applying the formula:

$$\frac{£x \times 100}{103}$$

The application of this formula *to the sum* so calculated will produce the sums needed to produce £x after *two* years of investment. The calculation then needs to be continued back to the date of the testator's death. See Parker and Mellows, *Modern Law of Trusts* (6th ed.), pp. 465–466.

[36] *Hinves v. Hinves* (1884) 3 Hare 609; *Alcock v. Sloper* (1833) 2 Myl. & K. 699; *Re Pitcairn* [1896] 2 Ch. 199.

[37] *MacDonald v. Irvine* (1878) 8 Ch.D. 101 at p. 124; *Re Wareham* [1912] 2 Ch. 312 at p. 315.

[38] *Gibson v. Bott* (1802) 7 Ves.Jr. 89.

[39] Key & Elphinstone, *Precedents in Conveyancing* (15th ed.), Vol. 2, pp. 926–928; (1943) 7 Conv.(N.S.) 128 (S. Bailey).

indication. Such a provision does not entitle the life tenant to the income produced by unauthorised investments.[40]

(b) *No Express Trust to Convert.* Here it is necessary to examine whether the will indicates an intention to retain the asset; or to permit the life tenant to retain the whole income. Either such intent will exclude apportionment. In *Gray v. Siggers*[41] the trustees were given power to retain any portion of the testator's property in the same state in which it should be at his decease, or to sell and convert the same *as they should in their absolute discretion think fit.* Such a power excluded the duty to convert.

An indication that the life tenant is to enjoy the whole income of the property also prevents apportionment and has the effect of excluding the duty to convert.[42] It may also have the effect of authorising the investments. A power to retain investments or to postpone conversion is thus more likely to exclude the duty to convert and to apportion in cases where there is no express trust to convert. But it may be so framed that it is intended to do no more than allow a suitable time to be selected for the sale.[43] Such a power, being merely administrative, will neither prevent conversion nor apportionment.

(c) *Reversionary Interests.* Similarly the rule in *Re Earl of Chesterfield's Trusts*[44] may be excluded.[45] A clause expressly excluding the rule in *Howe v. Earl of Dartmouth*[46] usually operates to exclude the rule in *Re Earl of Chesterfield's Trusts* also[47]; but it is the general practice to add a special clause for this purpose.

v. Leaseholds. The rule in *Howe v. Earl of Dartmouth*[48] applied before 1926 to leaseholds. After 1925 leases with 60 years or more to run were authorised investments for trustees of land,[49] so the rule could not apply to leases of that length. In the case of shorter leases, it was held in *Re Brooker*,[50] which involved in *express* trust for sale of leaseholds, that there was no duty to apportion because the effect of the Law of Property Act 1925[51] was to entitle the tenant for life

---

[40] *Re Chaytor* [1905] 1 Ch. 233; *Re Berry* [1962] Ch. 97.
[41] (1880) 15 Ch.D. 74; *Alcock v. Sloper* (1833) 2 Myl. & K. 699; *Re Pitcairn* [1896] 2 Ch. 199.
[42] *Alcock v. Sloper, supra; cf. Re Evans' W.T.* [1921] 2 Ch. 309; *Re Gough* [1957] Ch. 323.
[43] As with the ships in *Brown v. Gellatly* (1867) L.R. 2 Ch.App. 751, *ante,* p. 541.
[44] (1883) 24 Ch.D. 643; *ante,* p. 541.
[45] *Re Pitcairn* [1896] 2 Ch. 199.
[46] (1802) 7 Ves.Jr. 137.
[47] See *Rowlls v. Bebb* [1900] 2 Ch. 107.
[48] (1802) 7 Ves.Jr. 137; *ante,* p. 538.
[49] S.L.A. 1925, s.73; L.P.A. 1925, s.28(1) (now repealed).
[50] [1926] W.N. 93.
[51] s.28(2) (now repealed).

to all of the rents and profits until sale. It was unclear whether the rule in *Howe v. Earl of Dartmouth* still applied to residuary short leaseholds where there was no express trust for sale, but the better view was that the rule had gone.[52]

As trustees of land now have power to purchase a legal estate in any land, without any restrictions as to the length of any lease,[53] it appears that even if the rule in *Howe v. Earl of Dartmouth* in relation to leases survived the 1925 legislation, it can no longer apply. Thus the tenant for life is entitled to all the income from a short leasehold included in a trust of a residuary estate.

vi. Howe v. Earl of Dartmouth Today.[54] The rules relating to conversion and apportionment demonstrate basic principles of equity. But they should be understood in their proper perspective.

(a) *Exclusion of Duty to Apportion.* The duty to apportion is in practice nearly always excluded, both in respect of income from unauthorised securities and in respect of reversionary interests. The duty to convert, where it exists, thus appears in the context of a duty to change the investments.

(b) *Effect of Current Investment Situation.* The utility of the rules of conversion and apportionment varies according to the current investment situation. "At a time when investment in equities may be the only way in which the capital value of the fund can in fact be maintained the traditional theory that re-investment is necessary to protect those interested in the capital no longer holds good. Conversely, the yield on fixed interest investments is now such as to provide the tenant for life with an income which is as high and may be higher than the average yield on authorised equities."[55] Thus the life tenant wants fixed interest investments when they provide a high income; the remainderman wants unauthorised securities for the preservation of the real value of the capital. It is the life tenant who will be pressing the trustees to convert urgently into gilt-edged securities at times when they can being an income in excess of the mere 4 per cent allowed to the life tenant by the rule of apportionment.

(c) *Reform.* The apportionment rules were reviewed by the Law Reform Committee,[56] whose conclusion was that, rather than complete abolition, the rules in *Howe v. Earl of Dartmouth* and *Re Earl*

---

[52] *Re Trollope* [1927] 1 Ch. 596 at p. 601.

[53] Trusts of Land and Appointment of Trustees Act 1996, s.6(3); *ante*, p. 517.

[54] (1952) 16 Conv.(N.S.) 349 (L. Sheridan).

[55] Law Reform Committee, 23rd Report, *supra*, para. 3.31 (writing in 1982).

[56] *Supra*. The matter is under review by the Trust Law Committee. Proposed investment reforms should produce higher income without eroding capital.

of Chesterfield's Trusts should be subsumed into a statutory duty to hold a fair balance between the beneficiaries. The trustees should have express power to convert income to capital and vice versa. They should have regard to the whole investment policy of the trust, and should convert and apportion to the extent necessary to maintain an even hand.

Another way of resolving some of the problems discussed in this chapter might be the use of the "percentage trust",[57] under which all receipts (capital and income) are paid into the trust fund and all outgoings (capital and income) are paid out. The fund is valued annually and a percentage of it (fixed or variable) as specified by the settlor is given to the life tenant each year. The balance goes to the remainderman on termination of the life tenant's interest. Thus equality between the beneficiaries is maintained.

B. Other Methods of Apportionment

Apportionment is necessary in other situations, and these will be mentioned in outline only.

i. Apportionment Act 1870. When a testator or a life tenant dies, the question arises of the entitlement to periodical income, such as rents, interest and dividends, earned in whole or in part, but not paid, at the time of the death. That which is treated as being earned before the death will be added to the estate, and that earned afterwards is payable as income to the income beneficiary under the will or, in the case of the death of a life tenant, to the next life tenant, or to the capital.

The division is governed by the Apportionment Act, section 2, which provides that "all rents, annuities, dividends, and other periodical payments in the nature of income . . . shall . . . be considered as accruing from day to day, and shall be apportionable in respect of time accordingly." It is necessary therefore to ascertain the proportion of the earning period which expired prior to the death, and to divide the payment, when received, in the same proportion.[58] When rent is due, or a dividend earned, but not paid prior to the death, the whole income is paid to the testator's estate or to the life tenant. The Act may be excluded by an expression of an intention to do so. This is now common in order to avoid the complications which are introduced into the administration of an estate. Reform has been proposed.[59]

---

[57] See Moffat, *Trusts Law, Text and Materials* (2nd ed.) pp. 380–381; (1990) 106 L.Q.R. 87 at 94 (D. Hayton).

[58] For class gifts, see *Re Joel* [1967] Ch. 14.

[59] Law Reform Committee, 23rd report, *supra*. See paras. 3.40, 3.41.

ii. The Rule in Allhusen v. Whittell. This rule attempts to strike a fair balance between life tenant and remainderman in respect of the payment of the debts of an estate. The life tenant under a will is entitled to income earned after the testator's death. The debts of the testator must also be paid; and it may take some time to do so. In the meantime the assets of the estate are earning income for the life tenant. He should, in fairness, only have the income from the net estate. The rule in *Allhusen v. Whittell*[60] provides that the life tenant shall make a contribution.

Romer L.J. in *Corbett v. Commissioners of Inland Revenue*[61] laid down the rule as follows:

> "For the purposes of adjusting rights as between the tenant for life and the remainderman of a residuary estate, debts, legacies, estate duties, probate duties and so forth, are to be deemed to have been paid out of such capital of the testator's estate as will be sufficient for that purpose, when to that capital is added interest on that capital from the date of the testator's death to the date of the payment of the legacy or debt, or whatever it may have been, interest being calculated at the average rate of interest[62] earned by the testator's estate during the relevant period."[63]

The rule may be excluded by an expression of contrary intent, or where its application would in the circumstances be inappropriate.[64]

Witnesses to the Law Reform Committee described the rule as "complex, fiddlesome and resulting in a disproportionate amount of work and expense," adding that where the rule was not excluded it was often simply ignored.[65] The committee accordingly recommended that, as in the case of the rules in *Howe v. Earl of Dartmouth* and *Re Earl of Chesterfield's Trusts*,[66] it should be subsumed into a new statutory duty to hold a fair balance between the beneficiaries, as described above.[67]

---

[60] (1867) L.R. 4 Eq. 295.

[61] [1938] 1 K.B. 567.

[62] *Re Wills* [1915] 1 Ch. 769.

[63] Assuming a debt of £50, an average rate of income of 10 per cent, income tax at 25 per cent, and payment of the debt one year from the death, the apportionment will be:

$$\text{From Capital: } 46.47 \left(\text{being } \frac{100}{107.16} \times 50\right)$$

$$\text{From Income: } 3.53 \left(\text{being } \frac{7.6}{107.6} \times 50\right)$$

[64] *Re McEuen* [1913] 2 Ch. 704; *Re Darby* [1939] Ch. 905.

[65] 23rd Report, *supra*. See para 3.31.

[66] *Supra*.

[67] 23rd Report, *supra*, para. 3.36. See *ante*, p. 545.

iii. The Rule in Re Atkinson. Where an authorised mortgage security is sold by the trustee mortgagees and the proceeds are insufficient to satisfy the principal and interest in full, it is necessary to determine the way in which the loss is to be shared between life tenant and remainderman. The sum realised must be apportioned between the life tenant and the remainderman in the proportion which the amount due for the arrears of interest bears to the amount due in respect of the principal.[68]

iv. Interest on Damages. Where loss of the trust fund results in an award of compensation, interest will be payable on the sum awarded from the date of the writ until judgment. The interest should be apportioned between life tenant and remainderman. In *Jaffray v. Marshall*,[69] a fair apportionment was considered to be half and half, taking a broad view.

v. Purchase or Sale of Shares Cum Dividend. One of the factors which affects the price of shares is the date of payment of the next dividend. A share whose dividend will be paid tomorrow is worth more than it would be if the dividend has been paid yesterday. It would seem reasonable to require an apportionment when shares are bought or sold cum dividend, but the general rule is that there is none.[70] In this respect, the beneficiaries take "the rough with the smooth."[71] This is probably more convenient overall than an insistence on an apportionment in every case. But an apportionment will be required if there would otherwise be "a glaring injustice."[72]

vi. Company Distributions. Questions can also arise as to the entitlements of life tenant and remainderman to certain distributions by companies. The question of entitlement and that of the liability of the distribution to income tax are related questions, but are not identical.[73] The tax aspect is the reason for the attraction to shareholders generally of distributions as capital. The question whether the life tenant or remainderman is entitled (or whether an apportionment must be made) will arise, for example, where the company has taken steps to capitalise profits,[74] or where shareholders are given

---

[68] *Re Atkinson* [1904] 2 Ch. 160.
[69] [1993] 1 W.L.R. 1285 (overruled as to the assessment of damages in *Target Holdings Ltd v. Redferns (a firm)* [1996] 1 A.C. 421).
[70] *Bulkeley v. Stephens* [1896] 2 Ch. 241; *Re Ellerman's S.T.* (1984) 81 L.S.Gaz. 430, where the decision to the contrary in *Re Winterstoke's W.T.* [1938] Ch. 158 was regarded as wrong; (1986) 1 *Trust Law & Practice* 62 (I. Pittaway). See also Law Reform Committee, 23rd Report, *supra*.
[71] *Re Maclaren's S.T.* [1951] 2 All E.R. 414 at p. 420.
[72] *Ibid.*
[73] *Re Bates* [1928] Ch. 682; *Re Doughty* [1947] Ch. 263; *Re Sechiari* [1950] 1 All E.R. 417; I.C.T.A. 1988, ss.209–211, 234, 254.
[74] *Bouch v. Sproule* (1887) 12 App.Cas. 385.

the right to choose between a cash dividend and an allotment of shares. The modern context in which the question arises is the company demerger, where a company in effect splits into two, and shares in the new company are given to shareholders in the original company. Whether these shares are to be treated as income or capital is relevant to beneficial entitlement and, as mentioned above, to taxation. When ICI transferred its bioscience business to a new company, Zeneca, and shares in the latter were given to ICI shareholders (the ICI shares being reduced in value by the demerger) in satisfaction of a dividend, it was held in *Sinclair v. Lee*[75] that the new shares were capital assets, and hence did not pass under a gift by will of income from the ICI shares. The effect of the reconstruction was that two capital assets replaced one. Investment philosophy had greatly changed since the older cases,[76] and any other result would not reflect reality. The Revenue view, however, is that shares distributed under a "direct" demerger are treated as income. This view has been described as absurd, and reform has been called for.[77]

2. Duty to Provide Accounts and Information

A. Accounts

i. Extent of Duty. A trustee must keep accounts and be constantly ready to produce them for the beneficiaries.[78] It seems that a beneficiary is entitled only to see and inspect the accounts; if he wants a copy himself, he must pay for it; but it is common practice to provide a copy for each of the beneficiaries.[79] An income beneficiary is entitled to full accounts, but a remainderman is entitled only to such information as relates to capital transactions.[80] A member of a class of discretionary beneficiaries is entitled to accounts,[81] but a person who is merely a potential object of a discretionary trust has no such right, at any rate where there is a large number of possible beneficiaries.[82]

---

[75] [1993] Ch. 497.

[76] Such as *Hill v. Permanent Trustee Co. of N.S.W.* [1930] A.C. 720.

[77] (1995) 9 *Trust Law International* 55 (P. Duffield). The demerger in *Sinclair v. Lee* was "indirect", as to which see Parker and Mellows, *The Modern Law of Trusts* (6th ed.), p. 478.

[78] *Pearse v. Green* (1819) 1 Jac. & W. 135, *per* Plumer M.R. at p. 140.

[79] *Ottley v. Gilby* (1845) 8 Beav. 602; *Kemp v. Burn* (1863) 4 Giff. 348.

[80] Mellows, *The Trustee's Handbook* (3rd ed.), p. 52.

[81] *Chaine-Nickson v. Bank of Ireland* [1976] I.R. 393.

[82] *Hartigan Nominees Pty Ltd v. Rydge* (1992) 29 N.S.W.L.R. 405. It has been held in the Cayman Islands that the right to see accounts is not absolute: *Lemos v. Coutts & Co.* [1992–93] Cayman I. L.R. 400 at pp. 518–519.

ii. Audit. Apart from the case of pension trusts and charitable trusts,[83] it is neither necessary nor, except in large and complicated trusts or where trouble with a beneficiary is foreseen, usual to have trust accounts audited. However, trustees may, in their absolute discretion, have the trust accounts examined and audited by an independent accountant, and may pay the costs out of income or capital. Audit should not be effected more than once in every three years, except in special cases.[84]

Any trustee or beneficiary may apply for the accounts of any trust to be investigated and audited by such solicitor or public accountant as may be agreed upon, or in default of agreement by the Public Trustee or by some person appointed by him.[85] The costs are usually borne by the trust, but the Public Trustee may order that the appellant or the trustees must pay them or share them.[86]

B. Information. Trust Documents

The beneficiaries are entitled to be informed about matters currently affecting the trust.[87] Beneficiaries of pension trusts have a statutory right to information.[88] A large trust will keep many documents, such as the minutes of trustees' meetings. Documents connected with the trust are trust documents, and prima facie the property of the beneficiaries, and as such open to their inspection.[89]

We saw, however, in Chapter 17, that trustees are not bound to give reasons for the exercise of their discretions. The policy of that principle has already been discussed.[90] In the present context, the problem is to reconcile that principle with the principle that beneficiaries are entitled to see the trust documents. If reasons for the

---

[83] Pensions Act 1995, s.41 and regulations thereunder; *ante*, p. 465; Charities Act 1993, ss.42–44; *ante*, p. 449.

[84] T.A. 1925, s.22(4). For the audit by the court of the accounts of a judicial trustee, see Administration of Justice Act 1982, s.57; Judicial Trustee Rules 1983 (S.I. 1983 No. 370). By r. 2 there is to be no automatic audit by the court of the accounts of a "corporate trust," meaning the Official Solicitor, Public Trustee or a corporation appointed by the court to be a trustee, or which is entitled to be a custodian trustee by the Public Trustee Act 1906, s.4(3).

[85] Public Trsutee Act 1906, s.13. The Law Reform Commitee recommended the repeal of s.13, which is rarely used and is ineffective because there are no powers to enforce the findings of the Public Trustee. (23rd report, 1982, Cmnd. 8733, para. 4.48).

[86] See *Re Oddy* [1911] 1 Ch. 532.

[87] But this does not go so far as to put the trustees "under any duty to proffer information to their beneficiary, or to see that he has proper advice merely because they are trustees for him and know that he is entering into a transaction with his beneficial interest with some person or body connected in some way with the trustees, such as a company in which the trustees own some shares beneficially.": *Tito v. Waddell (No. 2)* [1977] Ch. 106 at p. 243, *per* Megarry V.-C.; questioned at (1977) 41 Conv.(N.S.) 438 (F. Crane).

[88] Pensions Act 1995, s.41 and regulations thereunder; *ante*, p. 471.

[89] *O'Rourke v. Darbishire* [1920] A.C. 581 at pp. 619, 626.

[90] *Ante*, pp. 505–507.

exercise of discretionary powers are recorded in documents relating to the trust, are the beneficiaries entitled to see the documents?

In *Re Londonderry's Settlement*,[91] the donees of a power under a discretionary trust decided to distribute the capital. One member of the discretionary class was dissatisfied with the sum which they intended to give her. She asked for copies of the minutes of trustees' meetings, documents prepared for the meetings, and correspondence between various interested persons. The trustees were willing only to show her documents giving the intended distributions and the annual trust accounts. They declined, in the general interest of the family, to disclose further documents, and brought a summons to determine the nature and extent of their duties in relation to disclosures.

The Court of Appeal found great difficulty in defining in general terms what were the "trust documents" which a beneficiary prima facie had a right to see. Salmon L.J. said that the category of trust documents could not be defined. They have however "these characteristics in common: (1) they are documents in the possession of the trustees as trustees; (2) they contain information about the trust, which the beneficiaries are entitled to know; (3) the beneficiaries have a proprietary interest[92] in the documents and, accordingly, are entitled to see them. If any parts of a document contain information which the beneficiaries are not entitled to know, I doubt whether such parts can be truly said to be integral parts of a trust document."[93] Applying this reasoning, it was held in *Hartigan Nominees Pty Ltd v. Rydge*[94] that the beneficiaries were not entitled to see the settlor's confidential memorandum of wishes, a document of no legal force setting out how he wished the trustees to exercise their discretions. It was also doubted whether a potential beneficiary of a discretionary trust had any right to information, at any rate if one of a large number of such persons.

Subject to the above, a trustee's duty is not merely one of answering questions; but also to provide beneficiaries with information concerning their interests under the trust; or, in the case of an infant beneficiary, to inform him of his entitlement on coming

---

[91] [1965] Ch. 918; (1965) 81 L.Q.R. 192 (R.E.M.). See further *Trends in Contemporary Trust Law* (ed. A. Oakley) at pp. 49 *et seq.* (D. Hayton).

[92] The right to information does not, however, depend on the beneficiary having a proprietary right. It extends to beneficiaries of an unadministered estate; *Att-Gen. for Ontario v. Stavro* (1994) 119 D.L.R. (4th) 750. Likewise a discretionary beneficiary, as in *Londonderry* itself.

[93] *Ibid*, at p. 938.

[94] (1992) 29 N.S.W.L.R. 405; [1994] 3 J.Int.P. 60 (J. Lehane).

of age.[95] There is, however, no duty to search out possible objects of a discretionary trust and inform them of their position.[96] Executors are under no positive duty, as a will is a public document.[97]

---

[95] *Hawkesley v. May* [1956] 1 Q.B. 304; including, it seems, his rights under the rule in *Saunders v. Vautier* (1841) Cr. & Ph. 240; *post*, p. 612; (1970) 34 Conv.(N.S.) 29 (A. Samuels).
[96] *Hartigan Nominees Pty Ltd v. Rydge* (1992) 29 N.S.W.L.R. 405.
[97] *Re Lewis* [1904] 2 Ch. 656; *Re Mackay* [1906] 1 Ch. 25.

CHAPTER 20

POWERS OF TRUSTEES

1. Trustees of Land 554
2. Power of sale 555
   A. Land 555
   B. Chattels 556
   C. Other Property 556
   D. Sales by Trustees 556
3. Power to Give Receipts: Section 14 557
4. Power to Insure: Section 19 557
   A. Insurance 557
   B. Reinstatement 558
5. Power to Compound Liabilities: Section 15 558
6. Power in Regard to Reversionary Interests: Section 22 559
7. Power to Delegate 559
   A. The Early Rule in Equity 559
   B. Trustee Act 1925: Section 23(1) 560
   C. Trustee Act 1925, s.30(1) 563
      i. Scope of Section 30(1): "Wilful Default" 563
      ii. Capital and Income 564
   D. Delegation of Discretions 565
   E. Reform 567
   F. Delegation under the Enduring Powers of Attorney Act 1985 568
8. Powers of Maintenance and Advancement 570
   A. Maintenance. Trustee Act 1925, s.31 . 571
      i. Subsection (1) 571
         (a) Prior Interests 571
         (b) Minority 571
         (c) Adult Contingently Entitled ... 572
      ii. Subsection (2) 572
         (a) Surplus Income to be Accumulated for Minors 572

   (b) Entitlement to Accumulation 572
   iii. Gifts Carrying Intermediate Income 574
      (a) Contingent Residuary Bequest 574
      (b) Contingent or Future Specific Gifts of Personalty or Realty and Contingent Residuary Devises of Freehold Land 574
      (c) Contingent Pecuniary Legacy 575
   iv. Aggregation of Income of Children with that of their Parents 575
   v. Gifts to Classes 576
   B. Advancement 576
      i. The Meaning of Advancement 576
      ii. Original Meaning of Advancement 577
      iii. Express Powers 577
      iv. The Statutory Power. Trustee Act 1925, s.32 578
      v. Problems in the Application of Section 32: *Pilkington v. I.R.C.* 579
         (a) Benefit 580
         (b) Settlement of Funds Advanced. Sub-Trusts 580
         (c) Delegation 581
         (d) Perpetuity 582
      vi. The Provisos 582
   C. The Court's Inherent Power to Provide Maintenance and Advancement 583
   D. Responsibility of the Trustees to See to the Application of the Money Advanced 583

TRUSTEES may exercise such powers as are given to them by the trust instrument or by statute. A power, as has been seen,[1] is to be distinguished from a duty, in that its exercise is not compulsory. In the absence of bad faith, the court will not interfere with the exercise of discretions. At most, the holder of a fiduciary power is under a duty to consider its exercise.[2]

[1] *Ante*, p. 59.
[2] *Ante*, p. 169. As to whether trustees can fetter their powers by deciding in advance how to exercise them, see (1993) 7 *Trust Law International* p. 69 (H. Arthur).

Originally, it was necessary to spell out a trustee's powers in detail in the trust instrument. Now, however, the Trustee Act 1925 (as amended) provides the basic powers needed by trustees. They may unless otherwise stated be excluded or amended as desired.[3]

1. TRUSTEES OF LAND

Trustees of land have in certain respects wider powers than trustees of personalty. Section 6(1) of the Trusts of Land and Appointment of Trustees Act 1996 provides that "For the purpose of exercising their functions as trustees, the trustees of land have in relation to the land subject to the trust all the powers of an absolute owner." Where the trust includes land and personalty, these powers are thus confined to the land. The width of the statutory powers is reduced by an important proviso: the powers conferred by section 6 "shall not be exercised in contravention of, or of any order made in pursuance of, any other enactment or any rule of law or equity."[4] The trustees, in exercising their powers under section 6, must also have regard to the rights of the beneficiaries,[5] and they have a general duty to consult adult beneficiaries with an interest in possession.[6] Thus trustees of land remain subject to the general duties imposed by equity on trustees and to restrictions on the statutory powers of trustees contained in other legislation or in other sections of the 1996 Act.[7]

Section 6 applies whether the trust of land is express, implied, resulting or constructive, and whether arising before or after the commencement of the 1996 Act; trusts for sale and bare trusts are also included.[8] In the case of an expressly created trust of land, however, section 6 may be excluded by the settlor or the powers made exercisable subject to consent.[9] In such a case the trustees must take all reasonable steps to bring the limitation to the notice of any purchaser of the land from them, but the conveyance is not invalid if the purchaser had no actual notice of the limitation.[10]

---

[3] T.A 1925, s.69(2). The 1925 Act is outdated in some areas. The Trust Law Committee is working on a proposed statutory list of modern "default powers" for the benefit of trustees who do not have sufficient express powers.

[4] s.6(6). See also s.6(7).

[5] s.6(5). A purchaser of unregistered land is not concerned to see that this duty has been complied with; s.16(1).

[6] s.11(1). This duty may be excluded by the settlor.

[7] See s.6(8). If a conveyance of unregistered land by the trustees (other than charity trustees) contravenes s.6(6) or (8), it is not invalid if the purchaser had no actual notice of the contravention; s.16(2).

[8] s.1. The Act came into force on January 1, 1997. For the application of the Act to personal representatives; see s.18.

[9] s.8. The settlor of a charitable trust may not exclude s.6.

[10] s.16(3). This is confined to unregistered land.

In addition to the general powers described above, the 1996 Act confers certain specific powers on trustees of land. Under the general law, beneficiaries who are of full age and capacity and together absolutely entitled may call for a transfer of the trust property.[11] In the case of land, section 6(2) gives the trustees power to convey to such beneficiaries provided each is absolutely entitled,[12] even though they have not required the trustees to do so. If the beneficiaries do not co-operate, the court may order them to do whatever is necessary to secure that the land vests in them. Where the trustees convey unregistered land to persons they believe to be such beneficiaries, they must execute a deed declaring that they are discharged from the trust of that land, and a purchaser of it is entitled to assume that the land is no longer subject to the trust unless he has actual notice that the trustees were mistaken in their belief.[13]

Where beneficiaries of full age are absolutely entitled as tenants in common, the trustees may partition the land or any part of it, obtaining the consent of each beneficiary and providing (by mortgage or otherwise) for the payment of any equality money.[14] This power may be excluded or made subject to other consents in an expressly created trust of land.[15]

The delegation powers of trustees of land are dealt with later in this Chapter. Their power to purchase land was discussed in the context of investment in Chapter 18.[16]

2. POWER OF SALE

A. Land

Land is held either by an owner absolutely entitled or under a trust of land or, in the case of a settlement created before the commencement of the Trusts of Land and Appointment of Trustees Act 1996, under a strict settlement. In the latter case the tenant for life has the legal estate and a power of sale.[17] In the case of a trust of land, the legal estate is vested in the trustees, and they have a power of sale.[18] Where an express trust for sale is created, the trustees have power to postpone the sale indefinitely in the exercise of their discretion,

---

[11] *Saunders v. Vautier* (1841) Cr. & Ph. 240; *post*, p. 612.
[12] *i.e.* they are equitable co-owners. That their interests together add up to the whole does not otherwise suffice.
[13] Trusts of Land and Appointment of Trustees Act 1996, s.16(4), (5).
[14] *Ibid.*, s.7. A purchaser of unregistered land is not concerned to see that the beneficiaries have consented; s.16(1).
[15] *Ibid.*, s.8.
[16] *Ante*, p. 517.
[17] S.L.A. 1925, s.38(1).
[18] Trusts of Land and Appointment of Trustees Act 1996, s.6(1); *supra*. This includes bare trusts; s.1(2). Personal representatives on intestacy have a power to sell land; A.E.A. 1925, s.33, as amended by the 1996 Act.

despite any provision to the contrary in the trust instrument.[19] The receipt of at least two trustees or of a trust corporation is required for all capital money arising under a trust of land or strict settlement,[20] and the same rule applies to the overreaching of the beneficial interests.[21]

B. Chattels

Where chattels or other personalty are held upon trust for sale, the position is the same as with land except that the receipt of a sole trustee is sufficient discharge to a purchaser.[22] The trust for sale may arise expressly or be implied, as we have seen, under the rule in *Howe v. Earl of Dartmouth.*[23] Personal representatives have power to sell chattels (and other property) on intestacy.[24]

C. Other Property

In the case of many other forms of property, a power of sale, if not given expressly, will usually be implied. Unauthorised investments, investments which the trustees think are not suitable for the trust, and trust property which is not in a state of investment at all, should be sold and invested in accordance with the express terms of the relevant investment power, or with the provisions of the Trustee Investments Act 1961.[25]

Whenever trustees are authorised to pay or apply capital money for any purpose or in any manner, they have power to raise such money by sale, mortgage, etc., of the trust property then in possession.[26] But this does not authorise trustees to raise money by charging existing investments in order to purchase others.[27]

D. Sales by Trustees

The detailed provisions relating to sales by trustees are contained in the Trustee Act 1925, s.12.[28] Trustees may sell all or any part of the property, by public auction or by private contract, subject to any

---

[19] *Ibid.*, s.4.
[20] T.A. 1925, s.14; L.P.A. 1925, s.27(2); S.L.A. 1925, s.94(1).
[21] L.P.A. 1925, s.2.
[22] T.A. 1925, s.14; *post*, p. 557.
[23] (1802) 7 Ves.Jr. 137; *ante*, p. 538.
[24] A.E.A. 1925, s.33, as amended by Trusts of Land and Appointment of Trustees Act 1996, Sched. 2.
[25] *Ante*, pp. 519 *et seq.*
[26] T.A. 1925, s.16(1).
[27] *Re Suenson-Taylor* [1974] 1 W.L.R. 1280 (land).
[28] As amended by Trusts of Land and Appointment of Trustees Act 1996, Sched. 3.

such conditions respecting title or other matter as the trustee thinks fit.

As we have seen, trustees are under an overriding duty to obtain the best price for the beneficiaries.[29] If they fail to do so, the beneficiaries may seek an injunction restraining the sale.[30] But if the sale has taken place, it may not be impeached by a beneficiary on the ground that any of the conditions of the sale were unduly depreciatory, unless it also appears that the consideration for the sale was thereby rendered inadequate.[31] A purchaser will not be affected unless he was acting in collusion with the trustees.[32]

3. Power to Give Receipts: Section 14

By the Trustee Act 1925, s.14, the written receipt by a trustee for money, securities, etc., is a sufficient discharge to the person paying, and effectually exonerates him from being answerable for any loss or misapplication of the money. The section applies notwithstanding anything to the contrary in the trust instrument,[33] and applies to sole trustees, except in the case of proceeds of sale or other capital money arising under a trust of land or under the Settled Land Act where, unless the trustee is a trust corporation, the receipt of at least two trustees is necessary.[34] Where there is more than one trustee, all must sign, in accordance with the rule that they must act together.[35]

4. Power to Insure: Section 19

A. Insurance

There is no duty upon trustees to insure the trust property. The rule is that they are not liable if the property is destroyed; and if the trustees differ on the question whether the property should be insured, it seems that nothing can be done to compel them.[36] However, it is difficult to see how, in some circumstances, failure to insure would be consistent with their general duty of caring for the

---

[29] *Buttle v. Saunders* [1950] 2 All E.R. 193; *ante*, p. 513. See also *Sergeant v. National Westminster Bank* (1991) 61 P. & C.R. 518. As to whether trustees can sell at a valuation to be determined by a third party, see [1985] Conv. 44 (G. Lightman).

[30] *Wheelwright v. Walker* (1883) 23 Ch.D. 752.

[31] T.A. 1925, s.13(1); *Dance v. Goldingham* (1873) L.R. 8 Ch.App. 902. The trustee may, of course, be liable.

[32] T.A. 1925, s.13(2).

[33] T.A. 1925, s.14(3).

[34] *Ibid.* s.14(2) as amended by Trusts of Land and Appointment of Trustees Act 1996, Sched. 3.

[35] *Ante*, p. 485; charitable and pension trustees may act by a majority.

[36] *Re McEacharn* (1911) 103 L.T. 900.

trust property. A power to insure up to three fourths of the value of personal property against loss or damage, and to pay the premiums out of income, is contained in section 19 of the Trustee Act 1925.[37] This does not apply where the beneficiaries are absolutely entitled and *sui juris*, and so can end the trust at any time.[38] Trustees of land may insure the land up to its full value by exercising the powers of an absolute owner under section 6(1) of the Trusts of Land and Appointment of Trustees Act 1996.

The policy moneys must be treated as capital and applied in accordance with the terms of the trust.[39]

B. Reinstatement

Trustees may apply the policy money relating to land or other property in reinstatement, subject to the consent of any person whose consent is required by the trust instrument,[40] and without prejudice to the statutory or other right of any person to require the money to be spent in reinstatement.[41] Persons interested under the trust can, therefore, insist on having the premises rebuilt if they wish; or, if they do not wish it, can prevent the trustees from using the money for that purpose, but in any case the money is capital money.

5. POWER TO COMPOUND LIABILITIES: SECTION 15

Trustees are given a wide discretion in settling claims which may be made by third persons against the trust estate, or by the trust estate against third persons. Adult beneficiaries who are under no disability may, of course, make any arrangement that they wish among themselves. Until the Variation of Trusts Act 1958[42] was passed, the court had no general power to approve adjustments in the beneficial interests. But the dividing line is difficult to draw. The Court has inherent power to compromise a genuine dispute between beneficiaries[43] and section 15 has been held to authorise the settlement of a dispute with a person claiming to be a beneficiary,[44] and also litigation between the trustees and beneficiaries on the question

---

[37] As amended by Trusts of Land and Appointment of Trustees Act 1996, Sched. 3, para. 4.
[38] T.A. 1925, s.19(2).
[39] T.A. 1925, s.20.
[40] T.A. 1925, s.20(4).
[41] *Ibid.* s.20(5).
[42] *Post,* Chap. 22.
[43] *Re Barbour's Settlement* [1974] 1 W.L.R. 1198; *Re Downshire S.E.* [1953] Ch. 218.
[44] *Eaton v. Buchanan* [1911] A.C. 253; *cf. Abdallah v. Rickards* (1888) 4 T.L.R. 622.

whether certain property was subject to the trust or not.[45] It was no objection to the jurisdiction under section 15 that the proposed compromise involved an adjustment of interests among the beneficiaries.[46]

Personal representatives and trustees may accept compositions for debts; allow time for payment of debts; compromise, abandon, submit to arbitration or otherwise settle any claim; and may enter into such agreements and execute such instruments as may be necessary for the efficient performance of these duties.[47] A wide power of this nature is of great practical importance in enabling the trustee to make a reasonable compromise instead of being obliged to litigate in respect of every possible claim, or risk liability for breach of trust if he fails to do so.[48] Trustees are not liable for loss caused by any act done by them in the exercise of the powers conferred by this section as long as it is done in good faith, and they have reached their decision by exercising their discretion and not by failing to consider the matter.[49] They may apply to the court to sanction a compromise. The court must consider what is the best from the point of view of everybody concerned, paying especial attention to the interests of minors.[50]

6. POWER IN REGARD TO REVERSIONARY INTERESTS: SECTION 22

Where part of the trust property consists of choses in action or reversionary interests the trustees may, on such interests falling into possession, "agree or ascertain the amount or value thereof in such manner as they think fit," without being responsible for any loss, if they act in good faith. But nothing in the section is to be construed as relieving trustees from the duty of getting in such interests as soon as possible after their falling into possession, for this is one of their primary duties.[51]

7. POWER TO DELEGATE

A. The Early Rule in Equity

The basic rule is that a person entrusted with a fiduciary duty does not fulfil it if he delegates it to someone else; he remains liable for

---

[45] *Re Earl of Strafford* [1980] Ch. 28.
[46] *Ibid.*
[47] See *Re Shenton* [1935] Ch. 651.
[48] *Re Brogden* [1948] Ch. 206; *ante*, p. 512.
[49] *Re Greenwood* (1911) 105 L.T. 509.
[50] *Re Ezekiel's S.T.* [1942] Ch. 230; *Re Earl of Strafford (supra)*.
[51] See *ante*, p. 511.

the other person's default.[52] But this rule was never, even in the times when the most rigorous views were being taken of the standard of conduct required from a trustee, inflexible. Indeed, there are certain things which a businessman would always delegate to a skilled agent. Thus, the employment of solicitors for legal, and brokers and bankers for financial, business is sanctioned by the ordinary business practice. This was recognised as early as 1754, by Lord Hardwicke in *Ex p. Belchier*,[53] and the trend of judicial decision, fortified by occasional statutory provisions, grew more and more tolerant of delegation in cases of commercial necessity. Following the two famous decisions of the House of Lords in *Speight v. Gaunt*[54] and *Learoyd v. Whiteley*,[55] it could be said that delegation was permissible if the trustees could show that it was reasonably necessary in the circumstances or was in accordance with ordinary business practice. The trustees had to exercise proper care in the selection of the agent, employ him in his proper field,[56] and exercise general supervision.[57] Trustees who delegated without authority remained vicariously liable for any resulting loss.[58] They were not vicariously liable for the acts of authorised agents, but incurred personal liability for failing to act prudently in matters of supervision and so forth. A trustee's discretions could not, however, be delegated.[59] Further, exemption clauses expressly limiting his liability to cases of "wilful default" did not relieve him from the responsibility of acting as a prudent man of business.[60] Nor did the statutes of 1859 and 1893, the predecessors of the Trustee Act 1925, s.30(1), which restricted the liability of trustees to cases of wilful default, do more than change the onus of proof; these statutes placed the onus on "those who seek to charge an executor or trustee with a loss arising from the default of an agent, when the propriety of employing the agent has been established."[61]

B. Trustee Act 1925: s.23(1)

Under the Trustee Act 1925 trustees are no longer required to show a need to delegate. Delegation as such is accepted as a normal method of performing the duties incidental to trusteeship; but the

---

[52] *Turner v. Corney* (1841) 5 Beav. 515 at p. 517, *per* Lord Langdale.
[53] (1754) Amb. 218.
[54] (1884) 9 App.Cas. 1.
[55] (1887) 12 App.Cas. 727.
[56] *Fry v. Tapson* (1884) 28 Ch.D. 268.
[57] *Rowland v. Witherden* (1851) 3 Mac. & G. 568.
[58] *Clough v. Bond* (1838) 3 My. & Cr. 490 at pp. 496–497; *Speight v. Gaunt, supra*; *Target Holdings Ltd v. Redferns (a firm)* [1996] 1 A.C. 421 at p. 434.
[59] *Speight v. Gaunt, supra*; *post*, p. 565.
[60] *Re Chapman* [1896] 2 Ch. 763; *Re Brier* (1884) 26 Ch.D. 238. Exemption clauses are discussed at p. 483, *ante*.
[61] *Per* Lord Selborne in *Re Brier, supra*, at p. 243; *Re Chapman, supra*, at p. 776.

overall duties of trusteeship remain of course in the trustees. The effect of the statutory powers upon the responsibilities of a trustee is a matter of dispute. The question turns on the proper construction of section 23(1) which provides:

"Trustees or personal representatives may, instead of acting personally, employ and pay an agent, whether a solicitor, banker, stockbroker, or other person, to transact any business or do any act required to be transacted or done in the execution of the trust, or the administration of the testator's or intestate's estate, including the receipt and payment of money, and shall be entitled to be allowed and paid all charges and expenses so incurred, and shall not be responsible for the default of any such agent if employed in good faith."

This provision was considered by Maugham J. in *Re Vickery*.[62]

An executor (the defendant) employed, to wind up a small estate, a solicitor named Jennens, who, unknown to him, had twice been suspended from practice. The beneficiaries (the plaintiffs) objected to his appointment, and also the defendant's permitting the money to be under the control of the solicitor. The defendant pressed the solicitor for payment and was promised that this would come shortly. Eventually the plaintiffs instructed a different solicitor, and Jennens absconded and the money was lost. Maugham J. held that the defendant was not liable. His decision was based upon two separate sections of the Act: sections 23(1) and 30(1), which raise quite separate issues, but which do not appear to have been kept separate in the case or in some of the comment upon it.

Section 23(1) was new in 1925. It widened the powers of trustees to delegate. Indeed, Maugham J. said[63] "it revolutionises the position of a trustee or an executor so far as regards the employment of agents. He is no longer required to do any actual work himself, but he may employ a solicitor or other agent to do it, whether there is any real necessity for the employment or not. No doubt he should use his discretion in selecting an agent, and should employ him only to do acts within the scope of the usual business of the agent."

It is sometimes suggested that the only requirement of a trustee now is one of subjective good faith in the original appointment of the agent.[64] So long as he appoints an agent whom he thinks to be

---

[62] [1931] 1 Ch. 572.
[63] *Ibid.* at p. 581.
[64] (1931) 47 L.Q.R. 330 (H.P.) and 463 (W.S.H.); *Steel v. Wellcome Custodian Trustees Ltd* [1988] 1 W.L.R. 167 at 174. For varying views of the effect of *Re Vickery*, see Parker & Mellows, *Modern Law of Trusts* (6th ed.), p. 405; (1959) 22 M.L.R. 381 (G. Jones).

suitable, he is absolved from any further responsibility; so that a trustee who negligently leaves money in the hands of an agent, employed in good faith, is free of liability, however long the money is left, and however inadequate the supervision of the agent. It is submitted that there is no need to reach this conclusion, either on the judgment of Maugham J. or on the words of the section.

Although regarding the issue of "good faith" as a subjective matter, Maugham J. saw no reason to suppose that the pre-1926 rules relating to the requirement of discretion in selecting the agent and the limitation of the agent to the usual scope of his business should not still apply. Section 23(1) clearly allows delegation in circumstances in which it would not have been permitted before. It is submitted that the section can be construed so as to apply the pre-1926 rules to the wider area of post-1925 delegation, and thereby to reach a result which is more consistent with the need to protect the beneficiaries.[65] The Act is a consolidating Act, and should be construed so as to effect as little change in the law as possible.[66] The words "shall not be responsible for the default of any such agent if employed in good faith" were included simply to make it clear that the trustee was not *vicariously* liable for the defaults of the agent in the era of widened delegation powers. They were not intended to affect his *personal* liability for failure to act prudently. He would be liable for the acts of the agent only if the act of employment involved bad faith, or if the loss resulted from his own "wilful default" within section 30(1), discussed below.[67] He would remain liable for his own failings according to the pre-1926 rules, in particular with regard to supervising the work of agents to whom proper delegation had been made.[68] Such a construction is not inconsistent with the actual decision in *Re Vickery*.[69] There was there no disapproval of the original delegation, nor is it clear that the executor was in breach of his duty to supervise. Once the matter was in the hands of the solicitor, it is difficult to see what the executor could have done beyond pressing him to account. As Maugham J. thought,[70] the executor may not have been liable under the pre-1926 law.

This narrower construction is also consistent with section 23(3), which, without prejudice to section 23(1), permits the delegation of certain tasks to solicitors or bankers. A proviso to subsection (3) retains the trustee's pre-1926 liability if he permits money or property to remain under the control of the solicitor or banker for longer

---

[65] See *Green v. Whitehead* [1930] 1 Ch. 38.
[66] *Re Turner's W.T.* [1937] Ch. 15.
[67] *Post*, p. 563.
[68] (1959) 22 M.L.R. 381 (G. Jones).
[69] [1931] 1 Ch. 571.
[70] *Ibid.* at pp. 584–585.

than is reasonably necessary[71] to enable it to be transferred to the trustee.

The pre-1926 principles were applied in *Re Lucking's Will Trusts*.[72] The fault of Mr Lucking was that he failed adequately to supervise the activities of Lt Col. Dewar, the managing director.

> The trust assets consisted of a majority holding of shares in a private family company. Mr Lucking and another were trustees. They could not run the business themselves, and Lt Col. Dewar, an old and trusted friend of Mr Lucking, was appointed managing director.[73] With the aid of blank cheques signed by Mr Lucking, he appropriated nearly £16,000 of company funds for his own purposes (causing the trust shareholding to decrease in value), and became bankrupt. Mr Lucking had trusted him implicitly throughout. Cross J. held Mr Lucking liable for "failing adequately to supervise Mr Dewar's drawings" on the funds after the time at which there was reason to suspect Dewar's honesty. The standard applied was that in which "an ordinary prudent man would conduct a business of his own."[74] The other trustee, however, was not liable. Unlike Lucking, he was not a director of the company, and was in no position personally to supervise the drawings.

C. Trustee Act 1925, s.30(1)

The relationship between sections 23(1) and 30(1) now needs to be examined.

> "A trustee shall be chargeable only for money and securities actually received by him notwithstanding his signing any receipt for the sake of conformity, and shall be answerable and accountable only for his own acts, receipts, neglects, or defaults, and not for those of any other trustee, nor for any banker, broker, or other person with whom any trust money or securities may be deposited,[75] nor for the insufficiency or deficiency of any securities, nor for any other loss unless the same happens through his own wilful default."

i. Scope of Section 30(1): "Wilful Default." It should first be noted that the protection given by this subsection is limited to the

---

[71] See *Re Sheppard* [1911] 1 Ch. 50.

[72] [1968] 1 W.L.R. 866; [1979] Conv. 345 at p. 358 (J. Stannard).

[73] He was appointed not by the trustees but by the company, hence s.23(1) was inapplicable.

[74] *Ibid.* at p. 874.

[75] s.30(1) was held inapplicable in *Re Lucking's Will Trusts* [1968] 1 W.L.R. 866, *supra*, because Lt Col. Dewar was not a person with whom trust money had been deposited.

situations mentioned therein. The words "for any other loss" are construed *ejusdem generis.*[76]

The extent of the protection given by the subsection depends upon the construction of the phrase "wilful default." We have seen that this phrase, when inserted into express exemption clauses, did not excuse a trustee from acting as a prudent man of business, and that the incorporation of the clause in the predecessors of Trustee Act 1925 had the effect only of changing the burden of proof.[77] It is submitted that Maugham J. in *Re Vickery*[78] should have so construed section 30(1). However, he introduced a subjective construction to the phrase "wilful default" which had been applied to the construction of these words in *Re City Equitable Fire Insurance Co.*,[79] where Romer J. said that a person is not guilty of wilful default "unless he knows that he is committing and intends to commit a breach of his duty, or is recklessly careless in the sense of not caring whether his act or omission is or is not a breach of duty."[80] Romer J. was there construing a set of articles of association dealing with directors' liability, and his definition has no bearing upon the construction of the Trustee Act. The technical meaning in equity is that of "failure to do what is reasonable" and involves no intentional misconduct.[81] Maugham J.'s application of the meaning applied in the common law cases to a case dealing with the liability of a trustee is as little justified by authority as by principle. A return to the earlier test of the prudent man of business,[82] coupled with the narrow construction of section 23(1) proposed above, would produce consistency in the interpretation of sections 23(1), 23(3) and 30(1).

ii. Capital and Income. Section 30(1) includes a reference to receipts, and this raises an important distinction between receipt of capital and receipt of income. The basic rule is that capital should be received by all the trustees unless some of them have power under statute or under their trust deed to give good receipts and discharges.[83] Similarly, investments of trust moneys should be made in the joint names of the trustees. If two trustees divide investments, and invest separately, and one trustee commits a breach of trust, the other will be liable to make good the loss.[84]

---

[76] *Re Vickery* [1931] 1 Ch. 572 at p. 582, *per* Maugham J.
[77] *Re Brier* (1884) 26 Ch.D. 238; *ante,* p. 560.
[78] [1931] 1 Ch. 572.
[79] [1925] 1 Ch. 407.
[80] *Ibid.* at p. 434; quoted in the Court of Appeal by Warrington L.J. [1925] Ch. 407, 523–524.
[81] [1979] Conv. 345 (J. Stannard).
[82] *Cf.* the views of the Law Reform Committee, *post,* p. 567.
[83] See *Lee v. Sankey* (1873) L.R. 15 Eq. 204 and Trustee Act 1925, s.14; *ante,* p. 557.
[84] *Lewis v. Nobbs* (1878) 8 Ch.D. 591.

The receipt of income is, however, treated differently from the receipt of capital. In *Townley v. Sherborne*[85] it was decided that the duty of receiving rents may be delegated to one of several trustees, on the ground that a requirement of receipt by all the trustees would involve inconveniences that would outweigh all the advantages of such a course. In the case of an investment by trustees in shares in a limited company it will be found that the articles provide that trusts shall not be recognised,[86] and that, in the case of joint owner-ship, the dividend shall be paid to the first named who can give a valid receipt.[87] The practice is to pay the dividend to the first named "and another."

Where income payments are properly paid to one only of multiple trustees, the co-trustee may nevertheless be liable if he permits the payee to retain the money for a longer period than the circumstances of the case necessitate.[88]

D. Delegation of Discretions

The principles discussed above relate to the delegation of admin-istrative acts. Trustees cannot as a general rule delegate their discre-tions, for example the distribution of funds to beneficiaries of a discretionary trust, or investment decisions.[89] The delegation of discretions is permitted by sections 23(2) and 25 of the 1925 Act, and under section 9 of the Trusts of Land and Appointment of Trustees Act 1996, discussed below.

Section 23(2) empowers a trustee to appoint an agent for the purpose of administering any part of the trust estate situated outside the United Kingdom, "or executing or exercising any discretion or trust or power vested in them in relation to any such property," and authorises also the appointment of sub-agents. Section 25[90] enables a trustee to delegate to any person[91] by power of attorney for a period not exceeding 12 months "all or any of the trusts powers and discretions vested in him as trustee either alone or jointly with any other person or persons." The instrument must be attested by at least one witness,[92] and written notice must be given within seven days to each of the other trustees and to each person who has the power to

---

[85] (1634) J. Bridg. 35. Such a power may be excluded by the trust deed: *Brice v. Stokes* (1805) 11 Ves.Jr. 319.

[86] Companies Act 1985, s.360.

[87] Companies (Tables A–F) Regulations 1985, Table A, reg. 106 (S.I. 1985/805).

[88] *Carruthers v. Carruthers* [1896] A.C. 659.

[89] *Speight v. Gaunt* (1884) 9 App.Cas. 1.

[90] As amended by Powers of Attorney Act 1971, s.9; [1978] Conv. 85 (J.T.F.). For enduring powers of attorney, see *post*, p. 568. See also Law Com. No. 220 (1994), *Delegation by Individual Trustees*; *post*, p. 569.

[91] Including a trust corporation; but not to a sole co-trustee; subs. (2).

[92] Subs. (3).

appoint new trustees.[93] It seems that there is no power to pay the delegate out of the trust fund.[94]

These provisions should only be used when such delegation is essential, for the protection given is less than that provided by section 23(1). Under section 23(2), the trustees are not responsible for losses "by reason only of their having made any such appointment"; pre-1926 liability remains. Under section 25 the donor of the power of attorney remains liable for the acts and defaults of the donee.[95]

The position relating to trusts of land is now found in section 9 of the Trusts of Land and Appointment of Trustees Act 1996, which permits the trustees to delegate any of their functions as trustees relating to the land, including sale, to any beneficiary (or beneficiaries) of full age and beneficially entitled to an interest in possession.[96] The delegation may be for any period or indefinite,[97] and must be by power of attorney[98] given by all the trustees jointly. It is revocable by any one or more of them, and will also be revoked if another person is appointed trustee.[99] Where a beneficiary ceases to be beneficially entitled, the delegation is revoked so far as it relates to him, but the functions remain exercisable by the remaining beneficiaries in the case of joint delegation.[1]

Beneficiaries to whom functions have been delegated under section 9 are in the same position as the trustees in relation to the exercise of the functions, but are not regarded as trustees for any other purpose. In particular, they cannot sub-delegate or give a valid receipt for capital money.[2] The trustees are jointly and severally liable for any act or default of the beneficiary or any of the beneficiaries in the exercise of the delegated functions only if the trustees did not exercise reasonable care in deciding to delegate to the beneficiary or beneficiaries.[3] Neither section 9 nor the repeal of section 29 of the Law of Property Act 1925 affect the operation after the commencement of the 1996 Act of any delegation effected before it.[4]

---

[93] Subs. (4). But failure to give notice does not, in favour of a person dealing with the donee of the power, invalidate any act done by the donee.

[94] The Law Reform Committee in its 23rd Report, *post*, p. 567, recommends otherwise; para. 4.19. The delegate may be paid if the trustees are paid.

[95] T.A. 1925, s.25(5).

[96] Where the trustees purport to delegate to a person who is not such a beneficiary, third parties dealing with that person in good faith are protected by s.9(2).

[97] s.9(5).

[98] s.9(6) provides that this cannot be an enduring power within the Enduring Powers of Attorney Act 1985; *post*, p. 568.

[99] s.9(3). It is not revoked if any grantor ceases to be a trustee.

[1] s.9(4).

[2] s.9(7).

[3] s.9(8).

[4] s.9(9).

E. Reform

The power to delegate was reviewed by the Law Reform Committee.[5] The Committee recommended that section 23(1) should be amended so that the trustees should only be able to charge the trust with the cost of delegating if the charges are reasonably incurred, taking into account the trustees' knowledge, qualifications, experience and level of remuneration.[6] It was felt that the relationship between sections 23(1), 30(1) and 61 was not as clear as it should be. Section 23(1) was concerned with the trustee's vicarious liability for the misfeasance of an agent who was not employed in good faith. Section 30(1) was concerned with the trustee's personal liability where loss was caused by the acts of other persons, which could have been prevented but for the trustee's wilful default. While the wilful default test, requiring connivance, was correct here,[7] the standard in section 23(1) was not stringent enough. A trustee should be expected to keep a check on his agent. The reference to "good faith" should be replaced by a provision that the trustee should not be liable if it was reasonable to employ an agent and if reasonable steps were taken to ensure that the agent was competent and that the work was done competently.[8]

More recently it has been suggested that legislation is necessary to clarify the position as to delegation of investment powers by trustees.[9] Such legislation now exists in the case of pension trusts,[10] but other trustees may wish to delegate to an investment manager authorised under the Financial Services Act 1986 in order to get the benefit of a skilled professional service.[11] As this involves the delegation of discretions, it can only be done by power of attorney under Trustee Act 1925, section 25 or by application to court,[12] unless expressly authorised by the trust instrument. Where trustees delegate under section 25, they will remain liable for the acts of the manager. It would seem that they cannot pay him from the trust fund,[13] nor exempt him from liability, nor allow him to do things which the trustees cannot do, such as self-deal. These problems arise

---

[5] 23rd Report, *The Powers and Duties of Trustees* (1982 Cmnd. 8733).

[6] *Ibid.* para. 4.6.

[7] This view is out of line with the criticisms of the interpretation of s.30(1) in *Re Vickery* [1931] 1 Ch. 572, *ante*, p. 562. It also seems inconsistent with the other recommendations.

[8] *Ibid.* paras. 4.9–4.11; (1983) 133 N.L.J. 1096 (C. Emery). For liability for the defaults of co-trustees, see *ante*, p. 563.

[9] (1989) 3 *Trust Law & Practice* 110 (C. Francis); (1990) 106 L.Q.R. 87 (D. Hayton); *ante*, p. 000. The matter is under review by the Law Commission and the Trust Law Committee; Law Com. Press Release, November 21, 1995. A Consultation Paper is expected in 1997.

[10] Pensions Act 1995, s.34; *ante*, p. 466.

[11] If the trustees conduct investment business themselves, F.S.A. 1986, s.3 requires them to be authorised under the Act or exempted. See also Sched. 1, para. 22.

[12] *Post*, Chap. 22; *Anker-Petersen v. Anker-Petersen* (1991) 88/16 L.S.Gaz. 32.

[13] Unless there is a remuneration clause in the trust instrument.

also where the trustees act under an express power to delegate investment discretions which does not specifically cover these matters,[14] and hence clarifying legislation is required.[15] Such legislation should also clarify the extent to which trustees may properly vest trust property (such as shares) in the name of a nominee. This is a convenient practice which reduces delays in completing share transactions and which is commonly permitted by express clauses, but it is doubtful whether it is permitted under the general law of delegation.[16]

F. Delegation under the Enduring Powers of Attorney Act 1985

We have seen that section 25 of the Trustee Act 1925 permits a trustee to delegate all of his functions by power of attorney for a maximum of 12 months, subject to various procedural requirements.[17] This could be done, for example, if he was going abroad.

Until 1985 there was no possibility of a power of attorney which would continue in force after the donor had become mentally incapable, as such incapacity automatically revoked the power. The Enduring Powers of Attorney Act 1985 permits the creation of a power of attorney which will survive the donor's subsequent incapacity.

This Act is relevant to trustees in two respects. First, it is provided that a power of attorney granted by trustees of land[18] or granted under section 25 of the Trustee Act 1925 cannot be an enduring power.[19] The reasoning here is that mental incapacity is a ground for replacing a trustee.[20] Secondly, and inconsistently with the latter point, section 3(3) of the 1985 Act provides that the donee of an enduring power of attorney may "execute or exercise all or any of the trusts, powers or discretions vested in the donor as trustee" and may give a valid receipt for capital money. Thus a trustee cannot create an enduring power under the 1925 and 1996 Acts, but such a power may be created under the 1985 Act.

---

[14] These problems are fully analysed in the articles cited in n. 9, above.

[15] See Trusts (Guernsey) Law 1989, s.29(2); Belize Trusts Act 1992, s.34; Uniform Prudent Investor Act 1994, s.9 (U.S.A.)

[16] For charity trustees, see Decisions of the Charity Commissioners, Vol. 2 (1994), pp. 28–32.

[17] *Ante*, p. 565.

[18] Trusts of Land and Appointment of Trustees Act 1996, s.9(6).

[19] Enduring Powers of Attorney Act 1985, s.2(8). See *infra* for reform proposals.

[20] See Law Com. No. 122 (1983), *The Incapacitated Principal*, para. 4.2.

The purpose of section 3(3) was to enable a trustee of a co-owned house to delegate the power to execute a conveyance of the house to his co-trustee in such a way that the subsequent incapacity of the delegating trustee would not terminate the power.[21] The subsection, however, is not limited to this situation,[22] and appears to permit a trustee to delegate all his functions indefinitely.[23] The execution of an enduring power of attorney will have this effect whether or not the trustee has considered the matter. Unlike section 25, delegation to the only other co-trustee is permitted, there is no time limit, and no requirement of notice to co-trustees. The rule requiring payment of capital money to two trustees is also ousted. If this is correct, section 3(3) is a "legislative blunder."[24] If a trustee wants to delegate for more than 12 months and may become incompetent, he should retire.

The matter has been reviewed by the Law Commission.[25] It is proposed that section 3(3) be repealed[26] and that different rules should apply to trustees who have a beneficial interest (i.e. co-owners) and other trustees. Co-owners should be able to delegate to their co-trustee by enduring power of attorney without time limit. Purchasers in good faith would be able to rely on the statement in the power of attorney that the donor trustee has a beneficial interest.[27] Delegation to a sole co-trustee would not enable him to give a good receipt for capital money, but he could appoint a second trustee for the purpose.[28] Co-owners would continue to be able to delegate by ordinary (non-enduring) power of attorney or under section 25 of the 1925 Act (for 12 months only), and would be liable for the acts of the donee.[29]

Other trustees should be able to delegate by enduring power of attorney under section 25, subject to the 12 month time limit.[30] Section 22(2) of the Law of Property Act 1925, providing that a mentally incapacitated trustee of land should be discharged before the legal estate is dealt with, should be amended to make it clear that it does not apply where an enduring power of attorney has been

[21] Reversing *Walia v. Michael Naughton Ltd* [1985] 1 W.L.R. 1125.

[22] For the view that it is impliedly so limited, see (1990) 106 L.Q.R. 87 at 89 (D. Hayton).

[23] See (1986) 130 S.J. 23 (R. Oerton); (1986) 1 *Trust Law and Practice* 54. The provision was added by the Lord Chancellor's Department after the *Walia* decision, and was not considered by the Law Commission.

[24] (1986) 130 S.J. 23 at p. 25; (1988) 85 L.S.Gaz. No. 19, p. 4.

[25] Law Com. No. 220 (1994), *Delegation by Individual Trustees*; (1995) 92/12 L.S.Gaz. 18 (R. Oerton).

[26] *Ibid.*, para. 4.1.

[27] Para. 4.38.

[28] Para. 4.41.

[29] Para. 4.31.

[30] Para. 4.1. Thus s.2(8) of the 1985 Act would be repealed.

granted. On section 25 generally, it is proposed that delegation to a sole co-trustee should be permitted, for example for general management, although such a trustee would not be able to give a receipt for capital money.[31]

8. POWERS OF MAINTENANCE AND ADVANCEMENT

Where any person has a contingent interest in property the question arises as to the use which should be made of the income until the gift vests. Otherwise the income would not be put to any use during the period. The policy is to allow the gift to "carry the intermediate income" unless there are good reasons to the contrary. Generally speaking, all testamentary gifts except contingent pecuniary legacies carry the intermediate income unless it is otherwise disposed of.[32]

One of the most common contingencies is that of attaining the age of 21 or more. It is important to make provision for the use of the income for the maintenance and education of the beneficiary before the interest vests.

A similar question arises in the opposite case of a minor who has a vested interest in property; for it may then be desirable that he should not be entitled to draw the whole of the income. It is better that he should receive what is reasonably necessary for his maintenance and education, and that the balance should be invested for him. Again, it may be that capital sums may be needed to establish him in a profession or in business or on marriage.

These matters may be expressly provided for in the trust instrument. If not, the court has an inherent power to approve the use of income, or even of capital for the maintenance of minors.[33] But the statutory powers of maintenance[34] and advancement[35] about to be discussed are sufficient to meet the needs of most situations, and they can be amended as required to meet the needs of a particular trust. Such powers have commonly been used, not only, or mainly, for their original purposes, but rather for the fiscal advantages which they have been able to offer.[36]

---

[31] Para. 4.15, amending s.25(2) of the 1925 Act. Para. 4.46 recommends the repeal of s.25(3) as having been superseded by the witness rule of Law of Property (Miscellaneous Provisions) Act 1989, s.1(3).

[32] *Post*, p. 574.

[33] *Post*, p. 583.

[34] T.A. 1925, s.31.

[35] T.A. 1925, s.32.

[36] *Pilkington v. I.R.C.* [1964] A.C. 612. See (1994) 8 *Trust Law International* 49 (J. Brown).

A. Maintenance.[37] Trustee Act 1925, s.31

i. Subsection (1).

"Where any property is held by trustees in trust for any person for any interest whatsoever, whether vested or contingent, then, subject to any prior interests or charges affecting that property—
  (i) during the infancy of any such person, if his interest so long continues, the trustees may, at their sole discretion, pay to his parent or guardian, if any, or otherwise apply for or towards his maintenance, education, or benefit,[38] the whole or such part, if any, of the income of that property as may, in all the circumstances, be reasonable, whether or not there is—
    (a) any other fund applicable to the same purpose; or
    (b) any person bound by law to provide for his maintenance or education; and
  (ii) if such person attaining the age of [18][39] years has not a vested interest in such income, the trustees shall thenceforth pay the income of that property and of any accretion thereto under subsection (2) of this section to him, until he either attains a vested interest therein or dies, or until failure of his interest: ... "

(a) *Prior Interests.* The power of maintenance can only arise where a person is entitled to the income, whether by virtue of a vested interest, or by virtue of a contingent interest which carries the intermediate income.[40] If the income is applicable in favour of a prior interest, no question of its use for maintenance can arise. Similarly, a member of a discretionary class is not entitled to any income and the section does not therefore apply to payments made by the trustees in the exercise of their discretion.[41]

(b) *Minority.* The question of application of income for the minor's maintenance, education or benefit, whether his interest is vested or contingent, is a matter for the trustees' discretion. The decision to apply income for such minor's maintenance must be taken as a result of a conscious exercise of their discretion, and not automatically.[42] The trustees should, so far as practicable, arrange

---

[37] See (1953) 17 Conv.(N.S.) 273 (B. Ker) for a most helpful discussion of s.31.
[38] See *Re Heyworth's Contingent Reversionary Interest* [1956] Ch. 364; *Pilkington v. I.R.C. supra; Re Pauling's S.T.* [1964] Ch. 303; (1959) 23 Conv.(N.S.) 27 (D. Waters).
[39] Reduced from 21 by Family Law Reform Act 1969. See *Begg-McBrearty (Inspector of Taxes) v. Stilwell* [1996] 1 W.L.R. 951.
[40] T.A. 1925, s.31(3); *post*, pp. 574, 575.
[41] *Re Vestey's Settlement* [1951] Ch. 209.
[42] *Wilson v. Turner* (1883) 22 Ch.D. 521.

for maintenance payments to be shared proportionately among various funds available for the purpose.[43] The payments are usually made to the parent or guardian whose receipt is a sufficient discharge for the trustees.

(c) *Adult Contingently Entitled.* A beneficiary contingently entitled to the principal becomes entitled under paragraph (ii) of subsection (1) to the income at majority.[44] His entitlement to the capital must, of course, await the happening of the contingency. The entitlement to income at majority is subject to a contrary intention; and this has been found to exist where there is a direction to accumulate.

In *Re Turner's Will Trusts,*[45] a testator provided interests in favour of his grandchildren contingently on their attaining the age of 28, and expressly gave the trustees power to apply the income for their maintenance, education and benefit until that time, and instructed the trustees to accumulate the surplus.

One grandchild, Geoffrey, was 21 when the testator died; and himself died three years later aged 24. No income had been paid to him, and some £3,000 had been accumulated since the testator's death. The question was whether section 31(1) applied. If it did, Geoffrey's estate would have become entitled to the income. The Court of Appeal held that, in spite of the imperative terms of section 31, it gave way to an expression of a contrary intention in accordance with the Trustee Act 1925, s.69(2).

ii. Subsection (2).

(a) *Surplus Income to be Accumulated for Minors.* Subsection (2) provides that the residue of the income, not applied for maintenance, shall be accumulated by investment during the minority of the person contingently entitled. Income from such investments becomes available for future maintenance; and the accumulations themselves may be applied, during the minority, as if they were income arising in the then current year.

(b) *Entitlement to Accumulations.* On the majority (or earlier marriage) of a minor, the question arises whether or not any accumulations should be given to him. As would be expected, he is

---

[43] T.A. 1925, s.31(1), proviso.
[44] *Re Jones' W.T.* [1947] Ch. 48.
[45] [1937] Ch. 15; *Re Ransome* [1957] Ch. 348; [1979] Conv. 243 (J. Riddall); *Brotherton v. I.R.C.* [1978] 1 W.L.R. 610; *I.R.C. v. Bernstein* [1961] Ch. 399; *Re McGeorge* [1963] Ch. 544, where the contrary intention was shown by deferring the gift to a daughter until after the death of a widow; *Re Erskine's S.T.* [1971] 1 W.L.R. 162.

entitled to the accumulations if he had a vested interest during his minority (for he was entitled all along to the income)[46]; or if, on attaining his majority, he "becomes entitled to the property from which the income arose in fee simple, absolute or determinable, or absolutely or for an entailed interest." In short, he is entitled to the accumulations on his majority (or earlier marriage) if he is then entitled to the capital.[47]

The question arose in *Re Sharp's Settlement Trusts*[48] whether the provision covered the case where the children of the settlor became entitled, subject to an overriding power of appointment, to the capital on attaining the age of 21. Were they then entitled absolutely? Pennycuick V.-C. held that they were not: the fact that their interests could be defeated by the exercise of the power prevented their becoming entitled absolutely. It is anomalous that "a person having a determinable interest in realty should qualify to take accumulations at 21,"[49] but "a person having a like interest in personalty should not equally so qualify."[50] This is just another one of those curious instances where the 1925 legislation just did not go far enough in its expressed intention so far as possible to assimilate the rules relating to realty and personalty."[51] In all other cases, as for example the case of a contingent beneficiary whose interest never vests, or where the beneficiary, although having a vested interest, fails to reach majority, the accumulations are added to capital for all purposes.[52]

The provisions relating to the destination of accumulations in section 31(2) are also subject to a contrary intention in the trust instrument.[53] In *Re Delamere's Settlement Trusts*,[54] the trustees appointed income to beneficiaries "absolutely" in 1971. All the beneficiaries were then minors. By 1981, £122,000 had been accumulated. The question arose whether section 31(2) applied, so that the share of any beneficiary dying before majority would devolve with the capital, or whether there was a contrary intention, so that the accumulations were held indefeasibly for the appointees. It was held that the word "absolutely" in the 1971 appointment indicated

---

[46] For income tax liability, see *Stanley v. I.R.C.* [1944] K.B. 255.

[47] T.A. 1925, s.31(2)(i).

[48] [1973] Ch. 331; (1972) 36 Conv.(N.S.) 436 (D. Hayton). See also *Re Delamere's Settlement Trusts, infra.*

[49] The words "fee simple, absolute or determinable," applying only to realty.

[50] [1973] Ch. 331 at p. 346.

[51] (1972) 36 Conv.(N.S.) 436 at p. 438. The accumulations of income were added to the share of each child, subject to the exercise of the power: *Re King* [1928] Ch. 330; *Re Joel's W.T.* [1967] Ch. 14; *post,* p. 576.

[52] T.A. 1925, s.31(2)(ii). On the distinction between contingent interests and interests subject to defeasance, see *Phipps v. Ackers* (1842) 9 Cl. & F. 583; *Brotherton v. I.R.C.* [1978] 1 W.L.R. 610.

[53] T.A. 1925, s.69(2).

[54] [1984] 1 W.L.R. 813; [1985] Conv. 153 (R. Griffith).

indefeasibility, thus excluding section 31(2). Clearly the mere fact that the interest is vested is not sufficient to achieve this result.[55]

iii. Gifts Carrying Intermediate Income. Section 31 only applies to contingent interests which carry the intermediate income; that is to say, to gifts which entitle the donee to claim the income earned by, or interest upon, the subject matter of the gift between the date of the gift and the date of payment. Whether or not a gift should do so is not self-evident, and there are some complex and technical rules which do not provide any conceptual unity. Some rules are based on case law, and some on statute. It is unfortunate that there is not a single comprehensive code.

Vested gifts carry the intermediate income unless a contrary intention appears, as where the income is given to someone other than the donee for a period. A direction to accumulate the surplus income until majority, on the other hand, does not indicate that the gift does not carry the income, but merely that the power of maintenance is excluded.

With contingent gifts, the rules, subject always to an expression of contrary intention, are as follows.[56]

(a) *Contingent Residuary Bequest.* A contingent bequest of residuary personalty carries all income earned from the testator's death.[57] The undisposed of income "becomes part of the residue."[58] But it seems that, if a residuary bequest of personalty (whether vested or contingent) is postponed "to a future date which must come sooner or later,"[59] the intermediate income is undisposed of and therefore not carried by the gift.[60]

(b) *Contingent or Future Specific Gifts of Personalty or Realty and Contingent Residuary Devises of Freehold Land.* The Law of Property Act 1925, s.175 provides that a contingent specific bequest of personalty or devise of realty and a contingent residuary devise of freehold land, and a devise of freehold land to trustees on trust for persons whose interests are contingent or executory shall carry the intermediate income. It will be noticed that the section does not

---

[55] See T.A. 1925, s.31(2)(i)(a).
[56] (1953) 17 Conv.(N.S.) 273 (B. Ker); (1963) 79 L.Q.R. 184 (P.V.B.).
[57] *Re Adams* [1893] 1 Ch. 329.
[58] *Ibid.* at p. 334.
[59] *Per* Cross J. in *Re McGeorge* [1963] Ch. 544 at p. 551; such as the death of an annuitant.
[60] *Re Oliver* [1947] 2 All E.R. 161; *Re Gillett's W.T.* [1950] Ch. 102; *Re Geering* [1964] Ch. 136.

affect a residuary gift of a leasehold interest, which ranks as personalty.[61]

(c) *Contingent Pecuniary Legacy.* A contingent pecuniary legacy
does not carry the intermediate income.[62] To this rule there are three
exceptions, in which cases the contingent pecuniary legacy will
carry interest, and it will be available for the maintenance of a
minor.

First: Where the legacy was given by the father of the minor, or
by some person *in loco parentis*, so long as no other fund is provided
for his maintenance,[63] and the contingency is the attainment of
majority.[64]

Secondly: Where the testator shows an intention to maintain.[65]

Thirdly: Where the testator has set aside the legacy as a separate
fund for the benefit of the legatee.[66]

Section 31, having laid down that the section applies only to a gift
which carries the intermediate income, refers expressly to the first of
these exceptions, and provides that the rate of interest shall (if the
income available is sufficient, and subject to any rules of court to the
contrary) be 5 per cent.[67] Thus, the subsection refers only to the first
of the recognised exceptions, and the question arises whether that is
an indication that the other two are not intended to apply. The better
view is that they are unaffected by subsection (3), and that "the
specific mention of the rule in [the first exception] is only for the
purpose of establishing a suitable rate of interest.[68] The statute
widens the exception by making it applicable in the case of either
parent, and not only in the case of a father.

**iv. Aggregation of Income of Children with that of their
Parents.** It has been seen that an accumulation and maintenance
settlement[69] giving contingent gifts to minors with power to use the
income for maintenance, and to accumulate that not so used, offers
tax advantages, both in the context of income tax and of inheritance
tax, but that income so accumulated carries the income tax disadvantage of liability to the additional rate.[70] Where income is paid
to a minor who is the unmarried child of the settlor, the income is

---

[61] *Re Woodin* [1895] 2 Ch. 349.
[62] *Re Raine* [1929] 1 Ch. 716; *Re George* (1877) 5 Ch.D. 837.
[63] *Re George* (1877) 5 Ch.D. 837 at p. 843; *Re Moody* [1895] 1 Ch. 101.
[64] *Re Abrahams* [1911] 1 Ch. 108.
[65] *Re Churchill* [1909] 2 Ch. 431.
[66] *Re Medlock* (1886) 54 L.T. 828.
[67] *Cf.* R.S.C. Ord. 44, r. 10 (6 per cent where legacy ordered to be paid by the court).
[68] See (1953) 17 Conv.(N.S.) 273 at p. 279.
[69] *Ante*, p. 226.
[70] I.C.T.A. 1988, s.686.

treated as that of his parent.[71] In other cases, the income is treated as part of the minor's total income.

v. Gifts to Classes. Where there is a gift to a class contingently on attaining the age of 21, the trustees may treat separately, for these purposes, each person's presumptive share. That is to say, that when one member of the class attains 21 and becomes entitled to his share, the trustees may continue to exercise their powers of maintenance in respect of the other members.[72] Similarly, income may only be used for the maintenance of any member of the class if that income was earned during the lifetime of that member,[73] but if a member of a class dies without obtaining a vested interest, the accumulation of income representing his contingent share is added to the capital under section 31(2)(ii), although this means that future born members will thus benefit from it.[74]

B. Advancement

i. The Meaning of Advancement. We saw that maintenance was concerned with the payment of income for the benefit of minors. Advancement is concerned with the payment or application of capital sums to the beneficiary's advantage before the time comes when he is entitled to demand the fund. The scope of the power depends upon the terms of the instrument giving it,[75] and upon Trustee Act 1925, s.32.[76] Payments under such power have been made not only for the purpose of providing capital sums when needed, but also for the purpose of tax saving.

Thus, suppose a fund is held on trust for A, the capital being payable to him on attaining 25. If A marries, or sets up in business or in a profession before that time, a power of advancement makes possible the payment to him of some or all of the capital of the fund to help with such a project. There is a similar but more complicated question if A's interest is subject to a prior life interest in X; for X's income will be affected by any payments out of the capital fund which produces it. Likewise if A's interest is contingent on his

---

[71] I.C.T.A. 1988, ss.663, 664; F.A. 1990, s.82.
[72] *Re King* [1928] Ch. 330.
[73] *Re Joel's W.T.* [1967] Ch. 14.
[74] *Ibid.*; not following *Re King, supra,* on this point. The Law Reform Committee, 23rd Report, *The Powers and Duties of Trustees* (1982 Cmnd. 8733), para. 3.41, recommends the abrogation of the rule in *Re Joel.*
[75] See *Re Collard's W.T.* [1901] Ch. 293.
[76] *Infra.*

attaining 25; for if payments are made to A and A never attains 25 the capital payments will have been made to the wrong person.

The tax-saving question arises where trustees hold a large sum on trust for A for life and then to A's children equally at 21. Independently of the fund A is rich enough to provide the children with all they need. It may be advantageous to make transfers of capital from the trust for the children. Inheritance tax will be avoided if the advancement was made more than seven years before A's death.[77] Such a payment is certainly not an "advancement" within the usual meaning of the word, but no one could deny that the saving of tax on the trust is a benefit to the children. A further question arises, whether such sums must be held in trust for the children absolutely, or whether they may themselves be settled by the creation of sub-trusts for the benefit of themselves and also for other persons such as future dependants. These questions are dealt with below.

ii. Original Meaning of Advancement. "The word 'advancement' itself meant in this context the establishment in life of the beneficiary who was the object of the power or at any rate some step that would contribute to the furtherance of his establishment.[78] . . . Typical instances of expenditure for such purposes under the social conditions of the nineteenth century were an apprenticeship or the purchase of a commission in the Army or of an interest in business. In the case of a girl there could be advancement on marriage."[79]

iii. Express Powers. Until 1925 there was no statutory power of advancement. Express powers of advancement were given narrow scope consistent with the established meaning of the word.[80] So, "to prevent uncertainties about the permitted range of objects for which moneys could be raised and made available, such words as 'or otherwise for his or her benefit' were often added to the word 'advancement.' It was always recognised that these added words were 'large words'[81] and indeed in another case[82] the same judge spoke of preferment and advancement of being 'both large words'

---

[77] F.A. (No. 2) 1987, s.96.
[78] See *per* Jessel M.R. in *Taylor v. Taylor* (1875) L.R. 20 Eq. 155; *Lowther v. Bentinck* (1874) L.R. 19 Eq. 166 (payment of debts); *Roper-Curzon v. Roper-Curzon* (1871) L.R. 11 Eq. 452 (starting a career at the Bar); *Re Long's Settlement* (1868) 38 L.J.Ch. 125 (passage money to go to a colony); *Re Williams' W.T.* [1953] Ch. 138 (purchase of a house as a surgery); *Hardy v. Shaw* [1976] Ch. 82 (shares in family company), (1976) 126 N.L.J. 117 (F. Glover).
[79] *Per* Lord Radcliffe in *Pilkington v. I.R.C.* [1964] A.C. 612 at p. 634.
[80] *Per* Kennedy L.J. in *Molyneux v. Fletcher* [1898] 1 Q.B. 648 at p. 653.
[81] See Jessel M.R. in *Re Breed's Will* (1875) 1 Ch.D. 226 at p. 228.
[82] *Lowther v. Bentinck* (1874) L.R. 19 Eq. 166 at p. 169.

but of 'benefit' as being the 'largest of all.' "[83] The combined phrase "advancement or benefit" is read disjunctively,[84] it now means "any use of the money which will improve the material situation of the beneficiary."[85] The scope of an express power depends of course upon its own language. The standard form of express power has now been incorporated in the Trustee Act 1925, s.32; and express provisions on the question of advancement are now usually confined to extensions of the statutory power by making the power applicable to the whole of the beneficiary's presumptive share,[86] or by giving express powers to the trustees to create sub-trusts.[87]

iv. The Statutory Power. Trustee Act 1925, s.32.

Section 32—"(1) Trustees may at any time or times pay or apply any capital money subject to a trust, for the advancement or benefit, in such manner as they may, in their absolute discretion, think fit, of any person entitled to the capital of the trust property or of any share thereof, whether absolutely or contingently on his attaining any specified age or on the occurrence of any other event, or subject to a gift over on his death under any specified age or on the occurrence of any other event, and whether in possession or in remainder or reversion, and such payment or application may be made notwithstanding that the interest of such person is liable to be defeated by the exercise of a power of appointment or revocation, or to be diminished by the increase of the class to which he belongs:

Provided that—

    (*a*) the money so paid or applied for the advancement or benefit of any person shall not exceed altogether in amount one-half of the presumptive or vested share or interest of that person in the trust property[88]; and

    (*b*) if that person is or becomes absolutely and indefeasibly entitled to a share in the trust property the money so paid or applied shall be brought into account as part of such share; and

---

[83] *Per* Lord Radcliffe in *Pilkington v. I.R.C.* [1964] A.C. 612 at p. 634; *Re Halsted's W.T.* [1937] 2 All E.R. 570 at p. 571; *Re Moxon's W.T.* [1958] 1 W.L.R. 165 at p. 168.

[84] *Lowther v. Bentinck* (1874) L.R. 19 Eq. 166; *Re Halsted's W.T., supra,* at p. 571.

[85] *Per* Lord Radcliffe in *Pilkington v. I.R.C.* [1964] A.C. 612 at p. 635.

[86] By proviso (a) to T.A. 1925, s.32, the statutory power extends only to one-half of the beneficiary's presumptive share; *infra.*

[87] *Post*, p. 580; (1959) 23 Conv.(N.S.) 27 (D. Waters).

[88] The possible advancement of one half must be taken into account as resources for supplementary benefit purposes; *Peters v. Chief Adjudication Officer* (1989) 19 Fam. Law 318.

(*c*) no such payment or application shall be made so as to prejudice any person entitled to any prior life or other interest, whether vested or contingent, in the money paid or applied unless such person is in existence and of full age and consents in writing to such payment or application."

The section does not apply to capital money arising under the Settled Land Act 1925.[89] Its application is always subject to the expression of a contrary intention[90] and it has been held to be excluded by provision for accumulation.[91]

v. Problems in the Application of section 32. Pilkington v. I.R.C.[92] The wide construction of the phrase "advancement" or "benefit" must have been carried into the statutory power created by section 32, since it adopts without qualification the accustomed wording "for the advancement or benefit in such manner as they may in their absolute discretion think fit."[93] But this leaves open a number of questions; can payments be made for the "benefit" of a person who is not in any way in need? To what extent can an advancement re-settle the money advanced, the re-settlement changing the original trust? Can trustees, exercising the statutory power of advancement, delegate their discretion by giving a dispositive discretion to the trustees of the re-settlement; *i.e.* can they make an advancement on protective or discretionary trusts? These questions were discussed and largely settled in the long litigation over the will of William Pilkington.

The testator left a share of his residuary estate on trust for his nephew Richard upon protective trusts during his life and after Richard's death upon trust for such of his children or remoter issue as he should by deed or will appoint and in default of appointment in trust for such of Richard's children as attained 21 (or, if female, married under that age) in equal shares. Richard had three children all born after the death of the testator of whom a two-year-old daughter Penelope was one. Richard's father (brother of the testator and grandfather of Penelope) proposed to make a settlement in favour of Penelope, providing that the

---

[89] T.A. 1925, s.32(2), as substituted by Trusts of Land and Appointment of Trustees Act 1996, Sched. 3, para. 3(8).

[90] *Re Evans' Settlement* [1967] 1 W.L.R. 1294.

[91] *I.R.C. v. Bernstein* [1961] Ch. 399. This is so even if the direction for accumulation contravenes L.P.A. 1925, ss.164–166; *Re Ransome* [1957] Ch. 348; *Brotherton v. I.R.C.* [1978] 1 W.L.R. 610.

[92] [1964] A.C. 612.

[93] *Per* Lord Radcliffe in *Pilkington v. I.R.C., supra*, at p. 635; *Re Pauling's S.T.* [1964] Ch. 303.

trustees hold the property on trust to pay the income to Penelope at 21, and the capital for her absolutely at 30 and if Penelope died under 30 leaving children, on trust for such children at 21 with further family trusts in default. The trustees had power to apply the income for Penelope's maintenance until she reached the age of 21, and were to accumulate the surplus income.

The trustees proposed to advance, with the consent of Richard, one-half of Penelope's expectant share under the testator's will, and pay it to the trustees of Richard's father's settlement.

The House of Lords held that this proposal was within the trustees' power under section 32. They held also that the exercise of the power of advancement was analogous to the exercise of a special power of appointment and that in the circumstances the advancement would be void for perpetuity.

(a) *Benefit.* On the question of the benefit to Penelope, Lord Radcliffe held that it was immaterial that other persons, such as her future dependants, would benefit also. " . . . if the disposition itself, by which I mean the whole provision made, is for her benefit, it is no objection to the exercise of the power that other persons benefit incidentally as a result of the exercise."[94] The relief from anxiety about the future maintenance of a wife and a family has been held to be a sufficient benefit[95]; as has the performance of the obligation felt by a rich man to contribute to a charitable trust where it would be a great burden to do so out of taxed income[96]; and also the payment from a wife's fund to her husband to enable him to set up in business in England and prevent a separation of the family.[97] Similarly, there was no need to show that the benefit was "related to his or her own real or personal needs."[98] The estate duty saving was a sufficient benefit.[99]

(b) *Settlement of Funds Advanced. Sub-Trusts.* Nor was it any objection that the funds were being subjected to a settlement, and not paid for the sole benefit of Penelope; nor that her enjoyment was deferred. The settlement of advanced funds had many times been

---

[94] *Per* Lord Radcliffe in *Pilkington v. I.R.C.* [1964] A.C. 612 at p. 636; *Re Halsted's W.T.* [1937] 2 All E.R. 570.

[95] *Re Halsted's W.T., supra.*

[96] *Re Clore's Settlement Trust* [1966] 1 W.L.R. 955.

[97] *Re Kershaw's Trusts* (1868) L.R. 6 Eq. 322.

[98] *Per* Lord Evershed in *Re Pilkington's W.T.* [1961] Ch. 466 at p. 481.

[99] " . . . if the advantage of preserving the funds of a beneficiary from the incidence of death duty is not an advantage personal to that beneficiary, I do not see what is"; *per* Lord Radcliffe in *Pilkington v. I.R.C., supra,* at p. 640; see also Upjohn J. in *Re Wills W.T.* [1959] Ch. 1, 11–12; *Re Clore's S.T.* [1966] 1 W.L.R. 955.

approved[1] and this inevitably meant that the trusts on which the funds would be held under the advancement were different from those laid down by the original settlor.

(c) *Delegation.* Closely connected with the question of resettlement is that of the extent to which trustees, in making an advancement on new trusts, can give discretionary powers to the trustees of the new settlement. In general, *delegatus non potest delegare.*[2] However, "the law is not that trustees cannot delegate: it is that trustees cannot delegate unless they have authority to do so. If the power of advancement which they possess is so read as to allow them to raise money for the purpose of having it settled, then they do have the necessary authority to let the money pass out of the old settlement into the new trusts. No question of delegation of their powers or trusts arises. If, on the other hand, their power of advancement is read so as to exclude settled advances, cadit quaestio."[3]

This does not, however, solve all the problems. The statutory power allows trustees to advance money by paying it to other trustees to hold on new trusts. Such trusts may include a power of advancement[4]; and presumably section 32 applies to the new trustees. Further, acting on the analogy of cases on special powers of appointment, it seems that the new trusts may include a protective and forfeitable life interest[5]; but that the discretionary trusts which come into effect upon the determination of the life interest may be invalid, because the duties of trustees of a discretionary trust involve dispositive (as opposed to administrative) discretions,[6] and these cannot be delegated without express authority.[7]

If that is correct, section 32 appears to give trustees no power to make an advancement upon a new settlement which takes the form of discretionary trusts. Such a situation appears necessarily to raise questions of delegation; and not to be covered by Lord Radcliffe's dictum quoted above.[8] Whether a settlement on discretionary trusts would satisfy the test of "benefit" is another matter; for under such a trust no interest of course is technically given to the advanced beneficiary.[9] The delegation problem can be met by expressly

---

[1] *Re Halsted's W.T.* [1937] 2 All E.R. 570; *Re Moxon's W.T.* [1958] 1 W.L.R. 165; *Re Ropner's S.T.* [1956] 1 W.L.R. 902; *Re Wills' W.T.* [1959] Ch. 1; *Re Abrahams' W.T.* [1969] 1 Ch. 463; *Re Hastings-Bass* [1975] Ch. 25; (1974) 38 Conv.(N.S.) 293 (F. Crane).

[2] *Re May* [1926] 1 Ch. 136; *Re Mewburn* [1934] Ch. 112; *Re Wills' W.T., supra.*

[3] *Per* Lord Radcliffe in *Pilkington v. I.R.C.* [1964] A.C. 612 at p. 639.

[4] *Re Mewburn* [1934] Ch. 112; *Re Morris* [1951] 2 All E.R. 528; *Re Hunter's W.T.* [1963] Ch. 372.

[5] *Re Boulton's S.T.* [1928] Ch. 703; *Re Hunter, supra; Re Morris, supra.*

[6] See (1953) 17 Conv.(N.S.) 285 at p. 289 (A. Kiralfy).

[7] *Per* Eve J. in *Re Boulton's S.T. ante,* at p. 709.

[8] *Supra.*

[9] *Gartside v. I.R.C.* [1968] A.C. 553. This is not *per se* an objection; *Re Clore's Settlement Trust, supra.*

empowering the trustees of the original settlement to delegate their powers in that manner.[10]

(d) *Perpetuity.* For the purposes of the perpetuity rule, the exercise of a power of advancement is treated, as has been seen,[11] on the analogy of a special power of appointment. Where a sub-trust is created by an advancement, the limitation in the sub-trust is tested for validity by being read back into the original instrument under which the power was exercised.[12] The advancements made in *Re Abrahams' Will Trusts*[13] and *Re Hastings-Bass*[14] failed, in part, to comply; as the intended advancement would have done in *Pilkington v. I.R.C.*[15] In *Re Abrahams' Will Trusts*, the failure of the void parts of the sub-trust wholly changed the character of the benefit being conferred on the beneficiary, and the advancement was held void. In *Re Hastings-Bass*, however, the trustees' prime consideration was to create a life interest in the life tenant of the sub-trust in order to save estate duty on the death of his father, the life tenant of the original settlement. The fact that the interests in remainder in the sub-trust were void for perpetuity did not make the advancement itself void.

In the case of advancements made under powers coming into existence after July 15, 1964 the interests under the sub-trust would be treated as valid until it became known that they would in fact vest outside the perpetuity period.[16]

vi. The Provisos.[17] (*a*) Only half the presumptive share of each beneficiary may be advanced under the statutory power.[18] No doubt this is a wise limitation as a general rule; for if the contingent interest of the advanced beneficiary never vests, the fund in the hands of the person next entitled is reduced by the amount advanced. However, it may be advantageous to be able to advance the whole; and it is common to extend the statutory power so as to give the trustees power to advance the whole if they see fit.

---

[10] For the view that *Pilkington v. I.R.C.* ([1964] A.C. 612) does authorise the creation of discretionary trusts under the statutory power of advancement, see (1963) 27 Conv.(N.S.) 65; Parker and Mellows, *The Modern Law of Trusts* (6th ed.), pp. 512–513.

[11] *Pilkington v. I.R.C.* [1964] A.C. 612; *ante*, p. 580.

[12] *Re Paul* [1921] 2 Ch. 1.

[13] [1969] 1 Ch. 463.

[14] [1975] Ch. 25; *ante*, p. 507.

[15] [1964] A.C. 612.

[16] Perpetuities and Accumulations Act 1964, s.3.

[17] Set out *ante*, p. 578.

[18] See *Re Marquess of Abergavenny's Estate Act Trusts* [1981] 1 W.L.R. 843; [1982] Conv. 158 (J. Price); (express power to pay life tenant any part or parts not exceeding one-half in value of the settled fund was exhausted by the advance of one-half, even though the remainder subsequently increased in value).

(*b*) This attempts to effect an equality between the members of a class of beneficiaries, by requiring those who have received benefits in advance of other members of a class of beneficiaries to count the advancement against their ultimate share.[19] Of course it is otherwise if the share never vests.[20]

(*c*) By advancing some or all of the capital, the fund which provides the income of the tenant for life is reduced. The consent of the tenant for life is therefore requisite to the exercise of the power. The court has no power to dispense with this consent.[21] A member of a discretionary class is not, however, a person whose consent is required.[22]

C. The Court's Inherent Power to Provide Maintenance and Advancement

The court has inherent power to order provision to be made for a minor out of his property. This power is usually applied in respect of income,[23] but occasionally capital is used.[24] Also, the court has statutory power to make an order authorising a person to make use of a minor's property with a view to the application of the capital or income for the minor's maintenance, education or benefit.[25]

D. Responsibility of the Trustees to See to the Application of the Money Advanced

We have seen that the trustees must be satisfied that the proposed advancement is for the benefit of the beneficiary. The next question is whether the trustees, in making an advancement, are under an obligation to see that the money is applied towards the purposes for which the payment was made. In *Re Pauling's Settlement Trusts*[26] the Court of Appeal, dealing with an express power to advance one-half of an expected or presumptive share for the "absolute use" of a beneficiary, held that the power was fiduciary; the trustees could

---

[19] The advance is brought into account at its value at the date of advancement. In times of inflation this can have capricious results. A form of indexation was therefore recommended by the Law Reform Committee, 23rd Report, *The Powers and Duties of Trustees* (1982 Cmnd. 8733), paras. 4.43–4.47.

[20] *Re Fox* [1904] 1 Ch. 480 (express power).

[21] *Re Forster's Settlement* [1942] Ch. 199. See also *Henley v. Wardell, The Times*, January 29, 1988. (Power in will giving trustees "absolute and uncontrolled discretion" to advance whole capital did not give them power to dispense with the consent of the prior income beneficiary. The purpose of the clause was merely to enlarge the power as to the amount advanced).

[22] *Re Beckett's Settlement* [1940] Ch. 279.

[23] *Wellesley v. Wellesley* (1828) 2 Bli.(N.S.) 124.

[24] *Barlow v. Grant* (1684) 1 Vern. 255.

[25] *Post*, p. 617; T.A. 1925, s. 53.

[26] [1964] Ch. 303; *post*, p. 644.

hand over a sum of capital quite generally to a beneficiary if they thought that he was the type of person who could be trusted with the money. Or, if the trustees made the advance for a particular purpose, which they stated, they could quite properly pay it over if they reasonably thought that he could be trusted to carry it out. "What they cannot do is prescribe a particular purpose, and then raise and pay the money over to the advancee leaving him or her entirely free, legally and morally, to apply it for that purpose or to spend it in any way he or she chooses without any responsibility on the trustees even to inquire as to its application."[27]

[27] [1964] Ch. 303 at p. 334.

Chapter 21

THE FIDUCIARY NATURE OF TRUSTEESHIP

1. Remuneration and Reimbursement 585
   A. Remuneration Authorised by the Trust
      Instrument 586
   B. Remuneration Authorised by Sta-
      tute 587
   C. Remuneration Authorised by the
      Court 587
   D. Remuneration for Litigious Work by
      Solicitor-Trustees 588
   E. Authorisation by Contract 589
2. Trustees must not be Purchasers 589
   A. Purchase of the Trust Property 589
   B. Purchase of the Beneficial Interest 591
3. Incidental Profits 591

A. Trustees 591
   i. Rule in *Keech v. Sandford* 591
   ii. Purchase of the Reversion 592
   iii. Trustees as Company Directors ... 593
   iv. Other Profits by Trustees 594
   v. A Trustee must not be in Competi-
      tion with the Trust 595
B. Other Fiduciaries 595
   i. The Principle 595
   ii. Company Directors 598
   iii. *Boardman v. Phipps* 601
   iv. The Extent of the Fiduciary
      Principle 605
C. Personal and Proprietary Remedies 607

1. REMUNERATION AND REIMBURSEMENT

THE basic principle is that a trustee acts voluntarily and is not paid for his services.[1] It does not matter whether his services are of a professional nature, as where he is a solicitor, or whether they are personal. It follows, therefore, that a trustee can only claim remuneration if he can show a specific entitlement to it. The discussion that follows is essentially an account of how that entitlement can arise.

It is also a basic principle that a trustee may recover for his legitimate out-of-pocket expenses, which include the payment of agents' fees wherever their employment is permitted,[2] and the

---

[1] *Robinson v. Pett* (1734) 3 P. Wms. 249; *Re Barber* (1886) 34 Ch.D. 77; *Dale v. I.R.C.* [1954] A.C. 11 at p. 27. This rule is to the contrary in many of the American States. English executors were held to be entitled to retain a fee earned by taking out a grant of probate in New York in respect of American assets; *Re Northcote's W.T.* [1949] 1 All E.R. 442. For the views of the Law Reform Committee, see 23rd Report, *The Powers and Duties of Trustees* (1982) Cmnd. 8733) paras. 3.45–3.58; [1984] Conv. 275 (N. Parry). See generally (1983) 46 M.L.R. 289 (W. Bishop and D. Prentice); (1995) 9 *Trust Law International* 50 (P. Matthews).

[2] This must be borne in mind when considering the principle that the trustee's office is gratuitous. His burden is alleviated to the extent that he can properly delegate the work to agents; *ante*, p. 559.

proper costs of litigation.[3] Trustees should seek the court's author-isation before suing or defending, to avoid the risk that their costs are found to have been improperly incurred. Where there is hostile litigation between rival claimants to the trust fund, the trustee should not become involved but should offer to submit to the court's direction; where the trustee is sued successfully by the beneficiaries, his costs will not come out of the trust fund; but where the dispute is with a third party, the trustee's duty is to protect the trust and he will be indemnified so long as the proceedings are properly brought or defended for the benefit of the trust, whether or not successfully.[4] Trustees do not fail in their duty where they discontinue litigation against a third party because the trust fund is likely to be exhausted in indemnifying them, leaving them personally exposed as to any insufficiency.[5]

The right to reimbursement is now statutory,[6] and prevails against trust property generally, both capital and income, and in some cases against the beneficiaries personally.[7]

A. Remuneration Authorised by the Trust Instrument

While equity remains true to its basic principle in that it construes strictly clauses authorising remuneration,[8] it is equally true that such clauses are extremely common, and are frequently drafted in a very wide manner. Indeed, if it were not so, it would be difficult to persuade professional people to act as trustees in view of the many and complex matters that now fall to be considered. The remuneration may take the form of the income from a part of the estate[9] or capital under a power of appointment,[10] or the trustee may be given power to make use of trust money in other ways.[11] A clause in a will authorising remuneration is for many purposes equivalent to a legacy.[12]

---

[3] *Ante*, p. 513. See *Re Spurling's Will Trusts* [1966] 1 W.L.R. 920; *Holding and Management Ltd v. Property Holding and Investment Trust plc* [1989] 1 W.L.R. 1313 (costs not recoverable where trustees had acted in a manner hostile to the beneficiaries).

[4] *Alsop Wilinson v. Neary* [1996] 1 W.L.R. 1220. See also *McDonald v. Horn* [1995] 1 All E.R. 961.

[5] *Bradstock Trustee Services Ltd v. Nabarro Nathanson (a firm)* [1995] 1 W.L.R. 1405.

[6] Trustee Act 1925, s.30(2); R.S.C. Ord. 62, r. 6. Interest is not payable; *Foster v. Spencer* [1996] 2 All E.R. 672.

[7] See generally *Stott v. Milne* (1884) 25 Ch.D. 710; *Re Grimthorpe* [1958] Ch. 615.

[8] *Re Chalinder & Herington* [1907] 1 Ch. 58; *Re Gee* [1948] Ch. 284.

[9] *Public Trustee v. I.R.C.* [1960] A.C. 398. See (1988) 2 *Trust Law & Practice* 93 (J. Thurston).

[10] *Re Beatty's W.T.* [1990] 1 W.L.R. 1503.

[11] See *Space Investments Ltd v. Canadian Imperial Bank of Commerce Trust Co. (Bahamas) Ltd* [1986] 1 W.L.R. 1072 (settlement provided that bank trustee could deposit trust money with itself and use for own purposes, subject to normal obligation to repay).

[12] *Re Pooley* (1888) 40 Ch.D. 1; *Re Thorley* [1891] 2 Ch. 613; *Re White* [1898] 2 Ch. 217.

B. Remuneration Authorised by Statute

Statutory provisions enable fees to be charged by the Public Trustee,[13] by persons appointed to be Judicial Trustees,[14] and by corporations appointed as custodian trustees.[15] In this last case, the corporation concerned cannot also be a managing trustee.[16] But where a corporation is appointed to be a trustee by the court, the court has full discretion as to its fees, and is not restricted by this distinction.[17]

C. Remuneration Authorised by the Court

The court has an inherent jurisdiction, which is exercisable retrospectively[18] and prospectively, but in exceptional cases only, to authorise remuneration for trustees and other fiduciaries. The power has even been exercised in favour of a fiduciary who was guilty of undue influence. In *O'Sullivan v. Management Agency and Music Ltd*[19] a contract between a performer and his agent was set aside for undue influence and breach of fiduciary duty, but the agent was awarded remuneration (including a reasonable profit element) as he had contributed significantly to the plaintiff's success. The argument that the jurisdiction was exercisable only in favour of the morally blameless was rejected.

The jurisdiction extends to increasing the rate of remuneration authorised by the settlor.[20] The court in such a case would have regard to the nature of the trust, the experience and skill of the trustee, and the sums claimed in comparison with the charges of other trustees.

Factors in favour of the exercise of the court's discretion include the fact that the fiduciary's work has been of substantial benefit to

---

[13] Public Trustee Act 1906, s.9; Public Trustee (Fees) Act 1957; Administration of Justice Act, 1965, s.2; Public Trustee (Fees) (Amendment) Order, 1995 (S.I. 1995/1425). He is paid such salary as the Lord Chancellor determines; Public Trustee Act 1906, s.8(1A).

[14] Judicial Trustees Act 1896, s.1.

[15] Public Trustee Act 1906, s.4.

[16] *Forster v. Williams Deacon's Bank Ltd* [1935] Ch. 359; *Arning v. James* [1936] Ch. 158.

[17] Trustee Act 1925, s.42.

[18] *Re Worthington* [1954] 1 W.L.R. 526; *Re Jarvis* [1958] 1 W.L.R. 815; *Phipps v. Boardman* [1967] 2 A.C. 46; *Foster v. Spencer* [1996] 2 All E.R. 672. For the views of the Charity Commissioners on remuneration of trustees of a charitable trust, see Annual Report 1978, paras. 11–20; Annual Report 1981, paras. 61–64; *cf.* (1987) 50 N.L.J. Annual Charities Review 24 (H. Picarda).

[19] [1985] Q.B. 428; (1986) 49 M.L.R. 118 (W. Bishop and D. Prentice). See also *Warman International Ltd v. Dwyer* (1995) 69 A.L.J.R. 362 (share of profits of business); (1996) 55 C.L.J. 201 (R. Nolan).

[20] *Re Duke of Norfolk's S.T.* [1982] Ch. 61; (1982) 45 M.L.R. 211 (B. Green); (1982) 98 L.Q.R. 181 (P.V.B.); [1982] Conv. 231 (K. Hodkinson). See also *Re Barbour's Settlement* [1974] 1 W.L.R. 1198 (application for increase should be made directly and not included as a term of a compromise of an unconnected dispute); *cf. Re Codd's W.T.* [1975] 1 W.L.R. 1139.

the trust, as in *Boardman v. Phipps*,[21] and that if the work had not been done by the fiduciary it would have had to be done by someone else at the expense of the trust.[22] A recent example is where trustees (a surveyor and a building contractor) used special skills over many years to bring about a sale of trust land at a profit. They had not appreciated the extent of the task when appointed, otherwise they would have declined to act gratuitously. Remuneration was awarded for the work done, but not for remaining tasks, which required no special expertise.[23] The House of Lords in *Guinness v. Saunders*[24] refused a claim to remuneration by a company director who, it was assumed, had acted bona fide but in circumstances involving a clear conflict of interest and duty. It was doubted whether the jurisdiction would ever be exercised in favour of a director, as this would constitute interference by the court in the administration of the company's affairs. The company's articles gave the power to remunerate to the board of directors, to whom the claim should be addressed. Lord Goff considered that the jurisdiction could only be reconciled with the fundamental rule that a trustee is not entitled to remuneration to the extent that its exercise did not conflict with the policy underlying that rule. Such a conflict would only be avoided if the exercise of the jurisdiction was restricted to cases where it could not have the effect of encouraging trustees to put themselves in a position of conflict of interest and duty.[25] *Boardman v. Phipps*[26] was such a case. There the merits of the claim were overwhelming, but the present case was very different: the director had put himself in a position where his interests were in stark conflict with his duty. Also, he had received money which belonged to the company.

D. Remuneration for Litigious Work by Solicitor-Trustees

Under the rule in *Cradock v. Piper*,[27] a solicitor-trustee may charge costs if he has acted for a *co-trustee as well as himself*[28] in respect of business done in an action or matter *in court*, provided that his activities have not increased the expenses. It is not necessary that the court action should be hostile in character, but it must be

---

[21] [1967] 2 A.C. 46, *post*, p. 601.
[22] *Re Berkeley Applegate (Investment Consultants) Ltd* [1989] Ch. 32 at pp. 50–51.
[23] *Foster v. Spencer, supra.*
[24] [1990] 2 A.C. 663; (1990) 106 L.Q.R. 365 (J. Beatson and D. Prentice); (1990) 49 C.L.J. 220 (J. Hopkins). The facts are given at p. 599, *post.*
[25] *Ibid.* at p. 701; *cf. O'Sullivan v. Management Agency and Music Ltd* [1985] Q.B. 428, *ante,* p. 587, which was not referred to.
[26] *Supra.*
[27] (1850) 1 Mac. & G. 664. See (1983) 46 M.L.R. 289 at p. 306 (W. Bishop and D. Prentice).
[28] *Lyon v. Baker* (1852) 5 De G. & Sm. 622.

some form of litigious matter.[29] The rule will not be extended by analogies.

It may also be noted here that a solicitor-trustee may employ his *partner* in cases where it would be proper to employ an outside solicitor, provided that he himself will derive no benefit, direct *or* indirect, from such an employment.[30] There must be complete separation of the trust work from the firm's general work, so as to make it clear that the solicitor-trustee is not involved in the former. This power is not restricted to matters in court, but it does not enable a solicitor-trustee to employ his own *firm*.[31]

E. Authorisation by Contract

Trustees may contract for remuneration with those beneficiaries who are *sui juris*.[32] But such agreements may somewhat easily be brought under the head of undue influence,[33] and are not encouraged. Nor, in fact, are they at all common.

2. Trustees must not be Purchasers

A. Purchase of the Trust Property

This rule and those which follow are based on the principle that a trustee may not place himself in a position where his duty and his interest may conflict.[34] This means that trustees are not to become the owners or lessees of trust property. This rule is independent of any question of inadequacy of price, or unfairness, or undue advantage; the sale may have been at auction and the trustee may have taken the bidding well above the reserve price, but he is still caught by the rule, which derives from his status and position and not from his conduct in the particular case.[35] Nor does it matter that he left the decision to sell and the manner of sale wholly to his co-trustee; nor

---

[29] *Re Corsellis* (1887) 34 Ch.D. 675.
[30] *Clack v. Carlon* (1861) 30 L.J.Ch. 639.
[31] *Christophers v. White* (1847) 10 Beav. 523; *Re Gates* [1933] Ch. 913; *Re Hill* [1934] Ch. 623.
[32] No remuneration may be paid out of the trust property by agreement with the beneficiaries if they are not all *sui juris*. In such a case, application must be made to court, as in *Re Duke of Norfolk's S.T.*, *supra*, (living beneficiaries did not object, but some unborn).
[33] *Ayliffe v. Murray* (1740) 2 Atk. 58; *post*, pp. 828 *et seq.*
[34] *Boardman v. Phipps* [1967] 2 A.C. 46 at p. 123. This principle does not apply if it is the settlor who has placed the trustees in such a position; *Sargeant v. National Westminster Bank plc* (1991) 61 P. & C.R. 518.
[35] *Campbell v. Walker* (1800) 5 Ves.Jr. 678; *ex p. Lacey* (1802) 6 Ves.Jr. 625; *Movitex Ltd v. Bulfield* [1988] B.C.L.C. 104.

that he retired from the trust before making an offer.[36] His responsibility as trustee is such that he must not contemplate the purchase at all.

The rule was somewhat relaxed in *Holder v. Holder*,[37] involving an executor who had purported to renounce the executorship, but invalidly, as he had already done some minor acts in the administration of the estate. After his purported renunciation, the executor took no further part in the administration. He later purchased at auction for a fair price some farmland belonging to the estate, of which he had previously been tenant. The Court of Appeal declined to set aside the purchase. The circumstances were special, because the executor had not interfered in the administration of the estate; nor had he taken part in organising the auction; nor was there any conflict of interest and duty, as the beneficiaries were not looking to him to protect their interests; and finally, any special knowledge he had about the property was acquired as tenant and not as executor. In any event, the plaintiff beneficiary had acquiesced in the sale. As a general rule, however, a trustee or executor who has once involved himself in his office is affected by the rule for a considerable period after retirement.

The effect of the rule is that the purchase is voidable at the option of a beneficiary, who is allowed a generous time to discover the position.[38] The right to avoid the sale is effective against a purchaser with notice of the circumstances. The rule cannot be got around by sales to nominees,[39] for a repurchase by the trustee will be regarded as on behalf of the trust (unless the original sale was bona fide).[40] A sale to the trustee's wife is looked upon with suspicion,[41] and likewise a sale to a company in which the trustee has a substantial interest.[42]

The court may in certain circumstances prefer to order a re-sale, and, if the price is higher than the previous sale price, the trustee

---

[36] *Wright v. Morgan* [1926] A.C. 788; *Re Boles and British Land Co.'s Contract* [1902] 1 Ch. 244.

[37] [1968] Ch. 353. *Cf. Re Mulholland's W.T.* [1949] 1 All E.R. 460 (option to purchase acquired before trusteeship).

[38] For an illustration see *Re Sherman* [1954] Ch. 653.

[39] *Silkstone & Haigh Moor Coal Co. v. Edey* [1900] 1 Ch. 167.

[40] *Re Postlethwaite* (1888) 60 L.T. 514.

[41] See *Burrell v. Burrell's Trustees* 1915 S.C. 33, where the sale was upheld; *Tito v. Waddell (No. 2)* [1977] Ch. 106.

[42] See *Re Thompson's Settlement* [1986] Ch. 99; (1986) 1 *Trust Law & Practice* 66 (C. Sherrin), where the contract for sale to a company of which the trustee was managing director and majority shareholder was held unenforceable; *Movitex Ltd v. Bulfield* [1988] B.C.L.C. 104. A mortgagee is also debarred from selling the property to himself, but it has been held that he can sell to a company in which he has an interest if he acts in good faith and gets the best price reasonably obtainable; *Tse Kwong Lam v. Wong Chit Sen* [1983] 1 W.L.R. 1349. See also *Farrar v. Farrar's Ltd* (1889) 40 Ch.Div. 395.

must convey; otherwise he is held to his purchase. The trustee will not be allowed to bid at the new sale if this is objected to.[43]

The rule discussed above is subject to certain exceptions. The trust instrument may expressly permit the purchase by a trustee.[44] Secondly, the court has a discretion to allow such a purchase in a proper case,[45] or to permit the trustee to bid at an auction.[46] Finally, a tenant for life of settled land, which he holds on trust, is permitted by statute to purchase the property.[47]

B. Purchase of the Beneficial Interest

Equity's view is less stringent when dealing with a purchase by a trustee of the beneficial interest of a beneficiary.[48] This is a type of transaction which is carefully watched; the onus is on the trustee to show that he gave full value, and that all information was laid before the beneficiary when it was sold.[49] The principles of undue influence apply; but it is open to a trustee in this type of case to show that the whole transaction was conducted at arm's length. This must however be very distinctly proved.[50]

3. INCIDENTAL PROFITS

A. Trustees

The rules discussed below apply in full force to trustees. Many of them apply also to other fiduciaries. Although we are mainly concerned here with trustees, it will be convenient to mention also, where relevant, the application of the rules to persons who are not strictly trustees.

i. Rule in Keech v. Sandford.[51] This rule prevents a trustee from keeping for his own benefit a renewal of a lease which he was able to obtain for himself by reason of his being the trustee of the original lease; and even though the trustee had tried unsuccessfully

---

[43] See Cross J. in *Holder v. Holder* [1968] Ch. 353 at p. 371.

[44] See *Sargeant v. National Westminster Bank plc* (1991) 61 P. & C.R. 518.

[45] *Farmer v. Dean* (1863) 32 Beav. 327. Or the beneficiaries, all being *sui juris*, may agree to it.

[46] *Holder v. Holder, supra,* at pp. 398, 402.

[47] S.L.A. 1925, s.68; *Re Pennant's W.T.* [1970] Ch. 75.

[48] *Tito v. Waddell (No. 2) supra,* at p. 241; *Re Thompson's Settlement* [1986] Ch. 99.

[49] *Thomson v. Eastwood* (1877) 2 App.Cas. 215 at p. 236; *Hill v. Langley, The Times,* January 28, 1988.

[50] See generally *Coles v. Trecothick* (1804) 9 Ves.Jr. 234; *Morse v. Royal* (1806) 12 Ves.Jr. 355; *cf. Williams v. Scott* [1900] A.C. 499.

[51] (1726) Sel. Cas. t. King 61; (1969) 33 Conv.(N.S.) 161 (S. Cretney); *Re Edwards' W.T.* [1982] Ch. 30; *Chan v. Zacharia* (1984) 154 C.L.R. 178; *cf. Harris v. Black* (1983) 127 S.J. 224.

to obtain a renewal for the benefit of his beneficiary. In the leading case, from which the rule takes its name, the defendant held a lease of the profits of a market on trust for a minor. Before the expiration of the lease, the defendant asked the lessor to renew the lease in favour of the minor. The lessor refused to grant a lease to the minor on the grounds that, as the lease was of the profits of the market, he would be unable to distrain, and would be unable to enforce the covenant against the minor. The trustee then took a lease for his own benefit.

Lord Chancellor King held that the trustee must hold the lease on trust for the minor. "This may seem hard," he said,[52] "that the trustee is the only person of all mankind who might not have the lease; but it is very proper that the rule should be strictly pursued, and not in the least relaxed; for it is very obvious what would be the consequences of letting trustees have the lease, on refusal to renew to *cestui que use.*"

It is otherwise, however, where there is no fiduciary relationship.

> In *Re Biss,*[53] a lessor had refused to renew a seven-year lease of premises, and the lessee remained in possession as tenant from year to year. He died, leaving a widow and three children. The widow, who was his administratrix, and two of the children continued the business under the existing lease. The lessor terminated the lease, and then granted a three-year lease to one of the children. The Court of Appeal allowed him to keep the lease for his own benefit. Romer L.J. said that[54] "where the person renewing the lease does not clearly occupy a fiduciary position" he "is only held to be a constructive trustee of the renewed lease if, in respect of the old lease, he occupied some special position and owed, by virtue of that position, a duty towards the other persons interested."

ii. Purchase of the Reversion. Where the trustee acquires the freehold reversion, the position is unclear.[55] The trustee is liable if he has in any way made use of his position to get a personal benefit: thus if the lessor makes an offer to all his lessees giving them the right to enfranchisement on favourable terms, or if the lessee had any statutory right of enfranchisement, there could be no doubt that the trustee who sought to take the reversion for his own benefit

---

[52] (1726) Sel. Cas. t. King 61 at p. 62.
[53] [1903] 2. Ch. 40; *Brenner v. Rose* [1973] 1 W.L.R. 443. See also *Savage v. Dunningham* [1974] Ch. 181.
[54] [1903] 2 Ch. 40 at p. 61.
[55] The converse situation where a trustee of the reversion purchases the lease was left open in *Re Thompson's Settlement* [1986] Ch. 99.

would be liable. The courts have, however, vacillated in deciding whether there is any *absolute* liability in the absence of such abuse.[56] In *Protheroe v. Protheroe*[57] the Court of Appeal, without referring to the relevant authorities, held that the rule was applicable, without qualification, to purchases of the freehold. A husband held the lease of the matrimonial home on trust for his wife and himself in equal shares. After the wife had petitioned for divorce, he purchased the freehold reversion. When he sold, the wife was held to be entitled to a share of the proceeds.[58] In earlier cases the courts had limited the rule to cases where the lease, the reversion on which was being purchased, was renewable by law or custom.[59] The rationale of that limitation was that if the lease were normally renewed in practice,[60] the lessee would suffer if the lease passed to a third party who might not follow the custom (particularly if the lease, as was commonly the case with church leases, was generally renewed at less than the market rent). Thus it was wrong to allow the trustee, who ought to be protecting his beneficiary's interests, to damage them. Today, by statute, many lessees are given valuable rights of renewal or enfranchisement. It is submitted that the proper question in each case is: has the trustee taken advantage of his position to get a personal benefit? If so, he is liable, otherwise he is not. "It seems to me," said Pennycuick V.-C. in *Thompson's Trustee in Bankruptcy v. Heaton*,[61] "that apart from the fact that it binds me, this decision [*Protheroe v. Protheroe*], like the rule in *Keech v. Sandford*, is really in modern terms an application of the broad principle that the trustee must not make a profit out of the trust estate." The onus would be on the trustee to satisfy the court, and it can be a very difficult one to discharge.

iii. Trustees as Company Directors. The question has arisen several times in connection with the remuneration of directorships which trustees have obtained by virtue of their position as trustees.

---

[56] *Norris v. Le Neve* (1743) 3 Atk. 26; *Randall v. Russell* (1817) 3 Mer. 190; *cf. Phillips v. Phillips* (1885) 29 Ch.D. 673.

[57] [1968] 1 W.L.R. 519; (1968) 31 M.L.R. 707 (P. Jackson); (1968) 32 Conv.(N.S.) 220 (F. Crane); *Thompson's Trustee v. Heaton* [1974] 1 W.L.R. 605; (1974) 38 Conv.(N.S.) 288; (1975) 38 M.L.R. 226 (P. Jackson); *Popat v. Shonchhatra* [1995] 4 All E.R. 646.

[58] "It may be that there were facts in the case which indicated that the husband obtained the freehold by virtue of his position as leaseholder, but they are not apparent from the report"; (1968) 84 L.Q.R. 309 (L. Megarry).

[59] *Bevan v. Webb* [1905] 1 Ch. 620; *cf. Griffith v. Owen* [1907] 1 Ch. 195; *per* Wilberforce J. in *Phipps v. Boardman* [1964] 1 W.L.R. 993 at p. 1009.

[60] See generally (1969) 33 Conv.(N.S.) 161 (S. Cretney), where the history of the doctrine is traced.

[61] [1974] W.L.R. 605 at p. 606 Textbook criticisms of *Protheroe* were rejected.

In *Re Macadam,*[62] trustees had power under the articles by virtue of their office to appoint two directors of a company. They appointed themselves, and were held liable to account for the remuneration which they received because they had acquired it by the use of their powers as trustees.

On the other hand, the remuneration may be retained if the trustees were directors before they became trustees,[63] or if the trustees were appointed directors independently of the votes of the shares of the trust,[64] or if the trustee did not obtain the remuneration by the use of his position as a trustee, but by an independent bargain with the firm employing him.[65] Indeed, as Cohen J. said in *Re Macadam.*[66] " . . . the root of the matter really is: Did [the trustee] acquire the position in respect of which he drew the remuneration by virtue of his position as trustee?" Trustees will not be liable even within that test if the terms of the trust authorised them to appoint themselves and receive remuneration.[67]

iv. Other Profits by Trustees. Incidental profits come to trustees in a variety of ways and must always be disgorged. "Whenever it can be shewn that the trustee has so arranged matters as to obtain an advantage, whether in money or money's worth, to himself personally through the execution of his trust, he will not be permitted to retain, but will be compelled to make it over to his constituent."[68]

A few examples must suffice. A trustee who introduced to a firm, of which he was a member, business of the trust, was compelled to account for the profit[69]; similarly, a trustee who received a sum of £75 to induce him to retire[70] and a trustee who used trust funds in his own business was required to account for the profits he received[71]; and a trustee may be liable for profits which he ought

---

[62] [1964] Ch. 73; *Re Francis* (1905) 92 L.T. 77; *Williams v. Barton* [1927] 2 Ch. 9.

[63] *Re Dover Coalfield Extension Ltd* [1908] 1 Ch. 65. See also *Re Orwell's W.T.* [1982] 1 W.L.R. 1337.

[64] *Re Gee* [1948] Ch. 284.

[65] *Re Lewis* (1910) 103 L.T. 495, as explained in *Re Gee, supra.*

[66] [1946] Ch. 73 at p. 82. Harman J. accepted this test in *Re Gee, supra.*

[67] *Re Llewellin's W.T.* [1949] Ch. 225. The court may sanction the retention of the fees; *Re Keeler's S.T.* [1981] Ch. 156.

[68] *Huntingdon Copper Co. v. Henderson* (1872) 4 R. (Court of Session) 294 at p. 308. *Cf. Patel v. Patel* [1981] 1 W.L.R. 1342 (no breach where trustees sought to live in the trust property where the beneficiaries were young children adopted by the trustees on the death of their parents).

[69] *Williams v. Barton* [1927] 2 Ch. 9; *cf. Jones v. AMP Perpetual Trustee Company NZ Ltd* [1994] 1 N.Z.L.R. 690 (no breach where subsidiary placed trust business with parent company).

[70] *Sugden v. Crossland* (1856) 3 Sm. & G. 192; *Re Smith* [1896[1 Ch. 71.

[71] *Brown v. I.R.C.* [1965] A.C. 244 (a Scottish solicitor compelled to account for interest earned by deposits of clients' moneys).

reasonably to have received.[72] It has been suggested that trustees of pension funds who are also beneficiaries are excluded from benefit where they exercise a power to apply funds among a class of which they are members.[73] This over-strict interpretation of the principle, which has not been applied to trustee-beneficiaries of other trusts, has now been overturned by statute.[74]

v. Trustee must not be in Competition with the Trust. One possible area of conflict of interest and duty is where the trustee operates in business in competition with the trust. Such competition was inevitable in *Re Thompson*[75] where executors of a will were directed to carry on the business of the testator who had been a yacht broker. One of the executors was intending to set up on his own account as a yacht broker in competition. It was held that he must not set up in a competing business.

This rule applies to other fiduciaries who are not trustees. A partner is required by statute to "account for and pay over to the firm all profits made" by carrying on a business "of the same nature as and competing with that of the firm"[76] unless he has the consent of the other partners. It is a question of fact in each case whether or not the activity is in conflict with the fiduciary duty.[77]

B. Other Fiduciaries[78]

i. The Principle. A similar rule applies to profits made by other persons in breach of a fiduciary relation; indeed such persons are grouped with trustees in many formulations of the rule although there is no rule that they must act gratuitously. "It is an inflexible rule of a Court of Equity that a person in a fiduciary position, . . . is not, unless otherwise expressly provided, entitled to make a profit; he is not allowed to put himself in a position where his interest and

---

[72] *Re Waterman's W.T.* [1952] 2 All E.R. 1054.

[73] *British Coal Corp. v. British Coal Staff Superannuation Scheme Trustees Ltd* [1995] 1 All E.R. 912 at p. 925; *cf. In re Drexel Burnham Lambert U.K. Pension Plan* [1995] 1 W.L.R. 32; (1996) 10 *Trust Law International* 49 (J. Mowbray).

[74] Pensions Act 1995, s.39; *ante*, p. 463.

[75] [1930] 1 Ch. 203; *Aberdeen Railway Co. v. Blaikie Bros.* (1854) 1 Macq. 461; *Warman International Ltd v. Dwyer* (1995) 69 A.L.J.R. 362.

[76] Partnership Act 1890, s.30.

[77] *Moore v. M'Glynn* [1894] 1 Ir.R. 74.

[78] Goff and Jones, Chap. 33; (1968) 84 L.Q.R. 472 (G. Jones); (1976) 92 L.Q.R. 360 at p. 372 (R. Goode); Oakley, *Constructive Trusts* (3rd ed.), Chap. 3; (1981) 97 L.Q.R. 51 (J. Shepherd); Shepherd, *The Law of Fiduciaries* (1981); Snell, pp. 251–253. See Law Com. No. 236 (1995), *Fiduciary Duties and Regulatory Rules*, examining the mismatch between general law obligations and regulatory rules.

duty conflict."[79] But it is not safe to make the attractive over-simplification of saying that a fiduciary must always account for all gains which come to him by reason of his fiduciary position. Indeed, Lord Herschell in the paragraph containing the above quotation "plainly recognised its limitations."[80] But I am satisfied that it might be departed from in many cases, without any breach of morality, without any wrong being inflicted, and without any consciousness of wrong-doing. Indeed, it is obvious that it might sometimes be to the advantage of the beneficiaries that their trustee should act for them professionally rather than a stranger, even though the trustee were paid for his services."[81]

It is not always easy, however, to determine whether a particular relationship should be classified as fiduciary. While some examples are well established, the boundaries of the category of fiduciary relationships are not clear, and the category is not closed.[82] It includes certain agents,[83] (including "self-appointed" agents[84]), solicitors,[85] company directors,[86] partners,[87] confidential employees,[88] a pawnbroker,[89] and certain bailees,[90] but not a vendor of goods to which title has not yet passed to the purchaser.[91]

---

[79] Lord Herschell in *Bray v. Ford* [1896] A.C.44 at p. 51; see also Lord Cranworth in *Aberdeen Railway Co. v. Blaikie Bros.* (1854) 1 Macq. 461 at p. 471; *Regal (Hastings) Ltd v. Gulliver* [1942] 1 All E.R. 378; [1967] 2 A.C. 134n.

[80] Lord Upjohn in *Boardman v. Phipps* [1967] 2 A.C. 46 at p. 123.

[81] *Bray v. Ford* [1896] A.C. 44 at p. 52.

[82] *English v. Dedham Vale Properties Ltd* [1978] 1 W.L.R. 93.

[83] *De Bussche v. Alt* (1878) 8 Ch.D. 286; *N.Z. Netherlands Society v. Kuys* [1973] 1 W.L.R. 1126 at p. 1129. Not all agents are fiduciaries, although there may be a presumption that they are; *Aluminium Industrie Vaasen B.V. v. Romalpa Aluminium Ltd* [1976] 1 W.L.R. 676; *post*, p. 682. See Goff and Jones, p. 85, n. 74, suggesting that "much depends on whether the agent is under a duty to keep separate his own money from his principal's money." *Cf. Re Air Canada and M. & L. Travel Ltd* (1994) 108 D.L.R. (4th) 592.

[84] *English v. Dedham Vale Properties Ltd, supra.* (where the intending purchaser obtained planning permission in·the vendor's name); (1978) 41 M.L.R. 474 (A. Nicol); (1978) 94 L.Q.R. 347 (G. Samuel).

[85] *Brown v. I.R.C.* [1965] A.C. 244; (1964) 80 L.Q.R. 480; *Islamic Republic of Iran Shipping Lines v. Denby* [1987] 1 Lloyd's Rep. 367. See also *Hanson v. Lorenz* [1987] 1 F.T.L.R. 23 (no liability to account to client for his profits from a joint venture where client had understood the agreement). As to whether a head of chambers is in a fiduciary position to the members, see *Appleby v. Cowley, The Times,* April 14, 1982.

[86] *Regal (Hastings) Ltd v. Gulliver, supra; Industrial Development Consultants Ltd v. Cooley* [1972] 1 W.L.R. 443; *post*, p. 598. See also *Horcal Ltd v. Gatland, The Times,* April 16, 1984.

[87] *Featherstonhaugh v. Fenwick* (1810) 17 Ves.Jr. 298; *Clegg v. Fishwick* (1849) 1 Mac. & G. 294.

[88] *Triplex Safety Glass Co. v. Scorah* [1938] Ch. 211; *Att.-Gen. v. Guardian Newspapers Ltd (No. 2)* [1990] 1 A.C. 109 (The "Spycatcher" case; duty to account for profits). A former member of the security service does not owe a continuing fiduciary duty to the Crown; *Att.-Gen. v. Blake* [1996] 3 W.L.R. 741; (1996) 146 N.L.J. 727 (J. Stevens).

[89] *Mathew v. T.M. Sutton Ltd* [1994] 1 W.L.R. 1455; All E.R. Rev. 1994 p. 26 (N. Palmer). (Surplus proceeds of sale held on trust for pawnor and interest payable).

[90] *Aluminium Industrie Vaasen B.V. v. Romalpa Aluminium Ltd, supra; Re Andrabell Ltd (in liq.)* [1984] 3 All E.R. 407.

[91] *Re Goldcorp Exchange Ltd (in receivership)* [1995] 1 A.C. 74.

Indeed, it may sometimes appear that the defendant may be classified as a fiduciary, or not, in order to achieve the desired result.

In *Reading v. Attorney-General*,[92] a staff-sergeant in the British Army stationed in Cairo was bribed by Egyptians to ride in their civilian lorries carrying contraband goods, enabling the lorries to pass check posts without difficulty. The British authorities seized £20,000 from Reading; later he petitioned to recover it. He had obtained the money wrongfully, but he argued that this fact did not mean that the British Government was entitled to claim it. Reading failed, however, and one of the grounds for the decision in the House of Lords was that he, as a non-commissioned officer, was in a fiduciary relation to the Crown, and was therefore under a duty to account for the profit wrongfully made.

Illegal or secret commissions or bribes obtained by a confidential servant or agent are recoverable by the principal or employer regardless of any quantifiable loss by him.[93] If the fiduciary relationship in this case is accepted, the result merely follows the earlier cases on agents. The application of the rule to a policeman[94] and a staff-sergeant may be an extension; indeed it has been said that the speeches in the House of Lords in *Reading v. Attorney-General*[95] "confirm that the status of a fiduciary may ... be easily acquired."[96]

In *Swain v. The Law Society*,[97] on the other hand, the House of Lords declined to find such a relationship.

The Society negotiated a compulsory insurance scheme on behalf of all solicitors. It kept the commission on the policy, which it applied for the purposes of the profession. The plaintiff, a solicitor, objected to the scheme and claimed that the Society must account for the commission as a profit made out of a fiduciary position. The alleged conflict of interest and duty lay in the fact that it was in the interest of the Society to negotiate a high premium (resulting in a higher commission) while its duty to the

---

[92] [1951] A.C. 507.
[93] *Att.-Gen. for Hong Kong v. Reid* [1994] 1 A.C.; *post*, p. 608. See also *Brown v. I.R.C.* [1965] A.C. 244; *Mahesan v. Malaysia Government Officers Cooperative Housing Society Ltd* [1979] A.C. 374; (1979) 95 L.Q.R. 68 (A Tettenborn); *Logicrose Ltd v. Southend United Football Club Ltd* [1988] 1 W.L.R. 1256 (principal can recover from agent whether he affirms or repudiates the transaction between the agent and the third party); (1989) 48 C.L.J. 22 (G. Jones).
[94] *Att.-Gen. v. Goddard* (1929) 98 L.J.K.B. 743 (bribes received when on duty).
[95] *Supra.*
[96] Goff and Jones, p. 667.
[97] [1983] A.C. 598; [1982] Conv. 447 (A. Kenny).

solicitors was to obtain a low one. The House of Lords found in favour of the Society. It had not acted unconscionably, and there was no fiduciary relationship. The scheme was entered into with statutory authority.[98] The Society was acting in its public capacity. Private law concepts such as accountability and breach of trust did not apply.

ii. Company Directors.[99] Company directors are treated as fiduciaries[1] in so far as they are prohibited from making a profit out of their office[2] unless the articles permit it or the shareholders consent.[3] The leading case is the House of Lords decision in *Regal (Hastings) Ltd v. Gulliver.*[4]

R. Ltd set up a subsidiary, A. Ltd, to acquire the leases of two cinemas. A. Ltd had a share capital of 5,000 £1 shares. The owner of the cinemas was only willing to lease them if the share capital of A. Ltd was completely subscribed for. However, R. Ltd had resources to subscribe for only 2,000 of the 5,000 shares and it was therefore agreed that the directors of R. Ltd should subscribe for the rest. When the business of R. Ltd was transferred to new controllers the directors made a profit from their holdings in A. Ltd. The new controllers of R. Ltd caused the company to sue the ex-directors of R. Ltd for an account of the profit. The directors were held liable. They had made the profit out of their position as directors and, in the absence of shareholder approval,[5] they were obliged to account.

There are a number of noteworthy features of *Regal*. First, the directors were found by the court to have acted bona fide, but the liability of a fiduciary to account for a profit made from his office "in no way depends on fraud, or absence of bona fides."[6] Secondly,

---

[98] Solicitors Act 1974, s.37.

[99] See also, on insider dealing, Criminal Justice Act 1993, ss.52, 53; Parker and Mellows, *The Modern Law of Trusts* (6th ed.), pp. 459–460.

[1] The duty is traditionally regarded as owed to the company, not to the shareholders; *Percival v. Wright* [1902] 2 Ch. 421. But see (1975) 28 C.L.P. 83 (D. Prentice).

[2] The office of director should not, however, be equated with that of trustee. The assets of the company, unlike trust property, are not vested in the director but in the company which is a separate legal entity and, more importantly, directors "are . . . commercial men managing a trading concern for the benefit of themselves and of all other shareholders in it . . . ": *per* Jessell M.R. in *Re Forest of Dean Coal Mining Co. Ltd* (1878) 10 Ch.D. 450, at pp. 451–452.

[3] See *Neptune (Vehicle Washing Equipment) Ltd v. Fitzgerald* [1996] Ch. 274.

[4] [1967] 2 A.C. 134n.

[5] Lord Russell of Killowen considered that the shareholders could have ratified the director's breach of duty: [1967] 2 A.C. 134n. at p. 150. On this controversial aspect of the case, see (1958) 16 C.L.J. 93 at 102–106; (K. Wedderburn); *Prudential Assurance Co. Ltd v. Newman Industries Ltd (No. 2)* [1981] Ch. 257; (1981) 44 M.L.R. 202.

[6] [1967] 2 A.C. 134n. at p. 144.

the new controllers obtained a windfall.[7] Thirdly, it was arguable that the directors by purchasing the shares in A. Ltd had enabled R. Ltd to enter into a transaction which it was otherwise commercially impossible for the company to enter into. While there is some truth in this, the decision that R. Ltd did not have the necessary financial resources to enter into the transaction was made by the directors who were the very persons who benefited from this decision. Because of this a compelling argument can be made that a "reasonable man looking at the relevant facts and circumstances of the particular case would think that there was a real sensible possibility of conflict."[8]

A clear case of conflict of interest and duty arose in *Guinness plc v. Saunders*,[9] where a director (Ward) agreed to provide his services in connection with a proposed take-over of another company (Distillers), on terms that he would be paid a fee the size of which depended on the amount of the take-over bid if successful. The bid was successful, and the fee paid to Ward was £5.2 million. The claim by Guinness for summary judgment for the repayment of this sum was upheld in the House of Lords. Ward's interest in obtaining a fee calculated on the above basis conflicted with his duty as director, which was to give impartial advice concerning the take-over. The agreement for the fee, made with two other directors, but the not the board of directors, was void for want of authority. Ward had no arguable defence to Guinness's claim that he had received the money, paid under a void contract, as a constructive trustee.

The courts have imposed liability on directors to account where the directors have made the profit out of an economic opportunity, or information, even though they acquired it in a personal capacity, if it was information which could have been exploited by their company.[10]

In *Industrial Development Consultants Ltd v. Cooley*,[11] the defendant was a director and general manager of the plaintiffs, who provided construction consultancy services. He attempted to interest a public Gas Board in a project, but was unsuccessful because the Gas Board's policy was not to employ development companies. The defendant was a distinguished architect who had

---

[7] See (1979) 42 M.L.R. 215 (D. Prentice).

[8] *Boardman v. Phipps* [1967] 2 A.C. 46 at p. 124, *per* Lord Upjohn.

[9] [1990] 2 A.C. 663; (1990) 106 L.Q.R. 365 (J. Beatson and D. Prentice); (1990) 49 C.L.J. 220 (J. Hopkins); [1990] Conv. 296 (S. Goulding).

[10] See *Canadian Aero Service Ltd v. O'Malley* (1973) 40 D.L.R. (3d) 371 (S.C.C.).

[11] [1972] 1 W.L.R. 443; [1972] 2 All E.R. 162 (the reports on the case are not identical); (1973) 89 L.Q.R. 187 (A. Yoran); (1972A) 30 C.L.J. 222 (J. Collier); (1972) 35 M.L.R. 655 (H. Rajak); (1972) 50 C.B.R. 623 (D. Prentice).

worked in the gas industry for many years. For this reason the Gas Board decided to offer the contract to him personally, which he accepted, obtaining a release from the plaintiffs by falsely representing that he was ill. He was held to be liable to account to the plaintiffs for the profits of the contract.

The significance of the case is twofold. First, the court rejected Cooley's defence that the information concerning the Gas Board's contract came to him in his private capacity, and not as director of the plaintiffs; this "is the first case in which it was decided that the prohibition on exploiting a corporate opportunity applies also to an opportunity which was presented to the director personally and not in his capacity with the company."[12] Secondly, the decision whether or not the contract went to the company lay not with the fiduciary, Cooley, but with a third party, the Gas Board.[13] In *Cooley's* case there were special circumstances; this was exactly the type of opportunity which the company relied on Cooley to obtain; furthermore, the absence of bona fides was clear. Also, the imposition of liability will provide directors with an incentive to channel opportunities to their companies and not exploit them for their personal advantage.

There are other decisions which suggest a more benign attitude towards directors.

In *Queensland Mines Ltd v. Hudson*[14] the plaintiff company had been interested in developing a mining operation and the defendant, the managing director, was successful in obtaining for the company the licences necessary to enable it to do so. However, because of financial problems it could not proceed. Hudson resigned as managing director and, with the knowledge of the company's board, successfully developed the mines. The Privy Council held that Hudson was not liable to account, for either of two reasons: (a) the rejection of the opportunity by the company because of cash difficulties took the venture outside the scope of Hudson's fiduciary duties or (b) because Hudson had acted with

---

[12] (1973) 89 L.Q.R. 187 at p. 189.

[13] Roskill J. found that there was only a 10 per cent chance that the Gas Board would have awarded the contract to the plaintiff company. Thus the plaintiff company only benefited because Cooley had breached his duty.

[14] (1978) 18 A.L.R. 1; [1980] Conv. 200 (W. Braithwaite); applied in *Jones v. AMP Perpetual Trustee Company NZ Ltd* [1994] 1 N.Z.L.R. 690. See also *Island Export Finance Ltd v. Umunna* [1986] B.C.L.C. 460 (defendant not liable for developing a business opportunity after resigning as managing director because company was not actively pursuing the venture when he resigned, and his resignation was influenced not by any wish to acquire the business opportunity but by dissatisfaction with the company).

the full knowledge of the plaintiff company's board, they should be taken to have consented to his activities.[15]

This decision causes difficulties.[16] First, to argue that a board's rejection to the opportunity immunises a director against liability is difficult to reconcile with *Regal (Hastings) Ltd v. Gulliver.* Although in that case Lord Reid deliberately left open the question of the effect of board rejection,[17] it is difficult to see how there would still not be a serious conflict of interest if directors were permitted to acquire for themselves opportunities which they had rejected on behalf of the company. Secondly, only the shareholders could condone Hudson's breach, not the board.

iii. Boardman v. Phipps. Many of the difficulties relating to the application of the rule came to the fore in *Boardman v. Phipps.*[18]

The Phipps trust owned a substantial minority holding of shares in a private company. John Phipps, the plaintiff, was one of the beneficiaries under the trust, and the defendants were Boardman, a solicitor, and Tom Phipps, also a beneficiary. The trustees were an elderly widow who died in 1958, her daughter and an accountant. Boardman acted as solicitor to the trust.

In 1956 the defendants were dissatisfied with the way in which the company was managed. They made various inquiries on behalf of the trust, and in that capacity obtained confidential information about the company. They realised that it would be advantageous to sell some of the non-profit-making assets. They obtained control of the company by purchasing the remainder of the company's shares, and carried out the desired sales and reorganisation. The transaction was highly profitable. The trust gained in respect of its holding and the defendants gained in respect of the shares which they had purchased for the purpose of obtaining control.

Boardman had informed the beneficiaries and the two active trustees (the widow being senile and taking no part in the affairs of the trust) giving them an outline of the negotiations and asking them whether they had any objection to his taking a personal

---

[15] (1978) 18 A.L.R. 1 at p. 10. Lord Upjohn's reasoning in *Boardman v. Phipps* [1967] 2 A.C. 46 was adopted on the basis that he had "dissented on the facts, but not on the law." (p. 3).

[16] (1979) 42 M.L.R. 711 (G. Sullivan).

[17] [1967] 2 A.C. 137n. at pp. 152–153. In *Peso Silver Mines Ltd v. Cropper* (1966) 58 D.L.R. (2d.) 1, it was held that board rejection did immunise a director against any action to account; criticised in (1967) 30 M.L.R. 450 (D. Prentice); (1971) 49 C.B.R. 80 (S. Beck).

[18] [1967] 2 A.C. 46; (1968) 84 L.Q.R. 472 (G. Jones); [1978] Conv. 114 (B. Rider).

interest, bearing in mind that his initial inquiry had been on behalf of the trust. Boardman acted bona fide throughout and thought that he had made a full disclosure and had the beneficiaries' consent. Wilberforce J. however found that the plaintiff was justified in thinking that he had only been told half the truth. The trustees had been invited to consider whether the trust should find the money for the purchase of the shares; but the trustees were unable and unwilling to do so.

John Phipps then called upon the defendants to account for the profits which they had made. The House of Lords (3–2) held that they must do so; but having acted bona fide, they were entitled to payment on a liberal scale for their work and skill.[19]

A number of points of importance arise from the case. First, Boardman was not a trustee. The fiduciary relation arose from his employment as solicitor by the trustees. He was not, however, employed to act for the trust in the dealings in question and he claimed, as he stated at the time, to have been acting in a private capacity. The members of the House of Lords took different views on this issue. In the early negotiations with the company, the defendants, who were not shareholders in their own right, purported to represent the trust, although strictly they did not do so. Lord Cohen, in the majority, said[20] "that information and that opportunity they owed to their representing themselves as agents for the holders of the 8,000 shares held by the trustees." Lord Upjohn, dissenting[21]: "though they portrayed themselves as representing the Phipps Trust, it is quite clear the offer was made by these two personally."

Secondly, the liability of the defendants was unaffected by the fact that the trust had lost nothing; nor that the trust had greatly benefited; nor did it matter that the Phipps Trust could not have found the money; nor that the trustees would not have wished to use the money for that purpose even if they had it; nor that such user would have been in breach of trust, unless they had applied to the court and obtained consent to the investment.[22]

It is extremely difficult to determine the limits of this inflexible rule. Part of the difficulty stems from the lack of agreement as to whether the confidential information acquired by the appellants was

---

[19] *Ante*, p. 588.
[20] [1967] 2 A.C. 46 at p. 103.
[21] *Ibid* at p. 120; see also Viscount Dilhorne at p. 91; and *N.Z. Netherlands Society v. Kuys* [1973] 1 W.L.R. 1126, (1973) 37 Conv.(N.S.) 362.
[22] Lord Denning M.R. in the Court of Appeal mentioned this as a source of a potential conflict of interest and duty; [1965] Ch. 992, at p. 1020. The suggestion, however, seems unrealistic. See [1967] 2 A.C. 46 at pp. 92, 124; *cf.* Lord Cohen at pp. 103–104.

trust property, although this debate is less important since *Att.-Gen. for Hong Kong v. Reid*,[23] discussed below. The dissenting judges considered that it was not property. Of the majority, Lords Hodson and Guest considered that it was,[24] while Lord Cohen merely held that it was not property "in the strict sense of that word", so that liability to account for profits from its use depended on the facts of the case.[25] In *Aas v. Benham*,[26] Lindley L.J. laid down that information obtained in the course of a partnership business must not be used by the partners for their own benefit within the scope of the partnership business; but that they may make use of it for "purposes which are wholly without the scope of the firm's business . . . It is not the source of the information, but the use to which it is applied, which is important in such matters."[27] This was not disapproved in *Boardman v. Phipps*,[28] but it seems that a stricter view there prevailed; the defendants were held accountable because they had obtained the information by purporting to represent the trust; and although they were acting independently when they made the purchase. It is submitted that it is difficult to answer Lord Upjohn's argument in dissent[29]: "I think, again, that some of the trouble that has arisen in this case, it being assumed rightly that throughout he was in such a [fiduciary] capacity, is that it has been assumed that it has necessarily followed that any profit made by him renders him accountable to the trustees. That is not so. . . . It is perfectly clear that a solicitor can if he so desires act against his clients in any matter in which he has not been retained by them provided, of course, that in acting for them generally he has not learnt information or placed himself in a position which would make it improper for him to act against them. This is an obvious application of the rule that he must not place himself in a position where his duty and his interest conflict. So, in general, a solicitor can deal in shares in a company in which the client is a shareholder, subject always to the general rule that the solicitor must never place himself in a position where his interest and his duty conflict; and in this connection it may be pointed out that the interest and duty may refer (and frequently do) to a conflict of interest and duty on behalf of different clients and have nothing to do with any conflict between the personal interest and duty of the solicitor, beyond his interest in earning his fees." His

---

[23] [1994] 1 A.C. 324.
[24] Criticised (1968) 84 L.Q.R. 472 (G. Jones); Oakley, *Constructive Trusts* (3rd ed.), p. 170. See Goff and Jones, p. 684.
[25] [1967] 2 A.C. 46 at p. 102.
[26] [1891] 2 Ch. 244.
[27] *Ibid.* at p. 256.
[28] [1967] 2 A.C. 46.
[29] *Ibid.* at p. 126.

Lordship concluded "To extend the doctrines of equity to make the [defendants] accountable in such circumstances, is, in my judgment, to make unreasonable and inequitable applications of such doctrines."[30]

If this rule applies, the only escape of the fiduciary is that he made full disclosure, and obtained the consent of the other parties. It is not, however, clear whether the "other parties" are the trustees or the beneficiaries. In the straightforward case of a profit made by a trustee, the relevant consent must be that of the beneficiaries, to whom the duty is owed. Difficulties will arise if any of the beneficiaries are minors or unborn. *Boardman v. Phipps*,[31] however, was not such a case. Boardman was a fiduciary agent, the principals being the trustees. To whom did he owe his fiduciary duties? Presumably consent must be obtained from those persons. If the trustees had not consented, they would, as principals, have a right of recovery against their agent, any money thus recovered being held by them on trust for the beneficiaries. If the trustees had consented, the agent would nevertheless be liable to the beneficiaries if he owed fiduciary duties to *them*.[32] The result of *Boardman v. Phipps*[33] was that the beneficiary successfully sued the agent, but the basis of this is not clear. Their Lordships spoke, rather ambiguously, of his being a fiduciary "to the trust".[34] Lord Guest spoke of the "knowledge and assent of the trustees."[35] Lord Hodson held that the relevant consent was that of the beneficiary; Boardman "was in a fiduciary position *vis-à-vis* the trustees, and through them *vis-à-vis* the beneficiaries."[36] Viscount Dilhorne regarded the consent of the principals as necessary, but also referred to the fact that the beneficiary was not fully informed.[37] Lord Upjohn said that Boardman was "in a fiduciary capacity at least to the trustees. Whether he was ever in a fiduciary capacity to the [plaintiff] was not debated before your Lordships and I do not think that it matters."[38]

---

[30] *Ibid.* at pp. 133–134, quoting Lord Selborne L.C. in *Barnes v. Addy* (1874) 9 Ch.App. 244, at p. 251. See also *Chan v. Zacharia* (1984) 154 C.L.R. 178 at p. 204, suggesting that there should be no liability if it would be unconscientious to assert it, or if there was no possible conflict of interest and duty and it was plainly in the interest of the beneficiary that the fiduciary obtain the rights for himself that he was absolutely precluded from seeking or obtaining for the beneficiary.

[31] *Supra.*

[32] Presumably the beneficiaries could sue the trustees in such circumstances even if they could not sue the agent.

[33] *Supra.*

[34] [1967] 2 A.C. 46 at pp. 100, 104, 110.

[35] *Ibid.* at p. 117.

[36] *Ibid.* at p. 112. Lord Cohen also regarded the consent of the beneficiary as necessary; *ibid.* at p. 104.

[37] *Ibid.* at p. 93.

[38] *Ibid.* at pp. 125–126.

This raises the question whether trustees can, if acting unanimously, give consent to dealings by their agent which would otherwise be a breach of his fiduciary obligations.[39] In the present case Boardman had obtained the consent of the two active trustees, but did not inform the third because she was senile. Russell L.J. in the Court of Appeal[40] held that this was insufficient because two out of the three trustees "had no authority to turn this aspect of the trust property [the exploitation of the shares] over to the defendants, unless to be used exclusively for the benefit of the trust", and that the fiduciary could not "rid himself of the disqualification inherent in that position save with the informed consent of all three." It is submitted that the better view is that of Lord Upjohn, who replied that "not all the trustees acting together could do it for they cannot give away trust property."[41] On this view it is only the beneficiaries or the settlor (by express provision in the trust instrument) who can authorise such dealings.

Finally, it is important to determine what remedy was decreed in *Boardman v. Phipps.*[42] This is discussed below.

iv. The Extent of the Fiduciary Principle.

Essentially the problem is one of determining the limits of the rule. "Rules of equity have to be applied to such a great diversity of circumstances that they may be stated only in the most general terms and applied with particular attention to the exact circumstances of each case."[43] If a fiduciary obtains a benefit for himself at the expense of his beneficiary, there is no difficulty. The case is one of unjust enrichment. The position is more difficult where the beneficiary loses nothing; where he did not wish to make the profitable purchase which the trustee makes; where the fiduciary acted honestly; or even where the fiduciary conferred by his activities every possible benefit on the beneficiary, but received an additional benefit for himself. A windfall has been received through the exertions of the fiduciary; the beneficiary has risked nothing, and lost nothing; should he be entitled to the profits?[44] *Boardman v. Phipps* answers this question in the affirmative.

Such a principle might be criticised on the ground that it fails to draw any distinction between the honest and the dishonest fiduciary.

---

[39] See (1990) 106 L.Q.R. 87 at pp. 91–92 (D. Hayton), taking the view that prior specific (but not general) authority may be given if there is full disclosure by the agent and provided the "prudent businessman" test is satisfied.

[40] [1965] Ch. 992 at p. 1031.

[41] [1967] 2 A.C. 46 at p. 128.

[42] [1967] 2 A.C. 46.

[43] *Boardman v. Phipps* [1967] 2 A.C. 46 at p. 123.

[44] See generally (1968) 84 L.Q.R. 472 (G. Jones); Oakley, *Constructive Trusts* (3rd ed.), p. 178. A rigid application of the rule may lead to the unjust enrichment of the plaintiff; *Warman International Ltd v. Dwyer* (1995) 69 A.L.J.R. 362 at p. 369.

Both are liable. However, it should be borne in mind that the honest fiduciary may be remunerated by order of the court, as in *Boardman v. Phipps*.[45] A dishonest fiduciary, on the other hand, may be made to pay a higher rate of interest.[46]

But this still leaves open the question, to be determined on the facts of each case, whether the opportunity for profit arose by reason of the fiduciary position.[47] For example, a merchant banker, insurance broker, solicitor or company director learns through the proper course of his business information from a confidential source which may be of advantage to other clients in companies with which he is associated. Having satisfied the requirements of a particular client, is he precluded from making use of this information in respect of other trusts with which he is concerned or for himself? Similarly with the directors of several (non-competing) companies? Or, does his fiduciary duty to the second client place him under a duty to provide that client with the confidential information?[48] There is the danger that the rule, if applied inflexibly, may impose an impossible burden: As Lord Cohen said in *Boardman v. Phipps*,[49] " . . . it does not necessarily follow that because an agent acquired information and opportunity while acting in a fiduciary capacity he is accountable to his principals for any profit that comes his way as the result of the use he makes of that information and opportunity. His liability to account must depend on the facts of the case." Viscount Dilhorne[50] quoted Lindley L.J. as saying "to hold that a partner can never derive any personal benefit from information which he obtains from a partner would be manifestly absurd."[51]

It is difficult to formulate any single test which may be applied to determine whether a fiduciary has incurred liability. It is submitted that liability will arise if any of the following factors is present:

(a) The fiduciary has used trust property;
(b) The profit has been made by use of or by reason of the fiduciary position or of an opportunity or knowledge resulting from it, even though no trust property was used;
(c) There was a conflict (or a significant possibility of a conflict) of interest and duty, even if no trust property was used, and

---

[45] *Supra*. A fiduciary guilty of undue influence has, however, been remunerated by the court; *O'Sullivan v. Management Agency and Music Ltd* [1985] Q.B. 428, *ante*, p. 587.
[46] *Post*, p. 639.
[47] (1970) 86 L.Q.R. 463 (G. Jones).
[48] See [1978] Conv. 114 (B. Rider); *North and South Trust Co. v. Berkeley* [1971] 1 W.L.R. 470; (1972) 35 M.L.R. 78 (M. Kay and D. Yates); *Movitex Ltd v. Bulfield* [1988] B.C.L.C. 104 (fiduciary must not place himself in a position where his duty to X conflicts with his duty to Y).
[49] [1967] 2 A.C. 46 at pp. 102–103; see also Lord Upjohn at p. 126.
[50] *Ibid.* at p. 90.
[51] *Aas v. Benham* [1891] 2 Ch. 244 at pp. 255–256.

the opportunity did not arise from the fiduciary relationship.[52]

C. Personal and Proprietary Remedies

It is often said that a fiduciary who is required to account for profits becomes a constructive trustee. But a duty to account is a personal liability; a constructive trust is a proprietary remedy; the significance of the distinction appears where the fiduciary is bankrupt, or where the assets in question have been profitably invested. A related question is whether tracing is available, which is discussed in Chapter 23. Liability to account is not synonymous with constructive trusteeship, but the cases do not always maintain the distinction. Indeed, Lord Lane C.J. has said "We find it impossible to reconcile much of the language used in these decisions."[53]

In *Boardman v. Phipps*, Wilberforce J. had held that the shares were held on constructive trust[54] for the beneficiaries; and that Boardman was accountable for profits he made, less a sum for his skill and effort. The House of Lords did not distinguish between accountability and constructive trust. Lord Guest concluded that the defendants held the shares as constructive trustees, and were bound to account to the plaintiff.[55] The other members spoke of accountability only.

As submitted above, there is a difference between a duty to hold specific property on trust and a duty to account. Could Boardman have satisfied the judgment by payment of the value of the shares at that time, keeping any subsequent increase? Would a purchaser (with notice) have taken the shares subject to the same obligation? What would have been the position if Boardman had been bankrupt? None of these matters arose, and it was not necessary to discuss them.

If the fiduciary has used or received trust property, then any profits made are held on constructive trust for the beneficiaries.[56] Whether the remedy in other cases was personal or proprietary was not always clear, but until recently a special rule applied to bribes and secret commissions. It was laid down by the Court of Appeal in

---

[52] *Industrial Development Consultants Ltd v. Cooley* [1972] 1 W.L.R. 443. See also Stephenson L.J. in *Swain v. Law Society* [1982] 1 W.L.R. 17 at p. 31: there must be a possibility of a conflict of interest and duty, and a nexus between the fiduciary position and the profit made.

[53] *Re Att.-Gen.'s Reference (No. 1 of 1985)* [1986] Q.B. 491 at p. 503.

[54] [1964] 2 All E.R. 187; *cf* [1964] 1 W.L.R. 993.

[55] [1967] 2 A.C. 46 at p. 117. See (1990) 106 L.Q.R. 87 at 102 (D. Hayton), suggesting that the liability was personal only.

[56] *Guinness plc v. Saunders* [1990] 2 A.C. 663, *ante*, 588; *Neptune (Vehicle Washing Equipment) Ltd v. Fitzgerald* [1996] Ch. 274.

Lister & Co. v. Stubbs[57] that where an agent or other fiduciary took a bribe, the principal's remedy was personal. The fiduciary had to account for the bribe, but did not hold it on constructive trust. The result in that case was that the fiduciary could keep any profit made from investing the bribe money. This decision was long criticised[58] as contravening the principles of unjust enrichment and treating a dishonest fiduciary more leniently than an honest fiduciary such as Boardman in *Boardman v. Phipps*.[59] It was, however, affirmed by the Court of Appeal in *Re Att.-Gen.'s Reference (No. 1 of 1985)*,[60] although in a criminal law context, with the result that an employee who made a secret profit was not guilty of theft of his employer's property.

Lister & Co. v. Stubbs has now been disapproved by the Privy Council in a decision which concerned bribes but which is very significant in the wider area of profits made by fiduciaries.

> In *Att.-Gen. for Hong Kong v. Reid*[61] the defendant, a public prosecutor, took bribes of over $HK12 million to obstruct prosecutions, in breach of his fiduciary duty as a Crown servant. He failed to comply with an order to repay and was imprisoned. He had purchased three freehold properties with the money, which had since increased in value. The Privy Council decided that these properties were held on trust for the Crown.

Lord Templeman pointed out that bribes cause loss and damage to the principal, although it may not be quantifiable, as in the present case, where unquantifiable harm to the administration of justice had been done. A constructive trust of the bribe money arose because the fiduciary was under an immediate duty to pay it over to the principal. Applying the maxim "equity regards as done that which ought to be done", the money was the property of the principal in equity. The fiduciary's creditors should be in no better position than the fiduciary. If the bribe money was profitably invested, the profits belonged to the principal. If it decreased in value, the fiduciary was personally liable for the deficit. The constructive trust arose whether the fiduciary took property from the trust or from a third party in breach of duty. Any other result, it was said, would be inconsistent with the principle that a fiduciary must not profit from his office. There was no logic in treating a dishonest fiduciary more favourably

---

[57] (1890) 45 Ch.D. 1.
[58] Although supported in (1987) 103 L.Q.R. 433 (R. Goode).
[59] [1967] 2 A.C. 46.
[60] [1986] Q.B. 491.
[61] [1994] 1 A.C. 324. *Lister & Co. v. Stubbs* has been said to be still binding on the English High Court; *Att.-Gen. v. Blake* [1996] 3 W.L.R. 741 at 750.

than an honest fiduciary who had become liable as constructive trustee.

The decision has been welcomed so far as it prevents the unjust enrichment of a dishonest fiduciary, but certain difficulties remain. Instead of dealing with the policy issue of when proprietary remedies should be available, the Privy Council based its decision more narrowly on the equitable maxim, the application of which is controversial in that it is founded on the availability of specific performance, but an obligation to pay money is not normally specifically enforceable.[62] It might also be doubted whether the plaintiff's claim deserves priority over the defendant's unsecured creditors, who have not necessarily taken the risk of insolvency. So far as the bribe has increased in value, the increase is a windfall to the plaintiff. To balance the interests of creditors and the prevention of unjust enrichment, a compromise solution might be mere personal liability for any increase in value.[63] By allowing the plaintiff to assert ownership of the bribe money and any profits made from it, the decision amounts to "proprietary overkill".[64]

The Privy Council in *Reid*[65] answered some of the points discussed above in relation to *Boardman v. Phipps*.[66] Lord Templeman clearly regarded Boardman as a constructive trustee and not merely subject to a personal liability to account. He became such not by reason of any classification of confidential information as trust property but because he obtained the information by virtue of his office. The effect of the decision in the criminal law context remains to be seen.[67] Where the fiduciary retains neither the bribe nor any property deriving from it, then of course his personal liability to account remains.

Finally, a plaintiff cannot have an account of profits and also damages for what he would have received had he been able to use the property for the period in question. These remedies are alternative, not cumulative, and the plaintiff must elect between them at the time of judgment in his favour, by which time it will be clear which remedy is the more advantageous.[68]

---

[62] *Post*, p. 703; (1994) 53 C.L.J. 31 (A. Oakley); [1994] 2 R.L.R. 57 (D. Crilley); All E.R. Rev. 1994, p. 252 (P. Clarke); (1995) 54 C.L.J. 60 (S. Gardner).

[63] Birks, *An Introduction to the Law of Restitution*, p. 389; (1994) 110 L.Q.R. 178 (P. Watts); All E.R. Rev. 1994, p. 365 (W. Swadling); [1994] Conv. 156 (A. Jones); (1995) 58 M.L.R. 87 (T. Allen).

[64] [1994] 2 R.L.R. 57 (D. Crilley).

[65] [1994] 1 A.C. 324.

[66] [1967] 2 A.C. 46.

[67] *Re Att.-Gen.'s Reference (No. 1 of 1985)* [1986] Q.B. 491; (1994) 110 L.Q.R. 180 (J. Smith).

[68] *Tang Man Sit (Personal Representatives) v. Capacious Investments Ltd* [1996] 1 A.C. 514 (secret profits from wrongful lettings of houses in breach of trust); (1996) 112 L.Q.R. 375 (P. Birks); [1996] R.L.R. 117 (J. Stevens).

CHAPTER 22

VARIATION OF TRUSTS

1. The Background 611
2. Variations which Need the Approval of the
   Court 613
   A. Inherent Jurisdiction 613
      i. Salvage and Emergency 613
      ii. Compromise 614
   B. Statutory Provisions (other than
      Variation of Trusts Act 1958) 616
      i. Trustee Act 1925, s.57(1) 616
      ii. Settled Land Act 1925,
          s.64(1) 616
      iii. Trustee Act 1925, s.53 617
      iv. Matrimonial Causes Act
          1973 618
      v. Mental Health Act 1983 619
   C. Variation of Trusts Act 1958 619

   i. Persons on whose Behalf
      Approval may be Given 620
   ii. Parties 621
   iii. Applicants 622
   iv. Foreign Trusts 622
   v. Effect of Approval by the
      Court 623
   vi. Variation or Resettlement 624
   vii. Fraud on a Power 625
   viii. The Settlor's Intention 625
   ix. Benefit 626
      (a) Financial Benefit 627
      (b) Moral and Social Benefit 627
      (c) Postponing Vesting 628
      (d) Trouble in the Family 629
      (e) Taking a Chance 629

1. THE BACKGROUND

A TRUSTEE must administer the trust according to its terms. Any deviation is a breach of trust for which the trustee will be personally liable.[1] However, any adult beneficiary *sui juris* may deal with his equitable interest under the trust in any way he wishes; and may consent to the trustee dealing with the trust funds in a way which affects his interest. Further, adult beneficiaries who together are absolutely entitled to the trust property may terminate the trust and demand that the fund be handed over to them[2]; but not if any interests are outstanding.[3]

---

[1] *Ante*, p. 479; *post*, Chap. 23.

[2] *Saunders v. Vautier* (1841) Cr. & Ph. 240; *Re Chardon* [1928] Ch. 464; *Re Smith* [1928] Ch. 915; *Re Nelson* [1928] Ch. 920n; *Re Becket's Settlement* [1940] Ch. 279. See also Trusts of Land and Appointment of Trustees Act 1996, s.6(2); *ante*, p. 555.

[3] *Berry v. Green* [1938] A.C. 575; *Re Robb* [1953] Ch. 459; *Re Wragg* [1959] 1 W.L.R. 922.

They may wish to do this for various reasons. In *Saunders v. Vautier*,[4] the beneficiary wished to terminate an accumulation which was to continue until he reached 25; he was able to claim the fund at 21 (then the age of majority). If property is given to A for life and then to B, and both A and B are adult, they may each wish to have capital immediately available, and may agree to partition the fund. The main reason is the possibility of reducing tax liability and especially liability for inheritance tax on the death of A. Inheritance tax, an outline of which was given in Chapter 9, is chargeable on transfers on or within seven years before death. It is also chargeable on certain *inter vivos* transfers even if the transferor survives for seven years, for example the creation of a discretionary trust, although in such a case the rate is lower.[5] In the case of a non-discretionary trust, the advantage of partitioning the fund between life tenant and remainderman is that, provided the life tenant survives for seven years (which may be covered by insurance), no tax will be payable on the partition, whereas the whole capital is taxable if the life interest terminates on death.[6]

It may be advantageous in terms of income tax liability to share out the entitlement to income. Whether or not a variation is a disposal for capital gains tax purposes has never been decided.[7] As far as inheritance tax is concerned, trustees of a discretionary trust may wish to improve the tax position of the settlement by converting it to a trust where there is an interest in possession or to an accumulation and maintenance settlement.[8] Such a conversion will itself be taxable.[9] The tax saving aspect of the matter is emphasised here because it has been the motive force in the passing of the Variation of Trusts Act 1958, and the variations which have been made under it. "Nearly every variation" said Lord Denning M.R. "that has come before the court has tax-avoidance for its principal object."[10] Variations have, of course, been made for other purposes, as will be seen.

One particular tax exemption should be noted. Where, not more than two years after a death of a person, testate or intestate, the disposition of his property taking effect upon his death is varied by an instrument in writing, such a variation is not a transfer of value

---

[4] (1841) Cr. & Ph. 240. For the meaning of "absolutely entitled" in a tax context, see *Figg v. Clark (Inspector of Taxes)*, *The Times*, March 11, 1996 (class consisting of children of X not absolutely entitled until death of X, although X incapable of fathering more children).
[5] Inheritance Tax Act 1984, s.7.
[6] F.A. (No. 2) 1987, s.96. See *Gibbon v. Mitchell* [1990] 1 W.L.R. 1304.
[7] Harris, *Variation of Trusts*, pp. 97 *et seq.*
[8] *Ante*, p. 226.
[9] *Ante*, p. 225.
[10] In *Re Weston's Settlements* [1969] 1 Ch. 234 at p. 245.

for inheritance tax purposes,[11] nor a disposal for capital gains tax purposes,[12] and the variation takes effect as if made by the deceased. These provisions may be of great help where, for example, a wealthy testator has created a disadvantageous discretionary trust by will.[13] They clearly apply to an agreed variation by adult beneficiaries and to a variation under the Variation of Trusts Act 1958. A similar principle applies to an order under the Family Provision legislation.[14]

2. VARIATIONS WHICH NEED THE APPROVAL OF THE COURT[15]

We have seen that minors and persons not *sui juris* are not able to deal irrevocably with their property. If a situation arose where variations needed to be made to a trust in the interests of such persons, nothing could be done which involved any negotiation with or compromise by the persons under disability, without the approval of the court. The person under disability could be benefited at the expense of the adult parties. The life tenant may be willing to agree to an advancement by the trustees,[16] or to surrender his life interest. But if the life tenant wanted something in return, there was no way in which he could negotiate it.

Yet, especially in the tax context, it was in the interest of the remaindermen that the variation should be made. Adult remaindermen could agree to a variation; it was hard for infants, persons under a disability and unborn persons to be denied advantages which competent adults could obtain for themselves. The court, however, has no inherent jurisdiction to vary a trust in favour of infants and unborn persons.[17] But there are cases where the court can intervene, and these have been substantially increased by several statutes.

A. Inherent Jurisdiction

i. Salvage and Emergency. A court has inherent power in the case of absolute necessity to sanction the mortgage of an infant's property in order to protect the property which he retains. The

---

[11] Inheritance Tax Act 1984, ss.17, 142.
[12] Taxation of Chargeable Gains Act 1992, s.62(6).
[13] Inheritance Tax Act 1984, Part III, Chap. III, *ante*, p. 224.
[14] *Ibid.* s.146.
[15] (1954) 17 M.L.R. 420 (O. Marshall); Harris, *Variation of Trusts.*
[16] *Pilkington v. I.R.C.* [1964] A.C. 612, *ante*, p. 579.
[17] *Chapman v. Chapman* [1954] A.C. 429.

jurisdiction is very narrow and is usual where expenditure is necessary to save buildings from collapse.[18] An extension of this jurisdiction allows the court in an emergency, not foreseen or anticipated by
the settlor, to authorise the trustees to perform certain acts which are
beyond the powers given to them in the trust instrument, where this
is in the best interests of the trust estate and where the consent of all
the beneficiaries cannot be obtained because they are not in existence or are under a disability.

In *Re New*,[19] the court approved a scheme of capital reconstruction of a company, splitting the shares into different and smaller
denominations, and authorised the trustees to take the new shares,
subject to an undertaking to apply for further authorisation to retain
the shares after one year. This decision was said in *Re Tollemache*[20]
to be the "high water-mark" of the emergency jurisdiction. Kekewich J. and the Court of Appeal refused to sanction a widening of
the trustees' investment powers merely because this would be for
the advantage of the beneficiaries. There was no emergency. It is
clear that the jurisdiction applies to administrative matters only, and
does not cover schemes for the variation of beneficial interests.

ii. Compromise.[21] Until the decision of the House of Lords in
Chapman v. Chapman[22] in 1954, the courts had accepted a wide
definition of the word "compromise" as the basis of a useful
jurisdiction to approve a variation from the terms of a trust although
there was no dispute between the parties in any real sense of the
term. The cases were more akin to bargains or exchanges approved
by the court as being fair to infants or remaindermen, than to
compromised litigation. There was a question whether the jurisdiction effected a variation of beneficial interests as distinct from
varying the property subject to the trusts,[23] and the jurisdiction did
not extend to the redrafting of a settlement as such—there had to be
some element of composition of rights.[24] But this distinction was of
course paper-thin. Denning L.J., the minority judge in the Court of
Appeal in the *Chapman* case, would have got round the difficulty by
accepting for the courts a general jurisdiction to vary trusts on behalf
of those unascertained or not *sui juris*, but the House of Lords
preferred the other solution—that of limiting the jurisdiction to
sanction compromises to cases where there was a genuine dispute.

---

[18] *Re Jackson* (1882) 21 Ch.D. 786; *Conway v. Fenton* (1888) 40 Ch.D. 512; *Re Montagu*
    [1897] 2 Ch. 8 at p. 11, *per* Lopes L.J.
[19] [1901] 2 Ch. 534.
[20] [1903] 1 Ch. 457, affirmed, *ibid*, at p. 955.
[21] (1954) 17 M.L.R. 427 (O. Marshall).
[22] [1954] A.C. 429.
[23] *Re Downshire Settled Estates* [1953] Ch. 218.
[24] *Re Chapman's S.T.* [1953] Ch. 218.

Nor could matters that did not genuinely contain an element of dispute be made to look as if they did.[25] Where there is a genuine dispute, the court of course has power to sanction a compromise, even if the compromise solution contains tax-saving advantages for the beneficiaries.

In *Allen v. Distillers Co. (Biochemicals) Ltd*[26] the question was whether the court, in approving a settlement of the action of the child victims of the thalidomide drug, had jurisdiction to postpone the vesting of the capital in the children to an age greater than 18. Eveleigh J. held that the court had no inherent jurisdiction to order a postponement; a beneficiary with a vested interest under a trust was entitled to demand possession on majority.[27] Nor was there a trust to which the Variation of Trusts Act 1958 applied; the payment out to trustees of sums paid into court did not give rise to the kind of trust contemplated by that Act. However, it was found that the terms of the settlement of the action were wide enough to authorise a postponement of payment.

An attempt to invoke the court's compromise jurisdiction occurred in *Mason v. Farbrother*,[28] where trustees of a pension fund set up in 1929 for Co-operative Society employees had power to invest principally in the society itself and otherwise in authorised trustee securities. By 1982, as a result of inflation, the fund had increased to £127 million, and the trustees, who were anxious to have the wide powers of investment appropriate for modern pension funds, applied to the court for approval of an investment clause giving wider powers than those of the Trustee Investments Act 1961. The trustees were uncertain as to the proper construction of the original investment clause, one view being that the whole fund should be invested in the society, and the other that the whole should be invested under the 1961 Act. This was sufficient to give the court jurisdiction, as genuine points of difference existed. It was not necessary that there should be a contested dispute. While a compromise need not be something between the two views, it was doubtful whether the court could substitute an entirely new investment clause. Thus the variation was not permitted under the court's jurisdiction to approve a compromise. (It was, however, authorised by section 57 of the Trustee Act 1925).[29]

---

[25] *Re Powell-Cotton's Resettlement* [1956] 1 W.L.R. 23. Nor should the trustees, in their application to court for the exercise of the compromise jurisdiction, insert an unrelated claim for increased remuneration; *Re Barbour's Settlement Trusts* [1974] 1 W.L.R. 1198.
[26] [1974] Q.B. 384.
[27] *Saunders v. Vautier* (1841) 4 Beav. 115; *ante*, p. 612.
[28] [1983] 2 All E.R. 1078; All E.R. Rev. 1984, p. 308 (P. Clarke).
[29] *Infra.*

B. Statutory Provisions (other than Variation of Trusts Act 1958)

i. Trustee Act 1925, s.57(1).

"Where in the management or administration of any property vested in trustees, any sale, lease, mortgage, surrender, release, or other disposition, or any purchase, investment, acquisition, expenditure, or other transaction, is in the opinion of the court expedient, but the same cannot be effected by reason of the absence of any power for that purpose vested in the trustees by the trust instrument, if any, or by law, the court may by order confer upon the trustees ... the necessary power ... on such terms ... as the court may think fit ... "

This subsection overlaps the "emergency" jurisdiction discussed above, and widens it by making the statutory jurisdiction available in cases of expediency rather than emergency. It operates as if its provisions were read into every settlement.[30] It is clear from the opening words of the section that it is only available in questions arising in the *management* or *administration* of property; it is not therefore available for the purpose of remoulding beneficial interests or for tax saving generally.[31]

Applications are usually made in Chambers, and it is not possible to learn from reported cases the full scope of the operation of the subsection. It has however been effectively used to authorise the sale of land where necessary consents had been refused[32]; to authorise partition[33]; and to authorise the purchase of a residence for the tenant for life,[34] the sale of a reversionary interest which under the terms of the trust instrument was not to be sold until it fell into possession,[35] and wider investment powers.[36] It has been held that section 57 should be used in preference to the Variation of Trusts Act 1958 where wider investment powers are sought, provided the beneficial interests are not affected.[37]

ii. Settled Land Act 1925, s.64(1).

"Any transaction affecting or concerning the settled land, or any part thereof, or any other land ... which in the opinion of the court would be for the benefit of the settled land, or any part thereof, or the persons interested under the settlement, may, under an order of the court, be effected

[30] *Re Mair* [1935] Ch. 562; see also *Re Salting* [1932] 2 Ch. 57.
[31] *Re Downshire S.E.* [1953] Ch. 218; *cf. Re Forster's Settlement* [1954] 3 All E.R. 714.
[32] *Re Beale's S.T.* [1932] 2 Ch. 15.
[33] *Re Thomas* [1930] 1 Ch. 194.
[34] *Re Power* [1947] Ch. 572; (1947) 91 S.J. 541.
[35] *Re Cockerell's S.T.* [1956] Ch. 372.
[36] *Re Shipwrecked Fishermen and Mariners' Royal Benevolent Society* [1959] Ch. 220; *cf. Re Powell-Cotton's Resettlement* [1956] 1 W.L.R. 23; *Mason v. Farbrother* [1983] 2 All E.R. 1078.
[37] *Anker-Petersen v. Anker-Petersen* (1991) 77/16 L.S.Gaz. 32.

by a tenant for life, if it is one which could have been validly effected by an absolute owner."[38]

It will be seen that this subsection is wider than Trustee Act, s.57(1). "Transaction" is widely defined[39]; and there is no limitation restricting the court's powers to cases of management and administration.[40] The subsection enables the court to alter beneficial interests in such a way as to reduce tax liability[41] and was the most effective vehicle for this purpose before 1958. It applies however only to cases of settled land, and not to the ordinary case of a personalty settlement. In *Hambro v. Duke of Marlborough*[42] the Duke and the trustees considered that the second defendant, the Marquess of Blandford, who was tenant in tail in remainder, would be incapable of managing the Blenheim estate on the death of the Duke because of his "unbusinesslike habits" and lack of responsibility. They proposed a scheme whereby the estate would be conveyed to trustees of a new trust, to pay the income to the Duke for life, and then to hold on protective trusts for the second defendant for life, thereafter on the trusts of the existing settlement. This was held to be a "transaction" within section 64, which could vary the beneficial interests even where an ascertained adult beneficiary did not consent.[43]

iii. Trustee Act 1925, s.53.[44] Under section 53 the court is given power to authorise certain dealings with an infant's property "with a view to the application of the capital or income thereof for the maintenance, education, or benefit of the infant." As with section 57, the section overlaps and extends the inherent power to make provision for the maintenance of minors. The word "benefit" has been widely construed, and the court has authorised transactions whose object was the reduction of estate duty for the minor's benefit.[45] Thus, entails have been barred in order to exclude the interests of large numbers of remote beneficiaries with a view to raising money for the minor's benefit[46] or to simplifying an application to the court under the Variation of Trusts Act 1958[47]; and

---

[38] See also Settled Land and Trustee Acts (Court's General Powers) Act 1943. Settlements of land cannot be created after the Trusts of Land and Appointment of Trustees Act 1996.

[39] S.L.A. 1925, s.64(2). See *Raikes v. Lygon* [1988] 1 W.L.R. 281; *Hambro v. Duke of Marlborough* [1994] Ch. 158.

[40] It is used for such purposes. *Re White-Popham's S.E.* [1936] Ch. 725; *Re Scarisbrick's Re-Settlement Estates* [1944] Ch. 229.

[41] *Re Downshire S.E.* [1953] Ch. 218; *Raikes v. Lygon* [1988] 1 W.L.R. 281.

[42] *Supra*; [1994] Conv. 492 (E. Cooke).

[43] This was a preliminary issue. The scheme was subsequently approved; *The Times*, July 23, 1994.

[44] (1957) 21 Conv.(N.S.) 448 (O. Marshall).

[45] *Re Meux* [1958] Ch. 154.

[46] *Re Gower's Settlement* [1934] Ch. 365.

[47] *Re Bristol's S.E.* [1964] 3 All E.R. 939; *Re Lansdowne's W.T.* [1967] Ch. 603.

reversionary interests have been sold to the tenant for life.[48] However, the proceeds of sale should be resettled; this will be an "application" for the minor's benefit[49]; while an outright payment to him of the proceeds of sale will not be.[50]

iv. Matrimonial Causes Act 1973. The court has wide power to make orders affecting the property of parties to matrimonial proceedings. It may order capital provision to be made, by cash payment, or property transfer, or by the making of a settlement for the benefit of the other spouse and the children of the family.[51] It may also effect the variation of ante-nuptial or post-nuptial settlements,[52] and the variation of orders for settlements made under the Act.[53]

The jurisdiction to vary a "post-nuptial settlement" under section 24 of the 1973 Act enabled the provision of a pension for a wife on divorce in *Brooks v. Brooks*.[54] A company pension scheme of which the husband was the sole member provided that on retirement he could direct that part of his benefit should be used to make provision for his wife after his death, and that a lump sum would be payable at the discretion of the trustee to a class including the wife if he were to die prematurely. These factors made it a "marriage settlement", which had a wide meaning. The scheme could be varied so far as it constituted a settlement made by the husband. Under the scheme the surplus belonged to the employer company, and was thus not part of the settled property. The trust was varied by directing that an immediate annuity and a deferred pension were to be provided in priority to and, if necessary, in diminution of the husband's pension. Had there been any other scheme members, the court would not have ordered a variation to their detriment, nor would it sanction a variation with adverse tax consequences.[55]

This decision is of limited application and does not solve the problem of pension-splitting on divorce, which is dealt with by other legislation.[56]

---

[48] *Re Meux, supra, cf. Re Heyworth's Contingent Reversionary Interest* [1956] Ch. 364.

[49] *Re Meux, supra.*

[50] *Re Heyworth's Contingent Reversionary Interest, supra*; criticised (1957) 21 Conv.(N.S.) 448 at pp. 450–454 (O. Marshall).

[51] Matrimonial Causes Act 1973, ss.23 and 24. See also s.25, laying down the principles to be observed by the court in exercising its jurisdiction under ss.23, 24.

[52] s.24(1)(c), (d). See *E. v. E.* [1990] 2 F.L.R. 233.

[53] s.31(2)(e). Further details must be obtained from the Family Law books.

[54] [1996] 1 A.C. 375; (1995) 145 N.L.J. 1009 (M.Rae); [1997] Conv. 52 (M. Thomas).

[55] It was significant that the wife had once been employed by the company, otherwise the variation might have forfeited Inland Revenue approval (necessary for tax relief) by reason of an immediate payment to a non-employee.

[56] Provisions in the Family Law Act 1996 are expected to be implemented in April 2000. See also Pensions Act 1995, *ante*, p. 476, enacting limited reforms.

v. Mental Health Act 1983. Mental Health Act 1983, s.96(1)(*d*) gives to the Court of Protection a power to make a settlement of the property of the patient; and also, if any material fact was not disclosed when the settlement was made, or where there has been any substantial change in circumstances, to vary the settlement in such manner as the judge thinks fit.[57]

C. Variation of Trusts Act 1958[58]

The Variation of Trusts Act 1958 gives to the court a "very wide and, indeed, revolutionary discretion"[59] to approve on behalf of four groups of persons[60] "any arrangement . . . varying or revoking all or any of the trusts, or enlarging the powers of the trustees of managing or administering any of the property subject to the trusts."[61] On its terms, this provision covers not only administrative matters, but also variations in the beneficial interests; but the court may only approve such an arrangement if it would be for the benefit of the person on whose behalf the approval is given.[62]

The courts have approved a wide variety of variations, and, in addition to approving changes in the beneficial interests, have inserted a power of advancement,[63] terminated an accumulation,[64] inserted an accumulation period[65] and have widened the investment powers of trustees.[66] Investment clauses are rarely the subject of an application, for it became established that only in exceptional circumstances should a court give its approval to wider investment powers than those given to trustees in the Trustee Investments Act 1961.[67] The Act of 1961, however, has become outdated, and it seems that the courts are now willing to sanction an extension of

---

[57] M.H.A. 1983, s.96(3).
[58] Harris: *Variation of Trusts*, Chaps. 3 *et seq.*; (1958) 22 Conv.(N.S.) 373 (M. Mowbray); (1963) 27 Conv.(N.S.) 6 (D. Evans); (1965) 43 Can.B.R. 181 (A. Maclean). The jurisdiction given by the Act is independent of T.A. 1925, s.57, and S.L.A. 1925, s.64, *ante*. There may be technical reasons, *e.g.* difficulties as to representative parties, why it is not possible to invoke the 1958 Act. See *Mason v. Farbrother* [1983] 2 All E.R. 1078.
[59] *Per* Evershed M.R. in *Re Steed's W.T.* [1960] Ch. 407 at pp. 420–421.
[60] *Infra.*
[61] V.T.A. 1958, s.1(1). But see *Allen v. Distillers Co. (Biochemicals) Ltd* [1974] Q.B. 384, *ante*, p. 615.
[62] Except for persons in para. (*d*), *infra.*
[63] *Re Lister's W.T.* [1962] 1 W.L.R. 1441.
[64] *Re Tinker's Settlement* [1960] 1 W.L.R. 1011.
[65] *Re Lansdowne's W.T.* [1967] Ch. 603; *Re Holt's Settlement* [1961] Ch. 100.
[66] *Re Coates' Trusts* [1959] 1 W.L.R. 375; *Re Burney's S.T.* [1961] 1 W.L.R. 545.
[67] *Re Kolb's W.T.* [1962] Ch. 531; *Re Cooper's Settlement* [1962] Ch. 826; *Re Clarke's W.T.* [1961] 1 W.L.R. 1471. See also *Re Rank's S.T.* [1979] 1 W.L.R. 1242, where an arrangement included a power of appointment in terms wide enough to permit the donee to give wider powers of investment to the trustees for the benefit of the appointees.

investment powers.[68] It has recently been held that section 57 of the Trustee Act 1925 is more appropriate than the 1958 Act where wider investment powers are sought, provided the beneficial interests are not affected.[69] Under section 57 the court would consider the interests of the beneficiaries collectively in income and capital but would not need to consent on behalf of the various categories of beneficiaries as required by the 1958 Act, nor would it require the consent of adult beneficiaries.

It is of course in connection with schemes which vary beneficial interests for tax saving purposes that the 1958 Act has been mainly applied.

i. Persons on whose Behalf Approval may be Given. The principle is that the court is not asked to approve on behalf of ascertainable adults who can consent for themselves. The classes (as set out in Variation of Trusts Act 1958, s.1) are:

"(*a*) any person having, directly or indirectly, an interest, whether vested or contingent, under the trusts who by reason of infancy or other incapacity is incapable of assenting, or

(*b*) any person (whether ascertained or not) who may become entitled, directly or indirectly, to an interest under the trusts as being at a future date or on the happening of a future event a person of any specified description or a member of any specified class of persons, so however that this paragraph shall not include any person[70] who would be of that description, or a member of that class, as the case may be, if the said date had fallen or the said event had happened at the date of the application to the court, or

(*c*) any person unborn, or

(*d*) any person in respect of any discretionary interest of his under protective trusts where the interest of the principal beneficiary has not failed or determined."[71]

Paragraph (*b*) may well of course include adults; but because the class is ascertainable only at a future time, its members cannot yet be known. Under the proviso, however, those who would qualify if the future event happened at the date of the application to the court

---

[68] In *Mason v. Farbrother* [1983] 2 All E.R. 1078, *ante*, p. 530, concerning T.A. 1925, s.57, the effect of inflation and the fact that the trust was in the nature of a public fund were regarded as special circumstances; *cf. Trustees of the British Museum v. Att.-Gen.* [1984] 1 W.L.R. 418, [1984] Conv. 373 (H. Norman), where Megarry V.-C. preferred the view that the *Re Kolb* principle, *supra*, had gone. This was discussed in Chap. 18. See also *Steel v. Wellcome Custodian Trustees Ltd* [1988] 1 W.L.R. 167; [1988] Conv. 380 (B. Dale); Law Reform Committee's 23rd Report, *Powers and Duties of Trustees* (1982) Cmnd. 8733.

[69] *Anker-Petersen v. Anker-Petersen* (1991) 88/16 L.S.Gaz. 32.

[70] This presumably means any ascertained person; Harris, *op. cit.* pp. 39–40.

[71] For a recent example, see *Gibbon v. Mitchell* [1990] 1 W.L.R. 1304.

must themselves consent. If however they are infants, they come within paragraph (*a*).

In *Re Suffert*,[72] income was given under protective trusts to an unmarried woman for life, and, in the event of her having no issue, and subject to a general testamentary power, in trust for those who would become entitled under her intestacy. She had three adult cousins, who would be entitled in equal shares to her estate if she had died at the date of the application to the court. One cousin was made a party, and consented, but the others were not. In asking the court to approve the arrangement, it was argued that the court should approve on behalf of those who would be entitled on intestacy, as they came within paragraph (*b*). Buckley J. however held that the proviso applied and that he could not approve on behalf of the two cousins. Otherwise he approved the arrangement.

The meaning of the words "may become entitled" in paragraph (*b*) were examined in *Knocker v. Youle*.[73]

Property was held on trust for the settlor's daughter for life under a settlement in which her cousins had very remote contingent interests. It was not practicable to get the approval of the cousins to the proposed variation because they were very numerous, and some were in Australia.[74] Approval was therefore sought on their behalf under section (1)(1)(*b*). The question was whether paragraph (*b*) included persons with an existing contingent interest, however remote. Warner J. held that it did not. A person having a contingent interest was not a person who "may become entitled" to an interest. Paragraph (*b*) covered the case of a person who had a mere *spes* (an expectation) such as the prospective next of kin of a living person in *Re Suffert*,[75] or a potential future spouse.[76] The adult cousins were in any event excluded by the proviso to paragraph (*b*).

ii. Parties. In general, the settlor, if living,[77] and all beneficiaries under the trusts, both adult and minor, should be made parties. The

---

[72] [1961] Ch. 1.

[73] [1986] 1 W.L.R. 934; criticised [1987] Conv. 144 (J. Riddall), also discussing persons who are objects of mere powers and discretionary trusts.

[74] The Act does not deal with the problem of the beneficiary who must consent on his own behalf but who is untraceable. In such a case a *Benjamin* order (*ante*, p. 534) could be used. See (1986) 136 N.L.J. 1057 (P. Luxton).

[75] *Supra*; *Re Moncrieff's S.T.* [1962] 1 W.L.R. 1344. But see [1987] Conv. 144 at p. 146 (J. Riddall) for the view that such persons do have a contingent interest in the *settlement*, although not, of course, in the estate of their living relative.

[76] See *Re Clitheroe's S.T.* [1959] 1 W.L.R. 1159; *Re Lister's W.T.* [1962] 1 W.L.R. 1441.

[77] R.S.C., Ord. 93, r. 6(2).

minors, unless their interests coincide with those of adult beneficiaries who consent, should be separately represented,[78] and a
guardian *ad litem* must give full consideration to the way in which
the proposed variation will affect the minors' interests.[79] In the case
of a class, those who are members of the class at the date of the
application should be included[80]; but it is not necessary to join
persons who may become members later[81]; nor persons who may
become interested under discretionary trusts[82]; nor those who are
possible objects of a power.[83] Persons unborn cannot of course be
made parties, but their interests must be represented.[84] Where a
mental patient is involved the Court of Protection should be
informed as soon as the originating summons has been issued and
proceedings then taken in the Court of Protection to look after the
interests of the patient.[85]

iii. Applicants. The application should be made by a beneficiary, usually the person currently receiving the income. But the
settlor may do so.[86] It is not usually satisfactory for the trustees to
make the application because there might be an undesirable conflict
of interest between their interest as an applicant, and as guardian of
some of the beneficial interests for which they are responsible.[87]
They may apply if no-one else will do so, and the variation is in the
interests of the beneficiaries.[88]

iv. Foreign Trusts. The court will not approve an agreement
which provides for a settlement under the law of a foreign jurisdiction if the beneficiaries remain resident and domiciled in England;
nor, as in *Re Weston's Settlement*,[89] where the connection with
Jersey, the foreign jurisdiction, was recent and tenuous, and where
the court doubted whether the living beneficiaries really intended to
make Jersey their permanent home. Trusts have, however, been
"exported" in favour of a settlement with foreign trustees and
governed by foreign law where the beneficiaries have emigrated

---

[78] *Re Whigham's S.T.* [1971] 1 W.L.R. 831.
[79] *Re Whittall* [1973] 1 W.L.R. 1027.
[80] *Re Suffert's Settlement* [1961] Ch. 1.
[81] *Re Moncrieff's S.T.* [1962] 1 W.L.R. 1344.
[82] *Re Munro's S.T.* [1963] 1 W.L.R. 145.
[83] *Re Christie-Miller's Marriage Settlement* [1961] 1 W.L.R. 462; *Practice Direction* [1976]
     1 W.L.R. 884.
[84] The court must consider the position of any individual who may be born and become a
     beneficiary, not merely the class of unborn beneficiaries as a whole; *Re Cohen's S.T.* [1965]
     1 W.L.R. 1229.
[85] *Practice Direction* [1960] 1 W.L.R. 17; *Re Sanderson's W.T.* [1961] 1 W.L.R. 36.
[86] *Re Clitheroe's S.T.* [1959] 1 W.L.R. 1159.
[87] *Re Druce's S.T.* [1962] 1 W.L.R. 363.
[88] *Re Druce's S.T.* (*supra*) at p. 370.
[89] [1969] 1 Ch. 223.

permanently to the foreign country[90]; and approval has been given for the transfer of funds from a trust governed by English law to one governed by the law of Guernsey where the primary beneficiaries were resident and domiciled in France and the remainderman in Indonesia.[91] The advantages of trust exporting have been much reduced since the introduction of capital transfer and inheritance tax.[92]

It should be added that the appointment of a foreign trustee may be made in a proper case without the intervention of the court.[93]

Where the question is not one of exporting a trust to another jurisdiction but of varying a foreign trust, such a variation is governed by the applicable law of the trust.[94]

v. Effect of Approval by the Court. It appears that the arrangement is effective from the time of the approval by the court. The reasons why this is so are not clear; and the result may be due to the practice established by *Re Viscount Hambledon's Will Trusts*.[95] Several, and in some cases conflicting, accounts have been given of the effect of approval by the court.

In *Re Joseph's Will Trusts*[96] Vaisey J. included in his order approving the variation a direction that the variation should be carried into effect. In *Re Viscount Hambleden's Will Trusts*,[97] Wynn-Parry J. thought that he had no jurisdiction to make such a direction. Nor was it required. "I hold that the effect of my approval is effective for all purposes to vary the trusts."[98] In *Re Holt's Settlement*,[99] Megarry J. was unconvinced. Before him it was argued that the Act gives the court power to approve only on behalf of the persons mentioned in section 1(1); and the consent of the adults to a change in their beneficial interests was a "disposition," and ineffective unless in writing, as required by section 53(1)(c) of the

---

[90] *Re Seal's Marriage Settlement* [1961] Ch. 574 (Canada); *Re Windeatt's W.T.* [1969] 1 W.L.R. 692 (Jersey); see also *Re Whitehead's W.T.* [1971] 1 W.L.R. 833.

[91] *Re Chamberlain* (unreported) discussed in (1976) 126 N.L.J. 1034 (J. Morcom); (1976) 40 Conv.(N.S.) 295 (T. Watkin).

[92] See I.H.T.A. 1984, ss.48(3), 201(1)(d), 267.

[93] *Re Whitehead's W.T.*, *supra*. But application will often be made to the court, and a variation will be necessary if the form of the trust needs to be altered in order to comply with the foreign law, if there is no power in the trust instrument to do this. See Parker and Mellows, *The Modern Law of Trusts* (6th ed.), Chap. 22; (1990/91) 1 The Offshore Tax Planning Review p. 1 (R. Bramwell), discussing *Richard v. The Hon, A.B. Mackay* (1987, unreported), *ante*, p. 501.

[94] Recognition of Trusts Act 1987, Sched., Art. 8. The applicable law is determined by Arts. 6, 7; *ante*, p. 43.

[95] [1960] 1 W.L.R. 82; *Re Holt's Settlement* [1969] 1 Ch. 100 at p. 113.

[96] [1959] 1 W.L.R. 1019.

[97] [1960] 1 W.L.R. 82.

[98] *Ibid.* at p. 86.

[99] [1969] 1 Ch. 100; (1968) 84 L.Q.R. 162 (P.V.B.).

Law of Property Act 1925.[1] Megarry J. was reluctant to disturb what had become a very convenient practice based on *Re Viscount Hambleden*,[2] and searched for a theory to justify it. The suggestion that there was no "disposition" of the interests of the consenting adults, but a "species of estoppel"[3] operating against them was "unattractive." He was satisfied however that it could be explained on the ground that section 53(1)(c) was by necessary implication excluded; or that, where the variation was made for consideration, the consenting adults could be compelled to perform their contract and they held their original interests on constructive trusts, these being unaffected by section 53(1)(c).[4] The view that the variation obtains its effect by reason of the consent of the beneficiaries is supported by dicta in *I.R.C. v. Holmden*,[5] where however the question of section 53(1)(c) did not arise.

The arrangement coupled with the court's order is an "instrument" for the purposes of the Perpetuities and Accumulations Act 1964, s.15(5), and future interests or accumulations permitted by the Act may be provided for in an arrangement.[6] Because the variation does not owe its authority to the settlor, its provisions need not be such that the settlor could have created them.[7] In contrast with powers of appointment and advancement,[8] the perpetuity period does not relate back to the original settlement. A variation which is inconsistent with the continuous existence of a power operates as a release of a power.[9]

vi. Variation or Resettlement. The jurisdiction, as we have seen, is very wide. It is however a jurisdiction to "vary" and not to "resettle."[10] This is a difficult dividing line. In *Re Ball's Settlement*, Megarry J. laid down the general test as follows[11]:

"If an arrangement changes the whole substratum of the trust, then it may well be that it cannot be regarded merely as varying the trust. But if an arrangement, while leaving the substratum,

---

[1] *Ante*, p. 78; *Grey v. I.R.C.* [1960] A.C. 1.

[2] [1960] 1 W.L.R. 82.

[3] [1969] 1 Ch. 100 at p. 114; *Spens v. I.R.C.* [1970] 1 W.L.R. 1173.

[4] L.P.A. 1925, s.53(2); *Oughtred v. I.R.C.* [1960] A.C. 206; *Re Holt's Settlement* [1969] 1 Ch. 100 at pp. 115–116.

[5] [1968] A.C. 685; *cf.* T.A. 1925, s.57; *Re Mair* [1935] Ch. 562.

[6] *Re Lansdowne's W.T.* [1967] Ch. 603; *Re Lloyd's Settlement* [1967] 2 W.L.R. 1078; *Re Holt's Settlement, supra.*

[7] *Re Holt's Settlement, supra.*

[8] *Pilkington v. I.R.C.* [1964] A.C. 612, *ante*, p. 580.

[9] *Re Christie-Miller's Marriage Settlement* [1961] 1 W.L.R. 462; *Re Courtauld's Settlement* [1965] 1 W.L.R. 1385; *Re Ball's S.T.* [1968] 1 W.L.R. 899; *ante*, p. 183.

[10] *Re T.'s S.T.* [1964] Ch. 158; *Re Ball's S.T.* [1968] 1 W.L.R. 899; criticised (1968) 84 L.Q.R. 458 (P.V.B.); *Re Holt's Settlement* [1969] 1 Ch. 100 at p. 117; *Allen v. Distillers Co. (Biochemicals) Ltd* [1974] Q.B. 384.

[11] [1968] 1 W.L.R. 899 at p. 905.

effectuates the purpose of the trust by other means, it may still be possible to regard that arrangement as merely varying the original trusts, even though the means employed are wholly different and even though the form is completely changed."

vii. Fraud on a Power. Nor will the court approve a variation which involves a fraud on a power, as for example where property is held on trust for A for life and to such of A's children as he shall appoint, and A, in order to avoid tax liability on his death, appoints in favour of his living children, and does so with a view to partitioning the fund, with the court's approval, between his children and himself. Such an appointment has been held to be fraudulent and void on the ground that it was made so that the appointor may obtain a benefit for himself under the variation.[12]

viii. The Settlor's Intention. In giving approval, the court must be satisfied about the arrangement as a whole.[13] One relevant factor is whether or not the arrangement is consistent with the general plan of the settlor or testator.

In *Re Steed's Will Trusts*[14] a testator had left property to a faithful housekeeper for her life on protective trusts and after her death as she should appoint, the trustee having power to pay capital moneys to her as they should think fit. The property included a farm which was let to the housekeeper's brother. The terms of the will were designed to give the maximum benefit in the property to the housekeeper, without giving her an absolute interest, because of the danger which the testator "thought was real, of being, to use a common phrase, sponged upon by one of her brothers."[15]

The trustees decided to sell the farm. The housekeeper started proceedings to stop them, exercised the power of appointment in favour of herself, and applied under the Variation of Trusts Act, s.1, for the elimination of the protective element in her life interest. The result would be that the plaintiff would become absolutely entitled to the property, because she would then be the life tenant, having appointed to herself the reversion. The only persons who might be prejudiced by such a variation would be those who might benefit under the discretionary trusts which would arise if the protective life interests were forfeited[16]; and

---

[12] *Re Robertson's W.T.* [1960] 1 W.L.R. 1050; *Re Brook's Settlement* [1968] 1 W.L.R. 1661; *cf. Re Wallace's Settlement* [1968] 1 W.L.R. 711.

[13] *Re Burney's S.T.* [1961] 1 All E.R. 856.

[14] [1960] Ch. 407; *Re Michelham's W.T.* [1964] Ch. 550.

[15] [1960] Ch. 407 at p. 415.

[16] *Ante*, p. 189; assuming that she would not now have children, this was only a prospective husband, described in the case of the "spectral spouse."

under paragraph (*d*), the court is not concerned to see that they benefit from a variation. Was there any reason why approval should not be given?

The Court of Appeal refused. "It is the *arrangement* which has to be approved not just the limited interest of the person on whose behalf the court's duty is to consider it . . . the court must regard the proposal as a whole, and so regarding it, then ask itself whether in the exercise of its jurisdiction it should approve that proposal on behalf of the person who cannot give a consent . . . it was part of the testator's scheme . . . that this trust should be available for the plaintiff so that she should have proper provision made for her throughout her life, and would not be exposed to the risk that she might, if she had been handed the money, part with it in favour of another individual about whom the testator felt apprehension, which apprehension is plainly shared by the trustees."[17]

The question also arose in *Re Remnant's Settlement Trusts*,[18] where the proposed variation was the deletion of a forfeiture clause whereby beneficiaries who practised Roman Catholicism or married a Roman Catholic would lose their entitlement. The fact that the variation would defeat the settlor's intention was regarded as a serious matter, but not conclusive. As the forfeiture clause was undesirable in the circumstances of the family (unlike the disputed provision in *Re Steed's Will Trusts*,[19] which was not cited), it was fair and proper to delete it, notwithstanding the settlor's intention.

In *Goulding v. James*[20] the clear intention of the testatrix was that her daughter should have only a life interest and that her grandson should not have capital until aged 40 (because she mistrusted her son-in-law and her grandson had not "settled down"). A variation was sought whereby the daughter would have capital and the grandson would become entitled before the age of 40. As the proposed terms increased the financial benefit to unborn beneficiaries, approval was given by the Court of Appeal, even though the proposal was contrary to the intention of the testatrix. Her wishes carried little weight in these circumstances.

ix. Benefit. It is necessary that the variation should be for the benefit of the persons in categories (*a*) or (*c*) on whose behalf approval is sought. There is no such requirement of benefit in respect of persons under category (*d*).[21]

---

[17] [1960] Ch. 407 at pp. 421–422.
[18] [1970] Ch. 560, *post*, p. 628.
[19] *Supra*.
[20] February 7, 1997, distinguishing *Re Steed's Will Trusts, supra*.
[21] V.T.A. 1958, s.1, proviso. See *Re Van Gruisen's W.T.* [1964] 1 W.L.R. 449.

(a) *Financial Benefit.* There is usually no difficulty in showing financial benefit. But evidence must be presented to show that there is an advantage to each person required to be benefited.[22] Variations have commonly been made to save estate duty or inheritance tax,[23] capital gainst tax,[24] and income tax.[25] Any saving provides a larger sum for distribution, and remaindermen may also be benefited by the termination of an interest in possession as their interests will be accelerated. As stated above,[26] a partition of the settled fund between tenant for life and remainderman has inheritance tax advantages. Provided the tenant for life survives for seven years, no tax will be payable, whereas the whole capital is taxable if a life interest terminates on death. It is usual for the life tenant to pay the costs of the application.

(b) *Moral and Social Benefit.* But benefit is not only financial. The court must also consider the general welfare of the persons on whose behalf approval is sought; this does not necessarily coincide with their financial interest.

In *Re Weston's Settlements*,[27] two settlements had been made in 1964, one in favour of each of the settlor's sons (both young men and one still a minor) and their children. The settlor moved to Jersey in 1967, and the sons followed him. The application was for the appointment of new trustees under Trustee Act 1925, s.41,[28] and for the insertion into the settlement of a power for the trustees to discharge the trust of the settlements and to create almost identical Jersey settlements. The object was to take advantage of the favourable fiscal situation in Jersey. The Court of Appeal refused. The variation would make the beneficiaries richer but would not be for their benefit. "The court should not consider merely the financial benefit to the infant and unborn children, but also their educational and social benefit. There are many things in life more worthwhile than money. One of these things is to be brought up in this our England, which is still 'the envy of less happier lands.' I do not believe that it is for the benefit of the children to be uprooted from England and transported to another country simply to avoid tax . . . many a child has been ruined by being given too much.[29] The avoidance of tax may be lawful, but

---

[22] *Re Clitheroe's S.T.* [1959] 1 W.L.R. 1159 at p. 1163.
[23] *Re Druce's S.T.* [1962] 1 W.L.R. 363; *Gibbon v. Mitchell* [1990] 1 W.L.R. 1304.
[24] *Re Sainsbury's Settlement* [1967] 1 W.L.R. 476.
[25] *Re Clitheroe's S.T.* [1959] 1 W.L.R. 1159.
[26] *Ante*, p. 612.
[27] [1969] 1 Ch. 233.
[28] *Ante*, p. 497.
[29] A further objection concerned the absence of trusts legislation in Jersey. For the present position, see Matthews, *Jersey Law of Trusts* (3rd ed.), 1993.

it is not yet a virtue. The Court of Chancery should not encourage or support it—it should not give its approval to it—if by so doing it would imperil the true welfare of the children, already born or yet to be born."[30]

Similarly, as has been seen, with the housekeeper who wished to become the absolute owner of a farm which would then have been at the mercy of her brother.[31] In *Re C.L.*[32] it was held to be for the benefit of a mental patient to consent to the surrender of a protected life interest and a contingent remainder interest in favour of her daughter. It was what the patient would have done if she had been of sound mind. Mental patients should not be denied the opportunity of taking proper steps to preserve the family fortune.

(c) *Postponing Vesting.* It may be for the benefit of a minor that the date of vesting of an interest in the capital should be postponed.

In *Re T.'s Settlement Trusts,*[33] a female minor who was irresponsible and immature was entitled to a vested interest on attaining her majority, which she would do a few months after the application. The proposal was that her interest should be varied to become a protected life interest. Wilberforce J. could not regard such protection to the minor as a "benefit in its own right"; but he made an order postponing the vesting of the capital until a specified age and providing that the property should be held on protective trusts in the meantime.

(d) *Trouble in the Family.* Where a trust treats members of the family unequally, it may be for everyone's benefit, even for those who surrender a claim to property as a result, to vary the trust so as to treat each of them equally. Russell J. thought not in *Re Tinker's Settlement,*[34] where, owing to the draftsman's oversight, the settlement provided that the share of the settlor's son should accrue to his sister's share if he died under the age of 30 years, even if he left children. It was not for the benefit of the sister's children to surrender their contingent interest.

A broader view was taken in *Re Remnant's Settlement Trusts.*[35]

---

[30] [1969] 1 Ch. 233 at p. 245.
[31] *Re Steed's W.T.* [1960] Ch. 407; *ante,* p. 625.
[32] [1969] 1 Ch. 587.
[33] [1964] Ch. 158; *Re Holt's Settlement* [1969] 1 Ch. 100. See also *Allen v. Distillers Co. (Biochemicals) Ltd* [1974] Q.B. 384; *ante,* p. 615.
[34] [1960] 1 W.L.R. 1011.
[35] [1970] Ch. 560; (1971) 34 M.L.R. 98 (R. Cotterrell).

A trust fund gave contingent interests to the children of two sisters Dawn and Merrial, and contained a forfeiture provision in respect of any of the children who practised Roman Catholicism or was married to a Roman Catholic at the time of vesting, with an accruer provision in favour of the children of the other. Dawn's children were Protestant, but Merrial's were Roman Catholic.

Pennycuick J. approved the deletion of the forfeiture provision. This was clearly not for the financial benefit of Dawn's children, for they surrendered a very good chance of gaining by it. But it was overall for their benefit. "Obviously, a forfeiture provision of this kind might well cause very serious dissension between the families of the two sisters."[36] The forfeiture clause could also operate as a deterrent in the selection of a spouse. Freedom from such problems would be more important to the lives of the children than some more money.

(e) *Taking a Chance.* A difficulty arises where the proposed variation will almost certainly confer a benefit, but there may possibly be circumstances in which it will not. Thus, in *Re Cohen's Settlement Trust*,[37] an application was made to vary a settlement so as to make the interest of the grandchildren vest on a specified date, and not upon the death of a life tenant, in order to reduce estate duty. Although it was most unlikely (but not impossible) that the life tenant would live until the specified date, any children born after that date but before his death would lose their interests. Thus approval could not be given on behalf of unborn children. Where trustees wish to distribute on the footing that a middle-aged woman will not have further children, this may be sanctioned by court order without recourse to the 1958 Act.[38] Indeed, no application to court is needed where the woman is elderly.[39]

The question is one of degree. The court will not give its approval where the benefit is a matter of chance, but it will not require absolute certainty of benefit,[40] if the risk is one which a "prudent and well advised adult would be prepared to take."[41] Most risks can be covered by insurance.

---

[36] [1970] Ch. 560 at p. 566. Another benefit, of less weight, was to be freed from having to choose between one's religion and the entitlement under the will.

[37] [1965] 1 W.L.R. 1229.

[38] *Re Westminster Bank Limited's Declaration of Trust* [1963] 1 W.L.R. 820 (over 50). The order did not extinguish the rights of any future child.

[39] *Re Pettifor's S.T.* [1966] Ch. 257 (over 70); *cf. Figg v. Clark (Inspector of Taxes), The Times*, March 11, 1996 (presumption of fertility until death in context of capital gains tax).

[40] *Re Holt's Settlement* [1969] 1 Ch. 100; *Re Robinson's S.T.* [1976] 1 W.L.R. 806.

[41] (1960) 76 L.Q.R. 22 (R.E.M.).

CHAPTER 23

BREACH OF TRUST

1. Personal Liability to Beneficiaries 632
   A. General 632
      i. Liability is Compensatory 632
      ii. Liability is Personal, not
          Vicarious 632
      iii. Breaches before Appointment 632
      iv. Breaches after Retirement 633
      v. Trustee-Beneficiary 633
   B. Measure of Liability 633
      i. General Principles 633
      ii. Purchase of Unauthorised
          Investments 636
      iii. Improper Retention of
          Investments 636
          (a) Unauthorised Investments 636
          (b) Authorised Investments 637
      iv. Improper Sale of Authorised
          Investments 637
      v. Failure to Invest 637
      vi. Employment of Trust Funds in
          Trade 638
      vii. Mortgage of Land 638
      viii. Interest 638
      ix. Profit in One Transaction: Loss in
          Another 639
2. Liability *Inter Se*: Contribution and
   Indemnity 641
   A. Joint and Several Liability 641
   B. Liability *Inter Se*: Contribution 641
   C. Indemnity 642
      i. Fraud 642
      ii. Solicitor and Trustee 642
      iii. Beneficiary-Trustee 643
3. Criminal Liability 643
4. Protection of Trustees 644
   A. Participation in, or Consent to, a
      Breach of Trust 645
      i. Knowledge 645
      ii. Benefit 645
      iii. Freedom of Decision 646
   B. Release and Acquiescence 646
   C. Impounding the Beneficiary's Interest:
      Trustee Act 1925, s.62 647
      i. Inherent Power 647
      ii. Trustee Act 1925, s.62 647

   D. Statutory Relief: Trustee Act 1925,
      s.61 648
   E. Limitation and Laches 651
      i. Six-Year Period under Limitation
         Act 1980, s.21(3) 651
      ii. Exceptions to the Six-Year
          Rule 652
          (a) Limitation Act 1980, s.21(1) 652
          (b) Claim to the Personal Estate
              of a Deceased Person 653
          (c) Sections 28 and 32 654
      iii. Assignees 654
      iv. Where No Period is Applicable .. 654
5. Proprietary Remedies 656
   A. Personal and Proprietary Actions 656
   B. Unjust Enrichment. Restitution 656
   C. Tracing at Common Law 657
   D. Tracing in Equity 662
      i. Who is Entitled to Trace 662
         (a) Requirement of Fiduciary
             Relationship 662
         (b) Requirement of Equitable
             Proprietary Interest 663
      ii. Unmixed Funds 666
      iii. Mixed Funds 667
          (a) Position as Against the
              Trustee 667
          (b) Position as Between Two
              Trusts, or Trust and Third
              Party 669
          (c) Bank Accounts 670
      iv. Subrogation 674
      v. Increase in Value 676
      vi. The Innocent Volunteer 677
      vii. Loss of Right to Trace 678
          (a) The Property Ceases to be
              Identifiable 678
          (b) Bona Fide Purchaser 679
          (c) Change of Position 679
      viii. Retention of Title Clauses 681
          (a) Unmixed Goods 682
          (b) Incorporation into Manufac-
              turing Process 683
          (c) Proceeds of Sale 684
6. The Claim in Personam in *Diplock* 686

1. PERSONAL LIABILITY TO BENEFICIARIES

A. General[1]

i. Liability is Compensatory. A trustee who fails to comply with his duties is liable to make good the loss to the trust estate. Even if there is no loss, the trustee is accountable for any profit made in breach of trust.[2] The object of the rule is not to punish the trustee, but to compensate the beneficiaries. However, the court will, on suitable occasions, authorise acts which are technical breaches of trust; a trustee will not be liable for a technical breach which the court would have authorised[3]; but there is no need to take the risk; he should obtain the directions of the court before acting.[4] The effect of exemption clauses was considered in Chapter 17.[5]

ii. Liability is Personal, not Vicarious. The rule has always been that a trustee is liable for his own breaches and not for those of his co-trustees.[6] The dividing line however is extremely difficult to draw; for if there is a breach by a co-trustee, the trustee may himself be at fault by leaving the matter in the hands of a co-trustee without inquiry, or for standing by while a breach of trust is being committed,[7] or for allowing trust funds to remain in the sole control of a co-trustee, or for failing to take steps to obtain redress on becoming aware of a breach of trust.

Section 30 of the Trustee Act 1925, providing that a trustee shall not, unless guilty of "wilful default," be liable for the acts and defaults of any other trustee, has been examined elsewhere.[8]

iii. Breaches before Appointment. A trustee is not liable for breaches of trust committed before his appointment in the absence of evidence indicating a breach of trust.[9] On appointment, however, he should examine the books and documents relating to the trust, and should ensure that the trust property is vested in him. If in the course of his inquiries he discovers a breach of trust, he should take steps against the former trustees; unless for some reason he can show that such proceedings would have been useless.[10]

---

[1] See the definitions of breach of trust discussed by Megarry J. in *Tito v. Waddell (No. 2)* [1977] Ch. 106 at p. 247. As to costs, see *McDonald v. Horn* [1995] 1 All E.R. 961; *ante*, p. 460.
[2] See Chap. 21.
[3] *Lee v. Brown* (1798) 4 Ves. 362 at p. 369; *Brown v. Smith* (1878) 10 Ch.D. 377.
[4] *Ante*, p. 533.
[5] *Ante*, p. 483.
[6] *Townley v. Sherborne* (1643) J. Bridg. 35 at pp. 37, 38.
[7] *Bahin v. Hughes* (1886) 31 Ch.D. 390; *post*, p. 641.
[8] *Ante*, p. 563.
[9] *Re Strahan* (1856) 8 De G.M. & G. 291.
[10] *Re Forest of Dean Coal Co* (1878) 10 Ch.D. 450 at p. 452.

iv. Breaches after Retirement. A trustee remains liable after retirement for breaches committed by him during office; and similarly his estate remains liable after his death. He may on the other hand have been released by the other trustees, or by the beneficiaries being *sui juris* and in possession of all the facts. He will not usually be liable in respect of breaches committed after his retirement; but he may be if he retired in order to facilitate a breach of trust.[11]

v. Trustee-Beneficiary. Where the trustee in breach is also a beneficiary, his beneficial interest bears the loss against the other beneficiaries,[12] and, as we will see,[13] against the trustees[14]; and this liability applies although the beneficial interest was acquired by him derivatively, even by purchase.[15]

B. Measure of Liability

i. General Principles. In the case of an unlawful profit, the trustee must account for the profit, which will normally be held on constructive trust. Thus any increase in value belongs to the trust, while the trustee remains personally liable for the deficit if there is a decrease in value.[16] Indeed, he may be liable to account for the highest value between the date of breach and the date of judgment.[17] Thus the principle that liability is measured as at the date of judgment, applicable to other breaches, does not apply to profits.[18] Where a profit has been made from the wrongful use of property, the plaintiff must elect at judgment between an account of profits and compensation for loss sustained by the deprivation of the use of the property.[19]

With other breaches of trust or fiduciary duty, the measure of liability is the loss caused to the trust estate, directly or indirectly,[20]

---

[11] *Head v. Gould* [1898] 2 Ch. 250 at p. 272. This question came into prominence in the context of pressure upon English resident trustees to retire in favour of foreign resident trustees in order to allow a trust fund to escapte liability for capital gains tax: *Re Whitehead's W.T.* [1971] 1 W.L.R. 833; *ante*, p. 501.

[12] *Re Dacre* [1915] 2 Ch. 480; [1916] 1 Ch. 344. Assignees are also bound, unless they took for value and without notice.

[13] *Post*, p. 643.

[14] *Chillingworth v. Chambers* [1896] 1 Ch. 685.

[15] *Re Dacre, supra.*

[16] *Att.-Gen. for Hong Kong v. Reid* [1994] 1 A.C. 324; *ante*, p. 608.

[17] *Nant-y-glo and Blaina Ironworks Co. v. Grave* (1879) 12 Ch.D. 738 (liable to account for shares at previous value of £80 each although since fallen to £1 each).

[18] *Target Holdings Ltd v. Redferns (a firm)* [1996] 1 A.C. 421, *infra.*

[19] *Tang Man Sit (Personal Representatives) v. Capacious Investments Ltd* [1996] 1 A.C. 514; *ante*, p. 609.

[20] *Knott v. Cottee* (1852) 16 Beav. 77; *Bartlett v. Barclays Bank Trust Co. Ltd (No. 2)* [1980] Ch. 515.

and the onus is on the plaintiff to prove that there is a loss and that it would not have occurred but for the breach.[21]

The principles of equitable compensation have not yet been fully worked out.[22] Liability is restitutionary, and the principles are not identical to the common law rules for the assessment of damages.[23] Thus the rules of remoteness and foreseeability applicable in contract and tort are not relevant, but causal connection must be established. In *Canson Enterprises Ltd v. Boughton & Co.*[24] a solicitor committed a breach of fiduciary duty in a sale transaction in which he knew that the vendor made a secret profit. The purchaser (who would not have completed if aware of the facts) then built a warehouse which, due to the negligence of the builders, was defective. The purchaser's claim for compensation against the solicitor for the defective building was unanimously dismissed by the Canadian Supreme Court because there was insufficient causal connection between the breach and the loss, but different views were taken as to whether the common law rules of remoteness applied by analogy in equity.

The principles were reviewed in *Target Holdings Ltd v. Redferns (a firm)*[25]

> Target agreed to advance £1,525,000 to C Ltd, to purchase property valued (allegedly negligently) at £2m, to be secured by a mortgage. The arrangement, unknown to Target, was that the vendor would sell to P Ltd for £775,000, which would sell to K Ltd for £1.25m, which in turn would sell to C Ltd for £2m. This appeared to be a mortgage fraud by the three related companies. The defendant solicitors acted for the three companies and for Target. Target transferred £1,525,000 to the solicitors, who held it on a bare trust for Target. In breach of trust the solicitors paid away the money to P Ltd and K Ltd before completion of the purchase and the mortgage. The mortgage was in fact completed a few days later. On the insolvency of C Ltd the property was sold by Target as mortgagee, but, because of the property slump, raised

---

[21] *Re Miller's Trust Deed* (1978) L.S.Gaz. 454; *Nestlé v. National Westminster Bank plc* [1993] 1 W.L.R. 1260 (holding also that "loss" includes a gain which is less than the profit a prudent trustee would have made); *Target Holdings Ltd v. Redferns (a firm)* [1996] 1 A.C. 421 at p. 440.

[22] See (1994) 14 L.S. 313 (D. Capper). This is discussed in the context of "fusion"; *ante* p. 24.

[23] See *Re Bell's Indenture* [1980] 1 W.L.R. 1217 (trustee must restore turst property without deducting tax which would have been payable if it had not been misappropriated, in contrast with principles of assessing tort damages for loss of earnings).

[24] (1991) 85 D.L.R. (4th) 129. See also *Mahoney v. Purnell* [1996] 3 All E.R. 61; (1997) L.Q.R. 8 (J. Heydon).

[25] [1996] 1 A.C. 421; (1995) 9 *Trust Law International* 86 (J. Ulph); (1996) 112 L.Q.R. 27 (C. Rickett); [1996] L.M.C.L.Q. 161 (R. Nolan); [1997] Conv. 14 (D. Capper). The proceedings were interlocutory, as a result of which the defendants obtained leave to defend.

only £500,000. Target sued the solicitors for breach of trust in paying away the £1,525,000 and claimed that sum less the proceeds of sale. The House of Lords found for the solicitors. Target was in the same position as it would have been if the money had not been transferred until the security was in place and had thus failed to establish that the loss would not have occurred but for the breach.

Lord Browne-Wilkinson considered that it was wrong to apply rules developed in the context of traditional trusts to trusts arising in commercial dealings. In the case of a traditional trust for A for life then for B, each beneficiary was entitled to a restoration of the fund.[26] The present case involved a bare trust of a commercial kind. Before the transaction had been completed the solicitors could have been required to restore the money wrongly paid away. But "the clock did not stop" when the money was paid away. Once the transaction had been completed, equity required a trustee to make good a loss suffered which, using hindsight and common sense, could be seen to have been caused by the breach. The quantum of liability was to be assessed not at the date of the breach but at the date of judgment.[27] Although the principles underlying the common law and equitable rules were similar, the detailed rules were different. If it could be shown that the loss would not have occurred but for the breach,[28] the trustee would be liable even if the immediate cause of the loss was the dishonesty or negligence of a third party, as the common law rules of remoteness and causation would not apply. By way of exception, the *Target Holdings* principle does not apply where a fiduciary has made a representation or given a warranty which he knew or ought to have known was misleading. Thus a solicitor who has misled his mortgagee client cannot challenge the mortgagee's claim that it would not have proceeded with the loan but for the warranty or representation.[29]

It is important, however, to distinguish a breach of trust or fiduciary duty from other breaches of duty by a fiduciary. The special restitutionary principles of assessment of equitable compensation discussed above apply only where there is a breach of

[26] See *Clough v. Bond* (1838) 3 My. & Cr. 490.

[27] *Jaffray v. Marshall* [1993] 1 W.L.R. 1285, which measured the loss as the highest value of the property between breach and judgment, was overruled. See also *Re Dawson* [1966] 2 N.S.W.L.R. 211 (date of judgment equally applicable where this operates to the detriment of the trustees).

[28] Target would be able to prove this at trial if it could show that P Ltd could not have purchased from the vendor (and then sold on) without the funds advanced in breach of trust. Thus leave to defend was conditional upon paying £1m into court.

[29] *Bristol and West Building Society v. May May & Merrimans* [1996] 2 All E.R. 801, applying *Brickenden v. London Loan and Savings Co.* [1934] 3 D.L.R. 465. As in *Target Holdings*, the solicitor held the money on trust for the lender before paying it to a purchaser, the security later proving inadequate.

trust or fiduciary duty. A breach of fiduciary duty means a breach of
those duties which are special to fiduciaries, whose core obligation
is loyalty. Where a fiduciary (such as a solicitor) commits some
other breach, as where he acts incompetently, there is no reason why
compensation in equity should be assessed differently from common
law damages.[30]

The principle that equity does not require a trustee to compensate
for a loss which would have occurred had there been no breach is
surely correct. However, it is not clear exactly how the rules applicable to traditional trusts and commercial trusts differ. A more useful
distinction is that between breaches of fiduciary duty and other
breaches by fiduciaries, as mentioned above.

Subsidiary rules applicable to particular situations will now be
considered.

ii. Purchase of Unauthorised Investments. When trustees
make an unauthorised investment, they will be liable for any loss
incurred on the sale. This is so even if the sale is at a time chosen
by the court, and if the investments would have shown a profit if
they had been retained until the decision of the court holding them
to be improper.[31] The beneficiaries may, if they are *sui juris* and so
wish, adopt the unauthorised investment[32]; if they do so, there is
dispute whether that is the limit of their remedy,[33] or whether they
may claim the difference between the value of the investment and
the purchase price.[34]

iii. Improper Retention of Investments.

(a) *Unauthorised Investments.* A trustee who improperly retains
an unauthorised investment is liable for the difference between the
present value (or selling price) and the price which it would have
raised if it had been sold at the proper time. How hard this can be
on a trustee holding property in a falling market is shown by *Fry v.
Fry*[35] where trustees were liable for the difference between the price
offered for a hotel in 1837 which they refused as inadequate, and the
much lower price prevailing in 1859, the fall being largely due to the
diversion of road traffic by the building of a railway.

---

[30] *Bristol & West Building Society v. Mothew* [1996] 4 All E.R. 698. *Cf. Bristol & West
Building Society v. May May & Merrimans, supra,* where the breach was considered to be
of fiduciary duty, and *Target Holdings* itself, where breach of trust was conceded.
[31] *Knott v. Cottee, supra.*
[32] *Re Jenkin's and Randall's Contract* [1903] 2 Ch. 362; *Wright v. Morgan* [1926] A.C. 788
at p. 799.
[33] *Thornton v. Stokill* (1855) 1 Jur.(N.S.) 751.
[34] *Re Lake* [1903] 1 K.B. 439.
[35] *Fry v. Fry* (1859) 27 Beav. 144.

(b) *Authorised Investments.* Before 1961 a trustee was not liable for loss occasioned by the retention of an authorised investment, unless he was guilty of wilful default.[36] We have seen that the Trustee Investment Act 1961, s.6(2), requires advice to be taken on the question of retaining investments.[37] Trustee Act 1925, s.4[38] (no liability *by reason only* of continuing to hold an investment which has ceased to be authorised) has no application to such cases.[39]

iv. Improper Sale of Authorised Investments.

When an authorised investment is improperly sold, the beneficiaries may require the trustees either to account for the proceeds of sale or to replace the investment, valued as at the date of judgment.[40] Thus where trustees sold Consols and invested in an unauthorised investment, the whole matter was treated as a single transaction and the trustees were held liable to replace the Consols at the higher price then prevailing.[41] This is so even though the improper investment was realised without loss.[42]

v. Failure to Invest.

Trustees should invest within a reasonable time. Pending investment, moneys may be paid into a bank to a deposit or other account.[43] Interest should be obtained if possible; a trustee who unreasonably fails to find an investment will be chargeable with interest.[44]

If a trustee is required to make a specific investment and fails to make any investment, and the price of the specific investment has risen, he will be liable to purchase as much of that investment as would have been purchased at the proper time.[45] Similarly if he chooses an investment other than that specified,[46] profit in the unauthorised investment being surrendered, of course, to the trust.[47] Where, as is nearly always the case in practice, the trustees may select investments at their discretion, it is not practicable to base recovery upon the price of a particular investment. The beneficiary will be entitled to the difference between the actual value of the trust fund and the value which a prudent trustee is likely to have achieved

---

[36] *Re Chapman* [1896] 2 Ch. 763; *Rawsthorne v. Rowley,* [1909] 1 Ch. 409n.

[37] *Ante*, p. 525.

[38] *Ante*, p. 526.

[39] Advice requirements are to be modified; *ante*, p. 532.

[40] *Re Bell's Indenture* [1980] 1 W.L.R. 1217. But where the asset sold in breach of trust would have been properly sold at a later date, the trustee is liable to replace it at its value on that date, and not as at the date of judgment.

[41] *Phillipson v. Gatty* (1848) 7 Hare 516.

[42] *Re Massingberd's Settlement* (1890) 63 L.T. 296.

[43] T.A. 1925, s.11(1).

[44] *Att.-Gen. v. Alford* (1855) 4 De G.M. & G. 843.

[45] *Byrchall v. Bradford* (1822) 6 Madd. 235.

[46] *Pride v. Fooks* (1840) 2 Beav. 430.

[47] *Post*, p. 639.

(by considering the average performance of ordinary shares during the period in question).[48]

vi. Employment of Trust Fund in Trade. A trustee who employs trust funds in his trade or business is liable to account for the profits he makes,[49] or for the sums involved with interest, whichever is the greater. Difficult questions arise when he employs a mixed fund, being partly his own and partly trust money. Here the rule is that the beneficiaries may claim a proportionate share of the profits[50] or demand the return of the trust money with interest.[51]

vii. Mortgage of Land. We have seen that where trustees lend an excessive sum on a mortgage of land which would have been a proper investment for a smaller sum, the mortgage is treated as an authorised investment for the smaller sum and the trustees are liable only for the excess, with interest.[52]

viii. Interest. "It is well established in equity that a trustee who in breach of trust misapplies trust funds will be liable not only to replace the misapplied principal fund but to do so with interest from the date of the misapplication. This is on the notional ground that the money so applied was in fact the trustee's own money and that he has retained the misapplied trust money in his own hands and used it for his own purposes. Where a trustee has retained trust money in his own hands, he will be accountable for the profit which he has made or which he is assumed to have made with the use of the money. . . . The defaulting trustee is normally charged with simple interest only,[53] but if it is established that he has used the money in trade he may be charged compound interest. . . . Precisely similar equitable principles apply to an agent who has retained monies of his principal in his hands and used them for his own purposes.[54]"[55] If the trustee or agent has received a sum in excess of what the court

---

[48] *Nestlé v. National Westminster Bank plc* [1993] 1 W.L.R. 1260; *cf. Shepherd v. Moulis* (1845) 4 Hare 500 (trust fund plus interest).

[49] *Re Davis* [1902] 2 Ch. 314; *Re Jarvis* [1958] 1 W.L.R. 815.

[50] *Lord Provost, etc., of Edinburgh v. Lord Advocate* (1879) 4 App.Cas. 823; *Re Tilley's W.T.* [1967] Ch. 1179.

[51] *Heathcote v. Hulme* (1819) 1 Jac. & W. 122.

[52] T.A. 1925, s.9; *ante*, p. 530.

[53] *Belmont Finance Corporation Ltd v. Williams Furniture Ltd (No. 2)* [1980] 1 All E.R. 393.

[54] *Burdick v. Garrick* (1870) 5 Ch.App. 233.

[55] *Wallersteiner v. Moir (No. 2)* [1975] Q.B. 373 at p. 397; *Guardian Ocean Cargoes Ltd v. Banco do Brasil (No. 3)* [1992] 2 Lloyd's Rep. 193 (presumed used in investment business); *Mathew v. T. M. Sutton Ltd* [1994] 1 W.L.R. 1455; *cf. O'Sullivan v. Management Agency and Music Ltd* [1985] Q.B. 428, (1986) 49 M.L.R. 118 (W. Bishop and D. Prentice), *ante*, p. 587 (simple interest where profits used in trade, but trade benefited plaintiff, being in the nature of a joint venture).

would impose, he is accountable for what he has actually received, or the beneficiaries may adopt the investment.[56]

The rate of interest, and the choice between simple and compound,[57] is in the discretion of the court. The nineteenth century cases laid down 4 per cent[58] as the general rule, with an increase to 5 per cent where the trustee or other fiduciary was guilty of fraud[59] or active misconduct,[60] or where he ought to have received more than 4 per cent.[61] These rates are out of line with current commercial interest rates, and more recent decisions have charged 1 per cent above the London clearing banks' base rate in force at the time[62]; or that allowed from time to time on the court's short-term investment account (now called the court special account), established under section 6(1) of the Administration of Justice Act 1965.[63] Compound interest is charged where that fairly represents what the trustee may reasonably be treated as having received,[64] or where there is a duty to accumulate,[65] and sometimes in cases of fraud or misconduct.[66]

The question which arose in *Westdeutsche Landesbank Girozentrale v. Islington London Borough Council*[67] was whether the equitable jurisdiction to award compound interest could be invoked in a common law personal action. The House of Lords, by a majority, held that it could not. Lords Goff and Woolf, dissenting, held that equity should supplement the common law remedies to achieve full restitution, but the majority considered that this was a matter for Parliament.

ix. Profit in One Transaction: Loss in Another. Any gains made out of the trust property belong to the beneficiaries while a

---

[56] *Re Jenkins' and Randalls' Contract* [1903] 2 Ch. 362; *Wright v. Morgan* [1926] A.C. 788 at p. 799; *ante*, p. 636.

[57] With yearly rests (*Jones v. Foxall* (1852) 15 Beav. 388 at p. 393; *Guardian Ocean Cargoes Ltd v. Banco do Brasil (No. 3), supra; El Ajou v. Dollar Land Holdings plc (No. 2)* [1995] 2 All E.R. 213); and sometimes half-yearly rests (*Re Emmet's Estate* (1881) 17 Ch.D. 142).

[58] *Att-Gen. v. Alford* (1855) 4 De G.M. & G. 843; [1995] 2 All E.R. 213; *Fletcher v. Green* (864) 33 Beav. 426 at p. 430.

[59] *Att.-Gen. v. Alford, supra*, at p. 852.

[60] *Jones v. Foxall* (1852) 15 Beav. 388 at p. 393; *Gordon v. Gonda* [1955] 1 W.L.R. 885.

[61] *Jones v. Foxall, supra*, at p. 388 (calling in a mortgage which was returning 5 per cent.); see *Re Waterman's W.T.* [1952] 2 All E.R. 1054.

[62] *Wallersteiner v. Moir (No. 2)* [1975] Q.B. 373; [1982] Conv. 93 (J.T.F.); *Belmont Finance Corporation v. Williams Furniture Ltd (No. 2)* [1980] 1 All E.R. 393; *O'Sullivan v. Management Agency and Music Ltd* [1985] Q.B. 428; *Guardian Ocean Cargoes Ltd v. Banco do Brasil (No. 3)* [1992] 2 Lloyd's Rep. 193 (1 per cent above New York prime rate); *Rama v. Millar* [1996] 1 N.Z.L.R. 257.

[63] *Bartlett v. Barclays Bank Trust Co. Ltd (No. 2)* [1980] Ch. 515.

[64] *Wallersteiner v. Moir (No. 2), supra*.

[65] *Re Emmet's Estate* (1881) 17 Ch.D. 142.

[66] *Jones v. Foxall, supra; Gordon v. Gonda, supra; cf. O'Sullivan v. Management Agency and Music Ltd, supra*. As to costs, see Snell, p. 289.

[67] [1996] A.C. 669.

loss incurred by reason of a breach of trust must be made good by the trustee. A trustee cannot set off a gain in one transaction against a loss made in another unauthorised transaction.

In *Dimes v. Scott*[68] trustees retained an unauthorised mortgage returning 10 per cent all of which was paid to the tenant for life. When the mortgage was paid off, trustees were able to purchase more Consols than they would have done if the reinvestment had taken place at the end of a year from the testator's death. Lord Lyndhurst held the trustees liable for the excess interest paid to the tenant for life[69] over that which would have been payable if the capital of the unauthorised investment had been invested in Consols at the end of a year from the testator's death, and the trustees were unable to set against this the gain arising from the fall in the price of Consols.

The rule is harsh though logical. It has not been applied where the court finds that the gain and loss were part of the same transaction. There is often difficulty in determining whether the matter should or should not be regarded as a single transaction.

In *Fletcher v. Green*[70] trust money was lent on mortgage to a firm of which one trustee was a partner. The trustees reclaimed the money; the security was sold at a loss and the proceeds paid into court and invested in Consols. The question was whether the trustees' accounts should credit them with the amount of the proceeds of sale or with the value of the Consols, which had risen in price. They were held entitled to take advantage of the rise. No reasons were given. The case is usually explained on the ground that the whole matter was treated as one transaction. If that is so, they should logically have been at risk in relation to a possible fall in the price of Consols; the trustees can hardly be allowed to take advantage of a rise but not the burden of a fall; but it would be hard on the trustees if they have to run the risk of loss on an investment made by the court.

The difficulty of laying down a clear rule was recognised in *Bartlett v. Barclays Bank Trust Co. Ltd (No. 1)*[71] where the defendant bank was held liable as trustee for failing to exercise proper supervision of the board of directors of a private company whose shares were almost wholly owned by the trust. The board embarked

---

[68] (1828) 4 Russ. 195.
[69] The tenant for life was entitled only to 4 per cent under the rule in *Howe v. Earl of Dartmouth* (1802) 7 Ves.Jr. 137; *ante*, p. 538.
[70] (1864) 33 Beav. 426.
[71] [1980] Ch. 515; [1980] Conv. 155 (G. Shindler); *ante*, p. 527.

on speculative ventures in property development: the Old Bailey project was a disaster; the Guildford project was a success. In finding the bank liable, Brightman J. allowed the gain on the Guildford project to be set off against the Old Bailey. Without considering the case in detail, he said,[72] after recognising the general rule: "The relevant cases are, however, not altogether easy to reconcile. All are centenarians and none is quite like the present. . . . I think it would be unjust to deprive the bank of the element of salvage in the course of assessing the cost of the shipwreck." Thus a gain can be set off against a loss if, even though not arising from the same transaction, they resulted from the same wrongful course of conduct; in the present case a policy of speculative investment.

2. LIABILITY INTER SE: CONTRIBUTION AND INDEMNITY

A. Joint and Several Liability

Where two or more trustees are liable for a breach of trust, their liability is joint and several. Thus a beneficiary may claim the whole loss by suing all or some or any one of those who are liable; and may levy execution for the whole sum against any one.[73]

B. Liability Inter Se: Contribution

The rule used to be that the joint liability of trustees required an equal sharing of the liability, regardless of fault, and therefore that one trustee who had paid more than his share of the liability for a breach of trust was entitled to equal contribution from the other trustees who were also liable[74]; or from their estates after death.[75] The effect of this rule was shown dramatically in *Bahin v. Hughes*,[76] where the Court of Appeal held that a passive trustee was liable with the active trustee. Cotton L.J. said[77]: "Miss Hughes was the active trustee and Mr Edwards did nothing, and in my opinion it would be laying down a wrong rule to hold that where one trustee acts honestly, though erroneously, the other trustee is to be held entitled to indemnity who by doing nothing neglects his duty more than the acting trustee."

The Civil Liability (Contribution) Act 1978 gives the court a discretion in relation to the amount to be recovered against two or

---

[72] *Ibid*, at p. 538.
[73] *Fletcher v. Green* (1864) 33 Beav. 426 at p. 430.
[74] *Fletcher v. Green, supra; Ramskill v. Edwards* (1885) 31 Ch.D. 100; *Robinson v. Harkin* [1896] 2 Ch. 415.
[75] *Jackson v. Dickinson* [1903] 1 Ch. 947.
[76] (1886) 31 Ch.D. 390; *Bishopsgate Investment Management Ltd v. Maxwell (No. 2)* [1994] 1 All E.R. 261 (no defence that blindly followed co-director's lead).
[77] *Ibid*. at p. 396.

more defendants who are liable in respect of the damage. The amount recoverable against any defendant shall be "such as may be found by the court to be just and equitable having regard to the extent of that person's responsibility for the damage in question"[78]; and includes breach of trust as one of the forms of liability to which the Act applies.[79] It will be interesting to see how the passive trustee will fare under this provision. The Act does not apply to situations in which one trustee is entitled to an indemnity.[80]

C. Indemnity

There are a few cases where one trustee is not liable to contribute; where, that is, he is entitled to an indemnity from his co-trustee against his own liability. Such cases are rare; for such relief "would act as an opiate upon the consciences of the trustees; so that instead of the *cestui que trust* having the benefit of several acting trustees, each trustee would be looking to the other or others for a right of indemnity, and so neglect the performance of his duties."[81] The situations are:

i. Fraud. In some cases where one trustee alone is fraudulent, the other will not be liable at all, and so no question of contribution or indemnity will arise.[82] If both are in breach but one alone has made personal use of trust money, the latter must indemnify his co-trustee.[83] If all are fraudulent the rule used to be that the one who has paid the damages could not claim contribution from the others,[84] because a plaintiff should not base his claim upon his wrong. No specific exception, however, is made under the modern legislation authorising the court to determine how liability will be shared, and the Civil Liability (Contribution) Act 1978 is applicable.[85]

ii. Solicitor and Trustee. Many of the cases of indemnity are cases where one trustee is a solicitor and has exercised such a

---

[78] s.2(1). This may extend to a complete indemnity; s.2(2).

[79] s.6(1). See *Friends' Provident Life Office v. Hillier Parker May & Rowden (a firm)* [1996] 2 W.L.R. 123.

[80] s7(3); Law Commission Report on Contribution, No. 79 (1977), para. 26; *cf.* Snell, p. 296; Parker and Mellows, *The Modern Law of Trusts* (6th ed.), p. 592.

[81] *Per* Fry L.J. in *Bahin v. Hughes, supra,* at p. 398.

[82] *Re Smith* [1896] 1 Ch. 71 was an exceptional case of two trustees who acted together, but only one of whom was liable to the beneficiaries for the consequences. One trustee had chosen an investment honestly but the other had received a bribe in order to induce him to make it.

[83] *Bahin v. Hughes* (1886) 31 Ch.D. 390 at p. 395; *Thompson v. Finch* (1856) 25 L.J.Ch. 681 (where trustee also a solicitor).

[84] *Att.-Gen. v. Wilson* (1840) Cr. & Ph. 1 at p. 28.

[85] See *K. v. P.* [1993] Ch. 140 (not a case on trustees).

controlling influence that the other trustee has been unable to exercise an independent judgment.[86] There is no rule, however, that "a man is bound to indemnify his co-trustee against loss merely because he was a solicitor, when that co-trustee was an active participator in the breach of trust complained of, and is not proved to have participated merely in consequence of the advice and control of the solicitor."[87]

iii. Beneficiary-Trustee. When a person who is a trustee and beneficiary participates in a breach of trust, he may not claim any share of the trust estate until he has made good his liability as trustee.[88] He will be required to indemnify his co-trustee to the extent of his beneficial interest; but this does not take away his right to contribution from his co-trustee. The rule in *Chillingworth v. Chambers*[89] effects a compromise between these rules. A beneficiary trustee must indemnify his co-trustee to the extent of his beneficial interest. That property is taken first to meet the claims; after that, their liability is shared equally. The non-beneficiary trustee is thus given a partial indemnity; partial in that it extends only to the value of the beneficiary-trustee's interest.

3. CRIMINAL LIABILITY[90]

Breach of trust was not, at common law, a crime at all. The trustee was regarded as the owner of the trust property by the common law, which disregarded the rights of the beneficiary. But in 1857 breach of trust was made a statutory crime, and the law on the subject was incorporated in the Larceny Arts 1861 and 1916.

These Acts were repealed and replaced by the Theft Act 1968, which defines "theft" as the dishonest appropriation of property "belonging to another" with the intention of depriving the other of it permanently. By section 5(2) of the Act, "any person having a right to enforce the trust" is regarded as a person to whom the subject-matter of the trust "belongs." so that the criminal liability of trustees is in this way brought within the general law.[91] The objects

---

[86] *Re Partington* (1887) 57 L.T. 654.

[87] *Head v. Gould* [1898] 2 Ch. 250 at p. 265, *per* Kekewich J.; *ante*, p. 485; *Lockhart v. Reilly* (1856) 25 L.J. Ch. 697; *Re Turner* [1897] 1 Ch. 536.

[88] *Re Rhodesia Goldfields Ltd* [1910] 1 Ch. 239; *Selangor United Rubber Estates Ltd v. Cradock (No. 4)* [1969] 3 All E.R. 965.

[89] [1896] 1 Ch. 685; similarly if he becomes a beneficiary after the date of the breach, (1887) 37 Ch.D. 329, at p. 344.

[90] (1975) 39 Conv.(N.S.) 29 (R. Brazier). For guidelines on sentencing in trustee cases, see *R. v. Barrick* (1985) 81 Cr.App.R. 78.

[91] See *Re Att.-Gen.'s Reference (No. 1 of 1985)* [1986] Q.B. 491; *R. v. Clowes (No. 2)* [1994] 2 All E.R. 316 (misappropriation of money held on trust for investors was theft).

of a discretionary trust can presumably be regarded as having a sufficient right of enforcement to bring section 5(2) into operation for such trusts. Section 4(2)(*a*) also brings within the definition of "theft" an appropriation by a trustee of "land or anything forming part of it," and section 2(1)(*c*) makes a trustee guilty of theft if he appropriates property though he believes that the equitable owners cannot be discovered. A trustee cannot be convicted of theft on any evidence which has first been elicited from him in the course of civil proceedings instituted against him by the person aggrieved, but trustees have no privilege of refusing to incriminate themselves in civil proceedings.[92]

Finally, a trustee who is ordered to pay by a court of equity any sum in his possession or under his control, may be imprisoned in default of payment for a period not exceeding one year.[93]

4. Protection of Trustees

A trustee who has committed a breach of trust may be able to escape personal liability by bringing the case within one of the categories discussed below. Many of the relevant points arose in *Re Pauling's Settlement Trusts*.[94]

The children of the Younghusband family sued to recover from the trustees of their mother's marriage settlement various payments which were alleged to have been made in breach of trust. The Younghusbands were on many occasions in financial difficulties. Their main source of money was Mrs. Younghusband's marriage settlement under which she was tenant for life, and the trustees had power, with her consent, to advance up to one-half of the presumptive share of each child in the trust fund. Several advances were made under this power to the children when they had attained ages varying from 27 (in the case of Francis) to 21 (Ann and Anthony). In most cases the advances, although nominally made to the children, were, to the knowledge of everyone concerned, applied for family purposes and usually towards the reduction of Mrs. Younghusband's overdraft. On several occasions, but not on all, independent legal advice was obtained. The trustees relied on the consent and acquiescence of the advanced beneficiaries, and claimed an indemnity under Trustee Act 1925, s.62, and asked for relief under section 61. Several of the payments were held to be in breach of trust and the defences set up by the trustees are considered in the following sections.

---

[92] Theft Act 1968, s.31(1).
[93] Debtors Act 1869, s.4.
[94] [1964] Ch. 303.

A. Participation in, or Consent to, a Breach of Trust

A beneficiary who has participated in, or consented to, a breach of trust may not sue. "It is clear to us," said Willmer L.J. in *Re Pauling's Settlement Trusts*,[95] "that if the [trustee] can establish a valid request or consent by the advanced beneficiary to the advance in question, that is a good defence on the part of the [trustee] to the beneficiary's claim, even though it be plain that the advance was made in breach of trust." A reversioner is not "less capable of giving . . . assent when his interest is in reversion than when it is in possession,"[96] but he will not be treated as having given consent wherever he fails to take steps to remedy a breach of trust of which he has knowledge.[97]

i. Knowledge. "Consent is not a mere formality. It is a judgment of a person who is interested. . . . "[98] For, if mere knowledge and a passive assent constituted consent, then a trustee could always escape liability by informing a beneficiary of what he proposed to do. The consent must be given by an adult, *sui juris*, in circumstances in which he had a free choice. However, a minor beneficiary may exceptionally be taken to have assented to a breach, for instance where he fraudulently misstated his age.[99] "The court has to consider all the circumstances in which the concurrence of the *cestui que trust* was given with a view to seeing whether it is fair and equitable that, having given his concurrence, he should afterwards turn around and sue the trustees: that, subject to this, it is not necessary that he should know what he is concurring in is a breach of trust, provided that he fully understands what he is concurring in, and that it is not necessary that he should himself have directly benefited by the breach of trust."[1] Thus a beneficiary, who otherwise had a right to set aside a sale, was unable to do so when he had affirmed the sale, accepted part of the purchase money, and caused the purchaser to embark upon further liabilities which he could not repay.[2]

ii. Benefit. It is not necessary that the beneficiary should have been motivated to derive a personal benefit from the breach, nor that

---

[95] *Ibid.* at p. 335; *Re Bucks Constabulary Widow's and Orphans' Fund Friendly Society (No. 2)* [1979] 1 W.L.R. 936 at p. 955.

[96] *Life Association of Scotland v. Siddal* (1861) 3 De G.F. & J. 58 at p. 73.

[97] *Ibid.*

[98] *Re Massingberd's Settlement* (1890) 63 L.T. 296 at p. 299.

[99] See *Overton v. Bannister* (1884) 3 Hare 503.

[1] *Per* Wilberforce J. in *Re Pauling's S.T.* [1962] 1 W.L.R. 86 at p. 108, accepted by counsel in the Court of Appeal but not commented on by the Court [1964] Ch. 303, at p. 339; approved in *Holder v. Holder* [1968] Ch. 353 at pp. 394, 399, 406.

[2] *Holder v. Holder, supra.*

he actually received one.[3] Where a beneficiary may recover even though he has received a benefit he must give credit for any benefit which he has received from the breach.[4]

iii. Freedom of Decision. The decision must be freely taken by a person not under disability. Even where the beneficiary is adult and technically under no disability, it may be possible to show that the consent was due to undue influence. Thus, in *Re Pauling,*[5] the advancements were in each case delayed until the child had become 21; but several of the payments which had been made to, or indirectly for, the benefit of the parents were presumed to have been the result of undue influence exercised by them over the children. Indeed it was clear that the advances were all made to meet the financial needs of the father. The Court of Appeal refused to accept the trustees' argument that undue influence was only relevant as between the children and their parents where the parents had acquired the benefit; they suggested that "a trustee carrying out a transaction in breach of trust may be liable if he knew, or ought to have known, that the beneficiary was acting under the undue influence of another, or may be presumed to have done so, but will not be liable if it cannot be established that he so knew, or ought to have known."[6] It is impossible to say how long after the attainment of majority the presumption continues; this depends upon the circumstances of each case.[7]

B. Release and Acquiescence

These defences relate to the conduct of the beneficiary after the breach has taken place; where they apply, the become equivalent to consent *ex post facto*. A release may be, but need not be, formal; it may be inferred from conduct, as where a beneficiary accepted benefits under his mother's will which prohibited him from setting up any claim in respect of the administration of his father's estate.[8] Length of time in making a claim will not of itself be fatal, but will assist the trustee by requiring less evidence to establish a release.[9] Many of the points raised in connection with consent apply also

---

[3] *Fletcher v. Collis* [1905] 2 Ch. 24.
[4] *Re Pauling's S.T.* [1964] Ch. 303. (The £300 received by Ann; and the policies received by Francis and George). See p. 354 for the reasons why Anthony was not required to account for benefits received indirectly through his mother.
[5] [1964] Ch. 303.
[6] *Ibid.* at p. 338.
[7] *Huguenin v. Baseley* (1807) 14 Ves.Jr. 273; *Allcard v. Skinner* (1887) 36 Ch.D. 145 at p. 171.
[8] *Egg v. Devey* (1847) 10 Beav. 444.
[9] *Stackhouse v. Barnston* (1805) 10 Ves.Jr. 453; *Life Association of Scotland v. Siddall* (1861) 3 De G.F. & J. 58 at p. 77.

here. "I . . . agree that either concurrence in the act, or acquiescence without original concurrence, will release the trustees; but that is only a general rule, and the Court must inquire into the circumstances which induced concurrence or acquiescence."[10] There will be no release for the trustees where the beneficiary acquiesced without knowledge of the facts; but, as with consent, it is not necessary that the beneficiary should have been aware of his legal rights.[11]

C. Impounding the Beneficiary's Interest: Trustee Act 1925, s.62

i. Inherent Power. Independently of the Trustee Act 1925, s.62, the court has power to impound the interest of a beneficiary who has instigated or requested a breach of trust. The impounding of the beneficiary's interest means that it will be applied so far as it will go towards providing an indemnity to the trustee. The trustee must show that the beneficiary acted with knowledge of the facts, although he may not have known that these amounted to a breach of trust. If the beneficiary instigated or requested the breach, it is not necessary to show that the beneficiary received a benefit;[12] but where a beneficiary merely concurred in or consented to a breach of trust, it seems necessary that a benefit be shown.[13] The trustee, as has been seen, is protected against an action from the consenting beneficiary in respect of the breach.

ii. Trustee Act 1925, s.62. Section 62 extends this jurisdiction,[14] permitting the court to make an impounding order regardless of any question of benefit. As will be seen, consent, if it is to be effective, must be in writing.[15] Section 62(1) reads as follows:

> "Where a trustee commits a breach of trust at the instigation or request or with the consent in writing of a beneficiary, the court may, if it thinks fit, . . . make such order as to the court seems just, for impounding all or any part of the interest of the beneficiary in

---

[10] *Walker v. Symonds* (1818) 3 Swans. 1 at p. 64, *per* Lord Eldon; *Stackhouse v. Barnston, supra.*

[11] *Holder v. Holder* [1968] Ch. 353.

[12] *Fuller v. Knight* (1843) 6 Beav. 205; *Chillingworth v. Chambers* [1896] 1 Ch. 685 (a trustee beneficiary).

[13] *Booth v. Booth* (1838) 1 Beav. 125 at p. 130; *Chillingworth v. Chambers, supra.* It has, however, been said that, even in the case of a beneficiary who requests a breach, the indemnity is limited to the benefit received by the beneficiary: *Raby v. Ridehalgh* (1855) 7 De G.M. & G. 104.

[14] See Romer J. in *Bolton v. Curre* [1895] 1 Ch. 544 at p. 549.

[15] The requirement of writing applies only to consent; *per* Lindley M.R. in *Re Somerset* [1894] 1 Ch. 231 at pp. 265–266.

the trust estate by way of indemnity to the trustee or persons claiming through him."

The effect of an impounding order is not only that the beneficiary is unable to sue the trustee, but also that the liability to make up losses suffered by other beneficiaries will fall on him, rather than on the trustee. The liability cannot, however, be for a greater sum than the subsisting value of his own interest in the trust, and it is subject to the discretion of the court. The discretion is exercised in the light of the earlier cases on which section 62 is founded,[16] and generally speaking an indemnity will be given to a trustee against a beneficiary who has been at all active in inducing a breach. Again, however, the knowledge of the beneficiary must amount to a definite appreciation of what is being done. In *Re Somerset*,[17] an impounding order was refused to trustees who had invested trust funds on a mortgage of a particular property at the instigation of a beneficiary, since the beneficiary had no intention of being a party to a breach, which occurred only because the loan exceeded the authorised limit. He had left it entirely to the trustees to determine how much money to lend on the security.

The principle applies to a beneficiary who, only subsequently to the breach, became entitled to a beneficial interest.[18] The right to indemnity by impounding is available to former trustees after their resignation or replacement. The trustees in *Re Pauling's Settlement Trusts (No. 2)*[19] claimed an indemnity out of the life interest of the parents of the plaintiffs, and Wilberforce J. held that they were entitled to it, and would remain so entitled, although, as was intended, they would at a future time be replaced by new trustees.

D. Statutory Relief: Trustee Act 1925, s.61[20]

Under this section the court may excuse trustees from the consequences of a breach of trust. It reads:

"If it appears to the court that a trustee, . . . is or may be personally liable for any breach of trust . . . but has acted honestly and reasonably, and ought fairly to be excused for the breach of trust and for omitting to obtain the directions of the court in the matter in which he committed such breach, then the court may

---

[16] See Romer J. in *Bolton v. Curre* [1895] 1 Ch. 544 at p. 549.
[17] [1894] 1 Ch. 231; *Mara v. Browne* [1895] 2 Ch. 69; *cf. Raby v. Ridehalgh, supra.*
[18] *Evans v. Benyon* (1888) 37 Ch.D. 329.
[19] [1963] Ch. 576; *Re Bucks Constabulary Widow's and Orphans' Fund Friendly Society (No. 2)* [1979] 1 W.L.R. 936 at p. 955.
[20] (1955) 19 Conv.(N.S.) 420 (L. Sheridan); [1977] *Estates and Trusts Quarterly* 12 (D. Waters). The section also applies to executors; T.A. 1925, s.68(17).

relieve him either wholly or partly from personal liability for the same."

The courts have preferred not to lay down formal rules for the application of the section. "It would be impossible," said Byrne J., "to lay down any general rules or principles to be acted on in carrying out the provisions of the section, and I think that each case must depend upon its own circumstances."[21] The only way to show how the discretion has been exercised is to catalogue the cases; but there is inadequate space here. A few general rules, however, can be extracted.

The jurisdiction is available where a trustee "is or may be personally liable" for a breach of trust. There is thus no need to establish the liability; indeed it would put a trustee in a strange position if he had to prove his own liability in order to obtain relief. Several cases allowing relief have done so without reaching a conclusion on the question of liability.[22] However, " 'may be' has . . . been interpreted as indicating doubt, not futurity"[23]; the court will not commit itself in advance to giving relief in the case of a future breach of trust.[24]

In exercising the discretion three factors must be considered[25]; the trustee's honesty, reasonableness, and the question whether he ought "fairly" to be excused. There is little authority on honesty; dishonest trustees do not apply. But Kekewich J. once characterised as dishonest "a trustee who does nothing, swallows wholesale what is said by his co-trustee, never asks for explanation, and accepts flimsy explanations."[26]

There is some uncertainty as to the standard to be applied in determining reasonableness, but the usual standard is that of a prudent man of business managing his own affairs.[27] (Compliance with this standard may mean that there is no breach, but it is otherwise where, for example, payment has been made to the wrong person).[28] The amount of money involved will be a relevant factor.[29]

---

[21] *Re Turner* [1897] 1 Ch. 536 at p. 542; *Re Kay* [1897] 2 Ch. 518 at p. 524 (referring to the predecessor section).

[22] *e.g. Re Grindey* [1898] 2 Ch. 593.

[23] (1955) 19 Conv. (N.S.) 425.

[24] *Re Tollemache* [1903] 1 Ch. 457 at pp. 465–466; affirmed at p. 953; *Re Rosenthal* [1972] 1 W.L.R. 1273. The court may, however, authorise an act so as to prevent it being a breach.

[25] *Marsden v. Regan* [1954] 1 W.L.R. 423 at p. 434.

[26] *Re Second East Dulwich, etc., Building Society* (1899) 79 L.T. 726 at p. 727.

[27] See Chitty L.J. in *Re Grindey, supra,* at p. 601; *Re Turner* [1897] 1 Ch. 536 at p. 542; *Re Lord de Clifford's Estate* [1900] 2 Ch. 707 at p. 716; *Re Stuart* [1897] 2 Ch. 583 at p. 590; *Re Rosenthal, supra.* The trustees in *Bartlett v. Barclays Bank Trust Co. Ltd (No. 1)* [1980] Ch. 515, *ante,* p. 640, were unable to rely on the section because they had not acted reasonably.

[28] See *Eaves v. Hickson* (1861) Beav. 136.

[29] *Re Grindey* [1898] 2 Ch. 593; *Marsden v. Regan, supra*

In *Re Stuart*[30] it was said that, in connection with lending trust money on mortgage, the statutory procedure for valuations and reports[31] "constitute a standard by which reasonable conduct will be judged"; but failure to follow this is "not necessarily a fatal objection to the application of the section."

The distinction between conduct that is reasonable and that for which a trustee ought fairly to be excused is not easy to see. In *Davis v. Hutchings*[32] trustees, on the distribution of the trust fund, paid the share of one beneficiary to the solicitor to the trust (employed by them) in reliance upon the solicitor's statement that he was the assignee of the share. The share had in fact been mortgaged and assigned to him subject to the mortgage. Kekewich J. held that the trustees were liable to the mortgagee. They had acted honestly and reasonably in relying on the solicitor, but they should not be excused.[33] Fairness should be considered in relation to all the parties, the trustees, the beneficiaries and the creditors, and is "essentially a matter within the discretion of the judge."[34]

Little seems to be added to this section by the reference to omission to obtain the directions of the court. "I do not see how the trustee can be excused for the breach of trust without being also excused for the omission referred to, or how he can be excused for the omission without also being excused for the breach of trust."[35]

The onus of showing that he acted honestly and reasonably is on the trustee.[36] Applications for relief have most commonly arisen in connection with unauthorised investments.[37] A trustee will not usually be excused if he has "relied on a co-trustee, or on the testator's solicitor, or on some other adviser of the testator's, or on the testator's own course of conduct. . . . The honest taking of what is conceived to be reliable advice will be no ground for excuse if the court believe a prudent man of business would have acted differently in ordering his own affairs."[38] Another and common situation is that of payment of the funds to the wrong beneficiary,[39] or the

---

[30] [1897] 2 Ch. 583.

[31] *Re Stuart, supra,* at pp. 591–592; *Shaw v. Cates* [1909] 1 Ch. 389; *Palmer v. Emerson* [1911] 1 Ch. 758.

[32] [1907] 1 Ch. 356.

[33] Some of the dicta of Kekewich J. were disapproved in *Re Allsop* [1914] 1 Ch. 1 at pp. 11, 12; see also *Marsden v. Regan* [1954] 1 W.L.R. 423, at pp. 434–435.

[34] *Marsden v. Regan, supra,* at p. 435.

[35] *Perrins v. Bellamy* [1898] 2 Ch. 521 at p. 528.

[36] *Re Stuart* [1897] 2 Ch. 583.

[37] *Re Turner, supra; Re Stuart, supra; Re Dive* [1909] 1 Ch. 328; *Bartlett v. Barclays Bank Trust Co. Ltd (No. 1)* [1980] Ch. 515.

[38] (1955) 29 Conv. (N.S.) 420 at p. 427.

[39] *Re Allsop* [1914] 1 Ch. 1; *Re Pawson's Settlement* [1917] 1 Ch. 541; *National Trustees Co. of Australasia v. General Finance Co. of Australasia* [1905] A.C. 373; *Re Wightwick's W.T.* [1950] Ch. 260.

payment of void claims by creditors,[40] and relief may be given where the trustee's mistake was one of law.[41] The taking of legal advice is a relevant factor, but does not automatically entitle a trustee to relief.[42]

The section extends to professional trustees who are being paid for their services, but the court is less ready to grant relief in such cases.[43]

E. Limitation and Laches[44]

i. Six-Year Period under Limitation Act 1980, s.21(3).

Subject to exceptions discussed below, the Limitation Act 1980, s.21(3), provides a six-year limitation for the protection of trustees. The subsection reads:

"Subject to the preceding provisions of this section, an action by a beneficiary[45] to recover trust property or in respect of any breach of trust,[46] not being an action for which a period of limitation is prescribed by any other provision of this Act, shall not be brought after the expiration of six years from the date on which the right of action accrued.

For the purposes of this subsection, the right of action shall not be treated as having accrued to any beneficiary entitled to a future interest in the trust property, until the interest fell into possession."

In this subsection, "trustee" includes personal representatives[47] and also certain fiduciary agents,[48] company directors[49] and a mortgagee in respect of the proceeds of sale,[50] but not a trustee in

---

[40] *Re Lord de Clifford's Estate* [1900] 2 Ch. 707; *Re Mackay* [1911] 1 Ch. 300; *cf. Re Windsor Steam Coal Co. Ltd* [1929] 1 Ch. 151.

[41] *Holland v. German Property Administrator* [1937] 2 All E.R. 807.

[42] *National Trustees Co. of Australasia v. General Finance Co. of Australasia* [1905] A.C. 373; *Marsden v. Regan* [1954] 1 W.L.R. 423 at pp. 434–435.

[43] *National Trustees Co. of Australasia v. General Finance Co. of Australasia* [1905] A.C. 373; *Re Windsor Steam Coal Co.* [1929] 1 Ch. 151; *Re Waterman's W.T.* [1952] 2 All E.R. 1054; *Re Pauling's S.T.* [1964] Ch. 303 at pp. 356–359.

[44] See Preston and Newsom's *Limitation of Actions* (4th ed.), Chap. 7; Franks, *Limitation of Actions*, pp. 62–80; (1989) 48 C.L.J. 472 (H. McLean).

[45] The section does not apply to a claim by the Attorney General against the trustee of a charitable trust, which has no 'beneficiary"; *Att.-Gen. v. Cocke* [1988] Ch. 414; [1988] Conv. 292 (J. Warburton); (also holding the subsection inapplicable to an action for an account not alleging any breach of trust or claiming recovery of trust property).

[46] In *Tito v. Waddell (No. 2)* [1977] Ch. 106 at p. 249, Megarry V.-C. concluded that this provision did not apply to situations governed by the self-dealing and fair dealing rules applicable to trustees. Those cases are covered by the doctrine of laches.

[47] Limitation Act 1980, s.38(1); T.A. 1925, s.68(17).

[48] *Burdick v. Garrick* (1870) L.R. 5 Ch.App. 233.

[49] *Belmont Finance Corporation v. Williams Furniture Ltd (No. 2)* [1980] 1 All E.R. 393.

[50] *Thorne v. Heard* [1895] A.C. 495.

bankruptcy,[51] nor the liquidator of a company in voluntary liquidation.[52] It will also be noted that there is no distinction between the
protection given to an express trustee and that given to an implied or
constructive trustee; until Trustee Act 1888, s.8, no protection based
upon passage of time had been available to an express trustee.[53] It
will be seen that the subsection only applies to cases where an action
is brought by a beneficiary in respect of the trust property.[54] Under
the proviso, time only begins to run against remaindermen or reversioners when their interest falls into possession; and it has been held
that this does not occur when improper advancements are made in
favour of remaindermen.[55] If a beneficiary is entitled to two interests
in the property, one in possession and one in remainder, he does not
lose a claim in respect of the latter where time has run against him
in respect of the former.[56]

ii. Exceptions to the Six-Year Rule. There are some exceptions
to the six-year rule.

(a) *Limitation Act 1980, s.21(1).*[57]
   "(1) No period of limitation prescribed by this Act shall apply
to an action by a beneficiary under a trust, being an action—
   (*a*) in respect of any fraud or fraudulent breach of trust to which
        the trustee was a party or privy; or
   (*b*) to recover from the trustee trust property or the proceeds of
        trust property in the possession of the trustee, or previously
        received by the trustee and converted to his use."[58]

This subsection reproduces in the situations to which it applies
the rule of permanent liability which was applicable in equity to the
case of express trustees.

   In *North American Land Co. v. Watkins*,[59] an agent had been
sent to America to buy land for his company. He bought it, and it
was duly conveyed to the company, but the agent made and
retained a profit for himself. After the expiration of the period
applicable for the recovery of money had and received, the

[51] *Re Cornish* [1896] 1 Q.B. 99.
[52] *Re Windsor Steam Coal Co.* [1928] Ch. 609; affirmed on other grounds [1929] 1 Ch.
    151.
[53] Franks, *loc. cit.* p. 64.
[54] *Re Bowden* (1890) 45 Ch.D 444 at p. 451.
[55] *Re Pauling's S.T.* [1964] Ch. 303.
[56] *Mara v. Browne* [1895] 2 Ch. 69, reversed on another point [1896] 1 Ch. 199.
[57] See (1989) 48 C.L.J. 472 at 495 (H. McLean).
[58] But where a trustee is also a beneficiary and has received his share on a distribution of the
    trust property, paragraph (b) shall only apply in respect of the excess over his share, so long
    as the trustee acted honestly and reasonably in making the distribution; s.21(2).
[59] [1904] 1 Ch. 242; [1904] 2 Ch. 233.

company successfully recovered the money on two grounds, first that the agent was in the position of a trustee and had retained trust money, and secondly that this conduct had been fraudulent.

It seems that the fraud must be that of the trustee himself.

In *Thorne v. Heard*[60] a trustee was protected where he had negligently left funds in the hands of a solicitor who had embezzled them; for the trustee to come within section 21(1) he must be "party or privy" to the fraud.

No question of dishonesty arises where a trustee is in possession of the trust property.

In *Re Sharp*[61] trustees had paid to themselves annuities to which they were entitled, but had done so without deduction of tax and they were held to lose their protection within the provisions of the subsection in respect of the amount which should have been deducted for income tax.

In *Re Howlett*[62] a trustee, who was income beneficiary until remarriage, continued in possession of a wharf until he died, and the remainderman was held able to sue the life tenant's representatives after his death for an occupation rent for the premises.

Conversion to the trustee's own use requires some wrongful application in his own favour. A trustee was held to escape from the subsection where he applied the trust funds for the maintenance of a minor beneficiary,[63] or where the funds were dissipated by a co-trustee.[64]

(b) *Claim to the Personal Estate of a Deceased Person.* Under section 22, which is subject to section 21(1), an action in respect of any claim to the personal estate of a deceased person must be brought within the period of 12 years. Difficult questions on the inter-relation of this section and section 21(3) can arise where the personal representatives administering an estate would normally be treated as having become trustees. In that case the question is whether the 12-year or six-year rule is applicable.[65] The better view,

---

[60] [1894] 1 Ch. 599; [1895] A.C. 495; *Re Fountaine* [1909] 2 Ch. 382.
[61] [1906] 1 Ch. 793.
[62] [1949] Ch. 767.
[63] *Re Page* [1893] 1 Ch. 304; *Re Timmis* [1902] 1 Ch. 176.
[64] *Re Tufnell* (1902) 18 T.L.R. 705; *Re Fountaine* [1909] 2 Ch. 382.
[65] *Re Timmis* [1902] 2 Ch. 176; *Re Richardson* [1920] 1 Ch. 423; *Re Oliver* [1927] 2 Ch. 323; *Re Diplock* [1948] Ch. 465; [1951] A.C. 251.

it is submitted, is that the 12-year rule applies even though the personal representatives would for other purposes be treated as having become trustees.[66]

(c) *Sections 28 and 32.* Section 28 allows an extension of the period of limitation in cases in which the plaintiff has been under disability. Section 32 provides that where any action is based upon fraud or where the right of action is concealed by fraud or where the action is for relief from the consequences of a mistake, "the period of limitation shall not begin to run until the plaintiff has discovered the fraud, concealment or mistake ... or could with reasonable diligence have discovered it." This section applies to actions against trustees.[67]

iii. Assignees. A transferee from the trustee is in the same position as the trustee was[68]; unless he is bona fide purchaser for value without notice in which case he will presumably be treated as if he had purchased from someone who was not a trustee.

iv. Where No Period is Applicable. It has been seen that the Limitation Act 1980 deals comprehensively with the running of time in actions against trustees. In situations not covered, it is necessary to return to the law as it existed before the statutory protection was given. No provision is made, for example, either for claims for equitable relief by way of specific performance, rescission or rectification, or injunction,[69] or in cases of redemption of a mortgage of pure personalty,[70] or the setting aside of a purchase of trust property by a trustee.[71] The rule of equity is that either no period is applicable, or that the relevant common law period is applied by analogy. In any situation for which no period of limitation is expressly applicable to an equitable claim, the defendant may rely on the doctrine of laches.[72] Delay by a plaintiff in pursuing his rights "may furnish a defence in equity to an equitable claim."[73] Whether such a defence is available in a particular case is a matter for the discretion of the court, and will depend to a large extent upon

---

[66] See Pettit, *Equity and The Law of Trusts*, p. 499; Franks, *Limitation of Actions*, pp. 49–50; Preston and Newsom, p. 51; *Re Diplock* [1948] Ch. 465, *sub nom. Minister of Health v. Simpson* [1951] A.C. 251.

[67] See *Beaman v. A.R.T.S.* [1949] 1 K.B. 550; *Kitchen v. R.A.F. Association,* [1958] 1 W.L.R. 563; *Bartlett v. Barclays Bank Trust Co. Ltd* [1980] Ch. 515 at p. 537.

[68] See *Re Dixon* [1900] 2 Ch. 561; *Baker v. Medway Building and Supplies Ltd* [1958] 1 W.L.R. 1216; *Eddis v. Chichester Constable* [1969] 2 Ch. 345.

[69] See Limitation Act 1980, s.36(1).

[70] *Weld v. Petre* [1929] 1 Ch. 33.

[71] *Baker v. Read* (1854) 18 Beav. 398; *Morse v. Royal* (1806) 12 Ves.Jr. 355; Snell, p. 35.

[72] *Re Pauling's S.T.* [1964] Ch. 303. See also *Alec Lobb (Garages) Ltd v. Total Oil G.B. Ltd* [1985] 1 W.L.R. 173.

[73] *Re Sharpe* [1892] 1 Ch. 154 at p. 168; Franks, *loc. cit.*, pp. 233 *et seq.*

the hardship caused to the defendant by the delay, and the effect upon third parties; and generally upon the balance of justice in granting or refusing relief.[74] There is no maximum period beyond which the equitable relief cannot be sought but a period of 20 years may be taken as a convenient guide.[75] The defendant will be more likely to succeed if he can show not merely delay, but acquiescence. Both defences appear to have been retained by the Limitation Act 1980 which provides in section 36(2): "Nothing in this Act shall affect any equitable jurisdiction to refuse relief on the ground of acquiescence or otherwise."

These defences are therefore relevant to cases to which no period is applicable, including those within section 21(1). Prior to the Limitation Act 1939 the doctrine of laches applied differently in regard to express and other trustees; but it seems that there should no longer be a distinction,[76] and that the position of express trustees alone need be considered. The rule "seems to be that while the doctrine of laches applies to claims by beneficiaries, relief will only be refused in plain cases."[77]

A question which has recently arisen is whether any limitation period applies to an action for an account. Section 23 of the 1980 Act provides that "an action for an account shall not be brought after the expiration of any time limit under this Act which is applicable to the claim which is the basis of the duty to account." This confirms that the period applicable to a particular cause of action (*e.g.* copyright infringement) applies equally to the relief by way of account which flows from it.[78] In *Att.-Gen. v. Cocke*[79] an action for an account was brought in respect of an estate held upon charitable trusts. As there was no allegation of a breach of trust nor any claim to recover trust property (and also because there was no "beneficiary"), section 21(3) did not apply. It was held that in the case of an action for an account *simpliciter*, based on fiduciary relationship and nothing more, there would be no period of limitation under the Act and nothing for section 23 to operate upon. But where breach of a fiduciary's duty to account gives rise to a constructive trust, section 21 applies.[80]

---

[74] *Lindsay Petroleum Co. v. Hurd* (1874) L.R. 5 P.C. 221 at pp. 239–241; *Weld v. Petre* [1929] 1 Ch. 33 at pp. 51, 52.

[75] *Weld v. Petre, supra,* at pp. 54, 55; *Nelson v. Rye* [1996] 1 W.L.R. 1378 (no recovery for period before December 1985); *Kershaw v. Whelan (No. 2), The Times,* February 10, 1997.

[76] Franks, *loc. cit.* p. 260; *cf. Re Jarvis* [1958] 1 W.L.R. 815.

[77] Franks, *loc. cit.* p. 261. As to whether laches applies to a claim to an express trust, see *Orr v. Ford* (1988–89) 167 C.L.R. 316.

[78] *Nelson v Rye, supra.*

[79] [1988] Ch. 414; [1988] Conv. 292 (J. Warburton); All E.R. Rev. 1988, p. 183 (P. Clarke). See also *Tito v. Waddell (No. 2)* [1977] Ch. 106 at p. 251.

[80] *Nelson v. Rye, supra* (no period applied to action for account, either because outside Act or, if constructive trust, s.21(1)(*b*) applied).

5. PROPRIETARY REMEDIES

A. Personal and Proprietary Actions

Most actions at law and in equity are personal. We now have to consider the occasions on which a plaintiff has the right to proceed against a particular asset in the defendant's hands. Such proprietary claims exist to a very limited extent at law; and these, for convenience and for the sake of comparison, will be described here.[81] In equity the right to follow or trace property is more extensive. We will see that proprietary rights may be asserted where the plaintiff is making a claim at law or in equity to a specific piece of property, and also where he is making a claim in equity against a mixed fund to which property of his (in equity) has contributed. The tracing rules are also involved in personal actions based on receipt of property.[82]

There are two main advantages of a proprietary over a personal claim. First and foremost, satisfaction of the plaintiff's demand does not depend on the solvency of the defendant. If the property traced is the plaintiff's in equity, it escapes the defendant's bankruptcy.[83] Secondly, in some cases, the plaintiff will be able to take advantage of increases in the value of the property. This is obvious where specific property is treated as being the plaintiff's in equity, and was more recently established where a mixed fund is in question.[84]

Although the English and American rules on these matters are not identical, anyone who is faced with a question on tracing should be acquainted with paragraphs 160–162 and 202–215 of the *Restatement of Restitution*, whose authors have foreseen and provided solutions for most if not all the problems which have arisen in the English cases.[85]

B. Unjust Enrichment; Restitution[86]

Proprietary remedies cannot be fully understood without some appreciation of the doctrine of unjust enrichment. This is a doctrine which appears in nearly every system of law. It lays down as a general principle that where the defendant is unjustly enriched at the plaintiff's expense, the defendant must make restitution to the plaintiff.[87] Such a principle has its greatest scope in the area of quasi-

---

[81] *Post*, p. 657.
[82] *Ante*, Chap. 12.
[83] Insolvency Act 1986, s.283.
[84] *Re Tilley's W.T.* [1967] Ch. 1179; *post*, p. 676.
[85] Including that of the personal claim in *Re Diplock* [1948] Ch. 465; see *Restatement of Restitution*, para. 126, comment (c), and *Restatement of Trusts*, para. 199.
[86] Goff and Jones, *The Law of Restitution* (4th ed.); Birks, *An Introduction to the Law of Restitution; Restatement of Restitution*.
[87] *Restatement of Restitution*, para. 1.

contract, but it overlaps into many areas of equity. Even though there is no right to restitution in every case of unjust enrichment, all restitutionary claims are unified by the principle.[88]

Assume that A has a right to sue B on the ground that A has paid money to B by mistake, or under compulsion, or under a contract that was void, or in any other situation in which B is enriched at the expense of A. If B is solvent, a personal action will satisfy A's claim. What should be the effect on this situation if, (a) B is bankrupt, or (b) B invests the money and it doubles in value? In case (a) it is arguable that since B should never have had the money, nor should his creditors. In case (b) it can be argued that neither B nor his creditors should reap the full measure of the profit which B has made out of money which he should never have had. Should A have it? Would it make any difference if the invested funds were part A's and part B's? We might here pose a further case (c). If B uses the money to pay off a mortgage on his property and is insolvent, should A be placed in the position, by subrogation, of the mortgagee? These are all interesting and difficult questions, to most of which the English cases provide answers. The account which follows shows that different rules operate at law and in equity. While this is the present position, a unified restitutionary proprietary remedy may eventually evolve.[89]

C. Tracing at Common Law[90]

A proprietary remedy is one which entitles a claimant to treat specific property, or a portion thereof, as his own. If the common law had developed a real action for chattels which entitled a plaintiff to specific recovery, the claimant would be able to demand the return of the chattel. But although the court recognised the plaintiff as being the owner, there was no such action at common law. The defendant had the choice of paying damages or returning the chattel. A discretion to award specific recovery in an action in detinue was given to the court in 1854.[91]

The plaintiff's ownership was relevant however in that his entitlement was to the chattel or to its value—its full value that is, even if

---

[88] Goff and Jones (4th ed.), p. 15; *Woolwich Equitable Building Society v. I.R.C.* [1993] A.C. 70 at p. 196.

[89] *Agip (Africa) Ltd v. Jackson* [1990] Ch. 265 (on appeal at [1991] Ch. 547 a more conservative approach was taken); (1991) 107 L.Q.R. 71 (Sir Peter Millett). See also *Lipkin Gorman v. Karpnale Ltd* [1991] 2 A.C. 548, *post*, p. 659.

[90] (1966) 7 W.A.L.R. 463 (M. Scott); (1976) 40 Conv.(N.S.) 277 (R. Pearce); (1979) 95 L.Q.R. 78 (S. Khurshid and P. Matthews); (1976) 92 L.Q.R. 360 at pp. 364 *et seq.* (R. Goode); *Laundering and Tracing* (ed. Birks, 1995), p. 23 (P. Matthews). See Birks, *An Introduction to the Law of Restitution*, pp. 358 *et seq.*; Goff and Jones (4th ed.), pp. 75–83.

[91] Common Law Procedure Act 1854, s.78. Detinue has been abolished: Torts (Interference with Goods) Act 1977, s.2; but the discretionary power of the court to order specific recovery is retained by s.3.

the defendant was insolvent, and not merely to a dividend in the insolvency. In the case of a loan, the plaintiff's claim for the money lent to an insolvent defendant would abate; it was something owed. The position is different with the chattel; that was something owned.

The question then arises whether this right of the plaintiff's is limited to the case of a specific chattel. Should this right not continue if the defendant had exchanged one chattel for another; or the chattel for a sum of money; or had spent that money on another chattel? The answer was given by Lord Ellenborough in *Taylor v. Plumer*[92]: "It makes no difference in reason or law into what other form, different from the original, the change may have been made, whether it be into that of promissory notes for the security of the money which was produced by the sale of the goods of the principal, as in *Scott v. Surman*,[93] or into other merchandise, as in *Whitecomb v. Jacob*,[94] for the product of or substitute for the original thing still follows the nature of the thing itself, as long as it can be ascertained to be such, and the right only ceases when the means of ascertainment fail, which is the case when the subject is turned into money, and mixed and confounded in a general mass of the same description. The difficulty which arises in such a case is a difficulty of fact and not of law, and the dictum that money has no ear-mark must be understood in the same way; *i.e.* as predicated only of an undivided and undistinguishable mass of current money. But money in a bag or otherwise kept apart from other money, guineas, or other coin marked (if the fact were so) for the purpose of being distinguished, are so far ear-marked as to fall within the rule on this subject, which applies to every other description of personal property whilst it remains (as the property in question did) in the hands of the factor [the bankrupt] or his general legal representatives."

In *Taylor v. Plumer*,[95] the defendant handed money to a stock-broker, Walsh, to purchase bonds. Walsh instead purchased American investments and bullion and hurried off to Falmouth to sail to America. He was apprehended, and the investments and bullion were seized by the defendant. On Walsh's bankruptcy, his assignees in bankruptcy sought to recover them from the defendant. They failed. The investments were the ascertainable product of the defendant's money and owned by him. If the parties had been reversed, and the defendant had been suing for the recovery of the securities and bullion, his action would have succeeded, but the assignees would have had the choice of returning them or of

---

[92] (1815) 3 M. & S. 562 at p. 575.
[93] (1742) Willes 400.
[94] (1710) Salk. 160.
[95] (1815) 3 M. & S. 562; *Re J. Leslie Engineers Co. Ltd* [1976] 1 W.L.R. 292 at p. 297.

paying their full value in damages; just as if Walsh had taken the defendant's coach and horses and had them in his possession on his bankruptcy.

It is important to appreciate that the common law action of conversion and the action for money had and received are personal actions as was detinue, though, as has been seen,[96] the court may exercise a discretionary power to order the specific recovery of a chattel. Personal actions as a general rule abate in a bankruptcy, which is the normal situation in which tracing is attempted. In the conversion cases, however, full damages without abatement may be obtained against the trustee in bankruptcy if the chattel is not returned.[97] The plaintiff's proprietary rights are thus preserved to this extent.[98] A plaintiff who can establish by tracing that the defendant has received his money will be able to bring a personal action for money had and received, but, if he cannot identify his money or its product in the defendant's hands after receipt, he will not recover in full if the defendant is bankrupt. If he can still identify his money or its product, then he may assert a proprietary claim at common law against the defendant's trustee in bankruptcy on the basis of legal ownership.[99]

As Sir Peter Millett has emphasised, tracing a common law is neither a cause of action nor a remedy. Tracing is an identification process enabling the defendant to be identified as the recipient of the plaintiff's money.[1] Similarly in the case of tracing in equity.

The crucial question at common law was whether there was identifiable property, the title to which did not pass to the defendant.[2] In *Banque Belge pour L'Etranger v. Hambrouck*[3] money passing through substantially unmixed bank accounts was treated by the majority of the Court of Appeal as still identifiable. In *Lipkin Gorman v. Karpnale Ltd*[4] the House of Lords considered that the plaintiff firm could have traced at common law where money was drawn out of its client account by a partner, Cass, and paid to the

---

[96] *Ante*, p. 657.

[97] (1979) 95 L.Q.R. 78 (S. Khurshid and P. Matthews); (1966) 7 W.A.L.R. 463 (M. Scott). See *Giles v. Perkins* (1807) 9 East. 12; *Scott v. Surman* (1742) Willes 400.

[98] (1976) 40 Conv.(N.S) 277 (R. Pearce); Goff and Jones (4th ed.), p. 78, n. 34.

[99] *Jones (F.C.) & Sons (Trustee) v. Jones* [1996] 3 W.L.R. 703; *infra*.

[1] *Agip (Africa) Ltd v. Jackson* [1990] Ch. 265 at p. 285; (1995) 9 *Trust Law International* 35 at p. 39; *Jones (F.C.) & Sons (Trustee) v. Jones* [1996] 3 W.L.R. 703.

[2] See (1966) 7 W.A.L.R. 463 at pp. 481 *et seq*.

[3] [1921] 1 K.B. 321.

[4] [1991] 2 A.C. 548 (a personal action); (1991) 107 L.Q.R. 521 (P. Watts); [1992] Conv. 124 (M. Halliwell); (1992) 5 M.L.R. 377 (E. McKendrick); All E.R.Rev 1992, p. 262 (W. Swadling). It was conceded (p. 572) that the plaintiff's legal title to the money was not defeated by any mixing by Cass with his own money before payment to the club. Presumably mixing by the club would defeat a common law tracing claim. The plaintiff could have traced in equity, as Cass held the withdrawn money on trust for the firm.

Playboy Club. Although the plaintiff had no proprietary interest in the money in the account, the bank's debt was a chose in action which was the legal property of the plaintiff. This could be traced into its product, the money withdrawn (apparently even though Cass had legal title to that), and followed into the hands of the volunteer recipient. In *Jones (F.C.) & Sons (Trustee) v. Jones*[5] a partner withdrew £11,700 from a partnership account by cheques in favour of his wife after an act of bankruptcy on the part of the firm and the wife opened an account with a broker, into which the money was paid. The money was profitably invested and the wife received cheques from the broker for £50,760 which she paid into another account she had opened with R. Bank. The wife conceded that the trustee in bankruptcy was entitled to £11,700 but claimed to keep the profit. Her claim was rejected by the Court of Appeal. She had taken possession of money (£11,700) the legal title to which was vested in the trustee in bankruptcy under the insolvency legislation. He was entitled at common law not only to trace his property into its exchange product but also to trace any profit made from it.

It had been persuasively argued that *Taylor v. Plumer*[6] was in fact a decision on tracing in equity and thus not authority for the proposition that tracing into an "exchange product" is possible at common law.[7] It is clear, however, that *Taylor v. Plumer* has been accepted in the subsequent caselaw as authority for that proposition.[8] In the *Jones* case Millett L.J. acknowledged that *Taylor v. Plumer* was concerned with the rules of equity but held that this did not mean that the common law did not recognise claims to substitute assets or their products. Thus the trustee in bankruptcy could follow the chose in action constituted by the partnership account into the cheques drawn on it, and could follow those cheques into the account with the broker, the cheques from the broker, and ultimately the chose in action constituted by the account with R. Bank. He was entitled at law to the balance in that account, whether greater or less than the original amount withdrawn from the partnership account.

What the common law could not do was to provide full protection to the plaintiff in the most important type of case in which these questions arise: where the defendant has received the plaintiff's money, mixed it with other money in a bank account, and has gone

---

[5] [1996] 3 W.L.R. 703; (1997) 113 L.Q.R. 21 (N. Andrews and J. Beatson). Leave to appeal was refused; [1997] 1 W.L.R. 51.

[6] (1815) 3 M. & S. 562; *supra*.

[7] (1979) 95 L.Q.R. 78 (S. Kurshid and P. Matthews); [1995] L.M.C.L.Q. 240 (L. Smith); *Laundering and Tracing* (ed. Birks, 1995), pp. 49–51 (P. Matthews) and 297–298 (P. Birks).

[8] *Banque Belge pour L'Etranger v. Hambrouck, supra; Lipkin Gorman v. Karpnale Ltd, supra; Agip (Africa) Ltd v. Jackson* [1991] Ch. 547, *infra*.

bankrupt.[9] In *Agip (Africa) Ltd v. Jackson* the plaintiff claimed to trace money transferred to the defendants as a result of the fraud of the plaintiff's accountant, who had changed the names on payment orders. The money had been paid out (to B Co. and thence to the defendants) by a London bank on the telexed instructions of a Tunis bank (where the plaintiff maintained an account), which then instructed a New York bank to reimburse the London bank. The defendants had paid most of the money away, but part of it remained and was paid into court. Millett J.[10] rejected the common law tracing claim on the ground that no physical asset of the plaintiff (such as a cheque or its proceeds) could be identified in the defendant's hands. Nothing but a stream of electrons passed between the banks as a result of the telegraphic transfers. The London bank paid with its own money, subject to reimbursement, and not with anything identifiable as the product of the plaintiff's property. It was not possible to show the source from which the London bank was reimbursed without tracing the money through the New York clearing system. There it was mixed, which defeated the common law claim. The decision was upheld on appeal on the basis that mixing defeated the claim, although Fox L.J. (giving the only reasoned judgment) thought it did not matter that no cheque was involved.[11] Sir Peter Millett has restated the view that the common law cannot trace money transferred electronically both judicially and extra-judicially,[12] and it has found support elsewhere.[13] It may be, however, that such money remains traceable at common law if it has not been mixed by passing through an inter-bank clearing system.[14]

As we will see, mixing does not prevent tracing in equity, although other limitations upon the availability of the equitable remedy leave scope for tracing at common law. In practical terms, however, most of the situations in which a claim to trace arises are

---

[9] (1992) 45 C.L.P. 69 (P. Birks) For the position at common law in respect of mixed or improved goods, see (1981) 34 C.L.P. 159 (P. Matthews).

[10] [1990] Ch. 265 at p. 286; (1989) 105 L.Q.R. 528 (P. Birks); (1991) 107 L.Q.R. 71 (Sir Peter Millett).

[11] [1991] Ch. 547 at p. 565; (1991) 50 C.L.J. 409 (C. Harpum); [1992] Conv. 367 (S. Goulding); All E.R. Rev. 1992, p. 259 (W. Swadling). Tracing in equity was allowed; *post*, p. 663. In *Jones (F.C.) & Sons (Trustee) v. Jones, supra*, it was not necessary to trace the passage of the money through a clearing system.

[12] *El Ajou v. Dollar Land Holdings plc* [1993] 3 All E.R. 717 at p. 733 (not discussed on appeal at [1994] 2 All E.R. 685); (1991) 107 L.Q.R. 71 at p. 74; (1995) 9 *Trust Law International* 35 at p. 39.

[13] *Nimmo v. Westpac Banking Corporation* [1993] 3 N.Z.L.R. 218; *Bank Tejarat v. Hong Kong and Shanghai Banking Corporation (CI) Ltd* [1995] 1 Lloyd's Rep. 239; criticised (1995) 9 *Trust Law International* 91 (P. Birks). Where a payment is made between two bank accounts telegraphically, electronically or by cheque, one chose in action is reduced or extinguished and another created, thus no property of the payer is obtained by the payee within the Theft Act 1968; *R. v. Preddy* [1996] A.C. 815 (see now Theft (Amendment) Act 1996).

[14] (1995) 54 C.L.J. 377 (A. Oakley).

cases of money in mixed bank accounts, in which the common law remedy is not available. It has therefore limited practical importance at the present day.

D. Tracing in Equity

Equity has developed more sophisticated methods of tracing. The rules have developed, and are usually applied, in the context of property in the hands of trustees or other fiduciaries, and often on the bankruptcy of the fiduciary. But the rules apply also in a commercial context; as where a vendor, in order to protect himself in a customer's bankruptcy, provides expressly that property shall not pass in goods supplied until payment. Equity will assist in the location and preservation of traceable property by discovery and injunctions.[15]

i. Who is Entitled to Trace. The remedy in equity is not confined to claims between trustee and beneficiary. *Re Hallett*[16] decided that the remedy was not restricted to such a case but was available against other fiduciaries.[17]

(a) *Requirement of Fiduciary Relationship.* The courts have insisted that the existence of a fiduciary relationship is a prerequisite to tracing in equity, although this relationship need not exist between the parties to the action. In *Re Diplock*[18] the action was not against the executors, but against the innocent volunteers (the charities) to whom they handed the money.

By his will Diplock gave the residue of his property on trust for such "charitable or benevolent . . . objects in England as my . . . executors . . . may in their . . . absolute discretion select." He and the executors thought that this was a valid charitable gift, but it was not.[19] The executors distributed £203,000 among a considerable number of charitable institutions; and when the validity of the charitable gift was discovered, the next-of-kin claimed to recover the money from the charities. They succeeded in a personal claim[20] and were also entitled to trace, the Court of Appeal

---

[15] *Bankers Trust Co. v. Shapira* [1980] 1 W.L.R. 1274; *A. v. C.* [1981] Q.B. 956; *In re D.P.R. Futures Ltd* [1989] 1 W.L.R. 778.

[16] (1880) 13 Ch.D. 696 at p. 709.

[17] See Goff and Jones (4th ed.), p. 85, n. 74, where they point out how difficult it is to define precisely who is a fiduciary. They refer to the analogy of decisions on the Statutes of Limitation, which suggest that "much depends on whether the agent is under a duty to keep separate his own money from his principal's money."

[18] [1948] Ch. 465.

[19] *Ante*, p. 425, *Chichester Diocesan Fund v. Simpson* [1944] A.C. 341.

[20] [1951] A.C. 251. The appeal to the House of Lords concerned only the claim *in personam; post*, p. 686.

laying down as the test that[21] "equity may operate on the conscience not merely of those who acquire a legal title in breach of some trust, express or constructive, or of some other fiduciary obligation, but of volunteers provided that as a result of what has gone before some equitable proprietary interest has been created and attaches to the property in the hands of the volunteer." Although a beneficiary is not normally regarded as the equitable owner of assets in an unadministered estate,[22] the "equitable proprietary interest" was established for present purposes by the equitable claim by the plaintiffs as next-of-kin against the executors; and this gave the plaintiffs the right to trace against the charities.

The requirement of a fiduciary relationship has been much criticised,[23] but has been accepted in modern decisions of the Court of Appeal[24] and most recently by the House of Lords in *Westdeutsche Landesbank Girozentrale v. Islington London Borough Council*,[25] where the principles established in *Re Diplock* were approved.[26] But the position may be relieved by the apparent ease with which a fiduciary relationship may be recognised, as in most cases of commercial fraud.[27]

(b) *Requirement of an Equitable Proprietary Interest.* In the days before the fusion of the jurisdiction of law and equity, it was only possible to obtain equitable remedies if the litigation were "in equity." It is not therefore surprising that the test which has been laid down historically for the availability of equitable tracing is that the plaintiff should be entitled to an *equitable* proprietary interest; and this requirement of an equitable proprietary interest is distinct from absolute ownership at law.

There seems to be no reason at all on the merits why the equitable tracing remedy should not be available also to the beneficial legal owner. Indeed, it was arguable, before *Re Diplock*[28] was decided,

---

[21] [1948] Ch. 465 at p. 530.
[22] *Commissioner of Stamp Duties v. Livingston* [1965] A.C. 694; *ante*, p. 58.
[23] (1995) 9 *Trust Law International* 35 at p. 39 (Sir Peter Millett); *ibid.* 124 at p. 126 (P. Birks); Goff and Jones, p. 101; *Bristol and West Building Society v. Mothew* [1996] 4 All E.R. 698 at p. 716.
[24] *Aluminium Industrie Vaassen B.V. v. Romalpa Aluminium Ltd* [1976] 1 W.L.R. 676; *Agip (Africa) Ltd v. Jackson* [1991] Ch. 547; *Boscawen v. Bajwa* [1996] 1 W.L.R. 328 at p. 335; *Jones (F.C.) & Sons (Trustee) v. Jones* [1996] 3 W.L.R. 703.
[25] [1996] A.C. 669. See (1996) 55 C.L.J. 432 (G. Jones), pointing out inconsistencies.
[26] *Ibid.* at p. 714. But see [1997] Conv. 1 at p. 4 (A. Oakley).
[27] *Agip (Africa) Ltd v. Jackson, supra* (senior accountant and employer).
[28] [1948] Ch. 465; (1971) 34 M.L.R. 12 (F. Babafemi).

that this situation had been recognised by *Banque Belge v. Hambrouck.*[29] Atkin L.J. treated equitable tracing as a means of overcoming the common law's difficulty in identifying the plaintiff's money in a mixed fund.[30] "The question always was, Had the means of ascertainment failed? But if in 1815 the common law halted outside the bankers' door, by 1879 equity had had the courage to lift the latch, walk in and examine the books: *Re Hallett's Estate.*[31] I see no reason why the means of ascertainment so provided should not now be available both for common law and equity proceedings." It has been doubtful, since *Re Diplock*, whether equitable tracing will be available in the absence of some situation creating equitable as opposed to legal ownership.[32] In *Aluminium Industrie Vaassen B.V. v. Romalpa Aluminium Ltd*[33] however, the Court of Appeal permitted tracing by a legal owner to whom a fiduciary duty was owed, although this point was not discussed.

Consider this case; B owes £1,000 to his creditors and has only £100. He steals £1,000 from A and mixes that money in his account which now has £1,100. He now "owes" £2,000. Should the available money be shared rateably between A and the creditors, or should A get back first his £1,000, which B should never have had? Common law tracing is not available because the funds are mixed; nor equitable tracing if there is no fiduciary relation between a thief and his victim. Fortunately Lord Templeman in *Lipkin Gorman v. Karpnale Ltd*[34] has approved Australian authority[35] to the effect that a thief holds stolen money on trust for his victim, who can accordingly trace it. Similarly, Lord Browne-Wilkinson has confirmed that the money is traceable on the ground that equity imposes a constructive trust on a fraudulent recipient.[36]

---

[29] [1921] 1 K.B. 321.

[30] *Ibid* at p. 335; criticised in *Agip (Africa) Ltd v. Jackson, supra,* for treating common law and equitable remedies as the same. See also *Chief Constable of Kent v. V.* [1983] Q.B. 34 at p. 41, *per* Lord Denning M.R.: "It may be that 150 year ago the common law halted outside the banker's door, but for the last 100 years, since the fusion of law and equity, it has had the courage to lift the latch, walk in and examine the books: see *Bankque Belge pour l'Etranger v. Hambrouck* [1912] 1 K.B. 321 at p. 335, *per* Atkin L.J. and *Re Diplock's Estate, Diplock v. Wintle* [1948] Ch. 465, *per* Lord Greene M.R."

[31] (1880) 13 Ch.D. 696.

[32] For arguments to the effect that legal, as opposed to equitable, ownership is a sufficient basis for a right to trace, see (1975) 28 C.L.P. 64 (A. Oakley); (1976) 40 Conv.(N.S.) 227 (R. Pearce); Goff and Jones (4th ed.), p. 86.

[33] [1976] 1 W.L.R. 676, *post,* p. 681; *cf. Re Andrabell Ltd* [1984] 3 All E.R. 407. See Heydon, Gummow and Austin, *Cases and Materials on Equity and Trusts* (4th ed.), pp. 898, 906.

[34] [1991] 2 A.C. 548.

[35] *Black v. S. Freedman & Co.* (1910) 12 C.L.R. 105. See also *Lennox Industries (Canada) Ltd v. The Queen* (1987) 34 D.L.R. 297; *Bishopsgate Investment Management Ltd v. Maxwell* [1993] Ch. 1 at p. 70; *Ghana Commercial Bank v. C, The Times,* March 3, 1997.

[36] *Westdeutsche Landesbank Girozentrale v. Islington London Borough Council* [1996] A.C. 669 at pp. 715–716; *cf. Jones (F.C.) & Sons (Trustee) v. Jones* [1996] 3 W.L.R. 703 (No constructive trust nor fiduciary relationship where wife obtained possession of, but not title to, funds of bankrupt partnership. Thus only the common law tracing rules applied).

One question which came before the House of Lords in *Westdeutsche Landesbank Girozentrale v. Islington London Borough Council*[37] was whether the plaintiff bank retained an equitable proprietary interest in money paid to the defendant under a transaction (an "interest rate swap") which was *ultra vires* and void. Tracing would in any event have been impossible because the money had been mixed with other money in an account and used for general expenditure, the account having been subsequently overdrawn several times.[38] The defendant now conceded personal liability to repay, the issue being whether compound interest could be awarded to the bank. Their Lordships unanimously agreed that the bank retained no equitable proprietary interest in the money, which, according to the majority, meant that there was no jurisdiction to award compound interest.[39] *Sinclair v. Brougham*,[40] where the House of Lords had permitted tracing by creditors (depositors) of a bank whose business was *ultra vires*, was overruled. Although in the present case the bank's belief in the validity of the transaction was mistaken, it intended the money to become the absolute property of the defendant and had been prepared to take the risk of insolvency. As a general rule, property in money passes even though a contract is void, although there may be limited exceptions in the case of "fundamental mistake" in the orthodox sense.[41] Thus there was considered to be no moral or legal reason why, had there been an insolvency, the plaintiff should have had priority over general creditors. The defendant received the money neither as resulting trustee (because the property had passed, as intended) nor as constructive trustee (because it was unaware of the invalidity until after the money had been spent and its conscience was thus unaffected) but was merely subject to personal liability at common law to repay.

Grave doubt has been cast on the correctness of *Chase Manhattan Bank NA v. Israel-British Bank (London) Ltd*,[42] where the plaintiff's claim to trace money paid by mistake of fact to the defendant (now insolvent) was upheld on the basis that the plaintiff retained an equitable proprietary interest in the money. Lord Goff found it unnecessary to review that decision. Lord Browne-Wilkinson disagreed with the reasoning but considered that the result could be justified on the basis that the defendant bank became aware of the mistake within two days and retained the money in traceable form.

---

[37] [1996] A.C. 669; (1996) 112 L.Q.R. 521 (M. Cope); [1996] R.L.R. 3 (P. Birks); (1996) 55 C.L.J. 432 (G. Jones); (1996) 10 *Trust Law International* 84 (C. Mitchell).

[38] See *post*, p. 672.

[39] *Ante*, p. 638.

[40] [1914] A.C. 398. Lord Goff would have allowed it to stand in the confined area of *ultra vires* loans. The present case did not involve loans.

[41] [1996] A.C. 669 at p. 690 (Lord Goff); [1996] 55 C.L.J. 547 and [1996] R.L.R. 60 (D. Fox).

[42] [1981] Ch. 105; (1996) 16 L.S. 110 (W. Swadling); [1996] Conv. 86 (G. McCormack).

Thus its conscience was sufficiently affected to found a constructive trust.[43]

There has been some support for the view that in the case of a voidable transaction (for example, one induced by misrepresentation or undue influence) a plaintiff who elects to rescind can trace on the basis that the property, having initially passed to the defendant, revests in the plaintiff on rescission.[44] This argument is now difficult in the light of *Westdeutsche Landesbank Girozentrale v. Islington London Borough Council*.[45] On the other hand, a payment induced by forgery may be traced on the basis that equity imposes a constructive trust on a fraudulent recipient.[46]

Although some have taken the wider view that tracing should be permitted where necessary to prevent unjust enrichment,[47] the House of Lords has upheld the traditional rule that an equitable proprietary interest is a prerequisite for tracing in equity. As we have seen, the requirement is now satisfied in the case of bribes, on the basis that the defendant holds the bribe on constructive trust for his principal.[48] Finally, it should be said that an equitable proprietary interest normally goes hand in hand with a fiduciary relationship. A fiduciary relationship alone, however, is not a sufficient basis for tracing. Thus, assuming it is correct to call a person who dishonestly assists in a breach of trust a constructive trustee, no proprietary rights may be asserted against him if he has received no trust property.[49]

ii. Unmixed Funds. The easy case is that in which there has been no mixing of the trust funds with the trustee's own money. If the trustee has sold the trust property, the beneficiary may take the proceeds if he can identify them. (If the purchaser had notice, presumably the beneficiary may elect to take either the property or the proceeds.[50]) If the proceeds of sale have been used to purchaser other property the beneficiary may "follow" them and may "elect either to take the property purchased, or to hold it as a security for

[43] [1996] A.C. 669 at p. 715. The reasoning is criticised in [1996] R.L.R. 3 at p. 21 (P. Birks) and in (1996) 55 C.L.J. 432 (G. Jones). The correctness of *Chase Manhattan* had been left open by the Privy Council in *Re Goldcorp Exchange Ltd* [1995] 1 A.C. 74.

[44] *Daly v. Sydney Stock Exchange* (1986) 160 C.L.R. 371; *Lonrho plc v. Fayed* (No. 2) [1992] 1 W.L.R. 1; *El Ajou v. Dollar Land Holdings plc* [1993] 3 All E.R. 717 (not discussed on appeal at [1994] 2 All E.R. 685); *Halifax Building Society v. Thomas* [1996] Ch. 217.

[45] *Supra.* It was also doubted by the Privy Council in *re Goldcorp Exchange Ltd* [1995] 1 A.C. 74.

[46] *Bankers Trust Co. v. Shapira* [1980] 1 W.L.R. 1274, as explained by Lord Brown-Wilkinson in the *Westdeutsche* case, at p. 716.

[47] See Goff and Jones, p. 101.

[48] *Att.-Gen. for Hong Kong v. Reid* [1994] 1 A.C. 324; *ante*, p. 608.

[49] *Ante*, p. 294; (1995) 54 C.L.J. 377 at p. 383 (A. Oakley).

[50] See (1992) 45 C.L.P. 69 at p. 95 (P. Birks); *Jones (F.C.) & Sons (Trustee) v. Jones* [1996] 3 W.L.R. 703 (common law).

the amount of trust money laid out in the purchase; or, as we generally express it, he is entitled at his election either to take the property, or to have a charge on the property for the amount of the trust money."[51] Claims in equity will never, of course, be valid against a bona fide purchaser for value.[52] If, however, the property has come into the hands of an innocent volunteer, the tracing remedy lies against him while he retains it.[53]

iii. Mixed Funds. The position is more complicated where the trustee has mixed the trust funds with other money, and possibly converted the mixed funds into other property. The position differs according to whether the claim is against the trustee, or whether the ownership of the mixed fund must be apportioned between two trusts or a trust and an innocent volunteer. Also, there are special rules applicable to cases of mixed funds in bank accounts.

(a) *Position as Against the Trustee.* The rule here is that the beneficiaries have a first charge over the mixed fund or any property purchased with it. The onus is on the trustee to prove that part of the mixed fund is his own. " ... if a trustee amalgamated [trust property] with his own, his beneficiary will be entitled to every portion of the blended property which the trustee cannot prove to be his own."[54] It has been held that the trustee is not to be treated as having made any contribution where he uses trust money in part payment for a property and provides the balance by borrowing on mortgage on the security of the property. Thus the beneficiaries take the whole of any profit.[55] Even where the trustee has contributed his own money, the trust should take all the profit if the asset (such as a house) could not have been bought without the trust contribution, in contrast with the case where a trustee buys shares and could have bought fewer with his funds alone.[56]

An extremely wide view of tracing into mixed funds emerged from *dicta* of the Privy Council in *Space Investments Ltd v. Canadian Imperial Bank of Commerce Trust Co. (Bahamas) Ltd.*[57] A bank trustee deposited trust money with itself under an express

[51] *Per* Jessel M.R. in *Re Hallett's Estate* (1880) 13 Ch.D. 696 at p. 709.
[52] *Post*, p. 679.
[53] *Post*, p. 677. As to whether he has any personal liability, see *ante*, p. 300.
[54] *Lewin on Trusts* (16th ed.), p. 223, quoted in *Re Tilley's W.T.* [1967] Ch. 1179 at p. 1182; *Lupton v. White* (1808) 15 Ves.Jr. 432; *Indian Oil Corp. Ltd v. Greenstone Shipping S.A.* [1987] 2 Lloyd's Rep. 286; (1987) 46 C.L.J. 369 (P. Stein); *Coleman v. Harvey* [1989] 1 N.Z.L.R. 723; *Brinks Ltd v. Abu-Saleh* [1995] 1 W.L.R. 1478. Contrary views expressed in *Re Att.-Gen.'s Reference (No. 1 of 1985)* [1986] Q.B. 491 cannot stand in the light of *Att.-Gen. for Hong Kong v. Reid* [1994] 1 A.C. 324; *ante*, p. 608.
[55] *Davies (Paul A.) (Australia) Pty. Ltd v. Davies* [1983] 1 N.S.W.L.R. 440.
[56] See *Australian Postal Corporation v. Lutak* (1991) 21 N.S.W.L.R. 584; (1993) 13 L.S. 371 (L. Aitken).
[57] [1986] 1 W.L.R. 1072. See also *Ross v. Lord Advocate* [1986] 1 W.L.R. 1077.

power to do so, and was then wound up. It was held that if a bank trustee misappropriated trust money for its own benefit, tracing would be possible. But where the mixing was done lawfully, as here, the trust money became the bank's, subject only to a personal obligation to pay. Hence the beneficiaries had no interest in the bank's assets and were unsecured creditors. The settlor had accepted the risk of insolvency by allowing the deposit. Lord Templeman went on to discuss the position if tracing had been available, saying that if the beneficiaries could not trace their money into any partic-ular asset belonging to the trustee bank, equity would allow them "to trace the trust money to all the assets of the bank and to recover the trust money by the exercise of an equitable charge over all the assets of the bank.[58] The difficulty with this is that it suggests that if a commingled fund has been lost, the beneficiaries still have a proprietary claim to the trustee's remaining assets, which are impressed with a charge. Such a view would be unfair to the general creditors, and is supported neither by principle nor by policy.[59]

The point was discussed again by the Privy Council in *Re Gold-corp Exchange Ltd*,[60] where customers who had paid for bullion but had not taken delivery sought to trace into the assets of the now insolvent company. Save for one class of customers whose bullion had been segregated, the claim failed because the customers never had any proprietary rights in any bullion,[61] nor in the money paid over, which had never been impressed with any trust.[62] Thus they were simply unsecured creditors. As the customers had no proprie-tary rights in the purchase money, it was unnecessary to consider whether they could have traced into the company's assets. It was doubted, however, whether Lord Templeman's *dicta* in *Space Investments*[63] could overcome the difficulty that the money had been paid into an overdrawn account. The *dicta*, it was said, were con-cerned with tracing into a mixed fund, not a non-existent fund.

In the case of the customers whose bullion had been segregated, only a small amount could be traced because it had been mixed with other bullion, depleted by withdrawals, and not replaced by the addition of other bullion.[64] They could not improve their position by asserting an equitable lien over all the assets of the company in

---

[58] [1986] 1 W.L.R. 1072 at p. 1074.

[59] See the cogent criticisms in (1987) 103 L.Q.R. 433 (R. Goode); *cf.* Goff and Jones, p. 101.

[60] [1995] 1 A.C. 74 (on appeal from New Zealand); (1994) 110 L.Q.R. 509 (E. McKendrick); (1994) 8 *Trust Law International* 91 (N. Richardson); (1994) 53 C.L.J. 443 (L. Sealy); All E.R. Rev. 1994, p. 40 (N. Palmer); *ante*, p. 94.

[61] See now Sale of Goods (Amendment) Act 1995; (1996) 59 M.L.R. 260 (T. Burns); *ante*, p. 94 (co-ownership solution).

[62] In contrast with *Re Kayford Ltd* [1975] 1 W.L.R. 279; *ante*, p. 51.

[63] *Supra.*

[64] Applying *Roscoe v. Winder* [1915] 1 Ch. 62; *post*, p. 671.

reliance on the *dicta* in *Space Investments*. It was accepted, however, that where a bank uses all borrowed money as a mixed fund for lending or investing, any trust money unlawfully borrowed by a bank trustee could be said to be latent in property subsequently acquired by the bank so that an equitable lien could be imposed on that property.[65] In the present case there was no evidence that the bullion of these customers continued to exist as a fund latent in property vested in the company's receivers and no reason to favour them above other customers by the grant of a lien. Thus it was not appropriate to consider the scope of *Space Investments* nor its application to trustees other than bank trustees.

Although the Privy Council did not expressly reject Lord Templeman's observations (and it should be noted that his Lordship sat also in *Re Goldcorp Exchange Ltd*),[66] it has been said that after *Re Goldcorp* the *dicta* are "now as good as dead."[67] This is reinforced by *Bishopsgate Investment Management Ltd v. Homan*,[68] where Maxwell pension funds were wrongly paid into the overdrawn account of a company now found to be insolvent. The Court of Appeal confirmed that there could be no tracing into an overdrawn bank account (whether overdrawn at the payment or later) and that no equitable charge could be imposed on the company's assets in reliance on the *dicta* in *Space Investments*. The Privy Council in *Re Goldcorp Exchange Ltd*[69] had rejected a wide interpretation of those *dicta*, which related specifically to tracing into a bank's credit balances where a bank trustee had wrongfully deposited trust money with itself.[70]

(b) *Position as Between Two Trusts, or Trust and Third Party.* It may be, however, that the trustee has mixed the funds of two trusts, whether or not with his own,[71] or has transferred the funds to an innocent volunteer, who has mixed them with his own. The rule here is that the two trusts, or the trust and the volunteer, share *pari passu* (*i.e.* rateably) in the mixed funds or any property purchased out of them.[72] The position of the innocent volunteer is further dealt with below.

Where there have been several victims but there is no realistic possibility that other claimants will seek to assert a charge ranking

---

[65] Criticised (1994–95) 5 K.C.L.J. 143 (D. Hayton).
[66] *Supra.*
[67] (1995) 9 *Trust Law International* 43 at p. 45 (P. Birks). See also *ibid.*, p. 78 (P. Oliver); *Laundering and Tracing* (ed. Birks, 1995), pp. 82–88 (S. Moriarty) and 294 (P. Birks).
[68] [1995] Ch. 211; [1996] Conv. 129 (A. Jones); *infra*, p. 672.
[69] *Supra.*
[70] [1995] Ch. 211 at pp. 221–222.
[71] Any claim to ownership by the trustee will be governed by the principle discussed in paragraph (a) above.
[72] *Re Diplock* [1948] Ch. 465.

rateably with the plaintiff's, the plaintiff may be permitted to trace an amount in excess of that which he would obtain on a rateable division. Whether the rights of third parties may be raised as a partial defence to a tracing claim depends on the circumstances of each case.[73]

(c) *Bank Accounts.* The mixing is likely, however, to occur in the context of a banking account, to which special rules apply. Again, it is necessary to distinguish the position as between trustee and beneficiary and as between two trusts or trust and innocent volunteer. These rules govern the allocation of payments out of the mixed fund.[74] The principle as between trustee and beneficiary is that the trustee is presumed to spend his own money first.

> In *Re Hallett's Estate*,[75] Hallett, a solicitor, mixed with his own money certain funds from two trusts, one his own marriage settlement of which he was trustee, and the other a trust of which a client, Mrs Cotterill, was beneficiary. At his death there were insufficient funds to pay his personal debts and to meet these claims.
>
> Three questions arose; (i) whether Mrs Cotterill, not being a beneficiary of a trust of which Hallett was a trustee, was entitled to trace on the ground of the fiduciary relationship; (ii) (assuming that she was) how to allocate the payments from the fund as between Hallett and the claimants; and (iii) as between the claimants themselves.
>
> The Court of Appeal held that Mrs Cotterill was entitled to trace, and that the payments out must be treated as payments of Hallett's own money. This left sufficient to satisfy the claims of Mrs Cotterill and of the beneficiaries under the marriage settlement, so the third question did not arise.[76]

We are at present concerned with (ii). The other matters are discussed elsewhere.[77] The reason given by Jessel M.R. for allocating payments to Hallett's money and not to the trust is that wherever an act "can be done rightfully, [a man] is not allowed to say, against

---

[73] *El Ajou v. Dollar Land Holdings plc (No. 2)* [1995] 2 All E.R. 213.

[74] In the case of insuperable accounting difficulties, these rules will not be applied. See *Cunningham v. Brown*, 265 U.S. 1, 44 Sup.Ct. 424; 68 L.Ed. 873 (1923), where a tracing remedy was refused in respect of a mass of claims arising out of a fraud. Taft C.J. said "It would be running the fiction of *Knatchbull v. Hallett* into the ground to apply it here." The claimants shared equally.

[75] (1880) 13 Ch.D. 696; see (1975) 28 C.L.P. 64 (A. Oakley).

[76] In the court below, where, on the view taken by Fry J., the third question did arise, it was solved by applying the rule in *Clayton's Case* (1817) 1 Mer. 572.

[77] *Ante*, p. 662; *post*, p. 673.

the person entitled to the property or the right, that he has done it wrongfully."[78]

It should be appreciated, however, that this principle operates in the context of a claim against a balance in the account, and does not derogate from the general principle, described above, that the beneficiaries have a first charge on any property bought out of a mixed fund.[79]

In *Re Oatway*,[80] the trustee withdrew money from the mixed fund and invested it. Later he withdrew the balance of the fund and dissipated it. Joyce J. rejected the argument that the money drawn out first must be treated as his own, holding that the beneficiaries' claim must be satisfied from any identifiable part of the mixed fund before the trustee could set up his own claim. Thus the beneficiaries were entitled to the investments in priority to the creditors of the trustee.

It is submitted that *Re Oatway* merely gives the beneficiaries a charge over the property rather than a right to assert that it has been purchased with their money. On this approach, any increase in the value of the property will remain available for the claims of any other beneficiaries whose money may have been subsequently mixed in the account.[81] If the trustee is insolvent, this approach may also allow any increase in value to be available to the creditors, as there is little merit in permitting the beneficiaries to retrieve more than they have lost where the real contest is with the creditors.[82] This factor must always be borne in mind when considering whether, theoretically, the tracing remedy ought to be available. The question is essentially one of competition between the beneficiary and the creditors.

So far as claims against a bank balance are concerned, the rule is that tracing can succeed against a mixed fund in the bank account to the extent that the trust funds can still be shown to be there. If the account falls below that sum, that part of the trust money must have been spent.[83] Later payments in are not treated as repayments of the

---

[78] (1880) 13 Ch.D. 696 at p. 727.

[79] Thus it cannot be relied on in a criminal case to show that the accused was withdrawing his own money; *R. v. Clowes (No. 2)* [1994] 2 All E.R. 316.

[80] [1903] 2 Ch. 356; *Re Tilley's W.T.* [1967] Ch. 1179 at p. 1185.

[81] Such beneficiaries could not assert that the property was bought with their money because of *Clayton's Case, post*, p. 673.

[82] (1988) 37 King's Counsel 15 at p. 16 (G. Jones). The beneficiaries will be entitled to any profits if they can establish that the property was bought with their money; *post* p. 676.

[83] In *Roscoe v. Winder* [1915] 1 Ch. 62, 69 Sargant J. said that the tracing remedy applied to "such an amount of the balance ultimately standing to the credit of the trustee as did not exceed the lowest balance of the account during the intervening period."

trust fund unless the trustee shows an intention to do so.[84] It is essential therefore to ascertain from the accounts the lowest balance in the fund; to that extent the tracing remedy is available against that balance. Of course the personal claim remains as to any shortfall, in cases where the trust money withdrawn cannot be followed into other property. Where the money has been withdrawn from the account and paid into various different accounts, the beneficiaries can claim a charge over all such accounts and, as against the wrongdoer, are not bound to identify one.[85] This is because the payments derive from a fund which was subject to a charge in their favour.

We saw that the Privy Council in *Re Goldcorp Exchange Ltd*[86] held that there could be no tracing of money paid into an overdrawn account, confirming the principle that later payments in are not normally treated as repayments to the trust.[87] A related question is whether "backwards tracing" is possible, as where a trustee borrows money to buy a car and then repays the loan with trust money.[88] May the trust trace the car? In *Bishopsgate Investment Management Ltd v. Homan*[89] Leggatt L.J. firmly rejected the concept of tracing into an asset acquired by the trustee before the trust money was misappropriated and thus without its aid.[90] Dillon L.J., however, regarded it as arguable that the beneficiary could assert a charge over an asset if there was a connection between the misappropriated money and the acquisition of the particular asset, as where the asset was bought with borrowed money and at the time of the borrowing it could be inferred that the trustee intended to repay with trust money.[91] In this limited situation "backwards tracing" may be supportable, but to permit it on a wider basis would be contrary to the principles of tracing.[92]

There is little English authority on the question whether the beneficiaries may claim property purchased out of a mixed account when a sufficient balance remains to satisfy their claim. The point will be significant where the property purchased has increased in value, or it may be that the balance has been spent on a property

---

[84] *Roscoe v. Winder, supra.*

[85] *El Ajou v. Dollar Land Holdings plc* [1993] 3 All E.R. 717 at p. 735 (not discussed on appeal at [1994] 2 All E.R. 685); (1995) 9 *Trust Law International* 78 (P. Oliver).

[86] [1995] 1 A.C. 74; *ante,* p. 668.

[87] *Roscoe v. Winder, supra* (applied also in *Bishopsgate Investment Management Ltd v. Homan, infra*).

[88] If the loan was secured, subrogation to the security may assist; *post,* p. 674.

[89] [1995] Ch. 211; *ante,* p. 669. Henry J, agreed with both judgments.

[90] *Ibid.* at pp. 221–222.

[91] This view is favoured in (1995) 111 L.Q.R. 517 (Sir Peter Millett); *Laundering and Tracing* (ed. Birks, 1995), p. 18 (D. Hayton). See also (1995) 9 *Trust law International* 78 (P. Oliver); (1995–96) 6 K.C.L.J. 123 (D. Cowan).

[92] (1995) 54 C.L.J. 377 at p. 414 (A. Oakley); *cf,* p. 290 (L. Smith), taking a wider view.

which has made a smaller profit. Under *Re Hallett*[93] the first expenditure is presumed to have been the trustee's money. *Re Oatway*[94] is distinguishable because the balance has not been dissipated. *Re Tilley's Will Trusts*[95] suggests that the beneficiaries must be content with a claim to the balance (or the second property, as the case may be).[96] If the trustee is insolvent, the claims of the creditors must also be considered, as discussed above.

It remains to consider the position where the mixed funds in the bank account represent the funds of two trusts,[97] or of a trust and an innocent volunteer. Here the rule in *Clayton's* case[98] applies, which lays down that in the case of a current bank account, the first payment in is appropriated to the earliest debt which is not statute-barred; in other words, first in, first out. This is a rule which has some relevance and convenience in commercial matters. We have seen that it does not apply to accounts between trustee and beneficiary. Nor, it is submitted, should it appear in any aspect of the present subject,[99] but it has been applied as a means of determining entitlement in a mixed banking account between rival persons with a right to trace,[1] and also between a person with a right to trace and an innocent volunteer.[2] It never appears in any context other than that of a current bank account.[3] Although the rule has been much criticised, the Court of Appeal has recently confirmed it as settled law, although subject to a contrary intention, express or presumed, and subject to exceptions as established in the case law.[4]

---

[93] (1880) 13 Ch. D. 696.

[94] [1903] 2 Ch. 356.

[95] [1967] Ch. 1179, *post*, p. 676.

[96] See Pettit, pp. 512–513; Moffat, *Trust Law: Text and Materials* (2nd ed.) p. 427; Birks, *An Introduction to the Law of Restitution*, p. 370; (1995) 54 C.L.J. 377 at p. 416 (A. Oakley); *cf. Laundering and Tracing* (ed. Birks, 1995), pp. 6 *et seq.* (D. Hayton).

[97] If the trustee's own money is also mixed, the principle of *Re Hallett's Estate, supra*, will apply to determine withdrawals to be allocated to the trustee; *i.e.* he is presumed to spend his own money before that of either trust.

[98] (1817) 1 Mer. 572; (1963) 79 L.Q.R. 388 (D. McConville); (1965) 6 W.A.L.R. 428, at p. 437 (P. Higgins). *cf. Re British Red Cross Balkan Fund* [1914] 2 Ch. 419 (where later subscribers to a fund could not claim surplus to the exclusion of earlier subscribers).

[99] (1963) 79 L.Q.R. 401–402 (D. McConville); *Laundering and Tracing* (ed. Birks, 1995), p. 14 (D. Hayton). See the Report of the Review Committee on Insolvency Law and Practice (1982, Cmnd. 8558) paras. 1076–1080, preferring a rateable distribution.

[1] *Re Hallett's Estate* (1879) 13 Ch.D. 696 (Fry J.); *Re Stenning* [1895] 2 Ch. 433; *Re Diplock* [1948] Ch. 465 (the National Institute for the Deaf). It was not applied in *Re Ontario Securities Commission* (1986) 30 D.L.R. (4th) 1, or *Re Registered Securities* [1991] 1 N.Z.L.R. 545.

[2] *Re Stenning* [1895] 2 Ch. 433; *Mutton v. Peat* [1899] 2 Ch. 556 at p. 560, *per* Bryne J.; *Re Diplock, supra*.

[3] *Re Diplock* [1948] Ch. 465 at p. 554 (The Royal Sailors Orphan Girls' School and Home (Action 111C)).

[4] *Barlow Clowes International Ltd v. Vaughan* [1992] 4 All E.R. 22 (rule displaced by contrary intention where investors knew their money would be pooled); All E.R.Rev. 1992, p. 207 (P. Clarke); [1993] Conv. 372 (J. Martin); (1993–94) 4 K.C.L.J. 86 (A. Jones).

As has been said, the presumptions discussed above only work if
the withdrawals and deposits are modest in number and amount. If
millions of pounds flow daily into and out of a bank, equity's rules
and presumptions "conceived in the horse-and-buggy world of trifling sums paid into relatively passive banking accounts"[5] cannot
identify the plaintiff's money.

iv. Subrogation. This is a doctrine with common law and equitable origins whereby one person is entitled to stand in the shoes of
another and assert that other's rights.[6] The most common examples
are insurance and suretyship. An insurer who pays the loss is
entitled to stand in the shoes of the insured and assert his rights
against the wrongdoer. The House of Lords in *Napier and Ettrick
(Lord) v. Hunter*[7] held that an insurer's subrogation rights should
have proprietary protection in the form of a lien (rather than a more
onerous constructive trust) over damages paid to the insured by the
wrongdoer. Thus unsecured creditors would not benefit from the
double payment at the expense of the insurer on the bankruptcy of
the insured.

In the insurance cases the payer is subrogated to the rights of the
payee against third parties. In other cases the payer is subrogated to
the rights of third parties against the payee, as where the payee has
used the money to pay off creditors. Subrogation may assist where,
because of the *ultra vires* doctrine, no direct action lies against the
payee.[8] In such a case the payer cannot be subrogated to any
securities of the repaid creditors, otherwise he would be in a better
position than an *intra vires* creditor.[9]

In the context of tracing, the question is whether the plaintiff may
be subrogated to the position of a secured creditor paid off by the
defendant with the plaintiff's money. (If the creditor was unsecured,
subrogation will not improve the plaintiff's position). In *Re Diplock*[10] the next-of-kin's money had been wrongly paid to hospital
charities, two of which used it (innocently) to pay off secured and
unsecured debts. It was held that there was no right of subrogation,

---

[5] Goff and Jones (4th ed.), p. 98. The rule was not applied in *Re Eastern Capital Futures Ltd*
[1989] B.C.L.C. 371, where it was impossible to attribute particular sums to particular
claimants.
[6] See Mitchell, *The Law of Subrogation*; Goff and Jones (4th ed.), Chap. 31; (1995) 54 C.L.J.
290 (L. Smith).
[7] [1993] A.C. 713; [1993] Conv. 391 (A. Jones); (1993) 143 N.L.J. 1061 (J. Martin); (1993)
109 L.Q.R. 159 (W. Gummow). See also *Lonhro Exports Ltd v. Export Credits Guarantee
Department* [1996] 4 All E.R. 673 (if insurer recovers from the third party a sum greater
than its entitlement by subrogation, it holds the surplus on trust for the insured).
[8] See *Wenlock (Baroness) v. River Dee Company* (1887) 19 Q.B.D. 155.
[9] See Goff and Jones (4th ed.), p. 593; Birks, *Introduction to the Law of Restitution*,
pp. 390–393. A surety, on the other hand, is entitled to be subrogated to any securities on
paying the creditor.
[10] [1948] Ch. 465.

because that would require reviving debts and securities which had been extinguished. This has long been criticised as allowing the unjust enrichment of the charities at the expense of the next-of-kin. The position was reviewed by the Court of Appeal in *Boscawen v. Bajwa*,[11] which has been described as "the most important case on tracing in recent years."[12] A building society advanced money for the purchase of property and the discharge of a legal charge on that property. The society intended to have a first legal charge on completion. It sent the money to the solicitor[13] acting for itself and the purchaser, intending to retain the beneficial interest in the money until the security was in place, but its instructions were not carried out. The purchase was not completed, but the society's money was used to redeem the existing charge. It was held that the society was entitled to be subrogated to the position of the legal chargee. It would be unconscionable to assert that the charge had been redeemed for the landowner's benefit.

The application of the doctrine to a loan which is valid, intended to be secured, and which is used to pay off a secured loan, is not surprising.[14] However, the Court of Appeal took the opportunity to state that the doctrine applied in circumstances such as those of *Re Diplock*.[15] The passage in that case which denied the remedy was considered difficult and in need of review in the light of later developments in the law of restitution. It could not be objected that the creditor's security had been extinguished: that was not a bar to subrogation but a precondition. What had motivated the Court of Appeal to deny the remedy in *Re Diplock* was a desire to avoid injustice to a charity which had redeemed a mortgage which the bank was content to leave outstanding indefinitely. "It may be doubted whether in its anxiety to avoid injustice to the hospital the court may not have done an even greater injustice to the next of kin, who were denied even the interest on their money."[16] Instead of denying a remedy, the solution should have been to delay enforcement of the revived security until the charity had had a reasonable opportunity to obtain a fresh loan on suitable terms, which would now be possible as an application of the defence of change of position.[17]

---

[11] [1996] 1 W.L.R. 328. See also *Castle Phillips Finance v. Piddington* [1995] 1 F.L.R. 783.
[12] (1995) 9 *Trust Law International* 124 (P. Birks). See also (1996) 55 C.L.J. 199 (N. Andrews); [1997] Conv. 1 (A. Oakley).
[13] The sole partner was subsequently bankrupt.
[14] See Goff and Jones (4th ed.), p. 621.
[15] *Supra.*
[16] [1996] 1 W.L.R. 328 at p. 341 (Millett L.J.).
[17] *Post*, p. 679.

v. Increase in Value. We saw that Jessel M.R. said in *Re Hallett's Estate*[18] that where trust funds, unmixed, could be traced, the claimant could choose to take the property purchased with them, or to have a charge upon it for the amount; but that if property had been mixed with the trustee's own, and property purchased with the mixed fund, the claimant's remedy was that of a charge.

Such a rule would mean, however, that the beneficiary would be able only to claim the original money taken (with interest, and in priority to the creditors) and that the trustee would keep all the profits. This would be a startling result; all the more so in view of the extreme strictness with which the courts deal with cases of profits made by trustees.[19]

It appears that the appropriate remedy in such a situation is to allow the beneficiary to claim a share of the fund in the proportion which the original trust funds bore to the mixed fund at the time of the mixing. If the fund increased in value, it would be in his interest to do so. If the fund decreased in value, it would be to his interest to have a charge. This is the rule in the United States of America and in Australia.[20] The principle of proportionate entitlement has been applied in England as between two persons entitled to trace into a fund[21] but never between beneficiary and trustee. Its applicability was, however, conceded in *Re Tilley's Will Trusts*.[22]

The testator's widow and executrix had paid small amounts from the testator's estate (in which she had a life interest) into her own account which she then used so successfully in property purchases that the modest capital with which she started became worth £94,000 at her death. She made full use of overdraft facilities allowed her by the bank, and could have carried out her operations without the use of the trust money. The question on her death was whether those entitled in remainder could claim a share of the £94,000 in the proportion to which the trust money paid into her account bore to the balance in the account at the time; or whether they could claim only the return of the trust money with interest. In spite of the concession relating to the beneficiary's right to a proportionate share, Ungoed-Thomas J. allowed only the return of the trust money with interest; concluding, rather surprisingly, that "the trust moneys were not invested in properties at all, but merely went in reduction of Mrs. Tilley's overdraft which was in reality the source of the purchase-moneys."[23]

---

[18] (1880) 13 Ch.D. 696; *ante*, p. 670.
[19] *Boardman v. Phipps* [1967] 2 A.C. 46; *ante*, pp. 601 *et seq.*
[20] *Scott v. Scott* (1963) 37 A.L.J.R. 345.
[21] *Lord Provost of Edinburgh v. Lord Advocate* (1879) 4 App.Cas. 823.
[22] [1967] Ch. 1179 at p. 1189; (1968) 26 C.L.J. 28 (G. Jones).
[23] *Ibid.* at p. 1193.

Thus a beneficiary who can establish that property was purchased with a mixture of his own and the trustee's money should be able to claim a proportionate share of the property. This will enable him to share in the profits if the property has increased in value. If, however, it has decreased, he will be entitled to a charge for the sum expended. The fact that a beneficiary proceeding against a trustee has this choice of remedy does not mean that the choice should be available in every tracing situation; a dishonest trustee is in a very different situation from an innocent volunteer.[24]

vi. The Innocent Volunteer. The tracing remedy is never available against a bona fide purchaser for value. A volunteer of course is in a different position. The usual rule is that they take the property subject to any equitable interest affecting it. In the tracing situation, however, it appears from *Re Diplock*[25] that a person who receives a mixed fund bona fide[26] but without payment (the innocent volunteer) is raised to a position equal to that of the equitable owner who is entitled to trace. "But this burden on the conscience of the volunteer is not such as to compel him to treat the claim of the equitable owner as paramount. That would be to treat the volunteer as strictly as if he himself stood in a fiduciary relationship to the equitable owner which *ex hypothesi* he does not. The volunteer is under no greater duty of conscience to recognise the interest of the equitable owner than that which lies upon a person having an equitable interest in one of two trust funds of 'money' which have become mixed towards the equitable owner of the other. Such a person is not in conscience bound to give precedence to the equitable owner of the other of the two funds."[27] Thus the charities in *Re Diplock* were allowed to claim rateably with the plaintiffs; in other words, they were treated in the same way as they would have been if they had themselves been entitled to trace.

This principle of rateable sharing applies whether the mixed property has increased or deceased in value. So far as losses are concerned, it would seem preferable to say that the trust should share the loss only if (as will often be the case) the change of position defence[28] is available to the innocent volunteer.[29] In the case of profits, it has been argued that the beneficiaries should be

---

[24] *Restatement of Restitution*, paras. 202–204.
[25] [1948] Ch. 465.
[26] A recipient who, although not dishonest, ought to have known that the money was not his is not an innocent volunteer; *Boscawen v. Bajwa* [1996] 1 W.L.R. 328 at p. 337.
[27] *Ibid.* at p. 524.
[28] *Post*, p. 679.
[29] (1995) 54 C.L.J. 377 at p. 419 (A. Oakley). See also (1988) 3 *Trust Law & Practice* 7 (D. McNicol).

entitled only to a charge, enabling the volunteer to take all profit.[30] However, this seems too lenient on the volunteer, bearing in mind that the beneficiaries have been deprived of their property and must share losses rateably.[31] To the extent that the profit was created by the effort and skill of the volunteer, he should be recompensed by an allowance.[32]

We will see that, as far as the claim *in personam* in *Re Diplock* was concerned, the action against the volunteer could be brought only after the remedies against the personal representatives had been exhausted.[33] Any money recovered from them reduced the sum recoverable from the volunteer. It is not clear whether the action *in rem* against a third party is similarly limited. Without suggesting that there was any obligation to sue the executors before proceeding *in rem* against the volunteer, the Court of Appeal in *Re Diplock* took the preliminary view that "prima facie and subject to discussion"[34] the next-of-kin's proprietary claim should be reduced by any amounts recovered from the executors. It is difficult to see why this should be so. Of course, the beneficiary should not recover twice over, but "it should be no defence to the volunteer that the next-of-kin have recovered *in personam* against the executors. The executors should then be subrogated . . . to that part of the next-of-kin's fund which represents the difference between the total of the sums recovered from the executors and the volunteer and the loss suffered by the next-of-kin."[35] Another solution is to require the claimant to sue the volunteer before suing the executors, who are liable only for that which cannot be recovered from the volunteer.[36]

vii. Loss of Right to Trace. There are some situations in which the right to trace will be lost. Some of these have already been mentioned, but they will be included here for the sake of completeness.[37]

(a) *The Property Ceases to be Identifiable.* It is clear from the preceding discussion that tracing is not available to a plaintiff who

---

[30] *Laundering and Tracing* (ed. Birks, 1995) at pp. 12–13 (D. Hayton). See also (1995) 9 *Trust Law International* 78 (P. Oliver).
[31] (1995) 54 C.L.J. 377 at p. 420 (A. Oakley).
[32] [1983] Conv. 135 at p. 137 (K. Hodkinson).
[33] *Post*, p. 687.
[34] [1948] Ch. 465 at p. 556. The dictum may be confined to claims arising out of the administration of estates.
[35] Goff and Jones (4th ed.), p. 92.
[36] This is the rule adopted by the New Zealand Administration Act 1952, s.30B(5) and the Western Australia Trustee Act 1962, s.65(7); *cf.* Trusts Act (Queensland), s.109, whereby the trustee must be sued before the third party.
[37] See also Goff and Jones (4th ed.), p. 92, on the question how far the right to trace against an innocent volunteer is reduced by the amount recoverable from the trustee; *Re Diplock* [1948] Ch. 465 at p. 556.

cannot identify his property, for example where the trust funds or the proceeds of sale of trust assets have been dissipated.[38] Of course, the personal action remains.

(b) *Bona Fide Purchaser.* Where trust property has been transferred to a bona fide purchaser for value without notice, the latter must take free of the claims of the beneficiaries, which must be pursued against the proceeds of sale or against the trustee personally.[39] A purchaser in an arm's length transaction not involving investigation of title to land will not normally have constructive notice.[40] This is not a species of the change of position defence because the consideration does not need to be adequate.[41]

(c) *Change of Position.* The doctrine of change of position lays down that "the right of a person to restitution from another because of a benefit received is terminated or diminished if, after the receipt of the benefit, circumstances have so changed that it would be inequitable to require the other to make full restitution."[42] This doctrine, essential to any satisfactory system of restitutionary remedies, has now been accepted by the House of Lords in *Lipkin Gorman v. Karpnale Ltd.*[43] That case involved a personal action, but it is clear that the defence will be generally available. Indeed, their Lordships envisaged that it would encourage a more consistent approach to tracing at law and in equity. An earlier version of this defence can be seen in *Re Diplock*,[44] where innocent volunteers (charities) had spent the plaintiff's money on improvements and alterations to their own land. It was held that no charge should be imposed, because a charge is enforceable by sale and it would be harsh to make the volunteers sell their land. This has now been subsumed into the wider defence of change of position. Similarly where an innocent volunteer has spent his own money improving the plaintiff's property.[45]

The defence is available to an innocent defendant but not to a wrongdoer.[46] A defendant who, although honest, ought to have

---

[38] *cf. Space Investments Ltd v. Canadian Imperial Bank of Commerce Trust Co. (Bahamas) Ltd* [1986] 1 W.L.R. 1072, *ante*, p. 667.

[39] *Thorndike v. Hunt* (1859) 3 De G. & J. 563; *Thomson v. Clydesdale Bank* [1893] A.C. 282.

[40] The position is the same as in the case of personal liability for receipt of trust property; *ante*, p. 301.

[41] *Lipkin Gorman v. Karpnale Ltd* [1991] 2 A.C. 548.

[42] *Restatement of Restitution*, para. 142. It is no defence to the personal restitutionary claim that, because of transactions with third parties, the plaintiff has suffered no overall loss; *Kleinwort Benson Ltd v. Birmingham City Council* [1996] 3 W.L.R. 1139.

[43] [1991] 2 A.C. 548; (1993–94) 4 K.C.L.J. 93 (G. Jones); *ante*, p. 659.

[44] [1948] Ch. 465 at pp. 546–548.

[45] *Restatement of Restitution*, para. 178.

[46] *Lipkin Gorman v. Karpnale Ltd*, *supra*.

known that the property was not his may not be "innocent" for this purpose.[47] It will operate to eliminate or reduce the plaintiff's claim where the defendant has disposed of money or other property in an exceptional and irretrievable manner in reliance upon the validity of his receipt of the plaintiff's property. The defence is not available where a lender, at the direction of the defendant, pays money directly to a third party who then fails to repay the defendant, as in such a case the defendant has taken the risk of loss.[48]

Where it is plaintiff's property that has been disposed of, tracing will fail if neither the property nor anything representing it can be identified. The defence may then operate in the context of a personal claim against the defendant.[49] Where the defendant still has the plaintiff's property but has disposed of his own in reliance upon ownership of the plaintiff's property, the defence may operate in the context of tracing. The payment of debts cannot normally be relied on as a change of position, as the defendant was obliged to pay them in any event and there is no hardship sufficient to deny the plaintiff's claim.[50] Where the defendant has used the plaintiff's money to pay off a secured debt, we have seen that the plaintiff may recover by being subrogated to the position of the repaid creditor.[51] The defence of change of position should not be available in the usual sense of eliminating or reducing the plaintiff's claim, but any hardship may be avoided by delaying enforcement by the plaintiff until the defendant has had a reasonable opportunity to obtain a fresh loan on suitable terms.[52] The defence is not confined to cases of disposal of money or other property. It could apply where the defendant has performed services in reliance on entitlement to payment, although solicitors paid for services under the terms of an invalid will were not entitled to the defence when sued for recovery of the payment: they took the risk of invalidity in view of their knowledge of the law.[53]

The question which arose in *South Tyneside Metropolitan Borough Council v. Svenska International plc*[54] was whether the

---

[47] *South Tyneside Metropolitan Council v. Svenska International plc* [1995] 1 All E.R. 545 at p. 569; *Laundering and Tracing* (ed. Birks, 1995), p. 158 (R. Nolan) and 325 (P. Birks); *cf.* Goff and Jones (4th ed.), pp. 744–745; [1996] R.L.R. 103 (R. Chambers).

[48] *Goss v. Chilcott* [1996] A.C. 788. The case involved a restitutionary claim for money advanced under a mortgage instrument which had become unenforceable.

[49] *Ante*, p. 303.

[50] *Cf.* (1995) 54 C.L.J. 377 at p. 426 (A. Oakley).

[51] *Boscawen v. Bajwa* [1996] 1 W.L.R. 328; *ante*, p. 675.

[52] *Ibid.* at p. 341; (1995) 9 *Trust Law International* 124 (P. Birks).

[53] *Gray v. Richards Butler (a Firm), The Times*, July 23, 1996.

[54] *Supra*; criticised [1995] Conv. 490 (A. Jones); (1995) 3 R.L.R. 15 at p. 21 (A. Burrows); *Laundering and Tracing* (ed. Birks, 1995), p. 168 (R. Nolan) and p. 329 (P. Birks); All E.R. Rev. 1995, p. 455 (W. Swadling).

defence was available where the defendant had relied on the validity of certain *ultra vires* transactions (interest-rate "swaps") when entering into other irrevocable transactions ("hedges") *prior* to receipt of the plaintiff's money. It was held that the defence was not available, as, save in exceptional circumstances,[55] it required reliance on *actual receipt* and not merely on events before the receipt. Thus an employee who spent money on a holiday in reliance on the promise of a forthcoming bonus would have no defence if the bonus turned out to be *ultra vires* after payment, whereas an employee who spent an *ultra vires* bonus on a holiday would have.[56] To deny pre-enrichment reliance, although in accordance with the *Restatement of Restitution*,[57] places an unwarranted restriction on the flexibility of the defence. Indeed, reliance may not be necessary at all, as in the case where the plaintiff's property is lost or stolen after receipt by the defendant.[58]

viii. Retention of Title Clauses. In recent years the rules of equity have been utilised in the context of the supply of goods to manufacturers. By means of a retention of title clause, the supplier stipulates that the property in the goods shall not pass until payment.[59] He may also seek to reserve ownership where his goods have been mixed with others in a manufacturing process, or of the proceeds of sale by the manufacturer on a sub-sale. He may further, by means of an "all-monies" clause, stipulate that the property shall not pass until all the buyer's obligations to him have been satisfied, not merely as to the particular consignment.[60] Retention of title clauses are often called "*Romalpa* clauses," and take their name from the leading case, *Aluminium Industrie Vaassen B.V. v. Romalpa Aluminium Ltd.*[61]

---

[55] See *Lipkin Gorman v. Karpnale Ltd* [1991] 2 A.C. 548 (total receipts reduced by winnings paid to Cass regardless of order).

[56] [1995] 1 All E.R. 545 at pp. 564–565.

[57] para. 142, *supra*.

[58] (1995) 58 M.L.R. 505 (P. Key); *Laundering and Tracing* (ed. Birks, 1995), p. 147 (R. Nolan) and p. 330 (P. Birks).

[59] See Sale of Goods Act 1979, s.19.

[60] For the effect of such a clause in Scotland, see *Armour v. Thyssen Edelstahlwerke A.G.* [1991] 2 A.C. 339; (1991) 141 N.L.J. 537 (B. Avery); (1991) 54 M.L.R. 726 (R. Bradgate). The Review Committee on Insolvency Law and Practice (1982, Cmnd. 8558), para. 1645, proposed that such clauses should be regarded as creating a charge (and hence be registrable).

[61] [1976] 1 W.L.R. 676; (1976) 92 L.Q.R. 360, 528 (R. Goode); (1976) 39 M.L.R. 585 (R. Prior); (1977) 93 L.Q.R. 324 (D. Donaldson) and 487 (R. Goode); (1977) 36 C.L.J. 27 (J. Farrow and N. Furey); [1978] Conv. 37 (O. Wylie); (1980) 39 C.L.J. 48 (J. Thornley); (1980) 43 M.L.R. 489 (W. Goodhart and G. Jones); [1994] Conv. 129 (G. McCormack). See Smith, *Property Problems in Sale*; Goode, *Proprietary Rights and Insolvency in Sales Transactions;* McCormack, *Reservation of Title.*

The plaintiff vendor sold aluminium foil to the defendant, a manufacturing company. One clause in the contract provided that legal ownership in the foil was not to pass to the defendant until payment. Until that time, the defendant could be required to store the foil in such a way that it was clearly the property of the plaintiff. Other clauses dealt with the position where the foil was mixed with other materials. The defendant company got into financial difficulties and a receiver was appointed at a time when over £122,000 was owing to the plaintiff. The receiver certified that £35,152 in his hands represented the proceeds of sale of unmixed foil sold by the defendant to third parties. The plaintiff claimed priority in respect of that sum over the secured and unsecured creditors. The Court of Appeal, applying *Re Hallett's Estate*,[62] upheld the claim. Although the third parties acquired title to the foil sold to them,[63] the position as between the plaintiff and defendant was that the foil was the plaintiff's property, which the defendant was selling as agent. The defendant's position as agent and bailee gave rise to a fiduciary relationship,[64] which entitled the plaintiff to trace the proceeds of the unmixed foil and recover in priority to the secured and unsecured creditors.

It was conceded in *Romalpa* that the defendant held the goods as bailee.[65] Normally, however, the relationship of the parties under a title retention clause hardly fits the concept of bailment or agency. It has been held that if sub-sales are permitted, the normal implication is that the buyer will sell on his own account and not as fiduciary agent for the seller.[66] But where the sub-purchaser's contract also contains a reservation of title clause, the unpaid vendor may assert title against the sub-purchaser until the latter has paid the purchaser.[67]

(a) *Unmixed Goods.* Retention of title clauses have proved effective where, as in *Romalpa*, the property has retained its identity. In

---

[62] (1880) 13 Ch.D. 696.

[63] See also *Four Point Garage Ltd v. Carter* [1985] 3 All E.R. 12 (purchaser in good faith from buyer where resale in the ordinary course of business gets legal title even though, as between buyer and supplier, buyer did not get title); Sale of Goods Act 1979, ss.24, 25.

[64] Such relationships are not always fiduciary; *Hendy Lennox (Industrial Engines) Ltd v. Grahame Puttick Ltd* [1984] 1 W.L.R. 485; *Re Andrabell Ltd* [1984] 3 All E.R. 407; *Napier and Ettrick (Lord) v. Hunter* [1993] A.C. 713 at p. 744.

[65] See *Re Bond Worth Ltd, infra.*

[66] *E. Pfeiffer Weinkellerei-Weineinkauf GmbH & Co. v. Arbuthnot Factors Ltd* [1988] 1 W.L.R. 150; *Compaq Computer Ltd v. Abercorn Group Ltd* [1991] B.C.C. 484.

[67] *Re Highway Foods International Ltd* [1995] 1 B.C.L.C. 209; (1996) 55 C.L.J. 26 (A. Tettenborn).

Clough Mill Ltd v. Martin[68] the Court of Appeal held that a clause reserving legal title to yarn until payment entitled the seller, on the buyer's insolvency, to recover unused yarn which had not been paid for. As no title passed to the buyer, the buyer could not be regarded as having created a (registrable) charge over the yarn in favour of the seller. Similarly in *Hendy Lennox (Industrial Engines) Ltd v. Grahame Puttick Ltd*,[69] where the seller reserved title to a diesel engine which had been used by the buyer as a major component of a diesel generating set. The plaintiff's claim to ownership of the engine succeeded as the engine remained readily identifiable and could be disconnected quite easily from the generator. In *Re Peachdart Ltd*[70] on the other hand, where leather was supplied for the manufacture of handbags, it was not regarded as retaining its identity even though it remained recognisable in the product. Thus the claim fell to be considered under the following heading.

(b) *Incorporation into Manufacturing Process.* Vendors have been unsuccessful, however, where the property has been incorporated into a manufacturing process. In *Re Bond Worth Ltd*[71] the vendor supplied fibre to the purchaser, which was spun into yarn with other fibre and used in the manufacture of carpets, becoming an inseparable component of the yarn and the carpets. The contract provided that "equitable and beneficial ownership" should remain with the vendor until payment. If resold, the vendor's rights should attach to the proceeds. If converted to other products, the vendor's rights should extend to those products. Upon the purchaser's insolvency £587,397 was owing to the vendor. The receiver held little raw fibre but much yarn and carpets. Slade J. rejected the vendor's claim to priority. The contract was primarily a contract of sale, whereby the legal title and the risk passed to the purchaser, who was at liberty to resell or use the fibre in the manufacturing process. The purchaser was neither an agent nor a bailee. The retention of title clause, upon its true construction, did not reserve full equitable ownership to the vendor, but gave the vendor an equitable charge over the fibre or its products. This charge, which was created by the

---

[68] [1985] 1 W.L.R. 111, distinguishing *Re Bond Worth Ltd, infra,* as to unused material. See All E.R. Rev. 1984, p. 31 (N. Palmer); (1985) 135 N.L.J. 224, 271 (S. Jones); (1985) 36 N.I.L.Q. 165 (McKee); (1985) 44 C.L.J. 33 (J. Thornely); [1987] Conv. 434 (J. Bradgate).

[69] [1984] 1 W.L.R. 485. The plaintiff's proprietary claim to the engine was transferred to the proceeds of sale as the property in the engine had not passed to the defendant's customers at the time of receivership. As to other engines where the property had passed, see *infra.*

[70] [1984] Ch. 131; All E.R. Rev. 1983, p. 48 (N. Palmer); (1984) 100 L.Q.R. 35 (S. Whittaker); (1984) 43 C.L.J. 35 (J. Thornely); [1984] Conv. 139 (D. Milman). The contract expressly provided for a fiduciary relationship.

[71] [1980] Ch. 228. See also *Tatung (U.K.) Ltd v. Galex Telesure Ltd* [1989] B.C.C. 325. For the Australian position, see [1993] Conv. 375 (J. de Lacy).

purchaser company,[72] was void for non-registration under the Companies Act.[73] *Romalpa*[74] was distinguishable, primarily because there the clause reserved *legal* ownership to the vendor.[75]

The result was similar in *Borden U.K. Ltd v. Scottish Timber Products Ltd*,[76] where the vendor supplied resin to the purchaser, to be used in the manufacture of chipboard, of which it became an inseparable component. The contract reserved legal ownership in the resin to the vendor until payment, but did not purport to give the vendor rights over the chipboard. Upon the purchaser's insolvency, £318,321 was owing to the vendor. The Court of Appeal held that the clause merely reserved rights over the resin, which had disappeared, leaving nothing to trace. There was no fiduciary relationship, as the contract was a contract of sale, giving the purchaser liberty to use the resin in the manufacturing process, destroying its very existence. It was doubted whether the tracing remedy could ever apply when heterogeneous goods were mixed in a manufacturing process wherein the original goods lost their character.[77] If there was such a remedy, how could the value of the original goods be quantified? There had been no mixing in issue in *Romalpa*, where it was conceded that the defendant was a bailee of the foil. In the present case, even if the vendor had acquired rights over the chipboard, the claim would have failed for non-registration under the Companies Act. The vendor was similarly unsuccessful in *Re Peachdart Ltd*,[78] where leather was supplied for the manufacture of handbags. The retention of title clause was held to create a charge over the handbags or their proceeds, which was void for non-registration. The question of mixing was not in issue in *Clough Mill Ltd v. Martin*,[79] but the Court of Appeal there expressed the view that if the material is incorporated into other goods, it is assumed that they are owned by the buyer subject to a charge in favour of the seller, unless they are still in a separate and identifiable state.

(c) *Proceeds of Sale.* Even where the seller's goods have not been amalgamated with others, claims to proprietary rights in the proceeds of sale have been unsuccessful.

---

[72] See *Stroud Architectural Systems Ltd v. John Laing Construction Ltd* [1994] B.C.C. 18.

[73] s.95(1) of the Act of 1948. Companies Act 1985, ss.395–404, as substituted by Companies Act 1989, have not been brought into operation.

[74] *Supra.*

[75] Might the plaintiff in *Romalpa* have succeeded at common law?

[76] [1981] Ch. 25; doubted in (1992) 45 C.L.P. 69 at p. 98 (P. Birks).

[77] This view is not inconsistent with the retention of proprietary rights prior to such mixing; *Clough Mill Ltd v. Martin, supra.*

[78] *Supra.*

[79] *Supra.* See also *Specialist Plant Services Ltd v. Braithwaite Ltd* [1987] B.C.L.C. 1 (retention of title clause concerning parts incorporated into machines, and expressed to be as surety for debt, created charge which was void for non-registration).

First, the plaintiff may fail because he cannot establish a fiduciary relationship, which is necessary for tracing into a mixed fund.[80] Such was the case in *Re Andrabell Ltd,*[81] where a claim to the proceeds of sale of travel bags supplied by the plaintiff failed. The rights and duties of the parties were inconsistent with a fiduciary relationship and were merely those of debtor and creditor. Similarly in *Hendy Lennox (Industrial Engines) Ltd v. Grahame Puttick Ltd,*[82] where the plaintiff supplied engines for incorporation into generators. Where the property in the engines had passed to the defendant's customers, the plaintiff's claim to the proceeds failed, because the terms of the contract (in particular the granting of credit) were inconsistent with a fiduciary relationship.

Secondly, even if a fiduciary relationship can be established, the true analysis of the position is that the plaintiff has a charge over the proceeds,[83] which will fail unless registered under the Companies Act.

The reform of this area of the law, which has been called "a maze if not a minefield,"[84] was considered by the Review Committee on Insolvency Law and Practice.[85] Some of the Committee's proposals have been enacted by the Insolvency Act 1986 in the case of corporate insolvency. The Act provides that an administrator may be appointed to manage the affairs of a company which is in financial difficulties.[86] After the presentation of a petition for an administration order, no steps may be taken to enforce any security or to repossess goods under a retention of title agreement[87] without leave of the court.[88] Nor may any such steps be taken while an administration order is in force without the consent of the administrator or the leave of the court.[89] Where any property of the company is subject to a security or goods are subject to a retention of title agreement, the administrator may dispose of the property or goods as if they were not subject to the security or the agreement, if the court is satisfied that the disposal would be likely to promote the purposes specified in the administration order.[90] The net proceeds of the

---

[80] *Ante,* p. 662. The terms used in the documents are not conclusive; *Compaq Computer Ltd v. Abercorn Group Ltd* [1991] B.C.C. 484.

[81] [1984] 3 All E.R. 407.

[82] [1984] 1 W.L.R. 485; *ante,* p. 683.

[83] *Re Peachdart Ltd* [1984] Ch. 131; *Re Weldtech Equipment Ltd* [1991] B.C.C. 16, (1991) 54 M.L.R. 736 (J. de Lacy); *Compaq Computer Ltd v. Abercorn Group Ltd, supra*; (1992) 51 C.L.J. 19 (L. Sealy).

[84] *Hendy Lennox (Industrial Engines) Ltd v. Grahame Puttick Ltd* [1984] 1 W.L.R. 485 at p. 493.

[85] (1982 Cmnd. 8558), paras. 1587–1651.

[86] Insolvency Act 1986, s.8.

[87] Defined in s.251 as an agreement which does not constitute a charge but which gives the seller priority over other creditors.

[88] Insolvency Act 1986, s.10.

[89] *Ibid.* s.11.

[90] *Ibid.* s.15. See also s.43.

disposal must be applied towards discharging the sums secured by the security or payable under the retention of title agreement.[91] The object of these provisions is to enable the business to be kept as a going concern, for the benefit of all creditors.

The real question, however, is whether retention of title clauses are desirable as a matter of policy. Save where construed as creating charges and hence registrable, they effectively create a hidden security, enabling the seller to "leapfrog" other creditors.[92] This objection could be overcome if *all* retention of title clauses were registrable, but this is not yet the case.[93]

6. THE CLAIM IN PERSONAM IN DIPLOCK

It will be recalled that in *Re Diplock*[94] executors distributed large sums of money to numerous charities under the terms of a residuary bequest which was subsequently held to be invalid. The misapplied money belonged, therefore, to the testator's next-of-kin, whose claim to have the money *in rem* has already been considered.[95] The next-of-kin claimed alternatively that a direct action *in personam* lay against the innocent recipients in equity. This claim succeeded in the Court of Appeal, whose judgment was unanimously affirmed by the House of Lords.[96] Such an action may be brought by an unpaid or underpaid creditor, legatee or next-of-kin against the recipient, whether the latter is an overpaid creditor or beneficiary or a "stranger" having no claim to any part of the estate.[97] While the common law action for money had and received is, as a general rule, confined to mistakes of fact,[98] it was held that the action in equity lay whether the mistake was of fact or, as in the present case, of law. The mistake in such a case is not that of the plaintiff, but that of the personal representative, who is not a party to the action. The plaintiff has no way of finding out whether the mistake was of fact or law, nor whether it was a mistaken or deliberate misapplication,[99] hence "it would be a strange thing if the Court of Chancery, having taken upon itself to see that the assets of a deceased person were duly

---

[91] s.15(5).

[92] See [1987] Conv. 434 (J. Bradgate).

[93] See (1995) 54 C.L.J. 43 (S. Cowan, A. Clark and G. Goldberg).

[94] [1948] Ch. 465, [1951] A.C. 251. (Where the earlier authorities are extensively reviewed). For a historical survey, see (1983) 4 *Journal of Legal History* 3 (S. Whittaker).

[95] *Ante*, p. 662.

[96] [1951] A.C. 251 (*sub nom. Ministry of Health v. Simpson*).

[97] [1948] Ch. 465 at p. 502; [1951] A.C. 251 at p. 269.

[98] Legislation to permit recovery of payments made by mistake of law has been proposed; Law Com.No. 227 (1994). See generally *Woolwich Equitable Building Society v. I.R.C.* [1993] A.C. 70.

[99] It seems that the action will lie where the wrongful payment was deliberate: [1951] A.C. 251 at p. 270.

administered, was deterred from doing justice to a creditor, legatee or next-of-kin because the executor had done him wrong under a mistake of law."[1]

The action will not lie against a bona fide purchaser without notice, but, as far as a volunteer is concerned, it is no defence that he was unaware of the mistake,[2] "it is prima facie at least a sufficient circumstance that the defendant, as events have proved, has received some share of the estate to which he was not entitled."[3] But the claim will fail if the plaintiff has acquiesced in the wrongful payment,[4] or has failed to bring his action within the time permitted by the Limitation Act 1980.[5] It is not settled whether the action lies against the recipient's successor in title.[6]

The equitable claim *in personam* lies for the principal sum only, without interest,[7] and is subject to two further important qualifications. First, the direct claim against the recipient is limited to the amount which cannot be recovered from the personal representative, who is primarily liable.[8] Thus the recipient will only be liable in respect of the whole sum if nothing can be recovered from the personal representative, for example because he is insolvent, or acted under a court order,[9] or is protected by section 27 of the Trustee Act 1925.[10] This limitation has been criticised.[11] Why should the recipient's liability depend on the personal representative's solvency? The solution adopted in *Re Diplock*[12] benefits the recipient at the expense of the personal representative, who, on paying the plaintiff, should be subrogated to the plaintiff's right to sue the recipient. Another solution might be to require the plaintiff to exhaust his remedies against the recipient before suing the personal representative.[13]

---

[1] [1951] A.C. 251 at p. 270 (*per* Lord Simonds). But the personal representative cannot himself recover from the recipient unless the mistake was of fact (although he can deduct the mistakenly paid sum from any future payments to the recipient: *Livesey v. Livesey* (1827) 3 Russ. 287).

[2] This was, however, a defence to an alternative claim based on constructive trusteeship; [1948] 1 Ch. 465 at p. 478.

[3] [1948] Ch. 465 at p. 503 (*per* Lord Greene M.R.).

[4] [1951] A.C. 251 at p. 276.

[5] By s.22, the period is 12 years. (For creditors the period is six years). See [1948] Ch. 465 at p. 514.

[6] Goff and Jones (4th ed.), p. 585. This may depend on whether it becomes accepted that liability for receipt is not fault-based; *ante*, p. 300.

[7] *Re Diplock, supra*. This is described as "curious" by Goff and Jones, *loc. cit.* at p. 584.

[8] [1948] Ch. 465 at p. 503. Here the executors paid £15,000 under a compromise approved by the court. For the position concerning the action *in rem*, see *ante*, p. 662.

[9] For example, a Benjamin order (*Re Benjamin* [1902] 1 Ch. 723), giving him liberty to distribute on the footing that a particular person is dead.

[10] *Ante*, p. 535.

[11] See (1949) 65 L.Q.R. 37 at p. 44 (A. Denning); Goff and Jones, *loc. cit.* at p. 584; (1983) 4 Journal of Legal History 3 (S. Whittaker).

[12] [1948] Ch. 465, [1951] A.C. 251.

[13] See New Zealand Administration Act 1952; Western Australia Trustee Act 1962.

The second qualification is that the action appears to be limited to claims arising out of the administration of estates.[14] The action originated at a time when the Court of Chancery was attempting to acquire the jurisdiction then exercised by the ecclesiastical courts over the administration of assets,[15] and is not necessarily available to beneficiaries of *inter vivos* trusts.[16] But more recent cases indicate that the court is not unwilling to extend the action beyond the administration of estates. This approach is consistent with the doctrine of unjust enrichment.[17] In *Butler v. Broadhead*[18] it was suggested that the liquidator of a company had a sufficiently analogous position to that of an executor to allow a creditor of the company to recover from overpaid contributories in a winding-up, at any rate where the liquidator had not advertised for claims. But the action was held to be barred by the Companies Act 1948.[19] In *Re J. Leslie Engineers Co. Ltd*[20] Oliver J. was prepared to allow a personal action where a liquidator claimed recovery of money paid to X after the commencement of a winding-up (the transaction being void under the Companies Act). But the claim failed because the liquidator had not exhausted his remedies against the person primarily responsible, and, in any event, it appeared that X had given consideration for the payment.

Much criticism has centred around the apparent refusal of the House of Lords in *Re Diplock*[21] to recognise the defence of change of position. Where the volunteer has received the money in good faith, his liability to repay it could cause hardship if he has acted to his detriment by spending the money in an exceptional and irretrievable manner. It will be recalled that in *Re Diplock* money had been paid to a hospital charity, and used in the erection of new buildings. This, it was considered, made it inequitable to allow tracing,[22] but was no defence to the personal action.[23] Now that the House of

---

[14] See [1951] A.C. 251 at pp. 265–266 (*per* Lord Simonds).

[15] See (1990) 49 C.L.J. 217 at p. 219 (C. Harpum).

[16] Although if a trustee pays trust money under a mistake of fact, he may recover it, and may be compelled by the beneficiaries to do so: *Re Robinson* [1911] 1 Ch. 502.

[17] See (1989) 105 L.Q.R. 352 (P. Birks); (1991) 107 L.Q.R. 71 (Sir Peter Millett), suggesting strict liability, subject to change of position, for innocent receipt of another's property; *ante*, p. 300.

[18] [1975] Ch. 97. See also *G.L. Baker Ltd v. Medway Building and Supplies Ltd* [1958] 1 W.L.R. 1216; *Nelson v. Larholt* [1948] 1 K.B. 339; *Eddis v. Chichester Constable* [1969] 1 All E.R. 566 (affirmed, without discussing this point, [1969] 2 Ch. 345).

[19] Now Companies Act 1985, s.557.

[20] [1976] 1 W.L.R. 292.

[21] [1951] A.C. 251.

[22] *Ante.*

[23] The Court of Appeal rejected the claim that the volunteers were personally liable *as constructive trustees*, holding that they were not under any duty to investigate the validity of the gift and were entitled to assume that the executors were acting properly; *Re Diplock* [1948] Ch. 465 at pp. 477–479. A finding of constructive trusteeship would have resulted in liability to pay interest. See *Westdeutsche Landesbank Girozentrale v. Islington London Borough Council* [1996] A.C. 669.

Lords in *Lipkin Gorman v. Karpnale Ltd*[24] has accepted the defence of change of position, the *Diplock* personal action can develop on a fairer and more rational basis.

Finally, it seems that the action does not lie if there was a sufficiency of assets at the date of the payment to the defendant. Where the deficiency has arisen subsequently, the personal representative alone is liable.[25]

---

[24] [1991] 2 A.C. 548; (1991) 50 C.L.J. 407 (W. Cornish); *ante*, p. 679.
[25] See *Peterson v. Peterson* (1866) L.R. 3 Eq. 111.

PART IV

EQUITABLE REMEDIES

CHAPTER 24

SPECIFIC PERFORMANCE

1. General Principles	693	
A. Discretionary	694	
B. Common Law Remedies Inadequate	694	
C. Specific Performance is a Remedy in Personam	694	
D. Ensuring Observance	695	
E. The Enforcement of Positive Contractual Obligations	695	
F. Time for Performance	696	
G. Specific Performance and Damages or Compensation	696	
2. The Effect of a Decree of Specific Performance on Other Remedies	697	
A. Common Law Remedy not Excluded	697	
B. The Court's Discretion	698	
C. Subsequent Performance Regulated by Terms of Decree	698	
3. Specific Performance in Particular Situations	699	
A. Contracts for the Sale of Land	699	
B. Contractual Licences	700	
C. Contracts for the Sale of Personal Property	701	
D. Contracts to Pay Money	703	
E. Volunteers	704	
F. Contracts Requiring Supervision	704	
i. The Principle	704	
ii. The Construction Cases	706	
iii. Enforcement of Landlord's Covenants	707	
G. Contracts for Personal Services	707	
H. Contracts for the Creation of Transient or Terminable Interests	710	
I. Contracts to Leave Property by Will	711	
J. Contracts to Transfer Goodwill	712	
K. Contracts to Refer to Arbitration	712	
L. No Specific Performance of Part of a Contract	712	
4. Mutuality	713	
A. Refusal of Specific Performance for Lack of Mutuality	713	
B. The Time at which the Remedy must be Mutual	714	
5. Defences to Specific Performance	715	
A. Mistake and Misrepresentation	716	
B. Conduct of the Plaintiff	717	
C. Laches or Delay	718	
D. Hardship	720	
E. Misdescription of Subject-Matter	721	
i. Specific Performance Subject to Compensation	721	
ii. Refusal of Specific Performance	722	
iii. Conditions of Sale	722	
iv. Want of Good Title	723	
F. Public Policy	723	
6. Damages in Substitution for, or in Addition to, Specific Performance	724	
A. Chancery Amendment Act 1858. Lord Cairns' Act	724	
B. Measure of Damages under Lord Cairns' Act	726	
7. Specific Performance and Third Parties	728	
8. Jurisdiction	732	

1. GENERAL PRINCIPLES[1]

AN outline of the nature of equitable remedies has already been given.[2] Their characteristics, in relation to specific performance in particular, must now be examined.

---

[1] See Fry, *Specific Performance*; Spry, *Equitable Remedies*; Jones and Goodhart, *Specific Performance*; Sharpe, *Injunctions and Specific Performance*.

[2] *Ante*, p. 30.

A. Discretionary

Specific performance, like other equitable remedies, is only given as a matter of discretion, although the discretion is exercised in accordance with settled principles.[3] Thus there are some cases, notably contracts for the sale of land,[4] where the plaintiff may expect to obtain specific performance as a matter of course, and other cases, such as contracts for personal services,[5] where he may expect not to. The discretionary nature of the remedy is well illustrated by a consideration of the matters, such as the conduct of the plaintiff, which the court may regard as a bar to specific performance.[6]

B. Common Law Remedies Inadequate

Equitable remedies are only available where common law remedies are inadequate[7]; for example where the obligation is a continuing one, necessitating a series of actions at law for damages,[8] or where the loss would be difficult to quantify.[9] But specific performance will not be available if, on the true construction of the contract, the parties have agreed that a specific sum of money is to be paid as an alternative to performing the contract.[10]

C. Specific Performance is a Remedy in Personam[11]

A decree of specific performance issues against the individual defendant. If the defendant is within the jurisdiction of the court and can be compelled personally to carry out his obligation, the court may order him to do so even though the subject-matter of the contract is outside the jurisdiction of the court.

In *Penn v. Lord Baltimore*[12] the plaintiffs and defendant had entered into a written agreement fixing the boundaries of Pennsylvania and Maryland, the former of which belonged to the plaintiffs and the latter to the defendant. The plaintiffs sued the defendant in England to have the agreement specifically performed, and one of the objections taken by the defendant was to

---

[3] *Lamare v. Dixon* (1873) L.R. 6 H.L. 414; *Haywood v. Cope* (1858) 25 Beav. 140 at p. 151 (Romilly M.R.).

[4] *Post*, p. 699.

[5] *Post*, p. 707.

[6] *Post*, p. 715.

[7] *Beswick v. Beswick* [1968] A.C. 58, *post*, p. 729; *Tito v. Waddell (No. 2)* [1977] Ch. 106 at p. 327.

[8] *Ibid*. But see *post*, p. 730.

[9] *Co-operative Insurance Society Ltd v. Argyll Stores (Holdings) Ltd* [1996] Ch. 286.

[10] *Legh v. Lillie* (1860) 6 H. & N. 165; Pettit, p. 614.

[11] *Ante*, pp. 7, 18.

[12] (1750) 1 Ves.Sen. 444; *Richard West and Partners (Inverness) Ltd v. Dick* [1969] Ch. 424.

the jurisdiction of the court. This objection was overruled by Lord Hardwicke on the ground that "the conscience of the party was bound by this agreement; and being within the jurisdiction of this court, which acts *in personam*, the court may properly decree it as an agreement."[13] Although the land was not within the jurisdiction, the defendant was, and the court would hold him in contempt unless he complied.

But this jurisdiction is not, perhaps so wide as might at first appear. The land in question was subject at that time to the Crown. The court was invited in *Re Hawthorne*[14] to apply it to land in Saxony (not subject to the Crown) but refused to do so. It appears that the tendency of modern decisions is to restrict the limits within which this jurisdiction will be exercised.[15]

D. Ensuring Observance

Equitable remedies will never issue unless the court can ensure that they will be observed. As equity does not act in vain, specific performance will be decreed only where the defendant is in a position to comply with the order.

In *Jones v. Lipman*[16] the defendant entered into a contract to sell some land to the plaintiff, then sought to avoid specific performance by selling the land to a company acquired by him solely for this purpose and controlled by him. While specific performance would not normally be ordered against a vendor who no longer owned the property, here the defendant was still in a position to complete the contract, because the company was "the creature of the vendor, a device and a sham, a mask which he holds before his face in an attempt to avoid recognition by the eye of Equity."[17] This specific performance was decreed against the vendor and the company.

E. The Enforcement of Positive Contractual Obligations

Unlike injunctions, the remedy of specific performance is confined to the enforcement of positive contractual obligations. These obligations must be binding on the defendant.[18] A prohibitory

---

[13] *Ibid*. at p. 447.

[14] (1883) 23 Ch.D. 743.

[15] See *per* Parker J. in *Deschamps v. Miller* [1908] 1 Ch. 856, at p. 863; Dicey and Morris, *The Conflict of Laws* (12th ed.), pp. 952 *et seq.* See also Civil Jurisdiction and Judgments Act 1982, s.30.

[16] [1962] 1 W.L.R. 832. And see *Elliott v. Pierson* [1948] Ch. 452.

[17] *Ibid*. p. 836 (*per* Russell J.).

[18] For specific performance against a party estopped from denying the existence of a contract, see *Spiro v. Lintern* [1973] 1 W.L.R. 1002; *Worboys v. Carter* [1987] 2 E.G.L.R. 1.

injunction is appropriate to restrain the breach of a negative contract, while a mandatory injunction is used to force the defendant to take positive steps to undo an act already done in breach of contract. But this classification is not inflexible. Even where the plaintiff wishes to enforce a positive contractual obligation, he may ask for an injunction instead of specific performance. The advantage of such a course is that an injunction can be obtained on an interlocutory basis, while specific performance cannot.[19] It should also be added that specific performance does not lie against the Crown.[20]

F. Time for Performance

While specific performance is a remedy for breach of contract, it may in some circumstances be obtained before the time for performance has arrived. In *Marks v. Lilley*[21] the plaintiff issued a writ for specific performance of a contract for the sale of land after the contractual completion date but without first having served a notice making time of the essence of the contract. It was held that this action was not premature, as the equitable right to specific performance, based on the defendant's equitable duty to perform his contract, had already accrued. But the court would not normally interfere before the time for performance had arrived, and a premature plaintiff may be penalised in costs. In *Hasham v. Zenab*[22] specific performance of a contract for the sale of land was granted even before the contractual completion date where the defendant had been guilty of anticipatory breach of contract.[23] The decree would not, of course, take effect before the fixed date.

G. Specific Performance and Damages or Compensation

Damages may be awarded either in addition to or in substitution for specific performance.[24] Similarly, there are some cases, involving misdescription in contracts for the sale of land, where the court

---

[19] See *Sky Petroleum Ltd v. V.I.P. Petroleum Ltd* [1974] 1 W.L.R. 576; *Astro Exito Navegacion S.A. v. Southland Enterprise Co Ltd (No. 2)* [1983] 2 A.C. 787; *Peninsular Maritime Ltd v. Padseal Ltd* (1981) 259 E.G. 860; *Parker v. Camden London Borough Council* [1986] Ch. 162.

[20] Crown Proceedings Act 1947, s.21(1)(a). The proper remedy is a declaration.

[21] [1959] 1 W.L.R. 749. There is a breach of contract at law and in equity if completion does not occur on the contractual date, even though time has not become of the essence: *Raineri v. Miles* [1981] A.C. 1050, *post*, p. 718.

[22] [1960] A.C. 316; (1960) 76 L.Q.R. 200 (R.E.M.). This is similar to the position at law, where an immediate right to damages accrues upon an anticipatory breach of contract: *Hochster v. De la Tour* (1853) 2 E. & B. 678.

[23] Anticipatory breach is not essential, but there must be a sufficient likelihood of breach; Spry, *Equitable Remedies*, p. 76. See further *Oakacre Ltd v. Claire Cleaners (Holdings) Ltd* [1982] Ch. 197.

[24] Lord Cairns' Act 1858; Judicature Act 1873; *post*, p. 724.

may grant specific performance with compensation in the form of an abatement of the purchase price.[25]

2. THE EFFECT OF A DECREE OF SPECIFIC PERFORMANCE ON OTHER REMEDIES

If a decree of specific performance is attained, but enforcement subsequently becomes impossible, what remedies are available to the plaintiff?

A. Common Law Remedy not Excluded

In *Johnson v. Agnew*[26] the plaintiff, having contracted to sell mortgaged properties to the defendant, obtained a decree of specific performance. Subsequently, owing to the defendant's delay, the properties were sold by the mortgagees so that it became impossible to comply with the decree. The price obtained by the mortgagees was lower than the contract price, so the plaintiff sought damages from the defendant at common law for breach of contract[27] The defendant claimed that the plaintiff's election to seek specific performance was irrevocable, so that he could not claim damages at common law. The House of Lords found in favour of the plaintiff. Lord Wilberforce explained the vendor's position as follows:

If a purchaser fails to complete, the vendor can treat this as a repudiation and claim damages for breach of contract, or he may seek specific performance. If he proceeds for these remedies in the alternative, he must elect at trial.[28] If an order for specific performance is made, the contract still exists and is not merged in the judgment. If the defendant then fails to comply with the decree, the plaintiff may apply either to enforce or to dissolve the contract. It follows from the fact that the contract still exists that the plaintiff can recover damages at common law. The argument based on

---

[25] *Post*, p. 724 (damages), and p. 721 (compensation). See also *Seven Seas Properties Ltd v. Al-Essa* [1988] 1 W.L.R. 1272 (specific performance and damages combined with *Mareva* injunction).

[26] [1980] A.C. 367; (1979) 95 L.Q.R. 321 (P. Baker); [1979] Conv. 293 (F. Crane); (1979) 42 M.L.R. 696 (G. Woodman); (1980) 96 L.Q.R. 403 (M. Hetherington); (1980) 39 C.L.J. 58 (A. Oakley); (1981) 97 L.Q.R. 26 (D. Jackson).

[27] Or, alternatively, damages under Lord Cairns' Act, *supra*.

[28] See *Meng Leong Development Pte. Ltd v. Jip Hong Trading Co. Pte. Ltd* [1985] A.C. 511 (P.C.): P claimed in the alternative and was awarded damages. V appealed against the amount. P insisted that the damages be placed with a stakeholder, otherwise he would levy execution. It was held that P was estopped from later seeking specific performance. He was not bound to make an election at that stage, and could have retained the right to elect until after the appeal. Here, however, he had elected to take the benefit of the damages award, and thereby relinquished the right to seek specific performance. The reasoning is criticised at (1985) 101 L.Q.R. 309 on the ground that the damages had not come under P's control.

irrevocable election is unsound: "A vendor who seeks (and gets) specific performance is merely electing for a course which may or may not lead to implementation of the contract; what he elects for is not eternal and unconditional affirmation, but a continuance of the contract under control of the court, which control involves the power, in certain events, to terminate it. If he makes an election at all, he does so when he decides not to proceed under the order for specific performance; but to ask the court to terminate the contract."[29] If the plaintiff accepts a repudiation, he cannot afterwards seek specific performance, because the defendant has been discharged from further performance by the plaintiff's acceptance of the repudiation. But if the plaintiff attains a decree of specific performance, and enforcement becomes impossible, there is no reason why the plaintiff should be precluded from seeking a remedy at common law.[30]

B. The Court's Discretion

The control of the court is exercised according to equitable principles: the relief sought by the plaintiff will be refused if it would be unjust to the other party to grant it. In *Johnson v. Agnew*[31] it was the purchaser's fault that it had become impossible to enforce the decree, therefore the vendor was entitled not only to an order discharging the decree of specific performance and terminating the contract, but to damages at common law for breach of contract.

C. Subsequent Performance Regulated by Terms of Decree

Although the contract still exists after specific performance is granted and does not merge into the decree until the legal title has been conveyed, the rights under the contract may be affected by the decree. By applying for specific performance, the plaintiff puts into the hands of the court how the contract is to be carried out: the performance of the contract is regulated by the provisions of the order and not those of the contract. In *Singh v. Nazeer*[32] a purchaser was granted specific performance of a contract for the sale of land. The purchaser then delayed, so the vendor served a completion notice and claimed damages and forfeiture of the deposit. Megarry J. held that the completion notice was invalid. The machinery

---

[29] [1980] A.C. 367 at p. 398 (*per* Lord Wilberforce). See also *Hillel v. Christoforides* (1992) 63 P. & C.R. 301; *Homsy v. Murphy* (1997) 73 P. & C.R. 26.
[30] Damages are also available in lieu of specific performance under Lord Cairns' Act (*post*, p. 724); *Biggin v. Minton* [1977] 1 W.L.R. 701.
[31] *Supra.*
[32] [1979] Ch. 474; criticised in (1980) 96 L.Q.R. 403 (M. Hetherington). *Cf.* (1981) 97 L.Q.R. 26 (D. Jackson).

provisions of the contract, for example as to mode and date of completion, were intended to apply to performance out of court. Once specific performance was granted, they must yield to any directions in the order. Unless the parties agree, the working out, variation or cancellation of an order for specific performance is a matter for the court. Applying these principles, a vendor who obtains specific performance is not free to sell to a third party if the purchaser fails to comply with the decree. Unless the purchaser agrees to the resale, the vendor's remedy in such a case is to apply to court either for enforcement of the decree or for an order terminating the contract.[33]

3. SPECIFIC PERFORMANCE IN PARTICULAR SITUATIONS

It is a fundamental rule that specific performance will not be granted where the plaintiff would be adequately compensated by the common law remedy of damages.[34] There are some situations, few in number, in which it is settled that the plaintiff may expect to obtain specific performance.[35] There are also numerous situations in which it can firmly be said that the plaintiff will *not* be awarded specific performance. It may be that many of the arguments for restricting specific performance are no longer wholly convincing, and that the trend is towards expansion of the remedy.[36]

A. Contracts for the Sale of Land

A plaintiff seeking specific performance of a contract for the sale (or other disposition) of land must first satisfy the requirements of section 2 of the Law of Property (Miscellaneous Provisions) Act 1989.[37] These requirements apply also to a claim for damages. Section 2 provides that a contract for the sale or other disposition of an interest in land can only be made in writing incorporating all the terms which the parties have agreed. The document must be signed by or on behalf of each party. Under the previous law the contract needed only to be *evidenced in* writing, and an oral contract could

---

[33] *GKN Distributors Ltd v. Tyne Tees Fabrication Ltd* [1985] 2 E.G.L.R. 181. (Vendor's claim against purchaser for declaration, forfeiture of deposit and damages dismissed).

[34] *Hutton v. Watling* [1948] Ch. 26 at p. 36, affirmed [1948] Ch. 398. On the effect on the defendant's insolvency, see *Freevale Ltd v. Metrostore (Holdings) Ltd* [1984] Ch. 199; [1984] Conv. 446 (D. Milman and S. Coneys); *Amec Properties Ltd v. Planning Research & Systems plc* [1992] 1 E.G.L.R. 70 (insolvency of defendant before completion is no bar to specific performance).

[35] See *Haywood v. Cope* (1858) 25 Beav. 140, *per* Romilly M.R. at p. 151; *Lamare v. Dixon* (1873) L.R. 6 H.L. 414.

[36] Trietel, *The Law of Contract* (9th ed.), p. 919. See generally (1984) 4 L. S. 102 (A. Burrows).

[37] Replacing s.40 of the Law of Property Act 1925.

be enforced under the doctrine of part performance. The new rule leaves no scope for part performance, which can only cure *evidential* defects.[38] Estoppel could apply in situations previously covered by part performance, although specific performance would not necessarily be the remedy.[39]

Assuming section 2 is satisfied, specific performance is readily granted to enforce a contract to create or convey a legal estate in land (for example, to sell land[40] or to grant a lease) unless some special consideration arises to prevent it. It cannot however be said that the plaintiff is *entitled* to a decree; because the issue of a decree is always subject to the discretion of the court.

Each piece of land is unique, and it is accepted as a general rule that an award of damages is not adequate compensation for the purchaser or lessee.[41] If the purchaser does not acquire the fee simple he will not have to pay the price, thus "the damages for loss of such a bargain would be negligible and, as in most cases of breach of contract for the sale of land at a market price by refusal to convey it, would constitute a wholly inadequate and unjust remedy for the breach. That is why the normal remedy is by a decree for specific performance by the vendor of his primary obligation to convey, on the purchaser's performing or being willing to perform his own primary obligations under the contract."[42] The court, treating each party equally, will also give specific performance to the vendor or lessor,[43] although a monetary payment might be adequate compensation.

If a vendor fails to comply with the decree, the purchaser may apply to the court for an order nominating some person to execute the conveyance in the vendor's name.[44]

B. Contractual Licences

It was at one time thought that specific performance would not be granted of a contractual licence to occupy land, on the ground that

---

[38] *Cf. Singh v. Beggs* (1996) 71 P. & C.R. 120 at p. 122, where this point is not taken.

[39] Remedies in estoppel cases are flexible, but specific performance could be granted; *Spiro v. Lintern* [1973] 1 W.L.R. 1002. See (1990) 10 L.S. 325 (L. Bentley and P. Coughlan).

[40] On specific performance of options and rights of pre-emption, see *Pritchard v. Briggs* [1980] Ch. 338; *Sudbrook Trading Estate Ltd v. Eggleton* [1983] 1 A.C. 444. See also *Berkley v. Poulett* (1976) 120 S.J. 836, *ante*, p. 314 (sub-purchaser).

[41] *Cf.* Heydon, Gummow and Austin, *Cases and Materials on Equity and Trusts* (4th ed.), p. 946, preferring the explanation that "the process of looking for, negotiating for and completing the purchase of land is a lengthy and irritating one; . . . so that it is better to get specific performance . . . rather than get damages and use them to buy something similar." See also Law Com. No. 238 (1996), para. 9.3, n. 5.

[42] *Sudbrook Trading Estate Ltd v. Eggleton, supra*, at p. 478.

[43] *Cogent v. Gibson* (1864) 33 Beav. 557.

[44] Supreme Court Act 1981, s.39; Trustee Act 1925, ss.44(vi), 50; A.E.A. 1925, s.43(2). For other remedies, see *ante*, p. 697.

the licence created no estate in the land.[45] This view has now been seen to be inconsistent with the court's power to grant an injunction to restrain the wrongful revocation of a contractual licence.[46] Thus in *Verrall v. Great Yarmouth Borough Council*[47] the Court of Appeal affirmed the grant of specific performance to enforce a contractual licence whereby the National Front was to occupy the defendant's premises for the purpose of its annual conference. The remedy of damages would be inadequate as the plaintiff could not find any other premises. Roskill L.J. held it to be the duty of the court "to protect, where it is appropriate to do so, any interest, whether it be an estate in land or a licence, by injunction or specific performance as the case may be."[48]

C. Contracts for the Sale of Personal Property

Chattels and stocks and shares do not usually possess such individual character as land. Most commercial contracts for the purchase of goods,[49] or for a loan of money,[50] or contracts for the purchase of government stock, will not be specifically performed.[51] But if stocks or shares cannot always be bought in the market, the court may order specific performance[52]; or where a chattel has especial value by reason of its individuality, beauty or rarity.[53] Indeed, in such situations, there is an ancient jurisdiction to order the specific recovery of such a chattel if wrongly detained.[54] Where specific performance of a contract to sell a house is granted, the remedy is also available in respect of a related contract to sell the chattels in it.[55]

---

[45] *Booker v. Palmer* [1942] 2 All E.R. 674 at p. 677, *per* Lord Greene M.R.

[46] *Winter Garden Theatre (London) Ltd v. Millenium Productions Ltd* [1948] A.C. 173.

[47] [1981] Q.B. 202; [1981] Conv. 212 (A. Briggs). See also *Tanner v. Tanner* [1975] 1 W.L.R. 1346 at p. 1350.

[48] [1981] Q.B. 202 at p. 220. But the remedy of damages was adequate in *Webster v. Newham London Borough Council, The Times,* November 22, 1980, where, on otherwise similar facts, another hall had been hired.

[49] *Dominion Coal Co. Ltd v. Dominion Iron and Steel Co. Ltd* [1909] A.C. 293; *Cohen v. Roche* [1927] 1 K.B. 169; *Société Des Industries Metallurgiques S.A. v. The Bronx Engineering Co. Ltd* [1975] 1 Lloyd's Rep. 465. See the examples given by Goff L.J. in *Price v. Strange* [1978] Ch. 337 at p. 359.

[50] *South African Territories Ltd v. Wallington* [1898] A.C. 309.

[51] *Cud (or Cuddee) v. Rutter* (1720) 1 P.Wms. 570 (South Sea Bubble Stock); *Mason v. Armitage* (1806) 13 Ves.Jr. 25. For other reasons against the grant of specific performance, see Treitel, *The Law of Contract* (9th ed.), pp. 919, 922.

[52] *Duncuft v. Albrecht* (1841) 12 Sim. 189; (1953) 51 Mich.L.R. 408 (A. Neef).

[53] *Falcke v. Gray* (1859) 4 Dr. 651; *Philips v. Lamdin* [1949] 2 K.B. 33.

[54] *Pusey v. Pusey* (1684) 1 Vern. 273 (an antique horn, supposedly given by King Canute); *Duke of Somerset v. Cookson* (1735) 3 P.Wms. 390 (an altar piece); *Fells v. Reed* (1796) 3 Ves.Jr. 70; (the tobacco box of a club).

[55] *Record v. Bell* [1991] 1 W.L.R. 853.

Further, the Sale of Goods Act 1979, s.52 (re-enacting a similar provision in the 1893 Act) enables the court to decree specific performance of a contract for the sale of specific or ascertained goods, either unconditionally, or upon such terms as to damages, payment of the price or otherwise as to the court may seem just. The power is discretionary, and it must still be shown that the remedy of damages is inadequate.[56] It was intended to broaden the scope of the remedy of specific performance in connection with the purchase of chattels, but less use has been made of it than might have been expected.[57] In *Cohen v. Roche*,[58] the plaintiff agreed to purchase from the defendants a set of eight Hepplewhite chairs. This was a contract for the sale of specific goods; but McCardie J., finding that the chairs were "ordinary articles of commerce and of no special value or interest," refused to order specific performance and awarded damages. In *Behnke v. Bede Shipping Co.*,[59] Wright J. made an order for specific performance of a contract for the sale of a ship, being satisfied that the ship was of "peculiar and practically unique value to the plaintiff."

The boldest exercise of jurisdiction was in *Sky Petroleum Ltd v. V.I.P. Petroleum Ltd.*[60]

A contract had been entered into whereby the plaintiff company would buy all the petrol needed for its garages from the defendant company, which would supply the plaintiff with all its requirements. The defendant, alleging breach, purported to terminate the contract in November 1973, at a time when petrol supplies were limited, so that the plaintiff would have little prospect of finding an alternative source. An interlocutory injunction was granted to restrain the withholding of supplies.

Goulding J. acknowledged that it amounted to specific performance, the matter being one of substance, and not of form; but held that the court had jurisdiction to order specific performance of a contract to sell chattels, although they were not specific or ascertained, where the remedy of damages was inadequate. The usual rule that specific performance was not available to enforce contracts for the sale of chattels was well established and salutary; but it was based on the adequacy of damages, and was therefore not applicable

---

[56] *C.N. Marine Inc. v. Stena Line A/B., The Times,* June 12, 1982.
[57] [1969] J.B.L. 211; *Société Des Industries Metallurgiques S.A. v. The Bronx Engineering Co. Ltd, supra.*
[58] [1927] 1 K.B. 169.
[59] [1927] 1 K.B. 649 at p. 661; *cf. Hart v. Herwig* (1873) L.R. 8 Ch.App. 680.
[60] [1974] 1 W.L.R. 576. See also *Howard E. Perry & Co. Ltd v. British Railways Board* [1980] 1 W.L.R. 1375; (1980) 39 C.L.J. 269 (J. Thornely).

to the present case, where the plaintiff company might be forced out of business if the remedy was not granted.

D. Contracts to Pay Money

Contracts to pay money are normally not specifically enforceable, because damages will usually be an adequate remedy. So, for example, specific performance of a contract of loan will not be awarded against the borrower, because the remedy of damages is adequate.[61] Exceptionally, however, specific performance may be obtainable in the following situations:

i. Where the contract is to pay money to a third party, so that any damages awarded would probably be nominal;[62]

ii. Where the contract is for the payment of an annuity[63] or other periodical sums. This exception is based on two grounds: first that specific performance avoids the inconvenience of a series of actions for damages every time payment is not made; and, secondly, even if substantial damages were available, it has been suggested that the common law remedy would still be inadequate as the amount in the case of an annuity would be conjectural.[64]

iii. A contract with a company to take up and pay for debentures.[65]

iv. A contract of indemnity, if, on its true construction, the obligation is to relieve a debtor by preventing him from having to pay his debt. Instead of compelling the debtor first to pay the debt and perhaps to ruin himself in doing so, equity will order the indemnifier to pay the debt. It will be otherwise if the obligation is merely to repay the debtor a sum of money after he has paid it. Damages will then be an adequate remedy.[66]

v. As has been seen, in the case of a contract for the sale of land, the vendor will be granted specific performance of the purchaser's obligation to make a money payment. Although the remedy of damages may be adequate, specific performance is allowed because of the mutuality principle.

---

[61] See *Locabail International Finance Ltd v. Agroexport* [1986] 1 W.L.R. 657 (no mandatory injunction).

[62] *Beswick v. Beswick* [1968] A.C. 58; *post*, p. 729; *Gurtner v. Circuit* [1968] 2 Q.B. 587; *Woodar Investment Development Ltd v. Wimpey Construction U.K. Ltd* [1980] 1 W.L.R. 227. It was held in *Jackson v. Horizon Holidays Ltd* [1975] 1 W.L.R. 1468 that where one party contracts for the benefit of himself and others, he may recover substantial damages for the loss suffered by the others, but this was disapproved by the House of Lords in the *Woodar Investment* case, *supra*, but reform of the privity rule is proposed in Law Com. No. 242 (1996).

[63] *Beswick v. Beswick, supra.*

[64] *Adderly v. Dixon* (1824) 1 Sim. & St. 607 at p. 611. But see *post*, p. 730.

[65] Companies Act 1985, s.195.

[66] *McIntosh v. Dalwood (No. 4)* (1930) 30 S.R.(N.S.W.) 415 at p. 418.

vi. A contract to pay a debt out of specific property segregated by the debtor for that purpose is specifically enforceable, and creates an equitable interest in the specific property, unless there is evidence of a contrary intention.[67]

E. Volunteers

Specific performance will not be awarded to a volunteer. Indeed, unless the contract is by deed, consideration is necessary for the validity of the contract itself. Parties to a deed of covenant may sue at law, even though there is no consideration, but they will not be able to obtain specific performance.[68] Problems commonly arise in this connection in relation to covenants to make family settlements.[69] Inadequacy of consideration is not a bar to specific performance, but may be relevant to the exercise of the court's discretion.[70]

But it is no objection, provided that the party seeking specific performance is not a volunteer, that the decree will have the direct consequence of benefiting a volunteer[71]; nor, in the case of the due exercise of an option to purchase land, that the option was granted for a token payment or for no payment at all.[72]

F. Contracts Requiring Supervision

i. The Principle. It is settled law that a court will not order specific performance where the decree would require constant supervision by the court.[73] The reason is that supervision would be impracticable. Equity does nothing in vain; and will not issue decrees which it cannot be certain to enforce. Of course, the issue of a decree supported by a threat of imprisonment would be effective in many cases; but imprisonment of the defendant for contempt, if he proves recalcitrant, will not get the duty performed.

---

[67] *Swiss Bank Corporation v. Lloyds Bank Ltd* [1982] A.C. 584 at p. 613 (*per* Lord Wilberforce); *Napier and Ettrick (Lord) v. Hunter* [1993] A.C. 713.

[68] See *Cannon v. Hartley* [1949] Ch. 213; *cf. Gurtner v. Circuit* [1968] 2 Q.B. 587.

[69] *Ante*, p. xxx.

[70] Spry, *Equitable Remedies*, p. 57, See *post*, p. 720.

[71] See *Beswick v. Beswick* [1968] A.C. 58, *post*, p. 729.

[72] *Mountford v. Scott* [1975] Ch. 258, affirming on different grounds the decision of Brightman J., *ibid.*; (1975) 39 Conv.(N.S.) 270 (F. Crane); *Midland Bank Trust Co. Ltd v. Green* [1980] Ch. 590 C.A.; [1979] Conv. 441 (F. Crane).

[73] *Ryan v. Mutual Tontine Westminster Chambers Association* [1893] 1 Ch. 116; *Blackett v. Bates* (1865) L.R. 1 Ch. App. 117 (maintenance of railway); *Joseph v. National Magazine Co.* [1959] Ch. 14; *Malcolm v. Chancellor, Masters and Scholars of the University of Oxford, The Times*, March 23, 1990 (publishing contracts); *Re C (A Minor)* [1991] 2 F.L.R. 168 (schooling).

Decrees for the specific performance of contracts to create to convey a legal estate in land do not meet with this difficulty. All that the defendants needs to do to perform such a contract is to execute the document; and, as has been seen, if he refuses, he may be threatened with imprisonment for contempt; and if he still refuses, the court may nominate any person to effect the conveyance.[74]

Modern decisions indicate a relaxation of the principle.[75] The real question is whether there is a sufficient definition of what has to be done in order to comply with the order of the court.[76]

In *Posner v. Scott-Lewis*[77] a lease contained a landlord's covenant to employ a resident porter, whose duties were to clean the common parts, to look after the heating and to carry rubbish to the dustbins. Specific performance of this covenant was granted, to procure the appointment of a porter. The earlier decision in *Ryan v. Mutual Tontine Westminster Chambers Association,*[78] where a decree had been refused, was difficult to distinguish, but the authority of that case had been weakened by later decisions.[79] The relevant questions were: (a) was there a sufficient definition of what had to be done? (b) would an unacceptable degree of superintendence be involved? (c) what would be the respective hardship to the parties if the order was made or refused? The answer to these questions supported a grant of specific performance; the remedy of damages was clearly inadequate.

Thus the court now seems ready to grant the remedy more freely, circumventing the older cases, and accepting the principle that specific performance should be decreed where it is the appropriate remedy. Thus in *Co-operative Insurance Society Ltd v. Argyll Stores (Holdings) Ltd*[80] specific performance was granted of a covenant in a lease of a supermarket (which was the focal point of a shopping centre) to keep open during the usual hours of business, even though the supermarket had been trading at a loss and the lease had nineteen years to run. Although the usual practice had been to grant only damages in such cases, that remedy was inadequate because the loss to the landlord, although substantial, would be difficult to quantify. Millett L.J. dissented, however, on the ground that the decree would

---

[74] *Ante,* p. 700.
[75] See Treitel (9th ed.), p. 931; Heydon, Gummow and Austin, *Cases and Materials on Equity and Trusts* (4th ed.), p. 968.
[76] *Tito v. Waddell (No. 2)* [1977] Ch. 106 at p. 322, *per* Megarry V-C; (1977) 41 Conv.(N.S.) 432 at p. 436 (F. Crane).
[77] [1987] Ch. 25; (1987) 46 C.L.J. 21 (G. Jones).
[78] [1893] 1 Ch. 116.
[79] *Giles (C.H.) & Co. Ltd v. Morris* [1972] 1 W.L.R. 307 at p. 318; *Shiloh Spinners Ltd v. Harding* [1973] A.C. 691 at p. 724; *Tito v. Waddell (No. 2)* [1977] Ch. 106 at p. 321.
[80] [1996] Ch. 286.

be oppressive to the defendant and would defeat the commercial expectations of the parties at the date of the covenant. Other modern illustrations include *Beswick v. Beswick*[81] where specific performance was ordered of a contract to make a regular payment to the plaintiff for life. In *Sky Petroleum Ltd v. V.I.P. Petroleum Ltd*[82] an interlocutory injunction, which was regarded as tantamount to specific performance, was granted to enforce the defendant's obligation to supply petrol regularly to the plaintiff. In the analogous sphere of mandatory injunctions the requirement of supervision has not been regarded as an unsurmountable obstacle.[83] Specific performance is more likely to be granted, in spite of supervision difficulties, against a defendant who has had some or all of the benefit to which he was entitled under the contract.[84]

ii. The Construction Cases. The court does not, as a rule, order specific performance of a contract to build or repair[85]; but there are certain exceptional cases. "The first [requirement] is that the building work, of which he seeks to enforce the performance, is defined by the contract; that is to say, that the particulars of the work are so far definitely ascertained that the court can sufficiently see what is the exact nature of the work of which it is asked to order the performance. The second is that the plaintiff has a substantial interest in having the contract performed, which is of such a nature that he cannot adequately be compensated for breach of the contract by damages. The third is that the defendant has by the contract obtained possession of land on which the work is contracted to be done."[86]

In *Wolverhampton Corporation v. Emmons*[87] a plot of land had been sold by the plaintiffs, an urban sanitary authority, in pursuance of a scheme of street improvement, to the defendant, who agreed to erect buildings thereon, and went into possession. A later agreement provided for the erection of the buildings in accordance with detailed plans. The Court of Appeal made a decree of specific performance.

This exception is said to be based on a "balance of convenience." Historically it originates in a series of cases relating to the early days

---

[81] [1968] A.C. 58; *post.*
[82] [1974] 1 W.L.R. 576.
[83] *Redland Bricks Ltd v. Morris* [1970] A.C. 652; *Gravesham Borough Council v. British Railways Board* [1978] Ch. 379, *post*, p. 770.
[84] *Tito v. Waddell (No. 2), supra* at p. 322.
[85] *Wheatley v. Westminster Brymbo Coal Co.* (1869), L.R. 9 Eq. 538; *Haywood v. Brunswick Building Society* (1881) 8 Q.B.D. 403.
[86] *Wolverhampton Corporation v. Emmons* [1901] 1 K.B. 515 at p. 525, *per* Romer L.J.; *Hounslow L.B.C. v. Twickenham Developments Ltd* [1971] Ch. 233.
[87] [1901] 1 K.B. 515. See also *Price v. Strange* [1978] Ch. 337 at p. 359.

of railways.[88] Where a railway was built through a farmer's land and the railway company undertook to provide a bridge or tunnel to connect the separated parts of the farmer's land, it would have been most unjust to leave the farmer to a remedy in damages. These specialised cases have been given more general application, and the formulation in *Wolverhampton Corporation v. Emmons*[89] was further extended in *Carpenters Estates v. Davies*,[90] where Farwell J. held that it was sufficient that the defendant was in possession of the land, whether he came in by the contract or not. After all, the defendant's possession is the material factor; for the plaintiff cannot then enter to perform the construction or repair work himself.

iii. Enforcement of Landlord's Covenants. The "construction contracts" exception was extended to cover a landlord's repairing covenant in *Jeune v. Queens Cross Properties Ltd*,[91] where a balcony which was not part of the demised premises fell into disrepair. The three conditions laid down in *Wolverhampton Corporation v. Emmons*[92] were satisfied, as the landlord was in possession of the balcony, and the work involved was specific. There was a clear breach, and no doubt as to what was required to be done to remedy it. A mandatory order was much more convenient than an award of damages, leaving it to the plaintiff to do the work. The decision was extended by statute, now Landlord and Tenant Act 1985, s.17, which provides that the court may order specific performance of a landlord's repairing covenant relating to any part of the premises in which the tenant's dwelling is comprised, notwithstanding any equitable rule restricting this remedy. Neither this section nor the decision in *Jeune v. Queens Cross Properties Ltd*[93] will assist a landlord to get specific performance of a tenant's repairing covenant,[94] although the Law Commission recommends otherwise.[95]

G. Contracts for Personal Services

It is well established that contracts which are personal in nature or which involve the performance of personal services will not be

---

[88] *Ryan v. Mutual Tontine Westminster Chambers Association* [1893] 1 Ch. 116 at p. 128.
[89] [1901] 1 K.B. 515.
[90] [1940] Ch. 160.
[91] [1974] Ch. 97; *Francis v. Cowcliff Ltd* (1977) 33 P. & C.R. 368; *Gordon v. Selico Ltd* [1985] 2 E.G.L.R. 79; *Hammond v. Allen* [1994] 1 All E.R. 307. If the matter is urgent, a mandatory interlocutory injunction may be granted; *Parker v. Camden London Borough Council* [1986] Ch. 162 (boiler strike threatened tenants' health).
[92] [1901] 1 K.B. 515.
[93] [1974] Ch. 97.
[94] Although a mandatory injunction was suggested as a possibility in *Sedac Investments Ltd v. Tanner* [1982] 1 W.L.R. 1342.
[95] Law Com. No. 238 (1996), *Landlord and Tenant: Responsibility for State and Condition of Property*, para. 9.32, applying to all types of tenancy.

specifically enforced.[96] In this respect, it is necessary to distinguish contracts of employment from other contracts for personal services. The former are governed by a firm prohibition against specific enforcement by Trade Union and Labour Relations (Consolidation) Act 1992, s.236, which provides that "no court shall . . . by way of an order for specific performance . . . compel an employee to do any work or to attend at any place for the doing of any work." A contract of employment is defined in section 295(1).[97] Not every contract for personal services constitutes a contract of employment; for it may be a contract between an employer and an independent contractor; in other words, it may be a "contract for service" and not a "contract of service."[98]

In cases of contracts not covered by the Act, or where enforcement is sought against an employer,[99] the equitable principle applies. The reasons traditionally given for the rule are first, that such contracts would require constant supervision, and would in practice be impossible to enforce; and secondly, that it is contrary to public policy to compel one person to submit to the orders of another. "The courts," said Fry L.J., "are bound to be jealous, lest they should turn contracts of service into contracts of slavery."[1] Nor, as we will see, can the rule be avoided by seeking an injunction instead of a decree of specific performance, where the injunction would in effect compel performance.[2] Megarry J. hoped that the court might look again at this "so-called rule." It was not based on these difficulties alone; but was rather a question of human nature. "If a singer contracts to sing, there could no doubt be proceedings for committal if, ordered to sing, the singer remained obstinately dumb. But if instead the singer sang flat, or sharp, or too fast, or too slowly, or too loudly, to too quietly, or resorted to a dozen of the manifestations of temperament traditionally associated with some singers, the threat of committal would reveal itself as a most unsatisfactory weapon, for who could say whether the imperfections of performance were natural or self induced? To make an order with such possibilities of evasion would be vain, and so the order will not be made . . . the matter is one of balance and advantage and disadvantage in relation to the particular obligations in question, and

---

[96] Fry, *Specific Performance*, pp. 50–51; *Lumley v. Wagner* (1852) 1 De G.M. & G. 604, *post*, p. 787; *Thomas Marshall (Exports) Ltd v. Guinle* [1979] Ch. 227; *Provident Financial Group plc. v. Haywood* [1989] 3 All E.R. 298 at 302. See (1984) 4 L. S. 102 at pp. 112–114 (A. Burrows).

[97] "Contract of employment" means "a contract of service or of apprenticeship."

[98] See *Massey v. Crown Life Insurance Co.* [1978] 1 W.L.R. 676.

[99] If an employee is unfairly dismissed the Employment Rights Act 1996, ss.114, 115 empower an industrial tribunal to order reinstatement or re-engagement. But if the order is not complied with the sanction is an award of compensation; s.117.

[1] *De Francesco v. Barnum* (1890) 45 Ch.D. 430; *post*, p. 787.

[2] *Post*, p. 788.

the fact that the balance will usually lie on one side does not turn this probability into a rule."[3]

In *Giles (C.H.) & Co. Ltd v. Morris*,[4] a distinction was drawn between the performance of a contract of service and the execution of such a contract which provided for the plaintiff to be appointed managing director of a company for a period of five years. As we have seen, this approach was also adopted in *Posner v. Scott-Lewis*,[5] where specific performance was granted of a covenant in a lease to appoint a resident porter. Nor should it be assumed that as soon as any element of personal service or continuous services can be discerned in a contract, the court will always refuse an order. In *Beswick v. Beswick*,[6] Lord Upjohn said that a small element of personal services in a contract did not warrant the refusal of specific performance on the ground of want of mutuality.

In *Hill v. C.A. Parsons & Co. Ltd*[7]

The plaintiff was a senior engineer in the employment of the defendant. In May 1970 a trade union successfully introduced a closed shop, under which it became a term of employment that all the defendant's employees were to be members of the union. The plaintiff refused, and received a month's notice of dismissal. He obtained an interlocutory injunction restraining the termination. The circumstances were special, in that the notice was short; a reasonable notice would probably have given him protection under the Industrial Relations Act 1971; and the employee and employer retained their mutual confidence.

Lord Denning M.R. said[8]: "It may be said that, by granting an injunction in such a case, the court is indirectly enforcing specifically a contract for personal services. So be it. Lord St. Leonards L.C. did something like it in *Lumley v. Wagner*.[9] And I see no reason why we should not do it here." But Stamp L.J., dissenting, felt that the rule against specific performance of service contracts, while not without exceptions, was deeply embedded in the law.

---

[3] [1972] 1 W.L.R. 307 at p. 318. This passage was approved by Goff L.J. in *Price v. Strange* [1978] Ch. 337 at p. 359; *cf.* Buckley L.J., *ibid.* at p. 369. But the House of Lords in *Scandinavian Trading Tanker Co. A/B v. Flota Petrolera Ecuatoriana* [1983] 2 A.C. 694, concerning a time charter, took the view that there was no jurisdiction to grant specific performance of a service contract.

[4] [1972] 1 W.L.R. 307.

[5] [1987] Ch. 25; (1987) 46 C.L.J. 21 (G. Jones); *ante*, p. 705.

[6] [1968] A.C. 58 at p. 97.

[7] [1972] Ch. 305; *cf. Chappell v. Times Newspaper Ltd* [1975] 1 W.L.R. 482, where the employer "had every reason to suspect the plaintiff's loyalty"; *Wishart v. National Association of Citizens Advice Bureaux Ltd* [1990] I.C.R. 794. It seems that injunctions of the kind granted in *Hill v. Parsons* are no longer rare; see *Powell v. London Borough of Brent* [1987] I.R.L.R. 466, *Hughes v. London Borough of Southwark* [1988] I.R.L.R. 55, *post*, p. 790.

[8] *Ibid.* at p. 315.

[9] (1852) 1 De G.M. & G. 604; *post*, p. 787.

The rule, he said, was a salutary one, which benefited the employer and employee equally.[10]

H. Contracts for the Creation of Transient or Terminable Interests

As equity does not act in vain, specific performance will not be granted of an agreement for a lease which has already expired by the date of the hearing,[11] nor of an agreement for a tenancy at will or a partnership at will.[12]

An agreement for a tenancy from year to year is specifically enforceable,[13] but in *Lavery v. Pursell*[14] specific performance of an agreement for a lease for one year was refused, one ground being that, although rights should not be prejudiced by delays in litigation, it was normally impossible to get the action heard and the decree made within the year.

But the nineteenth century authorities on transient interests must now be treated with caution.

In *Verrall v. Great Yarmouth Borough Council*[15] the defendant council had granted a contractual licence to the National Front to occupy its premises for two days (on a date which had not yet occurred) for an annual conference. The defendant wrongfully repudiated the contract, but sought to avoid specific performance on the ground, *inter alia*, that the licence was a transient interest. This argument was rejected by the Court of Appeal. It was held that there was no reason why the court could not order specific performance of a contractual licence of short duration. Authorities to the contrary were inconsistent with the decision of the House of Lords in *Winter Garden Theatre (London) Ltd v. Millennium Productions Ltd*,[16] whereby an injunction could be granted to restrain the wrongful revocation of the licence. "In my judgment the old view, such as it was, that courts of equity would not

---

[10] [1972] Ch. 305 at p. 324.
[11] *Turner v. Clowes* (1869) 20 L.T. 214. But the doctrine of *Walsh v. Lonsdale* (1882) 21 Ch.D. 9, *ante*, p. 15, will govern the rights and obligations of the parties if specific performance of a contract for a lease would have been available during its currency, even though it has terminated by the date of the hearing: *Industrial Properties (Barton Hill) Ltd v. Associated Electrical Industries Ltd* [1977] Q.B. 580; *cf.* (1977) 40 M.L.R. 718 at p. 720 (P. Jackson). See also *Tottenham Hotspur Football and Athletic Co. v. Princegrove Publishers* [1974] 1 W.L.R. 113; (1974) 90 L.Q.R. 149 (M. Albery).
[12] *Hercy v. Birch* (1804) 9 Ves. 357. Even if not merely at will, a partnership agreement involves the difficulty of supervision; *ante*, p. 704.
[13] *Manchester Brewery Co. Ltd v. Coombs* [1901] 2 Ch. 608.
[14] (1888) 39 Ch.D. 508 at p. 519. See also *Gilbey v. Cossey* [1911–13] All E.R. 644 at p. 645.
[15] [1981] Q.B. 202, *ante*, p. 701.
[16] [1948] A.C. 173.

protect a so-called transient interest can no longer be supported, at any rate to its full extent."[17]

Thus while specific performance remains inappropriate in respect of an interest which has already expired or which is revocable at the will of the defendant, the mere fact that the interest is of short duration is no longer a bar to specific performance, which may be granted at the discretion of the court in an appropriate case.

I. Contracts to Leave Property by Will[18]

The remedy for breach of such a contract is normally damages, for any other result would amount to interference with testamentary freedom.[19] But specific performance might be decreed, as was indicated *obiter* by the Court of Appeal in *Synge v. Synge*,[20] where the contract is in consideration of marriage, and the marriage takes place on the faith of it. The court has power to order a conveyance of a defined piece of real property after the death of the contracting party, against those who have acquired it as volunteers. While the court could not order the defendant to make a will in any particular terms,[21] it could order the executor or devisee to convey to the plaintiff.

In *Schaefer v. Schuhmann*[22] Lord Cross treated it as established that where there is a contract to leave specific property by will, the plaintiff "can obtain a declaration of his right to have it left to him by will and an injunction to restrain the testator from disposing of it in breach of contract: *Synge v. Synge*.[23] No doubt if the property is land he could also register the contract or a caution against the title."[24] If the testator retains the property until his death, but dies insolvent, the promisee can only rank as a creditor for value in competition with other such creditors.[25]

Finally, it seems that specific performance will not be granted of a contract by the donee of a testamentary power of appointment to exercise the power in favour of the plaintiff.[26]

---

[17] [1981] Q.B. 202 at p. 220 (*per* Roskill L.J.). See also the comments of Lord Denning M.R. at p. 215.

[18] See (1971) 87 L.Q.R. 358 (W. Lee); A.R. Mellows, *The Law of Succession* (5th ed.); Chap. 3.

[19] *Ante*, p. 307.

[20] [1894] 1 Q.B. 466. See also *Wakeham v. Mackenzie* [1968] 1 W.L.R. 1175.

[21] *Re Dale (deceased)* [1994] Ch. 31 (mutual wills); *ante*, p. 307.

[22] [1972] A.C. 572 (P.C.): see also Inheritance (Provision for Family and Dependants) Act 1975, s.11; Law Com. No. 61 (1974), paras. 222–242.

[23] [1894] 1 Q.B. 466.

[24] [1972] A.C. 572 at p. 586. If the contract relates to land, it must be writing, in order to satisfy s.2 of the Law of Property (Miscellaneous Provisions) Act 1989.

[25] [1972] A.C. 572. See also *Beyfus v. Lawley* [1903] A.C. 411.

[26] *Re Parkin* [1892] 3 Ch. 510. The proper remedy is damages. See also *Robinson v. Ommanney* (1883) 23 Ch.D. 285.

J. Contracts to Transfer Goodwill

A contract to sell the goodwill of a business alone is not specifically enforceable, because the subject-matter of the contract is too uncertain.[27] But specific performance will be granted of a contract to transfer the goodwill together with the premises or other assets of a business.[28]

K. Contracts to Refer to Arbitration

Such a contract is not specifically enforceable.[29] But if the plaintiff sues on a contract which includes an arbitration provision, the defendant may ask for a stay of proceedings under Arbitration Act 1996, s.9 so that the plaintiff must proceed with the arbitration or be left with no remedy.[30] The court will, however enforce the arbitrator's award.[31]

L. No Specific Performance of Part of a Contract[32]

A court will not usually decree specific performance of any part of a contract unless it can decree performance of the whole. In *Ogden v. Fossick*,[33] an agreement between the parties provided that the defendant would grant to the plaintiff a lease of a coal wharf, and that the defendant should be appointed manager of the wharf. In a suit for specific performance of the agreement to grant the lease, specific performance was denied on the ground that the part of the agreement which the court could enforce was inseparably connected with the contract of employment which it would not.

But the rule is not absolute.[34] It may be possible to construe a contract which contains several parts as being in effect several separate and distinct contracts, so that the enforcement of one part is independent of the others.[35] This question often arises where

---

[27] *Darbey v. Whitaker* (1857) 4 Drew. 134.

[28] *Ibid.* at p. 140. And see *Beswick v. Beswick* [1968] A.C. 58; *post*, p. 730.

[29] *Doleman & Sons v. Ossett Corporation* [1912] 3 K.B. 257 at p. 268.

[30] See also s.86. As to the court's jurisdiction to intervene by way of injunction, see *post*, p. 804.

[31] *Wood v. Griffith* (1818) 1 Swans. 43. See also *Sudbrook Trading Estate Ltd v. Eggleton* [1983] 1 A.C. 444, as to the possibility of specific performance of a contract to appoint a valuer or arbitrator to fix the price in an option to renew a lease.

[32] Fry, *op. cit.*, Chap. 16. Compare the doctrine of partial performance; *Thames Guaranty Ltd v. Campbell* [1985] Q.B. 210.

[33] (1862) 4 De G.F. & J. 426.

[34] *Beswick v. Beswick* [1968] A.C. 58; *C.H. Giles & Co. Ltd v. Morris* [1972] 1 W.L.R. 307 at pp. 317–318; *Astro Exito Navegacion S.A. v. Southland Enterprise Co. Ltd (No. 2)* [1983] 2 A.C. 787.

[35] *Wilkinson v. Clements* (1872) L.R. 8 Ch. App. 96, *post*, p. 714. But specific performance of the one contract will not be granted if the plaintiff is in breach of his obligations in the other contract which are material to the transaction as a whole; *National & Provincial Building Society v. British Waterways Board* [1992] E.G.C.S. 149.

several lots of land are sold and the question is whether there is one sale of several lots,[36] or several sales of individual lots.[37]

4. MUTUALITY

A. Refusal of Specific Performance for Lack of Mutuality[38]

It has been seen that where equity will decree specific perform-ance in favour of a purchaser or lessee, the remedy will be available also in favour of the vendor or lessor.[39] Such a person can compel the other party to take the property or to accept a lease even though in many cases an award of damages would be adequate compensa-tion for his loss. He can obtain specific performance under a princi-ple of mutuality.

A similar principle applies to deny specific performance, on grounds of lack of mutuality, where the situation is one in which that remedy could not be available to the other party.[40] "It is not dis-puted," said Leach M.R., "that it is a general principle of courts of equity to interpose only where the remedy is mutual."[41] Thus one party is not compelled specifically to perform his obligation if he would himself be left with only a remedy in damages. In *Flight v. Bolland*,[42] a minor failed to obtain a decree of specific performance because a suit for specific performance could not be maintained against him.[43] Nor can a person whose own obligation is to perform personal services obtain a decree, for no decree could be obtained against him.[44]

There is, however, a statutory exception to the mutuality principle in the Landlord and Tenant Act 1985, s.17, which allows a court to order specific performance of a landlord's repairing covenant, not-withstanding any equitable rule restricting this remedy, "whether based on mutuality or otherwise."[45] It might be added that the plaintiff may be able to overcome the absence of mutuality by waiving the benefit of a term,[46] or submitting to perform an obliga-tion, which could not be specifically enforced against him.[47]

---

[36] *Roffey v. Shallcross* (1819) 4 Madd. 227.

[37] *Lewin v. Guest* (1826) 1 Russ. 325.

[38] See Spry, *Equitable Remedies*, pp. 7–12, 89–101.

[39] *Ante*, p. 700.

[40] This defence based on lack of mutuality may be waived by the conduct of the defendant: *Price v. Strange* [1978] Ch. 337.

[41] (1828) 4 Russ. 298 at p. 301.

[42] (1828) 4 Russ. 298.

[43] *Lumley v. Ravenscroft* [1895] 1 Q.B. 683.

[44] *Pickering v. Bishop of Ely* (1843) 2 Y. & C. Ch. 249; *Ogden v. Fossick* (1862) 4 De G.F. & J. 426; *ante*, p. 707.

[45] *Ante*, p. 707.

[46] *Heron Garage Properties Ltd v. Moss* [1974] 1 W.L.R. 148.

[47] *Scott v. Bradley* [1971] Ch. 850; (1951) 67 L.Q.R. 300 (R.E.M.)

Finally, the mutuality principle goes only to discretion, not to jurisdiction. Thus the absence of mutuality does not deprive the court of jurisdiction to award damages in lieu of specific performance under Lord Cairns' Act 1858.[48]

B. The Time at which the Remedy must be Mutual

Must the requirement of mutuality be satisfied at the date of the contract, or will it suffice that the remedy has become mutually available by some later date, such as the date of the hearing? This question has been the source of much academic disagreement. Fry's proposition was that, subject to certain exceptions, the contract must be mutual when entered into.[49] Ames, on the other hand, considered that "Equity will not compel specific performance by a defendant if, after performance, the common law remedy of damages would be his sole security for the performance of the plaintiff's side of the contract."[50]

The courts, it must be said, had never applied a principle as rigid as that propounded by Fry. It was laid down in *Hoggart v. Scott*[51] that a vendor may obtain specific performance if he can show a good title at the time of the hearing, even though he had none when the contract was made. We saw that there could be no specific performance of a contract where the obligation of one party was the performance of services. It was held, however, in *Wilkinson v. Clements*[52] that if the plaintiff has already performed the services, he may enforce the contract.

The formulation of Ames has been adopted by the Court of Appeal in preference to Fry's rule.

In *Price v. Strange*[53] D contracted to grant an underlease of a flat to P, and the agreement contained an undertaking by P to execute internal and external repairs. P did the internal repairs, and was ready and willing to complete the external; but D repudiated the contract, and did the external repairs herself. P sued for

---

[48] *Price v. Strange* [1978] Ch. 337. For Lord Cairns' Act, see *post*, p. 724.

[49] Fry, *Specific Performance*, p. 219.

[50] Ames, *Lectures in Legal History*, p. 370.

[51] (1830) 1 Russ. & M. 293; *Joseph v. National Magazine Co. Ltd* [1959] Ch. 14 (a case of personal property); *Price v. Strange* [1978] Ch. 337 at pp. 355 and 364. See (1977) 41 Conv.(N.S.) 18 (C. Emery).

[52] (1872) L.R. 8 Ch.App. 96. If the plaintiff has not performed all the obligations, justice can be done by granting specific performance on terms of a monetary readjustment. See also *Wakeham v. Mackenzie* [1968] 1 W.L.R. 1175.

[53] [1978] Ch. 337; (1978) 128 N.L.J. 569 (F. Glover); applied in *Sutton v. Sutton* [1984] Ch. 184 (wife agreed to consent to divorce and not to seek maintenance in return for a transfer of the home. Husband could not have enforced her promises, but once she had performed an appreciable part by giving formal consent to the petition, he could not rely on absence of mutuality).

specific performance of the contract to grant the underlease. D claimed that P was not entitled to specific performance because, relying on Fry's rule, there was no mutuality at the date of the contract: P's repair obligations were not specifically enforceable. It was held that Fry's rule was wrong; the time for considering mutuality was the date of the trial. If by that time those obligations which were not specifically enforceable had been performed, P could obtain specific performance.

Buckley L.J. said "I can discover nothing in principle to recommend the Fry proposition, and authority seems to me to be strongly against it. Accordingly in my judgment it should be regarded as wrong. The time at which the mutual availability of specific performance and its importance must be considered is, in my opinion, the time of judgment, and the principle to be applied can I think be stated simply as follows: the court will not compel a defendant to perform his obligations specifically if it cannot at the same time ensure that any unperformed obligations of the plaintiff will be specifically performed, unless, perhaps, damages would be an adequate remedy to the defendant for any default on the plaintiff's part."[54] Specific performance was, accordingly, granted on terms that P should pay compensation to D for the cost of the repairs done by D.

5. Defences to Specific Performance[55]

The situations discussed below are those in which the discretion of the court is unlikely to be exercised in favour of specific performance, although the contract is of a type to which the remedy is appropriate. Most of the illustrations relate to land, for, as we have seen, few contracts outside this area are specifically enforceable. It will be noted that, in some of the circumstances discussed below, such as hardship or delay, the contract is unaffected, and the defendant remains liable in damages; the plaintiff is merely denied specific performance. In others, as in some cases of mistake and misrepresentation, the contract may be rescinded in equity, which is of course a defence to specific performance, and which may or may not affect the parties' rights at law.[56] In cases of substantial misdescription or lack of good title, the vendor may be in breach; not

[54] [1978] Ch. 337 pp. 367–378.
[55] See also *BICC v. Burndy Corp.* [1985] Ch. 232; (1985) 101 L.Q.R. 145; (1985) 44 C.L.J. 204 (C. Harpum); All E.R.Rev. 1985, p. 36 (N. Palmer); discussing set-off as a defence to specific performance.
[56] *Ante*, p. 31.

only is the vendor unable in such circumstances to obtain specific performance; he may be liable in damages to the purchaser.

A. Mistake and Misrepresentation

There are situations in which equity, although refusing to rescind a contract or cancel a deed for mistake or misrepresentation, will not give the other party positive equitable help in enforcing it. The plaintiff will be left to his remedy in damages.[57] The court is not bound to decree specific performance in every case in which it will not set aside the contract, nor to set aside every contract that it will not specifically enforce.[58]

A defendant cannot usually resist specific performance by alleging merely his own fault and mistake,[59] nor on the ground that he was mistaken as to the legal effect of the agreement,[60] although "unilateral mistake may, in some circumstances, afford an answer to a claim for specific performance."[61] Generally, equity will hold the defendant to enforcement of his bargain unless it can be shown that this would involve real hardship amounting to injustice.[62]

In *Webster v. Cecil*[63] A, by letter, offered to sell some property to B. He intended to offer it at £2,250 but by mistake wrote £1,250. B agreed to buy at £1,250. A immediately gave notice of the error and was not compelled to carry out the sale.

In *Tamplin v. James*[64] an inn was offered for sale, and was correctly described with reference to plans. At the rear of the inn was a piece of land, not belonging to the vendors, and so not included in the sale, which had commonly been occupied with the inn. The defendant knew the premises, but did not consult the plans, and he agreed to purchase in the belief that he was buying

---

[57] See *per* Lord Eldon in *Mortlock v. Buller* (1804) 10 Ves.Jr. 292.

[58] *e.g. Wood v. Scarth* (1855) 2 K. & J. 33 (in equity); 1 F. & F. 293 (at law).

[59] *Duke of Beaufort v. Neeld* (1845) 12 Cl. & F. 248 at p. 286.

[60] *Powell v. Smith* (1872) L.R. 14 Eq. 85; *Hart v. Hart* (1881) 18 Ch.D. 670.

[61] *Per* Brightman J. in *Mountford v. Scott* [1975] Ch. 258 at p. 261; *Malins v. Freeman* (1837) 2 Keen 25; *Riverlate Properties Ltd v. Paul* [1975] Ch. 133, *per* Russell L.J. at p. 140; *Watkin v. Watson-Smith, The Times,* July 3, 1986.

[62] *Van Praagh v. Everidge* [1902] 2 Ch. 266; reversed on another ground [1903] 1 Ch. 434. The type of mistake that renders a contract liable to be set aside in equity though not at law would also be a defence to specific performance. See *Solle v. Butcher* [1950] 1 K.B. 671; *Grist v. Bailey* [1967] Ch. 532; *post,* p. 822; *Laurence v. Lexcourt Holdings* [1978] 1 W.L.R. 1128; [1978] Conv. 380 (F. Crane); *post,* p. 824.

[63] (1861) 30 Beav. 62; *Day v. Wells* (1861) 30 Beav. 220; *cf. Hartog v. Colin and Shields* [1939] 3 All E.R. 566. See also *Watkin v. Watson-Smith, The Times,* July 13, 1986, *post,* p. 836 (no specific performance where elderly vendor offered bungalow for sale at £2,950 by mistake, intending £29,500. There was no contract).

[64] (1880) 15 Ch.D. 215; *cf. Denny v. Hancock* (1870) L.R. 6 Ch.App. 1, where specific performance was refused because the mistake was induced unintentionally by the plaintiff.

both the inn and the land at the rear. Specific performance was ordered against him.

A case that goes further, and perhaps too far, is *Malins v. Freeman*,[65] where an estate was purchased at an auction and the defendant bid under a mistake as to the lot put up for sale. Specific performance was refused although the mistake was due entirely to the defendant's fault and not in any way caused by the vendor; and the defendant waited until the auction was over before declaring the mistake.

Where the mistake is in the written record of the contract, the plaintiff may obtain rectification and specific performance in the same action.[66]

B. Conduct of the Plaintiff

A plaintiff must come to equity with clean hands.[67] Before specific performance can be decreed in his favour, he must show that he has performed all his own obligations under the contract,[68] or has tendered performance, or is ready and willing to perform them.[69] Thus a person holding under an agreement for a lease is not entitled to a decree of specific performance of the lease if he is himself in breach of one of its covenants.[70] Nor could a purchaser obtain specific performance if he had taken advantage of the illiteracy of a defendant who was not separately advised.[71] The conduct in question must be connected to the contract of which specific performance is sought.[72]

If both parties have "unclean hands," there is no question of balancing the misconduct of the one against that of the other. The "clean hands" defence is concerned with the conduct of the plaintiff

---

[65] (1837) 2 Keen 25.

[66] *Craddock Bros. v. Hunt* [1923] 2 Ch. 136.

[67] This doctrine cannot be ousted by the terms of the contract; *Quadrant Visual Communications Ltd v. Hutchison Telephone (UK) Ltd, The Times,* December 4, 1991.

[68] Except the most trivial ones; *Dyster v. Randall* [1926] Ch. 932 at pp. 942–943. See also *Cross v. Cross* (1982) 12 Fam. Law. 182; *Sport International Bussum B.V. v. Inter-Footwear Ltd* [1984] 1 W.L.R. 776; *National & Provincial Building Society v. British Waterways Board* [1992] E.G.C.S. 149.

[69] *Lamare v. Dixon* (1873) L.R. 6 H.L. 414; *Australian Hardwoods Pty. Ltd v. Railways Commissioner* [1961] 1 W.L.R. 425; *Cornish v. Brook Green Laundry* [1959] 1 Q.B. 391; *National & Provincial Building Society v. British Waterways Board, supra.* See also *Ailion v. Spiekermann* [1976] Ch. 158.

[70] *Walsh v. Lonsdale* (1882) 21 Ch.D. 9; *Coatsworth v. Johnson* (1886) 55 L.J.Q.B. 220.

[71] *Mountford v. Scott* [1975] Ch. 258.

[72] *van Gestel v. Cann, The Times,* August 7, 1987 (no defence where alleged fraudulent expenses claims not connected to contract).

alone, although all the circumstances, including the conduct of the defendant, are relevant to the exercise of the discretion.[73]

C. Laches or Delay

Generally, in equity, time is not held to be of the essence of a contract,[74] thus specific performance may be decreed although the contractual date for performance has passed. Failure to complete on the contractual date may, however, render the delaying party liable to damages for breach of contract. The fact that time is not of the essence in equity does not negative a breach of contract in such a case. It means that the breach does not amount to a repudiation of the contract. Thus the delaying party, although liable to damages, does not lose the right to seek specific performance, nor will he forfeit his deposit, provided he is ready to complete within a reasonable time.[75]

There is no statutory period of limitation barring claims to specific performance or to the refusal of relief on the ground of acquiescence,[76] but a plaintiff who delays unreasonably in bringing an action for specific performance may lose his claim.[77] There is no rule to lay down what is meant by unreasonable delay. One relevant factor is the subject-matter of the contract. If it has a speculative or fluctuating value, the principle of laches will be especially applicable.[78] It was once thought that the plaintiff must normally seek specific performance well within one year,[79] but it now seems that this approach may be too strict.

In *Lazard Bros. & Co. Ltd v. Fairfield Property Co. (Mayfair) Ltd*[80] a contract was entered into on March 12, 1975. The plaintiffs issued a writ for specific performance on May 14, 1977. In

---

[73] *Sang Lee Investment Co. Ltd v. Wing Kwai Investment Co. Ltd, The Times*, April 14, 1983. See also *Wilton Group plc v. Abrams, The Times*, February 23, 1990 (no specific performance of "commercially disreputable" agreement).

[74] This rule now applies also at law; L.P.A. 1925, s.41. (Time may be made of the essence in a contract for the sale of land by the service of a notice to complete.)

[75] *Raineri v. Miles* [1981] A.C. 1050; *Oakacre Ltd v. Claire Cleaners (Holdings) Ltd* [1982] Ch. 197; *Canning v. Temby* (1905) 3 C.L.R 419; *cf. United Scientific Holdings Ltd v. Burnley Borough Council* [1978] A.C. 904 (as to rent review clauses). See (1980) 96 L.Q.R. 481; (1981) 44 M.L.R. 100 (A. Samuels).

[76] Limitation Act 1980, s.36(1), (2).

[77] *Southcomb v. Bishop of Exeter* (1847) 6 H. 213; *Eads v. Williams* (1854) 4 De G.M. & G. 674; *M.E.P.C. Ltd v. Christian-Edwards* [1981] A.C. 205. Even a delay for which neither party is to blame may be a reason for leaving the purchaser to damages; *Patel v. Ali* [1984] Ch. 283, *post*, p. 720.

[78] *Mills v. Haywood* (1877) 6 Ch.D. 196.

[79] *Huxham v. Llewellyn* (1873) 21 W.R. 570 (delay of five months in the case of commercial premises prevented specific performance); *cf. Wroth v. Tyler* [1974] Ch. 30, Farrand, *Contract and Conveyance* (4th ed.), p. 216.

[80] (1977) 121 S.J. 793; [1978] Conv. 184.

ordering specific performance, Megarry V.-C. said that if specific performance was to be regarded as a prize, to be awarded by equity to the zealous and denied to the indolent, then the plaintiffs should fail. But whatever might have been the position over a century ago that was the wrong approach today. If between the plaintiff and defendant it was just that the plaintiff should obtain the remedy, the court ought not to withhold it merely because the plaintiff had been guilty of delay. There was no ground here on which delay could properly be said to be a bar to a decree of specific performance.

An exceptional case where delay will not be a bar is where the plaintiff has taken possession under the contract,[81] so that the purpose of specific performance is merely to vest the legal estate in him. In *Williams v. Greatrex*[82] a delay of 10 years in such circumstances did not bar specific performance. But a significant factor there was that the transaction creating the proprietary interest was not in issue. It is otherwise where the contract itself is disputed. In such a case the doctrine of laches does apply.[83]

Where the plaintiff has delayed, but specific performance is refused for another reason, the effect of his delay may be that the date for assessing damages in lieu of specific performance under Lord Cairns' Act is moved back from the date of judgment to the date upon which the matter might have been disposed of.[84]

The situation discussed above is where the delay has occurred before the plaintiff has sought specific performance. Where the plaintiff issues the writ for specific performance promptly but then delays in bringing the matter to trial, he may, in a clear case, be disentitled to the remedy.[85] Where the plaintiff obtains a decree for specific performance but then delays in enforcing it for a long period, leave to enforce it[86] will be refused only if there is an insufficient explanation and detriment to the defendant. Thus, in *Easton v. Brown*,[87] a delay of eight years in seeking to enforce the decree was no bar where the defendant's former wife and children had remained in occupation and the plaintiff had been legally

---

[81] It is otherwise if possession has been taken other than pursuant to the contract: *Mills v. Haywood, supra.*

[82] [1957] 1 W.L.R. 31.

[83] *Joyce v. Joyce* [1979] 1 W.L.R. 1170.

[84] *Malhotra v. Choudhury* [1980] Ch. 52.

[85] *Du Sautoy v. Symes* [1967] Ch. 1146 at p. 1168. *Towli v. Fourth River Property Co. Ltd, The Times,* November 24, 1976 (delay of nine years between writ and hearing) was such a clear case. See also *Lamshed v. Lamshed* (1963) 109 C.L.R. 440 (specific performance refused where delay of over five years between commencement of action and setting down for trial); *Ridgeway Motors (Isleworth) Ltd v. Charles* [1996] E.G.C.S. 105.

[86] See R.S.C. Ord. 44, r. 2(1).

[87] [1981] 3 All E.R. 278. The plaintiff also obtained an order for inquiry as to damages arising from the defendant's failure to complete.

advised that it would be difficult to remove them. The plaintiff had an explanation for the delay and had acted reasonably; detriment to the defendant was not on its own a ground for refusing leave to enforce the order.

Finally, in cases where time is of the essence, specific performance is not normally available after the stipulated date. It has been held in Australia, however, that the court may, in the exercise of its equitable jurisdiction to relieve against forfeiture, grant specific performance to prevent the "forfeiture" of the purchaser's equitable interest under the contract.[88] The Privy Council has rejected the Australian approach, although leaving open the possibility of relief based on restitution or estoppel if injustice would otherwise result.[89]

D. Hardship

In general, specific performance may be refused in the discretion of the court where a decree would cause unnecessary hardship to either of the parties,[90] or to a third party.[91] Inadequacy of price is not, standing by itself, a ground for refusing specific performance; but it may be evidence of other factors, such as fraud[92] or undue influence,[93] which would render enforcement inequitable.

These matters arose in *Patel v. Ali*,[94] where the vendor and her husband were co-owners of a house which they contracted to sell in 1979. The husband's bankruptcy caused a long delay in completion, for which neither the vendor nor the purchaser was to blame. After the contract the vendor had a leg amputated. She later gave birth to her second and third children. The purchaser obtained an order for specific performance, against which the vendor appealed on the ground of hardship. She spoke little English, and relied on help from

---

[88] *Legione v. Hateley* (1983) 57 A.L.J.R. 292; (1983) 99 L.Q.R. 490.

[89] *Union Eagle Ltd v. Golden Achievements Ltd* [1997] 2 W.L.R. 341, applying *Steedman v. Drinkle* [1916] 1 A.C. 275.

[90] *Denne v. Light* (1857) 8 De G.M. & G. 774; *Warmington v. Miller* [1973] Q.B. 877 (no specific performance of contract to sublet if result would be to expose tenant to liability for breach of covenant against subletting); *Mountford v. Scott* [1975] Ch. 258; *Francis v. Cowcliff Ltd* (1977) 33 P. & C.R. 368; *Shell U.K. Ltd v. Lostock Garage Ltd* [1976] 1 W.L.R. 1187 at p. 1202; *Cross v. Cross* (1982) 12 Fam. Law. 182. For further details, see Fry, *Specific Performance*, Chap. 16; Spry, *Equitable Remedies*, pp. 193 *et seq.*

[91] *Earl of Sefton v. Tophams Ltd* [1966] Ch. 1140; *Sullivan v. Henderson* [1973] 1 W.L.R. 333; *Watts v. Spence* [1976] Ch. 165; *Cedar Holdings Ltd v. Green* [1981] Ch. 129 at p. 147; [1979] Conv. 372 (F. Crane); (1979) 38 C.L.J. 215 (M. Prichard). This case was disapproved on another point in *Williams and Glyn's Bank Ltd v. Boland* [1981] A.C. 487 at p. 507. See also *Thames Guaranty Ltd v. Campbell* [1985] Q.B. 210; *cf. Patel v. Ali* [1984] Ch. 283, *infra*, (interests of vendor's children in their own right not material, but relevant to hardship of vendor).

[92] *Coles v. Trecothick* (1804) 9 Ves.Jr. 234 at p. 246; *Callaghan v. Callaghan* (1841) 8 Cl. & F. 374.

[93] *Fry v. Lane* (1888) 40 Ch.D. 312 (sale set aside).

[94] [1984] Ch. 283; (1984) 100 L.Q.R. 337. There was evidence that the Muslim community would pay the damages.

nearby friends and relatives, hence it would be a hardship to leave the house and move away. Goulding J. held that the court in a proper case could refuse specific performance on the ground of hardship subsequent to the contract, even if not caused by the plaintiff and not related to the subject-matter. On the facts, there would be hardship amounting to injustice, therefore the appropriate remedy was damages.

E. Misdescription of Subject-Matter

i. Specific Performance Subject to Compensation.[95] If the property agreed to be sold is incorrectly described in the contract, the vendor cannot fulfil his promise to transfer property which corresponds exactly with that which he contracted to convey. A frequent instance is an inaccurate measurement in the plan.[96] A misdescription is a term of the contract; the vendor is therefore in breach. To deny him specific performance on that account would introduce a rigid rule capable of producing injustice. Equity adopts a more flexible approach; the circumstances may be such that justice will be done by compelling completion, notwithstanding the error, compensating the purchaser by allowing him a reduction in the price he had agreed to pay ("abatement").[97] This course will not be followed if it would prejudice the rights of a third party interested in the estate.[98] On the other hand the misdescription may be so serious that to decree specific performance would be in effect to force the purchaser to take something wholly different from what he intended.[99] If so, the only way of achieving justice may be to permit the purchaser to rescind; or to refuse to grant specific performance to the vendor.[1]

---

[95] See (1981) 40 C.L.J. 47 (C. Harpum), taking the view that this should not be distinguished from specific performance with damages under Lord Cairns' Act, *post*, p. 724.

[96] See, *e.g. Watson v. Burton* [1957] 1 W.L.R. 19; *Topfell Ltd v. Galley Properties Ltd* [1979] 1 W.L.R. 446 (inability to give vacant possession); [1979] Conv. 375 (F. Crane).

[97] If the misdescription goes against the vendor, he cannot increase the price: *Re Lindsay and Forder's Contract* (1895) 72 L.T. 832. (But specific performance might be refused on the ground of hardship, *ante*, p. 720.) See also *Seven Seas Properties Ltd v. Al-Essa* [1988] 1 W.L.R. 1272.

[98] *Cedar Holdings Ltd v. Green* [1981] Ch. 129.

[99] See *Cedar Holdings Ltd v. Green, supra.* (Specific performance with abatement not appropriate where vendor's interest merely a co-ownership share).

[1] Misdescription must be distinguished from non-disclosure. A vendor is under a duty to disclose latent defects in title; but not physical defects, where the doctrine of *caveat emptor* applies. Thus, in the case of latent physical defects, the purchaser can only resist specific performance if there has been a misdescription or misrepresentation; see *Re Puckett and Smith's Contract* [1902] 2 Ch. 258; Farrand, *Contract and Conveyance* (4th ed.), p. 67. The defence of hardship might perhaps apply. The *caveat emptor* doctrine has recently been reviewed; *Let the Buyer be Well Informed*, Conveyancing Standing Committee of the Law Commission (1990).

ii. Refusal of Specific Performance. The rule is thus that a purchaser will not be forced to take something which is *different in substance* from that which he agreed to buy.[2] Differences of quality or quantity will not *by themselves* suffice as a defence to an action for specific performance (although of course they will give rise to a claim for compensation) unless they can fairly be said to make the property, as it in fact is, different in substance from that contracted to be sold.[3] A misdescription is substantial for this purpose if it so far affects "the subject-matter of the contract that it may be reasonably supposed, that, but for such misdescription, the purchaser might never have entered into the contract at all."[4] This will always be a question of fact in each case: obviously A, who has contracted to sell Blackacre to B, cannot force him to take Whiteacre, even if Whiteacre is larger, more valuable, and better suited to B's purposes. It is often difficult to say whether a misdescription of the area of land involves a difference of substance or of quantity; the rule is "easy to be understood, though often difficult of application."[5] However, although the vendor cannot compel a purchaser to take something different from that contracted to be sold, it is only just to give the purchaser the option of insisting on completion, and being paid compensation[6] for what he has lost. If it were not so, a person in default could in effect take advantage of his own wrong. Thus the purchaser has a choice: he may elect to take the property,[7] notwithstanding that it may be substantially different from the contract description.

iii. Conditions of Sale. The above is true of "open" contracts, but the parties are free to make their own conditions to regulate what is to happen if there is a misdescription. In the case of contracts for the sale of land, most contracts prepared by a solicitor will now be made subject to the Standard Conditions of Sale. In every case, therefore, the first question must be: what does the contract provide? But even then caution is necessary, since the courts have been

---

[2] *Flight v. Booth* (1834) 1 Bing.N.C. 370; *Re Puckett and Smith's Contract* [1902] 2 Ch. 258; *Watson v. Burton* [1957] 1 W.L.R. 19.

[3] If a vendor contracts to sell a lease of Blackacre, a purchaser cannor be compelled to take an underlease; *Madeley v. Booth* (1845) 2 De G & Sm. 718; nor if he contracts to sell a "registered freehold property," can he compel the purchaser to take a possessory (as distinct from *absolute*) freehold title; *Re Brine and Davies' Contract* [1935] Ch. 388.

[4] *Per* Tindal C.J. in *Flight v. Booth* (1834) 1 Bing.N.C. 370 at p. 377.

[5] *Per* Lord Esher M.R. in *Re Fawcett and Holmes' Contract* (1889) 42 Ch.D. 150 at p. 156; *cf. Watson v. Burton* [1957] 1 W.L.R. 19.

[6] *Mortlock v. Buller* (1804) 10 Ves.Jr. 292 at p. 316. The compensation must generally be claimed before completion; *Joliffe v. Baker* (1883) 11 Q.B.D. 255.

[7] In the absence of special circumstances, *e.g.* if he was himself aware of the misdescription at the date of the contract; *Castle v. Wilkinson* (1870) L.R. 5 Ch. 534. See [1978] Conv. 338 at p. 340 (C. Emery).

reluctant to permit either party to contract out of the rights conferred on him by equity.[8]

iv. Want of Good Title. The court will not force a doubtful title on a purchaser. The phrase "defect in title" is loosely used in some of the cases to indicate that the vendor, through some material error in description, fails in effect to convey to the purchaser the property he intended to buy. In other cases the expression may be used in a more literal sense; where, for example, the vendor's land is burdened with restrictive covenants.[9] Yet there are other cases where there is not merely a defect in the vendor's title, but no title at all. Clearly the purchaser cannot be compelled to take a bad title, nor be allowed to refuse a good one. Between the good and the bad is an infinite variety of doubtful titles, and the question inevitably arises of drawing a line between those titles which a purchaser will, and those which he will not, be compelled to accept. The test is whether there is likely to be litigation.[10] If the doubt is one of law, the court will normally resolve it.[11] If the doubt is one of fact, it is the court's duty, unless there are exceptional circumstances, to decide the question of title as between the vendor and purchaser. If the circumstances are such that the court concludes that the purchaser will not be at risk of a successful assertion against him of an incumbrance, then the court should declare in favour of a good title, and should not be deterred by the mere possibility of future litigation by a claimant to an incumbrance who is not bound by the declaration.[12] But if good title is not shown, the purchaser will be entitled to rescind, unless the vendor removes the doubt. The court will not compel a party to purchase a law suit.[13]

F. Public Policy

The court will not decree specific performance of a contract where the result would be contrary to public policy.

---

[8] See *Topfell Ltd v. Galley Properties Ltd* [1979] 1 W.L.R. 446; [1979] Conv. 375 (F. Crane); *Rignall Developments Ltd v. Halil* [1988] Ch. 190. Conditions of sale are subject to the Unfair Contract Terms Act 1977; *Walker v. Boyle* [1982] 1 W.L.R. 495.

[9] *Re Nisbet and Potts' Contract* [1906] 1 Ch. 386; *Faruqui v. English Real Estates Ltd* [1979] 1 W.L.R. 963; [1979] Conv. 444 (F. Crane). See generally [1978] Conv. 338 (C. Emery).

[10] A vendor and purchaser summons to establish whether the title is good is not litigation for this purpose: *M.E.P.C. Ltd v. Christian-Edwards* [1978] Ch. 281, C.A.

[11] *Wilson v. Thomas* [1958] 1 W.L.R. 422.

[12] *M.E.P.C. Ltd v. Christian-Edwards* [1981] A.C. 205 (doubt as to abandonment of 1912 contract: good title established). See also *Re Handman and Wilcox's Contract* [1902] 1 Ch. 599; *Selkirk v. Romar Investments Ltd* [1963] 1 W.L.R. 1415.

[13] *Re Nichols and Von Joel's Contract* [1910] 1 Ch. 43 at p. 46. See also *Pips (Leisure Productions) Ltd v. Walton* (1981) 260 E.G. 601 (purchaser entitled to rescind contract for sale of lease which was already forfeited).

In *Wroth v. Tyler*,[14] a husband, the owner of the matrimonial home, entered into a contract to sell with vacant possession. Before completion, his wife registered a charge under the Matrimonial Homes Act 1967.[15] The purchaser sued for specific performance, and failed on two grounds:

i. The husband could only carry out his obligation by obtaining a court order terminating the wife's right of occupation, and this would depend on the discretion of the court. To grant a decree would compel the husband to embark on difficult and uncertain litigation. He had attempted to obtain the wife's consent by all reasonable means short of litigation, and it would be most undesirable to require a husband to take proceedings against his wife, especially where they were still living together.

ii. Nor could the purchasers get specific performance subject to the wife's right of occupation. The husband and daughter would remain liable to eviction by the purchasers, and the family would be split up. The court would be slow to decree specific performance in such circumstances.

6. DAMAGES IN SUBSTITUTION FOR, OR IN ADDITION TO, SPECIFIC PERFORMANCE

A. Chancery Amendment Act 1858. Lord Cairns' Act[16]

Section 2 of Lord Cairns' Act gave to the Court of Chancery discretionary power to award damages either in addition to or in substitution for specific performance, the damages to be assessed in such manner as the court shall direct.

Before this Act, it was only in the common law courts that damages were awarded.[17] The Act gave power to award damages where none would be available at law.[18] But it did not give the Court

---

[14] [1974] Ch. 30. See also *Malhotra v. Choudhury* [1980] Ch. 52 at p. 71; *Verrall v. Great Yarmouth Borough Council* [1981] Q.B. 202, *ante*, p. 701 (specific performance of contract to hire conference hall to National Front), where this defence failed: the risk of public disorder was outweighed by the freedom of speech and assembly and the sanctity of contract.

[15] Now Family Law Act 1996.

[16] See generally (1975) 34 C.L.J. 224 (J. Jolowicz); [1981] Conv. 286 (T. Ingman and J. Wakefield); [1994] Conv. 110 (T. Ingman); McDermott, *Equitable Damages* (1994).

[17] It appears that the Court of Chancery had inherent power to award damages in equity, but this was rarely exercised. See Spry, *Equitable Remedies*, p. 608; (1992) 108 L.Q.R. 652 (P. McDermott); *cf. Surrey v. Bredero Homes Ltd* [1993] 1 W.L.R. 1361 at p. 1368, where Dillon L.J. said that the Court of Chancery had "no power to award damages" before the 1858 Act. For the Court of Chancery's ancient statutory jurisdiction to award damages, see McDermott, *Equitable Damages*, p. 8.

[18] See *Johnson v. Agnew* [1980] A.C. 367 (Lord Wilberforce); *Price v. Strange* [1978] Ch. 337; *Oakacre Ltd v. Claire Cleaners (Holdings) Ltd* [1982] Ch. 197 (action for damages at law not accrued at date of writ).

of Chancery power to award common law damages.[19] It applied
only to cases where the court had jurisdiction to award specific
performance. Thus Lord Cairns' Act does not apply where the
contract is of a type which is not specifically enforceable[20]; but it
does apply where the contract is of a type which is, even though
specific performance is refused on some discretionary ground, such
as the absence of mutuality.[21] There is no jurisdiction under Lord
Cairns' Act if specific performance is no longer possible, as where
the land has been sold to a third party.[22] However, the jurisdiction
exists if, when the proceedings were begun, the court could have
granted specific performance, notwithstanding that thereafter, but
before judgment, specific performance has become impossible.[23]
But it has been held that the court has no jurisdiction to award
damages in lieu of specific performance under Lord Cairns' Act
where specific performance is not claimed by the plaintiff.[24]

It was not until the Judicature Act 1873 that common law damages were available in the Chancery Division. Today it is only
necessary to rely on Lord Cairns' Act if no damages would be
available at law.[25] It was at one time thought that it could be
advantageous to the plaintiff to rely on Lord Cairns' Act even where
common law damages were available, as the measure of damages
might be different.[26] This is now discredited.[27]

Lord Cairns' Act was repealed in 1883 by the Statute Law
Revision Act, but section 5 of that Act preserved its general effect,[28]

---

[19] But see *Price v. Strange* [1978] Ch. 337 at p. 358, where Goff L.J. said "One purpose and
a very important purpose of that Act was, of course, to avoid circuity of action by enabling
the old Court of Chancery to award damages at law. . . . "
[20] *Lavery v. Pursell* (1888) 39 Ch.D. 508 (tenancy for one year; *ante* p. 710). As to whether
contracts for personal services come into this category, see the different views expressed in
Price v. Strange [1978] Ch. 337 at p. 359 (Goff L.J.) and at p. 369 (Buckley L.J.). The
House of Lords in *Scandinavian Trading Tanker Co. A.B. v. Flota Petrolera Ecuatoriana*
[1983] 2 A.C. 694 took the view that there was no jurisdiction to grant specific performance
of a contract for services.
[21] *Price v. Strange* [1978] Ch. 337. Even where the contract concerns building or repair works,
the court has jurisdiction under the 1858 Act: *ibid.* at p. 359. See also *Wroth v. Tyler* [1974]
Ch. 30; *Malhotra v. Choudhury* [1980] Ch. 52, (1979) 38 C.L.J. 35 (D. Hayton); and the
cases on injunctions, *post*, pp. 776, *et seq.*
[22] *Surrey County Council v. Bredero Homes Ltd* [1993] 1 W.L.R. 1361.
[23] *Johnson v. Agnew* [1978] Ch. 176, C.A.
[24] *Horsler v. Zorro* [1975] Ch. 302. But see (1975) 91 L.Q.R. 337 (M. Albery) at pp. 352–353;
Jaggard v. Sawyer [1995] 1 W.L.R. 269 (injunction); [1995] Conv. 141 (T. Ingman). See
also *Malhotra v. Choudhury* [1980] Ch. 52. *Horsler v. Zorro* was overruled in part on a
different point in *Johnson v. Agnew* [1980] A.C. 367. Damages may be awarded under Lord
Cairns' Act, although not expressly claimed; (1985) 34 I.C.L.Q. 317 (A. Burgess); *Jaggard
v. Sawyer, supra.*
[25] See *Oakacre Ltd v. Claire Cleaners (Holdings) Ltd* [1982] Ch. 197 (writ for damages in
addition to specific performance not invalid although premature at law because issued
before breach).
[26] *Wroth v. Tyler* [1974] Ch. 30, *infra.*
[27] *Johnson v. Agnew, infra.*
[28] See *Leeds Industrial Co-operative Society Ltd v. Slack* [1924] A.C. 851.

although that section was unnecessary because section 16 of the Judicature Act 1873 had transferred all Chancery jurisdiction to the High Court.[29] Its provisions are now found in section 50 of the Supreme Court Act 1981.

B. Measure of Damages under Lord Cairns' Act

Where a purchaser claims damages for breach of a contract for the purchase of land, he is normally entitled to damages for any loss of bargain. In *Wroth v. Tyler*[30] the plaintiff contracted to buy a bungalow for £6,000. Contracts were exchanged on May 27, 1971, but on May 28 the vendor's wife registered a charge under the Matrimonial Homes Act 1967,[31] and refused to remove it. The vendor was thus unable to pass a clear title. At the date at which completion was due, the property was worth £7,500, but at the date of the judgment in January 1973, its value had risen to £11,500.

Megarry J. refused specific performance for reasons mentioned above.[32] Therefore the main issue was the measure of damages. It was "common ground" that the normal rule is that damages for breach of a contract for the sale of land are measured by the difference (if any) between the contract price and the market price at the date of the breach, which is normally the completion date (with interest from that date until judgment). Applying that rule, damages would be £1,500. Although Fry had said that "the measure would be the same under Lord Cairns' Act"[33] Megarry J. held that damages under the Act may be assessed on a basis which is not identical with that of the common law[34]: they should be a true substitute for specific performance, and must put the plaintiffs in as good a position as if the contract had been performed. Damages could be measured as at the date of judgment, and the plaintiffs were awarded £5,500.

It has since been doubted by the House of Lords[35] whether Lord Cairns' Act permits a departure from the common law rule on the quantum of damages, and, indeed, whether the damages awarded in *Wroth v. Tyler*[36] could not have been equally available at common law. There is no inflexible rule at common law that damages must be

---

[29] McDermott, *Equitable Damages*, pp. 41–44.
[30] [1974] Ch. 30; applied in *Grant v. Dawkins* [1973] 1 W.L.R. 1406. See also *Oakacre Ltd v. Claire Cleaners (Holdings) Ltd* [1982] Ch. 197 (damages awarded in addition to specific performance not limited to those accrued at writ).
[31] Now Family Law Act 1996.
[32] *Ante*, p. 724.
[33] *Op. cit.* p. 602.
[34] [1974] Ch. 30 at pp. 58–60.
[35] In *Johnson v. Agnew, infra*. The reasoning in *Wroth v. Tyler* is preferred in McDermott, *Equitable Damages*, p. 108; *cf.* [1994] Conv. 110 (T. Ingman).
[36] *Supra*.

assessed as at the date of the breach of contract.[37] The principle is that the plaintiff should be put in the same position as if the contract had been duly performed. The rule that damages are to be assessed as at the date of the breach evolved in times of financial stability when the subject-matter was unlikely to have increased in value between the breach and the judgment. The position at common law will be more readily appreciated by considering the doctrine of mitigation of damages. The principle that the plaintiff is to be put in the same position as if the contract had been performed is subject to the principle of mitigation.[38] Thus in the case of chattels, damages will usually be assessed at the breach, because at that date the plaintiff could have acquired an equivalent chattel elsewhere. But in the case of a specifically enforceable contract, such as a contract to buy land, the purchaser cannot reasonably be expected to mitigate the damages by seeking an equivalent property elsewhere as soon as the breach occurs, because he will normally wish to wait and see if specific performance is obtainable. In such a case, the common law principle of putting the plaintiff in the same position as if the contract had been performed is only adhered to in times of rising property prices by assessing the damages at a date subsequent to the breach.[39]

In *Johnson v. Agnew*[40] Lord Wilberforce rejected the view that damages under Lord Cairns' Act could be assessed on a different basis from that of the common law. Subject to the point that in some cases damages would be available under the Act where none at all would be available at common law, the quantum is the same. The words in section 2 that damages "may be assessed in such manner as the court shall direct" relate only to procedure.[41] *Wroth v. Tyler*[42] could not be supported in so far as it suggested that damages under the Act may be assessed on a different basis than at common law. Where, after the breach, the innocent party has reasonably continued to try for completion, the damages, however awarded should be

[37] *Wroth v. Tyler* [1974] Ch. 30 at p. 57; *Horsler v. Zorro* [1975] Ch. 302; *Radford v. De Froberville* [1977] 1 W.L.R. 1262, (1978) 94 L.Q.R. 327 (A. Zuckerman), [1978] Conv. 163 (F. Crane); *Malhotra v. Choudhury* [1980] Ch. 52, (1979) 38 C.L.J. 35 (D. Hayton); *Johnson v. Agnew* [1980] A.C. 367; *Suleman v. Shahsavari* [1988] 1 W.L.R. 1181.

[38] *Wroth v. Tyler* [1974] Ch. 30 at p. 57; *Radford v. De Froberville* [1977] 1 W.L.R. 1262; *Malhotra v. Choudhury, supra; cf. Kaunas v. Smyth* (1977) 75 D.L.R. 368.

[39] See generally (1979) 95 L.Q.R. 270 (D. Feldman and D. Libling); (1981) 97 L.Q.R. 445 (S. Waddams); (1982) 98 L.Q.R. 406 (I. Duncan Wallace); (1985) 34 I.C.L.Q. 317 (A. Burgess). If the market is falling, damages will be assessed at the date of breach; *Woodford Estates Ltd v. Pollack* (1979) 93 D.L.R. (3d) 350.

[40] [1980] A.C. 367. The facts have been given, *ante*, p. 697. See also *William Sindall plc v. Cambridgeshire County Council* [1994] 1 W.L.R. 1016 at p. 1037.

[41] This phrase does not appear in Supreme Court Act 1981, s.50.

[42] [1974] Ch. 30.

assessed as at the date the contract was lost.[43] This will normally be the date of the hearing, provided the proceedings have been conducted with due expedition: an earlier date will be substituted if the plaintiff has delayed.[44]

The assessment of damages under Lord Cairns' Act has been recently reviewed by the Court of Appeal in the context of injunctions,[45] and is further considered in Chapter 25.

7. SPECIFIC PERFORMANCE AND THIRD PARTIES

Claims for specific performance are usually made between the parties to the contract.[46] In such a case, all the parties to the contract must be parties to the suit.[47] Other difficulties arise where the issue is between assignees, or where the person to be benefited was not a party to the contract.

Difficulties have arisen as to whether the right to (or liability to) specific performance passes to an assignee of the agreement. These problems mainly arose in the context of agreements for leases, where the question was whether the assignee of either party could sue or be sued on the obligations of the agreed lease. These matters are now dealt with by the Landlord and Tenant (Covenants) Act 1995,[48] and will not be further discussed here. As far as contracts for the sale of land are concerned, such a contract confers an equitable interest on the purchaser. Whether specific performance is available against an assignee of the vendor will depend on the registration rules.[49]

A different question is whether specific performance may be obtained for the benefit of a third party, as where A has contracted with B to confer a benefit on C. Sometimes[50] C can enforce the contract in his own right, and obtain either an award of damages or specific performance according to the usual principles. If, however,

---

[43] This was the date on which the vendor's mortgagees contracted to sell the property; *ante*, p. 697. See also *Domb v. Isoz* [1980] Ch. 548; *Suleman v. Shahsavari* [1988] 1 W.L.R. 1181 (£29,500 awarded where property worth £76,000 at hearing but contract price £46,500); *Johnson & Co. (Barbados) Ltd v. N.S.R. Ltd* [1996] 3 W.L.R. 583.

[44] *Radford v. De Froberville* [1977] 1 W.L.R. 1262 (assuming a rising market); *Malhotra v. Choudhury* [1980] Ch. 52.

[45] *Surrey v. Bredero Homes Ltd* [1993] 1 W.L.R. 1361; *Jaggard v. Sawyer* [1995] 1 W.L.R. 269; *post*, p. 781.

[46] See generally Snell, p. 590. For the rights of a sub-purchaser to obtain specific performance of the head contract, see *Berkley v. Poulett* (1976) 120 S.J. 836, *ante* p. 314.

[47] See *Tito v. Waddell (No. 2)* [1977] Ch. 106 at p. 324 (Megarry V.-C.).

[48] The Act extends to agreements for leases and equitable assignments of leases; s.28(1).

[49] Land Charges Act 1972, s.2(4); Land Registration Act 1925, ss.49, 70(1)(g) (estate contracts).

[50] For instance, where there is a trust of a chose in action, *ante*, p. 124.

because of the usual "privity" rule,[51] C cannot enforce the contract himself, the question is whether B may obtain specific performance, compelling A to confer the benefit on C.

In *Beswick v. Beswick*,[52] one Peter Beswick, a coal merchant who wished to retire, made an arrangement with his nephew under which the business was transferred to the nephew, and the nephew promised to employ Peter as consultant for a weekly wage, and after his death to pay to Peter's widow £5 per week for her life. Payments were made to Peter during his lifetime, but soon after his death ceased to be paid to his widow. The widow took out letters of administration of Peter's estate and sued both as administratrix and in her own right under the contract.

The House of Lords held that she was entitled as administratrix to specific performance of the promise to make the weekly payments to her as Peter's widow. She was unable to sue in her own right because of the rule of privity.

The difficulties which faced the widow in her action as administratrix were essentially threefold: (a) Peter's estate, which she represented, had lost nothing by the breach; (b) the widow, in her own capacity, had suffered the loss but had no right of action; (c) the agreement was for the payment of money and was not the type of agreement where breach is usually remedied by a decree of specific performance.[53]

The widow, as administratrix, overcame them all. Lord Upjohn thought that (a) was an argument in favour of specific performance; " . . . the court ought to grant a specific performance order all the more because damages *are* nominal."[54] She had no other effective remedy; "justice demands that [the promisor] pay the price and this can only be done in the circumstances by equitable relief."[55] This disregards the principle that equitable remedies are available where the legal remedy is inadequate to compensate for the loss. It is not that equitable remedies are available where the plaintiff has suffered

---

[51] *Scruttons Ltd v. Midland Silicones Ltd* [1962] A.C. 466. *Cf. Trident General Insurance Co. Ltd v. McNiece Bros. Pty. Ltd* (1988) 165 C.L.R. 107. Reform of the privity rules is proposed in Law Com. No. 242 (1996); *ante*, p. 122.

[52] [1968] A.C. 58; Treitel, *The Law of Contract* (9th ed.), pp. 935–936; (1988) 8 L.S. 14 (N. Andrews).

[53] *Ante*, p. 703.

[54] [1968] A.C. 58 at p. 102; *cf. Re Cook's S.T.* [1965] Ch. 902; *ante*, p. 131. On damages for loss suffered by third parties, see also *Jackson v. Horizon Holidays Ltd* [1975] 1 W.L.R. 1468; *ante*, p. 125, *Woodar Investment Development Ltd v. Wimpey Construction U.K. Ltd* [1980] 1 W.L.R. 277.

[55] *Ibid.*

no loss,[56] nor where an independent person has suffered a loss for which there is no cause of action.

Their Lordships found no difficulty in treating the case as a suitable one for specific performance. "Had [the promisor] repudiated the contract in the lifetime of [the promisee] the latter would have had a cast-iron case for specific performance."[57] The orthodox view has been that specific performance will not be ordered in cases where the promise is to pay money unless the plaintiff is a vendor or lessor against whom the purchaser or lessee could have demanded specific performance. *Beswick v. Beswick*[58] may have been regarded as such a case, for the nephew "could on his part clearly have obtained specific performance of it if Beswick senior or his administratrix had defaulted."[59] That, it is submitted, is questionable; for the contract was essentially for the sale of the goodwill of the business; such a contract is not normally specifically enforceable, in contrast to a contract to sell premises along with the goodwill.[60]

It is said also that a contract to pay an annuity is specifically enforceable. In *Adderly v. Dixon*,[61] Leach M.R. gave the reason that the amount of damages would be conjectural. While such a proposition may have been sound in 1824, it is questionable whether it is sound today. The development of life assurance and of actuarial valuation of life interests has made an annuity and a capital sum in effect interchangeable. Annuities are freely purchased from insurance companies in exchange for capital payments and can similarly be freely sold for a capital sum. Thus the conjectural element is less marked than it was over a century ago. If the plaintiff was awarded damages, and desired the annuity, all he has to do is to buy one.

The cases on which their Lordships relied[62] to support the view that the contract to pay was specifically enforceable, at the instance of a personal representative, were all cases either of a contract to transfer land or contracts to pay an annuity. It is possible to treat *Beswick v. Beswick*[63] as consistent with authority by saying that there was mutuality, that the contract (being to pay an annuity) was

---

[56] *cf. Marco Productions Ltd v. Pagola* [1945] 1 K.B. 111; injunction available to restrain breach of negative covenant even though the breach causes no loss to plaintiff; or if only nominal damages would be available at law; *Rochdale Canal Co. v. King* (1851) 2 Sim.(N.S.) 78; *Wrotham Park Estate v. Parkside Homes Ltd* [1974] 1 W.L.R. 798; *post*, p. 780.

[57] [1968] A.C. 58 at p. 98.

[58] [1968] A.C. 58.

[59] *Ibid.* at p. 89, *per* Lord Pearce.

[60] *Baxter v. Connolly* (1820) 1 J. & W. 576; *Darbey v. Whitaker* (1857) 4 Drew. 134 at pp. 139, 140; *ante*, p. 712.

[61] (1824) 1 Sim. & St. 607 at p. 611; (1966) 29 M.L.R. 657 at p. 663 (G. Treitel).

[62] *Keenan v. Handley* (1864) 2 De G.J. & A. 283; *Hohler v. Aston* [1920] 2 Ch. 420; *Drimmie v. Davies* [1899] 1 Ir.R. 176; *Coulls v. Bagot's Executor and Trustee Co.* (1967) 40 A.L.J.R. 471; *ante*, p. 131.

[63] [1968] A.C. 58.

capable of specific performance, and that the common law remedy of damages (assuming them to be nominal) was inadequate. The plaintiff barely succeeds on the first two; and only on the third by relying on cases which uphold it without explaining the logical dilemma of holding an award of nominal damages inadequate where no loss was suffered by the party able to sue.

In spite of these criticisms, the House of Lords should be applauded for taking a broad equitable view of the situation. There was "an unconscionable breach of faith [and] the equitable remedy sought is apt."[64] Lord Pearce and Lord Upjohn both approved the dictum of Windeyer J. in *Coulls v. Bagot's Executor and Trustee Co. Ltd* in which he said[65]: "It seems to me that contracts to pay money or transfer property to a third person are always, or at all events very often, contracts for breach of which damages would be an inadequate remedy—all the more so if it be right (I do not think it is) that damages recoverable by the promisee are only nominal . . . I see no reason why specific performance should not be had in such cases . . . There is no reason today for limiting by particular categories, rather than by general principle, the cases in which orders for specific performance will be made." There were no technical or practical difficulties preventing an award of specific performance and "justice demands that [the promisor] pay the price and this can only be done in the circumstances by equitable relief."[66] Perhaps the correct explanation is that damages must be considered from the point of view of both plaintiff and defendant. Thus the remedy of damages is inadequate if it would lead to the unjust enrichment of the wrongdoer. Substantial damages have been awarded under Lord Cairns' Act for this reason.[67]

Beswick v. Beswick[68] was applied by the Court of Appeal in *Gurtner v. Circuit*,[69] concerning the Motor Insurers' Bureau's contract with the Minister of Transport. Under this contract, if an injured person's judgment against a motorist is not satisfied within seven days, the Bureau will pay the injured person.[70] While the injured person cannot sue, the Minister can get specific performance in his favour.

This chapter began by indicating how narrow was the scope of the remedy of specific performance in practice. Other systems of law tend to be much more free in their use of this type of remedy.

---

[64] *Ibid. per* Lord Hodson at p. 83.

[65] (1967) 40 A.L.J.R. at p. 487; (1978) 37 C.L.J. 301 (B. Coote).

[66] *Beswick v. Beswick* at p. 102, *per* Lord Upjohn.

[67] *Wrotham Park Estate Co. v. Parkside Homes Ltd* [1974] 1 W.L.R. 798. For further developments in the context of injunctions, see p. 781, *post.*

[68] [1968] A.C. 58.

[69] [1968] 2 Q.B. 587.

[70] It is the policy of the M.I.B. not to rely on absence of privity.

Beswick v. Beswick[71] indicates a willingness in the House of Lords to make freer use of the remedy in the interests of justice. The case is however concerned with its own particular problem of the contract to pay to a third party. Time alone will tell whether this more liberal approach will be applied to other, and more usual, aspects of the law of specific performance.

8. JURISDICTION

Both the High Court[72] and the county court have jurisdiction to grant specific performance, but the jurisdiction of the county court, in cases of specific performance of contracts to sell or to let land, is limited to cases where the purchase money, or the value of the property in the case of a lease, does not exceed the county court limit.[73]

The county court must give effect to every defence or counterclaim to which effect would be given in the High Court.[74] Thus, in *Kingswood Estate Co. Ltd v. Anderson*,[75] where the landlord brought an action for possession based on the termination of a common law periodic tenancy, the county court gave effect to the tenant's defence that she held the property under a specifically enforceable agreement for a lease for life, even though it had no jurisdiction to grant specific performance of that agreement. Similarly, in *Rushton v. Smith*,[76] the county court had no jurisdiction to grant specific performance of an agreement for a business tenancy where the value of the property exceeded the county court limit, but it nevertheless had jurisdiction to decide whether or not the tenant would be entitled to such a decree.

---

[71] [1968] A.C. 58.
[72] Where an expeditious procedure is available under R.S.C., Ord. 86, where the facts are not in dispute.
[73] County Courts Act 1984, s.23. The current limit is £30,000. See also *Joyce v. Liverpool City Council* [1996] Q.B. 252 (small claims).
[74] County Courts Act 1984, s.38.
[75] [1963] 2 Q.B. 169. See also *Cornish v. Brook Green Laundry Ltd* [1959] 1 Q.B. 394.
[76] [1976] Q.B. 480.

CHAPTER 25

INJUNCTIONS

1. Jurisdiction 734
  A. The High Court 734
  B. The County Court 735
2. Types of Injunction 735
  A. Prohibitory and Mandatory Injunctions 735
  B. Perpetual and Interlocutory Injunctions 736
  C. *Ex Parte* Injunctions 736
  D. Interim Injunctions 737
  E. *Quia Timet* Injunctions 737
3. Principles Applicable to the Issue of Injunctions 737
  A. General 737
    i. Discretionary Remedy 737
    ii. Remedy *in Personam* 738
    iii. The Public Interest 738
    iv. Contempt 739
    v. Crown Proceedings 740
  B. Protection of Rights 740
    i. *Locus Standi* 740
    ii. Legal and Equitable Rights 743
  C. Perpetual Injunctions 745
    i. Prohibitory Injunctions 745
    ii. Mandatory Injunctions 747
    iii. Suspension of Injunctions 750
  D. Interlocutory Injunctions 751
    i. General 751
      (a) *Ex Parte* Procedure 751
      (b) Discharge of Interlocutory Injunctions 752
      (c) Injunctions Pending Appeal ... 752
      (d) Complete Relief 752
      (e) Injunction Ineffective 753
    ii. Principles Applicable to the Issue of Interlocutory Injunctions 753
      (a) *American Cynamid Co. v. Ethicon Ltd* 754
      (b) Exceptional Cases 760
    iii. Mandatory Interlocutory Injunctions 765
    iv. Conditions and Undertakings 767
  E. *Quia Timet* Injunctions 769
4. Defences to Perpetual and Interlocutory Injunctions 771
  A. Delay 771
  B. Acquiescence 773
  C. Hardship 774

  D. Conduct of the Plaintiff 775
5. The Jurisdiction under Lord Cairns' Act . 776
  A. Award of Damages under Lord Cairns' Act 777
  B. The Measure of Damages under Lord Cairns' Act 780
6. Injunctions in Particular Situations 783
  A. To Restrain a Breach of Contract 783
    i. Contract Wholly Negative 783
      (a) Perpetual Injunctions 783
      (b) Interlocutory Injunctions 784
      (c) Mandatory Injunctions 784
    ii. Positive and Negative Terms 784
    iii. No Express Negative Stipulation 785
      (a) Contracts Affecting the Use of Land 786
      (b) Contractual Licences 786
    iv. Contracts for Personal Services 787
      (a) Restraining Breach by Employee or Independent Contractor 787
      (b) Compelling Employer to Employ 789
  B. To Restrain a Breach of Trust 791
  C. To Restrain the Commission or Continuance of a Tort 791
    i. Nuisance 791
    ii. Trespass 792
    iii. Libel 793
  D. Breach of Confidence 794
  E. Public Wrongs 797
  F. Family Matters 801
  G. Trade Unions, Clubs and Colleges 802
  H. Judicial Proceedings 803
  I. Legislative Proceedings 804
  J. To Prevent Removal or Destruction of Evidence: The "Anton Piller" Injunction 804
  K. To Prevent Removal of Assets: The "Mareva" Injunction 808
    i. General Principles 808
    ii. Guidelines for the Grant of the Injunction 810
    iii. The Jurisdiction of the Court 811
    iv. The English-based Defendant 812
    v. Assets Outside the Jurisdiction ... 812
    vi. Operation *in Personam* 814
    vii. Position of Third Parties 815

Injunctions

1. Jurisdiction

An injunction is an order by the court to a party to do or refrain from doing a particular act. Originally the Court of Chancery alone[1] had jurisdiction to grant an injunction. This inevitably led to much duplication of proceedings; as where the plaintiff required an injunction as a remedy for a legal right. The Common Law Procedure Act 1854 gave to common law courts a power to grant injunctions in certain cases. The present jurisdiction is governed by the Supreme Court Act 1981, replacing the Judicature Acts, which vested the jurisdiction of the Court of Chancery and of the common law courts in the High Court.

A. The High Court

Section 37(1) of the Supreme Court Act 1981 provides that "The High Court may by order (whether interlocutory or final) grant an injunction . . . in all cases in which it appears to the court to be just and convenient to do so."[2] The jurisdiction is however not so wide as would appear from a first reading of the section. It is exercised, not on the individual preference of the judge, but "according to sufficient legal reasons or on settled legal principles."[3] There have been differences of opinion as to whether section 25(8) of the Judicature Act 1873, which introduced the provision similar to that now contained in the Act of 1981, gave the court power to grant injunctions in cases where they had not previously been granted.[4] It has been said that the Act of 1873 "has not revolutionised" but "has to some extent enlarged" the jurisdiction.[5] The restrictive approach, namely that the court's jurisdiction has not been extended, was affirmed by the House of Lords in *Gouriet v. Union of Post Office Workers*.[6] Lord Edmund-Davies said that section 25(8) of the Act of

---

[1] Or the Court of Exchequer in its equity jurisdiction, *ante*, p. 4. See generally Sharpe, *Injunctions and Specific Performance*.

[2] This consolidates the previous legislation. Compare the wording of s.25(8) of the Supreme Court of Judicature Act 1873 and s.45 of the Act of 1925: "just *or* convenient"; *Day v. Brownrigg* (1878) 10 Ch.D. 294; *L. v. L.* [1969] P. 25.

[3] *Per* Jessel M.R. in *Beddow v. Beddow* (1878) 9 Ch.D. 89 at p. 93. Thus a plaintiff with no "rights" cannot obtain an injunction, however "just and convenient" it may be: *Gouriet v. Union of Post Office Workers* [1978] A.C. 435; *Paton v. Trustees of British Pregnancy Advisory Service* [1979] Q.B. 76, *post*, p. 744.

[4] See the different views of Lord Esher M.R. and Cotton L.J. in *North London Ry. v. Great Northern Ry.* (1883) 11 Q.B.D. 30. See also *The Siskina* [1979] A.C. 210; *Maclaine Watson & Co. Ltd v. International Tin Council (No. 2)* [1989] Ch. 286; *Channel Tunnel Group Ltd v. Balfour Beatty Construction Ltd* [1993] A.C. 334.

[5] *Cummins v. Perkins* [1899] 1 Ch. 16 at p. 20.

[6] [1978] A.C. 435. See also *Bremer Vulkan Schiffbau und Maschinenfabrik v. South India Shipping Corp.* [1981] A.C. 909.

1873 "dealt only with procedure and had nothing to do with jurisdiction."[7] But former rules of practice no longer hamper the exercise of discretion; thus enabling the merits of new situations to be dealt with as they arise.[8] A similar question is whether the Act of 1981 enlarged the previous jurisdiction, but the better view is that it did not.[9] A plaintiff with no cause of action cannot invoke section 37(1).[10]

B. The County Court

The jurisdiction of the county court, which is wholly statutory,[11] has been enlarged by the Courts and Legal Services Act 1990.[12] Under section 38 of the County Courts Act 1984 the court could only grant an injunction if it was ancillary to a claim for some other specific relief, such as damages, within its jurisdiction. The amended section 38 provides that (subject to exceptions) the court may make an order which could be made by the High Court. It appears, therefore, that no other relief need be claimed. The county court has no jurisdiction, however, to grant an *Anton Piller* injunction[13] or a *Mareva* injunction[14] (other than in family proceedings or in aid of execution of a county court judgment).[15]

2. TYPES OF INJUNCTIONS

A. Prohibitory and Mandatory Injunctions

The most common form of an injunction, as the name implies, is one which is prohibitory or restrictive. However, if the unlawful act has been committed and an order restraining its commission is therefore meaningless, justice can sometimes be done by issuing a mandatory injunction ordering the act to be undone. At one time the negative character of an injunction used to be insisted upon; if the court intended to order a party to pull down a building, the order

---

[7] *Ibid.* at p. 516. *cf.* the wider views of Lord Denning M.R. in *Rasu Maritima S.A. v. Perusahaan* [1978] Q.B. 644 at pp. 659–660.

[8] *Argyll v. Argyll* [1967] Ch. 302 at p. 345; *Rasu Maritima S.A. v. Perusahaan, supra.* See generally the *Mareva* and *Anton Piller* injunctions, *post*, pp. 804, 808.

[9] Contrast the views of Lord Denning M.R. with those of Donaldson and Slade L.JJ. in *Chief Constable of Kent v. V.* [1983] Q.B. 34; (1983) 99 L.Q.R. 1; (1983) 42 C.L.J. 51 (A. Tettenborn); All E.R. Rev. 1982, p. 205 (G. Zellick); *Richards v. Richards* [1984] A.C. 174. The wording of the 1981 Act and its predecessors is not identical.

[10] *Ainsbury v. Millington* [1986] 1 All E.R. 73; *Wilde v. Wilde* [1988] 2 F.L.R. 83.

[11] *D v. D (County Court Jurisdiction: Injunctions)*, The Times, July 29, 1993.

[12] s.3. In the case of land, its value must be within the county court limits (currently £30,000). See also *Joyce v. Liverpool City Council* [1996] Q.B. 252 (small claims).

[13] *Post*, p. 804.

[14] *Post*, p. 808.

[15] County Courts Remedies Regulations 1991 (S.I. 1991 No. 1222).

would be that he should refrain from permitting the building to remain on his land. Such an injunction may have a positive effect, as in *Sky Petroleum Ltd v. V.I.P. Petroleum Ltd*,[16] where an injunction restraining the defendant from withholding supplies of petrol was equivalent to specific performance of the contract. But a mandatory injunction is now couched in positive form,[17] but just for this reason it may be harder to obtain. For example, it has been held that it ought not to issue to compel a ferry owner to run a ferry when it could only be run at a loss.[18] But the fact that a local authority may have to borrow money, or get a building licence to comply with a mandatory injunction is a ground, not for refusing the remedy, but for granting it subject to a suspension.[19]

B. Perpetual and Interlocutory Injunctions

Prohibitory or mandatory injunctions may be perpetual or interlocutory. "Perpetual" does not mean necessarily that the effect of the order must endure for ever; it means that the order will finally settle the present dispute between the parties, being made as the result of an ordinary action, the court having heard in the ordinary way the arguments on both sides. But a plaintiff may not always be able to wait for the action to come on in the normal course; it may be that irreparable damage will be done if the defendant is not immediately restrained. If such is the case, the plaintiff will serve on him a notice that on the next motion day[20] his counsel will apply to the court for an injunction. The service of this notice will enable the defendant's counsel also to be heard, if he wishes, but the hearing will not be a final decision on the merits of the case. If the plaintiff's affidavit has made out a sufficient case, the judge will grant an interlocutory injunction, which is effective only until the trial of the action.[21]

C. Ex Parte Injunctions

If the urgency of the case is such that the plaintiff cannot even wait until the next motion day, he is still not without a remedy, for

---

[16] [1974] 1 W.L.R. 576.
[17] *Jackson v. Normanby Brick Co.* [1899] 1 Ch. 438.
[18] *Att.-Gen. v. Colchester Corporation* [1955] 2 Q.B. 207; *Gravesham Borough Council v. British Railways Board* [1978] Ch. 379; *Morris v. Redland Bricks Ltd* [1970] A.C. 652; *cf. Co-operative Insurance Society Ltd v. Argyll Stores (Holdings) Ltd* [1996] Ch. 286, *ante*, p. 705.
[19] *Pride of Derby Angling Association v. British Celanese Co.* [1953] Ch. 149.
[20] Every weekday in term is a motion day in the Chancery Division: *Practice Direction* [1980] 1 W.L.R. 751.
[21] *Jones v. Pacaya Rubber and Produce Co.* [1911] 1 K.B. 455 at p. 457, *per* Buckley J. For procedure, see *Practice Direction* [1983] 1 W.L.R. 433.

he can apply for an *ex parte* injunction, which will hold good until the next motion day, by which time notice can have been served on the defendant, who will then have a chance of opposing the plaintiff's application for an interlocutory injunction. The phrase "*ex parte*" signifies that the court has not had an opportunity of hearing the other side.

D. Interim Injunctions

An interim injunction restrains the defendant, not until trial, but until some specified date, if for some special reason it would be unjust to protect the plaintiff beyond that date. An interim injunction is usually, but not always, *ex parte*. For example, if notice has been served on the defendant, but he is not given sufficient time to prepare his case, then an interim injunction until the next motion day is more likely to be granted than a full interlocutory injunction until trial.[22]

E. Quia Timet Injunctions

A *quia timet* injunction is one which issues to prevent an infringement of the plaintiff's rights where the infringement is threatened, but has not yet occurred. The jurisdiction is one of long standing, and exists in relation to both perpetual and interlocutory injunctions, and to both prohibitory and mandatory injunctions. The plaintiff must show a very strong probability of a future infringement, and that the ensuing damage will be of a most serious nature.[23]

3. PRINCIPLES APPLICABLE TO THE ISSUE OF INJUNCTIONS

A. General

i. Discretionary Remedy. While the injunction is a much wider remedy than specific performance, the characteristics of the two remedies are similar. Thus, the injunction is a discretionary remedy,[24] based on the inadequacy of common law remedies. As will be seen, similar principles apply to the exercise of the discretion of the court. As in the case of specific performance, the court may award

---

[22] *Fenwick v. East London Ry.* (1875) L.R. 20 Eq. 544.

[23] *Fletcher v. Bealey* (1885) 28 Ch.D. 688; *Att.-Gen. v. Nottingham Corporation* [1904] 1 Ch. 673; *Redland Bricks Ltd v. Morris* [1970] A.C. 652; *post*, p. 770.

[24] Unless it is a statutory remedy; *Taylor v. Newham London Borough Council* [1993] 1 W.L.R. 444. Similarly, a plaintiff who has been totally dispossessed by trespass is entitled to an injunction as of right; *Harrow London Borough Council v. Donohue* [1995] 1 E.G.L.R. 257; *post*, p. 792.

damages under Lord Cairns' Act, either in lieu of, or in addition to, an injunction.[25]

ii. Remedy in personam.[26] Like specific performance, the injunction is a remedy *in personam*. It is possible to enjoin a defendant who is not personally within the jurisdiction, provided service out of the jurisdiction can properly be done under rules of court.[27] But, as a general rule, no injunction will be granted in connection with the title to land outside the jurisdiction, even if the defendant is within the jurisdiction.[28] It is otherwise in the case of chattels, and, even in the case of land, the rule is subject to exceptions.[29] Finally, an injunction may be granted against all the members of a class or organisation to restrain the unlawful acts of unidentified members.[30]

iii. The Public Interest. Divergent views have been expressed in the Court of Appeal on the question whether the court, in considering an application for an injunction to protect a private right, has a duty to take into account the interests of the general public. In *Miller v. Jackson*[31] a cricket club committed the torts of nuisance and negligence in allowing cricket balls to land on the plaintiffs' property. An injunction was refused by the Court of Appeal. The public interest in enabling the inhabitants to enjoy the benefits of outdoor recreation prevailed over the plaintiffs' private right to quiet enjoyment of their house and garden. But in *Kennaway v. Thompson*,[32] where the plaintiff sought an injunction to restrain a motor boat racing club from committing nuisance by excessive noise, the Court of Appeal granted the injunction, holding that the rights of the plaintiff should not be overridden by the interests of the club or of the general public. In considering whether to grant an injunction or

---

[25] *Post*, p. 776, Spry, pp. 610 *et seq.*

[26] *Ante*, p. 694. See the *"Mareva"* cases; *post*, pp. 808 *et seq.*

[27] R.S.C., Ord. 11. See *Re Liddell's S.T.* [1936] Ch. 365.

[28] *Deschamps v. Miller* [1908] 1 Ch. 856; *Re Hawthorne* (1883) 23 Ch.D. 743. See Dicey and Morris, *The Conflict of Laws* (12th ed.), pp. 945 *et seq.*, discussing also the effect of Civil Jurisdiction and Judgments Act 1982, s.30. This principle applies also to foreign intellectual property; *Tyburn Productions Ltd v. Conan Doyle* [1991] Ch. 75.

[29] One such exception is where there is "an equity between the parties": *Cook Industries Inc. v. Galliher* [1979] Ch. 439. See also *Penn v. Lord Baltimore* (1750) 1 Ves.Sen. 444, *ante*, p. 694; *Hamlin v. Hamlin* [1986] Fam. 11.

[30] *M. Michaels (Furriers) Ltd v. Askew*, The Times, June 25, 1983 (nuisance by members of "Animal Aid"); *E.M.I. Records Ltd v. Kudhail*, The Times, June 28, 1983; *cf. United Kingdom Nirex Ltd v. Barton*, The Times, October 14, 1986.

[31] [1977] Q.B. 966. For interlocutory injunctions, see *post*, p. 760. See also the cases on libel and breach of confidence, *post*, pp. 793, 794.

[32] [1981] Q.B. 88; (1981) 97 L.Q.R. 3; (1981) 44 M.L.R. 212 (R. Buckley); *Sevenoaks District Council v. Pattullo & Vinson Ltd* [1984] Ch. 211; *Elliott v. Islington London Borough Council* [1991] 1 E.G.L.R. 167.

damages in lieu under Lord Cairns' Act,[33] the public interest does not prevail over private rights. The views expressed in *Miller v. Jackson* ran counter to the well-established principles laid down in *Shelfer v. City of London Electric Lighting Co.*,[34] which was binding on the Court of Appeal.

iv. Contempt. Non-compliance with an injunction (or an undertaking given in lieu[35]) is a contempt of court,[36] punishable by imprisonment, sequestration of property (in the case of a corporation) or a fine.[37] Acts done in breach of an injunction are void for illegality.[38] As disobedience may lead to imprisonment, the injunction must be expressed in exact terms, so that the defendant knows precisely what to do, or refrain from doing.[39] As committal proceedings are equivalent to a criminal charge, the breach of injunction must be established beyond reasonable doubt.[40]

In matrimonial cases, committal orders should be made very reluctantly. As Ormrod L.J. said in *Ansah v. Ansah*,[41] "Committal orders are remedies of last resort; in family cases they should be the very last resort." It should be added that a power of arrest may be attached to occupation or non-molestation orders granted under the Family Law Act 1996.

A question which has recently been prominent is whether third parties commit contempt if they knowingly act contrary to an injunction. A third party who aids and abets a breach of injunction is guilty of contempt.[42] An agent of the party enjoined is also bound by the injunction.[43] The court has jurisdiction in wardship cases to make an injunction against the world at large, although a person

---

[33] *Post*, p. 776.

[34] [1895] 1 Ch. 287, *post*, p. 777. See (1982) 41 C.L.J. 87 (S. Tromans).

[35] *Hussain v. Hussain* [1986] Fam. 134; *Roberts v. Roberts* [1990] 2 F.L.R. 111.

[36] Contempt of Court Act 1981. See also *Parker v. Camden London Borough Council* [1986] Ch. 162. As to minors and mental patients, see *Wookey v. Wookey* [1991] Fam. 121.

[37] As to a company's liability for employee's breach, see *Re Supply of Ready Mixed Concrete (No. 2)* [1995] 1 A.C. 456. For liability of directors, see *Director General of Fair Trading v. Buckland* [1990] 1 W.L.R. 920; *Att.-Gen. for Tuvalu v. Philatelic Distribution Corporation Ltd* [1990] 1 W.L.R. 926. Non-compliance with an injunction may be an element in a subsequent award of exemplary damages: *Drane v. Evangelou* [1978] 1 W.L.R. 455.

[38] *Clarke v. Chadburn* [1985] 1 W.L.R. 78 (union rules); All E.R. Rev. 1985, p. 76 (C. Miller). Compliance with a statute affords a defence; *A. v. B. Bank (Governor and Company of the Bank of England intervening)* [1993] Q.B. 311.

[39] *Redland Bricks Ltd v. Morris* [1970] A.C. 652. The requirement has since been relaxed; *Channel Tunnel Group Ltd v. Balfour Beatty Construction Ltd* [1992] 1 Q.B. 656 at p. 678, C.A.

[40] *Re Bramblevale Ltd* [1970] Ch. 128; *Kent County Council v. Batchelor* (1977) 33 P. & C.R. 185.

[41] [1977] Fam. 138 at p. 144. See also (1977) 40 M.L.R. 220 (P. Pettit); *Brewer v. Brewer* [1989] 2 F.L.R. 251.

[42] *Acro (Automation) Ltd v. Rex Chainbelt Inc.* [1971] 1 W.L.R. 1676.

[43] *Cretanor Maritime Co. Ltd v. Irish Marine Management Ltd* [1978] 1 W.L.R. 966. See the *Mareva* cases, *post*, p. 808, particularly the "world-wide assets" cases.

who contravened the order in good faith and without notice of its terms would not commit contempt.[44] In *Att.-Gen. v. Times Newspapers Ltd*[45] newspapers which published confidential material which other newspapers had been enjoined from publishing were guilty of contempt. The House of Lords held that strangers who knowingly took action to damage or destroy confidentiality before the trial committed contempt by nullifying the purpose of the trial. The question was not whether third parties were bound by the injunction, but whether they could commit contempt even though they were not bound. As they were not parties to the order, the basis of the contempt would not be a breach of the order (unless they had aided and abetted a breach) but knowing interference with the administration of justice.

v. Crown Proceedings. One disadvantage is that an injunction will not normally lie against the Crown.[46] The proper remedy in such a case is the declaration, but this leaves the plaintiff without a remedy in situations where an interlocutory injunction would be desirable, as it seems that an interlocutory declaration cannot be made.[47] A final declaration may be made in interlocutory proceedings in rare cases, but not against the Crown.[48] The Law Commission has recommended that this gap be filled.[49] An interlocutory injunction may, exceptionally, be granted against the Crown to protect rights enforceable under European Community law.[50] Further, an injunction, final or interlocutory, may be granted against ministers and other officers of the Crown, and a minister can be liable for contempt.[51]

B. Protection of Rights

i. Locus Standi. "It is a fundamental rule that the court will only grant an injunction at the suit of a private individual to support a

---

[44] *Re X. (a minor)* [1984] 1 W.L.R. 1422; *Att.-Gen. v. Times Newspapers Ltd* [1992] 1 A.C. 191 at p. 224; *Re Z (a minor) (Identification: Restrictions on Publication)* [1997] Fam. 1.

[45] [1992] 1 A.C. 191 (the *Spycatcher* case). See also *Bank Mellat v. Kazmi* [1989] Q.B. 541; *Derby & Co. Ltd v. Weldon (Nos. 3 and 4)* [1990] Ch. 65; *Re C (Adult: Refusal of Treatment)* [1994] 1 W.L.R. 290; *Harrow London Borough Council v. Johnstone, The Times,* March 14, 1997.

[46] Crown Proceedings Act 1947, s.21; *R. v. Secretary of State for Transport, ex p. Factortame Ltd* [1990] 2 A.C. 85.

[47] *International General Electric Co. Ltd v. Commissioner of Customs and Excise* [1962] Ch. 784; *R. v. I.R.C., ex p. Rossminster Ltd* [1980] A.C. 952 at pp. 1000, 1007, 1014.

[48] R.S.C., Ord. 15, r. 16; *Clarke v. Chadburn* [1985] 1 W.L.R. 78.

[49] Law Com. No. 226 (1994), *Administrative Law: Judicial Review and Statutory Appeals.*

[50] *R. v. Secretary of State for Transport, ex p. Factortame Ltd (No. 2)* [1991] 1 A.C. 603; (1991) 107 L.Q.R. 4 (H. Wade).

[51] *M. v. Home Office* [1994] 1 A.C. 377; (1994) 57 M.L.R. 620 (C. Harlow); (1994) 53 C.L.J. 1 (T. Allen).

legal right."[52] The type of right which may be protected by injunction in the field of private law is dealt with below, but the question also arises as to who may seek an injunction to protect a public right. This requires a consideration of the extent to which the civil courts may restrain a breach of the criminal law by injunction. The general rule is that public rights are protected by the Attorney-General, acting either *ex officio* or on the relation of a member of the public. He may obtain an injunction to restrain breaches of the criminal law even if there is a statutory remedy, where that remedy is inadequate,[53] and the view of the court is that injunctions should be granted at his request to prevent clear breaches of the law irrespective of the weighing of benefits and detriments which characterises most other injunctions.[54]

By way of exception to this general rule, an individual may seek an injunction if interference with a public right, created by statute or existing at common law, would also infringe some private right of his or would inflict special damage on him,[55] save where statute has, for instance by providing an exclusive remedy, excluded it.[56] But an individual who does not come within the established exceptions has no remedy, for it is no part of English law that a person who suffers damage by reason of another person's breach of statute has a civil action against that person.[57] Thus a record company could not get an injunction against a defendant who traded in "bootleg" records in breach of statute, as there is no principle that a plaintiff can restrain a crime affecting his property rights by injunction where the statute was not designed for the protection of the class of which he is a member.[58]

Another important question is whether a private individual may obtain an injunction to restrain a threatened criminal offence which would interfere with a public right when the Attorney-General has

---

[52] *per* Lord Denning M.R. in *Thorne v. British Broadcasting Corporation* [1957] 1 W.L.R. 1104 at p. 1109. But compare the different views expressed in *Chief Constable of Kent v. V.* [1983] Q.B. 34.

[53] *Att.-Gen. v. Sharp* [1931] 1 Ch. 121; *Att.-Gen. v. Chaudry* [1971] 1 W.L.R. 1623.

[54] *Att.-Gen. v. Bastow* [1957] 1 Q.B. 514; *Att.-Gen. v. Harris* [1961] 1 Q.B. 74; *post*, p. 798.

[55] *Gouriet v. Union of Post Office Workers* [1978] A.C. 435; *Lonrho Ltd v. Shell Petroleum Co. Ltd* [1982] A.C. 173; *R.C.A. Corpn. v. Pollard* [1983] Ch. 135. An action also lies if the plaintiff can show that he is a member of the class for whose benefit the statute was passed and upon whom Parliament intended to confer a cause of action; *R. v. Deputy Governor of Parkhurst Prison, ex p. Hague* [1992] 1 A.C. 58. See also *Francome v. Mirror Group Newspapers* [1984] 1 W.L.R. 892; *Barrs v. Bethell* [1982] Ch. 294.

[56] *Stevens v. Chown* [1901] 1 Ch. 894; *cf. Meade v. London Borough of Haringey* [1979] 1 W.L.R. 637; Spry, pp. 357 *et seq.*

[57] *Lonrho Ltd v. Shell Petroleum Co. Ltd, supra*; *CBS Songs Ltd v. Amstrad Consumer Electronics plc* [1988] A.C. 1013; *P. v. Liverpool Daily Post and Echo Newspapers plc* [1991] 2 A.C. 370.

[58] *R.C.A. Corpn. v. Pollard* [1983] Ch. 135; *Rickless v. United Artists Corp.* [1988] Q.B. 40. See now Copyright, Designs and Patents Act 1988, s.194.

refused his consent to a relator action, the case not being one where private rights or special damage to the plaintiff are involved.[59]

In *Gouriet v. Union of Post Office Workers*[60] the plaintiff, a member of the public, sought an injunction to restrain a threatened boycott of postal communications between Britain and South Africa, in breach of statute. The Attorney-General had refused consent to a relator action, without giving reasons. It was unanimously held in the House of Lords that the court had no jurisdiction to grant such an injunction, nor to control the exercise of the Attorney-General's discretion in any way.

It was a fundamental principle that private rights could be asserted by the individual and public rights by the Attorney-General, and that "the criminal law is enforced in the criminal courts by the conviction and punishment of offenders, not in the civil courts."[61] Any interference by the civil courts exposes the defendant to "double jeopardy"; the penalty of imprisonment for contempt of court, if the offence is committed, is added to the criminal penalties fixed by Parliament.[62] Not only are the punishments different, but the contempt proceedings will be decided by a judge alone while the defendant may be entitled to a jury in the criminal proceedings.[63] These considerations are, of course, also present in cases where injunctions may be granted to enforce the criminal law. No doubt for this reason the House of Lords expressed the view that the cases where the Attorney-General can seek an injunction to restrain the commission of an offence are narrow and not to be extended. The jurisdiction is "of great delicacy and is one to be used with caution." The Attorney-General's power is "not without its difficulties and these may call for consideration in the future."[64]

The House of Lords affirmed that the Attorney-General is responsible to Parliament, not to the court. Any error he might make would

[59] The right to bring a private prosecution, once the offence is committed, is a different matter, but the Attorney-General has power to veto such proceedings.

[60] [1978] A.C. 435; (1977) 36 C.L.J. 201 (D. Williams); (1978) 94 L.Q.R. 4 (H.W.R.W.); (1978) 41 M.L.R. 58 (T. Hartley); (1978) 41 M.L.R. 63 (R. Simpson); (1979) 42 M.L.R. 369 (D. Feldman). See also Lord Denning's observations in *The Discipline of Law*, pp. 137 *et seq.*

[61] [1978] A.C. 435 at p. 490 (*per* Viscount Dilhorne). Although the case concerned criminal law enforcement, many statements in the House of Lords were wide enough to cover all public law actions. See also *Ashby v. Ebdon* [1985] Ch. 394; (1985) 44 C.L.J. 6 (J. Jolowicz).

[62] *Ibid.* at p. 498 (*per* Lord Diplock). See *Kent County Council v. Batchelor* [1979] 1 W.L.R. 213. But in other areas the civil court adds to the criminal penalty; see p. 315, *ante*, (forfeiture of property acquired by killing).

[63] But the standard of proof will be the same; see (1979) 42 M.L.R. 369 (D. Feldman).

[64] See also *Stoke-on-Trent City Council v. B. & Q. (Retail) Ltd* [1984] A.C. 754; *Waverley Borough Council v. Hilden* [1988] 1 W.L.R. 246; *Kirklees Borough Council v. Wickes Building Supplies Ltd* [1993] A.C. 227; *post*, p. 798.

be of political judgment, not law, and would not be appropriate for decision in the courts. Others have doubted whether responsibility to Parliament is a sufficient control to compensate for the exclusion of the court's jurisdiction.[65]

But the effect of the decision may not be so great as first appears. The prerogative remedies, with their broader concept of standing,[66] may be available where the defendant is a public authority.[67] Here the court feels able to judge on matters of public interest, even where there are political implications,[68] but the House of Lords has doubted the analogy.[69]

In the case of a crime which has already been committed, it has been held that the police have *locus standi* to seek an injunction to "freeze" money in a bank account which is reasonably believed to be the proceeds of a crime.[70] This principle is not without difficulty, and is confined to an asset which can be identified as the stolen item or as property representing it.[71] No such injunction is available in respect of moneys not themselves obtained by fraud but which were profits made by means of a loan obtained by fraud.[72]

Finally, the rule that only the Attorney-General may enforce public rights is subject to certain limited statutory exceptions, enabling a local authority to seek an injunction in its own name to protect public rights in the locality or to enforce planning control.[73]

ii. Legal and Equitable Rights. A right that is to be protected by an injunction must be one that is known to law or equity.[74] Thus it

---

[65] [1977] Q.B. 729 at pp. 758–759 (*per* Lord Denning M.R.); (1977) 36 C.L.J. 201 (D. Williams); (1978) 41 M.L.R. 58 (T. Hartley); (1979) 42 M.L.R. 369 (D. Feldman); *cf.* (1978) 41 M.L.R. 63 (R. Simpson).

[66] *Post,* pp. 799–801.

[67] See *R. v. Commissioner of Police of the Metropolis* [1968] 2 Q.B. 118; *R. v. I.R.C., ex p. National Federation of Self-Employed and Small Businesses Ltd* [1982] A.C. 617 at p. 640, *post,* p. 799; *R. v. Her Majesty's Treasury, ex p. Smedley* [1985] Q.B. 657.

[68] See, for example, *Secretary of State for Education and Science v. Tameside Metropolitan Borough Council* [1977] A.C. 1014.

[69] *Gouriet v. Union of Post Office Workers* [1978] A.C. 435 at p. 483.

[70] *Chief Constable of Kent v. V.* [1983] Q.B. 34; *West Mercia Constabulary v. Wagener* [1982] 1 W.L.R. 127; (1982) 98 L.Q.R. 190 (D. Feldman); All E.R. Rev. 1982, p. 205 (G. Zellick); (1983) 99 L.Q.R. 1; (1983) 42 C.L.J. 51 (A Tettenborn).

[71] *Chief Constable of Hampshire v. A. Ltd* [1985] Q.B. 132; (1984) 100 L.Q.R. 537 (G. Samuel). See also *Malone v. Metropolitan Police Commissioner* [1980] Q.B. 49.

[72] *Chief Constable of Leicestershire v. M.* [1989] 1 W.L.R. 20; *cf. Securities and Investments Board v. Pantell S.A.* [1990] Ch. 426.

[73] Local Government Act 1972, s.222; Town and Country Planning Act 1990, s.187B; *post,* p. 798.

[74] In *Chief Constable of Kent v. V.* [1983] Q.B. 34, Lord Denning M.R. considered that this was no longer the case after the Supreme Court Act 1981, but this was firmly rejected by the House of Lords in *P. v. Liverpool Daily Post and Echo Newspapers plc* [1991] 2 A.C. 370. See also *Zucker v. Tyndall Holdings plc* [1992] 1 W.L.R. 1127 (threatened breach of term of contract which is not presently performable does not suffice).

must not be one of which cognisance will be taken only in ecclesiastical law.[75] The point was firmly made in *Day v. Brownrigg*.[76]

The plaintiff lived in a house that had been called "Ashford Lodge" for 60 years. The defendant lived in a smaller neighbouring house called "Ashford Villa." The defendant started to call his house "Ashford Lodge" and the plaintiff sought an injunction to restrain him from doing so. The Court of Appeal took the view that there was no violation of a legal or equitable right in the plaintiff so that no injunction would be granted.[77]

Similarly, in *Paton v. Trustees of British Pregnancy Advisory Service*[78] it was held that a husband could not obtain an injunction to prevent his wife from having, or a registered medical practitioner from performing, a legal abortion: the husband had "no legal right enforceable at law or in equity."

Injunctions have proved valuable in protecting confidential material.[79] Before 1875, it was accepted that equity would, in suitable cases, restrain a defendant from revealing or distributing information or other material obtained in confidence,[80] regarding the breach of confidence as an equitable wrong needing protection by injunction. It has now been accepted[81] that the jurisdiction in this type of case does not depend on any notion of property or contract, but that an obligation of confidence can exist by virtue of the circumstances, and independently of any actual agreement to that effect. Confidential commercial information will be restrained from publication along similar lines.

Other rights which may be protected by injunction include the right (contractual or otherwise) not to be subjected to arbitration proceedings which could not lead to a fair trial[82]; the right (contractual or otherwise) not to be sued in a foreign court[83]; the right of the police to "freeze" money in a bank account which is reasonably

---

[75] *Att.-Gen. v. Dean and Chapter of Ripon Cathedral* [1945] Ch. 239.

[76] (1878) 10 Ch.D. 294; *Beddow v. Beddow* (1878) 9 Ch.D. 89 at p. 93.

[77] See also *Montgomery v. Montgomery* [1965] P. 46.

[78] [1979] Q.B. 276; (1979) 95 L.Q.R. 332 (J. Phillips); (1979) 30 C.L.P. 217 (C. Lyon and G. Benett). For a discussion of the position if the proposed abortion would be illegal, see (1979) 42 M.L.R. 324 (I. Kennedy); *C. v. S.* [1988] Q.B. 135; (1987) 103 L.Q.R. 340 (A. Grubb and D. Pearl).

[79] *Post*, p. 794.

[80] *Prince Albert v. Strange* (1849) 1 H. & T. 1 (copies of etchings made by the Prince and Queen Victoria: distribution restrained).

[81] See particularly *Argyll v. Argyll* [1967] Ch. 302 at p. 322; *Fraser v. Evans* [1969] 1 Q.B. 349 at p. 361; (1972) J.S.P.T.L. 149 (P. North).

[82] *Bremer Vulkan Schiffbau und Maschinenfabrik v. South India Shipping Corpn.* [1981] A.C. 909.

[83] *British Airways Board v. Laker Airways Ltd* [1985] A.C. 58; *South Carolina Insurance Co. v. Assurantie Maatschappij "De Zeven Provincien" N.V.* [1987] A.C. 24.

believed to be the identifiable proceeds of crime[84]; the right to restrain a breach of European Community law[85]; the right to restrain the export of works of art by means of forged documents[86]; the right to refuse surgery[87]; the right not to be harassed[88]; the right to have the status quo preserved pending trial of an action for a declaration[89]; and the right to ensure the effectiveness of a court order.[90] The latter right is the basis of the novel use of the injunction to prevent the defendant from leaving the country,[91] although this has been described as draconian and requiring careful examination.[92] Such an injunction may be granted even though there is no pre-existing cause of action.[93]

C. Perpetual Injunctions

It is axiomatic that the jurisdiction to grant injunctions is purely discretionary. But, as with specific performance, the court, in exercising its discretion, pays attention to certain factors established by the precedents as being of particular relevance.

i. Prohibitory Injunctions. If a plaintiff has established the existence of a right, infringement of that right should be restrained, but injunctions will not be granted where an award of damages[94] would be sufficient. Damages will not be an adequate remedy if they are not quantifiable, or if money could not properly compensate the plaintiff, as in the case of nuisance and other continuous or repeated injuries requiring a series of actions for damages, or even where the remedy would be ineffective because the defendant is a pauper.[95]

---

[84] *Ante*, p. 743.

[85] *Cutsforth v. Mansfield Inns Ltd* [1986] 1 W.L.R. 558; *Taittinger v. Allbev Ltd* [1994] 4 All E.R. 75.

[86] *Kingdom of Spain v. Christie, Manson & Woods Ltd* [1986] 1 W.L.R. 1120.

[87] *Re C (Adult: Refusal of Treatment)* [1994] 1 W.L.R. 290.

[88] *Burris v. Azadani* [1995] 1 W.L.R. 1372 (exclusion zone).

[89] *Re S (Hospital Patient: Court's Jurisdiction)* [1996] Fam. 1; *Newport Association Football Club Ltd v. Football Association of Wales Ltd* [1995] 2 All E.R. 87.

[90] *Maclaine Watson & Co. Ltd v. International Tin Council (No. 2)* [1989] Ch. 286 (unpaid judgment debt).

[91] *Bayer A.G. v. Winter* [1986] 1 W.L.R. 497 *post*, p. 810; *Arab Monetary Fund v. Hashim* [1989] 1 W.L.R. 565; *cf. Al Nahkel for Contracting and Trading Ltd v. Lowe* [1986] Q.B. 235 and *Allied Arab Bank Ltd v. Hajjar* [1988] Q.B. 787; (1988) 47 C.L.J. 364 (N. Andrews) (writ *ne exeat regno*). See also *Re I. (a minor), The Times*, May 22, 1987.

[92] *Bayer A.G. v. Winter (No. 2)* [1986] 1 W.L.R. 540; (1990) 20 U.W.A.L.R. 143 (J. Martin).

[93] *Re Oriental Credit Ltd* [1988] Ch. 204 (to prevent director leaving the country prior to examination under Companies Act 1985, s.561); criticised in (1988) 47 C.L.J. 177 (C. Forsyth); *Morris v. Murjani* [1996] 1 W.L.R. 848 (to prevent bankrupt leaving the country without complying with Insolvency Act 1986, s.333).

[94] The jurisdiction to award damages under Lord Cairns' Act is considered below, *post*, p. 776.

[95] *Hodgson v. Duce* (1856) 28 L.T.(o.s.) 155.

The extent of the damage is not the crucial point. An injunction may be granted even if only nominal damages would be recoverable at law.[96] The smallness of the damage suffered by a plaintiff and the fact that a monetary sum could easily be assessed to compensate for it, is no reason for withholding an injunction if the consequence is that the defendant is in effect compulsorily "buying" a right which is the plaintiff's to sell only if he wants to.[97] This principle was applied in *Express Newspapers Ltd v. Keys*.[98]

> Certain trade unions had issued instructions to their members to support a "Day of Action" in protest against Government policies. The plaintiffs sought an injunction to restrain the unions from inducing a breach of contract between the members and their employers. Griffiths J., in granting the injunction, held that damages would be inadequate. The plaintiffs did not want money; they wanted their newspapers to be published. To refuse the injunction would be giving a licence to the unions to commit an unlawful act merely because they could afford to pay the damages. It would not be fair to leave the plaintiffs to their remedy in damages, as there would be real difficulty in attributing any particular breach of contract to incitement by the unions as opposed to the voluntary act of the employees. "It is one thing to suffer damage and it is another to prove it."[99]

Similarly in cases in which the defendant has trespassed on the plaintiff's property: actual loss does not need to be shown before an injunction is granted.[1] But there may be cases in which injunctions will be refused, for example if the infringement is occasional or temporary, or if it is a trivial matter. One such case was *Armstrong v. Sheppard and Short*,[2] where the plaintiff had misled the court and had suffered no real damage. Lord Evershed M.R. said "A proprietor who establishes a proprietary right is ex debito justitiae entitled to an injunction unless it can be said against him that he has raised such an equity that it is no longer open to him to assert his legal or

---

[96] *Rochdale Canal Co. v. King* (1851) 2 Sim.(N.S.) 78; *Woollerton and Wilson Ltd v. Richard Costain Ltd* [1970] 1 W.L.R. 411.

[97] *Wood v. Sutcliffe* (1851) 2 Sim.(N.S.) 163. In *Express Newspapers Ltd v. Keys* [1980] I.R.L.R. 247, and *Patel v. W.H. Smith (Eziot) Ltd* [1987] 1 W.L.R. 853, it was held that this principle applied equally to interlocutory injunctions, and was not affected by *American Cyanamid Co. v. Ethicon Ltd* [1975] A.C. 396, *post*, p.753.

[98] [1980] I.R.L.R. 247. The injunction in this case was interlocutory but the judgment on this aspect is of general application.

[99] *Ibid.* at p. 250.

[1] *Goodson v. Richardson* (1874) L.R. 9 Ch.App. 221; *Trenberth (John) Ltd v. National Westminster Bank Ltd* (1979) 39 P. & C.R. 104. See also *Marco Productions Ltd v. Pagola* [1945] K.B. 111 on breach of contract.

[2] [1959] 2 Q.B. 384.

proprietary rights."[3] Similarly, in *Behrens v. Richards*[4] an injunction was not granted to restrain the public from using tracks on the plaintiff's land on an unfrequented part of the coast, causing no damage to the plaintiff. Such cases are, however, to be regarded as exceptional.[5]

It is obvious that these various factors are not to be considered in isolation and no complete list can be given of instances where an injunction will be refused. The principle applied by the courts is the protection of existing rights which are recognised by the law. But an injunction will not issue in every such case; it may be refused where damages are an adequate remedy, or where the plaintiff has by his conduct disentitled himself from injunctive relief,[6] or where the defendant gives to the court an undertaking not to do the act complained of[7]; or where, even if there is no other suitable remedy, the court considers that the plaintiff has suffered no injustice.[8]

ii. Mandatory Injunctions. These are governed by the same general principles as prohibitory injunctions, save that the problems of enforcement, supervision and hardship may be more acute. Mandatory injunctions are less frequently granted than prohibitory injunctions, and, as Lord Upjohn stated in *Redland Bricks Ltd v. Morris,*[9] are entirely discretionary, although it has been held that the court has no real discretion in cases involving trespass by total dispossession.[10]

There are two broad categories of mandatory injunctions: the "restorative" injunction, requiring the defendant to undo a wrongful act in situations where a prohibitory injunction might have been obtained to prevent the commission of the act[11]; and the mandatory injunction to compel the defendant to carry out some positive obligation. If the matter is one of contract, specific performance is

---

[3] [1959] 2 Q.B. 384 at p. 394. See *Harrow London Borough Council v. Donohue* [1995] 1 E.G.L.R. 257.

[4] [1905] 2 Ch. 614.

[5] *Patel v. W.H. Smith (Eziot) Ltd* [1987] 1 W.L.R. 853; *Anchor Brewhouse Developments Ltd v. Berkley House (Docklands Developments) Ltd* [1987] 2 E.G.L.R. 173; (1988) 138 N.L.J. 23 (E. McKendrick) and 385 (H. Wilkinson).

[6] Discretionary bars are considered below, *post*, p. 771.

[7] *Halsey v. Esso Petroleum Co. Ltd* [1961] 1 W.L.R. 683; *Att.-Gen. v. Times Newspapers Ltd, The Times*, June 27, 1975 (interlocutory injunction refused where defendant undertook not to publish Crossman diaries before trial); *British Broadcasting Corporation v. Hearn* [1977] 1 W.L.R. 1004.

[8] See *Glynn v. Keele University* [1971] 1 W.L.R. 487.

[9] [1970] A.C. 652 at p. 655. See also *Leakey v. National Trust for Places of Historic Interest or Natural Beauty* [1980] Q.B. 485; *Re C. (a minor)* [1991] 2 F.L.R. 168.

[10] *Harrow London Borough Council v. Donohue* [1995] 1 E.G.L.R. 257.

[11] *Charrington v. Simons & Co. Ltd* [1971] 1 W.L.R. 598; *Pugh v. Howells* (1984) 48 P. & C.R. 29. Failure to obtain a prohibitory injunction does not preclude the issue subsequently of a mandatory injunction: see *Wrotham Park Estate v. Parkside Homes Ltd* [1974] 1 W.L.R. 798, *infra*.

more usual in the latter situation, but an injunction may be granted.[12] We have already seen that the terms of an injunction must be certain. It follows from this that a duty which is itself uncertain cannot be enforced by injunction.[13]

Problems of supervision may arise with mandatory injunctions as with specific performance.[14] This will not normally prevent the grant of a "restorative" mandatory injunction, which merely requires an act of restoration, but a mandatory injunction is unlikely to be granted in cases involving the continuous performance of a positive obligation.

> In *Gravesham Borough Council v. British Railways Board*,[15] the defendant planned to curtail the services of its ferry. As this would cause inconvenience to some local workers, a mandatory injunction was sought to compel the defendant to maintain existing timetables, even though this would cause the ferry to be run at a loss. It was held that in fact there was no breach of the defendant's common law duty to operate the ferry, but even if there had been, a mandatory injunction would not be appropriate, because of enforcement difficulties and financial hardship to the defendant. Slade J. said that there was no absolute and inflexible rule that the court will never grant an injunction requiring a series of acts involving the continuous employment of people over a number of years. But the jurisdiction to grant such an injunction would be exercised only in exceptional circumstances.

As in the case of prohibitory injunctions, it is not necessary for the plaintiff to show grave damage or inconvenience. In *Kelsen v. Imperial Tobacco Co. Ltd*[16] a mandatory injunction was granted to enforce the removal of a sign which trespassed in the airspace above the plaintiff's premises, causing no real damage to the plaintiff, save in so far as he could have charged for the use of the space.

While the extent of the damage is not crucial, the question of hardship to the defendant is more significant.[17] In *Charrington v.*

---

[12] See *Evans v. B.B.C. and I.B.A., The Times*, February 26, 1974 (interlocutory); *SEDAC Investments Ltd v. Tanner* [1982] 1 W.L.R. 1342.

[13] *Bower v. Bantam Investments Ltd* [1972] 1 W.L.R. 1120 (interlocutory); *cf. Acrow (Automation) Ltd v. Rex Chainbelt Inc.* [1971] 1 W.L.R. 1676; *Peninsular Maritime Ltd v. Padseal Ltd* (1981) 259 E.G. 860.

[14] *Ante*, p. 704.

[15] [1978] Ch. 379. See also *Dowty Boulton Paul Ltd v. Wolverhampton Corporation* [1971] 1 W.L.R. 204 (no injunction to enforce a covenant to maintain land as an airfield); *cf. Co-operative Insurance Society Ltd v. Argyll Stores (Holdings) Ltd* [1996] Ch. 286 (specific performance of covenant in lease to keep open in trading hours as a retail shop).

[16] [1957] 2 Q.B. 334.

[17] *Gravesham Borough Council v. British Railways Board, supra*; *Jordan v. Norfolk County Council* [1994 1 W.L.R. 1353 (disproportionate cost). See also *Colls v. Home and Colonial Stores Ltd* [1904] A.C. 179, and other cases on Lord Cairns' Act, *post*, p. 778.

Simons & Co. Ltd,[18] Buckley J. thought that the criterion for the grant of a mandatory injunction was a fair result, taking into consideration the benefit which the order would confer on the plaintiff and the detriment which it would cause the defendant. But the Court of Appeal doubted the usefulness of the "fair result" test.[19]

In *Wrotham Park Estate v. Parkside Homes Ltd,*[20] the defendant had erected houses in breach of a restrictive covenant which it had thought was unenforceable. Although purchasers were now in occupation, the plaintiffs sought a mandatory injunction for the demolition of the houses. For various reasons, the plaintiffs had not sought interlocutory relief to prevent the erection of the houses, but this was not fatal to the grant of a mandatory injunction.[21] The fact that the writ was issued before much building had been done was a relevant but not a conclusive factor. The injunction was refused, as it would result in the unpardonable waste of needed houses. Instead, damages were awarded under Lord Cairns' Act.

Finally, it has been held that the court should be reluctant to intervene in industrial disputes by the grant of a mandatory injunction.

In *Harold Stephen and Co. Ltd v. Post Office,*[22] an industrial dispute had arisen whereby postal workers were suspended for unlawfully "blacking" the mail of a certain company (Grunwick). This resulted in the plaintiff company's mail being held up and its business seriously disrupted. The plaintiff sought a mandatory injunction against the Post Office to release its mail. The Court of Appeal refused the injunction, which would require the Post Office to take back the suspended workers, who would be likely to continue the unlawful action. The injunction would, therefore, have the effect of revoking the Post Office's disciplinary measures and making it appear that the court endorsed the continuance of the unlawful action. Geoffrey Lane L.J. said that "It can only be in very rare circumstances and in the most extreme circumstances that this court should interfere by way of mandatory

---

[18] [1970] 1 W.L.R. 725 at p. 730. See also *Shepherd Homes Ltd v. Sandham* [1971] Ch. 340.
[19] [1971] 1 W.L.R. 598, *post*, p. 784.
[20] [1974] 1 W.L.R. 798; (1974) 39 Conv.(N.S.) 289 (F. Crane); (1975) 34 C.L.J. 224 (J. Jolowicz); distinguished in *Wakeham v. Wood* (1982) 43 P. & C.R. 40, where the building was in flagrant disregard of the covenant.
[21] See also *Shaw v. Applegate* [1977] 1 W.L.R. 970 at p. 978.
[22] [1977] 1 W.L.R. 1172.

injunction in the delicate mechanism of industrial disputes and industrial negotiations." [23]

Such an extreme case was *Parker v. Camden London Borough Council*,[24] where a strike of boilermen employed by the landlord council meant that the tenants, many of whom were elderly or had young children, had no heating or hot water. In these exceptional circumstances, involving risk to life and health, the court was prepared to grant a mandatory injunction to turn on the boiler even though industrial action was involved.

The principles applicable to the grant of mandatory interlocutory injunctions and mandatory *quia timet* injunctions are discussed below.[25]

iii. Suspension of Injunctions. If it would be very difficult for the defendant to comply immediately with the injunction, he will not be made to do the impossible. The injunction may be granted but suspended for a reasonable period, particularly if such a course will not result in financial damage to the plaintiff. The defendant may be required to undertake to pay damages to the plaintiff for any loss. Suspension is not unusual where the defendant is a local authority, which must make alternative arrangements for the performance of its duties. Thus, in *Pride of Derby Angling Association v. British Celanese and Others*[26] an injunction was granted against a local authority to restrain the pollution of a river, but was suspended for a reasonable time, with the possibility of further suspension should the circumstances require it.

The courts have sometimes suspended injunctions not in order to give the defendant time to comply, but rather to enable him to continue his wrongful activity in cases involving no substantial injury to the plaintiff. Thus, in *Woollerton and Wilson Ltd v. Richard Costain Ltd*[27] an injunction to restrain aerial trespass (causing no danger or damage) by a crane during building works was granted but suspended until a date when the crane would no longer be needed. This was doubted by the Court of Appeal in *Charrington v. Simons & Co. Ltd*,[28] where a three-year suspension of an injunction to

---

[23] *Ibid.* at p. 1180. See also *Meade v. London Borough of Haringey* [1979] 1 W.L.R. 637.

[24] [1986] Ch. 162 (interlocutory).

[25] *Post*, pp. 765, 770.

[26] [1953] Ch. 149. See also *Halsey v. Esso Petroleum Co. Ltd* [1961] 1 W.L.R. 683 (suspension for six weeks in nuisance case); *Miller v. Jackson* [1977] Q.B. 966; *Waverley Borough Council v. Hilden* [1988] 1 W.L.R. 246.

[27] [1970] 1 W.L.R. 411; (1970) 33 M.L.R. 552 (G. Dworkin).

[28] [1971] 1 W.L.R. 598; and in *Jaggard v. Sawyer* [1995] 1 W.L.R. 269. See also *Trenberth (John) Ltd v. National Westminster Bank Ltd* (1979) 39 P. & C.R. 104; [1980] Conv. 308 (H. Street). A better solution might have been an award of damages under Lord Cairns' Act: see (1975) 34 C.L.J. 224 at p. 247 (J. Jolowicz).

reinstate a track (which had been resurfaced in breach of covenant) was held improper.

D. Interlocutory Injunctions

i. General. Interlocutory injunctions raise somewhat different considerations. The jurisdiction is related not to the most just method of protecting established rights, but to the most convenient method of preserving the status quo while rights are established. The object of an interlocutory injunction is "to prevent a litigant, who must necessarily suffer the law's delay, from losing by that delay the fruit of his litigation."[29]

Interlocutory injunctions may be prohibitory, mandatory, or *quia timet*. Normally such an injunction remains in force until the trial of the action, but an interim injunction may be granted, which endures for some shorter specified period. If the parties consent, the interlocutory hearing may be treated as a final trial if the dispute is of law. But this will not be possible if the dispute is of fact, as affidavit evidence is unsuitable for such issues.

As we have seen, failure to seek an interlocutory injunction to restrain the commission of a wrongful act will not necessarily preclude the plaintiff from later obtaining a final mandatory injunction to compel the defendant to undo the act.[30]

(a) *Ex Parte Procedure.* The plaintiff should give at least two clear days' notice, so that, when the motion is heard, the defendant can oppose it. But exceptionally an injunction may be granted *ex parte*, without serving notice on the defendant, if the matter is one of such urgency that irreparable damage would be caused if the plaintiff had to go through the normal procedure.[31] The *ex parte* injunction is usually an interim injunction, valid only until the next motion day,[32] for which formal notice can be given. An *ex parte* injunction may be granted even before the writ or summons has been issued. In *Re N. (No. 2)*,[33] an *ex parte* injunction was granted

---

[29] *Hoffman-La Roche (F.) & Co. v. Secretary of State for Trade and Industry* [1975] A.C. 295 at p. 355 (Lord Wilberforce).

[30] *Wrotham Park Estate v. Parkside Homes Ltd* [1974] 1 W.L.R. 798. But such an omission may be relevant to the defence of acquiescence: *Shaw v. Applegate* [1977] 1 W.L.R 970, *post*, p. 774.

[31] It is otherwise if the plaintiff had the opportunity to give notice; *Bates v. Lord Hailsham of St. Marylebone* [1972] 1 W.L.R. 1373. Where a trade dispute is involved, see the Trade Union and Labour Relations (Consolidation) Act 1992, s.221(2), *post*, p. 760.

[32] Every weekday in term is a motion day in the Chancery Division: see *Practice Direction* [1980] 1 W.L.R. 741. For procedure, see *Practice Direction* [1983] 1 W.L.R. 433.

[33] [1967] Ch. 512.

by a High Court judge at his residence on a Sunday, to prevent the applicant's husband from taking their children to Australia.

In family matters injunctions should not be granted *ex parte* unless there is "real immediate danger of serious injury or irreparable damage."[34] Only in the most exceptional circumstances will an injunction be granted *ex parte* requiring a spouse to leave the matrimonial home.[35]

In the commercial sphere, *ex parte* injunctions should not normally be granted which will prevent banks from honouring contractual obligations, such as payouts under letters of credit.[36]

The *ex parte* procedure has been found most useful in the *Anton Piller* and *Mareva* cases, where there is a danger that the defendant, if aware of the application, would destroy or remove vital evidence, or move assets out of the jurisdiction. These developments are discussed below.[37]

(b) *Discharge of Interlocutory Injunctions.* The court has inherent jurisdiction to discharge an interlocutory injunction, even when the defendant has not applied for its discharge.[38] Furthermore, where an injunction has been granted which affects someone who was not a party to the action, he can apply to court for the variation or discharge of the injunction.[39]

(c) *Injunctions Pending Appeal.* Where a claim for an interlocutory injunction is dismissed, the judge has jurisdiction to grant a limited injunction pending an appeal, on the plaintiff's *ex parte* application.[40] Such an injunction may be granted in order that the appeal, if successful, is not nugatory.

(d) *Complete Relief.* It is no objection that the grant of an interlocutory injunction gives complete relief to the plaintiff without requiring him to prove his case, so that he need bring no final action.[41] In

---

[34] *Practice Note* [1978] 1 W.L.R. 925; *Ansah v. Ansah* [1977] Fam. 138; *G. v. G.* [1990] 1 F.L.R. 395.

[35] *Masich v. Masich* (1977) 121 S.J. 645; (1977) 7 Fam. Law 245.

[36] *Bolivinter Oil S.A. v. Chase Manhattan Bank* [1984] 1 W.L.R. 392n.

[37] *Post*, pp. 804, 808.

[38] *R.D. Harbottle (Mercantile) Ltd v. National Westminster Bank Ltd* [1978] Q.B. 146 (*ex parte* injunction).

[39] *Cretanor Maritime Co. Ltd v. Irish Marine Management Ltd* [1978] 1 W.L.R. 966; *Iraqi Ministry of Defence v. Arcepey Shipping Co. S.A.* [1981] Q.B. 65, *post*, p. 815 (*Mareva* injunctions).

[40] *Erinford Properties Ltd v. Cheshire County Council* [1974] Ch. 261; *Chartered Bank v. Daklouche* [1976] 1 W.L.R. 107. See also *Ketchum International plc v. Group Public Relations Holdings Ltd* [1997] 1 W.L.R. 4 (jurisdiction to restrain disposal of assets pending appeal if good arguable appeal).

[41] As to whether the principle of *American Cyanamid Co. v. Ethicon Ltd, infra,* applies in such cases, see *post*, p. 762.

Woodford v. Smith,[42] Megarry J. granted an interlocutory injunction to restrain a residents' association from breaking its contract by holding a meeting without the plaintiff members. There was nothing to prevent the court in a proper case from granting on motion all the relief claimed in the action. It may be a more serious objection in the case of mandatory interlocutory injunctions,[43] where positive action is required, but in *Evans v. B.B.C. and I.B.A.*[44] a mandatory interlocutory injunction was granted to enforce the Welsh Nationalist Party's alleged contractual right to a Party Political Broadcast on television just before an election. The interlocutory injunction was thus a complete remedy, making it unnecessary to continue to trial and prove the case.

(e) *Injunction Ineffective.* As equity does not act in vain, an interlocutory injunction will not be granted where it would be of no effect.[45] In *Bentley-Stevens v. Jones*[46] a director was removed by irregular proceedings. This was not a case for an interlocutory injunction, as the irregularities could be cured by going through the proper processes; the result therefore would be the same.

ii. Principles Applicable to the Issue of Interlocutory Injunctions. As in the case of mandatory injunctions, the interlocutory injunction is discretionary and is never granted as of course. Prior to the decision of the House of Lords in *American Cyanamid Co. v. Ethicon Ltd*,[47] discussed below, it was well established that the plaintiff had to show a strong prima facie case that his rights had been infringed.[48] He was then required to show that damages would not be an adequate remedy if he succeeded at the trial, and that the balance of convenience favoured the grant. In other words, an interlocutory injunction would not be granted unless the plaintiff could show that it was more likely than not that he would succeed in obtaining a final injunction at the trial.

---

[42] [1970] 1 W.L.R. 806; see also *Manchester Corporation v. Connolly* [1970] Ch. 420, where there was plainly no defence.

[43] *Locabail International Finance Ltd v. Agroexport* [1986] 1 W.L.R. 657.

[44] *The Times*, February 26, 1974. See also *Shepherd Homes Ltd v. Sandham* [1971] Ch. 340 at p. 347, and *Acrow (Automation) Ltd v. Rex Chainbelt Inc.* [1971] 1 W.L.R. 1676 at p. 1683.

[45] Similarly with final injunctions; *Att-Gen. v. Guardian Newspapers Ltd (No. 2)* [1990] 1 A.C. 109. A declaration may be appropriate; *Love v. Herrity* (1991) 23 H.L.R. 217.

[46] [1974] 1 W.L.R. 638.

[47] [1975] A.C. 396; (1975) 38 M.L.R. 672 (A. Gore); (1976) 35 C.L.J. 82 (P. Wallington); (1975) 91 L.Q.R. 168 (P. Prescott); (1981) 40 C.L.J. 307 (C. Gray).

[48] See *J. T. Stratford & Son Ltd v. Lindley* [1965] A.C. 269, especially at p. 338 (Lord Upjohn). The contrary was not there argued. The decision was not cited in *American Cyanamid*.

(a) *American Cyanamid Co. v. Ethicon Ltd.*[49] The principles mentioned above were replaced by the rules laid down by Lord Diplock in *American Cyanamid*, which were designed to circumvent the necessity of deciding disputed facts or determining points of law without hearing sufficient argument.[50] The case concerned an application for a *quia timet* interlocutory injunction to restrain the infringement of a patent. It was unanimously held that there was no rule requiring the plaintiff to establish a prima facie case.[51] The rule is that the court must be satisfied that the plaintiff's case is not frivolous or vexatious and that there is a serious question to be tried. Once that is established, the governing consideration is the balance of convenience. The court should not embark on anything resembling a trial of the action. At the interlocutory stage it is no part of the court's function to resolve conflicts of evidence on affidavit nor to resolve difficult questions of law.[52] These are matters for the trial. At the interlocutory stage the facts may be disputed and the evidence incomplete and there is no cross-examination; the court's discretion would be stultified if, on untested and incomplete evidence, it could only grant the injunction if the plaintiff had shown that he was more than 50 per cent likely to succeed at trial.

While the balance of convenience is the governing consideration, a significant factor in assessing it is the inadequacy of damages to each party. If that does not provide an answer, then other aspects of the balance of convenience will arise. If the balance of convenience does not clearly favour either party, then the preservation of the status quo will be decisive. Only as a last resort is it proper to consider the relative strength of the cases of both parties, and only then if it appears from the facts set out in the affidavit evidence, as to which there is no credible dispute, that the strength of one party's case is disproportionate to that of the other.[53] Finally, other special factors may have to be considered in individual cases.

Thus it will be seen that there is a series of rules, most of which will apply only if the previous one has not afforded a solution. But, as Browne L.J. stated in *Fellowes & Son v. Fisher*,[54] the remedy is discretionary and the principles enunciated by Lord Diplock contain some elements of flexibility. The House of Lords cannot have

---

[49] [1975] A.C. 396.
[50] *Smith v. Inner London Education Authority* [1978] 1 All E.R. 411, at p. 426.
[51] But Lord Diplock himself had said that an applicant for an interlocutory injunction had to show a "strong prima facie case" that he would succeed at trial: *Hoffman-LaRoche (F.) & Co. v. Secretary of State for Trade and Industry* [1975] A.C. 295 at p. 360. For an explanation, see *Series 5 Software Ltd v. Clarke* [1996] 1 All E.R. 853.
[52] *Derby & Co. Ltd v. Weldon* [1990] Ch. 48.
[53] See *Cambridge Nutrition Ltd v. British Broadcasting Corporation* [1990] 3 All E.R. 523; cf. *Series 5 Software Ltd v. Clarke, supra.*
[54] [1976] Q.B. 122 at p. 139.

intended to lay down rigid rules.[55] They are best described as guidelines,[56] which "must never be used as a rule of thumb, let alone as a strait-jacket."[57]

But the new principles have not satisfied everybody. Lord Denning M.R. in *Fellowes & Son v. Fisher*[58] expressed a preference for the "prima facie case" approach, which had been required for a century, because most cases never went to trial,[59] as the parties usually accepted the court's prima facie view, which was a sensible and convenient practice. The other members of the Court of Appeal expressed the need for further guidance, as the new rules were a complete departure from previous practice. But the majority of the Court of Appeal in *Hubbard v. Pitt*[60] considered that the *American Cyanamid* principles were convenient and had often been adopted.

The principles laid down by Lord Diplock in *American Cyanamid* were these:

(i) PLAINTIFF'S CASE NOT FRIVOLOUS OR VEXATIOUS. This requirement was designed to remove "any attempt by plaintiffs to harass defendants, any case which was futile and any case which was misconceived or an abuse of the process of the court."[61] Such claims fail *in limine*. The plaintiff must also show that there is a serious question to be tried, which means that he must have a good arguable case,[62] or, in other words, a real prospect of success at the trial.[63]

(ii) THE BALANCE OF CONVENIENCE. This concept was well known before the decision in *American Cyanamid*,[64] thus the earlier cases remain useful illustrations, but it must be borne in mind that

---

[55] See *Hubbard v. Vosper* [1972] 2 Q.B. 84, advocating the flexibility of the remedy, and referred to with apparent approval by Lord Diplock in *American Cyanamid* [1975] A.C. 396 at p. 407; *Kirklees Borough Council v. Wickes Building Supplies Ltd* [1993] A.C. 227.

[56] *Cayne v. Global Natural Resources plc* [1984] 1 All E.R. 225.

[57] *Cambridge Nutrition Ltd v. British Broadcasting Corporation, supra*, at p. 535.

[58] [1976] Q.B. 122.

[59] See *British Broadcasting Corporation v. Hearn* [1977] 1 W.L.R. 1004; *Dunford & Elliott Ltd v. Johnson & Firth Brown Ltd* [1977] 1 Lloyd's Rep. 505 at p. 513; *Cayne v. Global Natural Resources plc.* [1984] 1 All E.R. 225.

[60] [1976] Q.B. 142. Lord Denning M.R. dissented.

[61] *Honeywell Information Systems Ltd v. Anglian Water Authority, The Times*, June 29, 1976 (Geoffrey Lane L.J.).

[62] *Morning Star Cooperative Society Ltd v. Express Newspapers Ltd, The Times*, October 18, 1978; *cf. Derby & Co. Ltd v. Weldon* [1990] Ch. 48; *post*, p. 813.

[63] *Re Lord Cable* [1977] 1 W.L.R. 7 at p. 20; *Smith v. Inner London Education Authority* [1978] 1 All E.R. 411; *Cayne v. Global Natural Resources plc, supra*.

[64] [1975] A.C. 396. The "balance of justice" was preferred in *Att.-Gen. v. Barker* [1990] 3 All E.R. 257 at p. 260.

this is now the governing consideration, assuming that the preliminary requirement outlined above is satisfied.

We have seen that the inadequacy of damages is a significant factor in assessing the balance of convenience. The court must first of all consider the adequacy of damages to each party, namely whether damages would adequately compensate the plaintiff for any loss caused by the acts of the defendant prior to the trial[65] and whether, should the plaintiff fail at the trial, any loss caused to the defendant by the grant of the injunction could be adequately compensated by the plaintiff's undertaking in damages.[66]

An example of irreparable loss is the distribution of a dividend to shareholders on the basis of supposedly erroneous calculations.[67] Another is the loss of trade when members of the public "picketed" the plaintiff's business premises,[68] or when a trade union proposed unlawfully to induce the plaintiff's employees to break their contracts by supporting a political strike[69]; the loss cannot be measured, but it may be great. Similarly, the publication of confidential material,[70] or the loss of a job with good prospects.[71] Damages will also be inadequate if the defendant is a foreign company whose government's exchange control may not permit the payment, or is a foreign company of unknown financial status so that the chances of any substantial damages being paid are questionable.[72] Likewise if an individual defendant does not have the means to pay any appreciable damages,[73] or if the damages would be unquantifiable,[74] as in the case of injury to goodwill[75] or reputation.[76]

---

[65] See *Lion Laboratories Ltd v. Evans* [1985] Q.B. 526.

[66] *Chancellor, Masters and Scholars of the University of Oxford v. Pergamon Press Ltd* (1977) 121 S.J. 758. See also *Laws v. Florinpace Ltd* [1981] 1 All E.R. 659 (injunction to restrain nuisance by running "sex shop" in residential area).

[67] *Bloxham v. Metropolitan Ry.* (1868) L.R. 3 Ch.App. 337.

[68] *Hubbard v. Pitt* [1976] Q.B. 142, *post*, p. 759. See also *Cutsforth v. Mansfield Inns Ltd* [1986] 1 W.L.R. 558.

[69] *Express Newspapers Ltd v. Keys* [1980] I.R.L.R. 247.

[70] *Att.-Gen. v. Times Newspapers Ltd, The Times,* June 27, 1975 (The Crossman Diaries); *Att.-Gen. v. Guardian Newspapers Ltd* [1987] 1 W.L.R. 1248 (*Spycatcher*). But the perpetual injunctions were refused: *Att.-Gen. v. Jonathan Cape Ltd* [1976] Q.B. 752; *Att.-Gen. v. Guardian Newspapers (No. 2)* [1990] 1 A.C. 109.

[71] *Fellowes & Son v. Fisher* [1976] Q.B. 122, *post*, p. 758; *Powell v. London Borough of Brent* [1987] I.R.L.R. 466.

[72] *Evans Marshall & Co. Ltd v. Bertola S.A.* [1973] 1 W.L.R. 349.

[73] *Morning Star Cooperative Society Ltd v. Express Newspapers Ltd, The Times,* October 18, 1978; *De Falco v. Crawley Borough Council* [1980] Q.B. 460 (no injunction where plaintiff could not give worthwhile undertaking in damages). See also *Thomas Marshall (Exports) Ltd v. Guinle* [1979] Ch. 227.

[74] *Morning Star Cooperative Society Ltd v. Express Newspapers Ltd, supra.* See also *Express Newspapers Ltd v. Keys, supra.*

[75] *Chancellor, Masters and Scholars of the University of Oxford v. Pergamon Press Ltd* (1977) 121 S.J. 758.

[76] *British Broadcasting Corporation v. Hearn* [1977] 1 W.L.R. 1004. (Injunction to restrain interference with plaintiff's broadcast of the Cup Final to South Africa); *Schering Chemicals Ltd v. Falkman Ltd* [1982] Q.B. 1.

While the adequacy of damages is a most significant factor, other considerations may be taken into account in assessing the balance of convenience. Where the dispute between the parties is a political one, the damage to both parties may not be calculable in monetary terms.[77] All the circumstances must be considered, including difficulties of compliance or enforcement, and the principle that the court should be reluctant to interfere in industrial disputes or political decisions by injunction.[78] In *Smith v. Inner London Education Authority*,[79] where an interlocutory injunction was sought to restrain an alleged breach of statutory duty, it was said that where the defendant is a public body, the balance of convenience must be looked at more widely; the court must consider the interests of the general public to whom the duty is owed. The public interest was also a relevant consideration in *Express Newspapers Ltd v. Keys*,[80] where an interlocutory injunction was granted to restrain a trade union from unlawfully inducing a breach of contract by the plaintiff's employees, by persuading them to support the "Day of Action," a political strike. Where it was clear that the defendant was acting unlawfully,[81] "it would require wholly exceptional circumstances to justify a proper exercise of the discretion to allow such conduct to continue." If the injunction was refused, the plaintiff would suffer unquantifiable damage, whereas if it was granted, the union would suffer no harm save political embarrassment. It was in the interest of the members of the union and of the public that the injunction be granted.

If the balance of convenience does not clearly favour either party, then, as we have seen, the deciding factor will be the preservation of the status quo,[82] which means the circumstances prevailing when the defendant began the activity which the plaintiff seeks to restrain.[83]

We have also seen that the relative strength of each party's case is a factor to be considered as a last resort, and only then if the

---

[77] See *Lewis v. Heffer* [1978] 1 W.L.R. 1061. Geoffrey Lane L.J., at p. 1078, found great difficulty in applying *American Cyanamid* in such a case.

[78] *Meade v. London Borough of Haringey* [1979] 1 W.L.R. 637, *ante*, p. 749; *Jakeman v. South West Thames Regional Health Authority and London Ambulance Service* [1990] I.R.L.R. 62.

[79] [1978] 1 All E.R. 411. (Injunction to restrain phasing out of grammar schools refused.)

[80] [1980] I.R.L.R. 247, *ante*, p. 746.

[81] See also *Thanet District Council v. Ninedrive Ltd* [1978] 1 All E.R. 703; interlocutory injunction granted to restrain plain breach of statute where defendant making profits by flouting the statute (Sunday trading).

[82] See *Lewis v. Heffer* [1978] 1 W.L.R. 1061; *Chancellor, Masters and Scholars of the University of Oxford v. Pergamon Press Ltd* (1977) 121 S.J. 758.

[83] *Fellowes & Son v. Fisher* [1976] Q.B. 122 at p. 141; *Garden Cottage Foods Ltd v. Milk Marketing Board* [1984] A.C. 130. But delay by the plaintiff will be taken into account in considering this principle: *Shepherd Homes Ltd v. Sandham* [1971] Ch. 340, *post*, p. 771.

strength of one party's case is disproportionate to that of the other.[84] Prior to the decision in *American Cyanamid*,[85] however, this was a vital consideration: the plaintiff had to show a strong prima facie case.[86] This departure from the previous practice was regarded as a source of difficulty by the Court of Appeal in *Fellowes & Son v. Fisher*,[87] where it was felt that the relative strength of the parties must be a factor in assessing the balance of convenience, and that sometimes the court could not do justice without considering the merits. The view was expressed that perhaps the House of Lords had not had all types of cases in mind.[88]

(iii) OTHER SPECIAL FACTORS. Lord Diplock in *American Cyanamid* concluded his exposition of the guiding principles by saying that "other special factors" may have to be considered in individual cases. A question which arises is whether these special factors are merely an aspect of the balance of convenience, or whether they justify a departure from the principles laid down in *American Cyanamid* and a return to the previous practice of requiring a prima facie case.

In *Fellowes & Son v. Fisher*,[89] the plaintiffs, a firm of solicitors, sought to restrain the breach of a restrictive covenant in the contract of a former employee. The covenant was of doubtful validity, but there was a serious question to be tried. As there was no evidence as to the adequacy of damages to either party, the decisive factor, according to the majority of the Court of Appeal, was the balance of convenience, which favoured refusal of the injunction.

Lord Denning M.R., refusing the injunction on different grounds, did not feel bound by *American Cyanamid*.[90] There were two escape routes from it. First, Lord Diplock had indicated that other special factors could be considered in individual cases. These "individual cases" were numerous and important, and included the present case. Secondly, the relative strength of the parties could be looked at

---

[84] Relative strength was decisive in *Cambridge Nutrition Ltd v. British Broadcasting Corporation* [1990] 3 All E.R. 523, where the timing of a broadcast was vital and a contract to restrain it was doubtful.

[85] [1975] A.C. 396.

[86] Relative strength is still a governing consideration in Scotland, where *American Cyanamid* does not apply. See (1980) 43 M.L.R. 327 (R. Simpson).

[87] [1976] Q.B. 122, *infra*. See further *Series 5 Software Ltd v. Clarke* [1996] 1 All E.R. 853.

[88] Possible special cases are dealt with below.

[89] [1976] Q.B. 122.

[90] [1975] A.C. 396.

where the court found that there was little difference in the uncompensatable disadvantages to both sides. Thus the injunction should be refused because there was no prima facie case.

The question next arose in *Hubbard v. Pitt*.[91]

> Certain members of the public disapproved of the extensive development which had taken place in Islington, and they picketed a leading firm of estate agents which had acted in connection with many developments in the area. The pickets held placards and distributed leaflets to passers-by, thus impeding access to the premises, and deterring potential clients. The estate agents obtained an injunction to restrain them and this was upheld by the majority of the Court of Appeal.

There was a serious question to be tried, and the balance of convenience favoured the grant. Damages could not compensate the plaintiffs for loss of business, even if the defendants could pay, whereas the injunction would not prevent a legitimate campaign. The majority held that there were no circumstances in which "special factors" would take a case out of the general rule that no prima facie case was required. "It appears to me clear beyond peradventure that Lord Diplock was there referring to special factors affecting the balance of convenience and not to special factors enabling the court to ignore the general principles laid down or, more particularly, to ignore ... the admonition not to require of a party seeking an interlocutory injunction that he should have made out a prima facie case."[92] But Lord Denning M.R. again held that "special factors" took the case out of the *American Cyanamid* rules. In his view a prima facie case was required. The appeal should be allowed because the injunction would interfere with free speech and the right to demonstrate and protest.

The better view, it is submitted, is that "special factors" are merely an aspect of the balance of convenience. In *Smith v. Inner London Education Authority*[93] it was held, as we have seen, that where the defendant is a public body, the balance of convenience must be looked at more widely, and the interests of the general public, to whom the defendant's duties are owed, must be considered. This was treated as a "special factor." Similarly where an injunction is sought to prevent a public authority from enforcing a law which is claimed to be invalid (as being incompatible with European Community law). In such an exceptional case an injunction should not be granted unless there is firm ground for the

---

[91] [1976] Q.B. 142; (1976) 35 C.L.J. 82 (P. Wallington).
[92] *Ibid.* at p. 185, *per* Stamp L.J.
[93] [1978] 1 All E.R. 411. See also *Lewis v. Heffer* [1978] 1 W.L.R. 1061, *supra; Bryanston Finance Ltd v. de Vries (No. 2)* [1976] Ch. 63, *infra.*

challenge, and the public interest must be considered when assessing the balance of convenience.[94]

It has long been established that interlocutory injunctions will rarely be granted in libel cases where the defendant intends to justify.[95] It has been held that *American Cyanamid* has not affected this principle,[96] which might, therefore, be regarded as a "special factor." Similarly the rule that a bank will not be enjoined from paying under a letter of credit unless there is a clear prima facie case of fraud by the beneficiary.[97] Special considerations affecting the grant of *Mareva* and *Anton Piller* interlocutory injunctions are discussed elsewhere.[98]

(b) *Exceptional cases.* The following are cases where the *American Cyanamid* principles do not apply, or apply in modified form. Other exceptional cases may arise outside these categories.[99] Thus it has been held that *American Cyanamid* is inapplicable to an order to give life-sustaining treatment to a child.[1] Nor does it apply where there is a clear statutory power to grant an injunction.[2] Indeed, the growing number of exceptions may indicate that the principles are flawed.[3]

(i) TRADE DISPUTES. After the decision in *American Cyanamid*, provisions now found in s.221(2) of the Trade Union and Labour Relations (Consolidation) Act 1992[4] were enacted, providing that where, in an application for an interlocutory injunction, the defendant claims that he acted in contemplation or furtherance of a trade dispute, the court in exercising its discretion is to have regard to the likelihood of the defendant's establishing at the trial any of the

---

[94] *R. v. Secretary of State for Transport, ex p. Factortame (No. 2)* [1991] 1 A.C. 603; (1991) 107 L.Q.R. 196 (A. Zuckerman).
[95] *Bonnard v. Perryman* [1891] 2 Ch. 269, *post*, p. 793. See also *Hubbard v. Vosper* [1972] 2 Q.B. 84 (similarly in copyright actions where reasonable defence of fair dealing).
[96] *J. Trevor & Sons v. P. R. Solomon* (1978) 248 E.G. 779 (*per* Lord Denning M.R.); *Bestobell Paints Ltd v. Bigg* (1975) 119 S.J. 678; *Herbage v. Pressdram Ltd* [1984] 1 W.L.R. 1160; *Att.-Gen. v. British Broadcasting Corporation* [1981] A.C. 303 at p. 342 (expressing a similar principle as to contempt in civil actions); *Gulf Oil (Great Britain) Ltd v. Page* [1987] Ch. 327.
[97] See *Group Josi Re v. Walbrook Insurance Co. Ltd* [1996] 1 W.L.R. 1152.
[98] *Post*, pp. 804, 808.
[99] *R. v. Secretary of State for Health, ex p. Generics (UK) Ltd, The Times*, February 25, 1997.
[1] *Re J (a minor) (medical treatment)* [1993] Fam. 15.
[2] *Runnymede Borough Council v. Harwood* (1994) 68 P. & C.R. 300 (Town and Country Planning Act 1990, s.187B).
[3] See (1993) 3 Carib. L.R. 76 and (1993–94) 4 K.C.L.J. 52 (J. Martin); (1993) 56 M.L.R. 325 at p. 328 (A. Zuckerman).
[4] The amendments have been said to have made little impact; (1987) 50 M.L.R. 506 (B. Simpson). See also s.221(1) (*ex parte* orders).

matters which, under the Act, confer immunity from tortious liability.[5] Thus *American Cyanamid* is modified in trade dispute cases by the opportunity for the defendant to prove a prima facie defence under the labour relations legislation.

The reason for this amendment was that applications for injunctions in industrial disputes rarely went beyond the interlocutory stage, and if *American Cyanamid* was applied without modification, the balance of convenience would invariably favour the plaintiff (*i.e.* the employer),[6] thus denying the trade unions their power to pressurise employers. Industrial action is unlikely to be effective if it has to be postponed, thus the unions' bargaining counter would disappear. In view of the immunity from liability in tort mentioned above, this might be thought to be unfair.[7] But trade dispute cases should not be approached on the basis that they will not go to trial.[8] Since the Employment Act 1982 the injunction may be sought against the union itself, as opposed to an office-holder personally, which increases the likelihood of a trial.[9]

A question which arises is whether the predecessor to section 221(2) restored the previous law, requiring a prima facie case, to interlocutory injunctions concerning trade disputes,[10] or whether it merely added an extra element to the *American Cyanamid*[11] principles. It is submitted that the latter is the correct approach.[12] Sometimes the likelihood of the defendant's establishing the defence of statutory immunity has been regarded simply as an aspect of the balance of convenience.[13] Perhaps the better view[14] is that it adds a third stage to the enquiry. Thus the court must consider first whether there is a serious question to be tried, secondly the balance of convenience, and thirdly the likelihood of the establishment of the defence of statutory immunity.[15]

---

[5] See s.219 of the 1992 Act.
[6] Especially in public service disputes, where public interest is relevant to the balance of convenience; see *Beaverbrook Newspapers Ltd v. Keys* [1978] I.R.L.R. 34.
[7] See *N.W.L. Ltd v. Woods* [1979] 1 W.L.R. 1294; (1980) 43 M.L.R. 327 (R. Simpson); (1980) 96 L.Q.R. 189 (A. Clarke and J. Bowers). *Woods* was regarded as of general application and not confined to trade disputes in *Cayne v. Global Natural Resources plc* [1984] 1 All E.R. 225; *post*, p. 762.
[8] *Hadmor Productions Ltd v. Hamilton* [1983] 1 A.C. 191; *Dimbleby & Sons Ltd v. National Union of Journalists* [1984] 1 W.L.R. 427; (1984) 100 L.Q.R. 342 (H. Carty).
[9] *Post*, p. 763.
[10] See *The Camilla M* [1979] 1 Lloyd's Rep. 26; (1979) 42 M.L.R. 458 (B. Doyle).
[11] [1975] A.C. 396.
[12] See *N.W.L. Ltd v. Woods* [1979] 1 W.L.R. 1294; *British Broadcasting Corporation v. Hearn* [1977] 1 W.L.R. 1004; (1978) 41 M.L.R. 80 (Lord Wedderburn); (1977) 127 N.L.J. 654 (R. Kidner); *Hadmor Productions Ltd v. Hamilton, supra*.
[13] *N.W.L. Ltd v. Woods, supra* (Lords Diplock and Fraser).
[14] So considered by Lord Wedderburn in (1978) 41 M.L.R. 80 and (1980) 43 M.L.R. 319. See also (1980) 43 M.L.R. 372 (R. Simpson).
[15] *British Broadcasting Corporation v. Hearn* [1977] 1 W.L.R. 1004 at p. 1016 (Scarman L.J.); *N.W.L. Ltd v. Woods, supra*, at p. 1315 (Lord Scarman).

Section 221(2) requires the court to "have regard" to the likelihood of the defence of statutory immunity succeeding at the trial. Thus the injunction will not normally be granted where the likelihood is that this defence would succeed.[16] But even in such a case the court retains a residual discretion which it may exercise in favour of granting the injunction, for example if the industrial action "endangers the nation or puts at risk such fundamental rights as the right of the public to be informed and the freedom of the Press,"[17] or "would probably have an immediate and devastating effect on the applicant's person or property" or would "cause immediate serious danger to public safety or health."[18] But such cases would be "altogether exceptional", because "When disaster threatens, it is ordinarily for the government, not the courts, to act to avert it."[19] Where it is unlikely that the defence of statutory immunity will be established, it does not always follow that an injunction is appropriate, for example if it would be of no practical use.[20]

(ii) WHERE TRIAL OF THE ACTION UNLIKELY OR DELAYED. We have seen that Lord Denning M.R. in *Fellowes & Son v. Fisher*[21] preferred the "prima facie case" approach to the principles laid down in *American Cyanamid* because most cases never went to trial; and also that amendment was required in the area of trade disputes for the same reason.[22] It has since been held by the Court of Appeal in *Cayne v. Global Natural Resources plc*[23] that the *American Cyanamid* principles do not apply to cases where no trial is likely to take place. Likewise in a restraint of trade case if the trial is unlikely to come on before the end of the period of the restraint.[24] Where the question is whether information can be published in spite of its confidentiality, delay in coming to trial could result in the stifling of legitimate comment until it is no longer important if only an arguable case is required.[25] In these cases it is best to decide on the basis of relative strength, otherwise the defendant might be effectively

---

[16] As to the degree of likelihood necessary to produce this result, see *Duport Steels Ltd v. Sirs* [1980] 1 W.L.R. 142; *Hadmor Productions Ltd v. Hamilton* [1983] 1 A.C. 191.

[17] *Express Newspapers Ltd v. MacShane* [1980] A.C. 672 at p. 695 (Lord Scarman). See also the views of Lords Diplock and Scarman in *N.W.L. Ltd v. Woods* [1979] 1 W.L.R. 1294.

[18] *Duport Steels Ltd v. Sirs* [1980] 1 W.L.R. 142 at p. 166 (Lord Fraser).

[19] *Ibid.* at p. 171. The existence of this residual discretion has been challenged; (1980) 43 M.L.R. 319 at p. 326 (Lord Wedderburn), and at p. 327 (R. Simpson).

[20] *Hadmor Productions Ltd v. Hamilton, supra*; (1982) 45 M.L.R. 447 (R. Simpson).

[21] [1976] Q.B. 122; *ante*, p. 758.

[22] *Ante*, p. 760.

[23] [1984] 1 All E.R. 225, applying *N.W.L. Ltd v. Woods* [1979] 1 W.L.R. 1294; *Thomas v. National Union of Mineworkers (South Wales Area)* [1986] Ch. 20; (1985) 44 C.L.J. 374 (K. Ewing); *Cambridge Nutrition Ltd v. British Broadcasting Corporation* [1990] 3 All E.R. 523.

[24] *David (Lawrence) Ltd v. Ashton* [1991] 1 All E.R. 385; *Lansing Linde Ltd v. Kerr* [1991] 1 W.L.R. 251 (treated as a "wider view of the balance of convenience").

[25] *Att.-Gen. v. Times Newspapers Ltd* [1992] 1 A.C. 191 at p. 226.

precluded at the interlocutory stage from disputing the claim at trial.

In the area of trade disputes, however, it is possible to obtain an injunction and damages against the union itself as opposed to an office-holder personally, and to obtain substantial damages.[26] This means that there is no reason for a judge to exercise his discretion on the assumption that the case will not proceed to trial in cases where the union itself is the defendant.[27]

(iii) WHERE NO ARGUABLE DEFENCE. It has been held that the *American Cyanamid*[28] rules do not apply where the defendant has no arguable defence.[29] In such a case it is not necessary to consider the balance of convenience. Thus the plaintiff may obtain an interlocutory injunction to restrain a clear trespass even where it causes no damage[30]; or to restrain a clear misapplication of union funds.[31] It is probable that the principle that the plaintiff is entitled almost as of right to an injunction to restrain a plain breach of a negative contract provides another example.[32]

(iv) INJUNCTIONS TO RESTRAIN THE PRESENTATION OF A WINDING-UP PETITION. It has been held that a prima facie case (of abuse of process) is still required where a company seeks to restrain a creditor from presenting a winding-up petition.[33] If a prospective petitioner intends to petition on the basis of a debt alleged to be presently due, and there is a bona fide dispute as to whether it is presently due, it has been held by the Court of Appeal that the company is entitled as of right to an interlocutory injunction

---

[26] Trade Union and Labour Relations (Consolidation) Act 1992, ss.20–23 (replacing 1982 legislation).

[27] *Dimbleby & Sons Ltd v. National Union of Journalists* [1984] 1 W.L.R. 427; (1984) 100 L.Q.R. 342 (H. Carty); (1984) 47 M.L.R. 577 (B. Simpson); *Hadmor Productions Ltd v. Hamilton* [1983] 1 A.C. 191.

[28] [1975] A.C. 396.

[29] *Official Custodian for Charities v. Mackey* [1985] Ch. 168; *Love v. Herrity* (1991) 23 H.L.R. 217.

[30] *Patel v. W.H. Smith (Eziot) Ltd* [1987] 1 W.L.R. 853; *Anchor Brewhouse Developments Ltd v. Berkley House (Docklands Developments) Ltd* [1987] 2 E.G.L.R. 173; *London & Manchester Assurance Co. Ltd v. O. & H. Construction Ltd* [1989] 2 E.G.L.R. 185.

[31] *Taylor v. National Union of Mineworkers (Derbyshire Area), The Times*, December 29, 1984.

[32] *Doherty v. Allman* (1878) 3 App.Cas. 709; *post*, p. 783, applied to interlocutory injunctions in *Hampstead & Suburban Properties Ltd v. Diomedous* [1969] 1 Ch. 248; *Att.-Gen. v. Barker* [1990] 3 All E.R. 257.

[33] *Bryanston Finance Ltd v. De Vries (No. 2)* [1976] Ch. 63. But Buckley L.J., at p. 78, regarded this as a "special factor." The other members of the Court of Appeal said that *American Cyanamid* did not apply. See (1976) 35 C.L.J. 82 at p. 86 (P. Wallington). *American Cyanamid* was applied, albeit with difficulty, in *Re Euro Hotel (Belgravia) Ltd* [1975] 3 All E.R. 1075.

restraining the presentation of the petition, other than on the basis of a contingent or future debt.[34]

Difficulty was also experienced in applying the *American Cyanamid* rules where a company sought an interlocutory injunction to restrain a takeover bid.[35]

(v) MANDATORY INTERLOCUTORY INJUNCTIONS. *American Cyanamid* itself involved a prohibitory injunction, but the principles there expressed were not in terms confined to such applications. But it may still be said that mandatory interlocutory injunctions, which are discussed below,[36] will be granted less readily than the prohibitory, as was the case before *American Cyanamid*,[37] because the balance of convenience is likely to favour the refusal more often than the grant.[38]

The *American Cyanamid* principles have been applied to mandatory injunctions,[39] but a strong prima facie case was required in *De Falco v. Crawley Borough Council*,[40] where the plaintiff sought a mandatory interlocutory injunction to secure the provision of housing by the defendant. The Court of Appeal, refusing the injunction, held that the plaintiff had to show a strong prima facie case that the defendant's decision was invalid. Lord Denning M.R. held *American Cyanamid* to be inapplicable because the plaintiff could not give a worthwhile undertaking in damages.[41] Bridge L.J. held that *American Cyanamid*, which governed the grant of prohibitory interlocutory injunctions, did not apply to the present case, which exhibited "sufficiently unusual features to make a comparison even with other types of litigation where a mandatory injunction may be granted on an interim application difficult and possibly misleading."[42] If the defendant was wrong, the plaintiff would suffer homelessness which was not compensatable in damages. But if the plaintiff was wrong, a heavy financial burden, with no prospect of recovery, would fall on the ratepayers, and there would also be a

---

[34] *Stonegate Securities Ltd v. Gregory* [1980] Ch. 576 (*American Cyanamid* was not cited).

[35] *Dunford & Elliott Ltd v. Johnson & Firth Brown Ltd* [1977] 1 Lloyd's Rep. 505. Lord Denning M.R. held that the *American Cyanamid* principles did not apply, but Lawton and Roskill L.JJ. preferred to apply those principles, notwithstanding the difficulties.

[36] *Post*, p. 765.

[37] [1975] A.C. 396.

[38] See *Shotton v. Hammond* (1976) 120 S.J. 780.

[39] *Meade v. London Borough of Haringey* [1979] 1 W.L.R. 637.

[40] [1980] Q.B. 460; overruled in *Cocks v. Thanet District Council* [1983] 2 A.C. 286, on another point; *post*, p. 800. The requirement of a strong prima facie case was upheld in *R. v. Kensington and Chelsea Royal London Borough Council, ex p. Hammell* [1989] Q.B. 518 and *R. v. Westminster City Council, ex p. Augustin* [1993] 1 W.L.R. 730, regarding *De Falco* as still good law on the point.

[41] [1980] Q.B. 460 at p. 478. This, it is submitted, might more properly be regarded as a factor in assessing the balance of convenience. See further Yates and Hawkins, *Landlord and Tenant Law* (2nd ed.), p. 631.

[42] *Ibid.* at p. 481.

detriment to others on the housing list.[43] Therefore such an injunction should be granted only if the plaintiff had a strong prima facie case. *De Falco* could be regarded as a special case because of the public law element. The Court of Appeal has stated, however, that the "high degree of assurance", required in *Shepherd Homes Ltd v. Sandham*[44] for the grant of mandatory interlocutory injunctions, was not affected by the *American Cyanamid* principles.[45]

Finally, the *Anton Piller* injunction,[46] which is partly mandatory, has been held to require an extremely strong prima facie case.[47] This, it is submitted, is an exceptional case because such applications are usually *ex parte*, and because of the "draconian" nature of the injunction.[48]

iii. Mandatory Interlocutory Injunctions.

These are less readily granted than prohibitory interlocutory injunctions,[49] especially on an *ex parte* application, because the mandatory order may be more drastic in effect. If the defendant has been required to do some positive act, it may not be easy to restore the parties to their previous position if the plaintiff turns out to be wrong at the trial.[50]

Mandatory interlocutory injunctions will be granted in a suitable case, for example, to compel the demolition of a building where the defendant has deliberately hurried on with the building,[51] to reinstate a wrongfully evicted occupier to possession[52]; to enforce the return of passports wrongfully detained by the police[53]; to compel performance of a landlord's obligations[54]; to enforce the planning legislation[55]; to compel surrender of an unlawful sublease[56]; or in the *Anton Piller* cases,[57] to compel the defendant to submit articles for inspection.

---

[43] This, again, might be regarded simply as an aspect of the balance of convenience, without departing from *American Cyanamid*.

[44] [1971] Ch. 340; *post*, p. 766.

[45] *Locabail International Finance Ltd v. Agroexport* [1986] 1 W.L.R. 657; *post*, p. 766.

[46] *Anton Piller K.G. v. Manufacturing Processes Ltd* [1976] Ch. 55.

[47] *Post*, p. 806. See also (1987) 103 L.Q.R. 246 (L. Anderson), suggesting likewise in the case of an injunction against leaving the country.

[48] See *Yousif v. Salama* [1980] 1 W.L.R. 1540, at p. 1544; *post*, p. 805; *Derby & Co. Ltd v. Weldon (No. 7)* [1990] 1 W.L.R. 1156 at p. 1173.

[49] *Daniel v. Ferguson* [1891] 2 Ch. 27; *Shotton v. Hammond* (1976) 120 S.J. 780.

[50] See *Shepherd Homes Ltd v. Sandham* [1971] Ch. 340 at p. 349.

[51] *Von Joel v. Hornsey* [1895] 2 Ch. 774; *London & Manchester Assurance Co. Ltd v. O. & H. Construction Ltd* [1989] 2 E.G.L.R. 185.

[52] *Luganda v. Service Hotels* [1969] 2 Ch. 209; *Parsons v. Nasar* (1991) 23 H.L.R. 1.

[53] *Ghani v. Jones* [1970] 1 Q.B. 693; *cf. Malone v. Metropolitan Police Commissioner* [1980] Q.B. 49.

[54] *Hart v. Emelkirk Ltd* [1983] 1 W.L.R. 1289; *Peninsular Maritime Ltd v. Padseal Ltd* (1981) 259 E.G. 860.

[55] *Croydon London Borough Council v. Gladden* (1994) 68 P. & C.R. 300 (removal of replica spitfire from roof).

[56] *Hemingway Securities Ltd v. Dunraven Ltd* [1995] 1 E.G.L.R. 61.

[57] *Post*, p. 804.

The court will be reluctant to grant such an injunction where the case involves an industrial dispute,[58] but will do so in exceptional circumstances if the balance of convenience so requires. Such a case was *Parker v. Camden London Borough Council*,[59] where a strike of boilermen was endangering the life and health of council tenants. The court was prepared to grant a mandatory interlocutory injunction to resume the supply of heating and hot water.

It has been held, in a case concerning trespass by building operations, that if the plaintiff could have got a prohibitory *quia timet* injunction to restrain the commission of the wrongful act, had he known about it in time, then the defendant should be in no better position if he in fact commits the act: a mandatory interlocutory injunction should be granted to enforce the removal of the building works.[60]

Modern decisions illustrate an increasing readiness to grant mandatory interlocutory injunctions. The principles were reviewed in *Shepherd Homes Ltd v. Sandham*,[61] where the defendant erected a fence in breach of covenant, which the plaintiff sought to have removed. Megarry J. said that the case has to be unusually strong and clear before a mandatory interlocutory injunction will be granted. The court must feel "a high degree of assurance" that at the trial it will appear that the injunction was rightly granted, and this is a higher standard than is required for a prohibitory injunction. In view of the plaintiff's delay, the injunction was refused.

The "high degree of assurance" test has been approved by the Court of Appeal,[62] holding that although the test was formulated before *American Cyanamid Co. v. Ethicon Ltd*,[63] it was unaffected by that case. It was added that the application should be approached with caution where the relief sought on the motion would amount to a major part of the relief claimed at the trial. Hoffmann J. has since held that in exceptional cases, where the refusal of the injunction carried a greater risk of injustice than the grant, then the injunction should be granted even though the "high degree of assurance" test was not satisfied. That test is a guideline which applies in "normal" cases.[64]

---

[58] *Meade v. London Borough of Haringey* [1979] 1 W.L.R. 637; (1979) 38 C.L.J. 228 (J. Griffiths). (No injunction to reopen schools closed by a strike.) See also *Harold Stephen and Co. Ltd v. Post Office* [1977] 1 W.L.R. 1172, *ante*, p. 749. *cf. Express Newspapers Ltd v. Keys* [1980] I.R.L.R. 247, where the dispute was political.

[59] [1986] Ch. 162; *ante*, p. 750.

[60] *Trenberth (John) Ltd v. National Westminster Bank Ltd* (1979) 39 P. & C.R. 104.

[61] [1971] Ch. 340. See also *Astro Exito Navegacion S.A. v. Southland Enterprise Co. (No. 2)* [1982] Q.B. 1248, C.A.

[62] *Locabail International Finance Ltd v. Agroexport* [1986] 1 W.L.R. 657.

[63] [1975] A.C. 396; *ante*, p. 753.

[64] *Films Rover International Ltd v. Cannon Film Sales Ltd* [1987] 1 W.L.R. 670; (1988) 47 C.L.J. 34 (N. Andrews). See also *Channel Tunnel Group Ltd v. Balfour Beatty Construction Ltd* [1992] 1 Q.B. 656 at p. 678, C.A.

The following are cases where a mandatory interlocutory injunction was clearly required:

In *Esso Petroleum Co. Ltd v. Kingswood Motors*,[65] the defendant agreed with the plaintiff not to sell a garage without first procuring that the purchaser would enter a solus agreement with the plaintiff. The land was sold to a purchaser who conspired with the defendant to effect a breach. A mandatory interlocutory injunction was granted to compel a retransfer of the land to the defendant. There could be no clearer case of inducing breach of contract, and damages would be wholly inadequate.

In *Sky Petroleum v. V.I.P. Petroleum Ltd*,[66] such an injunction was granted to enforce a contract to supply petrol to the plaintiff. As there was no alternative supply, damages would be inadequate, and the plaintiff might be forced out of business unless the court intervened.

In *Evans v. B.B.C. and I.B.A.*,[67] an order was made to compel the television authorities to show a party political broadcast. On the balance of probabilities[68] there was a contract with the Welsh Nationalist Party to broadcast it. Damages would be manifestly useless, as the election was about to take place. In such a case the court should take the risk of it turning out that there was no contract.

iv. Conditions and Undertakings. On the grant of an interlocutory injunction, the plaintiff is normally required to give an undertaking in damages[69] in the event that the injunction is discharged at the trial as having been granted without good cause[70]; but a defendant may also be put on similar terms as a condition of an injunction not being granted.[71] One reason for the practice of undertakings is that it aids the court in achieving its object of abstaining from expressing any opinion on the merits until the hearing.[72] While an undertaking by the plaintiff is exacted for the benefit of the defendant, it is not a contract with the defendant. The undertaking is given

---

[65] [1974] Q.B. 142; *Hemingway Securities Ltd v. Dunraven Ltd* [1995] 1 E.G.L.R. 61.
[66] [1974] 1 W.L.R. 576. (The injunction was negative in form, but mandatory in substance.)
[67] *The Times*, February 26, 1974.
[68] *cf.* Megarry J.'s requirement of a "high degree of assurance," *ante*, p. 766.
[69] Or to do some other act; *P.S. Refson & Co. Ltd v. Saggers* [1984] 1 W.L.R. 1025. See generally (1994) 53 C.L.J. 546 (A. Zuckerman).
[70] *Anton Piller* and *Mareva* injunctions, *post*, pp. 804, 808, provide good examples of the need for undertakings. See *Digital Equipment Corporation v. Darkcrest Ltd* [1984] Ch. 512.
[71] *Elwes v. Payne* (1879) 12 Ch.D. 468.
[72] *American Cyanamid Co. v. Ethicon Ltd* [1975] A.C. 396, at p. 407.

to the court, so that non-performance is a contempt of court and not a breach of contract.[73] Enforcement is at the court's discretion.[74] Damages will normally become payable if the plaintiff is unsuccessful at the trial, either because he cannot establish his case or because the judge who granted the interlocutory injunction took a wrong view of the law. The plaintiff may be required to give security or to pay the money into court. Any damages will be assessed on the same basis as damages for breach of contract.[75] A plaintiff's refusal to seek an interlocutory injunction, in order to avoid the need to give an undertaking, is not a ground for striking out his application for a final injunction,[76] but is a factor to be taken into account.[77]

Where interlocutory injunctions are sought in matrimonial and children's matters, undertakings may be required if the claim concerns the protection of property rights, but will not be required in respect of matters concerning personal conduct.[78]

In *Hoffman-La Roche (F.) & Co. v. Secretary of State for Trade and Industry*[79] the question arose whether the Crown should be required to give an undertaking as a condition of the grant of an interlocutory injunction to restrain the company from charging prices for drugs in excess of those specified in an order (which the company claimed was *ultra vires*). The House of Lords held that the undertaking should not be required.

A distinction had to be drawn between two cases: first, where the Crown was asserting a proprietary or contractual right,[80] the ordinary rule applied and the Crown should give an undertaking; but, secondly, where an injunction was sought to enforce the law, the defendant must show special reason why justice required that it should not be granted, or should only be granted on terms. The present case was within the second category. The reason for this distinction is that where a person is prosecuted and acquitted, he may suffer loss but cannot normally recover from the prosecutor.

---

[73] See *Hussain v. Hussain* [1986] Fam. 134. But the undertaking may include a contractual obligation to the other party; *Midland Marts Ltd v. Hobday* [1989] 1 W.L.R. 1143.

[74] *Cheltenham and Gloucester Building Society v. Ricketts* [1993] 1 W.L.R. 1545.

[75] *Hoffman-La Roche (F.) & Co. v. Secretary of State for Trade and Industry* [1975] A.C. 295 at p. 361, *per* Lord Diplock.

[76] *Oxy Electric Ltd v. Zainuddin* [1991] 1 W.L.R. 115, doubting *Blue Town Investments Ltd v. Higgs & Hill plc* [1990] 1 W.L.R. 696; All E.R. Rev. 1990, p. 201 (A. Zuckerman); (1991) 141 N.L.J. 243 (R. Chaplin). The final injunction in *Oxy Electric* was later refused; [1990] E.G.C.S. 128.

[77] *Snell & Prideaux Ltd v. Dutton Mirrors Ltd* [1995] 1 E.G.L.R. 259.

[78] *Practice Direction* [1974] 1 W.L.R. 576.

[79] [1975] A.C. 295. The statute in question expressly provided for the grant to the Crown of an injunction as the only means of enforcing the statute.

[80] Including the case where the Crown is asserting proprietary rights on behalf of a charity; *Att-Gen. v. Wright* [1988] 1 W.L.R. 164; All E.R.Rev. 1987, p. 190 (A. Zuckerman).

There is therefore no reason why the Crown should incur liability when an injunction is sought to enforce the law.

This principle applies also to a local authority seeking a law-enforcement injunction[81]; likewise where the Attorney-General acts *ex officio* to enforce the law by injunction. But where the Attorney-General brings the action under the relator procedure, the relator must give the usual undertaking,[82] as must a local authority acting as a relator.[83]

E. Quia Timet Injunctions

A *quia timet* injunction may be available where the injury to the plaintiff's rights has not yet occurred, but is feared or threatened.[84] The injunction may be perpetual or interlocutory, prohibitory or mandatory. It may further be subdivided into two broad categories: "first, where the defendant[85] has as yet done no hurt to the plaintiff but is threatening and intending (so the plaintiff alleges) to do works which will render irreparable harm to him or his property if carried to completion . . . those cases are normally, though not exclusively, concerned with negative injunctions. Secondly, the type of case where the plaintiff has been fully recompensed both at law and in equity for the damage he has suffered but where he alleges that the earlier actions of the defendant may lead to future causes of action . . . It is in this field that the undoubted jurisdiction of equity to grant a mandatory injunction . . . finds its main expression."[86]

How serious must the fears of the plaintiff be, and how grave the suspected damage? As Lord Dunedin has said, it is not sufficient to say "timeo."[87] The requirements have been described in the following terms: a strong case of probability[88]; proof of imminent danger,

---

[81] *Kirklees Borough Council v. Wickes Building Supplies Ltd* [1993] A.C. 227 (Sunday trading); criticised All E.R.Rev. 1992, p. 319 (A. Zuckerman); *Director General of Fair Trading v. Tobyward Ltd* [1989] 1 W.L.R. 517. See also *Securities and Investments Board v. Lloyd-Wright* [1993] 4 All E.R. 210. Company liquidators are not within this principle; *Re D.P.R. Futures Ltd* [1989] 1 W.L.R. 778.

[82] *Hoffman-La Roche (F.) & Co. v. Secretary of State for Trade and Industry, supra*, at p. 363.

[83] *Kirklees Borough Council v. Wickes Building Supplies Ltd, supra.*

[84] For different views on the meaning of *quia timet*, see (1975) 34 C.L.J. 224 (J. Jolowicz); *cf.* (1977) 36 C.L.J. 369, (1978) 37 C.L.J. 51 (P. Pettit); Spry, p. 369.

[85] The defendant must himself have threatened the act in question. See *Celsteel Ltd v. Alton House Holdings Ltd* [1986] 1 W.L.R. 512 (no injunction against freeholder where act threatened by tenant).

[86] *Redland Bricks Ltd v. Morris* [1970] A.C. 652 at p. 665, *per* Lord Upjohn. See also *Hooper v. Rogers* [1975] Ch. 43; *Allen v. Greenhi Builders Ltd* [1979] 1 W.L.R. 136 (registration as "pending land action").

[87] *Att.-Gen. for the Dominion of Canada v. Ritchie Contracting and Supply Co. Ltd* [1919] A.C. 999 at p. 1005.

[88] *Att.-Gen. v. Manchester Corporation* [1893] 2 Ch. 87 at p. 92.

and there must also be proof that the apprehended damage will, if it comes, be very substantial.[89] Thus in *Att.-Gen. v. Nottingham Corporation*[90] a *quia timet* injunction was not granted to restrain the corporation from building a smallpox hospital, as there was no proof of genuine danger to nearby residents.

The principles applicable to the grant of a mandatory *quia timet* injunction were laid down by the House of Lords in *Redland Bricks Ltd v. Morris*.[91]

The defendant company's digging activities caused landslips on the plaintiffs' adjoining property, which they used as a market garden. The plaintiffs' land, of which about one-tenth of an acre was affected, was worth about £12,000, but the cost of remedying the landslips would be about £30,000. The plaintiffs were awarded damages, a prohibitory injunction to restrain further withdrawal of support, and a mandatory injunction that the defendants "take all necessary steps to restore support within six months." But the House of Lords allowed the defendant's appeal against the grant of the mandatory injunction on the ground that it did not specify exactly what it had to do. Lord Upjohn set out the following four principles applicable to the grant of a mandatory *quia timet* injunction:

i. The plaintiff must show a very strong probability that grave damage will accrue to him in the future. It is a jurisdiction to be exercised sparingly and with caution, but, in the proper case, unhesitatingly.

ii. Damages will not be an adequate remedy if such damage does happen, applying the general principle of equity.

iii. Unlike the case where a negative injunction is granted to prevent the continuance or recurrence of a wrongful act, the cost to the defendant to do works to prevent or lessen the likelihood of a future apprehended wrong must be taken into account:

(*a*) where the defendant has acted wantonly and quite unreasonably, he may be ordered to do positive work even if the expense to him is out of all proportion to the advantage thereby accruing to the plaintiff;

---

[89] *Fletcher v. Bealey* (1885) 27 Ch.D. 688 at p. 698. *cf. Trenberth (John) Ltd v. National Westminster Bank Ltd* (1979) 39 P. & C.R. 104.

[90] [1904] 1 Ch. 673; *Att.-Gen. v. Guardian Newspapers (No. 2)* [1990] 1 A.C. 109 (no general injunction against publication of any material the media might obtain from Crown servants in breach of confidence). For libel, see *British Data Management plc v. Boxer Commercial Removals plc* [1996] 3 All E.R. 707.

[91] [1970] A.C. 652. See critical commentary in Heydon, Gummow and Austin, *Cases and Materials on Equity and Trusts* (4th ed.), p. 1050.

(*b*) but where the defendant has acted reasonably, although wrongly, the cost of remedying his earlier activities is most important. If it seems unreasonable to inflict such expenditure on one who is no more than a potential wrongdoer the court must exercise its jurisdiction accordingly. The court may order works which may not remedy the wrong but may lessen the likelihood of further injury. It must be borne in mind that the injury may never in fact occur, and that, if it does, the plaintiff may then seek the appropriate legal or equitable remedy.

iv. If a mandatory injunction is granted, the court must see that the defendant knows exactly in fact what he has to do.[92] A more recent statement is that, in the issue of mandatory *quia timet* injunctions, "what is aimed at is justice between the parties, having regard to all the relevant circumstances."[93]

4. Defences to Perpetual and Interlocutory Injunctions

A. Delay

As in the case of specific performance, laches may be a defence even though the plaintiff's rights have not yet become statute-barred.[94] But a smaller degree of delay will defeat a claim for an interlocutory injunction than is necessary in the case of a perpetual injunction.[95] This is because, if an interlocutory claim is dismissed, the plaintiff is not unduly prejudiced, as he can still seek a perpetual injunction. But the refusal of a perpetual injunction amounts to a final dismissal.

As we have seen, the plaintiff must come promptly in the case of an *ex parte* injunction, as any delay illustrates that his case is not urgent.[96] Where the plaintiff has delayed his motion for an interlocutory injunction, he is unlikely to establish that it would be unreasonable to make him wait until trial. An unexplained delay of five months prevented the grant of an interlocutory injunction in *Shepherd Homes Ltd v. Sandham*,[97] where Megarry J. explained that

---

[92] See also *Harold Stephen & Co. Ltd v. Post Office* [1977] 1 W.L.R. 1172; *Parsons v. Nasar* (1991) 23 H.L.R. 1.

[93] *Hooper v. Rogers* [1975] Ch. 43 at p. 50 (*per* Russell L.J.).

[94] See Limitation Act 1980, s.36.

[95] *Johnson v. Wyatt* (1863) 2 De G.J. & S. 18.

[96] *Bates v. Lord Hailsham of St. Marylebone* [1972] 1 W.L.R. 1373.

[97] [1971] Ch. 340; *ante*, p. 766; *cf Texaco Ltd v. Mulberry Filling Station Ltd* [1972] 1 W.L.R. 814; *Express Newspapers plc v. Liverpool Daily Post and Echo plc* [1985] 1 W.L.R. 1089; *Newport Association Football Club Ltd v. Football Association of Wales Ltd* [1995] 2 All E.R. 87 (explanation for delay).

if the injunction is also mandatory, any delay by the plaintiff will mean that the injunction, if granted, would disturb rather than preserve the status quo.[98] It may be otherwise, however, if there is no arguable defence.[99]

The authorities are not reconcilable on the question of delay in perpetual injunctions. It is sometimes said that laches is no defence,[1] or, to go to the other extreme, that mere lapse of time is a bar.[2] In *Kelsen v. Imperial Tobacco Co. Ltd*[3] a mandatory injunction was granted to restrain a trespass even though it appeared that the state of affairs had existed for seven years. In *Fullwood v. Fullwood*,[4] Fry J. held that a delay of two to three years was no defence, on the ground that mere lapse of time unaccompanied by acquiescence was no bar unless the legal right itself was barred.

In *H.P. Bulmer Ltd & Showerings Ltd v. Bollinger S.A.*[5] the appellants had described their products as "champagne perry" and "champagne cider" since 1950 and 1906 respectively. The latter usage had been known to the respondents since about 1930. Injunctions were granted in the High Court to restrain both descriptions. The defence of delay failed. This was a continuing wrong, and the right in question was legal. Whitford J. held that in such a case the delay must be "inordinate" if it is to prevent the grant of an injunction. Here it was not, because advice had to be sought, and interests consulted. There was no appeal against one injunction, but the other was discharged by the Court of Appeal because passing-off was not established, but their Lordships considered that the injunction would not have been refused on account of delay. Goff L.J. thought that "inordinate" delay would be a ground for refusing an injunction, even in the case of a legal right, but that delay in the present case was not of that order.

Laches may be regarded more strictly if third parties would be affected. It is possible that a plaintiff who has delayed will be awarded damages in lieu of an injunction under Lord Cairns' Act.[6]

---

[98] See *Shotton v. Hammond* (1976) 120 S.J. 780: mandatory interlocutory injunction granted in spite of delay of six weeks by the plaintiff, who was not legally aided.

[99] See *Patel v. W.H. Smith (Eziot) Ltd* [1987] 1 W.L.R. 853.

[1] *Archbold v. Scully* (1861) 9 H.L.C. 360 at p. 383.

[2] *Brooks v. Muckleston* [1909] 2 Ch. 519.

[3] [1957] 2 Q.B. 334.

[4] (1878) 9 Ch.D. 176.

[5] [1977] 2 C.M.L.R. 625, C.A. *cf. Vine Products Ltd v. McKenzie & Co. Ltd* (1969) R.P.C. 1 (no injunction to restrain description as "sherry," the usage having been common knowledge for 100 years). See also *Erlanger v. New Sombrero Phosphate Co.* (1873) 3 App.Cas. 1218 at pp. 1279–1280.

[6] *Shelfer v. City of London Electric Lighting Co.* [1895] 1 Ch. 287 at p. 322; see also *Bracewell v. Appleby* [1975] Ch. 408; *Gooden v. Ketley* [1996] E.G.C.S. 47.

It has been suggested that a longer delay is required before a plaintiff will be refused an injunction where the right is legal than where it is equitable[7]; or alternatively that a less strict view of laches might be taken as to matters within equity's exclusive jurisdiction, such as a breach of trust, where there is no alternative remedy at law.[8] But the Court of Appeal has described the distinction between legal and equitable rights in this context as archaic and arcane.[9]

Finally, where an injunction is sought in an application for judicial review,[10] it is provided that, in the case of "undue delay," the injunction may be refused if the granting of relief "would be likely to cause substantial hardship to, or substantially prejudice the rights of, any person or would be detrimental to good administration."[11]

B. Acquiescence[12]

Lapse of time will be taken into account in that it may indicate acquiescence. It is, of course, possible to find acquiescence without delay and delay without acquiescence but there is normally some overlap. As in the case of laches, a greater degree of acquiescence is needed to defeat a claim for a final injunction than an interlocutory injunction. It has also been suggested that acquiescence is easier to establish where the right in question is equitable only.[13] In *Richards v. Revitt*[14] it was said that the fact that the plaintiff has previously overlooked trivial breaches of covenant does not debar him, on the ground of acquiescence, from acting on a serious breach. A leading authority is *Sayers v. Collyer*,[15] where a house was being used as a beershop in breach of covenant. The plaintiff could not get an injunction, as he had known of the breach for three years, and, furthermore, had bought beer there. This was sufficient to bar any remedy. But a lesser degree of acquiescence, while not sufficient to bar the action completely, might be a reason for giving damages in lieu of an injunction under Lord Cairns' Act.

---

[7] *Cluett Peabody & Co. Inc. v. McIntyre Hogg Marsh and Co. Ltd* [1958] R.P.C. 335 at p. 354, *per* Upjohn J.; *H.P. Bulmer and Showerings Ltd v. J. Bollinger S.A., supra.*

[8] See Spry, *Equitable Remedies*, p. 428; *Knight v. Bowyer* (1858) 2 De G. & J. 421; *cf. Oxy Electric Ltd v. Zainuddin* [1990] E.G.C.S. 128 (final injunction to enforce restrictive covenant refused because of seven month delay).

[9] *Habib Bank Ltd v. Habib Bank A.G. Zurich* [1981] 1 W.L.R. 1265 at pp. 1285 and 1287; *cf.* Spry, p. 428.

[10] *Post*, p. 799.

[11] Supreme Court Act 1981, s.31(6); R.S.C., Ord. 53, r. 4.

[12] See Limitation Act 1980, s.36(2). The Act does not affect this defence.

[13] *Shaw v. Applegate* [1977] 1 W.L.R. 970 at p. 979 (the right in this case was legal). But see *Habib Bank Ltd v. Habib Bank A.G. Zurich, supra.*

[14] (1877) 7 Ch.D. 224 at p. 226.

[15] (1885) 28 Ch.D. 103.

In *Shaw v. Applegate*[16] the plaintiff sought to enforce a covenant entered into by the defendant in 1967 not to use his land as an "amusement arcade." Breaches of covenant occurred from about 1971. The plaintiff was aware of the facts but was unsure whether they constituted a breach of covenant. The plaintiff began proceedings for an injunction in 1973, but did not seek interlocutory relief, so that the defendant continued to carry on his business, investing money and building up goodwill, until the trial in 1976. It was held that the plaintiff was not guilty of such a degree of acquiescence as to bar all remedies, the real test being whether, on the facts of the particular case, it would be dishonest or unconscionable for the plaintiff to seek to enforce his rights.[17] This was not the case, because of the plaintiff's doubts as to his legal rights. But there was sufficient acquiescence to bar the remedy of an injunction because the defendant had been lulled into a false sense of security by the plaintiff's inactivity and failure to seek interlocutory relief. Thus the appropriate remedy was damages in lieu of an injunction under Lord Cairns' Act.

C. Hardship

Hardship to the defendant is a relevant consideration in injunctions as in specific performance.[18] It is perhaps of more weight in the case of an interlocutory injunction[19] than in the case of a final injunction, where the infringement of the plaintiff's rights has been established. Hardship may also carry more weight in the case of mandatory injunctions,[20] where it has been said that the benefit to the plaintiff in granting the injunction must be balanced against the detriment to the defendant.[21] As we shall see, damages may be awarded in lieu of an injunction under Lord Cairns' Act if the injunction would be oppressive to the defendant.[22]

---

[16] [1977] 1 W.L.R. 970; (1977) 41 Conv.(N.S.) 355 (F. Crane). See also on this point *Sayers v. Collyer* (1885) 28 Ch.D. 103 at p. 110.

[17] *Ibid.* at p. 978. See also *H.P. Bulmer & Showerings Ltd v. J. Bollinger S.A.* [1977] 2 C.M.L.R. 625 at p. 682; *Blue Town Investments Ltd v. Higgs and Hill plc* [1990] 1 W.L.R. 696.

[18] See *Shell U.K. Ltd v. Lostock Garages Ltd* [1976] 1 W.L.R. 1187. As to difficulty in compliance, see generally *Att.-Gen. v. Colney Hatch Lunatic Asylum* (1868) L.R. 4 Ch.App. 146.

[19] See the "balance of convenience" requirement, *ante*, p. 755.

[20] *Att.-Gen. v. Colchester Corporation* [1955] 2 Q.B. 207; *Gravesham Borough Council v. British Railways Board* [1978] Ch. 379 (A mandatory injunction would not be granted to compel the running of a ferry at a heavy loss, which would benefit few passengers); *cf. Co-operative Insurance Society Ltd v. Argyll Stores (Holdings) Ltd* [1996] Ch. 286, *ante*, p. 705.

[21] *Shepherd Homes Ltd v. Sandham* [1971] Ch. 340; *Charrington v. Simons & Co. Ltd* [1970] 1 W.L.R. 725.

[22] There are other conditions: see *Shelfer v. City of London Electric Lighting Co.* [1895] 1 Ch. 287. See also *Shaw v. Applegate, supra*, at pp. 978–979.

The element of hardship to the defendant might be overcome in appropriate cases by granting an injunction but suspending its operation.[23] Even if there is no hardship to the defendant, an injunction may be refused if it would prejudice an innocent third party.[24]

It has previously been noted that the disproportionate cost of complying with a mandatory *quia timet* injunction may be a ground for refusing the grant if the defendant has acted reasonably.[25] Lord Upjohn, however, thought that such considerations would not be taken into account in the case of a negative injunction to prevent the continuance or recurrence of a wrongful act; any argument by the wrongdoer that the injunction would be very costly to him, perhaps by preventing him from carrying out a contract with a third party, would carry little weight.

D. Conduct of the Plaintiff

The plaintiff must come to equity with clean hands.[26] If, therefore, he is in breach of his own obligations, or otherwise guilty of unfair conduct,[27] he will not be granted an injunction, although trifling breaches by the plaintiff may not disentitle him.[28] Similarly, he who comes to equity must do equity, therefore the plaintiff will not succeed if he is unable or unwilling to carry out his own future obligations.[29]

But the defence of "clean hands" must be related to the subject-matter of the dispute, and does not embrace the plaintiff's general conduct. Thus in *Argyll v. Argyll*,[30] the fact that the wife's conduct had caused the divorce was no answer to her claim to an injunction to restrain a breach of confidence by her husband. In *Hubbard v. Vosper*,[31] one reason for refusing the interlocutory injunction was that the plaintiff had not come with clean hands, in that he had protected his secrets by deplorable means, namely by a private criminal code for dealing with the "enemies" of scientology.

Similarly, the injunction may be refused if the court is not impressed with the plaintiff on the merits.[32]

---

[23] *Ante*, p. 750.
[24] *Maythorn v. Palmer* (1864) 11 L.T. 261; *cf. PSM International plc v. Whitehouse and Willenhall Automation Ltd* [1992] I.R.L.R. 279.
[25] *Redland Bricks Ltd v. Morris* [1970] A.C. 652 at p. 666.
[26] See *Malone v. Metropolitan Police Commissioner* [1980] Q.B. 49 at p. 71.
[27] *Shell U.K. Ltd v. Lostock Garages Ltd* [1976] 1 W.L.R. 1187.
[28] *Besant v. Wood* (1879) 12 Ch.D. 605.
[29] *Measures v. Measures* [1910] 2 Ch. 248; *Chappell v. Times Newspapers Ltd* [1975] 1 W.L.R. 482 (employees failed to obtain injunction to restrain their dismissal where they refused to give an undertaking not to strike).
[30] [1967] Ch. 302.
[31] [1972] 2 Q.B. 84.
[32] See *Glynn v. Keele University* [1971] 1 W.L.R. 487; *Shelfer v. City of London Electric Lighting Co.* [1895] 1 Ch. 287 at p. 317.

5. THE JURISDICTION UNDER LORD CAIRNS' ACT

The Chancery Amendment Act 1858[33] allowed damages to be awarded in lieu of, or in addition to, an injunction or specific performance. The Chancery Division has, of course, been able, since the Judicature Act 1873, to award damages in any case where the common law courts could have done so, but these are common law damages. It will still be necessary to rely on Lord Cairns' Act where no damages would be available at law, for example in lieu of a *quia timet* injunction where no legal injury has yet occurred[34]; or if some damage has occurred but may continue in the future, and damages are awarded to cover future loss[35]; or where the plaintiff's right is exclusively equitable, as in the case of a restrictive covenant.[36] In other cases, it will not be necessary to invoke Lord Cairns' Act, and damages may be awarded at common law; but there is no need to distinguish the ground of jurisdiction. The discretion exercisable under Lord Cairns' Act is similar to the discretion which the court has had since the Judicature Act to grant injunctions or damages at common law, in cases where they are available. The principle is the same; the court will not give damages instead of an injunction if damages will not be adequate to protect the plaintiff's rights. It seems that the court will consider the principles set out in *Shelfer v. City of London Electric Lighting Co.*[37] governing the award of damages under Lord Cairns' Act even where the plaintiff has a cause of action at law, and there is jurisdiction to award damages at law.[38]

Lord Cairns' Act enables the award of damages in lieu of a final (not interlocutory) injunction only if there is *jurisdiction* to grant one,[39] in the sense that the plaintiff has established a prima facie case for equitable relief. It does not matter that the injunction is refused on some discretionary ground, such as, for example, delay

---

[33] *Ante*, p. 724; repealed and replaced by Statute Law Revision Act 1883 and Judicature Act 1873. The jurisdiction now derives from Supreme Court Act 1981, s.50. In *Leeds Industrial Co-operative Society v. Slack* [1924] A.C. 851 Viscount Finlay suggested that the repeal may have been a mistake, made under the false impression that it dealt only with common law damages, and was therefore redundant after the Judicature Act 1873. The better view is that s.16 of the 1873 Act, which transferred all Chancery jurisdiction to the High Court, made the 1858 Act redundant. See McDermott, *Equitable Damages* (1994), pp. 44–45.

[34] *Leeds Industrial Co-operative Society v. Slack, supra*; establishing the point after some doubt; *Hooper v. Rogers* [1975] Ch. 43; *Johnson v. Agnew* [1980] A.C. 367 at p. 400.

[35] See *Kennaway v. Thompson* [1981] Q.B. 88.

[36] *Baxter v. Four Oaks Properties Ltd* [1965] Ch. 816; *Wrotham Park Estate Ltd v. Parkside Homes Ltd* [1974] 1 W.L.R. 798.

[37] [1895] 1 Ch. 287; *infra*.

[38] See *Kelsen v. Imperial Tobacco Co. Ltd* [1957] 2 Q.B. 334; *Woollerton and Wilson Ltd v. Richard Costain Ltd* [1970] 1 W.L.R. 411.

[39] *Hooper v. Rogers* [1975] Ch. 43; *Wrotham Park Estate Ltd v. Parkside Homes Ltd, supra*; *Surrey County Council v. Bredero Homes Ltd* [1993] 1 W.L.R. 1361.

or acquiescence.[40] If, on the other hand, the plaintiff has no case at all for an injunction, then damages cannot be awarded under Lord Cairns' Act, but, as we have seen, such a plaintiff can be awarded common law damages, provided he has a cause of action at law. Lord Cairns' Act applies even though the plaintiff does not seek an injunction, but the pleadings should make it clear whether he seeks damages at common law for past injury or under the Act in lieu of an injunction.[41]

A. Award of Damages under Lord Cairns' Act

If the plaintiff can establish that his rights have been infringed, he is prima facie entitled to an injunction. Damages will only be awarded in lieu in special circumstances; otherwise the defendant would be allowed to "buy" the right to continue the wrongful act.[42]

The leading case is *Shelfer v. City of London Lighting Co.*,[43] a case of nuisance. A.L. Smith L.J. laid down a "good working rule," that damages should only be awarded in lieu if all the following requirements were satisfied:

  (i) the injury to the plaintiff is small; and

  (ii) the injury is capable of being estimated in monetary terms; and

  (iii) the injury would be adequately compensated by a small payment[44]; and

  (iv) it would be oppressive to grant an injunction.[45]

Lindley L.J. said[46] that the injunction should not be refused merely because it would not greatly benefit the plaintiff, as the court is not

---

[40] *Shaw v. Applegate* [1977] 1 W.L.R. 970. Distinguish a case of *jurisdiction* being lost through the passage of time. See generally *Lavery v. Pursell* (1883) 39 Ch.D. 508 at p. 519. The position is the same for specific performance, *ante*, p. 725.

[41] *Jaggard v. Sawyer* [1995] 1 W.L.R. 269; criticised [1995] Conv. 141 (T. Ingman).

[42] See *Wakeham v. Wood* (1982) 43 P. & C.R. 40; *Sampson v. Hodson-Pressinger* [1981] 3 All E.R. 710; *Oxy Electric Ltd v. Zainuddin* [1991] 1 W.L.R. 115; *Elliott v. Islington London Borough Council* [1991] 1 E.G.L.R. 167; *Harrow London Borough Council v. Donohue* [1995] 1 E.G.L.R. 257.

[43] [1895] 1 Ch. 287. See Viscount Finlay's valuable account of the Act in *Leeds Industrial Co-operative Society v. Slack* [1924] A.C. 851 at pp. 856–863. Damages are not appropriate where the nuisance is actionable without proof of damage; *Sevenoaks District Council v. Pattullo & Vinson Ltd* [1984] Ch. 211 (right to hold market).

[44] The jurisdiction to grant injunctions is based on the inadequacy of common law damages. It might be argued that compliance with the third requirement should alone be sufficient to prevent the grant of an injunction. But common law damages may not be available, and cannot be awarded for the future; *Jaggard v. Sawyer* [1995] 1 W.L.R. 269. See (1975) 34 C.L.J. 224 (J. Jolowicz).

[45] See *Jaggard v. Sawyer, supra* (injunction would prevent access to defendants' house).

[46] [1895] 1 Ch. 287 at pp. 315–316.

a tribunal for legalising wrongful acts where the wrongdoer is able and willing to pay. Damages will not normally be substituted in a case of nuisance, as they cannot be easily estimated, but it was suggested that damages would be appropriate if it was a trivial or occasional nuisance, or if it is a vexatious case, or if the plaintiff has shown that he only wants money. If damages are awarded in a case where the wrong is continuing, they must include a sum for the future as well as the past.

Even if the above four principles are satisfied, an injunction may still be awarded if the defendant has acted in reckless disregard of the plaintiff's rights,[47] or has acted in a high-handed manner, or tried to steal a march on the plaintiff, or to evade the jurisdiction of the court.[48]

The Court of Appeal in *Redland Bricks Ltd v. Morris*,[49] while accepting the principles of *Shelfer's* case, disagreed on the question whether the injury could be regarded as small, or could be adequately compensated in money. The defendant's excavations caused damage by subsidence to the value of £1,500, but the correction of the situation, if an injunction was issued, would require expenditure of some £30,000. An injunction was granted, but the House of Lords reversed on a different ground, and Lord Upjohn rejected the applicability of Lord Cairns' Act to the case. But the reasons for his Lordship's rejection of the Act are unclear and, it is submitted, unconvincing.[50]

The four principles have not always met with approval, notably in cases concerning rights to light and trespass, where the burden of remedying the situation will often be out of all proportion to the injury to the plaintiff. In *Fishenden v. Higgs and Hill Ltd*[51] the defendant erected a building which obstructed the plaintiff's light in a manner that justified substantial damages, but not, by reason of the very high property values involved and the conduct of the defendant, an injunction. The Court of Appeal said that the principles of *Shelfer's* case were a useful guide, but not intended to be exhaustive or rigidly applied, and not a universal or even a sound rule in the case of rights to light.

---

[47] *Shelfer v. City of London Electric Lighting Co.* [1895] 1 Ch. 287; *Pugh v. Howells* (1984) 48 P. & C.R. 298.

[48] *Colls v. Home and Colonial Stores Ltd* [1904] A.C. 179 at p. 193, a case on an easement of light, where it was suggested that the court should incline to damages if there is any doubt, and the defendant has not acted in an unneighbourly spirit. See also *Pugh v. Howells, supra* (injunction to remove extension interfering with easement of light, where built quickly over a bank holiday, although warning given).

[49] [1967] 1 W.L.R. 967; *ante*, p. 770.

[50] See (1975) 34 C.L.J. 224 (J. Jolowicz); (1977) 36 C.L.J. 369; (1978) 37 C.L.J. 51 (P. Pettit). See also *Hooper v. Rogers* [1975] Ch. 43.

[51] (1935) 153 L.T. 128; *Colls v. Home and Colonial Stores Ltd, supra; Lyme Valley Squash Club Ltd v. Newcastle under Lyme Borough Council* [1985] 2 All E.R. 405.

Similarly in the case of trespass, the injury to the plaintiff may bear no relationship to that imposed on the defendant by the grant of an injunction. It was assumed in *Kelsen v. Imperial Tobacco Co. Ltd*[52] that *Shelfer's* case applied to trespass. The question was whether the defendant should be required to remove an advertisement which trespassed upon the plaintiff's airspace. The injury was minimal, but an injunction was granted. In *Woollerton and Wilson Ltd v. Richard Costain Ltd*[53] Stamp L.J. doubted whether *Shelfer's* case could apply to trespass involving nominal damage, as the award of damages would amount to a licence to continue the trespass. An injunction was granted although the four principles were satisfied, but the injunction was suspended.[54] That decision was considered wrong in *Jaggard v. Sawyer*,[55] where *Shelfer's* case was applied to a trespass which caused little injury and the other conditions were satisfied. The damages could reflect the amount the defendants should have been prepared to pay for a right of way. Thus *Shelfer's* case remains good law in relation to trespass, and continues applicable to nuisance.

In *Kennaway v. Thompson*[56] the plaintiff sought an injunction to restrain a nuisance by excessive noise against a motor boat racing club. The High Court had awarded damages in lieu under Lord Cairns' Act. The Court of Appeal, in granting the injunction, held that the jurisdiction to award damages in lieu of an injunction should be exercised only in very exceptional circumstances in cases of continuing nuisance. *Shelfer's* case had been applied countless times over the last 85 years, and was binding on the Court of Appeal. In the present case the injury to the plaintiff was not small, nor was it capable of estimation in monetary terms, nor could the sum awarded in the High Court (£16,000) be called a "small payment." In considering whether to award damages in lieu of an injunction, the public interest does not prevail over the private rights of the plaintiff. Any statements to the contrary in *Miller v. Jackson*[57] ran counter to the principles of *Shelfer's* case and were based on old authorities decided before *Shelfer's* case and now subject to it.

---

[52] [1957] 2 Q.B. 334.
[53] [1970] 1 W.L.R. 411.
[54] *Ante*, p. 750; criticised in (1975) 34 C.L.J. 224 (J. Jolowicz). Trespass is an exception to the rule that damages require proof of loss; *Stoke-on-Trent City Council v. W. & J. Wass Ltd* [1988] 1 W.L.R. 1406.
[55] [1995] 1 W.L.R. 269; *post*, p. 782; *Gooden v. Ketley* [1996] E.G.C.S. 47.
[56] [1981] Q.B. 88; (1981) 97 L.Q.R. 3; (1981) 44 M.L.R. 212 (R. Buckley); *Elliott v. Islington London Borough Council* [1991] 1 E.G.L.R. 167.
[57] [1977] Q.B. 966; *ante*, p. 738. The principle of *Miller v. Jackson* was also rejected in *Webster v. Lord Advocate* (1984) S.L.T. 13. See also *Sevenoaks District Council v. Pattullo & Vinson Ltd* [1984] Ch. 211.

But there is much to be said for the view which regrets an attempt to reduce the court's function to "a series of inelastic rules."[58] "The general rule is . . . that . . . this substitution [of damages for specific relief] ordinarily occurs only when the hardship caused to the defendant through specific enforcement would so far outweigh the inconvenience caused to the plaintiff if specific enforcement is denied that it would be highly unreasonable in all the circumstances to do more than to award damages."[59]

B. The Measure of Damages under Lord Cairns' Act

In *Leeds Industrial Co-operative Society v. Slack*,[60] Lord Sumner said[61]: "No money awarded in substitution can be justly awarded, unless it is at any rate designed to be a preferable equivalent to an injunction and therefore an adequate substitution for it." This principle was re-echoed in *Wroth v. Tyler*[62] in respect of specific performance. This decision was once regarded as authority for the proposition that greater damages may be awarded under Lord Cairns' Act than would be available at law. But in *Johnson v. Agnew*[63] the House of Lords held, in a case concerning specific performance, that there is no difference in the measure of damages obtainable under Lord Cairns' Act and at common law. Of course, damages may be recoverable under Lord Cairns' Act where none at all would be obtainable at law,[64] but in general equity follows the law, and it may generally be expected that if only nominal damages would be available at law, then no more will be awarded in equity.[65] A different view had been taken in *Wrotham Park Estate Ltd v. Parkside Homes Ltd*,[66] a case where no damages were available at law.

> The defendant had erected houses in breach of covenant. There was jurisdiction to grant a mandatory injunction against the defendant and the purchasers, who had aided and abetted the breach; but the injunction was refused, in order to avoid the demolition of valuable houses. As a restrictive covenant was involved, damages were available only under Lord Cairns' Act. The value of the plaintiff's estate was not diminished by the breach, but it did not follow that only nominal damages were

[58] Spry, *Equitable Remedies*, p. 624.
[59] *Ibid.* p. 625.
[60] [1924] A.C. 851.
[61] *Ibid.* at p. 870.
[62] [1974] Ch. 30.
[63] [1980] A.C. 367, *ante*, p. 727.
[64] As in *Hooper v. Rogers* [1975] Ch. 43 (*quia timet*).
[65] *Johnson v. Agnew* [1980] A.C. 367.
[66] [1974] 1 W.L.R. 798; not cited in *Johnson v. Agnew, supra*.

available. It would not be right to leave the defendants in possession of the fruits of their wrongdoing. Brightman J. held that a just substitute would be such sum as the plaintiff could reasonably have demanded to relax the covenant, assessed at £2,500.

The question whether substantial damages may be awarded under Lord Cairns' Act (or at common law) in the absence of loss cannot be answered without distinguishing various causes of action. Clearly damages cannot be awarded on the *Wrotham Park* basis in all cases, because to do so would be inconsistent with the principle expressed in *Johnson v. Agnew*[67] that the measure of damages under Lord Cairns' Act is the same as at common law. The basic principle at common law is that damages are to compensate for loss suffered. One exception is trespass, where substantial damages may be awarded without proof of loss.[68] Thus an award of substantial damages (including such sum as the plaintiff might reasonably have charged to permit the otherwise tortious act) may be awarded in lieu of an injunction under Lord Cairns' Act.[69]

In cases of nuisance it is essential to prove damage, but once that is established, any damages awarded in lieu of an injunction may properly include such sum as the plaintiff could reasonably have charged to permit the nuisance.[70] Indeed, tort damages at common law may include this element.[71]

So far as contract actions are concerned, a plaintiff who cannot establish loss is not entitled to damages at common law to reflect the sum he might have charged to release the defendant from the contract. As we have seen, such damages were awarded in *Wrotham Park Estate Ltd v. Parkside Homes Ltd*[72] for breach of a restrictive covenant which was enforceable only in equity.[73]

The *Wrotham Park* principle was reviewed by the Court of Appeal in *Surrey County Council v. Bredero Homes Ltd*,[74] where the defendant, a property developer, increased its profits by building

---

[67] [1980] A.C. 367.
[68] See *Inverugie Investments Ltd v. Hackett* [1995] 1 W.L.R. 713 (plaintiff entitled to reasonable rent for wrongful use whether or not he would have let the property to a third party or used it himself).
[69] *Bracewell v. Appleby* [1975] Ch. 408; *Jaggard v. Sawyer* [1995] 1 W.L.R. 269; *infra.* Doubts expressed in *Anchor Brewhouse Developments Ltd v. Berkley House (Docklands Developments) Ltd* [1987] 2 E.G.L.R. 173 were considered misplaced in *Jaggard v. Sawyer*. See also *Bosomworth v. Faber* (1995) 69 P. & C.R. 288.
[70] *Carr-Saunders v. Dick McNeill Associates Ltd* [1986] 1 W.L.R. 922; *Stoke-on-Trent City Council v. W. & J. Wass Ltd* [1988] 1 W.L.R. 1406.
[71] So considered in *Surrey County Council v. Bredero Homes Ltd* [1993] 1 W.L.R. 1361 and *Jaggard v. Sawyer* [1995] 1 W.L.R. 269, *infra.*
[72] [1974] 1 W.L.R. 798, *supra.*
[73] Doubted in *Wrotham Park Settled Estates v. Hertsmere B.C.* [1993] 2 E.G.L.R. 15, but see *Jaggard v. Sawyer* [1995] 1 W.L.R. 269, *infra.*
[74] [1993] 1 W.L.R. 1361, criticised in (1993) 109 L.Q.R. 518 (P. Birks); All E.R.Rev. 1993, p. 368 (W. Swadling); [1993] 1 R.L.R. 31 (R. O'Dair); [1994] Conv. 110 (T. Ingman).

five extra houses in breach of covenant. The plaintiff sued for damages, and did not seek an injunction because the defendant had sold all the houses. For that reason it was considered that Lord Cairns' Act did not apply.[75] The plaintiff could not establish that the breach of covenant caused it any loss, but sought such part of the profits made from the breach as would reflect a reasonable payment for release of the covenant, relying on *Wrotham Park*. It was held that only nominal damages could be awarded, under the ordinary contract principle. *Wrotham Park* was distinguished as a decision on Lord Cairns' Act. Dillion L.J. regarded it as inconsistent with *Johnson v. Agnew*,[76] but the other members of the Court of Appeal regarded it as correctly decided, although for different reasons. Steyn L.J. considered it to be based on sound restitution principles, while Rose L.J. emphasised the different conduct of the plaintiff in *Wrotham Park* and in the present case.

The matter arose again in *Jaggard v. Sawyer*,[77] where the defendant built a house in breach of covenant and trespassed upon a private road to gain access to it. The plaintiff sought an injunction to restrain the trespass (which caused little injury) or damages in lieu. The judge below refused the injunction, which would have rendered the property landlocked, and awarded a sum reflecting what the defendant should have paid for a right of way and a release of the covenant. This was upheld by the Court of Appeal, applying *Wrotham Park*. It was emphasised that damages assessed on that principle were compensatory, and that there was no inconsistency with *Johnson v. Agnew*[78] because the House of Lords there recognised that Lord Cairns' Act could apply where no action lay at common law or to compensate for future loss. Lord Wilberforce's statement that the measure of damages under the Act was the same as at common law was limited to the position where damages were recoverable for the same cause of action and did not mean that damages under the Act for a continuing or future breach must be assessed in the same way as damages at common law for a past breach.[79] Sir Thomas Bingham M.R. regarded *Wrotham Park* as a case of continuing invasion of rights. Millett L.J., on the other hand, considered it to be a case of a single past breach, so that the measure of damages under the Act was the same as at common law, but approved the decision on the basis that the damages there awarded could have been awarded at common law. Thus the authority of

---

[75] See the discussion of this aspect in *Jaggard v. Sawyer* [1995] 1 W.L.R. 269.

[76] [1980] A.C. 367.

[77] [1995] 1 W.L.R. 269; [1995] 3 R.L.R. 3 (W. Goodhart); All E.R.Rev. 1995, p. 453 (W. Swadling).

[78] *Supra.*

[79] [1995] 1 W.L.R. 269 at p. 291. See also *Lawson v. Hartley-Brown* (1996) 71 P. & C.R. 243 at p. 249.

Wrotham Park Estate Ltd v. Parkside Homes Ltd[80] has been restored in spite of earlier criticisms, but further clarification is required.

6. INJUNCTIONS IN PARTICULAR SITUATIONS

A. To Restrain a Breach of Contract

An injunction is the appropriate remedy to restrain the breach of a negative undertaking in a contract. In some measure it corresponds to specific performance in the area of positive undertakings.[81] But, as will be seen,[82] the jurisdiction to grant an injunction is wider.

i. Contract Wholly Negative

(a) *Perpetual Injunctions.* Where the essence of the contractual undertaking is negative, the court will grant an injunction to restrain a breach almost as a matter of course. As Lord Cairns L.C. explained in *Doherty v. Allman and Dowden*,[83] if the parties "contract that a particular thing shall not be done, all that a Court of Equity has to do is to say, by way of injunction, that which the parties have already said by way of covenant, that the thing shall not be done . . . " It is not necessary even to prove damage,[84] except where the action is by a reversioner.[85]

But the *Doherty v. Allman* principle must be applied "in the light of the surrounding circumstances in each case,"[86] and it does not prevent the court from considering the effect of delay or other supervening circumstances.[87]

Thus an injunction was refused in *Baxter v. Four Oaks Properties Ltd*,[88] where the defendants, innocently, but in breach of the covenant, intended to use a new building as flats. "The effect of granting such an order would . . . be to put the plaintiffs in a very strong bargaining position, for unless the defendants were prepared to leave the building unused, they would be forced to buy a release of

---

[80] [1974] 1 W.L.R. 798.

[81] *Ante,* pp. 695 *et seq.* Mandatory injunctions may also be available.

[82] *Post,* p. 785; *Donnell v. Bennett* (1883) 22 Ch.D. 835.

[83] (1878) 3 App.Cas. 709 at p. 720; *Sefton v. Tophams Ltd* [1967] A.C. 50; *Sutton Housing Trust v. Lawrence* (1988) 55 P. & C.R. 320 (granted to prevent tenant keeping dog in breach of covenant).

[84] *Grimston v. Cuningham* [1894] 1 Q.B. 125; *Marco Productions Ltd v. Pagola* [1945] K.B. 111, where dancers agreed not to perform for another producer; injunction granted although the plaintiffs could not show that they would suffer greater damage if the dancers performed elsewhere than if they remained idle; *cf. Provident Financial Group plc v. Hayward* [1989] I.C.R. 160.

[85] *Johnstone v. Hall* (1856) 2 K. & J. 414; *Martin v. Nutkin* (1724) 2 P.Wms. 266 (injunction to restrain ringing of church bells at 5 a.m.).

[86] *Shaw v. Applegate* [1977] 1 W.L.R. 970 at p. 975 (*per* Buckley L.J.).

[87] *Ibid.* at p. 980 (*per* Goff L.J.).

[88] [1965] Ch. 816.

the injunction . . . what the plaintiffs would get in the end would be damages—though, no doubt, more damages than they would get if no injunction were granted."[89]

(b) *Interlocutory Injunctions.* Interlocutory injunctions are not granted as a matter of course, but it was said in *Hampstead and Suburban Properties Ltd v. Diomedous*[90] that the *Doherty v. Allman*[91] principle applied where there was a plain breach of a clear negative covenant. In such a case, there was no reason why the defendant "should have a holiday from the enforcement of his obligation until the trial."[92] But where the validity of the covenant is in dispute, *Doherty v. Allman* cannot apply to interlocutory injunctions.[93]

(c) *Mandatory Injunctions.* Mandatory injunctions are entirely discretionary, and can never be granted automatically, even if a negative covenant is involved.[94] It is not possible to give precise guidance as to the way in which the discretion will be exercised. In *Shepherd Homes Ltd v. Sandham*,[95] Megarry J. said of *Doherty v. Allman*[96] that "a court of equity which says by way of injunction 'that which the parties have already said by way of covenant that the thing shall not be done,' is not thereby in the same breath adding 'and what is more, if it has been done, it shall be undone.' "[97] The application of the principle of *Doherty v. Allman* is tempered by a judicial discretion which withholds a mandatory injunction more readily than a prohibitory injunction, even where the plaintiff is blameless. Benefit to the plaintiff must be balanced against detriment to the defendant. But the search is not merely for "a fair result."[98]

ii. Positive and Negative Terms. Where a contract contains both positive and negative stipulations, and the positive ones are not susceptible to specific performance, the question arises whether the

---

[89] *Ibid.* at p. 829, *per* Cross J.
[90] [1969] 1 Ch. 248 (excessive noise made in breach of covenant by restaurant).
[91] (1878) 3 App.Cas. 709.
[92] [1969] 1 Ch. 248 at p. 259; *Att.-Gen. v. Barker* [1990] 3 All E.R. 257 (proposed publication, in breach of contract, of book about royal family).
[93] *Texaco Ltd v. Mulberry Filling Station Ltd* [1972] 1 W.L.R. 814 at p. 831.
[94] See *Wrotham Park Estate Ltd v. Parkside Homes Ltd* [1974] 1 W.L.R. 798. But the plaintiff may obtain summary judgment in a flagrant case; *Chelsea (Viscount) v. Muscatt* [1990] 2 E.G.L.R. 48.
[95] [1971] Ch. 340; *Sharp v. Harrison* [1922] 1 Ch. 502, at p. 512.
[96] (1878) 3 App.Cas. 709.
[97] [1971] Ch. 340 at p. 346.
[98] *Charrington v. Simons & Co. Ltd* [1971] 1 W.L.R. 598 at p. 603, *per* Russell L.J.

plaintiff can restrain the breach of the negative stipulation by injunction. In suitable cases, this can be done. The jurisdiction to grant an injunction is wider than that to order specific performance.[99]

The principle is that an injunction will not be granted if that would amount to indirect specific performance of the positive terms. Thus, it used to be said with confidence that no injunction would lie to restrain the termination of employment in breach of contract, for this would indirectly enforce the contract.[1] It has been seen, however, that in the special circumstances of *Hill v. C.A. Parsons & Co. Ltd*,[2] where an employer was reluctantly obliged to terminate the employment of a senior engineer who refused to join a trade union operating a closed shop principle, an interim injunction was issued to restrain the termination.

iii. No Express Negative Stipulation. Where a contract, drafted in positive form, contains no express negative stipulation, it may be possible to discover in the contract, on its proper construction, an implied negative undertaking which can be remedied by injunction.[3] This is especially important where the positive obligation is not specifically enforceable. It is not possible to lay down a rule to determine the circumstances in which an injunction may be obtained. The question in each case depends upon the construction which the court places upon the particular contract.

The principle was laid down by Lord Selborne in *Wolverhampton and Walsall Railway Co. Ltd v. L.N.W. Ry. Ltd*[4] as being that the court should "look in all such cases to the substance and not to the form. If the substance of the agreement is such that it would be violated by doing the thing sought to be prevented, then the question will arise, whether this is the court to come to for a remedy. If it is, I cannot think that ought to depend on the use of a negative rather than an affirmative form of expression."

A negative stipulation is rarely implied in contracts of personal service, for to do so might allow the indirect enforcement of a contract which is not specifically enforceable.[5] Thus, it will not be implied although the servant has contracted to devote the whole of

---

[99] See *Thomas Marshall (Exports) Ltd v. Guinle* [1979] Ch. 227 at p. 243.
[1] *Davis v. Foreman* [1894] 3 Ch. 654.
[2] [1972] 1 Ch. 305; *C.H. Giles & Co. Ltd v. Morris* [1972] 1 W.L.R. 307; (1975) 34 C.L.J. 36 (B. Napier).
[3] *Tulk v. Moxhay* (1848) 2 Ph. 774; *De Mattos v. Gibson* (1859) 4 De. G. & J. 276, Pettit, p. 579; *Catt v. Tourle* (1869) L.R. 4 Ch.App. 654; *Clegg v. Hands* (1890) 44 Ch.D. 503; *Jones & Sons Ltd v. Tankerville* [1909] 2 Ch. 440. Breach of an obligation imposed by law can be restrained by injunction even though the contract contains no express negative term: *Hivac v. Park Royal Scientific Instruments* [1946] Ch. 169; *Provident Financial Group plc v. Hayward* [1989] I.C.R. 160 (confidential information).
[4] (1873) L.R. 16 Eq. 433 at p. 440; *Whitwood Chemical Co. Ltd v. Hardman* [1891] 2 Ch. 416 at p. 441, *per* Lindley L.J.; *Bower v. Bantam Investments Ltd* [1972] 1 W.L.R. 1120.
[5] *Ante*, p. 707.

his time to his employer,[6] nor where there was a contract to sell to a purchaser all the "get" of a colliery for five years[7]; nor where a boxer agreed that his manager should have the "sole arrangements" for his boxing and other engagements.[8] However, in *Metropolitan Electric Supply Co. v. Ginder*,[9] the defendant applied for a supply of electricity on terms which provided that the defendant agreed to take all the electricity required by his premises from the plaintiff for a stated period. The plaintiff was not bound to supply, nor the defendant to take, any electricity. The contract was construed as an undertaking not to take electricity from any other persons, and the defendant was restrained by injunction from doing so. In *Manchester Ship Canal v. Manchester Racecourse Co.*[10] the grant of a "first refusal" was construed as an undertaking enforceable by injunction, not to sell to anyone else in contravention of the undertaking.

It is established that a negative term may be implied in the following types of case:

(a) *Contracts Affecting the Use of Land.* A covenant which touches and concerns the land so as to be binding in equity upon successors in title under the doctrine of *Tulk v. Moxhay*[11] will be construed as negative and subjected to an injunction if it is negative in substance although positive in form. Indeed, in *Tulk v. Moxhay* itself, the covenant was to "keep and maintain the said piece of ground in its then form, and in sufficient and proper repair . . . in an open state, uncovered with any buildings in neat and ornamental order."[12] The fact that a court was powerless to interfere against third parties except by the use of an injunction no doubt encouraged the courts to extend its use of the concept.

(b) *Contractual Licences.* After a long search for the proper solution to the problem of the revocation by a licensor of a contractual licence in breach of contract, the courts found it in the issue of an injunction to restrain the breach of contract.[13] Where the wrongful revocation occurs before the licensee has entered, the

---

[6] *Whitwood Chemical Co. Ltd v. Hardman* [1891] 2 Ch. 416; *Bower v. Bantam Investments Ltd* [1972] 1 W.L.R. 1120.

[7] *Fothergill v. Rowland* (1873) L.R. 17 Eq. 132.

[8] *Mortimer v. Beckett* [1920] 1 Ch. 571. See also *Fraser v. Thames Television Ltd* [1984] Q.B. 44.

[9] [1901] 2 Ch. 799. See also *Sky Petroleum Ltd v. V.I.P. Petroleum Ltd* [1974] 1 W.L.R. 576.

[10] [1901] 2 Ch. 37. See also *Gardner v. Coutts & Co.* [1968] 1 W.L.R. 173 (implied term in right of pre-emption that property will not be given to another); *cf. Pritchard v. Briggs* [1980] Ch. 338.

[11] (1848) 2 Ph. 774.

[12] *Ibid.* at p. 775.

[13] *Post,* p. 873.

court may, in an appropriate case, grant specific performance or a mandatory injunction to compel performance of the licensor's obligations.[14] A contractual licence is commonly in positive form—permitting the licensee to occupy premises. But where the licence on its proper construction gives no right to the licensor to revoke in the way in which he has purported to do, the court will treat the matter as one in which the licensor has contracted not to revoke inconsistently with the terms of the licence, and will restrain him from doing so.[15]

iv. Contracts for Personal Services. It has been seen that contracts for personal services would not be specifically enforced either by specific performance or by an injunction.[16] In the case of contracts of employment, the Trade Union and Labour Relations (Consolidation) Act 1992, s.236 provides that "no court shall . . . by way of . . . injunction . . . restraining a breach or threatened breach of [a contract of employment] compel an employee to do any work or to attend at any place for the doing of any work." This provision, as with the corresponding provision relating to specific performance, applies only to contracts of employment[17] and only to enforcement against an employee. The equitable principle which denies specific enforcement of contracts of service has in appropriate circumstances permitted the issue of an injunction to restrain a negative undertaking in a contract for personal services, and this may have the effect indirectly of causing a contract to be performed. It remains to be determined whether and how far the provision now found in section 236 affects the operation of this principle. Two aspects of the question of the issue of an injunction in this circumstance need to be examined.

(a) *Restraining Breach by Employee or Independent Contractor.*

In *Lumley v. Wagner*,[18] Miss Wagner, an opera star, had agreed with Lumley that she would sing at Her Majesty's Theatre during a certain period, and would not sing anywhere else without his written permission. She made another engagement with Gye to sing at Covent Garden and abandoned her previous commitment to Lumley, who sought an injunction to restrain her from singing for Gye. Lord St. Leonards held that an injunction should be

---

[14] *Verrall v. Great Yarmouth Borough Council* [1981] Q.B. 202, *ante*, p. 701.
[15] See *Jones (James) and Sons Ltd v. Earl of Tankerville* [1909] 2 Ch. 440.
[16] *Ante*, p. 707.
[17] *Ante*, p. 708.
[18] (1852) 1 De G.M. & G. 604. The injunction may be granted even though it interferes with the contractual rights of innocent third parties; *PSM International plc v. Whitehouse and Willenhall Automation Ltd* [1992] I.R.L.R. 279; *cf. Maythorn v. Palmer* (1864) 11 L.T. 261. See also *Thomas Marshall (Exports) Ltd v. Guinle* [1979] Ch. 227 at pp. 240–242.

granted to restrain the breach of the negative stipulation; it would not of course have been possible to obtain specific performance of the promise to sing.

The principle of *Lumley v. Wagner* has been much criticised.[19] It is said that the issue of an injunction in this situation is the equivalent of specific performance; and that a number of principles are thereby disregarded, especially the rule that the court will not supervise the performance of contracts; and the principle that the contracting parties must not become tied together in a relationship involving a status of servitude. On the other hand, the carrying out of agreements must be encouraged by the courts, whatever remedy is used.[20]

It is submitted that the correct approach in these situations, as in other cases of injunctions, is that the injunction should issue to restrain the breach of a negative undertaking, unless the defendant can show that the court should in its discretion refuse on the ground that undesirable consequences may follow. Each case, in other words, should be treated on its merits.

Thus an employee should not be put into a position in which he must either perform the contract or do nothing.

In *Rely-a-Bell Burglar and Fire Alarm Co. v. Eisler*[21] the employee had contracted to serve the employer and to take no other employment for the period of the contract of service. An injunction was refused, and damages awarded.

In *Warner Bros. v. Nelson*,[22] a well-known actress, Bette Davis, contracted to work for the plaintiffs and not to work as a film actress for any other film company for the period of her contract, "or to be engaged in any other occupation." The term was not void under the restraint of trade doctrine,[23] and the question was whether an injunction was an appropriate remedy. "[I]t would, of course, be impossible to grant an injunction covering all the

---

[19] Ames, *Lectures on Legal History*, p. 370; *per* Lindley L.J. in *Whitwood Chemical Co. v. Hardman* [1891] 2 Ch. 416 at p. 428; "I think that the court . . . will generally do much more harm by attempting to decree specific performance in cases of personal service than by leaving them alone; and whether it is attempted to enforce these contracts directly by a decree of specific performance, or indirectly by an injunction, appears to me to be immaterial."

[20] *Lane v. Newdigate* (1804) 10 Ves.Jr. 192.

[21] [1926] Ch. 609.

[22] [1937] 1 K.B. 209.

[23] *Per* Russell L.J. in *Instone v. A. Schroeder Music Publishing Co. Ltd* [1974] 1 All E.R. 171 at p. 178, C.A. He also criticised Branson J. who suggested in *Warner Bros. v. Nelson* [1937] 1 K.B. 209 at p. 214 that the doctrine of restraint of trade could not apply during the continuance of the contract; see also *Clifford Davis Management Ltd v. W.E.A. Records Ltd* [1975] 1 W.L.R. 61.

negative covenants in the contract. That would, indeed, force the defendant to perform her contract or remain idle; but this objection is removed by the restricted form in which the injunction is sought. It is confined to forbidding the defendant, without the consent of the plaintiffs, to render any services for or in any motion picture or stage production for any one other than the plaintiffs."[24] An injunction was given on these terms.[25] Miss Davis was still free to earn a living in other ways, even if they were less lucrative.

In *Evening Standard Co. Ltd v. Henderson*[26] an employee had failed to give the required notice. The Court of Appeal was prepared to grant an interlocutory injunction to prevent him from working for a rival paper during the notice period. As the employer had undertaken to pay his salary for that period even if he did not work ("garden leave"), the injunction did not compel him to perform the contract or starve, but was rather a means of enforcing the notice requirement. It may be otherwise if the "garden leave" is so long that the employee may lose his skills.[27]

(b) *Compelling Employer to Employ.*

In *Page One Records v. Britton*,[28] a group of musicians appointed the plaintiff as their manager for five years, contracting not to engage anyone else as manager. They wished to change, and the plaintiff sought an injunction to prevent the employment of another manager, arguing, on the lines of *Warner Bros. v. Nelson*[29] that the defendants could retain him or continue without a manager. The injunction was refused, as it would *persuade* them to retain the plaintiff, which would be undesirable in a personal and fiduciary relationship in which the defendants had lost confidence in him.

Although the group could have earned their living in another way, just as Bette Davis could have done, it would be unrealistic to expect any of them to do so. Unless the period of the injunction is short, it puts economic pressure on the defendant to perform an obligation

---

[24] [1937] 1 K.B. 209 at p. 219, *per* Branson J.
[25] *Robinson & Co. Ltd v. Heuer* [1898] 2 Ch. 451.
[26] [1987] I.R.L.R. 64; (1989) 139 N.L.J. 1716 (J. Hand and P. Smith).
[27] *Provident Financial Group plc v. Hayward* [1989] I.C.R. 160.
[28] [1968] 1 W.L.R. 157.
[29] [1937] 1 K.B. 209.

which is not specifically enforceable. The Court of Appeal has now held in *Warren v. Mendy*[30] that *Page One Records* is preferable to *Warner*. The plaintiff was refused an injunction which in effect would have compelled a boxer to retain him as manager for at least two years. In relationships involving skill or talent and a high degree of mutual confidence,[31] the court should not enforce negative terms of a contract if this would in effect compel performance of the positive terms.

In *Hill v. C.A. Parsons & Co. Ltd*,[32] we saw that the Court of Appeal granted an injunction restraining an employer from acting on a wrongful dismissal. This amounted to indirect specific performance of a service contract; but the circumstances were special. Personal confidence still existed between the parties; a proper length of notice would have safeguarded the plaintiff's right under the Industrial Relations Act 1971; and the plaintiff was due to retire in two years, and his pension depended on his average salary during the last three years of employment. Stamp L.J. dissented, and would have allowed the pension claim to be included in an award of damages. The question arose again in *Chappell v. Times Newspapers Ltd*,[33] where employees sought an injunction to restrain their dismissal during an industrial dispute. As mutual confidence no longer existed between the parties, the case was not within the *Hill v. Parsons* exception. The fact that unfair dismissal was unlawful did not mean that a service contract was enforceable by injunction. That would be a "plain recipe for disaster."[34]

It appears that the grant of an injunction within the *Hill v. Parsons* exception is no longer a rarity. Although the plaintiff must normally show that mutual confidence still exists,[35] this is not inevitably precluded by the fact that the employer opposes the claim. It suffices

[30] [1989] 1 W.L.R. 853; (1990) 49 C.L.J. 28 (H. McLean); (1990) 140 N.L.J. 1007 (A. Burrows).
[31] The obligation of the plaintiffs in *Warner Bros. v. Nelson, supra*, and *Lumley v. Wagner*, *ante*, p. 787, was merely to pay money.
[32] [1972] Ch. 305; *ante*, p. 709. See also *Jones v. Lee* [1980] I.R.L.R. 67. For the position where the employment is protected beyond the common law by procedural requirements relating to dismissal, see *R. v. British Broadcasting Corporation, ex p. Lavelle* [1983] 1 W.L.R. 23.
[33] [1975] 1 W.L.R. 482; see also *G.K.N. (Cwmbran) Ltd v. Lloyd* [1972] I.C.R. 214; *Sanders v. Ernest A. Neale Ltd* [1974] I.C.R. 565; *Ali v. London Borough of Southwark* [1988] I.R.L.R. 100; *Wishart v. National Association of Citizens Advice Bureaux Ltd* [1990] I.C.R. 794.
[34] *Ibid.* at p. 506. See also the Employment Rights Act 1996, s.117: an industrial tribunal may order reinstatement, but the sanction in the event of non-compliance is an award of compensation.
[35] *cf. Robb v. London Borough of Hammersmith and Fulham* [1991] I.R.L.R. 72 (no dismissal prior to disciplinary procedure even though loss of confidence); *Jones v. Gwent County Council* [1992] I.R.L.R. 521.

to establish that the employer has no rational ground to lack confidence, as where there has been no friction at the workplace.[36]

B. To Restrain a Breach of Trust

There are many examples of the issue of an injunction to restrain a breach of an equitable obligation, and a few must suffice here. Trustees have been restrained from distributing an estate inconsistently with the terms of the instrument,[37] or from selling under depreciatory conditions of sale[38]; or for a price below that offered firmly by a prospective purchaser[39]; or selling land without appointing a second trustee and without consulting the beneficiary.[40] Where the plaintiff has a claim to trace property in equity,[41] an injunction may be granted to restrain the defendant from disposing of the property.[42]

C. To Restrain the Commission or Continuance of a Tort

In each of the many cases in which an injunction issues to restrain the commission of a tort, equity is exercising its "concurrent" jurisdiction. Equity plays no part in determining whether a wrong has been committed; that is a matter solely of law. It is the remedy alone that is equitable. Thus the plaintiff must first establish the commission or threat of something which constitutes a tort at law. If it is, the court may, in its discretion, grant an injunction. The rules and practice vary with the tort in question. The tort of harassment should now be added to the list.[43]

i. Nuisance.[44] The act complained of must constitute a nuisance at law. "There is no such thing as an equitable nuisance."[45] The interference must cause or threaten damage.[46] No injunction will

---

[36] *Powell v. London Borough of Brent* [1987] I.R.L.R. 466; *Hughes v. London Borough of Southwark* [1988] I.R.L.R. 55; (1988) 85/5 L.S.Gaz. 28 (J. Hendy and J. McMullen); (1989) 48 C.L.J. 28 and (1993) 52 C.L.J. 405 (K. Ewing); (1989) 52 M.L.R. 449 (H. Carty).

[37] *Fox v. Fox* (1870) L.R. 11 Eq. 142.

[38] *Dance v. Goldingham* (1873) L.R. 8 Ch.App. 902.

[39] *Buttle v. Saunders* [1950] 2 All E.R. 193 (*ante*, p. 513) where the trustee had promised (but not in binding form) to sell land to another purchaser.

[40] *Waller v. Waller* [1967] 1 W.L.R. 451.

[41] *Ante*, p. 662.

[42] *A. v. C.* [1981] Q.B. 956n.; *Polly Peck International plc v. Nadir (No. 2)* [1992] 4 All E.R 769.

[43] *Burris v. Azadani* [1995] 1 W.L.R. 1372.

[44] See generally (1982) 41 C.L.J. 87 (S. Tromans).

[45] *Per* Kindersley V.-C. in *Soltau v. de Held* (1851) 2 Sim.(N.S.) 133 at p. 151.

[46] It is otherwise where the nuisance is actionable without proof of damage; *Sevenoaks District Council v. Pattullo & Vinson Ltd* [1984] Ch. 211; *Halton Borough Council v. Cawley* [1985] 1 W.L.R. 15 (right to hold market).

issue to deal with a trifling interference[47]; and even if damage is proved, equity will not grant an injunction in every case in which the common law would award damages. The remedy is discretionary, and is particularly appropriate in cases of nuisance.[48] Damages may be awarded in lieu under Lord Cairns' Act.[49]

It was held in *Miller v. Jackson*,[50] by a majority of the Court of Appeal, that the court should weigh the interests of the public against those of the individual, and should refuse the injunction if, on balance, it was felt that the interest of the public should prevail. This proposition was doubted in *Kennaway v. Thompson*[51] by the Court of Appeal. It was there held that, when considering whether to award damages in lieu of an injunction under Lord Cairns' Act in a nuisance case, the public interest does not prevail over the private interest of the plaintiff.[52]

ii. Trespass. An injunction will issue to restrain a threatened or existing trespass. In minor cases, the court will leave the plaintiff to such remedy as he has at law; as where a clergyman of the Church of England held services on the seashore between high and low water mark which was leased by the Crown to the Corporation[53]; or where collectors chased a butterfly on to the plaintiff's land.[54] Where, however, the defendant entered the plaintiff's wood, cut down trees and clearly intended to cut more, he was restrained.[55] Indeed, there is no real discretion to refuse in cases of total dispossession.[56]

Where the defendant has no arguable defence, the plaintiff may be granted an interlocutory injunction even where the trespass has caused no damage.[57]

---

[47] *Ankerson v. Connelly* [1907] 1 Ch. 678.

[48] *Halsey v. Esso Petroleum Co. Ltd* [1961] 1 W.L.R. 683; *Leakey v. National Trust for Places of Historic Interest or Natural Beauty* [1980] Q.B. 485; *Laws v. Florinpace* [1981] 1 All E.R. 659; *Pugh v. Howells* (1984) 48 P. & C.R. 298.

[49] *Ante*, p. 776.

[50] [1977] Q.B. 966, *ante*, p. 738; *Tetley v. Chitty* [1986] 1 All E.R. 663.

[51] [1981] Q.B. 88. It was also rejected in *Webster v. Lord Advocate* (1984) S.L.T. 13. See also *Sevenoaks District Council v. Pattullo & Vinson Ltd, supra; Rosling v. Pinnegar* (1987) 54 P. & C.R. 124.

[52] Authorities supporting the contrary proposition were decided before *Shelfer v. City of London Electric Lighting Co.* [1895] 1 Ch. 287, *ante*, p. 777.

[53] *Llandudno Urban District Council v. Woods* [1899] 2 Ch. 705. Refusal terminates self-help remedies; *Burton v. Winters* [1993] 1 W.L.R. 1077.

[54] *Fielden v. Cox* (1906) 22 T.L.R. 411; *Behrens v. Richards* [1905] 2 Ch. 614.

[55] *Stanford v. Hurlstone* (1873) L.R. 9 Ch.App. 116. See also *League Against Cruel Sports Ltd v. Scott* [1986] Q.B. 240 (persistent trespass by hunt).

[56] *Harrow London Borough Council v. Donohue* [1995] 1 E.G.L.R. 257.

[57] *Patel v. W.H. Smith (Eziot) Ltd* [1987] 1 W.L.R. 853; *Anchor Brewhouse Developments Ltd v. Berkley House (Docklands Developments) Ltd* [1987] 2 E.G.L.R. 173.

A mandatory injunction will be granted where necessary, for example requiring the removal of an advertising sign which projected into the airspace above the plaintiff's single storey shop.[58]

iii. Libel. The granting of injunctions to restrain the publication of a libel has caused particular difficulty, partly because of the complexity of proof of the tort, but largely because of the importance of allowing to be said things that ought to be said. It was not until *Quartz Hill Consolidated Gold Mining Co. v. Beall* in 1882[59] that the courts positively asserted a jurisdiction to restrain publication. The matter is usually one of urgency, requiring an interlocutory injunction, and Jessel M.R. was careful to point out the need for great caution in its exercise.

The plaintiff must satisfy the court of the falsity of the statements and, where they are privileged, the presence of malice. "The court will not restrain the publication of an article, even though it is defamatory, when the defendant says that he intends to justify it or to make fair comment on a matter of public interest. . . . The reason sometimes given is that the defences of justification and fair comment are for the jury, which is the constitutional tribunal, and not for a judge; but a better reason is the importance in the public interest that the truth should out."[60] The interest of the public in knowing the truth outweighs the interest of a plaintiff in maintaining his reputation.[61] Thus, it was laid down in *Bonnard v. Perryman*[62] as a working rule that an interlocutory injunction ought never to be granted except in the clearest cases, in which, if a jury did not find the matter complained of to be libellous, the court would set aside the verdict as unreasonable. Lord Denning M.R. stated that all requests for "gagging injunctions" which seek to prevent true and fair comment on matters of public interest should fail.[63] But in *Hubbard v. Pitt*[64] the Court of Appeal upheld the grant of an interlocutory injunction to restrain, *inter alia*, the display of allegedly libellous placards and leaflets outside the plaintiffs' business

---

[58] *Kelsen v. Imperial Tobacco Co. Ltd* [1957] 2 Q.B. 334. See also *Trenberth (John) Ltd v. National Westminster Bank Ltd* (1979) 39 P. & C.R. 104; *London & Manchester Assurance Company Ltd v. O. & H. Construction Ltd* [1989] 2 E.G.L.R. 185 (interlocutory).

[59] (1882) 20 Ch.D. 501.

[60] *Fraser v. Evans* [1969] 1 Q.B. 349 at p. 360, *per* Lord Denning M.R.; *Bryanston Finance Ltd v. de Vries* [1975] Q.B. 703 (privileged occasions); *Crest Homes Ltd v. Ascott, The Times*, February 4, 1975 (no injunction when defendant chose "flamboyant and vulgar method of airing his complaints"); *Khashoggi v. I.P.C. Magazines Ltd* [1986] 1 W.L.R. 1412; *Att.-Gen. v. News Group Newspapers Ltd* [1987] Q.B. 1.

[61] *Woodward v. Hutchins* [1977] 1 W.L.R. 760, at p. 764 (*per* Lord Denning M.R.).

[62] [1891] 2 Ch. 269. See also *Hermann Loog v. Bean* (1884) 26 Ch.D. 306; *Harakas v. Baltic Mercantile & Shipping Exchange Ltd* [1982] 1 W.L.R. 958.

[63] *Att-Gen. v. British Broadcasting Corporation* [1981] A.C. 303 at p. 311, C.A.

[64] [1976] Q.B. 142; (Lord Denning M.R. dissenting). See (1976) 35 C.L.J. 82 (P. Wallington).

premises. The necessity of preserving the freedoms of speech, assembly and demonstration should "not constrain the court to refuse a plaintiff an injunction to prevent defendants exercising these liberties in his front garden."[65] The injunction may also be granted if there is a clear case that publication is part of a concerted plan to inflict deliberate damage without just cause.[66] In *Monson v. Tussaud's*,[67] an injunction was refused because it appeared that there might be a question at the trial whether the plaintiff had agreed to the publication. The court will only intervene where the issue is clear and certain. It "will not prejudice the issue by granting an injunction in advance of publication."[68] It has been held that the principles laid down in *American Cyanamid Co. v. Ethicon Ltd*[69] governing the grant of an interlocutory injunction have no application to libel injunctions, thus preserving the rule in *Bonnard v. Perryman*.[70]

Once libel has been proved at the trial, the plaintiff may obtain an injunction to restrain its repetition.

D. Breach of Confidence

An injunction will be available to restrain a breach of confidence, whether arising out of a personal, commercial or other relationship.[71] Many of the questions which arise are similar to those discussed in connection with the cases on libel, but the principle of freedom of speech plays a less dominant part here. Unlike libel, the truth of the statement is no defence to a breach of confidence. As will be seen, the *Anton Piller*[72] injunction has evolved to protect the victims of commercial malpractice and espionage.

An obligation of confidence exists in respect of communications between husband and wife. "It is the policy of the law (which is the basis of the court's jurisdiction) to preserve the close confidence and

---

[65] *Ibid.* at p. 187, *per* Stamp L.J.
[66] *Gulf Oil (Great Britain) Ltd v. Page* [1987] Ch. 327 (airborne sign over Cheltenham racecourse); *Femis-Bank (Anguilla) Ltd v. Lazar* [1991] Ch. 391.
[67] [1894] 1 Q.B. 671. The plaintiff, who had been tried in Scotland for murder, where the jury had returned a verdict of "not proven," complained of the exhibition of a figure of himself in a room next to the "Chamber of Horrors."
[68] *Fraser v. Evans, supra,* at p. 361, *per* Lord Denning M.R.
[69] [1975] A.C. 396, *ante,* p. 753.
[70] *Bestobell Paints Ltd v. Bigg* (1975) 119 S.J. 678; *J. Trevor & Sons v. P. R. Solomon* (1978) 248 E.G. 779 (*per* Lord Denning M.R.); *Herbage v. Pressdram Ltd* [1984] 1 W.L.R. 1160; *Gulf Oil (Great Britain) Ltd v. Page* [1987] Ch. 327; *Kaye v. Robertson* [1991] 18 F.S.R. 62; [1993] Conv. 347 (M. Thompson).
[71] See generally (1977) 30 C.L.P. 191 and (1976) 92 L.Q.R. 180 (M. Bryan); Goff and Jones, *The Law of Restitution* (4th ed.), Chap. 36.
[72] [1976] Ch. 55, *post,* p. 804. See *Lock International plc v. Beswick* [1989] 1 W.L.R. 1268.

mutual trust between husband and wife."[73] Other kinds of confidential information will be restrained from publication along similar lines,[74] and even, in some cases, where the information is available from other public sources,[75] but not if it has been disseminated worldwide, for in such a case the injunction would be futile.[76] It is necessary that the plaintiff should himself have an interest in preventing the disclosure,[77] although he need not show that the use of the information would cause him detriment.[78] Even where the injunction is granted, it may be that the defendant is enjoined from making use of the confidential information only for a limited period rather than for all time.[79]

As the right to the preservation of confidence is an equitable interest, third parties with notice may be bound by the duty of confidence.[80] Injunctions may, therefore, be granted against third parties, such as the press, who seek to publish confidential information knowing it to be such.[81] The third party, however, is not necessarily in the same position as the original confidant, as their respective duties may be different.[82] But worldwide publication releases third parties[83] (but probably not the original confidant[84]) from any duty of confidence.

The injunction will be refused if the public interest in the preservation of confidence is overridden by some other public interest. While the precise scope of the "public interest" defence remains

---

[73] *Argyll v. Argyll* [1967] Ch. 302 at p. 332.

[74] *Saltman Engineering Co. Ltd v. Campbell Engineering Co. Ltd* [1963] 3 All E.R. 413n; *Peter Pan Manufacturing Corporation v. Corsets Silhouette Ltd* [1964] 1 W.L.R. 96; *Seager v. Copydex* [1967] 1 W.L.R. 923; *Thomas Marshall (Exports) Ltd v. Guinle* [1979] Ch. 227; *Fraser v. Thames Television Ltd* [1984] Q.B. 44; (1983) 42 C.L.J. 209 (A. Tettenborn). See generally (1977) 9 Patent L.Rev. 271 (J. Berryhill); (1979) 95 L.Q.R. 323 (W. Braithwaite).

[75] *Schering Chemicals Ltd v. Falkman Ltd* [1982] Q.B. 1; *Att.-Gen. v. Guardian Newspapers Ltd* [1987] 1 W.L.R. 1248 (*Spycatcher* at the interlocutory stage).

[76] *Att.-Gen. v. Guardian Newspapers Ltd (No. 2)* [1990] 1 A.C. 109 (*Spycatcher* final injunction refused). The European Court of Human Rights held that the Government had violated Article 10 of the Convention in maintaining the injunctions after publication abroad.

[77] *Fraser v. Evans* [1969] 1 Q.B. 349; *Hubbard v. Vosper* [1972] 2 Q.B. 84.

[78] *X. v. Y.* [1988] 2 All E.R. 648. See the varying views in *Att.-Gen. v. Guardian Newspapers Ltd (No. 2), supra.*

[79] This is the "springboard" doctrine. See (1979) 42 M.L.R. 94 (W. Braithwaite); (1976) 92 L.Q.R. 180 (M. Bryan); *Bullivant (Roger) Ltd v. Ellis* [1987] I.C.R. 464.

[80] *Att.-Gen. v. Guardian Newspapers Ltd (No. 2), supra* (*Sunday Times* liable to account for profits of publication). See also *Printers and Finishers Ltd v. Holloway* [1965] 1 W.L.R. 1; *Goddard v. Nationwide Building Society* [1987] Q.B. 670.

[81] *Att.-Gen. v. Guardian Newspapers Ltd* [1987] 1 W.L.R. 1248, and *(No. 2)* [1990] 1 A.C. 109 (*Spycatcher*); (1989) 52 M.L.R. 389 (J. Michael); (1989) C.L.P. 49 (G. Jones).

[82] *Att.-Gen. v. Guardian Newspapers Ltd (No. 2), supra.*

[83] *Ibid.* (*Spycatcher* final injunction refused). See also *Lord Advocate v. The Scotsman Publications Ltd* [1990] 1 A.C. 812.

[84] *Ibid.*; the reasoning being that he must not profit from his own wrong.

uncertain,[85] it is clear that matters such as confidentiality or national security[86] must be balanced against the public interest in freedom of speech and the press and the right to receive information. More particularly, there is no confidence as to the disclosure of "iniquity." This principle was discussed by the House of Lords in *Att.-Gen. v. Guardian Newspapers Ltd (No. 2)*,[87] where the question was whether newspapers should be enjoined from publishing *Spycatcher* (the Peter Wright memoirs). It was said that the "iniquity" defence was subject to two limitations. First, the disclosure of confidential information revealing wrong-doing should in some cases be to interested parties such as the police rather than to the public at large.[88] Secondly, the duty of confidence was not overridden by mere allegations of wrong-doing. While the wrong-doing need not be proved, there must be at least a prima facie case. Further, it was not the case that *any* breach of the law was within the "iniquity" defence. In the present case, the publication of the entire book or substantial extracts could not be within this defence when the allegations of "iniquity" covered only a few pages. The final injunction was, however, refused because the information was by this time within the public domain.

Where there is no wrong-doing by the plaintiff the public interest defence will succeed only in exceptional cases. Such a case was *Lion Laboratories Ltd v. Evans*,[89] where the plaintiff failed to restrain the publication of confidential documents concerning the accuracy of a "breathalyser" device manufactured by the plaintiff. The public interest in confidentiality had to be weighed against its interest in the accuracy of a device upon which depended liability to criminal penalties. There might be circumstances where it was right to publish confidential material even if unlawfully obtained in flagrant breach of confidence, and irrespective of the motive of the

---

[85] Goff and Jones, *op. cit.*, pp. 696–702. See also *Att.-Gen. v. Jonathan Cape Ltd* [1976] Q.B. 752; *Schering Chemicals Ltd v. Falkman Ltd* [1982] Q.B. 1; (1982) 41 C.L.J. 40 (G. Jones); (1982) 98 L.Q.R. 5 (A. Tettenborn).

[86] *Att.-Gen. v. Guardian Newspapers Ltd* [1987] 1 W.L.R. 1248, and *(No. 2)* [1990] 1 A.C. 109 (*Spycatcher*). The latter decision, however, is not based on the balancing of public interests but on the fact that no further damage could be caused by publication. See generally *X. Ltd v. Morgan Grampian (Publishers) Ltd* [1991] 1 A.C. 1.

[87] *Supra.* The "iniquity" involved alleged plots to overthrow the Wilson government and to kill President Nasser. See also *Finers v. Miro* [1991] 1 W.L.R. 35 (fraud).

[88] See *Francome v. Mirror Group Newspapers* [1984] 1 W.L.R. 892 (injunction to restrain publication of illegally taped telephone conversations revealing possible criminal offences and breaches of Jockey Club regulations. Public interest could be served by making tapes available to police or Jockey Club); *cf. Cork v. McVicar, The Times*, October 31, 1984 (Exposure of corrupt practices in the administration of justice not to be restrained by injunction, although clear breach of contract and confidence. Argument that disclosure should only be to the appropriate authorities rejected). See also *Re a Company's Application* [1989] Ch. 477; (1990) 106 L.Q.R. 42 (E. Lomnicka); (no injunction to restrain disclosure to tax and regulatory authorities).

[89] [1985] Q.B. 526 (interlocutory); (1984) 100 L.Q.R. 517; (1985) 44 C.L.J. 35 (Y. Cripps); (1985) 48 M.L.R. 592 (N. Lowe and C. Willmore).

informer. But, it was added, what is interesting to the public should not be confused with the public interest.

Other cases where the public interest defence has succeeded include *Woodward v. Hutchins*,[90] where "publicity seeking" pop singers failed to restrain the publication of newspaper articles revealing "discreditable incidents" about them, and *W. v. Egdell*[91] where a prisoner in a secure hospital failed to enjoin the disclosure by a doctor to the authorities having power to discharge him of a confidential report on his mental state. In *X. v. Y.*,[92] on the other hand, the defence failed when a health authority sought to restrain publication of the identity of two doctors suffering from AIDS, disclosed by its employee in breach of contract and confidence.

In the sphere of judicial proceedings, the public interest requiring the truth to be disclosed in the administration of justice does not override the confidentiality of matters disclosed in other proceedings, which may be protected by injunction.[93]

E. Public Wrongs

Although an injunction normally issues to prevent a breach of the plaintiff's own rights, it is available, at the suit of the Attorney-General, to restrain an act which is illegal or detrimental to the public. Thus the Attorney-General may obtain an injunction to restrain a public nuisance, either on his own initiative, or on the relation of some other person.[94] A private individual may only sue in respect of public wrongs where a private right of his own is interfered with,[95] or where he suffers special damage from the interference with the public right.[96] We have seen that, subject to this exception, the individual cannot sue in his own name to enforce a public right. He must bring a relator action, with the consent of the Attorney-General.[97]

---

[90] [1977] 1 W.L.R. 760 (interlocutory); criticised in Goff and Jones, *op. cit.*, p. 700. See also *Stephens v. Avery* [1988] Ch. 449; (1989) 105 L.Q.R. 37 (P. Sparkes); (1990) 53 M.L.R. 43 (W. Wilson); *Hellewell v. Chief Constable of Derbyshire* [1995] 1 W.L.R. 804.

[91] [1990] Ch. 395.

[92] [1988] 2 All E.R. 648; All E.R. Rev. 1988, p. 214 (A. Grubb).

[93] *Medway v. Doublelock Ltd* [1978] 1 W.L.R. 710. See also *Distillers Co. (Biochemicals) Ltd v. Times Newspapers Ltd* [1975] Q.B. 613; *Goddard v. Nationwide Building Society* [1987] Q.B. 670. But the Banking Act 1987 overrides the duty of confidence; *A. v. B. Bank (Governor and Company of the Bank of England intervening)* [1993] Q.B. 311.

[94] *Att.-Gen. v. P.Y.A. Quarries* [1975] 2 Q.B. 169.

[95] *Lyon v. Fishmongers Co.* (1876) 1 App.Cas. 662.

[96] *Meade v. London Borough of Haringey* [1979] 1 W.L.R. 637; *Gravesham Borough Council v. British Railways Board* [1978] Ch. 379; *Barrs v. Bethell* [1982] Ch. 294; *Lonrho Ltd v. Shell Petroleum Co. Ltd* [1982] A.C. 173; *Ashby v. Ebdon* [1985] Ch. 394; *Rickless v. United Artists Corp.* [1988] Q.B. 40; *CBS Songs Ltd v. Amstrad Consumer Electronics plc* [1988] A.C. 1013; *P. v. Liverpool Daily Post and Echo Newspapers plc* [1991] 2 A.C. 370; *R. v Deputy Governor of Parkhurst Prison, ex p. Hague* [1992] 1 A.C. 58.

[97] *Gouriet v. Union of Post Office Workers* [1978] A.C. 435, *ante*, p. 742.

An injunction may issue in circumstances where it is the only effective way of protecting the interests of the public, or where the criminal penalty has proved inadequate to prevent continuous breaches of the law. It should be added that where the Attorney-General brings such an action, the injunction is almost always granted. Thus injunctions were issued where the defendant ran buses in Manchester without licence and in defiance of the corporation's objections, the profits being greater than the fines,[98] and where the defendant operated a hotel without a fire certificate, causing danger to the public.[99]

We have already seen that the view of the House of Lords is that the cases where the Attorney-General can invoke the aid of the civil courts to restrain the commission of a criminal offence are narrow and not to be extended, and may require reconsideration.[1]

Some statutory provisions enable local authorities to seek injunctions in their own name to enforce public rights, without the concurrence of the Attorney-General. For example, the Local Government Act 1972, s.222[2] enables the local authority to act where it is "expedient for the promotion or protection of the interests of the inhabitants of their area." Applications under section 222 are usually successful. Although the Attorney-General's power to seek injunctions to restrain criminal offences is limited to cases of emergency or inadequate criminal penalty, it has been held that the local authority's power under section 222 is not limited in this way: the only limitation is that the action must promote or protect the interests of the inhabitants.[3] But the court will be reluctant to grant an injunction if the sanctions for disobeying it would be more onerous than the criminal penalty.[4] Where the defendant is flouting a statute, an injunction may be sought before the statutory remedies have been exhausted.[5] In exceptional cases, involving a plain breach and a clear intention to continue with it, the injunction may be

---

[98] *Att.-Gen. v. Sharp* [1931] 1 Ch. 121; *Att.-Gen. v. Harris* [1961] 1 Q.B. 74 (selling flowers illegally from stalls); *Att.-Gen. v. Bastow* [1957] 1 Q.B. 514; *Att.-Gen. v. Smith* [1958] 2 Q.B. 173. Such cases could now be dealt with by an action by the local authority under the Local Government Act 1972, s.222, *infra*.

[99] *Att.-Gen. v. Chaudry* [1971] 1 W.L.R. 1623.

[1] *Gouriet v. Union of Post Office Workers* [1978] A.C. 435.

[2] This exception was described as "limited" in *Gouriet v. Union of Post Office Workers, supra*. See also the wider provisions of Town and Country Planning Act 1990, s.187B; *Runnymede Borough Council v. Harwood* (1994) 68 P. & C.R. 300.

[3] *Kent County Council v. Batchelor* [1979] 1 W.L.R. 213 (breach of tree preservation order); (1979) 95 L.Q.R. 174 (D. Feldman). See also *Thanet District Council v. Ninedrive Ltd* [1978] 1 All E.R. 703 (Sunday trading); *Solihull Metropolitan Borough Council v. Maxfern Ltd* [1977] 1 W.L.R. 127 (Sunday trading); *Hammersmith Borough Council v. Magnum Automated Forecourts Ltd* [1978] 1 W.L.R. 50 (nuisance).

[4] *Stoke-on-Trent City Council v. B. & Q. (Retail) Ltd* [1984] A.C. 754.

[5] *Runnymede Borough Council v. Ball* [1986] 1 W.L.R. 353.

granted before proceedings for the statutory remedy have even been commenced.[6]

Although injunctions under section 222 are typically granted in cases of deliberate flouting or where the criminal penalty is inadequate, the jurisdiction is not confined to these circumstances.[7] Flagrant breaches of the criminal law need not be shown where there is clear evidence of persistent and serious conduct.[8] However, an injunction in aid of the criminal law is a remedy of last resort and should not be granted if a less draconian means of securing obedience is available.[9]

In the sphere of public law an injunction, declaration or prerogative order may be sought, with leave of the court, in an "application for judicial review."[10] The court may grant the injunction or declaration if, in all the circumstances, it is "just and convenient" to do so.[11] On the question of *locus standi*, it is provided that the applicant must have a "sufficient interest" in the matter.[12] In a case concerning a declaration and an order of mandamus, it has been held that one taxpayer has no sufficient interest to ask the court to investigate the tax affairs of another taxpayer or to complain that the latter has been under or over-assessed.[13] Order 53 has not removed the established requirements for *locus standi* by giving the court a discretion, although the test is not the same for all the remedies.[14]

The question soon arose whether, in the field of administrative law, the "application for judicial review" was an exclusive remedy, so that the plaintiff could not seek an injunction in the ordinary way. In *O'Reilly v. Mackman*[15] the House of Lords held that, as a general rule, it would be contrary to public policy and an abuse of process for a plaintiff complaining of a public authority's infringement of his public law rights to seek redress by an ordinary action and thus avoid the protection afforded to statutory tribunals.[16] It is otherwise

---

[6] *Stafford Borough Council v. Elkenford Ltd* [1977] 1 W.L.R. 324; *Stoke-on-Trent City Council v. B. & Q. (Retail) Ltd, supra,* (Sunday trading).

[7] *Runnymede Borough Council v. Ball* [1986] 1 W.L.R. 353; *Kirklees Borough Council v. Wickes Building Supplies Ltd* [1993] A.C. 227.

[8] *City of London Corporation v. Bovis Construction Ltd* [1992] 3 All E.R. 697.

[9] *Waverley Borough Council v. Hilden* [1988] 1 W.L.R. 246; *Newport Borough Council v. Khan* [1990] 1 W.L.R. 1185.

[10] R.S.C., Ord. 53, codified by Supreme Court Act 1981, s.31. See (1978) 41 M.L.R. 437 (J. Beatson and M. Matthews); (1978) 94 L.Q.R. 179 (H.W.R.W.). See also Ord. 15, r. 16.

[11] S.C.A. 1981, s.31(2).

[12] Ord. 53, r. 3(5); S.C.A. 1981, s.31(3). See the comments of Lord Denning in *The Discipline of Law,* p. 133.

[13] *R. v. I.R.C., ex p. National Federation of Self-Employed and Small Businesses Ltd* [1982] A.C. 617; (1982) 45 M.L.R. 92 (D. Feldman); (1982) 41 C.L.J. 6 (J. Griffiths). *cf. R. v. Her Majesty's Treasury, ex p. Smedley* [1985] Q.B. 657.

[14] *Ibid.* at p. 631, *per* Lord Wilberforce.

[15] [1983] 2 A.C. 237; (1983) 99 L.Q.R. 166 (H.W.R.W.); (1983) 42 C.L.J. 15 (J. Jolowicz); (1983) 46 M.L.R. 645 (M. Sunkin); (1987) 103 L.Q.R. 34 (J. Beatson).

[16] Which includes the requirement of leave of the court, and a three-month time limit.

where the plaintiff's private law rights have been infringed.[17] Neither Order 53 nor section 31 of the Supreme Court Act 1981 provides that judicial review is an exclusive remedy. Where an action is begun as an application for judicial review but it transpires that it involves a private law right, it can be treated as if begun by writ,[18] but the converse is not the case.[19]

An ordinary injunction is appropriate where the defendant is a domestic body with no public role. Where the defendant is a public body, a distinction is drawn between its public and private law functions. Thus a local authority's decision as to whether it has a duty to house a homeless person is a public law function, while its executive functions once it has decided that there is such a duty are matters of private law.[20]

This has been described as "an area of the law where the forms of action abolished by the Common Law Procedure Acts in the nineteenth century appear to be in danger of returning to rule us from their graves.[21] Lord Denning M.R., discussing the distinction between a public authority's private and public law functions, said, "But the division is very difficult to make. So difficult indeed that I can foresee an infinity of trouble arising from it. It makes me regret that the dichotomy was ever made."[22] The House of Lords has since favoured a broader approach, namely that a litigant can seek to enforce a private law right by ordinary action, notwithstanding that the proceedings involve a challenge to a public law act or decision, judicial review being necessary only when private law rights are not at stake.[23] This approach, favoured by the Law Commission,[24] would get rid of a "procedural minefield."[25] It was concluded that, unless the procedure was ill suited to dispose of the question at issue, "there is much to be said in favour of the proposition that a

---

[17] No private right was involved in a decision as to remission of a prison sentence. There may be other exceptions, such as where none of the parties objects.

[18] Ord. 53, r. 9(5). See *R. v. Secretary of State for the Home Office, ex p. Dew* [1987] 1 W.L.R. 881.

[19] Thus cases may be lost by the wrong choice of procedure, defeating the purpose of Ord. 53; see (1983) 99 L.Q.R. 166 (H.W.R.W.); *cf. Roy v. Kensington and Chelsea and Westminster Family Practitioner Committee* [1992] 1 A.C. 624, *infra.*

[20] *Cocks v. Thanet District Council* [1983] 2 A.C. 286. See the review by the House of Lords in *X (Minors) v. Bedfordshire County Council* [1995] 2 A.C. 633.

[21] *Doyle v. Northumbria Probation Committee* [1991] 1 W.L.R. 1340 at p. 1348. See also (1985) 44 C.L.J. 415 (C. Forsyth); (1985) 101 L.Q.R. 486 (A. Grubb); (1991) 107 L.Q.R. 298 at p. 315 (S. Fredman and G. Morris).

[22] *The Closing Chapter*, p. 125.

[23] *Roy v. Kensington and Chelsea and Westminster Family Practitioner Committee* [1992] 1 A.C. 624; (1992) 108 L.Q.R. 353 (S. Fredman and G. Morris); (1992) 51 C.L.J. 201 (I. Hare); *Mohram Ali v. Tower Hamlets London Borough Council* [1993] Q.B. 407.

[24] Law Com. No. 226 (1994), *Administrative Law: Judicial Review and Statutory Appeals*; (1994) 144 N.L.J. 1527 (R. Gordon); (1995) 111 L.Q.R. 591 (S. Fredman).

[25] [1992] 1 A.C. 624 at p. 653.

court having jurisdiction ought to let a case be heard rather than entertain a debate concerning the form of the proceedings."[26]

F. Family Matters

The court has a statutory jurisdiction to grant injunctions to restrain a husband from dealing with property so as to defeat his wife's claim to maintenance.[27] Injunctions are commonly granted in relation to occupation of the home under the provisions of the matrimonial homes legislation.[28] Thus injunctions have been granted to restrain a husband from installing his lover in the matrimonial home,[29] or to exclude the husband from the home,[30] or to restrain a man from living near his former wife,[31] or, in a grave case, to exclude an adult child from his parents' home.[32] But the jurisdiction is sparingly exercised; it must be necessary to protect the applicant or a relevant child and should never be regarded as routine.[33]

Orders may be made under the Family Law Act 1996 (replacing and extending earlier legislation) to regulate the occupation of the family home.[34] The jurisdiction extends to spouses, former spouses, cohabitants and former cohabitants, but the details are outside the scope of this book. Non-molestation orders may be granted under the 1996 Act,[35] and under the court's general jurisdiction. They should not be granted against mental patients, nor against minors where there is no effective means of enforcement.[36] It should be added that injunctions of this kind should not be granted *ex parte* unless there is real danger of serious injury or damage.[37]

The remedy of injunction is also employed in the protection of minors[38]; for example, to restrain persons who had enticed a girl of 16 away from her father, from continuing to harbour her[39]; in

---

[26] *Ibid.* at p. 655.
[27] Matrimonial Causes Act 1973, s.37; Matrimonial and Family Proceedings Act 1984, s.24.
[28] Now the Family Law Act 1996.
[29] *Pinckney v. Pinckney* [1966] 1 All E.R. 121.
[30] *Hall v. Hall* [1971] 1 W.L.R. 404; *Phillips v. Phillips* [1973] 1 W.L.R. 615.
[31] *M v. M* (1983) 13 Fam.Law 110; *Burris v. Azadani* [1995] 1 W.L.R. 1372.
[32] *Egan v. Egan* [1975] Ch. 218 (a clear history of assaults, and threats of more).
[33] *Des Salles d'Epinoix v. Des Salles d'Epinoix* [1967] 1 W.L.R. 553; *Wiseman v. Simpson* [1988] 1 W.L.R. 35; Family Law Act 1996, ss.33, 35, 36.
[34] See ss.33, 35, 36.
[35] See ss.42, 45 (*ex parte* orders), 47 (power of arrest).
[36] *Wookey v. Wookey* [1991] Fam. 121.
[37] *Practice Note* [1978] 1 W.L.R. 925; *Ansah v. Ansah* [1977] Fam. 138. See Family Law Act 1996, s.45 (risk of significant harm).
[38] For the practical limitations on the exercise of the jurisdiction, see *Re C. (a minor)* [1991] 2 F.L.R. 168.
[39] *Lough v. Ward* [1945] 2 All E.R. 338.

support of a custody order[40]; to protect a minor from publicity (although press freedom should not be restricted any more than is essential[41]); or to restrain the mother of a ward from leaving the jurisdiction before submitting to a test to establish its paternity.[42] It is in connection with equity's special care concerning minors that most risks are taken with regard to the issue of injunctions against persons outside the jurisdiction.[43]

As we have seen, a husband cannot obtain an injunction to prevent his wife from having an abortion.[44]

Finally, the use of *Mareva* and *Anton Piller* injunctions in family matters is dealt with below.[45]

G. Trade Unions, Clubs and Colleges

Some use of the injunction has been made as a remedy against trade unions.[46] Perhaps the most important use of the injunction in this field has been to restrain the expulsion of a member by his union where such expulsion is contrary to the rules of the union,[47] or the rules of natural justice.[48]

The right of a member of an association to invoke the assistance of the courts in resisting expulsion is essentially a contractual right.[49] Modern decisions have established that the right to an injunction is not confined to cases where the plaintiff has some proprietary right. A member may seek an injunction, for example, to protect his "right to work,"[50] or where matters of public importance

---

[40] *Re W. (a minor)* [1981] 3 All E.R. 401; doubted (1982) 45 M.L.R. 468 (G. Douglas). As to adoption orders, see *Re D. (a minor)* [1991] Fam. 137.

[41] The authorities are reviewed in *Re Z (a minor) (Identification: Restrictions on Publication)* [1997] Fam. 1.

[42] *Re I. (a minor)*, The Times, May 22, 1987.

[43] *Re Liddell's S.T.* [1936] Ch. 365; *Harben v. Harben* [1957] 1 W.L.R. 261; *Re O.* [1962] 1 W.L.R. 724. See also *Practice Direction* [1983] 1 W.L.R. 558 (injunctions to restrain removal of child from jurisdiction).

[44] *Paton v. Trustees of British Pregnancy Advisory Service* [1979] Q.B. 276; *ante*, p. 744; *C. v. S.* [1988] Q.B. 135.

[45] *Post*, p. 805.

[46] See also Trade Union and Labour Relations (Consolidation) Act 1992, s.176, providing additional remedies against unreasonable exclusion or expulsion.

[47] See *Osborne v. Amalgamated Society of Railway Servants* [1911] 1 Ch. 540; *Lee v. Showmen's Guild* [1952] 2 Q.B. 329. The plaintiff should normally, however, first exhaust other remedies available under the rules: *White v. Kuzych* [1951] A.C. 585; but *cf. Lawlor v. Union of Post Office Workers* [1965] Ch. 712.

[48] *Edwards v. SOGAT* [1971] Ch. 354; *Breen v. A.E.U.* [1971] 2 Q.B. 175; *Shotton v. Hammond* (1976) 120 S.J. 780.

[49] *White v. Kuzych, supra*; *Bonsor v. Musicians' Union* [1956] A.C. 104.

[50] *Edwards v. SOGAT, supra*; *cf. Gaiman v. National Association for Mental Health* [1971] Ch. 317 (no injunction as membership involved no question of property, livelihood or reputation).

are concerned.[51] But the mere fact of membership is not, in the absence of these special considerations, sufficient to found a claim to an injunction.[52] Equity will not compel persons to remain in continual and personal relations with one another.[53]

Injunctions have also been granted to professional people who have been dismissed contrary to the rules of their profession, though usually only where improper motive or bad faith can be shown,[54] and to members expelled by social clubs, either in breach of the rules of the club, or where the club has acted in breach of natural justice. Thus, in *Labouchere v. Earl of Wharncliffe*,[55] the general meeting of a club, summoned without proper notice, expelled the plaintiff without full inquiry, without giving him notice of any definite charge, and by a resolution carried by an insufficient majority. The court granted an injunction against such purported expulsion.

Injunctions are sometimes sought by students or teachers dismissed from a university without a fair hearing, in breach of the rules of natural justice, to restrain the university authorities from acting on the dismissal.[56] This raises the question of the visitor's jurisdiction which was discussed in Chapter 15.[57]

H. Judicial Proceedings

In proper cases, judicial proceedings in inferior courts,[58] administrative tribunals,[59] and private prosecutions[60] may be restrained. So also the initiation of proceedings in the High Court,[61] but once commenced, proceedings in the High Court are not subject to injunction; indeed interference with such proceedings may itself be

---

[51] *Woodford v. Smith* [1970] 1 W.L.R. 806, concerning membership of a ratepayers' association, where an injunction was granted to restrain the holding of a meeting without permitting the plaintiff members to attend and vote.

[52] *Baird v. Wells* (1890) 44 Ch.D. 661.

[53] *Lumley v. Wagner* (1852) 1 De G.M. & G. 604.

[54] *Hayman v. Governors of Rugby School* (1874) L.R. 18 Eq. 28; *Cassel v. Inglis* [1916] 2 Ch. 211; *Weinberger v. Inglis* [1919] A.C. 606.

[55] (1879) 13 Ch.D. 346; and see *Harington v. Sendall* [1903] 1 Ch. 921; cf. *Dawkins v. Antrobus* (1881) 17 Ch.D. 615.

[56] *Glynn v. Keele University* [1971] 1 W.L.R. 487; *Herring v. Templeman* [1973] 3 All E.R. 569; cf. *R. v. Senate of the University of Aston, ex p. Roffey* [1969] 2 Q.B. 538 (where certiorari was thought appropriate).

[57] *Ante*, p. 445.

[58] *Re Connolly Bros. Ltd* [1911] 1 Ch. 731 (Lancaster Palatine Court); *Thames Launches v. Trinity House Corporation (Deptford Strond)* [1966] Ch. 197 (magistrates' court); *Murcutt v. Murcutt* [1952] P. 266 (county court).

[59] de Smith, *Judicial Review of Administrative Action* (5th ed.), pp. 730–731.

[60] *Thames Launches v. Trinity House Corporation (Deptford Strond)* [1966] Ch. 197.

[61] *McHenry v. Lewis* (1882) 22 Ch.D. 397; *Ellerman Lines v. Read* [1928] 2 K.B. 144; *Orr-Lewis v. Orr-Lewis* [1949] P. 347; *Settlement Corporation v. Hochschild* [1966] Ch. 10. See also *Bryanston Finance Ltd v. de Vries (No. 2)* [1976] Ch. 63 (winding-up petition).

restrained by injunction as a contempt of court.[62] It might be added that arbitration proceedings may, in certain cases, be restrained by injunction.[63]

Judicial proceedings in foreign courts may be restrained by injunction, where this is appropriate to avoid an injustice, but this is a jurisdiction to be exercised with great caution. Such an injunction will only be issued against a party who is amenable to the jurisdiction of the English court. It is directed not to the foreign court, but to the parties.[64]

I. Legislative Proceedings

It is very doubtful whether an injunction will lie to restrain the introduction or enactment of a Bill,[65] or to restrain the making of a subordinate legislative instrument.[66] It is, however, possible that an injunction may be granted to restrain the breach of contractual obligations not to promote or to petition against a private Bill,[67] or to restrain unauthorised expenditure of public funds in promoting or opposing a private Bill.[68] But no injunction will lie to restrain any procedure concerning a public Bill.[69]

J. To Prevent Removal or Destruction of Evidence: The "Anton Piller" Injunction[70]

This type of injunction is designed to secure that pending trial[71] the defendant does not dispose of any articles in his possession

---

[62] *Att.-Gen. v. Times Newspapers Ltd* [1974] A.C. 273. But this decision was held by the European Court (April 26, 1979) to infringe Art. 10 of the European Convention on Human Rights, which guarantees freedom of expression. See (1979) 95 L.Q.R. 348 (F. Mann); (1979) 38 C.L.J. 242 (C. Gray); Lord Denning, *The Due Process of Law*, pp. 45–49. See also *Att.-Gen. v. London Weekend Television Ltd* [1973] 1 W.L.R. 202.

[63] Mustill and Boyd, *The Law and Practice of Commercial Arbitration in England* (2nd ed.), pp. 518 *et seq.*

[64] See Dicey and Morris, *The Conflict of Laws* (12th ed.), p. 397; *Société Nationale Industrielle Aerospatiale v. Lee Kui Jak* [1987] A.C. 871. See also Civil Jurisdiction and Judgments Act 1982, s.49.

[65] Bill of Rights 1688, s.1, Art. 9; see de Smith, *op. cit.* pp. 722 *et seq.*

[66] *Harper v. Secretary of State for Home Affairs* [1955] Ch. 238; see also *Bates v. Lord Hailsham of St. Marylebone* [1972] 1 W.L.R. 1373.

[67] *Bilston Corporation v. Wolverhampton Corporation* [1942] Ch. 391.

[68] *Att.-Gen. v. London and Home Counties Joint Electricity Authority* [1929] 1 Ch. 513.

[69] *Att.-Gen. for New South Wales v. Trethowan* [1932] A.C. 526; doubted in *Hughes and Vale Pty. Ltd* (1954) 90 C.L.R. 203 at p. 204.

[70] See generally Dockray, *Anton Piller Orders*; Sheridan, *Chancery Procedure & Anton Piller Orders*.

[71] Or after judgment, in aid of execution; *Distributori Automatici Italia SpA v. Holford General Trading Co. Ltd* [1985] 1 W.L.R. 1066.

which could be prejudicial at the trial.[72] It is "an illustration of the adaptability of equitable remedies to new situations."[73] It is particularly useful to plaintiffs who are the victims of commercial malpractice, such as breach of confidence, breach of copyright and passing off. It has also been used in the family context, as in *Emanuel v. Emanuel*,[74] where a husband had been ordered in matrimonial proceedings to transfer properties to his wife. He failed to comply, and had sold a property and spent the proceeds. An *Anton Piller* order was granted to allow the wife's solicitors to enter his home to inspect documents relating to his finances. It is essential that such an order be available *ex parte*, so that the defendant is not forewarned: "If the stable door cannot be bolted, the horse must be secured. ... If the horse is liable to be spirited away, notice of an intention to secure the horse will defeat the intention."[75]

The *Anton Piller* order has been variously described as "a draconian power which should be used only in very exceptional cases",[76] and as "an innovation which has proved its worth time and time again."[77] The first reported decision was *EMI Ltd v. Pandit*,[78] where an *ex parte* order was made in a breach of copyright action to enable the plaintiff to enter the defendant's premises to inspect, photograph and remove infringing articles. The practice was confirmed by the Court of Appeal in *Anton Piller KG v. Manufacturing Processes Ltd*.[79]

The defendants had received confidential information and plans concerning the plaintiff's electrical equipment in their capacity as the plaintiff's selling agents in England. The plaintiffs had reason to believe that the defendants were selling the information to the plaintiff's competitors, but were unable to prove this without access to documents situated on the defendants' premises.

---

[72] The articles need not be the subject-matter of the action; *Yousif v. Salama* [1980] 1 W.L.R. 1540 (accounts and a diary); *Emanuel v. Emanuel* [1982] 1 W.L.R. 669 (documents relating to husband's finances).

[73] *Rank Film Distributors Ltd v. Video Information Centre* [1982] A.C. 380 at p. 439 (*per* Lord Wilberforce).

[74] [1982] 1 W.L.R. 669. See also *Law Society v. Shanks* [1988] 1 F.L.R. 504; *Shipman v. Shipman* [1991] 1 F.L.R. 250; *Ghoth v. Ghoth* [1992] 2 All E.R. 920 (*Mareva* injunctions). It remains a rare weapon in family cases; *Burgess v. Burgess* [1996] 2 F.L.R. 34.

[75] *Rank Film Distributors Ltd v. Video Information Centre* [1982] A.C. 380 at p. 418.

[76] *Yousif v. Salama* [1980] 1 W.L.R. 1540 at p. 1544 (*per* Donaldson L.J.). His Lordship, dissenting, regarded the order granted by the majority as a power to "take" discovery.

[77] *Rank Film Distributors Ltd v. Video Information Centre* [1982] A.C. 380 at p. 406 (Lord Denning M.R.).

[78] [1975] 1 W.L.R. 302.

[79] [1976] Ch. 55; Lord Denning, *The Due Process of Law*, pp. 123 *et seq.* See also *Vapormatic Co. Ltd v. Sparex* [1976] 1 W.L.R. 939; *Universal City Studios Inc. v. Mukhtar & Sons Ltd* [1976] 1 W.L.R. 568 (order to hand over unlicensed "Jaws" T-shirts); *EMI Ltd v. Sarwar* [1977] F.S.R. 146.

The Court of Appeal made an *ex parte* order,[80] requiring the defendants to permit the plaintiffs to enter their premises and inspect documents relating to the equipment. Such an order would only be made in exceptional circumstances, where it was essential that the plaintiff should inspect the documents to enable justice to be done between the parties, and there was a danger that vital evidence would otherwise be destroyed.

Unlike a search warrant, the order does not authorise the plaintiff to enter against the defendant's will. But it does order him to permit the plaintiff to enter, so that, if the defendant does not comply, not only does he commit a contempt of court,[81] but adverse inferences will be drawn against him at the trial. Ormrod L.J. laid down three conditions for the grant of the order.[82] The plaintiff must:

(i) have an extremely strong prima facie case;
(ii) show actual or potential damage of a very serious nature;
(iii) have clear evidence that the defendant has incriminating documents or things and a real possibility of their destruction before an *inter partes* application can be made.[83]

A further requirement was added by Lord Denning M.R.: the inspection will do no real harm to the defendant. However, it is no defence that disclosure could expose the defendant to the risk of violence from associates.[84] It might be added that the order should not be sought as a "fishing expedition."[85]

In the enforcement of the order, the plaintiff must act with circumspection. He should be attended by his solicitor,[86] and must undertake in damages (giving security in appropriate cases), so as to safeguard the defendant's rights. Because of the draconian nature of the order, the applicant is under a strict duty to make full and frank

---

[80] The practice was affirmed in a decision *inter partes*: *Rank Film Distributors Ltd v. Video Information Centre* [1982] A.C. 380. See also Supreme Court Act 1981, s.33(1). The order may relate to premises abroad; *Cook Industries Inc. v. Galliher* [1979] Ch. 439; *Altertext Inc. v. Advanced Data Communications Ltd* [1985] 1 W.L.R. 457.

[81] See, however, *Bhimji v. Chatwani* [1991] 1 W.L.R. 989.

[82] In *Anton Piller KG v. Manufacturing Processes Ltd, supra*. For further guidelines, see *CBS United Kingdom Ltd v. Lambert* [1983] Ch. 37; *Digital Equipment Corporation v. Darkcrest Ltd* [1984] Ch. 512.

[83] See *Yousif v. Salama, supra*.

[84] *Coca-Cola Co. v. Gilbey* [1995] 4 All E.R. 711.

[85] *i.e.* as a means of finding out what charges can be made; *Hytrac Conveyors Ltd v. Conveyors International Ltd* [1983] 1 W.L.R. 44.

[86] The solicitor should avoid arriving simultaneously with police executing a search warrant; *I.T.C. Film Distributors Ltd v. Video Exchange Ltd* [1982] Ch. 431; (1990) 106 L.Q.R. 173 (L. Collins).

disclosure of all relevant matters to the court.[87] Having obtained the order, he must neither act oppressively nor abuse his power in executing it.[88] Further and stricter requirements have since been added.[89] For example, the order must be executed in office hours so that legal advice is available; a woman must be present at a search of a private house where a woman may be alone; and a list of items must be prepared before they are removed, which the defendant may check. Where the plaintiff or his solicitor has acted improperly the court may set aside the order. Even if it is not set aside, the defendant may be entitled to exemplary damages,[90] and the solicitor may be found to be in contempt.[91]

In recent years grave disquiet has been expressed that the *Anton Piller* practice has gone too far in favour of plaintiffs,[92] and is "inherently oppressive."[93] An example of its abuse is *Lock International plc v. Beswick*,[94] where the plaintiff's solicitors searched the business premises and homes of the defendants and removed not only documents containing confidential information but nearly all their commercial papers, computer records and prototypes. The *Anton Piller* order, which should never have been granted, was discharged. Commentators have said that "an exceptional device intended to avoid injustice has become almost a routine method of creating it."[95] It seems that these warnings are being heeded, but further safeguards are required to prevent the .orders falling into disrepute.[96]

The utility of the *Anton Piller* injunction suffered a set-back when the House of Lords held in *Rank Film Distributors Ltd v. Video Information Centre*,[97] a copyright case, that the defendant could

---

[87] *Behbehani v. Salem* [1989] 1 W.L.R. 723; *Lock International plc v. Beswick* [1989] 1 W.L.R. 1268; *Tate Access Floors Inc. v. Boswell* [1991] Ch. 512.

[88] *Columbia Picture Industries Inc. v. Robinson* [1987] Ch. 38.

[89] *Universal Thermosensors Ltd v. Hibben* [1992] 1 W.L.R. 840; (1992) 142 N.L.J. 350; (1992) 108 L.Q.R. 555 (B. Davenport); *Practice Direction* [1996] 1 W.L.R. 1552. See also *Bhimji v. Chatwani, supra* (solicitor must explain effect to non-lawyers).

[90] *Columbia Picture Industries Inc. v. Robinson, supra.*

[91] *VDU Installations Ltd v. Integrated Computer Systems & Cybernetics Ltd, The Times*, August 13, 1988.

[92] *Columbia Picture Industries Inc. v. Robinson* [1987] Ch. 38; All E.R. Rev. 1986, p. 225 (A. Zuckerman); (1987) 46 C.L.J. 50 (N. Andrews); (1987) 1 *Trust Law & Practice* 146 (C. Bell).

[93] *Bhimji v. Chatwani* [1991] 1 W.L.R. 989 at p. 1002; All E.R. Rev. 1991, p. 263 (A. Zuckerman).

[94] [1989] 1 W.L.R. 1268; All E.R. Rev. 1989, p. 221 (A. Zuckerman).

[95] (1990) 106 L.Q.R. 601 at p. 620 (M. Dockray and H. Laddie); (1990) 20 U.W.A.L.R. 143 (J. Martin).

[96] *Universal Thermosensors Ltd v. Hibben* [1992] 1 W.L.R. 840, *supra*. Anton Piller orders have been put on a statutory footing by s.7 of the Civil Procedure Act 1997, which is not in force at the time of writing.

[97] [1982] A.C. 380. Templeman L.J. in the Court of Appeal, at p. 423, thought the court would award high damages where the defendant sought to rely on the privilege.

invoke the privilege against self-incrimination. But the privilege was subsequently withdrawn by section 72 of the Supreme Court Act 1981, in the case of proceedings to obtain disclosure of information relating to the infringement of rights pertaining to any intellectual property[98] or passing-off. Matters disclosed as a result of such proceedings are not admissible in evidence against the defendant in proceedings against him for a related offence.[99] The defendant may still invoke the privilege against self-incrimination in a case where the possible offence is not included in section 72,[1] but the House of Lords has suggested further reforms.[2]

K. To Prevent Removal of Assets: The "Mareva" Injunction

i. General Principles. This injunction takes its name from *Mareva Compania Naviera S.A. v. International Bulkcarriers S.A.*,[3] although the first reported exercise of this novel jurisdiction occurred in *Nippon Yusen Kaisha v. Karageorgis.*[4] It was described by Lord Denning M.R. as "the greatest piece of judicial law reform in my time."[5]

"A *Mareva* injunction is interlocutory, not final; it is ancillary to a substantive pecuniary claim for debt or damages; it is designed to prevent the judgment . . . for a sum of money being a mere 'brutum fulmen.' "[6] The usual purpose of a *Mareva* injunction is to prevent the dissipation or removal of assets before trial, so that if the plaintiff succeeds in the action, there will be property of the defen-

---

[98] Defined by s.72(5).

[99] s.72(3). It is otherwise in the case of proceedings for contempt or perjury, s.72(4). For the construction of s.72, see *Universal City Studios Inc. v. Hubbard* [1983] Ch. 241; All E.R. Rev. 1983, p. 266 (A. Zuckerman); *Crest Homes plc v. Marks* [1987] A.C. 829. See (1983) 46 M.L.R. 274 (A. Staines).

[1] *Emanuel v. Emanuel* [1982] 1 W.L.R. 669 (Revenue offences); *Tate Access Floors Inc. v. Boswell* [1991] Ch. 512; *IBM United Kingdom Ltd v. Prima Data International Ltd* [1994] 1 W.L.R. 719 (conspiracy).

[2] *Istel (A.T. & T.) Ltd v. Tully* [1993] A.C. 45. The position is not changed by the Civil Procedure Act 1997; s.7(7).

[3] [1975] 2 Lloyd's Rep. 509; (1978) J.B.L. 11 (D. Powles); (1980) 2 W.I.L.J. 60 (A. Bland); [1982] Conv. 265 (R. Horsfall); (1982) 99 L.Q.R. 7 (C. Hodgekiss); (1993) 56 M.L.R. 325 and (1993) 109 L.Q.R. 432 (A. Zuckerman).

[4] [1975] 1 W.L.R. 1093. See *The Siskina* [1979] A.C. 210 at p. 229, where Lord Denning M.R. described this injunction as a "rediscovery" of the procedure known as foreign attachment; *Z Ltd v. A–Z and AA–LL* [1982] Q.B. 558.

[5] *The Due Process of Law*, p. 134; *The Closing Chapter*, p. 225. See also Donaldson L.J. in *Bank Mellat v. Nikpour* [1985] F.S.R. 87 at 91–92, describing the *Mareva* injunction, along with the *Anton Piller* order, as "one of the law's two 'nuclear' weapons."

[6] *The Siskina* [1979] A.C. 210 at p. 253 (Lord Diplock). Compare the French "saisie conservatoire."

dant available to satisfy the judgment. It may also be granted after final judgment if the plaintiff can show grounds for believing that the defendant will dispose of his assets to avoid execution.[7] In such a case the injunction may even be granted against the defendant's wife.[8]

The *Mareva* injunction is always interlocutory, and usually *ex parte*: speed is of the essence.[9] It is frequently sought in conjunction with an *Anton Piller* order. The basis of the jurisdiction is now the Supreme Court Act 1981, s.37: the injunction may be granted whenever it is "just and convenient" to do so,[10] but with "great circumspection."[11] It is unlimited as to its subject-matter and the nature of the proceedings.[12] As in the case of interlocutory injunctions generally, the plaintiff must satisfy the conditions laid down by the House of Lords in *American Cyanamid Co. v. Ethicon Ltd*[13]: he must have a good arguable case and the balance of convenience must favour the grant.[14] The plaintiff must give an undertaking in damages in case he should be unsuccessful at the trial, and the defendant may apply at any time for the injunction to be discharged.[15] The defendant may be able to rely on the privilege against self-incrimination to avoid compliance with the injunction or a discovery order, unless he is adequately protected by a term of the order preventing the use of the disclosures in a prosecution. The House of Lords has said that the privilege should be abolished or modified by Parliament.[16]

---

[7] *Orwell Steel (Erection and Fabrication) Ltd v. Asphalt and Tarmac (U.K.) Ltd* [1984] 1 W.L.R. 1097; R.S.C. Ord. 29, r. 1; *Babanaft International Co. SA v. Bassatne* [1990] Ch. 13. For the similar jurisdiction to restrain the disposal of assets pending appeal (where good arguable appeal), see *Ketchum International plc v. Group Public Relations Holdings Ltd* [1997] 1 W.L.R. 4.

[8] *Mercantile Group (Europe) A.G. v. Aiyela* [1994] Q.B. 366.

[9] *Third Chandris Shipping Corp. v. Unimarine S.A.* [1979] Q.B. 645.

[10] *Mareva Compania Naviera S.A. v. International Bulkcarriers S.A., supra; Nippon Yusen Kaisha v. Karageorgis, supra; Third Chandris Shipping Corp. v. Unimarine S.A., supra; Rasu Maritima S.A. v. Perusahaan Pertambangan Minyak Dan Gas Bumi Negara (Pertamina)* [1978] Q.B. 644.

[11] *Mercedes-Benz AG v. Leiduck* [1996] 1 A.C. 284 at p. 297 (Lord Mustill).

[12] *Z Ltd v. A–Z and AA–LL* [1982] Q.B. 558. For matrimonial cases, see *ante*, p. 805, n. 74. It may be combined with specific performance; *Seven Seas Properties Ltd v. Al-Essa* [1988] 1 W.L.R. 1272.

[13] [1975] A.C. 396; cf. *Polly Peck International plc v. Nadir (No. 2)* [1992] 4 All E.R. 769 at p. 786.

[14] *Rasu Maritima S.A. v. Perusahaan, etc. supra; Third Chandris Shipping Corp. v. Unimarine S.A., supra; Allen v. Jambo Holdings Ltd* [1980] 1 W.L.R. 1252; *Derby & Co. Ltd v. Weldon* [1990] Ch. 48. See (1978) 41 M.L.R. 1 (M. Kerr) and n. 22, *infra*.

[15] *Mareva Compania Naviera S.A. v. International Bulkcarriers S.A., supra.* But a broad view must be taken of the plaintiff's ability to undertake in damages; see *Allen v. Jambo Holdings Ltd, supra* (legally-aided plaintiff).

[16] *Istel (A. T. & T.) Ltd v. Tully* [1993] A.C. 45 (where S.C.A. 1981, s.72, and Theft Act 1968, s.31, inapplicable). As to the incrimination of third parties, see *Arab Monetary Fund v. Hashim (No. 2)* [1990] 1 All E.R. 673.

It has been held that the old writ *ne exeat regno*[17] may be granted in support of a *Mareva* injunction,[18] or, if the requirements of that writ are not satisfied, an interlocutory injunction under section 37(1) of the Supreme Court Act 1981 to restrain the defendant from leaving the country.[19] While this development increases the efficacy of the *Mareva* injunction, it has been criticised as an unjustified restriction on individual liberty.[20]

ii. Guidelines for the Grant of the Injunction. While the discretion of the court is not fettered by rigid rules, Lord Denning M.R. suggested the following guidelines[21]:

(a) The plaintiff must have a good arguable case[22];

(b) Where the injunction applies to goods, caution is required to avoid bringing the defendant's business to a standstill[23];

(c) The court should favour the grant if it would be likely to compel the defendant to provide security;

(d) The plaintiff must make full and frank disclosure of all material matters[24];

(e) He should give particulars of his claim and its amount, and (in an *ex parte* application) he should fairly state the points made against it by the defendant;

(f) He should give grounds for believing that the defendant has assets in the jurisdiction[25];

(g) He should give grounds for believing that there is a risk of their removal and a danger of default if the assets were removed.[26] The mere fact that the defendant is abroad is not sufficient;

---

[17] *Ante*, p. 30.

[18] *Al Nahkel for Contracting and Trading Ltd v. Lowe* [1986] Q.B. 235; *cf. Allied Arab Bank Ltd v. Hajjar* [1988] Q.B. 787. This is doubtful, as the writ *ne exeat regno* is to assist prosecution of an action, not execution of a judgment.

[19] *Ante*, p. 745.

[20] (1986) 45 C.L.J. 189 (C. Harpum); All E.R. Rev. 1986, p. 225 (A. Zuckerman); (1987) 104 L.Q.R. 246 (L. Anderson); (1990) 20 U.W.A.L.R. 143 (J. Martin).

[21] *Rasu Maritima S.A. v. Perusahaan, etc.* [1978] Q.B. 644 (a decision *inter partes*); *Third Chandris Shipping Corp. v. Unimarine S.A.* [1979] Q.B. 645. See also *Barclay-Johnson v. Yuill* [1980] 1 W.L.R. 1259; (1981) 97 L.Q.R. 4; *Z Ltd v. A–Z and AA–LL* [1982] Q.B. 558; *Derby & Co. Ltd v. Weldon, supra.* See *Practice Direction* [1996] 1 W.L.R. 1552.

[22] See *Etablissement Esefka International Anstalt v. Central Bank of Nigeria* [1979] 1 Lloyd's Rep. 445; *Barclay-Johnson v. Yuill, supra.*

[23] As to chattels, see *CBS United Kingdom Ltd v. Lambert* [1983] Ch. 37.

[24] Failure to make full disclosure may result in discharge. See *Columbia Picture Industries Inc. v. Robinson* [1987] Ch. 38; *Lloyds Bowmaker Ltd v. Britannia Arrow Holdings plc* [1988] 1 W.L.R. 1337; *Brink's-MAT Ltd v. Elcombe* [1988] 1 W.L.R. 1350; *Behbehani v. Salem* [1989] 1 W.L.R. 723n.

[25] Having established this, the court has power to order discovery or interrogatories in aid of the injunction: *A.J. Bekhor & Co. Ltd v. Bilton* [1981] Q.B. 923; *Bankers Trust Co. v. Shapira* [1980] 1 W.L.R. 1274; *cf. R.H.M. Foods Ltd v. Bovril Ltd* [1982] 1 W.L.R. 661.

[26] See *Montecchi v. Shimco* [1979] 1 W.L.R. 1180; *Etablissement Esefka International Anstalt v. Central Bank of Nigeria, supra.*

(h) He must undertake in damages, giving security in suitable cases, in case he is unsuccessful in the action.

In relation to (f) and (g) above, it should be added that the plaintiff need no longer establish in all cases that there is a risk of removal of the assets from the jurisdiction, as section 37(3) of the Supreme Court Act 1981 provides that the injunction may be granted to prevent the defendant from removing from the jurisdiction "or otherwise dealing with" the assets. Thus a risk of dissipation within the jurisdiction[27] (or, in an extreme case, damage or destruction[28]) is sufficient. The developments as to foreign assets are discussed below.

Exceptionally, the injunction may be made against all the defendant's assets; but usually a limit will be specified.[29] In rare cases it may be made in respect of a joint account,[30] but not assets of the defendant's wife or another third party,[31] save in aid of enforcement of a judgment.[32] The injunction should rarely be granted where the defendant is a bank, otherwise its business could be irreparably harmed.[33]

iii. The Jurisdiction of the Court. The House of Lords in *The Siskina*[34] emphasised that the injunction had to be ancillary to substantive relief which the High Court had jurisdiction to grant; and that there was no power to grant the injunction save in protection or assertion of some legal or equitable right which the High Court had jurisdiction to enforce by final judgment. *The Siskina* was reversed for cases within section 25 of the Civil Jurisdiction and Judgments Act 1982,[35] and its correctness has been doubted.[36] The Privy Council has, however, confirmed that a *Mareva* injunction

---

[27] See *Z Ltd v. A–Z and AA–LL* [1982] Q.B. 558.
[28] *Standard Chartered Bank v. Walker* [1992] 1 W.L.R. 561.
[29] *Z Ltd v. A–Z and AA–LL, supra; Ghoth v. Ghoth* [1992] 2 All E.R. 920 (should not cover all assets in matrimonial proceedings). See also *Oceanica Castelana Armadora S.A. of Panama v. Mineralimportexport* [1983] 1 W.L.R. 1294. After-acquired assets may be included; *TDK Tape Distributors (U.K.) Ltd v. Videochoice Ltd* [1986] 1 W.L.R. 141.
[30] *Ibid.*
[31] *S.C.F. Finance Co. Ltd v. Masri* [1985] 1 W.L.R. 876; *Allied Arab Bank Ltd v. Hajjar* (1989) 19 Fam.Law 68; *cf. T.S.B. Private Bank International S.A. v. Chabra* [1992] 1 W.L.R. 231.
[32] *Mercantile Group (Europe) A.G. v. Aiyela* [1994] Q.B. 66.
[33] *Polly Peck International plc v. Nadir (No. 2)* [1992] 4 All E.R. 769; (1992) 108 L.Q.R. 559 (A. Zuckerman). See also *Themehelp Ltd v. West* [1996] Q.B. 84 (guarantee).
[34] [1979] A.C. 210; (1978) 37 C.L.J. 241 (K. Lipstein); (1978) 94 L.Q.R. 169 (P.V.B.); (1978) 41 M.L.R. 1 (M. Kerr). See also *Veracruz Transportation Inc. v. V.C. Shipping Co. Inc.* [1992] 1 Lloyd's Rep. 353; criticised (1992) 108 L.Q.R. 175 (L. Collins); holding that cause of action must have accrued; similarly *Zucker v. Tyndall Holdings plc* [1992] 1 W.L.R. 1127; *Department of Social Security v. Butler* [1995] 1 W.L.R. 1528.
[35] See *Haiti (Republic of) v. Duvalier* [1990] 1 Q.B. 202.
[36] See *Channel Tunnel Group Ltd v. Balfour Beatty Construction Ltd* [1993] A.C. 334; (1993) 109 L.Q.R 342 (L. Collins).

may not be granted to freeze assets in the United Kingdom of a
foreign defendant outside the jurisdiction pending the conclusion of
proceedings against him in a foreign state (which is not a party to the
Brussels or Lugano Conventions).[37] The claim had nothing to do
with the United Kingdom save for the presence of assets.

iv. The English-based Defendant. The *Mareva* injunction
evolved as a remedy against a foreign-based defendant having assets
within the jurisdiction. It was assumed in the earlier decisions that
there was no power to grant such an injunction against an English-
based defendant, although the merit of such a distinction was
questioned.[38]

The difficulty in the way of extending the *Mareva* injunction to
English-based defendants was the clear line of authority to the effect
that there is "no statutory or other power in the Court to restrain a
person from dealing with his property at a time when no order
against him has been made."[39] It must be said, however, that this
principle had already been eroded by the development of the
Mareva injunction against foreign-based defendants.[40]

Attempts to extend the scope of the *Mareva* injunction were made
in *Chartered Bank v. Daklouche*[41] and in *Barclay-Johnson v. Yuill*,[42]
and the jurisdiction to enjoin an English-based defendant became
established.[43] It was confirmed by section 37(3) of the Supreme
Court Act 1981, providing that the court's power to grant an interlocutory injunction restraining a party to any proceedings from
removing from the jurisdiction, or otherwise dealing with, assets
located within the jurisdiction shall be exercisable whether or not
that party is domiciled, resident or present within the jurisdiction.

v. Assets outside the Jurisdiction. The *Mareva* injunction was
originally confined to assets within the jurisdiction. It is now established that the injunction (and ancillary disclosure order) may be
granted against a defendant who is amenable to the jurisdiction[44] of
the court in respect of assets outside the jurisdiction, even on a
world-wide basis. The objections to extending the injunction to

---

[37] *Mercedes-Benz AG v. Leiduck* [1996] 1 A.C. 284 (Lord Nicholls dissenting); (1996) 112
L.Q.R. 8 (L. Collins); (1996) 55 C.L.J. 12 (N. Andrews).

[38] See *The Siskina* [1979] A.C. 210.

[39] *Jagger v. Jagger* [1926] P. 93 at p. 102 (*per* Scrutton L.J.). See also *Lister & Co. v. Stubbs*
(1890) 45 Ch.D. 1 (disapproved on another point in *Att.-Gen. for Hong Kong v. Reid* [1994]
1 A.C. 324).

[40] See *Malone v. Metropolitan Police Commissioner* [1980] Q.B. 49 at pp. 61, 68.

[41] [1980] 1 W.L.R. 107.

[42] [1980] 1 W.L.R. 1259 (*ex parte*); approved in *Rahman (Prince Abdul) Bin Turki Al Sudairy
v. Abu-Taha* [1980] 1 W.L.R. 1268 (*inter partes*).

[43] See *A.J. Bekhor & Co. Ltd v. Bilton* [1981] Q.B. 923; *The Due Process of Law*, pp. 147 *et
seq.*

[44] See (1989) 105 L.Q.R. 262 (L. Collins); (1994) 144 N.L.J. 932 (P. Friedman).

foreign assets were that the order would be oppressive and unenforceable, and that the territorial limitations were confirmed by section 37(3) of the Supreme Court Act 1981.[45] But the Court of Appeal held in *Babanaft International Co. S.A. v. Bassatne*[46] that section 37(3) did not restrict the scope, geographical or otherwise, of section 37(1). This case involved a post-judgment *Mareva* injunction. Such an order would more readily be made against assets abroad than in a pre-judgment case, but would nevertheless be rare. A personal order binding the defendant alone was made.

The issue next arose in the Court of Appeal in *Haiti (Republic of) v. Duvalier*,[47] which concerned the alleged embezzlement of $120m. from the Republic during the presidency of Jean-Claude Duvalier. No substantive relief in England was sought. The court granted a pre-judgment *Mareva* injunction in respect of world-wide assets, although recognising that this was a most unusual measure which should very rarely be granted. While the court would be more willing in a post-judgment case, or where the plaintiff had a tracing or other proprietary claim, the injunction could be granted in respect of a pre-judgment money claim such as the present case, where international co-operation was demanded. Previous limitations arose from practice rather than from any restriction on the court's power. The injunction was granted subject to a *"Babanaft* proviso"[48] in respect of the foreign assets, to protect third parties outside the jurisdiction save to the extent that the order might be enforced by the local court. Even stricter safeguards were required by the Court of Appeal in *Derby & Co. Ltd v. Weldon*,[49] where a pre-judgment world-wide *Mareva* injunction was granted. It was emphasised that the plaintiff must do more than satisfy the requirements for an internal *Mareva*. In addition to a good arguable case, he must show that any English assets are insufficient, that there are foreign assets, and that there is a real risk of disposal of the latter. The injunction will not be granted if it would be oppressive. The court must be satisfied, by means of undertaking or proviso, that (a) the defendant will not be oppressed by exposure to a multiplicity of proceedings[50]; (b) the defendant will be protected against misuse of information

---

[45] *Supra.* See *Ashtiani v. Kashi* [1987] Q.B. 888 (pre-judgment).

[46] [1990] Ch. 13; (1989) 48 C.L.J. 199 (N. Andrews); (1991) 54 M.L.R. 329 (D. Capper).

[47] [1990] 1 Q.B. 202; *cf. Rosseel N.V. v. Oriental Commercial Shipping (U.K.) Ltd* [1990] 1 W.L.R. 1287. It has been said that *Duvalier* "goes to the very edge of what is permissible"; (1989) 105 L.Q.R. 262 at p. 281 (L. Collins). For the position in Canada, see (1996) 59 M.L.R. 460 (J. Epp).

[48] Modified in *Derby & Co. Ltd v. Weldon (No. 3 and No. 4)* [1990] Ch. 65.

[49] [1990] Ch. 48. The approach in matrimonial cases may be broader; *Shipman v. Shipman* [1991] 1 F.L.R. 250.

[50] See *In re Bank of Credit and Commerce International S.A.* [1994] 1 W.L.R. 708; All E.R. Rev. 1994, p. 305 (A. Zuckerman).

gained from the order for disclosure of assets; and (c) third parties
are protected. The present case was sufficiently exceptional because
a very large sum was involved (£15m.), the English assets were
totally inadequate, and there was a high risk of dissipation of the
foreign assets through inaccessible overseas companies. In *Derby &
Co. Ltd v. Weldon (No. 3 and No. 4)*[51] a similar injunction was
granted against companies in Luxembourg and Panama which had
no assets within the jurisdiction. The Luxembourg company was
subject to the jurisdiction of a court which would enforce the orders
of the English court under the Civil Jurisdiction and Judgments Act
1982. Concerning the Panama company, the fact that the order could
not be specifically enforced was no bar. The order would not be
made if there was no effective sanction, but the sanction of being
debarred from defending in the event of disobedience normally
sufficed.[52] Finally, the court may, in exceptional cases, order the
transfer of assets from one foreign jurisdiction to another to prevent
their dissipation.[53]

vi. Operation in Personam. The usual subject-matter of a
Mareva injunction is a sum of money, often in a bank account. But
there is no reason why other assets, such as a ship,[54] or an aero-
plane,[55] should not be "frozen" by this method. It is important to
note, however, that the *Mareva* injunction, even if related to a
specified asset, operates only *in personam*.[56] It is not a form of pre-
trial attachment. It does not effect seizure of the asset, nor is it
analogous to a lien. It merely prohibits the defendant personally
from removing or transferring the asset. It gives no proprietary right
in the asset, nor priority over other creditors.[57] The plaintiff's right
is merely to have the asset preserved so that, if he succeeds in his
action, judgment may be executed against it, but the rights of a third-
party with an interest in the asset will not be prejudiced.[58] The
injunction may (initially or by variation) permit the assets to be used

---

[51] [1990] Ch. 65.
[52] See (1989) 105 L.Q.R. 262 at p. 296 (L. Collins).
[53] *Derby & Co. Ltd v. Weldon (No. 6)* [1990] 1 W.L.R. 1139.
[54] *The Rena K* [1979] Q.B. 377. There is no conflict here with the jurisdiction to arrest ships.
See [1982] Conv. 265 at p. 270 (R. Horsfall).
[55] *Allen v. Jambo (Holdings) Ltd* [1980] 1 W.L.R. 1252 (A fatal accident case).
[56] *Cf. Z Ltd v. A–Z and AA–LL* [1982] Q.B. 558 at p. 573, "it operates *in rem* just as the arrest
of a ship does."(*per* Lord Denning M.R.). This was *per incuriam; Att.-Gen. v. Times
Newspapers Ltd* [1992] 1 A.C. 191 at p. 215.
[57] See *Sanders Lead Co. Inc. v. Entores Metal Brokers Ltd* [1984] 1 W.L.R. 452; *Bank Mellat
v. Kazmi* [1989] Q.B. 541. Assets which the plaintiff claims to trace may be protected by
an ordinary interlocutory injunction and not a *Mareva; Polly Peck International plc v.
Nadir (No. 2)* [1992] 4 All E.R. 769.
[58] *Cretanor Maritime Co. Ltd v. Irish Marine Management Ltd* [1978] 1 W.L.R. 966.

for living expenses or to make payments in good faith in the ordinary course of business.[59]

vii. Position of Third Parties. As far as the liabilities of a third party are concerned, we have seen that a third party who aids and abets the breach of an injunction by the defendant is guilty of contempt.[60] So in the case of a *Mareva* injunction against a sum of money in a bank account, the bank, once it has notice, must not facilitate the disposal of the money without a court order.[61] It is clear that any expenses incurred by a bank or other third party in complying with the injunction must be met by the plaintiff.[62] Furthermore, a bank can exercise any right of set-off it had before notification of the injunction.[63]

Similarly, the injunction must not interfere with the convenience or freedom of action of a third party. So in *Galaxia Maritime S.A. v. Mineralimportexport*,[64] where a *Mareva* injunction had been obtained as to a ship's cargo, the shipowner obtained its discharge, as it would interfere with the crew's arrangements for Christmas.

The protection of third parties where a world-wide *Mareva* injunction is granted has already been considered.[65]

---

[59] *Iraqi Ministry of Defence v. Arcepey Shipping Co. S.A.* [1981] Q.B. 65; *A. v. C.* [1981] Q.B. 956n.; *A. v. C. (No. 2)* [1981] Q.B. 961n.; *P.C.W. (Underwriting Agencies) Ltd v. Dixon* [1983] 2 All E.R. 158; 697; *Z Ltd v. A–Z and AA–LL* [1982] Q.B. 558; *TDK Tape Distributors (U.K.) Ltd v. Videochoice Ltd* [1986] 1 W.L.R. 141; *Law Society v. Shanks* [1988] 1 F.L.R. 504; *Atlas Maritime Co. S.A. v. Avalon Maritime Ltd* [1991] 4 All E.R. 769 and *(No. 3)* [1991] 1 W.L.R. 917.

[60] *Ante*, p. 739. See *Bank Mellat v. Kazmi* [1989] Q.B. 541. A post-judgment *Mareva* injunction may be granted against the defendant's wife; *Mercantile Group (Europe) A.G. v. Aiyela* [1994] Q.B. 366; *ante*, p. 809.

[61] *Z Ltd v. A–Z and AA–LL* [1982] Q.B. 558; *cf. Law Society v. Shanks, supra.* The injunction should not be granted against a bank as defendant; *ante*, p. 811.

[62] *Rahman (Prince Abdul) Bin Turki Al Sudairy v. Abu-Taha* [1980] 1 W.L.R. 1268; *Searose Ltd v. Seatrain (U.K.) Ltd* [1981] 1 W.L.R. 894. Undertakings will normally be given in this respect; *Z Ltd v. A–Z and AA–LL, supra.*

[63] *Oceanica Castelana Armadora S.A. of Panama v. Mineralimportexport* [1983] 1 W.L.R. 1294; All E.R. Rev. 1983, p. 262 (A. Zuckerman).

[64] [1982] 1 W.L.R. 539. See also *Clipper Maritime Co. Ltd of Monrovia v. Mineralimportexport* [1981] 1 W.L.R. 262; *Arab Monetary Fund v. Hashim (No. 2)* [1990] 1 All E.R. 673 (where compliance with disclosure order might incriminate third parties abroad).

[65] *Ante*, p. 813.

CHAPTER 26

RESCISSION AND RECTIFICATION

1. Rescission	817	
A. General	817	
B. Grounds for Rescission	818	
i. Mistake	818	
ii. Policy Considerations	820	
iii. Modern Formulations of the Remedy	822	
iv. Other Grounds	825	
(a) Misrepresentation	825	
(b) Undue Influence	828	
(c) Unconscionable Bargains	836	
C. Loss of the Right to Rescind	837	

i. Affirmation	838	
ii. *Restitutio in Integrum* not Possible	838	
iii. Third Party Acquiring Rights	839	
2. Rectification	839	
A. Nature of the Remedy	839	
B. The Nature of the Mistake	841	
i. Common Mistake	841	
ii. Unilateral Mistake	842	
C. Proof of the Mistake	844	
D. Instruments which may be Rectified	844	
E. Defences	845	

1. RESCISSION

A. General

The right to rescind is the right of a party to a contract[1] to have it set aside and to be restored to his former position. The contract remains valid unless and until rescinded, so that, as we shall see, third parties may acquire interests under it in the meantime. This is rescission in the strict sense, and must be distinguished on the one hand from contracts void *ab initio*, for example on the ground of illegality, and on the other hand from contracts with no inherent invalidity which are subsequently discharged by breach.[2] Rescission is not a judicial remedy as such, for it may be achieved by act of the parties, nevertheless the assistance of the court is often invoked, for example to secure restitution of any property. The role of equity is, first, that equity might set aside a contract in circumstances where the common law would not; secondly, that equity is more flexible in its view of *restitutio in integrum*, and can effect what is necessary,

---

[1] Or voluntary deed; *Gibbon v. Mitchell* [1990] 1 W.L.R. 1304; *Dent v. Dent* [1996] 1 W.L.R. 683.

[2] See *Johnson v. Agnew* [1980] A.C. 367. On the right to rescind for fraud, see *Logicrose Ltd v. Southend United Football Club Ltd* [1988] 1 W.L.R. 1256.

for example by ordering accounts and inquiries[3] or an allowance for services rendered[4]; and thirdly, that equity can grant relief on terms, by applying the maxim "he who comes to equity must do equity."[5]

The party rescinding is entitled to be restored to the position he would have been in had the contract not been entered into. He cannot recover damages, as that would put him in the position he would have been in had the contract been performed.[6]

B. Grounds for Rescission

i. Mistake. While mistake alone may justify refusal of a decree of specific performance,[7] mistake alone is not an automatic ground for rescission, although a mistake induced by fraud, or by mis-representation, or deliberately not corrected in a situation that called for full disclosure[8] is a more compelling case than a mistake arising without the responsibility of the other party. If two parties enter into a contract and one makes a mistake concerning it, the general principle is that behind the maxim *caveat emptor*; a party who knows he is making a better bargain than the other is under no duty to divulge the fact. A party who wishes to secure a form of guarantee as to any aspect of the transaction must raise the matter at the time and have it dealt with on the basis of representation or a term of the contract. All this is inherent in freedom of contract; but it is subject to some limits even at common law. For instance, a party cannot remain silent when he knows the other party is mistaken as to what the actual terms of the contract are[9]; or in certain cases of mistake as to the identity of the person contracted with.[10]

Equity does not disturb these long-established principles. It is true that equity has limited their effect when it has granted rescission on a ground not recognised at law, but it does not grant rescission except on a recognised ground. Generally speaking, the mistake of a plaintiff is no ground as such for rescission, but only when coupled

---

[3] *Erlanger v. New Sombrero Phosphate Co.* (1878) 3 App.Cas. 1218. If all that was required was a return of money or other property without any adjustments, this could be achieved by the common law action for money had and received.

[4] *Guinness plc v. Saunders* [1990] 2 A.C. 663 at p. 698.

[5] See *Solle v. Butcher* [1950] 1 K.B. 671, *post*, p. 820; *cf. TSB Bank plc v. Camfield* [1995] 1 W.L.R. 430, *post*, p. 835. For "partial rescission", see *Vadasz v. Pioneer Concrete (S.A.) Pty Ltd* (1995) 184 C.L.R. 102; (1997) 113 L.Q.R. 16 (D. O'Sullivan).

[6] *Redgrave v. Hurd* (1881) 20 Ch.D. 1.

[7] *e.g. Wood v. Scarth* (1855) 2 K. & J. 33, *ante*, p. 716.

[8] *e.g. Gordon v. Gordon* (1816) 3 Swan. 400, *post*, p. 826.

[9] *Smith v. Hughes* (1871) L.R. 6 Q.B. 597; *Hartog v. Colin & Shields* [1939] 3 All E.R. 566.

[10] *Cundy v. Lindsay* (1878) 3 App.Cas. 459; *Ingram v. Little* [1961] 1 Q.B. 31; *Lewis v. Averay* [1972] 1 Q.B. 198.

with, for example, a misrepresentation that induced it. Thus there is no separate set of rules in equity relating to rescission for mistakes as to the person or mistakes as to the extent of the terms of a contract.[11] Of course, if the contract is void at law, no question of mistake in equity arises.

In the absence of misrepresentation, the general principle is that, in order to justify rescission, the mistake must be common to both parties.[12] The law concerning a mistake made in common by both parties is difficult to state due to common law's own ambivalent attitude to it.[13] It has been said at various times that such a mistake may be so fundamental as to render an apparent contract based on it necessarily void,[14] and at the other extreme that, if there is an apparent agreement on all points, then the contract can be avoided only be reference to the further intention of the parties or by equity.[15] This is a larger problem than can be solved here, but the cases in equity can be considered to a substantial degree apart from it.

In *Cooper v. Phibbs*,[16] A was the legal owner and trustee of land which, unknown to either party, belonged in equity to B. A improved the land and agreed to let it to B. On discovering the facts B sought to rescind the letting agreement. The House of Lords held that, subject to a lien for A's expenditure, it should be set aside: "If parties contract under a mutual mistake and misapprehension as to their relative and respective rights, the result is, that that agreement is liable to be set aside as having proceeded upon a common mistake."[17]

Equity's jurisdiction has been reaffirmed in subsequent cases, and in the widest language.[18] The jurisdiction has not been confined to

---

[11] The judgment of Denning L.J. in *Solle v. Butcher* [1950] 1 K.B. 671, at pp. 692–693 contains propositions asserting a wider equitable jurisdiction than is usually accepted. See (1961) 24 M.L.R. 421 (P. Atiyah and F. Bennion); Goff and Jones (4th ed.), p. 216; (1989) 9 L.S. 291 (A. Phang); *Grist v. Bailey* [1967] Ch. 532; *Magee v. Pennine Insurance Co. Ltd* [1969] 2 Q.B. 507; *post*, p. 822.

[12] See *Riverlate Properties Ltd v. Paul* [1975] Ch. 133; *post*, p. 842.

[13] See Heydon, Gummow and Austin, *Cases and Materials on Equity and Trusts* (4th ed.), p. 271: "In this field no case is certain, none hopeless, no advice given with assurance sufficient to foreclose a journey through the courts."

[14] *Bell v. Lever Bros.* [1932] A.C. 161; *Scott v. Coulson* [1903] 2 Ch. 249; *Associated Japanese Bank International Ltd v. Credit du Nord SA* [1989] 1 W.L.R. 255 (sale of machines which did not exist); (1989) 48 C.L.J. 173 (G. Marston).

[15] *McRae v. Commonwealth Disposals Commission* (1951) 84 C.L.R. 377; *Solle v. Butcher* [1950] 1 K.B. 671; (1954) 70 L.Q.R. 385 (C. Slade); (1957) 73 L.Q.R. 340 (P. Atiyah); *Magee v. Pennine Insurance Co.* [1969] Q.B. 507.

[16] (1867) L.R. 2 H.L. 149; (reversing (1865) 17 Ir.Ch.Rep. 73).

[17] (1867) L.R. 2 H.L. 149 at p. 170. See (1989) 105 L.Q.R. 599 (P. Matthews), explaining that the agreement was not void *ab initio* because B was not the legal owner.

[18] *e.g.* Lord Chelmsford in *Earl Beauchamp v. Winn* (1873) L.R. 6 H.L. 223 at pp. 233–234. See Goff and Jones, pp. 212–220.

mistakes of fact in any technical sense; it has been said that it should not be exercised in respect of mistakes as to public law such as the construction of a statute[19] and that it should not be exercised in cases where parties have finally settled their difference but on an assumption which has since turned out to be false in point of law.[20] Attempts to formulate the jurisdiction more precisely in terms of "mistakes as to private rights" have not proved successful.

In *Solle v. Butcher*,[21] a flat was leased for seven years on an erroneous assumption (made by both parties) that structural alterations had taken the premises out of the provisions of the Rent Restriction Acts imposing rent control. The lessee sued to recover rent paid in excess of the amount permitted by the Act. He failed. The landlord obtained rescission of the lease on "just and equitable" terms on the ground of mistake.

The judgments in the Court of Appeal reveal a variety of possible views on the nature of the mistake. It can be viewed as one of fact, of private rights, of misconstruction of a statute, of misapprehension of the legal consequences of an agreement; and this variety is not surprising, as it is not feasible to distinguish the causes, natures and effects of mistakes in this way. There are elements of each in the mistake as it is eventually made, so that the only question for the courts can be whether it is right in a general sense to remedy by rescission the particular mistake in question, and this jurisdiction cannot be limited by reference to the kind or type of mistake made.

ii. Policy Considerations. The question of the availability of rescission should therefore be answered only after considering the issues involved. For instance, would remedying a common mistake by rescinding a contract lead to insecurity of a certain type of contract, as in *Rogers v. Ingham*?[22] Further, the effect of the common law view of the question should be considered as a matter of

---

[19] Lord Westbury and Lord Chelmsford both appear mindful of the need to make this reservation.

[20] *Rogers v. Ingham* (1876) 3 Ch.D. 351; contrast the facts in *Gordon v. Gordon* (1816) 3 Swan. 400, *post*, p. 826.

[21] [1950] 1 K.B. 671, followed in *Grist v. Bailey* [1967] Ch. 532, and *Magee v. Pennine Insurance Co. Ltd* [1969] 2 Q.B. 507, *post*, p. 822. See Jackson, *Principles of Property Law*, pp. 334, 358–364; (1987) 103 L.Q.R. 594 (J. Cartwright); (1994) 110 L.Q.R. 400 (J. Smith).

[22] (1876) 3 Ch.D. 451; (estate divided among family in accordance with counsel's advice cannot be reopened even if division incorrect).

policy before deciding whether equity should intervene by rescission.[23] These wide aspects are in fact implicit in some cases in which rescission has been refused, for instance *Bell v. Lever Bros. Ltd*[24] and the contemporaneous case of *Munro v. Meyer*.[25] In the former case, the company gave Bell a "golden handshake" to compensate him for the early termination of his contract of service. The company then discovered that the contract of service was voidable by reason of Bell's breach of fiduciary duty, so that he could have been dismissed without compensation. There was no fraudulent concealment, as Bell's mind was not directed to his breach of duty at the time of the compensation agreement. The House of Lords declined to rescind the latter agreement.

It can be seen that this wide doctrine of rescission has less scope in ordinary commercial transactions. The common law is more disposed to examine such cases on their merits, and in many cases it will be best to let the loss lie where it falls. In such circumstances there is no need for the application of a doctrine like rescission which will readjust the loss. This can be perceived particularly well on the facts of *Oscar Chess v. Williams*.[26]

A car was disposed of to a garage without any warranty as to its age. Both parties had in fact relied on the log-book, on which the date of manufacture had been altered from 1939 to 1948, by some person unknown. Not only was there no term of the contract as to the car's age, but the garage had not been misled by anything said by the owner. The result was that the loss due to mistake fell on the garage; no ground of action was available against the former owner. But in a dictum,[27] Denning L.J. canvassed the possibility of rescission for common mistake. This seems an unsuitable case for rescission, which would make the former

[23] Thus the considerations discussed in *McRae v. Commonwealth Disposals Commission* (1951) 84 C.L.R. 377, based on the intentions and responsibilities of the parties, would seem to be a matter for determination prior to consideration of the question of rescission in equity. Yet the common law aspects are not fully discussed in cases such as *Solle v. Butcher, supra*, or *Grist v. Bailey* [1967] Ch. 532, *post*, p. 822. But see Winn L.J. (dissenting) in *Magee v. Pennine Insurance Co.* [1969] 2 Q.B. 507 at pp. 515–517.

[24] [1932] A.C. 161. "It is perhaps not fanciful to suggest that in *Bell v. Lever Bros. Ltd* a narrow doctrine of mistake corrected an injustice that would have flowed from the rule of law under which a relatively trivial breach, which caused the innocent party no loss, nevertheless gave that party a ground for rescinding the contract." (1988) 104 L.Q.R. 501 at 505 (G. Treitel). The position may be otherwise in the case of fraudulent concealment; *Sybron Corp. v. Rochem Ltd* [1984] Ch. 112; All E.R.Rev. 1983 p. 65 (D. Prentice), p. 115 (M. Furmston) and p. 176 (P. Elias); (1983) 42 C.L.J. 218 (S. Honeyball). See also *Horcal Ltd v. Gatland, The Times*, April 16, 1984; (1985) 44 C.L.J. 215 (M. Owen); *van Gestel v. Cann, The Times*, August 7, 1987.

[25] [1930] 2 K.B. 312 (Wright J., who tried *Bell v. Lever Bros.* a few days later).

[26] [1957] 1 W.L.R. 370.

[27] [1957] 1 W.L.R. 370, at p. 374; he did not proceed with this possibility as in his view too long a period of time had elapsed.

owner pay a sum of money to the garage which was in excess of the value of the car which he would get back in exchange. This is not different in effect from an award of damages, for which the court held there was no justification.

Despite, therefore, the very wide statement of the remedy to be found in some cases and the impossibility of limiting its width by reference to types or kinds of mistake, its exercise is to be associated with a comparatively narrow range of cases. These cases concern land more than commerce in the wider sense, and tend to involve mistakes as to private rights more than mistakes as to facts or to qualities. To be more exact than that, however regrettable, is not possible.

iii. Modern Formulations of the Remedy

In *Grist v. Bailey*[28] a freehold house was sold for £850 in a belief shared by both parties that it was subject to a protected tenancy; in fact no protected tenancy existed, in which event a fair price would have been £2,500. The vendor refused to complete the purchase and successfully claimed rescission of the contract for sale; but rescission was made subject to an undertaking that he would sell to the purchaser at a proper price. Goff J. treated *Solle v. Butcher*[29] as authority for the exercise on such facts of the remedy of rescission, subject to (1) the mistake being common and (2) sufficiently fundamental, and (3) the vendor not being at fault.

In *Magee v. Pennine Insurance Co. Ltd,*[30] the plaintiff obtained insurance cover for a car, having signed an application form, the details of which had been filled in by a third party. The form incorrectly stated that he had a provisional licence, and that the car would be driven by himself, his eldest son who was an experienced driver, and a younger son aged 18. In truth, Magee had no licence, and the car was for the younger son, who alone drove it.

The car was destroyed in an accident. The plaintiff's claim was compromised by an agreement to pay £385, the plaintiff not being

---

[28] [1967] Ch. 532; Jackson, *Principles of Property Law*, p. 361. The formulation of Goff J. in this case was applied in *Laurence v. Lexcourt Holdings Ltd* [1978] 1 W.L.R. 1128, *post*, p. 824, where a common mistake as to the availability of planning permission was sufficiently fundamental to allow rescission.

[29] [1950] 1 K.B. 671.

[30] [1969] 2 Q.B. 507; (1969) 85 L.Q.R. 454; (1969) 32 M.L.R. 688 (J. Harris). If, however, the company had paid out under the policy without entering into any contractual compromise, the money would have been recoverable in quasi-contract as having been paid under a mistake of fact; *Kelly v. Solari* (1841) 9 M. & W. 54 (where the insurance company made a payment under a policy, forgetting the policy had lapsed).

fraudulent in that he was not aware that the policy was voidable for non-disclosure. The insurer refused to pay, arguing that the compromise could not be enforced. The Court of Appeal, Winn L.J. dissenting, held that the action for the money failed.

The difficulty lies in reconciling this decision with that of the House of Lords in *Bell v. Lever Bros. Ltd.*[31] The compromise was an agreement whose basis was the validity of the insurance contract. The contract was voidable for misrepresentation, but not void. The compromise was therefore not void for mistake. But, said Lord Denning M.R.[32]: "A common mistake, even on a most fundamental matter, does not make a contract void at law[33]; but it makes it voidable in equity . . . it is clear that, when the insurance company and Mr Magee made the agreement to pay £385, they were both under a common mistake which was fundamental to the whole agreement." This view, if correct, would greatly increase the scope of equitable jurisdiction, but it appears inconsistent with many decisions on the effect of mistake.[34] It is doubtful whether *Bell v. Lever Bros. Ltd*[35] can be regarded as dealing only with the position at common law.[36] It is submitted, therefore, that there is much force in the dissenting judgment of Winn L.J.[37]

It is clear that the mistake must be one common to both parties; and that both parties must have acted on the common incorrect assumption; the mistake must result in something being contracted for where, but for the mistake, no such contract would have been made. A similar emphasis on the causative nature of the mistake appears in quasi-contractual actions for the recovery of money paid under mistake of fact.[38]

---

[31] [1932] A.C. 161. See Goff and Jones, p. 216.

[32] [1969] 2 Q.B. 507 at p. 514. Fenton Atkinson L.J. agreed with Lord Denning's decision, but it is not clear whether he did so on the basis that the contract was voidable in equity or void at law.

[33] Steyn J. in *Associated Japanese Bank International Ltd v. Credit du Nord SA* [1989] 1 W.L.R. 255 at p. 267 considered that Lord Denning's interpretation of *Bell v. Lever Bros.* did not do justice to the speeches of the majority. For a valuable commentary on this case, see (1988) 104 L.Q.R. 501 (G. Treitel).

[34] Treitel (9th ed.), p. 295.

[35] [1932] A.C. 161.

[36] Steyn J. in *Associated Japanese Bank International Ltd v. Credit du Nord SA, supra*, at p. 266 considered that it should be so regarded.

[37] See Heydon, Gummow and Austin, *Cases and Materials on Equity and Trusts* (4th ed.), p. 286, describing the decision as "indicative of the confusion which swathes the subject of common mistake in contract."

[38] *Barclay's Bank Ltd v. W.J. Simms Son and Cooke (Southern) Ltd* [1980] Q.B. 677; Robert Goff J. said, at p. 692, that money paid under mistake of fact was prima facie recoverable "provided the plaintiff's mistake is 'vital' or 'material,' which I understand to mean that the mistake caused the plaintiff to pay the money."

It was said in *Grist v. Bailey*[39] that the plaintiff should not be "at fault." This concept is more enigmatic; it appears to reflect the discretionary nature of the remedy, and permits of all the factors leading to the creation of the contract being taken into account. This was done in *Magee v. Pennine Insurance Co. Ltd*[40] for Magee had no claim under the policy, and "it is not equitable that he should have a good claim on the agreement to pay the £385. . . . "[41] If the vendor in *Grist v. Bailey*[42] had been at fault in any material way in not appreciating the circumstances of the tenancy, the loss might have remained on him, as common law would have ordained.[43] In *Laurence v. Lexcourt Holdings Ltd*,[44] where the parties had entered into a tenancy agreement under a common and fundamental mistake of fact as to the availability of planning permission, the tenants' claim to rescission succeeded even though they had made no enquiries or searches. They acted imprudently, but were not "at fault" within the formulation of Goff J. in *Grist v. Bailey*,[45] because they owed no duty of care to the landlord to make the searches, nor were they responsible for the landlord's mistake. However, both *Grist v. Bailey* and *Laurence v. Lexcourt Holdings Ltd* might have been decided differently if the court had considered the question of the contractual allocation of risk. The general principle is *caveat emptor* in the absence of an express warranty. Thus where the risk of the existence of an incumbrance is expressly allocated to the purchaser by the contract, there is no room to rescind for mistake.[46]

The discretionary character of the remedy is also emphasised by the rescission being granted in appropriate cases on the terms which appear to the court to be just and equitable,[47] the term in *Grist v. Bailey*[48] being the sale of the house at a fair price. A more precise account of the scope of the equitable jurisdiction to rescind on the ground of common mistake cannot be given; "In the present confused state of the authorities one can only conclude that the courts recognise the existence of the equitable jurisdiction; but no clear answer can be given to the question just when a contract which is

---

[39] [1967] Ch. 532.

[40] *Supra.*

[41] *Ibid.* at p. 515, *per* Lord Denning M.R.

[42] [1967] Ch. 532.

[43] In *Associated Japanese Bank International Ltd v. Credit du Nord SA* [1989] 1 W.L.R. 255 at p. 269 Steyn J. regarded the lack of fault requirement of equity as consistent with the principle that a party cannot rescind at law for common mistake if he had no reasonable grounds for his mistaken belief.

[44] [1978] 1 W.L.R. 1128.

[45] [1967] Ch. 532.

[46] *William Sindall plc v. Cambridgeshire County Council* [1994] 1 W.L.R. 1016 at p. 1035.

[47] *cf.* the much more complicated terms in the rescission decree in *Solle v. Butcher* [1950] 1 K.B. 671 at p. 697, *ante*, p. 820.

[48] [1967] Ch. 532. *cf. Magee v. Pennine Insurance Co. Ltd, supra*, where no terms were imposed, for example as to repayment of the insurance premiums by the company.

valid at common law will be rescinded in equity."[49] Evans L.J. has recently stated that there is a category of mistake which is "fundamental", so as to permit the equitable remedy of rescission, which is wider than the "serious and radical" mistake which makes a contract void at law. "The difference may be that the common law rule is limited to mistakes with regard to the subject matter of the contract, whilst equity can have regard to a wider and perhaps unlimited category of 'fundamental' mistake."[50] As Treitel has said, the differing results in the cases illustrate a conflict of policies, "respect for the sanctity of contract" and "the need to give effect to the reasonable expectations of honest men." "The fact that each policy has its own validity accounts for the interest of this branch of the law and for the impossibility of explaining the authorities by reference to any single set of sharp distinctions."[51]

iv. Other Grounds. In addition to mistake in the sense discussed above, the right to rescind may arise where the mistake results from a misrepresentation; similarly in a case of constructive fraud, which embraces the doctrines of undue influence and unconscionable bargains. These will be discussed below. The right to rescind may also be granted expressly by the terms of the contract, which will then govern its exercise.[52] The right to rescind where there has been a substantial misdescription in a contract for the sale of land has already been discussed.[53]

(a) *Misrepresentation.*[54] Where the misrepresentation was fraudulent, the contract could be set aside both at common law and in equity. "Fraudulent" here means that the misrepresentation was made knowingly or recklessly.[55] It must have been intended to be acted upon, and actually have had this result. Equity alone, however, gave relief where the misrepresentation was not fraudulent. Such an

---

[49] Treitel (9th ed.), p. 296. See also Goff and Jones, pp. 216–220. Steyn J. in *Associated Japanese Bank International Ltd v. Credit du Nord SA* [1989] 1 W.L.R. 255 at pp. 267–268 was more optimistic: "No one could fairly suggest that in this difficult area of the law there is only one correct approach or solution. But a narrow doctrine of common law mistake (as enunciated in *Bell v. Lever Bros. Ltd*), supplemented by the more flexible doctrine of mistake in equity (as developed in *Solle v. Butcher* and later cases), seems to me to be an entirely sensible and satisfactory state of the law."

[50] *William Sindall plc v. Cambridgeshire County Council, supra,* at p. 1042.

[51] (1988) 104 L.Q.R. 501 at 507, comparing *Bell v. Lever Bros. Ltd* [1932] A.C. 161 with *Associated Japanese Bank International Ltd v. Credit du Nord SA, supra.*

[52] See Snell, pp. 619–620.

[53] *Ante,* p. 721.

[54] Only an outline can be given here, and reference should be made to the standard works on contract.

[55] *Derry v. Peek* (1889) 14 App.Cas. 337. Damages for deceit are also available: *Archer v. Brown* [1985] Q.B. 401; *Saunders v. Edwards* [1987] 1 W.L.R. 1116.

"innocent misrepresentation" was not recognised at common law unless it had become a term of the contract.[56]

It should be noted that mere silence does not constitute a misrepresentation unless it creates a false impression by distorting the meaning of any positive statement.[57] Further, there is a duty of disclosure in the case of a contract *uberrimae fidei*,[58] such as contracts of insurance of all kinds,[59] and contracts for family settlements. Breach of such a duty of disclosure is not a misrepresentation within the Misrepresentation Act 1967,[60] nor does it sound in damages,[61] the proper remedy being rescission. Thus in *Gordon v. Gordon*[62] a deed of settlement of property within a family was entered into by an eldest son in the belief that he was illegitimate, though a younger son knew of a secret marriage of his parents by virtue of which the eldest son was legitimate. Lord Eldon held that a duty of candour recognised in equity had been breached so that the settlement should be set aside.

Similar duties may be owed to the court. In *Jenkins v. Livesey (formerly Jenkins)*,[63] a divorcing couple agreed that the husband would transfer his half-share of the home to the wife, who would give up all claims to financial provision. Shortly after this agreement, the wife became engaged to marry a man she had met before the agreement. This was not disclosed to the husband nor to her own solicitor. The agreement was then embodied in a consent order under section 25(1) of the Matrimonial Causes Act 1973. Two days after the husband conveyed his share of the home, the wife remarried. The House of Lords set aside the consent order. The remarriage ended the wife's right to financial provision, thus the husband would not have entered into the agreement had it been disclosed. Under section 25(1) the court must have regard to all the circumstances, and therefore a duty is owed to the court to make full and frank disclosure of material facts to the other party and to the court. But

---

[56] See *Heilbut Symons & Co. v. Buckleton* [1913] A.C. 30.

[57] *Oakes v. Turquand* (1867) L.R. 2 H.L. 325.

[58] Or where a fiduciary or other similar special relationship exists between the contracting parties; *van Gestel v. Cann, The Times*, August 7, 1987; *Guinness plc v. Saunders* [1990] 2 A.C. 663.

[59] Also company prospectuses. See *London Assurance Co. v. Mansel* (1879) 11 Ch.D. 363, and Kindersley V.-C.'s well-known judgment in *The New Brunswick and Canada Railway and Land Company v. Muggeridge* (1860) 1 Dr. & Sm. 363 at p. 381.

[60] *Banque Keyser Ullman S.A. v. Skandia (U.K.) Insurance Co. Ltd* [1990] 1 Q.B. 665 at pp. 789–790; affirmed [1991] 2 A.C. 249.

[61] *Ibid.*; *Bank of Nova Scotia v. Hellenic Mutual War Risks Association (Bermuda) Ltd* [1990] 1 Q.B. 818.

[62] (1816) 3 Swan 400.

[63] [1985] A.C. 424. See (1985) 44 C.L.J. 202 (R. Ingleby); All E.R.Rev. 1985, p. 175 (S. Cretney). The decision is based on the requirements of s.25, rather than the concept of *uberrima fides* in the agreement for a consent order.

not every failure to disclose would result in the setting aside of the order. The test was whether the order was substantially different from that which would have been made upon full disclosure.

As far as innocent misrepresentation was concerned, equity's jurisdiction depended on the force of the misrepresentation on the plaintiff's mind rather than the mental state of the defendant when he made it, or on the relative importance of the fact misrepresented to the contract as a whole. Thus a plaintiff seeking rescission on this ground did not have to prove negligence or any other degree of fault in the defendant but only the fact of his own reliance on the statement, and its untruth.

Until the Misrepresentation Act 1967 the plaintiff could rescind,[64] or possibly resist specific performance, but he could not recover damages on the basis of an innocent misrepresentation. Since that Act, however, the plaintiff may recover damages under section 2(1) for an innocent misrepresentation unless the defendant had reasonable grounds to believe and did believe that the statement was true.[65] The measure of damages is the same as that which applies to a fraudulent misrepresentation.[66] By section 2(2),[67] damages may be awarded in lieu of rescission wherever the court thinks it would be equitable to do so, having regard to the nature of the misrepresentation and the loss that would be caused by it if the contract were upheld, as well as the loss that rescission would cause to the defendant. Damages may be awarded under section 2(2) although the misrepresentation was wholly innocent, (*i.e.* non-negligent). The measure is as in contract, and is thus different from the measure of damages under subsection (1).[68] The result intended would seem to be that damages are the most suitable remedy in cases of misrepresentations inducing a contract, save where the facts reveal a real justification for there being rescission of the contract as well. A term in the contract purporting to restrict or exclude liability for misrepresentation is of no effect except insofar as it satisfies the

---

[64] See generally *Redgrave v. Hurd* (1881) 20 Ch.D. 1.

[65] See *Esso Petroleum Ltd v. Mardon* [1976] Q.B. 801 (negligent forecast of petrol sales); *Laurence v. Lexcourt Holdings Ltd* [1978] 1 W.L.R. 1128 (negligent misrepresentation as to permitted user); *Walker v. Boyle* [1982] 1 W.L.R. 495 (negligent statement by vendor that no boundary disputes); *Resolute Maritime Inc. v. Merchant Investors Assurance Co. Ltd* [1983] 1 W.L.R. 857.

[66] *Royscot Trust Ltd v. Rogerson* [1991] 2 Q.B. 297; (1991) 107 L.Q.R. 547 (R. Hooley). But the correctness of *Royscot* was left open in *Smith New Court Securities Ltd v. Scrimgeour Vickers (Asset Management) Ltd* [1996] 3 W.L.R. 1051. See also *East v. Maurer* [1991] 1 W.L.R. 461 (loss of profits); (1992) 108 L.Q.R. 386 (J. Marks); (1994) 110 L.Q.R. 35 (P. Chandler).

[67] (1967) 30 M.L.R. 369 (G. Treitel and P. Atiyah).

[68] *William Sindall plc v. Cambridgeshire County Council* [1994] 1 W.L.R. 1016; (1995) 111 L.Q.R. 60 (H. Beale); (1995) 54 C.L.J. 17 (A. Oakley).

requirement of reasonableness as stated in section 11(1) of the Unfair Contract Terms Act 1977.[69]

Equity's remedy of rescission now forms part of a hierarchy of remedies for misrepresentation that are available generally to a plaintiff, instead of being the only and not always very apposite remedy available in the absence of fraud. It is thus now more important as a supplementary than as a basic remedy. The history and rationale of the remedy are, however, of interest in considering rescission for mistakes not induced by misrepresentation, discussed in the earlier part of this section.

(b) *Undue Influence.*[70] Under the head of constructive fraud,[71] equity recognises a wide variety of situations in which intervention is justified by reason of a defendant's influence or dominance over a plaintiff in procuring his execution of a document (such as a settlement) or his entering into an obligation; equity's intervention here is independent of any question of the accuracy of information supplied to the plaintiff. Equity intervenes in such cases, not because, as is the case with misrepresentations, the defendant has positively (albeit innocently) misled the plaintiff on a particular and relevant point of fact, but because the defendant had caused the plaintiff's judgment to be clouded, with the result that the plaintiff has failed to consider the matter as he ought.

Actual threats, or physical duress, are remedied both at law and in equity, but equity's view is the wider. Where threats have made it impossible for a plaintiff either to consider the relevant matter normally or to feel a free agent, as when a son was threatened with disclosure to his sick father of the forging of the father's signature by his brother, equity will intervene.[72] But influence by means other than threats is the more usual type of case. It is possible for a defendant to have obtained almost complete domination over the mind of another,[73] but in most cases the undue influence is exerted only to secure a specific objective.[74] The varieties of methods are infinite also; they may range from developing a sense of complete confidence[75] over many years to quick seizure of an opportunity

---

[69] s.3, as amended by the 1977 Act. See *Walker v. Boyle* [1982] 1 W.L.R. 495.

[70] See generally Keeton and Sheridan's *Equity* (3rd ed.), pp. 255 *et seq.*; [1985] Conv. 387 (C. Barton and P. Rank); (1988) 2 *Trust Law & Practice* 98 (S. Foster).

[71] See Snell, pp. 550 *et seq*; *O'Sullivan v. Management Agency and Music Ltd* [1985] Q.B. 428, at p. 455.

[72] *Mutual Finance Co. v. Wetton* [1937] 2 K.B. 389; *Barton v. Armstrong* [1976] A.C. 104. See (1939) 3 M.L.R. 97 (W. Winder).

[73] *Smith v. Kay* (1875) 7 H.L.Cas. 750; *Morley v. Loughnan* [1893] 1 Ch. 736.

[74] *Lyon v. Home* (1868) L.R. 6 Eq. 655.

[75] *Tate v. Williamson* (1866) L.R. 2 Ch.App. 55.

presented by a defendant's weakness. In *Tufton v. Sperni*,[76] a plaintiff was prevailed upon to buy a house from the defendant at an over-value and at the same time to make it available to the defendant on a lease on absurdly favourable terms. The Court of Appeal, in rescinding the transaction, emphasised that these cases cannot be categorised, but are all variations on the one theme of undue[77] use of a mental domination possessed or gained over another. Undue influence may be exercised by a corporation, although there may be no special personal relationship with any individual representative.[78] The novel point as to whether undue influence could be exercised by an unincorporated association arose in *Roche v. Sherrington*,[79] where the plaintiff had been a member of Opus Dei (an international Roman Catholic association) for some years. After leaving, he sought repayment of gifts to the association on the basis of undue influence. Slade J. held it to be arguable that a transaction between an individual and an unincorporated association might give rise to a presumption of undue influence on the part of the members. But the plaintiff's action was dismissed as he had brought it against the defendant as representative of all present members, including many persons who were not members at the time of the gifts.

There are two categories of cases; first, those in which equity presumes undue influence. While the presumption does not apply to every relationship of trust and confidence,[80] it does arise in certain well defined cases such as parent and child, guardian and ward, doctor and patient, religious adviser and pupil,[81] and other situations where it is shown that a similar relationship of confidence existed.[82] Here equity requires positive evidence that no undue influence was

---

[76] [1952] 2 T.L.R. 516. See also *Langton v. Langton* [1995] 2 F.L.R. 890 (father pressured to make gift of house).

[77] It may be undue without being for personal gain, as where a parent's influence leads to an improvident settlement by a child that is only of marginal benefit to the parent: *Bullock v. Lloyd's Bank* [1955] Ch. 317.

[78] See *Lloyd's Bank Ltd v. Bundy* [1975] Q.B. 326.

[79] [1982] 1 W.L.R. 599.

[80] *National Westminster Bank plc v. Morgan* [1985] A.C. 686; *Goldsworthy v. Brickell* [1987] Ch. 378.

[81] *Allcard v. Skinner* (1887) 36 Ch.D. 145 (nun and mother superior); *Huguenin v. Baseley* (1807) 14 Ves. 273.

[82] *Re Craig* [1971] Ch. 95 (aged widower and secretary); *Lloyd's Bank Ltd v. Bundy (supra)*, (banker and aged customer); *O'Sullivan v. Management Agency and Music Ltd* [1985] Q.B. 428 (manager and entertainer); *Re Brocklehurst* [1978] Ch. 14 at p. 42; *Simpson v. Simpson* [1992] 1 F.L.R. 601 (incapacitated elderly husband and younger wife); *Goldsworthy v. Brickell* [1987] Ch. 378 (elderly farmer and manager); *Cheese v. Thomas* [1994] 1 W.L.R. 129 (elderly uncle and great nephew); *Langton v. Langton* [1995] 2 F.L.R. 890 (vulnerable ex-convict and son); *Mahoney v. Purnell* [1996] 3 All E.R. 61 (elderly father-in-law and son-in-law). See also *Mathew v. Bobbins* (1980) 41 P. & C.R. 1 (there is no presumption of undue influence arising from the relationship of master and servant or landlord and tenant, or a combination of the two).

in fact exerted. In cases outside this category equity requires positive proof of influence having actually been exerted.[83] But in all
cases the question is whether a defendant has taken advantage of his
position, or, *per contra*, has been assiduous not to do so. Many cases
turn on whether a defendant discouraged independent legal advice
or proceeded in such a way as to make it unlikely that the plaintiff
would think of taking it.[84] For, as with many of the flexible remedies
of equity, a defendant is not placed under an absolute bar by virtue
of this equitable obligation, but has to adopt proper steps, in view of
the obligation, if he wishes to proceed in certain ways. So a genuine
insistence on independent legal advice from a fully informed adviser
is a natural means of repudiating a charge of having exerted undue
influence, even in a case where the possibility of influence was
strong[85] and especially where there is a conflict of interest and
duty.[86] But the presumption of undue influence is not rebuttable only
by establishing insistence on independent legal advice (which, however, does not always suffice to rebut the presumption[87]); it may also
be rebutted by showing that the gift was a "spontaneous and independent act."[88] In any event, the presumption will not operate unless
the gift is so large or the transaction so improvident that it cannot
reasonably be accounted for on grounds of friendship, relationship,
charity or other motives.[89]

Most of the illustrations relate to situations of special relationship
existing between particular people, and often involve settlements of
property. The principle is less often seen in operation in commercial
matters, where it has had little impact in derogating from the more
widely applicable principle that lies behind the maxim *caveat emptor*.[90] Mere inequality of bargaining power, which is a relative
concept, does not justify interference with a commercial transaction.

---

[83] As in the case of gifts by will, where no presumption of undue influence arises by reason
of the relationship of the parties. See Mellows, *The Law of Succession* (5h ed.), pp. 53 *et
seq*. There is no presumption of undue influence between husband and wife, although a
transaction may be set aside if a relationship of confidence is shown to have existed, or
failing that, on proof of undue influence; *Bank of Montreal v. Stuart* [1911] A.C. 120;
Kingsnorth Trust Ltd v. Bell [1986] 1 W.L.R. 119; *Simpson v. Simpson, supra*; *Midland
Bank plc v. Shephard* [1988] 3 All E.R. 17; [1989] Conv. 63 (B. Dale).
[84] *Baker v. Monk* (1864) 4 De G.J. & S. 388; *Backhouse v. Backhouse* [1978] 1 W.L.R. 243;
Cresswell v. Potter (1968); [1978] 1 W.L.R. 255n.
[85] See *Zamet v. Hyman* [1961] 1 W.L.R. 1442 at pp. 1445–1446; *Banco Exterior Internacional
SA v. Thomas* [1997] 1 W.L.R. 221.
[86] *Lloyds Bank Ltd v. Bundy* [1975] Q.B. 326.
[87] *Credit Lyonnais Bank Nederland NV v. Burch* [1997] 1 All E.R. 144 (because the influence
may cause the advice to be disregarded); *cf. Banco Exterior Internacional SA v. Thomas,
supra*, at p. 230.
[88] *Re Brocklehurst* [1978] Ch. 14. See also *Simpson v. Simpson* [1992] 1 F.L.R. 601;
Goldsworthy v. Brickell [1987] Ch. 378.
[89] *Goldsworthy v. Brickell* [1987] Ch. 378; (1987) 104 L.Q.R. 160; All E.R.Rev. 1987, p. 311
(M. Furmston).
[90] "Extravagant liberality and immoderate folly do not provide a passport to equitable relief,"
per Evershed M.R. in *Tufton v. Sperni* [1952] 2 T.L.R. 516 at p. 519.

There is rarely absolute equality, and the court only interferes in exceptional cases as a matter of common fairness.[91] The principles of undue influence have generally been discussed in the types of transaction which attracted equity's particular attention in the nineteenth century, such as the cases on bargains with expectant heirs, and the modern form of such cases. These include cases where a beneficiary under a trust, who, although past the age of majority, is still subject to parental influence, and is persuaded to use his fortune to support the family finances[92]; or where a secretary companion takes advantage of her dominance of a weak, dependent and vulnerable old man[93]; or where an elderly farmer grants a tenancy on terms disadvantageous to himself to the manager upon whom he relies.[94] Bridge L.J. summarised these cases as those in which there is a "duty on the donee to advise the donor, or a position of actual or potential dominance of the donee over the donor."[95] But there was no such position of dominance in *Re Brocklehurst*,[96] where an "autocratic and eccentric old gentleman" made a valuable gift of shooting rights to the defendant, a "subservient garage proprietor." The relationship was not one of confidence and trust such as to give rise to a presumption of undue influence.

The House of Lords reviewed the doctrine in *National Westminster Bank v. Morgan*,[97] where a husband and wife mortgaged their home to the bank to secure a loan to the husband, who was in difficulties with his business. The wife claimed that the bank manager had exercised undue influence in obtaining her signature during a visit to the home. Although the wife had not received independent legal advice before signing, her claim failed because the relationship never went beyond the normal business relationship of banker and customer, nor was the transaction disadvantageous to the wife. The principle which justifies setting a transaction aside for undue influence is the victimisation of one party by the other. The party alleging undue influence must show, it was said, that the transaction was manifestly disadvantageous to him (which will, of course, be easier to establish in cases of gifts). While there are no precisely defined limits to the equitable jurisdiction to relieve against undue influence,

---

[91] *Alec Lobb (Garages) Ltd v. Total Oil G.B. Ltd* [1985] 1 W.L.R. 173; (1985) 101 L.Q.R. 306. The cases where a commercial transaction such as a mortgage may be set aside because the mortgagee has constructive notice of undue influence exerted by a third party are discussed below; *post*, p. 832.

[92] *Re Coomber* [1911] 1 Ch. 732 at pp. 726, 727; *Bullock v. Lloyds Bank Ltd* [1955] Ch. 317; *Re Pauling's S.T.* [1964] Ch. 303.

[93] *Re Craig* [1971] Ch. 95.

[94] *Goldsworthy v. Brickell* [1987] Ch. 378.

[95] *Re Brocklehurst* [1978] Ch. 14 at p. 41.

[96] [1978] Ch. 14 (Lord Denning M.R. dissented).

[97] [1985] A.C. 686; (1985) 101 L.Q.R. 305 and (1985) 44 C.L.J. 192 (N. Andrews); (1985) 48 M.L.R. 579 (D. Tiplady); All E.R. Rev. 1985, p. 20 (N. Palmer) and p. 89 (M. Furmston).

the doctrine is sufficiently developed not to need the support of a principle of inequality of bargaining power. This decision, in rejecting the broad approach of inequality of bargaining power, restricted the scope of the doctrine of undue influence.

The requirement of manifest disadvantage proved troublesome, especially where a wife was seeking to set aside (on the basis of undue influence) a charge over the matrimonial home to secure a loan made to assist the husband's business. If the loan was the only way to keep the business afloat, the wife had difficulty in showing that it was to her manifest disadvantage even though the business ultimately failed. The House of Lords has now held that manifest disadvantage need not be shown in cases of actual, as opposed to presumed, undue influence.[98] It was considered that *National Westminster Bank v. Morgan*[99] did not intend to lay it down as a universal requirement, and that there was no logic in requiring it in a case of actual undue influence, which is a species of fraud. The requirement of manifest disadvantage remains in cases of presumed undue influence,[1] but is open to review in the House of Lords.

An important question which has arisen in the context of mortgages and guarantees is whether the creditor should be prejudiced by any misrepresentation or undue influence exercised by the debtor over a third party who executes the mortgage or guarantee in favour of the creditor, or agrees to give priority to the mortgagee. As a general rule, a creditor owes no duty to the debtor's surety or guarantor to ensure that the third party understands the transaction and has given a free and informed consent. The transaction will, however, be set aside if the creditor had actual or constructive notice at the time of the execution of the security that the third party's consent was procured by the undue influence or misrepresentation of the debtor. Likewise in the very rare case where the creditor has made the debtor its agent in procuring the execution of the security by the third party (agency not being established merely by reason that the creditor has left it to the debtor to procure the execution), and the debtor has been guilty of undue influence or misrepresentation.

These propositions were confirmed by the House of Lords in *Barclays Bank plc v. O'Brien*,[2] where the principles were fully reviewed. In that case a wife (who was neither uneducated nor vulnerable) executed a charge securing her husband's unlimited

---

[98] *CIBC Mortgages plc v. Pitt* [1994] 1 A.C. 200.

[99] [1985] A.C. 686.

[1] See *Cheese v. Thomas* [1994] 1 W.L.R. 129, *post*, p. 839 (transaction set aside where elderly man aged 86 spent £43,000 to buy an insecure right to reside in a particular house for life); *Mahoney v. Purnell* [1996] 3 All E.R. 61.

[2] [1994] 1 A.C. 180. The bank had recovered £60,000, and the appeal did not deal with that. For Commonwealth views, see (1996) 16 L.S. 368 (M. Richardson).

guarantee of a company's liability to the bank. Owing to her husband's misrepresentation, she thought it was a temporary security for the sum of £60,000. The wife did not read the documents before signing. It was held that the bank could not enforce the charge because it had constructive notice of the wife's right to set aside the transaction. Such cases involved a consideration of two questions: was the creditor put on inquiry as to the existence of undue influence, misrepresentation or other legal wrong and, if so, had the creditor taken reasonable steps to ensure that the third party entered into the transaction freely and knowing the true facts? If reasonable steps had not been taken, the creditor would have constructive notice of the third party's right to set aside the transaction, which would be accordingly unenforceable by the creditor. Where a wife charged her property or stood surety for her husband's debt, the creditor would be put on inquiry by a combination of two factors: first, the transaction on its face was not to the wife's financial advantage; secondly, although there was no presumption of undue influence between husband and wife, there was a substantial risk that the husband had committed a legal or equitable wrong entitling the wife to set aside the transaction.[3] The principle was not confined to wives, but extended to cohabitants[4] (including homosexual couples), provided the creditor was aware of the cohabitation, and other relationships may be included.[5] It was emphasised, however, that the principle did not apply to a third party who merely misunderstood the transaction, without wrongdoing by the debtor.

Where the creditor is put on inquiry, the next question, as mentioned above, is whether it has taken reasonable steps to ensure that the third party has entered into the transaction freely. For transactions after *O'Brien* this means that, unless the circumstances are exceptional, the creditor must warn the third party, at a meeting not attended by the debtor, of the potential liability and risks, and must advise the third party to take independent advice. Cases involving transactions entered into before the House of Lords gave these guidelines are dealt with on their merits, as explained below.

Some older authorities had treated the wife as having a "special equity" deserving of extra protection. Lord Browne-Wilkinson in

---

[3] The decision has not been followed in Scotland on the ground that it achieves a presumption of wrongdoing by a husband against his wife; *Mumford v. Bank of Scotland* (1996) S.L.T. 392 (actual knowledge required); [1996] R.L.R. 100 (E. McKendrick).

[4] See also *Massey v. Midland Bank plc* [1995] 1 All E.R. 929 (couple not cohabiting but longstanding relationship); *Allied Irish Bank plc v. Byrne* [1995] 2 F.L.R. 325 (divorced but partly reconciled). This reflects the Code of Banking Practice.

[5] The House of Lords approved *Avon Finance Ltd v. Bridger* [1985] 2 All E.R. 281 (vulnerable elderly parents and adult son). See also *Credit Lyonnais Bank Nederland NV v. Burch* [1997] 1 All E.R. 144 (employer and employee whose relationship gave rise to a presumption of undue influence).

Barclays Bank plc v. O'Brien,[6] rejecting this theory, considered the true basis to be the doctrine of notice, which "lies at the heart of equity."[7] Although his Lordship spoke in terms of earlier rights prevailing against later rights, it must be emphasised that it is not the traditional doctrine of notice which is at work here, because there is only one transaction, and not a contest between a prior interest and a later one. The real issue is the validity of the transaction. The doctrine of notice is applied in its wider sense, and for that reason is equally applicable to cases of registered title.[8]

Lord Browne-Wilkinson was concerned to hold a fair balance between the vulnerability of wives (and others) and the practical problems of lenders. This factor was particularly significant in the contemporaneous decision of the House of Lords in *CIBC Mortgages plc v. Pitt*,[9] where a husband exercised undue influence in relation to a mortgage to secure a joint loan of £150,000 to himself and his wife. The loan application stated that the money was required to pay off an existing mortgage and to buy a holiday home. After paying off the prior mortgage the husband used the surplus in unsuccessful speculation on the stock market. The wife, who had not read the documents nor received separate advice, failed to set aside the mortgage. The bank was not put on inquiry because it was a joint loan and, in contrast with the surety cases, there was nothing to indicate that it was not for their joint benefit. To have decided otherwise would have had the detrimental result in practice of restricting the availability of joint mortgage loans for the purchase of homes. The mere fact that the loan is joint will not, however, automatically disapply the principle of *Barclays Bank plc v. O'Brien*,[10] if in substance the situation is one of suretyship,[11] or if the stated purpose is for the couple's joint benefit but the creditor knows that the money will be used for the husband's sole benefit,[12]

---

[6] *Supra.*

[7] [1994] 1 A.C. 180 at p. 195.

[8] *Ante*, p. 37. See All E.R. Rev. 1993, p. 367 (W. Swadling); (1994) 144 N.L.J. 765 (P. O'Hagan); [1994] Conv. 421 (M. Dixon and C. Harpum); [1995] Conv. 250. (P. Sparkes); (1995) 54 C.L.J. 280 (A. Lawson) and 536 (J. Mee); (1995) 15 L.S. 35 (G. Battersby); [1996] Conv. 34 (J. Howell). For the position where the debtor was not a party to the transaction in question, see *Banco Exterior Internacional SA v. Thomas* [1997] 1 W.L.R. 221.

[9] [1994] 1 A.C. 200; (1994) 57 M.L.R. 467 (B. Fehlberg); [1994] 2 R.L.R. 3 (S. Cretney). See also *Britannia Building Society v. Pugh* [1996] E.G.C.S. 128; *Scotlife Home Loans (No. 2) Ltd v. Hedworth* (1996) 28 H.L.R. 771 (not set aside where in fact used for joint benefit, contrary to stated purpose).

[10] [1994] 1 A.C. 180.

[11] *Allied Irish Bank plc v. Byrne* [1995] 2 F.L.R. 325 (joint loan but bank aware that for benefit of husband). See also [1994] Conv. 140 (M. Thompson); (1994) 53 C.L.J. 21 (M. Dixon).

[12] *Halifax Mortgage Services Ltd v. Stepsky* [1996] Ch. 207 (not set aside because knowledge of borrowers' solicitor acquired before instructed by lender not imputed to lender). See also *Dunbar Bank plc v. Nadeem, The Times*, November 13, 1996 (charge to secure loan partly for joint purchase of property and partly for husband's sole benefit).

or knows that the benefit to the wife is disproportionately small in comparison with her potential liability.[13]

It has since been held by the Court of Appeal in *TSB Bank plc v. Camfield*[14] that where a third party has established the right to set aside a transaction against the creditor, the right is absolute. The court will not impose terms which make the security or guarantee partially enforceable. Thus where the husband misrepresented that the security was limited to £15,000, but in fact it was unlimited, the wife had no liability even as to the £15,000. Although the court recognised the "abstract justice" of partial enforcement, the position was the same as any other case where a person was affected by notice of another's rights. The right to rescind is that of the third party, who does not need to ask the court for equitable relief, to which terms may be attached. Where, however, a joint mortgage on the home is set aside by the wife, it may take effect as a charge on the husband's equitable interest, and in any event the creditor may bring about a sale of the home by making the husband bankrupt.[15]

As stated above, the requirements laid down in *Barclays Bank plc v. O'Brien*, which a creditor with constructive notice must satisfy in order to establish that reasonable steps have been taken to ensure that the third party entered into the transaction freely, apply in their full rigour only to post-*O'Brien* transactions. Subsequent decisions have treated creditors somewhat leniently in this regard.[16] Creditors have been able to resist the third party's claim where she was not interviewed separately from the debtor[17] or where the solicitor who has advised her has been the solicitor of the debtor[18] or of the creditor.[19] Where the wife has signed a certificate stating that the solicitor has explained the matter to her, and the solicitor has signed a certificate for the bank stating the same, the bank is entitled to rely

---

[13] *Goode Durrant Administration v. Biddulph* (1994) 26 H.L.R. 625 (joint loan to spouses and company but wife entitled only to 2.5 per cent shareholding); (1994) 24 Fam. Law 675 (S. Cretney); *Barclays Bank plc v. Sumner* [1996] E.G.C.S. 65.

[14] [1995] 1 W.L.R. 430; [1995] Conv. 325 (A. Dunn); (1995) 111 L.Q.R. 555 (P. Ferguson); All E.R. Rev. 1995, p. 450 (W. Swadling); [1996] R.L.R. 71 (L. Proksch); *Castle Phillips Finance v. Piddington* (1995) 70 P. & C.R. 592. The point did not arise in *Barclays Bank plc v. O'Brien* [1994] 1 A.C. 180; *ante*, p. 832, n. 2. Terms have been imposed for the repayment of so much of a loan as was for the wife's benefit; *Dunbar Bank plc v. Nadeem, supra. Camfield* has been rejected in Australia; *Vadasz v. Pioneer Concrete (S.A.) Pty Ltd* (1995) 184 C.L.R. 102; (1997) 113 L.Q.R. 16 (D. O'Sullivan).

[15] *Zandfarid v. Bank of Credit and Commerce International S.A. (in liquidation)* [1996] 1 W.L.R. 1420. See also *Albany Home Loans Ltd v. Massey, The Times,* February 14, 1997.

[16] (1994) 24 Fam. Law 563 (S. Cretney); (1995) 111 L.Q.R. 51 (A. Chandler); [1995] Conv. 148 (J. Mee); [1995] 7 C.F.L.Q. 104 (M. Oldham); (1995–96) 6 K.C.L.J. 108 (P. Giliker); (1996) 59 M.L.R. 675 (B. Fehlberg).

[17] *Massey v. Midland Bank plc* [1995] 1 All E.R. 929.

[18] *Ibid.; Bank of Baroda v. Rayarel* [1995] 2 F.L.R. 376; *Banco Exterior Internacional v. Mann* [1995] 1 All E.R. 936; *cf. Bank Melli Iran v. Samadi-Rad* [1995] 2 F.L.R. 367.

[19] *Midland Bank plc v. Serter* (1996) 71 P. & C.R. 264.

on the solicitor having done his job properly.[20] The creditor need not stipulate the nature and extent of the advice to be sought.[21] On the other hand, the terms of the transaction may be so manifestly disadvantageous (as where a junior employee mortgaged her home to the bank to secure an unlimited guarantee of her employer's overdraft) that the creditor cannot be said to have taken reasonable steps unless it ensures that the third party actually receives independent legal advice, and even then the creditor will have no defence if it must have known that no competent solicitor could have advised the third party to enter into the transaction.[22]

The review of this area by the House of Lords in *Barclays Bank plc v. O'Brien*[23] leaves some matters still uncertain, in particular the relationship between cases of presumed undue influence, where "manifest disadvantage" is still required, and cases of breach of fiduciary duty, where transactions can be set aside without proof of disadvantage. Likewise the distinction between cases of actual undue influence and "unconscionable bargains", discussed below, needs to be clarified.[24]

(c) *Unconscionable Bargains.*[25] Equity intervenes to set aside unfair transactions made with "poor and ignorant" persons. The doctrine does not apply to gifts.[26] It is not enough to show that the transaction was hard and unreasonable.[27] Three elements must be established.[28] First, that one party was at a serious disadvantage to the other by reason of poverty, ignorance or otherwise,[29] so that circumstances existed of which unfair advantage could be taken[30]; secondly, that the transaction was at an undervalue; and thirdly, that

---

[20] *Ibid.*; *Bank of Baroda v. Rayarel, supra; Banco Exterior Internacional v. Mann, supra;* *Barclays Bank plc v. Thomson* [1997] 1 F.L.R. 156.

[21] *Massey v. Midland Bank plc, supra.*

[22] *Credit Lyonnais Bank Nederland NV v. Burch* [1997] 1 All E.R. 144; (1997) 113 L.Q.R. 10 (H. Tjio).

[23] [1994] 1 A.C. 180.

[24] (1994) 110 L.Q.R. 167 (J. Lehane), considering Lord Browne-Wilkinson's comments in *CIBC Mortgages plc v. Pitt* [1994] 1 A.C. 200; (1994) 110 L.Q.R. 238 at p. 249 (Sir Anthony Mason); *cf.* (1995) 9 *Trust Law International* 35 at p. 37 (Sir Peter Millett).

[25] See Keeton and Sheridan's *Equity* (3rd ed.), pp. 255 *et seq.* and 280–282.

[26] *Langton v. Langton* [1995] 2 F.L.R. 890 (set aside only if undue influence or equitable fraud); (1996) 26 Fam. Law 87 (S. Cretney); [1996] Conv. 308 (D. Capper).

[27] *Alec Lobb (Garages) Ltd v. Total Oil G.B. Ltd* [1985] 1 W.L.R. 173; *Boustany v. Piggott* (1995) 69 P. & C.R. 298; (1993) 109 L.Q.R. 530 (J. Cartwright); [1996] Conv. 454 (M. Pawlowski)

[28] *Fry v. Lane* (1888) 40 Ch.D. 312. The list is not exhaustive; *Cresswell v. Potter* [1978] 1 W.L.R. 255.

[29] See *Watkin v. Watson-Smith, The Times,* July 3, 1986 (old age with diminution of capacity and judgment, together with a desire for a quick sale, satisfied the requirement). See also *Mountford v. Scott* [1975] Ch. 259. The modern equivalent of "poor and ignorant" is a member of the lower income group or a "less highly educated" person; *Cresswell v. Potter, supra,* at p. 257, *Credit Lyonnais Bank Nederland NV v. Burch* [1997] 1 All E.R. 144.

[30] This requirement is not satisfied where, unknown to the purchaser, the vendor is of unsound mind; *Hart v. O'Connor* [1985] A.C. 1000; [1986] Conv. 178 (A. Hudson).

there was a lack of independent legal advice.[31] A similar principle applies in the case of unconscionable bargains with reversioners or "expectant heirs."[32] The Court of Appeal has recently stated that the doctrine needs careful confinement if it is not itself to become an instrument of oppression.[33] It was held that a bank guarantee could not be set aside on the basis of illiteracy or unfamiliarity with English in the absence of substantial unfairness in the transaction itself, otherwise banks would not lend to those in a weak bargaining position. An example of substantial unfairness readily justifying the setting aside of a transaction was where a junior employee mortgaged her home to secure an unlimited guarantee of her employer's debts to a bank without receiving independent legal advice.[34] It seems that the unconscionable bargain cases should now be treated as cases where a presumption of undue influence arises from the facts.[35]

There are also at the present time other types of situation which call for relief. Oppressive hire purchase contracts and other credit arrangements are controlled by legislation,[36] and statutory protection is now given to unfair contractual terms, especially in the field of exemption clauses, by the Unfair Contract Terms Act 1977.[37] Relief has long been given against oppressive provisions in mortgages,[38] and a similar general principle is evident in the protection of the weak against the strong in the context of relief against forfeiture, in the development of the principles of restraint of trade, and in certain other contexts.[39] The view of the House of Lords is that there is no need to erect a general principle of relief against inequality of bargaining power. Parliament has undertaken this essentially legislative task, and the courts should not formulate further restrictions.[40]

C. Loss of the Right to Rescind

Formerly a contract entered into in reliance upon an innocent misrepresentation could not be rescinded after execution of the

---

[31] See *Butlin-Sanders v. Butlin* (1985) 15 Fam. Law 126, where the claim was in any event barred by laches and acquiescence.

[32] Mere undervalue is not sufficient. See L.P.A. 1925, s.174(1).

[33] *Barclays Bank plc v. Schwartz, The Times*, August 2, 1995.

[34] *Credit Lyonnais Bank Nederland NV v. Burch* [1997] 1 All E.R. 144 (decided on the basis of undue influence) however.

[35] *Langton v. Langton, supra.*

[36] Consumer Credit Act 1974. See *Woodstead Finance Ltd v. Petrou, The Times*, January 23, 1986.

[37] See also Unfair Terms in Consumer Contracts Regulations 1994 (S.I. 1994 No. 3159).

[38] A modern example is *Cityland and Property (Holdings) Ltd v. Dabrah* [1968] Ch. 166; *cf. Multiservice Bookbinding Ltd v. Marden* [1979] Ch. 84.

[39] *e.g.* salvage agreements; *The Port Caledonia and The Anna* [1903] P. 184.

[40] *National Westminster Bank plc v. Morgan* [1985] A.C. 686, disapproving wider statements in *Lloyds Bank Ltd v. Bundy* [1975] Q.B. 326.

contract by the transfer of property under it. This rule was abrogated by the Misrepresentation Act 1967, s.1. However, the court has a discretion under section 2(2) to award damages in lieu of rescission in any case of innocent misrepresentation if it would be equitable to do so.[41] This discretion is more likely to be exercised where the contract has been executed than where it remains executory.

More generally, the right to rescind may be lost in any of three ways:

i. Affirmation. Where the party entitled to rescind affirms the contract, for example by taking a benefit under it, with knowledge of the facts giving rise to the right to rescind and of his legal rights,[42] he will be taken to have waived that right.[43] Affirmation may be shown by words or acts, or may be indicated by lapse of time, the remedy being subject to the doctrine of laches.[44]

ii. *Restitutio in Integrum* not Possible. A contract will cease to be capable of rescission if the parties can no longer be restored to their original position.[45] Any money paid or other property transferred under the contract must be restored. But a precise restoration is not required, particularly in cases involving fraud. Equity is concerned to restore the parties, and especially the defendant, to their former positions so far as practically possible.[46] This might be achieved by, for example, ordering an account of profits and making allowances for deterioration of the property,[47] or by ordering fair compensation in equity where it is not possible to restore the

---

[41] (1967) 30 M.L.R. 369 (G. Treitel and P. Atiyah).

[42] *Peyman v. Lanjani* [1985] Ch. 457; [1985] Conv. 408 (L. Anderson). (Mere knowledge of facts not enough. Plaintiff can rely on ignorance of law unless estopped from denying affirmation by unequivocal act showing intention to proceed with the contract coupled with detriment to defendant; or unless plaintiff's solicitor aware of right to rescind); *Stevens & Cutting Ltd v. Anderson* [1990] 1 E.G.L.R. 95; *cf. Goldsworthy v. Brickell* [1987] Ch. 378.

[43] *Clough v. London and North Western Rail Co.* (1871) L.R. 7 Ex.Ch. 26.

[44] *Life Association of Scotland v. Siddal* (1861) 3 De G.F. & J. 58; *Alec Lobb (Garages) Ltd v. Total Oil G.B. Ltd, supra.* In the case of company shares it seems that delay is viewed more strictly; *Re Scottish Petroleum Co.* (1883) 23 Ch.D. 434. See also *Leaf v. International Galleries* [1950] 2 K.B. 86. For the application of the Limitation Act 1980, s.32(1)(c), see *Peco Arts Inc. v. Hazlitt Gallery Ltd* [1983] 1 W.L.R. 1315.

[45] *Thorpe v. Fasey* [1949] Ch. 649; *Erlanger v. New Sombrero Phosphate Co.* (1873) 3 App.Cas. 1218.

[46] *Spence v. Crawford* [1939] 3 All E.R. 271; *Newbigging v. Adam* (1886) 34 Ch.D. 582. Where a principal rescinds a contract with a third party, there is no obligation to return a bribe paid by the third party to the agent and recovered by the principal, as it is not money paid under the contract; *Logicrose Ltd v. Southend United Football Club Ltd* [1988] 1 W.L.R. 1256.

[47] *Erlanger v. New Sombrero Phosphate Co., supra.* See also *O'Sullivan v. Management Agency and Music Ltd* [1985] Q.B. 428 (contracts between manager and entertainer rescinded for undue influence; *restitutio* principle not applied with full rigour in cases of breach of fiduciary relationship; practical justice achieved by ordering account of profits, giving credit for defendant's labour and skill).

property nor (because its value has since been lost) to account for profits.[48]

In *Cheese v. Thomas*[49] the plaintiff, aged 86, and the defendant, his great nephew, agreed to buy a house for £83,000 in the defendant's name, where the plaintiff would reside for life, after which it would belong to the defendant. The plaintiff contributed £43,000 and the defendant raised the balance on mortgage. When the mortgage payments fell into arrears, the plaintiff sought to set aside the transaction and to recover £43,000. The relationship of the parties was one of confidence, giving rise to a presumption of undue influence, but there was no evidence of impropriety. The lower court ordered a sale and division of the proceeds in the proportions of 43:40. Owing to the property slump, the sale realised only £55,000. The Court of Appeal held that the plaintiff was entitled only to a proportionate share, and not £43,000. Justice required each party to be restored to his original position so far as possible; it would be harsh to make the defendant stand all the loss.

iii. Third Party Acquiring Rights. The right to rescind is lost if an innocent third party acquires an interest under the contract for value before the plaintiff seeks to set it aside.[50] There is no bar to rescission if the third party is a volunteer, such as the defendant's trustee in bankruptcy.[51]

2. RECTIFICATION

A. Nature of the Remedy[52]

Rectification is a discretionary equitable remedy whereby an instrument[53] which does not accord with the intentions of the parties to it may be corrected. It operates as an exception to the "parol evidence rule," whereby oral evidence is not admissible to alter a

---

[48] *Mahoney v. Purnell* [1996] 3 All E.R. 61 (sale of shares in company now in liquidation); (1997) 113 L.Q.R. 8 (J. Heydon).

[49] [1994] 1 W.L.R. 129; (1994) 144 N.L.J. 264 (J. Martin); (1994) 53 C.L.J. 232 (M. Dixon); (1994) 110 L.Q.R. 173 (M. Chen-Wishart), considering change of position a preferable basis.

[50] *Oakes v. Turquand* (1867) L.R. 2 H.L. 325.

[51] *Re Eastgate* [1905] 1 K.B. 465.

[52] See Goff and Jones, pp. 222–228.

[53] Distinguish cancellation of an instrument that is void or voidable on some ground, *e.g.* forgery: *Peake v. Highfield* (1826) 1 Russ. 559. For the effect of an unexecuted alteration to a deed, see *Co-operative Bank plc v. Tipper* [1996] 4 All E.R. 366.

written instrument. It must be emphasised that the court does not rectify a mistake in the contract itself, but only a mistake in the instrument recording the contract. It must be very clearly shown that the parties had come to a genuine agreement and that the instrument had failed to record it. Thus where both a written agreement to sell land and the ensuing conveyance incorrectly described the land which it had been agreed to sell, it was possible to obtain rectification on proof of the real oral agreement.[54] Rectification may also occur where there are grounds for rescission and the court grants rescission on terms which include an option to the defendant to submit to rescission or rectification.[55]

It is no objection that the rectification may have the effect of saving tax[56]; nor that the mistake arose through the negligence of the plaintiff or his legal advisers[57]; nor that one of the parties has since died.[58]

When rectification is ordered, a copy of the order may be indorsed on the instrument. There is no need to execute a new document.[59] Rectification is retrospective, and affects steps taken by the parties in the meantime.[60] But the instrument remains binding in its uncorrected form until rectification is actually ordered. The plaintiff may obtain rectification and specific performance in the same action.[61]

Rectification must be distinguished from the court's power to correct an obvious error as a matter of construction. If an instrument contains a manifest mistake in its drafting, neither common law nor equity is prevented from discerning the fact and substituting the words that were intended to be there. But this is a limited jurisdiction for it applies only when the mistake is obvious from the instrument itself and what should have been written is obvious too.[62] Extrinsic evidence is not admissible. This jurisdiction is one based on the duty of the court to construe documents correctly and is not a jurisdiction to rectify as such.

---

[54] *Craddock Bros. v. Hunt* [1923] 2 Ch. 136.

[55] See the terms imposed in *Solle v. Butcher* [1950] 1 K.B. 671 and *Grist v. Bailey* [1967] Ch. 532. But where the mistake is unilateral, see *post*, p. 842.

[56] *Re Colebrook's Conveyance* [1972] 1 W.L.R. 1397; *Re Slocock's W.T.* [1979] 1 All E.R. 358; *Lake v. Lake* [1989] S.T.C. 865; *Seymour v. Seymour, The Times*, February 16, 1989.

[57] *Weeds v. Blaney* (1977) 247 E.G. 211 (discussing also the position as to costs); *Central & Metropolitan Estates Ltd v. Compusave* (1983) 266 E.G. 900 (rectification ordered on terms in such a case); *Boots The Chemist Ltd v. Street* (1983) 268 E.G. 817.

[58] *Johnson v. Bragge* [1901] 1 Ch. 28.

[59] *White v. White* (1872) L.R. 15 Eq. 247.

[60] *Malmesbury v. Malmesbury* (1862) 31 Beav. 407. See also *Freer v. Unwins Ltd* [1976] Ch. 288, contrasting rectification under the Land Registration Act 1925.

[61] *Craddock Bros. v. Hunt* [1923] 2 Ch. 136.

[62] *Re Bacharach's W.T.* [1959] Ch. 245; *Re Doland* [1970] Ch. 267; *Schnieder v. Mills* [1993] 3 All E.R. 377.

B. The Nature of the Mistake

i. Common Mistake. The general rule is that rectification requires a mistake common to both parties, whereby the instrument records the agreement in a manner contrary to the intention of both.[63] It must be shown that there was some prior agreement, although not necessarily an enforceable contract, whereby the parties expressed a common intention regarding the provisions in question.[64] It must also be shown that the common intention continued until the execution of the instrument. Rectification is not possible where the instrument departs from the prior agreement because the parties had agreed to vary the terms.[65] Next, it must be established that the instrument is not in accordance with the true agreement of the parties, and that, if rectified in the manner claimed, it will represent the agreement. But only the actual agreement of the parties is relevant, not what they would have agreed if they had not been under a misapprehension. Thus in *Frederick E. Rose (London) Ltd v. William H. Pim Jnr. & Co. Ltd*,[66] rectification was not possible where the parties agreed to buy and sell horsebeans, and the written contract referred to horsebeans, but the parties mistakenly believed that horsebeans were the same as feveroles. The mistake was made when entering into the contract in the first place. The crux of the remedy is proof of what the parties actually had decided at the time of reaching their agreement and not what they, or one of them, had thought at a later date, or what they might have thought if they had considered the matter in greater detail or in the light of more information than that available to them. In other words, the remedy exists to correct, but not to improve, an instrument.

The mistake is usually one of fact, but relief may be possible where the mistake is of law. In *Re Butlin's Settlement Trust*,[67] rectification was ordered where the settlor and his solicitor were mistaken as to the effect of a clause giving power to the trustees to decide by a majority. Rectification has been granted where the

---

[63] *Murray v. Parker* (1854) 19 Beav. 305. See also *Fowler v. Fowler* (1859) 4 De G. & J. 250.

[64] *Joscelyne v. Nissen* [1970] 2 Q.B. 86, (1970) 86 L.Q.R. 303 (P.V.B.), (1971) 87 L.Q.R. 532 (L. Bromley), arguing that an outward expression of accord is not *per se* a requirement. See also *Shipley U.D.C. v. Bradford Corpn.* [1936] Ch. 375; *Crane v. Hegeman-Harris Co. Inc.* [1939] 1 All E.R. 662, [1939] 3 All E.R. 68, [1971] 1 W.L.R. 1390n.; *C.H. Pearce & Sons Ltd v. Stonechester Ltd, The Times*, November 17, 1983 (a plaintiff who pleads two claims for rectification in the alternative based on inconsistent assertions of the parties' common intentions demonstrates at the outset that there was no certain intention which would found such a claim).

[65] *Breadalbane v. Chandos* (1837) 2 My. & Cr. 711.

[66] [1953] 2 Q.B. 450, described as a "hard case" in Goff and Jones, p. 224. See also *London Regional Transport v. Wimpey Group Services Ltd* (1987) 53 P. & C.R. 356.

[67] [1976] Ch. 251.

parties used the then ineffective phrase "free of tax" to carry out their agreement to pay such sum as after deduction of tax would leave the sum in question.[68] It is no bar to rectification that the parties are in agreement and there is thus no dispute, but there must be an issue capable of being contested between the parties.[69] The remedy was accordingly refused in *Whiteside v. Whiteside*[70] as the parties had already corrected the error by executing a supplemental deed.

ii. Unilateral Mistake. Where one party incorrectly records a term of the agreement, but it is bona fide accepted as it is written by the other party, the mistake is unilateral and there is no ground for rectification. Thus, the rent may be incorrectly stated, or the lessor's obligations, or the land or buildings incorrectly described. The party making the mistake can only obtain rectification if he can show that the mistake is due to the fraud[71] of the other party, or that the other party was aware of the mistake.

In *Riverlate Properties Ltd v. Paul*,[72] the plaintiffs, who were the landlords of property in London, intended to provide in the lease that the defendant should be liable to contribute one half of the landlord's expenditure on matters contained in clauses 6(a), (b), (c). By mistake, the lease referred to 6(b), (c), (d). The defendant and her solicitors were unaware of the mistake. The lease stood, as signed.

On the other hand, in *A. Roberts and Co. Ltd v. Leicestershire County Council*,[73] the plaintiffs had undertaken to build a school for the defendants. The agreement provided that the school should be completed within 18 months, but the officers of the Council altered the period to 30 months in the draft contract, not drawing the company's attention to the alteration. The company signed the contract without noticing the change, and one of the defendant's officials was aware of the mistake. Rectification was ordered.

---

[68] *Burroughes v. Abbott* [1922] 1 Ch. 86; *Jervis v. Howle & Talke Colliery Co. Ltd* [1937] Ch. 67; *Seymour v. Seymour, The Times*, February 16, 1989; *Lake v. Lake* [1989] S.T.C. 865.

[69] *Seymour v. Seymour, supra; Lake v. Lake, supra*; All E.R.Rev. 1989, p. 320 (J. Tiley); *Racal Group Services Ltd v. Ashmore* [1995] S.T.C. 1151.

[70] [1950] Ch. 65. The plaintiff's purpose in seeking the order was to improve his tax position. Such a motive is immaterial if the requirements of rectification are satisfied.

[71] Constructive fraud suffices. See *Lovesy v. Smith* (1880) 15 Ch.D. 655.

[72] [1975] Ch. 133; (1974) 90 L.Q.R. 439; (1975) 53 Can.Bar.Rev. 339 (S. Waddams); *Taylor v. Johnson* [1982–1983] 151 C.L.R. 422; [1985] Conv. 81 (H. Wilkinson); *Agip S.p.A. v. Navigazione Alta Italia S.p.A.* [1984] 1 Lloyd's Rep. 353.

[73] [1961] Ch. 555. See Goff and Jones, p. 225, expressing the view that the principle is akin to estoppel.

The Court of Appeal has held[74] that, in order for the *Roberts* doctrine to apply, it must be shown first that one party, A, erroneously believed[75] that the document sought to be rectified contained a particular provision; secondly, that the other party, B, was aware of the mistake and that it was due to an error on the part of A; thirdly, that B had omitted to draw the mistake to the notice of A; fourthly, that the mistake must be one calculated to benefit B.[76] Although it need not amount to sharp practice, the conduct of B must be such as to make it inequitable that he should be allowed to object to rectification. The graver the character of the conduct involved, the heavier the burden of proof, but the conduct must be such as to affect the conscience of the party who had suppressed the fact that he had recognised the presence of a mistake. Thus, rectification was ordered where a rent review clause in a lease failed to provide machinery for determining the rent in default of agreement. The landlord realised the omission only when the time for review arrived, whereas the tenant had been aware of the mistake at all times. An arbitration clause was ordered to be inserted into the lease, according to the original mutual intention of the parties. Similarly where the defendant "put up a smokescreen" during negotiations to divert the plaintiff from discovering its mistake.[77] In such a case it suffices that the defendant merely suspected the plaintiff's mistake, without proof of actual knowledge of it.

It was at one time thought that the court could give the defendant a choice of submitting to rescission or rectification, even though the mistake was unilateral and the court was unable to satisfy itself that the defendant was aware of the mistake. A practice developed of imposing such an option,[78] but this was firmly disapproved by the Court of Appeal in *Riverlate Properties Ltd v. Paul.*[79] Unilateral mistake can only give rise to rectification in cases of fraud or upon the principle of *A. Roberts and Co. Ltd v. Leicestershire County*

[74] *Bates (Thomas) & Son Ltd v. Wyndham's (Lingerie) Ltd* [1981] 1 W.L.R. 505; *Kemp v. Neptune Concrete Ltd* (1989) 57 P. & C.R. 369. See also *Central & Metropolitan Estates Ltd v. Compusave* (1983) 266 E.G. 900 (20 year lease rectified to include rent review clause. Negotiations contemplated such a provision, but mistakenly omitted from lease. Tenant aware of landlord's mistake. Rectification on terms that tenant should have opportunity to surrender lease after first review).
[75] The belief need not have been induced by any misrepresentation by the other party; *Commission for the New Towns v. Cooper (Great Britain) Ltd* [1995] Ch. 259.
[76] Or, *per* Eveleigh L.J., be detrimental to A.
[77] *Commission for the New Towns v. Cooper (Great Britain) Ltd, supra.*
[78] See *Paget v. Marshall* (1882) 28 Ch.D. 255.
[79] [1975] Ch. 133 at p. 145; in the absence of fraud or sharp practice, mere unilateral mistake was not a ground for rescission "either with or without the option to the [defendant] to accept rectification to cure the [plaintiff's] mistake." *Solle v. Butcher* [1950] 1 K.B. 671, *ante,* p. 820, was there distinguished as being a case of common mistake. Rectification may, however, be ordered on terms. See *Central & Metropolitan Estates Ltd v. Compusave, supra,* n. 74.

Council,[80] where rectification was particularly appropriate, for the school had been built at the time of the action; and if the contract had been rescinded or held void at law, the plaintiff would have been forced to sue in quasi-contract.

Where the transaction is unilateral, a unilateral mistake is sufficient. This is discussed below.

C. Proof of the Mistake

The burden of proof on the party seeking rectification is a heavy one. According to older authority, the plaintiff must establish the mistake with a "high degree of conviction."[81] A more recent description is "convincing proof."[82] Oral evidence is admissible to prove the agreement, and there is no need to show anything in the nature of error on the face of the instrument. It is no objection that the transaction is one required by statute to be evidenced in writing; it suffices that the rectified instrument will comply with the statute.[83]

In the case of a settlement, the settlor's evidence alone,[84] or even a mere perusal of the document[85] may suffice to establish the mistake, but the court is slow to act without the support of other evidence such as any written instructions given by the settlor prior to the execution of the settlement. In the case of a will (discussed below) extrinsic evidence of the testator's intentions is admissible but, although the standard of proof is the balance of probabilities, convincing proof is needed to rectify a formally executed will.[86]

D. Instruments which may be Rectified

The remedy is widely available, being applicable to leases and other conveyances of land,[87] insurance policies,[88] bills of exchange[89] and many other instruments; but not the articles of a company.[90]

---

[80] [1961] Ch. 555.
[81] *Crane v. Hegeman-Harris Co. Inc.* [1939] 4 All E.R. 68 at 71.
[82] *Joscelyne v. Nissen* [1970] 2 Q.B. 86 at 98. See also *Bates (Thomas) and Son Ltd v. Wyndham's (Lingerie) Ltd* [1981] 1 W.L.R. 505 at 514; *Brimican Investments Ltd v. Blue Circle Heating Ltd* [1995] E.G.C.S. 18; *Racal Group Services Ltd v. Ashmore* [1995] S.T.C. 1151.
[83] *Craddock Bros. v. Hunt* [1923] 2 Ch. 136.
[84] *Hanley v. Pearson* (1870) 13 Ch.D. 545.
[85] *Banks v. Ripley* [1940] Ch. 719.
[86] *Re Segelman* [1996] Ch. 171; [1996] Conv. 379 (E. Histed).
[87] *Bates (Thomas) and Son Ltd v. Wyndhams (Lingerie) Ltd* [1981] 1 W.L.R. 505.
[88] *Collett v. Morrison* (1851) 9 Hare 162.
[89] *Druiff v. Lord Parker* (1868) L.R. 5 Eq. 131.
[90] *Scott v. Frank F. Scott (London) Ltd* [1940] Ch. 794.

Rectification can also be obtained of a voluntary deed, such as a settlement, if the court is satisfied on the evidence that the donor's real intent at the time of entering into it was not accurately reflected in the instrument.[91] It is not necessary to show that the intent of the trustees was inaccurately reflected.[92] Clearly the requirement of a common mistake has no application to unilateral transactions.[93] Rectification of a settlement may be ordered not only at the instance of the settlor but also at the instance of a volunteer beneficiary, although this will not be done during the settlor's lifetime without his agreement.[94]

Formerly it was not possible to rectify a will except in the case of fraud,[95] although the court could, as a matter of construction, correct a manifest error in drafting.[96] It is now provided by section 20 of the Administration of Justice Act 1982[97] that a will may be rectified if the court is satisfied that it fails to carry out the testator's intentions in consequence of a clerical error or a failure to understand his instructions,[98] as where a solicitor failed to delete a clause for which the testator had not given instructions and which restricted the class of beneficiaries intended by the testator.[99] This statutory power does not permit rectification where the testator himself has misunderstood the legal effect of the wording used.[1]

E. Defences

The remedy of rectification, which, like other equitable remedies, is discretionary, will not be granted where a bona fide purchaser for value without notice has acquired an interest under the instrument.[2] Laches or acquiescence will bar the claim[3]; similarly if the contract

---

[91] *Lackersteen v. Lackersteen* (1864) 30 L.J. Ch. 5; *Bonhote v. Henderson* [1895] 1 Ch. 742; [1895] 2 Ch. 202 (where rectification was refused). Such a deed may be set aside for mistake if rectification would not be appropriate; *Gibbon v. Mitchell* [1990] 1 W.L.R. 1304.

[92] *Re Butlin's Settlement* [1976] Ch. 251 at p. 262.

[93] *Wright v. Goff* (1856) 22 Beav. 207.

[94] *Thompson v. Whitmore* (1860) 1 J. & H. 268; *Lister v. Hodgson* (1867) L.R. 4 Eq. 30.

[95] *Collins v. Elstone* [1893] P. 1.

[96] *Re Bacharach's W.T.* [1959] Ch. 245; *Re Doland* [1970] Ch. 267; *ante*, p. 840.

[97] For time limits and the position of the personal representatives, see s.20(2), (3). See generally (1983) 46 M.L.R. 191 at 201 (A. Borkowski and K. Stanton).

[98] See *Wordingham v. Royal Exchange Trust Co. Ltd* [1992] Ch. 412.

[99] *Re Segelman* [1996] Ch. 171.

[1] See *Collins v. Elstone* [1893] P. 1.

[2] *Smith v. Jones* [1954] 1 W.L.R. 1089; *Lyme Valley Squash Club Ltd v. Newcastle under Lyme Borough Council* [1985] 2 All E.R. 405. In the case of registered land, the right to rectify may be asserted against the purchaser as an overriding interest under s.70(1)(g) of the Land Registration Act 1925: *Blacklocks v. J.B. Developments (Godalming) Ltd* [1982] Ch. 183. The benefit of the right to rectify in cases concerning land will pass with the land; *Boots The Chemist Ltd v. Street* (1983) 268 E.G. 817; *Berkeley Leisure Group Ltd v. Williamson* [1996] E.G.C.S. 15; L.P.A. 1925, s.63.

[3] *Beale v. Kyte* [1907] 1 Ch. 564.

is no longer capable of performance,[4] or has been fully performed under a judgment of the court.[5] In the case of a voluntary settlement, it has been held that the court may decline to rectify if a trustee, having taken office in ignorance of the mistake, has a reasonable objection to the rectification.[6]

---

[4] *Borrowman v. Rossell* (1864) 16 C.B.(N.S.) 58.
[5] *Caird v. Moss* (1886) 33 Ch.D. 22.
[6] *Re Butlin's S.T.* [1976] Ch. 251 (where rectification was granted).

PART V

**MISCELLANEOUS EQUITABLE DOCTRINES AND
EQUITIES**

CHAPTER 27

EQUITABLE DOCTRINES OF CONVERSION, ELECTION, SATISFACTION AND PERFORMANCE

1. The Doctrine of Conversion 849
   A. Basis of the Doctrine 849
   B. Partial Abolition of the Doctrine 850
   C. Contracts for Sale and Options 850
2. Election 852
   A. Introduction 852
   B. Requirements for Election 853
      i. The Intent to Dispose of Property 853
      ii. The Property of Another that is Disposed of 854
      (a) Property Must be Alienable 854
      (b) Void Disposition 855
      (c) Appointment to Object with Proviso in favour of Non-Object 855

      (d) A's Title Independent of Instrument Raising Question of Election 855
      iii. The Gift of Property to the Person Electing 857
   C. Nature of Election and Conclusion 858
3. Satisfaction 859
   A. General 859
   B. Satisfaction of Debts by Legacies 859
   C. Satisfaction of Portion Debts by Legacies. The Rule Against Double Portions 860
   D. Ademption of Legacies by Portions ... 862
4. Performance 863
   A. Covenants to Purchase and Settle Land 863
   B. Covenants to leave Money on Death . 864

1. THE DOCTRINE OF CONVERSION

A. Basis of the Doctrine

The basis of the doctrine is the maximum "Equity looks on that as done which ought to be done." The classic example was the trust for sale of land, where equity regarded the land as money from the date the instrument creating the trust took effect.[1] Conversely, in the case of a trust of money to buy land, equity regarded the money as land from the outset. The significance of the doctrine lay in its effect on the devolution of the property on the death of its beneficial owner. Land held on trust for sale devolved as personalty even though no sale had yet occurred, while money (or other personalty) held on trust to buy land devolved as realty. This was particularly

---

[1] The leading case was *Fletcher v. Ashburner* (1779) 1 Bro.C.C. 497.

849

important before 1926, when different rules applied to the devolution of realty and personalty on intestacy.

B. Partial Abolition of the Doctrine

The rationale of the doctrine was that the devolution of beneficial interests should not be affected by any failure or delay by the trustees in carrying out their duty. Nevertheless, it had an air of artificiality and was not likely to be understood by non-lawyers. The basis of the doctrine, so far as it applied to trusts for sale imposed by statute (primarily in cases of co-ownership and intestacy) has gone, now that the trust for sale in those cases has been replaced by the new "trust of land", where the trustees have a power of sale, but no duty to sell. This is the effect of the Trusts of Land and Appointment of Trustees Act 1996, following the recommendations of the Law Commission.[2] Although a trust for sale may still be expressly created, the 1996 Act abolishes the doctrine of conversion in relation to trusts for sale. Section 3(1) provides as follows: "Where land is held by trustees subject to a trust for sale, the land is not to be regarded as personal property; and where personal property is subject to a trust for sale in order that the trustees may acquire land, the personal property is not to be regarded as land." This applies to trusts for sale arising before or after the commencement of the 1996 Act, save that the abolition of the doctrine does not affect trusts created by will if the testator died before the commencement.[3] Subject to the latter point, all interests under trusts of land, whenever created, are now treated as interests in land until any sale actually occurs.

The doctrine was not confined to trusts for sale, but applied also to certain contracts and options. This aspect of the doctrine, which is unaffected by the abolition, will now be briefly considered.

C. Contracts for Sale and Options

Conversion applies to specifically enforceable contracts for the sale of land. The vendor is under an obligation to convey, which is specifically enforceable. Again, equity looks on that as done which ought to be done, and regards the purchaser as the owner in equity.[4] He becomes owner at law when the conveyance is executed. If he should die between contract and completion, the property passes to those entitled to his realty, subject to the obligation to pay the

---

[2] Law Com. No. 181 (1989), *Trusts of Land*.
[3] s.3(2), (3).
[4] The vendor is said to be a constructive trustee for the purchasers; *ante*, p. 312.

balance of the purchase price.[5] Equity also regards the land in the vendor's hands as personalty; and if he should die before completion, those entitled to his personalty will receive the proceeds of sale.

The doctrine applies also to the exercise of an option under the unsatisfactory rule in *Lawes v. Bennett*.[6] If A grants B a lease of Blackacre containing an option to purchase the freehold and then dies, the rent must clearly go the the devisee of A's freehold pending the exercise of the option.[7] But the devisee does not take the purchase money on the exercise of the option, because under an unnecessary extension of the doctrine of conversion, the land is treated as personalty from the exercise of the option, even if it became exercisable only after A's death.[8] Thus A's residuary legatee is entitled to the money. Of course, there is no conversion if the option is never exercised.[9]

The rule in *Lawes v. Bennett*[10] is excluded where the will indicates that the testator's *entire* interest in the land is to pass to the devisee. Similarly where the will is made after or contemporaneously with the grant of the option, even though the will does not refer to the option.[11]

The rule has even been applied to an option to purchase personalty (shares), so that the residuary beneficiary was entitled to the purchase money instead of the specific legatee.[12]

More recently, in *Re Sweeting (deceased)*,[13] the doctrine of conversion was applied to a conditional contract, where the conditions were fulfilled after the testator's death. There the testator, having specifically devised a yard in his will of 1978, exchanged contracts for the sale of the yard three weeks before his death. The contract was conditional upon certain events, and was completed after his death. In fact the fulfilment of the conditions was within the testator's control at his death, but even if that were not so, the doctrine of conversion would still have applied. Although the doctrine as it related to options had been criticised, its application to conditional contracts was considered more justifiable because the contract

---

[5] A.E.A. 1925, s.35 (subject to any contrary intention).
[6] (1785) 1 Cox 167.
[7] *Townley v. Bedwell* (1808) 14 Ves.Jr. 591.
[8] *Re Isaacs* [1894] 3 Ch. 506.
[9] *Re Marlay* [1915] 2 Ch. 264. The *grant* of the option causes no conversion.
[10] (1785) 1 Cox 167.
[11] *Re Calow* [1928] Ch. 710; *Re Pyle* [1895] 1 Ch. 724.
[12] *Re Carrington* [1932] 1 Ch. 1; criticised (1933) 49 L.Q.R. 173 (H. Hanbury). The court seems to have confused the doctrine of conversion with that of ademption.
[13] [1988] 1 All E.R. 1016; criticised All E.R. Rev. 1988, p. 292 (C. Sherrin) as a lost opportunity to limit the doctrine.

existed at the death, unlike in the options cases. Thus the proceeds went to the residuary legatee.

2. Election

A. Introduction

The doctrine of election derives from the principle that a person may not take a benefit and reject an associated burden or, to put it in another way, a person may not choose between parts of a single transaction.[14] If T attempts to give property over which A has rights to B absolutely, and as part of the same transaction gives other property to A, A cannot take the latter without giving effect to the former.

The principle of election has become associated more with cases where a testator has made a mistake than where he has made an eccentric or ineffective disposition. It is established that election leads to compensation not to forfeiture, that an actual intent to cause an election need not be shown, and that oral evidence is not admissible to explain the disposition. A supportable basis for the doctrine in its developed form is, as will be apparent, hard to find.

A good modern statement of the doctrine is given by Jenkins L.J.[15] "The essentials of election are that there should be an intention on the part of the testator or testatrix to dispose of certain property; secondly, that the property should not in fact be the testator's or testatrix's own property; and, thirdly, that a benefit should be given by the will to the true owner of the property." This statement of the doctrine will need careful consideration, but first an example may be helpful. (The letters in the example will be used throughout the section). A is owner of Blackacre. T in his will devised Blackacre to B and bequeaths £10,000 to A. A cannot, of course, be compelled to transfer Blackacre to B. A is put to his election. This means that he can choose to take with the will or against the will. If A takes with the will, he will release Blackacre to B and get his £10,000. If A takes against the will, he will retain Blackacre but the £10,000 will be subject to an equity in B to claim compensation out of it to the extent of the value of Blackacre. If Blackacre is worth £12,000 at T's death, B will take the £10,000, but A is not obliged to find the extra £2,000 from his own money. If Blackacre is worth £6,000, B will take that much and A £4,000.

---

[14] For modern appearances of this principle, see *Halsall v. Brizell* [1957] Ch. 169; *Ives (E.R.) Investments Ltd v. High* [1967] 2 Q.B. 379; *Tito v. Waddell (No. 2)* [1977] Ch. 106 at pp. 289–311.

[15] *Re Edwards* [1958] Ch. 168 at p. 175. See also *Re Mengel* [1962] Ch. 791 at p. 797 (*per* Buckley J.); *Re Gordon's Will Trusts* [1978] Ch. 145 at p. 153 (*per* Buckley L.J.). The doctrine applies to deeds as well as to wills.

It is essential that the legacy to A should not have been *expressed* to be conditional upon A releasing Blackacre to B. If a condition attached to a legacy is not complied with, the legatee loses the legacy. If A does not comply with the condition, he gets nothing, B gets nothing, and the residuary beneficiary takes the legacy.

B. Requirements for Election

i. The Intent to Dispose of Property. Jenkins L.J., in the passage already quoted, talks of the intent as being to "dispose of certain property"; not to "dispose of another's property." This distinction goes to the heart of the matter. The courts do not examine the state of a testator's knowledge. The question is—does the will purport to dispose of property? Was that property the testator's to dispose of? That the testator did or did not realise that the property was or was not his to dispose of is irrelevant. This was clearly put by Lord O'Hagan[16]: "But what is the intention that the Court must apprehend upon clear evidence? Not an intention on the part of the testatrix that there shall be an election. . . . A . . . testatrix does not generally know or understand anything about the doctrine of election. . . . The intention that must be clearly demonstrated in evidence to the Court, is an intention to do the particular thing—to give the property which the party has not a right to give, and to give a benefit to a person who has an interest in the property. Those two intentions being ascertained upon clear evidence, the law draws the conclusion. It is a conclusion of equity, . . . and there is an end of the matter."

The first requirement is therefore that it should appear from the will that the testator was purporting to dispose of property which was not his to dispose of. But if this does so appear, then the requirement is satisfied though the testator may very well not have understood the position.[17]

Two considerations limit this strictness of construction, however. First, a disposition will not be construed as including another's property if it has a sensible effect when construed in some other way. The will of a testator who has a limited interest in property will only be construed as disposing of a larger interest in that property if the latter construction is the only reasonable one.[18] Secondly, a legacy which appears to dispose of another's property may have

---

[16] *Cooper v. Cooper* (1874) L.R. 7 H.L. 53 at pp. 74–75.
[17] See *Re Mengel's W.T.* [1962] Ch. 791, where the testator had overlooked his wife's rights under Danish law.
[18] *Parker v. Sowerby* (1854) 4 De G.M. & G. 321.

ceased to be operative by reason of an ademption. Thus no election will arise if T, having devised Blackacre to B and another property to A, subsequently sells Blackacre to A and dies, without changing his will; for the sale adeemed the legacy, which thereupon became inoperative.[19]

ii. The Property of Another that is Disposed of. A testamentary power of appointment is taken as an example, as many of the cases arise in that context.

T has power to appoint by will among the children of Z, the property to go to such children in default of appointment. T appoints half of the property to A, a child of Z, and the other half to B, a stranger. T also devises Greenacre to A. A will be put to his election. But the reason is not because T made an appointment of half of the property to A, but because A was one of the class entitled in default of appointment. Only A's share under the latter gift counts as A's prior property for the purpose of the doctrine.

(a) *Property Must be Alienable.* The property of A that T purports to dispose of must be alienable by A. If it is not alienable, A is not obliged to elect. He has no choice in the matter and election presupposes a choice. In such a case A takes his gift under the will without any obligation attaching to it. Thus, in *Re Lord Chesham*,[20] chattels were held upon trust to be enjoyed with settled land, of which A was tenant for life. T bequeathed the chattels to B, and his residuary estate to A. A was not put to his election, because he had no power to alienate the chattels.

An election does arise, however, where A has only a limited interest in the property which T has purported to dispose of absolutely. In *Re Dicey*,[21] T devised property to A, and purported to dispose of the entire interest in other property to B, which was in fact owned as to a half-share by A, and as to a quarter-share each by B and by C. The Court of Appeal held that A must elect and that, on an election to take with the will, must release his property to B so far as he was able; *i.e.* release his half-share to B.

---

[19] *Re Edwards* [1958] Ch. 168.

[20] (1886) 31 Ch.D. 466. But it is no objection that A's interest in the property was originally defeasible; see the cases on powers of appointment (where, of course, the default beneficiary's interest is no longer defeasible when the testator's will comes into operation, as, *ex hypothesi*, no valid appointment has been made). A similar rule as to alienability applies to T's gift to A, *post*, p. 857.

[21] [1957] Ch. 145. It is doubtful whether the doctrine applies to a purported disposition of property of which the testator was joint tenant, and which passes by survivorship to the other joint tenant (who also benefits from the will).

(b) *Void Disposition.* A more difficult problem arises if T's purported disposition of A's property to B is bad for a reason quite independent of it being A's property, for instance through the rule against perpetuities. It is tempting to argue that a disposition that is legally bad is non-existent for all purposes. However, the judges have varied in their views in the context of the rule against perpetuities. In *Re Oliver's Settlement*,[22] an infringement of the perpetuity rule was said to be "illegal," so that equity would not, through causing an election, help to effectuate it. This view was upheld by the Court of Appeal in *Re Nash*.[23] Nevertheless, Younger J. in *Re Ogilvie*[24] did not regard the matter as finally established. If A is put to his election, he is not asked to do more than *he* legally can; no perpetuity will attach to the manner in which A releases his property to B.

(c) *Appointment to Object with proviso in Favour of Non-Object.* If T, in making a valid appointment in A's favour, superadds some proviso in favour of B, (a non-object), there is no election. The proviso is simply ignored, and A takes the property validly appointed to him, together with any property to which he is entitled in default of appointment and any other property given him by T in his will.[25] The proviso is not treated as a purported gift of A's property but as non-existent.[26] But it is anomalous that this particular attempt to provide a benefit for B at A's expense should not put A to his election.

(d) *A's Title Independent of Instrument Raising Question of Election.* The property of A must be A's property independently of the will that raises the question of putting A to his election. The point was firmly taken in *Wollaston v. King*.[27]

Under a marriage settlement, T had a special power of appointment in favour of her children, who were also to take in default of appointment. By her will T appointed part of the fund to her son for life and the remainder to her daughters, A. The appointment included a general power of appointment given to the son. The appointments which the son made under it were void for perpetuity and consequently the property appointed by him was

---

[22] [1905] 1 Ch. 191.
[23] [1910] 1 Ch. 1.
[24] [1918] 1 Ch. 492 at p. 501, in a reserved judgment.
[25] *Carver v. Bowles* (1831) 2 R. & M. 301; *Churchill v. Churchill* (1867) L.R. 5 Eq. 44. *cf. Re Neave* [1938] Ch. 793.
[26] *Woolridge v. Woolridge* (1859) Johns. 63 at p. 69.
[27] (1869) L.R. 8 Eq. 165.

caught by the residuary appointment to the daughters, A. The daughters were also given other property by T's will.

James V.-C. held that the daughters were not put to their election between this other property and the windfall. They took the windfall not in *default* of appointment under the marriage settlement, but as the result of an appointment under T's will, and their rights accordingly arose *wholly* under this will. No property of theirs outside of this will had been disposed of. "The rule as to election is not to be applied as between one clause in a will and another clause in the same will."[28]

A different view was taken in *Re Macartney*.[29]

T purported to bequeath to B stock that T held as a trustee; the legacy of course failed. The beneficial interest in the stock was vested in a company, which was a subsidiary of a company the shares in which were held mainly by T. He bequeathed the shares in this latter company to his children, A, who in this way received the beneficial interest in the stock intended for B. No property previously vested in A was disposed of by T in his will. It was rather a case of T giving the same property to A and to B in the same instrument, but Neville J. nevertheless took the view that equity would intervene to subject the shares bequeathed to A to a charge under which B would be compensated for the loss of her legacy.

This result could be justified only if there existed in equity a wide principle of producing rough justice among beneficiaries, as indeed the judge realised when he placed reliance on the view that "A volunteer under a will cannot take the benefit and at the same time wilfully defeat the expressed intentions of the testator."[30] Logically this would mean that residuary beneficiaries or those taking on a partial intestacy would always have to compensate beneficiaries of specific gifts that failed. Further difficulties inherent in *Re Macartney*[31] include the fact that, contrary to the doctrine of election, A was given no choice in the matter: the decision was that A's shares were charged with compensation to B. This may have been because a transfer of the shares themselves to B would have been *ultra vires*

---

[28] (1869) L.R. 8 Eq. 165 at p. 174.
[29] [1918] 1 Ch. 300. A further criticism of this decision might be that Neville J. seemed to identify the shareholders with the company, a different legal entity.
[30] [1918] 1 Ch. 300 at p. 303.
[31] [1918] 1 Ch. 300.

the rules of the company, thus raising a further problem as to the alienability of the property.[32]

iii. The Gift of Property to the Person Electing.

The third requirement for election is that the testator should have given some property of his own to A. This can be neatly illustrated by a comparison of *Bristow v. Warde*[33] and *Whistler v. Webster*.[34] In the former case T, who had a power to appoint among children, A, appointed some of the property to them and some to strangers, B. It was held that A could set aside the appointment to B and take the whole property. Election did not arise even though A were entitled in default of appointment, as A received no other benefits under T's will. But in the latter case, on analogous facts, A were put to their election as they did receive other benefits under T's will.

It is essential that the property given to A is given beneficially and in such form as to be alienable; for the property has to be available to compensate B if A elects to take against the will.[35] The property need not be an absolute interest, but if it is a defeasible gift for instance, or a gift on protective trusts, so that it is not effectively alienable, no election will arise. A modern example is *Re Gordon's Will Trusts*.[36]

T and A owned the Old Rectory jointly, therefore A became absolutely entitled to it on T's death. T by her will purported to leave the Old Rectory to A and B in equal shares. T's will also gave A some furniture, a legacy of £1,000, and a life interest on protective trusts in half of the residuary estate. It was conceded that a case for election arose. A elected against the will by selling the Old Rectory and keeping the proceeds, but the furniture and the £1,000 legacy were insufficient to compensate B. The question arose as to whether A's interest under the protective trusts was subject to the doctrine of election, in which case his life interest would terminate, leaving no property from which to compensate B. The Court of Appeal held that the interest under the protective trusts was not subject to the doctrine of election, whose essential feature was compensation, not forfeiture. A's determinable life interest was inalienable, and "the doctrine does not require a beneficiary to surrender for the purpose of compensation an interest which would be destroyed by the very act of

---

[32] This requirement is discussed below.
[33] (1794) 2 Ves.Jr. 336. It would be otherwise if A was simply an object of a mere power of appointment, for such a person has no proprietary interest.
[34] (1794) 2 Ves.Jr. 367.
[35] *Re Vardon's Trusts* (1885) 31 Ch.D. 275; *ante*, p. 123. Presumably an interest under a discretionary trust created by T's will would not suffice. See (1977) 41 Conv.(N.S.) 188 at p. 196 (T. Watkin).
[36] [1978] Ch. 145.

surrender, and thereby rendered unavailable to make compensation."[37]

C. Nature of Election and Conclusion

Where A is under a duty to elect, the property which he is given under T's will is regarded as being subject to a form of equitable charge. This is most clearly shown by the situation that arises if A dies before he has elected. Where his own property and that given to him under T's will devolve on the same person, that person is in the same position as A with regard to election.[38] But if A's assets devolve so that no one person can elect in his place, the property given to him under T's will devolves subject to the charge, and can only be claimed by the person entitled if B is compensated, so far as is possible, out of it.[39]

Benefits passing as the result of an election are of a testamentary character; what B will receive will be a testamentary gift, and, where A elects to take with the will, A's prior property will become part of T's assets liable for the payment of his debts.[40]

An election may be express, or implied, as by receiving rents or selling the property,[41] but it must have been made with a full appreciation of the issues involved.[42] When made, it refers back to the date of the gift; for instance, the amount of compensation B will receive depends upon the valuation *at the date of T's death* of the property A elects to retain.[43]

An overall consideration of these rules reveals a doctrine far removed from the simple principle from which it derives. It has been described as a "mischievous doctrine" which should be abolished.[44] In its present form, election is too uncertain an instrument of equity. It does not even achieve a fair distribution. T must intend both A and B to benefit, but in fact A may get nothing, while B always takes something. We have seen that if T's legacy to A is worth no more than A's own property, A derives in reality no benefit from the will; indeed A benefits as much as B only if A's legacy is worth at least double the value of his own property. In all other cases the net benefit to B is greater than that to A, yet it is A alone who has an effective gift in the will. Is there an adequate rationale for it? In practice, most election cases arise not from eccentricity but from

---

[37] [1978] Ch. 145 at p. 162 (*per* Sir John Pennycuick).

[38] *Cooper v. Cooper* (1874) L.R. 7 H.L. 53.

[39] *Pickersgill v. Rodger* (1877) 5 Ch.D. 163; *cf. Rogers v. Jones* (1876) 3 Ch.D. 688.

[40] *Re Booth* [1906] 2 Ch. 321; *Re Williams* [1915] 1 Ch. 450.

[41] See *Re Gordon's W.T., supra.*

[42] *Kidney v. Coussmaker* (1806) 12 Ves. 136.

[43] *Re Hancock* [1905] 1 Ch. 16.

[44] (1990) 106 L.Q.R. 487 (N. Crago). But see *ibid.* p. 571 (P. Millett) and the reply at p. 572 (N. Crago).

mistake. Ordinarily, mistakes in a will are not remedied by equity, but in this context they are. Why? Because there is to hand a wide and ancient principle, not invented to cover mistakes, but which in this context has come to be more concerned with mistakes than with anything else. But the real question, and the only one in relation to which it is justifiable to consider the merits of election, is whether a more general jurisdiction to correct mistakes should exist.[45] There is limited merit in a doctrine that deals only in mistakes as to other people's property.

3. SATISFACTION

A. General

"Satisfaction," "ademption" and "performance" must be distinguished. Ademption in the present context means the cancellation of a legacy by a subsequent life-time advance, but in its strict sense ademption deals with the disappearance of the subject-matter of a specific legacy, through its disposal or destruction before the testator's death. Satisfaction and performance are based on the maxim "Equity imputes an intent to fulfil an obligation," and the principle of preserving equality amongst children. In performance, the act which the party was obliged to do is considered actually to have been done, while in satisfaction, something that is different from the act agreed to be done is taken as equivalent to it. Both doctrines are said to rest upon intention, but the courts do not allow much scope for subjective intention; presumptions are much relied on.[46]

B. Satisfaction of Debts by Legacies

Suppose a legacy is given to a person to whom the testator owed a debt (other than a portion debt[47]). Can the legatee claim the legacy and the debt? Equity's attitude to this question is certainly based on intention, for if the legacy is expressly said to be given in reduction of the debt, the legacy must be given that effect. But, generally, the question is decided on presumptions of intention. There is a presumption that if a debtor, without mentioning the debt in his will, gives a legacy to his creditor, then the legacy replaces the debt in the sense, of course, that the legatee has an option; he can choose to receive the legacy but he thereby admits that he can no longer enforce the debt.[48]

---

[45] See the limited measures in A.J.A. 1982, s.20, permitting rectification of wills in the case of certain mistakes. This has no application here.

[46] (1964) 38 A.L.J. 147 (M. Cullity).

[47] *i.e.* an obligation by a parent to make a payment to a child by way of an advancement; *post*, p. 861.

[48] *Thynne v. Glengall* (1848) 2 H.L.C. 131; *Chichester v. Coventry* (1867) L.R. 2 H.L. 71.

But the operation of this presumption is greatly circumscribed. First, the presumption only applies where the debt existed prior to the making of the will[49]; and the presumption does not apply to a running account, *e.g.* a trade account.[50] Secondly, the presumption does not apply if the will contains the usual direction to pay debts.[51] Thirdly, the presumption only applies if the legacy is as great as, or greater than, the debt and is in every circumstance as beneficial as the debt: there is thus no possibility of *pro tanto* satisfaction, as there is with performance. Thus there will be no satisfaction where the gift by will is of residue, nor where it is a gift of land or chattels, or a conditional gift, or an unsecured gift if the debt was secured.[52] There is doubt whether a legacy can be satisfaction of a debt due at a specific time prior to the probable date of distribution under the will,[53] or whether a legacy can be satisfaction of a debt of exactly similar amount at a rate of interest[54]; on these points it would seem sensible to deny satisfaction when there was a particular difference between the debt and the legacy, but not to deny it on grounds which merely reflect the differences in the manner of discharge of testamentary and *inter vivos* obligations.

In *Re Haves*[55] there was a covenant by the testator, made on the dissolution of marriage, to pay his wife £3 a week, charged upon specific assets. By his will he gave her an annuity of £3 a week, charged on the whole of his estate. The testamentary annuity was held to be in satisfaction of the covenant.

C. Satisfaction of Portion Debts by Legacies. The Rule Against Double Portions

In the absence of special circumstances, most parents would wish to share out the family capital in equal shares among the children. There is, of course, no obligation to do so; but it would be unsatisfactory if a grossly uneven division occurred unintentionally. This

---

[49] *Crammer's Case* (1702) 2 Salk. 508. If the debt is discharged between the date of the will and the death, the legacy is adeemed, at least where the sums are identical: *Re Fletcher* (1888) 38 Ch.D. 373.

[50] *Rawlins v. Powel* (1718) 1 P.Wms. 297. The reason being that the necessary intention is missing, as the testator would not know at the date of his will the amount of the debt, if any, at his death.

[51] *Bradshaw v. Huish* (1889) 43 Ch.D. 260; *Re Manners* [1949] Ch. 613.

[52] *Barret v. Beckford* (1750) 1 Ves.Sen. 519; *Crichton v. Crichton* [1895] 2 Ch. 853; *Re Van den Bergh's W.T.* [1948] 1 All E.R. 935.

[53] In *Re Rattenberry* [1906] 1 Ch. 667 the problem was solved by holding that a legacy in satisfaction of a debt carried interest from the date of death rather than from the end of the executors' year, and was therefore as beneficial as the debt.

[54] *Re Horlock* [1895] 1 Ch. 516; *Re Rattenberry* [1906] 1 Ch. 667; *Fitzgerald v. National Bank* [1929] 1 K.B. 394.

[55] [1951] 2 All E.R. 928.

could happen if a parent made a will providing for equal division, but then incurred an obligation to pay a portion, or made a distribution, to some of the children during his lifetime. "Equity leans against double portions," and provides for the satisfaction of portion debts by the legacy, or, in the case of *inter vivos* distributions, for the ademption of the legacy by the portion. A similar result was formerly achieved in cases of intestacy by the principle of "hotchpot."[56] Of course, if the portion has actually been paid, the doctrine cannot apply even though a legacy is subsequently given. But if the will was made before the portion was given, the question of ademption, discussed below, will arise.

To bring the rule into operation, there must be both an unsatisfied portion debt and a testamentary provision by way of portion. The two provisions must normally have been made by and for the same persons. Ordinary debts, even between father and child, are governed by ordinary rules. What then transforms a debt or a gift into a portion? It must be a gift made, or an obligation undertaken, by a parent or person *in loco parentis* to set the child up in life. This is a question of intent but, generally speaking, a portion must be substantial, though this is relative to the wealth of the parent and the age of the child.[57]

The presumption of satisfaction applies to father and legitimate child[58]; and otherwise where a person systematically acts in relation to a child so as to demonstrate the intention of making full provision for the child. This is easier to show in the case of a mother, or the father of an illegitimate child, than in the case of an uncle or a grandfather, but in *Pym v. Lockyer*[59] a wealthy grandfather was held to have placed himself *in loco parentis* to his grandchildren though their father was living.

The strength of the presumption in respect of portions can be illustrated in several ways. An ordinary debt cannot be satisfied *pro tanto* by a smaller legacy; but in the case of portion debts, a legacy may be satisfaction *pro tanto*.[60] Greater flexibility is also shown in evaluating differences between the portion debt and the legacy. In the case of an ordinary debt, small differences negative satisfaction, but this is not so in portions cases, where the differences must be of some substance.

---

[56] The principle is inapplicable as from January 1, 1996; Law Reform (Succession) Act 1995, s.1(2).

[57] *Re Hayward* [1957] Ch. 528.

[58] It does not seem that the Family Law Reform Act 1987, which generally abolishes the distinction between legitimate and illegitimate children in property matters, affects this proposition.

[59] (1841) 5 Myl. & Cr. 29. The result, sometimes, is that a child receiving a substantial provision in the ordinary way from his or her father is less favourably treated than other recipients of gifts.

[60] *Warren v. Warren* (1783) 1 Bro.C.C. 305.

The presumption of satisfaction may be rebutted by extrinsic evidence as well as by evidence of intent in the will itself.[61] But extrinsic evidence may only be used to rebut the presumption, not to raise it. The presumption is intended to produce equality among children, but it sometimes has a further effect. For instance, the fact that the presumption only affects children means that a legacy may in some cases be satisfaction of that part of a covenant that constitutes a portion debt in favour of a child while other beneficiaries, for instance the spouse of a child, can claim under the covenant and the will.[62]

D. Ademption of Legacies by Portions

The principle of ademption has been explained.[63] It is relevant here because the equitable presumption against double portions may adeem a legacy. Indeed, many of the cases cited in discussing the satisfaction of portion debts are ademption cases. This is distinguishable from satisfaction because there is no obligation to satisfy, but merely a legacy. The rule is that a legacy by way of portion is adeemed if, after the making of the will,[64] the legatee actually receives a portion, or obtains an enforceable right, *e.g.* by way of covenant, to receive one. The law relating to portions applies as discussed above. Thus the presumption of ademption applies only to portions between a parent (or someone *in loco parentis*) and a child; ademption can be *pro tanto*; and extrinsic evidence is admitted on the same principle. But there are some differences. First, ademption gives the legatee no choice; the *inter vivos* provision made for him prevails over his testamentary claim. Secondly, the presumption in favour of ademption is much stronger than the presumption in favour of satisfaction.[65] The presumption in favour of satisfaction of ordinary debts by legacies may be excluded by small differences between the two; the differences must be substantial in order to exclude the presumption of satisfaction of portion debts by legacies; but the presumption in favour of ademption will yield only to really considerable differences, for example, a devise of land will not be adeemed by a portion.

It is sometimes said that an ademption in this type of case must not benefit a stranger, as its aim is only to produce equality among children. This principle emerges from *Re Heather*[66] and *Re Vaux*,[67]

---

[61] *Re Tussaud's Estate* (1878) 9 Ch.D. 363.
[62] *Re Blundell* [1906] 2 Ch. 222.
[63] *Ante*, p. 859.
[64] If the portion is actually paid before the will is made, the child will take both.
[65] *Lord Chichester v. Coventry* (1867) L.R. 2 H.L. 71 at p. 87, *per* Lord Cranworth.
[66] [1906] 2 Ch. 230; *Meinertzhagen v. Walters* (1872) L.R. 7 Ch.App. 670.
[67] [1938] Ch. 581 (reversed on other grounds [1939] Ch. 465 (C.A.)).

where it was said that strangers could not benefit from an accretion to residue as a result of the presumption operating. But these were cases where the residue was divisible amongst children and strangers, so that there was an obvious method to hand of dealing with the accretion without benefiting the strangers. It is not easy to see how this method can be applied where the only residuary beneficiary is a stranger.

4. PERFORMANCE

The equitable doctrine of performance is closely related to the doctrines of satisfaction and ademption. All three doctrines depend on the maxim "Equity imputes an intention to fulfil an obligation." The principle of performance is that where A is bound in equity to do something for B but leaves that thing undone, equity may in appropriate circumstances feel able to regard something else that A has done as performance of the obligation. A similar principle operates where property subject, on it vesting in a covenantor, to an obligation to settle, may be regarded from the moment that it does vest as subject to the settlement.[68] The doctrine of performance, normally involving contests between the heir-at-law and the next-of-kin, has become less important since the property legislation of 1925.

A. Covenants to Purchase and Settle Land

The doctrine applied to covenants in a marriage settlement to lay out money on the purchase of land to be held on the trusts of the settlement, as in *Lord Lechmere v. Lady Lechmere.*[69]

Lord Lechmere covenanted on his marriage to lay out, within a year after his marriage and with the consent of the trustees, £30,000 in the purchase of freehold lands in fee simple in possession to be held on the trusts of the marriage settlement, whereby he was entitled in default of issue. He died intestate without issue, and without having complied with his covenants. Lord Lechmere's heir-at-law, who was entitled to all the realty on the death, claimed that the £30,000, which was to be considered as realty under the doctrine of conversion[70] should be raised from the personalty and laid out in accordance with the covenant. The next-of-kin claimed that, under the doctrine of performance, the value

---

[68] *Ante,* p. 122.
[69] (1733) 3 P.Wms. 211; (1735) Cas.T.Talb. 80.
[70] *Ante,* pp. 849 *et seq.*

of other realty devolving on the heir-at-law should be subtracted from that sum. At the time of marriage, Lord Lechmere owned estates in fee simple; after marriage he purchased, and contracted to purchase, more, some being in possession, some in reversion, and some for life only. But for none of these purchases did he seek the trustees' consent.

Lord Talbot held that the purchases of, and contracts to purchase, the estates *in possession* should be regarded as intended as a partial performance of the covenant to lay out £30,000, although they had not been entered into within a year of marriage, nor had the trustees' consent been obtained, nor had the estates been settled. Equity would, despite the difficulties, identify these estates as purchased in performance of the covenant, so that their value could be deducted from the sum of money devolving on the heir-at-law. He could not have these estates and their value in addition. But Lord Talbot refused to identify the purchases of the estates in reversion and those for life only as in performance of the covenant, as they were different in nature from the lands in fee simple in possession covenanted to be settled. Nor could estates already owned by Lord Lechmere at the time of his marriage be taken as intended performance of a covenant to purchase after marriage.

B. Covenants to Leave Money on Death

The second type of case with which the doctrine of performance is associated is that of performance through an intestacy. Where A covenants that he will leave by his will part of his personal estate to B, or that his executors shall pay a sum of money to B, and A dies intestate, and under his intestacy B becomes entitled to part of A's personal estate,[71] B cannot claim both the agreed sum or share and the intestacy entitlement, for the latter is deemed to be a performance, or *pro tanto* performance, of the covenant. This, like other aspects of the doctrine of performance, rests on presumed intention.

In *Blandy v. Widmore*[72] it was agreed that A should leave B £620 by will if B survived him. A died intestate and B became entitled thereon to more than £620. It was held that she had no separate claim for the £620 covenanted, as this covenant was deemed performed.

---

[71] Whether more or less than that covenanted; *Garthshore v. Chalie* (1804) 10 Ves.Jr. 1.
[72] (1716) 1 P.Wms. 323.

But the position is different if the covenant was one to be performed during the covenantor's life and not later.

In *Oliver v. Brickland*,[73] A covenanted that he would, within two years of marriage, pay to B a sum of money. The sum taken by B on A's intestacy some years later could not be deemed performance of A's obligation, which had simply been broken. Performance can, however, take place by intestacy of a covenant to leave by will *or* by deed.[74]

The doctrine of performance is sometimes said to extend to cases where a covenant is followed by a legacy[75] that yields a similar effect. Unfortunately the cases are confused in that, in them, performance is not kept sufficiently distinct from satisfaction. But the rules of performance are less inflexible than those of satisfaction, particularly in relation to performance *pro tanto*, so that the possibility of performance having a role to play in this situation should not be overlooked.[76]

---

[73] (1732) cited 3 Atk. 420; *Lang v. Lang* (1837) 8 Sim. 451.
[74] *Lee v. Cox and d'Aranda* (1747) 3 Atk. 419.
[75] Not a devise, or a bequest of other than money. Nor can a covenant to pay an annuity be performed by a bequest of a lump sum: *Salisbury v. Salisbury* (1848) 6 Hare 526.
[76] See Cullity in (1964) 38 A.L.J. 147, especially at p. 153.

CHAPTER 28

LICENCES AND ESTOPPEL

1. General 867	D. Contractual Licences and Third Parties 876
2. The Situation at Common Law 869	4. Constructive Trusts 879
A. Bare or Gratuitous Licence 869	5. Licences by Estoppel 882
B. Licence Coupled with a Grant (or an Interest) 869	A. Types of Estoppel 882
C. Contractual Licences 869	i. Estoppel by Representation 883
3. Contractual Licences After the Judicature Acts 870	ii. Promissory Estoppel 884
	iii. Proprietary Estoppel 885
A. Injunction to Restrain a Licensor from Breaking a Contractual Licence 871	(a) General Principles 885
	(b) Remedies 887
	(c) Judicial Formulations 890
B. The Licensee's Remedy for the Breach 872	B. Conveyancing Problems Caused by Licences by Estoppel 893
i. Damages 872	i. Status Prior to Court Order 894
ii. Injunction 873	ii. Registered and Unregistered Land 895
(a) The Judge at Your Elbow 873	iii. Other Problems Arising Under the Doctrine of Proprietary Estoppel . 895
(b) Discretionary Nature of the Remedy 873	(a) Necessity for Litigation 895
iii. Specific Performance 874	(b) Effect of Life Interest 896
C. Express or Implied Contracts 875	

1. GENERAL

A LICENCE is a permission. We are here concerned with licences to enter land.[1] The licence makes lawful what would otherwise be a trespass.[2] The licence may be express; or it may be implied; as in the case of a shopkeeper's invitation[3] to enter the premises to do business.

---

[1] A licence, however, may be a permission to a neighbour to do on his own land something which would otherwise be a wrong to the licensor; *Hopgood v. Brown* [1955] 1 W.L.R. 213; *Ward v. Kirkland* [1967] Ch. 194.

[2] *Thomas v. Sorrell* (1673) Vaug. 330 at p. 351; *Winter Garden Theatre (London) Ltd v. Millennium Productions Ltd* [1946] 1 All E.R. 678 at p. 680.

[3] *Davis v. Lyle* [1936] 2 K.B. 434 at p. 440, *per* Goddard L.J.

Express licences arise in a myriad of factual situations, as where the occupier invites guests to dinner; or to stay in a room in his hotel. Some of these situations will be expected to give minimal rights to a licensee. He has no interest in the land. The licence prevents him from being a trespasser, and no more. In other situations there will be a contract which gives certain rights to the licensee; and some situations create difficulties in determining whether a person is a contractual licensee or a lessee.[4] Different situations create different types of licences; and different levels of protection to the licensee.

The main question for discussion in this chapter is the protection of the licensee; as where the licensor purports to revoke the licence. The common law cases prior to the Judicature Acts will demonstrate what difficulties the common law met in dealing with this question; largely through the inadequacy of the remedies available at common law. If the licence was coupled with a proprietary interest, the licensor clearly could not revoke; but, as a licence was not a proprietary interest, it was difficult to see how the licensee could be protected. The common law judges found themselves saying that if a licence were granted by deed, it would not be revocable; which still leaves open the question of finding a proper remedy available to the licensee.

Equity provided the remedies. If the licensor could not lawfully revoke the licence, equity could grant an injunction to restrain him. The licence may be irrevocable for various reasons; most commonly because the terms of the contractual licence make it irrevocable; or because an estoppel has worked in favour of the licensee. Thus, the licensee would enjoy the licence for the period covered by the injunction.

The protection of the licensee against the licensor soon raised the question of whether the licensee should be protected against a third party; not being a bona fide purchaser of the legal estate for value without notice. Where the licensee is protected against third parties, the question arises whether the licence has, by this roundabout route, become an interest in land.

Another question is whether the licensee can only properly be satisfied by a permanent right, and not merely by an injunction. The doctrine known as "proprietary estoppel" has developed, allowing the courts to exercise a wide range of remedies in favour of the licensee, including the award to him of a proprietary interest in the land, with or without monetary compensation; and intended to provide the solution which is the most just and proper in all the circumstances.

---

[4] *Street v. Mountford* [1985] A.C. 809.

2. THE SITUATION AT COMMON LAW

The common law never reached a satisfactory solution to the problem of the protection of the licensee. Essentially, this was because the inquiry was to see what it was that the licensor had *granted* to the licensee; and a licence *grants* nothing. The true issue is the extent of the protection which should be given against the licensor or against a third party; and, without the remedy of an injunction to restrain interference, the common law had no adequate means of protection. A number of propositions were, however, established prior to 1875.

A. Bare or Gratuitous Licence

A simple permission to enter the licensor's land gives no contractual or proprietary right to the licensee. The permission may be withdrawn at any time by the licensor. On revocation, the licensee becomes a trespasser, but is allowed a reasonable time to leave the land.[5]

B. Licence Coupled with a Grant (or an Interest)

It has long been established that a licence coupled with a grant of a proprietary interest is irrevocable[6]; where for example an occupier sells some cut timber,[7] and expressly or by implication gives the purchaser permission to enter the land to collect it. Such a licence is irrevocable. Similarly where there is a grant of a right to take away part of the realty, as with a *profit à prendre*. The grant carries with it an irrevocable licence to enter. We do not speak of a licence coupled with a grant where the proprietary interest is one which itself includes a presence on the land; with a lease or an easement, the grantee enters by force of the grant and not under any licence.

C. Contractual Licences

Most of the difficulties which arose at common law were concerned with contractual licences. If the licensor (A) contracted to allow the licensee (B) to enter his land for a particular purpose or for

---

[5] *Canadian Pacific Ry. Co. v. R.* [1931] A.C. 414; *Winter Garden Theatre (London) Ltd v. Millennium Productions Ltd* [1948] A.C. 173 at p. 199; *Australian Blue Metal Co. v. Hughes* [1963] A.C. 74.

[6] *Webb v. Paternoster* (1619) Palm 71; *Wood v. Manley* (1839) 11 A. & E. 34; *James Jones & Son Ltd v. Tankerville* [1909] 2 Ch. 440.

[7] *James Jones & Son Ltd v. Tankerville, supra.*

a particular period of time, and A, in breach of contract, ordered B to leave, and perhaps forcibly ejected him, the common law held that B had become a trespasser and could be ejected.

In *Wood v. Leadbitter*,[8] the plaintiff purchased a ticket for the grandstand at Doncaster Racecourse. The defendant, on the orders of the steward, required him to leave. He refused to go, and was physically removed, no more force being used than was reasonably necessary. He sued for assault and false imprisonment, and failed. The Court of Exchequer distinguished between a mere licence, such as this, which was revocable; and a licence coupled with an interest, which was not.

In the circumstances, nothing was *granted* to the plaintiff. As Latham C.J. said in *Cowell v. Rosehill Racecourse Co.*[9]: "50,000 people who pay to see a football match do not obtain 50,000 interests in the football ground." An action for breach of contract no doubt lay,[10] but that was not the issue. Whether or not the defendant had the *right*, under the terms of the contract, to eject the plaintiff, he had a *power* to do so.[11]

The conclusion must be that the common law provided no adequate doctrine nor any adequate remedies to deal with the problem of protection of licensees.

3. Contractual Licences after the Judicature Acts

The treatment of contractual licences at common law was clearly unsatisfactory. This situation, and that of licences generally, has been transformed by the application of equitable remedies, not available to common law courts; by the recognition of the part that estoppel has to play; and finally by the willingness of modern courts to seek the most appropriate remedy for the particular situation. "It is for the court in each case to decide in what way the equity can be satisfied."[12]

---

[8] (1845) 13 M. & W. 838. See (1954) 12 C.L.J. 201 and (1955) 13 C.L.J. 47 (H. Hanbury).

[9] (1937) 56 C.L.R. 605 at p. 616.

[10] *Per* Viscount Simon L.C. in *Winter Garden Theatre (London) Ltd v. Millennium Productions Ltd* [1948] A.C. 173 at p. 190.

[11] *Per* Goddard L.J. in *Thompson v. Park* [1944] K.B. 408 at p. 410; later disapproved in *Verrall v. Great Yarmouth Borough Council* [1981] Q.B. 202.

[12] Lord Denning M.R. in *Ives (E.R.) Investments Ltd v. High* [1967] 2 Q.B. 379 at p. 395.

A. Injunction to Restrain a Licensor from Breaking a Contractual Licence

The reasoning of the common law, established in *Wood v. Leadbitter*,[13] was that a licence was revocable unless it validly granted a proprietary interest. In the absence of such a grant, it was said, even as late as 1944,[14] that, though the licensor had no *right* to revoke, he had a *power* to revoke, and could then turn the licensee into a trespasser. The opposite conclusion had been reached in 1915 in *Hurst v. Picture Theatres Ltd*,[15] but on grounds that show that the courts still thought that it was the grant of a proprietary interest which made the licence irrevocable. In that case the plaintiff paid to watch a cinema show in the defendants' theatre. The defendants mistakenly thought that he had entered without paying. On being requested to leave, he refused and was ejected. He sued for assault and false imprisonment and succeeded.

Buckley L.J. gave two grounds for distinguishing the case from *Wood v. Leadbitter*,[16] both based upon the availability of equitable doctrine, the first reason being, it is submitted, clearly wrong, and the second being the basis of the modern doctrine protecting contractual licensees. The first ground was that the plaintiff had a licence coupled with an interest—"the right to see"—and that the interest could now be granted in equity by a contract, whereas before 1875 a deed was required. The fallacy in this reasoning is that there was no identifiable proprietary interest to be granted.[17]

As a second ground for the decision, Buckley L.J. treated the matter as one of construing the parties' rights under the contract. Here "there was included in that contract a contract not to revoke the licence until the play had run to its termination".[18] This is the germ of the later development; and the significance of the Judicature Act in this context is that it makes available the equitable remedy of an injunction to restrain the breach of contract by the licensor. This precludes the argument that he has no right to revoke, but has a power to do so; he has no power if an injunction is available to restrain him.

[13] (1845) 13 M. & W. 838; which was distinguished in *Butler v. Sheffield and Manchester Rly. Co.* (1888) 21 Q.B.D. 207, where the plaintiff sued for assault on being forcibly ejected from a railway carriage, having paid the fare, but lost his ticket. The plaintiff succeeded in the Court of Appeal, the matter being dealt with on the basis of his rights under the contract. "The present case . . . has nothing to do with . . . any licence to go upon land." (*Per* Lopes L.J. at p. 214).

[14] *Thompson v. Park* [1944] K.B. 408 at p. 412.

[15] [1915] 1 K.B. 1.

[16] (1845) 13 M. & W. 838.

[17] These matters are demonstrated by Phillimore L.J. in his dissenting judgment; see *Hounslow L.B.C. v. Twickenham Garden Developments Ltd* [1971] Ch. 233 at p. 244; *cf. Cowell v. Rosehill Racecourse* (1937) 56 C.L.R. 605.

[18] *Hurst v. Picture Theatres Ltd* [1915] 1 K.B. 1 at p. 10; see also Kennedy L.J. at p. 14.

Winter Garden Theatre (London) Ltd v. Millennium Productions Ltd[19] finally established that the rights of the parties must be determined upon the proper construction of the contract. In that case, as the licence was held to have been revoked in accordance with its terms, the problem in *Hurst's* case[20] did not arise. In the Court of Appeal, however, the contract had been construed as irrevocable by the licensor. In that situation, they held, the licensee would be protected by the issue of an injunction to restrain a breach of contract by the licensor. Sir Wilfrid Greene M.R., in words referred to with approval in the House of Lords, explained that the revocation of the licence was a breach.[21] "It may well be that, in the old days, that would only have given rise to a right to sue for damages. The licence would have stood revoked, but after the expiration of what was the appropriate period of grace the licencees would have been trespassers and could have been expelled, and their right would have been to sue for damages for breach of contract . . . But the matter requires to be considered further, because the power of equity to grant an injunction to restrain a breach of contract is, of course, a power exercisable in any court. The general rule is that, before equity will grant such an injunction, there must be, on the construction of the contract, a negative clause express or implied. In the present case it seems to me that the grant of an option which, if I am right, is an irrevocable option, must imply a negative undertaking by the licensor not to revoke it. That being so, in my opinion, such a contract could be enforced in equity by an injunction."

B. The Licensee's Remedy for the Breach

i. Damages. The normal remedy for breach of contract is, of course, damages; and there is little doubt that this was recognised even in the old common law cases which held that the licensee could be evicted. The question did not arise in *Wood v. Leadbitter*,[22] because the form of action was for assault and not for breach of contract.

In *Tanner v. Tanner*,[23] the defendant was the mistress of the plaintiff, and bore him two daughters. She lived in a rent-controlled flat; which she left in 1970, when the plaintiff purchased a house for her and for the children. The relationship ended, and in 1973 the plaintiff offered her £4,000 to vacate. She refused, claiming that she could stay in the house until the children left school. The Court of

---

[19] [1948] A.C. 173.
[20] [1915] 1 K.B. 1.
[21] [1946] 1 All E.R. 678 at pp. 648 *et seq.*
[22] (1845) 13 M. & W. 838.
[23] [1975] 1 W.L.R. 1346.

Appeal would have permitted her to stay, but she had been rehoused by the local authority before the appeal. The defendant's remedy was compensation for the loss of the licence; expressed by Lord Denning M.R. as requiring the plaintiff to make restitution for the unjust benefit which he had received; or, by Brightman J., as the amount which might reasonably be payable for a surrender of the licence; which was quantified at £2,000.

ii. Injunction. The normal way of protecting a contractual licensee against improper revocation is by issuing an injunction to restrain the breach by the licensor. A number of questions arise:

(a) *The Judge at your Elbow.* It was said in 1915[24] in connection with *Hurst's* case, that an injunction would be a useless remedy unless a Chancery judge was sitting at your elbow, because the breach and ejection would take place before the injunction could issue. But the court will treat the licence as not revoked in circumstances in which an injunction would issue, and this will prevent the licensee from being a trespasser. As has been seen, monetary compensation was awarded in *Tanner v. Tanner*[25] where it was no longer practicable to issue an injunction. Moreover, a mandatory injunction may be obtained, in a suitable case, to enable the licensee to re-enter.[26]

(b) *Discretionary Nature of the Remedy.* An injunction, like all equitable remedies, is discretionary. An injunction will not therefore be available to a licensee who is himself in breach of the terms of the licence. A licensee who himself misbehaves will not be protected.[27] Further, an injunction will not be granted where it will have the effect of compelling persons to live together in circumstances which are intolerable. If this situation arises in the case of a licence, an injunction may be refused, and the parties may be left to their rights at common law to sue for breach of contract.[28]

---

[24] See (1915) 31 L.Q.R. 217 at p. 221 (Sir John Miles); and Lord Greene M.R. in *Millennium Productions Ltd v. Winter Garden Theatre (London) Ltd* [1946] 1 All E.R. 678 at p. 685.

[25] [1975] 1 W.L.R. 1346.

[26] As in *Luganda v. Services Hotels Ltd* [1969] 2 Ch. 209.

[27] *Thompson v. Park* [1944] K.B. 408. See also *Ivory v. Palmer* [1975] I.C.R. 340. For a consideration of the question of the circumstances in which misbehaviour by a licensee by estoppel will allow his licence to be terminated, see *Williams v. Staite* [1979] Ch. 291, [1986] Conv. 406 (M. Thompson), suggesting that termination is only possible where the previous court order was not the grant of an estate in the land. A smaller degree of misconduct will prevent an estoppel licence arising, under the "clean hands" principle, than will cause it to terminate; *J. Willis & Son v. Willis* [1986] 1 E.G.L.R. 62.

[28] *Thompson v. Park* [1944] K.B. 408, at 409.

iii. Specific Performance. The Court of Appeal had no hesitation in holding in *Verrall v. Great Yarmouth Borough Council*[29] that a contractual licence was enforceable by specific performance.

The National Front entered into a contract in April 1979 with the Council to hire a hall for a conference. In May 1979, after local authority elections, the new Labour controlled Council purported to revoke the licence; on the ground that the Front's extremist political stance would create unrest in the borough. Specific performance of the contract was granted.

The old argument that a licence can be revoked by the licensor on payment of damages was firmly and finally disposed of. The Front was entitled to the benefits of the contractual licence.

The issue of a decree of specific performance raised a number of questions of principle relating to the availability of the decree. It used to be said that a decree of specific performance would not issue in relation to a transient matter; because the issue may not come to the court in time.[30] That view was held to be out of date. Presumably, however, it would have been a defence if the date of the conference had passed before the issue was tried. Another possible difficulty might be the question of the continued supervision by the court, although, as we have seen,[31] inroads have already been made into the supervision principle. A further question is whether specific performance is available to enforce a contract which does not create a proprietary interest. The older view was that the decree would not issue in such a case.[32] But more recent authorities indicate that specific performance is a remedy based on the inadequacy of damages rather than on the vindication of some proprietary interest.[33] This, it is submitted, is the correct approach today; "it is the duty of the court to protect, where it is appropriate to do so, any interest, whether it be an estate in land or a licence, by injunction or specific performance as the case may be."[34] Such an approach is consistent with the court's power to grant a prohibitory injunction to restrain the wrongful revocation of a contractual licence, or to grant a mandatory injunction to re-instate a licensee whose licence has been revoked in breach of contract.[35]

---

[29] [1981] Q.B. 202; [1981] Conv. 212 (A. Briggs).

[30] *Ante*, p. 710.

[31] *Ante*, p. 705.

[32] *Booker v. Palmer* [1942] 2 All E.R. 674 at p. 677 (*per* Lord Greene M.R.). This was the view that prevailed at the time of *Hurst's* case.

[33] *Beswick v. Beswick* [1968] A.C. 58; *Tanner v. Tanner* [1975] 1 W.L.R. 1346 at p. 1350; *Hutton v. Watling* [1948] Ch. 26 at p. 36 (affirmed, *ibid.* p. 398); (1980) 96 L.Q.R. 483.

[34] [1981] Q.B. 202 at p. 220 (*per* Roskill L.J.).

[35] *Winter Garden Theatre (London) Ltd v. Millennium Productions Ltd* [1948] A.C. 173 (prohibitory); *Luganda v. Service Hotels Ltd* [1969] 2 Ch. 209 (mandatory).

C. Express or Implied Contracts

The contract may be express or implied. In the older cases, which dealt mainly with commercial transactions, it was not difficult to recognise the existence of a contract, though its terms may have been difficult to construe. Many of the recent cases concern arrangements within the family. These are situations in which the terms of an agreement are usually not spelled out; and a contract may in any case fail because of a lack of intention to create legal relations.

In these circumstances, it is not surprising that it is difficult to distinguish clearly between cases in which a contract has been found and those where it has not. As has been seen, a contractual licence was implied in *Tanner v. Tanner*.[36] That indeed was the only way to find an adequate remedy; and Lord Denning M.R., conscious of the difficulty of finding a contract in the circumstances, went so far as to say that the court should "imply a contract by him—or if need be impose the equivalent of a contract by him."[37] In *Coombes v. Smith*,[38] the court failed to find a contract in circumstances which were basically similar. There the defendant bought a house into which the plaintiff, his lover, moved. As she was pregnant, she gave up her job, the defendant assuring her that he would always provide for her. The defendant paid the outgoings, but the plaintiff did some decorating and gardening. When the couple separated 10 years later, the defendant offered the plaintiff £10,000 to move out, but she claimed a contractual licence for life. Her claim failed, as she had provided no consideration, and it was impossible to infer a contract. *Tanner v. Tanner*[39] was distinguished as the claimant there had provided consideration in giving up her rent-controlled flat and was not claiming a licence for life. The defendant, however, conceded that the plaintiff could remain until the child was 17. It is indeed easier to see why there was not a contract in *Coombes v. Smith*,[40] than it is to see how one could be implied in *Tanner v. Tanner*.[41]

In other cases the occupier has received protection by the court's finding that there was a contractual licence which was irrevocable for a period of time.

In *Hardwick v. Johnson*,[42] a mother purchased a house, on her son's marriage, for occupation by him and his bride. The young couple were to pay £7 a week as rent to the mother. But this soon

---

[36] [1975] 1 W.L.R. 1346; (1976) 92 L.Q.R. 168 (J. Barton).
[37] *Ibid.* at p. 1350.
[38] [1986] 1 W.L.R. 808; (1986) 45 C.L.J. 394 (D. Hayton); *post*, p. 887. See also *Horrocks v. Forray* [1976] 1 W.L.R. 230; (1976) 40 Conv.(N.S.) 362 (M. Richards).
[39] *Supra.*
[40] *Supra.*
[41] [1975] 1 W.L.R. 1340.
[42] [1978] 1 W.L.R. 683. See also *Chandler v. Kerley* [1978] 1 W.L.R. 693 ("mistress" entitled to remain for a period determinable upon 12 months' notice).

ceased to be paid, and the mother did not demand it because the couple had little money.

The son left his bride, now pregnant, for another woman. The mother sued for possession. The wife claimed to be entitled to remain in possession on payment of £7 per week.

The Court of Appeal found a contractual licence. The daughter-in-law was held entitled, subject to resuming the weekly payments, to protection by injunction for an indefinite period of time. Lord Denning M.R. thought, however, that no enforceable contract could arise in a family situation of this kind,[43] preferring to find a licence by estoppel. On the face of it, it would seem to be unlikely that the parties would intend to bind themselves contractually in a situation of this type.

D. Contractual Licences and Third Parties

Protection of the licensee against the licensor inevitably gives rise to the question whether a licensee will be protected also against an assignee of the licensor. On the one hand, protection given to a licensee is in many cases of little use if the licensor can transfer the land and leave the licensee helpless. On the other hand, if a licensee is protected against third parties, his licence begins to look like some sort of proprietary interest.[44]

The extent to which a licence is binding on a third party will vary with the type of licence. Bare licences are obviously not binding. The question whether a contractual licence can bind a purchaser under a constructive trust is considered later[45]; likewise whether an estoppel licence can bind third parties.[46] First the position as to contractual licences outside these situations will be examined.

It is important to appreciate that there is no principle which requires that the availability of an injunction against one contracting party will make it available against third parties coming to the land. The jurisdiction to apply an injunction against a third party was demonstrated by the development of the law of restrictive covenants from *Tulk v. Moxhay*.[47] The policy decision to refuse an injunction against third parties was shown by the unsuccessful attempts to make covenants run with chattels.[48]

---

[43] *Ibid.* at p. 688.
[44] See, however, (1986) 49 M.L.R. 741 (J. Dewar), suggesting that it is wrong to attempt to fit licences into traditional academic land law.
[45] *Post*, p. 879.
[46] *Post*, p. 894.
[47] (1848) 2 Ph. 774.
[48] *Taddy & Co. v. Sterious* [1904] 1 Ch. 354; *Port Line v. Ben Line Steamers* [1958] 2 Q.B. 146; *Lord Strathcona S.S. Co. v. Dominion Coal Co.* [1926] A.C. 108.

As far as contractual obligations are concerned, the estate of a deceased party to the contract is not properly a third party. The devisee of the licensor is a third party, but takes as a volunteer. One of the landmark cases on the enforcement of licences against third parties, *Errington v. Errington and Woods*,[49] is such a case; the report fails to say whether the licensor's widow, who was the devisee, was also his executrix; but both Lord Denning M.R. and Hodson L.J. refer to her as successor in title. Such a person is in a different position from a purchaser.

Authority leads to the conclusion that contractual licences are not ordinarily binding on third parties.

In *King v. David Allen & Sons, Billposting Ltd*,[50] the licensor agreed that the licensees should have the exclusive right of affixing advertisements upon a building. Later the licensor leased the building to a cinema company, no provision being made to protect the rights of the licensees. The licensees sued the licensor for breach of contract. The licensor was liable if the lease to the company deprived the licensees of their contractual right. The House of Lords held that it did.

In *Clore v. Theatrical Properties Ltd*,[51] a deed which was drafted in the form of a lease purported to grant the lessee the "front of the house" rights in a theatre; that is, the right to use refreshment rooms etc. to provide for the needs of patrons. The instrument provided that the terms "lessor" and "lessee" should include their executors, administrators and assigns.

It was held to be a licence and not a lease. The "lessor" and "lessee" both assigned; and the question was whether the "lessee's" assignee could enforce the right under the agreement. He failed; because the licence was a personal contract and enforceable only between the parties to it.

As has now been reaffirmed,[52] these cases lay down a correct doctrine relating to contractual licences. Licences were indeed treated as binding on third parties in a number of cases decided in the days when a deserted wife was treated as a licensee protected by injunction[53]; and these provided a very compelling case for applying the injunction also against the party to whom the deserting husband sold the house. But these cases were incorrect; because the House of

---

[49] [1952] 1 K.B. 290.
[50] [1916] 2 A.C. 54.
[51] [1936] 3 All E.R. 483.
[52] *Ashburn Anstalt v. Arnold* [1989] Ch. 1, *post*, p. 880.
[53] *Bendall v. McWhirter* [1952] 2 Q.B. 466; *Lee v. Lee* [1952] 2 Q.B. 489n; *Ferris v. Weaven* [1952] 2 All E.R. 233.

Lords decided that a deserted wife was not a licensee of her husband, and had no interest capable of binding the land.[54] Legislation
followed.[55] There are some cases in which a contractual arrangement, outside the context of a deserted wife, was held to bind a third
party, but they are best explained as being decided on other
grounds.

In *Errington v. Errington and Woods*[56] the father (A) of a
young man who was about to be married purchased a house
through a building society, made a down-payment and told the
young couple that the house would be theirs when they paid all
the instalments due under the mortgage. They went into possession and paid all the instalments which fell due. Nothing was
stated concerning the rights of the young couple during the
currency of the mortgage payments. A died, leaving all his property to Mrs A. The son returned to his mother, who took steps to
evict the daughter-in-law. She failed. The daughter-in-law was
held to be a licensee who was entitled to protection not only
against A in his lifetime, but also against Mrs A, taking as a
volunteer.

There was clearly a flavour of contract in the licence, and the case
is usually treated as one of contractual licence. But the wide views
expressed in the case as to the enforceability of such licences were
disapproved, *obiter*, by the House of Lords in *National Provincial
Bank Ltd v. Ainsworth*,[57] and have since been said by the Court of
Appeal in *Ashburn Anstalt v. Arnold*[58] to be neither practically
necessary nor theoretically convincing. They could not be reconciled with *King*[59] and *Clore*,[60] but the decision was, however,
correct on the facts. It could be justified on one of three grounds:
(i) there was a contract to convey on completion of the payments,
giving rise to an equitable interest in the form of an estate contract
which would bind the widow as a volunteer; (ii) the daughter-in-law
had changed her position in reliance upon a representation by the
deceased, the estoppel binding the widow; (iii) the payment of
instalments gave rise to a direct proprietary interest by way of a
constructive trust under the principle later formulated in *Gissing v.
Gissing*.[61] Thus the result could have been achieved without accepting Lord Denning's broad principles, which were unnecessary and

---

[54] *National Provincial Bank Ltd v. Ainsworth* [1965] A.C. 1175.
[55] Matrimonial Homes Act 1967 (now Family Law Act 1996).
[56] [1952] 1 K.B. 290; *Duke of Beaufort v. Patrick* (1853) 17 Beav. 60.
[57] [1965] A.C. 1175.
[58] [1989] Ch. 1, *infra*.
[59] *Supra*.
[60] *Supra*.
[61] [1971] A.C. 886, *ante*, p. 266.

per incuriam. The correct principle is that a contractual licence cannot bind a third party unless the circumstances are such that a constructive trust has arisen. Further examination of this principle will be deferred until the development of the constructive trust solution has been outlined.

4. CONSTRUCTIVE TRUSTS

A few cases in this field have been decided on the basis of a constructive trust. Lord Denning has described a constructive trust as one "imposed by law whenever justice and good conscience require it. It is a liberal process, founded upon large principles of equity, to be applied in cases where the legal owner cannot conscientiously keep the property for himself alone, but ought to allow another to have the property or the benefit of it or a share of it."[62]

In those terms, the constructive trust solution is at once too vague and too far-reaching. Too vague in that such broad statements provide no way of determining when such a trust will be held to exist.[63] It may be unobjectionable in cases such as *D.H.N. Food Distributors Ltd v. Tower Hamlets London Borough Council*,[64] where the issue was whether a contractual licensee could claim compensation for disturbance upon compulsory purchase. But it is not appropriate where title to land is at stake.

Lord Denning M.R. pioneered this solution in *Binions v. Evans*.[65]

> Mrs Evans was the widow of an employee of the Tredegar Estate. The trustees made an agreement with her, under which she would be allowed to reside in a cottage, free of rent and rates, for life. She undertook to keep the cottage in repair.
>
> Two years later, the trustees sold the cottage to Mr and Mrs Binions, expressly subject to the agreement, the purchase price being reduced accordingly. The purchasers claimed possession of the cottage. Lord Denning M.R. held that the purchasers were bound by Mrs Evans' contractual licence and also by a constructive trust in her favour, whereas Megaw and Stephenson L.JJ. relied upon the agreement as creating a life interest.[66]

---

[62] *Hussey v. Palmer* [1972] 1 W.L.R. 1286, at p. 1290.

[63] (1973) 32 C.L.J. 123 at p. 142 (R. Smith).

[64] [1976] 1 W.L.R. 852. See also *Pennine Raceway Ltd v. Kirklees Metropolitan Council* [1983] Q.B. 382 (Licensee a "person interested in the land" within Town and Country Planning Act 1971, s.164).

[65] [1972] Ch. 359; (1972) 88 L.Q.R. 336 (P.V.B.); (1972) 36 Conv.(N.S.) 266 (J. Martin); (1973) 32 C.L.J. 123 (R. Smith).

[66] Applying *Bannister v. Bannister* [1948] 2 All E.R. 133. See also *Costello v. Costello* (1995) 70 P. & C.R. 297.

Clearly, the case provides no support for the view that contractual licences generally are binding on third parties. Nevertheless, it was cited subsequently as authority for the proposition that a contractual licence is capable of binding a third party.

In *Re Sharpe*[67] an elderly aunt lent money to her nephew towards the purchase of a house on the understanding that she would live there with the nephew and his wife for the rest of her life. The nephew subsequently went bankrupt, and his trustee in bankruptcy contracted to sell the house to a purchaser. The trustee failed in his claim to recover possession of the house from the aunt. Her rights were held to be more than merely contractual, and gave rise to a constructive trust binding upon the trustee in bankruptcy. The purchaser was not a party to the action, and it was left open whether he would also be bound.[68] However, as the aunt had sold her home and paid for improvements to the nephew's house, a preferable basis for the decision might have been proprietary estoppel.

The position has now been clarified by the Court of Appeal in *Ashburn Anstalt v. Arnold*,[69] which has "put the *quietus* to the heresy that a mere licence creates an interest in land."[70] The plaintiff purchaser sought possession against the defendant, who was in occupation under an agreement with the plaintiff's predecessor in title. The plaintiff had been aware of the agreement and had purchased expressly subject to its provisions "so far as the same are enforceable against the Vendor." In fact it was held that the defendant had a tenancy which was binding on the plaintiff under the Land Registration Act 1925.[71] However, the Court of Appeal proceeded to consider the position if the defendant had been a contractual licensee. On the clear authority of *King v. David Allen & Sons, Billposting Ltd*,[72] the correct principle was that a contractual licence could not normally bind a third party. However, the law must be free to develop, and the finding of a constructive trust was considered a beneficial adaptation of old rules to new situations in

---

[67] [1980] 1 W.L.R. 219; [1980] Conv. 207 (J. Martin). See also *Midland Bank Ltd v. Farmpride Hatcheries Ltd* (1981) 260 E.G. 493; [1982] Conv. 67 (R. Annand).

[68] See further Murphy and Clark, *The Family Home*, pp. 199–204.

[69] [1989] Ch. 1; (1988) 51 M.L.R. 226 (J. Hill); (1988) 104 L.Q.R. 175 (P. Sparkes); [1988] Conv. 201 (M. Thompson); (1988) 47 C.L.J. 353 (A. Oakley); All E.R. Rev. 1988, p. 177 (P. Clarke).

[70] *IDC Group Ltd v. Clarke* [1992] 1 E.G.L.R. 187 at p. 189, upheld (1993) 65 P. & C.R. 172 (where the issue was not discussed).

[71] As an overriding interest under s.70(1)(g).

[72] [1916] 2 A.C. 54, *ante*, p. 877.

appropriate circumstances. But there could be no bare assertion that a licence gives rise to a constructive trust. It would arise only if the conscience of the third party was affected. Mere notice would not be sufficient,[73] nor the fact that the property was conveyed "subject to" the interest. Such a term does not mean that the grantee is necessarily intended to be under an obligation to give effect to the interest, but may be merely to protect the grantor against claims by the grantee (for example as in the case of an old restrictive covenant which may or may not be enforceable). The question is whether the grantee has acted in such a way that, as a matter of justice, a trust must be imposed on him. In the present case there would be no constructive trust because the transfer "subject to" the defendant's rights was done to protect the vendor, and the purchaser had not paid a reduced price. As far as the previous cases were concerned, *Binions v. Evans*[74] was a legitimate application of the constructive trust doctrine because the parties intended the purchaser to give effect to the interest and the price was reduced accordingly. Also approved was *Lyus v. Prowsa Ltd*,[75] where the intention had been similar and the purchaser had given assurances. The doctrine was not, however, appropriate in *Re Sharpe*,[76] where the aunt had not replied to the trustee in bankruptcy's enquiries as to her interest.

The Court of Appeal added that certainty was of prime importance as far as title to land was concerned, and it was not desirable to impose a constructive trust on slender materials.[77] One difficulty is that the imposition of a constructive trust, in the case of a fee simple, creates an equitable interest which is not registrable (in unregistered land).[78] If the interest protected by a constructive trust is for life only, problems once arose with the Settled Land Act, but settlements cannot now be created.[79] Similar points arise with the doctrine of proprietary estoppel, as discussed below.[80] In that context also the constructive trust has been invoked in order to achieve a just result.[81]

The new formulation, it is submitted, provides welcome guidelines as to the circumstances in which a constructive trust will be

---

[73] See *IDC Group Ltd v. Clark* [1992] 1 E.G.L.R. 187 at p. 190 (in the High Court); *Chattey v. Farndale Holdings Inc.* [1997] 06 E.G. 152.

[74] [1972] Ch. 359, *supra*.

[75] [1982] 1 W.L.R. 1044, *ante*, p. 322.

[76] [1980] 1 W.L.R. 219, *supra*.

[77] Reiterated in *IDC Group Ltd v. Clark*, *supra* (in the High Court).

[78] Formerly the interest of a beneficiary absolutely entitled under a constructive trust was not overreachable, but this has been changed by the Trusts of Land and Appointment of Trustees Act 1996; *ante*, p. 36. Overreaching, however, requires two trustees.

[79] Life interests now give rise to the less complex trust of land under the 1996 Act, *supra*.

[80] *Post*, p. 885.

[81] *Re Basham* [1986] 1 W.L.R. 1498, *post*, p. 892.

imposed, and thereby achieves a compromise between the sometimes divergent goals of certainty and justice.

5. LICENCES BY ESTOPPEL

The doctrine of estoppel has played a significant part in the modern development of the law of licences.[82] A situation in which a licensee has acted to his detriment in reliance upon a representation or promise by the licensor presents a compelling case for the intervention of equity in order to protect the licensee; more compelling, in a sense, than the case of a contractual licence, because the licensee by estoppel has no alternative remedy in damages.[83] The doctrine of estoppel by encouragement or acquiescence has found a fruitful area of operation in the field of licences, under the name of proprietary estoppel; its success in this area has been largely due to the fact that, unlike estoppel by representation or promissory estoppel, it can found a cause of action and, in the licence context, enables the court to award a proprietary interest to the licensee. In the enthusiasm for the application of this doctrine, it has become confused with other estoppels, and has been credited with the solution to many cases in which it is quite clear that the judges reached their decision on other grounds. The utility of the doctrine stems from the fact that the court will "look at all the circumstances in each case to decide in what way the equity can be satisfied"[84]; and the most suitable solution is often an award to the licensee of a proprietary interest, rather than merely an injunction. A sword and not a shield is sometimes required.

A. Types of Estoppel

There are many different types of estoppel at law and in equity. We are concerned with three of these, each having a separate origin and history.[85] The Australian courts have recently asserted that distinctions should not be drawn between the various categories of

---

[82] It seems that a licence by estoppel was first so referred to judicially in *Inwards v. Baker* [1965] 2 Q.B. 29 *per* Danckwerts L.J. at p. 38, *post*, p. 888.

[83] As to how far a contractual licence may also be a licence by estoppel, see [1983] Conv. 50 (M. Thompson) and 285 (A. Briggs).

[84] *Plimmer v. Wellington Corporation* (1884) 9 App.Cas. 699 at p. 714; *Greasley v. Cooke* [1980] 1 W.L.R. 1306 at p. 1312. It may be held that the claimant has already had sufficient satisfaction for his expenditure; *Appleby v. Cowley, The Times*, April 14, 1982; *Sledmore v. Dalby* (1996) 72 P. & C.R. 196.

[85] For estoppel by convention, *i.e.* by a course of dealing, see *Amalgamated Investment and Property Co. (in liquidation) v. Texas Commerce International Bank Ltd* [1982] Q.B. 84; *Pacol Ltd v. Trade Lines Ltd* [1982] 1 Lloyd's Rep. 456; *Troop v. Gibson* [1986] 1 E.G.L.R. 1; (1982) 79 L.S.Gaz. 662 (P. Matthews).

estoppel, nor between their common law or equitable origin.[86] The courts in this country have not yet reached this conclusion, although there have been *dicta* to the effect that it is undesirable to distinguish between types of estoppel.[87] If this view prevails, the existing differences (such as whether the type of estoppel operates as a sword or a shield) will have to be modified in order to achieve a coherent unified doctrine.[88]

i. Estoppel by Representation. Estoppel by representation operates over a wide field of common law and equity. The basic principle is that a person who makes an unambiguous[89] representation, by words,[90] or conduct,[91] or by silence,[92] of an existing fact, and causes another party to act to his detriment in reliance on the representation will not be permitted subsequently to act inconsistently with that representation. The doctrine was originally applied only where there was a representation of existing fact,[93] and not where the representation was one of law or of intention. The representor could not subsequently allege, in dealing with the representee, that the facts were different from those represented. Apart from a few long-established exceptions,[94] such an estoppel works negatively. It is not capable of creating a cause of action. It works like a rule of evidence, a rule which excludes a particular defence or line of argument.

This is not to say that estoppel is available only to a defendant. A plaintiff may take advantage of the doctrine if he has an independent

---

[86] *Waltons Stores (Interstate) Ltd v. Maher* (1988) 62 A.L.J.R. 110 at p. 123; (1988) 104 L.Q.R. 362 (A. Duthie); *Commonwealth of Australia v. Verwayen* (1990) 65 A.L.J.R. 540 at p. 546; (1991) 107 L.Q.R. 221 (M. Spence); [1992] Conv. 239 (M. Lunney). Likewise in New Zealand: *Gillies v. Keogh* [1989] 2 N.Z.L.R. 327 at p. 331.

[87] *Crabb v. Arun District Council* [1976] Ch. 179 at p. 193; *Amalgamated Investment and Property Co. Ltd (in liquidation) v. Texas Commerce International Bank Ltd* [1982] Q.B. 84 at p. 103; *Troop v. Gibson* [1986] 1 E.G.L.R. 1 at p. 5 (distinguishing, however, estoppel by representation and by convention). *Cf.* (1981) 97 L.Q.R. 513; [1988] Conv. 46 (P. Evans); *J.T. Developments Ltd v. Quinn* (1991) 62 P. & C.R. 33 at p. 45; *First National Bank plc v. Thompson* [1996] Ch. 231.

[88] See (1994) 14 L.S. 15 (M. Halliwell), suggesting the remedying of unconscionable conduct as the unifying factor. See generally Pawlowski, *The Doctrine of Proprietary Estoppel* (1996).

[89] *Low v. Bouverie* [1891] 3 Ch. 82.

[90] *Hunt v. Carew* (1649) Nels. 46; or through an agent; *Moorgate Mercantile Ltd v. Twitchings* [1977] A.C. 890.

[91] *Waldron v. Sloper* (1852) 1 Drew. 193.

[92] *Fung Kai Sun v. Chan Fui Hing* [1951] A.C. 489; *Pacol Ltd v. Trade Lines Ltd* [1982] 1 Lloyd's Rep. 456.

[93] *Jorden v. Money* (1845) 5 H.L.C. 185; not followed in Australia; *Legione v. Hateley* (1983) 57 A.L.J.R. 292; *Foran v. Wight* (1989) 168 C.L.R. 385.

[94] *e.g.* a tenancy by estoppel, M. & W., pp. 660 *et seq.*; see also *Stiles v. Cowper* (1748) 3 Atk. 692; *Ramsden v. Dyson* (1866) L.R. 1 H.L. 129; *post*, p. 890.

cause of action, and can show that the defence is inconsistent with a representation of the defendant on which he relies.[95]

A well-known example is *Roberston v. Minister of Pensions*,[96] where an officer claimed a pension, relying upon a statement by the War Office that his disability had been accepted as due to military service, and forbore to obtain an independent medical opinion. It was held that the Crown, through the Minister of Pensions, could not go back on the statement previously made. The officer was no longer in a position to supply the necessary evidence; but the Minister was estopped from denying that he qualified.

ii. Promissory Estoppel. The doctrine is expanded in equity, so as to include not only representations of fact, but also representations of intention; or promises. The doctrine came into prominence with the decision of Denning J. in *Central London Property Trust Ltd v. High Trees House Ltd* in 1947,[97] and became firmly established in later cases.[98]

Where, by words or conduct, a person makes an unambiguous representation as to his future conduct, intending the representation to be relied on, and to affect the legal relations between the parties,[99] and the representee alters his position in reliance on it, the representor will be unable to act inconsistently with the representation if by so doing the representee would be prejudiced.[1]

The doctrine emerged in *Loffus v. Maw*[2] and *Hughes v. Metropolitan Railway Co.*,[3] and developed through a line of cases which was little known until 1947. Denning J. then applied it in *Central London Property Trust Ltd v. High Trees House Ltd.*[4]

> The plaintiff company in 1937 leased to the defendant a block of flats for 99 years at a rent of £2,500 a year. Early in 1940, because of the war, the defendants were unable to find sub-tenants for the flats, and unable in consequence to pay the rent. The plaintiffs agreed to reduce the rent to £1,250 from the beginning of the term. By the beginning of 1945 all the flats were let, and the

---

[95] Similarly with promissory estoppel; *Amalgamated Investment and Property Co. (in liquidation) v. Texas Commerce International Bank Ltd* [1982] Q.B. 84; *Pacol Ltd v. Trade Lines Ltd* [1982] 1 Lloyd's Rep. 456.

[96] [1949] 1 K.B. 227; *Combe v. Combe* [1951] 2 K.B. 215 at p. 219, *per* Denning L.J. See also *Western Fish Products Ltd v. Penwith District Council* [1981] 2 All E.R. 204; *Rootkin v. Kent County Council* [1981] 1 W.L.R. 1186.

[97] [1947] K.B. 130.

[98] *Combe v. Combe* [1951] 2 K.B. 215; *Ajayi v. R.T. Briscoe (Nigeria) Ltd* [1964] 1 W.L.R. 1326; *W.J. Alan & Co. Ltd v. El Nasr Export and Import Co.* [1972] 2 Q.B. 189.

[99] *Foot Clinics (1943) Ltd v. Cooper's Gowns Ltd* [1947] K.B. 506.

[1] See *Combe v. Combe* [1951] 2 K.B. 215 at p. 220.

[2] (1862) 3 Giff. 592.

[3] (1877) 2 App.Cas. 439.

[4] [1947] K.B. 130.

plaintiffs claimed the full rent as from the middle of that year. They succeeded. Denning J., however, stated that they would have been estopped from claiming the full rent for the period from 1940 to 1945, on the ground that though not technically bound because of the lack of consideration, the plaintiffs had intended the defendants to rely on the promise and the defendants had acted on the faith of it.

Promissory estoppel contains a number of features which distinguish it from estoppel by representation of fact.[5] First, in that the representation may be one of intention and not one of fact; which raises the question whether it is inconsistent with the House of Lords decision in *Jorden v. Money*.[6] But the doctrine is now well established.[7] Secondly, the requirement of detriment to the representee is less stringent in the case of promissory estoppel. Financial loss or other detriment is of course sufficient; but it seems that it is not necessary to show more than that the representee committed himself to a particular course of action as a result of the representation.[8] Thirdly, the effect of the estoppel may not be permanent. The representor may escape from the burden of the equity if he can ensure that the representee will not be prejudiced.[9] But, consistently with estoppel by representation, promissory estoppel does not create a cause of action. It is a shield and not a sword.[10]

iii. Proprietary Estoppel.

(a) *General Principles.* This doctrine is applicable where one party knowingly encourages another to act, or acquiesces in the other's actions, to his detriment and in infringement of the first party's rights. He will be unable to complain later about the infringement, and may indeed be required to make good the expectation which he encouraged in the other party. Unlike other estoppels, therefore, this doctrine may, in some circumstances, create a claim, and an entitlement to positive proprietary rights; in others, it

---

[5] See generally (1947) 63 L.Q.R. 283 (G. Cheshire and C. Fifoot); (1951) 67 L.Q.R. 330 (J. Wilson); (1952) 15 M.L.R. 1 (Denning L.J.); (1952) 15 M.L.R. 325 (L. Sheridan).

[6] (1854) 5 H.L.Cas. 185. See *Foran v. Wight* (1989) 168 C.L.R. 385 at p. 411.

[7] But it "may need to be reviewed and reduced to a coherent body of doctrine by the Courts": *Woodhouse A.C. Israel Cocoa Ltd v. Nigerian Produce Marketing Co. Ltd* [1972] A.C. 741 at p. 758 (*per* Lord Hailsham).

[8] *Central London Property Ltd v. High Trees House Ltd* [1947] K.B. 130; *W.J. Alan & Co. Ltd v. El Nasr Export and Import Co.* [1972] 2 Q.B. 189; *Ajayi v. R.T. Briscoe (Nigeria) Ltd* [1964] 1 W.L.R. 1326.

[9] *Tool Metal Manufacturing Co. Ltd v. Tungsten Electric Co. Ltd* [1955] 1 W.L.R. 766.

[10] *Combe v. Combe* [1951] 2 K.B. 215 at p. 224. See generally (1983) 42 C.L.J. 257 (M. Thompson). *Cf. Waltons Stores (Interstate) v. Maher* (1988) 62 A.L.J.R. 110.

can operate negatively, or can produce a compromise situation appropriate to the particular circumstances. As far as interests in the home are concerned, the modern tendency is to assimilate proprietary estoppel and common intention constructive trusts.[11]

One question which arises is whether the courts should decree a remedy which fufils the expectations of the claimant[12] or one which merely reverses the detriment. The latter is all that is required to avoid unjust enrichment, whereas the former might be said to give a promise unsupported by consideration the effect of a contract. The better view is that the aim should be the reversal of detriment, as it would normally be inequitable to insist on a remedy which is disproportionate to the detriment.[13] There may, however, be special reasons for going further in some cases.[14]

Detrimental reliance need not involve the expenditure of money on the land.[15] In *Greasley v. Cooke*,[16] the plaintiff served notice to quit on the defendant, who had moved into the property as a servant, but had cohabited with the owner's son, K, and had stayed on after the owner's death, continuing to care for the family, which included a mentally-ill daughter. She had remained without payment since 1948, encouraged by K, now deceased, and his brother (the plaintiff) to believe that it was her home for life. The Court of Appeal held that she was entitled to remain as long as she wished. Lord Denning M.R. appeared to suggest that it was not necessary that the claimant should have acted to her detriment[17]: "it is sufficient if the party, to whom the assurance is given, acts on the faith of it—in such circumstances that it would be unjust and inequitable for the party making the assurance to go back on it. . . . There is no need for her to prove that she acted to her detriment or to her prejudice."[18] Subsequent cases, however, have made it clear that these comments

---

[11] *Ante*, p. 268.

[12] *Pascoe v. Turner* [1979] 1 W.L.R. 431, *post*, p. 890; (1984) 100 L.Q.R. 376 (S. Moriarty); [1986] Conv. 406 (M. Thompson); *Re Basham* [1986] 1 W.L.R. 1498, *post*, p. 892; *Durant v. Heritage* [1994] E.G.C.S. 134; *Wayling v. Jones* (1995) 69 P. & C.R. 170; *Price v. Hartwell* [1996] E.G.C.S. 98.

[13] *Waltons Stores (Interstate) Ltd v. Maher* (1988) 62 A.L.J.R. 110 at p. 126; *Commonwealth of Australia v. Verwayen* (1990) 64 A.L.J.R. 540 at p. 546. See also *Crabb v. Arun District Council* [1976] Ch. 179 at p. 198; *Baker v. Baker* [1993] 2 F.L.R. 247 (an unusual case where the detriment exceeded the value of the expected interest); *Sledmore v. Dalby* (1996) 72 P. & C.R. 196 (proportionality required).

[14] *Pascoe v. Turner*, *supra* (interest less than fee simple considered insecure against future purchasers).

[15] For the application of the doctrine to property other than land, see *Western Fish Products Ltd v. Penwith District Council* [1981] 2 All E.R. 204 at p. 218; *Moorgate Mercantile Co. Ltd v. Twitchings* [1976] Q.B. 225 at p. 242; (1981) 40 C.L.J. 340 (P. Matthews).

[16] [1980] 1 W.L.R. 1306; (1981) 44 M.L.R. 461 (G. Woodman).

[17] Here in any event the claimant had foregone wages and perhaps lost job opportunities.

[18] *Ibid.* at pp. 1311–1312. This resembles the requirements of promissory estoppel (*supra*, note 8).

related only to the burden of proving reliance. In *Coombes v. Smith*[19] (the facts of which have already been given[20]) Lord Denning's statement was interpreted as meaning merely that where the plaintiff has adopted a detrimental course of conduct after the defendant's assurances, there is a rebuttable presumption that this was done in reliance upon the assurances. Here the claim based on proprietary estoppel failed. The plaintiff had no mistaken belief that she had a right to remain indefinitely, and in any event there was no detrimental act. Her acts in leaving her husband, becoming pregnant and looking after the house were not done in reliance on any expectation of an interest and were not detrimental.[21] Other decisions have shown more lenience on "reliance". In *Matharu v. Matharu*[22] a married couple had improved property owned by the husband's father, who had encouraged the wife to believe that it belonged to her husband. She was granted a licence to occupy for life even though some of the improvements were done after she discovered the truth. In *Wayling v. Jones*[23] the plaintiff helped the deceased, with whom he cohabited, to run a café merely for pocket money, and acted as his chauffeur and companion. The deceased promised to leave him a house and business, but all he received by will was a car and furniture. The café had been sold and at his death the deceased owned a hotel. The plaintiff was awarded the proceeds of sale of the hotel (over £72,000), even though his evidence was that he would have stayed with the deceased if no promise had been made. It was held that the promise did not need to be the sole inducement for the plaintiff's conduct.

(b) *Remedies.* Early illustrations of the doctrine dealt with the protection of a lessee; as where a life tenant granted a 30 year lease, to the knowledge of remainderman who "stood by and encouraged" the tenant to take the lease and incur expenditures. Lord Hardwick confirmed the tenant in the balance of his lease after the life tenant's death.[24]

Other cases deal with activities on a party's own land which require facilities from a neighbour; allowing that party to acquire a

---

[19] [1986] 1 W.L.R. 808; (1986) 45 C.L.J. 394 (D. Hayton); *Wayling v. Jones* (1995) 69 P. & C.R. 170. See also *Stevens & Cutting Ltd v. Anderson* [1990] 1 E.G.L.R. 95, suggesting that the headnote in *Greasley* is wrong: the decision was on the burden of proof of reliance, not of detriment.

[20] *Ante*, p. 875 (the contract claim).

[21] *cf. Grant v. Edwards* [1986] Ch. 638, *ante*, p. 263.

[22] (1994) 68 P. & C.R. 93; (1994) 24 Fam. Law. 625 (J. Dewar); [1995] Conv. 61 (M. Welstead); (1995) 58 M.L.R. 411 (P. Milne); [1995] 7 C.F.L.Q. 59 (G. Battersby).

[23] *Supra*; (1995) 111 L.Q.R. 389 (E. Cooke); [1995] Conv. 409 (C. Davis); (1996) 16 L.S. 218 (A. Lawson).

[24] *Huning v. Ferrers* (1711) Gilb.Eq. 85; *East India Co. v. Vincent* (1740) 2 Atk. 83; *Stiles v. Cowper* (1748) 3 Atk. 692; *Jackson v. Cator* (1800) 5 Ves. 688 (tenant making alterations to landlord's knowledge).

right in the nature of an easement; as where a millowner erects a mill on the understanding, to the knowledge of a canal owner, that he could use canal water to generate steam[25]; or where the defendants constructed a sewer over a strip of the plaintiff's land, and the plaintiff failed to complain until the construction of the sewer was complete,[26] or where a landowner subdivides his land in reliance on a right of way being granted by a neighbour (the local authority) through a specified outlet[27]; or where one party with the knowledge and consent of his neighbour, builds so as to encroach on the neighbour's land.[28] The doctrine does not, however, apply where the claimant does acts on his own land which are not done in the expectation of acquiring rights over the land of another.[29]

The most extreme cases are those where a non-owner, in reliance upon a gratuitous promise of a gift of the land, has built on or improved the land. Clearly some remedy is required. In some cases the licensee has been protected from eviction without obtaining a proprietary interest in the land.

In *Inwards v. Baker*,[30] Mr Baker's son, Jack, decided to build a bungalow upon land which he hoped to purchase, but the project proved to be too expensive. Mr Baker suggested that Jack should put the bungalow on land already owned by him; that would save some expense, and Jack could build a bigger bungalow. This was done. Jack lived there some 40 years before the proceedings began in 1963. The father died in 1951, leaving a will dated 1922, under which the land was left to others.

The Court of Appeal held that the son should not be disturbed as long as he wished to stay. This is the first case, as far as is known, in which a licence is expressly referred to as one "created by estoppel."[31] Negative protection only was considered, because "proprietary estoppel" had not yet been introduced into the licence cases.

---

[25] *Rochdale Canal Co. v. King* (1853) 16 Beav. 630.
[26] *Armstrong v. Sheppard & Short Ltd* [1959] 2 Q.B. 384.
[27] *Crabb v. Arun D.C.* [1976] Ch. 179.
[28] *Hopgood v. Brown* [1955] 1 W.L.R. 213; *Ives (E.R.) Investments Co. v. High* [1967] 2 Q.B. 379.
[29] *Western Fish Products Ltd v. Penwith District Council* [1981] 2 All E.R. 204 (no estoppel where plaintiff spent money on own land relying on planning officer's assurance that planning permission would be granted; doctrine in any event not available against statutory body exercising statutory discretion or performing statutory duty; *Rootkin v. Kent County Council* [1981] 1 W.L.R. 1186); *Lloyd's Bank plc v. Carrick* [1996] 4 All E.R. 630; [1996] Conv. 295 (M. Thompson). *Cf. Lim Teng Huan v. Ang Swee Chuan* [1992] 1 W.L.R. 113 (co-owned land).
[30] [1965] 2 Q.B. 29; *Jones v. Jones* [1977] 1 W.L.R. 438; *Matharu v. Matharu* (1994) 68 P. & C.R. 93.
[31] By Danckwerts L.J. at p. 38.

On other occasions, the non-owner has been given a lien on the land for his expenditure[32]; or compensation for the value of the improvements[33]; or awarded the improved land on payment of a reasonable price for the site[34]; or a right to occupy until expenditure on improvements has been reimbursed[35]; or a non-assignable lease at a nominal rent, determinable on death.[36] A monetary award may be given where a right to occupy would be oppressive or unworkable,[37] or where the land in question has been sold.[38] In some cases, however, the minimum equity to do justice may have expired, so that it is no longer inequitable to enforce legal rights.[39] In other cases a conveyance of the freehold has been ordered.

In *Dillwyn v. Llewelyn*[40] a father encouraged his son to build a house on the father's land, and signed a memorandum purporting to convey the land to the son; but it was not by deed. The father's will left all his real estate upon certain trusts in favour of others. The son spent some £14,000 in building a house on the land, with his father's knowledge and approval. On the father's death, it was held that the son was entitled to a conveyance of the land.

On its face, the decision is inconsistent with two basic rules, namely that a gratuitous promise is not enforceable, and that an incomplete gift will not be completed in favour of a volunteer.[41] Detrimental reliance is not consideration under English law. Further, the solution is not just and equitable. There was no reason why the son should have a transfer of the land at the expense of the father's estate. Too much has been read into this case. It has been regarded as the origin of the doctrine of proprietary estoppel[42]; though that phrase would have meant nothing to Lord Westbury.[43]

---

[32] *Unity Joint Stock Mutual Banking Association v. King* (1858) 25 Beav. 72.

[33] *Raffaele v. Raffaele* [1962] W.A.R. 29. See also *Plimmer v. Wellington Corporation* (1884) 9 App.Cas. 699.

[34] *Duke of Beaufort v. Patrick* (1853) 17 Beav. 60; *Lim Teng Huan v. Ang Swee Chuan* [1992] 1 W.L.R. 113 (house built on land co-owned by parties, but contract to build house void for uncertainty).

[35] *Dodsworth v. Dodsworth* (1973) 228 E.G. 1115.

[36] *Griffiths v. Williams* (1977) 288 E.G. 947.

[37] *Baker v. Baker* [1993] 2 F.L.R. 247.

[38] *Wayling v. Jones* (1995) 69 P. & C.R. 170.

[39] *Sledmore v. Dalby* (1996) 72 P. & C.R. 196 (rent-free occupation for past 18 years sufficient recompense for improvements).

[40] (1862) 4 De G.F. & J. 517; *Chalmers v. Pardoe* [1963] 1 W.L.R. 677; *Raffaele v. Raffaele, supra*; (1963) 79 L.Q.R. 238 (D. Allen).

[41] See (1980) 96 L.Q.R. 534 at pp. 539–542 (S. Naresh).

[42] See *Sen v. Headley* [1991] Ch. 425 at p. 439.

[43] Dawson & Pearce, p. 34.

Perhaps the most extreme of the cases on proprietary estoppel, resulting in an extraordinary windfall for the licensee, is *Pascoe v. Turner*.[44]

The plaintiff and defendant lived together in the plaintiff's home. Later the plaintiff purchased another house and the couple moved in. When the relationship ended he told the defendant that the house was hers and everything in it. In reliance on this gratuitous promise, she expended, to the plaintiff's knowledge, her own money on repairs, improvements and redecoration, and also on furniture. Later the plaintiff gave the defendant two month's notice to determine the licence. Even though the defendant never sought to establish that she had spent more money on the house than she would have done had she believed that she only had a licence to live there for her lifetime, the Court of Appeal felt that protection for her lifetime was insecure, and awarded a conveyance of the house.

Finally, the court will not make an order which would be unworkable in view of family discord. In such a case a clean break may be the best solution, involving an award of compensation rather than a proprietary interest.[45] Thus the equity may be satisfied in a different way from that which the parties intended when on good terms.

(c) *Judicial Formulations.* Two early judicial formulations of the doctrine come from statements of Lord Kingsdown and Fry J. Lord Kingsdown, with the old cases of disappointed lessees in mind, explained the doctrine as follows[46]:

"If a man, under a verbal agreement with a landlord for a certain interest in land, or, what amounts to the same thing, under an expectation, created or encouraged by the Landlord, that he shall have a certain interest, takes possession of such land, with the consent of the landlord, and upon the face of such promise or expectation, with the knowledge of the landlord, and without objection by him, laid out money on the land, a Court of Equity will compel the landlord to give effect to such promise or expectation."

Fry J. in *Willmott v. Barber*[47] laid down the principle in more specific detail, in what have been called the "five probanda." He said:

---

[44] [1979] 1 W.L.R. 431; *Voyce v. Voyce* (1991) 62 P. & C.R. 290.

[45] *Burrows v. Sharp* (1991) 23 H.L.R. 82; [1992] Conv. 54 (J. Martin); *Baker v. Baker* [1993] 2 F.L.R. 247; (1994) 144 N.L.J. 264 (J. Martin).

[46] *Ramsden v. Dyson* (1866) L.R. 1 H.L. 129 at p. 170. It would be otherwise if the expectation was not created nor encouraged by the landlord; *ibid.*, p. 171.

[47] (1880) 15 Ch.D. 96 at pp. 105–106.

"In the first place the plaintiff must have made a mistake as to his legal rights.[48] Secondly, the plaintiff must have expended some money or must have done some act (not necessarily upon the defendant's land) on the faith of his mistaken belief. Thirdly, the defendant, the possessor of the legal right, must know of the existence of his own right which is inconsistent with the right claimed by the plaintiff. If he does not known of it he is in the same position as the plaintiff, and the doctrine of acquiescence is founded upon conduct with a knowledge of your legal rights. Fourthly, the defendant, the possessor of the legal right, must know of the plaintiff's mistaken belief to his rights. If he does not, there is nothing which calls upon him to assert his own rights. Lastly, the defendant, the possessor of the legal right, must have encouraged the plaintiff in his expenditure of money or in the other acts which he has done, either directly or by abstaining from asserting his legal right."[49]

Modern judicial formulations of the doctrine have moved away from the inflexibility of the "five probanda." In *Taylors Fashions Ltd v. Liverpool Victoria Trustees Co. Ltd,*[50] Oliver J. held that estoppel by acquiescence was not restricted to cases where the defendant knew his rights. There were many circumstances of estoppel, and it was not possible to lay down strict and inflexible rules. The application of the *Ramsden v. Dyson*[51] principle "requires a very much broader approach which is directed to ascertaining whether, in particular individual circumstances, it would be unconscionable for a party to be permitted to deny that which, knowingly or unknowingly, he has allowed or encouraged another to assume to his detriment rather than to inquiring whether the circumstances can be fitted within the confines of some preconceived formula serving as a universal yardstick for every form of unconscionable behaviour."[52] "The inquiry which I have to make therefore . . . is simply whether, in all the circumstances of the case, it was unconscionable for the defendants to seek to take advantage of the mistake, which, at the material time, everybody shared. . . . "[53]

---

[48] The claim failed on this ground in *Att.-Gen. of Hong Kong v. Humphreys Estate (Queen's Gardens) Ltd* [1987] A.C. 114 (expenditure in reliance upon "subject to contract" agreement which was never finalised).

[49] See *Brinnand v. Ewens* (1987) 19 H.L.R. 415 (tenant had no claim for voluntary improvements where no reliance on any interest and no encouragement or acquiescence by landlord).

[50] [1981] 2 W.L.R. 576; [1982] Q.B. 133n.; [1982] Conv. 450 (P. Jackson).

[51] *Supra.*

[52] [1981] 2 W.L.R. 576 at p. 593. See also *Ives (E.R.) Investments Co. v. High* [1967] 2 Q.B. 379; *Shaw v. Applegate* [1977] 1 W.L.R. 970 at pp. 977–978, 980.

[53] *Ibid.* at p. 596. It was suggested that the "five probanda" might be necessary in a case of "standing by," where the defendant has done no positive act. The "five probanda" were, however, applied in *Coombes v. Smith* [1986] 1 W.L.R. 808 and *Matharu v. Matharu* (1994) 68 P. & C.R. 93.

This broad approach was adopted in *Amalgamated Investment and Property Co. Ltd (in liquidation) v. Texas Commerce International Bank Ltd*,[54] where Robert Goff J. said that "Of all doctrines, equitable estoppel is surely one of the most flexible . . . it cannot be right to restrict [it] to certain defined categories."[55] Similarly, Lord Denning M.R., in the Court of Appeal, considered that:

"The doctrine of estoppel is one of the most flexible and useful in the armoury of the law. But it has become overloaded with cases. . . . It has evolved during the last 150 years in a sequence of separate developments: proprietary estoppel, estoppel by representation of fact, estoppel by acquiescence, and promissory estoppel. At the same time it has been sought to be limited by a series of maxims: estoppel is only a rule of evidence; estoppel cannot give rise to a cause of action; estoppel cannot do away with the need for consideration; and so forth. All these can now be seen to merge into one general principle shorn of limitations. When the parties to a transaction proceed on the basis of an underlying assumption—either of fact or of law—whether due to misrepresentation or mistake makes no difference—on which they have conducted the dealings between them—neither of them will be allowed to go back on that assumption when it would be unfair or unjust to allow him to do so. If one of them does seek to go back on it, the courts will give the other such remedy as the equity of the case demands."[56]

It seems that we have moved away from the basic rule that an estoppel is a shield and not a sword. If an injunction suffices as the remedy, the estoppel operates in the traditional way as a shield and not a sword. But if something more is needed, like the grant to the licensee of a proprietary interest, then we call it a case of proprietary estoppel, and make use of the additional remedies. The constructive trust has even been called upon to fill in possible gaps in the estoppel doctrine.

In *Re Basham*[57] the plaintiff's mother married her stepfather in 1936 when the plaintiff was aged 15. The plaintiff lived with them until her marriage in 1941, helping to run the business without

[54] [1982] Q.B. 84; *Pacol Ltd v. Trade Lines Ltd* [1982] 1 Lloyd's Rep. 456; *Lloyd's Bank plc v. Carrick* [1996] 4 All E.R. 630.

[55] *Ibid*. at p. 103.

[56] *Ibid*. at p. 122. See also *Att.-Gen. of Hong Kong v. Humphreys Estate (Queen's Gardens) Ltd* [1987] A.C. 114; *Lim Teng Huan v. Ang Swee Chuan* [1992] 1 W.L.R. 113 (where both parties wrongly assumed they had a contract); [1993] Conv. 173 (S. Goo); *John v. George* (1996) 71 P. & C.R. 375.

[57] [1986] 1 W.L.R. 1498; *Durant v. Heritage* [1994] E.G.C.S. 134; *Wayling v. Jones* (1995) 69 P. & C.R. 170; *Price v. Hartwell* [1996] E.G.C.S. 98.

pay on the understanding that she would inherit from her step-father. He dissuaded the plaintiff's husband from taking a job with a tied cottage, saying he would help them to get a house. After the mother's death in 1976, the plaintiff and her husband helped her stepfather in his house and garden, prepared his meals, bought carpets for the house, and paid solicitors for advice over a boundary dispute. The stepfather constantly assured the plaintiff that the house would be hers, but he died intestate. The plaintiff, who did not benefit under the intestacy, succeeded in her claim to the whole estate under the doctrine of proprietary estoppel. It was held that the doctrine was not confined to a case where the plaintiff's belief related to an existing right and to specific assets.[58] Where the belief related to a future right, a species of constructive trust arose. The doctrines of estoppel, mutual wills[59] and secret trusts[60] had a common theme, and thus reliance could be placed on cases such as *Re Cleaver*,[61] where an expectation of inheritance of non-specific assets gave rise to a constructive trust under the mutual wills doctrine. The proper remedy was an award of the entire estate, to satisfy the expectations encouraged by the deceased.

Clearly the plaintiff should have some remedy, however it is doubtful whether the introduction of the constructive trust is either necessary or desirable.[62] Under the modern flexible approach to proprietary estoppel,[63] the plaintiff may succeed without a con-structive trust. If that is not so, the plaintiff should not succeed under estoppel but should look to other remedies.[64]

B. Conveyancing Problems Caused by Licences by Estoppel[65]

The question to be considered in this section is whether a licence by estoppel has the status of a proprietary interest prior to the litigation, and, if so, how it may be protected against successors in

---

[58] *cf. Layton v. Martin* (1986) 16 Fam. Law. 212, where the deceased's assurances that he would provide for the plaintiff by will could not found a claim to proprietary estoppel, which arose only in connection with specific assets. See [1996] Conv. 193 (C. Davis).

[59] *Ante*, p. 305.

[60] *Ante*, Chap. 5.

[61] [1981] 1 W.L.R. 939, *ante*, p. 306. If the analogy with the surviving testator in *Re Cleaver* is taken too far, a finding that the estopped party holds his estate on constructive trust seems to restrict the choice of discretionary remedies open to the court.

[62] See [1987] Conv. 211 (J. Martin); (1987) 46 C.L.J. 215 (D. Hayton); All E.R.Rev. 1987, p. 156 (P. Clarke) and p. 263 (C. Sherrin); (1988) 8 L.S. 92 at pp. 101 *et seq.* (M. Davey). See, however, *Sen v. Headley* [1991] Ch. 425 at p. 440.

[63] *Supra*.

[64] For example, under the Inheritance (Provision for Family and Dependants) Act 1975.

[65] See generally (1984) 100 L.Q.R. 376 (S. Moriarty); [1981] Conv. 212 (A. Briggs) and 347 (P. Todd); [1983] Conv. 50 (M. Thompson) and 285 (A. Briggs); (1988) 51 M.L.R. 226 (J. Hill).

title of the estopped party. If it is incapable of binding successors, then the licensee (unless the licence is contractual[66]) has no remedy.

i. Status Prior to Court Order. Clearly a recognised proprietary interest may be conferred by the court, such as the conveyance of the fee simple or the grant of a life interest. More difficult is the question whether the estoppel licensee has an interest capable of binding a third party prior to the order of the court. What would have happened, for example, if the legal owner in *Pascoe v. Turner*[67] had conveyed the house to a purchaser before the matter came to court? One view is that the estoppel interest is too uncertain and unstable to qualify as a proprietary interest, even a "mere equity", before the court's decree.[68] Another view is that the interest is a "mere equity" capable of binding third parties, at any rate volunteers and purchasers with actual notice.[69] Another is that it can bind third parties under the ordinary rules of priorities, even though the interest is inchoate and does not "crystallise" until the court order.[70]

There is little authority on the point. Estoppel interests have been held binding on volunteers[71] and purchasers with actual notice.[72] In *Voyce v. Voyce*[73] the Court of Appeal held that the estoppel was binding on a donee taking with notice from the estopped party, and ordered the donee to convey the fee simple to the claimant. Dillon L.J. held that the claimant was the equitable owner before the conveyance (in the context of a dispute between the parties concerning a right to light), because his equitable right (an "equity") had accrued long before the conveyance.[74] Similarly Nourse L.J. in *Sen v. Headley*[75] said that in estoppel cases where the promisee had a right to a conveyance, an implied or constructive trust arose once all

---

[66] In which case he may sue the licensor. He cannot sue a third party unless a constructive trust has arisen; *Ashburn Anstalt v. Arnold* [1989] Ch. 1; *ante*, p. 880.

[67] [1979] 1 W.L.R. 431; *ante*, p. 890.

[68] (1990) 106 L.Q.R. 87 at p. 97 and [1990] Conv. 370 at pp. 380–384 (D. Hayton); [1991] Conv. 155 (P. Evans); (1992) 22 Fam. Law. 72 (P. Clarke); (1993) 109 L.Q.R. 114 (P. Ferguson); (1996) 16 L.S. 325 at p. 342 (N. Glover and P. Todd).

[69] Warburton, *Sharing Residential Property*, pp. 156–157; (1991) 5 *Trust Law International* 9 (J. Warburton).

[70] [1991] Conv. 36 and (1995) 58 M.L.R. 637 at pp. 640–643 (G. Battersby); (1993) 3 Carib.L.R. 96 at p. 109 (R. Smith); (1994) 14 L.S. 147 (S. Baughen); [1996] Conv. 34 (J. Howell) and p. 193 (C. Davis).

[71] *Dillwyn v. Llewelyn* (1862) 4 De G.F. & J. 517 and *Inwards v. Baker* [1965] 2 Q.B. 29 (trustees of will); *Voyce v. Voyce* (1991) 62 P. & C.R. 290, *infra*.

[72] *Ives (E.R.) Investments Ltd v. High* [1967] 2 Q.B. 379; *Duke of Beaufort v. Patrick* (1853) 17 Beav. 60. A purchaser was bound in *J.T. Developments Ltd v. Quinn* (1991) 62 P. & C.R. 33, but the point was not argued. See also *Hopgood v. Brown* [1955] 1 W.L.R. 213 (estoppel by representation); *Lloyd's Bank plc v. Carrick* [1996] 4 All E.R. 630 at p. 642.

[73] (1991) 62 P. & C.R. 290; [1992] Conv. 56 (J. Martin).

[74] *Ibid.* at p. 294.

[75] [1991] Ch. 425 at p. 440; *Re Basham* [1986] 1 W.L.R. 1498.

.

the requirements of the estoppel doctrine were satisfied. All this suggests that a proprietary interest capable of binding a third party does arise before the court order, although presumably this cannot be so where the expectation did not relate to specific property.[76]

ii. Registered and Unregistered Land. Assuming that estoppel interests are capable of binding successors in title, the difficulty is that they do not readily fit into the conveyancing system. They are not overreachable by a disposition by two trustees.[77] In unregistered land they are not registrable under the Land Charges Act 1972[78] and, therefore depend on the doctrine of notice, under which occupation gives constructive notice. The position would be unsatisfactory if they were registrable, as they arise under informal arrangements without legal advice and would not be registered, and hence void against purchasers.

In the case of registered land the doctrine of notice does not apply. Interests are binding only if protected on the register or if over-riding. It seems that estoppel interests could be protected by regis-tering a caution,[79] although this would rarely be done. More useful is the possibility that an estoppel licensee in occupation has an overriding interest under section 70(1)(g) of the Land Registration Act 1925. This provision requires not only occupation but a property right of some kind.[80]

Thus conveyancing complications will be increased if an estoppel interest is capable of binding a successor prior to the order of the court which crystallises the interest. However, the difficulties seem no greater than those which arise in respect of other informally created interests, such as shares in the family home under con-structive trusts.[81]

iii. Other Problems Arising Under the Doctrine of Pro-prietary Estoppel.

(a) *Necessity for Litigation.* The problems here are the same as those met in the context of licences giving rise to a constructive trust. No one knows, without the court's decision, whether or not the licensee is entitled to have an interest in the land transferred to him,

---

[76] *Re Basham, supra; ante,* p. 892.

[77] They are not within L.P.A. 1925, s.2.

[78] s.2 (easement, right or privilege, being merely equitable) has been narrowly construed; *Shiloh Spinners Ltd v. Harding* [1973] A.C. 691. As to registration as a pending land action, see *Haslemere Estates Ltd v. Baker* [1982] 1 W.L.R. 1109.

[79] See Ruoff and Roper, *Registered Conveyancing* (6th ed.), para. 8.02; [1983] Conv. 99 (T. Bailey); (1985) 44 C.L.J. 280 (M. Thompson).

[80] *National Provincial Bank Ltd v. Ainsworth* [1965] A.C. 1175.

[81] *Ante,* Chap. 11. The tendency to assimilate the doctrines of estoppel and constructive trusts has been mentioned, *ante,* p. 886.

nor what the interest will be. If the court orders the transfer of any interest, the documentation will be completed. Until then, a third party's position is as discussed above.

(b) *Effect of Life Interest.* Where the expectation of the licensee was to occupy the licensor's property for life, as is not uncommon in the family context, the award of a life interest to the licensee caused problems until recently. The difficulty was that such a life interest brought the complex provisions of the Settled Land Act 1925 into play, under which the life tenant acquired the legal estate and extensive powers of sale and leasing. Thus in *Ungurian v. Lesnoff*[82] a life interest under the Settled Land Act arose (either on the basis of estoppel or a common intention constructive trust[83]) in favour of the defendant, who had given up her flat, nationality and career to live with the plaintiff. He bought a house for them to live in, which the defendant improved, but they separated after four years. An irrevocable licence was considered inadequate, but an outright conveyance would have gone beyond what the parties intended.

Most modern cases, however, have avoided a solution involving the Settled Land Act. In *Dodsworth v. Dodsworth*[84] the defendants had spent over £700 on improvements in the belief that they would have a right to occupy for life. They were held entitled to occupy until the expenditure had been reimbursed. Similarly in *Griffiths v. Williams*,[85] where a daughter looked after her mother and spent money on repairs and improvements to the house in the belief that she had a home there for life, but the house was left to another relative. In order to avoid the complications of the Settled Land Act, she was awarded a non-assignable lease at a nominal rent, determinable on death.

Since the Trusts of Land and Appointment of Trustees Act 1996 came into operation it is no longer possible to create a settlement under the 1925 Act. The problem discussed above has diminished because the award of a life interest will now bring into play the less complex "trust of land", which was explained in Chapter 11.

---

[82] [1990] Ch. 206. The 1925 Act was also applied in *Costello v. Costello* (1995) 70 P. & C.R. 297, where a deed provided that parents could occupy rent free for life.
[83] *Ante*, p. 263.
[84] (1973) 228 E.G. 1115.
[85] (1977) 248 E.G. 947.

INDEX

ACCOUNT,
  audit of trustees', 549
    pension fund, 465, 471
  joint bank, 247, 255
  liability to,
    agent, 595
    fiduciaries, 30, 595 *et seq.*
    trustee, 30, 591 *et seq.*, 655
  trustees' duty to keep, 548
    final, 535

ACCUMULATION,
  maintenance trusts, and, 226
  minors, for, 198, 572
  periods of, 199
  powers of, in trustees, 198, 203,
    206
  termination of, 612, 619
  Trustee Act 1925, s.31, under, 198,
    572
  V.T.A. 1958, and, 612, 624

ACQUIESCENCE. *See also* LACHES.
  beneficiary by, to breach of trust,
    646, 655
  equitable claims, 655
  estoppel by, 141, 885
  injunction, 773
  rectification, 845
  release of trustees from liability,
    646

ADEMPTION,
  performance and, 859
  satisfaction distinguished, 859, 862,
    863

ADMINISTRATOR. *See* PERSONAL
  REPRESENTATIVES.

ADVANCEMENT,
  meaning of, 576 *et seq.*

ADVANCEMENT—*cont.*
  power of,
    court, inherent, of, 583
    trustees', of, 570, 576 *et seq. See
      also* POWERS OF TRUSTEES.
  presumption of, 231, 246–249, 255,
    264, 272
    children, 248, 255
    engaged couple, 247
    evidence, 249 *et seq.*
    father and child, 248, 255
    husband and wife, 246–248, 255,
      264, 272
    loco parentis, in, 230, 248, 255
    purchase in name of another, 231,
      254 *et seq.*
    resulting trust, displacing, 230,
      246
  protective trust, 193
  satisfaction of legacy or debt,
    860–863
  variation of trust, for purposes of,
    613, 619

AFTER-ACQUIRED PROPERTY,
  constitution of trust of, 133
  covenant to settle, 121 *et seq.*
  performance and, 863–865
  trust of, 133–135

AGENCY,
  death, cannot arise on, 365, 370
  distinguished from trust, 47

AGENT,
  appointment of, by trustees,
    559–570
    See also POWERS OF TRUSTEES,
    delegation
  fiduciary position of, 292, 595 *et
    seq.*

AGENT—*cont.*
interest charged to, 638
liability of, 47, 292, 303, 595
limitation, period of, 651
trustee's liability for defaults of,
559–570

ALIENATION,
conditions in restraint of, 186, 332
pension rights, 472
perpetuity rule, and, 334–337

ALLHUSEN *v.* WHITTELL, Rule in, 546

ANIMALS,
trusts for, 348, 355, 400, 406

ANNUITY,
specific performance of contract to
purchase, 703, 730

ANTE-NUPTIAL AGREEMENT, 122n. *See
also* COVENANT, property, to
settle.

APPOINTMENT,
new trustees, of, 492 *et seq.*
power of. *See* POWER OF
APPOINTMENT.

APPORTIONMENT,
Act, 545
Allhusen v. Whittell, rule in, 546
Atkinson, Re, rule in, 547
capital and income, 538
capital payment, 547–548
Chesterfield's Trusts, Earl of, rule
in, 541, 543
convert, duty to, 538
debts, 546
generally, 540 *et seq.*
Howe v. Earl Dartmouth, rule in,
538 *et seq.*
leaseholds, 543
life tenant, death of, 545
mortgaged property, 547
reversionary interests, 541
shares cum dividend, 547
trustees' duty of, 540 *et seq.*
wasting assets, 540

ARRANGEMENT,
court, approval of, by, 613–629
deed of,
creditors, 342, 489
family, 826

ASSENT, 53–57

ASSIGNMENT OF EQUITABLE INTEREST,
78

ATTORNEY-GENERAL,
charitable trust, 46, 351, 379, 429,
447, 452
injunction to restrain public wrongs,
741, 797
relator actions, 741, 769, 797

AUDIT,
pension fund, 465, 471
trust accounts, of, 549

AUTHORISED INVESTMENTS, 518–520
See also INVESTMENT BY TRUSTEES.

BAILMENT,
distinguished from trust, 46

BANK ACCOUNT,
joint, 247, 255
tracing into, 670

BANKER,
employment of, trustee by, 561, 563
liability for trust funds, 293–304

BANKRUPTCY,
ante-nuptial,
settlement, 122n., 339
benefits to bankrupt, 188, 194
determinable interest on, 186, 188
discretionary trusts,
arising on, 188, 189, 194
of beneficiary under, 194, 196
forfeiture of life interest on, 188,
189, 194
pension fund, 472
settlor, of,
protective trust, under, 187
voluntary settlement, under,
342–344
trustee, of, 493, 497
voluntary settlements on, 342–344

BARE TRUSTS, 36, 69, 273

BEARER BONDS,
transfer to new trustees, 499n.

BENEFICIARY,
ascertainable, must be, 63, 97 *et
seq.*, 198, 351
breach of trust by, 633
consent to breach of trust, 645, 647
consultation of, by trustees, 280
control of trustees, by, 496, 498,
611

BENEFICIARY—*cont.*
  equitable ownership of, 17, 45, 47,
    59, 111, 203, 323
  impounding beneficial interest of,
    647
  infant. *See* MINOR.
  information concerning trust, 471,
    548–551
  minor, 570–576
  overpaid, 533
  principal, 189, 190, 193, 194
  sale by, to trustees, 591
  sui juris, all, 64, 204, 496, 498,
    555, 611
  termination of trust by, 64, 204,
    555, 611
  trustee, 633, 643
  unaware of trust, 121

BENJAMIN ORDER, 534, 687n.

BILL OF EXCHANGE,
  transferable by indorsement, 115,
    120

BONA FIDE PURCHASER FOR VALUE
    WITHOUT NOTICE. *See*
    PURCHASER.

BONA VACANTIA,
  surplus funds, 233–241, 429, 443,
    470

BREACH OF TRUST,
  acquiescence by beneficiary, 646,
    655
  after retirement, 633
  authorised by court, 632
  beneficiary trustee, 633, 643
  compensatory liability, 632
  contribution, 641
  criminal liability, 643
  exemption clauses, 483
  fraudulent, 639, 642
  indemnity, 642, 647
  injunction to restrain, 791
  interest charged, 638
  joint and several liability, 641
  laches, 651, 654
  liability *inter se*, 641
  limitation, 651–655
  measure of, 633–641
    failure to invest, 637
    mortgage of realty, 638
    profits not balanced against
      losses, 639

BREACH OF TRUST—*cont.*
  measure of—*cont.*
    retention, improper, of
      investments, 636
    sale, improper, 637
    trade, employment of funds in,
      638
    unauthorised investments,
      purchase of, 636
  pension fund, sanctions for, 462
  personal liability, 632
  prior to appointment, 632
  proprietary remedies. *See*
    PROPRIETARY REMEDIES.
  protection of trustees, 644–655
    acquiescence by beneficiary, 646,
      655
    authorisation by court, 632
    consent to breach, 645
    impounding beneficiary's interest,
      647
    laches, 651, 654
    limitation of action, 651–655
    participation in breach, 645
    release, 633, 646
    T.A. 1925, s.61, 482, 483, 648
  retirement to permit, 633
  solicitor trustee, 642
  third party, assisting in 293, *et seq.*
  trustee beneficiary, 633, 643
  vicarious liability, 560, 562, 567,
    632

BUSINESS,
  investment in, 518 *et seq.*
  sale of, specific performance of,
    712, 730
  use of trust funds in, 638

CANCELLATION OF DEEDS, 30, 839n.

CAPACITY,
  settlor, to be, 73–75
  trustee, to be, 451, 464, 486–490

CAPITAL AND INCOME,
  Allhusen v. Whittell, rule in, 546
  Atkinson, Re, rule in, 547
  apportionment, 540 *et seq.*
  Chesterfield's Trusts, Earl of, rule
    in, 541, 543
  demerger, 548
  Howe v. Earl Dartmouth, rule in,
    538 *et seq.*
  life tenant and remainderman, 538
    et seq.

CAPITAL AND INCOME—*cont.*
receipt of, by trustees, 564
testator, death of, 545

CAPITAL GAINS TAX, 215–216, 515, 633n.

CAPITAL MONEY,
receipt for, 55, 276, 490, 491, 556, 557, 564, 569

CAPITAL TRANSFER TAX, 216, 217. *See also* INHERITANCE TAX.

CERTAINTY,
conditions, 90, 102, 109, 328, 333
powers, in, 63, 371
conceptual, 101, 328
evidential, 101
trusts, in,
charitable, 90, 379
discretionary, 64, 99
fixed, 64, 98
intention, 90
objects, 97 *et seq.*, 351
subject-matter, 93, 271, 309–310

CESTUI QUE TRUST. *See* BENEFICIARY.

CESTUI QUE USE, 9, 10, 32

CHANCELLOR, 5–9, 12–14

CHANCERY,
court, composition of, 14
Division, matters assigned to, 38
history of, 5–17
jurisdiction, 38

CHANGE OF POSITION, 301, 303, 679–681, 689

CHARGE,
distinguished from trust, 52, 241
land, registration of, 35, 895

CHARITABLE TRUSTS,
accumulation for, termination of, 380
administration of, 444 *et seq.*
accounts, 449
advice, 447
Annual Reports, 444, 447
Charities Official Investment Fund, 450
Charity Commissioners, 384, 386, 399–400, 444, 448
powers of, 448
charity proceedings, 448
Common Deposit Scheme, 450

CHARITABLE TRUSTS—*cont.*
administration of—*cont.*
Official Custodian for Charities, 445
pooling of trusts, 450
register, the, 446
reviews of charities, 453–454
Services, State, and, 453
advantages of, 378
aged, 401
animals, gifts for, 400, 406, 436
Attorney-General, 46, 351, 379, 429, 447, 452
beneficial to the community,
purposes, 398 *et seq.*, 419
animals, 400, 406, 436
environment, 407, 410
impotent and sick, 401
locality trust, 411, 422
overseas trusts, 384
political trusts, 393, 407
public benefit, 419
recreational trusts, 391, 402
social trusts, 402
certainty, not necessary, 90, 351, 379
Charities Act 1960, 430, 439, 444
— 1992, 444
— 1993, 439 *et seq.*
Charity Commissioners, 384, 386, 399–400, 444, 448
classification, 347, 376, 383, 398
cy-près, 430 *et seq. See also* CY-PRES.
definition, 347, 376, 383, 398
disaster appeals, 429
discrimination, 327, 328, 332, 387n., 392n., 430
disjunctive construction, 425
education,
advancement of, 388 *et seq.*
art, 390
closed scholarships, 414
independent schools, 394
personal nexus, 414
political propaganda, 393
professional bodies, 392
public benefit in, 413
recreation, 391
research, 389
sport, 391
endowment, 387, 443
environment, 407, 410
ex gratia payments, 452

CHARITABLE TRUSTS—*cont.*
exclusivity of charitable intent, 352,
384, 423
failure of. *See* CY-PRES.
fiscal privileges, 381
gift over to non-charity, 370–371,
380, 438
health, 401
hospitals, 402
international co-operation, trusts for,
384, 394, 399, 408n.
interpretation, 421 *et seq.*
investment of funds of, 450. *See
also* INVESTMENT BY TRUSTEES.
locality, for benefit of, 411, 422
main and subsidiary object, 423
masses, for, 356, 419
motive of donor, 422
overseas, 384
Pemsel's case, 383
perpetuities, rule against,
as applied to, 337, 380
gift over from charity to non-
charity, 370–371, 380, 438
personal nexus, 414, 420
political trusts, 393, 407
poverty, relief of, 386, 412
immediate distribution, 387
meaning of, 386
poor employees, 412
relations, 412
public benefit, 412
preamble to 43 Eliz. 1, 376, 383,
398
professional bodies, 392
public benefit, 384, 411 *et seq.*
rates, remission of, 382
recreation, 391, 402
register of, 446
religion, for the advancement of,
395
contemplative orders, 361, 417
masses, 356, 419
non-Christian religions, 396
public benefit, 417
related purposes, 397
scheme, 430 *et seq.*, 448
severance, 426
sign manual, 379, 430n., 433
social welfare, 404
spirit and intendment, 376, 383, 398
sport, 391, 402
taxation, freedom from, 381
tomb, maintenance of, 397

CHARITABLE TRUSTS—*cont.*
trustees,
charitable status of, 423
number of, 451, 491
removal of, 451
uncertainty, 379
validation by statute, 427
visitor, jurisdiction of, 445, 803
youth, 391, 402

CHATTELS,
ascertained, 702
contract for purchase of, 701
specific, 702
transfer of, 115, 138
unique, 701

CHEQUE,
death, not payable after, 136
donatio mortis causa, 138
endorsement, 115, 120
gift of, 115, 120

CHILD. *See also* MINOR.
accumulation for, 198, 572
advancement, presumption of, 230,
248, 255
illegitimate, 248, 326
income of, aggregation of, 214n.,
227, 575
undue influence over, 829, 831

CHOSE IN ACTION,
donatio mortis causa, 137, 138
trust of, 46, 93, 111, 124 *et seq.*

CLASS,
beneficiaries, 62–63, 203, 204
certainty of, 63, 97 *et seq.*

CLASSIFICATION OF TRUSTS, 64–70

CLAYTON'S CASE, RULE IN, 671n., 673

CLUBS AND ASSOCIATIONS,
expulsions from, 802
gifts to, 48, 359 *et seq.*, 370
property of, 235–241, 359 *et seq.*

COMMON INJUNCTION, 11, 16

COMMON LAW,
conflict with equity, 15–17
equitable rules prevail over, 15–17
remedies, inadequacy of, 30, 694,
737, 868, 869, 870

COMPANY,
directors of, 292, 593, 596, 598 *et
seq. See also* DIRECTOR.

COMPANY—*cont.*
  investment in shares of, 518 *et seq.*
  reduction of capital, 547
  transfer of shares in, 115, 117
  trustee as, 490

COMPENSATION,
  beneficiaries of, for breach, 631 *et seq.*
  pension fund, 471
  specific performance, subject to, 696, 721

COMPROMISE,
  approval of court for, 614
  family, fraud affecting, 826
  trustee's power of, 558

CONDITIONS,
  alienation, against, 186, 332
  appointment, attached to, 855
  certainty of, 90, 102, 109, 328, 333
  marriage, against, 329
  precedent, 109, 328, 333
  racial, 326, 332
  religious, 331
  subsequent, 186, 328, 333
    distinguished from determinable interest, 186, 328, 438
  trust, distinguished from, 52

CONDITIONS OF SALE, 722

CONFIDENTIAL INFORMATION, 23–24, 598 *et seq.*, 744, 794, 805
  injunction to protect, 744, 794 *et seq.*, 804

CONSCIENCE, CONCEPT OF, 4, 7, 32, 295–297, 317, 677, 881

CONSIDERATION,
  contract to create a trust requires, 113 *et seq.*
  defence to setting aside of settlement, 339, 341, 343
  marriage, 113, 122, *et seq.*, 339
  specific performance, necessary for, 121, 704

CONSTITUTION OF TRUSTS, 66, 111 *et seq.*, 492
  administrator, appointment of intended donee as, 135
  chose in action, trust of, 46, 93, 111, 124 *et seq.*
  contract to convey, 113, 121 *et seq.*
  conveyance to trustee, 112, 114–119
    bill of exchange, 115

CONSTITUTION OF TRUSTS—*cont.*
  conveyance to trustee—*cont.*
    chattels, 115
    copyright, 115
    equitable interests, 46, 78 *et seq.*, 111, 113, 115, 116
    land, 115, 118
    legal interests, 114
    shares, 115, 117–118
  covenant to settle, 113, 121 *et seq.*
    consideration, 113, 121, *et seq.*
    specific performance of, 121, 130
  damages, action for, 124, 125
  declaration,
    of self as trustee, 79, 112, 119
    of trust, 111
  donatio mortis causa, 137
  estoppel, 141
  exceptional cases, 135–141
  executor, appointment of intended donee as, 135
  future property, 133
  gift, imperfect, 112, 135–141
  marriage, consideration of, 113, 122 *et seq.*
  next-of-kin, 123
  secret trusts, 149, 159 *et seq.*
  Strong v. Bird, rule in, 135
  volunteer, equity will not assist, 67, 111 *et seq.*, 704

CONSTRUCTIVE FRAUD. *See* FRAUD.

CONSTRUCTIVE NOTICE. *See* NOTICE.

CONSTRUCTIVE TRUST, 31, 42, 68, 77, 85, 285 *et seq.*, 607–609, 879
  accountability, contrasted with, 288, 293, 294, 607–609
  classification of, 68, 285
  duties of constructive trustee, 287, 290
  estoppel,
    assimilation, 268, 886
  formalities, not necessary for, 76, 85, 162
  fraud, conveyance by, 314
  licensee, for, 320, 879
  matrimonial home, 261 *et seq.*, 318
  mutual wills, 65, 287, 305 *et seq.*
    agreement necessary for, 305
      remedy on, 307
    create constructive trust, 65, 307
    property effected by trust, 309
    receipt of benefits, 308–309
    survivor as trustee, 311

CONSTRUCTIVE TRUST—*cont.*
mutual wills—*cont.*
vested interests, beneficiaries
have, 308
when trust arises, 308
nature of, 285
proportionate share, and, 676
registered land, 322
remedy, 289
accountability, 288, 607–609
proprietary, 288, 323, 607–609
remedial constructive trust, 69,
289, 323
resulting trust, and, 67, 231, 264,
286
secret trusts as, 162, 314
terms of, 287
third parties, liability of, 293 *et seq.*
tracing, 288, 662 *et seq.*
trustee, constructive, duties of, 287,
290
de son tort, 298n.
knowledge of trust, 293
limitation, period of, 652
unjust enrichment, 69, 289–291,
300, 315, 317–324, 605,
608–609, 656, 675, 679, 688
volunteer, innocent, 289, 301, 677
when trust arises,
fraud, conveyance by, 314
intermeddler, 293 *et seq.*
killing, acquisition by, 315
licences, 320, 879
mutual wills, 305
profit by trustee or fiduciary, 292,
591 *et seq.*
renewal of lease, 292, 591
reversion, purchase of, 292, 592
vendor under specifically
enforceable contract for sale,
85, 312
writing, not necessary for, 76

CONTEMPT OF COURT, 7, 704, 739,
804, 806, 815

CONTINGENT INTEREST,
advancement from, 578, 582
income from, 574
maintenance from, 571, 574
pecuniary legacy, 575

CONTRACT,
co-existence with trust, 48, 49
Conditions of Sale, 722
divisible, 712

CONTRACT—*cont.*
for sale of land,
estate contract, 699
specific performance of, 699. *See*
SPECIFIC PERFORMANCE.
vendor as constructive trustee,
312
writing, necessity for, 85, 699
fraud, effect upon, 825 *et seq.*
implied, 875
injunction, to restrain breach of,
783, 871, 873
insurance, 826
mistake and misrepresentation,
affecting, 716, 818, 825, 839
negative provisions of, 783 *et seq.*,
872
open, 722
option, 850
quasi, 289–291, 533, 605, 656, 823,
844
rectification of. *See* RECTIFICATION.
rescission of. *See* RESCISSION.
services, personal, for, 707, 787
shares, 84–88, 701
specific performance of, 693–732.
See SPECIFIC PERFORMANCE.
trust, distinguished from, 48
to create, 48, 113, 121 *et seq.*
uberrimae fidei, 826
unincorporated association, 235 *et
seq.*, 359 *et seq.*, 370

CONVERSION, 849–852
contract to sell, under, 850
option to purchase, 850
trustee by, 652–653

CONVEYANCE,
constituting a trust, 111, 112,
114–116
fraudulent, 314
overreaching by, 36, 273, 276
personal representatives, by, 54–55
rectification of, 844
rescission of, 817 *et seq.*
undervalue, 338–345
voidable, 337–345

CO-OWNERSHIP, 272 *et seq.*
joint tenancy, 273–274
occupation, right to, 274
tenancy in common, 273–274
unincorporated associations, 359 *et
seq.*

COPYRIGHT,
assignment of, 115
convert, duty to, 539

CORPORATION. *See also* COMPANY.
charitable, 379, 433
sole,
Official Custodian for Charities
is, 445
Public Trustee is, 488
trust, 55, 490, 495n., 502n.
trustee, as, 480, 490, 495n., 502n.,
587

COSTS,
judicial trustee, 487, 587
pre-emptive costs order, 460
public trustee, of, 88, 587
reimbursement to trustees, 585–586
solicitor trustee, 588

COURT. *See also* HIGH COURT.
administration by, 504
appointment of trustees by, 497
county,
injunction to restrain proceedings
in, 803
jurisdiction to grant injunction,
735
jurisdiction in specific
performance, 732
payment into, 181, 534
sale, order for, 279–283
trust, enforced by, 60, 63, 98, 351
trustees,
application to, 533, 632,
648–651, 687
control of, by, 505–509

COURT OF PROTECTION, 74–75
settlements by mental patients,
74–75, 619, 622, 628

COVENANT,
property, to settle, 48, 113, 121 *et
seq.*
action by trustees, 124 *et seq.*
ante-nuptial, 122n.
damages for breach of, 124
specific performance of, 121, 130
third party rights, 48, 124, 728

CREDITORS,
bankruptcy of settlor, 187, 338
fraud on, 249 *et seq.*, 337 *et seq.*
preference of, 342
subrogation of, 674
trusts for, 49, 342

CRIME,
injunction to restrain, 741, 798
killing testator, 315
theft by trustee, 643

CROWN,
bona vacantia, 235–240, 429, 443,
470
charity and 430, 445
fiduciary relationship to, 596, 597
trustee, as, 70, 486
undertaking by, 768

CUSTODIAN TRUSTEE, 489

CY-PRES,
Charities Act 1960, 430
Charities Act 1993, s.13, 439
s.14, 442
form different, continuation in, 432
impracticability, 430
incorporated charity, 433
initial failure of trust, 431
general charitable intent, 431
several gifts, not all charitable,
436
specific charity never existed, 435
judicial, 430
meaning of, 430
non-charity, gift over to, 438
paramount charitable intent, 431
prerogative, 430
schemes, 430 *et seq.*, 448
small charities, 443
spirit of the gift, 439–441
subsequent failure of trust, 436
unincorporated charity, 433

DAMAGES,
breach of trust, for, 632 *et seq.*
Cairns', Lord, Act, 14, 724, 776
effect of decree of specific
performance on right to, 697
equitable compensation, 633–636
injunction, in substitution for, 776
licence, 872
misrepresentation for, 827
trustee, in action by, 125
undertakings as to, 756, 767, 811
Crown, by 768

DEATH,
gift in contemplation of, 137
inheritance tax on, 218–221
trustee, of, 492, 493

DEBT,
advertisement for, 535
distinguished from trusts, 49
executor, debt due to, 135
legacy, when satisfaction for, 859
portion, 860 *et seq.*
specific performance of contract to
pay, 701, 703
subrogation, 674
trust for payment of, 342

DECLARATION,
equitable origin, 31
injunction and, 740, 799
judicial review, application for, 799
of self as trustee, 76, 84, 111, 113,
119
of trust, 66, 76, 82, 84, 90,
111–121, 159–162, 360

DECLARATORY JUDGMENT, 740, 799

DEED,
appointment by, 172, 174
attestation of, 174
cancellation, 30, 839n.
conveyance of land, necessary for,
115
gift of, 115
parties, rights of, 121–124
rectification of, 844
rescission of, 817
variation of, 611 *et seq. See*
VARIATION OF TRUSTS.

DELAY. *See* LACHES; LIMITATION OF
ACTIONS.

DELEGATION,
donee of power, by, 174, 581
testamentary power, of, 352
trustees, by, 200, 450, 525, 559 *et
seq.*, 581. *See also* PENSION
FUND, POWERS OF TRUSTEES.
trustees of land, 566

DELIVERY,
chattels, of, 115
document, 30
donatio mortis causa, 137

DEMERGER, 548

DETERMINABLE INTEREST, 186, 328,
333

DEVISEE, NATURE OF INTEREST OF, 57

DIRECTOR,
accountability of, 292, 598

DIRECTOR—*cont.*
fiduciary position of, 598
limitation of action against, 651
trustee, as, 593

DISABILITY. *See also* MINOR; MENTAL
PATIENT.
settlements made by persons under,
73–75
variation of trusts affecting persons
under, 619, 622, 628

DISCLAIMER,
formalities, 88
trustee, by, 158, 491

DISCLOSURE,
beneficial interest, purchase by
trustee, 591
contracts *uberrimae fidei*, 826
fiduciaries, by, 601–607

DISCOVERY, 30, 507, 805n.

DISCRETION,
control by court of trustee's,
505–509
donee of power, 59, 165 *et seq.*
duty, distinguished from, 481
remedies, in
injunction, 737, 747, 753, 873
rectification, 839
rescission, 824
specific performance, 694
trustees, of, 481. *See also*
DISCRETIONARY TRUSTS;
POWERS OF TRUSTEES.

DISCRETIONARY TRUSTS, 59–64, 99 *et
seq.*, 188, 189, 190, 194, 195 *et
seq.*, 224
accumulations under, 198
advancement on, 581–582
advantages of, 196
beneficiaries,
bankruptcy of, 196
certainty of, 64, 99 *et seq.*
class of, 62–64, 99, 204
creditors of, 196
nature of interest of, 62–64, 109,
202 *et seq.*
benefit to settlor, 200, 220
duration of, 198
exhaustive, 61, 199, 203, 206
form of, 197
inheritance tax, 224
nature of, 60, 195, 202 *et seq.*
non-exhaustive, 61, 199, 203, 206

DISCRETIONARY TRUSTS—*cont.*
perpetuity period and, 198, 225
power,
accumulation of, 198, 201
delegation of, 200
distinguished from, 60, 205 *et seq.*
foreign trustees, to appoint, 200
protective trusts, under, 188, 189, 190, 194, 228
termination of, 64, 198, 205
trustees, selection of, 201

DISPOSITION,
assignment, 79
beneficial owner, consent of, 82
conveyance by trustees, 80
direction to hold on other trusts, 79, 114
equitable interests, of, 78 *et seq.*, 114, 115, 623–624
pension fund, nomination under, 88
specifically enforceable contract, by, 84
sub-trust, 84, 114
variation under V.T.A. 1958, 88, 623–624
will, by, 89
writing, requirement of, 75

DIVIDENDS,
apportionment of, 545, 547
capital payments, distinguished from, 547

DIVORCE,
conditions relating to, 329
injunction in proceedings for, 801
pension rights, 476, 618
settlements, variation of, on, 618

DOCUMENTS,
delivery up, 30
discovery, 30

DONATIO, MORTIS CAUSA, 137–140
chattels, 137, 138
choses in action, 137, 138
contemplation of death, 137
delivery, necessity for, 138
land, 137, 139
requirements of, 137
revocation, 140

DUTIES OF TRUSTEES. *See also*
PENSION FUND; TRUSTEE.
accepting office, on, 511
accounts, 548

DUTIES OF TRUSTEES—*cont.*
assets, duty to collect in, 511
audit, 549
capital and income, receipt by trustees of, 564
discretionary trusts, under, 205
distribution, 532–536
advertisement, 535
application to court, 533
Benjamin Order, 534
discharge after, 535
doubtful claims, 533
fund, setting aside, 535
overpayments by, 532
payment into court, 534
wrongful payments, liability for, 532, 535
equality between beneficiaries, to maintain, 514 537 *et seq.*
Allhusen v. Whittell, rule in, 546
apportionment, 540 *et seq. See also* APPORTIONMENT.
Atkinson, Re, rule in, 547
Chesterfield's Trusts, Earl of, rule in, 541, 543
convert, duty to, 538 *et seq.*
Howe v. Earl Dartmouth, rule in, 538 *et seq.*
impartiality. *See* EQUALITY.
information,
dealings with property, 549
interests under trust, 550–551
pension scheme members, 471
successors to, 512
trust documents, 549
investment, 514 *et seq. See also* INVESTMENT BY TRUSTEES.
leaseholds, 518, 543
litigation, 513
mortgaged property, 547
price, best, must obtain, 513
reversionary property, 541
trust documents, 549
authorised investments, 518, 538

EDUCATION,
minor, of, 571
trust for advancement of, 388 *et seq.*, 413. *See also* CHARITABLE TRUSTS.

ELECTION, DOCTRINE OF, 123, 852 *et seq.*
ademption and, 854
alienability of property, 854, 857

ELECTION, DOCTRINE OF—*cont.*
condition, distinguished from, 853
death before, 858
debts, property available for, 858
intent, 853
nature of, 858
perpetuities, rule against, and, 855
power of appointment and, 854,
855, 857
protective trusts, gift on, 857
time for, 858
title independent of instrument
raising question of, 855
void disposition, 855

ENDOWMENT, 362, 387, 443

ENTAILED INTERESTS, 273n.

EQUALITY,
beneficiaries, among, 537 *et seq.*
charitable trusts, severance of, 427
children, among, 63, 859, 860, 862
is equity, 28, 63, 93, 99, 271, 427
pension scheme members, among,
475

EQUITABLE,
doctrines, 849 *et seq. See also*
CONVERSION; ELECTION;
PERFORMANCE; SATISFACTION.
interests. *See* EQUITABLE INTERESTS.
maxims, 25–29
remedies, 30–32
rights, nature of, 17–19

EQUITABLE INTERESTS,
disposition of, 78 *et seq.*, 114, 115
mere equities, 33
nature of, 17–19, 45, 47, 111, 202
origin of, 8–9
purchase, bona fide, of, 32
registration of, 35
trust of, 46, 84, 111, 114, 116

EQUITABLE ESTOPPEL. *See* ESTOPPEL.

EQUITABLE LEASE, 15–16

EQUITABLE MORTGAGE,
trustee investments, 528

EQUITIES, 33
distinguished from equitable
interest, 33
investment in, 516, 518 *et seq.*
purchase of equitable interest, 33
third parties, whether binding on,
32–38

EQUITIES—*cont.*
where equities equal, first in time
prevails, 27
where equities equal, law prevails,
27

EQUITY,
acts *in personam*, 7, 12, 17–19, 29,
30, 77, 504, 694, 738, 814
conflict with law, 15–16
conscience and, 7, 32, 677
Court of Exchequer, jurisdiction in,
4n.
delay defeats, 29, 654, 718, 771,
838, 845
does not act in vain, 695, 753
equality is, 28, 63, 93, 99, 271, 427
follows the law, 25, 66, 780
fraud in, 76, 176, 828
fusion with law, 20–25
he who comes to equity must come
with clean hands, 26, 250, 717,
775
he who seeks equity must do equity,
26, 775
history of, 5–17
imputes an intention to fulfil an
obligation, 27, 859, 863
licences, effect upon, 870 *et seq.*
See also LICENCES.
looks on that as done which ought
to be done, 16, 27, 312, 849,
850
looks to intent rather than form, 28
maxims, 25–29
mere, 33
mistake in, 818 *et seq.*
subject matter of, 38
will not assist a volunteer, 48, 67,
111 *et seq.*, 704
will not suffer a wrong to be
without a remedy, 25

ESTATE DUTY, 217

ESTOPPEL,
acquiescence, by, 141, 885 *et seq.*
cause of action, 882, 883, 885, 892
common law, 882
constitution of trust by, 141
constructive trusts,
assimilation, 268, 886
conveyancing problems, 893 *et seq.*
detriment, 883, 885 *et seq.*
effect of, 141, 883 *et seq.*

ESTOPPEL—*cont.*
equitable, 22, 882, 883, 884, 885 *et seq.*
lease by, 887
licence by, 141, 882 *et seq.*
negative operation of, 141, 883, 885, 888
promissory, 22, 884
proprietary, 22, 43, 141, 268, 320, 885 *et seq.*
  litigation, necessity for, 895
  registered land, 895
  requirements of doctrine, 885
  S.L.A. 1925, application of, 896
  status prior to court order, 894
  unregistered land, 895
registrable, not, 895
representation,
  fact, of, 883
  intention, of, 883, 885
  unambiguous, 883

ETHICAL INVESTMENTS, 521, 523–525

EVIDENCE,
advancement, rebutting presumption of, 249 *et seq.*
contracts concerning land, 699
secret trusts, 149, 162
trustee by, to support beneficial claim, 156
undue influence, 829–830
writing, 76 *et seq.*, 162, 262, 699

EXECUTED AND EXECUTORY TRUSTS, 65

EXECUTOR,
assent by, 54–57
imperfect gift to, 135
limitation, 651, 653
office, not assignable, 493n.
retirement, 55
sale, power of, 54
title of, 56
trustee and, 54 *et seq.*, 653
vesting of estate in, 56
year, 540

EXEMPTION CLAUSES,
trustees, 467, 483, 560, 564

EXPECTANCY, ASSIGNMENT OF, 133–135

EXPRESS TRUST, 65, 76, 162

FAMILY HOME, TRUSTS OF, 259 *et seq.*

FAMILY LAW, INJUNCTION IN, 801

FATHER,
advancement to child, 230, 248, 255
undue influence of, 829, 831

FIDUCIARY,
bribes, 608, 666
directors, 292, 593, 596, 598 *et seq.*
disclosure, by, 598 *et seq.*
liability of, 292, 595 *et seq.*
limitation of action, 651
meaning of, 292, 595
powers, 61, 166
profits by, 292, 595 *et seq.*
relationship, 292, 595 *et seq.*, 662 *et seq.*, 829
tracing, 662
trusteeship, nature of, 585 *et seq.*

FOLLOWING TRUST PROPERTY. *See* PROPRIETARY REMEDIES.

FORFEITURE,
protected life interest of, 190–194

FORMALITIES,
bill of exchange, indorsement of, 115, 120
chattels, assignment of, 115
constructive trust, 76, 85, 162
copyright, assignment of, 115
declaration of trust, 75
disclaimer, 88
disposition of equitable interest, 78 *et seq.*, 114, 115, 623–624
land,
  contract for sale of, 699
  conveyance of, 115
power of appointment, 171–174
resulting trust, 76, 230
shares, transfer of, 115, 117–118
trust of land, 75, 143 *et seq.*, 162, 230, 244, 254 *et seq.*, 261, 262
will, 89, 143 *et seq.*

FRAUD,
constructive, 828
conveyance by, 314
creditors, on, 337 *et seq.*
equity, in 76, 176, 828
limitation, effect on, 652, 653
meaning of, in equity, 828
misrepresentation, 23, 825
mutual wills, 309
power, on a, 176, 625
secret trusts, 143, 148 *et seq.*, 158–163
trustee, by, 68, 639, 642, 652, 653

Fraud—*cont.*
uberrimae fidei, in contracts, 826
undue influence, 828

Frauds, Statue of,
assignment of equitable interest, 78
et seq.
trusts of land, 76 *et seq.*, 143 *et
seq.*, 162

Fund Manager,
delegation, 525, 567
pension fund, 466

Fusion of Law and Equity, 20–25

Future Property,
assignment of, contract for, 133
performance, 863–865
trust of, 133, 309

Gift,
executor, to, 135
imperfect, 112, 115–116, 117–119,
135 *et seq.*
method of effecting, 111, 112, 114
et seq.
mortis causa, 137
undue influence, under, 828 *et seq.*

Half-Secret Trusts, 144, 153–156,
157, 158, 160, 162. *See also*
Secret Trusts.

Hardship,
defence to specific performance,
720
defence to injunction, 774

Heir,
expectant, 837

High Court of Justice,
establishment of, 15
jurisdiction of, Chancery Division,
38
jurisdiction to grant injunction, 734
jurisdiction in specific performance,
732

Howe v. Earl of Dartmouth, Rule
in, 538 *et seq. See also* Duties
of Trustees.

Husband and Wife,
advancement, presumption of,
246–248, 255, 264, 272
inheritance tax exemption, 218
injunction, 801

Husband and Wife—*cont.*
marriage consideration, 113, 122 *et
seq.*, 339
matrimonial home, 246, 259 *et seq.*,
318, 801. *See also* Family
Home, Trusts of.
protective trusts, under, 189
trusts facilitating separation of, 329

Illegal Trusts, 249, 325 *et seq.*
alienation, in restraint of, 332
bankruptcy, 338 *et seq.*
conditions precedent and
subsequent, 328, 333
creditors, fraud on, 337 *et seq. See
also* Voluntary Settlement.
determinable interests, 328, 333
duration, 334
husband and wife, separation of,
329
immorality, 325, 326
marriage, in restraint of, 329
parent from child, separation of,
330
perpetuity, 334
public policy, 325, 326
religion, 326, 331
unlawful discrimination, 326, 327,
331, 332, 387n., 392n., 430,
475

Impartiality,
trustee's duty of, 537 *et seq. See
also* Duties of Trustees.

Imperfect Gift, 111 *et seq.*

Imperfect Obligation, Trust of, 354
et seq. See also Purpose Trusts.

Implied Trusts, 65

Impossibility,
charitable purpose, of, 430 *et seq.*

Impounding Beneficial Interests,
beneficiary, of, 647
beneficiary-trustee, 643

Improvident Bargains, Relief from,
836

Imputed Notice, 34

In Loco Parentis, 122, 230, 248,
255, 575

In Personam, Equity Acts, 7, 12,
17–19, 29, 30, 77, 504, 694, 738,
814

INALIENABILITY, 334, 337, 472

INCOME,
  aggregation of children's with
      parents', 214n., 227, 575
  intermediate, gift carrying, 574
  trust of, 198

INCOME AND CAPITAL. *See also*
    CAPITAL AND INCOME; DUTIES OF
    TRUSTEES.

INCOME TAX,
  accumulation trust, under, 227
  additional rate, 213, 214, 227
  basic rate, 213, 214, 227
  discretionary trusts, under, 214
  outline of, 213
  pension funds, 474
  planning, 211–212, 214
  trust,
      liability to, 213

INCORPORATION BY REFERENCE,
    145–147, 155. *See also* SECRET
    TRUSTS.

INDEMNITY, 641, 647. *See also*
    BREACH OF TRUST.

INFANT. *See also* MINOR.

INFORMATION,
  confidential, 23–24, 598 *et seq.*,
      744, 794, 805
  pension funds, 471
  trustee's duty to provide, 548–551

INHERITANCE TAX, 216, 218 *et seq.*,
    612
  accumulation and maintenance
      settlements, 226
  charities, and, 219, 224, 225, 228,
      381
  death, on, 218–221
  decennial charge, 225, 227
  disabled persons, 228
  discretionary trusts, 224
  excluded property, 218, 222
  exemptions, 218–219, 223, 224, 225
  exit charge, 225, 227
  foreign property, 218
  interests in possession, 222–224
  liability for, 219
  lifetime, 218–221
  pension funds, 474
  planning, 211–212, 220
  potentially exempt transfer, 219
  protective trusts, 228

INHERITANCE TAX—*cont.*
  rates of, 219, 225, 226
  reliefs, 219, 224, 225
  reservation of benefit, 220–221
  reversionary interests, 222, 223
  settlements, 222
  spouses, transfers between, 218, 224
  superannuation schemes, 228
  transfer of value, 218, 220

INJUNCTION, 11, 30, 42, 733 *et seq.*,
    871, 873
  acquiescence, 773
  Anton Piller order, 32n., 42,
      804–808
  assets to restrain removal of,
      808–815
  breach of contract, to restrain, 783
      et seq., 871, 873
    contractual licence, 701, 786,
        871, 873
    employment, 787–791
    land affecting, 786
    negative and positive terms, 784
    service, contract of, 787–791
  clubs, 802
  colleges, 802
  common, 11, 16
  confidential material, protection of,
      744, 794 *et seq.*, 804
  contempt, non-compliance is, 739,
      804, 806, 815
  criminal law, to prevent breach of,
      741, 798
  Crown, 740, 768
  damages,
    in addition to, or in substitution
        for, 14, 738, 776 *et seq.*
    insufficient remedy, 30, 737, 753
    smallness, 746
    undertaking as to, 756, 767–769,
        811
  declaration, 740, 799
  delay, 771, 776
  discretionary remedy, 30, 737, 747,
      753, 873
  evidence, to restrain removal of,
      804–808
  ex parte, 736, 751, 806, 809, 810
  expulsion from club, to restrain, 802
  family matters, in relation to, 801
  foreign courts, to restrain
      proceedings in, 804
  hardship, 747, 774
  husband and wife, 801, 805

INJUNCTION—*cont.*
in personam, is remedy, 29, 738, 814
industrial disputes, 749, 760, 766
interlocutory, 736, 751 *et seq.*, 784, 804 *et seq.*
appeal, injunction pending, 752
balance of convenience, 755 *et seq.*
complete relief by, 752
discharge, 752
ex parte, 736, 751, 806, 809, 810
mandatory, 764, 765
prima facie case, 754 *et seq.*, 806
principles applicable, 753
special factors, 758
undertakings, 767
judicial proceedings, to restrain, 803
jurisdiction, 734, 811
legal and equitable rights, 743
legislation, promotion of, 804
libel, 760, 793
licences and, 701, 786, 871, 873
locus standi, 740
Lord Cairns' Act, under, 14, 738, 776 *et seq.*
mandatory, 735, 747, 764, 765, 769, 873
Mareva injunction, 32n., 42, 808 *et seq.*
minors, 801–802
perpetual, 736, 745 *et seq.*
plaintiff, conduct of, 775
principles applicable to issue of, 737 *et seq.*
professions, 803
prohibitory, 735, 745
public interest, 738
public wrongs, to restrain, 797
quia timet, 737, 769
relator actions, 741, 769, 797
restrictive covenants and, 786
rights, to protect, 740, 743
specific performance,
indirect, 787
wider jurisdiction than, 737
suspension of, 750, 775, 779
third parties and, 739, 752, 775, 795, 809, 811, 813, 814, 815, 876
tort, to restrain commission of, 791
trade unions, 760, 802
trespass, 778–779, 781–782, 792
trivial injury, 777, 792

INJUNCTION—*cont.*
trust, breach of, 791
charitable, 452
types of, 735
undertaking, 756, 767–769, 811
Crown, by, 768
winding-up petition, to restrain, 763

INNOCENT MISREPRESENTATION. *See* MISREPRESENTATION.

INQUIRIES, PURCHASER'S DUTY, 34

INSOLVENCY,
defendant, of, 47, 51n., 288, 290, 338, 607–609, 656 *et seq. See also* BANKRUPTCY.
settlor, of, 338 *et seq.*

INSURANCE,
application of money, 558
contracts of, 826
lien, 28, 674
purchaser's risk under contract of sale, 312
reinstatement, 558
subrogation, 53, 674
trustees' powers to effect, 557
V.T.A. 1958, under, 629

INTENTION,
charity, general or paramount, of, 431 *et seq.*
election in, 853
manifestation of, to declare trust, 65, 76, 90, 111, 119–121, 127–130, 149, 159–162, 360

INTEREST,
breach of trust, 638, 687
compound, 30, 638–639
concurrent, 272 *et seq.*
conditional, 109, 186, 328, 333
determinable, 186, 328, 333, 438
duty and, conflict of, 480, 589 *et seq.*
equitable. *See* EQUITABLE INTERESTS.
licensee, coupled with, 869
proprietary, beneficiary's interest is, 17, 45, 47, 59, 111, 203, 323
proprietary remedies, 607, 656 *et seq.*
traced assets, on, 687

INTERLOCUTORY INJUNCTION, 736, 751 *et seq.*, 784, 804 *et seq. See also* INJUNCTION.

INTESTACY,
  interest under, distinguished from
    trust, 53 *et seq.*

INVESTMENT BY TRUSTEES,
  advice, 520, 525, 532
  authorised by T.I.A. 1961, 519 *et
    seq.*, 637
  charitable trust, 450
  controlling interest in company,
    trustees holding, 526
  dated stocks, 515
  debentures, 515
  delegation, 525, 567
  derivatives, 515
  diversification, 522
  equities, 516, 517, 518, 519, 520,
    532
  ethical investments, 521, 523–525
  express powers of, 517
  extension of powers, 530, 619
  financial services legislation,
    466–467, 514n., 525, 567
  fixed interest, 515
  futures, 515
  gilt-edged, 515, 519
  investment trusts, 516
  joint names, in, 564
  life tenant and remainderman, 514,
    522, 537 *et seq.*
  meaning of, 514
  mortgages of land, 528
  narrower range, 519
  pension funds, 465
  portfolio theory, 522, 532
  power, variation of, 530, 619
  preference shares, 516
  prudent man rule, 521
  purchase of land, 517
  retention of investments, 526, 637
  selection, 521
  special range, 521
  types of, 515
  unit trusts, 516
  wider range, 519

INVESTMENT TRUST, 516

JOINT ACCOUNT, 247, 255

JOINT TENANCY,
  matrimonial home, 264, 271
  secret trusts and, 151
  severance, 28, 273–274, 361
  survivorship, right of, 28, 274
  trustees hold on, 492

JOINT TENANCY—*cont.*
  unincorporated associations, 361

JUDICATURE ACT, 1873, 14–17, 870

JURISDICTION,
  auxiliary, 15n.
  Chancellor, 5–9
  Chancery Division, 38
  concurrent, 15n., 23, 791
  equitable, 3–5
  exclusive, 15n.
  injunction,
    county court, 735
    High Court, 734
  land abroad, 18, 694, 738
  specific performance,
    county court, 732
    High Court, 732

KEECH V. SANDFORD, RULE IN, 591,
  593

LACHES, 29, 651, 654, 718, 771, 776,
  838, 845
  equitable claim, 654–655
  injunction and, 771, 776
  rectification and, 845
  rescission and, 838
  specific performance and, 718
  trustees and, 651–655

LAND,
  abroad, specific performance of
    contract for, 18, 694
  contract for sale of, 85, 312, 699,
    705, 850
  conveyance of, 115
  lease, contract for, 699
  registered, *See* REGISTERED LAND.
  trust of, 75, 76–78, 162, 244, 259 *et
    seq.*, 312, 318 *et seq. See also*
    TRUST OF LAND.
  vesting in trustees, 498–499

LAND CHARGES, 35, 895

LAPSE, 160, 161, 308, 431

LEASE, LEASEHOLD,
  contract for, 15–16, 699
    specific performance of, 699
  Howe v. Earl Dartmouth, rule in,
    and, 543
  investment in, by trustees, 517, 528
  mistake in, 820, 839 *et seq.*
  option to purchase freehold,
    conversion and, 850

LEASE, LEASEHOLD—*cont.*
renewal of, 591
reversion, purchase of, by trustee,
592

LEGACY,
ademption of, 859
intermediate income, carrying,
574–575
satisfaction by, 859 *et seq.*

LEGATEE,
attesting witness, 159
killing testator, 315
lapse, 160, 161, 308, 431
nature of interest of, 57

LIBEL, INJUNCTION TO RESTRAIN, 760,
793

LICENCES,
bare, 869
common law, at, 869
constructive trust, 320, 879
contractual, 49, 320, 700, 786, 869
et seq.
conveyancing problems, 881, 893 *et
seq.*
damages, 872
deed, by, 868
equity, intervention of, 868, 870 *et
seq.*
estoppel, 141, 882 *et seq.*
grant, coupled with, 869
improvements to land, 885 *et seq.*
injunction protecting licensee, 701,
786, 871, 873
interest, coupled with, 869
licensee,
remedies available to, 700, 786,
871 *et seq.*
registered land, and, 895
registrability, 895
specific performance of, 700, 874
third parties and, 320, 876 *et seq.*,
894 *et seq.*
wives, deserted, 877

LIEN,
insurer's, 28, 674
trustee's, 585–586
vendor's, 313

LIFE INTEREST,
determinable, 187 *et seq.*, 332
mutual wills, under, 305, 309, 310
protected, 185 *et seq.*

LIFE INTEREST—*cont.*
remainderman, and. *See* DUTIES OF
TRUSTEES.

LIMITATION OF ACTIONS,
disability of plaintiff, 654
equitable remedies, 29, 651, 654,
718, 771
exceptions to six-year rule, 652
fraud, 652, 653
permanent liability, cases of,
652–653
personal representatives, against, 54,
651, 653
possession, trustee in, 652
remainderman and reversioner,
651–652
trustee, 54, 651 *et seq.*
vendor and purchaser, 313

LOCO PARENTIS, 122, 230, 248, 255,
575

MAINTENANCE,
accumulation, and, trusts, 226
power,
court, of, 583
trustees, of, 570 *et seq. See also*
POWERS OF TRUSTEES.

MANDATE, 364, 370

MANDATORY INJUNCTION, 735, 747,
764, 765, 769, 873. *See also*
INJUNCTION.

MARRIAGE,
articles, 66
consideration of, 113, 122 *et seq.*,
339
trusts in restraint of, 329

MASTER OF THE ROLLS, 14

MATRIMONIAL HOME, 246, 259 *et seq.*,
318, 801
improvement, 269
injunction, 280, 801

MAXIMS OF EQUITY, 25–29

MENTAL PATIENT. *See also* COURT OF
PROTECTION.
inheritance tax and, 228
settlements by, 74–75
variation of trusts affecting, 75,
619, 622, 628
will of, 75

MINOR,
  accumulation for, 198, 572
  advancement, presumption of, 230,
    248, 255
    to, 576 *et seq.*
  capacity to create settlement, 73
  consent to breach of trust, 645–646
  income of, under trust, 571
  injunction to protect, 801–802
  legal estate, cannot hold, 73, 141
  limitation of actions, and, 654
  maintenance of, 571 *et seq.*
  majority, age of, 73
  settlement by, 73
  specific performance and, 713
  trustee, as, 230, 245, 246, 486, 493
  undue influence, 829, 831
  variation of trust, 613, 617, 620

MISDESCRIPTION,
  refusal of specific performance, 722

MISREPRESENTATION, 23, 31, 716, 825
  Act of 1967, 23, 827
  damages for, 827
  rescission for, 825–828
  specific performance, refusal of, 716

MISTAKE, 31, 818 *et seq.*
  common to both parties, 819, 841
  drafting, in, 840
  payment by mistake, 532, 649–651,
    665, 686–689
  policy relating to, 820
  private right, as to, 820
  rectification for, 839 *et seq. See
    also* RECTIFICATION.
  rescission for, 818 *et seq.*
    terms on, 818, 820, 822, 824, 835
  specific performance, refusal of,
    716, 818
  terms of contract, as to, 818
  unilateral, 842

MONUMENT, TRUST FOR, 46, 348, 354,
  366, 369, 371, 397

MORALITY, TRUSTS CONTRARY TO, 325

MORTGAGE,
  contributory, 528
  equitable, 528
  investment in, 528, 638. *See also*
    INVESTMENT BY TRUSTEES.
  limitation of action, 651

MUTUAL WILLS, 65, 97, 161, 305 *et
  seq. See also* CONSTRUCTIVE
  TRUST.

MUTUALITY,
  specific performance and, 713

NE EXEAT REGNO, 21, 30, 810

NEXT-OF-KIN,
  limitation of actions, 653
  marriage consideration, not within,
    123

NOMINEES, 69–70, 568

NOTICE, 32 *et seq.*, 276–277, 295–297,
    298–302, 679, 894–895
  actual, 34, 35, 296, 298
  constructive, 34–35, 37–38, 276 *et
    seq.*, 295, 298–302, 832–836
  constructive trustee, 294, 298–302
  imputed, 34
  purchaser of,
    equitable interest for value
      without, 33
    voluntary settlement, 341, 343
    legal estate for value without,
      18–19, 32 *et seq.*, 276 *et
      seq.*, 894, 895. *See also*
      PURCHASER.
    personalty, 35
  registered land, 38, 277–279, 322,
    832–836, 895
  registration of land charges
    constitutes, 35
  title deeds, contents of, 34

NUISANCE,
  injunction to restrain, 778, 779, 781,
    791

OPTION TO PURCHASE,
  conversion, effecting, 850
  specific performance, 704

ORDERS,
  Benjamin, 534, 687n.
  impounding, 643, 647
  vesting, 499

OVERREACHING, 36–37
  overreachable interest, 36
  trust of land, 273, 276

OVERRIDING INTEREST, 245, 277 *et
  seq.*, 895

PARENT AND CHILD. *See* FATHER; CHILD.

PAROL EVIDENCE. *See* EVIDENCE.
secret trusts, 78, 144, 156, 162. *See* SECRET TRUSTS.

PARTNERS, 292, 304, 589, 596, 603

PAYMENT INTO COURT, 181, 534

PENSION FUND,
alienability of pension, 472
bankruptcy,
employer, 456, 469, 470, 472
member, 473
compensation scheme, 471
delegation, 466
divorce, 476
equal treatment, 475
information to members, 471
investment, 465
delegation, 466
policy, 466, 523, 530, 615
minimum funding, 468
nomination under, 88
ombudsman, 462
perpetuity rule, 473
professional advisers,
actuary, 465
auditor, 465
fund manager, 465, 466
quasi-public nature, 461, 520
regulatory authority, 461
role of trust, 39, 455
surplus, 66, 239, 469
tax relief, 228, 473
trustees, 462
disqualification, 464
independent trustee, 463, 471
majority decision, 464
member trustee, 463
types of scheme, 456
earnings-related, 457
funded, 457
insured, 457
money-purchase, 458
winding up, 470

PERCENTAGE TRUSTS, 545

PERFORMANCE,
doctrine of, 863–865
ademption, distinguished, 859
covenants to purchase and settle land, 863
intestacy on, 864
satisfaction and, 859

PERFORMANCE—*cont.*
part, 700
specific. *See* SPECIFIC PERFORMANCE.

PERPETUITIES, RULES AGAINST, 198, 334–337, 353, 360–363, 365–368, 380, 438, 473
advancement, power of, 580, 582
animals, 355–356, 366
charity, as applied to, 380, 438
condition, 334n.
discretionary trusts, 198, 225
duration of trusts, 198, 334–337, 353, 365–368
election, doctrine of, 855
fixed period of years, 335, 367
gestation, 335
gift over, 370, 380, 438
inalienability, 334, 337, 353
measuring lives, 335–337, 366
old rule, 335
pension trusts, 473
period of, 335
possibility of reverter, 370, 438
purpose trusts and, 337, 353, 354–356, 362, 365–368, 370–373
resettlement by trustees, 200–201
resulting trusts and, 370, 438
rule stated, 335
unincorporated associations, 360–363
variation of trusts, on, 624
vesting, 335
wait and see, 335, 366, 438

PERSONAL REPRESENTATIVES. *See also* EXECUTOR.
assent by, 53–57
disposition, power of, 54 *et seq.*
fiduciary duties of, 54, 56, 57
imperfect gift to, 135
limitation of actions, 54, 651, 653
retirement, 55
title of, 56
trustee and, 54 *et seq.*
vesting of property in, on death, 56, 67

PERSONALTY,
contract, specific performance of, 701
constructive notice and, 35
presumption of resulting trust on voluntary conveyance, 245

PERSONALTY—*cont.*
  trust of, 114–118

PERSONAM, RIGHTS IN, 17–19, 29, 30,
  77, 504, 694, 738, 814

PETITIONS TO THE CHANCELLOR, 5

PORTIONS,
  ademption of legacies by, 862
  debts, 860 *et seq.*
  double, rule against, 860

POVERTY,
  trust for relief of, 386, 412

POWER. *See also* POWER OF
    APPOINTMENT.
  bare, 166, 183
  capricious, 106
  certainty, requirement of, 63, 97, 99
    et seq.
  delegation of, 174, 352, 559 *et seq.*,
    581
  discretionary nature of, 59, 166
  disposition of, by, personal
    representatives, 54 *et seq.*
  distinguished from trusts, 59–64, 97
    et seq., 165, 168–171, 202,
    352, 371, 553
  ex officio, 166
  fiduciary, 61, 166, 168–171, 208
  foreign trustees, power to appoint,
    200
  fraud on a, 176, 625
  personal, 166, 183
  purposes, to apply for, 171, 352,
    371
  release of, 180 *et seq.*
  sale, of,
    personal representatives, by 54 *et
      seq.*
    trustee, by, 555
  testamentary, validity of, 352
  trust, in the nature of, 62, 109
  trustee of. *See* POWERS OF
      TRUSTEES.
  variation of, 183
  virtute officii, 166, 182
  wide, 104–106

POWER OF APPOINTMENT,
  categorised, 167
  certainty, requirement of, 63, 97, 99
    et seq.
  contract to exercise, 174, 711
  default, persons entitled in, 167

POWER OF APPOINTMENT—*cont.*
  exercise of,
    defective execution, 173
    excessive execution, 172
    formalities for, 171–174
  fiduciary, by, 166
  general, 167
  hybrid, 167
  intermediate, 167
  purposes, in favour of, 171, 352,
    371
  special, 167
  trustees of, 166, 197–201, 492

POWER OF ATTORNEY,
  trustee by, 525, 565, 566, 567,
    568–570

POWERS OF TRUSTEES,
  advancement, 570, 576 *et seq.*
    application of money advanced,
      583
    benefit, 576–578, 580
    contrary intention, 579
    delegation, 581
    express power, 577
    half of presumptive share, 578,
      582
    inherent power, 583
    meaning of, 576
    perpetuity rule, 582
    statutory power, 578
    sub-trusts, 580
    trustees' responsibility to see to
      money advanced, 583
  compounding liabilities, 558
  compromising claims, 513, 558
  consultation of beneficiaries, 280
  delegation, 200, 525, 559 *et seq.*,
    581
    abroad, 565
    capital and income, 564
    discretions, 525, 565–566, 567,
      568–570
    enduring power of attorney,
      568–570
    exemption clauses, 467, 483, 560,
      564
    good faith, 561, 562, 567
    pension trust, 466
    power of attorney, by, 525, 565,
      566, 567, 568–570
    pre-1926, 559, 562, 563, 566
    primary and vicarious liability,
      560, 562, 567
    supervision, 560, 562, 563

POWERS OF TRUSTEES—*cont.*
  delegation—*cont.*
    trustees of land, by, 566
    wilful default, 560, 562, 563,
      564, 567
  insurance, 557
    re-instatement, 558
  investment. *See* DUTIES OF
    TRUSTEES.
  maintenance, 570 *et seq.*
    accumulation, 572–574
    class gifts, 576
    contingent interests, 570, 571,
      572, 574–575
    inherent power, 583
    intention of settlor, 572, 573
    intermediate income, 574–575
    minority, 571
    prior interests, 571
    surplus income, 572
  receipt, 55, 276, 490, 491, 556, 557,
    564, 569
  reversionary interests dealing with,
    559
  sale, 555
    chattels, 556
    land, 555
    method of, 556
    order for, 279–283
    postponement of, 273, 279–283,
      540, 541, 542, 543, 555
  trustees of land, 554

PRECATORY WORDS, 90

PRE-EMPTION, RIGHT OF, 700n., 786

PREFERENCE OF CREDITORS, 342

PRESUMPTION,
  advancement, of, 231, 246–249,
    255, 264, 272
  resulting trust, 244 *et seq.*, 254, 264
  satisfaction, of, 859 *et seq.*
  undue influence, of, 829

PRINCIPAL AND AGENT. *See* AGENT.

PRINCIPAL BENEFICIARY, 189, 190, 193,
  194

PROMISSORY ESTOPPEL, 22, 884

PROPRIETARY ESTOPPEL, 22, 43, 141,
  268, 320, 885 *et seq.*

PROPRIETARY REMEDIES, 288, 293,
  607, 656 *et seq.*
  advantages of, 288, 607, 656

PROPRIETARY REMEDIES—*cont.*
  bank accounts, 670–674
  change of position, 301, 303,
    679–681, 689
  charge, 667, 678
  Clayton's Case, rule in, 671n., 673
  constructive trust, 288, 323,
    607–609
  defences, 678
  equitable proprietary interest
    requirement of, 663
  fiduciary relation, 662
  improvements to land, 679
  mixed fund, 667
  pari passu, sharing, 669, 677
  proportionate shares, 669, 677
  purchaser, bona fide, for value, 667,
    679
  restitution, 69, 289–291, 300, 315,
    317–324, 605, 608–609, 656,
    675, 679, 688
  retention of title, 681
  subrogation, 674
  tracing,
    backwards, 672
    common law, at, 657
    equity in, 288–289, 662 *et seq.*
  unjust enrichment, 69, 289–291,
    300, 315, 317–324, 605,
    608–609, 656, 675, 679, 688
  unmixed funds, 666
  volunteer, 289, 669, 673, 677

PROTECTION, COURT OF, 74–75, 619,
  622

PROTECTIVE TRUSTS, 185 *et seq.*, 228,
  332
  advancement, 193
  bankruptcy, protection of settlor on,
    185–188
  condition subsequent, 186
  determinable interests, 186
  doctrine of election, 857
  forfeiture,
    effect of, 193
    events causing, 190–193
  inheritance tax, 228
  order under Matrimonial Causes
    Acts, 192
  order under T.A. 1925, s.57, 192
  self-protection, 187
  T.A. 1925, s.33, 188, 332
  variation and, 620, 625–626

PROTECTOR, 373n., 480

PUBLIC BENEFIT,
 charity, element in, 384, 411 *et seq.*

PUBLIC LAW,
 injunction in, 740, 797

PUBLIC POLICY,
 trusts, contrary to, 325 *et seq.*

PUBLIC TRUSTEE, 480, 488, 587

PURCHASE MONEY,
 matrimonial home, 254 *et seq.*, 264
  et seq.
 receipt for, 55, 276, 490, 491, 556,
  557, 564, 569
 resulting trusts, 254 *et seq.*, 264 *et
  seq.*

PURCHASER,
 bona fide, for value, without notice,
  9n., 18–19, 32–38, 47,
  276–277, 287, 289, 301, 341,
  343, 667, 669, 687, 876 *et
  seq.*, 894
 contract under, 84, 312
 defective exercise of power, 173
 fraud on a power, after, 180
 inquiries, duty to make, 34
 of equitable interest, 33
 of interest under voidable
  settlement, 341, 343
 personal representatives, from, 54 *et
  seq.*
 root of title, 34
 trustee as, 589

PURPOSE TRUSTS, 41, 46, 171, 326,
  347 *et seq.*, 378
 animals, for, 355, 366
 beneficiary principle, 351
 capricious purposes, 368
 certainty, 101, 350, 358, 370
 charitable trusts distinguished, 347,
  359, 378
 delegation of testamentary power,
  352
 duration of, 353, 362, 365
 masses, 356
 methods of effecting, 369–373
 monumnets, for, 354, 366
 non-Christian private ceremonies,
  356
 objections to, 351–354
 perpetuities, rule against, 337, 353,
  354–356, 362, 365–368,
  370–373
 persons and purposes, 348

PURPOSE TRUSTS—*cont.*
 power, compared with, 171, 352,
  371
 tombs, 354, 366
 unincorporated associations, 349,
  359 *et seq.*, 370

QUASI-CONTRACT, 69, 289–291, 533,
  605, 656, 823, 844

QUIA TIMET INJUNCTION, 737, 769. *See
 also* INJUNCTION.

RATES,
 charity, remission of, 382

REALTY,
 assent to, 55, 56–57
 conversion of, 849 *et seq.*
 investment in, 514, 517, 528

RECEIPT,
 capital money, for, 276, 490, 491,
  556, 557, 564, 569
 personal representatives, by, 55
 trustee, by, 276, 490, 491, 556, 557,
  564, 569
  conformity, for sake of, 563

RECEIVER, 30

RECOGNITION OF TRUSTS, 43

RECREATIONAL CHARITY, 391, 402

RECTIFICATION, 30, 839 *et seq.*
 defences to, 845
 drafting, mistake in, 840
 instruments capable of rectification,
  844
 intention, to accord with, 839
 rescission, alternative to, 840
 standard of proof, 844
 unilateral mistake, for, 842
 voluntary deed, of, 845

REGISTRATION,
 charitable trusts, 446
 licence, 895
 notice, constitutes, 35
 registered land, 277–279, 280, 322,
  895
  overriding interest, 277–279, 895
  trust of land, 277–279
 spouse, interest of, 277
 vesting in new trustees, 499

REIMBURSEMENT,
 trustee, of, 585

RELEASE,
power, of, 179, 180–183, 625
trustee, of, 646

RELIGION,
conditions relating to, 331
trust for the advancement of, 395 *et
seq.*, 417. *See also* CHARITABLE
TRUSTS.

REM,
right in, 17–19

REMAINDERMAN,
apportionment of income, 537 *et
seq.*
entitled to capital, 538

REMEDIES. *See also* FRAUD;
INJUNCTION; LICENCES;
MISREPRESENTATION; MISTAKE;
RECTIFICATION; RESCISSION;
SPECIFIC PERFORMANCE.
equitable, 30–32, 693 *et seq.*
injunction, 30, 733 *et seq.*
legal and equitable, 15–16
personal, against trustee, 607, 632
et seq.
proprietary, 288, 293, 607, 656 *et
seq.*
specific performance, 30, 693 *et
seq.*

REMUNERATION,
judicial trustee, 487, 587
public trustee, 480, 488, 587
trustees, of, 480, 482, 490, 585 *et
seq.*

REPRESENTATION,
estoppel by, 883

RESCISSION, 30, 31, 817 *et seq.*
damages in lieu of, 827
loss of right to rescind, 837
misrepresentation for, 825
mistake for, 818
specific performance and, 716–717
terms, on, 818, 820, 822, 824, 835

RESTITUTION, 69, 289–291, 300, 315,
317–324, 605, 608–609, 656,
675, 679, 688

RESULTING TRUST,
advancement, presumption of,
230–231, 246–249, 255, 264,
272
engaged couple, 247

RESULTING TRUST—*cont.*
advancement, presumption of—*cont.*
father and child, 248, 255
husband and wife, 246–248, 255,
264, 272
illegitimate children, 248
intention, evidence of, 244, 246,
249 *et seq.*, 261 *et seq.*
loco parentis, 230, 248, 255
mistress, 247
mother, 248–249
rebuttal, 247
automatic, 67, 230, 243
charitable trusts, and, 431, 436, 438
classification, 67
constructive trust, and, 67, 231,
264, 286
failure of trust, 231–233
bona vacantia, 233–241
charitable trusts, of, 233n.
to dispose of beneficial interest, 67,
81, 92, 230, 231–233
formalities unnecessary, 76, 230
illegality, 249–254, 333
implied, 65, 230
intention, 65, 67, 244, 245, 246,
249 *et seq.*, 261 *et seq.*
evidence of, 247, 249–254
just result, to reach, 231
matrimonial home, 246, 259 *et seq.*
common intention, 261, 263
constructive trust, 261, 263, 264,
318–320
conveyance to one spouse only,
261
direct contributions, 264
express agreement, 262
improvements, 269
indirect contributions, 266
legal estate in both spouses, 271
mistress, 247
mortgage payments, 264–265,
270
resulting trust, 254, 264
share, size of, 270
valuation, date of, 271
minor as trustee, 230, 245, 246,
486, 493
nature of, 67, 229
option, of, 242–244
perpetuity, rule against, 371, 438
presumption of, 244 *et seq.*, 254,
264

RESULTING TRUST—*cont.*
property undisposed of, 230, 231 *et seq.*
purchase in name of another, 231, 254 *et seq.*
by several in name of one, 254
purpose, transfer for, 50–52
surplus, 233 *et seq.*
not available to trustee, 53, 156, 241
surplus funds, disposal of, 233–241
tax implications of, 242–244
unincorporated association, 235–241
voluntary conveyance and, 230, 244 *et seq.*
Wills Act 1837, non-compliance with, 245, 254

RETENTION OF TITLE CLAUSES, 681

RETIREMENT OF TRUSTEE, 451, 493, 502–503

REVERSIONARY INTEREST,
consent to breach, 645
duty to convert, 539, 541 *et seq.*
interitance tax, and, 222, 223
purchase of, by trustee, 591
sale of, 539, 616
trustees' powers in relation to, 559

ROOT OF TITLE, 34

SALE, POWER OF. *See* POWERS OF TRUSTEES, power of sale.

SATISFACTION, 859 *et seq.*
adeption, distinguished from, 859, 862, 863
debts by legacies, 859 *et seq.*
intention, significance of, 859
performance, distinguished from, 859
portions, 860–863
pro tanto, 860, 861, 862

SAUNDERS v. VAUTIER, Rule in, 555, 612

SCHEMES. *See* CHARITABLE TRUSTS; CY-PRES.

SECRET PROFIT,
fiduciary agents, 292, 595 *et seq.*, 666
trustees, 292, 591 *et seq.*

SECRET TRUSTS. *See also* TRUST.
additions to, 150

SECRET TRUSTS—*cont.*
communication,
before or after death, 147, 149, 150
before or after will, 150, 152, 154–156
methods of, 150
express or constructive trust, 162, 314
fraud, 143, 148 *et seq.*, 158–163
fully secret, 144, 147–153, 158–163
half-secret, 144, 153–156, 157, 158, 160, 162
incorporation by reference, 145–147, 155
joint tenants, 151
land, secret trusts of, 162
mutual wills, and, 161
policy concerning, 163
proof, 149
reasons for making, 144
revocation of gift, 161
surplus after performing trust, 156
tenants in common, 151
theoretical basis of, 158 *et seq.*
trustee as beneficiary, 156
uncommunicated in testator's lifetime, 147
witness, in favour of, 159
writing, necessity for, 143, 162, 314

SECURITIES,
bearer, 499n.
equities, 516, 518 *et seq.*
gilt-edged, 515, 519
redeemable, 515

SERVICE, CONTRACT OF,
injunction restraining breach of, 787
specific performance and, 707

SETTLED LAND, SETTLED LAND ACTS,
contractual licences, whether applicable, 896
overreaching, 36
trust of land, replacement by, 36, 272–273
variation of settlements under S.L.A. 1925, s.64, 616

SETTLEMENT. *See also* CONSTITUTION OF TRUSTS; SETTLED LAND; SETTLED LAND ACTS.
ante nuptial, 122n.
capacity to create, 73–75
creditors, in fraud of, 337 *et seq.*

SETTLEMENT—*cont.*
definition of, for inheritance tax, 222n.
discretionary trusts, on, 195 *et seq.*
inheritance tax and, 222 *et seq.*
marriage, consideration of, 113, 122 *et seq.*, 339
rectification of, 845
variation of, 611 *et seq. See also* VARIATION OF TRUSTS.
voluntary, 338 *et seq. See also* VOLUNTARY SETTLEMENT; VOLUNTEERS.

SETTLOR,
appointment of trustees, by, 492, 502
protective trust, of, 187
resulting trust for. *See* RESULTING TRUST.

SHARES,
bonus issue of, 520
capital and income, 547–548
constitution of trust of, 115, 117–118
dividends. *See* DIVIDENDS.
donatio mortis causa, 140
electronic transfer of, 115
investment in, by trustees, 516, 518 *et seq.*
oral contract for sale of, 84
registration of title to, 115, 117–118, 499
rights issue, 520
specific performance of contract for purchase of, 84–88, 701
transfer of, 115, 117–118
vesting of, in trustees, 499

SIGN MANUAL, 379, 430n., 433

SOLICITOR,
appointment of, as trustee, 501
fiduciary, as, 596
trust money, possession of, 304, 561, 562, 670
trustee and, 642

SPECIFIC PERFORMANCE, 30, 85, 122, 123, 124, 130, 312, 693 *et seq.*, 874
annuity, contract to purchase, 703, 730
arbitration, 712
build, contract to, 706
clean hands, 717

SPECIFIC PERFORMANCE—*cont.*
common law remedies,
effect of decree upon, 697
inadequacy of, 694
compensation, when granted with, 696, 721
contract,
build or repair, 706
contractual licence, 700, 710, 874
goodwill, 712, 730
landlord's covenants, 707, 713
lease, 16, 699
money, to pay, 703
personal services, 707
positive obligations, 695
sale of goods, 701
sale of land, 85, 312, 699
shares, 84–88, 701
trust, to create, 122, 130
unique chattel, 701
will, to leave property by, 307, 711
damages,
common law damages not excluded by decree, 697
failure to complete on contractual date, 718, 720
Lord Cairns' Act, 14, 724 *et seq.*
when adequate remedy, 85, 130–133, 694, 702, 728–732
when title bad, 723
debt, contract to pay, 701, 703–704
defences to suit for,
delay, 718
hardship, 720
laches, 718
misdescription, 721
misrepresentation, 716
mistake, 716, 818
plaintiff in breach, 717
price, inadequacy of, 720
public policy, 723
title doubtful, 723
discretionary remedy, 30, 694, 702
in personam, is remedy, 30, 694
jurisdiction, 732
land abroad, contract for, 18, 694
lessor, in favour of, 700, 713
licence, 700, 710, 874
Lord Cairns' Act, 14, 724 *et seq.*
jurisdiction, 724
measures of damages, 726
minor, 713
misdescription, 721

SPECIFIC PERFORMANCE—*cont.*
money, contract for payment of, 703, 729
mutuality, 713
observance, 695
option, 700n., 704
part of a contract, 712
part performance, 700
personal services, contract for, 707
proprietary interest, whether required, 700–701, 874
refusal to comply, 697–699, 700, 705
repair, contract to, 706–707
shares, contract to sell, 84–88, 701
supervision, 704, 874
terms of decree, subsequent performance regulated by, 698
third parties and, 130–133, 728–732
time for performance, 696
transient interest, 710, 725n., 874
vendor, in favour of, 700, 713
vesting order, 700
volunteer, 121, 130, 704, 729

STAMP DUTY, 79, 80, 84–86

STATUTE OF FRAUDS. *See* FRAUDS, STATUTE OF.

STRONG V. BIRD, RULE IN, 135. *See also* CONSTITUTION OF TRUSTS.

SUBROGATION, 674

SUB-TRUSTS, 84, 114, 580

SUPREME COURT OF JUDICATURE, 14–17
Chancery Division, 38

SURPLUS,
charitable trusts, 437–438, 439
pension funds, 469
resulting trusts, 67, 233, 235 *et seq.*
trustee not entitled to, 53, 90–91, 156, 241

TAX. *See also* CAPITAL GAINS TAX; INCOME TAX; INHERITANCE TAX.
avoidance and evasion, 211–212
charities, 381
pension funds, 473
planning, 211–212, 214–215, 220
trusts, of, 222 *et seq.*

TENANCY IN COMMON,
sale, order for, 279–283
secret trusts, 151

TENANT FOR LIFE,
apportionment of income, 538 *et seq.*
on death of, 545
survivor under mutual wills, 305, 310

THING IN ACTION. *See* CHOSE IN ACTION.

THIRD PARTY. *See also* CONSTRUCTIVE TRUST; INJUNCTIONS; NOTICE; PURCHASER, bona fide, for value, without notice; REGISTRATION.
covenant to settle, rights under, 48, 124 *et seq.*, 728
equitable rights, 32 *et seq.*, 876 *et seq.*, 893–895
liability of trustees, 484
specific performance, for benefit of, 130–133, 728–732

TITLE,
doubtful, 723
lessor, 34
personal representatives, of, 54–55, 56–57
retention of, 681
root of, 34

TOMB, REPAIR OF, 46, 348, 354, 366, 369, 371, 397

TRACING, 288, 657 *et seq. See also* CONSTRUCTIVE TRUST; PROPRIETARY REMEDIES.
at common law, 657
in equity, 662 *et seq.*

TRADE,
secrets, 23–24
injunction to protect, 744, 794 *et seq.*, 804
Union, injunction relating to, 760, 802

TRESPASS,
injunction to restrain, 778–779, 781–782, 792

TRUST,
ascertainable beneficiaries, 63, 97 *et seq.*, 198, 351
bare, 36, 69, 273
capacity to make,
mental patient, 74
minors, 73

Trust—*cont.*
  certainty, requirement of, 63, 89 *et
    seq.*, 198, 350
  intention, 90
  objects, 63, 97 *et seq.*, 198, 351
  precatory words, 90
  subject matter, 93, 271, 309–310
  charitable, 375 *et seq. See*
    Charitable Trusts.
  chose in action of, 46, 93, 111, 124
    et seq.
  classification of, 64–70
  constitution of, 66, 111 *et seq.*, 149,
    159 *et seq.*, 492. *See*
    Constitution of Trusts.
  constructive, 31, 42, 68, 77, 85, 285
    et seq., 607–609, 879. *See also*
    Constructive Trust.
  contract to create, 48, 113, 121 *et
    seq.*
  corporation, 55, 490, 495n., 502n.
  creation of,
    beneficial owner, by, 84, 114
    formalities. *See* Formalities.
    intention, 65, 76, 90, 111,
        119–121, 127–130, 149,
        159–162, 360
    minors, by, 73
  creditors, for the benefit of, 50–52,
    342
  debts, for payment of, 342
  declaration of, 66, 76, 82, 84, 90,
        111–121, 159–162, 360
    self as trustee, 76, 84, 111, 113,
        119
  definition of, 45
  discretionary, 59–64, 99 *et seq.*,
        188, 189, 190, 194, 195 *et seq.*
        224. *See also* Discretionary
        Trusts.
  disposition of equitable interest, 78
    et seq., 114, 115, 623–624
  distinguished from,
    agency, 47
    bailment, 46
    charge, 52, 241
    condition, 52
    contract, 48
    debt, 49
    interest under will or intestacy,
        53–59
    power, 59–64, 97 *et seq.*, 165,
        168–171, 202, 352, 371, 553
  documents, 549–551
  executed and executory, 65

Trust—*cont.*
  express, 65
  fixed, 64, 98, 205
  formalities for, 75 *et seq.*
    dispositions, 78 *et seq.*
    inter vivos, 75 *et seq.*, 159, 162,
        230, 254, 261, 262
    will by, 89, 143 *et seq.*, 245, 254
  future property, of, 133, 309
  governmental obligation, contrasted
        with, 70
  higher sense, trust in the, 70
  illegal, 249, 325 *et seq. See also*
    Illegal Trusts.
  imperfect obligation, of, 354 *et seq.*
    See Purpose Trusts.
  implied, 65
  land, of, 75, 143 *et seq.*, 162, 230,
        244, 259 *et seq.*, 312, 318 *et
        seq. See also* Trust of Land.
  lower sense, trust in the, 70
  mental patient, 74
  minor,
    legal estate in land, cannot hold,
        73
    settlement by, 73
    T.A. 1925, s.31, 571 *et seq.*
  oral, of land, 76, 162, 312
  pension funds, 455 *et seq. See also*
    Pension Fund.
  percentage trusts, 545
  power, distinguished from, 59–64,
        97 *et seq.*, 165, 168–171, 202,
        352, 371, 553
    in nature of, 62, 109
  precatory, 90
  private, 65, 347
  proprietary nature of beneficial
        interest under, 17, 45, 47, 59,
        111, 203, 323
  protective, 185 *et seq. See also*
    Protective Trusts.
  purposes, for, 347 *et seq. See also*
    Purpose Trusts.
  recognition of, 43
  requirements of, 73 *et seq.*
  resulting, 67, 76, 92, 93, 229 *et
        seq.*, 264. *See also* Resulting
        Trusts.
  secret, 143 *et seq.*, 314. *See also*
    Secret Trusts.
  spendthrift, 185
  sub-trusts, 84, 114, 580
  taxation of, 211

TRUST—*cont.*

termination of, 64, 198, 204–205, 555, 611–612

testamentary, 89, 143 *et seq.*, 245, 254

gift to existing, 146

unincorporated associations, 48, 235–241, 349, 359 *et seq.*, 370, 433

variation of, 611 *et seq. See also* VARIATION OF TRUSTS.

voidable, 73, 337 *et seq. See also* VOLUNTARY SETTLEMENT.

writing, when necessary, 75 *et seq.*, 159, 162, 230, 314

TRUST CORPORATION, 55, 490, 495n., 502n.

TRUST FOR SALE, 36, 272–273, 849

TRUST OF LAND, 36, 272 *et seq.*, 554–556

capital money, 55, 276, 490, 491, 556, 557, 564, 569

co-ownership, 272 *et seq.*

definition, 273

joint tenancy, 273–274

occupation, right to, 274–276

overreaching, 36–37, 273, 276

powers of trustees,

absolute owner, powers of, 554

consultation of beneficiaries, 280, 554

delegation, 566

sale, 555

purchaser from single trustee, 276

registered land, in, 277–279

rent, whether payable, 275

sale, order for, 279–283

tenancy in common, 273–274

trustee, single, 276–279

TRUSTEE,

abroad, 200, 216, 493, 500, 501, 504, 633n.

advancement, 570, 576 *et seq. See* ADVANCEMENT, POWERS OF TRUSTEES.

advertisement for claimants, 535

agent of, 293 *et seq.*, 559 *et seq.*

application to court for directions, 533, 632, 648–651, 687

appointment of, 492 *et seq.*

additional, 495

by beneficiaries, 496

by continuing trustees, 494

TRUSTEE—*cont.*

appointment of,—*cont.*

by court, 497, 499

by settlor, 492, 502

consent of surviving or continuing trustee to, 494

pension trust, 463

power of. *See* POWER OF APPOINTMENT.

statutory power, 493

beneficially, may not claim, 53, 90–91, 156, 241

beneficiary trustee, 633, 643

Benjamin Order, 534, 687n.

breach of trust by, 631 *et seq. See also* BREACH OF TRUST.

capacity to be,

corporation, 490

minor, 230, 245, 246, 486, 493

pension trust, disqualification, 464

charitable trust, of, 451

conflict of interest, 292, 504, 589 *et seq.*

constructive, 285

control by court of, 505–509

co-trustees, liability, 512, 563, 641

Crown as, 70, 486

custodian, 489

de son tort, 298n.

death of, 492, 493

decision, power to make, 508

delegation, 559 *et seq. See* DELEGATION; PENSION FUND; POWERS OF TRUSTEES

deviating from trust. *See* VARIATION OF TRUSTS.

directors, as, 593

discharge of, 535

disclaimer of office, 491

discretions of, 481

cannot surrender, 534

conscious exercise, 170, 513, 559

disclosure to beneficiaries, 505, 549

disposition, power of, 54 *et seq.*, 555

duties of, 481, 511–551. *See* DUTIES OF TRUSTEES.

exclusion of court's jurisdiction, 507, 508–509

executor, compared with, 53 *et seq.*, 653

exemption clauses, 467, 483, 560, 564

TRUSTEE—*cont.*
expenses of, 585
fiduciary nature of office, 585 *et seq.*
foreign, 200, 216, 493, 500, 501, 504, 633n.
impounding beneficial interest, 647
incapable, 493, 494, 496n.
income tax, assessable to, 213
judicial, 487, 587
Keech v. Sandford, rule in, 591, 593
laches and, 651
land, of. *See* TRUST OF LAND; TRUSTEES OF LAND.
liability of. *See* BREACH OF TRUST; PROPRIETARY REMEDIES.
  application of money advanced, 583
  contribution, 641
  criminal, 462, 464, 643
  discharge on distribution, 535
  exemption clauses, 467, 483, 560, 564
  indemnity, 633, 642
  inter se, 641
  joint and several, 641
  measure of, 633–641
  third parties, 484
  vicarious, 560, 562, 567, 632
limitation period, 651
maintenance, 570 *et seq. See* MAINTENANCE; POWERS OF TRUSTEES.
managing, 489
minor, as, 230, 245, 486, 493
number of, 451, 463, 491, 495
onerous nature of office, 479
paid, 480, 482, 490, 585 *et seq.,* 651
payment of funds into court, 534
pension trust, of, 462
personal representatives and, 54 *et seq.,* 651, 653
  when becomes, 54 *et seq.,* 59
powers of, 481, 553 *et seq. See* POWERS OF TRUSTEES.
professional, 202, 480, 482, 585 *et seq.,* 651
profits by, 68, 292, 589 *et seq.*
protection of, 467, 482 483, 644 *et seq.*
public, 488, 587
purchase of,
  beneficial interest by, 591
  trust property by, 589

TRUSTEE—*cont.*
reasons, giving of, 460, 549
receipt by, 55, 276, 490, 491, 556, 557, 564, 569
removal of, 449, 451, 503
  pension trust, 461, 464
remuneration of, 480, 585–589
  effect of payment on liability, 482
resident abroad, 200, 216, 493, 500, 501, 504, 633n.
retirement, 493, 502
  breach of trust, to permit, 502, 633
  liability on, 502, 633
sale, 555. *See* POWERS OF TRUSTEES, Power of Sale.
selection of, 201, 499
sole, 491
solicitor trustee,
  liability, 482, 642
  remuneration of, 585, 588
standards applicable, 481
  professional trustees, to, 482
successor, 512
trust corporation as, 55, 490, 495n., 502n.
unanimity, 54, 279, 485, 534n.
  charitable trustees, 451
  pension fund trustees, 464
unfit, 464, 493, 494
vesting of property in,
  declaration, 498
  exceptional cases, 498
  orders, 499
who may be, 451, 464, 486 *et seq.,* 501
  appointment by court order under T.A. 1925, s.41, 499
  appointment by donee of power, 492, 500
  appointment by settlor, 492, 502
  persons resident abroad, 200, 216, 493, 500, 501, 504, 633n.

TRUSTEE IN BANKRUPTCY, 185 *et seq.,* 196, 282–283, 342 *et seq.*
bankruptcy of life tenant, 188 *et seq.*
  member of class of beneficiaries, 196
voluntary settlement, 342

TRUSTEES OF LAND,
consultation of beneficiaries, 280, 554

TRUSTEES OF LAND—*cont.*
  delegation by, 559 *et seq.*
  overreaching by, 36–37, 273, 276
  powers of, 554
  sole,
    conveyance by, 276

UBERRIMAE FIDEI, CONTRACTS, 826

UNCONSCIONABLE BARGAINS, 836

UNDUE INFLUENCE, 147, 828 *et seq.*
  agent, by, 832
  examples of, 828 *et seq.*
  in consent to breach of trust, 646
  independent advice, 830, 831, 833,
    835, 836
  inequality of bargaining power, 832,
    837
  manifest disadvantage, 832, 836
  mortgagee, position of, 832 *et seq.*
  presumption, 829
  specific performance, defence to,
    720

UNINCORPORATED ASSOCIATIONS, 48,
    235–241, 349–350, 359 *et seq.*,
    370, 433
  charitable purposes, 359, 433
  dissolution, 235–241
  gifts to, cosntruction of, 48,
    349–350, 359 *et seq.*, 370, 433
  meaning, 359
  members, rights of, 235–241, 359 *et
    seq.*
  perpetuity rule, 360–363

UNIT TRUSTS, 516

UNJUST ENRICHMENT, 69, 289–291,
    300, 315, 317–324, 605,
    608–609, 656, 675, 679, 688

USES(S),
  active duties, 10
  origins of, 8–9
  resulting, 244
  Statute of, 10, 244
  use upon a, 10

VALUATION,
  pension funds, 468
  reversionary interests, of, 540, 559
  share in home, 271
VARIATION OF TRUSTS, 611 *et seq.*
  compromise, 614
  court, approval of, 613
  dispute, 614

VARIATION OF TRUSTS—*cont.*
  divorce, on, 618
  emergency, in, 613
  inherent jurisdiction, 613
  investment powers, 530, 619
  Matrimonial Causes Act 1973, 618
  Mental Health Act, 1983, 74–75,
    619
  pension fund, 476
  powers and, 183
  salvage, 613
  S.L.A. 1925, s.64, 616
  T.A. 1925,
    s.53, 617
    s.57, 616
  Variation of Trusts Act 1958, under,
    619 *et seq.*
    approval, effect of, 623
    benefit, 626–629
    costs of application, 627
    foreign trusts, 622
    fraud on a power, 625
    insurance, 629
    mental patients, 74–75, 619, 622,
      628
    parties, who should be, 621
    perpetuity period, 624
    persons or whose behalf court
      approves, 620
    principles applicable to, 619 *et
      seq.*
    resettlement, 624
    settlor, intention of, 625
    tax implications, of, 612–613,
      615, 617, 618, 620, 622, 627
    vesting, postponement of, 615,
      628

VENDOR AND PURCHASER,
  conditions of sale, 722
  constructive trust, 312
  misdescription, 721
  misrepresentation, 716, 825
  rescission of contract, 817
  root of title, 34
  specific performance, 699, 705
  undue influence, 828
  vendor's title defective, 723

VESTING,
  assent, 53–57
  declaration, 498
  order, 499
  perpetuity rule, for purpose of, 335
  personal representatives, in, 53 *et
    seq.*

VESTING—*cont.*
trustees, in, 114–119, 498–499

VISITOR, 445, 803

VOLUNTARY CONVENIENCE. *See also*
SETTLEMENT.
conveyance for value, after, 341, 343
personalty, of, 230, 245
rectification of, 845
resulting trust, 230, 244 *et seq.*

VOLUNTARY SETTLEMENT, 338 *et seq.*
bankruptcy of settlor, 342
consideration, 339, 341, 342, 343, 344
corporate insolvency, 344
creditors,
future, 338, 340
intent to defraud, 338–342
preference, 342, 344
family provision, 345
good faith, 341, 343, 344
matrimonial causes, 345
purchaser for value of interest under, 341, 343
rectification of, 845
trustee in bankruptcy, 342 *et seq.*
undervalue, 339, 342

VOLUNTEERS,
beneficiaries as, 121
bound by equities, 289, 677

VOLUNTEERS—*cont.*
equity will not assist, 48, 67, 111 *et seq.*, 704. *See also*
CONSTITUTION OF TRUSTS.
estoppel and, 141, 889, 894
innocent, liability of, 289, 300, 669, 673, 677, 686
next-of-kin, as, 123
specific performance, 704
tracing, 669, 673, 677

WARDSHIP OF MINORS, 39, 739, 802

WASTING ASSETS, 539, 540

WILL,
ambulatory, 154
contract to leave by, 307, 711
form of, 89, 143
attestation, 89
signature, 89
witnesses, presence of, 89
incorporation by reference, 145–147, 155
interest under, distinguished from trust, 57
lapse, doctrine of, 160, 161, 308, 431
mental patient, 75
mutual, 305 *et seq. See also*
CONSTRUCTIVE TRUST.
power of appointment, exercise of, 172, 174
public document, is, 144, 551
rectification of, 845
witnesses, attesting, 89, 159